A DESCRIPTIVE

DICTIONARY

OF THE

INDIAN ISLANDS & ADJACENT COUNTRIES

A DESCRIPTIVE

DICTIONARY

OF THE

INDIAN ISLANDS & ADJACENT COUNTRIES.

BY

JOHN CRAWFURD, F.R.S.

GYAN

Published by

Gyan Publishing House
5, Ansari Road
Daryaganj, New Delhi-110002
Phone: 011-47034999, 9811692060
E-mail: books@gyanbooks.com

Distribution Network
gyanbooks.com
India, USA, Canada, UK, Australia

ISBN: 978-81-212-7045-8 (PB)
First Published, 1856

2nd Impression 2024

Printed at: Gyan Press, Delhi.

A DESCRIPTIVE DICTIONARY OF THE INDIAN ISLANDS & ADJACENT COUNTRIES
Author: JOHN CRAWFURD

A DESCRIPTIVE DICTIONARY OF THE INDIAN ISLANDS & ADJACENT COUNTRIES.

BY

JOHN CRAWFURD, F.R.S.

LONDON:
BRADBURY & EVANS, 11, BOUVERIE STREET.
1856.

PREFACE.

It was my first intention to publish a second edition of a work which I gave to the public six-and-thirty years ago, but, on mature consideration, I have come to the conclusion that a subject so multifarious as a general description of the Indian and Philippine Archipelagos would be most conveniently and compendiously treated by an alphabetic arrangement. The result is the present work; the fruit of seven years' additional local experience of India, and of a study of the subject continued with little interruption from the publication of the History of the Indian Archipelago, in 1820. Some of the articles are meagre from want of materials, and others, without doubt, imperfect and unsatisfactory from defective knowledge or skill in the writer; but, upon the whole, the book will probably be found the most comprehensive and accessible which has yet been published on the extensive region of which it treats, while it will, at all events, lay the foundation for a more perfect superstructure by those who may follow the Author in the same direction.

A DESCRIPTIVE DICTIONARY,

ETC. ETC.

ABACA. This is the Musa textilis of Botanists, a species of banana, a native of the Philippine and of some of the more northerly of the Molucca Islands. On account of its filaments it is extensively cultivated in the first of these, particularly in the provinces of Camarines, and Albay in the great island of Luzon, and in several of the Bisaya Islands, or range lying south and east of it. The name abaca belongs to the Tagala and Bisaya tongues, but is not the generic name of the banana in either of them. By the Spaniards of the Philippines the plant is known under the name of arbol de cañamo, or the hemp tree, from which, no doubt, is derived our own commercial one for the filament "Manilla hemp." The abaca, like other bananas, is propagated easily by the suckers which spring up at the roots of the old plant when it dies. A measure of 5000 square yards of land will grow 1000 abaca plants. It grows to the height of 13 or 14 feet exclusive of the leaves. The fruit is small, of a disagreeable taste, and not edible. When it is about to form, the plant is cut down, and the stem being cut open longitudinally, is found to contain a great quantity of filaments of various thickness, and usually a couple of yards in length. These are extracted, hackled after the manner of flax, and then sorted. Some of the finest are as slender as a hair of the head, and these are reserved for the manufacture of cloth, while the coarser are appropriated for cordage, from the smallest rope to a ship's cable. In the husbandry of the Philippines, the abaca is of more importance than cotton. When or how its culture came to be first introduced is not known. In his enumeration of the plants of the Philippines on their first discovery in 1521, Pigafetta does not include the abaca, although he mentions cotton and the esculent banana; but it is possible enough that so peculiar a production may have escaped his notice. Dampier, in his account of Mindano, where he resided for six months in 1686, not only mentions the textile banana, but gives an ample and accurate description of the mode of extracting the thread from the trunk. "As the fruit of this tree," says he, "is of great use for food, so is the body no less serviceable to make clothes, but this I never knew till I came to this island. The ordinary people of Mindano do wear no other cloth." After this follows the account of the process of extracting the fibres, which is well worth perusal. The Dutch have of late years introduced the culture of the abaca into the northern or volcanic peninsula of Celebes, where it seems to be indigenous, and with a fair prospect of success. There is a large exportation of abaca in the forms of raw hemp and cloth, but especially of cordage, from Manilla.

ABANG. Pulo-abang, the name of two islets of the vast group, of various sizes, extending from the coast of the Malay peninsula to that of Sumatra at the eastern entrance of the Straits of Malacca. They lie about 30 miles to the north of the equator.

ABANG-ABANG. The name of a mountain of Sumatra towards its western side, within the territory of Achin, and in north latitude 4° 20′, computed to be 10,200 feet high above the level of the sea.—The word abang signifies "elder brother," but also from the Javanese "red."

ABRA; or, at full length, Centro del Abra, one of the thirty-four provinces into which the government of the Philippines is divided, and one of the twenty of these contained in the main island of Luson. The name is taken from the river which runs through it. It extends between north latitude 16° 6′ and 17° 50′, and is divided from the neighbouring provinces by high ranges of mountains, to the north from Ilocos-norte; to the east from Cagayan and Nueva Viscaya; to the south from Pangasinan, and to the west from Ilocos-sur. The whole province is mountainous and rugged, a branch of the great Cordillera of Caraballos passing through the centre of it. It has, however, a few fertile valleys. In the mountains, metallic ores, gypsum, and coal are said to exist. Deep forests of tall trees cover most of the province, some of which yield strong and durable timber. Game abounds, the most remarkable of which are the buffalo, the hog, deer, and the common fowl. In 1849, the total population subject to the Spanish rule was 28,971, of which 42 only were Spanish, and 122 mestizo Chinese. Of these no more than 3763 were assessed to the poll-tax, which yielded only 37,633 reals of plate. The mountains of Abra are inhabited by the following wild and generally unconverted and unsubdued tribes—the Ibalaos, the Guimanes, the Busaos, the Igorrotes, and the Tinguianes. These are all distinct from each other in language and manners, and are supposed by some Spanish writers, although doubtless erroneously, to be various crosses of the brown and negro races.

The first Catholic mission was established in Abra in 1698, twenty-eight years after the arrival of the Spaniards in Luzon, but it was not until 1720, or a century and a half after that event, that the conversion and subjugation of the inhabitants began in earnest; and, as elsewhere in the Philippines, the merit of both works belongs chiefly to the priesthood. It was only in 1846 that Abra was erected into a distinct and independent province, previous to which it had formed a part of Ilocos-sur.

ABRA. The river which gives name to the province just described. It has its source in the highest part of the western branch of the Cordillera of Caraballos, which terminates on the west coast in the promontory of Namagpacan. After passing through the province of Abra, it enters that of Ilocos-sur, receiving in its passage through both, several affluents. In the last-named province it divides into three branches, and thus disembogues on the western coast. In its course it irrigates much land, and is navigable for the light boats of the natives up to the elevated tracts.

ACHIN. The name of an independent state, occupying a small part of the north-western end of Sumatra, being the nearest portion of the Archipelago to continental India and Western Asia. The native name is correctly Acheh, but this word, which means "a wood-leech," does not, although naturalised, belong to any of the Malayan languages, but to the Telinga or Telugu of the Coromandel coast. The Portuguese, to whom the country was first known, corrupted the native term into Achem, and hence the Dutch Atsjin, and our own Achen, Acheen, and Achin, Europeans invariably laying the accent on the last instead of the first syllable. The town of Achin, which, with the valley in which it is situated, is the chief seat of the Achinese population, lies in north latitude 5° 56′, and east longitude 95° 26′. The boundaries of the state have oscillated with its power, but its nominal ones are Barus on the western coast, and Batubara on the eastern. Its real dominion is at present confined to the narrow valley just mentioned. When the most extensive, indeed, it never comprised more than a small portion of the great island in which it is situated. The valley of Achin is bounded by mountainous land; and one mountain, called by Europeans "Golden Mount," but by the natives Ya Murah (the generous or bountiful), rises to the height of 5000 feet, being visible at sea in clear weather at the distance of 92 miles. It bounds the valley to the north-east, its base reaching to within five or six miles of the town. The valley itself is narrow, and so low as to be partially inundated in the season of the rains. A small river runs through it, which falls into the sea by several mouths. The mountains are as usual in these latitudes covered with forests of tall trees, in which are found the usual wild animals of Sumatra.

The roadstead of Achin, formed by the main land and several islands, is safe for shipping at all seasons, by changing their berths according to the winds. The town, now a poor place, is situated on both banks of the river, about two miles from the sea, and is accessible by the main branch for small native vessels. The Achinese are distinguished from the other Sumatrans by their taller persons and darker complexions, ascribed to a large intermixture with the natives of continental India. Although generally speaking the Malay language, their own is a peculiar tongue. The animals domesticated by them are the elephant, the buffalo, the ox, and goat, with a few sheep brought from India, as their Sanscrit name, "biri," implies. Their poultry are confined to the common fowl and duck. All the fruits common to the western Malayan countries are cultivated in abundance.

That the soil, however, is not fertile, in so far as concerns the most important part of human food—corn—is sufficiently testified by the fact that it has at all times been an article of importation. The celebrated Dampier, who visited Achin in 1688, and whose account of it continues even now to be the most full and accurate we possess, observes that the Achinese had of late, encouraged by the example of the Indians, who in consequence of a great famine on the Coromandel coast had been largely imported as slaves, commenced the cultivation of rice, but that the consumption was chiefly furnished by importation. He quotes the prices of this grain as fluctuating between 12*s.* and 70*s.* a quarter, a range of prices affording sure evidence of a sterile soil and a rude agriculture and commerce.

The population of Achin, confining this to the proper Achinese race, can only be guessed at. Mr. Logan, in his excellent account of Sumatra, makes the rate of population to the square mile no more than twenty, and estimating the area of the territory at 2260 miles, the whole population in round numbers not more than 45,200, which is probably its utmost amount.

Achin being the nearest part of the Malayan Islands to the continent of Western India, the distance from shore to shore at the narrowest point not exceeding 750 miles, and possessing a safe harbour, the probability is that it formed for many ages one of the chief marts at which the maritime nations of Hindustan obtained pepper, fine spices, gold, tin, and other commodities, in exchange for their cotton fabrics and salt. Such a commerce existed on the first appearance of the Portuguese in the waters of the Archipelago, and still exists, although in greatly diminished amount. In their own annals the Achinese are stated to have been converted to the Mahommedan religion in the year of the Hegira 601, corresponding to the year 1204 of our time, and this seems to have been the earliest conversion of any of the Malayan nations. There can be little doubt but that the Arabs and Persians with the Mahommedans of Hindustan who had been settled in that country for two centuries before this event, must have traded with the Achinese and other people of the Archipelago much earlier. On the arrival of the Portuguese, Achin was tributary to the conterminous Malay state of Pedir, and De Barros (decade 3, bk. v. c. 1), enumerates it only as one of the twenty-nine little kingdoms of the coast of Sumatra, exclusive of those of the interior of the island. Its rise to commercial importance is curious, and worth describing as an illustration of the manners and state of civilisation of the Malayan race. The King of Pedir had appointed a favourite slave to the government of Achin, and in succession to him his son. The last was a man of talent and ambition, and the founder of the state as it existed in the 16th and 17th centuries. The slave's son assumed the title of Saleh Udin, the same which is familiar to us as Saladin in the history of the Crusades. His reign began in 1521, ten years subsequent to the conquest of Malacca by the Portuguese, and in the course of eighteen years he conquered Pedir and all the neighbouring states, and made Achin the chief emporium of the commerce of the western portion of the Archipelago, the country speedily attaining an amount of prosperity and power remarkable for so small a country and so rude a people. This seems to have lasted for at least a century and a half, but to have attained its greatest height in the reign of a prince who took the name of Sekander muda, a title half-Arabic and half-Malay, which may be translated "Alexander the Younger." This person ascended the throne in 1606, and after a reign of thirty-five years died in 1641, having in that year assisted the Dutch in the conquest of Malacca, against which he himself and his predecessors had fitted out many costly but fruitless expeditions. One of these, as described by Faria-y-Souza, may be quoted as an example of the resources of the state of Achin at the time. The fleet consisted of five hundred sail, a hundred of which were of greater size than any then constructed in Europe, and the warriors or mariners which it bore amounted to 60,000, commanded in person by the king. This great expedition, destined for the conquest of Malacca, was encountered and defeated by a Portuguese squadron, losing 50 vessels and 20,000 men in a combat which lasted from morning to midnight. But the Portuguese themselves were greatly disabled in this action with a native armament which a single stout steam sloop-of-war would, in our times, have more effectually defeated.

The Achinese prince in question was the correspondent of our King James the First, and his letter in reply to the peace-loving monarch's epistle is to be found in Purchas. Here is a sample: "This great king sendeth this letter of salutation to James, King of Great Britain, viz. England, Scotland, France, and Ireland, to signify the great content he hath received from his Highness' letter, delivered by the hands of Arancaya puto, Thomas Best, his Majesty's embassadour, at the receipt whereof his eyes were surprised with a celestial brightness and his spirits ravished with a divine ray,—the opening whereof rendered a savour more fragrant than the most odoriferous flowers or sweetest perfumes in the world. For which cause I the great King of Sumatra do profess myself to be of one heart, of one mind, and of one flesh, with the most potent King James of England, and do earnestly desire the league begun may be continued to all posterity." The style of this letter shows that it was not Malay, and in fact, it was written in Arabic, as was the letter of King James to his brother of Achin. Capt. Best, the ambassador of King James, was honoured by the Achinese king with a title of nobility, viz. "Orang-kaya-putih," which means "white nobleman," and this is the title contained in the letter as Arancaya puto.

In one of the narratives of Best's voyage and mission, the following description is given of the King of Achin in 1613: "The King of Achin is a proper gallant man of warre, of thirty-two years, of middle size, full of spirit, strong by sea and land, his country populous; his elephants many, whereof we saw one hundred sixty, or one hundred eighty at a time. His gallies and frigates carry in them very good brasse ordnance, demi-cannon, culverine, sakar, minion, &c. &c. His building is stately and spacious, though not strong; his court at Achen pleasant, having a goodly branch of the main river about and through his palace, which branch he cut and brought, six or eight miles off, in twenty days, while we continued at Achen. . . He (the king) desired the general (Captain Best) to commend him to the King of England, and to entreat him to send him two white women. For," said he, "if I beget one of them with child, and it prove a sonne, I will make him King of Priaman, Passaman, and of the coast from whence you fetch your pepper; so that you shall not need to come any more to me, but to your own English king for these commodities." The pious and moral English monarch would hardly have approved of the project of bigamy contained in the last sentence of this extract, and more especially when coming from a confirmed tobacco-smoker, which the Indian prince was, even in this early period of the Asiatic history of the plant; for the narrative tells us that "hee all this while" (during a festival of six hours' continuance) "drinkes tobacco in a silver pipe, given by his women, which are in a close roome behind him."

The English made their first appearance at Achin in 1602, with a squadron of four merchant-ships, under the command of Sir James Lancaster, who was furnished with a letter from Queen Elizabeth to the king. The reigning monarch had been a fisherman, and by his talents and skill had raised himself to the command of the forces. On the demise of his sovereign and the accession to the throne of his grandson, he became his guardian,—put his ward to death, and ascended the vacant throne. The common enmity of the Queen of England and King of Achin to the Portuguese assured to Lancaster a most favourable reception. The Queen's letter is given, and is highly complimentary to her royal brother, the fisherman, while it is full of excellent sense. "We for them" (the East India Company) "do promise, that in no time hereafter you shall have cause to repent thereof, but rather to rejoice much, for their dealing shall be true, and their conversation sure, and we hope that they will give such good proofe thereof that this beginning shall be a perpetual confirmation of love betwixt our subjects on both parts, by carrying from us such things and merchandise, as you have need of there. So that your Highness shall be very well served, and better contented than you have heretofore been with the Portugals and Spaniards our enemies, who only and none else of these regions have frequented those your and the other kingdoms of the East; not suffering that the other nations should do it, pretending themselves to be monarchs, and absolute lords of all those kingdoms and provinces, as their own conquest and inheritance, as appeareth by their lofty titles in their writings. The contrary whereof hath very lately appeared unto us, and that your Highness and your royal family, fathers and grandfathers, have, by the grace of God and their valour, known, not only to defend your own kingdoms, but also to give war unto the Portugals in the lands which they possess, as namely, in Malacca, in the year of the human redemption 1575, under the conduct of your valiant captain, Ragamacota" (Raja Makuta, two Sanscrit words, long naturalised in Malay, meaning "prince" and "tiara") "with their great loss and the perpetual honour of your Highness' crown and kingdom. And now, if your Highness shall be pleased to accept into your favour and grace, and under your royal protection and defence, those our subjects, that they may freely do their business now and continue yearly hereafter, this bearer who goeth chief of the fleet of four ships, hath order, with your Highness' license, to leave certain factors with a settled house of factory in your kingdom, until the going thither of another fleet which shall go thither on the return of this,—which left factors shall learn the language and customs of your subjects, whereby the better and more lovingly to converse with them."

A curious scene is enacted at the ambassador's audience of leave, which is thus related : "And when the general took his leave, the king saith unto him, 'Have you the Psalms of David among you?' The general answered, 'Yea, and we sing them daily.' 'Then,' said the king, 'I and the rest of these nobles about me will sing a psalm to God for your prosperity,' and so they did very solemnly. And after it was ended, the king said, 'I would have you sing another psalm, although in your own language.' So, there being in the company some twelve of us, we sang another psalm. And after the psalm ended, the general took his leave of the king, the king shewing him much kindness at his departure, desiring God to bless us in our journey, and to guide us safely into our own country, saying, that if hereafter your ships return to this port, you shall find as good usage as you have done." It is to be noticed that not only the intercourse of the English mission, but the correspondence of the two sovereigns, was carried on in the Arabic language by means of a Jew interpreter brought by Sir James Lancaster with him from England.

Such was the first humble appearance of our nation in India, and such the condition of the kingdom of Achin in the first years of the seventeenth century. Two hundred and fifty years have wrought a wonderful change. The successor of Queen Elizabeth is mistress of India with its hundred and fifty millions of people, and the successors of the merchants for whom she besought protection are her delegates in its administration, while the reigning King of Achin is the son of a mestizo Arab, a subject of Queen Victoria, and called to the throne on account of the wealth acquired by his father under British protection in the small out-settlement, Penang.

The rapid rise and fall of Achin deserve a few observations. Its territory was small, and its soil more sterile than fertile, so that it must have owed its prosperity almost wholly to commerce. Its published laws are liberal, but these, judging by the results, must also have been administered in a manner to insure a tolerable amount of security to life and property, and it seems certain that the Achinese government abstained from the common practice of Malayan states, that of monopolising in its own hands all foreign trade. The probability is, that the large number of Arabs and Indians settled among the Achinese contributed in some degree to liberalise their commercial policy. The whole foreign trade of the subdued neighbouring states came to centre in Achin, which must also have benefited largely by the violence of the Portuguese, which drove trade from Malacca. That the trade was large for the times, is at all events certain. In 1603, Sir James Lancaster informs us that he found in the roads from sixteen to eighteen ships of divers nations, some from Gujrat, some from Bengal, some from Calicut and other ports of Malabar, and some from Pegu and the eastern coast of the Malay peninsula. Eighty-five years later Dampier says, that the roads are "seldom without ten or fifteen sail of ships of several nations," and that from ten to twelve Chinese junks came yearly to Achin. "This town," says he, "consists of 7000 or 8000 houses, and in it there are a great many merchant strangers, viz., English, Dutch, Danes, Portuguese, Chinese, Gusrats, &c. &c. The houses of this city are generally larger than those I saw at Mindano and better furnished with household goods. The city has no walls, nor so much as a ditch about it. It has a great number of mosques, generally square-built and covered with pantile, but neither high nor large. The queen has a large palace here, built handsomely with stone, but I could not get into the inside of it." According to Dampier's statement the town of Achin must have contained in 1688 forty-five or fifty thousand inhabitants, a number at least equal to the whole of the present population of the principality.

Nearly all this has disappeared. No doubt the violence and injustice of the paramount European governments, the Dutch and English, in their efforts to establish their respective monopolies, contributed largely to the decay of Achin ; but the main cause has been the disorder and anarchy inherent in the government of an essentially barbarous people, whose fits of prosperity must be always inconstant and ephemeral. For a century and a half, the country was exhausted by wars and expeditions wholly disproportioned to the resources of so small a state. The extent of anarchy which prevailed is shown in a few words by the short duration of the reigns of its princes.

From the year 1621 to the present time no fewer than four-and-twenty princes have reigned, which gives an average duration for each reign of less than ten years. Of these, one half were either deposed or assassinated. Four of the Achinese sovereigns in succession, over a period of sixty years, were women, the puppets of an oligarchy of the nobles.

ADANG. A wild tribe of the island of Luzon, of the brown-complexioned race, with peculiar manners and a peculiar language, inhabiting the craggy recesses of the Cordillera of Caraballos, in about the latitude of 18° 30′ north, and within the province of Ilocos-norte. The tribe is also known to the Spaniards under the different names of Adangino, Adane, Adanite, and Adangta. "The blind love of all the Philippine islanders," say the authors of the Geographical Dictionary, "for their savage independence, aided by the nature of the country in which the Adantas hold their miserable abode, has prevented religious zeal, the civiliser of the Philippines, from reaching them, and kept them long in their stupid ignorance, and physical and moral destitution."

ADENARA. The name of one of the five small islands lying between Floris and Timur, and the nearest to the first of these. Its area is computed at 144 square geographical miles.

AETA, and also ITA. This is the name by which the negro race of the Philippine Islands is most commonly known. They are a short, small, but well-made and active people, with the nose a little flattened, soft frizzled hair, a complexion less dark, and features more regular than those of the African negro. The Spanish expression is, "less black and less ugly." From their diminutive stature, their average height not exceeding four feet eight inches, and resemblance to the Africans, the Spaniards call them negritos, or "little negroes." The Aetas are described as being in the rudest state of social existence; without other covering than a strip of bark to hide their nakedness; and without fixed dwellings, but wandering over the forest in quest of the wild roots, fruits, and game, on which they subsist. The bow is their only weapon, but they use it with much dexterity. With the brown-complexioned race they live in a state of constant hostility. They are usually seen only in the sequestered recesses of the mountains, and have been found by the Spaniards far less amenable to civilisation than the wildest of the brown-complexioned race. According to the Spanish statements, the negritos are found only in the five islands of Luzon, Negros, Panay, Mindoro, and Mindano; and in these, those subjected to the Spanish rule, or to some extent tamed, amount, for Luzon to 8309; for Negros to 3475; and for Panay to 4903, making the total number, in the three islands, 16,887; no account existing of those of Mindoro and Mindano. Throughout the whole Philippines, the total number of the negritos has been estimated not to exceed 25,000. No adequate specimens of the languages of the Philippine negroes has been published, but each tribe is supposed to have its own peculiar idiom, and all of them to be different from, although in many cases mixed with, the languages of the brown-complexioned race.

AGAR-AGAR. The Malay name for a species of marine alga, the Fucus saccharinus of botanists; growing on the rocky shores of many of the Malayan islands, and forming a considerable article of export to China by junks. It is esculent when boiled to a jelly, and is also used by the Chinese as a vegetable glue.

AGILA, the Eagle-wood of commerce. Its name in Malay and Javanese is kalambak or kalambah, but it is also known in these languages by that of gahru, or kayu-gahru, gahru-wood, a corruption of the Sanscrit Agharu. The perfumed wood thus named has been immemorially used as an incense throughout all the civilised countries of the East; and at least from the first appearance of the Portuguese in India, by the nations of Europe. In 1516, Barbosa (Ramusio, vol. i. p. 317) mentions it under the two names, of Aloe-wood and Agila; quoting the price of the first, which he characterises as "fine black," at 1000 fanams the farasuola, and the last at 300 only. There can be no doubt but that the perfumed wood is the result of disease in the tree that yields it, produced by the thickening of its sap into a gum or resin. In the mission to Siam and Cochin China in 1821 and 1822, I saw myself the wood in both states as it was freshly brought from the forest, and preparing for the market in the island of Kodud, on the coast of Camboja, between the latitudes of nine and ten degrees north. The tree yielding the genuine agila has not been ascertained by botanists, but it probably belongs to the natural order of Leguminosæ, in which it has been placed by the celebrated botanist Decandolle.

The perfumed wood is found in greatest perfection in the mountainous country to the east of the gulf of Siam, including Camboja and Cochin-China, between the 8th and 14th degrees of N. lat. It is found, however, although of inferior quality, as far north as Sylhet, in Bengal, and as far south as the Malay peninsula and Sumatra; and in all this wide extent the tree, a tall forest one, is probably either the same or of the same natural family. Castanheda mentions its existence in Campar, on the eastern side of Sumatra, and opposite to Malacca. "It (Campar)," says he, "has nothing but forests which yield aloes-wood, called in India Calambuco (kalambak). The trees which produce it are large, and when they are old they are cut down and the aloes-wood taken from them, which is the heart of the tree, and the outer part is agila. Both these woods are of great price, but especially the Calambuco, which is rubbed in the hands, yielding an agreeable fragrance; the agila does so when burned."

AGNO-GRANDE, one of the largest of the rivers of the island of Luzon. It has its source in the province of Abra, near its confines with that of Nueva Viscaya, and in the highest valley of the Cordillera of Caraballos, in lat. 16° 49′, and long. 121° 50′. After receiving some twenty affluents, and pursuing a tortuous course through a mountainous country, it passes through the province of Pangasinan, and disembogues in the deep gulf of Lingayen, on the western coast. In its course the Agno-Grànde expands into the formation of several lakes. The most remarkable of these is that of Ladiavin, in the district of San Carlos, which abounds in fish, especially in that called the dalag, a large article of trade in the Philippines. During the season of the rains, another lake of great extent is formed by the overflowing of the Agno-Grande at its confluence with three other streams in the low plain of Mangabol. When the water recedes, small lagoons remain, and in these also the fishery of the dalag is carried on; while in other parts of the land which had been inundated grasses spring up, on which are fed many oxen for the market of Manilla. The banks of the Agno-Grande abound in useful timber, bamboos, and ratans, which are transported by it directly to the Spanish dock-yards. In the plain of Asingan the sands of the Agno-Grande are washed for gold, an employment which affords the natives occupation for several months of the year. The soapy juice of a tree called the gogo is used to precipitate the gold from the earth and clay, every hundred pounds' weight of which are said yield thirty grains weight of gold.

AGUNG (GUNUNG); that is, in the Malay and Javanese languages, "great or chief mountain." A mountain of the island of Bali, with an active volcano, reckoned by the Baron Melvil de Carnabee at 11,600 English feet above the level of the sea.—A mountain of the country of the Sundas, in Java, bears the same name, but seems hardly entitled to it, since it is but 7000 feet high, while some of those in its neighbourhood rise to 8000 and 9000 feet.

AGUTAYA. A small island of the Philippines, in the Sea of Mindoro, forming one of the group called the Cuyos, which belongs to the province of Calamianes. It lies in north latitude 11°, and east longitude 121°; and is about 72 leagues distant from Manilla. It is about two leagues in length by one in breadth, with a rocky surface, of which very little is fit for cultivation. In 1849, the whole population was 2011. The inhabitants are remarkable for their industry, which chiefly consists in rearing the coco-nut, in fishing the tripang or holothurion, called in the Philippine languages, balaté, for the Chinese market; in breeding oxen, and what is more remarkable, considering their climate, sheep. The different objects of their industry are exchanged by them in Manilla, and in the fertile island of Panay, for rice and other necessaries.

ALABAT, an island lying in 7° north latitude, on the eastern coast of Luzon, within the deep bay of Lamon, and fronting the isthmus which divides the main body of that island from the peninsula of Camarines. It has an area of about eight square leagues, but on account of the barrenness of its soil, and the dangerous navigation of its coasts, it remains uninhabited. Spanish writers describe it as looking like a bit cut out of the main island.

ALAS. Name of a village on the shore of the island of Sumbawa, fronting the island of Lomboc, and which gives name among European navigators to the Strait, that forms the safest passage for shipping, between the Indian Ocean and China Sea on one side, and the Pacific on the other. The name in Javanese, with the accent on the first syllable, means "forest or wilderness," and alludes, no doubt, to the position of the village.

ALBAY, anciently called Ibalon, a province of Luzon, one of the twenty into which it is divided, and forming the south-eastern end of the island. To the south, it is divided from the island of Samar by the Straits of San Bernadino, and to the north by the province of Camarines Sur, the river Ugot being here the boundary. The portion of Albay on the main land of Luson extends in its greatest length 90 geographical miles from north to south, and in its greatest breadth from east to west 35 miles. Its area will be about 1265 geographical miles. But the province includes, besides, the considerable islands of Masbate and Ticao, with several smaller ones. The coast of the main land is broken, irregular, and of difficult approach. It is indented by three deep bays, those of Langonay and Albay on the eastern side, and that of Sorsogon on the western. The last forms the best harbour, and is the place where were, in former times, built and equipped the celebrated Acapulco galleons. Albay is generally a mountainous country, a portion of the great cordillera which traverses Luzon, passing through it. Two of the mountains of this chain within its boundaries, Bulusan and Mayon or Albay, both active volcanoes, are of great elevation, especially the last, which is visible far at sea and a landmark for mariners. The principal rivers are the Calaunan, which falls into the bay of Sorsogon; the Langonay, which falls into the bay of the same name; and the Ugot already named.

The mountains of Albay abound in building timber and fancy woods, ebony and sapan-wood. The most remarkable of the wild animals are the buffalo, the wild hog, several species of deer and monkeys, with the common fowl. The mountains are inhabited by the wild tribe called Igorrotes, a brown-complexioned people, and by the Aeta or negritos; but the civilised inhabitants, forming the bulk of the population, do not differ essentially from those of the rest of the island. Their language, called the Vicol, is peculiar.

The province of Albay is eminently fertile in soil, and well watered. The inhabitants are peaceable and industrious, but their industry has been too often disturbed by destructive earthquakes and volcanic eruptions. It produces rice, maiz, sesame, indigo, some cacao and coffee, the coco-nut palm, and the palm called by the natives the buri, the pith of which yields a sago, and the leaves a material for fine mats. It produces also some cotton and the abaca-yielding banana which is an important object of culture. The province is traversed by roads which, although hilly, are passable for wheel-carriage.

In 1735, the total population of the province of Albay was no more than 28,469; in 1799, it had increased to 80,203; and in 1810, to 118,533. But the volcanic eruption of Mount Mayon, or Albay, in 1814, having destroyed four out of its five towns, including the capital, it was found by a census taken in 1818, that the population had decreased to 92,065. Since that year it has sustained an extraordinary increase, for by the enumeration of 1849 it was found to amount to 219,740. This great increase, however, seems to have been produced chiefly by an exchange of territory with Camarines in 1846, by which it gained 41,369 inhabitants. In 1849, the number of marriages was 1046; of births, 4872; and of deaths, 2121. In 1847, the number of these, respectively, was 950, 6176, and 5621; the population of that year being 225,154. In 1850, the number of persons assessed to the poll-tax was 38,896, and the population being reckoned at 238,177, no fewer than one person in six was assessed. The total amount of poll-tax (tributo) in that year was 378,969 reals of plate, or 7958*l.*; thus each contributor paid about 49 pence.

ALBAY. Name of the chief town in the last province, latitude north 13° 24′, and longitude east 124° 28′. Albay lies on the shore of the bay of the same name, on the left bank of a river also of the same name, and at the foot of the volcanic mountain of Mayon, and in a direction south-west of it. The old town was totally destroyed by a violent eruption of the mountain in 1814, and the present built at a short distance from it. Most of the houses are built of slight materials, but a few are of stone, as the government-house, the town-hall, the office of the wine and tobacco farms, and a church. It has a preparatory school, supported by funds furnished by the Commune. By a recent census, the total number of houses was found to be 3257, and the population 19,546.

ALBAY. Name of a wide bay of the province above described, on its eastern coast. In its greatest extent from north to south it is three leagues and a half in breadth. To the north-east it is closed in by many islets, the largest of which are Datan, Rapurapu, and Pingan. In its centre there is very deep water, and towards the coasts rocks and shoals, but in some situations anchorage and shelter for vessels of small burden.

ALBINO. Persons born without the colouring matter of the skin, eyes, and hair, and thus far imperfect, are occasionally to be seen in every race and every nation and tribe of the Malayan and Philippine Archipelago, as they are of those of Europe, Asia, Africa, and America.

ALBOQUERQUE AFFONSO, or, as his name is more usually written, Alfonso Albuquerque, was the second son of Gonsalvo de Alboquerque, lord of Villaverde, and an illegitimate descendant of the royal family of Portugal. He was born in 1452. In 1503, only six years after the discovery of the passage to it by the Cape, he made his first voyage to India in the joint command of a fleet with his relative Francisco Alboquerque. Returning home in 1503, he was appointed to the command of a squadron bound for India, forming part of a fleet under the orders of Tristan da Cunha, who proceeding himself to India left Alboquerque to carry on a desultory and unprofitable warfare with the little Mahommedan states on the eastern coast of Africa. Tired by this kind of predatory war, he resolved on the conquest of the island of Ormus in the Persian Gulf,—took it, but was quickly driven out of it. In 1508, he acquired the government of India. In 1510, he attacked, and after a first unsuccessful attempt, succeeded in capturing Goa, which has ever since continued the capital of the Portuguese possessions in India. In 1511, he undertook and achieved the conquest of Malacca, the enterprise which connects his name with the present work. His last achievement was the conquest of Ormus, soon after which he fell sick, returned to India, when he found himself superseded, and died a few days after, in the 63rd year of his age.

Alboquerque unquestionably possessed all the qualities of a great captain and conqueror,—intrepid courage, a strong will, ambition, enterprise, and an unscrupulous conscience. His character seems much to have resembled that of Cortes, to whom he was in no respect inferior. His means, indeed, were better, but the enemy he had to deal with was far more civilised, and better armed than the Mexicans. Malacca was said to be defended by 30,000 men, having fire-arms and artillery, and the king in person led his forces. Alboquerque, at the head of his 800 Portuguese, and of 200 Indians of Malabar, armed only with swords and shields, stormed it in broad day, and although baffled in the first attack, took it in a second, after a desperate resistance. The Portuguese historians represent the capture of Malacca as his greatest achievement. "Surely," says Castanheda, who had himself served in India, "down to this day, since we began our Indian conquests, no enterprise has been undertaken so arduous, or in which so much artillery was brought against us."

In the civil administration of the conquest thus bravely achieved, there is little evidence of wisdom, but much of violence, bigotry, and injustice. The only discoverable exception consists in the coining of money. With the exception of tin counters, for the small traffic of the market, the Malays had no coin, but, like the Burmese at present, estimated gold and silver by weight and assay. Alboquerque struck a gold and silver coinage, stamped with the arms of Portugal. He erected a fortress to secure his conquest, the materials of which were supplied by rifling the tombs of ancient kings. He built a church, which he dedicated to "Our Lady of Annunciation," the chapel of which he ornamented with a carved cupola, taken from the same tombs, dragged to its new destination by the labour of elephants. There was in Malacca a wealthy Javanese, the chief, as is expressly stated, of 10,000 settlers of his countrymen. This person had assisted Alboquerque in the conquest, and was afterwards employed by him in civil office. Shortly before his departure for India, the conqeror caused this man, his son, his grandson, and his son-in-law, to be publicly executed. Their alleged crimes were peculation and extortion, but it is admitted that the execution was a mere measure of precaution against their wealth and influence. The wife of the chieftain offered a ransom amounting to 2800 pounds weight of gold for the life of her husband and children, engaging, at the same time, that they and their followers should quit Malacca and retire to Java. "Alboquerque," says De Barros, "replied that he was the minister of the justice of his king, Don Emanuel, who was not accustomed to sell justice for money, for justice was the most precious thing in the world;" and the same writer adds, "this was the first act of justice by our laws in the city, and the execution took place on the 27th day of December, 1511." The Mahommedan traders of Western Asia were the chief supports of the commerce of Malacca. But under the denomination of Moors, the Portuguese, under the auspices of Alboquerque, attacked and plundered their shipping, massacring their crews, in the same manner as they would have done those of the Moors of the Mediterranean. The only excuse for all this was the treachery of the king of Malacca towards a Portuguese squadron that had visited Malacca two years before his own attack.

The result of the policy thus pursued was, that the Portuguese came quickly to be considered, as they well deserved to be, as mere corsairs, and the common enemy of all the trading nations of Asia. Malacca was blockaded, even during the stay of Alboquerque himself, and being a sterile territory, which was supplied with corn from Java, a frightful famine ensued, which carried off many of the garrison and thousands of the inhabitants. The conqueror, in short, seems to have laid the foundation of that policy which brought on the Portuguese the hostility of all the surrounding nations,—which led to many invasions during the 130 years of their rule, and finally contributed to its overthrow. It must, however, be admitted, that the state of society and manners in Europe in the 16th century was not such as to have admitted of any of its nations governing an Asiatic people with justice and moderation, which may be pleaded in extenuation of the conduct of Alboquerque and his countrymen.

ALFORAS. This word, which has been variously corrupted, Alforias, Alfores, Alfours, Alforen, Arafuras, and Harafuras, and supposed to be the native name of a people inhabiting the interiors of the larger islands in the Molucca Sea, is not a native word at all, nor is it the generic name of any people whatsoever. It is a word of the Portuguese language, apparently derived from the Arabic article al, and the preposition fora, "without." The Indian Portuguese applied it to all people beyond their own authority, or who were not subdued by them, and consequently to the wild races of the interior. It would seem to be equivalent to the "Indios bravos" of the Spaniards, as applied to the wild and unconquered tribes of America and the Philippines.

ALLIGATOR, or CROCODILE; in Malay buwaya, and in Javanese baya. This reptile is found in all the rivers of the Malay and Philippine Archipelagos, but the most ordinary species of it being equally of fresh and salt water, generally at the mouths of rivers, or in the sea in their neighbourhood. The Malays of the peninsula reckon three species of alligator, which they distinguish as the labu or "gourd," the katak or "frog," and the tambaga or "copper" alligator. The species found in Sumatra and Java is the same,—the Crocodilus biporcatus of naturalists. In the rivers of Borneo the same species exists, but in these there is also another, partaking of the character of the Biporcatus and the Gavial of the Ganges, formidable by its size and rapacity. The Crocodilus biporcatus is also found in the rivers of Celebes, and extends even to the Moluccas. No alligator, however, has been found in New Guinea, and it is certain this reptile does not exist in Australia.

ALMAHERA, or GILOLO. The word Almahéra is said to mean, in one of the local languages, "mainland," referring to the great extent of the island of which it is the name, in comparison with the islets on its coast, constituting the true Moluccas. Gilolo, or, in the Dutch orthography, Djilolo, and correctly Jilolo, is the name of a bay, and, according to the early Portuguese writers, of a kingdom on the western side of the northern limb of the island. Almahéra has, on a small scale, the same whimsical configuration as Celebes, consisting of four long peninsulas proceeding from a nucleus. The two largest of these run, one to the north, and one to the south; and the two smaller, one to the north-east, and the other to the south-east. The equator passes through the island, and over its south peninsula. Its extreme northern point is in north latitude 2° 12′, and its extreme southern is 50 miles across the equator. The area of Almahéra has been computed at 5018 geographical square miles, so that it is less than one-tenth the size of Celebes, about half the size of Timur, and about equal in size to Ceram. Its surface is broken and mountainous, and several of its mountains and volcanoes often in a state of activity. The most remarkable of them is Kanoré, which rises to the height of 6500 English feet. The mountains are as usual covered with a tall forest, in which it is singular that the clove is not found, although a native of the small islands on its western coast, the true Moluccas. De Barros, who published his second decade, which contains his account of the Moluccas, 42 years after their discovery, expressly states this fact. The ascertained wild animals are hogs and deer; the latter so numerous that the natives kill them for jerked beef, which is their chief article of export. The native inhabitants are of the brown-complexioned race, speaking peculiar languages; but the coast is occupied by Malays, the original settlers having, most probably, been the Orang-lant, or Sea-Gipsies, whose wanderings extend, even at the present day, over the whole Archipelago. The aborigines seem to be a rude but inoffensive people.

De Couto, the Portuguese historian, says of them, that they were savages, without laws, and without kings or towns, dwelling in the forests. The low state of civilisation of the inhabitants of Almahéra is probably to be attributed to the want of a sufficiency of water for perennial irrigation, and to the absence of the clove, which brought commerce and civilisation to the Molucca Islands on its coast. Through this civilisation the princes of these mere islets have always been masters of Almahéra, and at present the prince of Tidor is sovereign of the south-eastern limb, and the prince of Ternate of the rest of the island, both subject to the Dutch. Almahéra has three great bays, formed by its peninsulas, all lying to the east, but no good harbours, which, however, are the less necessary in seas never troubled with storms.

ALUM (in Malay and Javanese, tawas). This substance, the principal mordant employed by the dyers of the Archipelago, is not a product of the Eastern islands, but imported from China, and the origin of the native name, for such it seems to be, is unknown.

AMBERGRIS. This substance, supposed to be a product of the sperm whale, was probably not known to the inhabitants of the Archipelago as a perfume before they were made acquainted with it by the Arabs. This is inferred from its having no native name, and its being known only by its Arabic ones of Sahabiri and Ambar. It is stated to be cast up by the sea on the shores of some of the more easterly islands of the Archipelago, the only part frequented by the sperm whale.

AMBLAU. Name of a small island in the Molucca Sea, lying between Boeroe and Amboyna, towards the southern coast of the former. It has an area of about 70 square geographical miles, and a population of 689; but its geological constitution and productions are not stated. South latitude 3° 15′, east longitude 125° 15.

AMBOYNA. This well-known island lies in the Molucca Sea, but is not one of the five islands strictly called the Moluccas, which are by four degrees further north. It is the largest of a group of five islands lying off the southern coast of the large island of Ceram, and towards its western end. Its native name is Ambun, said to be derived from that of its chief town, the island itself being called by its inhabitants Hitoe, or Hitu. Amboyna may be described as consisting of a main body and a narrow peninsula running parallel with it, the isthmus which joins them not exceeding a mile and a half in breadth. This peninsula is called Ley-timur, which is probably from the Malay lai-timur, meaning "eastern sheet or leaf." Between the main body of the island and peninsula there runs a bay 14 miles in depth, divided into an outer and inner portion, both affording good shelter for shipping; but the last, a good harbour, which cannot be used on account of the malaria proceeding from the marshes which surround it. The outer portion of the bay has such deep water as to afford no anchoring ground, except on a narrow bank which fronts the town, which is situated on the shore of the peninsula.

The geological formation of Amboyna is plutonic, consisting of granite and serpentine; but there are a few calcareous hills of recent formation. The whole island is hilly, but none of its mountains rise to any considerable elevation. Most of the land is covered with forest, of which the trees differ generally from those of the western islands of the Archipelago. The only wild animals of considerable size are the hog and deer,—even the tribe of monkeys being absent, as they are in the other islands of the Molucca Sea. The proper native inhabitants are of the brown-complexioned race, short in stature but active. They appear, when first visited by Europeans, to have possessed a peculiar language, now superseded by Malay. The plants chiefly cultivated are the clove, maiz, yams, the usual fruits, and the sago-palm, which yields the main sustenance of the people. Rice, as an object of culture, is hardly known, and, indeed, from the hilly nature of the land and the uncertainty of the supply of water, the island is unsuited to its production. The total population of Amboyna, as given in the Dutch returns, is 29,660. Of these 13,000 are computed to be in the town, a mixed population of strangers, while that of the country consists of the aboriginal inhabitants. The last have been converted to Christianity, and belong to the Dutch Lutheran church. They are regularly taught in public schools to read and write the Malay language in Roman characters, and are allowed to be the most moral, well-conducted, and peaceable people of the whole Archipelago.

AMPÂNAN. The name of a bay in the island of Lomboc, and on the strait which divides this island from Bali, one of the thoroughfares between the Indian and Pacific oceans. A village of the same name lies on the shore of this bay in south latitude 8° 32′ and east longitude 116° 9′, and is the principal place of trade in the island. This village is distant from the chief town of Lomboc, called Mataram, three miles inland, by a good road, having throughout an avenue of Indian fig-trees. The wide bay of Ampânan is but an open roadstead, on the shore of which a heavy surge frequently rolls, cutting off all communication with shipping. Within it, however, and sixteen miles distant from the village, there is a land-locked harbour, called Labuhan-pring (Bamboo anchorage), where shipping can take shelter, but which, from the prevalence of malaria on its shore, arising from want of ventilation, cannot be used permanently.

AMUK. The muck of the writers of Queen Anne's time, who introduced the word into our language. In Malay it means a furious and reckless onset, whether of many in battle, or of an individual in private. The word and the practice are not confined to the Malays, but extend to all the people and languages of the Archipelago that have attained a certain amount of civilisation. Running a-muck with private parties is often the result of a restless determination to exact revenge for some injury or insult; but it also results, not less frequently, from a monomania taking this particular form, and originating in disorders of the digestive organs.

ANAMBAS. The name given by European mariners to a numerous cluster of islands in the China Sea in about the 3° of north latitude, and 130 miles from the eastern entrance of the Straits of Malacca. The name, which is unknown to the natives, may possibly be a corruption of the Malay numeral anamblas—sixteen; but if this be so, the islands have not been correctly reckoned, for the natives estimate their number at no fewer than 50. The largest of them are, Jâmajah, towards the western part of the group, said to be 30 miles in circumference, having an area of 56 square geographical miles; and Siantan, towards its north-eastern, having two good harbours. These islands are mountainous, sterile, but covered with forest. Their own productions, or those of the sea and rocks which surround them, are sago-palms, agar-agar, coco-nuts, tripang, and fish, particularly the shark, which is killed for its fins, an article of trade for the Chinese market. These productions the natives convey in their own vessels, and dispose of in Singapore. The inhabitants are Malays of the class called Orang-laut, or "Men of the Sea," and had at one time an evil reputation for piracy; but since the establishment of Singapore they have become peaceful traders and fishermen. Nominally, at least, the Anambas islands are subject to the kings of Jehore.

ANAI. The Malay name for the termes, or white-ant. This destructive insect is found in every country of the Archipelago and Philippines, and being known by the same name in all their languages, a suspicion may arise that they have been disseminated by commerce and migration, especially when it is considered that the timber of ships is a favourite object of their depredation.

ANAM. See Cochin-China.

ANDMAN ISLANDS. These islands, situated in the midst of the Bay of Bengal, are no part of the Malayan Archipelago, and have no kind of affinity with it, except in being inhabited by a race of small squat negroes, bearing a likeness to those of the Malay peninsula. Their language, however, is not known to have any connection with that of the latter, nor does it contain a single word of Malay.

ANJIER. (Javanese, añar, new, or, to complete the sense, Desa añar, that is, "new village, or town.") A small town, with a fortress, on the coast of Java, where the strait which divides it from Sumatra is at the narrowest. The town is in the country of the Sundas, and in the kingdom which was once Bantam. It is highly convenient for shipping to refresh at, from its lying on the main thoroughfare of the Archipelago. The anchorage, however, is a mere open road, much exposed during the westerly monsoon; and therefore it is not a place of permanent trade, although the town furnishes abundant refreshments with wood and water.

ANONA. This is the name applied in the Philippines to the Anona reticulata, or Custard apple, and which the Malays have abbreviated Nona. It is a plant of tropical America. The Anona squamosa, or sweet-sop of the West Indies, is called by the Malays, Srikaya, from the name of a kind of custard, and is probably a native plant. Both species are easily raised, but little esteemed. In the Philippines, however, there seems to be another species, called, in the languages of the country, Ate represented as a fruit of excellent flavour.

ANTIMONY. This metal, until lately unknown to the natives of the East, as it was to Europeans until the fifteenth century, was found for the first time in Borneo, in 1823, on the north-western coast of that island. It exists in several places there, but mines of it have been worked only in Sarawak. The ore is, as usual, a sulphuret in a matrix of quartz, and at present furnishes the chief supply of Europe, being exported, from the emporium of Singapore, to the yearly amount of about 1500 tons.

ANTIQUE. One of the three provinces into which the large and fertile island of Panay, one of the Philippines, is divided. It occupies the western portion of the island, and has a population of 84,570, of whom 15,343 are assessed to the poll-tax, contributing 153,420 reals of plate.

ANTIQUE. Name of a town of the last-named province, and formerly its capital, having a population of 4219. It was founded in 1581, and has a church and a public school of primary instruction.

AOR PULO. See AWAR.

APARRI. The name of a town and harbour in the island of Luzon and province of Cagayan, situated on the left bank of the river Aparri (the Tajo, or Philippine Tagus,) at its disemboguement into the sea at the northern end of the island. Latitude north, 18° 23′ 15″, longitude 121° 33′. The town contains 1910 houses, all, with the exception of the public buildings, of frail native materials; and the population amounts to 5990. The harbour is the only one at the northern end of the island, that portion of the Philippines in which tempests and hurricanes are most frequent.

APAYO. Name of one of the wild tribes of Luzon, of the lank-haired race, inhabiting the mountains lying between the provinces of Cagayan and Ilocos. This tribe has made some progress in civilisation, for they have permanent dwellings of substantial houses, and cultivate roots and maiz. Their chief occupation seems to be the contraband trade in tobacco.

APO. Name of a lake of great extent in the island of Mindano, the centre of which is represented to be in latitude 7° 47′ north, and longitude 123° 52′ east. It communicates with the lake of Nusingan, lying south-west of it, and discharging itself into the Lagune of Panguil, a continuation of the Bay of Iligan. These lakes are in the territory of the Illanos, or Lanuns, and about the centre of the isthmus which divides Mindano into two quasi-peninsulas.

ARABIA. This country has been familiarly known to the inhabitants of the Malayan islands for six centuries, the majority of them, embracing nearly all the civilised nations, having, within that time, adopted its religion and laws, and engrafted much of its language on their own.

ARACHIS. The Arachis hypogæa, or ground pea, is known in the Malayan countries under the several names of kachang-tanah, kachang-China, and kachang-Jâpun, meaning, ground, Chinese, and Japan pulse. The two last of these names would seem to imply, what is probable, that the plant is an exotic, and was introduced either from China or Japan, with both of which the inhabitants of the Archipelago had maintained a commercial intercourse before the arrival of Europeans in India. With the exception of the coco-palm, it is, of all the oil-yielding plants, the most extensively cultivated in the Archipelago.

ARAYAT. The name of a volcanic mountain of the province of Pampanga, in the island of Luzon, with an extinct crater, and which rises solitary from an extensive plain. From its summit there issue seven different rapid torrents, one of which, about midway down, forms a lake, from which issues a fine cascade, the waters of which eventually fall into the "little river" of Pampanga. From the mountain there is a fine view of the town and bay of Manilla.

ARAYAT. The name of a town on the southern side of the mountain just named, containing 1100 houses and 7765 inhabitants. The "great river" of Pampanga passes through it; and within a quarter of an hour's walk of it is the spacious lake of Buracan, abounding in fish. The locality is considered by the Spaniards as one of the choicest of the Philippines.

ARCHIPELAGO (ASIATIC). Comprehending under this name both the Malay and Philippine Archipelagos, the whole Archipelago extends from about the 20th degree of north to the 11th of south latitude, and from the 95th to the 150th of east longitude, thus embracing 31 degrees of latitude and 55 of longitude. The islets to the north of Luzon are its northern, Timur its southern, Sumatra its western, and New Guinea its eastern limit. It is bounded to the north by the China Sea, to the east and south by the Pacific, and to the west by the Indian Ocean and Bay of Bengal. It forms by far the most extensive Archipelago in the world, for it contains three islands of the first magnitude, Borneo, Sumatra, and New Guinea; five if we include a peninsula of the second, Celebes, Luson, Java, Mindano, and the Malay Peninsula; fourteen of the third, Banca, Sumbawa, Bouton, Floris, Timur, Ceram, Gilolo, Panay, Mindoro, Negros, Cebu, Leyte, Samar, and Palawan; and ten of the fourth, Billiton, Bali, Lomboc, Sumba, Boeroe, Timur-laut, Taliabo, Bohol, and Masbate. Without reckoning other islands and islets, which some have computed at no fewer than six thousand, these thirty-two alone have an area of at least 700,000 square geographical miles, or above seven times the extent of Britain and Ireland!

The equator passes through nearly the centre of the Archipelago, thus leaving half of it in the northern and half in the southern hemisphere. By far the largest part of it lies within ten degrees of the equator, and this decides the character of the climate. The year throughout is one warm summer, the thermometer, at the level of the sea, varying from 80° to 90°. The only distinction of seasons is into dry and wet, about two-thirds of the year belonging to the first and one-third to the last. The whole region is within the influence of the monsoons. To the north of the equator, the wind blows half the year to the north-east, and the other half to the south-west: while the monsoons of the southern hemisphere are the south-eastern and north-western. All those parts of the Archipelago which are within 10° of the equator are free from hurricanes, and they prevail in no part of it except the northern portion of the Philippine group.

The geological formation of countries of such vast extent is, of course, very various. It may, however, be generally stated that a plutonic formation, consisting chiefly of granite, sienite, and porphyries, with a sedimentary one of sandstones and lime, characterise the countries north of the equator, and a volcanic, those to the south of it. The plutonic and sedimentary formations are found in the peninsula of Malacca, the greater part of Sumatra, all Borneo, the greater part of Celebes, and in all the smaller islands near them. A volcanic band, the most extensive in the world, runs west and east from about 100° to the 130° of east longitude; and then, taking a northerly direction, it reaches up to the 20° of north latitude. This embraces a part of Sumatra, the whole of Java, and the chain of islands east of it, as far as the islets lying west of Timur,—most of the islands in the Molucca Sea, a small part of Celebes, and much of the Philippines, from Mindanao to Luzon inclusive. The Archipelago may be described as eminently a mountainous region, the highest peaks existing in the volcanic band. In the volcanic portion of Sumatra, these rise to the height of 10,000 and 11,000 feet; while in the plutonic portion, they attain only from 5000 to 6000, or, in a few instances, to between 10,000 and 11,000. In Java, they range from 8000 to 12000 feet high, and in Lomboc there is one which reaches to 12,500. The highest mountain of the Malay peninsula reaches only to 4320 feet; of the plutonic portion of Celebes, to 8000, and of Timur, 6000. Borneo, alone, has one plutonic mountain which attains the height of 11,000 feet, the rest not exceeding 6000.

The volcanos of the Archipelago, in more or less activity, exclusive of mountains with extinct craters, are very numerous. Sumatra has five; Java, fifteen; Bali, Lomboc and Sumbawa, seven; the islands of the Molucca Sea probably not fewer than ten; Luzon, eight; and Mindanao, at least two.

The useful minerals of the Archipelago, so far as they have been ascertained and used, are gold, iron, tin, antimony, coal, sulphur, and the diamond. Gold exists in the Malay peninsula, Sumatra, Borneo, Celebes, Mindano, and Luzon. Iron ore, in sufficient abundance for use, does not exist in any part of the volcanic band; but in all the secondary formations, and, perhaps, most abundantly in Borneo. Tin is found in the Malay peninsula and several of the adjacent islands, extending from the 13° of north to, at least, the 3° of south latitude, constituting by far the most extensive known formation of this metal. Ores of antimony have been discovered on the north-western coast of Borneo in two situations, and are worked to advantage in one. Fossil coal has been found in many situations, as in parts of Sumatra, the Malayan peninsula and its islands, in Java, and Luzon, but, as far as known, in the greatest abundance and of the best quality in Borneo, where fields have been found and worked on the north and south coasts, which very probably extend across the island. Sulphur is found about the craters of all the volcanos; but is said to be most abundant in those of Mindano, and Leyte in the Philippines. The diamond appears to be confined to the western and south-western sides of Borneo.

In fertility of soil, it should be added, that the volcanic formation far excels the plutonic and sedimentary formations. Within it are to be found the majority of the population, and the people most advanced in civilisation, of which the most remarkable examples are the volcanic portion of Sumatra, Java, and the two islands immediately to the east of the latter, with the larger islands of the Philippine group. To elicit this fertility, nothing is wanting but an abundant perennial supply of water, and it is thus furnished in the islands now quoted.

As to the vegetable kingdom, as a general rule, the land from the sea-shore to the mountain-tops, is covered with an ever-verdant primeval forest of tall trees; naked rocks, brush-wood, grassy savannahs, and cultivated plains being, in most of the islands, the exceptions. The vegetation is of great variety, varying not only with the elevation of the land, but being often different even in islands in the same parallels. Thus the teak tree (*Tectona grandis*) is confined to some districts of Java, Sumbawa, and Mindano. The clove and nutmeg are confined to a few islands in the Molucca Sea; while the durian (*Durio zibethinus*) and mangostin, the most prized fruits of the western portion of the Archipelago, do not exist in the Moluccas, nor in any of the Philippines, except Mindano, the most southerly of them.

The zoology of the Archipelago is still more restricted to localities than its botany. The royal tiger is confined to the Malay peninsula, Sumatra, and Java. The only feline animal of considerable size in Borneo is a small leopard (*Felix macrocelis*). In Celebes, there is no feline animal at all, as far as it has been explored. In the Molucca Islands, feline animals are equally wanting; and in the whole range of the Philippine group there is but one carnivorous animal, the musang of the Malays, or *Paradoxurus musanga* of naturalists, a large weazel, a fact which goes far to account for the extent to which the ox, the buffalo, the horse, and goat—all imported,—have multiplied and run wild. Of the canine family, there is but a single representative throughout the Archipelago, and it is confined to Sumatra and Java; the hyena, the wolf, jackal, fox, and common dog, having no existence; the latter in the domestic state excepted. The elephant and tapir are confined to Sumatra and the Malay peninsula. Elephants, indeed, are found in a remote nook of Borneo; but, most probably, the wild descendants of those kept by the princes of Brunai, who are ascertained to have done so, when the island was first visited by Europeans. The rhinoceros exists only in the Malay peninsula, Sumatra, and Java. In Sumatra there are two species of it; and in Java, one, which is distinct from those of Sumatra. A wild ox (*Bos sondaicus*) exists in Java, Borneo, and the Malay peninsula; but not in Sumatra or any other island of the Archipelago. In the peninsula, however, there is another species, which has not yet been described. Sumatra is the only island of the Archipelago that has an antelope (the *Antilope Sumatrensis*), or wild goat of the Malays. In Celebes, and there only, there is a quadruped partaking of the characters of the ox and antelope, the *Antilope dipressicornis* of naturalists. There is but one bear in the Archipelago, an animal of small size, *Ursus Malayanus*, and it is confined to the Malay peninsula, Sumatra, and Borneo. The tribe of monkeys is numerous and various in the western islands of the Archipelago; the species, however, frequently differing in the different islands, but they are wholly absent in the islands of the Molucca Sea, while they appear again in the Philippines. The wild hog alone is widely diffused throughout the Archipelago, from Sumatra to the Philippines inclusive. But even in this case, the species will probably be found to be different. There are two distinct species of the family in Java, one in Sumatra, and one in Borneo; and in Celebes and some of the islands of the Molucca Sea, besides one resembling the common hog, that singular animal the Babirusa, which in Malay signifies literally "hog-deer." Marsupial quadrupeds, unknown in the western islands of the Archipelago and in the Philippines, are first time seen in Celebes, and from thence exist in several islands as far as New Guinea, in which there is an opossum and a tree-kangaroo.

Birds, with the exception of those that are migratory, are nearly as limited in their geographical distribution as quadrupeds. Thus, for example, the birds of Java and of Sumatra, parted by a strait not exceeding fifteen miles broad, and with islands like stepping-stones in the channel, differ with few exceptions, and even when the species are the same, it is found that those of Sumatra have more brilliant plumage and are of greater size. This is the conclusion of Temminck, the greatest living ornithologist. Peacocks are only found in the Archipelago, in the Peninsula, Sumatra, and Java; but in the two first, besides the one common to them with Java, which itself differs from the Indian species domesticated in Europe, there exists a small and beautiful double-spurred one. The Gallus Bangkiva, the supposed original of our common poultry, is alone widely disseminated, being found in all the considerable islands, including those of the Philippine group. Java however has, besides this, a second species confined to itself, the Gallus furcatus. The Cassowary, the suwari of the Malays, exists only, as far as known, in the island of Ceram, in the Molucca Sea. The birds of Celebes differ almost wholly from those of the great islands to the west of it. In Borneo first occur the Megapodes, or birds that, like reptiles, leave their eggs to be hatched by the heat of fermentation and the sun. They occur again in the Mindoro, one of the Philippines, and in New Guinea. The family of parrots, of a great many species, are spread over the whole of the Indian islands, from Sumatra to the Philippines and New Guinea, but the species often differ even in contiguous islands. In those of Celebes, for example, the predominant colour of the parrots (in Malay, nuri or loory) is green, but in the adjacent islands of the Molucca Sea it is a bright red or a crimson. The cockatoos exist only in New Guinea and the islets on its coast. The birds of paradise (manuk-dewata, birds of the gods) are confined to the same locality. Of the familiar birds of Europe and continental India, the only one usually met with, and it pervades the whole of the islands, is the common carrion crow. The house-sparrow, which is abundant in Siam, down to the thirteenth degree of north latitude, is found in the islands only in a few spots, introduced by Europeans.

The seas of the Indian and Philippine islands, and their rivers and lakes, abound in fish and reptiles. Among the most remarkable of these are several species of alligator, several of tortoises, land and sea, including the esculent and that which yields the tortoise-shell; the pearl, and mother-of-pearl oyster; the tripang, or hulothurion, and several species of sharks, the fins of which are an object of trade. The ordinary esculent fish are numerous, the species often differing on the coasts of the different islands. Thus of 108 species found in the Sea of Celebes and described, (probably not more than one-eighth of those that exist,) 64 only are found on the coast of Java. In the markets of Celebes, it is said that not fewer than 300 different species are, at one time or another, offered for sale. A few of them are of excellent quality, equalling, if not surpassing, in delicacy and flavour those of the European seas. Some frequent the rivers in the spawning season like salmon; and other sea-fish are multiplied in stews, a practice carried to a large extent in Java. The curing of ordinary fish and the pickling of prawns forms a considerable business on all the coasts, and cured fish is a considerable branch of trade between the coast and interior. The only sea mammal known west of Celebes is the Dugong, or Lamentine of naturalists, the first of these names being a corruption of the Malay Duyong. The spermaceti whale frequents only the southern portion of the Molucca Sea, where it is pursued by the Anglo-Saxon fishermen. The inhabitants of Solor, a volcanic island east of Floris, are the only people of the Archipelago that fish the whale. To the Malays and Javanese the animal is unknown, except by its mythic name borrowed from the Sanscrit, gajah-mina, "the elephant fish." The phoci or seals are unknown in the Archipelago.

Two distinct races of man are the original inhabitants of the Indian islands; a brown-complexioned, lank-haired people, the Malayan; and a black frizzle-haired one, the Negro. The first of these constitutes the great bulk of the inhabitants of most of the islands, and it is only among the nations composing it that any respectable amount of civilisation has been attained. It constitutes the entire population of Sumatra, Borneo, Java, and Celebes, and of several of the considerable islands of the Philippine group. The Malayan race is of a short squat form, with high cheek-bones, large mouth, and flattened nose; the hair of the head long, lank, and strong, and with very little beard. With the exception of New Guinea and some of the islands on its coast which are wholly peopled by them, the Negro race is found only in a few localities among the brown-complexioned. They occur first in the mountains of the Malay peninsula, and next in the Philippine group, being here confined to the mountains of Luzon, Panay, Negros, Mindoro, and Mindano. Under the common name of Negros, several different races of black men with frizzled hair seem to exist. The negros of the peninsula are a small race, under five feet high, and those of the Philippines are shorter and slenderer than the brown race of the same islands, while the negroes of New Guinea are an athletic people, at least equal in stature to the Malay race. All these negros agree in having dark complexions, frizzled hair growing in distinct tufts, but not woolly, in flat noses and much obliquity of fascial angle. At the same time they differ widely from the African, the Madagascar, and the Australian negros, the hair of the head although frizzled not being woolly, the skin being less black, and the lower portion of the face less protuberant. There is, of course, no common native name by which all these negros are known. The Malays call them Orang puwa-puwa, the last of these words, which Europeans have corrupted into Papua, being an adjective meaning "frizzled," and the first "man." The brown-complexioned people of the Philippines call them Aeta, or Ita, a term the origin of which is unknown. The Spaniards call those of the Philippines negritos, or little negros, from their diminutive size in comparison with the negros of Africa. This, however, could not be applied to the whole race, for it would exclude the most numerous section, the negros of New Guinea. Sometimes they have been called Austral negros, but neither will this designation answer, since they equally exist in the northern as the southern hemisphere. Papua negros would probably be the best designation, since it would include both themselves and the negros of the Pacific Islands, without including Africans or Australians.

The two broad distinctions of the man of the Asiatic islands, is into a brown race with lank, and a black one with frizzled, hair; but in reality it will probably be found that there are five distinct races,—the Malay, the Negro-Malay, the Papuan or New Guinea Negro, the Negrito or Little Negro of the Malay Peninsula, and the Negrito of the Philippines; for there is really nothing to show that these different negros belong to one and the same family of man.

Among the tribes of the Archipelago, some have attained a considerable amount of civilisation, one far more advanced than that of any nation of America on its discovery; others remain still in a savage condition. The civilisation of the more advanced nations is shown by the domestication of animals applicable for labour and food; by a knowledge of the precious and useful metals, and especially of malleable iron; by the culture of corns, pulses, and palms; by the growth of textile materials, with the arts of spinning, weaving, and colouring fabrics made from them; by the invention of letters, and by the possession of forms of polity calculated to afford a certain degree of security to life and property. The nations who have made this advancement, although in a very unequal degree, are five of Sumatra, two of Java, two of Celebes, and ten of the Philippines. Of these, by far the most distinguished, and those who have exercised the greatest influence on the rest, are the Malay and Javanese. The condition of the less advanced tribes is very various. Some wander in the forests in quest of a precarious subsistence, without fixed habitations, as some of those of Borneo, Sumatra, Luzon, and Mindano; others, as some of the tribes of the same islands, and the negros of New Guinea, have fixed habitations, have domesticated hogs and poultry for food, but no animals for labour, and grow roots and corn: others again have, by the assistance of trade, although possessing no domestic animals for labour, and no knowledge of the art of making malleable iron, or having invented letters, attained a higher degree of civilisation than the last. The condition of several of the inhabitants of the islands of the Molucca Sea, on their discovery by Europeans, is an example of this last state.

The total population of the Malay and Philippine Islands may be reckoned at twenty millions, of which seventeen are in the islands within the volcanic band; namely, in Sumatra, which may have 2,000,000; in Java, which has about 10,000,000; in the Philippines, which have 4,000,000; and in Bali and Lomboc, which may have between them about 1,000,000. This, of course, is but a rough estimate, for, with the exception of the European possessions, no census has ever been attempted.

The story of a people who have no history, and who indeed, are incapable of writing history, can only be gleaned from the records of the strangers who have settled among them, or by an examination of their own languages. The strangers who have from time to time settled in the Indian islands, or held intercourse with them for trade, have consisted of Hindus, Arabians, Persians, Chinese, and Europeans, chiefly Portuguese, Spaniards, Dutch, and English. Of these, the largest influence on the manners of the native inhabitants was unquestionably exercised by the Hindus. Their intercourse in a direct form was probably confined to the two islands of Sumatra and Java, but chiefly to the last of these, where they built splendid temples, the ruins of which remain,—where they introduced their calendar, and one of their epochs, and into the language of which they infused a considerable amount of their sacred tongue, the Sanscrit, with some portion of their literature and legends, a small admixture of the Telugu, a living vernacular language of Southern India. When or how the first intercourse of the Hindus with the Malayan countries commenced, is unknown; for of historical records the Hindus are nearly as destitute as the Malayan nations themselves. The Hindu records of Java will not, with any certainty, carry us back further than the year 1117 of the era of Salivana, corresponding with the year of Christ 1195, not quite a century before the celebrated Venetian traveller, Marco Polo, was passing through the Archipelago in a fleet of

Chinese junks, under the auspices of a grandson of Jengiz Khan. The Sanscrit names of many places in the Archipelago attest the influence and power of the Hindus, although it is probable that some of these were bestowed, not directly by themselves, but by those they converted—the Malays and Javanese. Such names are by far the most frequent in Java, where they are often borrowed from the Hindu legends. Here we find such names as Madura, the Madura or Mathura of India; Ayugya, its Ayudya or Aude; Indrakila, bolt of Indra; Indramaya, illusion of Indra; Talaga, the name of a place, a corruption of Taraga, a reservoir; Janggala, the thicket, the name of an ancient kingdom; Pranaraga, the desire of life, the name of a province; Jayaraga, desire of victory; Wirasaba, hall of heroes, also names of provinces; and Sumeru, Arjuna, and Brama, the names of mountains. In Sumatra, we have Indrapura, the city of Indra; and Indragiri, the mount of Indra; in Bali Swetyanagara, the city of well-being; and Sukawati, city abounding in pleasure: and in Borneo, Sukadana, parrot's gift; Kuti (Coti), little fortress; and Darmapati, king's bounty. Even as far as Celebes, we have an example in Andagili, which is evidently, although much mutilated through the imperfect pronunciation of the inhabitants of that island, Indragiri, or the mountain of Indra. See HINDU and HINDUSTAN.

On the arrival of Europeans in the Archipelago in the first years of the sixteenth century, they found the Malays and Javanese along with Arabs and other Asiatic nations, with their descendants who used the Malay language, conducting the whole of its internal commerce, and they seem to have been so engaged for ages. The extent of their trade and navigation is indicated by the names which they bestowed on the places they visited, even up to New Guinea and the Philippines, in which last Malay was spoken as the medium of communication with all strangers. The Malay words Tanjung, promontory, Ujung, point, Pulo, island, Sungai and Ayar, river, Batu, rock, Lant, sea, and Tanah, land, with the Javanese words Nusa, island, Sela, rock, and Kali, river, are of frequent occurrence throughout the Archipelago, usually prefixed to the names of places. These terms are found in parts of the Archipelago where Malay and Javanese are not vernacular, conjoined with other words of these languages, or with Sanscrit or local ones. Thus we have in the islands east of Java, and extending to New Guinea, such names of places as the following—Pulo-buru (Boeroe), hunting island; Pulo-wayang, shadow island; Pulo Timur (Timor), castor island; Nusa-lant, sea island; Nusa-kumba, elephant's trunk island; Nusa-ringgit, puppet island; Pulo arau (Aroes), cassuarina islands; Pulo-ubi (Pulo obi), yam island; Pulo-lata, creeping island; Pulo-gaja, elephant island; Pulo-putar, turning island; Nusa-manuk, bird island; Batu-china (a name of Gilolo), mark or signal rock; Ayar-aji, king's creek; Tanah-bugis, land of the Bugis, Celebes; Tanah-keke, land of sorcerers, name of a small island off the south-western peninsula of Celebes; Tanah-puwa-puwa, land of frizzle-haired people, New Guinea; Pulo pandan, Pandanus islets in the Philippine group; Pangasinan, salt or saline plain, a province of Luzon; Pulo-nila, indigo or blue island, in the Molucca Sea; Kuta-waringin, in Borneo, fortress of the Indian fig tree; Mas-sela, golden rock, in Sumatra; and the name of the island of Solor, lying immediately east of Floris, from the Javanese sulur, the sucker as of a fig-tree, which spontaneously strikes root, and figuratively a proxy or representative.

The ancients, it may be safely averred, were nearly as ignorant of the existence of the Indian Islands as they were of the islands and continent of America, and the European nations of the middle ages knew almost as little of them. The extent of the knowledge of the latter may be judged from the fact that it was a moot question with them whether Sumatra or Ceylon was the Taprobane of the ancients, although the one was distant from the other by a navigation of 1000 miles. Even the names of the principal islands had never reached them down to the moment of actual discovery. They had a vague notion that there existed some far countries beyond India that produced spices, gold, and tin, but this was in reality the extent of their knowledge of the Archipelago. The Arabians of the middle ages had a far earlier and better acquaintance with it, although the written records be very imperfect. They had navigated its seas, traded with it, and settled on it many centuries before the arrival of Europeans. The earliest account we possess of their intercourse is contained in the travels of the two Arabian merchants of the ninth century. The manuscript of the earliest of these is dated in the year 851, and of the latest in 903. The first of these dates carries us back 440 years before the visit to the Archipelago of Marco Polo, and 768 years before the actual discovery by the Portuguese. The two Arabian travellers make no mention of any trade with the

Indian islands conducted by their countrymen; but as they give very authentic accounts of the Arabian trade with China, they must, of necessity, have passed through them, and at least touched at them for wood and water. The earliest of the two travellers indeed indicates, although very obscurely, that the usual route was through the Straits of Malacca, the countries on each side of which were, probably, at the time in a barbarous state, for the ancient Singapore and Malacca had not yet been founded. The Arabian commerce with China, at the time, was conducted with the Persian Gulf, the trades of Bagdad, Basra, and Oman centering at the island of Kis, and afterwards at Ormus on the Persian side, towards the entrance of the Gulf, owing to the difficult navigation of its upper portion. The trade was in fact carried on both by Persians and Arabs, and this fact will account for the number of Persian words intermixed with Arabic that are found in the Malay language. Of the settlement of the Arabs in the Archipelago, the earliest date we possess is that of the conversion of the Achinese to the Mahommedan religion, which is recorded to have happened in the year of the Hegira 601, corresponding with 1204 of Christ, or 353 years subsequent to the voyage of the earliest of the Mahommedan travellers. The progress of conversion through the rest of the Archipelago was gradual and slow. The Malays of Malacca were not converted until 1276, the inhabitants of the Moluccas not until 1465, the Javanese not until 1478, and the people of Celebes not until 1495, the year before Vasco de Gama passed the Cape of Good Hope, and only fourteen years before the discovery of the Archipelago by the Portuguese. With the exception of a few of the more southerly islands of the Philippine group, the inhabitants of the rest continued unconverted down to the arrival of the Spaniards in 1521.

The Arabs, unlike the Hindus, have imposed no names on places within the Archipelago, for their work was that of mere trade and propagandism. It is certain, however, that Arabian intercourse gave a great impetus to the civilisation of the inhabitants, and that Mahommedan merchants, of Arabian, Persian, and Indian origin, carried on trade in the waters of the Archipelago long before the arrival of the Portuguese. The Spaniards and Portuguese, in fact, seem to have been indebted to them for their first rough knowledge of the geography of the Archipelago—a knowledge, indeed, which they could not have acquired so early as they are found to have done, nor have acquired from any other source, since the native inhabitants could not supply it. Some examples are worth quoting: Ludovico Barthema, a native of Bologna, who states that he was at Cairo on his way to the East in 1503, and who, at all events, visited Malacca before its conquest by the Portuguese, describes it as situated on the mainland of Asia. He mentions Sumatra by its name, as it is now written, and is probably the first European that did so. He calls it an island and gives it an exaggerated circumference, and he refers to the strait which divides it from the continent, but underrates its breadth. He also names Borneo by its correct name of Burnai. This island he had visited, and he describes it as being by 200 miles larger than Sumatra. He also mentions Java, in a passage worth transcribing, from the curious account it renders of Mahommedan navigation. "Here" (in Borneo), says he, "my companion freighted a small vessel for a hundred ducats. Being provisioned we took our course towards the fine island (bella isola) of Giuva, where we arrived in five days, sailing southward. The master of the vessel carried a compass with magnet after our manner, and had a chart marked lengthwise and across with lines."—Ramusio, vol. i.

Barbosa, the most accurate and intelligent of all the early Portuguese travellers, gives not only the names of many places in the Archipelago, but describes also their productions. His narrative is dated 1516, but his travels evidently refer to a period some years previous to the conquest of Malacca and discovery of the Moluccas. He describes Malacca, which he had seen, with fidelity, and he names all the spice islands with their productions. His account of Sumatra is even surprisingly accurate, while he shows the source from which he derived it. "Having passed," says he, "the above-mentioned island (Navacar, Nicobar), there is a very great one called Sumatra, which is in circuit 700 leagues, equal to 2500 miles, as reckoned by the Moors who have sailed all round it. It runs north-west and south-east, and the equinoctial line passes through the middle of it." He mentions, moreover, several of the neighbouring countries, and nearly by the same names by which they are still known to Europeans, these names being unknown to the inhabitants themselves, although still employed by foreign Mahommedan nations. In this manner he gives us Pegu, Verma (Burma), Ternasseri (Tenasserim), Siam and China.—Ramusio, vol. i.

Pigafetta, the companion of Magellan, seems to have given to several of the

Philippine Islands the names by which they are still known, although still unknown to the native inhabitants, such as, Loson (Luson), Sebu (Çebu), Maingdano (Mindano), Solo (Sulu), Palaoan (Palawan). The surviving companions of Magellan were certainly the first Europeans that discovered Borneo, which Pigafetta writes correctly, Burné. "The island," says he, "is so large that it takes three months to sail round it in a prau," which it certainly would, since half the voyage must of necessity be performed against the monsoon. He gives their correct names to the five Molucca Islands, and to Amboyna, Buru, Buton, and Banda; and passing through the Archipelago in returning to Spain, he names Timur, Eude, Bali, Madura, and Java, and in the last of these islands names such places as Magepaher (Majapait), Dabadama (Damak), Cîpara (Japara), Tuban, Cressi (Garsik), and Cirubaïa (Surabaya). Pigafetta's knowledge of such of the Philippines as he had not visited, must have been obtained from the Mahommedan merchants whom he met at Cebu; and he states himself that his acquaintance with the Malayan islands was derived from the Mahommedan pilot furnished to the squadron by the King of Tidor. From all the facts now stated, there can be no question but that the Mahommedan merchants and navigators of the Archipelago were the parties who furnished the European nations with their earliest knowledge of its geography and history.

The Portuguese first entered the waters of the Archipelago in the year 1509, twelve years after the arrival of Vasco de Gama in Calicut, and must be looked upon as the real European discoverers of countries of which even the very names were unknown to the Europeans of antiquity or the middle ages. "The country and land of Malacha," says Barbosa, writing seven years only after the event, "was discovered by Lopez de Sequiera, a Portuguese gentleman." In 1511, the Portuguese reached Sumatra, conquered Malacca, and at length, in 1512, found their way to the Moluccas, the chief object of the long search of themselves and the Spaniards, and, in fact, the bait that led to the discovery of the New World. The great group of the Philippines was discovered by Magellan in 1521; but their occupation and conquest were not commenced until 1565. Down to Magellan's discovery, they had been unknown even by name to the western world, although the Malays and Javanese seem for ages to have traded with them, and even communicated to them a considerable portion of their languages. It is remarkable that even the Portuguese, after ten years' possession of Malacca, scarcely suspected the existence of countries that are hardly now five days' voyage from that place, and still nearer to the Moluccas. The Dutch, just freed from the yoke of Spain, made their first appearance in the Archipelago, under Houtman, in 1596, eighty-five eventful years after its discovery by the Portuguese. The English did not appear in it until 1602, six years later than the Dutch. Of these four nations, which have all obtained possessions, although of very unequal extent, by far the greatest benefit has been conferred on the native inhabitants by the Spaniards, who have converted the greater number of those they subdued to Christianity, and advanced the people thus converted in civilisation far beyond what they found them. The dominion of the Portuguese has been nearly extinguished for above two centuries, and has left little valuable trace behind it. All the four nations, for three long centuries, acting on a false and rapacious commercial theory, in so far as that theory is concerned, may safely be said to have marred instead of promoting the industry and civilisation of the native inhabitants; and it is only within the present century that a wiser and more generous policy, not fully carried out by some of the parties even now, has been adopted.

ARECA. The Areca catechu, a slender graceful palm, is an object of extensive culture in all tropical India, and grows freely in all the islands, from Sumatra to the Philippines, in which it seems to have as many distinct names as there are languages. Thus in Malay it is called Pinang, in Javanese Jambi, in Bali Banda, in Bugis Rapo, and in Tagala and Bisaya Bongo. Judging by this, the probability is that the tree is indigenous in each country. With a tolerably attentive culture, and in a suitable soil, it bears in about six years, and yields about a hundred nuts. Thus prolific and easily reared, the produce is cheap. Like tea, coffee, and tobacco, the areca would seem to stimulate the nervous system, and hence, probably, its general use. In the fresh or green state it is an object of general domestic consumption, and in the dry, of large exportation to China and India. The most productive countries in this article are the northern and southern coasts of Sumatra, towards its western extremity.

ARJUNA. The name of one of the heroes of the Hindoo poem of the Mahabarat, one of the five sons of Pandu, a personage familiar in the legends of the Malays and Javanese.

ARJUNA (GUNUNG). The name of one of the highest mountains of Java, reckoned to be 11,500 feet above the level of the sea, with an active volcano. It lies between the provinces of Surubaya to the north, Pasuruhan and Malang to the east, Rawa to the south, and Kadiri to the west. South latitude 7° 48′, and east longitude 112° 35′.

ARMS; in Malay and Javanese, Sânjata, a word found in the language of all the civilised nations as far as the Philippines. The earliest weapons of the Indian islanders, after clubs, were most likely spears, for which their almost universal forests would yield a ready supply. The inhabitants of the island of Matan, scarcely exceeding an area of two leagues and a half, who defeated and slew the first circum-navigator of the globe, with his band of sixty Spanish cavaliers, were armed with hardly any other weapons than wooden or cane spears sharpened and hardened in the fire, with wooden bucklers. The spear is still a favourite weapon with all the tribes of the Archipelago. The Javanese use spears from twelve to fourteen feet long, but shorter ones, or javelins, for throwing, are occasionally employed. The common name for the first is tumbak, and for the last lâmbing; but these names do not extend to the Philippine Islands.—The sling, in Malay ali-ali, and in Japanese bandring, although well known, seems never to have been much used. The chief missile in use before the introduction of fire-arms, was a small arrow ejected from a blow-pipe by the breath, called a Sumpitan, meaning the object blown through. This instrument is at present in general use by most of the wild tribes of Sumatra, Borneo, and Celebes.—The bow for discharging arrows is well known to all the more advanced nations of the Archipelago, but does not seem, at any time, to have been generally employed, the blow-pipe probably superseding its use, although a far less effectual weapon. It is found represented on the sculptures of some of the ancient monuments of Java, of the 12th and 13th centuries. The common name for it, panah, extends over the whole of the islands; and, it is remarkable, is found in the language of the Tonga Islands, but in no other dialect of the Polynesian tongue. But of all weapons, the greatest favourite of the Malayan nations is the kris, the native word for a dagger or poniard. Men of all ranks wear one, and men of rank two, and even three and four when full dressed, the quality of the party being shown by the richness of the hilt, scabbard, and belt. The preference given to the kris over the more effectual sword had most probably its origin in the high price of iron in early times, and when there was no supply from abroad. In such times, a kris manufacturer, called a pande, cutler or blacksmith, was in Java a person of distinction, as the same artificer is represented to have been in the Ossianic poems, and the names of several have been handed down by tradition. The word kris belongs equally to the Malay and Javanese, and is to be found in the languages of all the more advanced nations, expressing the same object, with the exception of those of the Philippines, in which it means "a sword," in the corrupted form of kalis. In some of the languages, however, as the Javanese, there are other names for it, and especially names to designate the different forms which it takes. It is not found represented on the more ancient and better temples of Java, but is seen in the ruder ones of the 14th century. The sword is said to have been introduced about the year 1580, which is near 70 years after the Portuguese conquest of Malacca. It is found, whenever represented, on the best and most ancient monuments of Java; but as the sculptures of these represent only the legends of a foreign mythology, the fact cannot be adduced as evidence of its use as a weapon. Yet on the first arrival of Europeans, the Malayan nations had a tolerably active intercourse with the more advanced nations of the west, and even with the Chinese and Japanese, who would not have failed to introduce the sword had there been any demand for it. (See SWORD.) Bucklers were largely used by the Malayan nations before the introduction of fire-arms, and in the Malay language there are no fewer than eight names for them, sometimes synonymes, and sometimes expressing their different forms.

De Barros enumerates the different weapons generally used by the Malays of Malacca when it was attacked by Alboquerque. "They consisted," he says, "of daggers of from two spans and a half to three spans long, straight in the blade and two-edged (the kris), bows and arrows, blow-pipes, which discharged very small arrows, barbed and poisoned, with short spears for throwing, and bucklers of two kinds, the one short, and the other long enough to protect the whole body of the wearer." Barbosa says that the Malays of Malacca obtained arms from Java. "They" (the Javanese), says he, "bring many arms for sale, such as lances, bucklers, and swords (krises), having hilts wrought in marqueterie, and blades of the finest steel."—Ramusio, vol. i.

But besides the arms thus enumerated, the Portuguese and Spaniards, when they first arrived, found the most advanced of the Malayan nations in possession of fire-arms. This is De Barros' account of the artillery captured by Alboquerque in Malacca. "And of artillery," says he, "we found no more than 3000 out of 8000 pieces, which Ruy de 'Arajo (a prisoner of Sequiera's fleet) had stated to be in the city. Among those taken were many of great size (muy grossas), and one very beautiful piece which the King of Calicut had lately sent."—Book vi. c. 2. De Barros incidentally mentions the existence of match-locks in the defence of Malacca. The Portuguese had manned a captured junk with cannon, and sent her forward to batter the defences of a bridge, and this is his account of the action which took place: "As soon as the junk had passed the sand-bank and had come to an anchor, a short way from the bridge, the Moorish artillery opened a fire on her. Some guns discharged leaden balls at intervals, which passed through both sides of the vessel, doing much execution among the crew. In the heat of the action Antonio d'Abreu, the commander, was struck in the cheek from a fusil (espingardão), carrying off the greater number of his teeth." The son of Alboquerque, in his Commentaries, is still fuller on the subject of the captured artillery and the weapons of defence used by the Malays. "There were captured," says he, "3000 pieces, of which 2000 were of brass, and the rest of iron. Among them there was one large piece sent by the King of Calicut to the King of Malacca. All the artillery with its appurtenances was of such workmanship that it could not be excelled, even in Portugal. There were found also match-locks (espingardão), blow-pipes for shooting poisoned arrows, bows and arrows, lances of Java, and divers other arms, all which created surprise in those that captured them."—Commentarios do grande Afonso d'Alboquerque; Lisboa, 1576. The greater number most likely consisted of the small pieces called by the natives rantaka or hand-guns. Castanheda also mentions match-locks (espingardão), and while he reduces the captured cannon to 2000, he says that they threw balls, some of stone, and some of iron covered with lead. The cannon (bombardia) were some of them of brass and some of iron. By his account the bridge, the chief scene of combat in the storm of Malacca, was defended by seventy-two pieces of ordnance. In Borneo, the companions of Magellan found cannon, and Pigafetta thus alludes to them: "In front of the king's residence there is a rampart built of large brick, having barbicans in the manner of a fortress, and on it were planted sixty-two pieces of cannon (bombarde), fifty-six of brass, and six of iron. During the two days we passed in the city they were often discharged."—Primo viaggio intorno al mondo. Cannon had reached even as far as the Philippines. Magellan, indeed, did not find them in Çebu; on the contrary, the natives were astonished and terrified at the sound of those discharged from the admiral's ship in compliment to them. When, however, Legaspi discovered the main island of Luson, he not only found cannon, but a foundry of them at Manilla and Tondo in that island, the knowledge of fire-arms having been introduced by the Mahommedan Malayan nations of the west, along with their religion.

The name by which fire-arms are usually called is bâdil, a general one for any missile, and mariam, which is Arabic and in that language signifies "the Virgin Mary," which would seem to imply that the knowledge of artillery was derived by the Arabs themselves from the Christians, as without doubt it was. Smaller ordnance are called by various names, such as rantaka, lela, &c. &c. &c. The native term bâdil extends to the languages of all the more cultivated nations, although sometimes corrupted, as in the example of the Philippine tongues, in which it is pronounced baril. The Arabic name, mariam, is also of general acceptance. The name of the match-lock is satingar, a corruption of the Portuguese espingardão, and the fire-lock is called sânapang, a corruption of the Dutch snappaan.

A knowledge of gunpowder must have been, at least, as early in the Indian islands as that of cannon. It is not improbable that it may have been even earlier known through the Chinese, for the manufacture of fire-works, known to the Malays under the name of mârchun, a word of which the origin is not traceable. The principal ingredients of gunpowder are sufficiently abundant over many parts of the Archipelago, and known by native names, sândawa being the name of saltpetre, and bâlirang, or walirang, of sulphur. The names for gunpowder itself are a little singular. In Malay it is called ubat-bâdil, which literally means "missile-charm:" in Javanese it is ubat, or "charm" alone.

The parties who introduced the knowledge of fire-arms among the Malayan nations cannot be mistaken. They were certainly the Mahommedan nations of Western Asia, and most probably the Arabs. Cannon were in full use by European nations for military purposes in the middle of the 14th century, and nearly at the same time by the Arabs of Spain, who had a frequent intercourse with their eastern countrymen, and these, at the time, with the Oriental nations as far as China. Between the time when cannon were in general use in Europe and the first appearance of the Portuguese in the Archipelago, a century and a half had elapsed, ample time for the transmission of the new invention to the Malayan nations, and even to China, where also it was, most probably, first made known by the Arabs. The earliest reliable date which we possess of the use of artillery in continental India is the year 1482, when Mahommed Shah, King of Gujrat, employed cannon in a fleet during a war with pirates. In such cases the cannoniers are stated to have been Turks and Europeans. This seems to have been the case even after the arrival of Europeans; for in the great battle which secured to Babar the possession of Northern India, it is represented by the historian Farishta, that "he ordered his park of artillery to be linked together with leathern ropes made of raw hides, according to the practice of the armies of Asia Minor." On the arrival of the Portuguese on the western coast of India, they found all the maritime nations, whether under Mahommedan or Hindu rule, in possession of fire-arms, and employing them both on land and sea, and they found the same to be the case from the Arabian to the Persian Gulf. The handsomest piece of ordnance captured by them at Malacca, as has been already stated, had been a gift to the Malay prince from the King of Calicut, the Hindu prince called by the Portuguese the Zamorin. Of the actual year in which fire-arms were first made known to the inhabitants of the Archipelago there is no record, but, considering the frequent intercourse which subsisted between them and the maritime parts of Western India, we may safely conclude that the event did not take place earlier than fifty years before the arrival of the Portuguese, that is, about the middle of the fifteenth century, or about a century after they had been in common use in Europe.

On the first arrival of the Portuguese in the Archipelago, the Javanese appear to have been the great manufacturers of arms of all descriptions. De Barros, in rendering an account of an expedition of 12,000 men, which the Javanese sent against Malacca after its possession by the Portuguese, says that it was provided "with much artillery made in Java; for the Javanese are skilled in founding or casting, and in all works in iron, over and above what they have from India." At present a regular manufacture of cutting weapons, match-locks and cannon, is carried on by the Malays of Banjarmassin in Borneo, and this with a skill surprising for their state of society. As this part of Borneo was long subject to the Javanese, it seems probable that it was this people that introduced the art. For many generations the Malays of Menangkabo have been the manufacturers of all kinds of arms for Sumatra. But the skilful manufacture of arms is by no means confined to these places, and I have myself seen match-locks in Bali, with twisted barrels, inlaid all over in very good taste with gold and silver.

AROE. The correct name is Pulo-Aräu, that is "the islands of the Cassuarina trees." These form a chain of islets 100 miles in length and 50 in breadth, lying off the south-western coast of New Guinea, and having a computed area of 1040 geographical square miles. The western side of the chain, viewed from sea, presents the appearance of a single low island with numerous small openings, which more closely examined are found to be several islands, straits dividing them from each other, and which occasionally widen into broad sheets of water, connected by narrow gorges, producing eddies and whirlpools dangerous to native vessels. The islands are low throughout, on the western side hardly rising above the level of the sea, with the exception of a few hummocks of lime-stone, some 15 or 20 feet high. The Aroes are of lime-stone formation, and the land which rises towards their eastern side abounds in caverns, the resort of the swallow furnishing the esculent nest. They are, as usual, covered with tall trees, among which the most prominent is the cassuarina, which gives them name. The native inhabitants are of a quasi-negro race, and said to bear more resemblance to the northern tribes of Australia than to the Papuas of New Guinea. They would seem to have acquired a larger measure of civilisation than any other tribe of the insular negros. But besides the Aborigines, many strangers, Malays, Javanese, and natives of Celebes and the Moluccas, are settled in the islands. The total population, although we have no actual enumeration, has been computed at 80,000. The agriculture of the Aroes is confined to the culture of maiz, yams, the sago-palm, and some fruits; but sago is not much in use, the people being well supplied with rice from Java and Celebes, in the course of trade. The products of their fisheries are what give importance to the Aroes. A bank extending along the whole eastern coast is rich in the shell-tortoise, two kinds of mother-of-pearl shells, and in pearl oysters, with the tripang or holothurion. The principal port is Dobbo, near the north-western extremity of the chain of islands, in south latitude 5° 45′ 45″, and east longitude 134° 20′, where, in the season, may be seen, 100 small square-rigged vessels and large native craft with Chinese junks, bringing rice, cotton goods, and necessaries, with Batavian arrack, to exchange for the produce of the fisheries, and for loories and cockatoos with birds of paradise, of which these islands furnish the chief supply.

ARRACK; in Arabic Arăk, ardent spirit. Most probably the Arabs taught the Indian islanders, as they did the nations of Europe, the art of distillation. From Sumatra to the Philippines the one name for spirits is this Arabian one. The art might, indeed, have been introduced by the Chinese, who have immemorially possessed it, but there is no evidence that this was the case. The name for a still or alembic in Malay and Javanese is Kukusan; from the Javanese kukus, smoke or steam; but this composed word is no evidence of original invention. The Javanese have an intoxicating beverage, exclusive of the sap of palms, called brâm, prepared from the fermentation of rice, but this is a beer and not the produce of distillation. The fine arrack of Batavia is an invention and manufacture of the Chinese, of which the materials are boiled rice, molasses, and palm wine.

ARSENIC; is known by a native name, but is not a native product. It was probably brought to the islands originally from Siam and Burma, of which it is a product. Orpiment, or the sulphuret, goes under the name of Warangan, or barangan, and the epithet putih or "white" is added for the white oxide. Warangan is derived from Warang, which means the process of applying a compound, of which orpiment is a main ingredient, to a kris blade in order to preserve it. Arsenic is the only poison used by the Indian islanders for assassination, but even this very rarely, the kris being the means generally had recourse to.

ARTOCARPUS. Of this genus of plants three are cultivated in the Indian islands—the bread-fruit, the jack, and the champâda. The bread-fruit, Artocarpus integrifolia, is known to the Malays by the three different native names of sukun, kluwi, and tâmbul, and is probably an indigenous plant. As an article of food, however, it is held in no esteem, and the varieties cultivated are greatly inferior to that of the South Sea Islands. The jack, Artocarpus incisa, is extensively cultivated throughout the Archipelago, and its name, Nangka, extends all the way to the Philippines. Rumphius justly concludes that it is only a corruption of the Tamil or Malaylam word Jaka, which we have ourselves adopted with less change. The jack fruit grows occasionally to the weight of 70 lbs., and is then a good load for a woman going to market. It is rather an article of food than a fruit. The tree attains the height of 40 or 50 feet, and its yellow close-grained timber is a handsome fancy wood.

The Champada is a smaller fruit than the jack, but more delicate in flavour, and far more esteemed. It is exclusively a native of the Archipelago, and chiefly of Sumatra and the peninsula.

ASAHAN. The native name is Asäan, and it most probably means "place of hope," from the Sanscrit word Asa, hope, in frequent use with the Malays. It is the name of a river and Malay state on the north-eastern side of Sumatra. The river has its source in a mountain range and plateau called Tubah, in the country of the Bataks, and falls into the Straits of Malacca in north latitude 3° 1′ 30″, and east longitude 99° 52′. At its mouth it is about 1600 yards wide, but seven miles further up, where it receives a tributary called the Silau (dazzling), it narrows to one-third of this breadth. Fronting its embouchure there is an extensive mud flat, and at low water spring tides, the depth in the channel of the river itself does not exceed two fathoms. The lower portion of the country is part of the extensive alluvial plain which runs along nearly the whole eastern side of Sumatra, and is covered with a tangled and almost impenetrable forest, containing the usual wild animals of the island. The ruling people of Asahan are Malays, but much mixed with the nation of the Bataks. The cultivated corns are rice and pulses. The sea and rivers are replete with excellent fish, which form, unless occasionally, the chief animal food of the inhabitants. The exports consist of pulses, lakka a red dye-wood, bees'-wax, horses, and slaves usually Bataks, young women selling at 40*s*., children at 20*s*., and men at from 12*s*. to 15*s*. A prince of Menangkabo, the supposed original seat of the Malay nation, was the founder of the present principality of Asahan, and the prince who ruled the country in 1822 was the seventh in descent from him, which in the usual mode of reckoning would not carry us farther back than 110 years. Many ages before this, according to the tradition of the natives, a Javanese colony had settled in Asahan, and 70 miles up the river there are still to be seen the ruins of a fortress which goes by this name, Kuta-jawa.

ASS. This quadruped is wholly unknown to the inhabitants of the Indian islands, except by name. It goes in their writings under the name of Kâlda, which may be a corruption of the Persian Khăr, or possibly of the Indian Gâddah, for it is not traceable to any Arabic name.

ASTINA, and ASTINAPURA, is the Sanscrit name of the country of the Pandus in the poem of the Mahabarat, of which the Javanese have a paraphrase. These have transferred the locality from Upper India to the province of Pakalongan in their own island, as they have done to other places other scenes of this poem, and of the Ramayana. The name of Astina is also familiar in the legendary writings of the Malays.

AUSTRALIA. The northern coast of this continent is alone known to the natives of the Archipelago, and among these only to the Macassars of Celebes and the gipsy Malays, who frequent it yearly for the fishery of the tripang or holothurion. This they seem to have done so for ages, although seen there for the first time by Flinders in the beginning of the present century. Of the time when this fishery first commenced there is, of course, no record, but it is certain it could not have been before the first arrival of the Chinese, since these are the only people that consume the tripang, and still the only parties who furnish funds for carrying on the fishery.

AVERRHÖA. There are two species of this fruit tree cultivated in the Archipelago; the blimbing-bâsi, or iron blimbing, possibly from the rusty colour of its coat, and the blimbing-manis or sweet blimbing. The first is the Averrhoa blimbi, and the second, the Averrhoa carambola of botanists. The fruit of both, growing strangely from the trunk of the tree, is acid or sub-acid, and little esteemed.

AWAR (PULO); vulgarly Pulo Aôr or Awar Island (Awar being the name of a large species of bamboo). It is the most southerly of a chain of islets lying off the eastern coast of the Malay peninsula, and distant from it 30 miles. Pulo Awar, a mass of granite, is about 3 miles long and 1½ broad. It has two peaked mountains, one 1521 feet and the other 1852 feet high. The inhabitants, amounting to 1400, are Malays; and, whatever their character in former times, have, since the establishment of a commercial intercourse with Singapore, become peaceable traders and industrious fishermen. The only article cultivated by them is the coco-nut palm, which grows luxuriantly even as high as 1000 feet above the level of the sea. The nuts and their expressed oil are exported to Singapore to be exchanged for rice, clothing, and other necessaries. The island is subject to the Raja of Pahang, himself nominally subject to the Raja of Jehore. It is the landmark of shipping in taking a departure from and making the Straits of Malacca. North latitude 2° 30′, east longitude 104° 35′.

AYAR, is the Malay word for water, and sometimes for a river, and consequently for a district seated on a river. Adopted by the Javanese it becomes er, and it is most probably the same word that we find corrupted in the language of Celebes into we, and in Polynesian into wai. Of places having this word combined with another, we have at least a score in our maps and charts, as Ayar-itam, black water or river; Ayar-dâkat, near river; Ayar-bâsar, great river; Pulo-ayar, water island; and Pulo-we, which we write Pulo-way, having the same meaning.

B.

BA. A town of the island of Mindano, in the territory of the Sultan or independent Mahommedan chief. It is said to be situated on the left bank of a certain river, where it joins one which issues from the Lake of Ligassin, when the united streams take a north-western diversion, disemboguing in the Bay of Bongo, lying on the eastern side of the great bay of Llano, on the southern side of the island. The town is in north latitude 5° 1′ 40″, and east longitude 124° 34′.

BABI, the hog (Sus). In all likelihood originally a Malay word, but introduced into all the advanced languages, even into some, as the Javanese and Sunda, which have native terms besides. From Sumatra to the Moluccas it occurs frequently as the name of small islands, imposed most probably by Malayan navigators, and from some fancied resemblance in form to the animal.

BABI (PULO), "Hog Islands," a cluster on the western coast of Sumatra, consisting of one large island about 60 miles in length and from 10 to 15 in breadth, with an area of 480 square miles, and a number of small ones, the northern end of the larger island being in north latitude 2° 50′, and east longitude 95° 32′. The name given to the larger island by the Malays is Simalu, that is "Shame or modesty island," and to the inhabitants of the whole group, on what account I do not know, Maros or Maruwe. These speak a peculiar language, and have been converted to the Mahommedan religion. The chief products are coco-nuts and buffalos.

BABUYANES. A group of volcanic islets lying off the extreme northern end of Luzon. The largest of these are Calayan, and Babuyan which gives name to the whole, is only the second in extent. After it follow Carmiguin, Dalupiri, and Tuga, the others being mere islets. The whole group abounds in hogs, and is supposed to take its name from this circumstance. The Malay word Babi is pronounced in the Philippine languages Babuy, as it is written in the Spanish orthography. Babuyan means "place of hogs," and with a Spanish plural we have Babuyanes. These islands are liable to terrific hurricanes at the equinoxes, and being surrounded by shoals are difficult of approach. They form a part of the province of Batangas in Luzon.

BABUYAN, called by the Spaniards Claro Babuyan, the second island in magnitude of the above group, is in length three leagues, in breadth about two, and has an area of five square leagues. The centre of the island is in north latitude 19° 34′, and in east longitude 122° 51′.

BACHIAN, written more correctly by the Dutch Batjan, and in the orthography of this work Bachan, is one of the five original Molucca or Clove Islands, and the most southerly of them. Like the other four, it is of volcanic formation. Its area is 800 square geographical miles. Its most easterly point is in south latitude 48′ 30″, and longitude 127° 54′. Of late, fossil coal has been discovered in this island, stated to be of good quality.

BACOLOR. The name of an estuary at the north-western angle of the great bay of Manilla, into which falls a river of the same name.

BACOLOR. The chief town of the province of Pampanga, in the island of Luzon, in north latitude 18° 13′, and east longitude 120° 32′; distant ten miles from Manilla. It lies in a fertile plain, on the left bank of a river of the same name, where a brook called the Gogo falls into it. It has a population of 8737, of which 1298 are assessed to the capitation-tax. The place has some reputation in the annals of the Philippines, on account of the gallant stand made at it by Don Simon de Andé y Salazar, against the English invaders of 1762, the latter assisted by Chinese and insurgent Indians.

BADONG. A principality of the island of Bali, occupying its most southern part, and said to have a population of 130,000. In a commercial view, it is the most important state of the island. See BALI.

BAGLEN. A central province of Java, having Bañumas to the west, Pakalongan to the north, Mataram to the east, and the Southern Ocean to the south. This fine province, ceded by the native princes to the Dutch in 1830, has an area of 923 square miles; and, in 1850, had a population of 528,718, of which 238 were Europeans, 342 Arabs and other foreign Asiatic Mahommedans, 1594 Chinese, and six slaves. Its horned cattle amount to 120,000, and its horses to 9000.

BAGU, in Malay; and Wagu, in Javanese; the *Gnemium gnetum* of botanists, a tree of the fibrous bark, of which a coarse cordage is made, in extensive use by the natives of the Archipelago.

BAJAU. This is one of the most frequent of several names given to wandering maritime Malays, of gipsy manners, and from whose questionable habits, the word has become a synonyme for pirate. Some of this people have fixed dwellings on the sea-coast; and others have no other habitations than the boats, in which they are born, live, and die. All are fishermen, engaged in taking ordinary esculent fish, or the shell turtle, the tripang, the mother-of-pearl and pearl oyster. All speak the Malay language, although rude and various dialects of it. Many of them have embraced the Mahommedan religion; their observance of its tenets, however, being for the most part confined to submitting to circumcision, and abstaining from the flesh of swine.

The Bajaus are found on most of the coasts of the islands of the Archipelago, from

Sumatra to New Guinea and the Moluccas; their fishing voyages occasionally extending even to the northern coast of Australia. The various names which they bear have sometimes a reference to their habits or origin. Among the numerous islands at the eastern end of the Straits of Malacca, and on the opposite coast of Borneo, they are called Orang-lant, literally "men of the sea;" sometimes Orang-rayah, "men of plunder;" and also Rayat, which is the Arabic word for "subjects," meaning, no doubt, subjects of the kingdom of Jehor. On the south-eastern coast of the Peninsula, they go under the name of Orang-jehor, or men of the country or kingdom of Jehor. In Borneo they are called Sika, the meaning of which I do not know. The Macassars of Celebes call them Tau-ri-jene, which is but a translation of the Malay name, "men of the sea." The Bugis of the same island it is that have given them the name of Bajau, or, as they pronounce the word, Waju, and which is said to signify "men that go in troops." The Javanese call them Wong-kambang, or "floating people;" and among the Moluccas they are distinguished from the aboriginal inhabitants by the name of Orang Malayu, or Malays. Always speaking the Malay language, and always fishermen, we naturally seek for the origin of this people where the Malay language is indigenous, and where manners like theirs prevail; and as these conditions exist only in the more southern portion of the eastern coast of Sumatra, from the river of Palembang to that of Siak, we may reasonably fix on this as the parent country, not only of the gipsy Malays, but also of the more advanced tribes of the same nation, whose fortune, in placing them in more auspicious localities, enabled them to attain a higher civilisation, such as the agricultural Malays of the interior of Sumatra. See MALAY.

BAKA. The name of an ancient king of Java, said by tradition to have reigned at Brambanan, and to have built the temples of that place, except Boro-budor, the most remarkable of all the Hindu ruins of Java. If this account be true, the antiquity of the temples is not great, for to the earliest, the date given is 1266, or about 30 years before Marco Polo passed through the Archipelago.

BALABAC. One of the Sulu islands, about midway between Borneo and Palawan, and 60 miles distant from the former. The island is about 15 miles long and 10 broad, with an area of 420 geographical square miles, and its centre is in north latitude 8°, and east longitude 114° 40′. On its eastern side there is a bay, called Dalawan, which affords shelter to shipping. Little more than these naked facts is known about it.

BALABALAGA. The name of a group of islands in mid-channel between Borneo and Celebes, or Straits of Macassar, estimated to contain in all about 96 square geographical miles.

BALACHONG. This is the name of a condiment made of prawns, sardines, and other small fish, pounded and pickled. The proper Malay word is bâlachan, the Javanese trasi, and the Philippine bagon. This article is of universal use as a condiment, and one of the largest articles of native consumption throughout both the Malay and Philippine Archipelago. It is not confined, indeed, as a condiment to the Asiatic islanders, but is also largely used by the Birmese, the Siamese, and Cochin-Chinese. It is, indeed, in great measure essentially the same article known to the Greeks and Romans under the name of garum, the produce of a Mediterranean fish.

BALAMBANGAN, correctly Blâmbangan. The word blâmbang, in Malay, means a plank cut from a palm; and the name, therefore, signifies "place of palm-planks." The island is situated in the Sulu Sea, and distant from the most northerly point of Borneo 13 miles. Its most northern extremity is in north latitude 7° 3′, and east longitude 116° 50′. Its greatest length is about five leagues, its greatest breadth about one, and its circumference about 300 miles. The land is hilly, without any mountain of considerable elevation. To the south-east it is divided from the larger island of Banguey by a strait, at one point not exceeding a league in breadth. On this strait Balambangan has two harbours, the northern in latitude 7° 16′, and longitude 116° 58′, but both difficult of access on account of shoals. The sovereign that laid claim to this island, the Sultan of Sulu, ceded it to the English in 1762, as a reward for liberating him from his captivity at Manilla. In 1775, it was taken possession of by the East India Company; but soon after, the garrison and establishment were driven out by a marauding party of the donor's subjects. In 1803, it was again taken possession of, but speedily and justly abandoned on an experience of its worthlessness; for the island is itself sterile, uninhabited, and in the most piratical and barbarous neighbourhood of the whole Archipelago.

BALAMBUANG. Name of a deep and well-sheltered bay in the province of Banyuwangi, in Java, on the strait which divides that island from Bali. This place was in former times frequented by shipping; but, on account of its insalubrity, abandoned for Banyuwangi on the same strait.

BALANGUINI. One of the Sulu islands, but claimed by Spain as part of the province of Zamboanga, in the island of Mindano. It lies in north latitude 5° 57′ 30″, and east longitude 121° 39′, and between two other islets somewhat larger than itself, called Samusa and Parul. Its length is about a league, and its breadth a quarter of a league. This small spot gives name to the most daring and enterprising pirates of the Archipelago. In 1848, it was attacked and captured by a Spanish force of 650 infantry and artillery, with a squadron of three war-steamers and sixteen smaller armed vessels, under the governor-general of the Philippines; and the resistance made will show the formidable character of these pirates. The Spaniards had 1 officer and 20 men killed, and 10 officers and 150 men wounded. They stormed four redoubts, captured 124 cannon, mostly of small calibre, and burnt 150 praus. 450 of the enemy were killed, refusing to take quarter; 200 captives were rescued from slavery. The forts and the houses of the inhabitants were levelled to the ground, and in order to make the place uninhabitable, the coco-palms were cut down to the number of between 7000 and 8000. This was the most signal punishment ever inflicted on Malayan pirates by an European power.

BALI. The next island east of Java, and divided from it by a strait not exceeding a mile and a half broad. The name in Malay and Javanese signifies "to return," but how or why imposed is unknown. It is situated between south latitude 8° 3′ 30″, and east longitudes 114° 26′ and 115° 40′. Its greatest length is 74 geographical miles, and its greatest breadth 50. Its area is estimated at 1685 square geographical miles, so that it is about one twenty-second part only of the extent of Java, and not superior in size to some provinces of the latter. Its form is triangular, narrowing to the south, where it forms an attenuating projection. Its western side runs nearly due east and west. With the exception of a few calcareous ridges, its whole formation is volcanic. A chain of volcanic mountains, seemingly a continuation of that of Java, runs through it from west to east, leaving plains and valleys north and south of it of more or less extent. The mountain chain is of great elevation, commonly from 4000 to 10,000 feet. That called in our charts the Peak of Bali, in the language of the country Gunung-agung, or the great mountain, attains the height of 12,379 feet above the level of the sea, which makes it 433 feet higher than the Peak of Teneriffe. One mountain of the chain, called Batur, 6168 feet high, is an active volcano. From another there was a destructive eruption in 1804; and from a third, a more calamitous one in November, 1815, or within seven months after the memorable one of Tambora in the island of Sumbawa. Bali has many small rivers, navigable however for native vessels only, and as far as the reach of the tide. In respect to its supply of water, its most remarkable feature is its mountain lakes, situated at an elevation of several thousand feet. The most extensive of these are as much as 12 miles in circumference, and all are of great depth, some of them of 40 and 50 fathoms, and some of from 300 to 400. These lakes from their position afford a perennial supply of water, easily applied, even by a rude people, to irrigation, and they are the main cause of the extensive culture of corn, and hence of the great population of Bali, despite barbarism and misgovernment. The mountain lakes of Bali may in part, on a small scale, be compared to the lakes of Lombardy and Piedmont in reference to irrigation, and the fertility of which it is the result.

The plants of Bali, with the exception of a small number peculiar to itself, are the same as those of Java. Those which form the chief objects of cultivation, are rice, maiz, pulses, cotton, tobacco, and the fruits of Java. Recently coffee has been cultivated in the mountains, but the quality, probably from unskilful growth, is inferior. As to the Fauna, the tiger is found only in the western part of the island, opposite to Java. The elephant, the rhinoceros, the tapir, are all wanting; and the only wild animals of considerable size are the hog and some deer. The domestic animals are the ox and buffalo, both of them large and numerous; the hog very numerous; and the goat, with abundant poultry consisting of the common fowl and duck.

The Balinese are of the same race of man as the Malays and Javanese, and indeed, but for some difference of costume, it would be difficult to distinguish one of these nations from another. Some, however, have fancied that the Balinese are more athletic than the Javanese, which as they are more amply fed is probable. As to the amount of the population, all accounts of it can be no better than estimates. One reporter, a native of the Archipelago, who had lived among them, makes it 2,000,000; a Dutch authority, in 1818, above 900,000; while Baron Melvill De Camebée reduces it to no more than 700,000, which may be accepted as by far the most likely. Even this makes the relative population half again as much as that of Java, or near 480 to the square mile, being the greatest density of population throughout the whole Malayan and Philippine islands.

The Balinese live in villages of from 500 to 3000 inhabitants, surrounded by walls built of clay, without stone or brick. Within these walls are their dwelling-houses, or rather huts, with their clay-built walls and roofs thatched with grass or palm-leaves,—their temples, their stables, their granaries, and their pig-sties. In civilisation, the Balinese are among the most advanced of the nations of the Archipelago. Their agriculture is said to be superior to that of Java, otherwise the best of the Archipelago; their manufacture of arms, including fire-arms, is tasteful and comparatively skilful, and their textile fabrics from cotton are substantial and cheap. They have (in the Javanese character, however) a written language of their own, divided into an ancient or theological, a vulgar, and a ceremonial dialect; but they are ignorant of the manufacture of paper, which the Javanese had acquired before their intercourse with Arabs or Europeans, and their manuscripts are scratched on slips of palm-leaf. They have, moreover, a coined money, such as the Javanese possessed before their acquaintance with Europeans, and they possess a calendar and an epoch, the Indian one of Salivana beginning 78 years after Christ. The Balinese dress is a striped or tartan cotton cloth, in the shape of a sack open at both ends; this secured at the top with a girdle or careless knot, covers the lower part of the body, leaving the upper stark naked with both sexes,—a barbarism, at least in the costume of women, unknown to the Malays and proper Javanese, although occasionally to be seen among the lower orders of the Sundas. The hair of the head is cropped with the lower orders, but preserved by the upper, who tie it in a knot at the crown, and this is a mark of distinction strictly maintained. Neither of them wear any kind of head-dress, whether men or women; nor have they shoes or sandals.

The Balinese are a home-keeping people, which may be ascribed to their being more an agricultural, and less a maritime and piscatory race than any other nation of the Archipelago. The few strangers settled among them are Malays, Javanese, mestizo Arabs, and Chinese. The government is rude and arbitrary, making small account of the persons and property of the lower classes, confiscating the last without scruple, and condemning to death or slavery the first. Some degree of security to the middle and upper classes must, however, exist to have brought about the degree of industry which is certainly found to exist. A country cannot be utterly lawless where, on a comparatively small spot, food is raised to support 700,000 people, and which yields a surplus for above 100,000 more. The trade of the island is more considerable than might have been expected, but it is, in a good measure, the creation of recent years. The exports consist of rice, said to amount yearly to 20,000 tons, of pulses, oil, cotton-wool, and cotton fabrics, tobacco, and coffee. The imports are iron and English cotton cloths. The trade is chiefly with Singapore, Java, and, recently, with our Australian colonies.

The Hindu religion which once prevailed, to a greater or less extent, among all the more advanced nations of the Archipelago, and which was extinguished among the most considerable of them, the Javanese, in the year 1478 of Christ, at present exists only in Bali, and in a more partial degree in the neighbouring island of Lomboc. The Balinese are divided, as books divide the Hindus in their own country, into four great orders or castes: the priest, the soldier, the merchant, and the labourer, called respectively, with a slight corruption, by the Sanscrit names, Bramana, Satriya, Waisya, and Sudra. The Bramins are distinguished into those who perform the offices of the priesthood, called Ida, and those who are Bramins by lineage but do not engage in the functions of the priesthood, and have the title of Dewa, that is "Gods." The Satriya, or military order, is more generally known by the title of Gusti, which is a Balinese and also a Javanese word, meaning "a lord." The third order or Waisya comprises not only traders but such artisans as goldsmiths and cutlers; and the fourth, the Sudra, comprehends husbandmen, ordinary artisans, and slaves. The second order, of course, comprises the princes, and it is usually forbidden to the different orders to intermix; but it has happened, notwithstanding, that several of the rulers of Bali and Lomboc have risen to power from the third or mercantile order,—that is, from the middle class of society; and when such is the case, not much distinction is made between the second and third order. A Waisya prince may even happen to take a fancy for the daughter of a Bramin, when it becomes expedient that he should be gratified. Mr. Zollinger, in his interesting account of Lomboc, gives an example. The young raja of Mataram in that island, a Balinese, fell in love with the daughter of the chief dewa. In order to possess her, a friendly legal ceremony became necessary. The Bramin went through the form of expelling his daughter from his house, denouncing her as "a wicked daughter." By this she lost her rank as the daughter of a Bramin; but received into the raja's house, she became a Waisya, but at the same time a princess. The Balinese burn their dead; but as the ceremony is expensive, the poorer classes often bury them in the first instance, with the hope of having in time the means of disinterring the bones for cremation. The wealthy, like the Buddhist nations of Burma and Siam, embalm the corpse and keep it for weeks, or even months, before the rite of cremation is performed. The self-immolation of the widow is practised by the Balinese, with some difference from the practice of the Hindus of India. The suicide is most frequently practised by stabbing with the kris, when the body is afterwards thrown into the fire. The wives of the priests, or Bramins, never immolate themselves for their husbands, which is entirely conformable to the practice of India. The rite is most frequently performed with the military order; and with the princes, the sacrifice of two or three women is indispensable. On such occasions the practice is not confined to wives, for concubines and slaves may equally sacrifice themselves.

Of the time when, or the manner in which the Hindu religion was introduced into Bali, there is no record. There is sufficient evidence, however, to show that it was not directly introduced from India, and that no considerable number of Indian Hindus, possessed of much influence, were probably ever established in the island. We find in it, for example, no inscriptions, such as are found in Java, in the Sanscrit alphabet, or in the character in which it is usually written,—indeed no inscriptions at all ancient or modern. In Java, the presence of Hindus of influence is attested by the ruins of many fine temples,—monuments which it is safe to say that genuine Hindus alone could have built, since no monuments comparable to them have been constructed since the overthrow of their religion. The temples of Bali, instead of being like the ancient ones of Java, structures of solid masonry on a grand scale, are mere clay huts; nor are there the remains of any of a better description. On the other hand, not only the religion but much of the civilisation of Bali may be clearly traced to Java. Thus the sacred language of Bali, the Kawi, is the same as that of Java, existing in the latter island on inscriptions on stone bearing dates at least as far back as the 12th century of our time. The present religious writings of the Balinese are identical with the ancient ones of Java. As to civilisation, this is proved by a large infusion of the language of Java into the vulgar tongue of the Balinese,—by the ceremonial language of Bali being almost identical with that of Java, itself so peculiar in its construction; and finally, by the existing written character of Bali being the same, with the absence of two immaterial letters, with that now in use in Java. When I visited Bali in 1814, the priests informed me that they were the tenth in descent from certain Bramins of the sect of Siwa, who on the overthrow of the last Hindu state of Java in 1478, fled to Bali and established themselves there; but this is but a comparatively recent event.

Bali, small as is its extent, is divided into no fewer than eight independent principalities, namely, Baliling, Karang-asam, Klongkong, Tabanan, Bangli, Mangiri, Gyanjar, and Badong. Such a division of authority in a small island, and over which one language only is spoken, is sufficient proof of rudeness and unskilfulness far beyond the example of Java; which, although it certainly never existed under one rule, whether Hindu or Mahommedan, frequently possessed states of considerable extent and power.

BÂLILING, correctly **BLELENG**, one of the principalities of the island of Bali, embracing most of its northern coast, and computed to contain a population of 80,000.

BAMBOO (BAMBUSA); in Malay, Bulu; and in Javanese, Preng. The word Bamboo itself is said to belong to the Indian language of Canara, and to have been introduced into the languages of Europe by the Portuguese. Some species of this gigantic grass rise to the height of 70 and 80 feet. The bamboo is found throughout all the islands, both in the wild and cultivated state, and of many species. The various uses to which it is put are well known. The most important are in the construction of houses, of which it forms the rafters and floors; and in boat-building, of which it forms the masts, yards, and deck. It forms the handles of spears, and, must before the invention of iron, have formed the first weapons of offence and defence. The bamboo is still fashioned into utensils for holding both solids and liquids; and before the invention of pottery, was no doubt the material of the only vessels of the natives. The young shoots are used as a culinary vegetable like with us asparagus, but asparagus on a gigantic scale, for a distinguished botanist compares these shoots in appearance to the trunk of an elephant.

BANAJO. A volcanic mountain of the island of Luzon, supposed to be the highest peak of the Philippine Islands. It has a crater but no active volcano. The measurement of a Spanish officer makes its height 6534 English feet, so that it is not more than half the height of the highest peaks of Java, Bali, and Lomboc. It is part of the great Cordillera, and divides the province of the Laguna from those of Batangas and Tayabas.

BANANA (MUSA). This prolific fruit is found, wild and cultivated, in every considerable island from Sumatra to the Philippines inclusive, and of its being indigenous there can be no question. The Malay name is pisang, and the Javanese gâdang, but in every language it has a different one; and besides these two, twelve more may be enumerated without, by any means, exhausting the number. The Malays reckon forty varieties of the cultivated banana, and the Philippine islanders carry them to fifty-seven, both people having a distinctive epithet for each variety. The qualities are as various as those of our apples and pears, the ordinary sorts being very indifferent fruit. The cultivated banana cannot be raised from the seed,—indeed the best varieties are seedless. The fruit is always either eaten raw or cooked, and never dried and preserved to be used as a substitute for bread-corn, as in tropical America. Rice, pulses, sago and farinaceous roots supersede its use, and are, no doubt, all of them preferable to it. See Abaca.

BANCA. The meaning of the word, which is correctly Bângka, is not, as far as I am aware, known, but it is applied with an epithet to several places about the south-eastern end of Sumatra. Thus the ancient name of Palembang is Bângka-palembang, and Bângka-ulu is the native name of the place which we have corrupted into Bencoolen, the annexed word in this last case meaning "head" or "fountain." The name of Banca itself, at full length, is Bângka-musuh, meaning "Bângka of the enemy." The extreme northern and southern parts of Banca are respectively in 1° 28′ and 3° 7′ south of the equator, and its western and eastern extremities in 105° 5′ and 106° 56′ of east longitude. Its northern and eastern shores are washed by the China Sea, and its southern by the Java Sea. To the south-west it is divided from Sumatra by the strait which bears its name, about thirty-six leagues in length, varying in breadth from three to eight. This strait forms the most frequented thoroughfare of the internal waters of the Archipelago. The form of Banca is irregularly oblong from south-west to north-east, its greatest length being 120, and its greatest breadth 60 geographical miles. Its area has been reckoned at 3568 square geographical miles, or about one-tenth part of that of Java. The coast is irregular in its outline, but not deeply indented, except at its northern end, where it has the bay of Klabat, about 20 miles deep. Along the coasts are many islets, the most considerable of which is Lipar, at its northern end.

Through the whole island there runs a chain of mountains, the highest peak of which, that of Maras, at the head of the bay of Klabat, is supposed to be 2000 feet above the level of the sea. The hill called Monopin in our charts, and which is a landmark for navigators, is only 967 feet. The island has no lakes, but many morasses, and numerous small rivers, tangled with mangroves and ratans, and not navigable except for native boats.

The mountain chain of Banca has the same direction as that of the Malay peninsula, and of the plutonic part of Sumatra, running from north-west to south-east, and it has the same geological formation. The main component of the mountains is granite, containing, tin, gold, and iron. Next to the granite, and in situations of less elevation, there occurs an extensive formation of red iron-stone, the laterite of geologists, and in the lowest lands an alluvial formation, intermixed with sandstones and breccias, among which occur the washings of tin and gold.

The plants of Banca are, with few exceptions, the same as those of that part of Sumatra in its neighbourhood. The whole island, even to a greater degree than usual, is covered with forest, the marshy parts of it being impenetrable from tangled underwood. The timber trees are of great size, and some of them useful. The teak does not exist, but there is stated to be an oak of great size. The most valuable products of the forest for trade, are agila-wood, ebony, and bees'-wax. The larger wild mammalia are two species of wild boar, the same as those of Java, numerous, and hunted by the Chinese, chiefly for their lard; a stag, cervus elephas; a roe, cervus manjac; and the pigmy deer, moschus pigmeus; with the Malayan bear. The elephant, the rhinoceros, and the tapir do not exist, and the largest rapacious quadruped is a kind of pole-cat. The birds are, for the most part, the same as those of Sumatra. The pigeon family is remarkable for numbers and variety, 30 species having been reckoned. Among reptiles the alligators are numerous and dangerous, being found on the coasts, and in the rivers and marshes. Esculent fish and molluscs are abundant and of good quality.

The aboriginal inhabitants of Banca are a rude but inoffensive people, of the same race and speaking the same language as the Malays, who call them Orang-gunung, literally mountaineers, but in their acceptation "savages," or wild men. These people live in separate families, and do not, like the more civilised tribes, congregate in villages. They cultivate a few patches of rice in a very rude way, and understand the smelting of iron. In race, language, and state of society, they are essentially the same as the wild inhabitants of the peninsula called the Bânuwa. On the coasts of the island are found, seemingly, the same people, but with different habits, the Orang-lant, or Sea-gipsies, sometimes called Sika. These dwell in their boats, having no other habitation, and live by fishing, and occasionally by a little piracy. The mass of the inhabitants of Banca, however, are colonists of comparatively recent times, Malays, Javanese, and Chinese. In 1840, the total population of the island was reckoned at 35,000, of which 18,000 were Chinese, which gives less than the poor ratio of 10 inhabitants to the square mile.

The soil of Banca must be considered as decidedly sterile. It consists of a layer of mould, from a foot and a half to two feet deep, generally lying over the iron-stone or laterite, already described. The only rural industry of the island consists in a few patches of rice culture, and in raising a few fruits and culinary vegetables. The only other industrious pursuit that deserves naming, consists in digging, washing, and smelting the alluvial tin ore. This is entirely in the hands of the Chinese, who receive advances from the Dutch government, which exercises a monopoly of the produce. In 1844, the quantity produced was 70,289 piculs, or about 4300 tons, a quantity equal to the produce of our Cornish mines, and, being all grain tin, superior to it in value. But even this large product has since been greatly increased, for the quantity produced in 1853 was no less than 5540 tons.

Banca has no trade worth naming, the only considerable export being tin, the produce of a public monopoly, and the only imports iron and other necessaries of life for its scanty population. The only place of trade is the only town in the island, Muntok, situated on the shore of the safest roadstead, which is on the strait, in south lat. 2°, and east long. 105° 15′, containing no more than 3000 inhabitants. The only considerable revenue arises from the profits of the tin monopoly, a precarious one, which even the government that exercises it can hardly calculate or reckon upon. The government pays to the miner, on an average, about eight Spanish dollars for each picul of the metal, this weight being equal to 125 Dutch, or about 134 English pounds. Now the ordinary Indian market-price of tin, for the weight in question is about 20 dollars, so that there seems a gross profit of 12 dollars. This is, however, subject to many deductions, as European superintendence at the mines and furnaces, transport of the metal to Java, where it is sold, public establishments there for storing and selling, and risk of competition with the free produce of the Malay peninsula and its islands, not to mention all the civil, military, and naval expenses of the island, kept up chiefly, if not wholly, on account of its tin. Leasing the mines to adventurers for a certain rent, as practised by the proprietors of mines of all descriptions in Britain, and as is practised by the British government with its tin mines at Malacca, would be a far more effectual means of securing a certain revenue, than a monopoly which substitutes the dolings of public revenue for the wholesome efficacy of capital. The freedom of such a system could hardly fail to increase the amount of the produce. If it be taken only at 75,000 piculs, or short of 5000 more than the produce of the monopoly in 1844, and a seignorage of 15 per cent. were levied on it, and realised by farming it, the net revenue would amount, at the value of 20 dollars a picul, to 225,000 dollars, equal to £48,730. This view is corroborated by the results of the system as pursued at Malacca. The tin mines of this place were only effectually worked for the first time in 1845, and in 1848 they yielded 7000 piculs of tin. Their inferior fertility to those of Banca, and even the inferiority of the metal produced, did not admit of a higher seignorage than 10 per cent., but even at this rate, they yielded a revenue of near 10,000 dollars a-year.

Of the history of Banca, all that is worth narrating may be briefly told. An island which was not known to contain tin, until the first years of the last century, which was unfertile in soil, without natural facilities of irrigation, and which had no coveted natural products, is not likely to have tempted the resort of strangers, and seems to have been left almost entirely to its rude inhabitants. The Javanese, who, according to their own chronicles, established themselves at Palembang, in Sumatra, about the year of our time 1378, appear to have formed some establishments on the western side of Banca, which may still be traced by their names derived either from the Javanese or Sanscrit language, as Kuta-waringin, "the fort of the Indian fig-tree;" Bângka-kuta, the fort of Banca; and Selan, the mythological Indian name of Ceylon. Two centuries, from the first appearance of Europeans in the Archipelago, had passed away, before Banca had attracted any other notice from them than as an appendage of Sumatra. A pure accident called attention to it. Some of the inhabitants in burning the forest, in their rude culture of rice, found that some superficial tin ore had been smelted in the process, and ore being sought for in the neighbourhood, it was found in abundance. This happened in the year 1709, and in 1711 the discovery was known at Batavia to the Dutch. The fact of the manner in which, and the time when the discovery was made, are well ascertained. It is a signal proof of the ignorance and incuriousness of the Malayan nations, that the Javanese, the most advanced of them, should have been, after 330 years, as sovereigns of Palembang, masters of Banca, without being aware that it had rich mines of an useful metal well known to them. That the European nations should have been in the same state of ignorance is to be accounted for, by their being wholly employed during that long time in no worthier pursuit than the attempt to establish commercial monopolies in such paltry commodities as cloves, nutmegs, and black-pepper. The tin of Banca was no sooner discovered than the Sultan of Palembang established a monopoly of it, and no sooner was it known to the Dutch that he had done so, than they forced an engagement on him, securing to themselves the right of pre-emption at a very mean price. This state of things continued for a whole century, and until the conquest of the Dutch possessions by the English in 1811, when the Sultan of Palembang, in the base hope of gratifying the conquerors, put the whole of the Dutch at Palembang and Banca to death. The return for this office was an invasion of Palembang, the defeat of the Sultan, his dethronement, and the acquisition of Banca, as a cession from his successor in 1812. The island continued a British possession until 1816, when, along with the rest of their possessions, it was restored to the Dutch. These in 1818 restored the old Sultan, whose treachery brought on a war of two years, which ended in 1821 by the conquest of Palembang, which, with Banca, have since continued in undisputed possession of the Netherland government.

BANCALIS. One of four low islands, of considerable size, separated from each other, and from the north-eastern coast of Sumatra, by narrow straits. These islands lie off the mouths of the rivers of Siak and Kampar, between the first and second degrees of north latitude. Bancalis, which belongs to the Malay state of Siak, is about 35 miles in length by 10 in breadth, mostly covered with forest and thinly inhabited.

BANDA. The Banda or Nutmeg Islands consist of a group of mere islets, said to be five in number, like the Clove Islands, but really amounting to ten, although some of them be uninhabited. Their names were probably given by the Malayan traders, who had frequented them for ages: Banda, correctly Bândan, means in Javanese the thing or things tied or united, or with the word Pulo, "united islands." Pulo Nera is the "island of palm-wine." Lontar, written by Europeans Lonthor, is the name of the palm, the leaf of which is used for writing on, the word being half Sanscrit and half Javanese. Pulo Ai, properly Pulo Wai, means "water-island;" Pulo Pisang, "banana island;" Pulo Run (Rung), "chamber island;" Pulo Suwanggi, "sorcery island;" Gunung-api, "fire mountain or volcano." A name which, with the Dutch pronunciation and orthography, cannot be traced to a Malayan language, is Rosingen. It is written by De Barros, however, Rosolanguim, and if this, as is likely, be nearer the true word, it may possibly be derived from the Javanese word roso, "strength," and langgâng, "firm, assured." And Pulo Kapal may either signify "ship island" or "horse island," for the annexed word means the first in Telinga, borrowed by the Malays, and the second in Javanese. The whole group lies between south latitudes 3° 50′ and 4° 40′, and the Dutch fortress of Belgica, on the island of Nera, is in east longitude 129° 54′ 20″." Lontar, called usually by Europeans the Great Banda, is the largest of the group, being about 7 miles long, with an average breadth of 2 miles, and having the form of a crescent. Nera, on which the principal settlement stands, is but a mile and a half long, and half a mile broad.

The whole Banda group, which has an area of no more than 17·6 geographical square miles, is of volcanic formation, and Gunung-api, is an entire volcanic mountain, the most active of the whole great volcanic band, although its height above the sea-level is only 2500 feet. The eruptions of this mountain have been frequent and destructive. The first of which we have any record took place in 1629. This was followed by eruptions in 1690 and the five following years,—in 1765, in 1775, in 1816, in 1820, and in 1852. In the months of November and December of this last year, a succession of fearful earthquakes, but unaccompanied by any eruption of Gunung-api, took place, which nearly overwhelmed the islands of Nera and Lontar, overthrowing houses, and destroying ships and nutmeg plantations. The eruptions of Gunung-api are accompanied by violent earthquakes, and by risings of the sea equally fatal. In the eruption of 1690, the sea rose 25 feet higher than high water at spring tides, and swept off every dwelling on or near the shore, and every vessel. A cannon weighing 3500 pounds was carried away from the quay on which it stood to the distance of 30 feet. In the eruption of 1691, the succession of earthquakes which took place was such as to terrify the inhabitants, many of them emigrating to Amboyna and Celebes. The eruption of 1852 seems to have been not less disastrous than that of 1690. The eruptions are invariably followed by fatal epidemics, which carry off many of the inhabitants.

The Banda Islands are, with small exceptions, covered, as elsewhere, with a luxuriant forest. Their most distinguished product is, of course, the nutmeg, Myristica moschata, not, however, confined to them, for it is equally a native of other islands lying east of them, as far as New Guinea inclusive. The mammal animals are few in number, and, as is always the case in islands of small extent, none of the larger are found, not even any species of hog or deer. Among the feathered tribe the most abundant and remarkable are the parrots and pigeons. Of the first of those, the red loory, Psittacus ruber, is the most singular; and of the last, Columba perspicillata and Columba ænea, both great depredators on the nutmeg, and the first of them good game.

The population of the Banda Islands, by an enumeration made in 1840, was found to be 5081, of which Nera had 1225; Lontar or the Great Banda, 372; Ai, 148; and Run, 42. These, amounting to 1687, constituted the free population; the rest were made up of 2183 slaves and 1029 convicts; for these islands are the place of transportation for the felons of Java, Sumatra, and Borneo. In 1725 the population was stated at 5000, so that in a period of 115 years, no increase had taken place: indeed, if we deduct convicts, which did not exist in 1725, there had been a decrease of about 1000, or one-fifth of the whole number.

Agriculture is confined to the raising of fruits and vegetables, and the rearing of the nutmeg. Of this there are reckoned to be 34 parks, as they are called by the Dutch. These contain among them about half a million of trees, which on an average of years are reckoned to produce 400,000 pounds of nutmegs and 130,000 of mace. The whole trade of the islands consists in the export of the produce of the nutmeg tree, and in the importation of corn and other necessaries for the maintenance of the population, the government being the sole exporter of the nutmegs, and the sole importer of the corn. The volcano of Gunung-api furnishes an abundant supply of sulphur, but it is not collected; the necessary labour and enterprise for such an undertaking not existing in the stagnant state of society which prevails. The town, which is the seat of administration, not only for the Banda but for other islands annexed to them, such as those of Goram and Aroe, estimated at a population of 200,000, is situated on Nera, and on the shore of a safe harbour formed between it, Lontar and Gunung-api. The scene presented on entering this harbour is represented to be quite unequalled for picturesque beauty in the Archipelago, and is the more striking from the total absence of all evidence of industry and civilisation until it appears in view.

The revenue of the Banda Islands consists in the profits of the nutmeg monopoly. The price paid to the proprietors of the nutmeg parks may be reckoned in round numbers, for the quantity above specified, at about 10,000*l.*, and the value at Batavia, to which they are transported at the cost of the government, is about 55,000*l.*, so that the gross profits of the monopoly would be thus about 45,000*l.* This is, however, subject to many deductions, as the cost of the establishment for superintending the culture, for curing and warehousing on the spot, transport of the produce to Batavia, expense of warehousing and selling it there, and the difference between the prime cost of rice in Java and in the Banda Islands, some 1500 miles distant. But besides this, the monopoly profits have to support the whole charges of the civil, municipal, ordnance, naval and military establishments, the last alone comprising 400 rank and file, with their officers, all kept up for no other purpose than the maintenance of the monopoly. The certainty is, that instead of profit, there must be a heavy loss. In fact this monopoly, which now existing for above two centuries, if the cost of its acquisition be reckoned, never could have yielded a real profit, and for many years back is well known to have been accompanied by a heavy loss. A perseverance in it, therefore, is a subject of much surprise both to enlightened Dutchmen and strangers.

The history of the Nutmeg Islands is as follows: They had been known to and often frequented by the two principal insular nations of the western part of the Archipelago, the Malays and Javanese, for many ages before the advent of Europeans. Hindoos most probably, and Arabs and Chinese certainly, had visited them long before the Portuguese. The latter, therefore, although the first to reach, cannot be said to have discovered them. Alboquerque, after his conquest of Malacca in 1511, obtained all the necessary information respecting the Spice Islands, and despatched Antonio d'Abreu, one of his lieutenants, to trade with and take possession of them in the month of December of that year. "Before him," says De Barros, "he sent a native of Malacca, one Nakhoda Ismael, in a trading junk, belonging to some Moorish Javanese and Malays of these parts, so that on d'Abreu's arrival he might be well received. Indeed, as our name was wonderful in this part of the world, there was little risk of his not being handsomely treated." On his way d'Abreu touched at Gressic in Java, and there took "Malay and Javanese pilots who had made the voyage" to the Spice Islands. Leaving Java, the first of the Spice Islands which he reached was Amboyna, from whence he proceeded to the Banda Islands. De Barros' description of them is this: "And as the Moluccas comprehend five islands, so under the name of Banda are also five islands, each with its own proper name. In truth, the chief of them is called Banda, to the principal port of which, Lutatam, all ships resort that come for the nutmeg trade. The other islands are called Rosolanguim, Ay, Rom, and Neira, and all of them lie within 4½° south altitude. Every year there repair to Lutatam Javanese and Malays to load cloves, nutmegs, and mace; for this place being in the latitudes most easily navigated, and where ships are most safe, and as the cloves of the Moluccas are brought to it by vessels of the country, it is not necessary to go to the latter in search of them. In the five islands now named grow all the nutmegs consumed in every part of the world." He afterwards adds that nutmegs produced in all the other islands were brought for the convenience of the foreign merchant to Lutatam in Lontar or the Great Banda, and that place, in short, seems to have been, on the arrival of the Portuguese, the local emporium of the nutmeg trade. De Barros describes the volcano of Gunung-api correctly, and is only wrong in his etymology of its name, making gunung, which signifies mountain, to mean "fire," and api, which means "fire," to be the proper name of the island. His account of the characters of the Bandanese is this: "The people of these islands are robust, with a tawny complexion and lank hair, and are of the worst repute in these parts. They follow the sect of Mahommedan, and are much addicted to trade, their women performing the labours of the field. They have neither king nor lord, and all their government depends on the advice of their elders; and as these are often at variance, they quarrel among themselves. The land has no other export than the nutmeg. This tree is in such abundance that the land is full of it, without its being planted by anyone, for the earth yields it without culture. The forests which produce it belong to no one by inheritance, but to the people in common. When June and September come, which are the months for gathering the crop, the nutmeg woods are allotted, and he who gathers most has most profit." This account would seem to show that the people of the Banda Islands lived under a sort of rude patriarchal republic, and in fact that they were, although few in number, a spirited and independent people, as indeed, the desperate resistance they afterwards made against both Portuguese and Dutch sufficiently shows. Their adoption of the Mahommedan religion is by no means a proof of barbarism, but the reverse, as it is only the most advanced nations of the Archipelago that have done so, while generally, the more savage tribes remain unconverted up to the present day. That the life and property of strangers was tolerably secure among them is sufficiently attested by the fact of their islands having been selected as the emporium of the whole spice trade. Even their reception of the Portuguese on their first arrival was friendly, as admitted by themselves. "Antonio d'Abreu," says De Barros, "after having set up pillars testifying his discovery, and loading his ships with mace and nutmegs, as well as with cloves, brought thither, as before mentioned, by the junks of Malacca, quitted the Isles of Banda well satisfied with his reception by the people of the country."

The Portuguese had been nearly a century in possession of the nutmeg trade, when the Dutch made their first appearance in the Banda Islands with an armament, and with the view of taking possession of them. The expedition consisted of three ships carrying 700 soldiers; an armament equal in strength to that with which Cortes had conquered the Mexican empire. This was in 1609. The Dutch attempted to construct a fort on the ruins of one which had belonged to the Portuguese. The natives resisted,—seduced the Dutch admiral and forty-five of his companions into an ambuscade, and massacred them. This led to a war of extermination, which was not closed until 1627, and had produced the necessity of the presence of the governor-general with a large fleet and seventeen companies of soldiers. The Bandanese lost 3000 in killed and had 1000 made prisoners, who were most likely expatriated for the safety of the conquerors. The remainder of the population sought safety by flight to the neighbouring islands, where mixing with other populations, they have lost their nationality and disappeared as a people, no vestige of their language and manners remaining. Their numbers before the Dutch conquest are said to have been 15,000, and if so, the conquest had destroyed above a fourth part of the whole number. In this manner the Dutch became undisputed masters of the nutmeg monopoly, but there was no one to cultivate the trees, and it became necessary to introduce slaves for this purpose. The nutmeg plantations were divided as hereditary property among the Dutch who assisted in making the conquest,—traders and military officers whose descendants hold them under the name of Parkeniers to the present day, on the condition of delivering the whole produce to the government at a fixed and low price, receiving in return any required number of slaves at about 9*l.* a-head, and rice at its first cost in Java. The abolition of the carrying trade in slaves, and the impossibility of keeping up the stock by natural increase, made it necessary to modify the terms of the contract, and at present convicts from Java, Sumatra, and Borneo are substituted for slaves.

BANDUNG, a district of the country of the Sundas, in Java; one of those collectively called Prayangan, written Prianger by the Dutch, and meaning "fairy land," or "country of sprites." Bandung is a picturesque and extensive valley, not unlike in aspect to some of the valleys of the Apennines. It lies about midway between the northern and southern coasts, its chief town of the same name lying in about south latitude 6° 50′, and east longitude 105° 35′. The district contained 721 villages, in 1814 and had a population of 56,122. In the returns of the population of Java made in 1845, this district is not distinguished from the other eleven that constitute the Prayangan province; but if its increase has kept pace with that of the rest, it ought now to exceed 190,000.

BANGLI. A principality of Bali, in the interior of the island, and estimated to have a population of 30,000.

BANJARMASIN. A principality and river on the southern side of Borneo, the embouchure of the river being in south latitude 3° 32′, and east longitude 114° 38′. The principality is estimated to comprise 280 square geographical leagues, or 4840 miles. The meaning of the word in Javanese is "salt or saline garden." The geological formation seems to be plutonic and sedimentary; and its only mineral products available to industrial purposes are the diamond and coal, mines of both being now worked. Ratans, canes, and pepper are the only products of the vegetable kingdom available for foreign trade; and the culture of pepper, which had been largely prosecuted before this commodity was monopolised by the Dutch government, is now nearly extinct. The forests do not produce the teak tree, nor the camphor, so valuable for its timber, and essential oil, concrete and fluid, and so abundant on the north-western side of the island. The larger animals are the same as in other parts of Borneo,—the ox, wild and domestic; the buffalo in the latter state, and the hog in both states. The total population subject to the Sultan of Banjarmasin is estimated at 120,000, chiefly Malays, with a few natives of Celebes and a small number of Chinese; but besides, it is computed that within the limits of the territory claimed by this prince, there are about half a million of the wild tribes that go under the common name of Dayak.

The sovereignty of Banjarmasin is said, in olden times, to have extended over the whole of the south-eastern portion of Borneo. Tradition assigns the foundation of the state to a personage called Ampu-jatmika, the son of a merchant of the coast of

Coromandel, called Mangkunbumi. Ampu-jatmika, with his family and followers, emigrated from India, and settled in Borneo, giving their new country the name of Nagara-dipa; and on a river, still called Nagara, there are at present to be seen the remains of stone edifices said to have been the residence of the first princes. This event is reckoned to have taken place about the end of the 12th century of our time, but no precise date is assigned to it. In the third generation, the only descendant of the founder was a princess, for whom a husband was sought and found in a prince of Majapait, in Java, who took the title of Raden Suryanata. From his time to the overthrow of Majapait, in the year 1478, Banjarmasin continued tributary to that Javanese state, which assisted it in extending its dominions eastward, so as to embrace the now independent states of Kuti and Pasir. The people professed a rude Hinduism, similar to that of Java, but about the beginning of the 16th century, they embraced Mahommedanism, having been converted by the state of Damak in Java, founded at the end of the 15th century, and immediately after the subversion of the Hindu state of Majapait. This event must have been nearly contemporaneous with the first appearance of the Portuguese in the Archipelago. It is stated that the people of Banjarmasin asked for assistance towards the suppression of a revolt, and that it was given on condition of the adoption of the new religion, when a host of priests militant came over from Java, who suppressed the rebellion and effected the conversion. The reigning prince, at the time referred to, bore the half-Indian, half-Javanese title of Raden Sumadra, which, according to custom in such cases, he changed for the Arabic one of Sultan. Such is the statement made on native authority, and although, no doubt, there is much truth in it, it will not bear a close examination. A succession of two-and-twenty princes is stated to have reigned in Banjarmasin from its foundation to the year 1846, which, at the average European estimate of 20 years for each reign, would give no more than 440 years, and this would carry us back only to the beginning of the 15th century, and not to the end of the 12th, for the foundation of the state. According to the chronology given, each reign must have averaged about 30 years, which is highly improbable. The Dutch had visited Borneo and traded with it as early as 1600, but their first political relations with Banjarmasin began in 1664, by a contract for the monopoly of pepper, rendered inoperative by the machinations of the Portuguese. The English, about the same time, were busy trading and intriguing, and in 1698 obtained leave to erect a fort in the territory of Banjarmasin, and to establish a factory, but the last was plundered, and the garrison of the first massacred in 1707. Various subsequent treaties were made between the Dutch and the princes of Banjarmasin, but in 1756, the country being in a state of revolt, the Dutch lent the reigning prince assistance by sea and land, by which peace was restored; and in reward for this service, a complete monopoly of the pepper trade was granted to them. The terms of this engagement are worth noticing for the results which followed. The Sultan engaged to extend the cultivation of pepper to the amount of 15,000 piculs, or about 2,000,000 pounds, and the utmost he ever succeeded in delivering to his allies was about 70,000 pounds. The price fixed was six Spanish dollars for each picul of 125 Dutch pounds, which was no doubt thought at the time a very good bargain for the purchaser, and yet it is about one-fifth more than the same commodity may, under the existing commercial freedom, be had for in any native port of the pepper-producing countries. Indeed, a cargo may be got in an hour's warning at less price in any European port of the Archipelago, and without the cost of treaties and garrisons. The result of the monopoly is what might be safely expected, the cessation of the culture of pepper in Banjarmasin.

In 1785, the reigning prince having rendered himself odious to his subjects, the country was invaded by 3000 natives of Celebes. These were expelled by the Dutch, who dethroned the Sultan, placing his younger brother on the throne, who, in reward for their services, ceded to them his entire dominions, consenting to hold them as a vassal. This is the treaty under which the Dutch claim the sovereignty of Banjarmasin, and whatever was once dependent on it.

BAÑAK (PULO); that is, "the many isles," a cluster of islands on the western coast of Sumatra, lying off Singkel, which is itself in 2° 15′ 15″ north latitude, and east longitude 97° 43′ 40″. The group consists of one considerable island, about 20 miles long, with, at least, a score of mere islets. The inhabitants, who have a peculiar language of their own, distinct from those of Sumatra, are said to be called by the Malays, Maros and Maruwi, words of which I do not know the origin. They have been converted to the Mahommedan religion, and are chiefly fishermen.

BANGUI. An island in the Sulu Sea, at the northern end of Borneo, and lying off the promontory formed between the bays of Maludu and Paitan. It is about six leagues long, and has a mountain peak in north latitude 7° 19′, and east longitude 117° 6′, which being visible in clear weather at the distance of 14 or 15 leagues, cannot be less than 5000 feet high. The island forms a portion of the territory of the chieftain, called the Sultan of Sulu, but very little more is known about it.

BANKALAN, a district of the island of Madura, comprehending its western portion. In 1814, it contained 447 villages, and a population of 63,714, which at present is probably more than double that amount; but being, with the rest of the island, mixed up with the province of Surabaya, I possess no means of distinguishing the number.

BANTAM; thus written by the Portuguese, whose example has been followed by other European nations: in the native languages it is Bantân, but the literal meaning of the word I have not been able to ascertain. Bantam, in the country of the Sundas, and formerly an independent kingdom, is now a Dutch province. It forms the western end of Java, and has an area of 2568 geographical square miles, and is a mountainous country of volcanic formation. Its highest mountains, however, are not above one-half the height of those of the centre and eastern portions of the island. Thus Gunung-karang (rocky mountain) is but 6000 feet high, while the next in elevation, Pulosari (island of sweet flowers), is no more than 4200 feet. Fossil coal has been found in the district of Lebak, towards the south-eastern part of the province. With the exception of the teak, which does not exist, the other trees and plants, wild and cultivated, are generally the same as in other parts of the island. The wild and domestic animals are also the same, and it may here be remarked that the dwarf poultry, called by us after the country, were imported from Japan, and received their name, not from the place that produced them, but from that where our voyagers first found them.

The mass of the population of Bantam is of the Sunda nation, and speaking its peculiar language; but on the coast this people is mixed up with Malays, Javanese, and others who speak Malay. In 1814, the number of villages in Bantam was 738, and its computed population 231,604. By the census of 1850, this population had increased to 470,381, giving about 184 to the square mile, not above one-half the density of the more fertile central and eastern provinces of the island. The principal industrial products of the province are rice, coffee, sugar, indigo, tea, cinnamon, and bay salt. With the exception of the first and last, all these articles are more or less exotics, and cultivated or produced for the Dutch government, through the corvée labour which prevails over Java. About 2000 families are stated to be engaged in the fisheries. Pepper, the staple product of Bantam, and chiefly on account of which it was frequented by the European merchants of the 17th and 18th century, has ceased to be produced.

Bantam, conveniently situated on the shores of one of the great thoroughfares of the Archipelago, naturally became one of the chief emporia of native trade before the arrival of Europeans, and was frequented by Malays and Javanese trading with the Moluccas; by Arabs, Persians, Hindus, and Mahommedans, from both coasts of India; and by Chinese and Japanese. The country of the Sundas was first visited in 1511 by the Portuguese, under Henrique Lemé, one of the captains of the adventurous Alboquerque. He seems, however, to have gone no farther than Jacatra, or Sunda-kalapa, the future Batavia. The Dutch did not present themselves at Bantam until 1596, and then, not under very favourable auspices, for the future lords of Java; for one of the two brothers, Houtman, who commanded the fleet, allowed himself to be taken prisoner, and obtained his release only on payment of a ransom. The English made their first appearance there in 1602, and in due course, the two monopolists became embroiled, disputing about privileges which neither ought to possess, and in the sequel, the English were expelled by the superior power and activity of their rivals. The Dutch, from time to time, increased their influence in Bantam, and in 1843, the last of its kings was banished to Surabaya, at the further end of Java, and the country taken possession of as a province.

BAÑUMAS (golden water or river). A central province of Java, on the southern side of the island, and consequently bounded on one side by the sea. Its area is computed at 1589 square miles. It has itself no mountains of remarkable elevation, but to the north it is bounded by the high range in which is the mountain of Tâgal, 11,250 feet high. It has, extending along the coast, one considerable lake, or rather morass, and some considerable rivers, valuable for the purpose of irrigation. The largest island on the southern coast of Java, Nusa-kambangan, (literally, floating island,) forms a part of this province. By the census of 1845, the population of Bañumas was estimated at 405,654, of which 150 were Europeans, 1640 Chinese, and the remainder natives, speaking the Javanese language; for this province borders on the country of the Sundas. Rice is the staple product; but it produces, also, like similar parts of Java, cotton and pulses, and, of late years, the Dutch have introduced the culture of coffee, sugar, and similar products, grown on account of the government by corvée labour. The province is purely an agricultural one, having no foreign trade, and its only port being that which lies between the island above named and the main, is an isolated and, therefore, an inconvenient one.

BAÑUWANGI (fragrant water or river). A district of Java, forming its eastern extremity, as Bantam does its western. In 1814, its total population was no more than 8873, which, in 1850, had risen to 30,634. In fact, it is the wildest portion of the island. Its natural advantages, however, are not inferior to those of the finest districts; for in the west and north of it are several high mountains, which supply it with many rivers for irrigation. One of these, Widadaren (abode of celestial nymphs), is about 8000 feet high; and Ijeng is above 10,500; both of them active volcanoes. The neighbourhood of Bali, and the invasions from it, with destructive volcanic eruptions have probably been the chief causes of its backwardness.

BARAM. The name of a river and district on the north-western side of Borneo, part of the territory of the state of Brunai. The mouth of the river is in north latitude 4° 30′, and east longitude 113° 50′, and 80 miles southward of the British settlement of Labuan. The entrance is obstructed by a sand bar, on which the depth is no more than a fathom and a half; but after crossing this obstacle, the river deepens to four, to five, and even to ten fathoms; and these depths extend to the distance of 100 miles. The breadth of the river at its embouchure is about half a mile, after which it varies from 500 to 200 fathoms. At the respective distances of 72 and 80 miles, the Baram receives two affluents, called the Chingir and Tutu. Its banks, towards its embouchure, are clothed with cassuarinas, instead of mangroves, indicating a dry and sandy, instead of a muddy soil. Further up are many open grassy plains, in which the wild hog, deer, and wild ox, called by the natives the Tuladan (the *Bos sondaicus* of naturalists), are found. Towards the upper portion of the Baram excellent iron-ore and coal-fields exist; and as the river is navigable for vessels drawing no more than eight or nine feet, coal and iron might become articles of export to the European emporium in the neighbourhood. The ruling tribe of the interior is the Kayan, the most advanced and powerful of all the wild races of Borneo. In 1851, the war iron-steamer "Pluto" ascended the Baram to the distance of 140 miles, and ascertained all the facts now stated, the Kayans receiving her in a very friendly manner; but, as may readily be supposed, with wonder. "I hear," says the intelligent narrator of the voyage, "that the exclamations of the Kayans, on first seeing us, were 'Here is a god;' others, 'A mighty spirit.'"

BĂRAPI (GUNUNG); literally "fire mountain" or volcano. It has the same sense as Mârapi, and both are the names of mountains,—one in Sumatra, and one in Java. The Sumatran mountain rises to the height of 6000 feet above the level of the sea. It is an active volcano, and lies towards the southern side of the island, about 45 miles south of the equator.

BARBOSA, ODOARDO or DUERTE. Barbosa, written Balbosa by the Spaniards, the author of the fullest, the most authentic, and most intelligent of all the early accounts of India, represents himself in the preface to his book, as translated by Ramusio, to have been a gentleman of Lisbon who, in his youth, travelled over many parts of India, and who, taking notes of what he observed himself, or what he learnt "from authentic sources, whether Christian, Mahommedan, or heathen," composed his work for the public advantage, bringing it to a conclusion in 1516. The account, however, contains internal evidence of the author's having visited Malacca before its conquest by his countrymen in 1511. Barbosa's work has been, I believe, of late years, published in Portuguese, from the original manuscript; but I have not had the good fortune to have met with it. In 1519, three years after he had completed his work, we find Barbosa in Spain, joining the fleet under Magellan, whose relative he was. On the death of his commander in 1521, we learn from Pigafetta that, in conjunction with Juan Serano, a Spaniard, he was elected to succeed to the command, which he did not long enjoy; for on the 1st of May, four days after the death of Magellan, he and his colleague, having been seduced to land under a false pretext, by the king of the island of Çebu, were treacherously murdered, with four-and-twenty of their companions. On this the Spanish ships set sail, and nothing more was ever heard of Barbosa. The singular knowledge which Pigafetta, who had never been himself in India, until he accompanied Magellan, displays respecting it may, in some measure, be accounted for, when it is considered that he was the shipmate of one so well informed as Barbosa.

BARON (NUSA). The island of Baron, the second in size of the few islands which skirt the southern coast of Java, forms part of the province of Besukie. Latitude south 3° 8′ 32″, and longitude east 113° 18′.

BARROS, JÃO DE, the author of the classical history of the Portuguese discoveries and conquests in India, was born in 1496, and died on the 20th of October, 1570. He had never visited any part of India, but placed in charge of the Indian records, under the name of Feitor da casa da India, he had the best means of obtaining accurate information; and, for the time in which he lived, certainly made a faithful and judicious use of his opportunities. His appointment to the charge of the Indian records took place in 1532, only 34 years after the first arrival of the Portuguese in India, and but 23 after their first appearance in the waters of the Archipelago. The first decade of De Barros' History was published in 1552, and the second, that which treats of the Indian Islands, in the following year. The third was not published until ten years after the second, and the fourth and last was posthumous. De Barros was 15 years of age when Malacca was conquered, and Java and the Spice Islands discovered, and 20 at the time of Alboquerque's death. He may, therefore, be considered as a contemporary of Alboquerque, whose achievements he narrates, and to stand pretty nearly in the same relation to him that the historian Orme does to the English conqueror Clive.

BARUS. The name of a place on the western coast of Sumatra, situated about a league up a small river, and within the territory of the nation of the Bataks, although Barus itself be a Malay colony. At one time, it seems to have been a place of some eminence for native trade; but at present is chiefly known for giving its name to the native camphor (kapur-barus), on which the Chinese set so high and, seemingly, so capricious a value. North latitude 1° 59′ 35″, east longitude 98° 23° 30″.

BASHEE ISLANDS. The name of a cluster of islets to the north of the Babuyanes Isles, at the northern end of Luzon. The celebrated Dampier and his buccaneering comrades gave them this name when they visited them in 1687. "These islands," says Dampier, "having no particular names in the drafts, some or other of us made use of the seaman's privilege to give them what names we pleased. Three of the islands were pretty large; the westernmost is the biggest. This the Dutchmen who were among us called the Prince of Orange's Island, in honour of his present majesty. The other two great islands are about four or five leagues to the eastward of this. The northernmost of them, where we first anchored, I called the Duke of Grafton's Isle as soon as we landed on it, having married my wife out of the duchess's family, and leaving her at Arlington House at my going abroad. The other great isle, our seamen called the Duke of Monmouth's Island. Between Monmouth and the south end of Orange Island, there are two small islands of roundish form, lying east and west. The easternmost island of the two, our men unanimously called Bashee Island, from a liquor which we drank there plentifully every day after we came to an anchor at it." He adds, "And, indeed, from the plenty of this liquor (a kind of beer), and their plentiful use of it, our men called these islands the Bashee Islands." Most probably, however, all this is a mistake on the part of Dampier. All the islands have native names, and the particular one which he thinks was called after a native liquor, is in reality Basay, while the one he names after his patron, the first Duke of Grafton, whose duchess condescended to let the great navigator have one of her maid-servants for a wife, is that which gives name to the whole group. (See BATAN and BATANES.)

BASILAN. A considerable island in the Sulu Sea, lying off the south-western portion of the great island of Mindano, and parted from it by a strait known to European navigators by its own name. It lies between the latitudes of 6° 42′ and 6° 26′ north, and longitudes east 121° 50′ and 122° 18′. Its length is about seven leagues, its breadth four, and it is computed to have an area of 355 square geographical miles. A chain of high mountains passes through its length. The inhabitants of Basilan, a scanty population, are of the same race and speak the same language as the other inhabitants of the Sulu Islands; that is, a language partaking more of the

Philippine than the Malay character, and much intermixed with the Bisaya, one of the most prevailing languages of the Philippine Archipelago. Basilan having long enjoyed the bad reputation of being a nest of the thieves and pirates of the neighbouring islands, the boldest and most expert of the Archipelago, was lately taken possession of and garrisoned by the Spanish government, annexing it to the province of Zamhoanga in Mindano.

BÂSISI. The name of one of the wild tribes of the interior of the Malay peninsula, inhabiting the country inland from Malacca, and in the territory of Naning. In physical form and language they are Malays, and the learned Mr. J. R. Logan, who first visited and described them, comes to the conclusion "that they are undoubtedly the original, or uncivilised, perhaps I may add with truth, the unadulterated Malays." The only essential difference between the Bâsisi with other wild tribes of the same race in the Peninsula, and the wild races of Borneo, is, that the first invariably have the Malay for their language, whereas the latter have their own distinct and many peculiar idioms.

BATÄAN, one of the twenty provinces of the great island of Luzon. Batäan consists of a peninsula, lying between the great Bay of Manilla and the open sea, and has a coast line of 68 miles, and an inland frontier of 29, and probably contains an area of 375 geographical square miles. At its southern extremity it has the tolerably convenient harbour of Mariveles, and at its north-western angle the bay or inlet of Olonapo or Olopando, at the head of which is the harbour of Sulio. A spur of the great cordillera of Zambales runs through the province, covered with forest, and in which are found marbles of many varieties, much used in the churches and other buildings of Manilla. The province generally is poor and rugged, in some years not producing food enough for its inhabitants. The rivers of the eastern coast, or that on the Bay of Manilla, too small for navigation, abound in fish, which forms a large part of the sustenance of the people.

The inhabitants of Batäan are of the Tagala nation, but the recesses of the mountains give refuge to tribes of the Aetas, negritos or little negros. "The least accessible mountains of this province," say the authors of the 'Geographical and Statistical Dictionary of the Philippines,' "are inhabited by hordes of negritos, who are frequently pursued to their forest recesses, and being captured, the youngest are taken, civilised, and instructed up to the age of reason, being employed meanwhile in various work, with the view of being eventually set at liberty." In 1810, the total population of Bantäan, which had been erected into a province in 1754, was 20,344; in 1818, it was 23,395; and in 1849, it had risen to 39,008; the parties assessed to the poll-tax in this last year being 8375, and their contribution 8375 reals of plate. Its relative population gives 104 to the square mile.

BATAG. An island about half a league off the north-eastern coast of Samar, the most northerly of the Philippine group, which goes under the designation of Visaya, or Bisaya. Its length and breadth are respectively two leagues and one league, giving it an area of two leagues. On its south-west coast, and within the strait which divides it from Samar, it has one village, forming a part of the district of Palapag, in Samar.

BATAK. One of the advanced nations of Sumatra, although among these the lowest in the scale of civilisation. They are bounded to the north by the Achinese, and to the south by the Malayan nation, the latter having encroached so much on their coasts as to leave them little communication with the sea, either on the eastern or western coast of the island, thus making them essentially an inland people. The country of the Bataks lies in that part of Sumatra which is the narrowest, and where the breadth does not exceed 100 miles. Its mountains are of no great elevation, the highest being from 4000 to 6500 feet only above the level of the sea. A portion of the interior consists of an extensive plateau, but of what elevation is not stated. The Dutch have of late years, extending their conquests into the interior of the island, which no European nation had before attempted,—wrested two provinces in the heart of their country from the Bataks, and the account they have given of these is the only reliable one we possess of the nature of the Batak country. Their names are Mandeling and Pârtibi, and the first of them, although it has rugged and sterile portions, has also a series or chain of fertile valleys under culture of rice by irrigation, lying between the mountains Bârapi and Mali. The first of these is about 5500 feet in height, and judging by its name is probably volcanic, and being such may account for the fertility of the valleys at its foot. The physical geography of the province of

Pârtibi is very different, and much of it marked by characters very singular in the Malayan Archipelago. A considerable portion of it consists of a dreary, treeless, and sterile plain, thus described by Mr. Willer, an officer of the Dutch government of Java. "Here," says he, "we see unrolled a plain without horizon and without variety; an unbounded carpet on which the more or less luxuriant growth of the Lalang (Andropogon caricosum), a coarse worthless grass, a most troublesome weed, and a sure sign of sterility, makes the only diversity, and on which not a single living creature appears to move,—where a tree is literally a rarity, and when it exists has an appearance of stunted dwarfishness; where at the distance of miles we descry, like an oasis in the desert, an insignificant thicket, or a small strip of brushwood, along the banks of a marsh or stream; where a fell scorching wind blows for months together, and from the numerous conflagrations of lalang grass, generally spreads a dull glow, through which the sunlight scarcely forces itself wavering and heavy; in short, where all nature seems to have gone to an eternal sleep. Such is the appearance of Padang-luwas (wide or spacious plain), as of the greatest part of Pârtibi. The naked and flat *terrein* of Padang-luwas offers no other diversity than the ravines and morasses with which it is intersected. The upper soil is of the most meagre and unfruitful kind, and is seldom more than half a foot in thickness: beneath it we soon come to layers of white clay limestone, sandstone, and other formations. The climate although not actually unhealthy is extremely rude. Frequently we have in the afternoon a temperature of 27° to 29°, and in the night from 14° to 15° of Reaumur. This heat is accompanied by a great dryness, which, however, for want of instruments cannot be correctly ascertained. The Gendeng, which blows over Probolingo in Java (a funnel-shaped pass at the eastern end of the island, of the same character with the pass of Coimbatore in Southern India), can give but a faint idea of the storm which for the greatest part of the year, day after day, bellows from the west over Padang-luwas. Like the mistral, the wind has a strong desiccating power, cracking the ground, and in a few minutes removing all traces of mud and rain."

The Bataks are of the same brown-complexioned, lank-haired race as the rest of the inhabitants of Sumatra. They are divided into many independent states, and in 1822 Mr. Anderson reckoned on the eastern side of Sumatra alone, no fewer than five-and-twenty, of which he gives the several names. The Dutch represent the inhabitants of the districts subject to them as a patient, truthful, laborious, and not unfrequently a parsimonious people; their chief vice being a passion for gambling. They understand the smelting and forging of iron, the growth of rice by irrigation, the culture, the weaving, and the dyeing of cotton, and have domesticated the ox, buffalo, horse, and hog. But they have gone much beyond all this, for they have invented alphabetic writing, having a peculiar character of their own, and a rude literature written on palm leaves or slips of bamboo. Thus advanced, the most remarkable circumstance connected with the manners of the Bataks is their undoubted practice of cannibalism, a fact now as well ascertained as it is of the New Zealanders. The victims are enemies, criminals, and now and then a slave. The skulls are preserved as trophies, or sold at a handsome price to the friends of the victimised. "I am fully justified then," says Mr. Anderson, "not only from what I witnessed, and the proofs now in my possession, but from the concurring testimony of the most respectable and intelligent natives whom I met, in asserting that cannibalism prevails, even to a greater extent on the east side of Sumatra than according to the accounts received it does on the west. For the sake of humanity, however, be it mentioned that it is rapidly decreasing, as civilisation and commerce are advancing. It is not for the sake of food that the natives devour human flesh, but to gratify their malignant and demon-like feelings of animosity against their enemies." Recent Dutch writers in like manner testify to the cannibalism of the Bataks, stating at the same time that those, subject to the Dutch authority, are readily dissuaded from it. The cannibalism of this people seems early to have been known to the Portuguese, for De Barros, speaking of the natives of the interior of Sumatra, says, "This was the race called Batas, who eat human flesh, the most fierce and warlike people of all the land."—Decade 3, book v.

The Bataks have no consistent system of religious belief, but an abundance of superstitions, such as belief in evil spirits, omens, and the like. Slight traces of Hinduism are discernible in their language. Thus their astrologers are called guru, the Sanscrit for a "spiritual guide;" and the main object of their worship is the Batara-guru of the Javanese, that is, avatara guru, which would signify "descended spiritual guide," that is, "heaven-descended guide." The burning, instead of interring the dead, concremation, division of castes, and the other prominent practices of Hinduism are unknown to the Bataks. It is indeed obvious that no form of the religion of the civilised Hindus, which has existed since the days of Menu, could ever have existed among a people systematically cannibals. It is not a little remarkable of the Bataks, that while all the other nations of Sumatra, possessed of a knowledge of letters, have adopted the Mahommedan religion, they have sturdily rejected it for centuries, although surrounded by those who profess it.,

The two provinces subject to the Dutch are reckoned to embrace an area of about 6600 square miles, and to have a population of 78,000, that is, between 11 and 12 inhabitants to a mile. The rate is, however, very unequal in the two districts. The bleak and desert Pârtibi, with a computed area of 4800 square miles, has a population reckoned only at 23,000, or barely 5 to the mile; while the more fertile Mandeling, with an area of 1800 miles, has one of 55,000, or 30 to the mile. Mr. Logan, in the elaborate and judicious sketch which he has given of Sumatra in his valuable journal, reckons the whole area occupied by the nation of the Bataks at 17,000 square miles, and its population at 311,860, which, small as it is, is probably the utmost of it.

The strange civilisation of the Bataks, one of lettered cannibalism, was most probably first developed in the table-land of the interior, called in the maps the Plateau of Tobah, probably of Tuba, the name of a plant used for poisoning fish, a species of dalbergia. On this plateau there is a lake some 20 miles in length, and 4000 feet above the level of the sea, called Eik Daho, in which the Singkel, the largest river of the western side of Sumatra, has its source, and on the borders of which the civilisation of the Batak nation is not unlikely to have been first developed. That it spread from one centre seems probable from the fact of one language, with dialectic variations only, being spoken throughout by the whole Balak nation.

BATAM. One of the largest of the many islands at the eastern end of the Straits of Malacca, and which seem almost to block up the channel between Sumatra and the peninsula. It lies opposite to Singapore, and with the larger island of Bintang, forms the southern side of the Straits of Singapore, the common route to and from the China and Java Sea. Batam is the Portuguese orthography of Batang, a word meaning "trunk," or "main part." The island is computed to have an area of 128 square geographical miles, and its geological formation is like that of the neighbouring countries, plutonic and sedimentary. The land is poor and little cultivated. The ruling inhabitants are Malays, but it has also a rude tribe unconverted to Mahommedanism, called Sabimba. It belongs to the prince of Jehor, under the usual superiority of the Dutch.

BATAN, and BATANES. Batan is the name of the island of the Bashee group which Dampier called Grafton; and Batanes, its Spanish plural, is the name given by the Spaniards to the whole. This group lies between north latitude 19° 57′ 30″, and 20° 28′ 30″; and east longitude 122° 41′ and 123° 1′. Batan, the chief island, is about 3½ leagues in length, and has two ports or roads, one of them, the Bay of Ibaya, on the shore of which is the town of San José, the chief place of the whole group, as also of the Babuyanes Islands. The other larger islands are Basay, Saptan, Hugos, and Itabayat; but besides these there are half-a-dozen more which are uninhabited. The Batanes and Babuyanes Islands form together one Alcaldia, their united population amounting to no more than 8000, and so poor that they are not called on to pay the poll-tax. The chief branch of industry in the principal islands seems to be the breeding of horses, of a race greatly esteemed in Manilla, but which it has been found impossible to multiply in the more fertile island of Luzon, although the experiment has been often tried. Hogs and goats are in great abundance. The inhabitants of the Bashee Islands seem to belong to the Malayan race, but have a peculiar language of their own. Dampier's description of their personal appearance is so truthful and perfect, that although written more than a century and a half ago it is worth quoting. "The natives of these islands are short, squat people; they are generally round-visaged, with low foreheads and thick eyebrows; their eyes are of a hazel colour and small, yet bigger than the Chinese; short low noses, and their lips and mouths middle-proportioned. Their teeth are white; their hair is black, and thick and lank, which they wear but short; it will just cover their ears, and it is cut round very even. Their skins are of a very dark copper colour." This is unquestionably the true Malay.

BATANGAS, sometimes called BALAYAN, and also the province of the Lake Taal, one of the twenty provinces of the island of Luzon. Batangas has the open sea to the west, the strait which divides Luzon from Mindoro to the south, the province of Tayabas to the east, the great lake of Bay to the north-east, and the wide Bay of Manilla to the north. Thus nearly surrounded by water, it is a peninsula with two isthmuses of no great breadth. Its outline is very irregular, its utmost length being 50 geographical miles and its greatest breadth 30. Its area will probably be about 860 geographical square miles. It contains two spacious bays, that of Batangas, which is the smallest, containing one good harbour, and that of Balayan two. Both these bays are on the Straits of Mindoro.

The geological formation of Batangas is eminently volcanic, and the active volcano of Taal, situated on an island of the lake of this name, is one of the most remarkable of the Philippine group (see TAAL). In the centre of the province is situated the lake of Taal just mentioned, with a circumference of 15 leagues,—navigable and having a valuable fishery. The rivers of Batangas are numerous, but many of them, although torrents in the wet season, are reduced to empty beds in the dry. The most remarkable of them is the Bombon, which empties the surplus water of the Lake Taal into the Bay of Balayan after a course of ten miles. In the mountains is found iron ore, and the mines of Argut are stated to yield an ore which produces a metal of a quality equal to that of Biscay.

The soil of Batangas is eminently fertile, but the labours of agriculture are liable to be interrupted by earthquakes and volcanic eruptions,—the most terrible of the last on record being that of 1754. The chief products of agriculture are rice and maiz, cotton, coffee, cacao, and black pepper. Wheat is produced in the more elevated districts, reminding one, for luxuriant growth, says a Spanish writer, of the harvests of Valentia. The pastures of Batangas feed numerous herds of swine, horses, oxen, and buffaloes. The buffalo is chiefly used for labour, and is of especial need in a country almost destitute of roads, and which, in the season of the rains, would be impassable without them. The horses are greatly esteemed in the market of Manilla.

The inhabitants of Batangas are of the Tagala nation, and among the most civilised of the Philippine islanders. In 1849 the province consisted of 17 districts, and comprehended a population of 221,021, of whom those assessed to the poll-tax amounted to 42,845, contributing 428,455 reals of plate.

BATANTA. Name of a considerable island lying off the most westerly part of New Guinea, and computed to have an area of 208 square geographical miles. The strait between it and the island of Salawati, called by navigators Pitt's, is navigable for large ships, but is not considered safe.

BATAVIA. The capital of all the Dutch possessions in India since its foundation in 1619. In 1610, the Dutch had built a fort, which they named Batavia. This was besieged by the Sunda princes of Bantam and Jacatra in 1619, and it was on their defeat in that year that it was resolved to build a town on the ruins of the native one of Jacatra, and this took the name of the fort. Batavia, consisting at present of what may be called an old and new town, is situated on the shore of a bay, some 60 miles wide, but of no considerable depth, studded with islets, in south latitude 6° 8′, and east longitude 106° 50′. The site of the old town, as already mentioned, is that of the old native capital, Sund-kalapa, or "Sunda of the coco-palms," called in the polite language, from the Sanscrit, Jayakarta, popularly Jacatra, meaning "work of victory." The land on which it stands is little above the level of the sea, and consists of a recent alluvial formation, which, bored to the depth of 270 feet, has been ascertained to consist of layers of clays, sands, and marls. The new town, originally suburbs of the old, lies inland from it, and is generally 30 feet above the sea level. Through both, there runs a river of no great size, but with a rapid current, having its source in the mountains of the interior, at the distance of some 50 miles. The native name of this stream is Chai-liwung, meaning "perplexed river." For some years after its foundation, the climate of Batavia had not been remarked for insalubrity; and certainly the ancient Jacatra had not been unhealthy, or it would have been speedily, as it would be easily and cheaply, removed. The European-built town, however, soon acquired a proverbial reputation for insalubrity. The Dutch, unmindful of a difference of some 45 degrees of latitude, determined on having a town after the model of those of the Netherlands, within six degrees of the equator and on the level of the sea. The river spread over the town in many handsome canals, lost its current, deposited its copious sediment, and generated pestilential malaria, which were transported by the land-wind even to the roads. Fatal remittent fevers followed. This state of things was aggravated, 80 years after the foundation of the city, by a succession of violent earthquakes, which took place on the 4th and 5th of November, 1699. These produced the fall of a portion of the mountain in which the river had its origin, which partially changed its course, and brought down with it such quantities of earth as completely to choke the canals of Batavia, covering their banks with mud.

The obvious remedy for the evil was not applied until the vigorous administration of Marshal Daendels, under the French rule, in 1809, and they were continued under the government of the restoration in 1817. Many of the canals were filled up, and the river was carried between piers for a mile into the bay. These operations, carried on by skilful engineers, restored its natural current to the river; and, at present, Batavia is not more unhealthy than any other tropical city similarly situated. The new town, or suburbs, has never had a bad reputation.

In 1814, during the British occupation, the population of Batavia and its suburbs was found to be no more than 47,217. Twenty years after, it was ascertained to have increased to 118,000, and a census taken in 1850 raised it to 348,325. These are great augmentations in so short a time, if the enumerations referred to the same localities. This population has always been of a very miscellaneous character, consisting of many races and nationalities. Along with the original natives, the Sundas, there are found in it, various nations of Sumatra, Javanese, with people of all the considerable islands east of Java,—Chinese and their mestizo descendants, with a few natives of Arabia and India, and a few Europeans of various nations, besides the Dutch. In 1814, the number of Chinese and their descendants was 11,854 ; in 1834, it was 25,000; and in 1850, it had risen to 40,578. The Europeans and their descendants in 1814, exclusive of military, amounted to 2028, in 1834 to 2800, and in 1850, to 3774. In 1814, the number of slaves, consisting chiefly of natives of Sumatra, Bali, and Celebes, was 14,239, which had diminished, in 1834, to 9500; and in 1850, to 7556. This decline took place through manumission, the cessation of the slave-trade, the cheapness of free labour, and the generous indisposition of the Dutch themselves to the continuance of slavery.

Commodore Roggewein, who visited Batavia in 1622, gives a truthful and graphic picture of its heterogeneous population, applicable at the present day; and, therefore, worth transcribing. "There cannot be anything more curious," says this intelligent old writer, "or any spectacle more entertaining, than to see in so large a city, such a multitude of different nations living—all of them at their own dwellings—after their own manner. One sees, every moment, new customs, strange manners, variety of habits, and faces of different colours—black, white, brown, olive. Every one lives as he pleases; every one speaks his own tongue. Notwithstanding such a variety of customs, so opposite to one another, one observes an union very surprising among these citizens, which is purely the effect of commerce, which is the common soul that actuates this great body of people; so that they move uniformly and harmoniously in every respect, and live easily and happily under the gentle and prudent laws established under the East India Company." The laws which our author here lauds for their prudence and gentleness ought, however, in his time, to be considered as questionable in this sense, when he himself tells us that, but a few months before his arrival, a great conspiracy for the overthrow of the Dutch government had been discovered, and the conspirators put to death by torture.

The population of Batavia, considerable as it is, and affording evidence of an amount of public prosperity which could never have sprung up under a native government, is yet far less than it ought to be, if we consider that it was founded on the ruins of a native capital—that its locality is peculiarly favourable to trade—that its neighbourhood is eminently fertile—that it is the capital of a population of probably not less than 15 millions of people—that the main portion of the commerce of the Archipelago has been forced to it as an emporium, and that it has existed for above two centuries. That such is really the case will appear sufficiently clear, if we compare Batavia with other European towns in India similarly circumstanced. Thus, Calcutta, which was a poor village 100 years after the foundation of Batavia, contains at present, probably, twice as many inhabitants, and wealth even in a larger proportion. The little island of Bombay, which was not a British settlement at all for near half a century after the founding of Batavia, and, when it became so, was but a poor, sterile, and scantily-inhabited spot, has, at present, also, at least double its population, and that, too, of a much superior class. Even Manilla, the Spanish capital of the Philippines, has a population at least equal to Batavia, excluding suburbs in both cases. Insalubrity has probably contributed, in some measure, to this unfavourable result, but a com mercial policy, unfavourable to the development of industry, infinitely more.

BATO. The name of one of several lakes in the province of South Camarines in the Island of Luzon. This lake is about 3½ miles in length, and 3 in breadth, deep, and abounding in esculent fish. The volcanic country which surrounds it is fertile and populous. On the borders of the lake, and at the mouth of a river which falls into it, there is a town of the same name, with a population of 2167, latitude N. 13° 20′, and longitude E. 123° 16′.

BATU in Malay, and Watu in Javanese, (a stone or a rock,) is a word frequently found throughout the Archipelago in the names of places, as Batu-gade, "pawn" or "pledge rock," Batu-titi, "bridge rocks," Batu-bara, "live-coal rock," and Batu-mandi, "bathing rock." To complete the sense the words pulo, islet, or tanah, land, must generally be prefixed.

BATU (PULO), "stone or rock islands," in Malay, compose a group of four considerable islands, with many islets of the 300 lying off the western coast of Sumatra, and running in a direction parallel with it. The equator runs through the Batu Islands, leaving the larger part of the group south of it. They are stated to contain an area of 30 square geographical leagues, with a reputed population of 3000. The names of the larger islands have evidently been given to them by the Malays, for they all belong to the language of that people. They are Pingi, Tâluk, Masa, and Bala, meaning respectively, "fair," "cove," "time" or "season," and "host" or "army" island. The inhabitants are of the Malayan race, and as a friendly intercourse is kept up between them and those of the Nias Islands, the latter frequently settling among them, it is supposed they are one and the same people. The inhabitants of the Batu Islands are in a much more advanced state than those of Engano, cultivating rice, understanding the use of iron, and domesticating some animals for food. On the largest island, Masa, there are settled 170 Malays, 50 Bugis, and as many Chinese, the two first being engaged chiefly in the fishery of the tripang and shell turtle, and the last having the whole trade in their hands.

BATUBARA. A river and district of the eastern side of Sumatra, subject to the Malay state of Siak. The mouth of the river, about 300 yards wide, has a bar dry at low water, and an extensive mud-bank before it. It is in N. latitude 3° 13′ 15″, and E. longitude 99° 36′ 45″. The coast of Batubara is occupied by the Malays, the ruling nation, but the interior by the Bataks. The principal town is about two miles up the river. The sea abounds in fish, and the people are, for the most part, fishermen.

BATU-GAPIT, or, at full length, Gunung-batu-gapit, literally "mountain of the gapped rock," the name of a mountain of the interior of Sumatra, in the territory of Achin.

BATUR (GUNUNG). A mountain in the centre of the island of Bali, 6000 feet high, and an active volcano. The word in Javanese, and most probably also in the language of Bali, means "a servant," possibly in reference to its small height in comparison with the mountains which surround it.

BAWÏAN, in Javanese, "place of swine," is an island lying off the northern coast of Java, at the distance of about 50 miles from the western end of the strait which divides that island from Madura. Bawïan contains an area of 350 geographical square miles, and the middle of the island is in S. latitude 5° 49′, and E. longitude 112° 44′. It is surrounded by reefs and rocks; and has no harbour, its best roadstead, Sangkapura, being on its southern coast and taking its Sanscrit name, meaning, "city of imagination," from the principal village, the seat of administration, lying on its shore. The geological formation, like that of Java and Madura, is volcanic, the rocks being composed of trachite and limestone. Hot springs are found all over the island, of which the temperature rises to 125° Fahr., and there is a fine waterfall of 70 feet, and a magnificent cave in the limestone, 200 fathoms long. The island is generally mountainous, but its highest peaks do not exceed 2000 feet. About the middle of the island, and at an elevation of 1000 feet above the level of the sea, there is a lake 2½ miles in circumference, and 30 fathoms in depth, having all the appearance of the extinct crater of a volcano. It is remarked that this considerable collection of potable water contains, with the exception of shrimps, no fish.

The plants of Bawïan are, generally, the same as those of Java and Madura, and even the teak-tree once existed, although now exhausted by the extent to which boat-building has been carried on of late years. Among wild mammals the whole feline family is wanting, and the only carnivorous quadruped is the civet cat. There is one species of deer, seemingly different from any of those of Java. The wild hog is abundant, but whether the same as either of the two species existing in Java is not certain. By a census of the population, taken in 1845, the number of inhabitants was found to be 29,121, of whom 38 were Europeans or their descendants, 50 Chinese or theirs, 426 Malays, 1393 natives of Madura or Celebes, and the remaining 27,224, native Bawïans. This gives the rate of near 662 to the square mile, an immense population for an island but very partially cultivated. The agriculture of Bawïan is of the same general character as that of Java, rice being its principal product, and grown by artificial irrigation, the land thus watered being the only one worth claiming a right of property in. A small variety of maiz, not above four or five inches high, and ripening its corn in two months from the time of sowing, is grown in dry lands. The coco-nut and areca-palms flourish, and of the nuts of the latter about three millions are annually exported. The true sago-palm is also grown, and the inhabitants use its pith as bread when corn is scarce before the rice harvest. Oxen and buffalos are numerous, and so are horses, a diminutive, but well-shaped and hardy breed. Although an ownership in horned cattle and horses is claimed, both are allowed to run wild in the woods. By an enumeration made in 1845, the horned cattle were found to amount to 4200, and the horses to 1600.

But the agriculture of Bawïan scarcely yields corn enough for the support of its inhabitants, and about 1500 tons of rice are yearly imported from Java and Bali. In fact, the islanders are more fishermen and traders than agriculturists. Eight hundred little canoes, each carrying a single fisherman, may be seen at once on the coast of Bawïan engaged in their calling. Besides these, the island has 300 stout trading proas, which make voyages to various parts of Java, to the country of the Lampungs in Sumatra, and to Singapore in the Straits of Malacca.

Like the Irish, the Chinese, and the Scotch Highlanders, the Bawïans are in the habit of migrating to the neighbouring countries in search of better wages than home can afford them; and, like these, they return after a few years' absence with their earnings. Upon the whole, they seem a peaceable and industrious race, among whom crimes against person or property are of rare occurrence. The objects which they exchange with strangers for iron and clothing, consist of mats made from the leaf of the Pandan, horses, and cured fish, especially the holothurion, or sea-slug, for the market of China. The Dutch authorities would seem to be anxious to divert the natives from their present lines of industry to the cultivation of the land; and they complain, especially, of their propensity to a maritime life. This, however, is obviously a mistake. The land, compared with the neighbouring ones, is sterile, and experience has taught the Bawïans that they can obtain food and clothing more cheaply and abundantly by trade and fishing, than by struggling with an ungrateful soil.

With the exception of one village, in which the Javanese language is spoken, the Bawïans speak, with little alteration, the language of the western end of the island of Madura; a fact from which it may be inferred that they are a colony from this island, and that the period of their settlement cannot be a remote one, or the difference of language must have been greater than it is found to be.

BAY (LAGO DE). The lake of Bay in the Island of Luzon, the largest collection of fresh water in the Asiatic Archipelago. It extends from north latitude 14° 9′ to 14° 33′, and has a circumference of 36 leagues. Two projections of the land jut into it; one at its northern end, and one at its western side, between which are formed two deep bays. The lake contains several islets, and one considerable one, named Talim, which is very likely to be taken from the Malay and Javanese talam, a tray or salver. The lake is 58 feet above the level of the Bay of Manilla. No fewer than 15 streams discharge their waters into it, while it is emptied by one, the Pasig, which, after a short course, disembogues in the great bay, passing through the town of Manilla. The fishery of the Lago de Bay is of great value, and furnishes the main supply of the town of Manilla. At the source of the Pasig are several reedy islands, on which are bred for the consumption of Manilla, and by a caste that does not intermarry with the rest of the native inhabitants, a prodigious number of ducks. The lake itself is frequented by several varieties of wild ducks and other water-fowl.

BAY. The name of a town and township at the southern end of the great Lake of Luzon, and which gives it its name. It is situated in the province of Laguna, in north latitude 14° 8′, and contains a population of 2195 inhabitants. See LAGUNA DE BAY.

BENCOOLEN. The Bângkaülu of the Malays, once a British and now a Dutch settlement on the western coast of Sumatra, in south latitude 3° 48′, and east longitude 102° 28′. The entire territory, composing the British possession, did not exceed ten square miles, composed chiefly of sedimentary rocks, the nearest mountain, Gunung-bengkok (crooked mount), about 3000 feet high, and 18 miles to the north-east, being the only mountain near it of considerable elevation. The soil, as described by the faithful and judicious historian of Sumatra, who had passed his Indian life at Bencoolen, is a stubborn, unfertile glebe. "I cannot," observes Mr. Marsden, "help saying that I think the soil of the western coast of Sumatra is, in general, rather sterile than rich. It is for the most part a stiff, red clay, burnt nearly to the state of a brick where it is exposed to the heat of the sun." He proceeds to add, that the soil in its natural state, with the exception of a few dells here and there, into which the mould of the hills had been washed down, would yield no useful plants, except by the creation of an artificial soil and the help of manures.

The buffalo is the only one of the large domestic animals known in the territory of Bencoolen, the horse and the ox being imported occasionally only. Black pepper was the only exportable produce of the country until in 1798 and 1803 when the clove and nutmeg were introduced from the Moluccas. Of these two plants, the nutmeg alone has thriven, but even this only by dint of being forced by a laborious and expensive culture.

The formation of the settlement of Bencoolen arose out of a dispute with the Dutch touching black pepper. During the 17th century, Bantam was the great emporium for this article of trade, most of which, however, was produced, not in Java, but on the western coast of Sumatra. From 1603, the English, as well as the Dutch, had a factory at Bantam for the purchase of pepper, and for 80 years the former seem to have enjoyed a fair share of this then much-envied traffic. About the end of this time, however, the throne of Bantam was disputed between a father and son, the English taking side with the first, and the Dutch with the last. By this time the Dutch had been established in considerable force at Batavia, of which they had been in possession for 60 years. They came from thence with a considerable force,—placed their protegé on the throne,—obtained a monopoly of the trade of the kingdom of Bantam, and expelled the English as interlopers, playing nearly the same part towards them that the English themselves did towards the French in the Carnatic some seventy years afterwards. Our countrymen resolving to have a share in the pepper trade, fixed on Bencoolen for this purpose, after being baffled at Achin. This happened in 1685, two years after their expulsion from Bantam. The first fort was built on the banks of the river of Bencoolen, in a low swamp, and this, in honour of the reigning sovereign, the afterwards expelled James the Second, was called Fort York.

The celebrated Dampier, who held the humble post of gunner of this fort, five years after it was built, says it was a sorry place, sorrily governed, and moreover very unhealthy. "The land-winds," says he, "coming over swamps, brought a stink with them. 'Tis in general an unhealthy place, and the soldiers of the fort were sickly, and died very fast." The insalubrity of the locality produced the necessity of removing the settlement about a mile and a half from the river, to a site somewhat higher; and to mark the change in English politics, the new fort, constructed in 1714, took the name of Marlborough, but even this locality was not beyond the reach of the malaria, for the place continued more or less unhealthy down to the cession of the settlement in 1825. In 1719, the natives of the country, provoked at the ill-usage of the Europeans, attacked the new fort, and took it, but fearing the Dutch, it would seem, even more than the English, invited our people to return. Mr. Marsden pleads for our countrymen that at this time they were not versed in the art of "managing the natives by conciliating methods." There was, however, no reason why they should not have been so, for at the time of this insurrection against them, they had been 116 years engaged in the pepper trade, and 24 years settled in Bencoolen itself. The enforcement of the pepper monopoly, in fact, brought about this and several other insurrections. "The fort," says Dampier, "was sorrily governed when I was there; nor was there that care taken to keep a fair correspondence with the natives in the neighbourhood, as I think ought to be, in all trading places especially.—When I came thither, there were two neighbouring rajahs in the stocks, for no other reason but because they had not brought down to the fort such a quantity of pepper as the governor had sent for." Bencoolen, and the factories dependent on it, were given over to the Dutch by the Convention of 1824, in exchange for Malacca and its territory, with some factories on the continent of India. And thus a bad possession, after an occupation of 140 years, was happily got rid of. Within the first dozen years of its occupation, it had already cost 200,000*l.*, and as it continued ever after a heavy burthen on the trade of the East India Company, or on the Indian territorial revenue, it must in all have cost several millions, without credit or profit to counterbalance.

The territory of Bencoolen is situated in the country of the nation of the Rejangs, and during its possession by the English was computed to contain 20,000 inhabitants, of whom one half, a mixed population of Rejangs, Malays, Bugis, natives of the island of Nias, and Chinese, with their descendants, were in the town. But at present the town contains only 6000 inhabitants, and the territory forms part of the government of Padang, so far as surface is concerned, a very extensive one, rendered so by large annexations from the countries of the Bataks and Malays of Meangkabo.

BENUA, or more correctly Bânuwa, is a Malay, but not a Javanese word, signifying "a land," "country," or "region," that has had a wide extension, although with some modifications of sense, for in the Philippine tongues it means "a village," and in the Polynesian, "land" or "earth." The Malays prefixing to it the word Orang, "men or people," use the compound as a generic term for all the wild tribes of the peninsula speaking the same language as themselves, and of the same race, but who have not adopted the Mahommedan religion. The literal meaning of the phrase is "men of the land;" and it may be fairly translated in the sense in which the Malays use it, "aborigines." Such people are found from the extremity of the Peninsula up to the 5° of latitude, but apparently not further north. They also exist in some of the larger islands of the Archipelago at the eastern extremity of the Straits of Malacca. Everywhere they are brown-complexioned and lank-haired,—are of the same stature as the Malays, have the same features, and speak the same language; in short, are Malays in a lower state of civilisation than the people known to us under that name.

Some of the Orang-bânuwa dwell on the seacoast, and some in the interior, always in small independent tribes. Jakun and Sakai are two names by which they are known to the Malays, but they are more generally named from the rivers on or near which they have their chief residence, as Sletar, Mintira, Sabimba, and Bâsisi. The Orang-lant, "men of the sea," or sea-gipsies, as they have been very appropriately called, evidently belong to the same class, although some of them have embraced Mahommedanism, or passed through the form of having done so. The state of advancement of the different tribes varies, some being far more civilised than others. Some of those of the interior practise a rude husbandry, grow rice by burning the forest for a dressing, and dibbling in the seed, cultivate some farinaceous roots, some fruits, as the banana and durian, and have fixed habitations. The only domesticated animals known to them are the dog, the cat, and common fowl. The Orang-bânuwa of the interior receive their iron and clothing from the Malays, in exchange for the spontaneous products of the forest, including of late years the well-known guttah-percha. "At the time of my visit," says Mr. Logan, speaking of a tribe of Jehor, "nearly every man in the country was searching for teban," that is, for the tree that produces the best of this article.

Much of the time of the wild races of the interior is spent in hunting and fishing. The chief object of the first is the wild hog, which abounds; and next to it various species of deer. Both are pursued with dogs and spears, but fire-arms are unknown. Ingeniously constructed traps and pit-falls are also had recourse to. The modes of taking fish which are plentiful are not less ingenious, and Mr. Logan gives the names of no fewer than fifty distinct species of fish existing in the rivers of the southern portion of the peninsula. In their manners the Orang-bânuwa are superstitious, but have no mischievous customs or sanguinary usages. Generally, they are in the same state of society as the Dayaks of Borneo, but without the head-hunting, skull-hoarding habits of the latter.

From the first appearance of Europeans in the peninsula, the existence of this wild people has been known, but they were never well and truly described until visited by Mr. Logan in 1847 and subsequent years. De Barros, in his second decade, mentions them in the following terms, as the precursors of the Malays who founded Malacca: "The habitation of the Cellates is more on the sea than on the land. On the sea, their children are born and reared without their making any settlement on the land. However, as they were hated by the people of Singapore and of the neighbouring islands, they did not return to these parts, but they came and fixed their location on the banks of a river where now stands the city of Malacca. The first settlement which they made was on a hill above the fortress, which we now hold, where they found some people of the land, half-savages in their manner of living, whose language was the proper Malay, understood by all the people, and with which, also, the Cellates were acquainted. At first there was alienation between the two tribes on account of difference in the mode of life. But through the women an accommodation was effected, and they agreed to live in one settlement, each party following that mode of life to which it had been accustomed, the one subsisting on the produce of the sea, and the other on the fruits of the earth."

The half-savages of De Barros are evidently the Orang-bânuwa, and his Cellates, the sea-gipsies, the word being an obvious corruption of the Malay sâlat, a strait or narrow sea, which with orang prefixed, and making "men or people of the straits," is still applied to the inhabitants of the innumerable islands which nearly choke up the eastern entrance of the Straits of Malacca. Whether the Orang-bânuwa be the aboriginal inhabitants of the peninsula, and the people from which the wide-spread Malayan nation is sprung, or settlers from another country, is a question which naturally arises. The whole peninsula is called by the Malays themselves Tanah Malayu, or the country of the Malays, in the same way in which they call Java, Tanah Jawa, and Celebes, Tanah Bugis, the land of the Javanese and the land of the Bugis; and this would seem to imply that they consider it their original mother country. But this may arise from the country having, except a few scattered mountain negros, no other inhabitants than Malays, and is, therefore, not conclusive. Had the wild people of the peninsula been really its aboriginal inhabitants, they would most probably, like the tribes of Borneo, Sumatra, and Celebes, be found speaking many languages instead of one. As far as Malayan emigration is authentically known, it has always been, not from, but to the Peninsula. Thus, their arrival in a comparatively civilised state, with a regular form of government, and with a knowledge of letters, in the 12th century, is stated to have been from Sumatra, and they are, in fact, at the present day, migrating from the same country and settling in the Peninsula. It is true, however, that even in the 12th and 13th centuries the civilised Malays found the sea-gipsies and rude people of the interior before them in the Peninsula, so that this leaves the question of the parent country of the Malay nation still doubtful. All that can safely be asserted, then, is that Malay civilisation did not originate in the Peninsula, but most likely in Sumatra. The probability is that the Malays were originally fishermen, occupying the mouths and banks of the great rivers of the eastern side of Sumatra, such as those of Palembang, Jambi, Indragiri, and Siak. Ascending these, after intermixing, as they are known to have done, with the more civilised inhabitants of Java, and reaching the rich volcanic table-lands and valleys of the interior, they would naturally become a fixed agricultural population, and acquire that civilisation and power which under the name of Menangkabo they are known to have attained. To this inland country, communicating by its rivers with the sea, both on the eastern and western sides of Sumatra, all the civilised Malay states, whether of the Peninsula or Borneo, trace their origin. From the wandering Malay fishermen, who did not partake of the civilisation of the interior, might naturally proceed the Orang-lant, or gipsies, and occasional stragglers from these may have given rise to the Orang-bânuwa, or rude tribes of the interior. See MALAY and MALACCA.

BENZOIN. The resin of the Styrax benzoin, obtained by wounding the bark. The plant, which is of moderate size, is an object of cultivation, the manner of culture being from the seed. The trees are ripe for the production of the resin at about seven years old, and the plant is the peculiar product of the islands of Sumatra and Borneo; in the first in the country of the Bataks, and in the last on the northern coast in the territory of Brunai. The Malay and Javanese names are written Kamâñan, kamiñan, and kamayan, and abbreviated mâñan and miñan, all obviously mere modifications of the same word, purely a native one. Barbosa gives us the price of the best benzoin in the market of Calicut in the beginning of the 16th century, and before the violence of the Portuguese had interfered with the natural course of the Indian trade. He states it to be from 65 to 70 fanams the farazuola, a weight of 22 pounds 6½ ounces of Portugal, 16 ounces to the pound. He furnishes, at the same time, the price of incense, by which, no doubt, he meant olibanum, now known to be the resin of a Boswellia, and this he makes, for the first quality, only 15 fanams for the same weight.—Does it not seem probable that benzoin may have been the malabathrum of the ancients of the finer quality, for two kinds of it are expressly stated to have been known in the European markets, and the varieties of quality to have been so great, that the price varied from one to three hundred deniers the pound? With respect to the plant, its native country, and the manner of its growth, it is certain that the ancients who had never seen them, nor communicated with any persons that had, could not possibly have rendered an account. But they saw the article themselves in the European market, and their description, although vague enough, seems essentially to agree with that of benzoin. Pliny says that its odour resembled that of Indian spikenard, that it was a mass not easily broken, and that in taste it was neither hot nor aromatic. Dioscorides says that the best came from India, that it was of a blackish colour, that it was externally rough, and that its odour was stronger than that of saffron. He adds, that when dissolved in wine it excelled all other perfumes. In the Periplus of the Erythræan Sea, malabathrum is stated to have been an article of commerce at Barakê, the principal emporium of the Malabar coast, just as benzoin was found to be on the first arrival of the Portuguese; but it is said expressly, not to have been a native product, but brought from a country further east. Dr. Vincent's opinion that malabathrum, which was a perfume, was the betel or areca, is wholly untenable, for the areca nut is odourless, and, moreover, eminently a native product of the western coast of India. Whether true benzoin was known to the ancients or not, it is probable it was well known in the middle ages, since we find it a regular article of commerce in the emporia of Western India, and an article of export to Western Asia, from which so costly an article would easily be transmitted to Europe through Egypt.

BESUKIE, or, in a better orthography, Bâsuki (in Javanese "prosperity"), a province of Java embracing the eastern end of the island for about 100 miles of its length, and having an area of 4126 geographical miles square. It includes the two districts of Prabalinga and Besukie, and on two sides is bounded by the sea, to the north by the strait which divides Java from Madura, and to the south by the Southern Ocean. On its southern coast it has one considerable island—Baron. Its geological formation, like that of the rest of the island, is volcanic, its hills and mountains consisting of travertine and limestone. Some of its mountains are among the highest in the island.

The physical aspect of the province of Besukie gives rise to a singular local wind, called by the Javanese the Angin gânding, which may be translated the "song wind" or "singing wind." This is produced by the passage of the south-east monsoon through a funnel-shaped gap between the high mountains in a part of the island not exceeding 40 miles in breadth. It is of the same nature with the gap of Coimbatore in Southern India, which gives passage to the south-west monsoon through the western Ghauts, although of greater extent, and the wind from the greater height of the mountains and of the pass itself, much colder. The best account of it is given by Mr. J. Rigg, a most intelligent traveller, who visited Besukie in 1846: "We set sail," says he, "from Prabalinga with a fresh breeze off the land, being a peculiar wind that blows here during the prevalence of the south-east monsoon, and known by the name of Ginding. In the course of a couple of hours we ran off 15 or 16 miles, and then sailing out of the tract of the wind suddenly got becalmed. The course and edge of the Ginding were clearly marked upon the sea; where the wind blew, the water was lively and breaking in waves, whilst beyond, it lay sluggish and smooth as a mill-pond. We could see the fate awaiting us: in less than five minutes from spanking along at a pleasant rate the breeze slackened, died away, and our sails flapped to the masts, whilst the original impulse threw us from the fretful to the placid water. The Ginding is occasioned by the south-east monsoon blowing right over the land from the Southern Ocean through the gap leading to Lumajang, between the lofty Iyang and Tengar mountains, which tower into the air right and left, some 8000 to 9000 feet, the gap between them at Klaka only reaching a height of 1000 feet. The Lamongan volcano, 8000 feet high, stands in this gap, but we had the Ginding blowing from each side of it, and were not becalmed till we got under the lee of the huge chain of the Iyang. I am told that the Ginding is as sharply defined to the westward as where we passed out of it on the east. The Ginding blows strongest and steadiest during July and August, and is not found to exercise any unwholesome effect upon the atmosphere; only persons much heated must be careful not to expose themselves to its chill current, and thus suddenly stop perspiration."

The same intelligent writer informs us that there is a similar wind experienced in the province of Pasuruhan, or that immediately west of Besukie, but apparently of less strength. This is produced by a gap 1400 feet above the level of the sea, which is formed between the Tengar and Arjuna mountains, the last an active volcano 12,000 feet high. A third wind proceeding from the same cause is experienced in the province of Kadiri. Here the south-east monsoon rushes through the gap formed between the mountains Klut and Wilis, the first between 5000 and 6000, and the last between 8000 and 9000 feet high. But in this case the breadth of the island being double what it is where the two previous winds prevail, the current does not reach from sea to sea, and the province of Surabaya is protected from it by the mass of the mountain Arjuna.

In 1815 the number of villages in the province of Besuki was 967, and its population 113,212. The census of 1845, if the enumeration of both years was reliable, showed an extraordinary increase of population for a period so short as 30 years; for it had risen to 502,087, the classes of the population being as follows—Europeans and their descendants, 530; Chinese and their descendants, 1373; Arabs and natives of Celebes with their descendants, 3078; and natives of Java and Madura, 497,106. The total number gives a relative population of little more than 121 inhabitants to a square mile, not above a third or even a fourth of the density of some of the central provinces of the island. In 1850 the population amounted only to 500,577, showing a small apparent decline, but this arose from the separation from it of a district containing 30,634 inhabitants. The teak forests of Besukie extend to 45 square leagues, and by an enumeration made in 1845, the number of horned cattle was found to be 147,000 and of horses 50,000. It contains two small towns, Besukie, the seat of administration, and Prabalinga, a more considerable and thriving place, but the amount of their population is not stated.

Besukie contains a few Hindoo remains. Of these the most remarkable is the temple of Jabon, which lies about midway between the towns of Besukie and Prabalinga, about 20 miles from each, and a mile from the sea. The base of the building is of a quadrangular form, with retiring angles, each side measuring 32 feet. This form it preserves for half its height, which in all is 50 feet, when it assumes a rounded shape. The structure is of large well-baked bricks, with the exception of the thresholds and lintels, which are of hewn trachyte. Like other similar buildings of Java it shows that the outside had been coated with plaster ornamented with flowers and figures of men and animals. The inside, at present, contains no image, nor is there a date or any other inscription. Most probably, however, the temple was dedicated to the worship of Siwa or of his consort Durga, and that it is not older than the 12th century. It is without rent or crack—a fact which seems to prove that it has resisted the earthquakes of several centuries.

There has lately been discovered a singular relic of antiquity in a very unexpected situation, which is thus described by Mr. Rigg, the traveller already quoted: "On the top of the Argapura (mountain of the palace), the pinnacle of the Iyang mountain, Messrs. Bosch and Zollinger, at a height of 9000 feet, lately discovered, on the site of an extinct crater, the remains of what appears to have been once a religious establishment. These consist of a number of rude terraces, set round with stones, and some enclosures, also formed of unhewn stones. Here is a well walled round with stones, and sunk 6 feet in the ground. The most extraordinary discovery in such an elevated and lonely place was that of a number of pots or jars, some broken, others whole. They stand about two feet high, have a mouth of about a foot wide, but belly out below. Externally, they are covered over with a bluish glazing, and have some ornamented work round the rim. No images were discovered." The place may be judged to have been a Hindu hermitage, and as no such manufacture as the jars appears ever to have existed in Java, the probability is that they were imported either from China or Japan.

During the last half of the seventeenth and first of the eighteenth century, the present province of Besukie, and most that portion of Java which has Madura in front of it, were harassed and depopulated by invasions from Madura, Celebes, Bali, and the central parts of Java; and it was not until the year 1767 that the Dutch expelled the people of Bali, who laid claim to the country as a conquest. It was at this time that the Madurese emigrating from their own comparatively poor but populous country crossed over and began to occupy the rich but deserted lands of Java, a process that has been going on ever since, and which will in a good measure account for the extraordinary increase of population which has taken place within the last thirty years, the majority of the inhabitants being Madurese and not Javanese.

BETEL. See Areca and Pepper.

BEZOAR. Bezoar stones, still believed among the nations of Asia, as they once were among those of Europe, to possess the virtue of expelling poisons, continue to be an article of trade. They are mostly brought from Borneo, where they are reputed to be obtained from the stomach and intestines of monkeys. In Malay, they go under the names of goliga, mântika, and mâtika; the two last words being probably corruptions of mâstika, "a gem."

BILA. The name of a considerable river on the north-eastern side of Sumatra, forming the eastern limit of the country of the Batak nation, and nearly the only place on that coast where this people have direct communication with the sea. The river consists of two branches, which unite shortly before the disemboguement, in latitude 3° 28′ north.

BILLITON; in Malay, BLITUNG. This island, of which the peak or highest land is in south latitude 3° 13′ and east longitude 108° 7′, is computed to have an area of 1904 square geographical miles; and is, therefore, better than one-half the size of Banca. Its geological formation is the same as that of this island; and by all accounts it is equally productive in iron and tin ore. The first of these has been long worked by the natives; and the last, of late years, by a Dutch association. Billiton is the extreme southern limit of the tin formation, and reckoning only from Tavoy, on the coast of Tenasserim, it extends over 20° of latitude, and is, therefore, incomparably the greatest in the world. The only inhabitants of Billiton, until occupied by the Dutch, were the Malay fishermen, called Orang-lant, or Men of the Sea; here, and at Banca, called Sika, a word the literal sense of which I have not ascertained.

BIMA. The name of one of six principalities of the large island of Sumabawa, and forming its eastern end. To this state belong also some islands in the Straits of Sapi, or those which divide Sumbawa from Floris; the portion of the latter island called Mangarai; and the island of Gunung-api, conspicuous by its active volcano. The territory is indented by a very deep inlet, known as the Bay of Bima, at the head of which is a small town with a Dutch fort. The entrance of this bay is in south latitude 8° 26′, and east longitude 118° 38′. The people of Bima speak a peculiar tongue, one of the several languages of Sumbawa; and they write it in the character of Celebes, although they had once a native alphabet now obsolete. In manners and character they bear the nearest resemblance to the more civilised nations of Celebes, but they are less energetic. The total population has been computed at 90,000. The products of Bima are sapan and sandal woods, bees'-wax, and horses. The horses are considered, although small, to be the handsomest and best bred of the Archipelago, and are largely exported to Java. The most esteemed of them are those of the island of Gunung-api. See SUMBAWA.

BINONDO. A suburb of the city of Manilla, on the right bank of the river Pasig, and communicating with the walled town by a stone bridge 149 Spanish yards, or 411 English feet in length, the most remarkable European structure ever erected in the Philippine or Malayan Archipelagos. The number of houses in this suburb in 1849 was 4853, most of them native dwellings, of frail materials. The population in the same year was 29,211, of whom 4817 were subject to the capitation-tax, of which the gross produce was 48,170 reals of plate.

BINTANG, correctly BENTÂN. The name is said to be taken from the highest hill of the island. Bintang is the largest of the crowd of islands lying between the peninsula and Sumatra at the eastern extremity of the Straits of Malacca, and has an area of 336 square geographical miles. Its geological formation is similar to that of the peninsula and Singapore. A mountainous chain runs through it, the highest summit of which is 1368 feet above the level of the sea. Bintang is drained by five rivers, navigable only for small boats. On its western side there is a wide bay studded with islands, on one of which, called Tanjung Pinang, literally "Areca promontory," divided from the main by a very narrow strait, stands the Netherland settlement of Rhio, in north latitude 54° 40′, and east longitude 124° 26′ 30″. Bintang, in so far as the production of corn is concerned, is, like Singapore, unfertile. But both soil and climate seem eminently well suited to the production of black pepper, and the nauclea gambir, the inspissated juice of which is the gambir of commerce so largely used in the East as a masticatory, and of late in Europe for dyeing and tanning. Bintang and the neighbouring islands are the principal places of the production of gambir.

Bintang and all the other islands south of the Straits of Singapore are nominally subject to the Sultan of Jehor, but substantially ruled by the Dutch. The native chief is the lineal descendant of the princes who ruled first in Singapore, and afterwards in Malacca; and who, after being driven from the latter by the Portuguese in

1511, establishing themselves at Jehor or at Bintang, continued to foster piracy and up to the establishment of the free ports of Singapore and Rhio,—that is, for upwards of three centuries.

BINTULU. The name of a river and district of the north-western coast of Borneo, in north latitude 3° 13′ 30″, and east longitude 113° 3′ 15″. The country on the banks of the river is stated to abound in iron and antimony ore, while it is included in the coal fields, which are said to extend from the river of Borneo in the fifth, to the Rajang in the second degree of north latitude. The river of Bintulu is of inconsiderable size, and, as usual, it has a bar on which at low water there is a depth of no more than 4 cubits, and at high of not above from 7 to 8. The exported produce consists of native camphor, bees'-wax, wood-oil, damar, eagle and laka wood; with bezoar or goliga, taken from the stomach of monkeys hunted for the purpose. These products are obtained from the wild inhabitants of the interior, who exchange them with the Malays for corn and clothing. The antimony and coal mines have not been worked.

BIRD OF PARADISE, the Burung-dewata and Manuk-dewata of the Indian islanders. Burung is "a bird or fowl" in Malay; and manuk, a word that has had a wider dissemination, the same thing in Javanese. Dewata is the Sanscrit for the gods of the Hindus. The word, of course, signifies "bird of the gods," of which the European name is, no doubt, a paraphrase. These appellations were given, not by the people of the countries in which the birds of Paradise are indigenous, but by the Malay and Javanese traders who conducted the commercial intercourse between the eastern and western parts of the Archipelago before the arrival of Europeans. In one of the many languages of New Guinea, the chief country of the birds of Paradise, they, or more likely the best known species of the family, we are informed by the naturalist Lesson, is called Mambefore.

Five different species of birds of Paradise have been described by naturalists, who, instead of ascribing any divine attributes to them, place them in the rather obscene family of crows. All these species are prepared for the market by the natives of the producing countries, who are chiefly the negroes of New Guinea and the islands near it. Birds of Paradise must have been found by the Portuguese on their conquest of Malacca in 1511, brought to that emporium by the Malay and Javanese merchants for the markets of China. At all events, they must have seen them on their arrival in the Moluccas in the same year, or the beginning of the following. But the earliest account we have of them is that given by Pigafetta, who was at the Moluccas ten years after the Portuguese had reached them. His description, taken from the publication of the original manuscript published in 1800, is as follows: "They gave us also for the king of Spain, two most beautiful dead birds. These birds are about the size of thrushes. They have a small head and a long bill; legs fine as a writing quill, a palm long. They have no wings, but in their stead, long feathers of various colours like great plumes. The tail resembles that of the thrush. All the feathers, except those of the wings, are of a dark colour (scuro). They never fly, except when the wind blows. They told us that these birds came from the terrestrial paradise, and they called them bolondinata (burung-diwata), that is, 'birds of God.'" It is probable, from this account, that the birds of Paradise sent by the king of Tidor, one of the five Moluccas, to Charles the Fifth, was not the great emerald bird with which we are most familiar, but one of those which are natives of the Moluccas. At present, the principal emporium for these birds to the East is the Aroe Islands; and to the west, Batavia and Singapore, being brought to the two last by the praus of the Bugis of Celebes.

BIRDS'-NESTS. The esculent nests of the Hirundo esculenta, the Lawit of the Javanese, a small dark-coloured swallow, with a greenish hue on the back, a bluish one on the breast, and no white mark. The nest consists of a marine fucus elaborated by the bird. In Malay the nest is called Sarang-burung, of which our own name is a literal translation; and the Javanese name, expressed by one word, Susuh, is equivalent to it. The swallow producing the esculent nest is found all over the Malay and Philippine Archipelagos, wherever there are caves to afford it shelter and protection, and these, as usual, are most frequent in the limestone formation. But Java and Borneo seem to be their chief resort. The celebrated caves of Karang-bolong (hollow rocks) situated in the province of Baglen in Java, and on the shore of the Southern Sea, may be taken as an example. The entrance into these caves is at the sea level, and at the foot of limestone rocks several hundred feet in height, in one place 200 perpendicular feet before coming to the first ledge. The mouths of the caves are about 18 feet broad and 30 high, while within they expand to breadths of from 60 to 114 feet, and to heights of from 420 to 480, the sea penetrating them to the extent of one-fourth of their length, and in rough weather rendering them inaccessible. The descent of the collectors to the caves is effected by narrow ratan ladders, usually about 74 feet in length, attached at top to a stout tree. Within the caves there are bamboo scaffoldings, in order to reach at the nests, which are detached from the sides by the hand, and from the roofs by hooks attached to long poles. There are three periods for making the collection—April, August, and December. The nest-gatherers are persons bred to their dangerous calling, and before the commencement of the first gathering, plays are acted in masks, and there is feasting on the flesh of buffaloes and goats to invoke the aid of the "lady queen of the south" (Nai ratu kidul), an imaginary being, without whose aid the work of robbing the nests would not prosper. After the crop has been taken, the caves are hermetically sealed against human ingress. The whole annual gathering, which is effected at little cost, amounts to from 50 to 60 piculs yearly, or on an average to 7370*l.* This, which is worth at Batavia about 18,000*l.*, forms a convenient and unobjectionable branch of the revenue of the Netherland government, since it is paid by strangers in the indulgence of a harmless folly.

Esculent swallows' nests are by no means confined, as in the instance now given, to the sea-coasts, for we find them in caves in the interior both of Java and Borneo, and no doubt they exist also in other islands. On the north-western side of Borneo, and not far from the banks of the river Baram, birds'-nest caves are found 140 miles from the sea by the course of the river. They consist of three chambers, one of which is reckoned to be no less than 200 fathoms in length. These are the property of the powerful tribe of the Kayan, and like those of Karang-bolong are carefully guarded.

BISAYA, or VISAYA; the name of one of the principal nations of the Philippines, of their language, and of the islands peopled by them. The Bisaya Islands include those lying between the two great islands of Luzon and Mindano, as Panay, Negros, Çebu, Leyte, and Samar. The name was given to them from the practice of painting or probably tattooing their persons, which obtained among their inhabitants when they were first seen by the Spaniards, the word bisaya signifying in their language "to paint." The Bisaya language is divided into several dialects, differing so much from each other that the parties speaking them are unintelligible to each other. It is spoken by about a million of the inhabitants of the Spanish Philippines, and is therefore, after the Tagala, the most current of their languages. But it is besides supposed to extend to the Sulu Islands.

BLORA. A district of Java, on the river Solo the largest stream of the island. It contains some of the most extensive and most conveniently situated teak forests. South latitude 7° 10′, and east longitude 111° 30′.

BOAT, or VESSEL. The generic name for a boat or vessel, large or small, is Prau, a word almost naturalised in the European languages. It belongs equally to the Malay and Javanese languages, and from these has been very widely spread to others, extending as a synonym to the principal Philippine tongues. The usual name for a canoe or skiff, both in Malay and Javanese, is sampan. The large vessels which the natives of the Archipelago used in war and trade were called by them jung, which is the word corrupted junk, that Europeans apply to the large vessels of the Chinese, of which the proper name is wangkang. For a square-rigged vessel or ship, the natives have borrowed the word kapal from the Telugu or Telinga. Names vary with the forms of vessels, and the uses to which they are put; and these again differ with nations or tribes so as to be innumerable.

BOELEKUMBA. The name of a district at the extremity of the south-western peninsula of Celebes, conquered by the Dutch from the Macassar nation. The mountain of Lompu-batang, which is within it, is supposed to be the highest land in Celebes, and reaches to 8000 feet.

BOEROE, in the Dutch orthography, or more shortly and perhaps correctly, BURU, is the name of an island in the Molucca Sea. In Malay and Javanese buru means "to chase or pursue," and also "to hunt," and with the usual word pulo prefixed, the name may be translated "hunting island." The Dutch establishment on the eastern side of this island is in south latitude 3° 22′ 30″, and east longitude 128° 11′. The area of Boeroe is calculated at 2625 square geographical miles, and therefore it is by little more than one half more extensive than Bali or Lomboc, either of which is a hundred times more valuable. With the exception of the broad bay of Kayeli, on its eastern side facing Ceram, it is a compact unbroken mass of land of an oval form. The interior is a congeries of hill and mountain, divided by narrow valleys or deep ravines. The formation is stated to be sedimentary, the chief rock being slate, intersected by veins of quartz. The highest mountain rises to the height of 10,000 feet, and is the most elevated land in the Molucca Sea. The coast is alluvial and marshy. No indications of metallic ores applicable to industrial uses have been discovered. The soil of the hills is a red clay. Nearly the whole island is one grand primeval forest, containing many useful woods if there were any use to put them to. The only peculiar exportable product of the forests is the oil derived from the distillation of the leaves of a myrtaceous tree, the Melaleuca cajeput. This is the cajeput, or correctly the miñak kayu-putih, that is "white wood oil." The clove and the nutmeg are not native products. The only animal of considerable size is the Babi-rusa or hog deer, and it would seem to be abundant. No domestic animal is known to be reared, and rice is not an object of culture, the inhabitants for the most part subsisting on sago. The coast of Boeroe is occupied by Malay fishermen, most probably settlers of the tribe of the Orang-laut, or Malays of gipsy habits of the west. The interior is occupied by the aboriginal inhabitants, men of brown complexion and lank hair, by all accounts a docile, inoffensive, but idle people, reduced to dependence on the Malays of the coast.

The rude unreclaimed condition of Boeroe proclaims its unfavourable physical formation and comparative barrenness of soil. It possesses neither native vegetable or mineral products for exchange, and a few Malayan fishermen constitute its most civilised inhabitants. This will appear plain enough if we compare it with any of the islands composing the Moluccas. Ternate and Tidor, for example, are but mere islets, hardly one-hundred-and-fiftieth part the size of Boeroe, but, from the single fact of their possessing the clove, they were found to have attained an amount of wealth and civilisation, when first seen by Europeans, which Boeroe has by no means reached after a lapse of three centuries and a half. In 1854, the Netherland government declared the port of Kayeli free to all nations without impost on ship or cargo. The deep bay on which it stands is an excellent harbour.

BOETON, correctly BUTUNG. A large island situated off the south-eastern peninsula of Celebes, divided from it in one place by a narrow strait, and in another by the island of Moena, called also Pangasini. Boeton has an area of 138 square geographical miles, and its chief town Bolio, at the southern entrance of the strait which divides it from Moena, is in south latitude 5° 28′, and east longitude 122° 33′ 30″. The coast-line, generally bold and rocky, is indented by one bay on its eastern side, that of Kalinsoesoe, from eight to nine leagues wide, and containing many islets. The strait which divides Boeton and Moena nowhere exceeds a mile in breadth, is free from dangers, and navigable for large ships. The general aspect of the island is hilly, without however any mountain of considerable elevation. The geological formation consists of recent limestone containing the remains of madrepores and shells. The vegetation is described as being less luxuriant than is usual in the Malay Islands so near to the Equator, which may arise from the peculiarity of its rock formation. The larger wild animals of the island are the hog, the buffalo, and the horse invariably of a dark brown colour; and both it and the buffalo are supposed to have become wild from the domestic state. The inhabitants of Boeton are of the brown, lank-haired race, and speak a language of their own, of the same family as to sound and structure with the languages of Celebes, and they write it in the character of the latter island. In civilisation, the people of Boeton are not below the chief nations of Celebes, the Macassar and Bugis, and possess the same knowledge of the arts that these do. The only product of their industry that deserves special notice is their cotton. This for fineness and length of staple excels every other variety in the Archipelago, and being in demand abroad, particularly in Celebes, is an article of exportation.

No recent census has been made of the population of Boeton, but the island is, at least, as well inhabited as any part of Celebes. An old estimate made the population 50,000. Boeton, with Moena and the Tukang-bessie islands, are subject to the same prince, who calls himself Sultan of Boeton, but who is in reality a tributary of the Dutch under treaties, the oldest of which goes as far back as 1667. The main object of all such compacts was to secure to the European power the privilege of buying cheap and selling dear, by the exclusion of all competition.

BOGOR (Javanese, a mat or carpet). The name of a district of Java, in the country of the Sundas. In it is the country-seat of the Governor-General of Netherland India, called Buitenzorg, distant from Batavia about 40 miles, a beautiful locality in the hills, and with a temperate climate.

BOHOL, or **BOJOL**, one of the Philippine Islands, called the Bisayas or Visayas, a designation that includes all the islands lying between the great islands of Luzon and Mindano. Bohol lies between the larger islands of Çebu and Leyte, the tenth parallel of north latitude passing through it. It is computed to have an area of 150½ square leagues, and a circumference of 43. Its surface is represented as hilly and rocky, and its soil of inferior fertility, but producing some rice, the coco-palm, cacao, tobacco, cotton, and the Abaca banana. The population, by the census of 1849, was 116,751, of whom 21,925 were subject to the poll-tax.

BONI. The name of a leading state of the nation of Celebes, called by themselves Wugi, and by the Malays Bugis. The seat of government, which gives its name to the state, is situated on the south-western limb of Celebes, and on the western shore of the great inlet called by European geographers the Bay of Boni. The town is in south latitude 1° 37′, and east longitude 126° 32′.

BONIRATI, the native name of an islet in the sea of Celebes, lying between Salayer and Kalatöa, and about a day's sail for a prau west of the latter. It is probably the smaller of two islets called in the maps Kalao. Bonirati is a settlement or colony of the Bugis, and a considerable native emporium. The settlement is on the shore of the strait which divides the island from a larger one called Lambego. The majority of the inhabitants of both islands are Bajaus or wandering Malay fishermen, who collect tortoise-shell, holothurion, and birds'-nests: but the carrying trade is conducted wholly by the Bugis, whose praus make yearly voyages to Bali, Batavia, and Singapore to the west, and New Guinea, the Moluccas, and Manilla to the east and north.

BONTHEIN, called Bonti by the natives, is the name of a district of the country of the Macassars of Celebes, embracingthe southern extremity of the south-western peninsula of the island. The town or settlement of the Dutch, on the shore of a bay having the same name, is in south latitude 5° 32′, and east longitude 121° 52′. On the slope of the mountain Lompo-batang, and within this territory, the American potato and European vegetables are grown: and the place itself, distant from Boele-kumba 15 miles, is connected with Macassar, the chief Dutch settlement in Celebes, by a post-road of 50 miles in length.

BOONTING, correctly Pulo-bunting, that is "pregnant island." There are four uninhabited islets off the coast of the Malay principality of Queda, and within four or five leagues of the British settlement of Penang, the names of which will give some notion of the character of the Malayan nomenclature of places. "Pregnant island" is the largest of them; the next to it Songsong, or "escort;" the third Panggil, "call-island;" and the fourth Bidan, "the midwife."

BORNEO is undoubtedly the largest island in the world that can properly be called so, New Guinea alone approaching to it in magnitude, for it has a coast-line estimated at 2000 miles, and an area computed at 12,743 geographical square leagues, or about 263,600 square miles, which will make it between six and seven times the size of Java, and between three and four times the size of Britain. The equator bisects it, leaving about one-half of it in each hemisphere, so that it is swept by the four monsoons, and is therefore strictly an equatorial region, hot and moist. Its form is that of an irregular pyramid, of which the base is at the south-west, and the apex at the north-east. The greatest length of the island is about 700 miles, and its greatest breadth, which is in the first degree of north latitude, 600; but from the second degree of north latitude to its northern extremity its breadth is contracted, and on an average does not exceed 200 miles. It has been conveniently divided into a southern side facing Java, a western facing the Malay Peninsula and Sumatra, a north-western washed by the China Sea and fronting Kambojia, Cochin-China, and Tonquin, a northern of small extent having the southern Philippines before it, a north-eastern exposed generally to the Pacific, and an eastern facing Celebes.

The coast of Borneo is very little indented by bays, and nowhere by deep inlets; and it contains no internal sea or great navigable lake. Allowance made for its peculiar vegetation, it has the physical character of a mass cut out of Africa or America about the equator, with the disadvantage of wanting the great navigable rivers of these continents. The few bays which it possesses are, for the most part, situated towards its northern extremity, and consequently in the vicinity of rude and predatory tribes, and remote from civilised intercourse. Such a form of the coast of Borneo, although inconvenient, is, no doubt, less so in temperate seas, beyond the reach of storms and typhoons, the last never coming within three degrees of it.

The geological formation of Borneo, as far as it is known, may generally be described as composed of plutonic and sedimentary rocks,—granites, sienites, sandstones, schists, and limestones. The great volcanic band is distant from it at least 200 miles, the nearest points of it being Java and Bali; and no volcano, active or quiescent, is known to exist in it. Its mineral deposits, as far as they have been ascertained, consist of iron, gold, antimony, coal, and the diamond. Tin, copper, and zinc have not, as yet, been found; nor silver, except alloyed with gold, which is always the case. Gold has not hitherto been found *in situ*, and only in alluvial deposits, and these confined to the parts of the island south of the second degree of north latitude. Antimony has been found only in two localities, both on the north-western coast,—Sarawak between the first and second degree of north latitude, and Bintulu between the third and fourth. Coal has been found cropping out in various places on the north-western side of the island, between the north latitudes 3° and 5°, and longitudes 113° and 115°; and again on the southern side of the island, between the 3rd and 4th degrees of south latitude. If these, as is probable, are the extremes of the same carboniferous formation, the coal-fields of Borneo extend over about 8° of latitude and 2° of longitude, and must be the largest in the world, except those of North America. Borneo is the only country of the Malay or Philippine Archipelago, indeed, the only country of Asia, except Southern India, in which the diamond is found, and even in Borneo, it is confined to the western and southern sides of the island, south of the first degree of north latitude, and from the 109° to the 114° of east longitude, corresponding, generally, with the region of the gold deposits.

Borneo, as far as it has been explored, is a mountainous country, having, generally, an alluvial band of from 30 to 50 miles broad round its coast. Its mountains, however, do not consist, as in the Peninsula, Sumatra, and Java, of one or two regular continuous chains, but of many small and irregular ones, with probably two of greater regularity and continuity than the rest. Mr. Burns, who penetrated the north-western side of the island, between the 3° and 4° of north latitude, and the 113° and 114° of longitude, gives the following account of the country he visited: "Thirty miles inland from the coast, the greater portion of the country is low and densely covered with forests, but generally not swampy. After this, it becomes very mountainous, and rises most irregularly in ridges to the centre of the island." The mountains of Borneo are of no remarkable elevation compared with those of Sumatra and Java, with the single exception of Kinibalu towards the northern extremity of the island, and in north latitude 6° 5′, an isolated mountain of granite and sienite, estimated to be 11,500 feet high, but which an English traveller, Mr. Lowe, who visited it in 1851, does not consider to exceed 10,000. In the Dutch maps of Borneo, two distinct ranges are laid down running in a direction from south-west to north-east, the highest point of the most southerly of which is 6000 feet, and of the most northerly 3500. The mountains on the western side, corresponding with the most productive part of the gold region, do not exceed 2000 and 2250 feet in height. Mr. Burns mentions a mountain in the centre of the island of great height, which he calls Tibang, but he did not see it. From it and its neighbourhood he considers to proceed most of the principal rivers of the southern side of the island, and one or two of those of the north-western. This probably forms one of the mountains of the southerly chain of the Dutch maps, named in them Kaminting.

No doubt, a country of such vast extent as Borneo will be found to contain lakes of considerable extent, but as yet we have authentic accounts only of one, and this visited for the first time as late as 1823. It is called Danu-malayu, or "the Malay lake;" and is in north latitude 1° 5′, and east longitude 114°20′, about 45 leagues from the western coast. It has a length of 8 leagues and a breadth of 4, with a depth in some places of 18 feet. Four other lakes of smaller extent are laid down in recent Dutch maps on the southern side of the island, and in the territory of Banjarmasin, between latitudes 1° 30′ and 2° 30′ south. It is singular that the existence of a great lake supposed to lie at the western foot of the mountain Kinibalu, has not even been verified; for the English traveller, Mr. Lowe, who ascended the mountain itself in 1851, could hear nothing of it.

The largest rivers of Borneo are those which fall into the Sea of Java, and the straits which part the island from Celebes, and these, according to the Dutch maps, have their source in the range of Kaminting towards the centre of the island. The largest are those of Kuti, Banjarmasin, and Pontianak. The most considerable rivers that disembogue in the China Sea are those of Sambas, the Rajang, the Bintulu, the Baram, and the river of Brunai. All of these have bars at their mouths, making them inaccessible to vessels of considerable burthen, the last excepted, which is navigable for large shipping for 15 miles up, and which, therefore, notwithstanding the apparent shortness of its course, must be considered the most useful river of the island.

The vegetation of Borneo is as luxuriant as that of any of the other islands of the Archipelago. The whole island is, indeed, covered with a rank verdure, or a primeval forest of gigantic trees; the cleared and reclaimed spots forming but exceptional specks in this wild and unvaried landscape. The existence, however, of this rich vegetation, is neither here, nor anywhere else, a reliable proof of real fertility; for the largest timber trees will grow among rocks with a few inches of mould, or in the arid sand, or even in the salt mud of the shore, according to their natures,—localities in which nothing useful to man, or to the animals domesticated by him for food or labour, will thrive. The indigenous exchangeable vegetable products of Borneo are benzoin, eagle-wood, native camphor, the sago-palm, and ratans; and it may be remarked of the last, being the produce of Banjarmasin on the southern side of the island, that in the general markets of the Archipelago they are more valuable by 70 per cent. than those of any other country.

Among the larger animals of the forests of Borneo, are several species of monkeys, the most remarkable of which is the orang-utan, the Simia satyrus, possessed only by this island and Sumatra. The only animal of the feline family found in it is a species of leopard, Felis macrocelis, less powerful and less ferocious than the common leopard of Java and Sumatra. No canine animal exists except in the domestic state; the dog, the jackal, fox, and wolf being all absent. Of the Viverra, Borneo has one species peculiar to itself, Viverra Boiei; and a singular-looking animal, intermediate between the polecat and otter, to which the indefatigable Dutch naturalists have given the name of Patamophilus barbatus. In common with Sumatra, Borneo has one small bear, the Ursus Malayanus, or bruwang of the Malays. Of the gnawers, it has the same species of porcupine as Sumatra and Java, the landak of the Malays, and several squirrels (tupai) peculiar to itself. No indication of the elephant and rhinoceros has been detected on the western and southern sides of the island, but there is now no doubt of the existence of the last on the north-western side; and of the first in the peninsula of Unsang, forming the north-eastern angle of the island. The hog seems to be found all over the island, a peculiar species which naturalists have called Sus barbatus, from its having a tuft of hair on each side of the face, which gives it a hideous and grotesque appearance. The ox, called by the Javanese banteng, the Bos sondaicus, is a denizen of the forests of Borneo, as well as of those of Java. Besides the pigmy deer of Java and Sumatra the two last islands and their two larger ones, it has a deer peculiar to itself, the Cervus equinus. Among reptiles, there are three crocodiles, two of which are peculiar to the island, one of them being intermediate between the common crocodile and the gavial of the Ganges. The birds of Borneo, although among them there are many new species, present none that are striking for size, use, or beauty. The peacock, the Argus pheasant, and the jungle fowl of Sumatra and the peninsula, seem to be all wanting.

The aboriginal man of Borneo, the Dayak or wild man of the Malays, is in race identically the same as the inhabitants of Java and Sumatra,—culture making the whole difference between them. The complexion is a yellowish-brown, the hair is black and lank, the eyes small and obliquely set, the nose short and small, the cheek-bones high, the mouth wide, and the average stature much below that of the Chinese or European. The aborigines of Borneo are thinly spread over the interior of the island, rarely reaching the sea-coast, which is in the occupation of foreign settlers. They are divided among themselves into many independent tribes or nations, each speaking its own distinct language. Fifty such tribes or nations may be easily counted, and this is probably below their actual number. These are in very various social states. A few of them are wandering savages, without fixed dwellings,—without more clothing than what is sufficient to cover their nakedness and this consisting of the bark of trees, subsisting precariously on the animal and vegetable products of the forest. The majority, however, have advanced far beyond this condition, for they have fixed and substantial dwellings, cultivate, although rudely, farinaceous roots—the sago-palm, rice, cotton, tobacco, the banana, the sugar-cane, and even the pine-apple. They moreover understand the fabrication of malleable iron and the art of spinning and weaving cotton, while they have domesticated the dog, the hog, and the common fowl, but no animal for labour; the ox, the buffalo, and the horse being unknown to them.

No aboriginal nation of Borneo has invented letters, as has been done by the inhabitants of the other great islands—Sumatra, Java, Celebes, and Luzon. Neither have any of them borrowed those of any of the other nations of the Archipelago. In a word, the most advanced of the tribes of Borneo are in the scale of civilisation much below the least advanced of the civilised nations of the other islands, a result which may be fairly ascribed to the inaccessible physical form of the island, and to the virtual sterility of its soil compared to that of the countries within the volcanic band in which alone a reputable civilisation has sprung up. Such a state of society evidently bears a nearer resemblance to that of America on its discovery than to any thing Asiatic, with the advantage, on the side of the Borneans, of the knowledge of malleable iron, with which, however, they had not attained so high a civilisation as the Aztecs without it.

It would be instructive to know how much of the Dayak civilisation of Borneo is indigenous, and how much is derived from the strangers who have so long occupied the coast of the island. We can only guess at this from an examination of their languages. We possess a tolerably large vocabulary of the language of the Kayan, the most numerous and powerful native tribe of the island. This shows that the words for iron, gold, anvil, hammer, file, chisel, gimlet, axe, hoe, knife, needle, boat, oar, window, loft, floor, stairs, railing, beam, board, rafter, lath, thatch, pot, jar, areca-palm, banana, orange, and mangostin are all native, while those for brass, copper, whetstone, thread, cloth, chest, porcelain, cup, curtains, the balance, the durian, the coco-palm, the yam, sugar-cane, cotton, rice in the husk, rice freed from it and rice boiled, the hog and the dog, with all the numerals except the first, are Malayan. We may be disposed then to conclude from this enumeration that the making of malleable iron and whatever is formed from it, with the construction of houses, are native arts, while the taming of domestic animals, the growth of corn, and the weaving of textile fabrics, are arts which they have acquired from strangers.

No negro race is found in Borneo such as exist in the Malay peninsula, and in Luzon, Panay, and Negros in the Philippines. Nearly the whole coast is occupied by colonised strangers, the most remarkable of whom are the Malays, who are in possession of the debouchements of the rivers and territory adjoining them from the north-east angle of the island, including the whole north-western, western, southern, and eastern sides, up to about the third degree of north latitude. In these quarters, to the depth of about 100 miles, they have been settled for a time beyond the reach of history, holding the conterminous aboriginal inhabitants in a species of vassalage or helotism, and excluding them generally from maritime communication. Some fifteen such settlements, which either now form, or which once formed, so many petty independent states, may be counted. Of the time when, or the manner in which these colonies were planted, there is no record, but in their manner of formation it may be said that it bears, although in a rude way, no inconsiderable resemblance to that of the ancient Greek colonies of the shores of Italy, its islands, and the Mediterranean coast of France. The probability is that the original Malay settlers were not composed of premeditated emigrations, but of casual settlements of the wandering, warlike, and predatory people called the Orang-lant, or Men of the Sea, who finding convenient localities for settlement on the rivers of Borneo, assumed fixed habits from their position without altogether abandoning the occupations of fishermen and traders of the people from whom they were sprung. This seems a more reasonable mode of accounting for the Malay settlements in Borneo, than ascribing them to deliberate emigration, little compatible with the rude manners of such a people, and for which no sufficient cause could exist in a country never over-peopled, and therefore never under the necessity of migrating for more room. Settlements formed in this manner, with essentially maritime habits, would naturally maintain an intercourse with more advanced Malay nations, situated on the shores and islands of Sumatra, the parent country of this people, and by such an intercourse, acquire additional strength and civility.

The Malays of Borneo invariably ascribe their origin to those of Menangkabo, or to those of Malacca and Jehore, supposed to have sprung from these. This however is only tracing their source to the most powerful and civilised states which the Malays are known to have formed, or to the parties to have sprung from whom does themselves the greatest credit. Some merchants of Brunai or Borneo Proper, the most considerable state which the Malays ever established in the island, informed myself in 1824, while in Singapore, that the existing generation of their countrymen was the twenty-ninth in descent from the original founders, the Malays of Menangkabo, and in 1837 a similar account was given to a traveller who visited Borneo itself. In all probability the statement refers to the reigns of kings, and not to generations of men. Reckoning at the usual calculation of 20 years to a reign, this would make 580 years, and carry back the foundation of the state of Brunai to an era corresponding with the year 1243 of our time. Settlements of wandering Malay fishermen may, however, have taken place many generations before this date, which is little more than half a century before Marco Polo passed through the Archipelago, and but 278 years before the companions of Magellan visited Brunai itself, and found it a tolerably civilised country. The Malays of Brunai assert that the first settlers had not yet adopted the Mahommedan religion, and the date given corresponds with this statement, for their countrymen who had settled on the Malay peninsula had not embraced it until 30 years later.

That the Malay settlers of Borneo brought with them some portion of the civilisation of their parent country in Sumatra may be presumed, from at least, one curious fact. In 1840 two enterprising American travellers who penetrated Borneo to a considerable distance from its western coast, and by a tributary of the river of Pontianak, discovered an alphabetic inscription rudely engraved on a mass of sandstone, in an unknown character, but much resembling a similar one on the same material found in Singapore, the ancient seat of a Malay settlement. Since no aboriginal nation of Borneo now possesses, or seems ever to have possessed, the art of writing,—and since the inscription is not in the ancient or modern Javanese character, or in any other of the Archipelago,—it is natural to infer that it is in that in which the Malays wrote before it was supplanted by the modified Arabic now in use. It may be added, that when Brunai, the chief state of the island, was first visited by Europeans, and this was by the companions of Magellan in 1521, they found the Borneans in a state of civilisation hardly inferior to that of Malacca, considered, at the time, the most civilised Malay community. They had domesticated the buffalo, the horse, the goat, and even the elephant. They had adopted the money and the weights of China. Their chiefs, at least, were clad in silks and brocades. The fortress was mounted with both brass and iron cannon, and the art of writing (in the Arabic character) was practised for useful purposes. "He" (the king), says Pigafetta, "has ten writers, who register his transactions on fine bark, and they are called chiritoles" (jurutulis, "adepts in writing"). The horse is expressly named by Pigafetta as among the domesticated animals of the Borneans, and it is probable that a few were kept by the king for state; but it is to be observed that this animal, which abounds in Sumatra and Java, with several of the smaller islands, is, even at present, generally unknown in Borneo; a fact which attests the existence of a country of marshes, of many rivers, of forest-clad hills, and one without open plains, or bridges, or roads even to the extent of bridle-paths. Even the ox, less fitted to struggle against such difficulties than the semi-amphibious buffalo, is still confined to a few localities.

It is not to be concluded, that all the people of Borneo who go under the name of Malays, are the genuine descendants of the original settlers. Malays have intermarried with the aboriginal inhabitants; several tribes of the latter have adopted the Mahommedan religion and Malay language, and are now, consequently, not distinguishable from Malays, in the same manner that Scandinavian tribes settling in England, and adopting Christianity with the Anglo-Saxon language, are not distinguishable from the descendants of the companions of Hengist and Horsa.

The Javanese, like the Malays, formed settlements in Borneo, apparently at a much more recent period, in a different manner, and to a less extent. They were conquerors and propagandists rather than colonists. They are not distinguished in the population of Borneo by their language; but in the names of places, persons, and titles, abundant evidence exists of their presence and influence. They brought with them the Hindu religion, such as it existed in Java; and relics of it, in the form of monuments and images, still exist in that part of the island which is nearest to Java. The names referred to are sometimes Javanese; sometimes Sanscrit, in the form and sense of Sanscrit words in Javanese; and sometimes they are composed of the two languages. Of names of places entirely Javanese we have such examples as the following: Mogasari, "conspicuous flower;" Chandi, "the monument," or "the temple;" Banjarmasin, "saline garden;" Gunung-kumukus, "smoke or vapour mountain;" Danu-pamingir, "frontier lake;" Gunung-aji, "king's mount." Of names of places wholly Sanscrit, we have the following examples: Martapura, correctly Amartapura, "city of immortals;" Coti, correctly Kuti, "the little fortress;" Sukadana, "parrot's gift." With the two languages combined, we have the following: Kali-nagara, "river of the city;" Kuta-wringin, abbreviated Kotaringin, "fortress of the Indian fig-tree;" and Martalaga, correctly Amartalaga, "war of immortals." The line of princes, with their connexions that reigned over the state of Banjarmasin, furnish the Sanscrit names: Suryanata, "sun lord;" Suryawangsa, "offspring of the sun;" Gangawangsa, "offspring of the Ganges;" Sukarama, "delight of Rama;" and Sumadra, "he who gives great delight." The same list gives the Javanese names: Ampujatmika, "upholder of courtesy;" and Sâkar-sungsang, "inverted flower;" this last being the designation of an unfortunate princess. Titles are mostly Javanese; as Pangeran, "a prince;" Raden, "of royal blood;" Ratu, "king;" Panâmbahann, "object of reverence:" and Mangkurat, "nurser of the world." Mangkubumi, half-Javanese and half-Sanscrit, has the same sense as the last word; and Adipati is pure Sanscrit, and in Java the title of the highest nobility.

Words that are Javanese, without being at the same time Malay, have extended even to the languages of the aborigines. Thus, in the Kayan language, the name for the dog and common fowl, with several others, is purely Javanese.

Remains of Hindu temples and images have, of late years, been discovered both on the western and southern side of Borneo, bearing an entire resemblance to the similar relics of Java. Dutch travellers have identified among the images, the frequently found ones in Java of the elephant-headed god of wisdom, Ganesa; and that of the bull, Nandi, the vehicle of "the destroyer" of the Hindu triad. The English traveller, Dalton, who, in 1828 penetrated several hundred miles into the interior, by the river of Koti, and lived for several months among the wild tribe of the Kayan, assures us, "that in the very inmost recesses of the mountains, as well as all over the face of the country, remains of temples are to be seen," similar to those of India and Java. "In the country of Wagoo," says he, "400 miles from the coast, I have seen several of very superior workmanship, with all the emblematical representations so common in Hindu places of worship."

Over the western and southern sides of Borneo, the Bugis nation of Celebes has settled in considerable numbers; but they are nowhere much concentrated, and virtually independent, except on the rivers of Pasir and Koti, which have their debouchements in the strait which divides Borneo from Celebes. There, by their superior intelligence and enterprise, and the union and strength which spring from them, they have been enabled to dictate their own terms to the Malay princes, and have the entire trade of the rivers in their hands. The time of the first settlement of the Bugis, in Borneo, is unknown, but cannot be very remote, since this people themselves were nearly strangers to the commerce and navigation of the Archipelago when the latter first became known to Europeans. The northern end of Borneo, and a considerable part of its north-eastern side, are in the possession of the princes of the Sulu Islands; and the population appears to be a mixed one of tribes of aborigines, Malays, and Bugis, the ruling people being the Sulus, who are of the Bisaya nation of the Philippines. But, in truth, very little is known respecting this secluded portion of the island, which has rarely been visited by Europeans at any time, and not at all of late years.

The only other stranger people, who have settled in Borneo in large numbers, are the Chinese. They are found in scattered numbers in every part of the coast of Borneo, but it is only on the western side, attracted thither by its gold and diamonds, that they exist concentrated and in large numbers. A portion of these is subject to the Dutch rule, paying a capitation-tax; but the majority are virtually independent, living under a kind of rude republic, governed by elective chiefs who administer the laws of China. No females, as is well known, emigrate from China; but the settlers have found wives among the women of the Dayaks, and hence many of the present colonists are a mestizo or mixed race; the original blood being, however, to some extent kept up by annual immigrations from China. The original settlers, as well as the present immigrants, are natives of the province of Canton, and all of the lower or working classes of society. The Dutch authorities have estimated their numbers, on the western coast alone, at 130,000.

The trade of the Chinese with the Indian Archipelago is probably of considerable antiquity; but there exists no record of the time when, or the manner in which, it began. Their ships were found trading with Malacca when first visited by Europeans. Pigafetta does not mention their being in the port of Brunai, or Borneo Proper, when he visited it in 1521; but this may be accounted for by the time of the year, which was the month of July, which would be after the sailing of the Chinese junks on their return voyage with the south-western monsoon. He mentions, however, the silks and porcelain of China which he saw in Borneo; and he states the adoption, by the Borneans, of the weights and the money of China; facts sufficient to prove the existence of a trade which was afterwards known to have yearly employed four or five junks of large burden. Another curious fact attests the existence of the trade, and proves it to be of some antiquity. This is, our finding among the aboriginal inhabitants of Borneo, Chinese vases of ancient pattern which cannot now be imitated. These are preserved in the families of the Dayaks as sacred heir-looms, and bear extravagant prices, varying, according to size and quality, from 8*l.* up to 400*l.* each. The settlement of the Chinese in the Archipelago is certainly a much more recent event than their trading; and is, probably, coeval with that of European establishment and conquest. The narrators of the conquest of Malacca make no mention of Chinese settlers in that town, although they do of Javanese; of natives of continental India; and even of Pegu. Neither does Pigafetta mention Chinese settlers in Brunai; and from the peculiarity of their appearance they must have struck him had they existed.

The number of the different nations now named, or the total population of the island, must in the state of our knowledge, amount to little more than reasonable conjecture, and all that we can be sure of is that it must in reference to area be very small. "If," says Mr. Burns, speaking of the Kayans, the most powerful and numerous of the aboriginal tribes, "the amount and mode of cultivation practised throughout be taken as a criterion, the island must be very thinly inhabited indeed; and further, if the other divisions of the island be not more populous than that of the north-western, which is unlikely, the entire population of Borneo must fall far short of the surmises and highly exaggerated accounts already published." The public functionaries of the Netherland government have made computations of the population of that portion of the island over which the Dutch authority is paramount, reckoned at two-thirds of the whole, and this they make to amount to 1,348,000. If then we suppose the remaining third to be equally populous, we shall make the total population in round numbers 1,800,000. Even this would give but the poor relative population of less than 7 to the square mile. It is however, I am satisfied, far above the actual population, for the Dutch part contains most of the Malay, and nearly all the Bugis and Chinese inhabitants, the country occupied by whom must, from superior civilisation, be necessarily more populous than that of which the inhabitants consist only of Malays and aborigines. Even the population however of the Dutch portion of the island must itself be over-rated, and some of the facts adduced show that this is really the case. Thus in the Dutch statements we find the whole territory of Banjarmasin on the southern side of the island reckoned at 280 square geographical leagues, and as having a population of 120,000 souls. Yet the Dutch portion of it, the largest although not the most populous, has been found by enumeration to amount to no more than 20,115, leaving therefore near 100,000 for the smaller part. A population of 120,000 for the territory of Banjarmasin would in proportion to area give to the portion of Borneo under the supremacy of the Netherlands near three times the population which the Dutch authorities assign to it, while it would make the total population of the island near five millions and a half, a number which no one thinks of attributing to it. The essential sterility and rude condition of Borneo is shown by comparing its state of populousness with that of the great fertile volcanic islands according to area. Had it been proportionally as well peopled as Java, it ought to have contained some 65 millions of inhabitants, or had it even been as well peopled as Luzon, full twelve millions and a half. The populous and fertile volcanic islands of Bali and Lomboc have between them an area of 208 square geographical leagues, which is rather less than one-sixtieth part of the area of Borneo, and they are computed to contain a million and a quarter of inhabitants, and it is certainly more probable that they contain this population than that Borneo contains an equal number, yet the race of man is the same in both cases. In Bali and Lomboc, as in Java and Luzon, physical form and soil are favourable to the advancement of an early civilisation, and in Borneo they are adverse to it. A hardy, industrious, and enterprising population like that of China, fitted to labour under the equator, might with the help of its metallic wealth in a few generations make Borneo as populous as Java, but its natural difficulties are more than the Malayan race is competent to overcome. In some of the southern provinces of their own country, it is certain that the Chinese have overcome greater difficulties than any they would have to encounter in Borneo.

The earliest mention that I have met with of Borneo by an European writer is in the Itinerary of Ludovico Barthema. This traveller, a native of Bologna, whose narrative is to be found in Ramusio's Collection, visited most of the maritime countries of the East as far as the Molucca Islands, going by the route of Egypt, a country which he says he passed through in the year 1503. In 1507 he quitted Calicut on his way home, so that his visit to the Archipelago must have taken place in the intervening years, the last date being four years prior to the conquest of Malacca, when the active intercourse with Malayan countries commenced. Barthema visited of the Malayan countries, the Peninsula, Sumatra, the Banda and Molucca Islands, and Java. The Moluccas he seems to consider as one island, including probably under this name the great island of Gilolo, and it was from them that he sailed to Borneo in a native vessel. "Having," says he, "arrived at the island of Bornei, which is distant 200 miles (leagues) from Maluch, we found it to be somewhat larger than this last, and much lower." The next mention of it is by Barbosa, whose account of Malacca shows that he visited that place before its conquest by his countrymen. He does not seem to have visited Borneo, but he states its position, calls it an island, and writes the name, like Barthema, Bornei. Far more satisfactory than the notices of Barthema and Barbosa is that of Pigafetta, who, as one of the surviving companions of Magellan, visited Brunai, or Borneo Proper, in 1521, which was 10 years after the conquest of Malacca. He gives its latitude as 5° 15′, and its longitude from the first meridian as 176° 40′, the first being not above 10′ from its true position, but the last by the enormous amount of nearly 30°. He writes the name like his predecessors, and thus describes the island: "The island," says he, "is so great that it would take three months to sail round it in a prao." This account of its extent is probably not far from the truth, according to the manner of computation adopted. A native prau sailing round Borneo would necessarily encounter an adverse monsoon and calms in one half the voyage, to say nothing of delays for wood, water, and provisions. With these drawbacks, 20 miles a day would be a fair average rate of sailing, and at such a one it would certainly take three months to complete the circumnavigation of an island with a coast-line of 2000 miles.

The name of the island is obviously taken from the capital town of the chief native state in it, which is indifferently pronounced by the Malays, according to the dialect they happen to speak—Bruné, Brunai, Burné, or Burnai. This last is nearly the name given to it by Pigafetta and his predecessors. These European writers had no possible means of obtaining their knowledge of the name, the insularity, or the extent of the country, except from the native navigators of the Archipelago who preceded them. We may conclude, then, that the name of the town was not extended to the island by European writers, but by the Mahommedan navigators, who conducted the carrying trade of the Archipelago before the advent of Europeans. The word has not, like many other names of places, a specific meaning. Mr. Walter Hamilton, in his Gazetteer, derives it from Varuna, the Hindu god of the sea, but this seems to be the mere fancy of an oriental etymologist, for the name of the Indian deity in question is well known in the legends of the Malays and Javanese, and always pronounced Baruna or Waruna. It may be noticed that Borneo has been sometimes called by the Malays Kalamantan. This word is the name of a species of wild mango, and the word at full length would simply mean Isle of Mangoes. The name however is mythic, and neither a popular or well-known one.

I do not find that there was any formal taking possession of Borneo by its Spanish discoverers in the name of the King of Spain, as was usual in such cases. The first appearance of the Portuguese in Borneo, according to De Barros, was in 1526, fifteen years after their conquest of Malacca. They must have heard of it from the native merchants of that place immediately on that event; but it presented no commercial advantages like the Spice Islands, Sumatra, and Siam, which would tempt Alboquerque to open an immediate communication with it, as he had with these places. In order to get to the Moluccas by what was supposed to be a nearer route, it was resolved to sail to the north instead of the south of Borneo; and in the course of this voyage on one occasion the commander of a squadron, Don Jorgé de Menezes, appointed Governor of the Moluccas, touched at the port of Brunai, and exchanged gifts with the king. De Barros expressly states that until then, Borneo had been undiscovered by the Portuguese, and that the voyage which it was hoped would be shorter than the customary one, lasted eight months, and, like others, was conducted under the guidance of "Moorish pilots." The same Menezes, while exercising the government of the Moluccas, sent in 1527 one Vasco Laurenzo to Borneo in order to examine it more closely, with a view to the extension of Portuguese trade. The mission of this person was defeated by a strange, but by no means incredible incident, considering the character of those who sent it, and of those who received it. The Portuguese gift to the King of Brunai consisted of a piece of rich tapestry, on which was represented the marriage of Henry the Eighth of England with Katharine of Arragon.

When the king understood that Henry was a crowned prince, like himself, he became alarmed, fancying the Portuguese were practising an act of sorcery, and that the figures, springing into life from the tapestry, would take away his kingdom. He therefore ordered the tapestry to be removed, and the Portuguese forthwith to quit his country. He would even have proceeded to acts of violence against them, but for the intercession of some Moorish merchants. In 1530, however, a friendly intercourse between the Portuguese and the sovereign of Brunai was established, and during the continuance of the Portuguese supremacy, a fair trade seems to have been carried on between the different ports of Borneo and Malacca. The Portuguese had commercial factories in various parts of the island, but seem discreetly to have abstained from attempting conquests. This state of things lasted down to the year 1691, or for a period of 130 years.

The Dutch first made their appearance in Borneo under the celebrated navigator, Oliver Van Noort, in 1598, but it was not until 1606 that they began to trade with it, attracted by its gold, diamonds, and black pepper. Until, in comparatively late years, their relations were confined to its southern coast, and then chiefly with the state of Banjarmasin, which, at the time, ruled over the principal part of that side of the island. Their sole object, according to the commercial principles of the time, was to obtain, through arrangements with the native prince, the staple products of the country at prices below their natural cost, and to sell them above it. This kind of traffic went on until 1669, when, as alleged, through the treacherous conduct of the prince and his people, assisted by the intrigues of the English, who were pursuing the same discreditable commerce, the Dutch found themselves compelled to withdraw from the country. They did not return until 1733, when they entered into new arrangements with the reigning prince, having the same object in view. The result of these was the decline of the trade of Benjarmasin; its staple product, pepper, which had at one time been considerable, having become nearly extinct. In 1785, a disputed succession and a civil war having taken place in Banjarmasin, the Dutch interfered, dethroned the reigning prince, and placed his younger brother on the throne. In gratitude for their service, this prince ceded to them his entire dominions, which, with the exception of a portion to be held by themselves in full sovereignty, they restored to him to be held as a fief. It was thus that the Dutch first became possessed of territory in Borneo. Since the restoration of their Indian possessions in 1816, this territory has been vastly increased, through treaties with native princes on the western, southern, and south-eastern sides of the island; and their authority, in one form or another, is now asserted to extend over eight degrees of latitude and ten of longitude, embracing full two-thirds of the island, a territory by one-half larger than Great Britain and Ireland. This nominal sovereignty, however, is over a vast tropical wilderness, of no practical value to the possessors, but, on the contrary, a heavy incumbrance to them. In its present condition, it can neither feed its own scanty inhabitants, nor, unless the hog and buffalo, nourish any animal useful to man. As far as the published accounts will enable us to judge, the entire gross revenue of this monstrous territory falls short of 24,000*l*., out of which has to be maintained civil establishments, garrisons, and a naval force. Ever since 1816, the European power has waged a constant warfare with the Chinese of the western coast, endeavouring in vain to subject them to the payment of a capitation-tax, but with more success to place their commerce and immigration under restraints.

The English never had territorial possessions in Borneo, but, like the Dutch, they had factories on the southern coast, especially at Banjarmasin, where their intrigues to secure a monopoly of trade, had produced the expulsion of their commercial rivals. The factory consisted of the establishment which had been driven first from Chusan, in China, and afterwards, in 1704, cut off by a mutiny of its own native garrison in Pulo Condove, on the coast of Kamboja. In 1707, or within three short years of its establishment, it was forcibly expelled by the native prince, and justly so, if the account of the transaction given by Captain Alexander Hamilton, in his New Account of the East Indies, be correct. "Their factory," says he, "was not half finished before they began to domineer over the natives, who passed in their boats up and down the river, and, very imprudently, would needs search one of the king's boats which was carrying a lady of quality down the river, which so provoked the king that he swore revenge, and accordingly gathered an army, and shipped it in large praus to execute his rage on the factory, and shipping that lay in the river." The factory, however, had notice of the king's design, and embarked in two large vessels in the river, from which they successfully defended themselves, and effected their escape from the country, leaving some small craft belonging to private English merchants to be destroyed, and their crews massacred. This was the end, and nearly the beginning also, of our trade with Borneo under the system of monopoly. A British trade with it exists at present of a very different description, which is carried on chiefly with the free port of Singapore, and which not only far exceeds in value the Dutch and English trade of the 18th, but the trade of the Dutch in the 19th century, although exercising sovereign authority over two-thirds of the island.

All attempts on the part of European nations to establish a permanent territorial dominion in Borneo, we may rest assured, will, in the long run, be baffled by the insuperable obstacles of an uncongenial climate, a stubborn soil, a rude and an intractable population, and the absence of all adequate financial resources. Such dominion, no doubt, has been established in Java, the Philippines, and Hindustan, with fertile soils, dense and docile populations, and large financial local resources; but that is no reason for imagining it should be established in a sweltering jungle, occupied either by savages, or by rude, idle, and intractable barbarians.

BORNEO PROPER. See BRUNAI.

BORO-BUDOR. The name of the remains of an ancient temple, situated about the centre of Java, and in the fertile and picturesque province of Kadu, itself a valley lying between four volcanic mountains, the lowest of which is 9000 feet above the level of the sea, and the highest 11,000. This temple, the largest and most perfect of all similar buildings in Java, stands on the right bank of the river Praga, or Progo as pronounced by the Javanese, at an elevation of 800 feet above the level of the sea, in a small tract of country uncultivated, because beyond the reach of irrigation. It occupies the summit of a small hill fashioned to receive it, the hill itself, indeed, forming as if it were, a part of the edifice. It consists, first, of six quadrangular walls, diminishing as the hill is ascended, and having terraces between them: then, of three circular rows of latticed niches adapted to receive images, and finally of a dome. Each side of the base of the building, or lower wall, measures 426 English feet; and the height of the whole building in its present imperfect state is 116 feet. A part of the dome has fallen, but what remains of it is 20 feet high, and its diameter 50. Each of the latticed cages is a fane, and the several walls contain niches for images. All these are statues of Buddha or Jain, in the usual sitting posture, looking outward, and larger than life. There are four gates or entrances to the temple, facing the cardinal points of the compass. The dome is the only hollow part of the building, and this consists of a chamber, without an image, or pedestal to show that there had been one. The walls are profusely sculptured in low relief; the sculptures representing religious and other processions, battles, and sea views. The total number of images is about 400. There is no inscription of any kind on the temple to show when, by whom, or for what purpose it was built. The traditional chronology of the Javanese, contained as usual, after the example of the Hindus, in enigmatical verse, ascribes the date of its construction to the year of Salivana, or Saka, 1266, corresponding to the year of Christ 1344. This seems not an improbable date, for the perfect state of the building, notwithstanding the destructive nature of the climate, points at no great antiquity. Several of the terraces were, until lately, incumbered with volcanic ashes, from an eruption of the mountain Mârapi, one of the four alluded to, but of the time when this took place there is no record.

No image of the usual gods of the Hindus is to be seen in the temple of Boro-budor, but there are many in its immediate neighbourhood; and neither here, nor in any other part of Java, is there any evidence of the hostility supposed to have existed between the sectaries of Buddha and Brama; for what would seem to be the worship of these two deities is often to be met with, even in the very same temple. Buddha, at least under this name, is unknown to the Javanese, and is not even to be found in any of their writings. It is probable, therefore, that Boro-budor, as well as other temples in the island which we have fancied to be Buddhist, are in reality temples of Jain, which would admit the ordinary Hindu gods as objects of worship. The name is probably a corruption, and affords no clue as to the origin or object of the building. Boro is, in Javanese, the name of a kind of fish-trap, and budor may possibly be a corruption of the Sanscrit buda, "old."

BOUTON. See BOETON.

BOW AND ARROW. In Malay and Javanese, the bow is called Panah, and the arrow is expressed by words which literally signify "child of the bow." The Javanese also use the word gândewa as a generic, although in Sanscrit it properly applies only to the bow of the demigod Arjuna. The wild inhabitants of the Philippines have a knowledge of the bow, but it is remarkable that it is unknown to those of Borneo, the Peninsula, and Sumatra, who, instead, use the less effectual blow-pipe. The bow is named among the weapons used by the Malays in their defence of Malacca in 1511, but even with them, the blow-pipe seems to have been in more general use. Among the more advanced nations, both have been long displaced by fire-arms.

BOYAN, the name of a deep bay within the great one of Illano, on the south side of the island of Mindano. Its entrance is to the south-west, in north latitude 4° 47′, and longitude 124° 57′ east. Here, it is about a league broad, but it gradually widens, and about the middle has a breadth of four leagues. It is described as safe, well-sheltered, and capacious.

BRAMA, the creating power of the Hindu triad, frequently occurs in Javanese legend, and images of him in brass and stone occur in Java; but no temple has been found in which this deity appears to have been the chief object of worship.

BRAMA. The name of a mountain of Java, situated in the province of Pasuruhan, and forming a portion of the Tengger range. It springs out of an extinct crater, three miles in diameter, and rises to the height of about 7000 feet above the level of the sea. (See TENGGER.) The name is taken from that of the Hindu god, whose emblem is fire. The word brama, indeed, in the Javanese language, is one of several synonyms for fire; and the name complete, gunung-brama, literally signifies "mountain of fire, or volcano," and is equivalent to the more frequent one, gunung-api, applied as a proper name to several of the volcanos of the Archipelago.

BRAMANA, a Bramin or Hindu priest, frequently occurs in the writings of the Malays and Javanese.

BRAMBANAN. The name of a village on the high road between the two native Javanese capitals of Yugyakarta and Surakarta, about 10 miles distant from the first, and 30 from the last. Within a radius of two miles of it are the most remarkable Hindu remains of Java, usually called by Europeans the "Ruins of Brambanan." These consist of two buildings which have the appearance of having been monasteries, and of six separate single temples or groups of temples. All these buildings are constructed of huge blocks of hewn trachyte, without any cement whatever. The temples are of a pyramidal form, richly sculptured in relief, and had been originally coated thinly with plaster, which is still perfect in some places. All have chambers or fanes to receive images, a few of which are still seen in their places, while others are scattered about the neighbourhood.

One group of temples is known under the name, Lara-jonggrang, and is guessed to have originally consisted of twenty separate buildings. The central and principal temple is, for the most part, still standing, and when complete is supposed to have been ninety feet in height. It contains, still perfect, the well-known image of the Hindu goddess Durga, standing on a buffalo and in the act of slaying the demon Mahesasura, or personification of vice. The Hinduism of this group, therefore, is so far certain.

The most remarkable group of the whole, however, is that called by the natives Chandi-sewu, which means "the thousand temples." This is a quadrangle, measuring 540 by 510 feet, and consists of one grand temple in the centre, surrounded by five rows of smaller temples or chapels, amounting in all to no fewer than 296, all of the same size and the same architecture, and differing only in the sculptures. In the whole group, with its numerous fanes and niches, there remain but five images, and these represent, what appears to be Buddha, in the usual sitting posture; but none of the special gods of the Hindu Pantheon.

No part of the ruins of Brambanan contain a date or inscription of any sort; and the names of the temples are all in modern Javanese, hardly giving a hint of the nature of the buildings. They are chiefly named after the localities near which they are found: as Chandi Kalasan, "the temple of the village of Kalasan;" and Chandi Kali-sari, "the temple of Kali-sari," or literally, "of the flowery brook." The group of Lara-jonggrang, correctly Lara-jongkrang, has reference to the image of the goddess Durga, which it contains; the words in Javanese meaning "the tall or the exalted virgin;" the initial liquid of the first word, which signifies "a maid or virgin," being, according to a frequent practice, converted from an *r* to an *l*. The name of the village and district containing the ruins is most frequently written and pronounced Prambanan, and is reasonably thought to be an euphonic corruption of Bramanäan, which would signify "place of Bramins." Tradition assigns the building of the temples and other edifices of Brambanan to a prince called by the Javanese Raja Baka, or Boko as they pronounce it; but of this personage nothing is known but his name, and his connection with the buildings. Tradition expressed, not in numeral characters, but as usual in rhythmical verse, assigns to the building of the oldest of the temples of Brambanan the year of Saka, or Salivana, 1188; and to the latest 1218, corresponding with the years 1266 and 1296 of Christ; and there is no good ground for assigning to them an earlier date, nor is there any evidence of decay in the buildings which the heat, rain, and rank vegetation of more than five centuries would not account for. The thin coating of plaster which seems originally to have belonged to all the buildings, still remains in some of the parts least exposed to the weather; and the edges of the blocks of stones are as sharp as when originally hewn. The destruction of the buildings has, in fact, been chiefly produced by a species of fig, the young shoots of which insinuating themselves into the interstices of walls without mortar, and swelling with their growth, to the size of a ship's cable, have easily dislocated and overthrown the buildings. Converts to the new faith which was introduced into Java in the 15th century, would, no doubt, assist in defacing the temples, and overthrowing or removing their images.

BRATAYUDA. The name is derived from Barata, the ancestor of the Pandawa and Kurawa, and Yuda, "war," from the Sanscrit. The Javanese poem of this name is an abstract or paraphrase of the Sanscrit poem, the Mahaba-barat, composed in the Kawi or ancient language of Java, but there is, also, a translation in the modern idiom. The work is attributed to a Javanese bramin, named Ampusâdah, abbreviated Pusâdah; and said to have been written in the year of Saka, or Salivana, 1117, corresponding to the year of Christ 1195. It exhibits, at all events, more vigour of thought than any other literary composition of the Archipelago; and with a similar abstract of the Ramayana, forms the chief source of Javanese and Malay mythological legend.

BRUNAI, BRUNÉ, or BURNAI, the name of the town and state which European geographers have called Borneo Proper. The territory extends from Cape Datu, where it borders on the Malay state of Sambas, to the Bay of Sandakan, where it is bounded by the portion of Borneo claimed by the sultan of Sulu. Nominally, therefore, it extends over the whole north-western side of the island, and a portion of its northern, embracing a coast-line, bays included, of not less than 1000 miles. Its extent inland, where it is bounded by the lands of wild tribes, is unknown; but, probably, no where much exceeds 50 miles. If this be so, as it extends from the 2nd to the 7th degree of north latitude, the area of the whole state will not be less than 15,000 geographical miles, or about half the size of the kingdom of Ireland. Besides this continental territory, the sovereign of Borneo lays claim to the following considerable islands: Malawali, Banggi, Balambangan, Balabak, Mantanani, and Mangkalăan, with the south-western end of the large island of Palawan. With slender exceptions, his Bornean majesty, whether on continent or islands, is only lord of a vast primeval forest.

For 30 miles inland from the coast, the territory of Borneo is represented to consist of low, but generally not marshy land, after which it becomes mountainous, containing, however, but one mountain of great elevation, Kinabalu, estimated at about 10,000 feet above the sea level. The geological formation is plutonic and sedimentary, consisting, as far as it has been ascertained, of granites, sienites, sand and limestones. The minerals which have as yet been discovered are iron and antimony ores, but neither gold or diamonds, as on the western and south-western sides of the island. Its coal-fields, however, so far as they have been traced, promise to be the best and most extensive in the Indies. The Bornean territory contains no well-ascertained lake of any magnitude, but it contains many rivers—twelve of them of considerable size, and two, the Rajang and that of Brunai, being navigable to some distance from the sea for large shipping.

Of its useful indigenous plants, the most remarkable are the camphor-tree, *Dryobalanops camphora*, and the sago-palm. It has been represented to produce, like some parts of Sumatra, the benzoin; but this seems not to be well ascertained. The teak does not exist here, nor in any other part of the island; but five or six of its forest trees have been found fit, at least for the construction of the large ships of the Chinese. The wild quadrupeds are the elephant and rhinoceros, both confined to the districts of Paitan and Sandakan at the northern end of the island; the wild ox, the same as that of Java, called by the Malays of Borneo, tambadau; several species of monkeys, two of which furnish the bezoar stones; the Malayan bear, and one species of leopard peculiar to the island. Neither the buffalo nor the royal tiger are found in the forests. Among birds, it does not appear that the common fowl or peacock, which exist in the Peninsula, Sumatra, and Java, exist in the forests of this part of Borneo; but it is stated by the natives that a handsome gallinaceous bird, resembling the latter, does exist, which they name kruwi, probably a pheasant.

The cultivated plants of the Bornean territory are generally the same as those of the other countries of the Archipelago, namely, rice, some pulses, and farinaceous roots, the sago, coco, areca and gomuti palms, sugar-cane, cotton, and black pepper. The domesticated animals are the ox, the buffalo, goat, hog, dog, and cat; and among birds, the common fowl and duck only. The horse, small, like all those of the Archipelago, is bred only by the settled Bajaus and Lanuns of the districts of Tampasok and Pandasan, at the northern end of the island, and was probably there introduced from the Sulu Islands. They are not used in any other part of the state.

The tribes or nations inhabiting the Bornean territory are almost innumerable. The more advanced consist of the proper Malays, the ruling people; the Bajau Malays, divided into the settled and roving; the Lanuns, emigrants from Mindano; and the Sulus, from the Sulu Islands. The ruder tribes amount to at least 40, differing from each other in language and in their state of civilisation. A few tribes have adopted the Mahommedan religion, and parts of others have been converted to it; but the great majority are heathens, and all retain their own language. The Chinese have been long settled in the territory of Borneo; and, at one time, are said to have been numerous. At present, their number is thought not to exceed 500, and these scattered over the districts in which pepper is grown, of which they are the chief cultivators. The Malays of Borneo themselves assert that not above one tithe of the population of the state is Mahommedan. The total population of the state can only be guessed at, and all that we can be sure of is, that it must be very scanty. Fifteen inhabitants to the computed acre would give a total of 225,000 for the continental part of the territory, probably fully more than it contains; and as to the islands, they are either very scantily peopled or uninhabited.

The government of Borneo is, as usual, a despotism, the throne being hereditary in the reigning family, which traces its origin through 30 generations to the more civilised Malays of Sumatra. The proper title of the monarch, as of all other Malay princes, is Yang di Pârtuan, which may be translated "the lord or ruler." But, like some other petty Malayan princes, he has adopted the Arabian title of Sultan, first used by the first Mahommedan invader of India, and afterwards worn by the well-known Saladin. The revenue is precarious and trifling, consisting rather of aids and subsidies, irregularly levied, than of certain and fixed imposts. Altogether, the government, as at present exercised, is more rude than that of any other Malayan state. Under the sultan, it is administered by four ministers, who form a council. There exists, however, and it seems to be peculiar to this state, an hereditary nobility, which would seem to exercise considerable power. These amount to from 30 to 40 in number, and go under the Javanese title of Pangeran, which is equivalent to prince.

The articles composing the export trade of Borneo are the following: camphor, pepper, raw sago, ratans, and canes; tinder, from the gomuti palm; laka and ebony wood, bees'-wax, swallows' esculent nests, seed-pearls, pearl-oysters, tortoise-shell, and bezoar stones. To these may now be added, fossil coal and antimony ore. The imports consist of Indian and European cotton cloths (plain and coloured blue), coarse Chinese pottery, saltpetre, sulphur, fire-arms, unwrought iron, iron caldrons—the manufacture of China or Siam,—gambier, tobacco, and salt. It is remarkable that no part of the coast of Borneo is fit for the manufacture of salt, so that the whole consumption of the island is imported, on the southern side from Java, and on the western and northern from Siam and Cochin-China, through Singapore. The whole commerce of the state of Borneo is carried on by a kind of barter, the standards of value consisting of pieces of foreign cloth, or of bundles of native iron weighing a Chinese cattie or pound and a third. Gold and silver do not form a medium of exchange, even by weight, and counters for small change are unknown; so that in this matter Borneo is in a more backward state than Malacca was near 350 years ago.

The trade of the state is, at present, chiefly with Singapore, but praus occasionally also traffic with Sambas and Pontianak on the western side of the island, and with Pahang, Tringano, and Kalanten on the eastern side of the Malay peninsula. Down to the end of the last century a considerable trade was carried on with the Chinese ports of Shanghai, Ningpo, Amoy, and Canton, by junks, amounting in all to six, and with Macao by square-rigged vessels to the annual number of two. The junks in which this commerce was conducted were built in the river of Brunai of the timber of the country, among which was that of the Camphor, the builders being Chinese, and the principal owners also resident Chinese, a fact which shows that life and property enjoyed a degree of security which they are far from having had in later times. Borneo had also a considerable trade with Manilla, but all this has ceased, and chiefly owing to the violence and rapacity of the government, which had become the protector and associate of the corsairs of Mindano and Sulu.

All that is known of the history of the state of Borneo is matter of mere tradition, or induction from their language, for the people have neither written annals nor monuments to tell their story. At no great distance from the present town, there are some ancient ruins, and about seven days' journey from it in the interior, and in the country of the wild tribe called Murut, there are others. These are called by the Malays kuta, the Sanscrit for "a fortress," and are described as having been constructed of large blocks of hewn stone, but without inscription or image. Certain ambassadors from Borneo, as before alluded to, informed myself in 1824, that the present race of Borneans were then the twenty-ninth generation in descent from the first emigrants, who, at the time of their settlement, had not yet adopted the Mahommedan religion. If by a generation be meant a period of some 32 years, this would carry us back 928 years, or to the year of Christ 896; but, as is more probable, it refers to the reigns of the Bornean princes, and if these be taken at 20 years, the first emigration would go back only 580 years, making its date 1244. The true history of the state begins with the visit of the companions of Magellan, in 1521, before which the very existence of the island to which it belongs was as little known to Europeans as Mexico before the expedition of Cortes.

BRUNAI-TOWN, is situated on the river of the same name, not the largest of the island, but for the purposes of trade and navigation, perhaps the best. The town is about 14 miles from its mouth, the western side of which is formed by Pulo Muära, that is, "embouchure island," and 10 miles from an islet in the channel, called Cârmin, or "mirror island," in which a rich bed of coal crops out. The town is in latitude 4° 55′ north, and its longitude 114° 55′ east and extends to both sides of the river. The houses of wood and canes, thatched with palmetto, are erected on tall posts in the water or marsh, and run in lines at right angles with the river, so that at flood-time, instead of streets, we have what Forrest, who visited the place 80 years ago, calls water-lanes. Brunai is, in fact, an aquatic town, and all communication between one part of it and another, and even from house to house, is by boat. Even the public markets are held in boats, and Forrest's account of them conveys a graphic one of the character of the place. "In those divisions of the town," says he, "made by the water-lanes, it is neither firm land nor island; the houses standing on posts, as has been said, in shallow water, and the public market is kept, sometimes in one part, sometimes in another part of the river. Imagine a fleet of London wherries, loaded with fish, fowl, greens, &c. &c., floating up with the tide, from London bridge towards Westminster, then down again with many buyers floating up and down with them, and this will give some idea of a Borneo market. These boats do not always drive with the tide, but sometimes hold by the stairs of houses, or by stakes driven purposely into the river, and sometimes by one another. Yet, in the course of a forenoon, they visit most parts of the town where the water-lanes are broad. The boat people (mostly women) are provided with large bamboo hats, the shade of which covers great part of the body, as they draw themselves up under them, and sit, as it were, on their heels."—Voyage to New Guinea.

Pigafetta's account of the town, as he saw it in 1521, is worth quoting for its fidelity. "The city," says he, "is entirely built in the salt water, the king's house and those of some chieftains excepted. It contains 25,000 fires or families. The houses are all of wood, and stand on strong piles to keep them high from the ground. When the flood tide makes, the women, in boats, go through the city selling necessaries. In front of the king's palace there is a rampart constructed of large bricks, with barbacans in the manner of a fortress, on which are mounted fifty-six brass, and six iron cannon. During the two days we passed in the city many of them were discharged."—Primo Viaggio intorno al Globo.

The only part of this statement that is questionable is that which refers to the population. Some Malay courtier, it is likely enough, told Pigafetta that the town contained 25,000 dwelling-houses, which, at the usual estimate of five persons to a family, would give a population of 125,000, a number which most probably never existed in any town of the Archipelago under a purely native government,—a number, indeed, which it may safely be asserted, the rude policy, even of the most advanced of the Malayan nations, could neither gather together, nor hold together if gathered. The highest population assigned by recent visitors to the town of Borneo is 12,000.

The town, however, in the time of Pigafetta, was evidently a place of much more consequence than it is in ours, and his reliable narrative contains satisfactory evidence that such was the case. The king, like the princes of Malacca, before the conquest, had his elephants, and he and his courtiers were clothed in Chinese satins and Indian brocades. He was in possession of artillery, and the appearance of his Court was, at least, imposing. I shall transcribe Pigafetta's description of the latter, as giving the only authentic account we possess of a Malay court when first seen by Europeans, and before their policy, or impolicy, had affected Malayan society. He himself, with seven of his companions, ascended the river from the squadron which was at anchor at its mouth, for the purpose of making presents to the king, and asking permission to wood, water, and trade. One of the king's barges had been sent to convey them to the Court. "When," says he, "we reached the city, we had to wait two hours in the prau, until there had arrived two elephants, caparisoned in silk-cloth, and twelve men, each furnished with a porcelain vase, covered with silk, to receive and to cover our presents. We mounted the elephants, the twelve men going before, carrying the presents. We thus proceeded to the house of the governor, who gave us a supper of many dishes. Here we slept for the night on mattresses stuffed with cotton (bambagio), and cased with silk. Next day, we were left at our leisure until twelve o'clock, when we proceeded to the king's palace. We were mounted, as before, on elephants, the men bearing the gifts going before us. From the governor's house to the palace the streets were full of people armed with swords, lances, and targets : the king had so ordered it. Still mounted on the elephants we entered the court of the palace. We then dismounted, ascended a stair, accompanied by the governor and some chiefs, and entered a great hall full of courtiers, whom we shall call barons of the realm (baroni del regno). Here we were seated on carpets, the presents being placed near to us.

"At the end of the great hall, but raised above it, there was one of less extent hung with silken cloth, in which were two curtains, on raising which, there appeared two windows, which lighted the hall. Here, as a guard to the king, there were 300 men with naked rapiers (stocchi nudi) in hand resting on their thighs. At the farther end of this smaller hall, there was a great window with a brocade curtain before it, on raising which, we saw the king seated at a table masticating betel, and a little boy, his son, beside him. Behind him, women only were to be seen. A chieftain then informed us, that we must not address the king directly, but that if we had anything to say, we must say it to him, and he would communicate it to a courtier of higher rank than himself within the lesser hall. This person, in his turn, would explain our wishes to the governor's brother, and he, speaking through a tube in an aperture of the wall, would communicate our sentiments to a courtier near the king, who would make them known to his Majesty. Meanwhile, we were instructed to make three obeisances to the king with the joined hands over the head, and raising, first one foot and then the other, and then kissing the hands. This is the royal salutation.

"By the means pointed out, we made it to be understood by him that we belonged to the King of Spain, who desired to live in peace with his Majesty, and wished for nothing more than to be able to trade in his island. The king answered, 'that he would be much pleased to have the King of Spain for his friend, and that we might wood, water, and trade, in his dominions, at our pleasure.' This done, the presents were submitted, and as each article was exhibited, the king made a slight inclination of the head. To each of us was then given some brocade, with cloth of gold and of silk, which were placed on one shoulder and then removed, to be taken care of. After this, we had a collation of cloves and cinnamon, when the curtains were drawn and the window closed. All the persons present in the palace had their loins covered with gold-embroidered cloth and silk, wore poniards with golden hilts, ornamented with pearls and precious stones, and had many rings on their fingers."

The presents offered will give the reader some notion of what things were thought fit offerings to oriental princes in the beginning of the sixteenth century. Pigafetta describes those offered to the king and queen as follows : "The present for the king consisted of a vest of green velvet in the Turkish fashion, a chair of purple velvet, five yards of red broad-cloth, one cap (beretto), a gilded glass goblet, a glass vase with a lid, three quires of paper, and a gilded inkstand. We brought for the queen three yards of yellow broad-cloth, a pair of silver-embroidered shoes, and a silver case filled with pins."

The return of the Spanish gentlemen to the house of the governor, and their entertainment there, as described by Pigafetta, are worth quoting: "We remounted the elephants," says he, "and returned to the house of the governor. Seven men preceded us, bearing the presents which had been given to us, and as soon as we had reached the house, to each of us was given his own, the cloths being laid on the left shoulder, as had been done in the king's palace. To each of these seven men we gave in recompense for their trouble a couple of knives. After this there came to the house of the governor ten men, with as many large wooden trays, in each of which were ten or twelve porcelain saucers with the flesh of various animals, that is, of calves, capons, pullets, peafowls (?), and others, and various kinds of fish, so that of meat alone there were thirty or two-and-thirty dishes. We supped on the ground on mats of palm-leaf. At each mouthful we drank a porcelain cup full, the size of an egg, of a distilled liquor made from rice. We eat also rice and sweetmeats, using spoons of gold shaped like our own. In the place where we passed the two night, there were always burning two torches of white wax, placed on tall chandeliers of silver, and two oil lamps of four wicks each, while two men watched to look after them. Next morning we came on the same elephants to the sea-side, where, forthwith, there were ready for us two praus, in which we were re-conducted to the ships."

This is no doubt a faithful representation, as far as it goes, of the manners of a Malay court in the beginning of the sixteenth century, and shows a very considerable advancement in civilisation. We have cannon, a fortress, courtiers clothed in silk, secretaries preparing court circulars, and a tolerable cookery decently served. The free use of ardent spirits shows plainly enough that the Mahommedanism of the Malays, at the time, was not of a rigid character. In another place Pigafetta tells us that the distilled liquor was so strong that the Spaniards became inebriated from it, and he gives its Arabic name "arach," to show from whom it was that the Malays acquired the art of distillation.

This auspicious beginning of European intercourse with Borneo had a very unlucky ending. After the reception at court, the King of Borneo sent a fleet to attack some of his heathen neighbours, and the Spaniards, fancying it came to attack themselves, opened fire on it. "On the 29th of July," says Pigafetta, (a fortnight after the reception,) "being Monday, we saw coming towards us more than a hundred praus, divided into three squadrons, and with them an equal number of Tungulis,(?) which are their smallest barks. Seeing this, and apprehensive of treason, we anxiously made sail, and in our haste left an anchor in the ground. Our suspicion increased when we observed that behind us, there were certain junchi (jung, junks) which had come there the day before. Our first business was to disengage ourselves from the junks, and we opened fire on them, capturing four and killing many persons. Three or four other junks ran aground to save themselves. In one of those which we took was found the son of the king of the island of Loson (the chief island of the Philippines), who was the captain-general of the King of Burné, and who had come with the junks from the conquest of a great city called Laoe, situated at the end of that island opposite to Java Maggiore (probably some place in Banjarmasin). He had made that expedition and sacked that city, because the inhabitants wished to obey the King of Java in preference to the Moorish King of Bruné. The Moorish king having heard of our bad treatment of his junks, made haste to inform us through one of our people who was ashore trading, that the praus went by no means to do us harm, but to make war on the Gentiles, in proof of which they showed us some heads of those of them whom they had killed." I have thus quoted at some length from Pigafetta, because his account of the Malays is the first authentic one we have by an European eye-witness, and because it contains abundant internal evidence of intelligence and truthfulness.

BRITISH. We ourselves and our country are called by the natives of the Malayan Islands, Ingris or Inglis, a corruption, the origin of which is obvious. The word is an adjective, and for the first, requires to be preceded by a word signifying men or people, and for the second, by one signifying land or country. The English first appeared in the Archipelago in 1602, the last year of the reign of Elizabeth, six years after the Dutch, and 107 after the Portuguese. The first place visited by us was Achin, under Sir James Lancaster, the same commander having in 1603 visited Bantam.

The great superiority of the Dutch of the 17th century in commercial and nautical enterprise, and in fact in substantial power over the Portuguese, Spaniards,

French, and English, is shown by results in India. They expelled the Portuguese and Spaniards out of almost all their possessions in the Malay Archipelago, drove ourselves out of the Spice Islands in 1620, and from Bantam and Jaratra, in Java, in 1683. Expelled by their influence from Bantam we established ourselves in the sterile land of Bencoolen in Sumatra in 1685, our sole and humble object being to secure a share in the pepper trade. Bencoolen, with some neighbouring establishments, continued for a hundred years, or up to the foundation of Penang in 1785, to be our sole territorial possessions in the Malay Archipelago; for our other attempts at such acquisitions were ephemeral. In 1819 we founded Singapore, and in 1824 we received by convention Malacca and its territory from the Dutch, giving them Bencoolen and our other possessions in Sumatra in return.

At present our whole territorial possessions embrace four small settlements only, namely, Penang, Singapore, Malacca, and Labuan, containing between them 1300 geographical or 1496 square statute miles, with a population of about 225,000 souls, that is, about 166 to the square statute mile. But the great mass of this population is concentrated in three commercial towns, the rest of the territory being either thinly peopled, or an uninhabited jungle. Our possessions are, indeed, only valuable as commercial emporia, and in this sense are eminently so, as may be seen by the value of the imports and exports, the first of which in the year 1854-55 amounted to 4,923,237*l*., and the last to 4,347,219*l*.

BUCKLER. In the Malay language there are six different names for a buckler, or shield, according to form or material, a fact which proves the importance anciently attached to this weapon of defence. Pigafetta and the Portuguese historians inform us that bucklers were largely employed when Europeans first became acquainted with the Malayan nations, a sufficient proof that fire-arms had then been but little used. At present they are only used by a few of the rudest tribes.

BUDDHA. The name of this Indian deity, either in this its most frequent form, or as Gautama or Sakya, or any other shape, is not found either in the ancient language of Java, or in any of the living languages of the Archipelago. The nearest approach to it in form is the Sanscrit word Buda, "old or ancient," which is a naturalised one in Javanese. Coupling this with the facts that neither the secular nor sacred eras of Buddha are known to the Javanese, while they have an era purely Hindu, that of Salivana, and moreover that the images, which seem to be those of Buddha, are found in the same temples with those of the Braminical religion, the inference would seem to be that the Buddhist religion, such as we find it in Ceylon, Ava, Siam, and even Tartary and Tibet, never existed in Java or in any other island of the Archipelago, but that what has been taken for it is the worship of Jain. This is not a new opinion, for it was embraced as early as 1811 by my friend Colonel Colin Mackenzie, who was so well acquainted with the temples of Jain in Southern India, the country from which the Indian islanders are pretty well ascertained to have derived whatever of Hinduism existed among them.

BUFFALO, the Bos bubalus of naturalists, the same useful, powerful, ugly, sluggish, and unwieldy animal which exists in all the warm countries of Asia, and which was introduced into Greece, Egypt, and Southern Italy in the middle ages. It is only, however, within ten or twelve degrees of the equator that it is found of great size, strength, and vigour. Compared with that of the Malayan countries, the buffalo of Southern Italy is certainly an inferior animal, and that of Northern India even a puny one. The buffalo is the principal beast of draught and burden throughout the Archipelago and Philippines, the ox being chiefly reserved for the tillage of dry upland grounds. The buffalo is larger and more powerful than the ox, but much slower and with less capacity of enduring toil. The flesh of this semi-aquatic animal is coarse, and its milk poor in quality, compared with that of the cow. Its courage is indomitable, and united to its great strength, makes it an overmatch for the royal tiger. It has a repugnance to strangers, but with its friends is thoroughly docile. I have seen a boy of ten years of age part two enraged bulls with a switch, mount that which was his own by one of its horns, and ride home on it. The domestic buffalo is very scantily covered with hair, the colour of the skin appearing through it. It is either black or white, without any other variety, the black in nine cases out of ten predominating, and being considered, perhaps without much foundation, preferable to the white. Wherever the buffalo is found in the domestic state, it is also found in the wild one; and this makes it exceedingly difficult to determine whether this animal be a native of the Archipelago, or a domesticated stranger. Naturalists, I know not on what ground, have come to the latter conclusion, and the natives of the country would seem to entertain the same opinion, for they call all buffalos found in the forest by an epithet which implies this, and which in Malay is jalang, meaning "stray" or "vagabond." The names given to the animal, however, afford no warranty for this conclusion. With one exception, they are native, and not traceable to any foreign tongue. The Malay name is Kârbo, or Kârbau, and this with very slight variations extends over, at least, ten different languages of the Archipelago and Philippines. It is not, however, the only native name, for in the Sunda of Java we have the word munding, and in the Bugis and Macassar of Celebes, tedung. The only foreign name is the Sanscrit Maisa, restricted to the polite language of Java. That the domestic buffalo, however, has often escaped from servitude and become wild, is certain. This, for example, is probably the only source of the wild buffalo of the Philippines, for the buffalo of these islands was the only domesticated beast of burden in them before the arrival of the Spaniards. It seems then, to have been confined to Luzon, although it has since spread to the other large islands; and invariably, it is known by the Malay name kârbo only, even the Spaniards themselves having adopted it, although at the same time expressing the inconsistent opinion that the buffalo was introduced into the Philippines from China. It is easy to see how readily it might have been introduced by the nearest Malays, those of Borneo; for even in native craft, the voyage from Brunai to Manilla, in the proper season, is performed in seven days.

BUGIS, the name given by the Malays to the dominant people of Celebes, who call themselves Wugi, of which, no doubt, it is a corruption. The native country of the Bugis is the south-western limb of Celebes. The Macassar, or Mangkasara nation occupying the most southerly part of this peninsula, borders the Bugis to the south, and the Mandar nation to the north. Like the Malays, they are, for the most part, a maritime people, and it may be suspected that the original seat of their civilisation was the shores of the interior lake Labayo, or Tâparang-danao, a collection of navigable water said to be about 25 miles in length, surrounded by fertile land, at present well cultivated and peopled. See Tâparang.

The people who speak the Bugis language are, at present, divided into many small states, and seem never to have been united under one government. Several of these little states are united into confederations for general purposes. Each state is under the government of its own prince, elected by the chiefs of the tribe from the members of a family in which the office is hereditary, and women are not excluded from the choice. The princes so elected form a council, which must be unanimous for the decision of all matters of common concern. The confederacy of Boni consists of eight princes, and that of Waju of no fewer than forty.

The Bugis are among the most advanced people of the Archipelago. They have long possessed all the domesticated animals, and cultivated the useful plants known to the civilised inhabitants of the more westerly islands. They understand the working of the useful metals, the rearing of cotton, and the manufacture of cloth from it. They had framed a native calendar, although they had no epoch. The year of the calendar is solar, consisting of 365 days, and divided into 12 months, each with a native name. It commences with the 16th day of May of our time; eight of its months containing 30 days, three of them 31, and one 32. But, above all, they possessed the art of writing, having invented an alphabet which expresses with adequate precision the native sounds of their own language, a language that is softer than the Malay, for even its liquids do not coalesce with other consonants, and every word must end either in a vowel, an aspirate, or the soft nasal *ng*.

The Bugis, to judge by their language, would seem to have been indebted to the Malays and Javanese for a large amount of their civilisation. Thus the names of cultivated plants and domesticated animals are, for the most part, taken from the languages of these people; so are the names of the metals, terms connected with the useful arts, navigation, numeration, and even law and religion.

It is remarkable that the Bugis, now the most enterprising of all the native tribes of the Archipelago, are never mentioned by the earlier European writers. Thus Barbosa, who describes the Javanese, the natives of the Coromandel coast, and the Chinese whom he met at Malacca, never alludes to the Bugis, who, had they existed there in his time, could hardly have failed to attract his attention, were it only for the very peculiar build of their vessels. De Barros' enumeration of the people trading to Malacca is even more full than that of Barbosa, for he adds to his list the Peguans and the Japanese, but he makes no allusion to the Bugis. The inference is, that this people were unknown as traders in the beginning of the 16th century, and that the commercial enterprise by which they are now distinguished is of comparatively recent origin. Even their native country, according to De Barros, was not discovered until 1525, and when that happened, the country, instead of being considered by the Portuguese as one great island, was thought to be an aggregation of many islets, the people of which were thought to be in a very rude state,—clothed in the bark of trees, and unacquainted with all the metals except gold.

The first distinct notice we have of the Bugis is derived from native authority, and this assigns the year 1366 to the commencement of the reign of one of their princes. Their early commercial enterprises do not seem to have extended beyond the neighbouring Spice Islands. In the native annals of the state of Malacca, they and the people of Macassar are represented as harassing the trade of Malacca by their piracies in the time of a prince called Munsur Shah, whose reign began in the year 1374. Even the name of the piratical leader, Kraing Samerlak, is given, which proves, however, that he was not of the Bugis, but of the Macassar nation which had acquired notoriety before it. No traces whatever of the Hindu religion, in the shape of temples, images, or inscriptions, such as exist in Java and Sumatra, have been discovered in the country of the Bugis, or in any other part of Celebes. Their language, however, shows that the people speaking it had been slightly tinctured with Hinduism, but no more. It contains a considerable number of theological terms, palpably enough Sanscrit, but identical with those contained in the Malay and Javanese, and obviously introduced with other words of these languages.

Of all the more advanced nations of the Archipelago, the Bugis were the latest converts to Mahommedanism. Even the Macassar nation, although in this respect in advance of them, did not adopt it until as late as 1605, or 94 years after the arrival of the Portuguese, and even a few years subsequent to that of the Dutch and English. It was this people, at the time the most potent in Celebes, that by force of arms enforced the Mahommedan religion on the Bugis about the year 1640. It was, most probably, the adoption of the new religion that moved the Bugis, as it did the Arabs, although in a different direction, to action, and which in the sequel has made them what they now are, at once the bravest men and the most enterprising merchants and navigators of the Archipelago.

The enterprising character of the Bugis belongs more especially to the tribes which go under the common name of Waju. The trade of this people extends, at present, to every country of the Archipelago, from Sumatra to New Guinea. They are, in fact, the carriers of the internal trade, and now, what the Malays and Javanese were on the arrival of Europeans. The exports from the eastern ports of the Archipelago to the western are chiefly composed of cotton fabrics of their own manufacture, of gold-dust, holothurion, esculent roots, tortoise-shell, pearl-shells, rice from Java and Bali, and, of late years, tobacco and coffee. From the European emporia, they take back, to be distributed far and wide, the produce and manufactures of Europe and India. The Bugis are not only traders, but also settlers in many of the countries with which they carry on trade. The largest number of such settlers are probably on the western, and especially the eastern, coast of Borneo, on the strait which divides this island from their own country. On the large rivers of Pasir and Coti, there is supposed to be about 1600 families of them, in a state nearly independent of the Malay princes. The Waju Bugis have also established themselves in the territories of Mandar and Kaili in their own island, and the Bugis of Boni formed a colony in the little island of Bonirati, between Celebes and Floris. In the European settlement they form considerable communities, living in separate quarters, and preserving their own manners and language. Thus, in Singapore, by the census of 1849, they were found to number 2269.

Altogether, the number of the Bugis praus, usually known by the name of Padewakan, carrying on foreign trade, is thought not to be short of 800, of the burden of about 50 tons each. In their navigation they use charts and compasses, the former from European originals, with the names in the Bugis character, and the last made for them by the Chinese of Batavia. The account which Mr. Marsden gives of this people as he saw them at Bencoolen, above 80 years ago, is worth quoting. "The Macassar and Bugis people," says he, "who come annually in their praus from Celebes to trade at Sumatra are looked up to by the inhabitants as their superiors in manners. The Malays affect to copy their style of dress, and frequent allusions to the feats and achievements of these people are made in their songs. Their reputation for courage, which certainly surpasses that of all other people in the eastern seas, acquires for them this flattering distinction. They also derive part of the respect paid them from the richness of the cargoes they import, and the spirit with which they spend the produce in gaming, cock-fighting, and opium-smoking."—*History of Sumatra*, page 209.

BUHI or **BUJI.** The name of one of several lakes in the volcanic province of South Camarines, in the island of Luzon. It is about three miles long, and two broad, and its neighbourhood is fertile and highly cultivated with rice, the abaca banana, indigo, sesame, cacao, and sugar-cane. The lake is a rich fishery; and on its southern shore is a native town, of the same name, with 6304 inhabitants. This stands near the source of a river, also of the same name, which empties the surplus water of the lake in the sea, in north latitude 13° 24′, and east longitude 123° 25′.

BUITENZORG. The name of the country-palace of the Dutch Governor-General of India. The word is equivalent to the French *Sans Souci*. The native name of the palace is Bogor, which, in Javanese, means a mat or carpet. Buitenzorg is in the country of the Sundas, about 40 miles from Batavia, and 865 feet above the level of the sea. The climate of the place is temperate, and the surrounding country at once fertile and beautiful. Buitenzorg also gives name to a Dutch province of Java, having an area of 1064 square miles, and which, by the census of 1847, contained a population of 260,311; of which 662 were Europeans, 7462 Chinese, 172 slaves, and the rest Sundas or natives of the country. By the census of 1850, this had risen to 281,896; of which 545 were Europeans, 8135 Chinese, and 146 slaves.

BUKIT, in Malay, is "a hill or mountain," and equivalent to Gunung in Jayanese. Both words are of very frequent occurrence in the names of places.

BULACAN, anciently called Mecaüayan, one of the 20 provinces of the island of Luzon. The word means, literally, the sweet potato, convolvulus, batatas, in the Tagala language. It lies between north latitudes 14° 40′ and 15°, and east longitudes 120° 36′ and 121° 8′. It is bounded by the province of Tondo to the south-east, by Nueva Ecija to the east, by Pampanga to the north-west, and by the bay of Manilla, to the length of six leagues, to the west. Its greatest extent from east to west is 30 geographical miles, and its greatest breadth, from north to south, 20. Its area is about 575 geographical miles. It is, therefore, one of the smallest provinces of the Philippine Archipelago; but it is, at the same time, considered to be, beyond dispute, the richest, the most agreeable, the most salubrious, and the best-cultivated of the whole. The Spaniards call it "the garden of the Philippines."

Bulacan is mountainous to the east, being there penetrated by some spurs of the eastern Cordillera of Caraballos. It is rich in iron-ore, obtained with little labour near the surface. The produce of the mines of Sampang-bacal yield an ore which is said to give 90 per cent. of iron, equal in quality to that of Biscay in Spain. It has, also, beds of mineral coal, and gold is obtained by washing the sands of the rivers. Copper is supposed to exist in the mountains. At a place called Panig, there is an accumulation of masses of alabaster, some of them ten yards in height, in which is a curious grotto.

The province has many rivers, the most considerable of which are the Quingua, and that of Pampanga, which disembogue in the bay of Manilla by several mouths. The whole coast is a labyrinth of creeks, some of which are navigable for boats to a considerable distance inland. It has also several lakes, the most remarkable of which is that of Hogonoy, an extensive sheet of water, in the season of the rains, from the overflowing of the river of Pampanga; but in the opposite one, wholly dry, and an immense meadow, covered with rich herbage, on which numerous herds of different cattle, but especially of oxen, are pastured.

The mountainous parts of the province yield several kinds of useful timber for house and ship building, and the shores of the creeks abound in the nipa-palm (*nipa fruticans*), of which the leaves furnish the chief material for thatch, while from the sap, and this is peculiar to the Philippines, is made palm wine, ardent spirits, vinegar, and sugar. Bulacan, from the abundance of its flowering plants, is rich in bees'-wax, the produce of wild bees. Its cultivated plants are rice, maiz of which two, and sometimes three crops are produced yearly,—the sesame and ground-pulse, both for the production of oil,—cotton, tobacco, sugar-cane, indigo, cacao, and coffee, the last introduced for the first time in the year 1793. The fisheries of the coast give employment to many persons, and the province has no fewer than 1500 looms for the manufacture of silk and cotton fabrics, the women appearing to be the weavers, as in most rude countries of the East.

The inhabitants of Bulacan are, for the most part, of the Tagala nation, speaking the language of this name. They are described as a simple, credulous, and religious people, wholly under the government of their priests, whom they consult in every concern of moment: they look also with reverence to the public authorities. The white colour alone, say Spanish writers, is sufficient to secure respect, being that of the men under whom they have advanced to civilisation. In their habits they are regular and sober, but indolent and addicted to gaming. As among the Javanese, all buying and selling is the province of the women.

In 1849, the total native population of the province of Bulacan was 213,498, of whom 38,961 were subject to the poll-tax, its total amounting to 389,610 reals of plate. Besides these there were, in the same year, 15 Spaniards, 691 Spanish mestizos, and 9572 Chinese mestizos, with 84 pure Chinese, making a total population of 223,860. The relative population gives no less than 389 to the square mile, which is equal in density to some of the most populous parts of Java. In 1799, the total population was only 83,671, and in 1818, it had risen to 125,021. In fifty years' time it had, therefore, increased, if these figures can be relied on, by no less than 167 per cent.

BULACAN, the chief town of the province of the same name, situated on a creek of the bay of Manilla, and distant from the city five and a half leagues. Bulacan contains 1832 houses, and a population of 11,292, of whom 2219 are subject to the capitation-tax, the sum of which is 22,190 reals of plate. It was founded in 1572, or about 50 years after the discovery of the Philippines, and is regularly laid out with straight and spacious streets. Many of the houses belonging to the Spanish and Chinese mestizos are of stone and well built, but the majority are of wood or bamboo, thatched with nipa-leaf. The most remarkable buildings are the house of the chief alcalde, the hotel of the wine and tobacco revenues, a preparatory school-house, supported by the funds of the commune, a magnificent convent of the Augustines, and a fine church built by the same fraternity. In the neighbourhood there are many pleasant walks, and excellent roads connect it with the different parts of the province it belongs to, as well as with the neighbouring ones.

BULOAN. The name of a lake in the island of Mindano, and territory of the sultan of that island. It is laid down in the maps as being in north latitude 6° 40′, and east longitude 124° 38′,—described to be 12 leagues in circumference, and represented to be connected with the larger lake of Linao.

BUNWUT. The name of a small island fronting the bay of Bongo, itself within the great bay of Illano, on the southern side of the island of Mindano. It is about two leagues in length and one in breadth, and has therefore an area of two leagues. Latitude north 7° 8′, longitude east 124°.

BURACAN. The name of a lake in the province of Pampanga, and island of Luzon, formed by the perennial torrents which proceed from the neighbouring volcanic mountain of Arayat. It abounds in fish and water-fowl, and its neighbourhood is richly cultivated with rice, sesame, and tobacco.

BURIAS. The name of a considerable island of the Philippine Archipelago, lying on the southern coast of Luzon, and forming part of the province of South Camarines. It contains an area of 220 square geographical miles, but its surface is mountainous, rocky, and uneven. Its chief products are rice, maiz, and the abaca, or textile banana, and it is poorly cultivated and thinly inhabited, having but one town, and this, which is on the shore fronting Luzon, with no more than 602 inhabitants, being the whole population of the island.

BURI, or BULI. The name of a Philippine palm, probably the Corypha gebanga of botanists, and the Gâbang of the Malays and Javanese. The Philippine islanders make much use of the several parts of this palm. From the leaves they make mats, from the sap both sugar and a distilled spirit, from the pith a sago, and from the seeds rosaries, while the spines boiled in water yield a thread from which a coarse cloth is woven, called Sagoron.

BURIK. The name of one of the wild and independent tribes of the island of Luzon, and province of Abra, inhabiting the northern portion of the Western Cordillera. The Buriks belong to the same brown-complexioned and lank-haired race as all the more civilised people of the Philippines. In their persons they are robust, and they have received a considerable amount of culture, for they raise rice by irrigation, and rear herds of cattle. They tattoo the whole of the upper portion of the body, so as to represent the figure of a coat-of-mail, on which slender fact some Spanish writers have jumped to the conclusion that they are the descendahts of islanders of the Pacific, driven by storms on the coast of Luzon.

BUSAO. The name of one of the wild and independent tribes of the island of Luzon, and province of Abra, neighbours of the Burik and other similar tribes. Their locality is a spur of the Western Cordillera, called Saguey. They are of the brown-complexioned race, and of a tolerably peaceable character. They tattoo the person with the figures of flowers, and wear ear-pendants, commonly of wood, a slender foundation for believing them, as some Spanish writers have done, to be a mixed race of South-Sea islanders and men of Luzon.

BUSÜAGAN. The name of the largest of the cluster of islands called the Calamianes, from the name of one of their number. Its centre is in north latitude 12° 8′ and east longitude 122° 54′. Its length is three leagues, its breadth two, and its circumference ten leagues. The land is represented as fertile, and capable of producing abundantly, but the seed and crop are said to be devoured by inuumerable animals, such as deer, wild hogs, porcupines, squirrels, rats, parrots, and pigeons. For this reason the natives content themselves with raising a small quantity of rice, and live chiefly by the fishery of the holothurion, or sea-slug, called in the Philippine languages Balate, and in the perilous labour of collecting the esculent nests of the swallow in the caverns which are frequent in the Calamianes Islands.

BUTUAN. A large bay on the northern side of the island of Mindano, the innermost part of which is in latitude 8° 64′ north, and longitude 124° 5′ east. This bay receives the surplus water of the large lake of Sapongan, which issues from it in a single river, which divides into three branches before falling into the sea.

BUTUAN. The name of a Spanish town and district lying on the bay of the same name, and in the province of Caraga. The town is situated on the right bank of one of the branches of the river which proceeds from the lake of Sapongan. As far as the town, a distance of a league and a half, the river is navigable for vessels not exceeding 100 tons' burden. The town is situated in an open plain, and has a temperate and salubrious climate. Along with the district annexed to it, it contains 1634 houses of perishable materials, and a population of 9804 souls. The only product of the country that is abundant is the sago-palm.

BUYO. The name given in the Philippine Islands to the betel pepper, the sirih of the Malays, and piper betele of botanists.

C.

CACOA (THEOBROMA). The chocolate plant is unknown as an object of cultivation in every part of the Asiatic Archipelago except the Philippines, and of late the northern peninsula of Celebes. In most of the Philippines it is cultivated, but only for home use, and the quality produced is inferior to that of Guayaquil and other parts of America. That of the island of Çebu is the best, being worth from 15 to 20 per cent. more than the produce of the other islands.

CAGAYAN. One of the 20 provinces of Luzon, and occupying a large part of the northern end of the island. It is bounded by the province of Nueva Ecija, which was formerly a part of it, by Abra, Nueva Viscaya, and the sea. It extends from 17° 10′ to 18° 40′ north latitude. From east to west its extent is 26 leagues, and from north to south 25, and it is estimated to contain an area of 7585 square geographical miles. The Cordillera of Caraballos, and the Sierra Madre, with several minor ranges of mountains, pass through it from south to north. Cagayan has one large lake of the same name, 2¾ leagues in length, 2 in breadth, and twelve in circumference. Of this, the surplus waters are conveyed to the sea by a considerable river, having a course nearly due north. It has many other rivers, five or six of which are of considerable size. Its largest, and also the largest river of the island, is that which the natives, after the places it passes by, call the Sallo and the Aparri, but to which the Spaniards have given the name of Tajo, after the celebrated Iberian stream, the Tagus. This has its source on the northern acclivities of the chain of mountains called the Caraballos sur, and after passing through the provinces of Nueva Ecija and Nueva Viscaya, it traverses that of Cagayan. Its whole course, until it empties itself in the sea, where it forms the port of Aparri, is reckoned at 55 leagues. It is navigable for vessels of about 200 tons' burden for a considerable distance, but in the season of the rains the navigation is rendered dangerous by frequent drifted timber. The Tajo and its many tributaries abound in fish, which everywhere form so large an amount of the sustenance of the inhabitants of Luzon.

This province has abundant mines of iron-ore and gypsum, and gold is collected by washing the sands of several of its rivers. The mountains are covered with forests, which contain much useful timber for building, with ebony and sapan-wood. The wild game of these forests are deer, buffalos, hogs, and the common fowl. The climate, as might be expected from its locality, is the coldest of the Philippines, frequent hail-showers being experienced. It is also humid and stormy, and being subject to malaria in several situations, is considered the least healthy of the island of Luzon.

Notwithstanding the generally mountainous character of Cagayan, it has many fertile valleys, which produce rice, wheat, maiz, indigo, sugar-cane, and tobacco, the last considered the best of the Philippines. It has also some extensive plains, on which are bred herds of horses and oxen for the market of Manilla. Maiz is the principal crop and chief bread-corn of the inhabitants, a fact which indicates the general prevalence of high and mountainous land. The people have the reputation of being brave, superstitious, and honest, possessing the last quality more especially in so eminent a degree that thefts and robberies among them are of very rare occurrence. They are considered to make the best soldiers for the military service of the government, and are in repute as domestic servants in Manilla, to which they repair, poor and half-naked, in search of employment, much as the labouring population of Ireland does to the towns of Britain. Within this province are situated many of the wild tribes, both brown-complexioned and negro. Of the first, for example, there are, the Igorrotes, called also the Apayos, the Calauas or Calanes, the Aripa, and several less numerous tribes. Some of these are supposed by Spanish writers to be of the Malay race, and others of the Chinese; the last, most probably, without any good foundation. Exclusive of these wild tribes, the province in 1849 contained a population of 85,839 souls, of whom 15,522 were subject to the capitation-tax, which amounted to 155,225 reals of plate. This gives the relative population of no more than 11·3 to the square geographical mile, a very poor one compared to that of other provinces of the island. This is accounted for by the mountainous character of much of the land, the remoteness of the country, the absence of roads, and the tempestuous and dangerous character of its sea, with the turbulence and indocility of the many wild independent tribes contained within it. The population, however, appears to be rapidly increasing; for in 1818 it amounted to no more than 61,322, which would show an increase of nearly 40 per cent. in about 30 years.

CAGAYAN SULU, the Cagayan de Jolo, that is, the Cagayan belonging to Sulu of the Spaniards, is an island lying to the north of Borneo, and about 17 leagues distant from the Cape of Sugut in that island. It is about 10 miles in length by 7 in breadth, and lies in north latitude 7°, and east longitude 118° 36′. Cagayan is surrounded by several islets, but it alone is inhabited. The whole group is claimed as part of the dominions of the Sultan of Sulu.

CAJEPUT. A corruption of the Malay words kayu-putih, literally "white wood," from the colour of the bark of the tree which produces the well-known essential oil, the Melaleuca cajeput of botanists. It most abounds in the island of Boeroe in the Molucca Sea, where the essential oil is obtained by the distillation of the leaves.

CALAMBUCO. The name of one of the best timber-trees of the Philippine Islands, the wood of which is largely employed by the natives in the fabrication of domestic utensils and agricultural implements.

CALAMIANES. The name of a group of islands among those called the Bisayas or Visayas, and forming one of the 35 provinces constituting the Spanish Philippines. It extends from north latitude 10° 11′ to 12° 28′, and comprehends the northern portion of the great island of Palawan or Paragua, the island of Calamian which gives name to the province, Busuagan or Busbagan, Lutaya or Ayutaya, Culiong, Coron, Linacapan, Ilog, Dumaran, and Cuyo, with a great many smaller islands. The whole group seems to be without the limits of the volcanic band, and the province is the poorest and least populous of the Philippines, for the total population in 1849 was no more than 15,027. The soil, compared to that of the large islands of the Archipelago, is evidently sterile and intractable, while the climate is hot, humid, and, generally, not salubrious,—circumstances which will readily account for the smallness of the population. This, however, had increased very greatly, for by the census of 1818 it was no more than 5530.

CALAMUS. The scientic name of the class of plants which botanists have agreed to consider as belonging to the family of palms, although in appearance more like to rank grasses,—popularly "canes and ratans." These abound in all the forests of the Asiatic

Islands, particularly in low and swampy lands, which they contribute by their density and numerous prickles to render nearly impenetrable. They vary in size from a few lines to a couple of inches in diameter, and creeping along the ground or climbing trees they often extend to the length of several hundred yards. By the natives they are used for almost every purpose of cordage. The greater number of those exported are the produce of Sumatra and Borneo. The Malays, with a generic name for the whole family, distinguish the different kinds, which are probably distinct species, by adding an epithet to them. The general name is rotan, of which the European ratan is an obvious corruption. It is thought to be derived from the verb rawat, which in Malay means "to pare or trim," in reference to the process by which the canes are prepared for use.

CALANTAN. The name of a Malay state on the eastern side of the peninsula. See KALANTAN.

CALASUNGAY. The name of a wild or infidel tribe of the island of Mindano, in the Spanish province of Misamis, lately brought under subjection by the Spaniards, and among whom a Christian mission was established in 1849.

CALINGAS. The name of one of the many wild tribes of the island of Luzon inhabiting a range of mountains lying between the rivers Apayo and Tajo within the province of Cagayan. The Calingas, a brown-complexioned people, with lank hair, are among the most numerous and advanced of the wild tribes of the Philippines, cultivating rice and raising fine tobacco. They are of a peaceful and docile character, and by the indefatigable zeal of the Spanish missionaries a few of them have been converted to Christianity.

CAMARINES. A province of the island of Luzon, divided in 1829 into two, a northern and southern. The name is taken from the Spanish word Camarina, "a closet or dressing-room," which, in Manilla, is applied to the porch or portico of a house. The nipa-palms used in the construction of these, when Manilla was first built, were obtained from that part of Luzon which now bears the name. The Camarines constitute the principal portion of the peninsula which makes the southern end of Luzon; the province of Albay forming its extremity, and that of Tayabas the isthmus. It has three great bays, that of Ragay to the south, and of Lamon or Sogod to the north-west, between which lies the isthmus while to the south and south-east are the spacious gulfs of San Miguel and Logonay. The chain of the Caraballos mountains which run from north to south through the whole island, necessarily traverses it, and several of its peaks are active volcanos, the volcanic formation prevailing throughout the whole of the two provinces. Within them are the large lakes of Bato, Buhi, and Baao, and many rivers, of which the Naga is the largest. This receives the waters of the lakes just named, empties itself in the bay of San Miguel, and is navigable to a considerable distance by vessels of 200 tons' burden. On the north-eastern coast, there are many small islands, but none of any considera-tion, for Catanduanes belongs to the province of Albay. The two provinces of North and South Camarines contain between them an area of 2845 geographical square miles.

The climate of the Camarines is considered by the Spaniards agreeable and healthy. The soil is fruitful, yielding abundantly all the usual products of the Philippines, but rice and the textile banana or abaca are the staple products. The more active ox is substituted for the heavy and slow buffalo generally used in agricultural labour in the other provinces, a proof of a light and dry soil, as well as of improved husbandry. The Camarines are traversed by good roads, and their rivers well bridged, the bridges being sometimes of stone, but more frequently of bamboo.

In 1849 the province of North Camarines contained 28,329 inhabitants, of whom 3965 were subject to the capitation-tax, which amounted to 39,650 reals of plate. In the same year the much more extensive province of South Camarines contained 115,575 inhabitants, of whom 26,649 paid the capitation-tax, which amounted to 266,490 reals of plate. By the census of 1818 the population of the two provinces was only 113,893, so that in 30 years an increase of about one-fourth had taken place. Taking the two provinces together, the rate of population to the square mile gives 50·5.

CAMBOJA, or CAMBODIA, in Malay, correctly Kamboja, which is believed to be a name derived from the Sanscrit. This is the same country which is better known to the Malays under the name of Champa. The Proper Cambojans are a people distinct in manners and language from those of Lao and Siam to the north, and from those of Anam to the south and east of them. Their proper country extends along the eastern coast of the gulf of Siam up to the 12° of north latitude, and along the shore of the China Sea up to about 107° of east longitude. When the Portuguese first arrived in the Indian Seas, the Cambojans are described as being the most potent people between Pegu and Tonquin. They have long ceased to be so, most of their country having been wrested from them by the Cochin-Chinese from the south, and the Siamese from the north, so that as far as the sea-coast is concerned, they are at present reduced to the single port of Kâmpot, lying on a small river which falls into a bay, the head of which is in about 11° of north latitude. Much of Camboja is an alluvial country, productive in rice. Its forests yield in greater perfection and abundance than any others, the eagle wood or agila, and they alone furnish the well-known drug gamboge, the name of which is a corruption of that of the country. In the early period of the commerce of Europeans with India, when from imperfect navigation, the cost of transport was high, such commodities as these were of more import than the substantially more valuable ones of sugar, cotton, and corn, which from their bulk could not bear the expensive freights of the time.

CAMEL. This quadruped, fitted for the dry sands of the Desert, is wholly unsuited to the humid climate and forest-clad islands of the Asiatic Archipelago. It is in fact unknown to the natives, except by its Sanscrit name Unta, just as is the case with the lion.

CAMOTES. The name of a group of islets in the strait between the two large Philippine islands of Çebu and Leyté. They are included in the province of the latter name, but they are inconsiderable both in size and value. They take their name from the Bisaya word for the sweet potato, or Convolvulus batatas.

CAMPAR. The name of a Malay state on the north-eastern side of Sumatra, and nearly opposite to Malacca. See KAMPAR.

CAMPHOR. The Malay camphor tree, the Dipterocarpus, or Dryabalanops camphora, of botanists, is a large forest tree, as far as is known, confined to a few parts of the islands of Sumatra and Borneo, but in these abundant. The oil, both in a fluid and solid state, is found in the body of the tree where the sap should be, but not in all trees. The liquid oil, which is abundant, and little appreciated, but the concrete bears a very high price, which depends wholly on its scarcity and the fancy of the Chinese and Japanese, who ascribe high medicinal virtues to it, which it probably possesses in no higher degree than the cheap article which they themselves obtain by the distillation of the wood of the Cinnamomum camphora, and which may be had in the same markets for about "one hundredth" part of the price. The Malay name is a slight corruption of the Sanscrit one, Karpura. To distinguish it from the camphor of China and Japan, the word Barus is annexed, being the name of the sea-port of the western coast of Sumatra, from which the article was principally exported from that island. From what Barbosa says, it is to be presumed that both the Malay and Chinese camphor were in use by the Hindus before the arrival of Europeans. The prices of the different sorts reduced to present Indian weights and moneys will be as they existed in Malabar and Calicut in the beginning of the sixteenth century, as follows: coarse camphor, in cakes (canfora grossa in pani), from 40 to 45 Spanish dollars, the picul of 133⅓ pounds, which is about double the present price at Singapore; camphor, to use internally, and for the eyes (canfora da mangiar, e per gl' occhi) 1360 dollars the picul, which is probably no more than 35 per cent. above existing prices in the Singapore. There was also a sort used for anointing the idols (per ugner gl' idoli) at half the price of the last. These two must have been Malay camphor, while the first, from its low price, must have been Chinese or Japanese. The wood of the camphor tree is good timber, suited for house and ship-building.

CANAREN. The name of a lake in the island of Luzon, and lying between the provinces of Pampanga and Pangasinan, in latitude 15° 40′. In the dry season it is about 6 miles in length, and 5 in breadth; but in the wet, it becomes an extensive sheet of water. Like the other lakes of Luzon it abounds in fish.

CANDABA. A temporary lake, or Pinag as such collections of water are called in the Philippines, situated in the province of Pampanga, in the island of Luzon, on the left side of the river of Pampanga. It is formed in the rainy season by the overflowing of the Pampanga river, and of four of its tributaries. It is then 4¾ leagues in length, and 2¼ in breadth, and described by Spanish writers as a little fresh-water sea. In October the waters begin to abate, and by the end of January, the whole bed of the lake, with the exception of a few pools, is dry land, on which spring up rich crops of grass, on which are pastured many herds of horses, oxen, and buffaloes. While the inundation lasts, the lake affords a large supply of fish, especially of the favourite one called the dalag. From these, the whole neighbourhood of the lake is supplied, and some, fresh as well as cured, are exported to Manilla and other parts of the island. Some fish, also, are found during the dry season, in the pools above-named.

CANNON. See Arms.

CAPIS. One of the thirty-five provinces of the Spanish Philippines, and one of the three into which the fine island of Panay is divided, forming the northern part of it. Its average length is 68 geographical miles, and its breadth 20, so that it has an area of 1400 square geographical miles. The land of Capis is eminently fertile and well watered, but being low, some portions of it are liable to be inundated in the rainy season. It is the most productive in rice of all the Philippine provinces, the seed, according to some Spanish writers, returning from 150 to 200 fold. The mass of the inhabitants of Capis are of the Bisaya nation, speaking the Bisaya language; but in the mountains are found some tribes of Aetas, or negritos. In 1849, the population of the province amounted to 186,587; of whom 34,660 paid the capitation-tax, which came to 316,600 reals of plate.

The principal town of Capis, which bears the same name, lies between the two branches, into which the river Panay divides itself before falling into the sea in a small bay. It contains 2840 houses, and a population of 10,948. It is a place of large native trade, the staple export being rice. Latitude 11° 30′, longitude 122° 28′.

CAPSICUM. This, and not any of the genus Piper, is the universal peppery condiment of all the inhabitants of the Asiatic islands. The latter, indeed, are little used, being mostly raised for exportation. From its native names in Malay and Javanese, there can be little doubt of the capsicum being a native product; these are, chabé for the first, and lombok for the last. Foreign species or varieties, however, have been introduced. Thus we have Chabé China, the Capsicum of China; and Chabé sábrang, the Capsicum of India, literally, of "the other side of the water."

CAPUL. The name of an island lying off the large one of Samar, in the Philippines, at its north-western extremity, and belonging to the province of this name. It lies in north latitude 12° 38′, has an area of about 5 leagues, and a town of the same name on its eastern coast.

CAPULAN. The name of an island lying off the southern end of the main body of the island of Luzon, and the northern end of that of Marinduque. It lies in latitude 13° 52′, is about a league in length, and half that in breadth, and is distant from the province of Tayabas, to which it belongs, about half a league.

CAR, CART, CHARIOT. The name, in Malay and Javanese, for a car or cart for ordinary use, is pâd-ati, a word the origin of which I do not know. Wheel-carriages are hardly in use among the Malays, for the boat takes their place; and even with the agricultural nations they are little used, except where European power has been established. For a carriage for luxury, the terms used are káreta and rata, both Sanscrit. In Malayan romances we frequently read of a particular carriage of this description; and the Portuguese historian, Castagneda, has described one taken or rather destroyed at the capture of Malacca. His account of it is as follows; and it will give the reader some notion of the kind of barbaric pomp in which a Malay prince indulged three centuries and a half ago. "There was also set on fire a great wooden house placed on a car, which had thirty wheels, every one of them equal in size to the end of a hogshead. This chariot was made by command of the king of Malacca, in order to convey in procession through the city the king of Pam (Pahang), to whom he had given one of his daughters in marriage. He had prepared a great festival for the nuptials, and this chariot was one of the contrivances for the purpose. It was hung with silk inside, and adorned with banners without." Vol. iii., p. 194.

CARABALLOS. The Cordillera of Caraballos, is the common name given by the Spaniards to the chain of mountains which runs through the whole island of Luzon, over six degrees of latitude. It attains its greatest height, which however is not stated, and its greatest breadth, which is about 15 leagues, in latitude 16° 7′, and longitude 120° 50′. From this point, proceeding northward, it divides into two chains, one terminating in the Cape of Engaño, and the other in that of Pato, at the northern end of the island. From the same elevated point, the Caraballos runs in a single chain to the south end of the island, terminating in the volcano of Buluran, in the province of Albay. This last portion is known by the name of Cordillera del Sur, the more easterly of the two northern branches by that of the Sierra Madre, and the more westerly in its more early course by that of the Cordillera del Centro, and towards its termination by that of the Cordillera del Norte.

CARAGA. One of the thirty-five Spanish provinces of the Philippines, and of the four into which the Spanish portion of the island of Mindano is divided. It forms the north-eastern and projecting angle of the island where it is divided from the island of Leyté by the strait of Surigao. It is bounded inland by the territory of the sultan of Mindano, and the Spanish province of Misamis. To the east and west it has the sea. Its land frontier extends over 37 leagues, and its coast line over 94. On its western coast it has the great bay of Butuan, the long eastern side of which goes under the name of the coast of Aran. On its eastern coast it has some small bays and harbours, as that of Bislig. The province extends from latitude 6° 15′ to 9° 50′, and from longitude 125° to 125° 53′. Its extreme length from north to south is 235, and its breadth from east to west 58 geographical miles; but its area is computed not to exceed 7000. The land is generally mountainous, but of the height or the direction of its mountain-ranges no account has been rendered. For the most part the mountains are said to afford evidence of a volcanic formation. The most considerable river of the province is the Butuan, which falls into the spacious bay of the same name. This has a sand-bank at its entrance, but is navigable for small vessels for a considerable distance. Altogether the province appears to be naturally ill-drained, and abounds in stagnant water and marsh.

The climate is hot, humid, and stormy, and the country liable to violent earthquakes, especially during volcanic eruptions in other parts of the island. On account of the prevalence of malaria, it is unhealthy.

The greatest part of the province is covered with a stupendous forest; the trees, of which the teak, Tectona grandis, is one, and would be most useful, were there any economical means of transport to the coast. Another product of it which deserves notice, is a species of Cinnamon, which cannot be the Cinnamomum iners of the western Malayan islands, if what is stated of it be true, that it yields by distillation more essential oil than the cinnamon of Ceylon, although of inferior flavour. The forests, also, are said to contain wild buffaloes, wild hogs, deer, the civet cat, and several other animals of the same family yielding musk.

Caraga appears to be one of the poorest parts of the Spanish Philippines. The cultivated parts of the province are mere specks. Rice is little cultivated, most of what is consumed being imported from Luzon and Çebu; and the inhabitants, for the greater part, subsisting on roots, frequently of spontaneous growth, and on Sago. Their favourite employment is washing gold, which appears to be more abundant here than in any other part of the Philippines.

The bulk of the population of Caraga is of the Bisaya nation, speaking a dialect of the Bisaya language, from which it is to be inferred that they are strangers from some of the other islands. But there exists in the province also several wild tribes, having their own distinct tongues. The names of some of these, and it is all that is known respecting them, are the Mandaya, the Nanobo, the Talacaogo, the Taga-baloyo, and the Mamamanua. The first four are of the Malayan race, but the last is described as "very black negroes." The Mandaya are said to be so much fairer than the other inhabitants of Mindano, that some Spanish writers have come to the fanciful conclusion that they are a mixed race descended from shipwrecked Dutchmen. In the same fashion, the origin of the tribe called Taga-baloyo, from some imagined resemblance to Japanese, is traced to shipwrecked mariners of that nation. Exclusive of these wild tribes, the population of Caraga, all Christian, amounted by the last census to no more than 31,963 souls, or 4·76 inhabitants to the square mile. A great increase, however, has taken place since 1818, if the enumeration in both cases is to be trusted, for then the population amounted to no more than 15,987.

CARANG-ASAM. The name of one of the nine principalities into which the island of Bali is at present divided. See KARANG-ASAM.

CARDAMOMS. These are known in the Malay and Javanese languages by two names, kapulaga and puwar, which have every appearance of being native words, and yet the plant is neither indigenous nor cultivated in the Indian islands. It is the exclusive product of three countries only, Malabar, Ceylon, and Kamboja, and in these the spontaneous product of the forest incapable of cultivation. An immemorial commercial intercourse has existed between these and the Malayan countries.

Cardamoms were well known to the ancients, and Pliny describes their price in the market of Rome at 12 denarii the pound, equal to 11*s.* 4*d.* the pound avoirdupois, or about five times their present cost.

CARIMATA, in Malay, Kurimata, the name of an island on the south-western coast of Borneo, about three leagues in length, and of which the north-west end is in south latitude 1° 33′, and east longitude 108° 49′. Its highest hill is 2000 feet above the level of the sea, and visible at the distance of 15 or 16 leagues. Between it and Borneo are several islets and rocks, the largest named Surutu, two others Pulo Dua or "the two islets," and a group named Pulo Lima or "the five islets." Between Carimata and the island of Billiton is the Carimata passage, a route for large shipping at certain seasons of the year. Carimata is uninhabited, but occasionally visited by the itinerant Malays, the Orang-laut or sea-gypsies, for the fishing of tripang and tortoise-shell, and the collection of esculent swallows' nests. The whole group is estimated to have an area of 128 square geographical miles.

CARIMON ISLANDS, in Malay, Pulo Krimun, the name of two islands called by navigators the Great and Little Carimon; situated towards the eastern extremity of the Straits of Malacca. The smaller island is about two miles in length, and high land throughout, the highest part about 500 feet above the level of the sea. The larger island is about 12 miles in length and 5 in breadth, and its most elevated part rises to 2000 feet. Both are of granitic formation, and the smaller island, and probably both, contain ores of tin. In a visit which I made to the Little Carimon in 1824, I procured the finest specimen of alluvial tin that I have ever seen, a round mass of about 15 pounds weight, which had been very little rolled, for the surface was covered with perfect crystals of the oxide. The smaller island is uninhabited, but the larger has a population of about 400 Malay fishermen. Both form part of the State of Jehor, and are within the limit of which paramount sovereignty belongs, by the Convention of 1824, to the Dutch.

CARIMON JAVA, or the Javanese Carimon, a name given to it by European mariners to distinguish it from the last-named islands, is, in Javanese, Krimun. It is the largest of a group of islets on the northern coast of Java, opposite to the Promontory of Japara. The inhabitants are Javanese, simple, inoffensive, and poor. South latitude 5° 50′, and east longitude 110° 34′.

CASSOWARY. This bird erroneously supposed to be a native of the Sunda Islands, is known to the inhabitants of these countries only as an imported stranger. The Malay name is Suwari, from which, most probably, the European one is taken. Most probably it will be found to be a native of Ceram and New Guinea only, and like the cockatoos, crown pigeons, and birds of Paradise, of the last island, made known to the inhabitants of the west through the Malay and Javanese, who have immemorially carried on a trade with the country of the Papuans.

CAT. The domestic cat of the Malays has the same form, colour, and habits, as the European, except in one respect, that the tail seldom exceeds three or four inches in length, and always ends in a kind of crook, a peculiarity, however, not confined to it, for the same characteristic belongs to the Burmese cat. The origin of the Malayan domestic cat is equally obscure with that of the European. It is well known to all the civilised inhabitants. Its most common name throughout the Asiatic Islands, with slight corruptions, is kuching, but sometimes it takes its name from its cry. Thus mëong is, along with kuching, a synonyme for it in Javanese; and in Bugis, the only name for it mëau. In Javanese, while there are several foreign epithets for the dog, the hog, the horse, and the elephant, there is not even one for the cat. So far, then, as language indicates, the type of the domestic Malay cat will probably be found to be indigenous.

CATANDUANES. An island on the eastern coast of the great island of Luzon, and distant 2½ leagues from that of the province of South Camarines, lying between north latitudes 13° 30′ and 14° 7′, and east longitudes 123° 57′ and 124° 24′. Its extreme length from north to south is 12½, and its extreme breadth, from east to west, 7½ leagues, its area being computed at 55 square leagues. The heat of the climate is tempered by the sea breezes, and by the high mountains which it contains, and two chains of which run through it from north to south. It is, however, subject to storms, and has no harbours to afford shelter from the north-east monsoon. It is abundantly supplied with small rivers, from the sands of which the natives obtain gold dust. The soil is fertile and productive in rice, maiz, sesame, indigo, cotton, and abaca, and it has good pastures for rearing horses and oxen. The abundant forests of its mountains yield good timber for ship-building, while the building of boats, which are sent for sale to Mindoro and other places, is one of the principal branches of native industry. The total population of Catanduanes, by the census of 1850, was 20,910, the tribute payers being 3900, and the amount of the tribute 39,000 reals of plate. The first Spanish missionaries sent to this island were put to death by the then rude natives, who are now among the most peaceable and docile of the Philippine Christians.

CATECHU, the Cutch of European trade, and the kachu of the Malays, is the inspissated sap of several species of Acacia, obtained by the simple process of boiling the wood. The article is brought from Pegu to the European emporia, but I am not aware that any is produced in the Malayan countries themselves. In common with Gambier, the produce of the leaves of a nauclea, it is now largely exported to Europe and America for its tannin, to be used in tanning and dyeing.

CAUTO. Diogo de Cauto, the author of the Asia Portuguesa, was born in Lisbon in 1542, and died at Goa in 1616, at the age of 74. He seems to have gone to India at the early age of 14, and after passing ten years there in a military capacity, to have returned to Portugal. Soon after, however, he went back to India, so that he passed the greater part of his life in that country. His Indian experience, however, does not seem to have extended to any of the Asiatic Islands, as is evident from the palpable mistakes into which he falls in respect to the sense and orthography of Malayan words. Writing later than De Barros, he furnishes some additional information, but is greatly inferior to him, both in authenticity and intelligence.

CAVITÉ, anciently Cauit, one of the 20 provinces of the island of Luzon, and of the 35 of the Spanish Philippines. It has the metropolitan province of Tondo to the north and the provinces of Batangas and Laguna to the south, with the Bay of Manilla to the west. It contains the high mountain called the Pico de Loro, a portion of the southern Cordillera, towards its western side, and has an area of 408 square geographical miles. Cavité is generally a champaign country, watered by no fewer than 34 different streams, each with its proper name. The land, although a good deal of it is still unreclaimed, is in general well cultivated, the cultivation extending even to a considerable height on the slopes of the Cordillera. Its agricultural products are, rice, wheat, cacoa, coffee, and pepper, with the usual palms. By the census of 1850 it contained a population of 126,627, of whom 21,153 were subject to the capitation-tax, which amounted to 211,530 reals of plate. In this population the Spanish mestizos amounted to 418, the Chinese mestizos, called Sangley, to 5694, and the unmixed Chinese to no more than 103. Among the inhabitants of this province are the descendants of some Christians of Ternate, located in the district of Marigondo. These parties followed their instructors, the Jesuit fathers, when the Spanish and Portuguese were driven from the Moluccas by the Dutch, and settled in Luzon in 1660. The people of Cavité are a mixture of different Philippine tribes, but the prevailing nation and language are the Tagala. So far as the amounts given of the population can be trusted, it seems to have rapidly increased, for in 1735, it amounted to no more than to 5904. In 1799 it had risen to 33,302, and in 1818 to 51,665.

CAVITÉ, the name of the naval arsenal of Manilla, within the province last-named, and on the southern shore of the great bay, 3 leagues by sea and 6 by land, over a good carriage road, distant from the city of Manilla. Latitude 14° 29′, and longitude 120° 49′. The shelter of a low tongue of land, running for a league into the bay forms, with the southern shore, a harbour, secure from every wind except the north-east. The arsenal, fortifications, and town, are on the eastern side of the tongue of land. The town contains only 265 houses, and 1595 inhabitants. The fortifications, which were completed in 1819, are described as of great strength.

CAVITÉ EL VIEJOÉ, or OLD CAVITÉ, is a town and district within a league of the Arsenal, and to the south of it, with 1612 houses, and 9676 inhabitants.

ÇEBU. The name of an island, town, and province of the Philippines. The ancient name seems to have been Sogbu, which Pigafetta, who first described it, writes Zubu, evidently a corruption, since he makes the word to begin with a letter which does not exist in any of the Philippine tongues. Çebu is one of the islands called by the Spaniards the Visayas, or Bisayas. It lies between Negros to the west, and Leyté to the east; being divided from the first by a narrow strait, and from the last by a broader one. To the north it has Masbate, and to the south Mindano;

the first about 161, and the last 41 geographical miles distant. In form Çebu is long and narrow, its northern half being its broadest. Its length from north-east to south-west is 80 geographical miles, its average breadth 15, and its superficies 1843 square miles. A chain of mountains traverses the island through its whole length, and in it are stated to be found veins of gold and beds of mineral coal. The northern and broadest end of Çebu terminates in two projecting head-lands; between which is a deep and spacious bay, which gives occasional shelter to the coasting vessels of the Philippines. But the best harbours are those of the chief town of Dalagueté, and of Argao—both on the eastern coast. The rivers are numerous but small, and generally unfit for navigation or irrigation. The climate is healthy, but the heat would be suffocating but for the regularity of the sea breezes; for the quantity of rain which falls in Çebu is ascertained to be less than in any other of the islands of the Archipelago.

The surface of this island is generally sandy, stony, and uneven; and from this, and the unfitness of its rivers for irrigation, the produce of its soil does not answer to the extent of its surface. With the exception of a few fertile valleys, cultivation is generally confined to the sea-board. Of the geological formation of the island nothing is stated, but there is no indication of any portion of it being volcanic. In the history of the Philippines it is celebrated as the first place in which Christianity was preached to the natives. The people are of the Bisayan nation, and speak a dialect of the far-spread language of this name. It contains no wild races, negro or brown-complexioned.

ÇEBU, the chief town of the province of the same name, is situated on the eastern shore of the island of Çebu, opposite to the little island of Mactan, celebrated for the death of Magellan. It lies on a small river, or rather estuary, which divides it into two parts. Its situation is picturesque, but the climate sultry, though healthy. It contains 929 houses and 5576 inhabitants. The principal buildings are the episcopal palace, the cathedral, and the beautiful church of San Augustine, called also the Church of "the Holy Infant of Çebu," after an image discovered by a Biscayan soldier of the army of Miguel Lopes de Legaspi, the conqueror of the Philippines. This is supposed to have been the very image of Christ given to the natives of Çebu by Magellan, and miraculously preserved for four-and-forty years. The natives call it Batala, which, in their language, means "a god." The word seems to be an easy corruption either of the Malay word barala, "a graven image;" or of the Sanscrit one Avatara, "a descent," which the Malays and Javanese write batara, and is a genuine term with them for any of the principal Hindu gods. Besides this image, the Çebuans have preserved the first cross, erected by Magellan in 1521, which they venerate as a holy relic.

The town of Çebu is a place of considerable trade, carried on with almost all parts of the Philippines. This is in the hands of a few Chinese, but especially of the Spanish mestizos of the place, amounting to 500, who live in a quarter of the town apart from the rest of the inhabitants. Çebu, besides being the seat of the civil and military administration, is also that of a bishopric, the bishop having ecclesiastic jurisdiction over 13 out of the 35 provinces of the Philippines. The bishopric was founded in 1592, and the town itself in 1574.

ÇEBU. The province of this name, besides the principal island, includes the considerable island of Bohol or Bojol, with those of Sigujor or Isla del Fuego, Mactan, Olango, Davis or Dauis, Mino, and Panglao. The total population of the province in 1850 was 389,073, of whom 67,309 paid tribute, which amounted to 678,295 reals of plate. According to the Spanish enumerations, a great increase has taken place since the first of them was made in 1735, when the population was no more than 39,702. In 1799 it was 100,000; and in 1818 it rose to 154,902.

CELEBES. The fourth island in magnitude of the Malay, and the fifth of the Asiatic Archipelago. It lies between latitudes 1° 45′ and 5° 45′ north, and longitudes 113° 10′ and 116° 45′ east. Its greatest length from north to south has been computed at 768 geographical miles; its greatest breadth at 100; and its area at 57,250 square geographical miles, which makes it by above one-half part larger than Java. Deeply indented by three spacious gulfs, it consists of an irregular central body and of four long peninsulas, which gives it a grotesque appearance on the map, very unlike any other island, except the neighbouring one of Gilolo. The Portuguese historian, De Couto, compares its form to that of a grasshopper. Two of these gulfs penetrate the island from the east; Gorongtalu or Tomini, and Tolo or Tomaikoo, the first or most northerly to the extent of about 3½°, and the second to 2½°. The third gulf, that of Boni, penetrates it from the south to the depth of 3°. These names, it may be noticed, are not native ones, but such as have been imposed by European navigators from the names of places on their coasts. The peninsulas have no names, either native or European; but from their position may be designated the northern, the eastern, the south-eastern, and the south-western.

The Northern Peninsula, reckoning from the Bay of Palos to its extremity, extends over 6° of longitude,—being a long and narrow strip of land, in some places not exceeding 10 miles in breadth, and nowhere exceeding 40. A range of mountains runs through it, the general height of which does not exceed 2000 feet, while some peaks rise to 4000, 5000, and even 6000. The great volcanic band passes through this part of Celebes alone, but to what extent is not ascertained; although, most probably, to a small portion only of its extremity, in which several volcanic craters, some extinct and some in activity, exist. The whole of this peninsula is rugged and mountainous. Most of its valleys are transverse; and it is said to contain no more than three longitudinal ones of any extent, and but a single plateau, 300 feet above the level of the sea. The volcanic portion contains one lake, seemingly the crater of an extinct volcano. This, which is 2000 feet above the level of the sea, is about three leagues in length, and from one-third of a league to a league in breadth, varies in depth from 90 to 100 feet. The rivers are numerous, but small and of short course so as not to be navigable even for native boats. See MENADO.

The least known of the peninsulas of Celebes is the eastern, or that which has the Gulf of Tomini to the north, and that of Tolo to the south. Its length extends to four degrees of longitude, and its average breadth is probably not less than 80 miles. A chain of mountains is represented as passing through it, but of its geological formation or height nothing is known. Both its coasts are unbroken by considerable bays or inlets. Towards its junction with the body of the island an extensive lake is stated, on native authority, to exist. The south-eastern Peninsula, or that which has the Gulf of Tolo and the Molucca Sea to the east, and the Gulf of Boni to the west, extends over 2½ degrees of latitude, and is from 30 to 80 miles in breadth. On its eastern shore it has many islets, and at its extremity are the large islands of Boeton, Muna, and Wowoni. A range of mountains is represented as passing through it, but of its nature nothing is known; and the same thing is true of its interior, the most recent Dutch maps of Celebes being hardly marked by a single name.

By far the best known and the most important of the Celebesian peninsulas is the south-western, or that which has the Gulf of Boni to the east, and the strait which divides Celebes from Borneo to the west. Reckoning from the bottom of the Bay of Boni, its length is not less than 180 miles, but its average breadth does not exceed 70, giving thus an area of 12,600 square geographical miles. A chain of mountains runs through this, as through the other Peninsulas, which towards its southern extremity, contains the peak of Lompo-bàtang, 8200 feet high above the level of the sea and said to be the most elevated point of the whole island. The geological formation of this range is not stated, but probably it is plutonic and sedementary, and, at all events, is known to exhibit no traces of volcanic action. About the centre of this Peninsula is found the large lake called that of Labaya or Tâparang-dano, which discharges its waters by a river navigable for native vessels into the Bay of Boni. It is reported to be about 25 miles in length, with a breadth varying from 8 to 10, and having an average depth of 30 feet. This portion of Celebes is distinguished from Sumatra and Borneo by the existence of extensive prairies or grass plains, unencumbered with heavy timber, and yielding pasture for horses and oxen, some of the first of which are wild.

On the western side of Celebes there is no deep gulf as on the eastern, so that the last-named peninsula may be considered as part of the main body of the island; but reckoning the latter as only from the Bay of Mandar to that of Palos, and from the western shore to the head of the Gulf of Tolo, it is 4 degrees in length and 2½ in breadth. Little is known of it except its western coast, and that washed by the head of the Bay of Boni, and even of these our information is chiefly founded on native authority.

The rivers of Celebes are of short course, none of them navigable for vessels of burden, and few of them even for native craft. The largest is the Sadang, said to have its source in the mountains in the northern part of the south-western peninsula, and which falls into the Straits of Macassar, but it does not seem to be of much value to industry, either for navigation or irrigation. The most useful river is the Chinrana, which has its source in the lake of Labaya and falls into the Bay of Boni. This is navigable up to the lake by native vessels of 40 tons burthen.

Of the metals, copper and tin are stated to be found in Celebes, and mines of both to be wrought, but iron and gold are the only two that are abundant, and respecting which we have reliable information. The last of these is very widely disseminated over the northern part of the island, and procured by the rude washings of the natives: more of it is exported than from any other island, except Borneo. A deep forest covers the mountains of Celebes, as those of the other islands, some of the trees of which (but the Teak is not one of them) yield useful building timber. The sago, coco, and gomuti palms appear to be natives of the island, but neither black pepper, cloves, nutmegs, camphor, nor benzoin, those commodities which so early attracted the commerce of strangers to some of the other islands.

The zoology of Celebes is remarkable for the absence of all the larger animals of prey which characterise that of the Malay Peninsula, Sumatra, Java, and even to some extent of Borneo. It has neither tiger nor leopard, and of the whole feline family only one small cat. The elephant, the rhinoceros, and the Tapir are also wanting, and of this class the hog, the Babi-rusa or hog-deer, and the horse are the only representatives, the last, most probably a stranger, become wild. The wild ox, the Bos Sondaicus of the Peninsula, Sumatra, Java, and Borneo is not found in Celebes, but a small animal, forming the link between the ox and antelope, takes its place. In Celebes, proceeding eastward, are found for the first time representatives of the marsupial or pouched animals, which continue through the Molucca and New Guinea, until they become the leading type of the quadrupeds of Australia.

The people of Celebes are throughout of the same race with all the inhabitants of Java, Sumatra, and Borneo, men of short stature, of a yellowish brown complexion and lank strong hair, with scanty beard. No negro race exists, nor any race intermediate between the Negro and the Malay. The social state presents every variety, from savages, and it is alleged cannibals, to men possessing a knowledge of letters. The languages are as numerous as the tribes of the island. Three of them only have acquired any amount of cultivation, the Bugis, the Macassar, and the Mandar, or four, if we include the language of the neighbouring island of Boeton. Wherever the languages of Celebes are written the character is the same, a peculiar one, which differs from all other alphabets, and the invention of which is ascribed to the Bugis or Wugi nation. The most civilised tribes are found in the south-western peninsula, on the western shore of the main body of the island, and on the large islands of Boeton and Muna, both of which may be considered as parts of Celebes. They consist of the Bugis, the Macassar, the Mandar, and the Butung nations. An inferior civilisation belongs to the inhabitants of the more easterly part of the long and narrow northern peninsula, where we find the nations speaking the Menado and Gorongtalo languages. The mountains of the interior of the island, generally, are inhabited by wild races, whom the Malays call Dyaks, as they do the people of Borneo and Sumatra in the same state of society. The very centre of the island is occupied by a people, called by the more civilised inhabitants Turaja, which, however, is probably only a native term for "savage." Like the wild races of Borneo, these are professed head-hunters, and some of them, it is alleged, even cannibals. All the wild races are supposed to be divided into many tribes, each with its own distinct tongue, as is the case with the inhabitants of Borneo, but, in fact, little or nothing is known respecting themselves or their languages. Besides the indigenous population, there are settled on many of the coasts of the island, as fishermen, numbers of the wandering Malays called the Bajau, the same people that are to be traced in similar situations from Sumatra to New Guinea.

The more advanced nations of Celebes practise all the useful arts known to the Malays and Javanese, but, generally, with less skill than, at least, by the latter. The soil of Celebes is obviously unfruitful compared with that of Java and the other volcanic islands, and its agriculture greatly inferior as the consequence. It is stated that the arable land of Celebes must lie fallow for five or six years, before it is fit to yield a second crop, while that of Java, in so far as regards irrigated land, is cultivated from year to year without interruption, and this is certainly proof at once of the inferior skill and inferior fertility of the former. The only part of Celebes which produces a surplus of corn for exportation is the eastern portion of the northern peninsula, where the volcanic formation prevails. The crops grown, and the animals domesticated for food or labour in Celebes, are the same as in the western islands. In recent times the culture of coffee has been introduced by the natives themselves, and in the northern peninsula of the caco. The only manufacture in which the civilised inhabitants excel is that of checked cottons distinguished for their durability, and for the permanence, although not the brilliancy, of their colours. The raw materials are their own, and the women, the spinners, weavers, and dyers. These cloths are largely exported to the European and other emporia of the west, and maintain their place in competition with the manufactures of Manchester and Glasgow.

But the chief bent of the civilised inhabitants of Celebes is to maritime enterprise, impelled perhaps in this direction from the stubborn nature of the soil, and the physical form of the island, with so extensive a coast, and no part of the land very remote from a sea unusually productive in human food. From whatever causes it proceeds, the inhabitants of Celebes are, at present, the most adventurous and skilful native mariners and merchants of the Archipelago. Their little vessels of peculiar build, called Padewakan by the Malays, and of the burden of from 40 to 50 tons, conduct the carrying trade from one end of the Archipelago to the other, their outward and homeward voyages being guided by the monsoons. Besides the trade conducted from Celebes itself, the people of this island are to be found as settlers in every part of the Archipelago where there is trade and protection, and many vessels belonging to them sail from such settlements, so that altogether probably not fewer than 800 vessels belong to them. Their outward cargos consist of such articles as the following, cotton cloths, gold dust, birds-nests, tortoise-shell, tripang, scented woods, coffee, and rice.

The total population of a great island, most of which has never been explored by Europeans, or even trodden by them, must be a matter of mere estimate. A computation of that portion of it under the direct sovereignty of the Netherlands, made in 1838, gave the number at 410,000. Of this, the northern peninsula, and some portion of the eastern, amounted to 178,272, the rest being contained in the southern part of the south-western peninsula. The Dutch possessions are estimated to contain 1674 geographical leagues, and if the rest of the island be equally well peopled as these, it follows that the total population would amount to 888,297. It has been loosely estimated at 3,000,000, which a careful and judicious writer, M. Melville de Carnbée, considers an extravagant estimate, and reduces to 1,104,000, although, on what foundation, I am not aware. If we estimate the total population at 900,000 in round numbers, we shall, probably, not underrate it, when it is considered how much of the island is known to be in the possession of rude and savage tribes, and how much of it is an absolute wilderness. Were Celebes as well peopled as Java, it ought, according to the census of the latter, to contain above 14,000,000 inhabitants, but its population in proportion to area is, probably, not above one-fifteenth part of this number, or in other words, every square mile of Java contains as many inhabitants as 15 square miles of Celebes. This comparison gives a tolerably fair notion of the relative fertility and civilisation of the two islands.

With respect to the history of Celebes, it is hardly necessary to say that it was utterly unknown to the European nations of antiquity, or the middle ages. It seems even to have been very little, if at all, known to the Asiatic strangers who frequented the Archipelago long before Europeans, for it yielded none of the productions which attracted them to the other islands. These parties had given names to Sumatra, to Java, to Borneo, but they had bestowed none on Celebes. Barbosa is the first European writer who makes mention of the island, but he evidently thought that the country which he so called was not one island, but many. "Passing," says he, "the islands of Maluco (the Moluccas), there exist other islands to the west, from which occasionally come (to the Moluccas) a fair people, naked from the waist upwards. Yet they have cloth woven from a certain material like straw, with which they cover their nudities. They speak a language of their own. Their barks are ill-constructed, and in them they come to the aforesaid Maluco Islands to load with cloves, copper, tin, and cloths of Cambay. They bring for sale, swords very long and broad, of one edge" (at present well known to the Malays under the name of klewang), "with other works in iron, and much gold. These people eat human flesh, and if the king of Maluco has a criminal to execute, they ask for him as a favour to eat, as if asking for a hog. The islands from which these people come are called Celebe."—Ramusio, vol. i., p. 318.

De Barros gives the name as we now write it, not, however, as of one island, but like Barbosa, of many, and he informs us that "the islands" of Celebes were discovered in the year 1525, by a native vessel, manned by Portuguese, sent from the Moluccas in search of gold, which the islands in question had the reputation of producing. The Portuguese had thus been fourteen years in commercial intercouse with the Moluccas before they discovered Celebes, although only 60 leagues distant.

The account of Celebes given by the historian De Couto, which refers to the year 1540, or fifteen years after its discovery, is more full than that of De Barros, but it is somewhat confused, as well as, in some particulars, inaccurate. This is his account :

"At the same time," (1640) "there came to Ternate ambassadors from the islands of the Macaças (Macassars), which lie west of the Moluccas about 60 leagues. These islands (*estas ilhas*) are many, and extend in a direction north and south to the length of 100 leagues. This island (*esta ilha*) resembles in form a huge grasshopper, of which the head stretches to five degrees and a half of south latitude, and constitutes the Celebes (*os Cellebes*). This has a king of its own. The tail, which is next to the Moluccas, crosses the equinoxial, and runs a degree north of it. These islands (*estas ilhas*) are ruled by many kings, and have different languages, and separate rites and customs. Commencing with the tail, the extremity of which is cut by the equator, there is the kingdom of the Bogis (Bugis). Its principal city is called Savito, which is large, consists of storied houses, beautiful, but all of wood. There they burn the dead, and collect the ashes in urns, which they inter in separate fields, where they erect chapels, and for a year the relatives bring food, which they place on the tomb, which dogs, cats, and birds carry off. The viands thus placed, consist of such as the deceased eat of while living. These people have no temples, but pray, looking up to the skies with their hands raised, from which it may be seen that they have a knowledge of the true God. The common people have but one wife, but the kings three or four. Then comes the kingdom of Macaça. Its principal city is called Goa, and here they inter the dead. Near this is another kingdom called Dirapa, its principal town having the same name. The people of this country have the same rites and customs as the Bugis, and their kings are relations. To the kings thus named there are many petty princes subject. In these islands there is cotton, copper, iron, lead, and much gold, made into bracelets for the women. There are also red gems, which are made into ornaments, with sandal-wood and sapan-wood, and the people manufacture much good cloth of silk of many sorts. These islands are rich in rice, legumes, fruits, and salt, and they have horses, elephants, common fowls, sheep, buffaloes, deer, hogs, partridges, and all kinds of forest game, but no oxen. They have ships of many kinds, some of them called pelang (Malay, a barge or pinnace), which are fast.running vessels for war. They have others, called lopi, which are for cargo, and still larger ones, which are called jojoga. All these people are of a tawny complexion, like the inhabitants of the Moluccas. The men are well-made and handsome, but foul in their lives, and much addicted to heinous sin: the women are handsome and laborious. All of these people that have fallen into the hands of the Portuguese have been prisoners of war. Every year there is taken of them for sale a great number to Malacca."—Decade V. book vii. chapter 2.

There is some truth and much error in this description. The country of the Bugis and the town of Savito are not on the northern, but the south-western Peninsula. No such kingdom as Dirapa is traceable, and there is nothing but the assertion of the writer to show that the elephant ever existed in Celebes. He refers only to the northern and south-western Peninsulas, and most probably considered the eastern and south-eastern to be islands like Boetou, Muna, Wowoni, and Salayer. It is evident, however, from his account, that the people of Celebes were not yet converted to the Mahommedan religion, and it is probable, from their modes of prayer, and the burning of the dead, that they professed some rude form of Hinduism. It is evident that the parties who furnished De Couto with his statements derived their information, not by direct communication with the people of Celebes, but through the Malays of Malacca or of the Moluccas, and this is shown by the use of the Malay and not native proper names.

The accounts of the Portuguese historians may assist us in offering some conjectures respecting the name of the island. It is one wholly unknown, even at present, to the natives of Celebes itself, or to the other people of the Archipelago, and indeed, has not the sound of a native word, being one which the former could not pronounce. The island, in fact, has no native name any more than the other great islands. A land, by the inhabitants of the Archipelago, is considered only in reference to the people who inhabit it, and no effort is made at a geographical generalisation which would embrace the aggregate of many parts. They speak of the land of the Bugis and of the Macassars, as they speak of the land of the Malays, of the Bataks, of the Javanese, and of the Sundas, and it is highly probable that Celebes was not known to its inhabitants to be an island at all, until it was ascertained for them by Europeans. The name of Celebes then was, in all likelihood, imposed by the Portuguese, and as we have seen, they seem to have considered it rather as a group of islands than a single island. I have no doubt, therefore, but that the last syllable of the word is a Portuguese plural. The rest of the word is by no means so certain, but it seems very probable that the first syllable is the frequent initial and inseparable Malay particle Si, in its

Portuguese orthography. This is frequently prefixed by the Malays to the names of persons and to those of islets or rather of groups of islets, of which we have examples in the islands Sbiru, Simalu, and Sipora, on the western coast of Sumatra. These names may be literally translated, "the blue," "the shame," and "the dissembling" islands. The chief difficulty is with the medial syllable, or principal word, which, however, may be the Malay word lâbih or lebih, "more" or "over and above." Pulo Salâbih would, then, signify "the islands over and above," and in their explanations to the Portuguese such a vague name may have been given by the Malays, which with the Portuguese plural would approach to the word Celebes. We have a somewhat similar proceeding in the Cellates of De Barros, which he gives as the proper name of a people inhabiting the islands at the eastern end of the Straits of Malacca, and "whose vocation," he says, "it was to rob and fish" (cuyo officio he rubar y pescar.) The word thus fabricated into the name of a nation is the Malay word sâlat, "a strait or narrow sea," with the Portuguese plural, the people referred to being no other than the roving Malays spread over the coasts of the Archipelago, to the present day, and known as the Orang-laut, "men of the sea," or Orang-sâlat, "men of the straits."

That the people of Celebes had an early intercourse with the Malays and Javanese, and that they received from them some portion of their civilisation, is sufficiently testified by the evidence of language. Of the Bugis, the most copious and improved of the Celebesian languages, about one-fifth is either Malay or Javanese. Among words of these languages we find the names of such cultivated plants as rice, the yam, the sugar-cane, the mango, and the mangostin, but not the banana or the cocoa-nut, or the sago-palm, or the bread-fruit. All domesticated animals bear Malay or Javanese names, except the buffalo. The greater number of tools, implements, and weapons, but not all, have the same origin. Thus, saw, adze, knife, shears, file, chisel, sword and bow are Malayan, but not spear, javelin, shield, dagger, and hanger. Iron, tin, and silver are Malay and Javanese, but not gold. In the terms connected with the useful arts, while spin, thread, weave, shuttle, sew, nail, bolt, plank are Malayan, house, door, lime, and cloth, are native.

Language alone testifies that the more cultivated of the nations of Celebes had a slight tincture of Hinduism, but to judge by the form, sense, and identity of the words, evidently through the Malays and Javanese. Thus the words religion, worship, adoration, fast, ascetic devotion, heaven, infernal regions, deity, spiritual guide, goblin, and soul, are either Malay or Javanese, or Sanscrit through them. Independent, indeed, of theological terms, there are a good many Sanscrit words indicating progress in civilisation which have found their way into the Bugis, through the medium of the Malay and Javanese, such as cotton, copper, pepper, sugar, nutmeg, indigo, diadem, fortress, &c., &c.

When the Portuguese first visited Celebes, they found a few foreign Mahommedan settlers at Goa, the chief town of the Macassar nation, but the natives as yet unconverted. This was in 1540. The king of this state is said to have adopted Mohammedanism about the year 1603, but his people generally not until 1616. This great change in the manners of the people of Celebes did not begin, for the Macassars were the first converts, until a whole century after the Portuguese had been in occupation of Malacca and the Moluccas; nor, indeed, until some years after the arrival in the Archipelago of French, Dutch, and English. This fact proves how small had been the intercourse of the western nations of Asia with Celebes, down to so late a period as the beginning of the 17th century; especially when it is recollected that most of the Sumatrans had been converted four centuries before, and even the Javenese near a hundred and forty years.

The Dutch began to carry on some trade with Celebes as early as the year 1607, but did not enter into political relations with its princes until 30 years later, when they formed a treaty with the leading state of the island, the Macassars of Goa. In 1660, they conquered the Macassars, aud expelled their allies, the Portuguese. The period which has since elapsed of near two centuries, has been one of long, frequent, and costly wars, engaged in, as the results prove, for no other purpose than the establishment of a profitless supremacy, substantially nominal. It is certain that the occupation by an European nation of such a country as Celebes, with a scanty population, chiefly of fishermen, traders, or, still worse, of savages, can not only not be profitable, but must be wasteful. In such a state of society there is no real land-rent, and consequently no land-tax; neither is there a population by wealth or numbers to contribute revenue by indirect taxation: hence, the means of obtaining a revenue sufficient to maintain the expensive establishments of an European nation, such as are found in the dense populations of Java and Hindustan, have no existence. The entire computed population of the Netherland portion of the Celebes is no more than 410,000, and it would be unreasonable to expect that such a one armed and poor, should be either able or willing to furnish to the government of foreign conquerors a revenue adequate to their own efficient administration and at the same time to the control of as many more independent parties who make no contribution at all. The chief source of native revenue is a tithe on corn, and this also is exacted by the Dutch government. Where, however, there is no rent, such a tax is a virtual excise on bread, and can neither be a productive or expedient impost in a country where the majority of the people are not cultivators of the soil, and which hardly produces corn sufficient for its own consumption. What the revenues and expenditure of the Celebes are I have not seen in any public statement; but it is probable that the latter is greatly in excess, and that the balance is supplied from the revenues of Java.

It is to be presumed that it is a conviction of the truth of this state of things that has led the Netherland authorities, of late years, to establish free ports in Celebes, on the same principle as the British settlement of Singapore. In 1846 such a port was established with eminent success at Macassar, on the south-western peninsula; and at Menado and Kema in 1849, on the northern and southern shores of the northern peninsula.

CERAM. This is the Portuguese orthography for the Serang of the Malays, an island in the Molucca Sea, having New Guinea and its islands to the east, Boero to the west, Amboyna and the Banda Isles to the south, and Gillolo with the Moluccas to the north of it. It lies between south latitudes 2° 45′ 30″ and 3° 36′ 30″, and between east longitudes 129° 30′ and 130° 53′. Its length is about 162 geographical miles, but its greatest breadth does not exceed 40: its area has been computed at 4945 geographical square miles. It is thus the largest island of the Malay Archipelago next to Celebes, although very far from being of value proportioned to its extent. A chain of mountains runs through it from east to west, or rather the island is itself one mountain range with little exception,—some of the peaks rising to the height of 6000 and 8000 feet above the level of the sea; and the highest, Nusa-keli (in Javanese "drift island,") to as much as 9250. The eastern coast is bold, precipitous, and difficult of access; and although both sides contain some spacious bays, there seems to be no good harbour on either. Its geological formation has not been ascertained, but probably is the same as that of the neighbouring island of Amboyna, or composed of plutonic and sedimentary rocks. It has certainly no active volcano, or extinct crater, that has been ascertained. Numerous rivers, or rather torrents proceeding from the mountains, fall into the sea on both the eastern and western coasts; but none of them are of the least importance to agriculture or navigation. The country is generally covered with a stupendous forest, none of the trees, however, it has been ascertained, being fit for the purpose of ship-building. Neither is the forest known to contain the clove or the nutmeg. Hogs, deer, and the civet cat are the reported wild animals.

The coast of Ceram is occupied by Malay settlers, an active and enterprising race of fishermen, who pursue their chief game, the tripang or holothurion, and the shell-tortoise as far as the coast of New Guinea, and even Australia. The inhabitants of the interior are the aboriginal people of the island, divided into many small independent tribes, distinguished by the difference of their languages. The state of society among them resembles that of the fixed wild inhabitants of Borneo, although less civilised than the more advanced of these. Like the wild Borneans they live in villages, and practise a rude husbandry. Like them, too, they are stealers and hoarders of human heads, and exhibit these as trophies in their private and public dwellings,—the only historical records of their deeds of arms. Their husbandry consists in the culture of the banana, the sago-palm, some farinaceous roots, and some mountain rice. The growth of rice by irrigation, and the rearing of the ox and buffalo are unknown to the Ceramese,—evidence sufficient of the sterility of the soil, and of the barbarism and poverty of the people. Of the population of the island no conjecture has been made. Ten inhabitants to every square mile would give a population of 25,000, which probably exceeds the actual number. Bali and Lomboc are each about one-third part of the size of Ceram; and the first has a computed population of 700,000, and the last of 450,000,—one of many proofs that in these countries, even under the same parallels, mere extent of land counts for little or nothing in appreciating the value.

CERAM-LAUT, correctly SERANG-LAUT, that is "Ceram to sea," is the name of a cluster of islets, the largest of which are named Serenri, Gesir, Kaliwaru, Gorong, and Malongi. They lie in south latitude 3° 55′, and east longitude 133°, and off the south-east end of Ceram. The inhabitants, in physical form, belong to the Malayan and not to the Negro race. They practise a little agriculture, the chief object of which is the culture of the sago-palm, which yields their bread. They are chiefly fishermen, and their principal game the tortoise and holothurion. Their voyages extend to New Guinea, and the islands on its south-western coast. At these, they obtain seed-pearls, scented woods, nutmegs, stuffed birds of paradise, a great variety of birds of the parrot family, and the crown pigeon; with a considerable quantity of sulphur, but from what volcano obtained is not known. The Bugis traders repair to the Ceram-laut Islands and there purchase the different commodities thus collected, and convey them to the western emporia. The first of the islands above named, Serenre, appears to be that to which they resort for this purpose.

CHAI, abbreviated CHI, means water, and also river in the language of the Sundas; and exists as the first syllable of many names of places in the western part of Java, such as Chitarum, literally "Indigo-plant river;" Chimanuk, "bird-river;" Chiasam, "tamarind-river;" and Chiñur, "river of coco-nuts."

CHAMPA. The name of an ancient Malay settlement on the eastern side of the Gulf of Siam, in the country of Camboja. See CAMBOJA.

CHÂMPÂDAH. The *Artocarpus polypheme* of botanists, a fruit of the same natural family with the jack and bread-fruit; smaller than the first, but of more delicate flavour, and greatly esteemed by the Malays. It seems to be an indigenous plant of the Archipelago, and even here to be limited to the western parts of it, such as Sumatra, the Malay Peninsula, and their adjacent islands.

CHERIBON. A large province of Java, situated on the northern side of the island, and having the province of the Preanger Regencies to the west and south, that of Tâgal to the east, and the sea to the north. The western portion of it is peopled by the Sundas, and the eastern by the Javanese; and hence, perhaps, its name correctly Charuban, which in Javanese means "mixture." Its total area is estimated at 2043 geographical square miles. It contains a large proportion of mountain land; and one of its mountains, Chârmai, rises to the height of 10,000 feet above the level of the sea, and is an active volcano. Like the rest of the island, Cheribon is of volcanic formation. It has one beautiful mountain lake, which gives its Sanscrit name, Talaga, literally, the "cistern" or "reservoir," to one of its principal subdivisions.

Cheribon is divided into 13 districts. In 1815, its population was reckoned at 216,000, which, by the census of 1845, had risen to 616,523. By that of 1850, the number had declined, from causes not explained, to 574,730. In 1815, the number of its horned cattle was reckoned at 42,866, and of its horses, at 6623. In 1845, the cattle had increased to 115,000, and the horses to 30,000.

Previous to the conversion to Mahommedanism, Cheribon and the districts adjacent to it were under the rule of several petty independent princes. About the year 1480 of our time, an Arabian adventurer, called Shekh Maulana, better known to the Javanese by the name of the place of his residence and title Susunan Gunung-jati, signifying the "holy man of the hill of teak wood." This person subdued the petty princes of the country, and sent his son to Bantam, who performed the same office of conversion and subjugation for the Bantamese. From the father and son are descended the Sultans of Bantam and Cheribon, both now abdicated kings and pensioners of the European government, although a predecessor of the first named of these potentates once sent an embassy to the most powerful monarch of his time, Louis the XIV.

CHESS. The game of chess is supposed to have been an invention of the Hindus, and, through them, to have been made known to the Malayan nations. This opinion, however, is not supported by the terms of the game in the Malay language. Had it been received directly from the Hindus, these terms, as in other cases, would have been wholly Sanscrit. They are not so, for some of them are Persian, some native, and one belongs to the Telinga; while those that are Sanscrit are but words long naturalised in other departments of the insular languages. It seems probable that the Malays, who alone are familiar with the game, borrowed it in comparatively modern times, from the Mahommedans of the Coromandel coast, who themselves had learnt it, directly or indirectly, from the Persians.

CHETTO, CHATO, or JATO. The name of certain extensive but rude temples, situated on the eastern acclivity of the mountain Lawu, in Java, about the centre of the island, and in the country of the proper Javanese nation. The buildings, which are at the height of 4220 feet above the level of the sea, consist of eight ascending terraces, paved with hewn trachite, and communicating with each other by flights of steps of the same material. On the terraces are the remains of temples and monstrous images, having just sufficient resemblance to those of the Hindus to show that they were dedicated to their religion. Unlike most of the other monuments of Java, they are in a rude and grotesque style, evincing the absence in their construction of foreign guidance. An inscription in Javanese numerals gives the year of their building, and this is 1361 of the Hindu era of Saka, corresponding to 1439 of Christ, which was about 40 years only before the final subversion of the Hindu religion in Java. I had myself described these temples, the only ones of the kind in Java, except those of Suku, on the opposite side of the same mountain, many years ago, but they were visited in 1838, and a far better account given of them by M. Junghun, a gentleman to whose industry, enterprise, and ability the geography of Java is more indebted than to any one living.

CHINA. This word, which in the Malayan languages, in conformity to its practice in all such cases, is an adjective, is pronounced as an Italian would pronounce it. When the country is alluded to, the Sanscrit word nagri, or the native one, bânüa, are required. It is difficult to determine from what source the natives of the Archipelago have derived a word now so familiar to them. They may have received it from the Persian and Arabian merchants who passed through the Archipelago on their way to China, as early as the ninth and tenth centuries, or it may be the Malayan pronunciation of the word Tsin, the ancient name of China, north of the Yang-che-kiang, received directly from the Chinese themselves.

That an early intercourse existed between China and the islands of the Asiatic Archipelago is certain, but there is, at the same time, no ground for ascribing a very remote antiquity to it. In the ancient language, literature, and monuments of Java, the only country of the Archipelago boasting of an ancient civilisation, there is certainly no allusion whatever to China or the Chinese. There is, however, other evidence, which attests an intercourse of many centuries. Ancient Chinese coins have been discovered in various parts of the Archipelago; and as these, with the exception of those of Java, are known to have been the only coined money of the Archipelago before the arrival of Europeans, they are sufficient to prove the existence of the intercourse. Thus, several such coins were dug up in 1827, from the ruins of the ancient Malay settlement of Singapore, said to have been founded in 1160, and destroyed by the Javanese in 1252 of Christ. These coins have been deposited in the Museum of the Royal Asiatic Society, and bear the names of emperors whose deaths correspond with the years of our time, 967, 1067, and 1085. Besides this evidence, which carries us back to the tenth century, Chinese porcelain, of antique forms—no longer manufactured—has either been dug up, or found preserved as heirlooms. The wild aborigines of Borneo, for example, preserve many of the latter description; and it is hardly necessary to add, that the natives of the Archipelago are ignorant of the manufacture of porcelain, but that it now forms, and at all ascertained times has formed, a main object of the export trade of the Chinese. In 1844, a singular discovery of pottery, glazed porcelain vases, was made in Java, amidst the relics of antiquity in a mountain towards the eastern end of the island, at an elevation of 9000 feet above the level of the sea, which could hardly be other than Chinese. The name of the place in which the vases were found, some of them broken and some entire, is Argapura, a word partly Javanese and partly Sanscrit, and importing mountain palace, or city.

Such testimony is, unquestionably, far more satisfactory than anything that can be gleaned from the literary records of the Chinese, which, however, are not wholly silent on the subject of the intercourse between China and the islands of the Archipelago. In 1815, there were given to me by a highly intelligent Creole Chinese of Java, whose family had been for several generations settled in the island, a volume printed at Pekin, in the reign of the Emperor Kanghi, which contained some curious notices on the question. This work, now in the library of the British Museum, attributes the first intercourse with a country, supposed to be Java, to an era corresponding with the year of Christ, 421. After a long interval, it states that it was renewed in the year 964; a period, it will be observed, corresponding with the date of the earliest coins already alluded to, and, respecting such coins, it makes the following curious and instructive remark. "In this traffic they use the money of China, but of a coinage older than the present times, and the coin bears a value double what it does in China." The work refers to the unsuccessful expedition which Kublai Khan, the son of the celebrated Jengis, fitted out against some islands, which De Guignes supposes to be Borneo, but which the Chinese of Java consider to have been this last-named island, and which indeed, according to their interpretation, is expressly named. According to De Guignes, this expedition was undertaken in 1292. The last notice which the work gives of an intercourse with the Malayan islands refers to the sixteenth year of the reign of the third prince of the native dynasty, the Ming, which superseded the Moguls, and, which in its turn, was superseded by the Manchoos. This brings us down to the year 1420, only 89 years before the arrival of Europeans in the Archipelago. It states that in the fifth year of the reign of the same prince, the country alluded to, and supposed with reason to be Java, being divided between two princes, the prince of the western invaded and conquered the eastern territory. The year referred to corresponds with 1409 of Christ; and Mr. Marsden infers that the transaction thus alluded to is the conquest by the Mahommedans of the Hindu kingdom of Majapahit, which is probable, but if it really does, there is a chronological error on the part of the Chinese writer of near 70 years; for the event in question took place in 1478. In truth, Chinese accounts of foreign countries are but of slender value, owing to the national vanity of the people which attaches no importance to anything that is not Chinese, and to the imperfect means which the pictorial language of the Chinese affords of expressing the names of persons and places often leaving their identification a matter of mere conjecture.

When the Portuguese first made their appearance in the waters of the Archipelago, they found the Chinese carrying on trade with its emporia much in the same way as they do at the present day. Alboquerque, when he took Malacca, found their junks lying in the roads; and Barbosas' statement, which evidently refers to the condition of Malacca before its conquest, is so detailed and authentic as to be well worth quoting. "There assemble," says he, "at the above city many other merchants, Moor and Gentile strangers, in order to traffic with the ships of China, which have two masts. These ships bring hither great quantities of silk in hanks (raw silk), and many vessels of porcelain, damasked silks, brocades, and satins of various colours. They bring also coloured silk, much iron, saltpetre, fine silver, many pearls, large and small baskets, gilt fans, and incense. On the other hand, they take in return for these things—pepper, incense, cloths of Cambay, grained cloth (panni di grano), saffron raw and prepared, coral, many cloths of Pulicat of painted (printed) cotton, cinnabar, quicksilver amfiam, (opium), and other merchandise, with drugs of Cambay, among which there is one which we know not, but which they call pauchou (puchuk), and another, which they call cachou (Cutch terra-japonica)."

It deserves, however, to be noticed, that while there is abundant evidence of the trade and shipping of the Chinese, there is none whatever of their settlement in the Archipelago. Debarros specifies the different nations who were settled in Malacca under the Malay government,—Javanese, Siamese, Peguans, natives of Bengal, Coromandel, Gujrat, Arabia, and Persia; but he makes no mention of the Chinese as settlers. Barbosa's account of the persons and manners of the Chinese is taken from his account of China, given to him by others, and not from his own personal observation, which would have been the case had he seen them as settlers. It is wonderfully accurate, considering that it is derived from native authority. "Respecting," says he, "what is at present to be written, I have my information from four different persons (Moors and Gentiles), men worthy of credit and great merchants, who had been many times in the country of China." After giving a very graphic account of the Chinese and their arts, which includes their speaking a language like German, that is a guttural one, and their wearing shoes and stockings like the Germans and other inhabitants of cold countries, he adds, "They are also great navigators, who go to sea in great ships, which they call giunchi (Malay jung, a trading vessel), of two masts, and built in a fashion different from ours. The sails are of matting, and also the ropes. There are many pirates and robbers among the islands and ports of China, notwithstanding, which the Chinese go to Malacca, and carry thither iron, saltpetre, and the like."—*Barbosa* in *Ramusio.*

The probability seems to be that the native governments of the Archipelago were not sufficiently civilised to afford encouragement to the Chinese to settle in the country, and that their emigration from China with a view to settlement, dates only from the arrival of Europeans and the establishment of their power. Some circumstances connected with the condition of China itself, such as the increase of population, which is known to have followed the permanent establishment of the Manchoo dynasty about the middle of the seventeenth century, no doubt contributed largely to promote Chinese emigration, not only to the Asiatic Archipelago, but also to such countries as Tonquin, Cochin-China, and Siam.

The emigrants from China are all from the four maritime provinces of the empire, Canton, Fokien, Chekiang, and Kiangnan. Four-fifths of the whole number come from Canton, and about a tenth part from Fokien, the emigrants from the two more northerly provinces forming but a very small fraction. Nearly all the emigrants consist of the labouring classes,—fishermen, artisans, and common day-labourers. They usually arrive at their places of destination in great poverty, and are frequently obliged to mortgage their labour to their resident countrymen in consideration of their passage money.

Chinese emigration differs in two material respects from all other emigration,—that it consists entirely of adult males, to the exclusion of women and children, and that it never embraces either the upper or middle classes. I do not believe that the absence of the female sex arises from legal prohibition, for the prohibition to quit the country applies equally to both sexes. The real cause seems to be the reluctance of the Chinese to quit their native country, and the hope which those who emigrate always cherish of returning to it. The settlers, whenever it is in their power, form connections with the native women of the country; and hence has arisen a mixed race, numerous in the older settlements, known to the Malays under name of Pâranakan China, literally, "Chinese of the womb," that is, Chinese by native mothers; and called in the Philippines, Sangley, a word of which the origin is unknown, although it has been admitted into dictionaries of the Spanish language. These intermarrying, either among themselves or with native Chinese, a race of quadroons, and almost of creoles, has sprung up, differing little from the original Chinese,—perhaps, somewhat less energetic, but always possessed of more local knowledge. From the nature of Chinese emigration, the proportion of males to females is always great. In Singapore, a young settlement, the males are to the females in the proportion of 10 to 1. The result, of course, is that the increase of the Chinese population by natural means is very slow. The entire Chinese population of Java, after Chinese emigration has been directed to that island for two centuries and a half of European rule, consists of no more than 131,000 persons.

The annual number of Chinese immigrants into the Archipelago cannot be ascertained; but some notion of its amount may be formed from the number which lands in Singapore, the principal port to which emigration is at present directed. This, on an average of years, is above 10,000, of whom about one-fourth settle in the island, the majority being dispersed among the neighbouring ones. The number that returns yearly to China from the same port is about 3000, most of them parties resorting to it from neighbouring countries for the convenience of a passage.

As the Chinese are next to Europeans, and indeed, in many respects, before them, the most active and valuable agents in developing the resources of the Archipelago, it will be convenient to give some account of their employments. Here is an enumeration of them in Singapore, furnished by an intelligent chief of his nation, in reply to queries put by the indefatigable editor of the "Journal of the Indian Archipelago." "The different trades and professions of the Chinese in Singapore," says he, "are schoolmasters, writers, cashiers, shop-keepers, apothecaries, coffin-makers, grocers, goldsmiths, silversmiths, tin-smiths, blacksmiths, dyers, tailors, barbers, shoe-makers, basket-makers, fishermen, sawyers, boat-builders, cabinet-makers, achitects, masons, lime and brick burners, sailors, ferrymen, sago manufacturers, distillers of spirits, cultivators and manufacturers of gambier and of sugar, cultivators of pepper and of nutmegs, venders of cakes and fruits, porters, play-actors, fortune-tellers, idle vagabonds—who have no work, and of whom there are not a few,—beggars, and, nightly, there are those villains the thieves."

To this list must be added the general merchants and the parties engaged in the farming of all the branches of the public revenue, the last a department entirely in their own hands, and from which their superior skill and knowledge excludes all competitors. In the less populous parts of the Archipelago, such as the British settlements, they may be said to occupy the largest part of the field of common labour, while in the more populous, as Java, their industry is generally restricted to what may be called skilled labour, as the manufacture of sugar and indigo, and the distillation of spirits.

The total number of Chinese, including their descendants and families, throughout the whole Asiatic Archipelago can only be a matter of estimate. By the census of 1850, those of Java and the islands around it, amounted to 130,000. Those of Borneo have been variously computed at numbers varying from 30,000 to five times that number. Dutch authorities estimate them at 30,000 only, and this is far more probable than the larger numbers. In the three British settlements in the Straits of Malacca they amount in round numbers to 85,000. In the census of the Philippines the total Chinese population is returned at no more than 8000; but this does not include the mixed race, of whom the number in Luzon alone, the principal island, is 56,925. Besides these, there are a few in Sumatra, Celebes, and the Moluccas, and if we take these at 5000, we shall have a total Chinese population of 258,000. But as the mestizos of the Philippines are not included, and the Chinese of Borneo may be underrated, we may take the whole, in round numbers, at about 320,000.

The numbers of the Chinese in the different countries of the Asiatic Archipelago will always be found to be proportional to the encouragement held out to them by the character of the country and its government. In a large portion of the northern part of Borneo, in which no gold is found, and where there is no semblance of good government, the Chinese are not found at all. Neither do they exist under the rude and rapacious administrations of the islands of Mindano and the Salus, and not an individual of the nation is to be found in the unattractive islands of Ceram, Gilolo, and New Guinea. It is not mere land they emigrate in quest of, but employment for their labour, and protection for their lives and properties. With the exception, therefore, of the western coast of Borneo, where they are in sufficient strength and numbers to protect themselves, they are only to be found in the possessions of the European powers. In Java and the Philippines the ordinary labour-market is, in a great degree, pre-occupied by the native inhabitants, which necessarily operates as a natural discouragement to their settlement. In Java and in Borneo, under the Dutch rule, there is a tax on immigration and another on emigration, with a poll-tax. Under the native princes, the Chinese of Borneo, paying a nominal tribute, were allowed to govern themselves. Since brought under the Dutch rule, they are subjected to a fine of two guilders for leave to settle, to an annual poll-tax of the same amount, and to a fine of thirty guilders for permission to return to China. The consequence of this has been that the number of emigrants is said to have fallen off from 3000 a-year to one-third of that number.

The lot of the Chinese under the Spanish government of the Philippines is much worse than this. Before the year 1828, the poll-tax imposed upon them was six Spanish dollars a-year. This heavy contribution, however, was not thought a sufficient return for the great gains they were represented to make, and, as it was publicly alleged, at the expense of the Spaniards and Spanish mestizos. They were, accordingly, divided into the four classes of merchants, shop-keepers, artisans, and day-labourers, the first being subjected to a monthly payment of ten dollars, the second of four, the third of two, and the fourth of one dollar.

The effect of this law of extravagant ignorance and improvidence, so much like the enactments of the middle ages against the Jews, is described by Spanish writers themselves as deplorable. The leaders of the Chinese refused to assess or collect the tax, and the Spanish functionaries had to perform these duties themselves. At the time of its enactment, the Chinese, exclusive of mestizos, who were subjected only to double the native poll-tax, was 5708. Of these it was found that seven only belonged to the class of merchants, and 166 to that of shop-keepers, while the artisans were made to amount to 5509, and the day-labourers to 830, the remainder of 196 being exempted from the tax by old age. The collection of the taxes, according to the statement of the Spanish writers, was attended with the utmost difficulty. In order to escape it, 800 persons took advantage of the option which the law gave them, and returned to China. There fled to the mountains, where they were hospitably received by the native inhabitants, 1083 persons, and 453 who had not the means of defraying the cost of a passage to China, were seized and condemned to penal labour as defaulters.

The wages of a Chinese day-labourer in Singapore do not exceed three dollars a month, and probably are not higher in the Philippines. If this be the case, the Spanish poll-tax amounts to one-third of the whole wages of labour. A sensible Spanish author, writing in 1842, has the following observation on the subject of this oppressive tax : "The Chinese actually enrolled do not exceed 6000, and their capitation-tax is above 100,000 dollars a-year, while that of all the native inhabitants, exceeding 3,000,000, does not equal eight times that amount."—Informe Sobre el estado de las Islas Filipinas en 1842. Madrid.

In the British possessions the Chinese are on a footing of equality with all othe

British subjects, and pay no poll-tax, or fine on entering or quitting them. The result of the different causes enumerated is shown by the proportion which these people bear to the whole population in the different European settlements. In Java, they form the one-hundredth part and in the Philippines about the four-hundredth part of it. In the British possessions collectively, the Chinese constitute about one-third of the inhabitants, and in Singapore two-thirds.

The policy of persecution has certainly not succeeded, while that of toleration has been eminently successful. In Java, 10,000 Chinese were massacred in a day, and this was followed by an insurrection which involved nearly the whole island, and lasted several years. The Chinese of Borneo have been either in a state of active or chronic rebellion against the Dutch since the year 1816. The Spaniards had been only established in the Philippines eight-and-thirty years, when a revolt of the Chinese took place, followed, according to Spanish historians, by the destruction of 23,000 of their number. A second revolt followed, thirty-six years after, in which 30,000 are stated to have perished. Two others followed these, also with sanguinary results, in one of which the Chinese immediately and heartily joined the English invaders. The policy of equal treatment and toleration pursued by the English has certainly not had so long a trial as that of coercion and restriction by the Dutch and Spaniards, but it has been uniformly pursued since the establishment of Bencoolen in 1685, and neither insurrection or rebellion has been the result, while the only example, even of a dangerous tumult, occurred at Singapore in 1854. The Chinese are not, indeed, so docile and submissive as the Hindus, or the Javanese, or the Tagalas, and Bisayas of the Philippines. Their propensity to form secret societies has sometimes proved inconvenient, but on the whole they are peaceable subjects, and their co-operation might certainly be relied on by a British government, in the event of foreign invasion, a co-operation which experience shows that neither the Dutch or Spanish governments could reckon on.

CHRISTIANITY. It is probable that Christian traders of Syria and Egypt frequented the Archipelago along with Mahommedan; long before the arrival of the Portuguese, and Ludovico Barthema, in his Itinerary, alludes to having met persons of this description; but no Christian converts appear to have existed previous to the conquest of Alboquerque. The Portuguese during their dominion of 130 years, made a considerable number. The native Catholics, found throughout the different islands and settlements in which their power had been established, are the descendants of these converts. The native Christians of Malacca, probably the most numerous, amounted by the enumeration of 1847 to 2784, or about one-twentieth part of the whole population. all of the lower or labouring classes.

It is in the Philippines alone that the Christian religion has been effectually and extensively propagated. The work began, after a fashion, by the discoverer himself, for the great navigator was a zealous propagandist. This is Pigafetta's account of the manner of the conversion of the kings of the islands of Çebu and Massana, along with a crowd of their followers. "A great cross was then erected in the plain. The captain-general had previously advised all who desired to become Christians, that it was necessary to destroy all their idols and to substitute for them the cross, which they were to adore on their knees daily, morning and noon. He taught them also, how to make the sign of the cross on their foreheads, and admonished them to confirm these forms by good works. The captain-general, who was entirely clothed in white, said that he was habited in this colour in order to show his love and sincerity to them. Of this they appeared sensible, but without knowing what to answer. He then took the king by the hand and conducted him to a stage, where he, and those that were with him, were baptised. The king (of Çebu) who was before called Raia (Raja) Humabon, was named Don Carlo, after the emperor,—the prince, Don Ferdinando, after the emperor's brother,—the king of Massana, Giovanni, and one of the principal chiefs got the name of our captain, that is, Ferdinando. The Moorish merchant (master of a junk from Siam) was named Cristoforo, and others had other names given to them. Five hundred islanders were baptised before saying mass. The captain invited the king and some of his chiefs to dine with him: they excused themselves, but accompanied us to the beach, where they took leave. In the meanwhile, there was a general discharge of artillery from the ships. After dinner, the priest and many of us went ashore in order to baptise the queen and other ladies. We mounted the same stage where the queen was seated on a cushion, and the other ladies around her on mats. When the priest made his appearance, I called the attention of the queen to a portrait of Our Lady, and to a wooden statuette representing the Infant Jesus, and a cross, at the sight of which things she felt a movement of contrition, and weeping, entreated to be baptised. Other ladies of her train were baptised along with her. She was named Joanna, the name of the emperor's mother. Her daughter, wife of the prince, was named Catherine, and the queen of Massana, Elizabeth. A particular name was given to all the rest. We baptised that day, between men, women, and children, about eight hundred persons. The queen asked me to have the Bambino (the same alleged to have been found 44 years after by a soldier of Legaspi), in order to keep it in room of her own idols, and I gave it to her. At a later hour the king and queen came down to the sea-side, where we were assembled, and took pleasure in listening to the harmless discharge of cannon, which had before produced so much fear."—*Primo Viaggio intorno al mondo*, p. 87.

The sole interpreter in making these eight hundred converts in a day was a Sumatran slave, belonging to Magellan, who shortly after betrayed the Spaniards. In twelve days from the supposed conversion, Magellan himself lost his life in a foolhardy attempt to bring the petty chief of the little island of Mactan under subjection to the king of Çebu, and the Christianised king himself massacred all his companions that were within his power. The credulity of the bold and intelligent adventurers who were, at the moment, engaged in achieving the grand enterprise of the first circumnavigation of the globe, is shown in this singular transaction; but the quotation is chiefly of value for the insight it gives into the simple character of the Philippine islanders when they were first seen by Europeans. With the nations of the continent of India, or even with the more advanced ones of the western portion of the Archipelago, such an exhibition as that just described would not have succeeded, and, indeed, seems never to have been attempted by the Portuguese or any other European nation.

The real work of conversion commenced with the arrival of Legaspi, a man who possessed all the requisite talents, prudence, and zeal, for the purpose. A band of Dominicans, headed by Andres de Urdañeta, a priest possessed of all the qualities necessary to the successful apostle of a new faith, accompanied the conqueror of the Philippines, and the work of conversion was entered upon with zeal tempered by skill and discretion. Other religious orders followed the Dominicans, and the labour of conversion has been prosecuted, up to the present day, that is, for a period of near three centuries. The result has been, that out of a population, subject to the Spanish rule, amounting, according to the census of 1849, to 3,740,422, all are Roman Catholics, with the exception of 1555 Mahommedans, and 18,595 mountaineers of Mindano, with 8064 Chinese. Even a considerable number of the mestizo Chinese appear to have been converted to Christianity, an achievement accomplished in no other part of the Archipelago.

It must, however, be observed that the state of society among the Philippine islanders specially favoured the reception of a new religion. No organised system of native worship existed among them, nor had either Mahommedanism or Hinduism produced any material impression. Even, however, within the Philippines themselves, where serious obstacles happened to exist, the Spanish priesthood have met, either with very little success or with none at all. In the Sulu Islands, where the Mahommedans anticipated them, they have totally failed, and in the great Island of Mindano, from the same cause, their success has been very trifling, for they hold but a comparatively small portion of its territory, while the converts to Christianity do not exceed 60,000 in number.

Everywhere, the effect of the adoption of Christianity has been beneficial. Education, intelligence, morality, numbers, and physical comfort, have undoubtedly been promoted by it. Thus, to take agriculture as an example of the last of these benefits; the Spaniards have introduced among their subjects, maiz, wheat, the potato, the ox, and the horse. The Spanish priesthood have not only achieved a great intellectual victory, but they may be said to have contributed fully as much as the army itself to the conquest of the Philippines, a conquest, too, which they will probably be the cause of retaining for Spain, long after she has lost all her other colonies.

Christianity can hardly be said to have made any progress at all in the great islands of the Malayan Archipelago. The two most numerous and civilised nations, the Malays and Javanese, had accepted the Mahommedan religion before the arrival of the Portuguese. Even the inhabitants of the Spice Islands had done so. In Celebes alone the Portuguese had a fair field, for none of its inhabitants had embraced the Mahommedan religion until a whole century after their arrival, but they made no use of the opportunity. One cause militated against the success of the Portuguese, and afterwards of the Dutch and English, which did not affect the Spaniards in the Philippines.

The Philippines produced neither spices nor perfumes to divert attention from better objects, while their rapacious pursuit engrossed the attention of the other nations,—essentially demoralised, and rendered them very unsuitable missionaries for the propagation of a new creed.

The only Protestant native Christians of the Archipelago of any account are the inhabitants of the Island of Amboyna, amounting to about 30,000. These belong to the Lutheran reformed church, and are, with justice, considered as the most moral, best educated, and best conducted people of the whole Archipelago. They are poor and somewhat indolent, but their being so is little to be wondered at, when the only staple product of their soil has, in one form or another, been a subject of public monopoly for nearly three centuries and a half.

ÇIMARRONES. The name of one of the many tribes of the negros of the Philippines, and said to be among the wildest of this race. They inhabit the mountain of Isaroc, in the province of South Camarines, in the Island of Luzon, and also certain mountains of the Island of Samar.

CINNAMON, the kayu-manis, or sweet-wood of the Malays. The true cinnamon of Ceylon is certainly not a native plant of any island of the Asiatic Archipelago, nor are the cinnamons of Cochin-China and China. Most of the large islands, however, produce one, or perhaps several species, with little aroma, and consequently of little value. A cinnamon of this description is produced in Java, Sumatra, Borneo, and Luzon, but is described as most abundant in Mindano. Of late years, however, the cinnamon of Ceylon has been cultivated with some success in Java, and in the British settlements in the Straits of Malacca, and as the climate is suitable and the plant a hardy one, requiring but a moderate fertility of soil, it seems to be one of the exotics most likely to succeed.

CIRCUMCISION. Circumcision in male children, and even excision in female, seem to have been very generally practised by the more civilised nations of the Philippines before the introduction of Christianity, and what is more strange, it is still secretly practised, after near three centuries' conversion, among the same people. There is, however, no proof of the existence of such practices among the nations of the Malayan Archipelago before their conversion to the Mahommedan faith, and now the rite is confined to males. The singular practice universal among the wild tribes of Borneo seems to be akin to circumcision.

CITRON. Many species and varieties of this genus of plants are cultivated through the Asiatic Archipelago, from Sumatra to Luzon. As far as can be judged by their names, and we have no other evidence, some of these would appear to be indigenous and some exotic. The practice of the native languages in this, as in similar cases, is to give a generic name to the whole family, and to add an epithet for each species or variety. In the Malay and Javanese languages the generic term is Jârok, equivalent to the Citro of botanists. Thus the Shaddock or Pumplenoose is called "the great orange," or "the tiger orange," or "the orange of Bali; the common orange," "the sweet orange," or "the orange of China or of Japan," and the lime, the "slender or minute orange." The generic term, in this case, is a native word, and differs in the different classes of languages. Thus in the Philippine tongues it is wholly different from that in the Malayan, as in the Tagala where it is luoban, and the Bisaya, where it is kayeli. Sometimes the Persian word limau, which has also been adopted in the European languages, is used, as a synonym for the native one. It may be inferred from all this, that the shaddock, and probably some varieties of the sweet orange, are indigenous, while most of the latter have been introduced from China and Japan. The lime may have been brought in by Mahommedan traders from Persia or India.

CITY. In the languages of the Archipelago there are three native words and one Sanscrit for village, but none for city or town, except nagara or nagri and kut'a or kut'i, with pura in composition, which are all Sanscrit. It would seem from this that prior to the arrival of the Hindus, no assemblage of dwellings existed that deserved to be distinguished from a mere village. See Town and Village.

CIVET. In Malay and Javanese this perfume is known by the native names of rasé and d'ed'es, but the Sanscrit one kasturi, and the Arabic zabad, corrupted jâbad, are also used as synonyms. This article is produced by two distinct species of Viverra, rasé and zibetha, which are kept in a half domesticated state for the purpose of yielding it. The first is a native of Java, and the last of the other large islands. The natives of rank are great consumers of this perfume, not generally acceptable to Europeans.

CLOVE. Caryophyllus aromaticus. The clove belongs to the natural order of Myrtles, and is pronounced by Rumphius, who lived and died in Amboyna, in his time seat of the growth and trade of cloves, "the most beautiful, the most elegant, and the most precious of all known trees." The grace and beauty of the tree, which resembles a handsome and gigantic myrtle, will be readily admitted by all who have seen it. Its superior value, however, had only reference to a factitious state of things which no longer exists, for in point of true value it is greatly excelled even by the coco and sago palms which grow almost side by side with it,—which feed the inhabitants of the countries which produce the clove, while they decline to use itself, even as a condiment. The inflorescence of the clove consists of terminal clusters, and it is not the fruit but the unexpanded flower-buds that chiefly contain the aromatic oil, and are the objects of commerce.

The clove is remarkable for its limited geographical distribution. It is only in its native localities, the five small islets on the western coast of the large island of Gilolo, that it is easily grown, and attains the highest perfection. There, it bears in its seventh or eighth year, and lives to the age of 130 or 150. Rumphius informs us, that shortly before the arrival of the Portuguese it had been carried to and reared in Amboyna, where, however, it does not bear until its fifteenth year, and where the average duration of its life does not exceed 75 years. He informs us further that large islands are not favourable to its growth—that it succeeds indifferently even in such islands as Gilolo and Ceram, and that the natives of Celebes and Java who had attempted to grow it in their own country had obtained plants which bore no fruit. Europeans, however, have succeeded somewhat better. The clove has been long transferred by them from the Moluccas to Sumatra,—to the islands in the Straits of Malacca,—to Bourbon,—to Zanzibar, on the eastern coast of Africa, and to Cayenne. In some of these places the culture has virtually failed, even where that of the nutmeg has succeeded, and everywhere the produce is of inferior quality to that even of Amboyna. A suitable soil seems to be as indispensable as a suitable climate. The soil of the Molucca Islands is volcanic, which is not the case with any of the countries to which the tree has been transferred, except the Island of Bourbon, and here the suitable climate seems to be wanting. "The cloves," says De Barros, "which are used all over the world grow in the five islands which we have named, and are not found to any extent in the others; and the trees which produce them, as they are of comparatively small value to the nations at large, so God, the distributor of created things, has confined them to the five islands in question." Rumphius expresses himself to the same effect. "Hence it appears," says he, "that the great disposer of things in His wisdom, allotting His gifts to the several regions of the world, placed cloves in the kingdom of the Moluccas, beyond which by no human industry can they be propagated or perfectly cultivated." HERB. AMB., v. 2, p. 4.

It is very difficult to understand how the clove could have come first to be used as a condiment by foreign nations, considering the well-ascertained fact that it has never been used as such, and indeed hardly in any other way, by the inhabitants of the countries which produce it. Their first use, as with many other commodities, must have been a matter of pure accident. The wild clove must have been first used, but the supply of this, which has comparatively little aroma, would soon be unequal to the demand, and hence the cultivation of the tree which is shown by the superior aroma of its produce, and like most cultivated plants, by the production of several varieties.

The first strangers who acquired a taste for the clove would most probably be the nations of the western portion of the Archipelago, the Malays and Javanese, who, on the arrival of the Portuguese, were found conducting the first stage of the spice trade, and who had been doing so for ages. From these the Hindus, Chinese, and Arabs who frequented the Archipelago would learn its use. The different current names of the clove connect them immediately with these strangers, their principal consumers. Not one of these belongs to the native languages. The most frequent of them is câugkek, and this which has not the sound of a native word is said to be the corruption of the Chinese name tkeng-hia, which literally means "odoriferous nails." Another name is lawang, to which the Malays, as in many similar cases, prefix the words "flower" or "fruit." This is the name of the clove with the loss of the final vowel in the language of the Tâlugus or Telingas, the people of India, who in all ages as at present, have conducted the largest share of the trade between India and the Malayan countries. A third name is gaumedi, and this is that used by the natives of the Moluccas themselves. I have the authority of my friend Professor Wilson for saying that this word is Sanscrit, and means, literally, "cow's-marrow."

The time when cloves were first brought to India, and from India to Europe, can be a matter of little better than reasonable inference. In the detailed list of Indian commodities given in the Periplus of the Erythræan Sea, as existing at the ports of Western India, the clove is not included, and from this negative evidence it is to be inferred that it did not, at the period when this compilation was made, exist in the Indian markets, or at least did not rank as a staple commodity. The information of the Periplus is supposed to refer to about the tenth year of the reign of Nero, or the 63rd of Christ. Granting all this to be true, it follows that cloves were unknown in India, and consequently in Europe, about the middle of the first century. A celebrated law of the digest of the reign of Aurelian first names cloves among the Indian commodities imported into Alexandria. This law refers to the time between 176 and 180, so that there can be no doubt but that cloves were known both in Europe and in India towards the close of the second century. Thus we have a connexion existing between Continental India and the Malayan Archipelago of seventeen centuries duration.

Some, however, have fancied that the clove was known in Europe a century earlier and this seems to have been the opinion of the early Portuguese historians of India. "The knowledge of cloves," says De Cauto, "is so ancient that already Pliny, who lived in the time of the Emperor Domitian, takes notice of them, for in his twelfth book, chapter vii., he says there is in India a seed like pepper, except that it is longer, which is called cariofilum by some, while others call it gariofilum." The passage in Pliny referred to is literally as follows. "There is also in India a commodity like grains of pepper called gariophyllon, but larger and more fragile. It is said to be produced in an Indian sacred grove (Indico luco). It is brought on account of its perfume." Had cloves really existed in the Roman markets at the time, no one would have thought of describing them as resembling pepper, that is, as globular grains. Instead of being spherical, their resemblance to a small iron nail was so obvious that all the Europeans named them on this account.

The names given to the clove by European nations, or by the Asiatic ones through whom they received it, although they may not much assist us in tracing its commercial history, are, at least, a subject of curiosity. The historian, De Cauto, in continuation of the passage above quoted, says, "The Persians call the clove calafur, and speaking on this matter, with permission of the physicians, it appears to us that the cariofilum of the Latin is corrupted from the calafur of the Moors, for they have some resemblance. And as this drug passed into Europe through the hands of the Moors, with the name of calafur, it appears that the Europeans did not change it. The Castilians called cloves gilope, because those which they got came from the island of Gilolo. The people of the Moluccas call them chanqué. The Brahmin physicians first called them lavanga, but afterwards gave them the Moorish name. Generally all nations give them a name of their own as we have done, for the first of us that reached these islands (the Moluccas), taking them in their hands, and observing their resemblance to iron nails called them cravo, by which they are now so well known in the world." Decade iv., book vii., chapter 9.

The Persian calafur of the author is probably the Arabic karnafil, and therefore comes nearer to the Latin word. If this, then, be the true derivation of the latter, and Pliny's name really referred to the clove, although inaccurately described, the fact would carry us back in the history of the clove trade to the time of the Sabeans. The strange corruption of the word Gilolo, which De Cauto states was the name adopted in his time by the Spaniards, is not now to be found, that I am aware of, in any Spanish dictionary. If the Arabic word karnafil be the origin of the Latin word, it follows that it is so also of the Italian garofane, and of the French girofle. The striking resemblance of cloyes to tackets or small nails is so obvious that it has suggested most of their European names, as the Portuguese cravo, the Spanish clavo, the French clou-de-girofle; or clove-nails, our own clove from the last, the German kloben, and the Dutch kruid-nagel or herb-nails. Even the Chinese have their "odoriferous nails," as already mentioned.

India was no sooner visited by intelligent modern Europeans, than the clove, as well as every other Indian product, is accurately described for the first time; forming a complete contrast with the vague and uncertain knowledge of antiquity and the middle ages, a proof how very little was known before the actual arrival of the Portuguese by the new route. Barbosa is as usual wonderfully correct in his account of the clove, although it is not certain that he visited the Moluccas. In one place he describes the tree, which he compares to a laurel. He accurately describes the clove harvest, and he names the places of production. In another, he describes the nature and course of the trade with the fidelity and intelligence of an educated merchant of our own times. It is as follows: "The clove grows in the islands called Molucche, and from these it is brought to Malacca, and thence to Calicut, a country of Malabar. It is worth in Calicut, the bahar (712 small pounds of Venice), from 500 to 600 fanoes (about 50 gold scudi, or 12 marchette per pound), and cleaned from sticks and chaff 700 fanoes, the export duty being 18 fanoes the bahar. In Maluccha, where the clove grows, it is sold at from one to two ducats the bahar (equal to from four to six pounds the marchetta) according to the number of purchasers who come for it. In Malacca it sells at from 10 to 14 ducats, according to the demand of the merchants." RAMUSIO.

Pigafetta's account of the clove is a good popular one, even at the present day. "I landed," says he, "the same day, (November 17th, 1521), in order to see how the cloves grew, and this is what I observed. The tree from which they are gathered is tall, and its trunk about the size of a man's body, more or less, according to the age of the plant. Its branches spread at the middle of the tree, but at its top form a pyramid. The bark is of an olive colour, and the leaf is like that of the laurel. The cloves come out at the end of the smaller branches, in little clusters of from ten to twenty. These trees bear fruit more on one side than the other, according to the season of the year. The cloves, on their first appearance, are white; but when they ripen they become red, and being dried they become black. They are gathered twice a year; once, at the Nativity of our Lord; and once, at that of St. John the Baptist. In these times the air is more temperate than in others;—most so in December. When the year is sufficiently hot and there is little rain, there are gathered in each of these islands from 300 to 400 bahars of cloves. The clove tree will only live in the mountains, and if transported to the plains it dies. The leaves, the bark, and even the wood itself, as long as they are green, have the strength and fragrance of the fruit itself. If the fruit be not gathered when it is properly ripe, it becomes large and hard, so that no virtue remains in it. It is alleged that the clouds perfect the cloves; and, in fact, we daily saw a cloud to descend, and surround one or other of the mountains. Among these people every one possesses some of these trees, and each person guards his own, and gathers the fruit, but no labour is bestowed on their cultivation. The clove-tree will not flourish except in the mountains of the five islands of Maluccha. There are, no doubt, a few plants in Gilolo, and in a small island between Tidor and Mutir, called Mare, but the fruit is not good." Primo Viaggio intorno al Globo, p. 144.

The clove appears, from Pigafetta's statement, to have been private property, and entirely free in culture and trade; Malays, Javanese, Chinese, Macassars, and Arabs, all competing for it in an open market. The annual quantity produced, according to him, in the five islands, seems to have been from 1500 to 2000 bahars; and the bahar is an Arabian weight, computed in the Moluccas at about 590 pounds. The companions of Magellan themselves loaded two ships with cloves at a single island, Tidor, after a stay, from their arrival to their departure, of no more than forty-four days. De Cauto, whose information is more recent than that of Pigafetta, and, in such a matter, it may be presumed more correct, says, that the yearly product was 6000 bahars of ungarbled, and 4000 of garbled or clean cloves; which reduced to pounds would give 3,540,000, and 2,360,000. The prices quoted by Barbosa for the Moluccas, supposing the money he mentions to be the gold ducat of Venice, are 14*d.* and 28*d.* a cwt. At Malacca they rise to from 11*s.* to 15*s.* 6*d.* At Calicut, Barbosa's quotations, taking the fanoes or fanam at 4½*d.*, are 35*s.* 8*d.* and 42*s.* 8½*d.* We may trace these cloves from Calicut to one of their most remote consumers. In England, before the discovery of the passage by the Cape of Good Hope, a pound of cloves cost 30*s.*, or 168*l.* per cwt. Thus many unskilful sea voyages and tedious land journeys, with shipments and trans-shipments, loadings and unloadings, many custom and many transit duties, brought a commodity of which the first cost was not worth a penny a pound, to be sold to the consumer 360 times this amount. This is a picture of the rudest state of a remote commerce. Our ancestors must have ascribed curative virtues to the clove which it does not possess, or they never could have been tempted to give the enormous price quoted for a mere condiment.

The Portuguese made their first appearance in the parent country of cloves, in the year 1512; and having been expelled by the Dutch in 1605, they had the principal share of the clove trade for ninety-three years,—a period of rapine, violence, and bigotry. Their main object was the exclusive monopoly of spices, by the expulsion of all rivals. Their successors pursued the same object in a manner still more rigorous. They extirpated the clove trees in their native islands, and endeavoured to limit their growth to the five Amboyna islands, in which the clove is an exotic. Periodical expeditions for the extirpation of young plants that might spontaneously have sprung up, or been propagated by birds, formed part of this system.

The clove monopoly still exists, but in a very tottering condition. The periodical exterminating expeditions have been merely nominal during the present century; and for the last thirty years, although the monopoly be persevered in in the five Amboyna islands, where the parks, as they are called, are the property of the government, the culture and trade are legitimate everywhere else.

The annual produce of the monopoly has been estimated at from 300,000 to 400,000 pounds weight; but this is evidently an over-estimate, for the quantity, at present, frequently falls short of 200,000 pounds. De Cauto informs us that the quantity produced yearly, under the native governments, was 18,000 quintals of garbled, and 27,000 of ungarbled cloves, equal to 2,204,000, and 3,756,000 of pounds avoirdupois. The total gross value of 400,000 pounds of cloves is reckoned by the Dutch government at 80,000*l.*; and the profits of the monopoly at about 70,000*l.*, which is less than the rents of several English estates, or than the profits of several English merchants and manufacturers. As, however, the actual produce is not more than one-half of this, the actual profits drop to the poor sum of 35,000*l.* In the course then of about three centuries and a half, the produce of cloves in the Moluccas has been reduced by monopoly to less than one-tenth of what it was under native rule and free trade. No especial blame can be attached to the Portuguese and Dutch of the 16th and 17th centuries for the policy they pursued in regard to the clove and nutmeg, for any of the other nations of Europe would certainly have followed the same course. The Spaniards and the English, indeed, made strenuous endeavours to do so, and had only the good fortune to escape being involved, by being defeated by their rivals. Our ancestors, in fact, mistook the high prices which were the necessary result of a rude commerce and navigation for intrinsic value, and they acted on their error. A low-priced article, like salt or tobacco, the consumption of the many, may be made the subject of a profitable fiscal monopoly; but that is impossible with cloves, or any other articles, the consumption of the few. It was pardonable to the ignorance of the 16th, 17th, and even of the 18th centuries, to impose a monopoly of cloves, and to persevere in it; but perseverance in an exploded error is not excusable in the middle of the 19th century. Fiscal necessity is pleaded in extenuation by the government of the Netherlands, but this is evidently a mistake. An ample revenue can only be expected from a prosperous people; and the experience of more than three centuries has proved, that the monopoly of the sole staple of their country has impoverished and enervated the people over whom it has been established. Thorough freedom and security in production and trade are certain, in due time, to produce substantial wealth, the only fund from which taxes, respectable in amount, are ever paid; and when it exists, no government is so dull as not to understand the art of exacting a share of it for the public exigency. In the free settlement of Singapore a revenue of 50,000*l.* a year is obtained without oppressive taxation and without any custom duties, a larger sum than all the Spice Islands ever yielded to the Dutch.

Evidence of the beneficial effects of freedom in production and trade is discoverable, even under the rude governments of the natives themselves. When the Moluccas were first reached by Europeans, the inhabitants were found in a far more advanced state of civilisation than the neighbouring tribes that had no cloves. The resources of trade gave them power. Their princes were lords of the great island of Gilolo, on one of the coasts of which the five clove islets were mere specks. They had colonised Amboyna, before uninhabited, and they had even extended their dominion to parts of Celebes and New Guinea.

There seems no good reason to doubt but that the consumption of cloves might, with equal cheapness and freedom, become co-extensive with that of pepper. The taste for the clove is as universal as for pepper; for there is no civilised nation in the world that does not consume more or less of it. At present, to judge by the consumption of the United Kingdom, that of pepper is twenty-fold that of cloves. This result seems to be entirely a matter of price. The cost of Amboyna cloves is four times that of the best pepper, and yet there is no good ground for supposing that the one ought, with free production, to be more costly than the other, each being grown in the soil and climate best adapted to it. Pepper is so grown, but the majority of the cloves brought to market is the forced produce of unsuitable soils and climates, and the rest an object of monopoly. Rent affects neither cloves nor pepper, for in the lands in which they are grown, from their abundance, none exists. It might, then, as reasonably be expected that wheat should be raised with as little labour on the poorest as on the richest lands of America, as that cloves should be as cheaply produced in uncongenial as in congenial soils and climates. According to Barbosa, the price of cloves in the Moluccas, before the existence of the monopoly, was even lower than that of pepper in Calicut or Malacca. Even in Calicut, the price of cloves brought by two different voyages, in a rude and therefore costly navigation extending over ten degrees of latitude and fifty of longitude, was little more than double that of pepper grown near the spot. The experience of our own consumption proves that the consumption of cloves is capable of increase with reduction of cost. In 1820, the custom duty was between three and four shillings a pound, and it is now one shilling, or double only what it is on pepper, and the result has been that the consumption has increased by 118 per cent., while the increase in our population has been only 22 per cent. The Dutch government has only to pursue a course exactly the reverse of that which it has followed for two centuries and a half, and it will be right. If the five Molucca islets, which at present produce no cloves at all, should be found in time not to yield a sufficient supply, there are other volcanic islands in their immediate neighbourhood, of far greater extent, which may be resorted to, and even the great island of Gilolo itself, which once produced some cloves, may be had recourse to.

COAL (FOSSIL), in Malay, Arâng-tanah, literally, "earth-charcoal," has been found in the Malay peninsula, Sumatra, Java, and Luzon, but as yet nowhere but in Borneo of good quality and suited to economical uses. A seam of the Bornean coal was first discovered in one of the islands in the river of Brunai, where it crops out. It was afterwards found in the mainland, near the banks of the same river, and subsequently in the island of Labuan, about 12 miles from its embouchure. In these places it is at present mined by European skill and capital, and been found, on ample trial, superior to any Asiatic coal hitherto tried. The coal on the left bank of the Borneo river has been traced for several miles into the interior. On the southern coast of the island coal has been found in the territory of Banjarmasin, and mined by the Dutch. This, from all accounts, is of the same quality as the coal of the northern side, and may be a continuation of the same fields, which would make the Bornean coal-fields the largest in the world, after those of North America. Steam navigation has given a value to the coals of Borneo, which, without it, in a country inhabited by rude people and covered with forest, might have lain for ages as useless as the lime and sand-stones in which it is imbedded.

COCHIN-CHINA. This is a name given by the Portuguese, and is probably taken from Kuchi, the name by which the Malays designate the country, and by the latter most probably from the Anam name of the capital city of Tonquin, Kechao or Kachao. The Malays, however, give the same name of Kuchi, which the Portuguese write as Cochin, to the Hindu principality so called, on the Coromandel coast, and, to distinguish the eastern from the western country, they added to the first the epithet China or Chinese. Such seems to be the origin of the lumbering name by which European geographers designate the kingdom which at present comprehends Tonquin, Cochin-China, and a considerable portion of Kamboja, or in our old orthography, Cambodia.

The kingdom of Cochin-China extends from the promontory of Kamboja, in latitude 8° 25′ north to about latitude 23°,—that is, over a length of 875 geographical miles. The sea bounds it everywhere to the east; but its western limits are unknown to Europeans. The widest part of the kingdom is Tonquin, and this is supposed to have from east to west a breadth of about 180 miles. Cochin-China proper is but a narrow strip of land, said, on an average, not to exceed 24 miles in breadth, while Kamboja varies from 50 to 140, giving an average of 95 miles, with an extent from north to south of about 85 miles. Tonquin is stated to extend from latitude 17° 25′ to 23°, and therefore to have a length of 335 miles, and this multiplied by its breadth will make its area 60,300 square miles. Cochin-China extends from Cape St. James, in 10° 15′ latitude to 17° 25′, or is in length 430 miles, and this multiplied by its breadth of 24 miles, gives an area of no more than 10,320 square miles. The area of Kamboja will be 8075 miles. These different sums will give the whole kingdom an area of 78,695 square geographical miles, which would make it about one-fifth less than the British Islands.

The countries which bound Cochin-China to the east are the Chinese provinces of Quanton and Quangse. To the north, it has the great Chinese province of Yunan, far more extensive than itself, with the country of the Laos or Shans, and in one small part Kamboja. East, south, and west it is compassed by the sea, over a coast line, without reckoning indentations, of about 1100 geographical miles, of which about 120 are on the Gulf of Siam, and the rest on the China Sea.

In the extensive coast line thus mentioned, there have been reckoned no fewer than 57 ports or harbours, of which at least 10 have been ascertained to be among the safest and most commodious of eastern Asia. The finest are those of Saigon, in about latitude 10° 15′, and Turon in about 16°.

That portion of the kingdom, more especially called Cochin-China, is a mountainous country, a range of considerable elevation running through it from north to south. This throws out many spurs extending to the sea, and between them lie valleys and plains of greater or less extent, constituting the peopled portion of this part of the kingdom. To the north of this range lies the plain of Tonquin, and to the south of it, that of Kamboja.

The kingdom of Cochin-China is well watered, being reckoned to contain no fewer than 14 rivers of considerable size. Two of these are fine streams, the Mekon or river of Kamboja, and the Songka, or that of Tonquin. The Mekon, with its affluents and branches, waters the whole of Kamboja, forming a net-work over a tract of country little above the level of the sea, and, in a great measure, submerged in the season of the rains. Of the four branches by which it falls into the sea, the finest and most navigable is that which has its debouchement west of Cape St. James, in latitude 10° 25′. This, unusual in Asiatic rivers, is without a bar at its mouth, and navigable, therefore, for ships of considerable burden for 15 miles above the town of Saigon, itself about 45 miles from the sea. According to native accounts, it is navigable for trading boats for 20 days voyage above Saigon, which would make its whole navigable course about 450 miles. Much of it, however, is beyond the bounds of the kingdom of Cochin-China. The river of Tonquin is supposed to have a course of about 180 miles, and falls into the sea by two mouths, between latitudes 20° and 21°. The most northerly of these, which is about a mile broad at its embouchure, was safely navigated in the seventeenth century by European shipping; but is now described as being no longer accessible to vessels of burden. With regard to the sources of all the rivers of the kingdom, or the length of their courses, Europeans are really in possession of no trustworthy knowledge.

The climate of the kingdom of Cochin-China varies materially, both on account of latitude and physical geography. The whole country is subject to the north-east and south-west monsoons; but the low and level countries of Kamboja and Tonquin have, as in Bengal, the rainy season in the south-western, while Cochin-China proper, on account of its range of mountains, has it, as in southern India, in the north-eastern monsoon. At the capital city, Hüe, the greatest summer heat is about 103° Fahrenheit, and the lowest winter cold, 57°. Cochin-China, and more especially Tonquin, are subject to those fearful equinoxial storms called typhoons; but Kamboja wholly exempt from them, its climate in this, and several other respects, much resembling that of the Malay Archipelago, north of the equator.

The minerals of the kingdom applied to economical uses are marble, iron, silver, and gold. The productive mines of the two last are in Tonquin, and are worked by Chinese, but their locality is unknown to Europeans. Copper, tin, lead and zinc are asserted to exist, but are probably not worked, for none of these metals are exported.

The vegetable products of the forests of the kingdom put to use, are two species of cardamoms, eagle-wood, gamboge and stick-lac, all of which are productions of Kamboja only. Some good timber is produced in all parts of the kingdom, and teak is said by the botanist Loureiro to be one of them. The cultivated plants are those usual in other tropical countries of the same latitudes, rice and maiz being the staple corns. Cochin-China produces one plant peculiar to itself in these regions, a true cinnamon, largely exported to China, and held in the market of that country in greater esteem than that of Ceylon. In the same part of the kingdom and in Tonquin, the mulberry is cultivated for the production of silk, an article inferior in quality to the lowest quality of that of China. In the same parts of the kingdom the tea-plant is reared, but its produce is coarse and tasteless in comparison with the lowest qualities of that of China, its virtues, such as they are, being obtained, not by maceration but by boiling.

The larger animals of the forests of the kingdom are the elephant, the rhinoceros, the hog, a bear, the buffalo, the ox, several species of deer, and the royal tiger and spotted leopard. The wolf, fox, and jackal do not seem to exist. The domesticated quadrupeds are the elephant, large and fine; the buffalo, as large and powerful as in the Malayan countries, in the southern parts of the kingdom, but smaller in the more northerly; the ox, a small animal; the goat the same; the hog, a very fine breed; and the dog, a small animal resembling that of China. The buffalo is the chief animal used in agriculture, but neither the flesh of this nor the ox is used as food, and milk, as such, is considered with abhorrence. The hog, and as in China, the dog, are the chief source of their animal food, poultry excepted. In their proper seasons, Cochin-China is visited by numerous flocks of birds of passage, especially ducks and snipes. I never, indeed, saw the latter so numerous as in the rice-fields near the capital. The domestic poultry are chiefly the duck and common fowl, the first inferior to the European, and kept in large flocks, chiefly on account of the eggs. The last, certainly not the breed called Cochin-Chinese in this country, is the finest poultry I have ever seen. They are reared, not for food, but cock-fighting, an amusement to which the Cochin-Chinese are much addicted. The breed is probably derived directly from the jungle-fowl of the country, which is abundant, for passing through but a small part of the country, I had myself an opportunity of seeing flocks, close to the road-side, and even to the villages.

The seas and rivers of Cochin-China appear to be well stored with fish, and much of the food of the inhabitants of the coast is derived from this source. In 1822, we were abundantly supplied at Saigon with the celebrated Indian luxury, the mango-fish, which had been supposed to be peculiar to the Ganges.

The inhabitants of the kingdom of Cochin-China consist of two nations, the Anam, or civilised people, which occupies Tonquin and Cochin-China proper, and the Kambojan, the principal inhabitants of Kamboja, with several wild races inhabiting the mountains known to the civilised inhabitants under the common name of Ke-moi. The Anam, or dominant people, may be described as men of short stature, as compared with the Chinese, with well-formed limbs, features of the Chinese form, and a cheerful expression. It is probable that they are, in fact, of the same race with their neighbours the Kambojans and Siamese, although to strangers their appearance be disguised by their wearing the ancient costume of China.

Of the population of the kingdom, little better can be offered than a reasonable conjecture. The latest estimate that I have seen of it is by M. Lefevre, Bishop of Isauropolis and Vicar-Apostolic of Lower Cochin-China, which is for the year 1847. This makes it amount to 16,000,000, composed of 13,000,000 of the Anam or dominant people, and 3,000,000 of Kambojan and other dependent nations. This, which gives 187 inhabitants to the square mile, is most probably a great exaggeration. Most of the country is mountainous, and inhabited by rude races, always few in number, and much that is level, covered with forest, and also consequently thinly peopled. Tonquin is well known to be the most populous, as it is the largest section of the kingdom. If, then, we suppose it to be as densely inhabited as the neighbouring Chinese province of Quangsi, which has an area of 78,520 square miles, and a population of 7,313,895, it will contain in round numbers about 6,500,000. If we compare the population of the less populous sections of Cochin-China proper and Kamboja with that of another neighbouring Chinese province, that of Yunan, which has an area of 107,969 square miles, and a population of not more than 5,561,320, we shall make their inhabitants to amount in round numbers to no more than 1,200,000, so that the entire population of the kingdom would thus be only 7,700,000, or a good deal less than one-half the computation of M. Lefevre. That this is not under-rating the population of the kingdom, may be inferred by comparing that of Cochin-China proper and Kamboja with that of Ceylon, a country of which the people much resemble those of these two sections in their state of society. The population of Ceylon is barely 50 inhabitants to the square mile, which would give to Cochin-China proper and Kamboja, little more than 1,000,000. About six millions and a-half, therefore, may be assumed as the probable population of the whole kingdom. It is to be observed, however, that since the first year of the present century, Cochin-China has enjoyed peace and freedom from insurrection, and relieved from the long and devastating rebellion which had afflicted it immediately before, it is reasonable to believe that it must have sustained a great increase of population. M. Chaigneau, a French gentleman, who held a high office in Cochin-China, and whose acquaintance I had the pleasure of making when I visited the country in 1822, makes the following observation on the population in a manuscript description of the kingdom, of which he furnished me with a copy:—"The low price of food is the cause that no one fears to become a father, since there is a certainty of being able to support the most numerous offspring. A Cochin-Chinese scarcely ever emigrates. In fine, honour itself attaches to the paternal relation. In the eyes of his children, a father is sovereign during his life, and they make him almost a god after his death."

The principal strangers settled in Cochin-China, or sojourning in it, are the Chinese, of whom the total number throughout the kingdom, the greater part in Tonquin, it is supposed may amount to about 40,000. The iron, gold, and silver mines of Tonquin are worked chiefly by them, and they conduct the greater part of the foreign trade of the country. This number is trifling compared to that of the same people in the remoter country of Siam, a fact to be accounted for by the less favourable nature of Cochin-China, and the greater jealousy of strangers entertained by its government.

The civil divisions of the kingdom are into provinces, of which Tonquin contains 14, Cochin-China proper 15, and Champa and Kamboja 7, making, in all, 36. Each province is divided into districts, called, in the Anam language, Phu, and these into smaller ones called Kwen, composed of a certain number of villages. Within the whole kingdom, there are said to be no more than five places which deserve the name of town, a certain indication of the absence of wealth and industry. These towns are Cachao, or Kecho, the capital of Tonquin, said to have a population of 150,000; Hüe, the imperial capital, with 50,000 inhabitants; Saigon, the chief town of Kamboja, with 30,000; Kean, in Tonquin, with 10,000; and Calompé, the old capital of Kamboja, of which the population is unknown.

In character, the Cochin-Chinese are a mild and docile people. The manners of the lower classes are mild and sprightly beyond what is usual in the east, while the higher imitate the solemn and formal demeanour of the Chinese. In their habits and persons, the Cochin-Chinese are an uncleanly people: their diet is indiscriminate, for no kind of animal food comes amiss to them: it includes the flesh and eggs of the alligator, and hatched eggs are a dainty with them. Their national vanity at least equals that of the Siamese: they consider themselves the first people in the world, the Chinese being the only foreign nation that they are disposed to consider respectable. Their rude condition is implied by their treatment of women, of which Mons. Lefevre gives the following account: "The rich regard them as destined to serve as the instruments of their pleasure, and the poor of their wants. For this reason, they are devoted to offices which require the greatest bodily fatigue, and are under such a submission to the lords of creation, that they cannot have a will of their own. The labours of the field are ordinarily their portion; they guide the plough, and handle the spade and mattock. From morning to evening they wade in the water, transplanting rice. They carry provisions to market; they cultivate and manufacture the cotton and silk for the use of their families; and they often take the principal share in commercial affairs."

The dress of the Cochin-Chinese is the same for both sexes, and is generally the same as that of the Chinese, or rather what that of the Chinese was before its innovation by the Manchoo Tartars. Thus they wear the hair long and entire, tying it in a knot at the back of the head, and the head is covered with a turban.

The following faithful picture of the state of the arts among the Cochin-Chinese is given by M. Chaigneau, as the fruits of a long experience: "All the arts of first necessity are exercised in Cochin-China. The art of smelting and working metals is understood, as well as to spin cotton and to weave it; to construct ships, and manufacture their equipments. You find goldsmiths, blacksmiths, carpenters, joiners, &c., but none of their arts have risen beyond mediocrity. The iron which they smelt will not yield of good metal when wrought above 40 per cent. in small, and 30 in large work. The Cochin-Chinese have some knowledge of the art of tempering iron and steel, but their tools are always either brittle or too soft. They work better in copper, because this metal is always prepared for them by the Chinese. If, however, in these and other arts not necessary to name, they are little advanced, it is not for want either of intelligence or address. They want only models. We must not expect invention from them, but their talent for imitation is never at fault. It is thus, that instructed by us (the French), they have perfected to an extraordinary degree their naval and military architecture. Their cannon-foundry is a proof of the sagacity with which they know how to profit by instruction and example. The reigning monarch, Gialong, desiring to leave to posterity some memorial of his reign, caused nine cannon to be cast carrying each about a ninety-pound ball, and the experiment was completely successful."

The cannon alluded to by M. Chaigneau, I saw in the royal arsenal in 1822, and they certainly appeared to me to be splendid and beautiful ordnance. It may be added, on the subject of the state of the arts among the Cochin-Chinese, that they understand neither the manufacture of porcelain, glass, or paper, receiving all these from their far more skilful neighbours, the Chinese.

The Anam language, or that of Tonquin, and Cochin-China proper, is wholly monosyllabic, agreeing in this respect with all the oral languages of China, as well as with the dialects of Kamboja, Lao, Siam, Pegu, and Burma, in so far as these last are indigenous, and not derived from foreign sources. The Anam language, notwithstanding this general agreement, is a peculiar tongue, differing from all the neighbouring ones. From its nature, it is devoid of inflections, to express gender, number, and case in the noun, and time and mode in the verb, all these being represented by auxiliary words. The Anam has every consonant sound expressed by the Roman alphabet, except F and Z. From its monosyllabic character, it has little variety of sound, except what it derives from the vowels, which however are numerous. Thus the syllable which an European would write MA, has, according to the different intonations given to its vowel, the six following very different meanings, namely, "a spectre," the conjunctive "but," the verb "to gild," "a horse," "a tomb," and "the cheek."

The Cochin-Chinese never seem to have invented or possessed phonetic writing. Their only writing is the symbolic character of China, which they have adopted with little material change. They have no national literature, all their books being Chinese.

The kalendar of the Cochin-Chinese is that of the Chinese, and so are their weights and measures. The current coin is also in imitation of that of China, consisting, like it, of bits of zinc, with a square hole in the middle for filing. This coin is called a Sa-pek. Sixty of them make a mas, and ten mas a kwan, or quan, as the name has been usually written by Europeans. The two last denominations which are intended to represent the tail and mas of China, are only moneys of account. The kwan, or 600 sa-peks, is by law valued at about 55 centimes of a Spanish dollar, or nearly 28*d.*; but as the zinc coins are mere counters, their value is constantly varying with the supply. Gold and silver are considered only as merchandise, and bought and sold by weight and assay.

Two forms of religion exist in Cochin-China, that of Buddha or Fo, and that of Confucius. Of these, M. Chaigneau has given the following sensible outline. "The religion of Cochin-China is, with little difference, the same as that of China. The lower orders, the women, the ignorant, follow the worship of Buddha; while persons of rank and men of letters are of the sect of Confucius. The temples dedicated both to the religion of Buddha and Confucius, are remarkable for their simplicity; and no form of worship in Cochin-China is distinguished either for the splendour of its temples, or the pomp of its ceremonies. The opinions, the prejudices, the superstitions of the Chinese, are to be found amongst the Cochin-Chinese. This resemblance, their laws digested in Chinese, the books of the learned written in the same tongue, all reveal to us by whom it was that Cochin-China was first civilised. Marriages, funeral ceremonies, the worship of ancestors, festivals, and eras, are all, with slight deviations, the same as in China." I may add to this, that the temples which I myself saw during my visit, were small and mean buildings, and that the talapoins, or priests of Buddha, were either so few in number, or so little distinguishable from the laity, that neither my companions or myself could identify them. The religion of Buddha is certainly that of the majority of the people, and is said to have been introduced from China in the year of Christ 540. The name of this Indian teacher is pronounced in the Anam language Phât, as it is in the dialects of China, Fo, both probably monosyllabic corruptions of the true Sanscrit word.

The domestic trade of Cochin-China is chiefly conducted by its water communications, consisting of its rivers and sea-board. It is facilitated, however, by a highway which runs from north to south throughout the length of the kingdom. In many parts, this road is broad and well constructed, and at the distance of every ten miles there is a caravanserai, or house for the accommodation of travellers. It passes, however, over steep mountains, over rivers that are not bridged, and is interrupted by many arms of the sea, so that it is unfit for wheel-carriage. The principal external commerce is with China, and for the most part conducted by Chinese in Chinese shipping. I estimated the amount of this branch of commerce in 1822, at about 20,000 tons yearly; and even now it probably does not exceed this amount. Since the establishment of the British settlement of Singapore, a considerable trade has sprung up between it and Cochin-China, and this is conducted by native Cochin-

Chinese. In 1851, the value of this had risen to near 100,000*l*., but the piracy which arose out of the rebellion in China had reduced it in 1854, to less than one-fourth part of this amount.

The articles exported from Cochin-China are various, but not of great value. They are the following, namely, rice and pulses, cinnamon, black pepper, cardamoms, areca nuts, gamboge, eagle-wood, cotton, cane sugar, timber, dying drugs, Tonquin varnish, dried fish, esculent swallows' nests, ivory, elephant and rhinoceros hides, and elephant and buffalo bones, with bay salt, gold and silver. From China there are imported, porcelain, paper, tea, dried fruits and confectionery, raw and wrought silk, and toys. From the western world Cochin-China receives, woollens, iron, and opium, through Singapore. It has little commercial intercourse with Siam, the native productions of the two countries being nearly the same, and much jealousy subsisting between their governments.

The government of Cochin-China is a patriarchal despotism, on the model of that of China, but more arbitrary, and far less enlightened. "The power of the king," says M. Lefevre, "is absolute and without restriction. He can make all laws that seem proper to him, for he is the sole legislative authority. He cannot, however, entirely abrogate the ancient laws, on account of the respect which he believes himself bound to show to the memory of the kings his ancestors; and because these laws have acquired a sacred character, according to the opinion generally received by the nation, and against which the most absolute power could not struggle. But he is able, in many circumstances, to mould them to his own laws, and to elude them in a thousand ways, without expunging them from the Code."

The nobility of Cochin-China is purely official and personal. As in China, it is composed of two classes, a civil and a military. The first, the most important, is composed of nine different orders, beginning with a clerk or scribe, and ending with a minister of state. The king clothed in yellow, (the royal colour, but in countries exclusively Buddhist, the restricted one of the priesthood,) immured in his palace, and surrounded by eunuchs and women, carries on the supreme administration through a council or cabinet, consisting of six ministers, one for the examination of candidates for office, one for finance, one for ceremonies and customs, one for war, one for justice, and one for public works. "The power of all the officers of government," says M. Lefevre, "is so restrained and so limited, that they are always in dread of being found in fault, and of losing their places. The duration of their administration in the same post does not go beyond three or four years. They cannot exercise any important functions in the quarter where their parents reside. They take a wife or buy lands in the country under their jurisdiction. Any one can accuse the mandarin before a great tribunal erected for this purpose, and called Tam-phap. Justice is there done in all complaints brought against them. Thus a magistrate has to felicitate himself if he goes out of office without being accused."

The revenue of Cochin-China is derived from the following sources: a capitation tax, levied on the heads of families; a land-tax, assessed according to the quality and extent of the land, sometimes paid in money, but for the most part in kind; imposts on foreign trade, and corvées. All persons in the service of the state, civil and military, are exempt from taxation. Of all the taxes, the corvées are by far the most onerous, for they include every male inhabiatant of the age of 19 and upwards. No one has ventured to state the money-value of the whole revenue, which must, from the nature of a great part of it, be unknown even to the government itself.

The laws of Cochin-China are in principle the same as those of China, but in practice more arbitrarily and less skilfully administered. In matters of evidence they permit the use of torture. The chief punishments are imprisonment, fetters, the wooden ruff or collar, which prevents the wearer from lying down horizontally; but above all, flagellation by the bamboo, which is universal, both for domestic and public offences. Fathers and mothers inflict it on their children, husbands on their wives, and every officer, civil and military, on all below him. It is evident that no dishonour is attached to the punishment. The offender receives the punishment lying down, and held in this position by assistants. During my own visit to the country I saw several examples of it inflicted in this fashion. Capital punishments are inflicted for murder, treason, robbery, adultery, and, occasionally, for official malversation; but they do not appear to be frequent. "The police," says M. Chaigneau, "is exercised by the chiefs of villages. They can also impose a slight fine, inflict a few strokes of the rattan, and even, in certain cases, condemn to the cangue or wooden collar. Severity is almost inevitable in the midst of so numerous a population. Should the person convicted consider himself unjustly condemned, he can appeal from the jurisdiction of the village chief to that of the chief of the Huyen, and from this again to the governor of the province. When the penalty is small, the judgment of the governor of the province is final; but in all affairs of consequence, whether civil or criminal, an ultimate appeal lies to the royal council. It can scarcely fail but that an affair brought before the last tribunal, especially if the accusation be of a capital nature, should not be judged with the utmost impartiality. The eyes of the master are at hand. Besides, the most scrupulous precautions are taken, in order that the life of the accused may not be exposed to danger, through the ignorance or prejudices of the judges. The documentary evidence is reviewed with the most strict attention; the witnesses are heard anew; all is weighed and discussed gravely and deliberately. In fine, at the moment of pronouncing sentence, the judges are forbid to communicate. Each considers the case by himself, and signs and seals his vote. These votes, placed on the council board, without being opened, are jointly put under the seal of the council, and carried into the interior of the palace, where the king takes cognisance of the affair." Death is inflicted by decapitation with the sword, and, sometimes, it is certain, by the trampling of elephants.

The Cochin-Chinese have a regular army, disciplined in imitation of an European organisation, which they owe to the French officers who, from 1790 to 1801, effected the restoration of the dethroned King Giâlong. This army consists of infantry and artillery with elephants, but no cavalry, Cochin-China furnishing no horses fit for this purpose. When I visited Cochin-China, in 1824, the army consisted of the Royal Guard, amounting to 15,000 men, and the line, to 40,000. Each of these has its quota of artillery and elephants; the latter amounting for the entire army to 800 in number. Besides this regular army, each province has its militia or constabulary force. The artillery, as has been found to be the case with other Asiatic nations following the tactics of Europe, is the most effective part of the force.

The marine of Cochin-China is levied from the inhabitants of the coasts, and like the army, formed into companies, regiments and divisions. The vessels of war consist of corvettes, carrying from 16 to 22 guns,—of large row-galleys of 70 oars, carrying one large gun with many swivel cannon, and of small row-galleys of about 40 oars, with swivel guns and a cannon of four or six pound calibre. The total number of the corvettes was given to me as 200; of the large galleys, at 100; and of the smaller at 500.

Cochin-China possesses several fortified places, constructed on technical principles under the direction of French engineers; and the fortification of Hüe, the capital, is at once the most regular and extensive in Asia, next, probably, to Fort William, in Bengal. The courage of the Cochin-Chinese soldiery, however, does not correspond with their specious organisation. The character given of them by M. Lefevre, amounts simply to this, that, "in spite of their cowardice, they are somewhat less faint-hearted than the Chinese, whom," he states, "they have often beaten,"—it may be presumed in collisions on the frontier of Tonquin.

The history of the present kingdom of Cochin-China is but very imperfectly known to Europeans. Tonquin long formed the most important part of the Empire. The first historical fact of any apparent authenticity is obtained from the annals of China, which describe the Chinese as having effected the conquest of Tonquin in the year before Christ, 214, when they planted colonies among the people of Anam, then a rude race. That an early conquest by China took place seems sufficiently attested by the universal adoption by the people of Anam, but by none of the nations further west, of the manners, laws, written language, and costume of the Chinese. That the country, indeed, did not become a province of the Chinese empire while so close to it, seems only to be explained by the supposition that its inhabitants are a distinct race of men from those of China. Anam after having been for 477 years an integral part, or at least a dependency of China, is stated to have become a separate state, and virtually independent in the year of Christ 263. In 540 it is stated to have received the religion of Buddha from China. China would seem to have made several attempts for the re-conquest of Tonquin; one in 1280, under the Mongols; one in 1406; and one in 1540. All of these were baffled; but the last terminated in a convention, by which the kingdom of Anam consented to consider itself nominally as a lordship of China, the king consenting to receive on his accession an investiture from the Chinese emperor, and to send him triennially an embassy with tribute. This arrangement still subsists.

In the year 1570, a chief of Tonquin, in charge of certain provinces which the Tonquinese had conquered from the kingdom of Champa, declared his independence, and thus founded the present kingdom of Cochin-China. From that time to the year 1777, there reigned of this new dynasty, nine kings, when a formidable rebellion broke out under the leadership of three brothers, called the Tai-son, which lasted twenty-four years; ending only in 1801 by the re-establishment of the legitimate monarch, the celebrated Gialong, on his throne. The restored king was a man of firmness and talents, but chiefly owed his restoration to M. Pigneau, the titular bishop of Adran, and the able French officers who assisted him. These organised for him a disciplined army, against which the rabble of the rebel brothers could make no effectual resistance. The same army which put down the rebellion, enabled the restored sovereign to effect the conqest of Tonquin in 1802, and eventually of a considerable portion of Kamboja. Gialong died in 1819, and was succeeded by his son, the prince who sat on the throne during my own visit to the country in 1822. He died in 1841, and was succeeded by his son, the reigning king. Reckoning from the year 1570 to 1841, ten princes of the existing dynasty have reigned in Cochin-China, which gives the large duration of twenty-seven years for each reign. With the exception of a war with Siam in 1834, confined to the Kambojan frontier, and without result, the kingdom of Cochin-China has enjoyed, up to the present time, an uninterrupted peace of fifty-five years.

The partial introduction of Christianity into Cochin-China, forms at least in an European view, an important part of its history. The first attempt was made by a Spanish Franciscan friar, Bartholomew Ruis, in the year 1583. This missionary obtained permission to reside in the country, but achieved no conversions. It was not until 1615, or two-and-thirty years later, that the work of conversion began under some Spanish and Portuguese Jesuit and Franciscan missionaries. In 1658, Louis XIV. appointed two French bishops, one for Tonquin, and one for Cochin-China, these two countries forming at the time separate kingdoms. The first French missionary reached Cochin-China in 1662, and Tonquin in 1666. Down to the year 1846, there have been in all seventeen French bishops in Cochin-China, and sixteen in Tonquin. According to the statement of M. Lefevre, there are in Cochin-China and Kamboja 80,000 Christians, and in Tonquin 360,000; making for the whole kingdom 440,000.

During the reign of Gialong, Christianity and its European missionaries had been not only tolerated, but even encouraged. He had sent his son and heir to France, and the young prince is said to have embraced the Christian religion. This prince dying, however, was succeeded by another son, a persecutor of the Christians. Under him both lay and ecclesiastical Europeans were expelled from the kingdom, and an edict published denouncing the punishment of death against the propagation of Christianity,—a punishment in several cases carried into effect. This persecution is admitted to have had its origin, not in religious jealousy, but the fear of European invasion, and the apprehension that the followers of the new faith would adopt the cause of hostile strangers. In consequence of this state of things, which has now subsisted for above thirty years, Cochin-China may be considered as being as much closed against Christianity as Japan itself.

COCHINEAL. This insect was introduced into Java a few years ago, as a government experiment, and apparently with more success in its production than in British India, for as long ago as 1844 it was exported from Batavia to the estimated value of 93,319 guilders.

COCK. One species of the genus Gallus is found in the wild state in the Malay Peninsula, two in Sumatra, two in Java, and one in the Philippine Islands. It is remarkable, however, that no bird of the genus in the wild state is to be found in Borneo, Celebes, or any island of the Molucca Sea. Several of these supposed species are probably the same. The two of Java are distinct species; they will pair, but the progeny is a mule, a beautiful bird kept by the wealthy Javanese as an ornament of their poultry-yards, under the name, well known to them, of Pakiser. The wild fowl of the Philippines is sometimes tamed, and by the courage it displays, shows that it is of the true game breed, and probably identical with the domesticated bird. This is what the authors of the Spanish Geographical Dictionary say of it in their introduction:—"In the woods there are beautiful wild cocks. These are very brave in the combat, and always come off victors with the large but cowardly cocks of China, and not with these alone, for they will contend with the famous gallant band of the Laguna."

Nearly everywhere, even among the rudest tribes, the common fowl is found in the domestic state, and in this condition bears a close resemblance to the species called by naturalists Gallus bankiva, which is one of those found wild in Sumatra, and Java, and the sole one of the Malay Peninsula and the Philippines. Most likely, then, this is the origin of the domestic bird of the Asiatic Archipelago. The names by which it is known in the native languages are the only clue to the history of its introduction and dissemination. In Malay it is called ayam, and in Javanese manuk, pitik, and pâksi. The word pitik alone is the specific name of the domestic poultry, the others being generic terms, equivalent to our own word "fowl," but specially applied to the domestic bird when used without an epithet. The wild bird is expressed by adding the Malay word utan, or the Javanese alas, meaning "forest." All the names are native, except pâksi, which belongs to the ceremonial language of Java, and is Sanscrit. From the mere names, then, there is no ground for supposing that the domestic fowl is of foreign introduction. Among the nations of the Malay Peninsula, Sumatra, and Borneo, the Malay word ayam prevails, but every where else, even among the Philippine nations, who have a wild fowl of their own, called in the Tagala labuyu, the Javanese word for the domestic fowl, manuk, is universal. It may, perhaps, be argued from this that the bird was first domesticated by the Malays and Javanese, and by them conveyed to the other nations and tribes of the Asiatic Archipelago.

The Malay domestic cock is of the true game breed, full of courage, but inferior in size to the game cock of Continental India, which is larger than our own, and more powerful. Indeed, among the Malayan nations, there is no distinction, as with us, into game and dunghill fowls, all being of the first description. It, moreover, as to colour, sports less than with us. The dwarf variety, which we have received from the Archipelago, the Bantam, is no exception. There is no such breed in Bantam, but our Indian traders of the beginning of the 17th century, found it in that country, brought there by the junks of Japan which then traded freely with the emporia of the Archipelago, and they gave them the name of the only country in which they saw them. They are still occasionally imported by the Dutch ships into Batavia, where I have seen them.

The Gallus bankiva, or the imagined variety of it called the Malay gigantic cock, is supposed by M. Temminck, who is followed by other naturalists, to be the source from which our European poultry are derived. This Malay gigantic cock I have never seen, nor do I believe that any such native variety exists. Neither does it seem to me reasonable to fancy that our poultry is derived from any Malay breed whatsoever, seeing that in the remote antiquity in which it was introduced into Europe, no communication whatever is ascertained to have existed, direct or indirect, between Europe and the Asiatic Archipelago. The introduction of the common fowl into Europe is beyond the reach of all record, even in Greece. It is faithfully represented on the walls of ancient Etruscan tombs, and, even among the rude inhabitants of Britain, it was found near 2000 years ago. All that is pretty well ascertained is, that it never existed in the wild state in Europe or in Africa, or in any part of Asia west of Hindustan. From this last country to China, including the islands, the wild fowl is very generally distributed, and has been immemorially domesticated. The least distant of these countries, India, is that which is most likely to have furnished Europe, and in the nearest parts of it, the north-western provinces, there exists in abundance a wild cock, resembling, if not identical with, the Gallus bankiva, and also very like the least-improved varieties of our European poultry. Some of these provinces were occasionally under Persian rules, and through Persia, the Greeks in frequent communication with that country, might easily have received from it a bird of hardy constitution that lives, thrives, and multiplies in any climate from the equator to sixty degrees beyond it. The Greeks appear to have sometimes called the cock the "Persian bird," which would seem to point to the quarter from which it came to them.

Most of the advanced nations of the Asiatic Islands are gamblers, and the favourite shape which gaming takes with them is cock-fighting. This includes the people of Bali, Lomboc, Celebes, and all the Philippine Islands, the only material exception being the Javanese. The passion for cock-fighting is impressed on the very language of the Malays. Thus there is a specific name for cock-fighting, one for the natural spur of the cock, and another for the artificial; two names for the comb, three for the crow, two for a cock-pit, and one for a professional cock-fighter. The passion is nowhere carried further than in the Spanish dominions in the Philippines. There, it is licensed by the government, which derives from it a yearly revenue of about 40,000 dollars, or about 10,000*l*.

COCO-PALM (COCOS-MUCIFERA). This palm, so generally diffused over the tropical world, old and new, would appear to be a native of several of the islands of the Asiatic Archipelago, while to others, it seems to have been conveyed by currents or by man. The two most frequent names for it are, the Malay, ñur, and the Javanese, kâlapa. These, with some corruptions, have a very wide circulation, especially the first. The Javanese name extends to the languages of Celebes, and even to some of those of the islands of the Molucca Sea, but the Malay, to the Philippine tongues, to the language of the South Sea Islands, and even to that of Madagascar.

The coco-palm is in a good measure a littoral plant, attaining earliest maturity, greatest size, and most fruitfulness close to the sea, although growing also, and yielding fruit at a considerable distance from it. The natives are well aware of this fact, according to the following apt quotation from Marsden's Sumatra. "Here, said a countryman at Laye, if I plant a coco-nut, I may expect to reap the fruit of it, but in Labun (an inland district) I should only plant for my great grand-children." Many uninhabited islets, on the western coast of Sumatra, afford examples of the mode in which the coco-palm has been conveyed by currents, and of the partiality of the plant for the immediate neighbourhood of the sea. "This island, Tristé," says Dampier, "is not a mile round, and so low, that the tide flows clear over it. It is of a sandy soil, and full of coco-nut trees. The nuts are but small, yet sweet enough, full, and more ponderous than I ever felt any of that bigness, notwithstanding that at every spring-tide the salt-water goes clear over the island."—Vol. i. p. 474. The island thus referred to is the Pulo-Mega, or "Cloud Island," of the natives, a name taken from Sanscrit, and is distant from the shore of Sumatra fifteen leagues. From this account, it is evident that the nut may be conveyed a long way by sea without losing its vitality. The same judicious observer narrates the following fact in illustration. "The tenth day, being in latitude 5° 10′, and about 7 or 8 leagues from the island of Sumatra, on the west side of it, we saw abundance of coco-nuts swimming in the sea, and we hoisted out our boats and took some of them, as also a small hutch or scuttle, rather belonging to some bark. The nuts were very sound, and the kernel sweet, and in some, the milk or water in them was yet sweet and good."—Vol. i. p. 474. The coco-nuts, in this case, were no doubt the produce of a wreck.

By far the best account of this important palm, that I have seen, is to be found in the 4th vol. of the Journal of the Indian Archipelago, written by Mr. J. T. Thomson. "The habit of this tree," says this experienced and intelligent writer, "is on the sea-shore, fringing the beach. In such a position, should the soil be loose and friable, though of the most meagre description, such as sea-sand and shells, it grows luxuriantly without the concomitant aids of cultivation, manure, or the proximity of inhabited houses; but this only obtains within one or two hundred feet of the beach. Its bending stem, inclined towards the sea, causing its fruit to be received into the bosom of that element, appears to have peculiarly fitted it for extension to the various islands and atolls of the Indian and Pacific Oceans, to which the nut is floated by the winds and tides, and to whose inhabitants it affords both shelter and food. When planted in other localities than these, it neither grows well nor affords fruit, unless it be on rich soil, or in the proximity of dwellings, and in average soils it requires both considerable manuring and cultivation. . . . A good coco-nut tree, when in full bearing, will yield 140 to 150 nuts per annum. It commences to bear in damp, low, rich soils in the 4th or 5th year, in sandy soils, of middling height, in the 6th and 7th year, and on high ridges in the 9th and 10th year and the last, though slow in growth, are wholesome good trees. From the time the blossom shows, three months elapse before the formation of the fruit, and the fruit requires six months more to come to full growth, three months more to ripen, and it will remain other two months before it drops. Thus fourteen months elapse between the blossoming and the falling of the ripe fruit."

The accounts usually given of the almost innumerable uses to which the different parts of the coco-palm are put are in a good measure exaggerated. The only parts essentially valuable are the albumen of the nut for its oil, and its husk for a textile material. In the Asiatic Archipelago, the wood, the leaves, the sap, and the pith of other palms, are either better in quality or cheaper. In whatever manner the first inhabitants of other regions of the earth may have obtained their earliest subsistence, it is certain that those of which the coco-palm is a native, had at once from it, a spontaneous supply, both of food and drink. Its presence on the coast, probably contributed, with the easy supply of fish, to determine, from the first, that maritime character which still belongs to so many of the tribes of the Archipelago.

COCOS. The name of four small, coral-girt islets on the western coast of Sumatra, off the south-western end of the large island Simalu, the Hog-island of the charts, and lying in the third degree of north latitude. They are uninhabited, but covered with coco-nut palms, and hence their name imposed, no doubt, by the Portuguese.

COFFEE (COFFEA ARABICA). The Arabian name of this plant, kăwăh, is not unknown to the inhabitants of the Archipelago, but the European one corrupted, kopi, is more generally used. This really hardy plant, a native of Africa of the region between the 10th and 15th degrees of north latitude, thrives anywhere in a suitable soil and locality within the tropics. It was only brought across the Red Sea from Abyssinia and cultivated in the mountains of Arabia, as late as about the year 1450, less than half a century before the discovery of America and the passage to India by the Cape. Neither the Arabs, nor Portuguese, attempted to introduce the coffee plant into the islands of the Archipelago. This was reserved for the Dutch, who effected it in 1690, or some forty years after coffee had come to be used as a beverage in Europe. The event was, in a good measure, accidental, for it could hardly have been foreseen that a native plant of the dry climates of Abyssinia and Arabia would have flourished in the humid ones about the equator. The manner of its introduction and dissemination to remote regions is curious and instructive. The Dutch East India Company carried on some trade from Java with the ports of the Arabian Gulf, and about the year 1690 the governor-general Van Hoorne caused some ripe coffee seeds to be brought to him to Java. These were planted in a garden near Batavia, where they grew and produced fruit. A single plant so grown was sent by the governor-general to Holland, as a present to Nicholas Witsen, the governor of the East India Company. This, after the tedious voyage of the time, arrived safe,—was planted in the botanic garden of Amsterdam, where it flourished, bore fruit, and the fruit young plants. Some of these plants were sent to the colony of Surinam, the planters of which began to cultivate coffee as an object of trade in 1718, twenty-eight years after the introduction of the parent plants into Java. About the year 1728, coffee plants were carried from Surinam to the English and French West India Islands. From Java, the cultivation of coffee has been extended to Sumatra, Celebes, Bali, and several of the Philippine Islands, and the Asiatic Islands produce, at present, probably about one fourth part of all that is consumed. The hardihood of the coffee plant is proved by the facility with which it is raised, even under the careless husbandry of the natives, by which neither sugar nor indigo can be produced, except under European or Chinese direction. All the coffee of Celebes and Bali, and much of that of Sumatra, are the produce of native industry.

COMODO. The largest of the three islets, the other two being Gunung-api and Galibanta, lying in the Straits of Sapi, or those which divide Sumbanca from Floris. All that is known of it is that it is high, steep—of volcanic formation, and that it is part of the Principality of Bima, in the Island of Sumbawa. Its area, including other islands in the Straits of Sapi, is computed at 256 square geographical miles.

COMPASS. The compass, for nautical purposes, is, at present, used by the principal native traders of the Archipelago. The Bugis of Celebes, for example, use small rude compasses, made expressly for them by the Chinese of Batavia, at the very moderate cost of from one shilling to eighteen-pence a-piece. The directive power of the magnet is said to have been known to the Chinese for many ages,—by their own account, no less than 2634 years before the birth of Christ. The mere acquaintance with the directive quality of the magnet, and the practical application of this quality to the purposes of navigation, are two very different things; and there is certainly no evidence to show that the Chinese had put the magnet to the last of these uses. In Europe, the compass began to be used for nautical purposes about the beginning of the 14th century. Now, towards the close of the previous century, Marco Polo had made a long voyage in a fleet of Chinese junks, from China to the Persian Gulf, and never mentions the compass; which, as it must have been a novelty to him, he would hardly have failed to have done, had the Chinese fleet been steered by it. The voyage, in fact, was a coasting one. From a northern port of China to Ormus, in the Persian Gulf, it lasted eighteen months; and, in its course, the fleet touched at many places. The pilots seem to have steered by observation of stars and land-marks; and the navigation was only bolder than that of the Greeks and Romans, because it had the advantage of the monsoons. One easterly monsoon was expended in the performance of the part of the voyage from China to the north-eastern coast of Sumatra; for the voyagers had to wait five months for the return of another, before venturing to cross the Bay of Bengal. They must, indeed, have waited at some Indian ports for a third easterly monsoon, before they could reach the Persian Gulf. It seems highly probable that the Chinese were, for many ages, acquainted with the directive power of the compass, without using it for nautical purposes; just as they were acquainted with the explosive quality of gunpowder, without using it for propelling missiles. It seems not improbable, that both the Hindus and Arabs may have been acquainted with the directive power of the magnet, before it was known to Europeans, and perhaps they even used it on land for determining the cardinal points; but there is certainly no evidence of their employing the compass for nautical purposes any more than the Chinese; and the Italian name used by the Arabs sufficiently attests that they, at least, learnt the use of it in modern times, from Europeans.

In the Malay languages, the name for the magnet, and for the compass and its divisions, are almost exclusively native words. That for the magnet is batu-brani, or bâsi-brani, literally "powerful stone," or "powerful iron." The compass is called pandoman or padoman, a word, of which the Javanese word dom, "a needle," seems to be the radical part, the compound signifying "place of the needle," or "object with a needle." The Malay compass is divided into sixteen parts, twelve of which are multiples of the four cardinal points. For the cardinal points the different nations have native terms; but for nautical purposes, those of the Malay language are used throughout, as in the case of the nations of Celebes, the most expert native navigators of the present day. It may be here remarked, that all the ancient Hindu temples of Java are found to face the cardinal points of the horizon with surprising correctness, the principal façades being to the east and west; a fact from which we may be disposed to infer, that the builders, most probably Hindus, had availed them-selves of the directive property of the magnet.

When the Portuguese first arrived in India, they found the Mahommedan traders to the east of the Cape of Good Hope in possession of the mariner's compass, of astrolabes and charts. De Barros does not expressly name the compass as being pos-sessed by them; but he mentions other objects still less to be expected, and the use of which would seem to imply the presence of that instrument. "A Moor of the kingdom of Gujrat," he says, "visited Vasco di Gama on board his ship, while at Melinda, on the east coast of Africa; and to the great satisfaction of the Portuguese commander, showed him a chart of the whole coast of India, dressed in the manner of the Moors, with minute meridians and parallels. Vasco di Gama showed this person, whom he calls a pilot, his own astrolabes in wood and metal, at which he expressed no surprise, saying, 'that the pilots of the Red Sea used instruments of brass, of a triangular and quadrangular form, for taking the sun's altitude, but espe-cially the altitude of the stars, which it was that they chiefly employed in their navigation.' The pilot added, however, 'that he himself, and the mariners of Cam-bay, and indeed of all India, did not make use of such instruments, but of others, which he showed; and also that they sailed by certain stars.'"—Decade 1. Lib. 4. cap. 6. The compass is expressly named by Barthena as being used by the mari-ners of the Archipelago about the years 1505 or 1506. "Here," says he, (Borneo), "my companion freighted a small vessel for 100 ducats, which being provisioned, we took our course towards the fine island of Java, (bella isola de Giava,) where we arrived in five days, sailing southward. The master of the vessel carried a compass with magnet, after our manner, and had a chart marked with lines, lengthways and crossways."—Ramusio, vol. i. p. 168. Unfortunately Barthena does not tell us the quality of his companion, or of the master of the vessel, but still there can be no doubt of the fact he states.

COPPER. Ores of this metal have been found in Sumatra, Celebes, and Timur, and most probably in time will be found in Borneo. In Sumatra and Celebes, mines of it are said to be worked, but if such be the case, even their locality has certainly never been shown. The probability is that this metal has always been, as it now is, imported. The prevailing name for it is tambaga, a corruption of the Sanscrit tamra, and this corrupt form of the word extends from Sumatra to the Philippines, a fact from which its dissemination may be traced to a single nation, most probably the

Javanese. To the use of this foreign name there are a few exceptions in comparatively rude tongues, but they are not material ones. Thus in the languages of Floris, it is called by a word which in Malay and Javanese means a gem, and in the language of the Kisa Islands the name seems a corruption of that which signifies silver in Malay. The use of copper in Java, chiefly in the formation with tin and zinc of alloys, is attested to have been of considerable antiquity by the discovery in old ruins of many statues and utensils of bronze, and even of copper itself. A Hindu cup, with the signs of the zodiac, in the collection of Sir Stamford Raffles, bears the date, according to the era of Salivana, 1220, and two in my own possession, those of 1241 and 1246. The oldest of these carries us back to the year 1298 of Christ. Copper is not used to the same extent by the Indian Islanders as it is by the Hindus, coarse Chinese porcelain for culinary purposes having immemorially taken the place of brass vessels. Its principal use at present is in the manufacture of musical instruments and cannon.

COWRY SHELLS. The Cypræa moneta, of naturalists, is found in the Asiatic Archipelago in considerable quantity, only on the shores of the Sulu group of islands, but the cowry seems never to have been used for money among the Indian islanders as it has immemorially been by the Hindus. The Malay and Javanese name however is Sanscrit, beya, and is also one of the synonyms which express duty, impost, or toll.

CUBEB PEPPER. This article, as it appears in commerce, is stated to be the fruit of two different species of pepper—the Piper cubeba, and Piper caricum, both natives of Java, to which island their cultivation appears to be confined. In the Javanese language its name is kumukus, and this is its only specific one, for the Malay name lada bârekor, meaning "tailed pepper," is a factitious one derived from the appearance of the dried fruit, which has always the foot-stalk adhering to it. Cubebs are used in Java, only as a condiment, but in Hindustan, besides being applied to this purpose, they have long been used as a remedy in certain sexual maladies. In the early periods of the European commerce with the Archipelago, cubebs appear to have been an export to Europe. Barbosa names them as one of the articles brought by the Javanese traders to Malacca, and they are included in his Calicut price current where he calls them "cubebas, which grow in Java, and are there sold at a mean price without being weighed." Their importation into Europe had been long discontinued, but began again in 1815, upon their medicinal virtues having been brought to the knowledge of the English medical officers serving in Java, who had obtained their acquaintance from their Hindu servants. The present price of the cubeb is about three times that of black pepper: the article still continues to be the exclusive production of Java, and it is largely exported to Europe as well as to Continental India.

CUPANG. The name of a possession of the Dutch in the island of Timur. See Timur.

CUYOS. The name of a group of islets, said to amount to thirty-six in number, lying between the large islands of Panay and Palawan in the Philippine Archipelago, and forming part of the province of Calamianes. The largest of them called by the Spaniards the Gran Cuyo lies between north latitudes 10° 46′ and 10° 53′, and east longitudes 121° 1′ and 121° 7′. Its greatest length from north to south is 3½ leagues, and its greatest breadth about 1½; its medium length and breadth however not exceeding 2½ and 1 league respectively, and its circumference being no more than 8½ leagues. This little island has been long celebrated for its considerable population,—for supplies of all sorts of provisions, and for the agreeable manners of its inhabitants, who differ from those of the surrounding islands in physical form, by a clearer complexion, by taller persons, and even by a more agreeable dialect. The trading vessels of Panay touch at Cuyo, as the most convenient port in their voyages to and from Paragua in Palawan and the Calamianes Islands. The soil appears to be poor, for the agriculture chiefly consists in the culture of mountain rice, a sure sign everywhere of inferior fertility. It seems chiefly adapted to the growth of the coco-palm, the sap of which forms the chief article of exportation. The women manufacture fabrics from the abaca and cotton, which are exported, but the men are mostly employed in the fisheries, which include that of the Balaté or holothurion. They also find employment in gathering the esculent nests of the swallow. On the west side of the island there is a town of the same name, consisting of 1256 houses, for the most part native huts, with a population of 7540 inhabitants. This is defended by a fine stone fortress with four bastions, mounted with heavy cannon, built at the cost of the clergy, as a protection against the corsairs of Sulu and Mindano. The town was founded in 1622, and in the same year the Catholic religion was first preached to the inhabitants.

D.

DÄA, pronounced by the Javanese DÖO, an ancient kingdom of Java, corresponding with the modern province of Kadiri. The most celebrated of its kings, well known in Javanese story as Jayabaya, is stated to have begun his reign in the year of Salivana 1117, corresponding with 1195 of Christ. The country contains many relics of the ancient religion of Java.

DAMAR. The meaning of this word in Malay and Javanese is "resin." The substance usually known under this name is the produce of several forest trees, and is the sap which exudes spontaneously, and being exposed to the air acquires a flinty hardness from which the epithet batu, or stone, is given to it to distinguish it from a softer substance, kruïn or wood-oil. The damar is found either in large masses at the foot of the trees which yield it, or floating in rivers, drifted to them by the floods of the rainy season. It is produced in such abundance, and gathered with so little labour, that its market price seldom exceeds four or five shillings a hundredweight. The natives of the country apply it to most of the uses to which we put tar, pitch, and resin, and it forms an article of exportation to Continental India. Most of the family of Dipterocarpeæ yield resinous balsamic juices, those of the genus Dipterocarpus the wood-oils, and of Valeria, indurated damar. The natural order abounds in Sumatra, Java, and Borneo, which are the chief sources of the damar of commerce.

DAMAR. (Pulo). This is the name of two islets, one lying off the western coast of Borneo, and the other off the extreme end of the southern peninsula of Gilolo.

DAMPIER. William Dampier, the greatest of our naval discoverers after Cooke, was, like him, a man of humble origin, having been, as he himself informs us, the son of a small farmer in East Coker, near Yeovil, in Somersetshire. He is said to have been born in 1652. "My friends," says he, "did not originally design me for the sea, till I came to years fit for a trade. But upon the death of my father and mother they who had the disposal of me took other measures, and having removed me from the Latin school to learn writing and arithmetic, they soon after placed me with the master of a ship at Weymouth, complying with the indications I had very early of seeing the world." He made voyages to France, to Newfoundland, and to Bantam, in Java, as "a man before the mast." He afterwards attempted to settle as assistant to planters in Jamaica, but dissatisfied with this mode of life, he joined the log-wood cutters in the Bay of Campeachy, and eventually the buccaneers, who crossed the continent and carried on their depredations on the western shore of America. In 1684 he went on a privateering expedition round Cape Horn, and after committing depredations on the coasts of Chili, Peru, and Mexico, the ship to which he belonged crossed the Pacific, and brought him into the Asiatic Archipelago in 1686, where he passed four years.

The style of Dampier's writings is well known as being at once graphic and simple. It was the model for his narrative which Swift adopted in the celebrated "Travels of Gulliver," and as his first voyage was published in 1691, it may be suspected that De Foe was under obligations to him for his "Robinson Crusoe." That he was a keen, accurate, judicious, and even enlightened observer, his voyages afford ample evidence. The parts of the Archipelago, or its neighbourhood, which he chiefly describes, are the island of Mindano, Achin, and Tonquin, and of these, at an interval of 170 years, his accounts are the fullest and the best we possess. The fame which he acquired by his voyage round the world recommended him to the command of a sloop of war, the Roebuck, in which he made his discoveries on the coast of New Holland and its neighbourhood. This voyage was published in 1703, but he seems to have gone again to sea in 1711, since which time nothing of him is known, not even the time or manner of his death. His voyages are dedicated to noblemen, successive First Lords of the Admiralty, in terms of sufficient humility, and he expresses his obligations to a third nobleman equally unknown to fame, because he had his wife—most probably a maid-servant—out of his lordship's family.

DEER. In the Asiatic Archipelago there are found eight species of the genus Cervus, and three of the genus Moschus, or pigmy deer. Of the first, there are the Cervus manjac, the Cervus Kuhlii, the Cervus equinus, the Cervus hippelaphus, the Cervus axis, or spotted deer, the Cervus Moluccensis, and the Cervus babi-rusa, or hog-deer. The second genus consists of Moschus memina, Moschus Javanicus, and Moschus kanchil, hornless animals, of less bulk and weight than an European hare. Besides these there is one antelope, or at least an animal approaching to the character of the antelopes, the Antilope depressicornis. With the exception of one species, the Cervus Moluccensis, all the Cervi and all the Moschi are confined to the islands of the Malay Archipelago, west of Celebes. Cervus Kuhlii is restricted to Java and its islands, Cervus axis to Sumatra, and Cervus equinus to Borneo. The single antelope belongs to Celebes only. The most frequent of all these deer are Cervus rusa, the rusa of the Malays, and the mânjangan of the Javanese, and the Cervus manjac, the kijang of the Malays and kidang of the Javanese. These are common to all the large islands, and to many of the small ones west of Celebes. Such is also the case with the three species of pigmy deer called by the Malays and Japanese napuh, kanchil, and pâlandok. The babi-rusa is not found west of Celebes.

DELLI, in Malay DILI. The name of a Malay state on the north-eastern side of Sumatra, opposite to the state of Perak, in the Peninsula. The mouth of the small river on which the chief town lies is in north latitude 3° 46′ 30″, and east longitude 98° 42′ 30″. The embouchure is a quarter of a mile broad, but four miles up, the river, where the town stands, narrows to forty yards. The river is a shallow stream throughout, and on its bar the depth at high water is no more than four feet, so that it is only navigable for small native craft. It has its source at the base of two lofty mountains called Kwali and Sukanalu, visible in clear weather from the coast.

The territory of Delli extends for about sixty miles along the coast, and to an unknown extent inland, including the dependent states of Butu-china and Langkat. It forms a part of the great alluvial plain which embraces nearly the whole north-eastern side of Sumatra. Near the coast the land is almost on a level with the sea, but inland rises a few feet above it. The soil near the coast is described as a deep black mould, which with skill and industry would be fertile, but for the present the land, with the exception of a few spots, is covered with a deep forest, and most likely has been so from the creation. The inhabitants consist of the ruling people, the Malays, of Bataks, and Achinese, with a few Javanese, Bugis, and Chinese. Of the number of the population nothing is known, except that it is very scanty. The productions of the country are the usual ones, the principal being rice, black pepper, and gambier. Of the first hardly enough is produced for domestic consumption, but the pepper is a large produce, which Mr. Anderson, the source of most of our information respecting the country, estimated in 1822 at as much as 5,500,000 pounds, all exported to the British possessions in the Straits of Malacca.

When or how the Malays settled in this part of Sumatra is unknown to themselves. There exist, however, in the country some remains of antiquity, indicating the former presence of strangers more advanced than the Malays. On the river of Butu-china, about three days' sail up, there is at a place called Kuta-bangun, a stone building sixty feet square, having the figures of men and animals sculptured on its walls, most probably a Hindu temple. On the Delli river there are the remains of a stone fortress, said to be in some parts thirty feet in height, with a circumference of 200 fathoms, an earthen entrenchment of the extent of a mile or a mile and a quarter, called Kuta-jawa or the Javanese fortress, and a large stone with an inscription in a character unknown to the present inhabitants. According to the tradition of the Malays, a Javanese colony of 5000 persons was once settled in this part of Sumatra, and the probability is that the monuments in question were erected by this people. The inscription will probably be found to be in the Kawi, or ancient character of Java, and similar to those which Sir Stamford Raffles found in the neighbouring inland country of Menangkabo. The account of these relics is on native authority, for no European traveller has ever seen them. Delli, as an independent state, is most probably of modern origin, for it does not appear to have existed as such on the first arrival of the Portuguese, as may be seen from De Barros, who names the nine-and-twenty kingdoms of Sumatra, among which it is not found.

DEMPO. The name of a mountain in Sumatra, in the territory of Pasâman-lebar, and latitude 4° 10′ south, computed to have a height of 10,250 feet above the level of the sea. It is an active volcano—the most southerly and easterly of those of that island.

ḌENḌENG. The Malay name for the jerked beef of commerce, that is, of animal muscular fibre, preserved by drying in the sun, nearly the only mode of curing flesh in the Archipelago. Ḍenḍeng is made of the flesh of deer, oxen, and buffalos, and by the Chinese of that of the wild hog. It is a considerable article of native trade.

ḌESA. This word, taken from the Sanscrit, signifies "the country," as distinguished from "the town," or rather from the seat of government, and it is also a synonym for a "village." It occurs, not unfrequently, in the names of places.

DIAMOND. In Malay and Javanese intân, and sometimes kumala. The diamond has been found in no part of the Asiatic Archipelago except Borneo, and even in that island only in a comparatively small part of it, a portion of its western coast. The principal diamond mines are in the district of Landak, in the territory of Pontiyanak, in the longitude of 109° east, about forty miles north of the equator, and they occur from thence as far as Banjarmasin, in south latitude between three and four degrees, and longitude between 114° and 115° east. The mines are worked by the wild Dayaks and the Malays, but with far superior skill by the Chinese. The gems are found in a yellow-coloured rubble or gravel which occurs at various depths, the greatest to which a shaft has been known to be sunk being between fifty and sixty feet. When a shaft of such a depth is sunk, six different alluvial strata occur before reaching the diamond-yielding one, which the Malays call the Areng. These strata are,—a black mould, a yellow sandy clay, a red clay, a blue clay, a blue clay intermixed with gravel, called by the Malays "ampir," or "near at hand," and lastly, a stiff yellow clay, in which the diamonds are imbedded. The largest diamond found in the Bornean mines of late years, was only of thirty-two carats. The prince of Matan, however, has long had in his possession, a rough diamond of 367 carats, but its genuineness has been suspected. At present the Dutch government are the owners of the diamond mines, and make advances to the miners, who are bound to deliver all stones at twenty per cent. below their market value, which is equivalent to a seignorage of twenty-five per cent. Under this management there were delivered in 1824 no more than 1900 carats, and the quantity in the two subsequent years was still less.

DÏENG. The name of a mountain in Java, lying between the provinces of Pakalongan and Baglen, having an altitude of 6300 feet above the level of the sea. In the plateau between it and the adjacent mountain Prau, which is 7870 feet high, there are one-and-twenty small temples, each of about 30 feet high, tolerably entire; with the ruins of many others, all built of blocks of hewn trachyte. This is the most elevated locality in which Hindu remains are found in Java. The temples of Dïeng are said to be purely Braminical, without any intermixture of the worship of Buddah, or Jain, such as occurs in the ruins of Brambanan. No dates or other inscriptions have been found in these temples; but, most probably, like Brambanan and Borobudor, they were built in the 12th or 13th centuries.

DILI. The name of a Portuguese settlement on the northern side of the island of Timur. The name is exactly the same as that of the Malay state on the north-eastern side of Sumatra, which is written in our maps Delli; and as Malays have been immemorially settled in this part of Timur, and as the current language is still Malay, it seems probable that the place was a colony of the Malays of Sumatra. See TIMUR. The small town and harbour of Dili are in south latitude 8° 35′ 36″, and east longitude 125° 40′. The harbour would be exposed nearly to every wind, except the south, but for the coral reef, bare at low water, which forms it, and through which there are but two navigable channels, the widest of which is only from a cable and a half to two cables length broad. The Portuguese claim the sovereignty of all that part of Timur which lies east of Dili, but their authority, beyond the limit of this place itself, is for the most part nominal. This poor possession, then, is all that remains to the nation of the insular empire, so gallantly established and so badly managed in the 16th century.

DISEASES. In the Malay and Javanese languages the same words express disease and pain. The most frequent word in both languages for this purpose, is sakit; but the Javanese have three synonyms, gâring, lara, and gârah, the last, however, signifying also "heat." The ordinary diseases to which the natives of the Indian islands are subject, are those arising from malaria, namely, fevers, remittent and intermittent and dysentery. The epidemics are small-pox, measles, hooping cough, and Asiatic cholera. The last was introduced in 1820, three years after its first appearance in Bengal. This, therefore, they owe to ourselves, as more than three centuries ago they did syphilis to the Portuguese and Spaniards. The Turkish pest has never reached them, any more than it has other countries east of Persia. Leprosy, the disease of filth and barbarism, is common to them as to other Asiatic nations. I have seen many examples of it in Java, where the sufferers have, as elsewhere, been considered as outcasts. Inflammatory diseases, and tubercular ones, are less frequent than in temperate and cold regions, but the inhabitants are by no means exempt from them. Diseases of the skin are very frequent, more especially among the fish-eaters of the coasts. In the mountainous parts of the country, goïtres are to be seen, and this too, close to the equator, and in countries where there is no snow.

In so far as concerns their native inhabitants, there is no reason to believe that the Indian islands generally, are in climate less salubrious than other parts of the world. Every place that is tolerably dry, and, above all, well-ventilated, is healthy; while localities even when dry, but not well-ventilated, are sure to be unhealthy. The town of Singapore, although a part of it be built in a salt marsh and on the level of the sea, is as salubrious as any tropical country, because thoroughly ventilated by land and sea-breezes, by the north-eastern monsoon, and by occasional squalls from the west. But within two miles of it is a beautiful and picturesque land-locked harbour, which although dry, has a climate that is pestilential from malaria. High lands are generally more healthy than low ones, but it must be presumed chiefly because they are better ventilated. In proof of the salubrity of the climate of the Indian islands, it may be stated that longevity among its native inhabitants is as frequent as in temperate regions. In the Spanish Philippines, there were living in 1850, sixty-two persons of the age of 100 or upwards, the oldest of them having attained the age of 137. This fact is stated in the population returns.

DISTILLATION. The probability is, that the Indian islanders were unacquainted with the art of distilling an ardent spirit, until they acquired it either from the Arabs or the Chinese. The Javanese have a fermented liquor made from rice, which they call brâm, and the Malays another called gilang, but these are not obtained by distillation; and all the current names which both nations have for ardent spirit are of foreign origin. These are the Arabic aräk, the Chinese chu, and the Dutch soopije, a dram, corrupted into sopi. The Javanese have, indeed, terms for the verb to distil, and for the noun a still, or alembic, but they are only derivatives from the word kukus, smoke or vapour. The distilled spirit obtained from a mixture of rice, molasses, and palm wine, so well known under the name of "Batavian arrack," seems to have been an invention of the Chinese, who are still its only manufacturers.

DJILOLO. The Dutch orthography of the word which we should write Jilolo. This name for the whole island of Halmahera, seems to be taken from a bay on its western coast, nearly opposite to the island of Ternate, one of the five clove islets. See ALMAHERA.

DJOCJOCARTA. This is the cumbrous and not very correct orthography in which the Dutch write the name of the capital town of one of the two existing tributary princes of Java,—and which may be more accurately written Ayuga-karta, or abbreviated, Yugyakarta. See YUGYAKARTA.

DOG. The dog is found in all the islands of the Archipelago, in the half-domestic state in which it is seen in every country of the East, except China, Tonquin, Cochin-China, and the islands of the Pacific, in which it is kept for food. Some of the rudest tribes alone use it in hunting. It is the same prick-eared cur as in other Asiatic countries, varying a good deal in colour,—not much in size or shape,—never owned,—never become wild, but always the common scavenger of every town and village. Its origin is as obscure as in other parts of the world. As the wolf, the fox, and the jackal do not exist in any part of the Archipelago, it cannot, locally at least, have sprung from any of these. There is, however, one species of wild dog in Sumatra, the Malay Peninsula, Borneo, and Java, which some naturalists have called the Canis Sumatrensis, and others Canis rutilans; and from this the half-domesticated dog may have sprung, although there is certainly no evidence that it has done so. At the same time there is none that points at a foreign origin. In Sumatra there are several names for the dog, all native, as anjing, in Malay, and kuyo, in the languages of the Rejangs and Lampungs. In Javanese, there are five names,—three of them native, and one Sanscrit; which last, however, turns out to be a name for the jackal in that language. The usual Javanese name is asu; and it is remarkable, that this word is the name for the dog in the languages of tribes remote from Java; being those too of countries having themselves no wild dog, as Floris, Timur, and the Philippine Islands. This fact seems, at least, to show that Java was the source from which these countries derived the domestic dog. It may be added that neither this word, nor any other Malayan name for it, has reached Australia or the Polynesian islands. A wild dog exists in Napal, and a variety of it in some of the southern parts of Continental India, the Canis primævus; and this seems to me by far the most likely to have formed the stock from which, not only the half-domesticated dog of the islands, as well as those of Hindustan itself and the neighbouring countries have sprung, but even all the varieties of the European dog. I have seen the Napal wild dog, which certainly very much resembles that of the domesticated one of Hindustan.

DONGALA. The name of the principal place and port of the state of Kaili, in Celebes, situated in a bay on the shore of the Straits of Macassar, in latitude south 2° 20′. Much of the gold of Celebes is collected at this place for exportation by the Bugis traders of Waju.

DORY HARBOUR. This is the name of the most frequented part of the northern coast of the great island of New Guinea, and the chief place within the great bay of Geelvink, so called from the name of a Dutch ship which surveyed it in the year 1705. This bay itself may be thus briefly described. Its entrance is in south latitude 2° 20′, and in east longitude 140° 47′. From cape to cape, east and west, it is full 200 miles broad, while its extreme depth is 180. Thus it so deeply indents the island as to make it to consist of two peninsulas, leaving a connecting isthmus not exceeding 20 miles in breadth. The coast line of the bay extends over at least 500 miles, and contains the debouchements of many rivers, some of which seem to proceed from the eastern or larger peninsula, and to be of considerable size. Within the bay are many islands, two of which, Jobi and Mysori, are of large size.

The inhabitants of the islands and shore of the Bay of Geelvink appear all to be of one race, and nearly in the same state of society as those which are best known, those of Dory; an account of which, therefore, will in a good measure serve for all the rest. In the year 1849, the Dutch government of India sent a mission to inquire into the condition and resources of the northern coast of New Guinea, of which, M. Kops, a most intelligent officer of the Netherlands navy, has given a faithful and sensible narrative, from which I take my account of Dory. This place is situated only 5 miles within Hut Point, the north-west angle of the bay, which is itself 46 miles south of the equator, and east of the meridian of Greenwich 132° 15′. The harbour consists of a succession of three bays connected with each other; the two innermost of which are safe harbours, with sufficient water, good anchorage, and a sandy beach. The outermost is protected by the two islets of Masinama and Nasmapi, as well as by two isolated reefs. Dory consists of two villages only, the number of houses in one of which only is given, and this is 33, but they are large and capable of accommodating twenty persons each. If every house then were full, we should have a population of this, the principal village, of 660. If the smaller village contain half as many inhabitants as Lonfabi, for that is the name of the larger, then we shall have a population for Dory short of 1000 at the utmost.

Of the personal appearance of the inhabitants of Dory, M. Kops gives the following account, omitting particulars that are not essential. The stature of the men is in general short, the greater number not exceeding 5 feet 3 inches, and very few attaining 5 feet 6 inches. Thus, then, the Papuas are about the average stature of the Malay race, and about 5 inches short of the height of Europeans, in so far as the race is represented by the people of Dory. Their colour is a dark brown, inclining in some individuals to black. The hair is black and frizzled, and wearing it usually to the full length that it will grow to, it makes the head seem, at a distance, of twice the natural size; while from no care being bestowed upon it, it has a disorderly appearance, which gives the wearer a wild aspect. The beard is crisp, but short; the forehead high, but narrow;—the eyes dark brown or black. The nose is flat, the mouth large, the lips thick, and the teeth fine. M. Kops, however, states an apparent anomaly in the physical form of this people, which has also been noted of the Papuans in other parts of New Guinea, that notwithstanding the prevalence of negro features, many of them are found with arched noses and thin lips, giving them an European physiognomy.

The people of Dory are properly fishermen, and but partially agriculturists. Their dwellings are on posts in the water, which at flood tide reaches nearly to their floors, and they are connected with the shore by bridges. Their patches of cultivation are at a distance in the forest, surrounded by hedges to protect them from the wild hog. In these are raised a little rice, without irrigation; maiz, millet, with yams and tobacco. The palms reared are the coco and the sago; and the chief fruits the banana, the pine-apple, and oranges, the latter abundant. The only domestic animals are the hog, and the crown-pigeon, but both rare. The people of Dory have boats with out-riggers, and are constantly in these or in the water, for they are bold swimmers and expert divers. They understand the smelting and the forging of iron; making their own implements, although preferring those of strangers. Their food consists chiefly of fish and sago. The first, which are caught in nets or killed with the spear, are abundant. The chief employment consists in the fishery of the tripang, the tortoise, and the pearl oyster, to exchange with strangers for rice, iron, or clothing. They are ignorant of letters, native or foreign, and have no substitute for them. "Their religion," says M. Kops, "consists in the worship and consultation of a wooden image, called Harwar, which every man makes for himself, and which is considered the protector of the owner. This image, of the height of a foot and a half, rudely carved in a human form, stands behind a carved shield. When worshipping, they place the image before them,—sit down,—raise the hands together to the forehead,—bow before it, and relating what they intend to do, ask its advice. It surprised me," says M. Kops, "that while they gave to all the human figures on their praus, shields, and houses the character of a Papuan with bushy hair, they did not do so with the images of their deities, for all had the head smooth, or covered with a kerchief." The head was in these unnaturally large; the nose long and sharp at the point; the mouth wide and furnished with numerous teeth; and every part of the body disproportioned." Besides these penati they had other images, such as wooden figures of alligators, lizards, and snakes.

The moral characters, not only of the men, but of the inhabitants of the islands of the bay which he visited, is summed up by M. Kops in the following few words. "Gentleness even to timidity, good nature, chastity, and a sense of justice appear to be general, and to form the ground-work of their character." In another place he observes: "Theft is considered by them as a very grave offence, and is of very rare occurrence. They have no fastenings to their houses, and yet the chiefs assured us that seldom or never was anything stolen. Although they were on board our ship, or along-side the whole day, we never missed anything." Except that they are less softened by intercourse with strangers, the state of society among the tribes of the coast and islands of Geelvink, does not probably differ materially from that of the Dorians. The race is the same, and the manners and habits similar. They are divided into many small independent tribes, speaking languages which, to all appearance, differ among themselves to such a degree at least, that the parties are not intelligible to each other. They are at perpetual war, the object of which is to get heads as trophies, or to make prisoners to sell or to ransom. The whole bay and its islands have been for ages tributary to the petty kings of Tidor, one of the five true Moluccas; the power obtained by the sale of cloves to the nations of the West having enabled this mere islet to effect conquests, at the distance of at least 700 miles. All the tribes referred to are maritime; but of those of the interior we only know, and this from the captives that are brought for sale to the coast, that they are essentially the same Papuan negros as those of Dory.

DRAGON'S-BLOOD. This colouring substance is a granular matter adhering to the ripe fruit of a species of ratan, Calamus draco, and obtained by beating or thrashing the fruit in little baskets. Within the Archipelago, the principal place of production is Jambi, on the north-eastern side of Sumatra. The plant is the wild produce of the forest, and not cultivated, although some care is taken to preserve it from destruction. The collectors of dragon's-blood are the wild people called Kubu, who dispose of it to the Malays, at a price not much exceeding a shilling a pound. The whole quantity produced in Jambi is said to be about 1000 hundredweights. The article is often adulterated by a mixture of damar. The best kind imported into Europe in reeds, is manipulated by the Chinese. The canes of the male plant used in former times to be exported to Batavia, and very probably formed the "true Jambees," commemorated in the Spectator as the most fashionable walking-sticks in the reign of Queen Anne.

DRAMA (in Javanese, RINGGIT), a word which literally signifies a deputy or representative, and thence also a play or dramatic representation. The more advanced of the nations of the Archipelago have the rudiments of a drama, the origin of which, it is certain, from the terms connected with it, and from its subjects, was in Java. There exists, however, in Javanese, no written dramatic performance in the form of dialogue; and, indeed, the actors do not, except occasionally a few sentences, speak at all, so that the plays are really pantomimes. A practised artist, called the D'alang, reads the story before the audience, which the performers act in pantomime. Men perform both male and female parts, and usually in masks (topeng), and in the ancient costume of Java. The subjects of the drama are taken either from the Javanese versions of the Hindu poems, the Mahabaret, or Ramayana, or from the ancient legends of Java itself, and this always, whether the performance take place in the island itself, or in countries beyond it. A Javanese play consists of one continuous exhibition without scenes or acts. Jesters or drolls (badud and bañol) are introduced on the stage without any observance as to time or subject; and a band of music, consisting of the usual staccato instruments, which make a wild and plaintive music, is played throughout the performance.

Another kind of acting substitutes a sort of puppets for living actors: these puppets consist of pieces of leather richly painted and gilt, and always representing the same personages, celebrities of ancient story. They are put in motion behind a screen of white cloth, having a lamp behind, so as to resemble the figures from a magic lantern. The same master of the revels, the d'alang, moves the figures, and furnishes the dialogue or story, something after the manner of Punch. Of all these performances, the buffoonery is by far the best part.

DRESS. A mere outline of this subject will suffice to give the reader a general notion of it. In the hot climate of the Asiatic islands, the trees of the forest most probably furnished the raw materials of the first scanty clothing of its inhabitants, and that would consist of a mere covering for the loins. The fibrous inner bark of some trees furnishes, even at present, among the more civilised races, a main portion of the dress of the poorer classes. Cotton, however, has immemorially formed the staple of the clothing of all the more advanced races. Silk was found to form a portion of the dress of the upper classes on the first arrival of Europeans, imported wrought or raw from China; and since a direct intercourse with Europe, woollen cloths have been used to a very considerable extent by the same classes. To these are added, in the Philippine islands, fabrics of the Abaca, or textile banana, and of the Piña, or pine-apple leaf fibre; the first no doubt of native origin, but the last, from the nature of the material, certainly of American, through Europe.

Among all the more civilised nations, the most important portion of dress is that which covers the lower portion of the body, and this is the same for both sexes. It consists of a short web of cotton cloth, sown at the sides, and forming a sack open at both ends. Its usual Malay name, sarung, which literally signifies a case or sheath, has reference to its use. This is loosely secured by tucking the upper end into its own folds, or by a girdle. This kind of petticoat forms generally the only dress of the male sex of the working classes, and within doors of all classes; and on this account we find the early Portuguese writers, always representing the Indian islanders as "going naked from the waist upwards." The dress for the upper portion of the body consists of a jacket coming below the hips, called in Malay, baju, and in Javanese, rasukan; and the classes in easier circumstances wear under it a tight vest with a single row of buttons. The head is always bare with the women, but the men cover it with a small handkerchief, saputungan, literally, "hand-wiper." This is evidently an imitation of the turban, the Persian name for which, dástár, is only known to the learned. The Javanese, indeed, down even to the arrival of the Portuguese, seem to have used no head-dress, for Barbosa informs us that the people of this nation, whom he met at Malacca, "wore nothing on the head, but had their hair either arranged with art, or cropped." The Javanese, contrary to the usage of the Mahommedan nations of Western Asia, still continue to wear their long hair under the handkerchief. Trowsers are occasionally used under the sarung by the richer classes, and this portion of dress, like the imitation of the turban, seems to have been borrowed from the Arabs, as is implied by its Arabian name, sarual, corrupted saluwar.

Such is, generally, the dress of the more advanced nations of the Malayan Archipelago; but there are some distinctions of national costume, which consist chiefly in the manner of wearing the head-handkerchief, and in the pattern of the cloth of which the dress is made, and which last with the Malays and nations of Celebes is always a tartan, and with the Javanese a fabric of various colours, the dye being given by an expensive and tedious process, and not to the yarn but the web. The dress of the Philippine islanders is an exception to that of the rest of the inhabitants of the Archipelago, for it is modified by the costume of Spain. The men wear trowsers fastened at the waist by a running cord, and the women a petticoat, saya, and over these both sexes wear a shirt. The women use no head-dress, but the men hats of light native material. Of the costume of the Indian islanders generally, it may be remarked, that although sufficiently convenient and well adapted to the climate, it is wholly wanting in the flowing grace of the Arabian, Persian, or Hindu costumes.

DUCK. A species of duck has been immemorially domesticated by the more civilised nations of the Archipelago, but the bird is unknown to the ruder. Of the time or manner in which it was first introduced, it is impossible to form any reasonable conjecture. The name for the domestic duck in Malay is itik, and in Javanese bebek, both of them native words. The duck of Java is of a dirty-brown colour, that sports little in colour, that stands erect like a penguin, and that is not comparable in size or goodness of flesh to the European mallard. That it is not derived from any native wild species is certain, since no large wild duck exists in the western islands of the Archipelago; and, indeed, no wild duck at all except one teal, called by the Malays and Javanese mâliwis, the *Anas arcuata* or dendroygna of naturalists, a bird that is sometimes kept in tealeries, but has not been, and is probably not capable of being domesticated. The Malay name for the domestic duck, it may be remarked, extends to the cultivated languages of Celebes and the Philippine islands, from which it may be conjectured that like the common fowl, the dog, hog, and buffalo, it was introduced into Celebes and the Philippines by the Malayan nations, who are so well known to have frequented them immemorially as traders. In the Philippine Islands, or at least in the most northerly of them, Luzon, where a true wild duck is abundant, this is called by a native name, papan, while the domestic duck goes under the Malay one, itik. In Java and the principal Philippine islands, large flocks of ducks are kept for their flesh and eggs; the first being preserved by drying, and the last when salted forming a principal part of the stock of animal food in native sea voyages.

DUGONG. The Helicore dugong of naturalists is an inhabitant of the shallow seas of the Archipelago, but it is not numerous, or at least is not often caught by the fishermen. It is the duyong of the Malays, which naturalists mistaking a *j* or *y* for a *g*, have corrupted into dugong. During my residence in Singapore, a few were taken in the neighbouring shallow seas, and I can testify that the flesh of this herbivorous mammifer is greatly superior to that of the green turtle.

DUKU. The Malay and Javanese name of a tree and fruit of the genus Lansium, and natural order Meliaceæ of botanists. To the same genus belong the langseh, langsat or langsab, for in all these forms the word is written, the rambeh and the ayar-ayar, probably all four but varieties of the same species. The duku is the most esteemed of them, and to the European palate is the best of the native fruits of the Archipelago, after the mangostin. The natives class it after the durian and mangostin. It is of the size of a pigeon's egg, of a globular form, and covered with a coriaceous skin of the colour of parchment. The species seems to be indigenous in the western portion of the Archipelago, but to have been introduced into the Philippines where one variety of it, the langseh, is cultivated.

DUMARAN, the name of a small island forming part of the province of Calamianes in the Philippines, situated 3¼ leagues from the eastern coast of Paragua, in Palawan, and between north latitudes 10° 23′ and 10° 39′, and east longitude 119° 41′ and 120° 4′. It is computed to have an area of 151 square geographical miles, and in its greatest breadth and length to extend to 205 miles. Between it and Paragua lie innumerable islets, which make the navigation dangerous even for small boats. The coast of Dumaran itself is steep, and has no harbours for large ships, and even for boats there is shelter only in the favourable season. On the eastern coast of the island there is a small town of about 1750 inhabitants, and a Catholic mission. The interior is covered with a forest, which contains the wild buffalo, wild hog, and deer: its human inhabitants are unconverted. The people of the coast chiefly employ themselves in the fishery of the balate, or holothurion, the shell-tortoise and pearls, and in the search of the esculent swallows-nests.

DURIAN, the Durio Zibethinus of botanists, a large tree of the natural family of Bombaceæ, and itself the only plant of the genus. This famed fruit is about the size and form of a large melon, and contains esculent seeds resembling chestnuts, which are enveloped in a large quantity of a pale yellow pulp, which is the esteemed part of the fruit. This is of the consistence of clotted cream, and has the taste of fresh cream and filberts. Although possessing an offensive odour, resembling that of over-ripe apples, so powerful and diffusive as to taint the air of a whole town when it is in season, the pulp is rich without being cloying. The natives of the countries yielding the durian, prize it beyond all other fruits. In countries with a suitable climate, it flourishes without care or culture. It is most abundant in the western portion of the Archipelago, and extends east as far as the island of Mindano, the only one of the Philippine group in which it is known. It is abundant in Siam, however, up to the 13th and 14th degrees of north latitude; and again it is found on the coast of Tenasserim, in about the 14th degree of latitude, which is the furthest distance from the equator to which it has been successfully propagated. All attempts to cultivate it in any part of Hindustan have failed; nor has it, like some other Asiatic fruits, been transferred to tropical America. I did not find that it was grown in Cochin-China, although I think it most likely that it is so in some parts of Kamboja. A hot, moist, and equable climate would seem to be indispensable to the darian, but soil seems to be indifferent to it, for it thrives in the granitic, in the sandstone, and in the calcareous ones of the Peninsula and Sumatra, in the volcanic soil of Java, and in the rich alluvium of the valley of the Menam in Siam.

The name, which is perhaps most correctly written durian, is pure Malay, and is a derivative from the word duri, a thorn or prickle, in reference to the sharp tubercles with which the rind is covered. This name, with trifling variations, is that of the fruit in every country in which it is found from Java to Siam, and it has no other. From this, therefore, I think it may be inferred that the tree is a native of the country of the Malays, viz., Sumatra, the Peninsula, and their adjacent islands, and that through the Malays it was more widely disseminated. It may even be stated to grow wild in some, at least, of the countries named. An intelligent writer in the Journal of the Indian Archipelago, thus incidentally refers to the subject in a paper rendering an account of the wild inhabitants of the interior of the Malay peninsula. "In several places in the interior of the forest are found durian trees, always in a body together, to the number of about ten or twelve trees. Such places are for the Jakuns an object of great attention, and matter of work. They cut with the great axe all the other trees which surround the durians, that these, by receiving more air, may grow up more easily, and give finer and a greater quantity of fruit. They build there a small house, of which I will hereafter speak; and they then return to their ordinary habitations, which are sometimes distant from such places one or two days' journey." Another party, in the same publication, writes to the same effect respecting the durian, as it is seen to grow spontaneously in one of the small islands off the eastern coast of the peninsula, and which is nearly one entire forest down to the margin of the sea. "At Pulo tingi," says he, "we found orang-laut, or sea-gypsies, assembled. A large crop of durians, this season, had attracted tribes of them from the coasts of the peninsula, as well as from the islands of the Jehore Archipelago. Six boats from Moro, an island of that group, we found on their way to Pulo tingi; they had travelled by sea a distance of 180 miles, to partake of the fascinating fruit."

DURIAN ISLANDS. The name of two islands of the vast group at the eastern end of the straits of Malacca, between which is the passage into the China sea, called by European mariners the straits of Dryan, the last word being a corruption of durian. Like the rest of the group, these islands are of granitic and sedimentary formation, and both have peaks,—that of the largest being of the height of 656 feet above the level of the sea. Their coasts only are inhabited by Malay fishermen.

DUSUN, in Malay and Javanese means a village; and also the country distinguished from the town. It is the native synonym of the Sanscrit d'esa.

DUSUN. The name of one of the many wild tribes of the north-western side of Borneo. It inhabits the upper portion of the river of Brunai.

DUTCH. (In Malay and Javanese, OLANDA, a corruption of Holland.) The first appearance of the Dutch in the Archipelago was in 1596, seventy-six years after that of the Portuguese. Although their enterprise ended in the formation of an empire, their first sole object was the pursuit of the spice trade. In 1600, the Dutch East India Company, the model on which our own was formed two years later, was established; and in 1610, the Company appointed its first governor-general, Peter Both. Of the many that succeeded him, by far the most eminent was John Pietrsoon Koen, the real founder of the empire, the Clive of Netherland India, a man of talent, energy, resource, and strong will. The Dutch authorities at home had made the mistake of establishing the seat of government in the remote and sterile island of Amboyna; but Koen, on his own authority, placed it in Java, and in 1619 founded the city of Batavia, from which time may be dated the formation of the Dutch Indian empire. Many able governors-general succeeded Koen, but neither of him or of his most eminent successors, can it be said that they acquired an European reputation, which can for a moment be compared to several of the men of corresponding rank who founded the Spanish empire in America, or the British in India. Yet this cannot fairly be ascribed to any inferiority on the part of the Dutch officers, but rather to their talents having been exercised on a narrower and obscurer field. In comparing the Dutch with the English functionaries, one cause, the sordid, vulgar, and worthless object of pursuit, a commercial monopoly, militated alike against the fame of both; but in a far greater degree against that of the Dutch, who, dealing with ruder tribes, pushed the principle to a degree of rigour which was wholly impracticable with the English, having to do with far more civilised nations, whose country, moreover, yielded few or none of the products which stimulated the cupidity of the nations of Europe in the 16th, 17th, and 18th centuries.

The commencement of territorial acquisition by the Dutch preceded that by the English by at least 120 years, and has now been in progress for about 236 years. At present, the Netherland possessions are stated to extend from the third degree of north to the eleventh of south latitude, and from the ninety-fifth to the hundred and thirty-fourth of east longitude.

The area of the territory claimed by the Dutch, including tributaries, is estimated at 413,952 geographical square miles, of which 38,585 are in Java and Madura, and 375,367 in the other islands. In 1849, the population was stated as follows, namely, Java and Madura, 9,584,130; Sumatra, 3,430,000; Banca and Belliton, 50,000; Rhio and its Archipelago, 70,000; Borneo, 1,200,000; Celebes, 3,000,000; the Moluccas and their dependencies, 718,000; Timur and its dependencies, 800,000; Bali and Lomboc, 1,205,000. This gives a total population of 20,057,630. The relative population is therefore no more than 48·4 to the square mile, which shows that the far greater part of the vast region is unoccupied. The four islands of Java, Madura, Bali, and Lomboc, although embracing little above one-tenth of the whole area, contain better than one-half the whole population. The four islands in question have a relative population of 257·3 inhabitants to the square mile; while the rest of the islands have no more than 25, or less than a tenth part of the more fertile and civilised. With the exception of Java and Madura, the numbers here given are evidently mere computations, and most probably exaggerated ones. Considered as territorial possessions, Java alone is valuable in so far as concerns the maintenance of power, and the rest but an incumbrance. Java is, in fact, to the Netherlands what the valley of the Ganges is to Britain, for, like it, it yields the revenue by which all the other conquests or acquisitions have been made and are maintained.

DYAK, more correctly Dayak, is a word used by the Malays as a generic term for all the wild races of Sumatra and Celebes, but more especially of Borneo, where they are most numerous. It seems to be equivalent with them to the European word "savage." The word is most probably derived from the name of a particular tribe, and in a list of the wild tribes of the north-western coast of Borneo, furnished to me by Malay merchants of the country, one tribe of this name was included. In Borneo, the names given to the different tribes of this people seem, for the most part, to be derived from the rivers near which they dwell, as the Kayan or Dyaks of the river Kayan. The names of not fewer than fifty tribes of this people, inhabiting the north-western side of Borneo, were furnished to me by intelligent native merchants of Brunai. They are, perhaps, less numerous in the other quarters of the island, but between the territory of Sambas and that of Banjarmasin, ten different tribes are reckoned, and, probably, their whole number, including those of the interior, does not fall short throughout of one hundred. As these differ from each other in language,—in some respects in manners and customs, and to a considerable degree in social advancement,—we have here a condition of things far more resembling the wildest parts of Africa and America than of any portion of Asia.

The Dyaks of Borneo are in very different states of civilisation. Some of them are wanderers in the forest, without fixed habitation, living precariously on the produce of the chace, or collecting the spontaneous products of the woods, to be exchanged for food, with their more advanced neighbours. Others have fixed dwellings, consisting of great barn-like houses, accommodating many families,—cultivate corn and roots,—rear the cotton plant, spin and weave it,—manufacture malleable iron and steel, and breed the hog, common fowl, and dog, but no large quadruped for labour. Letters are wholly unknown to the Dyaks, for they have neither invented alphabetic writing themselves, nor adopted that of any of the other nations of the Archipelago. In whatever state of society, the Dyaks are all of one and the same race, and this race is the true Malayan,—brown complexioned men with lank hair, and of short stature.

The most numerous, powerful, and civilised of all the Dyaks, is the tribe of the Kayan, which extends across the island nearly from sea to sea, between the third degree of north and the first of south latitude. These have been described by two English travellers, who penetrated the interior of the island for several hundred miles, —Mr. Dalton in 1828 from the southern coast, and Mr. Burns in 1848 from the north-western. Both lived among the Kayans, and had the best opportunities of observing them. As this people are little known, I shall, therefore, copy some of these gentlemen's observations, most of which are equally applicable to the other less powerful tribes of Dyaks. This is Mr. Dalton's account of the distribution of the wild tribes over Borneo generally. "Borneo," says he, "is intersected with rivers of greater or less magnitude: every river has a distinct people, who will associate with no other, but wages continual war with all. The entrances of the rivers are the scene of unceasing warfare, as parties always lie in ambush about these parts, in hopes of surprising individuals who may be found fishing, or straying too far from their campongs (villages), where they may be cut off without notice or alarm. Every river has a raja, and a large one several. In particular parts, many of these chiefs are united under one great raja, the better to consolidate their strength, and insure protection by mutual support."

Mr. Dalton thus describes one of the ravaging expeditions of his host Selji, one of the principal chiefs of the Kayans. "The ravages of these people are dreadful: in August, 1828, Selji returned to Marpao from an excursion. His party had been three months absent, during which time, besides detached huts, he had destroyed seventeen campongs, with the whole of the men and old women. The young women and children were brought prisoners. The former amounted to 113 and the latter to about 200. He had with him about 40 war boats or large canoes, none less than 95 feet in length. The one set apart for Selji and his women was 105 feet long. I was nearly two months in this boat in various directions with him when Selji was in search of heads. The swiftness of these canoes is incredible: when going down the river with the stream, they have the appearance of a bird skimming the water. The sensation is such that I invariably fell asleep. The perseverance of the Dyaks during an expedition is wonderful; they generally get information of distant campongs from the women taken prisoners (no man ever escapes to tell the tale), who soon become attached to the conquerors. In proceeding towards a distant campong the canoes are never seen on the river during the day-time. They invariably commence their journey about half an hour after dark, when they pull rapidly and silently up the river close to the bank. One boat keeps immediately behind another, and the paddles are covered with the soft bark of a tree, so that no noise whatever is made. In Selji's last expedition, it was forty-one days before a campong was surprised, although several canoes were cut off in the river, owing to the superior sailing of his boats. After paddling all night without intermission, about half an hour before daylight, they pull the boats up upon the banks, amongst the jungle and thick trees, so that from the river it is impossible to see them, or discover the least trace of their route. Here they sleep, and feed upon monkeys, snakes, or any other animals they can reach with their sumpits (blow-pipes): wild hogs are their favourite food, and they are in abundance. If these fail them, the young sprouts of certain trees and wild fruit will answer the purpose. Nothing comes amiss to the stomach of a Dyak. Should the rajas want flesh and it cannot be procured with the sumpit, one of their followers is killed, which, not only provides them with a good meal, but a head to boot. Whilst part of the people are employed in hunting and cooking, others ascend the highest trees to examine the country, and observe if a campong or hut be near, which they discover by the smoke. Should it be a solitary hut, they surround it and take care no one escapes, but should it be a considerable campong, they go much more warily to work. When the boats have arrived within about a mile of a campong, they prepare themselves: about a third of the party are sent forward, who penetrate the thickish part of the jungle, arriving at night near the houses. These are surrounded, and men are placed in every footpath leading from them, for the purpose of intercepting all who may attempt to escape into the woods. In the meantime, the remainder of the party, in their boats, arrive a few hours before day-light, in perfect silence, within a few hundred yards of the campung, when most of the warriors put on their fighting dress, and creep slowly forward, leaving a few men in each boat; likewise, about a dozen men with the women who remain in the jungle. About twenty minutes before day-break, they commence operations by throwing on the ataps (thatch) of the huts lighted fire-balls made of the dry bark of trees and damar (resin), which immediately involves the whole in flames. The war-cry is then raised, and the work of murder commences. The male inhabitants are speared, or more commonly cut down with the mandow (cutlass) as they descend the ladders of their dwellings in attempting to escape the flames, which Selji remarked to me gave just sufficient light to distinguish a man from a woman. The women and children endeavouring to gain the jungle by the well-known paths find them already occupied by an enemy, from whom there is no escaping. They, of course, surrender themselves, and are collected together on the appearance of day-light. When the signal is first given (always by the raja), the people in the boats pull rapidly. Some boats are placed in the river above the campung, some below it, and the remainder abreast of the huts, so that should any of the unfortunate beings gain their sampans (canoes), they are certainly cut off in the water. The principal object is to prevent a single person escaping to give intelligence to other campungs, and to arrange the time, so that the day shall dawn about ten or fifteen minutes after the slaughter begins, which enables them to take their stations and fire the houses in the midst of darkness, and afterwards affords sufficient light to seize their prey. After the women and children are collected, the old women are killed, and the heads of the men cut off. The brains are then taken out and the heads held over a fire, for the purpose of smoking and preserving them. The women and children are only secondary considerations: the heads are what they want, and there is no suffering a Dyak will not cheerfully endure to be recompensed by a single one. From the last excursion, Selji's people brought with them 700, of which 250 fell to the share of himself and his sons. The women and children all belong to him in the first instance. Many of Selji's people are cannibals. Some, however, will not eat human flesh, while others refuse to do so, except on particular occasions, as a birth, a marriage, or a funeral. All these events are celebrated with fresh heads. Nothing can be done without them. All kinds of sickness, particularly the small-pox, are supposed to be under the influence of an evil spirit, which nothing can so well propitiate as a head. A Dyak who has taken many heads, may be immediately known from others who have not been so fortunate: he comes into the presence of the raja and takes his station without hesitation, whilst an inferior person is glad to creep into a corner to escape notice."—Moore's Indian Archipelago, p. 48.

The same writer describes the arms of the Dyaks and their manner of fighting very graphically. "On going to war they wear defensive armour made of the skins of wild beasts, generally of the black bear, which is very numerous, but the raja will have a tiger's skin. They are put over the head, and effectually cover the breast and back, leaving the arms naked. This, with a helmet curiously wrought with bamboo, is proof against the sumpit, spear, or sword. Each man carries a shield, which is made of light hard wood, covered with skin. It is adapted to the height of the wearer, generally about five feet in length and two in breadth, turned inwards and held with the left hand. When the chiefs engage hand to hand, they, after the spirit of chivalry, throw these away. After skirmishing with the sumpit, they usually come to close quarters. What the chiefs principally aim at is a surprise, but the adverse party, knowing his enemy is in the field, always provides against this, and as one side is as cunning as the other, they usually in the end, come to open blows. Their personal combats are dreadful: they have no idea of fear, and fight until they are cut to pieces. Indeed, their astonishing strength, agility, and peculiar method of taking care of themselves, are such that I am firmly of opinion a good European swordsman would stand little chance with them, man to man, as, except at their arms, he could not get a cut at them. The temper of the steel with which they make their mandows is such that it does not require a powerful man to cut through a musket-barrel at a single blow. The Dyaks, in fighting, always strike and seldom thrust. Indeed, their mandow is not calculated for it, but the small sword would be useless against them, as it would not penetrate the thick skin in front, over which, above the navel, they attach a very large shell. I have been present when Selji has taken two campungs: the inhabitants were surprised, and the fighting, consequently, all on one side, but in a few instances resistance was offered. I did not observe them attempt to parry the blows with their weapons. These were either received on the shield, or met by the bamboo cap. As the men of the campungs had no time given them to cover themselves, they were easily cut down. The noise is terrific during the massacre, for it can be called nothing else, and joined in by all the raja's women, who accompany him in his excursions. I was always stationed amongst them, far from any danger."—Ibid.

It is strange enough that with a long and almost daily familiarity with inter-tribal warfare, conducted in their own ruthless manner, the Dyaks should, down to the present day, have as great a dread of fire-arms as the Aztec nations on the invasion of Cortes. Such, however, is the case, for the fact is attested by several independent witnesses, of whom Mr. Dalton is the best. "What these people most dread," says he, "is the musket. It is inconceivable what a sensation of fear comes over the bravest of the Dyaks when they have an idea that a few muskets may possibly be brought against them. No inducement will prevail on them, however numerous, to go forward. Hence the Bugis, with a handful of men act towards them as they think proper, making them deliver over, not only the produce of the country for a trifling exchange, but a certain number of their children yearly, whom they sell as slaves. Selji can bring together 12,000 fighting men, and yet the Bugis, with fifty muskets and a few boat-swivels will not hesitate to meet them. The fact is, they no sooner hear the report of a gun, than they run deep into the jungle. If they are in boats, they leap into the water, and after gaining the shore, never stop until they are out of hearing of the report. The most sensible of the Dyaks have a superstitious idea of fire-arms. Each man, on hearing the report, fancies the ball is making directly towards himself. He therefore, runs, never thinking himself safe as long as he hears the explosion of gunpowder. Thus a man, hearing the report of a swivel five miles off, will still continue at full speed with the same trepidation as at first. They have not the least conception of the range of gun-barrels. I have been frequently out with Selji and other chiefs shooting monkeys, birds, &c., and offended them by refusing to fire at large birds at the distance of a mile or more. They invariably put such refusal down to ill-nature on my part. Again, firing at an object, they cannot credit it is missed, although they see the bird fly away, but consider that the shot is yet pursuing it, and it must fall at last. The Bugis take great care to confirm them in their great dread of fire-arms."

The testimony of Sir James Brooke, who had been often engaged in hostilities with the boldest of the Dyaks of the north-western side of Borneo, is to the same effect. "The Saribas," says he, "are by no means so warlike as the others" (the Sakarans), "and from their dread of fire-arms may be kept in subjection by a comparatively small body of Malays. The sound of musketry or cannon was enough to put the whole body to flight, and when they did run, fully the half disappeared, returning to their own homes."—Journal, vol. i. p. 237. 1848.

It would appear, however, that the Kayans of the northern coast, who have advanced as conquerors from the southern, have in some measure conquered their superstitious fear of fire-arms. These tribes occupy the country situated on the two great rivers, Baram and Rajang, and have emancipated themselves from the control of the Malays, and even captured their cannon. "Knipa Batu," says Mr. Burns, "is a chief of considerable power and influence: he rules the lower districts of the river" (the Rajang). "His residence is situated above the great rapids, and is strongly barricaded with thick planks, in front of which are placed an old iron six-pounder, two brass Dutch-made two-pounders, and upwards of twenty brass lelahs of different sizes" (long swivel guns of small calibre). "At the house of the chief, Batu Dian, which is about ten miles further up, there are also fifteen guns similar to the above. The majority of these guns were captured during the wars with the people of the coast" (the Malays).

The human heads, so ardently sought after and so carefully preserved by the Kayans and other Dyaks, it is certain are chiefly esteemed as trophies of victory and evidences of personal prowess, and this is satisfactorily shown by the fact that no value is attached to the heads of women and children. The practice, indeed, is similar to, and has the same origin as, the head-preserving of the New Zealanders, and of the hairy scalp by the North American Indians. In fact, the Dyaks preserve heads as we preserve banners, and for the same reason. It would appear, however, that the deeds of which they are memorials are apt, in the lapse of time, to be forgotten, for Mr. Burns tells us that among the Kayan tribes that he visited, he found only four-and-twenty heads, and that the chiefs informed him that when they were quitting their former locality for their present, they threw an accumulation of no fewer than 700 into the river, not choosing to be encumbered with them on their march.

On the subject of religion, Mr. Dalton observes, "I cannot ascertain that the Dyaks have any religion amongst themselves, or entertain an idea of future rewards and punishments. They have no fear whatever of dying in battle, or otherwise, provided they are in no danger of losing their heads. They have, however, the utmost dread of such an event occurring, which they conceive the greatest, and, indeed, the only misfortune that can befall them; and this feeling seems to emanate from the knowledge of the triumph their enemies enjoy from getting possession of this greatest of all treasures; for all Dyaks in every part of Borneo, and likewise in Celebes, have the same predilection for cutting off the heads of their enemies, and every stranger is regarded as an enemy. It is, however, most certain, they have some idea of a future state. This not only appears in their burials, but on other occasions."

Mr. Burns adds to this, that "they have no idols, nor any apparent representation of the Deity,—no priests,—no castes,—nor any ostensible ceremonial system of religion." This is, no doubt, all true of the Dyaks, as it is of all people in the same state of society. But, although without any organised religion, or, as the Malays express it, "without book," they have an abundance of superstitions which take its place. They believe in malignant spirits, and have names for some of the most potent of them, as Tanangan, Tâpa, Jaruwang, &c., &c., and they have even adopted the butas, or goblins of the Malays and Javanese, and through these parties the dewata, or gods of the Hindus. They believe, moreover, and to a remarkable degree, in omens and the flight of birds. Their funeral rites attest that they have some obscure notions of an existence after death. "The burials of these people," says Mr. Dalton, "are no less singular than their marriages. The old men have every attention paid to them whilst living, and, indeed, long after they die. On the death of a chief or raja, they dress him out in his war habiliments, and carry him to the grave, after keeping him in the house a certain time, according to his rank, seldom longer than ten days, on a large litter, enveloped in a white cloth. They lay the body in a place prepared, without a coffin. By his side are deposited his arms, particularly his shield, spear, and mandow (sword). A quantity of rice and fruit are likewise interred, with such other articles of food as the deceased was most partial to. The grave is then closed up, a high mound raised, and this is encircled with strong bamboo, upon which fresh heads are placed, as the most acceptable offering to the deceased. No warrior would dare to appear before the family of the chief without at least one head as a consoling present. These heads are thickly studded round the grave, and occasionally renewed during the first year or two, the old ones being considered the property of the succeeding chief."

Mr. Burns's account is somewhat different, although generally agreeing with that of Mr. Dalton's; the difference probably arising from variation in customs between tribes of the same nation living far apart from each other. "After death," says he, "the Kayans very stupidly keep the body in the house from four to eight days, and even sometimes longer. Generally, the first day after death, it is put into a coffin scooped from the trunk of a tree, and carved according to the importance or means of the relatives. Day and night during the time the body is kept in the house, lights are placed at each side of the coffin, and, should they happen to get extinguished, it is considered most unfortunate. Also, during four or five days after the corpse has been removed, torches are kept at the place where it lay. Previous to its removal, a feast is prepared, and part of the food is placed beside the corpse; the relatives devour the remainder. Removal takes place soon after, and although the body is invariably much decomposed, the nearest relatives, especially women, express their grief in a most inconsolable manner, and with cries most pitiable,—long and affectionately hug the coffin, and, with their faces on it, inhale the odour, and continue doing so until it reaches the place of disposal, which is in the loft of a small wooden house on posts about twelve feet high. The tombs of the chiefs are built of hard wood, supported by nine massive posts from twelve to fourteen feet high, and which, with the other parts, are elaborately carved. Several articles, which belonged to the dead person, are conveyed to the tomb with the corpse, but are not deposited with it. On the death of a person, the relatives directly lay aside all apparel of foreign manufacture, and wear only a kind of bark cloth instead, for a prescribed number of days after the funeral."—Journal of the Indian Archipelago, page 149.

The sacrifices offered to appease evil spirits take the form of immolation, or the shedding of blood in some form or another, among the Dyaks, and must be considered as part of their religion. All diseases are considered to be caused by these evil genii, and Mr. Burns gives us an example of the sacrifices performed in a case of this kind:

"It is the blood only," says he, "that is prized, or considered efficacious. That blood is considered to be so by them, the following might tend to show. During my stay in the house of Knipa Batu, one of his children, a little boy, was at the point of death from fever. After exhausting all their skill in applying remedies, as a last resource the chief took a young chicken, and passed it a number of times over the face of the child. Then, with his most valued war-sword, killed it at the window, and threw it upwards from him, in the direction of the setting sun. The sword, with the blood on it, he then held over the face of the child as before, with a fervent invocation, desiring that his child might not die; and, laying himself down beside the unconscious little sufferer, he indulged in the wildest paroxysm of grief."

The victim, however, it would appear, is not always of so harmless a description. "Regarding human sacrifice, the Kayans strenuously deny," says the same writer, "the practice, at the present day; but it would seem to have been prevalent amongst them formerly, especially on the occasion of the king or principal chief taking possession of a new-built house, and also on the occasion of his death. They acknowledge that an instance of this most revolting custom took place about two years ago, on the occasion of the chief Batu-dian taking possession of his new house. The victim was a Malay slave girl, brought from the coast for the avowed purpose, and sold to the chief by a man who was also a Malay. It is said to be contrary to the Kayan custom to sell or sacrifice one of their own nation. In the case alluded to, the unfortunate victim was bled to death. The blood was taken and sprinkled on the pillars, and under the house, but the body was thrown into the river."

The singular custom of swearing a solemn friendship may be considered a religious ceremony, and is stated to be peculiar to the Kayans. Both the authors cited underwent the ceremony, and describe it in nearly the same terms. This is Mr. Dalton's account of it. "During my detention in Borneo, altogether fifteen months, I experienced much attention and kindness from many Dyak chiefs, particularly from Selji, with whom I was some months. Indeed, I was always of opinion that I was unsafe elsewhere. Being the first and only European he had ever seen, we no sooner met than I informed him, through an interpreter, as he could not speak a word of Malay, that I had come on the part of the Europeans to make friends with him; and trusted he and his people would do me no harm. I mentioned this at once, fearing the Sultan of Coti (a Malay prince) had given some previous orders by no means favourable towards me. Selji replied that he was incapable of such an act, but for our future good understanding it was proper that all his followers should know on what footing we were, and therefore requested I would make friendship. On my gladly consenting, he went in person and stuck a spear into the ground above his father's grave. This being the signal for a general assembly, each of the chiefs sent a person to know the rajah's pleasure. It was that every warrior should assemble around the grave by twelve o'clock the next day. Some thousands were present; a platform of bamboo was raised above twelve feet above the grave, and on this Selji and I mounted, accompanied by an Aji, his high priest. After some previous ceremony, the Aji produced a small silver cup which might hold about two wine-glasses, and then, with a piece of bamboo made very sharp, drew blood from the raja's right arm. The blood ran into the cup until it was nearly full. He then produced another cup of a similar size, and made an incision in my arm, a little above the elbow, and filled it with blood. The two cups were then held up to the view of the surrounding people, who greeted them with loud cheers. The Aji now presented me with the cup with Selji's blood, giving him the other one with mine. Upon a signal we drank off the contents, amidst the deafening noise of the warriors and others. The Aji then half filled one of the cups again from Selji's arm, and with my blood made it a bumper. This was stirred up with a piece of bamboo, and given to Selji, who drank about half. He then presented the cup to me, and I finished it. The noise was tremendous: thus the great raja Selji and I became brothers. After this ceremony I was perfectly safe, and from that moment felt myself so during my stay among his people. Drinking the blood, however, made me ill for two days, as I could not throw it off my stomach. The raja took his share with great gusto. Great festivities followed, and abundance of heads were brought in, for nothing can be done without them. Three days and nights all ranks of people danced round the heads, after being, as usual, smoked, and the brains taken out, drinking a kind of toddy, which soon intoxicates them. They are then taken care of by the women, who do not drink—at least I never observed them."

Although it be stated by Burns that the Kayans have no priesthood, it will be seen from the account now given, that parties performing at least some of its functions, do really exist. Most probably they will be found to be persons professing to heal by charms and incantations. The name applied to them, Aji, is Sanskrit, and means incantation. In all likelihood, the Kayans received it through the Javanese, whose monuments of the times of Hinduism are described by Mr. Dalton as being frequent throughout their country. See Borneo.

The Kayans believe in the existence of birds of good and of ill omen, regulating their conduct especially by the manner of flight of such birds, and this, probably, in a greater degree than any people since the days of the Romans. Mr. Dalton gives the following account of a bird of ill omen, which may probably be the Kâdasih of the Javanese, a species of cuckoo, the Cuculus flavus of naturalists, whose plaintive, pleasing, but monotonous note is considered by this people as ill-boding. "There is a certain bird of which they stand in great awe. When they hear the note of this bird, no inducement can urge them further on the same line of road. I have been frequently out shooting when we heard it. On such occasions they would invariably stop and tremble violently, and immediately take another road. I never could obtain a sight of this bird of ill-omen, for such it is considered. If I attempted to advance a single step nearer the sound, they took hold of me, and pointing towards the sky with gestures of apprehension, forced me a contrary way. The notes are very similar to those of our blackbird—equally sweet, but much stronger. Notwithstanding my becoming brother to the great raja, I always entertained an impression that I should be murdered, if by mischance I happened to shoot one of these birds. It is evidently a superstitious feeling, this particular bird being looked upon as an evil genius."—page 53.

The following is Mr. Burns's account. "The custom of drawing omens from the direction of the flight of birds is common to most of the tribes of Borneo, but with the Kayans it is not connected with their ideas of the Deity. The birds that are held as ominous by them are about ten in number. From the flight of the rhinoceros horn-bill they draw omens of success, or the reverse, in war; and any of the ominous kind flying from the right to the left bank of the river, is considered inauspicious, but the reverse favourable and a prognostic of success. Journeying on the rivers, should one of the ominous sort cross from the right, they immediately halt,—kindle a fire on the shore,—smoke their leafy cigars, and generally wait till a bird less vindictively inclined crosses from the opposite direction. If this does not happen, they very often return to the place from which they started. One instance I experienced from the whim of a pretty little bird called lukut, from its being spotted or streaked, taking its flight from the right to the left bank of the river. I was obliged to retrace a considerable distance to the place we slept at the previous night, and recommence our journey the following morning. On another occasion, in descending the upper part of the Tatau river, one of the birds of fate crossed from the unlucky side. The party immediately halted,—went on shore,—kindled a fire and betook themselves to their accustomed smoking over it, but were not disposed to move onward, unless one more favorably disposed should take its flight from the opposite side. However, on reminding them of their belief, that fire is efficacious in appeasing the hate of birds, and that they had observed their usual custom of kindling a fire and smoking, they were prevailed on to resume an onward course." Vol. v., p. 147.

The strangest of the customs of the Kayans, and it extends to several of the other wild tribes of Borneo, is in some degree analagous to circumcision, although far more painful, dangerous and preposterous. It is called in the language of the Kayans utang, and the operation is performed at the age of puberty. The people themselves can give no account of its origin, nor assign any reason for it. Both the writers whom I have so frequently cited, describe the operation fully. "There are certain people," says Mr. Dalton, "who perform this operation on boys arriving at the age of puberty.—The pain is such that many are affected, and die of lock-jaw; whilst many others die from mortification taking place. It is shocking to observe the state to which many of them are reduced in consequence of this singular and absurd custom." It is remarkable that this custom, however absurd, does not appear to have been peculiar to the wild tribes of Borneo, for it extended to the Philippines, or at least to the large island of Çebu before the conversion of the inhabitants to Christianity; and Pigafetta describes the operation almost in the same terms and details as our recent English travellers.—Primo Viaggio intorno al Globo, p. 94.

The practice of perforating the lobes of the ears, and distending them by the use of ponderous ear-rings, so that they shall reach to the shoulders, and sometimes even the bosom, and that of tattooing, exist among the wild inhabitants of Borneo as among many other savage nations, but there is nothing peculiar about them. Mr. Dalton's account of the use of poisoned arrows is curious, although I must consider the effects he ascribes to them as exaggerated, "Of the sumpits," says he, "I need not say much; they are similar to those used in various parts of the island. The darts are of various sorts: those used in war are poisoned by dipping them in a liquid taken from a young tree, called by the Dyaks, upo. The effects are almost immediately fatal. I have seen in Selji's boat, when a man was struck in the hand, the poison ran so quickly up the arm, that by the time the elbow was green the wrist was black. The man died in about four minutes; the smell from the hand was very offensive. Each man carries about with him a small box of lime juice. By dipping the dart into this before they put it into the sumpit, the poison becomes active, in which state they blow it. They will strike an object at forty yards, and will kill a monkey or bird at that distance. When the darts are poisoned they will throw them sixty yards, as in war, or at some large ferocious animal, which they seldom eat. However, I have seen them eat of the flesh notwithstanding it was killed with a poisoned dart. In such cases they boil it before roasting, which, they say, extracts the poison."—Vol. v., p. 51. The word sumpit, used by Mr. Dalton, is correctly sumpitan, the first two syllables making a Malay verb, meaning to perflate with the mouth; and the last, the tube or instrument through which perflation is performed. The upo of the Kayans is most probably a corruption of the Javanese word upas, poison or venom.

Such, then, are the manners and customs of the most advanced and most powerful of the native tribes of Borneo. The Kayans cultivate corn and cotton; rear the common fowl, the hog, and the dog; and by the help of an excellent ore, fabricate the best iron and steel of the whole Archipelago, They have extended their conquests nearly from sea to sea; and if we would credit the statements of Mr. Dalton, their numbers cannot be fewer than a quarter of a million. This, however, is the utmost extent of power and civilisation to which any indigenous tribe of Borneo seems ever to have reached; while in all the large islands, except New Guinea, and in many of the smaller ones, a far higher civilisation has sprung up. The race of men in Borneo is one and the same with that of the other islands, and I imagine the difference in social progress can only be ascribed to the obstacles which the physical geography of Borneo has opposed to the development of an indigenous civilisation. These consist in the absence of untimbered plains, the universal presence of a deep and almost impenetrable forest, a comparative sterility or stubbornness of soil, and a density of land which precludes an easy communication with more civilised strangers. The only advantage which Borneo possesses over the other large islands, consists in its mineral wealth,—its gold, iron, and coal; but this would not be available to any effective extent, in the promotion of an early civilisation. The result has been, that even the most improved of the aboriginal inhabitants of Borneo are still unlettered savages, and sometimes cannibals. Even the small advancement which they have made, may, on the evidence of language, be traced, in no small degree, to their communication with strangers; as in the instances of the cultivation of corn, roots, cotton, the manufacture of textile materials, and of iron. Few of the savages of Borneo are in so low a state as the majority of those of tropical America; but notwithstanding the great advantage possessed by them in a knowledge of iron, the most advanced have not attained, by any means, so large a measure of civilisation as that which sprung up on the elevated and open plateaus of that continent.

A few of the Dyaks of Borneo have adopted the Mahommedan religion. These consist of such tribes as have been long in immediate communication with the Malay settlers of the coasts. This conversion is followed by the adoption of the manners, customs, and even language of the Malays; so that, in time, they are merged into Malays, and come to be considered as such. The Dyak passion for pork is reasonably stated to prove a serious obstacle to conversion. When this conversion does not take place, the subjugated Dyaks are always found to be living in a state of Helotism.

DYEING. The Javanese, who of all the Malayan race, have certainly made the highest progress in all the useful arts, have a specific term for dyeing or tinting,—mâdal; but the Malays express it only by the word for dipping,—châlup. Yet the only generic words which either of them possess for "colour," are the Sanscrit, warna; and the Portuguese, tinta. Their colours are usually sombre,—little varied, but generally fast. Blues are always produced from indigo, yielded for the most part by the Indigofera tinctoria, as in other parts of India; but in Sumatra, occasionally, from the Marsdenia tinctoria, a plant of the natural order of the Asclepiadeæ. Yellows are produced from the woods of two species of Artocarpus, the jack and châmpädah, and from turmeric; and reds from the bark of the roots of the mangkudu, the Morinda umbellata,—from the kusumba-jawa, safflower or Carthamus tinctorius, from the kusumba-kling, which is the arnotto, or Bixa orellana, from the sâpang, or sapan-wood, Cæsalpinia sappan, and from the nidus of the lac insect. Black is produced from the rinds of the mangostin fruit, and of the kâtapang, Terminalia catappan, with sulphate of iron. Sails and nets are dyed, and perhaps also tanned with a wood called in Sumatra ubar, which is the Ricinus tanarius of botanists. The mordants used are rice-bran, alkalis from the combustion of some vegetable matters, as the fruit stalks and mid-ribs of the coco-nut palm, and alum brought from China.

Most of the dyeing materials, but not all, are probably native products. The name of the indigo-plant, the Indigofera tinctoria, is a native word to all appearance. In Malay it is tarum, and this, with some corruptions, as talum in the Lampung, tom in Javanese, tayum in Tagala, and tayung in Bisaya, is universal. This would seem to indicate that the culture of it, at least, had been spread from Sumatra to the Philippines. The drug, however, is as universally known by the Sanscrit name nila, or blue, from which it may be conjectured that the art of extracting the dye was taught the islanders by the Hindus. It is always manufactured in the Archipelago in a liquid, and therefore in a rude, form, yet in this state there is a considerable exportation of it from Java. Safflower and arnotto are, no doubt, both exotics, the last, in all likelihood, made known by the Portuguese. The name of both is the Sanscrit kasumba; the safflower having annexed to it the epithet "Javanese," and the arnotto "kling," or Hindu, to distinguish them, although the last be undoubtedly American. Copperas and alum trusi and tawas are native words, yet the articles nowhere produced within the Archipelago. They are now imported from China, but probably were so in earlier times from India.

E.

EAGLE-WOOD. See AGILA.

EARTHENWARE. See POTTERY.

EARTHQUAKE. See VOLCANO.

EBONY. The kayu-arâng, literally, "charwood" in Malay and Javanese, and so called, of course, from its blackness, is found in most of the countries of the Asiatic Archipelago, from the Peninsula and Sumatra to the Philippine Islands. It is probably the produce of several species of Diospyrus, but chiefly of Diospyrus melanaxylon. It is greatly inferior in quality to the ebony of Ceylon and the Mauritius, the produce of Diospyrus ebenus.

ECLIPSE. The names for an eclipse of the sun or the moon are all that is known about eclipses by the Indian Islanders. The word for an eclipse is the Sanscrit one, grahana. An eclipse of the sun is, therefore, called grahana-mata-ari, and of the moon grahana-bulan, in Malay. But eclipses of both luminaries represent them as "sick," and so we have sakit-mata-ari and sakit-bulan, "sickness of the sun," and "sickness of the moon." An eclipse of the moon is also expressed by the native phrase bulan-makan-rahu,—the moon eaten by the dragon. The word rahu is Sanscrit, and the name of a monster supposed to aim at devouring the moon. During an eclipse the rice-stampers are clattered in their mortars, in order to frighten the monster from his meditated mischief. In Java, for example, there is not a rice-mortar among ten millions of people that is not put in requisition on such an occasion.

ELEPHANT. The elephant is found in abundance, in the wild state, in almost every part of Sumatra, where they are seen in troops of 30 and even of 60, and in the Malay peninsula, especially towards its northern portion. It was long supposed to be confined to those two countries of the Archipelago; but there is now no question but that it exists also in parts of Borneo, namely, the districts of Pahitan, and the Sandakan at its northern end, with the peninsula of Unsang forming its north-eastern extremity. This had been long insisted on by the natives of Borneo; and although no European has yet seen the animal itself, the fact of its tusks having been brought as an article of trade from the places in question to the British settlement of Labuan, would seem to settle the question of its existence. Considering, however, that the elephant does not exist in any other part of Borneo than those named, there is room to suspect that the individuals found in these may be the descendants of those which were found in the domesticated state on the first arrival of Europeans in the island, and which were seen and described by Pigafetta, in 1521.

The learned and indefatigable Netherland naturalists of India have lately made an unexpected discovery respecting the elephant of Borneo. They have found it to be a species distinct both from the African and Asiatic, and hence have given it the name of Elephas Sumatrensis. It approaches nearest in form to the Asiatic elephant, but differs from it very materially. The ribbon-formed ridges on the crown of the teeth are larger and more prominent. The dorsal vertebræ, instead of 19, amount to 20; but the sacral vertebræ, instead of being five, amount to four only; while, instead of 19 pairs of ribs, it has 20. Whether the elephant of the Malay peninsula be the same with the Sumatran, or with the common Asiatic, or whether it be different from either, is a point which has not been ascertained.

Both the elephant of Sumatra and of the peninsula are, like the Asiatic species, and as the African once was, amenable to domestication. In the northern states of the Malay peninsula they are, in fact, domesticated and employed as beasts of burden; and in Sumatra, they were once tamed and used by the kings of Achin for parade. From both countries they are occasionally caught, tamed, and exported by the Telingas to the Coromandel coast. I have no doubt, also, that in old times they were exported to Java; for they are abundant in the nearest part of Sumatra to that island, the country of the Lampungs. For the purposes of court ceremonies or for war, the elephant was found by the Europeans, on their first arrival in the Archipelago, in places where they no longer exist. Thus, at the capture of Malacca, the king and his son, each on their elephants carrying a wooden tower, charged the Portuguese, and in the pursuit of the fugitive king after the capture, mention is made by the Portuguese historians of the taking of seven elephants. And when the companions of Magellan touched at Borneo, and visited the king, in 1521, Pigafetta informs us that he himself and his associates were conveyed from the river side to the palace on caparisoned elephants.

It seems highly probable that the natives of the Asiatic Archipelago were ignorant of the art of taming the elephant until instructed by the Hindus. This is to be inferred, not only from the prevalence of Sanscrit names for the elephant itself, but from matters connected with its domestication. The usual name in Malay is the Sanscrit one, gajah; and, indeed, it was long before I myself found out that it had a native one. This is beram, although now obsolete. The Sanscrit name, gajah, prevails all over the Archipelago,—even where the elephant is known only by repute. Thus, in the Tagala of the Philippines, we find it in the corrupt form of gaya, and in the Bisaya of the same group, as garya. In the language of Java, an island in which the animal could only be an exotic, it has no fewer than seven names, all Sanscrit, although some of them be only epithets. Among the terms connected with the domestication of the elephant that are taken from the Sanscrit, are the elephant driver, or attendant, gâbala-gaja, literally, "elephant groom," bâlanggu, the fetters, and kusa, the driving-crook. The names of the tusks, of the decoy elephant, and of the elephant trap are, however, pure Malay.

ENGANO. The most southerly, and one of the largest, of the chain of islands which runs along the western coast of Sumatra, and reckoned to be, in all, no fewer than 300 in number. The origin of the name is uncertain, but is probably from the Portuguese word, engaño, fraud or deception, which, joined to the Malay word, pulo, as usual in such cases, would make "Deception Island." The western end of Engano is in south latitude 5° 21′, and its east end in longitude 102° 7′ 15″. Along with some small islands near it, it is computed to have an area of 400 geographical square miles. It is surrounded and girdled by a coral reef, on which a heavy surf breaks, making landing difficult. The soil is red clay, most probably the produce of the decomposition of sandstone. It does not appear to contain any mountain of considerable elevation; but the whole land is of sufficient height to be visible at sea, at the distance of seven or eight leagues. As usual, it is covered with large timber. On the south-east side of the island there is a safe harbour, formed by a bay fronted by four islets. The inhabitants of Engano are of the genuine Malayan race, but in a very rude state. Their chief subsistence is the coco-nut, yams, and the banana, with fish. They have no knowledge of any textile material, going naked, with the exception of a shred of prepared bark or dried banana-leaf at the waist; and no knowledge of iron, their weapon being a spear tipped with fish-bone. They have canoes, however, which are capable of accommodating five or six men. Of the language of Engano, we have no specimens. It is, however, wholly unintelligible to the Malays, and will probably be found to be a peculiar and distinct tongue. The people appear to be the rudest of all the inhabitants of the chain of islands to which it belongs, attributable, no doubt, to its distance from the mainland of Sumatra, twenty leagues, its coral-fortified shore and its sterility of soil. Here, indeed, we find the true unmixed Malayan race, the same from which has sprung up the civilisation of Java and Sumatra, in a much lower condition than tribes of the Polynesian race in the islands of the Pacific.

ERA. The only people of the Asiatic Archipelago who possessed an era before the conversions to Mahommedanism and the advent of the Portuguese, were the Javanese and the Balinese. This era was not a native one, but derived from the Hindus of Southern India,—that of Saka or Salivana, which commences with the 78th year of Christ. It is still in use in Bali, but only nominally so in Java. Down to the year of our time, 1633, or for 155 years after the last Hindu dynasty, it seems to have been preserved in Java with its solar or sidereal reckoning, but in that year, lunar time was adopted, and as no intercalation is practised, the Javanese era and that of Salivana no longer correspond. Thus the year of 1820 of Christ was the year of Salivana 1742, but of Java, 1747. By the Javanese this era is called Saka-warsa and Saka-kala, terms which are Sanscrit, and signify year and time of Saka,—that is, of Salivana, a personage made in their story to be the first foreign sovereign of Java, under the appellation of Aji Saka, or "King Saka." There is no evidence to show that the Malays had any era, native or foreign, before their adoption of the Hejira. They seem, however, to have had a solar year, and, like the Chinese, to have reckoned in it by the reigns of their kings, the number of years of each reign being always specified in their annals. Thus, although the Malays of Malacca did not adopt the religion of Mahommed until the year of Christ, 1276, we find them alleging themselves to have founded Singapore in 1160, and giving various intermediate dates, which they could only have arrived at by reckoning backwards, with the duration of their princes' reigns as their guide, unless, indeed, which is not improbable, that the era alluded to was that of Salivana, borrowed from Java. The chronology of the Bugis of Celebes appears to have been of the same nature.

F.

FARIA Y SOUSA. This Portuguese writer was born in 1590, and died in 1649. The work which connects him with the history of the Asiatic Archipelago is his "Asia Portuguesa," which is the Portuguese history of India from its commencement in 1497, to its virtual termination in 1649. This work is posthumous, and written in Spanish. It is a hasty compilation, of which neither the facts nor reasonings are reliable; and the author is, in every way, greatly inferior to the earlier historians—De Barros, De Cauto, and Castaghneda—who lived nearer the most important events, and had better sources of information. There is an English translation of the "Asia Portuguesa," dedicated to the Princess of Modena, second wife of James the Second.

FIRE-ARMS. See Arms.

FISH and FISHERIES. There are assuredly no seas in the world more abundant in esculent fish than those of the Asiatic Archipelago, and a few of them are of excellent flavour. The fish of rivers and lakes, although, perhaps, less abundant and of very inferior quality, are of importance in some of the islands, particularly in those of the Philippine group. Fish constitutes the chief animal aliment of all the inhabitants, and everywhere of those of the sea-coast who are by profession fishermen. In most of the languages the same word expresses both fish and flesh. The greatest plenty of fish, and also the best quality of it, is found in the comparatively shallow seas, bordering the granitic and sedimentary formations, and the least abundant in the deep seas close to the volcanic. Among the best fisheries are those of the eastern coast of the Malay Peninsula, those of the entire straits of Malacca, of the northern coast of Java, and of all the coasts of Borneo and Celebes, with those of the Philippine Islands.

The variety of fish which is found may be judged by the fact previously mentioned respecting the Ichthyology of the island of Celebes. The learned Dr. Bleeker, the director of the Batavian Society of Arts and Sciences, has named and described no fewer than 108 species belonging to that island, and yet expresses himself satisfied that he has not described above one-eighth part of the whole number which exists. Out of the 108 species so described, it was found that 64 only were common to Celebes and Java. A people who have derived from the sea or river a main portion of their sustenance from their first existence, may well be expected to have acquired some skill in the capture of fish, and fishing is indeed the art in which the greater number of them excel the most. Fish are caught by them by hook and line—by a great variety of nets—by weirs and traps—by spearing and by stupefying those of rivers by narcotic juices. Notwithstanding their long experience, the Chinese excel them even in their own waters, and are the constructors and owners of all the weirs on a large scale which are so frequent on the banks in the neighbourhood of European settlements, and in which are caught the greatest quantity and best quality of fish. The taking of the mother-of-pearl oyster, the pearl-oyster in a few places,—of the holothurion or tripang, and of the shell tortoise, forms valuable branches of the Malayan fisheries.

FLORIS, called also Endé and Mangarai, is an island of the third magnitude in the Malayan Archipelago, and forming one of the long volcanic chain, which may be said to constitute the southern barrier of the Archipelago. It lies between south latitude 7° and 9°, and east longitudes 120° and 123°. Its form is long and narrow, its length extending to 200 geographical miles, with a breadth running from 42 to 50 miles. Its area has been computed at 4035 geographical square miles. Like all the other islands of the same chain, the formation is volcanic, and it has several peaks, two of which are active volcanoes, one of them 7000 feet high. The natives state that the country produces copper, but neither gold nor iron in sufficient quantity to be worked. The mountains, which are forest-clad, yield abundance of sapan-wood, called in the language of the country usu, and a yellow dye wood, the kayu-kuning of the Malays. The aboriginal inhabitants are a frizzle-headed people, with features intermediate between the Papuan and Malay race, yet apparently not an intermixture of these, but a distinct race. Their manners are simple and inoffensive. They dwell in houses built on the ground, and not elevated on posts like those of the Malays. They cultivate mountain rice, maiz, and roots, and some of the best cotton of the Archipelago exported to be manufactured in Celebes. Floris produces none of the larger wild animals, but the hog in great plenty. The domesticated animals are the buffalo, ox, goat, dog, duck, and common fowl. The inhabitants are divided into many distinct nations, speaking different languages, of which I received from the Bugis merchants settled among them the mames of six, and vocabularies of two. The principal places of trade are Mangarai, on the northern, and Endé, on the southern coast, the last being the most considerable place, the town or village of the same name containing about 200 houses, and its territory about 5000 inhabitants. Close to it is an active volcano 1500 feet high. At both are settled some Bugis and Malays, the former trading to Batavia and Singapore in vessels of considerable size, and in smaller ones to Sumba or Sandal-wood Island. At a place called Pota, on the northern coast, the Dutch have a fort and small post, the chief object of which is protection against piracy. Towards the south-eastern end of the island the Portuguese have a small settlement on a bay, in front of which are the islands of Solor and Adinara. This is named Larantuka, and here they have converted a few of the natives to Christianity. The origin of two of the names of this island is obvious enough, and the most current is most probably a Portuguese word—the plural of flor, a flower, the same name which the Portuguese have given to one of the Azores.

FORMOSA. The Iha formosa of the Portuguese, called Tai-wan by the Chinese, a word signifying as I am informed by my very acute friend Mr. H. Parkes, her Majesty's Consul at Amoy, "The Terraced Harbour," and applied by them to the port and chief town, and thence to the whole island. Near to and inhabited, as far as its aboriginal people are concerned, by the same race as the Philippines, it has some claim to be considered as part of them. It lies between north latitudes 21° 58′ and 25° 15′, and east longitudes 120° and 122°. It is of an oval form, its length being from north to south, its western side fronting the main land of China. The strait which lies between, called after the island, is in its narrowest part 80 miles broad, and in its widest 150. The total area of Formosa has been estimated at 14,000 square miles, so that it is by about one-fifth part larger than the classic island of Sicily. Its situation is in the very heart of the region of typhoons, and it is moreover, amenable to severe earthquakes.

A range of high mountains runs through the island from north to south, the summits of which are clad in perpetual snow, from which it is concluded that they cannot be less than 12,000 feet above the level of the sea. An undulating plain, extending from the foot of the range to the sea, forms the western side of the island, leaving a large portion of the eastern a mountain mass. What its geological formation is has not been ascertained, but that a portion is volcanic is certain from the existence of craters yielding a large supply of sulphur, which is one of the staple exports of the island.

The population of Formosa is of two descriptions, an aboriginal and a Chinese, the first for the most part confined to the fastnesses of the mountains, and the last occupying the extensive plain already named. The aboriginal inhabitants are of the same race as the fairer people of the Philippines—that is, of the Malay race—but whether divided into different tribes, speaking one language, or having many tongues, has not been ascertained. The Dutch, during their short occupation of the island, obtained a vocabulary of a Formosan language, which, on examination, is found to contain a few words of Malay and of Philippine languages, implying the probability that the first came through the medium of the last. The natives of Formosa are evidently in a very rude state, never having obtained that degree of civilisation which even the principal nations of the Philippines had reached when discovered by Europeans. A few of them have been tamed by the Chinese, and reduced by them to a kind of predial servitude. The Chinese settlers are for the most part emigrants from the province of Fokien, the inhabitants of which are known to be the most industrious, ingenious, and enterprising of the empire. It is remarkable that Formosa, although its existence must have been sufficiently known to the Chinese from an early period, was never colonised by them until they were driven to take shelter in it by the invasion of the Manchoo Tartars at the beginning of the seventeenth century. The Spaniards appear early to have formed a small settlement on the island, and when the Dutch in 1624 began their establishment, they found a colony of Chinese said to amount to 200,000. The present Chinese population is said to number two millions and a half. This, however, must be a great exaggeration, for supposing them to occupy one half the area of the island, and it is not likely that they occupy so much, the number would give 375 to the square mile, which would amount to the density of an old country, and not of a colony yielding the products of the earth cheaply, as Formosa is known to do.

The Dutch, after occupying a large part of Formosa for 34 years, were expelled from it in 1662 by a powerful Chinese pirate who had infested and invaded it. This catastrophe was the result of sheer incapacity and neglect, and it is remarkable that it should have happened at a time when their energy and enterprise were at their greatest height. Considering its temperate climate and its favourable geographical position, it is certain that Formosa might, under happier auspices, have become a great and prosperous European colony.

The soil of the plains and mountain slopes of Formosa is described as being of eminent fertility, and it may fairly be concluded from the height and magnitude of its mountains that this fertility is promoted by an abundant irrigation. The chief products of its agriculture are rice, wheat, pulse, millet, and sugar-cane. Its chief exports are rice, sugar, camphor, timber, bay-salt, and sulphur. Formosa forms part of the province of Fokien, the dense population of which is said to draw a large part of its supplies of food from it.

FOW. This is the name of an islet on the south-western coast of the island of Gebi in the Molucca Sea, and which forms with it a fine and secure harbour. Fow, itself, is deeply penetrated by an inlet of the sea, which makes it to consist of two peninsulas, the isthmus between them consisting of land from 350 to 400 feet high. This inlet is a cone with a very narrow entrance, but which widens after entering, has a depth of from 5 to 10 fathoms, and although a small, is a safe harbour, easily made defensible.

FUNERALS. The funerals of the Malays, Javanese, and other nations converted to Islamism, are in conformity to the usages of the Mahommedans. The body, within twenty-four hours after death, in a shroud, without coffin, is buried; and the word which expresses this simple ceremony literally signifies to place in the earth, and is the same which means to plant or put seed in the ground. At the bottom of the grave on one side there is a lateral excavation to receive the body. A simple mound marks the grave without monumental stone or tomb, except in the case of kings and reputed saints, the tombs of the latter being considered holy under the Arabic name of kramat, or sacred. The cemeteries of the Javanese are usually on small hills or rising grounds at a short distance from the villages, and lying in a grove of the Samboja tree (Plumeria acutifolia) are exceedingly picturesque.

We have examples of the funerals of tribes that have not embraced either the Mahommedan or Hindu religions in the instances of the inhabitants of the island of Nias on the western coast of Borneo, and of the Kayan Dyaks of Borneo. Those of the first of these are thus described by a writer in the Malayan Miscellany, published under the auspices of Sir Stamford Raffles in 1822, and believed to be a distinguished botanist, the late Dr. Jack. "The mode of burial in the southern division of the island," (that most remote from Malay influence) "is peculiar. The body is not committed to the earth, but is inclosed in a wooden shell or coffin, which is elevated on four posts, and then given to enjoy the free winds of heaven. Flowering shrubs and creepers are generally planted beneath, which soon climb up and cover the coffin with foliage. These cemeteries are at some little distance from the villages, and when not quite recent, have nothing unpleasant or disgusting in their appearance. On the contrary, there is something almost poetic in the idea of placing the remains of their friends, as it were, beyond the reach of the worm, suspended in the air amid verdure and flowers; and if they might be supposed to have had further a moral object in view, what could be more forcible than to see the very sepulchres hastening to decay amid the wild luxuriance, and unfading freshness of the shrubs they had supported."

The funerals of the Kayan Dyaks of Borneo are thus described by Mr. Robert Burns. "After death, the Kayans very stupidly keep the body in the house from four to eight days, and sometimes even longer. Generally, the first day after death, it is put into a coffin, scooped from the trunk of a tree, and carved, according to the importance or means of the relatives. Day and night, during the time the body is kept in the house, lights are placed at each side of the coffin, and should these happen to get extinguished, it is considered most unfortunate. Also, during the four or five days after the corpse has been removed, torches are kept at the place where it lay. Previous to its removal, a feast is prepared, and part of the food is placed beside the corpse: the relatives devour the remainder. The removal of the body takes place soon after, and, although it be invariably much decomposed, the nearest relatives, especially the women, express their grief in a most inconsolable manner, and with cries most pitiable, long and affectionately hug the coffin, and with their faces on it inhale the odour, and continue doing so, until it reaches the place of disposal, which is on the loft of a small wooden house on posts, about twelve feet high. The tombs of the chiefs are built of hard wood, supported by nine massive posts, from twelve to fourteen feet high, and which, with the other parts of the building, are elaborately carved. Several articles which belonged to the deceased are conveyed to the tomb with the corpse, but are not deposited with it. On the death of a person, the relations directly lay aside all apparel of foreign manufacture, and wear only a kind of bark cloth instead, for a prescribed number of days after the funeral."—Journal of the Indian Archipelago, vol. iii. p. 149.

The only people of the Archipelago who continue to follow Hinduism are those of Bali, and such of the inhabitants of this island as have recently settled in the neighbouring one of Lomboc as conquerors, and of their funerals a very interesting account has been given by Mr. Zollinger in the Journal of Netherland India. "The Balinese of Lomboc," says he, "burn their dead. This is accompanied by very many ceremonies, which cost incredible sums of money. The poor, for this reason, often bury their dead, but always so that they can recover the bones, should it ever happen that they can gather together enough of money to meet the expenses of a cremation. The rich after death are embalmed, because months and even years often elapse before they are burned. Wives may suffer themselves to be burned after the death of their husbands, but they are not compelled to do so. Such an event very seldom occurs, and during my stay, there was only a single widow who allowed herself to be krised. They have the choice of allowing themselves to be either burned or krised. The first is the more rare. The wives of the rajas, however, must suffer themselves to be burned. When a raja dies, some women are always burned, even should they be but slaves. The wives of the priests never kill themselves. Having been present at one of these horrid spectacles, I shall relate how it was conducted. A gusti (lord) who died at Ampanan, left three wives. One of them resolved to let herself be krised in honour of him, and that against the will of all on both sides of her family. The woman was still young and beautiful; she had no children. They told me that a woman, who, under such circumstances, suffered herself to be killed, had, indeed loved her husband. She intended to accompany him on his long journey to the gods, and she hoped to be his favourite in the other world. The day after the death of the gusti, his wife took many baths, she was clothed in the richest manner, and passed the day with her relatives, drinking, chewing betel, and praying. About the middle of a space before the house, there were erected two scaffoldings or platforms of bamboo, of the length of a man, and three feet above the ground. Under these a small pit had been dug, to receive the water and blood that was about to flow. In a small house at one side of and opposite to these frame-works were two others, and entirely similar. At four o'clock in the afternoon, the body of the gusti was brought out, wrapped in fine linen, and placed on the left of the two central platforms. A priest of Mataram (the capital) removed the cloth from the body, while young persons hastened to cover the private parts of the dead with their hands. They poured much water over the corpse, washed it, combed the hair, and covered the whole body with champaka and kanangega flowers (Michelia champaka and Uvaria odorata). A white net was then produced. The priest took a silver cup with holy water, called chor, on which he strewed flowers. He first sprinkled the deceased with this water, and then poured it through the net on the body, which he blessed, praying, singing, and making various mystical and symbolical motions. He finally powdered the body over with flour of coloured rice and chopped flowers, and placed it on dry mats. Women then brought out the wife of the gusti on their crossed arms. She was clothed in white linen only. Her hair was crowned with flowers of the Chrysanthemum Indicum. She was tranquil, and betrayed neither fear nor regret. She placed herself, standing before the body of her husband, raised her arms on high, and prayed in silence. Women approached her and presented to her small bouquets of the Hibiscus rosa-sinensis and other flowers. She took them, one by one, and placed them between the fingers of her hands raised above her head. On this, the women took them away and dried them. On receiving and giving back each bouquet, the wife of the gusti turned a little to the right, so that when she had received the whole, she had turned quite round. She prayed anew in silence, went to the corpse of her husband, kissed it on the head, the breast, below the naval, the knees, the feet, and then returned to her place. They took off her rings; she crossed her arms on her breast. Her brother (on this occasion one by adoption), placed himself before her, and asked her with a soft voice if she was determined to die, and when she gave a sign of assent with her head, he asked her forgiveness for being obliged to kill her. At once, he seized his kris, and stabbed her on the left side of the breast, but not very deeply, so that she remained standing. He then threw away his kris and ran off. A man of consideration then approached her, and buried his kris to the hilt in the breast of the unfortunate woman, who sunk down, at once, without a cry. The women placed her on a mat, and sought by rolling and pressure to cause the blood to flow as quickly as possible. The victim being not yet dead, she was stabbed again with a kris between the shoulders. They then laid her on the second platform near her husband. The same ceremonies that had been practised with him began for the wife. When all was ended, both bodies were covered with resin and cosmetics, enveloped in white linen, and placed in the small lateral house on the platform. There they remain, until the time arrives for their being burned together.

"It is always a near relation who gives the first wound, but never father or son. Sometimes dreadful spectacles occur: such was one at which Mr. King was present. The woman had received eight kris stabs and was yet quite sensible. At last, she screamed out, impelled by the dreadful pain, 'Cruel wretches, are you not able to give me a stab that will kill me?' A gusti who stood behind her, on this, pierced her through and through with a kris.

"The native spectators, whom I had around me, saw in the slaughter, which took place before our eyes, nothing shocking. They laughed and talked as if it was nothing. The man who had given the three last stabs wiped his kris, and restored it to its place in as cold-blooded a manner as a butcher would have done his knife after the slaughter of an animal.

"Only the wives of the most considerable personages of the land allow themselves to be burned, because the ceremony is attended with much more expense than krising. They make on such an occasion a very high platform of bamboo. The woman ascends, after many ceremonies, and when the fire is at its greatest heat, she springs from above into the middle of the flames. Mr. King (an English merchant long resident in Lomboc) thinks that they do not suffer much, because during the leap they are stifled, and, at all events, the fire strengthened by fragrant resins, is so fierce that death must speedily ensue."

It will be seen by these statements that the ordinary funeral rites of the Balinese much resemble those of the Buddhists of Siam and Ava,—that the concremation is a modification of the Hindu Suttee, and the bloody ceremony of krising, a barbarism peculiar to the people of Bali themselves.

G.

GADDANÉ. The name of one of the wild tribes of the island of Luzon. They are not negritos, but are described as having darker complexions than the other brown tribes in the same condition,—as being of shorter stature, having round eyes and flat noses, speaking a language of their own, and in their manners dull and filthy. Brought within the pale of christianity by the missionaries, they have proved serviceable in converting the neighbouring savages.

GÂDEH or GEDEH (GUNUNG), literally, "the great mountain," is the name of one of the highest mountains of the western part of Java. It is situated in the district of Chanjor, in the country of the Sundas,—has the same base as another large mountain, called Pangarango,—rises to the height of 10,500 feet above the level of the sea, and is an active volcano.

GAMBIER. This is the Malayan name of the terra-japonica, and of the plant that yields it, the Uncaria gambier of botanists. The plant is a straggling shrub, from eight to ten feet high, and an object of extensive cultivation. A gambier plantation generally extends to about 30 acres, and, when full grown, has the appearance of a coppice. The drug is the inspissated juice of the leaves, obtained by boiling to the consistence of a syrup, which is poured into moulds, and, when dry, cut into cubes of an inch and a half to a side. The leaves are pulled three or four times a year, and the plantation is exhausted in fifteen years, when it is abandoned, and new land had recourse to. In Singapore, where the cultivation was established on its first occupation, in 1819, there are 800 plantations; but the culture has been largely extended to the neighbouring continent. It is, however, carried on to a much greater extent in the islands of Batang, Bintang, and Linga. Although originally a Malay manufacture, it is at present almost wholly carried on by the Chinese, who conduct the cultivation of gambier in combination with that of black pepper, the refuse leaves of the first being found an useful manure for the last. The gambier plant appears to be a native of all the countries on the shores of the Straits of Malacca, but especially of the numerous islands at its eastern end. From the last, it has been immemorially exported to Java and the islands east of it, to be used as a masticatory, being one of the ingredients in the betel preparation. It does not seem to be a production of any of the islands of the volcanic band. Gambier contains from 40 to 50 per cent of pure tannin, and hence it has been of late years largely imported into Europe, to be used in the purposes of dying and tanning, the quantity imported yearly into England being not less than 6000 tons. This is one of the striking results of the freedom of commerce, and the progress of the arts among us.

GAMBLING, in Malay and Javanese, Judï. All the more advanced nations of the Asiatic Archipelago are greatly addicted to gaming, the passion for which is very far from being confined to the nations that have adopted the Mahommedan religion; for the Hindus of Bali and Lomboc, and the Christians of the Philippines are as great gamblers as the Malays, and greater than the Javanese. Cock-fighting is everywhere the normal shape which it takes; but card-playing, and other games, have been acquired from the Chinese, who are themselves even more determined gamblers than any of the native nations.

GAMBOGE. Our name for this article of commerce is a corruption of the Malay name of the chief country which produces it, Kamboja. The plant which produces it is a large forest tree, supposed to be a Garcinia, or a species of the same genus which produces the celebrated mangostin fruit, on the rind of which last is frequently seen a yellow pigment, having all the appearance of gamboge. The drug is the inspissated sap of the tree, obtained by wounding the bark. It quickly dries in the sun, is formed at once into rolls, and undergoes no other preparation. Both the tree and its sap must be abundant in the forests of Kamboja, judging by the moderate price at which the article is sold at the chief emporium, Singapore, where the price does not exceed from 55*s.* to 65*s.* a hundred weight. The Malay name of the drug seems to be taken from the language of Kamboja. This is rong, which the Portuguese have adopted, writing the word, rom.

GEBI. The name of an island of the Molucca Sea, lying between Gilolo and Waigyu, one of the Papuan Islands. It is long and narrow, running in a direction from north-east to south-west, and is in length from six to seven leagues, the western extremity being only four miles north of the equator, and in east longitude 129° 19′. The geological formation is not volcanic, but probably sandstone much impregnated with iron. The land is generally hilly; but the highest point does not exceed 500 feet. The aboriginal inhabitants are Papuans: but there are also settlers from the Moluccas, and these are the ruling party, the king of Tidor, one of the clove islands, claiming the sovereignty. Some of the Papuans have been converted to the Mahommedan religion by the intrusive party, while the rest still continue pagans. The cultivated products of Gebi are a little rice, the coco, and sago-palms, yams, and the banana. The mammalia of the forest are only the hog and two marsupial animals; and the chief birds, several species of the pigeon and parrot families. The chief employment of the natives is the fishing of tripang and pearl oysters. Between Gebi and the islet Fow, at its south-western end, is a harbour, safe in all winds, with good anchorage and depth for a ship of the line. See Fow.

GEELVINK. The name of the great bay or gulf which deeply indents the northern side of New Guinea, converting it into a western and eastern peninsula. See DORI HARBOUR and NEW GUINEA.

GILIBANTAH. The name of an islet lying between the islands Gunung-api and Comodo, in the Straits of Sapi, or those which divide Sumbawa from Floris. It is like those in its neighbourhood, of trachytic formation, and its highest point rises to the elevation of 1200 feet. The name may probably be Javanese, in which gili signifies "a highway," and bantah "to dispute," that is, the islet disputing or interrupting the highway.

GINGER. The Zingiber officinalis of botanists, is produced almost everywhere throughout the Asiatic Archipelago, and is more used by the natives as a condiment than any other spice, except the capsicum. Its native name in Malay is alya, and in Javanese, jait; but it has almost as many different names as there are languages; from whence it is to be inferred that it is indigenous in most parts of the Archipelago, the names being everywhere native, and not foreign. Ginger was an article of the Indian trade of the Romans, most likely in their case the produce of Malabar. Pliny gives its price in the Roman market at six denarii the pound, which, at the usual estimate of 8½*d.* the denarius, would make 5*s.* 9¼*d.* the pound avoirdupois. The price in the London market just now is about two-pence.

GLUGA. This is the Broussonetia papyrifera of botanists, popularly called the paper mulberry tree, the same plant from which a kind of paper is made in China and Japan, and clothing in the islands of the Pacific. The Javanese are the only people of the Archipelago who manufacture a paper from the liber or inner bark of this plant, and this is by a process very similar to that by which the ancients manufactured papyrus. The raw material, however, is of a better quality, and the process of manufacturing it far less expensive; for the ordinary Javanese paper, instead of being costly, like the papyrus, is a very cheap commodity. Its colour is that of parchment; it is very tough, and, except that it is liable to be preyed on by insects, owing to the rice-water used in its preparation, it is very durable. The name of the plant, and the vulgar and polite names of the paper, dâluwang and dâlambang, are all native Javanese words; and it may be concluded that the art of manufacturing paper from the gluga plant is a native one, and of long standing; for the few ancient manuscripts found in Java, and which, belonging as they do, to the times of Hinduism, cannot be of later date than the year 1478, that in which Hinduism was finally subverted. The gluga is an object both of culture and manufacture, chiefly carried on in the province of Kadiri, once an extensive seat of Hinduism, and the parties conducting them are the Mahommedan priests; in this matter very likely the successors of the Bramins.

GOAT. The domestic goat, a small animal kept for its flesh, but not for its milk any more than is the cow, is pretty generally distributed over the Archipelago; but its origin is as obscure here as in other countries. In Malay it has two names, kambing and bebek, the last being oddly enough the name for the domestic duck in Javanese. In this last language it has also two names, meda and wâdus; but they are local only. The first Malay name extends as far as the Philippines, and the second has also a wide currency; either the one or the other being nearly the only names in the other languages of the Archipelago. The goat was not found, any more than the ox and buffalo, in the Polynesian islands; and in the language of Madagascar it has a native, and not a Malayan, name, usi. All the names now given are native words, and through them, therefore, a foreign origin for the goat cannot be traced. In Sumatra and the Malay Peninsula there exists a species of antelope, the Antilopa Sumatrensis, a denizen of the deepest recesses of the mountain forests; but I do not think this likely to be the source of the domestic goat, although the Malays have no other name for it than "the wild goat," kabing-utan, and, notwithstanding its native names, it seems more probable that the Hindus brought it from Southern India, than that it is indigenous.

GOGA. The name of a tree very generally found in most of the Philippines (Ensenada Philippensis), the woody filaments of which yield a soapy matter much used in washing linen, and in the process of gold washing for the purpose of precipitating the metal from the sand. It is a shore or littoral plant, formerly ranked by botanists as an Acacia.

GOLD. This metal, in sufficient abundance to be worked, is found in the Malay Peninsula, Sumatra, the western and southern sides of Borneo, the northern and south-western peninsulas of Celebes, and in a few parts of the great Philippine islands of Luzon and Mindano. In none of the islands of exclusively volcanic formation does it exist in such quantity as to be worth working. The qualities of the gold vary greatly in the same country. Thus, on the western side of Borneo there are reckoned to be twelve different qualities, designated by the localities which produce them, and which range in fineness from 16 up to 22 carats. The finest gold brought to market is that of the principality of Pahang, on the eastern side of the Malay Peninsula, which brings a higher price than even that of Australia by better than three per cent. The gold of the places mentioned is all obtained by washings, and the metal has never been worked and scarcely even traced to the original veins. It is mostly in the form of powder or dust—the mas-urai of the Malays, literally "loose, or disintegrated gold." Now and then lumps of considerable size are found, but compared to the nuggets of California and Australia, mere pebbles. The Prince of Sambas, on the western side of Borneo, keeps as a curiosity a mass weighing 22 ounces, and lumps of double this weight are said to have been found. The alluvial bed which contains the gold is found by digging a shaft to depths varying from 15 to 60 feet. The miners of Borneo are the Dyaks or wild natives, the Malays, and the Chinese, and it is by these last that the mining is conducted with the greatest effect. The mining of this people, however, is confined to Borneo, for in all the other countries it is carried on by the natives of the country.

Attempts have been made to estimate the total quantity of gold produced throughout the Archipelago, but all estimates, from the nature of things, can be no better than conjectures. Some of the metal is consumed in the countries producing it in trinkets; no record of the produce is anywhere kept, and much is clandestinely, or at least not avowedly, exported. The produce of the western side of Borneo, by far the largest, I have seen estimated as low as 52,000 ounces, and this by parties reckoning the Chinese population of the same country, most of it engaged in gold washing, as high as 125,000. On the other hand Sir Stamford Raffles estimated the total annual produce of the western part of Borneo as high as 225,335 ounces, which at the value of 3*l.* 17*s.* the ounce, would give a total value of 867,539*l.* Mr. Logan estimates the total produce of the Malay Peninsula at no more than 20,000 ounces. I have never heard of any attempt at estimating that of Sumatra, Celebes, or the two Philippine Islands. If all of them put together yield a million sterling's worth, it will certainly be their utmost produce, and even this will not exceed a twelfth part of the produce of California or Australia.

Gold has, no doubt, been known in the parts of the Archipelago which now produce it from the rudest and earliest times, and through early traffic must have soon been conveyed to such as do not,—the islands within the volcanic band. In all the producing countries it has a native name, and this in the Malay language, that of the most productive prevails in all the non-producing ones. This name is amas, usually abbreviated both in speaking and writing, mas; and it is the current one in the Javanese, Bali, Sunda, Lomboc, and Floris. In the two first of these tongues there are two Sanscrit synonyms, kanchana and rukmi, but they belong to the polite and recondite dialects. In the language of the Bugis, whose country produces gold, we find a native word, ulawang, and this is again the case in the language of the Tagalas of the Philippines, where we have the indigenous name balituk, while in the language of the volcanic Bisaya Islands we find the word bulawang, most probably a corruption of the Bugis word.

Gold has never been coined for money in any part of the Archipelago, except Achin, where there is a small coin of it worth about 1*s.* 2*d.* called a mas, after the Malay name of the metal. Gold-dust has been, however, used as a medium of exchange, and occasionally is so still. The natives have even an empirical skill in the art of assaying gold. This however they have acquired from the Tâlugu settlers, as may be seen by the name and character of the scale, called mutu, and divided into 10 degrees, the fineness being ascertained by the touchstone. A small colony, indeed, of this people still professing Hinduism, and whose special calling it is to assay gold, still exists in Malacca.

Gold ornaments of considerable beauty are made by most of the civilised nations of the Archipelago. The neck chains of Manilla are examples of very delicate workmanship, and the filagree work of the Malays of Sumatra is still more remarkable. In all these cases what is most striking is the beauty of the work compared with the rudeness and simplicity of the workmen and their tools.

GOLO. The name of an island forming part of the province of Batangas, in the island of Luzon. It is about three leagues in length, and half a league in breadth, mountainous, but thickly inhabited. Its coast is surrounded by rocks and shoals, and very difficult of access.

GOMUTI. The palm (Borassus gomuti), to which Europeans have given this name, derived from one of its products, is one of importance, second only to that of the coco in the rural economy of the Asiatic Archipelago, from one extremity of it to the other. It takes the place of the Tal or Borassus flabelliformis of the continent of India. It is readily distinguished from other palms by its thick, rough, and wild aspect. Its favourite locality is the dry uplands of the interior, and not like that of the coco-palm, the vicinity of the sea. Its chief and most valuable product is its sap, obtained by bruising and cutting the inflorescence. From this liquid, and not from the juice of the cane, is made nearly all the sugar consumed by the natives, while the sap itself, which runs rapidly to the vinous fermentation, is their chief intoxicating beverage. The sap, however, is not the only product of this palm which is put to use. Between the trunk and the fronds there are found three different useful materials, a black horse-hair-like substance, which makes the best cordage of the western islands of the Archipelago,—a fine cottony substance, which makes the best tinder and is exported for this purpose, and strong stiff spines, from which are made the pens of all the nations that write on paper, with the arrows for the blow-pipe of the rude tribes that still use this weapon. The pith furnishes a sago, although an inferior one. The seeds have been made into a confection, while their pulpy envelope abounds in a poisonous juice, a strong infusion of them being used in the barbarian wars of the natives. This is the fluid to which the Dutch gave the appropriate name of "hell-water."

The Gomuti palm appears to be a peculiar product of the Asiatic Archipelago, but of many parts of it. This is to be inferred from its having a distinct name in each language, and all its names being native ones. Thus, in Malay, the name is anau, in Javanese, aren; in Amboynese, nawa; in Macassar, monchono; and in Mandar, akel. It is the palm which the Portuguese have called sagwire, and the Spaniards saguran, both words probably derivatives from sago. The different parts of the tree have also their separate native names in each language: gomuti, the name of the species adopted by botanists, is the name in Malay for the material of the cordage above mentioned, and not of the tree itself.

GOOSE. The goose has been domesticated, although in very scanty numbers, in the western islands of the Archipelago. Here there exists no wild species, and from this circumstance, and its Sanscrit name 'angsa, sometimes corrupted gangsa, there can be little doubt of its origin being Hindu. It has been stated that the goose will not breed or even lay eggs in Manilla and its neighbourhood. This is, I believe, an undoubted fact, but no reason has been assigned for it, and it is singular that such should be the case when all other kinds of poultry thrive to a remarkable degree. A similar fact has been observed with respect to the turkey in Singapore. It will not only not multiply but even live in that island, although hardy and prolific in Java and the Philippines.

GORONGTÂLO. The name of a country on the southern side of the northern peninsula of Celebes, and of the gulf which lies between that peninsula and the eastern. (See CELEBES and MENDANO).

GRESSIE. In Javanese correctly Gârsik, that is, "dry land" or firm land, distinguished from muddy or marshy, is the name of a district of the province of Surabaya, in Java. It lies along the shore of the narrow strait which divides Java from Madura, towards the western end of the latter. The Solo river, the principal one of Java, disembogues within it. Gressie is remarkable for its production of bay-salt, its sea-fishery, with its stews or fish-ponds, the property of the government, and the source of a considerable public revenue. It was in Gressie that the Mahommedan strangers who eventually overthrew the ancient religion of Java, first established themselves in the 14th century, and the tomb of one of these apostles of Islam, who died in 1391, is still pointed out. Gressie was the first spot of Java seen and visited by the Portuguese, Antonio d'Abreu, the European discoverer of the Moluccas, having touched at it on his way to these islands in 1511, although in the Portuguese orthography of De Barros, it is hardly recognisable in the strange corruption of Agaçim.

GROBOGAN. The name of a district of the province of Japara, in Java. This inland district and the neighbouring one of Blora, contain some of the finest teak forests of the island, but the most remarkable thing connected with Grobogan is its brine springs, which yield a considerable supply of culinary salt. These are found in that portion of the district which consists of lime-stone. They are thus described by my friend, Dr. Horsfield: "These wells are dispersed through a district of country several miles in circumference, the base of which, like that of other parts of the island which furnish mineral and other saline waters, is lime-stone. They are of considerable number, and force themselves upwards through apertures in the rocks, with some violence and ebullition. The waters are strongly impregnated with sea-salt, and yield upon evaporation very good salt for culinary purposes, in quantity not less than 200 tons a-year. About the centre of this lime-stone district is found an extraordinary volcanic phenomenon. On approaching it from a distance, it is first discovered by large volumes of smoke rising and disappearing, at intervals of a few seconds, resembling the vapours arising from a violent surf; while a dull noise is heard like that of distant thunder. Having advanced so near that the vision is no longer impeded by the smoke, a large hemispherical mass is observed, consisting of black earth, mixed with water, about sixteen feet in diameter, rising to the height of twenty or thirty feet in a perfectly regular manner, and, as it were, pushed up by a force beneath, which suddenly explodes with a dull noise, and scatters about a volume of black mud in every direction. After an interval of two or three, or sometimes four or five seconds, the hemispherical body of mud or earth rises and explodes again. In the same manner this volcanic ebullition goes on without interruption, throwing up a globular body of mud, and dispersing it with violence through the neighbouring plain. The spot where the ebullition occurs is nearly circular, and perfectly level. It is covered only with the earthy particles impregnated with salt water which are thrown up from below. Its circumference may be estimated at about half an English mile. In order to conduct the salt water to the circumference, small passages or gutters are made in the loose muddy earth, which convey it to the borders, where it is collected in holes dug in the ground for the purpose of evaporation. A strong, pungent, sulphurous smell, somewhat resembling that of earth-oil, is perceived on standing near the explosion, and the mud recently thrown up possesses a degree of heat greater than that of the surrounding atmosphere. During the rainy season, these explosions are more violent, the mud is thrown up much higher, and the noise is heard at a greater distance. This volcanic phenomenon is situated near the centre of the large plain, and the large series of volcanos, and owes its origin to the general cause of the numerous volcanic eruptions which occur in the island."—Transactions of the Batavian Society of Arts and Sciences, vol. ix. This singular phenomenon is known to the Javanese under the name of Kuwu, as is also the village of salt-makers near it. In Javanese the word simply means "place of abode, or residence." But in Javanese legend the eruption is supposed to be produced by a fabulous monster snake, of which the place is alleged to be the dwelling. Grobogan was also the seat of an ancient Javanese kingdom.

GUADALUPÉ. The name of a monastery and sanctuary of the island of Luzon, about two leagues south-east of the city of Manilla, and situated on the summit of a high rock on the left bank of the river Pasig. Its height is such that it takes several hundred steps of a stair cut in the rock to reach it. The monastery and the church which belongs to it were built as early as 1601, and are under the direction of the shod Augustine friars. The view from the top is one of the most extensive in the Philippine islands, embracing the whole metropolitan province of Tondo, with the city and spacious bay of Manilla. The climate has such a reputation for salubrity that many convalescents repair to it. The sanctuary is dedicated to Saint Nicolas, and on the 10th day of September, his birth-day, vast crowds repair to it to pay their devotions and make offerings at his shrine. Among these votaries the most remarkable are the heathen Chinese of Manilla. With this people the saint has obtained the reputation of being the special protector of merchants and mariners. On his anniversary, the river Pasig is covered with their noisy procession on the way to make offerings, and to purchase pictures of Saint Nicolas, one of which is possessed by every infidel Chinese in Manilla, placed side by side, say the Spanish clergy, with those of Confucius.

GUAVA. Several species of the genus Psidium yield this fruit, a native of tropical South America, and most probably brought by the Portuguese from Brazil. This hardy and easily-reared fruit, little prized by natives or Europeans, is to be found in every part of the Archipelago, even growing wild in the jungles. The Malays, in their rough botanical arrangement, class it with the jambu, calling one species of it jambu-biji, the seedy jambu; another jambu china, or the Chinese jambu; and a third jambu-bol, the meaning of which I am unacquainted with.

GUIMANES. The name of one of the wild tribes of the island of Luzon, of the brown-complexioned race, inhabiting the Great Cordillera, between the provinces of South Ilocos and Abra. They are represented as being among the most savage of the wild races, living in the recesses of the mountains, and descending from them only to commit depredations on their more civilised, but still infidel neighbours, the Tinguianes.

GUIMARAS. The name of a considerable island of the Philippines, lying in the channel between the large islands of Panay and Negros, and forming a part of the province of Iloilo in the first. It is about 27 geographical miles in length, and 10 in breadth, and has an area of 210 square geographical miles. It is four leagues distant from Negros, and three-quarters of a league from Panay. Guimaras is mountainous,—contains forests of useful timber, and its soil is fertilised by many streams. Its productions are rice, maiz, the coco-nut palm, cacoa, tobacco, cotton, and abaca. The inhabitants manufacture coarse and fine cloths, and besides their agricultural labours, find employment in hunting and fishing. On the western side of the island there is a town of 994 houses, or rather Indian huts, and the total population is 5964, paying a tribute of 9335 reals of plate.

GUN and GUNPOWDER. See Arms.

GUNTUR (Gunung) is the name of a mountain of Java, in the country of the Sundas, and district of Bandung, having an active volcano. It rises to the height of 7000 feet above the level of the sea, and 5000 above the plain of Bandung. The name signifies "Thunder-mountain," no doubt derived from its eruptions.

GUNUNG. This is the Javanese word for mountain, the corresponding Malay one being bukit. It has, however, been introduced into many languages of the Archipelago. It is always prefixed to the names of considerable mountains, and indeed, forms an integral part of the name of most of them, as Gunung-gâdé, the name of a mountain in Java, signifying "great mountain," and Gunung-agung, the name of the highest mountain of Bali, meaning "chief or principal mountain."

GUNUNG-API, literally "fire-mountain," is the usual name for a volcano, but is also the proper name of some islets with active volcanos, as of one at the eastern end of Sumbawa, and of another in the Banda group. The first of these, which has an elevation of 5800 feet, is inhabited, and famous for horses of the best blood of the Archipelago. The last has a height of 2500 feet above the sea, and is celebrated for its frequent and formidable eruptions.

H.

HALMAHERA. See Almahera.

HARAFORA. See Alfora.

HAROEKOE or HARUKU, called also OMA and BUWANG-BASI (iron-ejecting), is the name of one of the islands of the Amboyna group, and lies between the main island Ambun and Saparoewa, in south latitude 3° 40′, and east longitude 128° 33′, having a length of twelve and a breadth of eight leagues. Like the rest of the group, it is of Plutonic formation. It has twelve villages, with a total population of 5000 inhabitants, nearly all protestant Christians.

HEMP. The Indian variety of the Cannabis sativa has been introduced into a few parts of the Archipelago, where there are settlers from the Continent of India. It is not cultivated for its fibre, but for its intoxicating juice, the Bang of the Hindus, and the Hashashin of the Arabs, the last being the supposed origin of the European word Assassin. It was not the Arabs, however, who made the people of the Archipelago acquainted with this plant, but the Tâlugus, or Telingas, as its native name Ganja demonstrates. The earliest account of hemp as a product of the Archipelago is by the observant Dampier, who saw it at Achin, in 1688. "They have here," says he, "a sort of herb or plant called Ganga or Bang. I never saw it but once, and that was at some distance from me. It appeared to me like hemp, and I thought it had been hemp, till I was told to the contrary. It is reported of this plant that if it be infused in any liquor, it will stupify the brains of any man that drinks thereof. But it operates diversely, according to the constitution of the person. Some it makes sleepy, some merry, putting them into a laughing fit, and others it makes mad; but after two or three hours they come to themselves again. I never saw the effects of it on any person, but have heard much discourse of it."—Vol. ii. p. 126. Although this account is chiefly from hearsay, nothing can be more faithful in so far as regards the effect of the hemp juice on the nerves. The natives of the country have not taken to the use of the intoxicating sap of this plant, and its consumption is almost wholly confined to strangers and settlers from India, Persia, and Arabia.

HINDU—HINDUSTAN. These are words hardly known to the natives of the Indian Islands. The name by which the people of India, without reference to their faith, is known to them, is that of the nation with which they have immemorially had most intercourse, the Tâlugu, whom they call Kâling. For Hindustan, or the country of the Hindus, they prefix the word for land or country of this nation, as in Malay, Tanah Kâling, and in Javanese, either this or Siti Kâling, from the Sanskrit, having the same import. The name Kâlinga, with the elision of the final vowel, it deserves notice, is the Sanskrit name of the northern part of the Coromandel coast, and, as my friend Professor Wilson informs me, the Calingarum Regio of the Romans. Frequently, however, the Indian islanders refer to the country of the Hindus under the appellation of "the country across the water"—Tanah-sabrang, an expression similar to the Italian Tramontana—beyond the mountains—applied to the countries of Northern Europe.

The time and manner in which the Hindu religion was first introduced into the Indian islands is, to say the least, a matter of very great curiosity. Without doubt the monsoons had a very large share in bringing about this event. Favoured by these, the timid Hindus could early accomplish voyages of a length impracticable to their more intrepid and adventurous contemporaries of Greece and Italy. It is probable that they were performing, with ease and safety, voyages from the Coromandel coast to Sumatra and Java, when the Greeks found a voyage to the eastern coast of the Euxine an adventure of hazard and difficulty, although not of one-half the length. The trade which the Hindus would conduct in the Malay Archipelago, under the auspices of the monsoons, would naturally lead in time to partial settlement, and, of course, to an acquaintance with the manners and languages of the people among whom they settled. The introduction of the Hindu religion would follow, and with it its indispensable concomitants, the Sanskrit language and literature. The Hindus who effected this were, no doubt, the most active, intelligent, and enterprising nation of the Coromandel coast, the Tâlugus, well known to Europeans as Gentoos and Chuliahs, and to the Malays and Javanese, as Kâlings or Klings, as already stated. These are the only people of Hindustan who at present carry on a regular trade with the Indian islands, or who, indeed, in any time, are known to have carried on such an intercourse. The intelligent Barbosa, who describes Malacca before its conquest by the Portuguese, in 1511, represents this class of traders very much as we at present find them, only more important from the absence of the competition of Europeans. "There are here," says he, "many great merchants, Moor as well as Gentile strangers, but chiefly of the Chetis, who are of the Coromandel coast, and have large ships which they call giunchi" (junks).—Libro de Odoardo Barbosa. Ramusio, Vol. i. p. 318. The word Cheti, here supposed to be the name of the nation, is, in fact, only the Tâlugu and Tamil corruptions of Chethi, a trader, itself a corruption of the Sanskrit Sreshti, having the same signification. It is, moreover, the same word which we have ourselves written Set, well known in our early Indian history. The trade thus alluded to by Barbosa has gone on for the period of nearly three centuries and a-half since he wrote, and most probably had been carried on for many ages before it. It was in fact, the second stage of that tedious transit which brought the clove and nutmeg to Western Europe, the first being the home trade of the Malays and Javanese, which brought them from the eastern to the western ports of the Archipelago.

Neither the Malays, the Javanese, nor the Tâlugus have any record of the time or manner in which this commercial intercourse commenced, any more than the ancient Britons had of their trade in tin with the Carthaginians. Circumstantial evidence, therefore, is all that is available on the subject, and even the amount of this is but scanty. When Europeans first visited the Archipelago, they found the Malays and Javanese carrying on what may be called its internal carrying trade, acting, in fact, the same part which is now in a great measure performed by the principal nation of Celebes. They collected the native products of the Archipelago, and conveyed them to the emporia of the west, where they bartered them with the traders of western Asia, for the manufactures and produce of Hindustan, Persia, and Arabia. They, themselves, however, it is certain, never went, any more than they do at the present day, beyond the limits of their own waters. Barbosa enumerates the commodities which the Malays and Javanese brought to Malacca, then, probably, the most considerable emporium of the Archipelago. They consisted of camphor, aloes-wood, benzoin or frankincense, black pepper, cubeb pepper, the clove and nutmeg, honey, bees-wax, gold, tin, and slaves. He adds, that the native vessels which sailed from Malacca went as far as Timur and the Moluccas, in quest of those articles, touching at various intermediate places for trade. Such, then was the state of the internal trade of the Archipelago when the islands were first seen by Europeans, and such, to all appearance, it had been for many ages. It is remarkable that several of the most distinguishing products of the Archipelago are known, and this, too, even in many cases to the natives themselves, by names which are obviously Sanskrit. Thus, camphor is kapur, from karpura; aloes-wood or eagle-wood, garu, from aguru; the nutmeg, pala, abbreviated and corrupted from jatipahla; the clove, in Javanese, gomeda, from gomehda, meaning "cow's marrow;" and black pepper, maricha, which is unaltered. From this it is to be inferred that it was the trade of the Hindus that first gave importance to these commodities, none of which are, even in the present day, much esteemed by the natives themselves, considered as articles of consumption. Thus, the clove and nutmeg, as Rumphius long ago observed, are not used as condiments in the Molucca and Banda islands, and black pepper is hardly more so by the natives of Sumatra.

In the Javanese chronologies the Hindu religion is alleged to have been introduced into their island by an Indian king, whom they call Aji Saka. This is a pure myth, for the name of the personage thus referred to is Sanscrit, the first part of it signifying king, and the last being one of the names of Salivana, who introduced an era prevalent in the South of India, which goes by his name. In fixing the commencement of this era, there is a discrepancy of one year between the Tâlugu and Tamil nations, the first making it 78, and the last 79 years after Christ. It is the first of these that was adopted by the insular Hindus, and which continues to exist in the island of Bali up to the present time, and does so also in Java nominally, although in that island lunar having been substituted for solar time, in the year of our time, 1633, the time no longer corresponds with the original. This fact determines the introduction of the era of Saka to the Tâlugus, the people whom I suppose to have introduced Hinduism into the islands. We may add to this the adoption by the Malay and Javanese of the name of the Tâlugu nation for the whole country of the Hindus.

In order to be able to form a reasonable conjecture respecting the time in which the intercourse of the Hindus with the Archipelago commenced, and the Hindu religion was introduced into it, we must have recourse to circumstantial evidence of a different description. Among the commodities which the Malays and Javanese brought to the emporia of the western parts of the Archipelago, to barter with the foreign traders that resorted to them, the only two not liable to be confounded with similar products of other parts of the east, are the clove and nutmeg. These, it is known, are not mentioned in the minute list of merchandise given in the Periplus of the Erythræan Sea, thought to have been written in the sixty-third year of Christ. Neither are they named by Pliny, who wrote about the same time. Down, therefore, to the first century after Christ, the clove and nutmeg were unknown in Europe, and if known even in the markets of Western India, they would not have been enumerated in the Periplus. Little more than a hundred years later, however, we find them enumerated in the Digest of the Roman Laws. At this time, then, the Hindus must have been carrying on a commercial intercourse with the Archipelago, for they were the second link in the chain of transport by which the clove and nutmeg were conveyed, and there is no other apparent means by which the native products of the remote Molucca and Banda Islands could have reached the Western world. In so far, then, as the clove and nutmeg are concerned, the Hindu intercourse with the Archipelago may be said to have existed for at least seventeen centuries. But it may have existed, and most probably did exist, much earlier; for besides the clove and nutmeg, the Malayan Archipelago produces several other commodities much in demand in the country of the Hindus, such as benzoin or frankincense, camphor, cubeb pepper, gold and tin, none of which are yielded by any part of Hindustan. Tin, in particular, is one which they could hardly have obtained from any other quarter, and which, as we now understand the state of society among the Hindus, they could hardly have dispensed with.

It may be objected to the hypothesis of the Tâlugus being the people who introduced the Hindu religion and its language into the Archipelago, that if such had been the case, Sanscrit would have found its way into the vernacular languages along with the idiom of the Tâlugus, and not in the state of comparative purity in which we find it. But if it came in with, and had been intermixed with that language, such a fact would have implied either a conquest by the Tâlugu nation and an extensive settlement; and of this there is certainly no trace. It is not true, however, that no Tâlugu words are found in Malay or Javanese, for there is a considerable number co-extensive with the influence exercised by this people,—some pure Tâlugu, and others Sanscrit, bearing evidence of their having passed through the medium of that language. The settlers, few in number, would naturally have acquired the language of the natives, but religion would be taught in the sacred tongue.

The Hindu religion and Sanscrit language were, in all probability earliest introduced in the western part of Sumatra, the nearest portion of the Archipelago to the continent of India. Java, however, became eventually the favourite abode of Hinduism, and its language the chief recipient of Sanscrit. Through the Malays and Javanese, Sanscrit, with some tints of the Hindu religion, appears to have been disseminated among the other nations of the Archipelago, extending even to those of the Philippines. This is to be inferred from the greater amount of Sanscrit in the Malay and Javanese than in the other tongues, especially in the Javanese,—from the Sanscrit existing in greater purity in Malay and Javanese, and from the errors of these two languages, both in sense and orthography, having been copied in all the other tongues. An approximation to the proportions of Sanscrit existing in some of the principal languages of the islands will show that the amount is constantly diminishing as we recede from Sumatra and Java, until all vestige of it disappears in the Polynesian dialects. In the ordinary written language of Java the proportion is about 110 in a 1000; in Malay, about 50; in Sunda, about 40; in the Bugis of the Celebes, about 17; and in the Tâgala of the Philippines, about 1½. To show the superior purity of the Sanscrit, as it exists in Malay and Javanese, and the adoption of the errors of these two languages by the others, I shall adduce a few examples. Kut'a is a wall or a house in Sanscrit; but in Malay and Javanese, it is a fortress, and so it is in every other language of the Malay and Philippine Archipelagos. Sutra, in Sanscrit, is a thread; but in Malay, Javanese, and all the other tongues, it signifies silk. Avatara, in Sanscrit, is a descent, or a coming down; but in Malay and Javanese, it signifies a principal Hindu deity, and so it does in all the other languages. This word, in Malay and Javanese, is corrupted into bat'ara, written with a palatal *t*. In the other tongues the *t* is a dental, and in the language of the Philippines we have an *l* for it; so that the word becomes batala. In Sanscrit, the word laksa is a hundred thousand; but in Malay and Javanese, followed by all the other languages, it is ten thousand. Tapas, in Sanscrit, signifies ascetic devotion, and has the same sense in all the insular languages; but the Malays and Javanese elide the sibilant, making the word tapa, and in this they are followed by all the other languages. Guda is sugar; ghura, a horse; tamraka, copper; and karpasa, cotton, in Sanscrit: but in Malay and Javanese, followed by the other tongues, they become gula, kuda, tambaga, and kapas. Sanscrit words are found in greatest purity in Javanese, and, next to it, in Malay; corruption increasing as we recede from Java and Sumatra. The word wartta, news or intelligence, in Sanscrit, is in Javanese warta; in Malay, bârita; and in Tagala balita. The Sanscrit swarga, heaven, is the same in Javanese; in Malay, surga; and in Bugis, suruga. Charitra, a narration, is written correctly in Javanese; but in Malay, it becomes charita; and in the Tagala of the Philippines, salita. See History.

HISTORY. In the sense of a rational narrative of public events, history is a species of composition unknown to the most civilised nations of the Asiatic Archipelago. They may, indeed, be said to have no more idea of it than they have of the mechanism and construction of the steam engine. The nearest approach to a chronicle of events is made by the Javanese, in the writings which they called babad, sâjarah, and pakâm; the first of these words signifying, literally, the hewing or cutting down of a forest. Narratives of this description are all in verse, and have all, more or less of the cast of romance, their object being to amuse and not to instruct. They are hardly to be relied on beyond the era of the conversion of the principal nations of Java to the Mahommedan religion, the year of our time, 1478. The Javanese possess, however, bald chronological lists of events, which go as far back as the era of Saka or Salivana, corresponding to the year 78 of Christ. These are incontestable fabrications, often differing widely from each other, and containing gaps of whole centuries.

The presence of the Hindus in Java, and to a less extent in Sumatra, is attested by the remains of temples, and by inscriptions on stone and brass, and some of these contain real dates in figures; for the most part, however, going no further back than the 13th century of our time. These monuments include many inscriptions, containing a considerable infusion of the language of the Hindus, and even the modern language contains from 10 to 12 words of Sanscrit in every 100; and these facts point to an intercourse with the Hindus of an antiquity far beyond what actual dates will carry us.

It was through the medium of commerce that the Hindus found their way into the Archipelago; and a few incidental facts can be adduced to show that this intercourse must have been of considerable antiquity, although it is impossible to determine how or when it originated. In its character it did not, probably, differ greatly for several centuries from what it was when the Portuguese first arrived in India, towards the end of the 15th century. The commodities peculiar to the Malay Archipelago, which were at this time found at the emporia of the western coast of India were, benzoin, nutmegs, cloves, cubeb pepper—perhaps Malay camphor, and tin. If benzoin was the Malabathrum of the ancients, this peculiarly Malayan product is named in the Periplus of the Erythræan Sea as an article found at the emporia of Malabar, about 63 years after the birth of Christ; and thus we have evidence of a trade between India and the Malay Archipelago, nearly 15 centuries before the arrival of the Portuguese in the waters of the latter.

The question as respects the article of tin is, however, of a more decisive character. This is stated in the Periplus to have been an article of export at two of the emporia of Western India, and to have been brought to these from countries further east,—that is, not to have been local products. India now, and at all known times, has been supplied with tin from the Malayan countries only. It has no tin of its own. nor do any of the countries in its immediate neighbourhood furnish it. The tin, referred to could, therefore, be no other than Malayan, imported most probably into the emporia of the Coromandel coast, and conveyed by land to those of Malabar, to be from thence carried to Western Asia and Egypt. This fact, then, proves the existence of a commercial intercourse between India and the tin-producing countries of the Archipelago in the first century of the Christian era.

But we can go much further back by means of the same commodity. The ancient Egyptians used tin some 15 centuries before the Christian era, as is shown by their tools and implements of bronze, which are known to be of this antiquity; and Sir Gardner Wilkinson is reasonably of opinion that this tin was far more likely to have been Indian—that is, Malay—than British or Iberian. This commodity would be received by the traders of the western ports of Malabar; so that we have here by this single link the indication of a direct trade between the Malay countries and India, and of an indirect intercourse between them and Egypt of three-and-thirty centuries standing.

The Periplus of the Erythræan Sea names another, although not a peculiar product of the Malayan Archipelago, as being found at the emporia of Malabar. This is tortoise-shell, which, although the produce also of other parts of India, is produced in largest quantity and of the best quality in the Archipelago. The Periplus states the article to be brought from Khrusé or the Golden Islands. This would apply to Sumatra and the Peninsula, which produce gold, but could not well refer to the Maldive or Laccadive Islands, as some have supposed, since neither of these yield gold; and are, in fact, little better than coral banks.

As before observed the clove and nutmeg are not named in the Periplus of the Erythræan Sea, as among the commodities found at the emporia of the western coast of India. This may, however, refer to their not being articles dealt in by the western nations; but does not preclude their having been used in the first century as condiments by the Hindus, although their presence even for this purpose is doubtful.

The annals of the Malay nation are still more barren than those of the Javanese. The very names by which their histories are known proclaim their character, and indicate the light in which the people themselves view them. These are, either the Sanscrit word, charitra, or the Arabic, hakayat, both of which signify story, tale, or romance. Until they adopted the Mahommedan religion, the Malays had no era, and reckoned time only by the duration of the reigns of their very obscure princes, not one of whom has left a name deserving of remembrance by posterity. Respecting their intercourse with the Hindus, we possess no recorded fact whatever. The earliest date that can be quoted for their intercourse, even with the Arabs, is the period of the conversion of the Achinese of Sumatra, and this corresponds to the year 1204 of our time. No doubt, however, their mere commercial intercourse was far earlier, and will probably go as far back as the first establishment of the Arabs in Egypt, and the coasts of the Arabian and Persian Gulf, which would correspond with the seventh and eighth centuries.

HOG. One or more species of hog exists, in the wild state, in every great island of the Asiatic Archipelago, from Sumatra and the peninsula to New Guinea and Luzon, and in many, also, of the smaller. Thus, there are abundance of hogs, even in so inconsiderable an island as Singapore. There is, at least, one species in great plenty in the Malay peninsula, three in Sumatra, two in Java, two in Celebes and in some of the smaller islands east of it, including the Babirusa, literally, the "hog-deer." In Java and Sumatra there exist the Sus vittatus and the Sus verrucosus, and in the last of these a third species, not yet named by naturalists. In Borneo, there is a fourth species, the Sus barbatus. All the Philippine islands, also, abound in wild hogs, although the particular species has not been described. The hog, too, exists in the domestic state in the Philippine islands, and in the Hindu islands of Bali and Lamboc, where they are used for food, and in the islands of which the inhabitants have embraced Mahommedanism, they are found, like the dog, in the semi-domestic state, acting as scavengers.

All the wild hogs that I have seen are small animals, compared with the wild boar of Europe, or even with that of continental India. The Sus verrucosus, so called from the fleshy excrescence on the sides of the cheeks, has a grotesque and a formidable appearance, but is in reality a timid animal. The number of them in Java is immense, and in passing along the highway, in particular districts, scores of them are to be seen. I lately read in a Java newspaper an account of a two days' hunt, and the number killed was 1760, chiefly, I believe, taken in nets or destroyed by poison. At particular seasons the crops of rice and sugar-cane have to be watched all night against their depredations. Their habits appear to differ in some respects from those of the European and Indian wild hog, for they come frequently to the sea-shore to feed on crabs, and they will greedily devour carrion.

Whether any of the wild species be the origin of the domesticated hog of the Archipelago is a question not easily solved. The popular names for the hog are all native words. The most frequent of them is babi, which, with slight modifications, is found in many languages from the peninsula and Sumatra to Timur and the Philippines. This name, I have no doubt, belongs to the Malay language, which has no other. It is not, however, the only name in other languages of the Archipelago. The Javanese have a popular name of their own, cheleng, besides five synonyms, namely, the Malay name, two belonging to the polite dialect, and three to the recondite one. The three last are Sanscrit, dârwila, wijung, and sukara. Those for the polite dialect have evidently been framed after the adoption of the Mahommedan religion. They are châmângan and andapan, "the black object," and "the low or mean object." The Sundas of Java have also a name for the hog distinct from the Malay one, badil, and in the language of Endé in Flores, there is also a native name, la. Indeed, the great probability is, that all the languages had originally a native name for an animal so widely diffused, and so useful, until superseded by the Malay one. In most of the languages the name of the domestic and wild hogs is the same, the first only having such words as utan and alas annexed, making "hog of the forest." The languages of the Philippines, however, are an exception, for in these the wild hog has a distinct name from the tame. Thus in the Tagala, while the domestic has the Malay name, the wild is called pagil, a native word. From the prevalence of the Malay name, it may fairly be inferred, that the domestic hog was disseminated by the Malays over the islands remote from their own parent country, Sumatra. This name, however, will not account for the existence of the domestic hog beyond the limits of the Archipelago, and in countries to which the Malayan languages have reached, for it is not to be found in the Polynesian or Madagascar languages. It should be noticed that the flesh of the hog must have formed a principal part of the animal food of the nations and tribes of the Archipelago before the conversion to Mahommedanism. It did so with the people of the Philippine islands on the arrival of the Spaniards, and it does so still with all the rude tribes, and even with the Hindus of Bali and Lomboc.

HONEY and WAX. Honey is found in every country of the Archipelago, the produce of wild bees, which make their hives in the crevices of trees, but no species of bee has ever been domesticated, which would probably be difficult or impracticable in countries which have no distinction of summer and winter,—where every season produces flowers, and where, consequently, there is no necessity for laying up a large store of food. The honey of the Archipelago is a thin syrup, very inferior in flavour to that of temperate climates. It is chiefly sought on account of the wax, which forms a large article of exportation to Europe, India, and China. In Malay, the honey-bee has a specific name, lâbah: so has the wax, lilin, and the hive, tuwalan. The native name for honey is manisan-lâbah, "the sweet of the honey-bee," but the Sanscrit name madu is of more frequent use.

HONGOTES. The name of a wild tribe of the island of Luzon, inhabiting the Cordillera, chiefly within the province of Nueva Ecija. They are of the brown-complexioned, lank-haired race, like the majority of the Philippine islanders, but described physically, as short of stature and weakly,—mischievous and predatory in their manners, and using their poisoned arrows with a skill only inferior to that of the Negritos.

HORSE. The horse has been immemorially domesticated by most of the more advanced nations of the Malay Archipelago, wherever it could be made use of. The chief exceptions are the Malay peninsula, the eastern sea-board of Sumatra, and nearly the whole of Borneo, countries in which the people dwell on the marshy banks of rivers, in which there is not even a bridle-path, and fit, therefore, only for the boat and the buffalo. The native horse is always a mere pony, seldom reaching 13 hands high, and more generally of about 12 hands. There are many different breeds, every island having at least one peculiar to itself, and the large islands, several. Beginning with Sumatra, we have here at least two distinct races,—the Achin and Batubara, both small and spirited, but better adapted to draught than the saddle. Of all the countries of the Archipelago, Java is that in which the horse most abounds, and here we find several different breeds, as those of the hill countries, and those of the plains. Generally, the Java horse is larger than that of Sumatra, but in the language of the turf has less blood and bottom. The lowland horses, the great majority, are somewhat coarse and sluggish, but the upland spirited, smaller, and handsomer. According to the statistics of the Netherland government, the total number of horses in the island in 1842 was 291,578, and at present probably exceed 300,000. The horse, although of a very inferior breed, is found in the islands of Bali and Lomboc, but the next island to these eastward, Sumbawa, produces the handsomest breeds of the whole Archipelago. They are the Arab of the Archipelago, yet the blood is not the same as the Arab, for the small horse of Sumbawa, although very handsome, wants the fine coat and the blood head of the Arabian. There are in this island, and adjacent islets, three different races, that of Tambora, of Bima, and of Gunung-api, the last being most esteemed. Next to Java, horses are most abundant in Celebes. These are inferior in beauty to those of Sumbawa, but excel all others of the Malayan portion of the Archipelago, in combining the qualities of size, strength, speed, and bottom. A very good breed is produced in Sumba, called in our maps Sandalwood Island. But perhaps the best breed of the whole Archipelago, although still but a pony, is that of the Philippines. It is superior in size to any of the breeds of the western islands, which it may owe to the superior pastures of the Philippines, and, possibly, to a small admixture of the Spanish horses of America, although this last is, by no means, an ascertained point.

In the Archipelago, as in other parts of the world, the colour of the horse is singularly connected with quality, temper, and locality. The prevailing colour with the horse of Achin is pye-ball, which becomes more and more rare as we proceed eastward. The most frequent colours of the Batak or Batubara horse are bay and mouse. In Java, the best and the most prevailing colours are grey, bay, and mouse, and the worst black and chestnut. To the last colour, indeed, the Javanese have such an antipathy, that a chestnut horse is expressly forbidden to enter the precincts of the royal courts, or to join in the public tournaments. In the Bima and other ponies of Sumbawa, bays, greys, and duns, are the most frequent and most approved. Blacks and chestnuts are rare, and a pye-ball is as rare as a black among Arabs. Among the Malays, the highest breed of horses is designated by the name of Sâm-brani, but what that means no one can tell, and it must be concluded that it is a purely mythical name.

Generally, the horses of the Archipelago are hardy, surefooted, and docile. The horses are all entire, and the mares used only to breed and as beasts of burden. By the natives of the Archipelago the horse is only used for the saddle or to carry burdens, and never for draught, either for plough, or wheel-carriage. To see horses drawing a native carriage, except in imitation of Europeans, we must go to the sculptures on ancient temples in Java, where they are thus represented. The Javanese have used them in war, and where there were no real horses, they might have been formidable, but against a cavalry mounted on the latter, they are of course worthless. On the invasion of Java in 1811, the French government of the island had a corps mounted on native horses, but it never thought of meeting the charge of a squadron of British dragoons, mounted on the large and active horses of southern India.

The origin of the horse of the Malay Archipelago is as obscure as that of the same animal in other parts of the world, America, Australia, and the islands of the Pacific excepted. Its name in Malay, and the only one it has in that language, kuda, is a corruption of the Sanscrit ghura, and this might lead to the belief that it was brought originally from some Hindu country. In this case, however, we must suppose that no other horses were brought than ponies, which is improbable,—or that the race has degenerated as to size, which is not likely, since it has not degenerated either in spirit or symmetry, but on the contrary is in fact superior in these respects to the continental horse. This hypothesis is made still more improbable when we find that, in the Javanese language, the popular name for the horse, jaran, is a native word. It is true that the Javanese has also four synonyms, but these are all foreign words. Thus, in the polite dialect the name is kapal, which, in the Tâlinga language, is the name for a ship, here probably used in a similar figurative sense to that by which the Arabs designate the camel the "ship of the desert." The three other synonyms are all Sanscrit, and belong to the obsolete and recondite language, namely, turongga, waji, and kuda, the last being the same which has become the popular name in Malay, having, most probably, superseded a native one. The popular Javanese name has extended, unchanged, to the language of the Lampungs of Sumatra, and it is found in the Bugis of Celebes in the corrupt form of añarang, and in the Rotti the language of a small island adjacent to Timur, as dalan. In the other languages of countries in which the horse is found, the Sanscrit name kuda prevails, and from its form evidently derived through the Malays.

In two islands only of the Archipelago is the horse found in the wild state—Celebes and Luzon—the only ones that are known to have extensive grassy plains fit for its pasture, and in these it is caught by the lasso and broke in as in the Llanos of America. In such situations it is certainly far more likely to have become wild from the domestic state than to be indigenous. In so far as Celebes is concerned this view is rendered probable by the name being a corruption of the Javanese in one language of that island, the Wugi, while in another, the Macassar, the horse is called "the buffalo of Java." In the Philippines it is not even alleged that the wild horses are anything else than domesticated ones become so. In Pigafetta's enumeration of the domestic animals of Çebu, he makes no mention of the horse, nor do the Spaniards who followed Magellan allege that they found the horse in Luzon or any of the other islands. In none of the languages of the Philippines, in fact, does there exist any native or any Asiatic name for it, the only one throughout being the Spanish one, cavallo. The horse, then, is neither indigenous in the Philippines, nor was it introduced like the buffalo by the Malayan nations before the arrival of the Spaniards. But from what quarter it was brought, or at what time, it is not easy to say. Most probably it was early introduced, and the countries from which it could be most easily brought would be Celebes, Mindano, and the Sulu Islands. It seems probable that the horse so introduced might have been improved by a few Spanish horses brought from America, but even this supposition is not necessary to account for the superiority of the Philippine horses over those of the western and southern islands, for the better pastures of the Philippines would be quite sufficient to do so. Some Spanish writers have fancied that the horse introduced into the Philippines was

Spanish, degenerated in time by the soil and climate. This hypothesis, however, is not tenable; for the Spanish horse, although neglected, has not degenerated at least in size in similar latitudes and even worse soils in America. The theory of degeneration as to size must, indeed, be given up, when we find that since the time of the English occupation of Java very good full-sized horses have been bred in that island, a much less favourable situation than Luzon.

It might at first sight be supposed that the horse may have been introduced into the countries of the Archipelago from those parts of the continent nearest to them—Siam and Cambodia—in which, as with themselves, small horses or ponies only are found. This hypothesis, however, is only plausible. Between the countries in question and the islands of the Archipelago not much intercourse has existed at any time, and in the peninsula, the nearest part to them, the horse does not exist at all. Even in the parts of Siam and Cambodia, nearest the islands, the horse is not used, and its monosyllabic names in the languages of these countries bear no resemblance to any of those of the insular tongues. We must come then to the conclusion that the horse of the Asiatic Archipelago cannot be traced to any foreign stock, nor to any native wild one now in existence. All that can safely be asserted is, that it seems to have been tamed for many ages, and that its first domestication belongs to a time beyond the reach of history or reasonable conjecture.

In the city of Manilla a pair of good riding horses costs from 100 to 120 dollars, and a pair of carriage horses from 20 to 30. Of course they are much cheaper in the provinces where they are reared. The horses of Sambawa, Celebes, and Sumba, are largely exported to Java, to the British settlements in the Straits of Malacca, and even as far as the Mauritius. In Batavia a good Bima or Batak horse is worth from 10*l*. to 15*l*.

I.

IJEN. The name of one of the highest mountains of Java, rising to the height of 10,000 feet above the level of the sea. It is situated in the province of Buñuwangi, directly opposite to the island of Bali, where the strait is narrowest. It is the last mountain of Java in an eastern direction that has an active volcano. The name seems to signify "sole" or "unique."

ILIM. The name of an island lying off the south-western end of the large island of Mindano, in the Philippines, and parted from it by a strait about a quarter of a league broad. It is about 9·4 geographical miles in length, and 3·4 in breadth, with an area of 29 square geographical miles, mountainous, and naked of timber. It forms a part of the province of Mindoro, and on its western coast it has a small town or village of the same name.

ILOC. The name of one of the islands of the Calamianes group in the Philippines, lying south of that of Linacapan, and north-east of Paragua, or the northern portion of the great island of Palawan. It is 10 miles in length and 5 in breadth, with a superficies of 35 square geographical miles. Iloe is mountainous, covered with forest, and the fisheries of its coast are very productive, but that coast is surrounded, especially on the western side, by many rocks and islets, which make access to it difficult and dangerous, and hence it is little frequented.

ILOCOS (from the Tagala word Iloc, a river). The name of an old province of the island of Luzon, forming a considerable portion of its north-western end. It is bounded by the sea to the west, by the great cordillera of Caraballos to the east, and extends from north latitude 16° 39′ to 18° 30′. This great province, conquered by Juan Salcedo, the brother-in-law of Legaspi, the discoverer and first governor of Luzon, was divided in 1818 into two provinces—a north and a south.

ILOCOS-NORTE, or northern Ilocos, is bounded to the east by the province of Cagayan, to the south by Ilocos-sur, and to the west by the Chinese Sea. On the land side it has a boundary of 83·7, and by the coast, one of 88·9 geographical miles. It is computed to have an area of 1388 square geographical miles. Two mountain chains pass through it, and its surface is generally broken and uneven. Its mountains are covered with forest, producing valuable timber and dye-woods, among which the sappan wood or Cæsalpinia sappan is abundant. Its principal agricultural products are rice, wheat, cotton, sesame, sugar-cane, coffee, and cacoa. Horses are largely bred in it. The climate is moist, cloudy, and for the Philippines cold, for Reaumur's thermometer frequently falls to 8° in winter, and hail is occasionally experienced.

The province is, however, sheltered from the severity of the north-eastern monsoon by the high chain of the Caraballos, and therefore considered agreeable and salubrious. Its communications both by land and water with Manilla are stated to be convenient. In 1818 the population was 135,748, and in 1850, 157,558, paying a poll-tax of 315,125 reals of plate. The relative population is 112 to the square geographical mile.

ILOCOS-SUR. The area of this province, one of the most fertile and populous of the Philippines, is 676 square geographical miles. Its surface is broken by spurs proceeding from the chain of Caraballos, which forms its eastern boundary, dividing it from Abra by glens, valleys, and rivers, the last being numerous, the principal of them being the Abra, which disembogues on its coast. This province has several harbours, the safest and the best of which are Salomaque and Currimao, which have sufficient depth of water for frigates, and are the most commodious of Luzon, north of the bay of Manilla. Its climate is temperate, less moist than that of the northern province, and like it sheltered from the violence of the north-eastern monsoon by the Caraballo mountains. There is one volcano within this province, but it is probable that some part of its formation is Plutonic, as a considerable quantity of gold is washed from the sands of its rivers by the wild tribe—the Igorrotes. The mountains are covered with an almost impenetrable forest, containing a vast supply of useful building timber and dye-woods, and in which the wild hog and buffalo, with several deer, are found. The bulk of the inhabitants of this and the northern province are of the same race with the other civilised inhabitants—men with lank hair, olive complexions, large eyes, and flat faces. Their customs and manner of living are also generally the same, but in one respect they differ from them and the other civilised inhabitants of the Philippines, in living in agglomerations of huts or villages remote from the fields they cultivate. Thus Laog, in the northern province, contains a population of above 20,000 inhabitants, while the lands they till are at a distance of two or more leagues. The main people of Ilocos speak a peculiar language called after them, distinct from the Tagala, although having many words in common with it. Besides this main population Ilocos-sur contains the wild races called the Igorrotes and Tinguianes, with a few Negritos. In 1818 its population was said to be 135,743, and in 1850 it was 192,272, paying a poll-tax of 385,175 reals of plate. In this last enumeration was included 4354 Igorrotes, 1898 Tinguianes, 144 Negritos, 15 Chinese, 2118 mestizo Chinese, 100 Spaniards, and 471 mestizo Spaniards. The relative population rises to the high figure, for the Philippines, of 284·4 to the square geographical mile.

ILOILO, called also OGTONG, one of the three provinces into which the large and fine island of Panay is divided, and embracing the south-eastern angle of it. Its coast is broken by many estuaries, from which at high tides the sea flows into its rivers almost to their sources. The whole area of the province on the island of Panay is 155 leagues, and including Guimaras and some other islands which form part of it, 185. Its population in 1849 was 321,049. The mass of its race belongs to the Bisaya nation, so widely spread over the Philippines. But, besides, there were the following inhabitants in 1849—15 Spaniards, 470 Spanish mestizos, 11 Chinese, 663 Chinese mestizos, 5000 mountaineers called Mundos, and 500 Negritos. A brisk coasting trade is carried on between this province and most parts of the Philippines, the principal export being rice, and the chief port, which bears the same name as the province, being formed between the island of Guimaras and the main island. See PANAY.

INDIAN CORN. See MAIZ.

INDIGO. The plant generally cultivated for this dye in the Archipelago is the Indigofera tinctoria, the same usually grown for the same purpose on the continent of India. It is said to be indigenous, at least in several islands, and this would seem to be confirmed by its having everywhere a native name. This name is generally the same in all the languages, for there can be little doubt but that the tarum of the Malay, the tom of the Javanese, the tayum and the tayung of the Tagala and Bisaya, are one and the same word. But the case is different with the dye or drug, for this is always called by a foreign name,—the well-known Sanscrit one, nila, literally "blue." From these two facts it may be at least conjectured that the Hindus taught the inhabitants of the Archipelago the art of extracting the dye and using it,—that the plant is indigenous, and that the culture of it, along with the art of manufacture, were conveyed from the western nations of the Archipelago, those nearest to the Hindus and most in communication with them, to the more remote tribes, as in the instance of the people of the Philippines. All the indigo manufactured by the natives of the Archipelago is in a liquid and fetid form, and the process of drying the pure fecula is entirely one of European introduction, conducted nowhere but in Java and the Philippines, and then always under European or Chinese superintendence.

INDRA. The name of the Hindu god of the air, and in Malay and Javanese that also of a class of aërial beings. It is found in the names of places, as in the three subsequent examples :

INDRAGIRI, in Sanscrit, "the hill of Indra;" the name of a Malay state on the north-eastern side of Sumatra, lying between that of Jambi and Kampar, and within the alluvial plain which extends from the eastern slopes of the mountain chain to the sea. The river, which has the same name, is one of the largest of Sumatra, having its source in the mountains, and disemboguing in the Straits of Malacca, opposite to the islands of Linga and Singkep. About the year 1252, Indragiri is said to have been conquered by the Javanese, and to have been afterwards made over by them to the kings of Malacca. Very little is known respecting it, except that it is a vast forest, with a sprinkling of inhabitants along the banks of the river and its affluents.

INDRAMAYA, in Sanscrit "the illusion of Indra;" the name of a district on the northern side of Java, in the country of the Sundas, and forming a part of the modern province of Krawang. It is low, alluvial, and scantily peopled and cultivated.

INDRAPURA, in Sanscrit "the city of Indra;" is the name of a Malay country on the western side of Sumatra, said to have been an offshoot from the inland kingdom of Menangkabo, and to have been once a state of some consequence, although now, and for a long time, of none whatever.

INDRAPURA. This is also the name given to a mountain in the same country. This is in south latitude 1° 2′, and rises to the height of 8500 feet above the level of the sea.

INTEREST OF MONEY: in Malay, bunga-mas, or shortly bunga; and in Javanese, kambang-mas, or in the polite dialect, sâkar-kânchana. These expressions signify "flower of gold," that is, profit of money. By the strict letter of Mahommedan law, interest and usury are one and the same, and are expressly prohibited, so that the legitimate profits of capital in gold and silver are held to be sinful. Except by a few rigid observers of the precepts of the Koran, this foolish law is disregarded by the Mahommedan inhabitants of the Archipelago.

IRON. Most of the nations of the Archipelago,—even many of those in a very rude state of society, have immemorially possessed the knowledge of malleable iron, and even of steel. How they came by it, it is impossible to imagine, but, judging by language, the only evidence we have on the subject, the invention appears to have been a native one, and not borrowed from any foreign people. All the names for iron, and all those for steel, with the exception of one synonym, are native words. The countries in which iron ore, fit for smelting, are most abundant, are the Peninsula, Sumatra, and Borneo; and those in which it is least so, Java, and the other islands within the great volcanic band. Even at present, when abundance of foreign iron is cheaply imported, native iron is still made in Sumatra and Borneo; but there is none made in Java, with a more civilised population, nor is there any evidence of its ever having been made in that or any other of the volcanic islands. It is to be inferred, therefore, that the process of smelting malleable iron and making steel, must have been first discovered in the non-volcanic countries; and among these, Sumatra, or at least the non-volcanic part of it, in which we find the most improved nations, would, probably, be among the earliest in which the invention would be made. In the language of the Malays, the leading nation of that island, the name for iron is bâsi, and it has extended to a great many of the languages of the Asiatic Archipelago, including nearly all those within the volcanic band. Thus we have it in the Javanese with one commutable consonant changed into another, as wâsi. This is the only name for it in this language, so frequently abounding in synonyms, excepting in the polite dialect, where we have the factitious one, tosan, meaning the "firm or hard object." The Malay name, however, although very prevalent over the Archipelago, is not the only one. In the language of the Kayan, the most powerful and advanced of the wild tribes of Borneo, and great manufacturers of iron, the name is titi. Iron ore abounds in the Philippines, and the natives, on the first discovery by Europeans, were found in possession of the knowledge of malleable iron. In the two principal languages of these islands, we find, therefore, names for it distinct from the Malay one; for in the Tagala it is called balakal, and in the Bisaya, salsalon. The Malay name for steel, baja, is even more general through the Archipelago than that for iron. In Javanese it is the only name, with the exception of a factitious one for the polite language, which signifies "perverse or refractory." But here, as in the case of iron, the Malay name is not the only one, for the Kayan of Borneo, and the Bisaya of the Philippines, have national ones. With respect, however, to both iron and steel, it is to be observed that the Malay names seem to have superseded native ones, where the influence of the Malays and their language have been extensive, as in the examples of most of the wild tribes of Borneo. Seemingly in the same manner, the Spanish word for steel, acero, has superseded a native one in the Tagala of the Philippines; while the original one has been preserved in the Bisaya of the same islands. The names of the tools and implements connected with the manufacture of iron, and of its productions, such as bellows, anvil, hammer, tongs, file, chisel, saw, nail, knife, kris, of the Malay language, extend to the principal languages of Java, Bali, Lomboc, and Celebes; and a few of them even to the languages of the Philippines. In the latter, however, most of them are native words, and all of them seem to be so in the language of the Kayans of Borneo. The inference then to be drawn from all these facts is, that the fabrication of iron and steel are native inventions,—that these metals were first manufactured in the non-volcanic countries, and that the discovery was made at several independent points, as Sumatra, Borneo, and Luzon in the Philippines.

The countries of the Archipelago in which iron ore seems to be most abundant, are, as already stated, Sumatra, in the interior country of Menangkabo, where iron has been immemorially smelted and manufactured for all Sumatra, and even for some of the other islands,—the Malay Peninsula,—its adjacent islands, and Borneo. In the Peninsula the ore, although not smelted at least to any extent, is very abundant; and for this we have the authority of a personal observer and a man of science. Mr. J. R. Logan, in his account of the physical geography of the Peninsula, informs us that "Iron ores are everywhere found, and in the south they exist in vast profusion. In some places the strata have been completely saturated with iron; and here, the bare surface of the ground, strewed with blackish scoriform gravel and blocks, presents a strange contrast to the exuberant vegetation of surrounding tracts, appearing as if it had been burnt and blasted by subterraneous fires. Much of the ordinary forms of iron-masked rocks, which are common, and so little regarded for their metallic contents that in Singapore they are used to macadamise the roads, contain often near 60 per cent. of pure metal."—Journal of the Indian Archipelago; Vol. ii., p. 102. In the islands of Banca and Billiton iron ore is very abundant; and in the last of them, good iron appears to have been manufactured, at one time, by its Malay inhabitants. But of all the Archipelago, the country in which iron ore is best in quality and most abundant is Borneo. On this subject we have the testimony of several different and competent observers; and as the subject is of importance, in an economic and commercial view, I shall quote their opinions at some length, premising that the ore is found and worked from the fifth degree of north latitude on the north-western side of the island to the equator on the southern, and to the 4th degree of south latitude on the western; and smelted at many points within this wide range. "The Dusun iron ore," says a writer on the manufacture of iron, in the Moniteur des Indes, whose information is drawn from an essay on this subject in the Transactions of the Batavian Society: "is found in the ravines, the rivers, and even in the plains of the province which gives its name; and in which whole families are to be seen almost constantly employed in searching for, extracting and smelting it. In general the ore is found at the depth of a mètre (39·37 inches) from the surface, but in the dry season it is obtained from the bed of the main river, the Dusun. This mineral, contains much ferruginous acid, and appears to have particular properties which give it much analogy with the wotz of continental India. The Malays of Banjarmasin distinguish two kinds of the ore,—that of the river, and that of the mountains; the last characterised by its hardness and its brown-coloured fracture."

The process of smelting is thus described by the same authority. "In order to smelt this ore, the Dusuns (the name of one of the wild tribes,) make a clay furnace 1·25 mètres in height, and 1·5 in diameter. This, of which the walls are 62 centimes of a mètre in thickness, is furnished with a chimney and a pair of bellows, with an opening having an iron grating for the flow of the slag. They begin by roasting the ore on a wooden fire; and having broken it, they place it in the furnace between two beds of charcoal. A workman then begins to blow the bellows, at first gently, and then with more force, so as to raise the heat to the greatest possible degree. When the metal is considered sufficiently reduced, it is allowed to run on the ground, more of the consistence of a paste than a fluid. In this state it is stirred about, scummed, and the impurities, which it still retains, passed into a gutter under a grating. The metal is then replaced in the furnace, and kept there until sufficiently cool to be subjected to the hammer. Finally, it is cut into small bars of 62 centimes of a kilogramme on an anvil, similar to that of our own blacksmiths. The price of a cattie (1⅓lb. English,) is from 30 to 35 centimes of a franc, if of the first quality; and 25 if of the second. On the spot, the value of Dusun iron compared with English, is as 25 to 21; and of Dusun steel to English, as 25 to 20." The country of the Dusuns, who manufacture this iron, lies between the first and second degrees of south latitude; and the 115th degree of east longitude runs through it."

Mr. Robert Burns, who visited the tribe of the Kayans from the north-eastern coast, gives a very similar account of the manufacture of iron among them. He says they are industrious, and among other examples adduces "their knowledge of the manufacture of iron and steel from the native ore." "This knowledge must," he adds, "have greatly tended to keep them independent and superior in power to the other aboriginal tribes of the islands. From the native ore they make their wood-cutting implements, spears, and swords, and many other articles in use. Commonly, at every village, there is a place for smelting iron, in all the process of which the community mutually partake. Covered by a shade, the rude furnace consists of a circular pit, formed in the ground 3 feet deep and 4 feet in diameter. Previous to the smelting process, the ore is roasted and broken into small pieces. The coals (charcoal) in the furnace being set fire to and well kindled, the prepared ore is placed over them in alternate layers with coals. The ventilators used consist of wooden tubes, 10 to 12 in number, about 6 feet long, and placed vertically round the furnace. The bore of each is about 7 inches in diameter, and the pistons to correspond are armed with cloth or soft bark. Attached to the piston rods are others of considerable length, to which weights are made fast and balanced on the cross-beams of the shed. By this contrivance the pistons are moved up and down, and a constant blast produced, which is led by clay pipes from the orifice at the bottom of each tube into the furnace. In the smelting process there is no flux used with the ore which yields about 70 per cent. of iron. The iron manufactured from the ore of the above district is much preferred to that of Europe by the Malays and other natives of Borneo as being superior." Journal of the Indian Archipelago, vol. iii., p. 151. The district referred to in the last sentence, and which equally abounds in fossil coal as in iron ore, extends from the river Baram to that of the Pajang, or from about 2° 30′ north latitude to 4° 50′.

Mr. Dalton, an English traveller, who visited the Kayans in 1828, and lived for several months among them, gives the following account of their manufacture on the southern side of the island about the equator, and the 117° of east longitude. "Having but briefly mentioned the excellence of the iron and steel of these people, it may not be amiss to say something more on the subject, it being little understood how much the Dyaks excel in these articles. The iron found all along the coast of Borneo is of a very superior quality, which every person must know who has visited Pontianak and Sambas. At Banjarmasin, however, it is much superior; they have there a method of working it which precludes all necessity of European steel, excepting for cock's-spurs, which they prefer when made from a razor. But the best iron of Banjarmasin is not equal to that worked by the rudest Dyaks. All the best kris blades of the Bugis rajahs and chiefs are manufactured by them, and it is a most singular but an undoubted fact, that the further a person advances, the better will be found all instruments of iron. Selji's (the native chief with whom the traveller resided) country is superior in this respect to all those nearer the coast, his goloks (cutlasses), spears, and kris-blades being in great demand. I have counted 49 forges at work merely in the campung of Marpao (the chief village), but the Mandaos (swords) and spears which he uses himself and gives to his favourite warriors are obtained, iron-made, further north. Instruments made of this last will cut through overwrought iron and common steel with ease. I have had several pen-knives shaved to pieces with them by way of experiment, and one day having bet a wager of a few rupees with Selji that he would not cut through an old musket barrel, he without hesitation put the end of it on a block of wood and chopped it to pieces without in the least turning the edge of the mandao. This favourite weapon he presented to me as the greatest and most acceptable present he could bestow, and I gave it to the governor of Macassar who, I believe, sent it to his excellency the Commissioner of Java. I may here mention another proof of their power. In the Sultan of Coti's house I have myself seen three muskets belonging to Major Muller's detachment, which were each cut half through in several places by the mandaos of the party which destroyed them. I once mentioned this circumstance to Selji : he laughed and assured me the mandaos used on that occasion were not made of his iron, otherwise the barrels would have been cut through at every stroke." Moor's Notices of the Indian Archipelago, p. 51.

A similar iron ore and manufacture exist on the western side of the island in the neighbourhood of the equator, and in about the 110° of east longitude, being 7° west of that described in the last paragraph, is described by an anonymous but very judicious traveller, whose account is to be found in the compilation above quoted. "Iron," says he, "is principally procured from Jellé in the interior of Matan (a Malay principality) in sufficient quantities to form an article of export, when it is known by the name of bâsi-ikat (faggot iron) from the manner in which it is made up. The pieces, each about 8 or 9 inches long, 1½ broad, and half an inch thick, form a small bundle, and five of these a large one, which weighs about 19 or 20 catties, and sells at Matan for about three Spanish dollars. It is collected by the Dyaks, and is of superior quality, as tools made of it are not steeled. It is in great demand among the natives, and is imported advantageously at Pontianak, both from Matan and from Banjarmasin, at which places it is known by the name of bâsi-desa (country iron)" page 8.

The price of the native iron, as quoted in the last paragraph, is about 50*l.* a ton, and that given for the best quality of that of Banjarmasin, previously mentioned, about one-half that amount, both being of course retail prices. We have here, then, the testimony of four independent witnesses to prove a very wide dissemination of rich iron ore over Borneo, and that superior iron and steel are made from it by different rude races, and by processes exceedingly simple. To judge by the rude methods by which the ore is picked up, rather than mined, it seems also to be abundant, and if we believe one of the travellers, it is rich in metal. Considering the rude nature of the process of manufacture, it is more than probable that the good quality of the metal produced depends chiefly on the superiority of the ore, and that it will be found, when subjected to scientific analysis, a magnetic oxide, such as yields the best iron and steel of Sweden, and the wotz steel of Southern India. Most of the iron and steel manufactured in other Asiatic countries by civilised nations, including even that of the ingenious Chinese, is not above one-half the value of English iron and steel, while that of the wild Dyaks is by from near 20 to 25 per cent. superior to them.

If the ore should turn out of the quality described, it might perhaps be imported to advantage for the use of our English foundries. The most eligible quarter for obtaining it, would probably be the north-western side of Borneo, which is penetrated by several rivers, navigable to a considerable distance for coasting craft, such as the Baram, the Bintulu, and the Rajang. If found near the banks of any of these, it might be conveyed to Labuan or Singapore, as dead weight for ships returning to England. With any tolerable security for life and property, the mining would be effectually conducted by the Chinese. Coal and antimony are found in the same localities as the iron ore. The whole subject deserves inquiry, and the first point ought to be a scientific analysis of the iron ore.

ISINAYES. A wild tribe of the island of Luzon, resembling in physical form the Igorrotes, but by the exertions of the Spanish clergy converted to Christianity They inhabit the mountains lying east of the province of Ilocos-sur.

ISLAM. An Arabic word adopted by all the nations converted to Mahommedanism, and signifying that religion. Although properly a noun, it is much more frequently employed, conformably to the practice of the insular languages in all such cases, as an adjective, as in the examples, "orang-islam," a Moslemman, and "agama-islam," the Mahommedan religion, being united in the first instance with a native, and in the last with a Sanscrit word.

ITANEGS, called also, Tinguianes, one of the unconverted wild tribes of the island of Luzon, of the Malayan race, inhabiting the mountains between the provinces of Ilocos-sur and Abra. This is the most civilised of all the wild tribes of the Philippines, practising a husbandry of considerable skill, carrying on some ingenious manufactures, trading with the inhabitants of the coast, dwelling in villages and being decently clad. From their fairer complexions, and more industrious habits, the Spaniards imagine them to be derived from Chinese settlers from the province of Fokien, but this notion is probably without any foundation.

ITAPANES, the name of one of the wild tribes of the island of Luzon, inhabiting the recesses of the mountains of the northern portion of the island. They are described as short of stature, but well-made, and with darker complexions than their neighbours, the Igorrotes, the Guimanes, the Busayas, and the Gaddanes—having large flat noses, and round eyes. In stature, complexion, and shape of the nose, they are described as resembling the Aetas or negritos, but in texture of hair and form of the eyes, the Tagalas and other civilised inhabitants. From this seeming union, the Spaniards infer that the Itapanes are a mixture of the negrito and Malay races, a notion, however, for which there is, probably, no substantial foundation. They have been equally difficult to civilise as the Negritos themselves, with whom they have many customs in common.

ITAS, or AETAS, the native name by which the diminutive negros of the Philippines are usually known. See NEGRO and AETAS.

J.

JACATRA. An European corruption of the compounded Sanscrit word, Jaya-karta, signifying "work of victory," and the name of a town of the Sunda nation of Java, on the site of which now stands the Dutch city of Batavia, founded in 1619.

JACK-FRUIT. See ARTOCARPUS.

JAKUN. This is a name of unknown origin and meaning, which the Malays apply, seemingly as a generic term, to the wild tribes of the interior of the peninsula, from Malacca, southward to Johor. All the men that go under this name have the same physical form as the Malays, speak the same language in a ruder form, and seem, in short, to be Malays, without the Mahommedan religion, and in a much lower state of civilisation. The notion of some writers, founded on certain resemblances of physical form, that the Jakuns are of Tartar origin, is, in the absence of all historical or philological evidence, and when the two parties, supposed to be the same people, are separated from each other by at least forty degrees of latitude, too whimsical for serious consideration. The Malays of Sumatra continue, down to the present day, to emigrate to and settle in the interior of the peninsula, and the great probability seems to be, that in remote times, the peninsula was without any other inhabitants than the negros of the mountains, and that all its brown-complexioned, lank-haired people, whether of the sea-board or the interior, were emigrants from Sumatra, or the islands lying between it and the peninsula.

JAMBI. The name of a Malay state on the north-eastern side of Sumatra, and entirely within the great alluvial plain, which extends from the central chain of mountains to the Straits of Malacca. This state was visited in 1820 by my friend, the late Captain Crooke, a skilful surveyor, and a most careful and judicious observer, and we possess, consequently, more correct knowledge of it than of any other portion of the same side of Sumatra. To the north-east, Jambi is bounded by the sea, having in front the great group of islands which nearly blocks up the strait between Sumatra and the continent,—to the north-west by the Malay state of Indragiri,—to the east by the inland Malay states of Korinchi and Menangkabo, and to the south-east by forests thinly peopled by the wild race of the Kubu, lying between Jambi and Palembang. One large river of the same name as the state, and having several considerable affluents, runs through the whole country, having its origin in the mountains. It bifurcates at 50 miles from the sea, and falls into it by two mouths. The most easterly of these, shallow at its entrance, is in south latitude 1° 2′ 30″, and is called in the Malay language kwala-sâdu, literally, "embouchure of sobs." The most westerly, in Malay, kwala-ñur, or "coco-palm mouth," is in 1° south, and, although the smallest, is the most navigable. The face of the country is flat and even, being nowhere diversified by mountains or hills. Towards the sea-coast it is low, swampy, and subject to inundation, but, as it recedes from the shore, it becomes proportionally elevated and dry. The land rises in an inclined plain from the sea towards the great central chain of mountains, and at the town of Jambi, 60 miles from the coast, in a direct line, it is 20 feet above the level of the river in the dry season, but only 5 feet during the rains, when the river is swollen by 15 feet. The soil, at the town, is composed of a rich vegetable mould, over a bed of clay mixed with fine sand. At the depth of 11 or 12 feet there is a stratum of peat of various depth, containing trunks of trees of different dimensions, the undecayed bark, and the fibres of the wood retaining much of their natural colour, strength, and elasticity. The stratum below this is a fine light-coloured clay, slightly mixed with decayed vegetable matter in specks, where the stratum of peat disappears. Neither stone or gravel are found in the soil, though pebbles of quartz and fragments of iron-stone are washed down by the river from the interior and deposited on the sand-banks. Below the town, the banks continue to exhibit the same strata, till their height is considerably reduced, when the stratum of peat entirely disappears.

For full 30 miles from the sea in a straight line, or 50 by the course of the main river, the country of Jambi is uninhabited and uninhabitable, being in fact, a wooded marsh. "The banks of the Kwala-ñur," says Mr. Crooke, who sailed up this branch, "are throughout uninhabitable from their lowness, and present one uniform character of wooded and impenetrable loneliness. . . . Along the banks and in the neighbourhood of the streams and rivers only, is there any open ground or cultivation, a thick forest extending in every other quarter."

From this description of the country, it is certain that the population must be extremely scanty in relation to the area, which is probably not less than 15,000 square geographical miles. In ascending the river to the town of Jambi, Mr. Crooke counted only twelve villages, the total number of houses among them being only 118, with about perhaps from six to seven hundred inhabitants. The principal place or seat of government, called also, like the country and river, Jambi, is estimated by Mr. Crooke, including the villages just named, to have a population not exceeding 6000, but of the population of the upper portion of the Jambi and its affluents, nothing is known.

The following is Mr. Crooke's account of the chief town, which, by the course of the river, and reckoning from its western branch, is about a hundred miles from the sea. "The town of Jambi is about three quarters of a mile in extent on both banks of the river, to which it is nearly confined, the natives occupying the whole of the right bank, and the Arabs and other strangers, who are settled there, a part of the left. Many of the houses, especially those of the Arab kampong (quarter), are sided and partitioned in a neat manner with planks, and roofed with tiles, shaped with a waving line cross-ways, of excellent manufacture. A few are covered with a thatch of gomuti, which forms a durable roof, and some have their sides constructed of large thick pieces of bark. But the greater number are huts of mat and ataps (palmetto leaves), built on posts in the usual Malay style. Besides these descriptions of buildings, there is also a number of houses upon rafts composed of huge trunks of trees, clumsily put together, which, during the periodical swelling of the river, are afloat and moveable, but in the dry season are, generally, especially the larger ones, lodged on a sandy flat, which becomes dry and confines the stream on the right. There is also a number of little rafts supporting a small hut, attached to the better class of houses, and used for the convenience of bathing, of which the women, in particular, seem to be very fond. In fact, there is an appearance of cleanliness in the persons and houses of the inhabitants, rather unusual in Malay towns. They have a mosque, but it is in a neglected and ruinous condition. A burying-ground, about three quarters of a mile below the town, appears to claim more attention: many of its tombs are carved and gilded and inclosed by a tiled building."—Anderson's Mission, Appendix. At the town, which is destitute of all defence, the river, in the dry season, is 450 yards broad and has a depth of three fathoms, but in the rainy season its breadth is doubled, and it gains 15 feet in depth. All the way from the sea to the town the depth in the dry season ranges from 12 to 15 fathoms, with the exception of one spot below the town where it is only 8 feet.

As to roads, properly speaking, there are none. "The mode of communication," says Mr. Crooke, "between villages, as well as distant parts of the country, is almost exclusively by water, there being few habitations that are not situated on the rivers, or near them; and such routes as do exist are mere foot-paths through the woods. They extend, however, to Padang, Bencoolen, and other parts on the western side of the island, with which they are the means of commercial intercourse."

The climate, at the town of Jambi, is considered by the inhabitants healthy and agreeable, but the lower parts of the country subject to agues. In the beginning of July, the nominal winter, the thermometer of Fahrenheit, in no very favourable situation, stood, at sunrise, at from 76° to 77°; from two to three o'clock at 86°; and at eight at night, at 79°. Jumbi is subject to the monsoons that blow south of the equator, namely, the south-east and north-west, the same which blow in Java and the seas which surround it.

The bulk of the inhabitants of Jambi are genuine Malays, and besides those who dwell on "dry land," there are, towards the embouchures of the river, some of those Malays whose whole dwellings are their boats, the orang-laut, or "men of the sea," the same people whose migrations extend even as far as the Moluccas. In the town are to be found a few Javanese, and persons of Arabian descent. Formerly there were some Chinese, and their abandonment of the country is, here as elsewhere, a sure sign of anarchy. "The lower orders," says Mr. Crooke, "are generally below the middle size in stature; but in shape, they are generally muscular and well-proportioned, and their complexions are ordinarily fairer than those of the Malays commonly seen at Prince of Wales Island. They are ignorant, poor, and indolent, but they have neither incitement or means to be otherwise. They do not appear to possess the character of vindictive treachery, so commonly ascribed to the Malays. Although the country has, for two or three years, been in a state of civil war, few lives are said to have fallen a sacrifice to this calamity, though the population has been reduced by the numbers who have fled to other countries."—page 403.

The history of Jambi is as obscure and uncertain as that of all other Malay countries. It is enumerated as one of the twenty-nine states which, independent of those of the interior, existed, according to De Barros, on the arrival of the Portuguese in the Archipelago. Before the introduction of the Mahommedan religion, it is certain the people professed some form of Hinduism. Mr. Crooke discovered near the town of Jambi, and at the village of Muwara-jambi, mutilated Hindu images. Among these were statues of the bull Nandi, the vehicle of Mahadewa, and of the elephant-headed god Ganesa. These indicate the worship of Siva, or the Hindu destroyer, the most frequent form of Hinduism in ancient Java. The images, however, were not of trachyte, like all those of that island, but of a small-grained granite. This would show that they were certainly not imported from Java; and as neither granite nor any other rock exists within the territory of Jambi, it is to be inferred that either the images themselves, or the stone of which they were made, were brought from the high lands of the interior, most probably from the most civilised portion of the country, and the cradle, by its own account, of the Malayan people, Menangkabo. Within three hours' journey of the town, according to statements made to me by natives of the country, there still stand the ruins of a Hindu temple, constructed of brick similar to some of those found in the more easterly parts of Java.

The productions of Jambi are the same generally as those of the other parts of Sumatra. Small quantities of gold are imported from the mountain region of the interior, and, as before mentioned, its canes, jambees as they were called, were of such reputation in England as to have added a new word to our language, still retained in our dictionaries. The trade is trifling. The Dutch, who claim a supremacy over the country, lately established a port to protect it, at a place called Muwara-kompek, forty-two miles below the town of Jambi, where, as the name imports, two branches of the river rejoin, but it is liable to inundation in the season of the rains.

JAMBU. A generic Malay name for several kinds of fruit of different botanic genera, but which is probably borrowed from the Jambu-kling, the Eugenia Malaccensis of botanists. This is a fruit, with a rose-coloured cuticle, a spongy white flesh, of an agreeable subacid taste, and about the size and shape of an ordinary pear. It is of considerable esteem for the table.

JANGGALA. The name of an ancient kingdom of Java, in the country of the proper Javanese nation. Javanese authorities are not agreed as to the time when this kingdom, of great reputation in Javanese story, flourished. One manuscript places it in the year corresponding with that of Christ, 818, and another in 1082, the discrepancy probably arising, however, from its rise being referred to in one case, and its fall in the other. Its locality, or at least that of its capital, was the modern province of Surabaya, a district of which, strewed with ancient relics, still retains the name.

JAPAN. In Malay and Javanese Jâpon, which is nearly our own old orthography, Japon. The name is, no doubt, taken from that of the principal island in the Japanese language, Nipon, and in Chinese Jipun, the corruptions being taken by the natives of the Archipelago from the Portuguese. The Japanese empire is said to have been discovered by the Portuguese, in 1542, and then only by the accident of a trading junk, manned and owned by Portuguese, having been driven by a storm on its coast.

Upwards of thirty years, therefore, had elapsed from the conquest of Malacca, and sixteen from their first reaching China, before they had made the discovery. Yet it is very plainly indicated by Marco Polo, and on the arrival of the Portuguese in Malacca, Japanese junks seem to have frequented it. The Japanese are not, indeed, named by De Barros, as among the strangers that resorted to this port, but they are so in the Commentaries of Alboquerque, written by his son, who thus describes them under the name of Goré. "The Gorés (according to the information which Alfonso Alboquerque received when he conquered Malacca) stated that their country was a continent, but by the common voice, it is an island, from which there come, yearly, to Malacca, two or three ships. The merchandise which they bring are raw and wrought silks, brocades, porcelain, a large quantity of wheat, copper, alum, and much gold in ingots (ladrillos), marked by their king's stamp. It is not known whether these ingots be the money of the country, or whether the stamp be attached to indicate that their exportation is prohibited, for the Gorés are men of little speech, and will render an account of their country to no one. The gold is from an island near them, called Perioco, which abounds with it. The country of these Gorés, they themselves call Lequea. They are a fair people. Their garment is like a baladrois without a hood. They carry long swords of the form of the cimeters of the Turks, but a little narrower in the blade, and daggers of two palms long. They are bold men, to be feared on land. At the ports they come to, they do not unload their whole cargoes at once, but by little and little. They speak the truth, and desire that it be spoken to them; and if any merchant of Malacca departs from his word, they forthwith arrest him. They strive to have their ships despatched in a short time, and do not dwell in foreign lands, for they are not men that love to go beyond their own. They leave their own country in the month of January for Malacca, and return to it in August and September."—Commentarios do Grande Alfonso D'Alboquerque, collegido por seu filho das cartas que elle escrivia al muito poderoso Rey Don Manuel O primiero deste nome. Cap. 17, p. 353. Lisboa: 1576.

Of the origin or meaning of the word Goré, as applied to the Japanese, I can offer no conjecture, but it was probably the name, from whatever source derived, which the Malays gave them; but that of Liquea, which the Javanese themselves gave to their country, is probably derived from the Li-u-ki-u or Loochoo Islands, the nearest portion of the Japanese empire to the Asiatic Archipelago. The articles which composed the cargos which the Japanese brought to Malacca, their stamped gold pieces which still exist, and the wheat which no other country to the east of the Archipelago and communicating easily with it produces, seem clearly enough to identify the Gorés with the Japanese. The Spanish historians of the Philippines also inform us that previous to the discovery and conquest of these islands they were frequented by the Japanese for the purposes of trade. But the intercourse of this people with the Archipelago was, probably, inconsiderable, until the establishment of Portuguese and Spanish influence in Japan, and from that time, for the best part of a century, it went on with considerable activity. Japanese junks visited Manilla, Jacatra, and Bantam, and the people themselves migrated and settled in various parts of the Archipelago, as do now the Chinese, and they were employed, as the Chinese never were, as soldiers at the European establishments. The island of Luzon, in the Philippines, seems to have been the chief place to which they resorted, and here their numbers appear to have been so considerable that they rose twice in insurrection against the Spanish government. Then came in 1637 the decree of the Japanese government which, for now above two centuries, has nearly isolated Japan from the rest of the world. Its trade and migration ceased at once, and there is now not a vestige to show that the Japanese ever existed in the Archipelago. The Spaniards, indeed, allege that one of the wild races of Luzon, the Ifugaos, are the mixed descendants of the Japanese; but this is a mere hypothesis for which there seems no good foundation. The whole external intercourse of the Japanese empire, with a computed population of 25,000,000, is limited to that of the Dutch of Batavia, and of the Chinese of the province of Chekiang. The trade of the first is now restricted to a single ship, not allowed to export any other staple commodities than camphor and copper, while the export and import cargos are not to exceed the sum of about 80,000*l.* in value. The trade of the Chinese is much more valuable, for their junks amount to from 10 to 12, while their imports and exports, less restricted as to commodities, may each amount to the value of about 250,000*l.* At length, in 1854, through the enterprise of the Americans, intercourse with the nations of Europe and America has been so far relaxed, as to allow their ships to wood, water, and refresh, with an express prohibition, however, of carrying on trade.

JÁPAN, with the accent on the first syllable, is the name of a Javanese district, now forming part of the Netherland province of Surabaya. This is an inland country, and a fertile and populous one. Within it is the district of Wirasaba, in which was situated the ancient Hindu Javanese capital of Majapait, destroyed by the Mahommedans in 1478.

JAPARA. The name of a province of Java, comprehending Juwana, situated in the country of the Proper Javanese. It contains 63 square miles of teak forest, and its fisheries are valuable. In 1814 its population was computed at 216,096, but this had increased to 421,420 in 1845, when it had 92,000 head of oxen and buffalos, and 6600 horses. The area being 672 square miles, it follows that the rate of population to the square mile is no less than 671, making Japara, therefore, the most densely peopled part of Java. It is remarkable, however, that this population, by the census of 1850, was only 341,140, or had declined by better than 80,000, supposing both enumerations to have been made with equal care.

JAVA, although only an island of the second magnitude among those of the Archipelago, is incomparably the greatest in importance, and that in which has sprung up the highest civilisation. The name which we apply to it is correctly Jawa, and is derived from that of the principal nation which inhabits it. The word cannot stand by itself, and like many similar ones in the languages of the Archipelago is as often an adjective as a noun. When the country is referred to, it is preceded by some word signifying "land," and when it is the people, their language, or anything else, by words having these meanings, as Siti-Jawa, the land of Java; Wong-Juva, people of Java or Javanese. It is however to be observed that the "land of Java," as comprehending the whole island, although sometimes thus used by them, is not the usual sense in which it is employed by the natives themselves, who confine it, for the most part, to that portion of the island inhabited by the proper Javanese nation, in contradistinction to that inhabited by the Sundas, and which the Javanese call Pasundan, the "place or country" of the Sundas. This mode of naming a country, it will be seen, is analogous to that which in many cases prevails in European languages, as in the examples—England and Englishman, Inghilterra, and Inglese, with many others.

The word Jawa has no other meaning in the Javanese language than those now attributed to it. The only word, changing one labial for another (a frequent practice), that is essentially the same with it, is the preposition, Jaba, "outside," or "without," and to connect it with this would require a large stretch of etymological ingenuity. A legendary tradition of the Javanese themselves derives Java from Juwawát, the native name of a millet, Panicum Italicum, which, according to them, was the first food of the original inhabitants. An European etymology, equally absurd and extravagant, derives Java from the Sanscrit name for barley, jau, but unluckily for this conjecture, the corn in question is unknown to the inhabitants, and what is still worse, never could have been known as a native product, since it will not grow in the island, unless in a few elevated spots where no one attempts to grow it.

The Arabs call the island Jawi, and although this be the form of the word in the polite Javanese, the term is far more likely to be a corruption of that people themselves. It is however, although taken obviously from the word Jawa, applied by them to the whole Archipelago, its language, and inhabitants. The Chinese call the island Haoa-oua, and Jou-wa, which is as near the true word as could be expected from their intractable language. By their own account, however, it would seem that anciently they had given it the name of Che-po, or Chapo, which is probably only another corruption of the true word. Java was unknown even by name to the civilised nations of ancient Europe, and even to those of the middle ages. It is first named by Marco Polo, who, in his junk voyage from China to the Persian Gulf, passed through the northern part of the Archipelago about the close of the 13th century. He gives the name, due allowance made for errors of transcription, with sufficient correctness, as Giaua or Java, but his information being mere hearsay is in other respects erroneous. Thus, mistaking probably the products of its commerce for its indigenous productions, he enumerates among the latter cloves and nutmegs, and gold in quantity "exceeding all calculation and belief," although producing none at all.

No sooner had the Portuguese reached India by the route of the Cape of Good Hope than the name became familiar enough to Europeans. Thus, according to the Italian orthography of Ramusio, it is called by Ludovico Barthema and Edoardo Barbosa, Giava. The first of these travellers visited the island and remained 14 days in it, but his account is obviously false or worthless, for he describes parents as selling their children to be eaten by the purchasers, and himself as quitting the island in haste for fear of being made a meal of. Not so Barbosa, although he had not visited it, for he describes its productions, its trade, its manufacture of arms, and the persons, dress, and manners of its inhabitants with much accuracy. Pigafetta also calls the island by the same name as the two last named travellers, and although his information respecting it was derived, as he tells us himself, from the old pilot who accompanied him from the Moluccas, it is even more correct than that of Barbosa. Thus he describes the concremation of women as still practised in Bali, and as it no doubt once was in Java. He states that it contained large towns, and he names several of them, such as the ancient capital of Majapait, Japara, Sidayu, Tuban, Gressik, and Surabaya. It is true that these names are fearfully mis-spelt, but this arises in a good measure, probably, from errors of transcription. Thus, in the edition published at Milan in 1800 from the original manuscript, the conterminous districts of Japara and Sidayu are run into one word and written Cipaparasidain, and those of Tuban and Gârsik as Tubancressi, while Majapait is written Magepaher. The neighbouring islands of Madura and Bali are correctly written, just as they are at present, and they are described as being only half a league distant from Java.

How very little, however, was really known of Java by the early Portuguese of India, is to be seen from what De Barros, master of all the Indian archives, says of it in his third Decade, published in 1663, no less than 52 years after the conquest of Malacca, and several years after his countrymen had visited China, discovered Java, and traded with both. He makes it to consist of two islands, Java and Sunda, and his work contains a rude map, in which a great river, or rather a strait of the sea, is represented as dividing them. This he calls the river Chiamo, which may possibly be the Chitando of the Sundas, a considerable stream at the eastern boundary of their country, and which, in their language, signifies, "boundary water or river." His description is taken, apparently, from the report of Henrique Lemé, sent to Bantam in 1522, by George Alboquerque, Governor of Malacca.

This is his account of Java : "The land of Jauha is an island, which lies to the east of Çamatra, or so near to it that the strait between them does not exceed the breadth of 15 leagues. Its direction is from east to west, and its northern end is in 6° of south latitude; its eastern in 7° 30′. The length of the island is 190 leagues, but of its breadth we have no certain knowledge; for our people have not yet navigated its southern coast. According to the information of the natives, the whole of the southern side, on account of the great gulf of the ocean, has few harbours; and those who inhabit the northern side of the island hold no intercourse with the Gentiles who inhabit the southern. Through the middle of the island, by its length, there runs a chain of mountains which interrupts all communication. The natives constantly assert that the breadth of Jauha is equal to one-third its length. Generally, the people are idolaters. They are called Jaos, from the name of the land, and are the most civilised people (gente de mais policia) of these parts."—Decade second, book ix. chapters 3 and 4.

The account given in the third Decade of the supposed joint islands varies considerably from that just quoted, and is as follows :—"We make of the land of Jauha two islands, the one facing the other. The direction of both is from west to east, and in the same parallels of from 7° to 8° of south latitude. As the mariners of the east have laid these islands down in their charts, they are in their length, more or less, 180 leagues; but they are not so much, as we shall show in our Universal Geography. The Javanese themselves do not make two islands of Java, but consider the whole as one. As to the western end, where Java approaches Sumatra, there is a channel between them from ten to twelve leagues in breadth, through which the intercourse of the western world with the east was conducted before Malacca was founded, as we have already written. Java, through its whole length, has in the middle a chain of mountains of great height, distant from the northern shore about 25 leagues; but as to their distance from the southern shores, the inhabitants have no recent knowledge, although they think it is the same. For about a third part of the length of Java, counting from its western end, is Sunda of which we have now to treat. Its inhabitants hold it to be an island, divided from Java by a river, little known to our navigators, and which they call Chiamo or Chenano. This intersects the whole of this part of the country as far as the sea, in such a manner that when the people of Java describe their own country, they say that it is bounded to the west by the island of Sunda, parted from it by the aforesaid river Chiamo; on the east by the island of Bali; to the north, by Madura; and to the south, by an undiscovered ocean. They hold that whoever passes by this strait (the river Chiamo) into the South Sea, is carried away by a violent current, and cannot return. For this reason, they do not navigate the South Sea, in like manner as the Moors, from Caffraria to Sofala, never pass the Cape for fear of the great current that prevails there. The inhabitants of Sunda, in praising their country and boasting of its superiority over Java, say that God established the aforesaid river Chiamo as a partition between them."—Decade third, book viii. chapter 1.

The island of Java lies between 105° 12′, and 114° 4′ east longitude, and 5° 52′ and 8° 40′ south latitude. It is the only great land of the old world of native civilisation within the southern hemisphere. In form it is long and narrow, its length being in a direction nearly east and west, with a slight inclination to the south. Its extreme length is 575 geographical miles, while its breadth varies from 48 to 117. Its area has been computed at 37,029 geographical square miles, which would make it about one-third part larger than Ireland. To the north, Java is separated from Borneo by the broad, but comparatively shallow, Java Sea; to the south, by the deep Indian Ocean, without a foot of land intervening between it and the Antarctic Pole, save towards its eastern extremity, a corner of the Australian continent. To the north-west, it is parted from Sumatra by a strait, at its narrowest part only 14 miles wide, and with islands between; and to the east from Bali, by a strait of no more than two miles broad. On its low, and in some measure, sheltered northern coast, Java has a good many islands, by far the largest and most important of which is Madura, so connected with it as to form almost a portion of itself; for although the strait which divides them is generally 30 miles broad, at the western end of Madura it is hardly one mile. On the bold precipitous southern coast there are very few islands, and two only of very considerable size, those of Baron and Kambangan.

The coast line of Java, which is about 1400 English miles in extent, has many bays on its northern coast, but it is not deeply penetrated by any one of them; so that it has properly no harbour but one, that of Surabaya, formed between the main island and Madura, where the strait that divides them is still narrow. The southern coast is still less indented. Here there are two harbours only, Pachitan—inconvenient and unsafe, and Chalachap, formed between the main island and Kambangan, or "floating island," out of the way of intercourse, and little, if at all frequented. On the coast of the deep and bold southern side there is no safe anchorage, while a heavy and dangerous surge rolls in on the shore in every season.

With the single exception named, the ports of the northern coast are but open roadsteads, with good anchoring ground; but the inconvenience of wanting land-locked harbours is not felt so near the equator, where hurricanes are never experienced, and where the weather is only tempestuous occasionally at the change of the monsoons.

The physical outline of Java may be divided into five different sections of various breadth. Beginning from the western end, and following the line of the northern coast, the first section ends with the eastern side of the bay of Batavia. This is about 75 miles in average breadth. The second extends east as far as Cheribon, in longitude 108° 36′, and is about 95 miles broad. Both these divisions are mountainous, the mountains being of less elevation than in the other parts of the island, but more crowded, and with narrower valleys. They constitute the proper country of the Sundas, who speak a distinct language, and are less advanced in civilisation than the Javanese, the nation which occupies all the rest of the island. The Sunda portion may be said to stand in the same relation to Java proper that Wales does to England, Lower Brittany to France, and the Basque Provinces to Spain. The third section extends from Cheribon to the western side of the promontory of Japara, in about longitude 110° 30′, and its breadth does not exceed 50 miles, the island being greatly narrowed by the bay which extends for 140 miles from the point of Indramaya to that of Japara. The fourth section extends from the promontory of Japara to that portion of the island which is opposite to the western end of Madura, and this has an average breadth of about 100 miles. The fifth section embraces the remainder of the island, and is no more than 50 miles in breadth. In the three last sections, the mountains are of greater elevation, the plains more spacious, and along their northern coasts there runs generally a belt of alluvial land, varying from five to fifteen miles in depth. These sections constitute the proper country of the Javanese nation, although in its fifth section, which is parallel throughout with the island of Madura, the Madurese, from recent settlemeut, constitute the majority of its inhabitants.

The geological formation of Java is eminently volcanic; for it forms, perhaps, the most material portion of that great volcanic band, which, beginning in Sumatra near the equator, extends for 30° of longitude to the Banda Islands, and then taking a north-western direction, embraces most of the Philippines up to the 20th° of north latitude. A range of mountains in a longitudinal direction runs through the centre of Java. The whole of this main range is volcanic, the peaks of which vary from the height of near 4000 to near 12,000 feet above the level of the sea. No fewer than 46 of these peaks are volcanos, 20 of which are in a state of more or less activity. The separate mountains of the range are of a conical form, having a central tube or chimney, ending in a crater. The craters are sometimes of great extent, and their walls illustrate the structure of the mountains, which is either vertical and irregularly columnar, or disposed in oblique or horizontal strata.

My friend, Dr. Horsfield, of whose account of the geology of Java I am now giving an abstract, renders the following account of the most remarkable crater in Java, that of the Tenger mountain, in the eastern part of the island. "This mountain," says he, "constitutes one of the most remarkable volcanos of the island. It rises from a very large base, in a gentle slope, with gradually extending ridges. The summit, seen from a distance, is less conical than most of the other principal volcanos, varying in height, at different points, from 7000 to 8000 feet. The crater is not at the summit, but more than 1000 feet below the highest point; and consists of a large excavation of an irregularly circular form, surrounded on all sides by a range of hills of different elevations. It is by far the largest crater in the island, and perhaps exceeds every other crater on the globe. It constitutes an immense gulf, the bottom of which is level, and denominated by the natives the dasar, (the floor). This is naked and covered with sand throughout; in one portion, near the middle, the sand is loose and blown by the wind into slight ridges, and to this the natives give the name of sâgara-wâdi, literally 'sea of sand.' The largest diameter of the crater is, according to my estimate, full three miles. From its interior, and towards the middle, there rise several conical peaks, or distinct volcanos. The chief of these, the mountain Brama, (from the Hindu god, Brama, whose emblem is fire,) is a perfectly regular cone, and still in partial activity, with occasional eruptions. It is surrounded on one side by the 'sea of sand,' above mentioned. Adjoining to it stands another conical peak, more than 1000 feet high, named Watangan, (hall of audience,) or Widadaren, (abode of celestial nymphs), covered externally with sand,—quite naked, and on account of its steepness, its top has never been examined. At a small distance from the Brama rises a smaller cone, called Butak, (the bald). The two last have not exhibited any volcanic activity in recent times.

"The Brama, which rises from the middle of the Dasar as a regular cone, is also covered with sand, and is marked with regular parallel grooves and ridges: its height is above 600 feet. The ascent, though arduous, is facilitated by steps which the natives have made in the sandy covering. On reaching the summit, I was surprised by finding myself suddenly at the brink of an immense funnel, having a circumference of about one mile, and a depth of above 600 feet. Its form is, on the whole, regular; the interior walls are stratified with undulating layers of sand, and volcanic débris of different colours, grey, reddish, and black. The sides converge to a small bottom, apparently about twenty yards in diameter, containing a greenish fluid, from which volumes of smoke ascend. While standing at the brink, several outbursts occurred which shook the mountain, and were accompanied by a rumbling noise resembling distant thunder.

"The range of hills surrounding the Dasar is very steep, and elevated to the north: at the opposite point it is lower, and affords a passage for men and horses; and while I was occupied in examining the Brama, my assistants amused themselves by galloping over the extensive sandy plain, 6000 feet above the level of the ocean, much to the gratification of the attendant natives. The soil of the Tenger (wide or spacious) hills is extremely fertile, consisting of a deep vegetable mould, accumulated for many ages on the sand and débris thrown up from the mountain. Vegetables of northern latitudes, potatos, cabbages, onions, &c., &c., are planted by the natives in great abundance for the supply of the markets of Pasuruhan and Surabaya. European fruits, as apples and peaches, are also raised; as well as wheat, and other northern grains. Rice refuses to grow, and the coco palm produces no fruit. Most of the plants of the higher regions of the island are also found, with several which appear to be peculiar to this mountain."—Map of the Island of Java, with the Geographical Preface, &c., of Plantæ Javanicæ Rariores, by Thomas Horsfield, M. D.

Several of the volcanic cones of Java are naked of vegetation at their tops, being covered with lava thrown out by late eruptions; but more generally, the successive eruptions have covered the declivities with débris arranged in regular strata, and vegetation has been going on for many ages. The great central chain itself consists of independent mountains connected by low ranges, forming aggregately, a consecutive series, single in some localities. The volcanos afford examples of every kind of volcanic product, as lava, tufa, obsidian, sulphur, and ashes in a high state of comminution.

To the south of the great central is a range of low mountains skirting the southern shore of the island, seldom exceeding 3000 feet high, called in Javanese, kandang, literally "war drums," possibly from the columnar form of the rock composing them. This is thought to have been produced by an agency distinct from that which gave rise to the central chain. In some places this low chain comes into contact with the high central one, and covers its basis; but it is not like it stratified, although consisting also of volcanic materials, chiefly basalt. Agates, chalcedony, flint, and petrified wood are found in it. The southern shore of the island is frequently bounded by steep and often precipitous piles of trap. Low ranges of limestone are seen in the low lands of the eastern parts of the island. In the western part of it, where it is nearest to Sumatra, a few boulders of granite are occasionally found; but, as a general rule, this rock forms no part of the geological constitution of Java.

Hot springs are frequent in many parts of the island, generally at the basis of the volcanos, and several of them strongly impregnated with carbonic acid. Mud volcanos exist in the low lands, yielding muriate of soda for culinary purposes, the most remarkable of which are mentioned under the head of Grobagan.

The valleys of Java are innumerable, but its extensive plains are not above six in number. In the first section of the island, or its eastern end, there is no considerable plain; in the second only one, that of Bandong. These two constitute the country of the Sunda nation, in which, therefore, there is but a single plain of great extent. In the third and fourth sections there are four great plains, those of Surakarta, Madiyun, Kâdiri, and Malang; and in the fifth, constituting the eastern portion of the island, there are two, those of Bandawasa and Pugar. All these plains of the country of the Javanese, are bounded to the east and west by mountains varying from 8000 to above 11,000 feet high, which furnish them with a perennial supply of water for irrigation, such as the Alps furnish to the plain of Lombardy. Although the valleys of Java be frequently narrow, some of them are spacious, and of at least equal fertility with the plains. That of Kadu, in the centre of the island, is an example. This lies between the mountains Sundara, (the beautiful,) and Sumbing, (the notched,) 9650 and 10,350 feet; and Mârapi, (the volcano,) and Mârbabu, (the nurse,) 8640 and 9590 feet high. It must also be added, that the long alluvial tract which runs along the greater part of the northern side of the island, is of the nature of an extensive plain.

Java is singularly deficient in lakes. It has no extensive collection of water, salt or fresh, and no large lagune connecting with the sea. There exist, however, a few beautiful mountain lakes. One of these lies within the mountain Wilis (the green), which parts the plains of Madiyun and Kâdiri, and is known by the name of Gâbal, literally, the slave or servant. There is a second in the province of Cheribon, known by the Sanscrit name of Tâlaga, or the reservoir, and this gives its name to the district in which it lies. A third is in the province of Pasuruhan and called Bañunila, or the blue-water. In Java, however, there are several extensive marshes in the native language rawa, which, in the season of the rains, become lakes, are navigated and have fisheries. The largest in the island is within the province of Bañumas, and close on the southern shore. This is called the Rawa-tuna, which literally signifies "deaf morass." Another considerable one lies in the district of Damak on the northern side of the island, under the range of hills called Prawata, a name, however, which is itself the Sanscrit for "mountain."

The rivers of Java, especially on its northern side, are almost innumerable, but from the form of the island, they are of comparatively small size, none of them navigable for vessels of burden, and few even for boats beyond the reach of the tide. All of them are, more or less, obstructed by mud or sand bars at their mouths. While, however, they afford but slender convenience to trade, they are excellently adapted for irrigation by their nimble flow and almost perennial supply of water, qualities to which Java probably owes more for its immemorial civilisation, than even to the great fertility of its soil. Few of the rivers of Java have specific names, taking their appellations generally from the places they pass by, and changing them with every new one, a circumstance which may, perhaps, be owing to their small size and great number. There are, however, a few exceptions in favour of some of the larger, as the Sâraya, a river of the province of Bañumas and the Praga, with its tributary, the Elo rivers of Kâdu, all debouching on the southern coast. In the Javanese part of the island we have such names as Kali-putih, the white river, Kali-pait, the bitter river, Kali-asam, tamarind river, and in the Sunda part, Chai-manuk, bird river, Chai-wulan, moon river, and Chai-tarum, indigo plant river.

The largest and most useful river of the island is that usually called that of Solo, from its passing the native capital, of which this is the popular name. This has its source in one of the low ranges of mountains towards the southern side of the island, and after a tortuous course of 350 miles, reckoning only from the native capital of Solo or Surakarta, empties itself in the sea by two mouths in the narrow strait formed between Java and the western end of the island of Madura. This river is usually known to the Javanese by the name of the Bangawan, but this word usually means "large river," is not a proper name, and may be applied to any considerable stream. Except for the three months beginning with August, being the three last of the dry season, it is navigable for large boats, and for the whole year for small ones. The second river in magnitude is called by the natives the Brantas, but usually by Europeans the river of Surabaya. This also has its origin in one of the low mountain ranges towards the southern coast, receives many affluents, and dividing itself into two branches enters the sea by two mouths, one in the province of Pasuruhan, and the other in the narrow part of the strait between the main island and Madura, passing by the town of Surabaya and contributing to form its harbour.

The climate of Java is what may be expected in a narrow sea-girt country between five and eight degrees south of the equator, having plains, almost on a level with the sea, habitable and inhabited land 5000 feet above it, with every variety between them. The wet season, or summer, begins with October and ends with March, and the dry, or winter, with April and ends with September. The monsoons are those of the southern hemisphere, the north-western corresponding with the wet season, and the south-eastern with the dry, instead of the south-western and north-eastern, which blow on the opposite side of the equator. The setting in of these monsoons is irregular, and, even during their prevalence, there is some dry weather in the wet and not unfrequent rain in the dry. At the equinoxes, when the monsoons change the weather is most unsettled, and most tempestuous at the commencement of the winter solstice in September and October. Thunder storms are then frequent, and in the vicinity of the hills often destructive to life. Land and sea breezes are experienced within fifteen miles of the northern and southern coasts, and in particular localities of its eastern and narrowest extremity, the south-eastern monsoon blows with great force across the whole island.

The temperature, so far as the seasons are concerned, is equable, that is, the whole year is one continued summer. Near the level of the sea, which is that of the great alluvial band, which runs along the northern side of the island, and of the wide plains of the interior, Fahrenheit's thermometer seldom falls below 70°, and seldom rises above 90°. According to the elevation of the land, every variety of temperature is experienced from this last heat to five degrees below the freezing point. Snow never falls, even on the highest peaks, but at the height of the nominal winter, in July and August, ice a few lines thick is formed, and hoar-frost is seen every morning, called by the natives, poison-dew (âmbun-upas), from its pernicious effect on vegetation. In the inhabited mountain valleys, at the height of 4000 feet, the thermometer is usually about 20° below what it is at the level of the sea, and here is experienced a climate agreeable and congenial to the European constitution, and where the corns, fruits, flowers, and esculent vegetables of temperate regions, have long been acclimated.

In point of salubrity, the climate of the high lands of Java is unexceptionable, and that of the low, containing the mass of the population, is generally equal to that of any other tropical country. In a few spots of the alluvial band of the northern coast, such as Batavia and Cheribon, deleterious malaria have occasionally prevailed, arising from the neglect of canals and water-courses, or from these being obstructed by volcanic débris; but these are exceptions, as are also a few forest tracts of the interior of the island. The extensive cultivation of rice by irrigation, might, as it is alleged to have done in temperate regions, have been expected to generate malaria, but such is not the case, nor has it ever been even supposed to do so in the country itself.

The botany of Java is rich and diversified. The whole island, in fact, presents throughout, few of the plants being deciduous, the same appearance at all times, as the most fertile temperate regions at the height of summer. Its villages and even its towns are, in a great measure, concealed from view, by the luxuriant abundance, and perpetual verdure of its vegetation. Patches of sandy shore and lava-covered peaks of mountains are the few exceptions. The vegetation varies a good deal with the soil, whether composed of the débris of volcanic matter, by far the most prevalent one, or of calcareous rock, or of sand-stone. But it varies far more, according to the elevation of the land, which gives rise to, at least, six different botanical zones: of these, the learned Dr. Bleeker gives the following succinct, but spirited description. "It is more especially on the low coast lands that we find superb palms, bananas, aroids, amaranthaceæ, poisonous euphorbiaceæ, and papilionaceous legumens. Scarce have we reached the height of 1000 feet, above the level of the sea, when our eyes are struck by the quantity of ferns which already preponderate over the other plants. Here, too, we are surprised by magnificent forests of slender bamboos growing spontaneously. The further we ascend, the greater is the change in the aspect of vegetation. Palms and leguminous plants become rare, and bamboos are less abundant. In recompense, we find forests of fig trees with their tall trunks, spreading branches and thick foliage, enveloping more lowly trees and humbler plants, and exhibiting a majesty which even surpasses the splendour of the palms of the coast. Here, too, the ferns increase in number and extent, often with trunks several yards in height. Orchideous plants also present themselves in considerable numbers. Sometimes, these are found solitary and independent, but more generally as pseudo-parasites, forming, in this case, along with an infinite variety of other plants, an additional vegetation on old trees, hardly distinguishable on this account on first view.

"At a height considerably higher, the vegetation still loses nothing of its imposing aspect. The figs here fraternise with gigantic rasimalas (Liquidambar astingiara) with white trunks. To the orchideæ are added Nepenthes, with calyciform flowers (Nepenthes gymnamphora), while numerous species of ferns are accompanied by Loranthaceæ and elegant Melastomas. The region of figs and rasimalas is bordered above by that of oaks and laurels, and here the Melastomas and orchideous plants become still more abundant, while the vegetation receives a new ornament in numerous Pandans, particularly the Frecinatias, which are found as pseudo-parasites, rubiaceous plants being at the same time abundant, growing by themselves and flourishing in the shade. There is but one region higher than that of oaks and laurels where the magnificence of the trees begins to decline. It would seem as if nature, at the height of 5000 and 6000 feet, having accomplished her master-piece, becomes powerless to maintain the tropical character of the vegetation. Therefore, rubiaceæ, heaths, coniferous and other plants familiar to countries beyond the tropics, present to us the Flora of higher latitudes. Cryptogamous plants, especially, are infinitely multiplied; mushrooms are abundant, and mosses cover the ground and invest the trunks and branches of trees. The ferns are now smaller in size, but play an important part, being of an infinite variety of forms, and constituting the mass of the vegetation." Such is the botanical character of the western or Sunda portion of the island, and although there be several plants peculiar to each, that of the central and eastern or Javanese portion does not materially differ from it.

The Fauna of Java is proportionally as varied as its botany. Of mammiferous animals, alone, it is thought to have no fewer than a hundred species, several of them peculiar to it. It has four species of monkey, each with its proper name, with no fewer than eight generic names for the family, whether belonging to the popular, the court, or the recondite language. It has one sloth peculiar to itself, the Kukang or Stenops Javanicus. The species of bats are numerous. One of these, the kalung of the Javanese, or Pteropus adulis, is remarkable for its size and numbers. A flock of these is easily mistaken by a stranger for crows, and they are chiefly to be distinguished by their larger size and heavier flight. They feed on fruit, and in the course of a night will devour the produce of several trees. Their flesh is considered esculent, but I never saw it eaten. The dung of another species, together with that of swallows that dwell in caves and old buildings, affords the only supply of saltpetre in Java and the other islands.

In Java, although the most populous and cultivated island of the Archipelago, wild feline animals are still numerous, and likely to continue so for indefinite ages. The tiger, known to the Javanese by the five different names, machan, mong, sima, uraga, and sradula, the same as that of Sumatra, of the peninsula, and of Continental India, abounds in all the forests of Java, from one end to the other, although nearly unknown in Bali, divided from it by a strait only two miles broad. The leopard, called in Javanese machan-tutul, that is, the "spotted tiger," is also common, the same litter sometimes producing a black variety of it, in which the spots can only be distinguished in a strong light,—the machan kumbang, or black-bee tiger of the Javanese. Two small species of leopard are also found, Felis minuta, and the Linsang gracilis, the last an anomalous animal with some of the habits of a weasel. Of the weasel family, Java has five species, two of which yield musk, and a third is the luwak of the Javanese, and the musang of the Malays—Viverra musanga—an animal of the size of an ordinary cat, and of very wide distribution, for it is found also in the Philippine islands. Of the dog, besides the half-domesticated race, there are two wild species, but the fox, the jackal, the wolf, and the hyena of the continent of India are unknown. There is one otter, Aonyx leptonyx, the wâlingsang of the Javanese, and the wargul of the Sundas.

The elephant is not found in Java, nor does there exist any evidence for its ever having been indigenous, and this is the more remarkable since it is abundant in Sumatra, even in those parts of it which are but a few miles distant. The animal, however, was sufficiently known to the Javanese for ages, and was probably imported occasionally for the use of its princes, for in the various dialects of their languages it has no fewer than seven different names, all of which however are borrowed from Sanscrit. Java has one rhinoceros peculiar to itself, and differing even from those of Sumatra, the warak and garnata of the Javanese, an animal easily tamed, and when so, gentle in its habits. Besides the domesticated hog, Java has two wild species—the Sus verrucosus and Sus vittatus. Both are more numerous than I have ever seen the wild hog in any other country, and their depredations are a serious impediment to agriculture.

A wild ox is found in the forests of Java, the same which is found in the peninsula and Borneo, but which is wanting in Sumatra. This is the banteng of the Javanese, and the Bos sondaicus of naturalists. The Dutch naturalists inform us that all attempts to tame it have been vain, as in the case of the buffalo of the American prairies. According to the Javanese, however, it will pair with the domesticated cattle, producing a fertile offspring, to which they attribute the largest breed of their oxen. The buffalo, Bos bubalus, is found wild in many of the forests of Java, but considered by naturalists to be derived from individuals in the domestic state that had escaped from servitude. The horse nowhere exists in Java, in the wild state, as it does in Celebes, but the numbers of this animal and of horned cattle in the domestic state throughout the island is very large, the Dutch returns reckoning the first at 320,000, and the last at about 2,000,000.

No wild goat exists in Java, but the domestic, the mendé and wâdus of the Javanese language, has been immemorially known, although of small importance in its rural industry. The sheep, usually known by its Sanscrit name biri, but sometimes called "the European goat," is very little known to the natives. Six different species of deer exist, the most numerous of which are the kidang, Cervus mantjac, and the mânjangan, Cervus rufa. These two will live and multiply in parks and paddocks, like our fallow and red deer, and are occasionally so kept. One species only of pigmy deer exists, the kanchil of the Malays and Javanese, and the Moschus kanchil of naturalists. One species of hare is found in the neighbourhood of Batavia, and to the distance of about 50 miles east of it, but in no other part of the island. It is a small animal, not exceeding a rabbit in size, and even of less speed, for a terrier will overtake it. It had been generally believed that it was originally imported from the continent of India, but the Dutch naturalists have lately described it as a distinct species, under the name of Lepus melanancha, from being black over the nape instead of red, as the European hare.

Among birds it may be noticed that the number of species is large, but that of individuals generally small. Dr. Horsfield, to whom I am indebted for most of this outline of the zoology of Java, has enumerated no fewer than 176 species. I shall notice a very few of them only. Of gallinaceous birds there is one species of peacock equally handsome with the Indian, but differing from it, the Pavo spicifer; but the small and beautiful double-spurred peacock of Sumatra and the peninsula does not exist in Java, nor does the Argus or any other of the pheasants of these two countries. Two species of Gallus, or cock, are found in the woods of Java, the ayam alas, or "fowl of the forest," the Gallus Bankiva of naturalists, probably the source in the Archipelago of the domestic poultry, and very widely diffused over it, and the Gallus furcatus or Javanicus, the Bâkekuk of the Javanese, a very beautiful bird and peculiar to Java. This will pair with the common poultry, but the progeny is a hybrid, which for its beauty is sometimes kept by the natives, and often named in their poetry under the appellation of pakiser. Two species of partridge are found in Java, the Perdrix Sinensis and Perdrix Javanica, and two small species of quail, the pugnacious propensities of the females of which, in the season of incubation, are availed of to produce a combat after the manner of fighting cocks. Of the pigeon tribe there are in Java no fewer than ten different species.

The family of birds which is most deficient is that of web-footed water fowl. There is but one species of duck, a teal, the Dendrocygna arcuata of naturalists, and no species of goose, nor of either kind, any migratory bird. There are however two indigenous species of pelican. The species of waders are numerous. The common snipe, the burchet of the Javanese, is more abundant, and at the same time of better quality than I have ever seen it in any other country, and unless we except hogs and deer, the best game of the island. Among the waders there are eleven species of stork or heron. Among smaller birds there are two species of cuckoo, one of which, the kâdasek of the Javanese, has a wild plaintive and monotonous note, not unpleasant to Europeans.

With the Javanese, however, the last is a bird of ill-omen, and whenever its note is heard attempts are made to drive it away. The mancho or Gracula religiosa, the speaking minor, is common. The Java sparrow, a great enemy of the rice crop, is but too frequent. It is the glatek of the Javanese, the Fringilla oryzivora, or rice-devouring finch of naturalists. The house sparrow is a stranger, introduced seemingly by Europeans. It is still, for the most part, confined to the European towns on the northern coast, and called by the natives manuk greja, that is, the "church bird," from its partiality for breeding under the eaves of churches. Birds of prey are very numerous, but none of them of great size. There are eight species of eagle or falcon, and seven of owls, but no vulture. One species of black crow is abundant.

Fish are plentiful along the whole northern coast of Java, and a few species are of excellent quality, but, upon the whole, the abundance and the quality are not equal to those of the shores of the Straits of Malacca. The fresh water fish is all of very inferior quality, and no migratory species frequent the rivers for spawning as they do on the rivers of the eastern side of Sumatra. Crustaceous fish are very abundant on the northern coast, especially oysters, of excellent quality, and prawns, the last contributing largely to the subsistence of the people in the shape of the condiment called by the Javanese trasi. The fisheries of the exposed southern coast of the island are unimportant. Whales never frequent either coast of Java, and are known to both Malays and Javanese generally by the Sanscrit name of gajah-mina, signifying "elephant fish."

Java, whether the inhabitants be of the Javanese or Sunda nation, is peopled by the same race, the Malayan. This is characterised by a short and squat person, the stature being about two inches short of that of the European, the Chinese, the Hindu, the Persian, or Arabian. The face is round, the mouth wide, the cheek-bones high, the nose short, small, never prominent as with the European, and never flat as with the African negro. The eyes are always black, small, and deep-seated. The complexion is brown, with a shade of yellow, not so dark as with the majority of Hindus, and never black as with some of them. Fairness is, indeed, in estimation with the Javanese and others of the same race. The hair of the head is abundant, always black, lank, and harsh, or at least never soft or silky. The hair on other parts of the body is either scanty or altogether wanting. The beard consists only of a few short straggling hairs, and there is none at all on the breast or limbs. The Javanese, personally, are not an agile people, and make very indifferent runners or wrestlers. Compared with the Hindus they are personally a slow people.

As to moral character, the Javanese of the present day may be described as a peaceable, docile, sober, simple, and industrious people. From my own experience of them, I have no difficulty in pronouncing them the most straightforward and truthful Asiatic people that I have met with. The practice of running a muck, so frequent with the other cultivated nations of the Archipelago, is of very rare occurrence with them. It is curious to contrast this character with that given of them by the Europeans who first observed them. Barbosa, who saw them at Malacca before its conquest, and of which, according to De Barros, they formed the majority of the population, renders the following account of them :—"These," says he, "are small thick-made men, with large faces, broad chests, and ill-favoured. They go naked from the waist upwards, and below it they wear a piece of cloth carelessly put on. They wear nothing on the head, but their hair is arranged with art; and some have the hair shaven or cropped. They are a people of great ingenuity, very subtle in all their dealings; very malicious, great deceivers, seldom speaking the truth; prepared to do all manner of wickedness, and ready to sacrifice their lives. Among them are some who, if labouring under any dangerous malady, will make a vow to God, that if restored to health they will choose a more honourable mode of death. When recovered, these persons will issue from their houses with dagger in hand. Then, they rush into the public squares and kill all the persons they meet, like rabid dogs. These are called amulos (amoks). When they are seen in this fury, all begin to cry out 'amulos, amulos,' so that people may protect themselves, and with knives and spears they forthwith slay them. Of these Javanese, many dwell in the city with their wives and children, who have much wealth."—Ramusio, Vol. i. p. 317. If this be a true representation of the character of the Javanese in the beginning of the 16th century, and considering the general accuracy of Barbosa, I am disposed, making due allowance for some exaggeration, to think that it is, all that can be said is, that three centuries and a-half have wrought a great change in the character of this people.

That Java was a populous and civilised country for many ages before it was known to Europeans that such a country existed, is a matter easily proved. De Barros describes the Javanese, at the arrival of the Portuguese, as what they still are, "the most civilised people of these parts" (gentes de mais policia). They were then found carrying on trade from Sumatra to the Moluccas; they furnished bread-corn and manufactures to the less advanced nations in return for their rude productions, and they had effected conquests or settlements in Malacca, Palembang in Sumatra, and in the two fertile islands of Bali and Lomboc. In fact, it is certain that the Javanese were, at this time, a far more civilised, probably even a more numerous people, than either the Mexicans or Peruvians, who became known to Europe nearly at the same time. The essential part of Javanese civilisation is, I am satisfied, of native origin, and sprang up in the island itself, although it subsequently received considerable accessions by intercourse with Hindus. It had its source in the fertility of the land, and in its natural capacity to supply water to augment that fertility, by irrigation. We may judge that these were the fundamental causes of the social advancement of Java, when we find that wherever similar facilities exist, as in the islands of Bali and Lomboc, and in a portion of the volcanic interior of Sumatra, a similar, although not an equal civilisation has sprung up; whereas in countries destitute of them, as Borneo, the people, although of the same race, and enjoying nearly the same climate, are in a very rude, or even savage condition.

With the exception of the people of Bali and Lomboc, the Javanese are the only nation of the Archipelago that can be said to be almost exclusively agricultural. With the exception of the fishermen of the northern coast, and a very small proportion of artisans, the computed ten millions of the population of the island is directly or indirectly engaged in agriculture, and have made a respectable progress in it; for their husbandry is equal, if not superior to that of any Asiatic people, the Chinese excepted. This is evinced by the neatness and cleanness of the fields, by the good condition of the cattle, by attention to the seasons of sowing and reaping; but above all, by a skilful irrigation, in which consists the chief improvement in all warm countries, and especially in those in which the main crop consists of rice. To regulate the processes of agriculture, the Javanese have a rural calendar still in use. This consists of a year of 360 days, beginning with the winter solstice of the southern hemisphere in the end of June, and divided into twelve seasons of unequal length, varying from 23 to 41 days each, in which the times for clearing and preparing the land,—of sowing, of transplanting, and for reaping the different crops are detailed. The native terms by which the seasons are named, are, for the most part, the ordinal numbers of the vernacular language, while the adaptation of the seasons to the latitude of Java, sufficiently show that this calendar is a Javanese invention, and not borrowed from strangers.

Irrigation, in so far as the rice crop is concerned, multiplies the productive powers of the same soil, from five to ten-fold, according to the abundance of water, and the facility of using it, and has been carried to such an extent in Java, that the majority of the arable land of the island consists of it, remaining thus a permanent inheritance to its inhabitants. The perennial streams and rivers, as they descend from the mountains, are, by means of embankments and trenches, diverted into small fields surrounded by low dikes, which can be flooded or drained at pleasure. The process of forming such lands is expensive and laborious, but when once formed, they are easily preserved. These watered lands are known by the native name of sawah, to distinguish them from dry-field, known by the names of tâgal and umah, all which terms, most probably taken from the language of Java, are found in all those of the western parts of the Archipelago.

When the water for irrigated lands is sufficiently abundant and continuous, two crops of rice are raised within the year, and in some cases even three within eighteen months, for the sun is hot enough to ripen rice in every season. In such cases, too, the husbandman may follow his convenience as to the time of sowing, and he does so, for in contiguous fields may frequently be seen sowing and reaping rice, with every intermediate stage of the growth of the plant. When the water is not sufficiently copious for two rice crops, the corn is sown in the wet or hot season, and in the dry, or cold, crops considered of secondary value are produced, such as pulses, oil-giving plants, and cotton. No manure is ever applied to irrigated lands, nor are fallows practised; but notwithstanding this, the system of cropping now described has been going on for ages, and, apparently, without diminution in the fertility of the land. The soil itself is, no doubt, of eminent fertility, but the water evidently goes for more than the soil.

Dry or upland arable, compared to irrigated land, is of small value; indeed, in unfavourable situations such is its abundance, that it is not worth appreciation. On the best dry lands rice is occasionally grown without the help of water, but more generally dry lands are used for such crops as pulses, oil-giving plants, cotton, sugar-cane, and tobacco, and, at present, on the mountain-slopes, at an elevation of two and three thousand feet, for coffee.

In the most fertile parts of Java, and these from the neighbourhood of the high mountains, are usually, also, the most picturesque, the scenery is at once agreeable and magnificent, and certainly for grandeur and beauty excels all that I have seen, even in Italy, that country which, in summer, bears the nearest resemblance to Java. In such situations we have mountains ten thousand feet high, cultivated to half their height, the valleys below having all the appearance of a well-watered garden, in which the fruit trees are so abundant as to conceal the closely packed villages.

When Java first became known to Europeans, its principal agricultural products were rice, pulses, sesame, ground-pea, and other oil-giving plants, indigo and cotton, with palms and indigenous fruits. European intercourse has added to these, two products of America, maiz and tobacco, and one of Arabia, or rather of Africa, coffee. The quantity of its great staple, rice, which it produces, can only be estimated. The statistical returns of the Netherland Government give the produce for some of the provinces only, so that no general view can be exhibited for the whole island. With the exception of a small quantity of maiz, rice is the only bread-corn of all the Javanese; and therefore, if we take the consumption per head at a quarter, or 448 lbs., this, on a computed population of ten millions, will make the total annual produce the same number of quarters. The export is, at present, too inconsiderable, materially to affect this computation, for in 1848 it amounted to no more than 217,000 quarters.

From the first appearance of Europeans, and no doubt for many ages before it, Java was the great granary of the other countries of the Archipelago. This fact is attested by De Barros, in so far as concerns Malacca, and the countries in its neighbourhood. He tells us truly that the territory of Malacca is naturally sterile; and that through an interruption of the communication with Java, a famine ensued almost immediately after the Portuguese capture. "At this time," says he, "on account of the troops that had come from India, and because the junks did not arrive from Java, which alone brought provisions to the city, the Laksimana, (the Malay admiral), intercepting them on the way, the town began to be in such want of them that our people were reduced to one meal a day, and this consisting of a very small quantity of rice boiled in water. And the famine was so great among the Moors, and other people of the land, that the poor were found dead in the streets; and those who escaped death by famine were killed by tigers in the woods, where these poor people had betaken themselves in search of wild fruits. The famine, indeed, was so great, that it produced a truce, for both parties were more intent on seeking food than on fighting. What led to this was, that the monsoon was adverse for our sending for provisions to Java, as Malacca and all the neighbouring countries depend on that island for them."—Decade II. Book vi., c. 2.

Java continued from its first discovery, until within a few years back, to be the granary of the Archipelago; but the extensive culture by corvée labour of such products as sugar, coffee, and indigo, under an idle and pernicious hypothesis that some peculiar commercial advantage to the state belonged to their culture, has greatly interfered with the production of corn. The export of it has consequently diminished, and the price materially risen; the consequence of which has been, that countries immemorially supplied by it, now draw their corn from other countries, such as Bali, Lomboc, Siam, and Arraccan.

The state of the mechanic arts among the Javanese is far below that of their agriculture, but still in advance of that of the other nations of the Archipelago; and with the exception of textile fabrics, not below that of the Hindus. In this respect, the Javanese are probably on a par with our Saxon forefathers a thousand years ago. About thirty different crafts may be enumerated as practised among them. We cannot be sure, however, how many of these have been immemorially practised; for by prefixing words (tukang or juru) equivalent to our own terms, smith, wright, workman, or artificer, to the object on which the calling is exercised, any craft may be created at pleasure. The most important, however, and these have specific names, are the blacksmith or cutler, the carpenter, the kris-sheathmaker, the coppersmith, the goldsmith, and the potter.

The manufacture of bricks, bata, and of tiles, gânding, is certainly a native art. Both bricks and tiles are, at present, largely made; and excellent bricks are found in the remains of many ancient temples, proving that the art of manufacturing them has been known for many ages. Coarse unglazed pottery, similar to that of Hindustan, is also made; and the names of the different sorts, all belong to the vernacular language. The potter is one of the artisans distinguished by a specific name, kundi; and we conclude, therefore, that the art is an ancient and indigenous one. Beyond the manufacture of this coarse article, the Javanese have not advanced,—all their better pottery having been for ages received from China. In this, however, they are no worse than the Hindus.

The chief exercise of the skill of the Javanese in carpentry, is displayed in house and boat building; in the fabrication of agricultural implements; and in that of the hilts, shafts, and scabbards of warlike weapons. The ordinary dwellings of the peasantry consist of a rough frame of timber, thatched on the coast with the leaves of the nipa palm, and in the interior with grass; having walls and partitions of split, flattened, and plaited bamboo work. They are always built on the ground, as are those of the people of Bali and Lomboc, which distinguishes them from the dwellings of the Malays, and other maritime tribes, always erected on tall piles, to suit the low and often marshy situations which they usually occupy. The dwellings of the upper classes differ, chiefly, in their greater size, with the exception of the palaces of the princes and higher nobility.

Boat building is an art extensively practised all along the northern coast of Java; and there are vessels of this description of all sizes and many forms, from mere fishing canoes to those of fifty tons, which navigate the principal rivers. In Javanese there are no fewer than four generic names for a ship or vessel: prau, jong, bäita, and palwa,—all native words. The first of these terms has been almost naturalised in the European languages. The second is that most generally applied by the Javanese to their larger vessels, which the Portuguese not improperly translated, "ships." They wrote the word as junca, and this is the term which, in the shape of junk, we apply to the large vessels of the Chinese, but which the Javanese and others denominate wangkang. The building of ships is, at present, conducted only under European direction, the workmen, however, being all Javanese. When Europeans became first acquainted with the Javanese, and found them engaged in the spice trade, they were possessed of vessels of large size, well entitled to the name of ships. Barbosa gives a curious, and to all appearance, a very accurate account of these vessels and their import cargoes. "There arrive here from Java," says he, "many vessels which have four masts, and are very different from ours. They are built of large timber, and when they become old they are covered with new planking, and sometimes there will lie three or four coatings of this description, one over the other. The sails are made of osiers (ratans), and the ropes of the same. These vessels bring great quantities of rice, flesh of oxen, hogs, and deer," (the dendong and balur of the Malays and Javanese, or jerk beef,) "common fowls, garlic, and onions. Also, they bring many arms for sale, such as lances, swords, shields with daggers, with hilts wrought in marquetry, and blades of the finest steel. Finally, they bring cubebas," (cubeb pepper,) "and a yellow colouring matter which they call casuba," (kasumba, "safflower,") "and gold. Among the mariners there are some whose wives and children never land, for in their vessels they are born, live, and die."—Ramusio, Vol. i., p. 317.

We have an example of the extent to which these vessels could be fitted out by the Javanese, in an expedition which they prepared against Malacca, before its conquest by the Portuguese, and in which they persevered even after that event. De Barros informs us that it was fitted out by the lord of Japara, a man who had "enriched himself by piracy;" and the same who afterwards became king of Sunda, that is, of Jacatra, or the modern Batavia. By the Portuguese, his name is written Pate Unus, the first part of which is Javanese from the Sanscrit for "lord," but the second, probably Arabic, is not intelligible. The force consisted of "12,000 men conveyed in juncas (junks correctly jungs) and smaller vessels, with much artillery;" the total number of the vessels of all kinds having been, according to Castaghnoda, 300. The expedition reached Malacca in 1513, two years after its conquest by the Portuguese, and was defeated and dispersed by a small Portuguese squadron, and a small garrison. In the neighbourhood of Japara where this fleet was equipped, it may be remarked, are situated the finest teak forests of Java.

The agricultural implements of the Javanese are like those of nearly all other Asiatic people, simple and rude. The plough, "waluku," consists of a single handle, a beam, a soc tipped with iron, and a mould board, in which last particular it is more perfect than the usual Hindu plough. It has no coulter, or cutting instrument,—no iron indeed in its construction, except the tip of the soc. It is drawn with a yoke, and always by one pair of oxen, or of buffalos, and no more. The harrow is only a great rake, with a single row of wooden teeth. The spade and shovel are unknown; and the universal substitute for them is the hoe, "pachul." These simple implements are not, however, so inadequate to their purpose as might, at first sight, be supposed; for the greatest and best part of the land is tilled when the soil, by flooding, is reduced to the condition of a soft mud.

The Javanese of the present day have no architecture that deserves the name, and apart from the temples of their ancient worship, most probably never had, for no relics remain of any kind of domestic architecture, of bridges, of reservoirs, or of embankments of rivers, such as are found in the country of the Hindus. The remains of the remarkable architecture connected with the Hindu religion are, as is well known, abundant; but it is singular that an improved architecture ceased with that religion, and that no Mahommedan structure of solid materials or beauty has been constructed since the adoption of the Mahommedan religion in the long period which has elapsed since the end of the 15th century.

It is in working the metals, however, that the Javanese have most excelled, and as they acquired this comparative excellence without possessing any of the metals themselves, but having all of them imported, the fact may be considered as evidence of a higher civilisation than was attained by any of their neighbours. According to the Javanese, the first rank among artisans is to be ascribed to the blacksmith, or at least to the cutler. In the native language this personage is called âmpu, but he has another designation, pandé, which signifies "cunning" or "skilful." The most esteemed product of his skill is the dagger, the well known kris, which, in the different dialects of the Javanese, has four different names, kâris, duwung, churiga, and wangkingan, and is alleged to have no fewer than one hundred different forms. Every man, and boy of fourteen wears, at least, one kris, as parcel of his ordinary dress, and men of rank two and sometimes four. Even ladies of high rank occasionally wear one, so that the total number throughout the whole island cannot be less than several millions. Swords, taking the different names, according to their form, of pâdang, klewang, badik, lamang, golok, and chudra, all native words except, perhaps, the first, are used only in native warfare, and are much less esteemed than the kris, the national weapon. The Javanese spear, a plain pike with an iron head, is a formidable weapon, from its long shaft, of from 12 to 14 feet. Some of the Javanese krises, from their antiquity, are highly appreciated, and when saleable bring enormous prices. They are fancied, in fact, to be charmed, but the temper of the best of them may be doubted, since the Javanese have no iron of their own, and the source and quality of what they had before their intercourse with Europeans is unknown. The Javanese had also before the arrival of the Portuguese, a knowledge of gunpowder and artillery. De Barros in describing the expedition already alluded to as having invaded Malacca in 1513, says, "that it was furnished with much artillery, made in Java, for," adds he, "the Javanese are skilled in founding or casting, and in all work in iron, besides what they have from India."

In works in gold and silver the Javanese display no peculiar skill, for, although they manufacture ornaments of considerable beauty, they execute nothing equal to the filagree work of Sumatra. In works in brass, their chief excellence consists in the fabrication of musical instruments, a full band of which is known throughout the Archipelago by the Javanese name of gamâlan. The instruments consist chiefly of bars, constructed after the manner of the Stauata, or of the gong, a word which has found its way into our dictionaries, and is genuine Javanese. Some of these gongs have been made three feet in diameter. Musical instruments of this description are still manufactured in Java, and form an article of exportation, as, indeed, they are described as having done, on the first arrival of the Portuguese.

The only textile material of native produce woven by the Javanese is cotton, rather a coarse article, and the only kind of cloth made from it is a stout durable calico, the muslins and other fine textures of continental India being unknown to the Javanese looms. The processes of cleaning and preparing the cotton, of spinning, weaving and dyeing are all carried on by women, and are purely domestic manufactures, as is the case with all the other nations of the Archipelago, and with the Burmese, Peguans, Siamese, and Kambojans, evidence with all of them of rudeness and semi-barbarism. The usual mode of giving variety of colours to the web is the simplest possible, consisting in weaving the previously coloured yarn, and always in stripes, chequered or tartan patterns, so frequent with the other tribes, being against the taste of the Javanese. Another mode of effecting the same object is peculiar to this people. It consists in covering with melted wax the part of the cloth not intended to be dyed before putting it in the vat, the process necessarily requiring repetition in proportion to the number of colours intended to be given. Cloths of this pattern go under the name of batik, which means painting or delineating, from the pattern being first delineated on the cloth with a pencil, and filled in with a painting tube having a bowl for the melted wax. The process is operose and expensive, and it may be adduced as proof how little beyond religion, the Javanese gained from their intercourse with the Hindu, since they did not instruct them in the art of calico-printing, immemorially practised by themselves.

To judge from its name, kapas, a corruption of the Sanscrit karpasa, the cotton plant was, most probably, introduced into Java by the Hindus. All the terms, however, connected with the art of converting the raw material into a textile fabric, are native words, such as, spinning, antik; yarn, bânang or lawé; weaving, tânun; warp, lungsen; and woof, pakan. So also are words connected with the decoration of the wrought fabric, as dom, needle; sewing, jait or jaib; embroidering, sulam. All these terms, including the foreign name of the plant itself, and always in its corrupted form, have been very widely diffused among the other languages of the Archipelago, a fact from which we are led to infer that the manufacture of cotton was spread from Java to the other islands. The same fact, may, however, lead us to conjecture that the Javanese, before the introduction of the cotton plant, may have possessed the art of weaving a cloth from some native material, in the same manner that the natives of the Philippines did from the fibre of the textile Banana.

The only material, besides cotton, from which cloth is made by the Javanese is silk, and as the art of rearing the silk-worm has never been introduced into Java, with any effectual result, the raw material has always been imported. The name by which it is universally known in the Asiatic Archipelago, the Philippines excepted, is sutra, which is the Sanscrit word for "thread," in which form it was most probably first introduced by the Hindu traders. At present, the raw material is imported from China, an inferior silk, from which a coarse cloth is wrought with the same implements as that of cotton.

Paper, known by the vernacular name dâluwang, is, as stated in another place, a manufacture peculiar to the Javanese. It is of the nature of the papyrus of the ancients, and not of the beautiful and ingenious fabric which the nations of Europe acquired from the Arabs of Spain, and so long known to the Chinese. The possession, however, of such a paper as that made by the Javanese, evinces a superiority in the arts over the other nations of the Archipelago, many of whom still continue to scratch their writings on palm-leaves.

The manufacture of glass is now, and has at all times been, unknown to the Javanese, to whom this article is known only by the Sanscrit name, kacha. The mirror is known by a native name, chârmin, and most probably, as in Europe, consisted of polished metallic plates, before the introduction of glass coated with tin.

In higher branches of knowledge, the little that is known to the Javanese is soon told. The Hindu system of noting numbers seems to have been introduced from India, and not by the Arabs, for we find it in ancient inscriptions, both on stone and brass. The Javanese, however, have little knowledge of arithmetic, and it can hardly be said to exist among them as an art. As connected with astronomy, they have a rural year, of 360 days, divided into twelve seasons of unequal length, two being of 23 days, two of 24, two of 26, and four of 41. The first ten of these seasons take their names from the ordinal numbers of the vernacular language. The meaning of the word, which is the name of the eleventh season, has escaped my enquiries, but the twelfth signifies, "certain," or "established," and corresponds with the dry season, when the rice harvest is completed, that is, with the height of winter, or June and July for the southern hemisphere. From the native names of the seasons in this rural calendar and their conformity with the climate and latitude of Java, there can be no question of this division of the year being of indigenous invention. The Javanese have also a native week of five days. By this, the market days are still designated. Each day has a native name, and these names are of such antiquity that their literal signification cannot be determined. The names for a day, a month or moon, and for a year, although they have each Sanscrit synonyms are all Javanese, and have had a wide dissemination over the other languages of the Archipelago.

To the native calendar, the Hindus superadded their own. They introduced the week of seven days with its Sanscrit names, and in the same sequence in which it is so general throughout central Asia and Europe. This, however, has been long obsolete, and is found only in old writings. They introduced, also, one of their eras, that of Salivana or Saka, known to the Javanese by the Sanscrit name of Saka-warsa, literally, the year of Saka. This era, which commences 78 years after the birth of Christ, still nominally prevails in Java, and did so in reality down to the year of our time 1633, or for 155 years after the overthrow of the Hindu religion. At that time, through the caprice of a reigning sovereign, solar time, with its intercalations, was changed for lunar, without adopting the year of the Hegira, so that the era of Salivana and that of Java no longer correspond. In all other respects, the Arabian calendar, with the names of the days of the week and of the months prevail in Java as in all Mahommedan countries. The native and the Hindu calendar of Java existed in no other country of the Archipelago, except the neighbouring islands of Bali and Lomboc, in which they are still found, and into which there is no question but that they were introduced from Java.

Music is, probably, of all others, the art in which the Javanese, compared with most other Asiatic people, have made the greatest progress. In common with all the other nations of the Archipelago, they have generally fine musical ears, and are passionate lovers of music. Javanese melodies are wild, plaintive, and beyond all other Asiatic music, not, perhaps, excepting that of the Persians, pleasing to the European ear. Most of their musical instruments, too, are superior to those of other Asiatic nations. They have wind and stringed instruments, both of them rude and imperfect however. Their best and most frequent are those of percussion. Some of these consist of a single gong, a Javanese word, or of a series of them representing different notes, and others of bars of brass or sonorous wood placed over troughs and representing so many keys, after the fashion of the harmonicon, called in Javanese, gândang. The late Dr. Crotch, a most competent judge, after inspecting the fine collection of instruments brought to England by Sir Stamford Raffles, favoured me with his opinion of them as well as of the general character of Javanese music. With respect to the single gongs, he thus expressed himself. "A pair of gongs was suspended from the centre of a most superb wooden stand, richly carved, painted, and gilt. The tone of those instruments exceeded in depth and in quality anything I had ever heard." Of the instrument consisting of a double series of small gongs, he thus spoke. "The tone of this instrument is at once powerful and sweet, and its intonation clear and perfect," and of the instruments of percussion, generally, he observed that he "was astonished and delighted with their ingenious fabrication, splendour, beauty, and accurate intonation." With respect to the character of Javanese music, generally, he made the following observations. "The instruments are all in the same kind of scale as that produced by the black keys of the piano-forte, in which scale, so many of the Scots and Irish, all the Chinese, and some of the best Indian and North-American airs were composed. The result of my examination is a pretty strong conviction that all the real native music of Java is composed in a common enharmonic scale. Some of the cadences remind us of Scotch music for the bag-pipe. Others in the minor key have the flat seventh, instead of the leading note or sharp seventh, one of the indications of antiquity. In many of the airs, the recurrence of the same passages is artful and ingenious. The irregularity of the rhythm or measure, and the reiteration of the same sound, are characteristic of oriental music. The melodies are, in general, wild, plaintive, and interesting." I may add, that a full band of Javanese musical instruments, which consists of flutes, drums, gongs and staccatas, will cost from 100*l.* up to 400*l.*

Two languages are spoken in Java, of the same general structure, belonging to the same class of tongues, and having many words in common, yet essentially differing from each other. These are, the Javanese, spoken in the central and eastern part of the island, and the Sunda spoken in the western part. A small river called the

Losari is, at least the nominal boundary between them, on the northern side of the island. In the ancient state of Cheribon, both languages are spoken, and it is probably from this circumstance that it takes its name, which is correctly Charuban or Charubin, which literally signifies "mixture." The Javanese, as already stated, call their own country Tanah or Siti Java, that is, "the Javanese land," and the region in which the Sunda language is spoken, Tanak Suda or Pasundan, signifying, "land" or "country" of the Sunda nation. In some respects, the two languages stand to each other in the same relation as English and Welsh, French and Armorican, Spanish and Basque, although, the two tongues, in this case, being of the same family, the distinction is by no means so broad.

The Javanese, by far the most cultivated tongue, has been immemorially a written language, and its alphabet has extended to the Sunda language, to that of Bali, of Lomboc, and of Palembung in Sumatra. Inscriptions on stone and brass will carry us back in its history to the 12th century. The time which has elapsed since then, however, undoubtedly forms but a very small portion of its history, for in the 12th century, the Javanese were probably the same advanced people that Europeans found them four centuries later. The written character is of two descriptions, that found in ancient inscriptions, and that at present current. They seem, however, to be essentially the same, and not to differ more than black letter from modern manuscript. The character is peculiar, essentially unlike that of the other alphabets of the Archipelago, and equally unlike any Hindu or other foreign character. It does not even, like several of the ruder alphabets of the Archipelago, follow the rhythmical arrangement of the Hindu alphabets. In fact it has all the appearance of being an indigenous invention. The consonants alone are considered substantial letters, and the vowels mere adjunctive signs to modify them, or as the Javanese designate them, their "clothing," sandangan. The consonants are nineteen in number, but the initial vowel *a* is considered a substantive letter. This vowel too, is inherent in, and follows every consonant, unless there be a contrivance to elide it. Independent of this letter, there are five other vowels. Javanese writing is neat and distinct, and so far as concerns native sounds, perfect, for every sound in the language has its representative character, and the same character has invariably the one power and no other.

There are three dialects of the Javanese, the vulgar tongue, the polite dialect, and the ancient or recondite. All of them are marked, in common with the other languages of the Archipelago, by simplicity of grammatical structure, a simplicity which appears to be innate and original, and not, as in the case of the modern languages of Europe, to have arisen from the breaking down of languages of complex structure, through an admixture of foreign tongues. The proof of this is that no language of complex structure now exists, nor is there any evidence to show that one ever did exist, while foreign words are adopted without change, and subjected to the same rules of grammar as native ones. The simple structure of the Javanese has, in fact, every appearance of being an original quality of it.

The polite, ceremonial, or court dialect of the Javanese is unique in the Archipelago, nor, indeed, does there exist anything like it in any Asiatic language whatever. It is what may be called a factitious language, and in framing it the object seems to have been to avoid every word that by frequent use had become familiar,—to adopt such as had not done so,—for this purpose to borrow words from other languages, and, for the same end, to change words of the vulgar tongue, by altering their terminations. The ceremonial language is that of the court, or, more correctly, that of courtiers; for the sovereign, and members of his family, address others in the vulgar tongue, while they themselves are addressed in this factitious language. In epistolary writing the ceremonial dialect is always used, even by superiors addressing inferiors, unless the party addressed be of very inferior rank indeed. In books it is used indifferently with the ordinary language, but all royal letters, edicts, and proclamations, are in the vulgar tongue,—that is, in the language of authority and command. A knowledge of the polite dialect is, of course, an indispensable accomplishment of a courtier.

One of the most frequent modes of converting words of the vulgar into the polite dialect may be given as an example. This consists in the permutation of vowels, usually of the final vowel of a word, and sometimes of a medial, but never of the initial one. For this purpose the low, or broad-sounding vowels, are exchanged for the high or sharp ones, in the following order: *u, o, a, â, e, i.* The vowel *u*, in this case, belongs to the vulgar tongue, and then we have a scale of ascending respect, according to the quality of the party addressed. The verb "to sit" is an example. In the vulgar tongue it is lunguh, and then follow these modifications, lungah, lângah, and lingih. There can, of course, be no record of the time when this singular language began to be framed, but we may be sure that its formation was gradual, and that, in its present shape, it is the accumulation of many ages. It contains many Sanscrit words, and therefore it must be concluded that it received a large increase after the introduction of Hinduism. It has even a few Arabic words, and hence it is to be inferred that it received some access, since the conversion to Mahometanism. The bare existence of such a language, it may safely be asserted, implies a very ancient civilisation, as well as the long existence of a thorough despotism.

The recondite language of Java may be said, in many respects, to bear the same relation to the popular one, that Sanscrit does to the current languages of Hindustan, Pali to the Hindu-Chinese languages and Singalese, or Zend to the modern language of Persia. In Bali and Lomboc it is still the language of the priesthood; but in Java, where, no doubt, it once was so also, and from which these small islands received it, it is, at present, entirely a dead tongue, found only in ancient inscriptions and manuscripts. The name by which it is usually known is kawi, which is, however, only the correlative of jawi, signifying in this sense "refined," in opposition to vulgar or common, the final vowel of both words being changed from *a* to *i*, so as to make them to belong to the polite dialect. The original word kawi seems to be the Sanskrit kavya, meaning "narrative," a sense in which it also occurs in Javanese. In Java, there are many ancient inscriptions on stone and brass in this dialect, written in an obsolete character, yet essentially the same as the modern, for the form and powers of the letters, and the vowel-marks and orthographic signs are mere modifications, the characters only ruder in form and less connected with one another. No ancient inscription in Java exists in the modern character, but this is no proof that it did not exist cotemporaneously with the ancient, for even in Bali and Lomboc kawi writings are in the modern character of Java. The ancient character was, indeed, probably, at all times, confined to the priesthood, and to inscriptions which have always more or less of a theological character. In corroboration, I may state that I found the same to be the case in Burmese inscriptions, which are invariably in the Pali character, even when in the popular language, and of modern date. Certain it is, at all events, that the modern character of Java is near 400 years old, for it is written in Palembang, in Bali, and Lomboc, with no material difference from what it is in Java, after a virtual separation since the year 1478.

The foreign languages which we find mixed with the Javanese are Sanscrit, Arabic, and Tâlugu, or Telinga. All these have found their way into it, not through foreign conquest, and the intermixture and settlement of men of strange race, but through the influence of religion and commerce. Of these languages by far the largest infusion is of Sanscrit. Of the first conversion of the Javanese to Hinduism, and consequent influx of its sacred language into Javanese, there is no record whatever; but it seems probable, from the extent of the influence exercised, that the connection is of great antiquity,—probably little short of twenty centuries. In the ordinary language of Java, the proportion of Sanscrit words is about 11 in 100, but in the kawi, or recondite, it is not less than 40 per cent. The proportion of Arabic in Javanese is comparatively small. Nineteen out of twenty of the words are nouns; none of them affect the grammatical structure of the language, and all that require it are altered in pronunciation, so as to suit the genius of Javanese prosody. The Tâlugu words introduced are very few in number, and most of them may be traced to the influence of commerce.

The literature of the Javanese is sufficiently abundant, and exists both in the ancient and modern languages. In both it is metrical throughout, the first being in different metres, borrowed from Sanscrit poetry, and the last in native stanzas, of many kinds, and in a peculiar rhyme. The principal portion of Javanese literature consists of romances, called in the native language, konda, and in Sanscrit, charitra, and of histories, partaking too much of the character of the romances, called babad, which signifies, literally, "clearing land of forest." The romances are founded, some of them, on Hindu legends, and others on ancient Javanese story. Of the Sanscrit poems, which describe the wars of the Pandus, and the adventures of the demi-god Rama, the Javanese possess abstracts both in the ancient and modern tongue. These two poems are to the Javanese, and through the Javanese to the other civilised nations of the Archipelago, what the poems of Homer were to the Greeks and Romans, and they have even laid the scenes of them in their own island. The poem which describes the wars of the Pandus is known to the Javanese by the name of the Bratayuda, a title which is composed of two Sanscrit words, signifying "the war of the descendants of Barat." This, the most meritorious production of Javanese literature, is said to have been composed in the 12th century (1195), by a Bramin of the name of

Ampusâdah, at the court of a Javanese prince of Kâdiri, about the centre and towards the southern side of the island, one of the most fertile, beautiful, and romantic parts of it.

It cannot with truth be said of Javanese poetry, for such all Javanese literature is, at least in name, that it possesses either vigour or fertility of imagination. On the contrary, although a few better passages now and then occur, its general character is that of inanity and childishness. At the same time, it is certainly of a higher order than that of any other people of the Archipelago, while it is much inferior to the literature of the Hindus, itself assuredly puerile in comparison with that of the Persians and Arabs.

The Sunda language, as already stated, differs from the Javanese, and is a ruder and less cultivated tongue. To judge by ancient inscriptions, it had once a peculiar character of its own, but is now written in the Javanese, with the omission of two letters, a palatal *d* and a *t*. It has no recondite, like the Javanese, and no ceremonial dialect, except in so far as it has borrowed, in the last case, a few words from that of the Javanese. Its literature, also, small in amount, is taken from the latter.

The native government of Java is, like that of every other government of the civilised nations of Asia, a pure despotism, and chiefly distinguished from that of the other advanced nations of the Archipelago by its greater power, derived from the superior civilisation and wealth of the people. The sovereign is the arbitrary lord of all, including, in theory at least, the religion and the property of his subjects. All titles are derived from him, and are annulled at his pleasure. He names his successor out of the members of his family; and there is nothing hereditary, save the royal family, for which there is a superstitious veneration, very like idolatry,—even here, however, scarcely extending beyond the first generation. Some notion of the prerogative of a Javanese king may be formed from the following translation of a patent of nobility, known by the name of a nuwala, or "royal letter," a word taken from the Sanscrit:—"Take notice! This, the royal letter of us the exalted monarch, we give in keeping to our servant (or slave). Be it known to all our servants, whether high lords or inferior chiefs of our royal city and provinces, that we have given this our rescript to our servant, in order that he may be made high from being low, and placed in our confidence by being raised to the rank of a noble (niyaka, Sanscrit). Moreover, we empower him to wear and use such dress, decorations and insignia as belong to a high noble (bopati, Sanscrit), giving for his subsistence, out of our royal property within a certain district, the quantity of land laboured by one thousand families."

The popular name for a king is ratu, most probably the same word which in some other languages of the Archipelago is written datu, meaning, literally, an ancestor, and figuratively a lord or seignior. But there are no less than nine synonyms, most of them compound epithets taken from the Sanscrit, as narendra, "lord of men," and naradipa, "lord of lords." The Javanese sovereign exercises his authority through a minister, pateh, which is Sanscrit, and he bears the Sanscrit title of adipati, meaning "excellent lord," with the native epithet, raden, prefixed, which signifies "royally related." Under him are four assistants, pateh or kliwon. These are the deputies of the first minister, as he himself is of the sovereign. Two of these are charged with the administration of the royal household and capital, and two with the administration of the provinces of which, in the Javanese portion of the island, when under native rule there were not fewer than forty. These were themselves under the administration of governors bearing the Sanscrit title of bopati, who had their assistants, so that a provincial government was a copy in miniature of the supreme administration. The province was divided into districts, administered by officers, called by the native name of dâmang, or the Sanscrit one of mantri. The district was composed of a certain number of villages, in Javanese, d'usum, and in Sanscrit, desa, each village having its head man, bâkâl or patingi, and his kliwon or deputy.

A brief account of the palace and the village, the most important subjects of Javanese government, will be a useful illustration of it. In Java there are no isolated cottages or farmhouses; the whole island is an aggregation of villages, and both the capitals and chief provincial towns are but assemblages of villages, with a palace in the midst of them. For a town there is, in fact, no native name; the only terms for it being the Sanscrit words nagara or nagari, and praja. The palace of the prince is called karaton, a derivative from ratu, a king, and meaning the royal residence. This may be considered a walled town. The actual palace occupies the centre, and is surrounded by the dwellings of the princes, and those of attendants and retainers. The spaces unoccupied by houses contain the gardens and reservoirs of the sovereign. The principal approach to the palace is invariably from the north, and through a square or court of considerable extent called the alun-alun, the sides of which are adorned by rows of fig trees (ficus benjamina), while a pair of these are invariably in its centre. It is here that the prince shows himself to his subjects with much ceremony once in every week, and that tournaments, public processions, and military exercises are exhibited. It is, in a word, the Javanese field of Mars. To the south side of the palace there is a similar court, but on a much smaller scale. After passing through the principal court we come to the actual entrance into the palace, called the paseban, a word of Sanscrit derivation, meaning "place of entry," and also named pagâlaran, or "place spread with mats." It is a pavilion, forming a waiting room for the courtiers before entering into the presence. A spacious flight of stairs leads from this to a terraced pavilion, the sitingil, literally, the "high ground," or terrace in which the prince gives audience on public occasions. From this spot winding passages through a variety of walled inclosures and gates lead to the different dwellings of the sovereign himself, and of the members of his family.

The external walls of the ancient kraton, were of hewn stone, or of excellent brick and mortar, without any other defence than round towers. At present they are imitations of European fortifications, with bastions, parapets, moats, and glacis, the form, however, being always the same in other respects. Of the extent of these walled towns we can judge from the modern one of Yugyakarta, which is three miles in circumference, and in my time, in 1816, contained a population of 10,000 inhabitants, exclusive of the kampung or quarters—properly villages—which surrounded it nearly up to the glacis. The extent of the Hindu capital of Majapait must have far exceeded this, for the two principal gateways, still standing, are distant three miles from each other. The residences of the governors of provinces, kabopaten, are counterparts in miniature of the palace of the sovereign.

The village community constitutes the most important part of the Javanese institutions. The Javanese village, like the Hindu, is an incorporation, in which the powers of self-government to a large extent are inherent. Its officers consist of the head man, his assistant or deputy, and the village priest, who are elected by the occupants of the land, and in a few cases, by its proprietors. With these village officers rests the collection of the public taxes, and the whole care of the police.

In the structure of Javanese society there is no other distinction of classes, except that of nobles and commonalty, or, as the Javanese express it, the head and the foot, or sometimes "the whole," and "the broken grains" of rice. There are several words for a slave, but they are obsolete, unless to express a servant or retainer, as batun and renchang, or as a pronoun of the first person in the polite or ceremonial dialect. Slavery is, in fact, at present unknown in Java, in so far as concerns its native inhabitants, nor is it known to have existed in any period of Javanese history, which is remarkable enough since it prevails more or less among all the less advanced nations of the Archipelago. That at a remote and early time it did exist in Java there can be no doubt. Its disappearance must be attributed to density of population, with its concomitant cheapness of labour, which made it more economical and convenient to employ free men than to breed and maintain slaves, and assuredly to no higher motive. The humbler order of the Javanese are sufficiently docile and servile without being bought or sold.

The main source of the revenue of a Javanese prince is derived from the rent of land, or consists of a tax on rent; and Java is probably the only country of the Archipelago, with the exception of Bali and Lomboc, in which, from the relation between land and population, a real land rent can be said to exist. This rent is chiefly found in the irrigated land, that is, in the land of the highest fertility, and is composed of two elements—the difference in the quality of different lands, and the value which in the course of ages has been invested in such lands in converting them into water-field, equivalent in a temperate region not only to clearing, draining, and fencing, but to the conversion of ordinary pasture into watered meadow—indeed, even to far more than all this, for the produce of irrigated in comparison with dry lands for the same amount of labour is usually from five to ten fold.

In the ruder country of Sundas there are some remains of a private and heritable property in the land, but in the country of the Javanese the sovereign has gradually taken the whole rent as tax, reducing the cultivators to the condition of mere occupants or tenants at will, he himself having become the virtual proprietor. This state of things is exactly parallel to the condition of land tenures in India, where more or less of a private right of property in the land exists, in proportion to the capacity of the ruling power to exact, and of the occupants to resist exaction.

The mode of registering the irrigated, for the dry land or upland is only supplementary to it and hardly worth reckoning, has reference to the families of the cultivators. The terms employed are chachah-siti, which literally means "census of the land," and gave-ning-wong, "a man's work or labour." But, practically, both terms signify the quantity of land cultivated by a family of peasants. The property in the land being thus in the sovereign, he deals with it by families, retaining a small portion as a domain in his own hands, and bestowing the rest in temporary trust as appanages to the members of his family and his chief officers, or in small allotments to inferior public functionaries down to those of the lowest degree. The land in fact, constitutes nearly the whole public exchequer.

All other sources of taxation than the land are, under the native government, comparatively trifling. In some cases a small capitation tax is levied, but this also is confined to the cultivators, and is sometimes called by them sarcastically pângawan, which means "air tax," pretty much in the same way in which we ourselves used to call our own "window tax" a tax on light. A property in the nests of the esculent swallow, and in certain fish-ponds or stews, formed another branch of the native revenue. Taxes on consumption in the shape of customs, transit duties, and market dues formed a third, but probably most of these are of comparatively modern origin, and will be presently considered.

The Javanese cannot, in any rational sense of the word, be said to possess any writing deserving the name of history; and no people in such a state of society as theirs ever indeed possessed such. The Hindus, even so much more advanced in the scale of civilisation, certainly had none until it was written for them by their northern conquerors. Something similar to this was the case with the Javanese, whose story began only to have some semblance of congruity from the time of their conversion to the Mahommedan religion, which all parties are agreed in asserting to have been consummated by the overthrow of the most potent Hindu state of the island in the year of Christ 1478. All that transpired previous to this date is more a matter of archaeology than of history or chronology. The Javanese possess chronological tables, but in these the earlier period is palpably fabulous, and dates after the manner of the Hindus being expressed, not in numeral characters, or in words representing numbers, but in mystical terms, differently interpreted by different parties, it follows that these lists often differ by whole centuries one from another. The character of these chronologies may be illustrated by a few examples. The commencement of most of them begins with the year 1 of the Javanese era, when a certain Indian chief is stated to have arrived in Java. This personage is called Aji saka, which in Sanscrit means "king Saka." Saka, however, turns out to be only another name for Salivana, the founder of an era prevalent in the southern part of the continent of India, that portion of the country of the Hindus from which the Javanese drew their religion, and with it this era. The certainty is that the real Sáka not only never emigrated to Java, but that in all probability, he was unaware even of the existence of the island. In Hindu records there is certainly no notice of the island, and still less of any emigration to it, the intercourse being, in all likelihood, confined to a few obscure traders, and Bramins following in their train. It is a favourite notion with Javanese chronologists that the islands of Sumatra, Java, Bali, Lomboc, and Sumbawa formed at one time a continuous land, and they assign precise dates preposterously modern, to the times in which they became so many different islands. Sumatra, according to these statements, was separated from Java in the year 1192, Bali from Java in 1282, and Lomboc from Sumbawa in 1350, that is above half a century after Marco Polo had passed through the Archipelago.

The same chronologists assign dates to the origin of certain islands on the coast of Java, and to some of its principal mountains. Thus the islands Buron and Baweyan are said to have first appeared in the year of Christ, 88; the mountains Brama and Sumeru, both Sanscrit names, in 158. From the 11th century, the Javanese chronology assumes an air of, at least, some feasibility; but even from that time down to 1478, there is much discrepancy between different statements, according as the mystic words in which dates are expressed, are interpreted. Thus, the "thousand temples" of Brambanan, the finest remains of Hinduism in the island, are said by one account, to have been built in 1096, and by another in 1266. The most celebrated work of Javanese literature is the Bratayuda, the epitome of the Hindu poem of the Mahabarat, before mentioned; and this is said by one account to have been written in 786; by another, in 1175; and by a third in 1195.

The great events of Javanese history are the respective conversions of the people to Hinduism and Mahommedanism. Of the time when the first of these took place, or the manner in which it was brought about, we have no positive information, either Javanese or Hindu. The ample evidence derived from language and ancient monuments, sufficiently attest the general prevalence, if not, indeed, the universality of some form or modification of the religion of the Hindus over the island; but anything beyond this is matter of inference or conjecture. One fact respecting Javanese history is sufficiently established,—that the whole island was never subject to the rule of a single power, constituting a permanent and undivided empire. Ancient states existed which had acquired a considerable amount of civilisation and power, as is shown by the ruins of palaces and temples; but none of them had any durability,—none of them ruled over the whole island, while several of them, according to tradition, existed at one and the same time.

Inscriptions on copper and stone have been found among the ruins thus alluded to; but, unfortunately, the earlier ones, instead of having dates expressed in plain writing, or numerical figures, have them all in the mystical words expressing numbers, already mentioned; so that the same terms being capable of several, or even of many, different interpretations, little or no reliance can be placed on them. The earliest dates we possess are the years of Saka, 505 and 506, or of Christ, 583 and 584, contained in two inscriptions on stone in the fine province of Kâdu. Supposing these dates to be authentic, which, however, is very improbable, the next to them, in point of time, is 735 of Saka, leaving thus a gap of 230 years without any recorded date at all. The next date to this last, in sequence, is 845 of Saka, and hence, therefore, there is here a dateless chasm of 110 years. This last date is followed by others of nearly the same time, 863 and 865. From this last named year up to 1220 of Saka, not a single monumental date occurs on brass or stone, leaving a chasm of 355 years. From the year 1220 now alluded to, the dates are expressed generally in numeral figures, and consequently are trust-worthy. They continue to be thus represented on various monuments, to within a short time of the conquest of the last Hindu state of any importance; an event which all parties seem to agree in placing in the year 1400 of Saka, or 1478 of our own time.

With the exception of the last event named, not one of the different dates now quoted refers to any historical event. In so far as the inscriptions containing them have been deciphered, they are found to be mere laudations of some pious chieftain, powerful, no doubt, in his time, but unknown even to Javanese fame. They are historical only from having been found amid the ruins of places well known as having been once the seats of independent governments.

The Hindus, it is highly probable, migrated to Java and established their religion in it, even at the earliest of the dates alleged to be those of the inscriptions, that is, in the 6th century; but it cannot at the same time be asserted, that there exists any precise or reliable evidence of their having done so. That the Hindus and their religion, however, existed in Java from the end of the 13th to that of the 15th century, is a matter of certainty, proved by monumental dates entirely reliable.

The history of the conversion of the Javanese to the religion of Mahommed, although even of this comparatively recent event much is enveloped in fable, is far more authentic than that of their adoption of Hinduism. The parties who effected this conversion were the mixed descendants of Arabs, Persians, Malays, and Mahommedans of Hindustan,—parties who had settled on its northern coast for the purposes of trade,—who were intimately acquainted with the natives of the country and their language; and who, in process of time, had acquired wealth and influence. Of such men, were the real missionaries of Islam in Java composed, and the work of conversion was certainly a slow one. As early as the year of our time, 1358, an unsuccessful attempt had been made by missionaries of this description to convert the Sunda nation. Another was made in 1391, to convert the proper Javanese; and the tomb of one of the reputed saints who made this attempt, one Maulana Ibrahim, still exists in Gressik, bearing the year of Salivana, 1334, or of our time, 1412. In the year of Christ, 1460, the Mahommedan converts assembled a force for the conquest of Majapait, the capital of the principal Hindu state, but were defeated; and it was not until 1478, eighteen years after, that they succeeded in capturing the capital, overthrowing the state, and establishing their own power and faith.

All authorities are agreed in assigning the year 1400 of Salivana, or 1478 of Christ, as that in which Majapait was overthrown; and in considering this event as the virtual overthrow of Hinduism. The Sunda nation appears to have been converted about the same time, the conquests proceeding from Cheribon, and ending with Bantam in 1480. The Mahommedan chiefs assumed the government of the respective states which they had subjugated, under the title Susunan, abbreviated Sunan, a spiritual title, meaning "object of reverence," which one of the native princes still retains.

According to these statements, the work of conversion ran over a period of at least 130 years. Even at the lapse of this time, however, it does not appear to have been completed; for according to De Barros, when Henrique Lemé visited the country of the Sundas 1522, forty-four years after the supposed final conversion of the Javanese, he found idolatrous temples, nunneries, and the practice of concremation still existing. For a century after the overthrow of Majapait, Java appears to have been split into many independent states. When first visited by the Portuguese, such was unquestionably its condition. "The island of Java," says De Barros, "is divided into many kingdoms;" and he enumerates no fewer than fourteen, most of which, notwithstanding much corruption of orthography, can be identified with the existing names of provinces. About the year 1578, however, a native chief, the governor of the province of Mataram, on behalf of the king of the neighbouring state of Pajang, raised himself to sovereign power, and founded the family from which has sprung the two existing native tributary rulers. In the course of the first four reigns of this dynasty, most of the proper country of the Javanese, with the island of Madura, were subjugated, and the princes of the Sunda country made tributary.

It was in the reign of the second prince of this dyhasty, that the Dutch made their first appearance in Java, under Houtman, in 1595. In 1610 they obtained permission from the Sunda prince of Jacatra, to build a fort near to the spot on which now stands the city of Batavia. In 1619 this fort was besieged by the joint forces of the princes of Jacatra and Bantam, aided and abetted by the English. It was relieved by a Dutch fleet under Admiral Koen, and the assailants defeated and driven off. It was after this event that the name of Batavia first given to the fortress was given to the town. In 1628, Batavia was besieged by a numerous army sent against it by the reigning prince of Mataram, with the hope of expelling the Dutch from the island; but by the skill and courage of the European garrison, the rude and disorderly host was baffled and routed. From this time the history of Java is properly that of its European conquerors. No considerable territorial acquisition, however, was made until 1677, when the Dutch obtained a cession of the principality of Jacatra. From that time up to the year 1830, every war carried on by them with the native princes, whether as principals or auxiliaries, invariably ended in a cession of territory to the former; so that, at present, hardly one-fourteenth part of the island is in possession of native rulers, and even that is entirely tributary and dependent, so that the government of the native principalities is, in fact, but a clumsy form of European rule, similar to that of our own in respect to some states of Hindustan.

From the year 1674 to 1830, the Dutch, as principals or auxiliaries, have been engaged in no fewer than four great wars, all of long duration. One which began in 1674, lasted for thirty-four years. One which began in 1718, lasted for five years; one which began in 1740, for fifteen years; and one which began in 1825, for five years; so that, of one-third part at least of a period of 156 years, civil war raged in the island. The history of Dutch aggression in Java is probably, on the whole, neither worse or better than that of English aggression in Hindustan. Indeed, although upon very different scales, they bear, in their general features, a very close resemblance. The English administration of its conquest has, however, been at least far more fortunate than that of the Dutch; for instead of the numerous rebellions which have sprung up in Java, there has not been a single serious revolt in Bengal, with four times its population, in a period approaching to a century; a result which, in fairness, must be chiefly ascribed to difference in the character of the subjugated parties. The inhabitants of the British provinces had been accustomed to foreign domination for many centuries, while those of Java had never been subjected to foreign rule until the Dutch began their conquests in the 17th century.

The Dutch have divided their possessions in Java into twenty provinces or residencies, each of which is administered by a Resident or Prefect. Six of these belong to the country of the Sundas, and fourteen to that of the Javanese. The two remaining native states, although administered by their own princes, are, as already stated, virtually Dutch provinces; and placed under the control of an officer, with the same title as those of the provinces under direct Dutch rule.

Attempts have been made, at various times, to estimate the total population of Java. The first of these was by the historian Valentyn, who, in his account of the island, says that down to his time, 1726, it had "never been described, and that the notions entertained of it were as vague as those of a man born blind respecting colours." His estimate made the population 3,199,750; and including Madura,

3,591,500. This estimate was made shortly after a civil war of five years' duration. In 1755, immediately after the finest parts of the island had been the theatre of a civil war of fifteen years, an estimate was made which gave Java only 1,941,911; or including Madura, 2,001,911. This would seem to show, that in less than thirty years a decrease had taken place exceeding a million and a quarter. At the close of the last century, estimates of the population were made, which raised the joint population of Java and Madura to 3,559,611. This was after a continued peace of forty-five years; and shows, compared to the last estimate, an increase exceeding a million and a half. In 1808, another estimate was made; and by this the number was made 3,730,000. In 1815, a census was attempted, during the temporary occupation of the English, which raised the population of Java to 4,39,661; or including Madura to 4, 615,270.

The Dutch, since the restoration of the island to them in 1816, have made no fewer than eleven different attempts at a census. The first of these was made in 1826; and the number it gave was 5,403,786. Ten years later another was made, and this raised the number to 7,861,551; and consequently gave a decennial increase at the rate of about 44 per cent. The census of 1845, made the joint population of Java and Madura, 9,530,781; or of Java alone, 9,235,033. The last census is that of 1850; and this made the joint population of Java and Madura 9,564,324. This, compared to previous increases, exhibits but a very trifling augmentation; and indeed in seven of the finest provinces there is an absolute decline: while in the provinces subject to native rule, there is an increase of from 14 to 15 per cent. The decrease in the Dutch portion is most probably attributable to the highly impolitic practice of raising revenue by the corvée culture of agricultural products for the markets of Europe, and the great rise in the price of corn, which has been the consequence of it. None of these enumerations can be considered as better than approximations; but it is probable that all of them err rather in omission than exaggeration. The last, as the most recent, taken with the most care, and with the best means, are the most reliable. The census of 1845 is considered rather to underrate than overrate the numbers, which the officers who made it consider ought to make the joint population of the two islands not less in round numbers than 10,000,000.

Taking the population of Java, exclusive of Madura, as it is given in the census of 1845, at 9,235,033,and its area at 37,556 English miles, its relative population is 248 inhabitants to the square mile; which would give it about the same density of population as Great Britain or Ireland; and consequently show that, with the exception of these, it is far more populous than any other great island in the world. The population is very unequally distributed over the different parts of the island. The mountainous country of the Sundas, including Cheribon, which is partly Javanese, has an area of 13,944 square miles, but a population of no more than 2,406,097 inhabitants, so that it has only 171 to the square mile. The inland districts, called Prayangan, or "fairy lands," have only 120 to the square mile, and Bantam but 154; while Cheribon, with its mixed population and wide valleys, has 301. The country of the Javanese has an area of 23,612 square miles, and a population of 6,933,696; which gives a relative population of 293 to the square mile. Even in this more populous portion of the island the density of population varies greatly. The province of Surabaya, with a harbour and two large rivers, has 461 to the square mile; Samarang, 528; and the highly fertile inland province of Kadu, a valley watered by the streams which pour down from four of the highest mountains of the island, 565. In the narrow section of the island which fronts Madura, and forms the most easterly portion of it, the density of population gradually decreases from west to east. Thus in the province of Pasuruhan it is 188 to the square mile; and in Besuki, which includes the extremity of the island opposite to Bali, it is only 121.

The inhabitants of Java, besides Javanese and Sundas, consist also of Madurese; for these are not confined to their own island, but form the larger part of the population of that section of Java which fronts Madura. This portion having been depopulated by the civil wars of the end of the 17th and beginning of the 18th centuries, the Madurese began to emigrate to it from their own less fertile land; and this emigration still goes on, so that the Madurese in Java are probably, at present, more numerous than in their parent country. For the whole island, including Madura, the proportions of the three nations, is supposed to be 66 in 100 of the Javanese; 26 of the Sundas; and 8 of the Madurese.

The most numerous class of stranger-settlers are the Chinese; the census of 1845 making their numbers 106,033, the greater number consisting of a mixed race. Of these, 31,764 are in the city of Batavia and its environs, which is fewer than the number of this people in the British settlement of Singapore. The small proportion of Chinese in Java is, of course, in a good measure attributable to the nature of the labour market, in so far as respects unskilled labour, that being already preoccupied by the native population: but it arises, also, from the restraints imposed by the policy of the Dutch government on their settlement. While in the British settlements, no restriction whatever is placed on them, in Java they pay a mulct for leave to enter, and a larger one for permission to quit, besides a poll-tax,—all of them imposts to which no other class of strangers is subjected. Jealousy of Chinese settlement is, indeed, a principle of the Dutch administration of Java of long standing. In the early part of the last century their numbers alarmed the government, and their wealth and prosperity appears to have excited the envy of the Dutch colonists. In 1723, the local government issued a decree against Chinese immigration, which, however, was never fully acted on. They were, however, prohibited from passing beyond the limits of the town of Batavia without a license; and all who could not render an account of themselves satisfactory to the European authorities, were imprisoned or sent back to China. These severities drove the Chinese to revolt; and on the 26th of September, 1740, the Chinese quarter of Batavia was attacked by a mob, consisting of soldiers, sailors, European settlers, and natives, and in the course of two days, 10,000 of the Chinese are stated to have been slaughtered, and their houses pillaged and burnt. The armed Chinese who escaped the massacre, retreated into the interior of the island; and the result was a civil war, which, in one form or another, lasted for fifteen years. The local government sent a letter full of excuses to the emperor of China, to which the emperor did not vouchsafe a reply. In justice to the Dutch nation it should be noticed, that the whole proceeding was condemned at home; and the weak and timorous governor, who was the cause of, or winked at the massacre, duly punished.

The other Asiatic people settled in Java, consist of Arabs, or rather, for the most part, of their mestizo descendants, and of natives of the other islands of the Archipelago. All these are grouped together in the census of 1845; and their total number, including slaves, is no more than 36,327. The number of slaves is but 5111. None of these are Javanese, but all natives of the other islands of the Archipelago, or their descendants, chiefly of Celebes, Sumatra, and Bali. All of them are domestics of Europeans or Chinese; and through the humanity of their owners, and without any legislative enactment, they are in rapid progress towards emancipation. In 1813, they amounted to no fewer than 20,452. The practice of employing free Javanese as domestic servants, was first introduced by the English during their temporary occupation of the island, and has been followed by the Dutch.

The class of bondsmen produced an adventurer, a kind of Javanese Spartacus, who gave rise to one of the most remarkable incidents in the history of Java. This person was a native of the island of Bali, from which he had been brought as a child. He became the slave of a Dutch citizen of Batavia, misconducted himself, and was imprisoned. He effected his escape from prison and bondage,—organised a small force,—baffled the pursuit of the European authorities, and became one of the dangerous and too frequent class of persons that have at all times disturbed the peace of Java, well known in the language of the country under the name of kraman, which signifies a rebel and pretender. Making his way to the eastern part of the island, he formed an alliance with the Susanan, or Emperor of Java, whom he seduced to join in his insurrection. In due time he established, and maintained for some years, an independent principality, and was at length killed in an action which he fought with the Dutch troops. This rebellion lasted, in all, nine years, having commenced in 1684, and not ending until 1705.

The revenue of the European government of Java is that of the whole island, including Madura; but except as to some taxes on consumption not of the territories, subject to the two remaining native princes, which embrace an area of 2229 square miles, and a reputed population of 850,000. It is derived from multifarious sources, and may be briefly described, taking the figures from the public accounts of 1843, as given by Mr. Temminck. These are the most recent that I have seen, but sufficient for a general view, as no material change has since been made in the fiscal system.

During the five years' temporary occupation of Java by the British government, from 1811 to 1816, nearly the whole ancient system of monopolies, forced deliveries, and corvée labour was overthrown, and free culture, open trade, and free labour substituted for them. The merit of this great revolution in the administration of the island belongs to the late Sir Stamford Raffles, the British Lieutenant-Governor of Java, under the supreme government of India; and he carried his bold and valuable innovations into effect with a courage, industry, and perseverance entitled to the greatest praise. The financial system which he adopted, however, was not so happy. In so far as the land-tax was concerned, the elaborate, vexatious, scourging, and impracticable system which proceeds on the principle of the States entering directly into an arrangement with each individual occupant of a few acres, in the case of Java probably not fewer than half a million, was at the time in vogue with the authorities in England, and he attempted the establishment of this pernicious innovation. Under this system, the tax was paid either in money or in land, at the option of the occupant; and being generally paid in the latter, it followed that the government was converted at once into a warehouse-keeper, and a corn-merchant. As in our own territories on the continent of India, the new system was found mischievous and impracticable. The land was over-assessed, and the hypothetical land-tax could not be realised.

After a two years' trial, the Dutch commissioners who received charge of the island, judiciously abandoned the Ryotwarrie system of 1814, and arranged with the heads of the village corporations for the land-tax, leaving its distribution among the occupants, to these corporations themselves. This natural and simple system, the only one suited to such a state of society as that of Java, after being in operation for fourteen years, was partially relinquished in 1832, and the old system of forced deliveries of certain agricultural products, and of corvée labour in raising them, was to some extent restored. The pretext for this was the hope of greater gain, and the assumption that, by the immemorial usage of the country, the state was entitled to take, at its option, its tax in money, in kind, or in corvée labour. Hindu and Mahommedan kings had done so three or four hundred years ago, and hence it was argued that it was just and proper that an enlightened European nation should do, in the 19th century, what barbarous native rulers had done in the 14th and 15th. Under this system a considerable portion of the tax on rent is remitted, and some of the best lands with the labour of its peasantry, was appropriated to the cultivation of products deemed peculiarly fitted for the markets of Europe, such as coffee, sugar, and indigo, with tea, cinnamon, and cochineal, the three last expressly introduced into the island for this special purpose. By this impolitic measure, the Dutch government has become, once more, a cultivator, a trader, and necessarily, from its position to a certain extent, a monopolist trader, the evil effects of which on that wealth, which is the only source of public revenue, must be obvious to every enlightened modern statesman.

The actual amount of the tax on rent or land-tax remaining to the Dutch government, after deducting exemptions, was, in 1843, allowing 20 pence to the florin, 835,551*l*. To this, however, is to be added a sum of 26,215*l*. for the quit rents of land sold at various times to Europeans, with other items partaking of the nature of a land-tax, as the rents of certain fish-ponds, or stews, amounting to 27,302*l*., making the total land-tax realised 889,128*l*. No account is rendered of remissions on account of land appropriated to the culture of produce for government, but a few facts are stated which will give a tolerable notion of the extent to which this very barbarous system is carried. The number of Javanese families from which corvée labour was exacted for the culture of coffee, in 1841, was 453,289, and for that of sugar, indigo, and cinnamon, 350,955, making the total number, exclusive of those employed in the cultivation of tea and cochineal, which is not stated, 704,244 families, equivalent to a population exceeding three millions and a-half, or 40 parts in 100 of the entire population of the European portion of the island. The quantity of land set aside for the cultivation of sugar, indigo, and cinnamon, amounted, in 1841, to 317,635 acres, and this consisted of the richest irrigated lands of the island, usually yielding two yearly harvests, and equal in value to ten times that of the average of all dry lands. The quantity of land, of an inferior description, appropriated to the culture of coffee and tea, all peculiarly fitted for the growth of maiz, is not stated, but some notion of it may be formed from the number of families employed, as above given and from the number of trees, which last, in 1841, amounted to 336,922,460.

The taxes on consumption are multifarious, consisting of monopolies, excises, customs, transit and market duties, taxes on fisheries, and on the slaughter of cattle. The chief monopolies are those of the vend of opium and salt. In 1843, the first of these amounted to 796,630*l*., and the last to 384,159*l*. The monopoly of opium is at once productive and unexceptionable in principle. That on salt, is, of course, a poll-tax, which amounts to about 4*s*. on each family, and is only less onerous than our own in Bengal, from the salt of Java, the produce chiefly by solar evaporation, of its northern coast, being better, cheaper, and more economically distributed to the consumers than that of Bengal. Another monopoly is that exercised in certain caves producing the esculent swallow nests, and this, as the birds are the chief manufacturers, and strangers the chief consumers, is as unexceptionable a source of revenue as any government ever possessed. In 1843, its amount was 24,271*l.* The sale of timber from the teak forests, which are the exclusive property of the government, constitutes another monopoly, of which the produce in the same year was 42,141*l.* These different items make the total revenues arising from monopolies 1,247,201*l.* In the public accounts, the monopoly of the tin of Banca is set down as Javanese revenue, and stated at the sum of 250,000*l.* As the revenue of Java alone supplies the funds with which the mining and smelting is carried on, this branch is correctly enough included in the financial resources of that island.[1]

The export and import duties of Java, in 1843, including port charges, amounted to 460,840*l.*, and the market, transit, and ferry dues, came to 262,672*l.* The tax on the slaughter of catile was 39,341*l.*, and that on fish and fisheries 27,911*l.* It is not necessary to add that these, as taxes on first necessaries of life, are injurious imposts. A very strange want of attention to an obvious principle is evinced by the European government of Java, connected with the slaughter of cattle. The slaughter of the buffalo is expressly prohibited, with the avowed object of increasing the number of this animal for the benefit of agriculture. The certain effect of the prohibition, however, must of course be, the very reverse of what is intended, for the rearing of these animals is surely discouraged, not promoted, by depriving the owners of a market for the old, imperfect, or superfluous ones.

The excise on distilled and fermented liquors, and on tobacco, yielded between them, in 1843, only 36,843*l.* The taxes on consumption yielded, in all, monopolies included, a revenue of 2,207,488*l.*

The direct taxes, land-tax excepted, are of very trifling amount. Stamp duties yielded 26,452*l.*, and taxes on transfers and successions, 19,470*l.*, plain proofs of the real poverty of the ten millions of people, and similar to those which are afforded from the same class of taxes in our own Indian possessions. The capitation tax paid by the Chinese yielded no more than 3,477*l.*, and that on slaves only 2,014*l.* A tax on gaming was far more productive than either of these, for it produced 37,101*l.* A duty on auction sales gave 24,173*l.*, and the profits on public pawnbrokers' shops, 27,905*l.* The tax on carriages and horses kept for private use gave the small sum of 5530*l.* only, and the post office and stage coaches no more than 18,226*l.* Printing is a monopoly in the hands of government, and is represented as yielding a profit of 4,533*l.* The tribute paid by native princes amounted only to 3,287*l.* To these items are to be added the sale of such articles as rice, packing sacks, gold-dust, and sundries amounting to 78,483*l.* The whole amount of these direct or miscellaneous taxes is 166,938*l.*, or, including the sale of produce, probably not the productions of Java, 245,421*l.*

The account of receipts contains, in all, forty-five different heads, without, however, any logical arrangement. The sums, too, are for the most part, gross receipts, not including charges of collection, which are not separately given. The total revenues of Java, in 1843, were 3,209,357*l.*, including the monopoly of tin, but exclusive of the profits of trade on commodities sold in Europe,—if there should be any. The rate of taxation per head on the population of Java, subject to European rule, is about 7*s.* 5*d.*, and would probably amount to at least 10*s.*, had not the resources of the island been dissipated in idle and wasteful governmental speculations agricultural and commercial. In the British settlement of Singapore, without land-tax, customs, port dues, salt monopoly, poll-taxes, gaming tax, or stamp duties, the rate of taxation per head is better than 18*s.*, or 142 per cent. more than that of Java. The difference is evidently owing to the superior industrial strength of the population of Singapore; its superior freedom in the exercise of that strength, and its comparative superior wealth.

The expenses of the government of Java in 1843 were given at the sum of 6,291,606*l.* Thus, then, the expenditure exceeded the amount of the taxes by the enormous sum of 3,082,249*l.*, to be made good, or otherwise, by the contingency of produce remitted to Europe. The civil charges came to 827,825*l.*, the military to 720,319*l.*, the naval to 138,846*l.*, and the extraordinary expenditure, on account of Sumatra, to 220,076*l.* The expense of despatching government produce, exclusive of freight and charges, amounted to 75,212*l.*, while the interest of the public debt, nearly all incurred in twenty-seven years' time, came to 1,018,463*l.*, or about half the amount of that of British India, with a hundred and ten millions of inhabitants, and which it has taken 80 years to incur.

The internal trade of Java embraces that of all the Netherland possessions in India, as it is the entrepôt for the whole of it. It includes also a large remittance for the public revenue in the shape of produce, as coffee, sugar, indigo, tin, and spices.

Java and the other Dutch possessions were delivered over by the English in 1816, with a considerably improved commerce, and certainly, at all events, with a clear field for the establishment of a liberal system. The opportunity has assuredly not been taken advantage of. Double duties have been imposed on all goods imported under a foreign flag, and other contrivances of the exploded mercantile system have been had recourse to, in order to give trade a direction to Holland, a costly expedient, injurious to the colony, and of no substantial value to the mother country. In 1824, and within eight years after the restoration, a new East India Company was set up as one of these contrivances, the Handel Maatschapij or trading association. This association, is merchant, shipowner, agent, for the sale of the government produce in Europe, carrier of this produce, and farmer of some branches of the public revenue of Java. Originally, there was guaranteed to it, a fixed and certain interest on its capital stock, and even the sovereign of the Netherlands was a sleeping partner of it. The false hypothesis on which this retrograde policy was adopted, was a supposed necessity for encountering what was called the over-grown capitals and enterprise of England and America, as if the free capital and enterprise of Holland, which under greater difficulties had not achieved much greater things, was unequal to carry on the trade of its own colony without pilling and bolstering. This company has been in existence for thirty years, and we may see by the result how little it has effected.

In 1851, the value of all the imports into the Dutch East India possessions, exclusive of government stores, was 2,512,893*l.*, but that of the exports 6,149,088*l.* Of the exports, no less than 3,996,750*l.* consisted of government produce, chiefly sent to Europe through the Handel Maatschapij or Commercial Association, leaving for the exports of private merchants no more than 2,152,300*l.*, a large portion of it the property of the privileged society itself. From this statement it will appear that the exports, instead of being nearly the same as the imports, as they ought in all fair trade, exceed them by the enormous sum of 363,619*l.*, or by 144 per cent. It is evident that the difference, whether it ever reaches the treasury of Holland or not, is mere tribute paid by Java, and this, too, in a form the most injurious. These figures will further show that of the export trade of the Dutch possessions in India, nearly two third parts are carried on by the government with the colonial revenue, while little more than one third of it is conducted by private capital and enterprise. This is assuredly the greatest violation of the sound principles of commercial policy, which has been perpetrated since the overthrow of Indian monopolies, and one which ought not to have been witnessed in our times.

In 1844, the total value of the imports of Java was 2,339,971*l.*, which shows that in the seven years ending with 1851 they had fallen off by no less than 172,922*l.* In 1842, the value of the exports was 5,034,529*l.* In the nine years, therefore, between 1842 and 1851, these had increased by the sum of 1,114,560*l.*

The government of Java and the other Netherland possessions of India is vested in a governor-general, named by the king, and answerable for his acts only to him. He is commander-in-chief of the military and naval forces, and possesses absolute legislative and administrative power. The liberty of the press does not exist; indeed, there is no press at all except that of the government, the political literature of Java consisting of two newspapers, the government gazette, and another equally under a rigorous censorship. In the three small British settlements, in the same quarter of India, there are six, as free as the journals of England or America.

For the administration of justice, there is a supreme court sitting at Batavia, which has a primary jurisdiction in a few cases, but is, generally, a court of appeal and cassation for the whole Netherland possessions in India. There are three provincial courts at the three principal European towns, Batavia, Samarang, and Sarabaya, for the administration of civil and criminal justice, one of the judges of which performs circuits. Justice to natives and Chinese is administered by the country courts in which the president or chief civil administrator presides, having native chiefs for assessors. In criminal cases, the jurisdiction of these courts is confined to offences not capital, and, in certain civil cases, appeals from them lie to the provincial courts.

The finances are under the management of a director-general, a director of receipts and domains, a director of produce and warehouses, and a director of cultivation, these officers constituting the finance board. For keeping and auditing the public accounts, there is a distinct department—the chamber of accounts. From the mixing up of cultivation and trade with governmental affairs, the duties of these two departments become sufficiently onerous, complex, and always greatly in arrears.

The tributary princes, of which the number of principal ones are no fewer than one and twenty, administer the civil governments of their own countries. Of these, there are five in Java, two of them only considerable; three in Madura, two in the group of islands at the eastern end of the Straits of Malacca, three in Borneo, two in the Moluccas, four in Celebes, one in Sumbawa, and one in Sumatra.

JAYAKUSUMA. The name of an ancient king of the state of Janggala in Java, situated in the present province of Surabaya. This prince is supposed to have reigned about the beginning of the 12th century, and is of great celebrity in Javanese and Malay romance, but nothing authentic is really known regarding him.

JIMAJA, correctly Jâmaja, the name of a small island, one of the group in the China Sea, called in our maps, the Anambas. See Anambas.

JOBIE. This is the name which European navigators have given to a long narrow island, extending east and west for ninety miles, and situated in the great bay of Geelvink on the northern side of New Guinea. The land is high and the inhabitants are negros, but this is all that is known about it, which is much less than we know of almost any small island of the Pacific.

JOHOL. The name of one of the small inland Malay states of the peninsula of Malacca, claiming to derive their origin from Menangkabo in Sumatra. It lies between the British territory of Malacca and the Malay state of Pahang on the eastern side of the peninsula. It contains a large lake, called that of Brau, alleged to be 50 miles in length, but probably with exaggeration. The waters of this lake are discharged into the China Sea, by the river on which stands the town of Pahang. The country produces gold and tin, but these are not washed to any extent, the working of them being confined to the native inhabitants. The whole population of this state, including that of Jompol, which is tributary to it, has been estimated not to exceed 4000.

JOHOR. The name of the Malay state, which embraces the southern end of the peninsula of Malacca, and which has to the north the British territory of Malacca for its boundary on the western coast, and that of the Malay state of Pahang on the eastern. The country takes its name from the town, which was founded by the Malays in 1512, after their expulsion from Malacca by the Portuguese in the previous year. Besides the continental territory, the state includes the many islands on its coasts, with the exception of the few belonging to England and Holland. The area of the whole territory is probably not less than 10,000 square miles, while its computed population does not exceed 25,000, or 2½ inhabitants to the square mile. The country, in fact, with the exception of here and there cleared paths on the banks of its rivers, is one immense jungle, and there is no evidence in the shape of temples, tanks, or other structures, to show that it was ever otherwise. Mr. J. R. Logan, who visited it in 1847, gives the following faithful and graphic account of its present condition. "The scene is not without its saddening aspect. Within eight and twenty miles of a vigorous and populous British settlement (Singapore), and at the entrance of a strait, through which 1500 vessels annually pass, the eye may search in vain all round for a single hut. Perfect solitude rests both on the sea and jungle. Not a single fisherman's canoe is to be seen afloat, not a single coco-nut tree rising along the beach. The chief town of Johor-lama is situated about 20 miles up a very considerable river, and what was once a capital is now a miserable village of five and twenty houses, of perishable materials, and without a vestige of any permanent buildings." The principal inhabitants of Johor consist of Malays, and the wild uncultivated tribes of the same race, and speaking the same language, known by the various names of Jakun, Bânua, &c. &c. The larger animals of the forest, namely, two species of the ox, the elephant, the tapir, the hog, the rhinoceros, and above all the tiger, are probably far more numerous than its human inhabitants. The only sign of vitality which it has of late years exhibited consists in the settlement of Chinese emigrants from Singapore in quest of fresh lands for the growth and manufacture of gambir or terra-japonica. The country produces alluvial gold and tin, but washed to a very small extent.

From 1512 to 1810, there reigned in Johor fourteen princes, giving an average duration of 21 years to each reign. The prince who died in the last of these years left two sons, who disputed the succession. It suited the policy of the English and Dutch governments to take, each, one of the rivals as its protégé, and hence the cession of Singapore to the first, and of Rhio to the last. Both princes are now pensioners, the protégé of the English claiming sovereignty over the forests north of the Straits of Singapore, and he of the Dutch, those to the south of it, as laid down by the convention of London of 1824.

JOLÓ. The name by which the Sulu or Suluk Islands are designated by the inhabitants of the Philippine Islands and Spaniards. See Sulu.

JUAN (San), called also Guajan and Guan by the Spaniards, the Guam of our maps, one of the Ladrone or Marianne Islands. See Mariannes.

JUAN (San). The St. John of our maps. The most easterly island of the Philippine group, lies on the eastern side of the great island of Mindano, and separated from it by a strait 3½ leagues broad in its narrowest part. It lies between north latitude 7° 51′ and 8° 57′, and east longitude 125° 50′ and 126° 40′. Its length from east to west is 22 leagues, and its average breadth 15, giving it an area of 330 leagues. Its northern and eastern coasts are rugged and precipitous, but its western has some roadsteads affording shelter during the north-easterly monsoon. The interior is rough, craggy, and covered with forest. San Juan appears to be eminently sterile, and it is remarkable that so large an island should be, as it is, uninhabited, and frequented only by a few fishermen during the north-eastern monsoon.

JUAN DEL MONTE. The name of a sanctuary of great celebrity in the island of Luzon and metropolitan province of Tondo, belonging to the order of the Dominicans. The building, of solid masonry, is situated on a hill on the banks of an affluent of the river Pasig. Near to it is a mineral spring of great reputation for its sanative qualities, and the surrounding country being beautiful and picturesque, the sanctuary, which is very spacious, is much frequented by the inhabitants of Manilla, who are conveyed to it all the way by water.

JUNK, from the Portuguese junca, a corruption of the Malay and Javanese word ajong, abbreviated jong, a ship or large vessel. Europeans have applied the name to the largest of the trading vessels of the Chinese, which are called by the Malays wangkang, while they designate the smaller vessels of the same people, top.

K.

KÂDIRI. The name of a province of Java in the proper country of the Javanese nation. It is bounded to the east by the provinces of Malang and Pasurahan, to the west by those of Madiyun and Pachitan, to the north by the province of Surabaya, and to the south by the ocean, the Sâgara-kidul or "south sea" of the Javanese. Kâdiri is a rich alluvial plain, lying between the mountains Walirang, Kawi, and Arjuna to the east, and Wilis to the west. The last is the lowest of these mountains, and has a height of 7957 feet, while the highest, Arjuna, is 10,350 feet above the level of the sea. The river Brantas, the second in magnitude of the island, has its origin in and passes through a great part of the province. Kâdiri has an area of 2054 geographical square miles, and by the census of 1850 had a population of 240,766 inhabitants;—therefore, a relative one of about 112 to the square mile. A great part of this province, in fact, is still covered with forests, 217 square miles of which consist of teak. The number of horned cattle has been reckoned at 58,600, and of horses at 14,000. Kâdiri was the seat of one of the most renowned of the ancient kingdoms of Java—Daä—renowned in Javanese story. That this state had attained a very considerable amount of civilisation is attested by the many Hindu remains which still exist in it, consisting of well-constructed temples—some of hewn trachite and some of brick, with images and inscriptions in the ancient Kawi. The time however in which it flourished cannot be correctly ascertained, but is with most probability to be ascribed to the eleventh and twelfth centuries of our time.

KÂDU, or in the Dutch orthography Kadoe, is the name of a beautiful, fertile, and highly cultivated province of Java. Kâdu, in Sanscrit, is "the dragon's tail," one of the nodes of the moon in Hindu astronomy, and hence probably the designation. The province is a valley lying between the mountains Mârapi and Râbabu to the east, and Sumbing and Sundara to the west, the lowest of these, Mârapi, an active volcano, being 9250 feet high, and the highest, Sumbing, 11,000. To the east it is bounded by the province of Pajang, to the south by Mataram, to the west by Baglen and Bañumas, and to the north by Pakalongan and Samarang. Kâdu has an area of 631 miles, and by the census of 1845 had a population of 457,035, giving 724 to the square mile, except Japara, another province of Java, probably the largest rural population of any country of Asia, unless of some parts of China. It is to be observed, however, that this population had by the census taken in 1850 declined to

400,057. I was myself in civil charge of this fine province, when it was delivered over to the British government in 1812, and although down to that time it had never been subject to any other than native rule, I can safely say that I have never since seen, although I have visited the plains of Belgium and Lombardy, so luxuriant a scene of cultivation—the result of a soil of wonderful fertility, of an easily practised irrigation at all seasons, and of near 60 years of uninterrupted peace. The number of its horned cattle has been reckoned at 126,000, and of its horses at 15,000. Its chief productions are rice and tobacco, both large articles of export. The Dutch in recent years have added coffee, indigo, and tea, produced as elsewhere on account of the government. Kâdu contains the largest and most perfect of the Hindu monuments of Java, the Buddhist or Jain temple of Borobudor with its 400 images.

KÆMPFER (Engelbert), the well-known author of the History of Japan, was a native of Lemgo, in the county of Lippe in Westfalia. He was born on the 16th of September, 1651, and highly educated for the medical profession. After some stay in Sweden he proceeded as Secretary of Legation to a Swedish mission to the court of Persia, in the year 1683, the ambassador being Fabricius. This mission, in its way to Ispahan, the then Persian capital, proceeded through Russia by the route of Moscow and the Caspian. Instead of returning to Europe with the ambassador, Kæmpfer resolved on continuing his stay in the East, and with this view accepted employment as chief surgeon to the Dutch fleet, which was at the time cruising in the Persian Gulf, and of which the chief station was Gomroon. After quitting this employment he proceeded to Batavia, which he reached in 1689, touching at various ports of Arabia and Western India on his way. In the following year, touching at Siam on his route, he went as surgeon to the Dutch mission to Japan, and in each of the two subsequent years visited the Court of Jeddo. In the year 1693 he returned to Europe, and passed the remainder of his life practising as a physician in his native town, dying in 1716 at the age of 65. It appears from this that Kæmpfer's whole residence in India did not exceed four years, three of which were passed in Japan. Of the Indian Islands he seems to have seen nothing beyond Batavia and the islets on the route between it and Siam. He does not appear to have acquired a knowledge of any oriental language, his whole information having been obtained through interpreters, and these not always competent ones. Of this a curious and amusing example is afforded in what he says of some of the Malay Islands in the China Sea. "Orang Kay," says he, "in the Malay language, signifies woodman, or a man entrusted with the care and inspection of woods and forests." The correct title is orang-kaya, which literally means "rich man," but properly a noble or person of rank. The author had mistaken the adjective kaya, "rich," for the noun kayu, "wood" or "timber," and he might have reflected that a conservator of forests was a needless office in countries covered with forest, and in which the great object is to get rid of it.

In 1711 Kæmpfer published his Amœnitates Exoticæ, but the History of Japan was not published until 1727, eleven years after his death. Sir Hans Sloane had purchased the manuscript from his heirs, and had it translated from the German into English, so that it was in this language that it first appeared, translations from it into French and Dutch having afterwards been made from the English version. Kæmpfer has contributed little or nothing to our knowledge respecting the Indian Archipelago, but for Japan he has been the principal source of our information for 130 years. He is a laborious, shrewd, and generally reliable observer.

KAILI, or KYELI. The name of a country of Celebes, situated on the main body of this winged island, and towards that side of it which lies on the Strait which separates Celebes from Borneo. The territory of Kaili consists of four separate and independent principalities—Dongala, Tuwaini, Sero, and Palu—the last of these being the most considerable. The country is generally mountainous, and most probably of granitic formation, for gold obtained by washing forms one of the staple exports. The ruling people are the Bugis of Tuwaju, but the interior contains many wild tribes, of whom nothing but their existence is known to Europeans. The principal port is Dongala, from which a number of praus trade with Java, Singapore, and other countries of the west. The exports, besides gold and the other commodities usually dealt in by the Bugis, have of late years included coffee of native growth.

KALANTAN. One of the four Malay states on the eastern side of the Malay Peninsula, being the fourth, counting from the south. It is bounded to the north by the Malay state of Patani, and to the south by that of Tringgano, the river Banara dividing it from the first, and the Bâsut from the last. It has the Malay state of Queda to the west, the great central chain of the peninsula being the boundary. The inhabitants are Malays, with a few tribes of Negritos in the mountains, and a considerable number of Chinese engaged in washing gold and in mining and smelting tin. The total population was estimated to me by some intelligent merchants of the country at 10,000 families or 50,000 inhabitants, which taking the area of the country at 7000 square miles, would give about seven inhabitants to the square mile. Mr. Newbold in his account of the Peninsula and its islands gives the same estimate, but, to judge from the natural sterility of the country and the barbarism of its government, I make no doubt but that it is much exaggerated. The staple exports are tin, gold, and black pepper, for the most part the products of Chinese industry. The chief town or residence of the raja, of the same name, is on a small bar river navigable only for boats, in north latitude 6° 16′. The principal trade is with Singapore, and chiefly conducted by the Chinese during the south-western monsoon, the coast of Kalantan being a lee shore in the opposite one. Kalantan existed as a state at the close of the fifteenth century and before the arrival of the Portuguese, but of the time or the manner in which it was founded nothing is known, or probably knowable. It is one of the five Malay states of the Peninsula, immemorially tributary to Siam, and which make a yearly acknowledgment of dependence by a small tribute called the "bunga-mas" or "gold flower."

KALI; in Javanese, a river. It frequently occurs in the names of places, and is equivalent to Sungai, in Malay; and Chai, in Sunda.

KAMBING (PULO), literally "goat-island," but the name is said to be given to it on account of the number of a small species of deer (Cervus Moluccensis), which are found in it. It lies off the northern coast of Timur, and opposite to the Portuguese settlement of Dili, between the islands of Ombai and Wetter. Its southern extremity is in south latitude 8° 21′, and east longitude 125° 39′. Its surface is hilly, with a peaked mountain; and the island is chiefly remarkable for a mud volcano on the top of this peak. This proceeds from pyramidal hillocks, twelve in number, united at the bottom, and at the apex of each of which there is a vent, from which, at regular intervals, there is a discharge of gas and liquid mud. The earth of this mud contributes to maintain the form of the cones, and the saline water trickling down their sides is licked by the deer, which resort to the place for the purpose.

KAMPAR. The name of a Malay state on the north-eastern side of Sumatra, and nearly opposite to the eastern extremity of the Peninsula and the British island of Singapore. It has Indragiri to the south-east; and Sïak, to which it is tributary, to the north-west. The principal river of the country extends inland all the way to the territory of Menangkabo, which bounds Kampar to the west; but it is shallow,—full of sandbanks—has a bar at its entrance, with a dangerous bore or tidal wave. The low island of Rantao, which is opposite to the mouth of the river, belongs to Kampar, and is famed for the quantity of raw sago which it produces for the manufactories of Singapore. The ruling people are Malays, all the way to the frontier of Menangkabo. There is, however, a wild people, in some respects distinct from them, who speak a jargon of their language, but have not embraced the Mahommedan religion. These are known to the Malays under the common name of Orang-utan, that is, literally, "men of the woods," but which, as they intend it, means "savages," or uncivilised men. These are represented as simple and peaceable: their chief employment is the cultivation of the sago palm. Kampar is said to produce a small quantity of tin and gold. No attempt has been made to estimate the number of its inhabitants; and little is known of its history. De Barros enumerates it as one of the twenty-nine states which existed on the sea-board of Sumatra on the first arrival of the Portuguese; and Castaghneda mentions its sovereign as the king of "a small country in Sumatra that consisted of nothing but forest," a description which equally applies to the principality at the present day.

KANGEAN. The name of a group of islands, consisting of one considerable one surrounded by many islets; lying north of Bali, and east of Madura, from which last it is distant about fifty miles.

KARANG-ASAM. The name of a principality of the island of Bali, occupying its north-eastern portion fronting Lomboc. Within it is the highest mountain of the island, the Gunung-agong, or "great mountain" of the natives, and the Peak of Bali of our mariners, which is of the height of 11,326 feet above the level of the sea. The most recent account of the population of this principality makes it 85,000. About the beginning of the present century this state effected the conquest of the island of Lomboc, which still continues to be ruled by a prince of the family of the conqueror. The name probably signifies, literally, "ornamented with tamarind-trees," from karang, "to arrange ornamentally," and asam, "the tamarind." See BALI.

KARIMON, correctly KRIMUN. There are two groups of islands of this name, one at the eastern end of the Straits of Malacca, and another on the northern coast of Java. See CARIMON.

KARTASURA. The name of the ruins of a place in the province of Pajang, in Java, once the seat of government of the dynasty of Mataram. Mataram having been destroyed by a rebellion two years before, the seat of government was removed to Kartusura in 1680; but in the course of two-and-sixty years, was again changed for its present site in 1742. The name is Sanscrit, and signifies "labour of valour;" the same words reversed in their order being given to the present capital, Surakarta. The ruins of a kraton, or palace, are still seen; and near to them a small but handsome lake.

KASUMBA; the Javanese and Malay name for Safflower, the Canthamus tinctorius of botanists. The name is from the Sanscrit, and as it has none in the native languages, it is probable that it was introduced into Java, the only country of the Archipelago in which it is cultivated, by the Hindus. The epithet "Javanese," is commonly added by the Malays in order to distinguish it from arnotto, the Bissa orellana, which is called Kasumba-kling, or the Telinga kasumba, although this last be an American plant.

KATI, frequently written by us Catty, a weight of 1⅓ pound avoirdupois; which contains 16 taïls, and 100 of which make a pikul, or picul, literally "a load." The taïl, the kati, and the pikul are native words, but the weights they express Chinese.

KAWI. In Java and Bali, but there only, there exists, as in northern and southern India, in Ceylon, in Birma, and in Siam, an ancient recondite language; and in Bali it is still the language of law and religion, as it was in Java before the adoption of the Mahommedan religion in the 15th century. This tongue is known by the name of kawi, a word which literally signifies "tale, or narrative;" and is not the name of any national tongue, but seems a corruption of the Sanscrit word, kavya. In Java there are found many ancient inscriptions in this language, both on stone and brass: and even two ancient manuscripts in it are still preserved. Such of the inscriptions as are not in the Devanagri, and these are but few, have been found to consist of various modifications of the present modern character. The consonants, vowels, and orthographic marks are essentially the same in number, power, and form, being only ruder in shape and less connected with one another. The ancient character is, at present, never used in Java, or even in Bali; neither is the modern ever seen on an ancient inscription. Such is the case in Birma and Pagu, with the Pali character of the Buddhist nations, which is confined to inscriptions and religious works, in which the modern character is never used. This leads to the conclusion that the Kawi, or ancient character of Java and Bali, was restricted to inscriptions, all of which are of a mythological character, and confined to religious uses. The modern character was, probably, used at the same sime for temporal purposes, as is at present the modern Burmese; and it may, therefore, be of great antiquity, although we have no positive evidence of it. It is certain, however, that it is written in Palembang and Bali at the present day, exactly as it is in Java, after a known virtual separation of near four centuries.

Some writers have supposed the Kawi to be a foreign tongue, introduced into Java at some unknown epoch; but there is, assuredly, no ground for this notion, as is sufficiently proved by its general accordance with the modern Javanese. Independent of its being the language of ancient inscriptions, it is that of the most remarkable literary productions of the Javanese. These consist of epitomes, or paraphrases of the celebrated epics of the Hindus,—the Mahabarat and Ramayana. The last of these appears in several different romances; but the first, which is the best, in a single poem, under the Sanscrit name of the Bratayuda, or the war of Barata, that is, of the descendants of Barat. In the text of this work we have the name of the author, and a date, an unique instance of authenticity in the literature of the Archipelago. The author's name is Ampusâdah, abbreviated Pusâdah; and he tells us that he lived at the court of Jayabaya, king of Däa, in the province of Kâdiri, in Java; and that he composed his work at the desire of the king, who was a great admirer of the character of Salya, the leader of the Kurawa. But the date is, unfortunately, not in numeral figures, or in ordinary writing, but in the mystic words representing numerals, in which dates are most usually given, and hence it is liable to several different interpretations. Among these, the latest gives the year of Saka or Salivana, 1117, corresponding with that of Christ 1195. A careful analysis of some stanzas of the Bratayuda, shows that about 80 in 100 of its words are modern Javanese; and of these about one-half, excluding proper names, is Sanscrit. In the Kawi, words common to the Malay and Javanese languages are found just as they are in the modern Javanese, the proportion only being fewer. Among the words common to the Kawi and modern Javanese are those essential to grammatical structure, as the prepositions and the particles employed in the formation of transitive, intransitive, and passive verbs, with the auxiliaries used in those of tenses. The names of plants, animals, metals, winds, and seasons are also the same in the ancient and modern tongues; and these, for the most part, are native and not foreign words. All this leaves little doubt that the Kawi is nothing more, both as to language and character, than an antique form of the vernacular language of Java.

The Kawi abounds more in consonants than the modern language. Thus, nusa, "an island," in Javanese, is nuswa or nusya in Kawi; dadï, "to become," is dadiya; kadaton, "a palace," is kadatyan; manusa, "man," is manuswa; and aja, "do not," is ajuwa. Many words in Kawi, although obsolete in the modern language, are sufficiently known to Javanese scholars, which is exactly analogous to what is the case in our own language. But the most satisfactory proof that Kawi is nothing more than an antiquated form of Javanese is, that whole passages of the Bratayuda now and then occur, which are easily understood by ordinary Javanese scholars. See LANGUAGE.

KAWI (GUNUNG). The name of a mountain of Java, in the provinces of Malang and Kâdiri, the summit of which is 8820 feet above the level of the sea. It has no active volcano.

KAYAN; the name of the most numerous, civilised, and powerful of the wild inhabitants of Borneo, called by the Malays, Dayak. The territory occupied by this nation extends, diagonally, across the island from the equator to the 5° of north latitude. See DYAK.

KEMA. The name of a port and district of the northern peninsula of Celebes, on its southern side, and northern coast of the Gulf of Gorongtalo. The port, which is an open road, is in north latitude 1° 22′, and east longitude 125° 19′; the volcanic mountain, Klobat, forming a conspicuous land-mark. Kema, and Menado on the opposite side of the same Peninsula, have, within the last few years, been declared free ports by the government of the Netherlands, to which the sovereignty of the whole Peninsula belongs.

KEI ISLANDS. The name of a group of islands lying west of New Guinea and the Aroe Islands, and estimated to contain an area of 960 square geographical miles. They consist of three large islands and many islets. The inhabitants are of the Malayan race, an industrious, peaceable, seafaring people.

KIDUL. "The South," in Javanese. It is applied as an epithet to the sea south of Java, Lant kidul, or Sagara kidul, that is, "the South Sea," and to a range of mountains extending along the southern shore of the island the Gunung-Kidul, called also Kândang, a range distinct from the great central volcanic one, and seldom exceeding one-third of its height.

KINABALAO. The name of the highest mountain of Borneo, situated towards its northern extremity, on the peninsula lying between the China sea and the bay of Maludu. By trigonometrical measurement its height has been made between 13,000 and 14,000 feet. This would make it the highest mountain of the Archipelago; but an English traveller, Mr. Lowe, who ascended it nearly to its summit, in 1851, did not make its height by barometer more than 9,500 feet. The mountain, in its lower parts, is composed of sandstone, and in its upper of sienitic granite. At the top it consists of bare rock, but the rest is covered with a tall forest, the character of the plants varying with the altitude. In the neighbourhood of Kinabalo there are other mountains, seemingly of the same formation, and some of them estimated at 6,000 feet high. Many new plants were discovered by Mr. Lowe on the mountain, such as orchises, rhododendrons, and myrtaceous plants. The inhabitants of the neighbourhood consist of four tribes of the Dayaks, or wild aborigines, each, as elsewhere, speaking a distinct language. These are the Murut, called also Idäan, the Murung, the

Kohom, and the Kïao. All these carry on a rude agriculture, and are of inoffensive manners. In all our maps, a large lake, called by the same name as the mountain, is laid down ; but Mr. Lowe, after diligent inquiry, could hear nothing of it, and came to the conclusion that no such lake exists.

KISA, called Kiser in the Dutch maps, is a small island off the east end of Timur, and distant from it 18 miles. It is no more than 16 miles in circumference, but well inhabited ; its population, in 1838, having been computed at 8000. One-third of the inhabitants are Christians of the Dutch Lutheran Church, and the rest idolaters. The people are peaceable and industrious, raising yams and batatas, and rearing poultry and hogs. Their language is peculiar, but intermixed with words of the languages of Timur, and of Malay and Javanese. They are of the Malayan race.

KLING. The name given by the Malays and Javanese to the Telinga nation of southern India, and which appears to be a corruption or abbreviation of the genuine name of the country of this people, Kalinga. Being the only Indian nation familiarly known to the nations of the Archipelago, the word is used by them as a general term for all the people of Hindustan, and for the country itself. The trade and intercourse of the Telingas with the Archipelago is of great but unascertained antiquity, and still goes on. Many Telingas have, from time to time, settled more particularly in the western parts of the Archipelago, as in Sumatra and the Malay Peninsula, and their mixed descendants are tolerably numerous. In Singapore, for example, the Telingas form about one-tenth of the population, and in Penang they are even more numerous. It was this people that, in all probability, introduced the Hindu religion into Java and the other islands, and they seem also to have contributed materially to the spread of Mahommedanism, the majority of the settlers being at present of this persuasion. In the beginning of the 16th century the Portuguese found them carrying on trade at Malacca, and Barbosa, who calls them Chetijs, describes them as " wealthy merchants of Coromandel, who traded in large ships." See HISTORY.

KLOBAT. The name of a mountain with an active volcano, 6,800 feet high, situated on the northern peninsula of Celebes, in north latitude 1° 32′. It is the highest of the volcanic mountains of Celebes, and consequently not much more than one-half the height of the highest of Java, Bali, and Lomboc.

KLONGKONG. One of the nine states into which the island of Bali is at present divided, and forming a portion of its southern side, between the principalities of Karang-asam, Giyanjar, and Bleleng. In 1842 its population was estimated at 50,000. See BALI.

KLUT. The name of a mountain of Java, in the province of Kâdiri, 7,500 feet high. Its name is taken from that of a wooden bell suspended to the neck of the buffalo, and to the form of which it is supposed to bear some resemblance. At the foot of the Klut are the remains of a Hindu temple, built of cubical blocks of trachite, highly sculptured, and still 18 feet high. It is known by the name of Chandi Pânataran, or the temple of Pânataran, taken from that of a neighbouring village.

KOEN (JOHN PETERSON), the fourth of the Dutch Governor-Generals of India, was born on the 8th of January, 1587, at Havre, in North Holland, the son of parents in easy circumstances. His education was wholly commercial, and to finish it, he was sent to Rome, where he served for several years in a large commercial establishment. On his return to Holland, in 1607, he entered the service of the East India Company, at the age of 20, and proceeded to India, where, having served for four years, he returned to Holland in 1611. Next year he went back to India, and was appointed chief of the Factory of Bantam, from which station he was promoted to that of Director-General of Trade, the next post in rank to that of Governor-General. At the early age of thirty-one he was made Governor-General.

Hitherto, the seat of government had been at Amboyna, in the Spice Islands, this locality, on account of the paramount value of the spice trade, being considered at the time the most appropriate and convenient. Koen's prescience soon discovered to him that a seat of government more central, and in a country of superior resources to the Moluccas, was indispensable for the consolidation of the Dutch power, and he naturally fixed on Java, and that portion of it which appeared accessible to him. The first site chosen was the mouth of the river Tangeran, three leagues west of Batavia, and within the same wide bay. This, however, belonged to the prince of Jacatra, who persistently refused to cede the necessary territory. The strong-minded Koen, nothing daunted, determined at once on fixing the future capital at Jacatra itself, where the Dutch had had a factory since 1611, and with this view he transferred the principal part of the commercial and military establishments from Bantam,—surrounded the factory of Jaratra with a rampart, and virtually founded the city of Batavia, in 1618 and 1619. From this time may be dated the foundation of the Dutch empire in the Archipelago, which, most probably, would never have come into existence had the seat of government continued in the remote Moluccas, or been established, according to the recommendation of the home authorities, in the barren island of Banca.

Koen surrendered the government in 1625, and once more returned to Holland, but, after a residence in Europe of four years, was again appointed Governor-General, the only example in the Dutch annals of a second nomination to this high trust. On his return to India, he had to defend his conquest, not only against the kings of Jaratra and Bantam, but against the Susunan of Mataram, by far the most powerful prince of Java, and lord of the most fertile and populous portions of it. In 1628 and 1629, this prince laid siege to Batavia, and in each year, with a host supposed to have amounted to a hundred thousand men. He was repeatedly defeated by a handful of Dutch, with a few Chinese auxiliaries, and assuredly the superiority of European courage, discipline, and power of combination over semi-barbarous Asiatic hordes, was never more conspicuous than in these contests. It was while the last of these sieges was in progress, and on the 20th of September, 1629, that the active and laborious life of Koen was brought to a close, by a sudden stroke of apoplexy, in the forty-second year of his age.

Koen was, without doubt, a man of great ability, full of resource, and secret, skilful, and bold in the execution of his projects. His countrymen describe him as a man of great integrity, and a lover of justice; but the patent parts of his administration attest that he was unscrupulous, even beyond the measure of other adventurers of the 17th century. One striking example given by his biographers sufficiently shows what were his notions of justice. In the suite of his wife was the illegitimate daughter of a councillor of the Indies, a girl of thirteen, who was detected in a love intrigue with a young Dutchman. The lover offered reparation by marriage, but the inexorable Koen directed the parties to be tried by a law of his own making, and by judges of his own nomination. They were condemned, the youth to be put to death, and the young woman to be severely whipped in public; and the Governor-General confirmed both sentences, and had them carried into execution. This was not justice, but barbarian ruffianism. In the Spice Islands he nearly exterminated the inhabitants of the Banda Islands, expatriating the remainder, and replacing the population by slaves. The expulsion of the English from Bantam, and the future Batavia, is quite justifiable, for it was the mere result of superior power and superior adroitness in intrigue. Had they themselves been successful, without a doubt they would have treated him and his countrymen in the same manner. His countrymen exonerate him from the tortures and massacre of Amboyna, in which ten Englishmen and as many of their followers lost their lives, because he had surrendered the Indian government a month before the massacre. This, however, is an untenable defence, for the local officers who perpetrated the massacre were of his own nomination, the system which they were carrying out, the eradication of all competition in the spice-trade, was his own, and on his return to power he never disavowed their act.

Koen was, undoubtedly, the greatest man that Dutch India has produced, and may be said to occupy in the Dutch annals the same place that Alboquerque does in the Portuguese and Clive in the English. He is the real founder of the Dutch empire in India, and although but a mere civilian, he was enabled, by the native strength of his character, to effect what those men had done, clothed with military reputation. His countrymen, however, are either insensible to his merits or negligent to reward them, for down to the present day, no monument has ever been erected to his memory.

KOMODO, or COMODO, a small island lying off the western end of Floris, and in the strait which divides this island from Sumbawa. It is surrounded by many islets, has a steep rocky coast, and an almost unfathomable sea. Like Sumbawa and Floris, Komodo is of volcanic formation, but beyond these few facts nothing more is known of it.

KOMRING. This is the name of a country and people within the territory of Palembang, at the north-eastern end of Sumatra. The language of the country is said to be peculiar and written in a national alphabet. The people are represented as industrious, independent in their manners, and pagans, believing in the transmigration of souls. Within their territory is a fine lake, which they call Ranau, a word, however, which seems only a modification of danau, the common name for a lake in Malay, or, perhaps, of ranu, water, in Javanese.

KORÉ is the Javanese name for Bima in the island of Sumbawa, but the origin of the word is unknown.

KORINCHI. The name of a valley of the interior of Sumatra, between the equator and the second degree of south latitude. Mr. Logan estimates its extent at 100 miles long and 50 broad, giving an area of 5,000 square miles, and he ascribes to it a population of 75,000, or 15 to the square mile. The inhabitants are a tolerably civilised people, practising a respectable agriculture, well clad in their own manufactures of cotton, and living in easy circumstances. Insecurity of life and property among them, however, is evinced by the form of their habitations, which consist, like those of the wild inhabitants of Borneo, of barn-like dwellings, capable of accommodating many families, sometimes to the number of forty. The people of Korinchi are of the Malay nation, speak the Malay language, and write it in an alphabet of their own, the same, very probably, in which it was written by all the Malays before the adoption of the Arabic character. The country contains several lakes, but one, the Danau-korinchi or lake of Korinchi, is of considerable size. On this, Mr. Charles Campbell, an eminent botanist, the only European who is known ever to have visited the country, sailed in 1800, and he and his companions estimated its breadth, without, however, rendering any account of its length, at seven miles. It abounds in good fish, especially in a species of mullet and of carp, and its borders are the chief seats of the agriculture and population of the country. The elevation of the valley above the level of the sea has not been ascertained, but as the coco-palm refuses to bear fruit in it, it is concluded that it must be considerable.

KORIPAN. The name of an ancient kingdom of Java, which was situated in the modern district of Grobogan, within the proper country of the Javanese. Koripan is of great celebrity in Javanese romance, but of its true history nothing is known.

KOTARINGIN, an abbreviation of Kota-waringin, literally, "fortress of the Indian fig-tree," a district of the kingdom of Banjarmasin in Borneo, and now of a Dutch residency. This name, partly Sanscrit and partly Javanese, was probably, like several others in the same part of Borneo, imposed by the Javanese princes of Majapait, when they acquired a supremacy over Banjarmasin, by the marriage of a Javanese prince with the heiress of the throne of that country. Kotaringin forms the most westerly district of the Residency of the Dutch Banjarmasin.

KRAMA. This is the name given by the Javanese to their ceremonial or polite dialect, also occasionally called bahasa. Both words are Sanscrit, the first meaning order or arrangement, and the last, speech or language. These names are applied to it in contradistinction to the word ngoko, applied to the vernacular tongue, and which signifies common or vulgar. The following is a brief account of this singular and unique dialect. The ceremonial language is that of the court, or more correctly of courtiers, for the sovereign and members of his family address others in the vulgar tongue, while they themselves are addressed in the ceremonial. In epistolary writing, the ceremonial dialect is always used, even by superiors to inferiors, unless the party addressed be of very humble rank indeed. The exception is the sovereign, for all royal letters, edicts, and proclamations are in the vulgar tongue, that is, in the language of command. In books, according to the nature of the subject, both dialects are used indifferently.

In framing the polite dialect, for it is obviously a factitious language, the object seems to have been to avoid every word that had become by frequent use familiar,—to adopt words that were not so, to borrow from other languages, and even to coin new words, or alter old ones, for these purposes. The distinction in words does not absolutely pervade the whole language, but there is a very near approach to it, for it extends to every word in frequent use, including even pronouns, prepositions, auxiliaries, particles, and numerals. In some cases, the words of the ceremonial language are native synonyms. Thus, bañu is water in the vulgar tongue, but toya in the ceremonial. The ceremonial language has borrowed largely from Malay and Sanscrit. Thus, wâdi, sand, is changed into the Malay pasir, and dawa, long, into panjang, of the same language. From the Sanscrit, we have asta, the hand, and akasa, the sky, substituted for the Javanese words tangan and langit. If, however, the Sanscrit word itself should have become familiar, it is rejected, and another word from the same language or from a native source is substituted for it. Thus, jagat, the world, belongs to the vulgar tongue, but buwana to the ceremonial,—manusa, a man, to the first, but jalma to the last, all being alike Sanscrit.

But besides synonyms taken from obsolete native words, or from foreign languages, the ceremonial dialect has other resources of wider application. It converts words of the vulgar tongue to its own purpose by a permutation of vowels and consonants, sometimes by a combination of both these means, and sometimes by substituting a syllable terminating in a consonant, when the word of the ordinary language happens to end with a vowel. Of these methods, the most frequent is the permutation of vowels, generally of the final vowel, sometimes of the medial, but never of the initial. For this purpose, the low and broad sounding vowels, u, o, and a, are exchanged for the high and sharp ones, â, e, and i. The vowel u, for example, belongs to the vulgar tongue, and, sometimes, we have a scale of ascending respect, according to the quality of the party addressed, ending as a climax in i. The verb, to sit, is an example, for it may be varied in four different ways, lunguh, lungah, lângah, and lingah. A single change, however, is more frequent, as in the case of swarga, heaven, which becomes swargi; mula, source, which becomes mila; and jajar, a row or rank, jejer.

When, however, a word of the vulgar tongue terminates in a slender vowel, or from other cause is not amenable to this kind of formation, another expedient is had recourse to. This consists in substituting for such slender vowel, a syllable ending in consonants, which are always nasals, liquids, or the sibilant. Euphony seems the object chiefly held in view in making these changes, as aji, to teach, becomes in this manner ayos, in the polite dialect; wâdi, fear, wâdos; sâgara, the sea, sâgantân; and apura, pardon, apuntân.

Sometimes the word in the ceremonial dialect is an epithet, or a translation, true or fanciful, of that in the vulgar tongue. Thus, the sugar-cane in the vulgar tongue is tâbu, and in the polite rosan, which is literally the object with joints. Bebek in the ordinary language is the domestic duck, which in the ceremonial becomes kambangan, which literally means the thing that swims or floats. For words of very frequent occurrence, the polite dialect has often several synonyms. Thus, for news, there are two, warti and wartos, and for the heart three, nala, manah, and galih.

Names of persons are not changed in the ceremonial dialect, but those of well-known places and even nations are. Thus the royal province of Matáram has two forms in the polite language, Matawun and Matawis. Frequently, the word of the polite language is a translation from that of the vulgar, as from Surabaya, Surapringa, and Surabangi. The word bali means "to return" in the vulgar tongue, and wangsul is its correlative in the polite and hence the last word is also the polite name for the island of Bali.

There is, of course, no record of the time or manner in which this singular dialect was introduced among, or framed by the Javanese, but we may be tolerably certain that its formation was gradual, and that in its present shape it is the accumulation of many ages. It contains many Sanscrit words, and we may therefore infer that it received a large accession after the introduction of Hinduism. It contains even a few Arabic words, and of course has gone on increasing ever since the comparatively recent time of 1478, the year of Javanese conversion. See JAVA and LANGUAGE.

KRAMAN. This word signifies in Javanese an impostor, pretending to some great secular or spiritual mission, or both united. The simplicity and credulity of the Javanese has, in all known periods of their history, rendered them peculiarly amenable to the impostures of persons of this description, and there are many examples of formidable and obstinate rebellions produced by them, such as that of Surapati, a Balinese slave, which lasted nine years; of Mangkubume, which lasted fifteen, and ended by splitting the kingdom of Mataram into two principalities, the rebel being rewarded with one of them; and, lastly, the rebellion of Dipa Nagara, which, after lasting four years, was brought to a conclusion only in 1830, by the cession of four provinces to the Netherland government, with an expenditure of, probably, not less than a million sterling. The mal-administration of a province, for any continued length of time, is pretty sure to give birth to such impostors, who, however, after an oriental fashion, are reckoned a kind of patriots.

KRAWANG. A province of Java in the country of the Sundas, and on the northern coast of the island. It is generally an alluvial tract, with many small streams, and one considerable river, the Chaitarum (indigo or blue river), which disembogues into the eastern side of the bay of Batavia. The area of Krawang is 1538 square miles, and its population in 1850 was 125,112, which, therefore, gives little more than 81 inhabitants to the square mile, or not above one-ninth part of the density of some of the proper Javanese provinces of the central and eastern portions of the island. By enumeration the number of horses in this province were computed at 5000, and that of its horned cattle 36,000.

KRIS, the abbreviation of Kâris, a dagger or poniard, the universal weapon of all the civilised inhabitants of the Archipelago, and of a hundred different forms, short or long, with a straight or serpentine blade, and with every variety in the shape and ornament of the hilt and scabbard. Men of all ranks, from the peasant to the prince, wear this weapon, and those of rank when full dressed, two or even four. In Java, even women of rank sometimes wear a small one. The word is probably Malay, but is now of general adoption through the Archipelago. The Javanese have three native names for it besides the Malay one, and it is found represented on several of the ancient temples of Java. The kris has even reached the Philippine Islands, for there is no doubt but that it is the same word of the Tagala and Bisaya languages which the Spaniards write calis, and translate "sword."

KROÉ, or **CROÉ**, as it is written in our maps, is the name of a district of the country of the Lampungs on the south-western coast of Sumatra. A British settlement existed here on a small river, navigable only for boats, until by the convention of 1824 it was made over with Bencoolen, of which it was a dependency, to the government of the Netherlands. Pepper-hunting was the unprofitable object of this poor and worthless settlement.

KUBU, in Malay, means a breast-work or redoubt, but it is also, for what reason I am unaware, the name of a wild people inhabiting the plain which extends from Jambi to Palambang, on the north-western side of Sumatra. Of this people little or nothing is known beyond the fact that they are of the Malayan race, and are possessed of even a smaller measure of civilisation than the most improved of the Dayaks of Borneo.

KUDUS. The name of a district of the Netherland province of Japara, in Java, lying between the districts of Damak and Pat·i.

KUPANG (in Malay, the name of a bivalve shell, a kind of mussell), or in the Dutch orthography, Koepang, is the name of the principal settlement of the Dutch in the island of Timur. The town and harbour are situated at the western end of the island, the fortress, Concordia, being in south latitude 10° 10′ 15″, and east longitude 123° 30′. The town lies on the south side of a spacious bay 12 miles wide at its entrance, and running into the country to the length of 20. The island of Semao, in some measure, protects the bay, which is a tolerable harbour, and at all events the best in the island of Timur. The population of Kupang and the surrounding country is 7000, and the dependent tribes are thought to amount to 40,000, so that the total inhabitants subject to the Dutch authority are but 47,000, although the Netherland government claims the sovereignty of one-half the island. The revenue derived by the Netherland government is stated to amount yearly to no more than 50,000 florins, or 4266*l.*, and this is all for the one half a great island! The exports, consisting chiefly of Sandal-wood, bees'-wax, and tripang, are reckoned to amount to 300,000 florins, or 25,000*l.*, and the imports, chiefly clothing, to about one-fourth more in value. These are but poor results for a country that has been near two centuries and a half in European occupation, and must be chiefly ascribed to the sterility of the land and the barbarism of its inhabitants. See TIMUR.

KURIMATA. The correct Malay name of the island which is in our charts Carimata. See CARIMATA.

KUT·I, generally written in our maps Coty, a Malay state on the eastern side of Borneo, fronting the south-western peninsula of Celebes. The name seems to be Sanscrit, and to signify "little fortress." Its boundaries and extent are not ascertained. The very little that is known of it is confined to its main river called by the same name. The embouchure of this large stream has in it many islands, so that it has several mouths. The most easily navigable of these is in south latitude 1° 10′, and east longitude 117°. Mr. Dalton, an English merchant and enterprising traveller, who visited Kut·i in 1827 and 1828, and resided fifteen months in the country or its neighbourhood, gives the following description of the river. At its most navigable mouth it has a bar on which at low water there are but 4 feet depth, but at the height of the flood 15 feet. It carries a breadth of from 200 yards up to 2 miles for a distance of at least 400 miles, with ample depth. The stream is rapid, often as much as 6 miles an hour, showing that it flows from high land. The inhabitants consist of Malays, Bugis, and Kayan Dayaks. The nominal rulers are the Malays, under a chief who takes the title of Sultan, and whose residence is at a place called Tongarong, on the right bank of the river, and in north latitude 1° 30′, and east longitude 115° 6′. The settlement of the Bugis, who are of the Tuwajos of Celebes, is at a place lower down the river, called by Mr. Dalton Semerindam, but by the Dutch, probably with more accuracy, Samarindé. Most of the houses of this place are built on floating rafts, as are some of those of Palembang in Sumatra, of Borneo in the island of this name, and of Bangkok the capital of Siam. The Bugis, who seem to be of comparatively recent establishment, exercise an independent authority, even controlling the Malay prince, and carrying on most of the trade of the country.

The Kayan Dayaks occupy the upper portion of the river, with the country far on both sides of it from a place called Markaman, which in the sketch map of the river given by Mr. Dalton is in nearly the second degree of north latitude. This place according to him has a mixed population of Malays and Dayaks, amounting to 3000. That the whole country must be very poorly inhabited is certain, since, with the exception of a few cultivated specks, it is one continuous jungle. Of one spot at which Mr. Dalton landed, and which is, nominally at least, a portion of the Kut·i territory, he gives the following description. "The country (Bagotta) under this pirate contains above 1200 square miles, without including the numerous islands. The intendant of the port told me the inhabitants might amount to 10,000 altogether, but from others, and what I consider to be much better information, the number was stated at 4000. The truth might probably lie between the two. It may appear strange that so large an extent of country should contain so few inhabitants. It must, however, be recollected that most of the country (indeed, the whole, with the exception of a few rice-fields) is little else than an impenetrable jungle, which nothing but a monkey can penetrate 50 yards from the banks of the rivers, which are very numerous." The traveller found the banks of the main river of more promising appearance, but equally unpeopled and uncultivated. "The higher," says he, "I ascend the country, the more beautiful it appears; hill and dale in pleasing variety, interspersed with clumps of the tallest trees. The verdure is rich beyond anything I have seen in India; indeed no country, however highly cultivated, can produce such views." Of this fine country to the eye, alligators, monkeys, and swarms of musquitoes are, however, the principal inhabitants.

The exports of Kut·i consist of bees'-wax, agar-agar or esculent sea-weed, esculent swallows'-nests, tripang, or holothurion, a small quantity of gold-dust, and slaves, consisting of the children of the Dayaks. Altogether, it is a poor and lawless place. In a more favourable state of the country, the commodities which might be expected to be profitably exported from Kut·i would be coal and iron ore. The history of the settlement of the Malays in this part of Borneo is wholly unknown, as it is in other parts of the island. Hindu temples and images are stated by Mr. Dalton to exist in the interior, within the country of the Kayan Dayaks. These were seen by him, but his information is not so precise as to enable us to determine their exact nature. He states, however, that they resembled those he had seen in Java and Southern India, and if this be the case, the probability is that they were the work of Javanese settlers, the same, probably, who first emigrated from Java to the neighbouring country of Banjarmasin. The Dutch lay claim to a paramount authority over Kut·i, but it seems to be neither exercised or acknowledged.

L.

LABO. The name of a high mountain, of a river, and of a town of the province of Camarines Norte in the island of Luzon. The highest peak of the mountain is in north latitude 13° 59′, and east longitude 123° 42′ 30″. The town is situated at the foot of the mountain in a spacious valley, and contains 400 houses, with a population of 2400. The valley itself is protected from the south-western monsoon by the central Cordillera, and from the north-eastern by the Sierra of Bagacay. Its products are rice, maiz, sugar-cane, indigo, and abaca. In the mountains which surround it are found a few wandering tribes of Negritos. Labo, in the Malay language, signifies a gourd, and was probably first given to the mountain.

LABUAN, correctly written Lábuhan, is a verbal noun, derived from the Malay and Javanese word labuh, to drop or let fall, hence to drop or cast anchor, and signifies anchorage or harbour. The name belongs to several places in the Archipelago, but is especially applied to the small island on the north-western coast of Borneo, now a British settlement. To complete the sense in this case, the word pulo or island must be prefixed, making "anchorage or harbour island." Labuan lies north-east of the estuary of the river of Borneo or Brunai, distant fifteen miles, with good anchoring-ground all the way. The island extends from north latitude 5° 11′ to 5° 25′, and from east longitude 115′ 10′ to 115° 25′. Its form is triangular, the base being to the south, and the apex to the north. Its greatest length is 12 miles, and its average breadth between 5 and 6, its area being about 40 square statute or 34 geographical square miles, and its coast line about 30. The highest land does not exceed 300 feet. The geological formation is sedimentary, consisting of sandstone, clay, and slate, much resembling the coal measures of England. The coal, which is found in several parts of the island, but chiefly towards the northern end, is a continuation of the great coal-field of the main island of Borneo. The main seam, which is now wrought by an English company, is 11 feet thick, and furnishes good coal for steam purposes. The base or south end of the island is six miles in length, and contains two bays, on the smallest and deepest of which, and on its eastern shore, is the site of the new town. Off the southern end of the island and extending towards Borneo there are no fewer than ten different islets, the largest of which, called Däat, forms a protection to the harbour and town. Some part of Labuan is covered with swamp, and some consists of sandy plain, but the greater part of the soil is a dark yellow loam, well adapted for cultivation. With the exception of the few spots recently cleared, the whole island is covered with forest, consisting in the marshy parts of mangroves, rattans, and palms, and in the higher grounds of a great variety of tall timber-trees, the most remarkable of which is that which yields the native camphor, the Dryobalanops camphora, the wood of which is used in house and ship-building.

Labuan had formed part of the principality of Borneo or Brunai, and like most of the rest of its territory had never been occupied, and was wholly destitute of inhabitants when we took possession, nor did it show any vestige of ever having been occupied. With its adjacent islands it was ceded to the British crown, and taken possession of on the 24th December, 1846. Its population does not exceed 1500, consisting principally of the parties engaged in the coal mines.

LAC. The colouring matter produced by the lac insect, or Coccus ficus, is known and used by the inhabitants of the Malay Islands, and the insect is found in the forests of Java, Sumatra, and the Peninsula. The produce however is neither so good nor so abundant as that of Hindustan, Burmah, or Siam, probably owing to the insect not being as in these countries domesticated and reared. The Malay name of the dye is ambalau, a native one.

LACCA, in Malay, Laka, the Tanarius major, a tree with a red-coloured wood, a native of Sumatra, used in dyeing and in pharmacy. It is an article of considerable native trade, and is chiefly exported to China.

LADRONE ISLANDS, or THIEVES' ISLANDS, so called by Magellan, their first discoverer. See MARIANES.

LAGONOY. The name of a spacious bay on the eastern coast of Luzon, and in the province of South Camarines. It is formed by an indentation of the coast of the main island, and by the considerable one of Catanduanes. It has two entrances, one narrow and dangerous from the north, between the main and Catanduanes; and the other a wide one, between this last and the islet of Bapurapu. Spanish writers describe the Bay of Lagonoy as a real open sea, and hence affording little shelter to shipping.

LAGONOY. The name of a town situated at the head of the above-named bay, in north latitude 13° 40′ 30″, and east longitude 123° 29′. Its population amounts to 7922 souls, of whom 969 contribute to the poll-tax. It lies on a small river, bearing also the same name. The level portions of the country near it are cultivated with rice, sugar-cane, sesame, and abaca, while in the pastures of the mountain sides are reared herds of horses, oxen, and hogs.

LAGUNA DE BAY, that is, "the lake of Bay," takes this name from a town called Bay, at its southern end. It is the largest collection of fresh water in the Philippines. Its greatest length is 34 miles; but its breadth is irregular, for towards its northern and north-eastern parts, through the interposition of two peninsulas, it spreads out into two spacious inlets or bays, so that its area will not exceed, probably, above 350 square geographical miles. Its coast line is reckoned to be 86 leagues,—its height above the level of the sea 58 feet; and its general depth from 15 to 16 fathoms. In a few places, however, it is shallow; while in others, it is said to be fathomless. Everywhere its water is sweet and potable. No fewer than fifteen different rivers contribute to form this lake; while it is emptied by one only, the Pasig, which, after a course of six leagues, falls into the great bay, near the city of Manilla. On its fertile shores there are no fewer than six-and-twenty townships. An east wind is the prevailing one on the lake, which has valuable fisheries, and an extensive boating traffic. In it there are several islands, the largest of them, named Talim, being three leagues in length by one in breadth: another, towards the southern end, contains within it a lake having all the appearance of having for its basin the extinct crater of a volcano. This last goes under the name of Los Caimanes, from the number of alligators which frequent it.

LAGUNA, PROVINCIA DE. This province, which takes its name from the lake above described, is bounded to the east by the sea at the Gulf of Lamon,—to the south by the provinces of Tayabas and Batangas,—to the west by the province of Cavité,—and to the north by the provinces of Tondo and Nueva Ecija. It contains thirty-six townships, the capital being Pagsanjan, on the eastern shore of the lake, in latitude 14° 15′ north. Exclusive of the great lake, the area of this province is estimated at 630 square geographical miles. Its productions are the usual ones,—rice, sugar-cane, and indigo; but it is remarkable besides for the extensive produce of the Nipa-palm, used for the distillation of spirits, and which affords a considerable branch of the public revenue. The inhabitants, in common with those of Batangas, Tondo, and most of those of the island of Mindoro, are of the Tagala nation. The following account has been given of the progress of its population. In 1735, it amounted only to 40,610 souls; in 1799, or in sixty-four years after, it had risen to 74,799. This, too, was without reckoning a township with 7314 inhabitants, which had been taken from Laguna and annexed to the neighbouring province of Batangas. In 1818, or in nineteen years more, the population was found to be 86,630; and in 1850, it had risen to 137,083, which gives a rate of 217 inhabitants to the square geographical mile, making it one of the most populous provinces of Luzon. It will appear, from the account above given, that in a period of 115 years the increase of population had been no less than 237 per cent.

LAKSAMANA. This is the name of the brother of the demi-god, and hero of the Hindu poem, the Ramayana; the adventures related in which are the frequent subjects of the romances and dramas of the Malays and Javanese. Laksamana, most probably borrowed from this personage, is also the appellation of the commander of the forces in several Malay states; and as that force is, for the most part naval, the word may be translated "admiral." It was so in the state of Malacca before the arrival of the Portuguese. Thus De Barros, mistaking the title of the office for a proper name, tells us that, on one occasion, the Portuguese under Alboquerque, after having landed,—attacked the town and been repulsed,—found it necessary to re-embark in order to protect their own fleet from being set fire to by the Malayans, of which the commander was "a valiant man, called Lacsamana;" and Castaghneda talks of the same personage as the king's admiral, who was called Lacsamana, "a discreet man, and a good cavalier, of eighty years of age." It is the same person, indeed, that is specially distinguished by the Malays themselves as "the laksamana," and whose name of adolescence was Hang-tuah. Although his story be little more than three centuries old, he has been long the favorite hero of Malay romance; which is about the same thing as if we were to consider the adventures of Sir Walter Raleigh the subject of a myth.

LAMON. The name of a deep gulf on the eastern side of Luzon, which mainly contributes to the formation of the Isthmus of Tayabas, and the Peninsula of Camarines; thus dividing that great island into two parts,—a main body to the north, and a peninsula to the south. Reckoning from the Island of Calabete, the length of the gulf is about 61, and its average breadth about 7 miles, making its area 427 square geographical miles.

LAMPUNG. The name of one of the nations of Sumatra, and of its country which forms the south-eastern end of the island. The territory of the Lampungs has the Straits of Sunda to the south, the Java Sea to the east, the country of Palembang to the north, and that of the Rejang nation to the west. Its southern coast, or that washed by the Straits of Sunda, is mountainous,—indented by numerous islets and by two large bays,—those of Lampung and Samangka; while along it are scattered no fewer than thirty-four islands, the most considerable of which are Samangka, Lagundi, Besi, and Krakatoa. The eastern coast, or that washed by the Java seas, differs remarkably from the western, for it forms a low, continuous, unbroken line, without inlets or islands.

The country of the Lampungs lies between 3° 48′ and 4° 59′ south latitude, and is computed to have an area of 8560 square geographical miles. Its southern portion is mountainous, and its geological formation volcanic; corresponding, in this respect, with that of Bantam, in Java, which lies opposite to it. Its northern or inland portion, on the contrary, is a level plain. The islands in the Straits of Sunda are composed of high land of volcanic formation, and some of them have extinct craters. The highest peaks of the mainland, those of the mountains called Tangamus and Lampung, rise to the height of 7500 feet above the level of the sea; and the peak of the island Krakatoa, which has been an active volcano in comparatively recent times, to that of 2700. In the volcanic part of the country there exist numerous hot springs, in which the heat rises to 180° of Fahrenheit. The rivers are numerous, but none of them large; and none adapted for navigation.

The vegetation of the volcanic portion of the country of the Lampungs agrees generally with that of the opposite shore of Java, but its zoology presents some singular discrepancies. Thus, there are three species of ape; and two feline animals in the first, unknown to the last. The elephant, the tapir, and the Malay bear are found in the country of the Lampungs, while they are unknown in Java. The Sunda ox is found throughout Java, but does not exist in the Lampungs. The peacock, which is abundant in Java, is not seen in the Lampungs; but instead, there are two pheasants, the Argus and another, both unknown to Java. These are strange differences in two countries, of which the geology and vegetation, at the nearest points, are similar; and which are divided from each other by a strait only a few leagues broad, having islands in the channel forming so many stepping-stones. "The whole phenomenon," says the judicious M. Zollinger, from whom this account of the Lampungs is taken, "is, in my opinion, evidence against the notion that Sumatra and Java, and indeed all the Sunda Islands, have been part of a continent, and united Asia with Australia. Geological grounds, indeed, ought long ago to have been sufficient to refute such an opinion."

The Lampung nation constitutes a distinct people from the other inhabitants of Sumatra; agreeing with the rest only in race, and differing from them in language, in manners, and in social state. The language is a peculiar one, and has been immemorially a written tongue in a peculiar character of its own. About one-third of it has all the appearance of an original tongue; the remaining part consisting principally of Malay and Javanese, with the usual small admixture of Sanscrit and Arabic, consequent on the peoples having adopted, successively, the religions associated with those two languages. Compared with the Malays and Javanese, the Lampungs are a rude people; and their backwardness is most probably to be ascribed to the unfavourable physical character of the country they inhabit, the volcanic portion of which is not peculiarly favourable to agriculture, while the alluvial is either sterile, or covered with morass and forest, beyond the power of a rude people to redeem. This rudeness of the Lampungs is evidenced by the almost total absence of irrigation; carried to so great an extent in Java, and the two islands immediately to the east of it, and even in several parts of Sumatra itself. Instead of the economical and productive husbandry which is the result of artificial irrigation, the Lampungs, generally, do no more than snatch an occasional crop of corn from the virgin land, using the ashes of the felled and burnt timber as a dressing, and abandoning the soil so cultivated for a new piece of forest, to be abandoned in like manner in its turn;—a practice which seems but one step above that of subsisting on the wild produce of the forest. The whole population of the Lampung country is not computed at more than 83,000. This gives the poor rate of from 6 to 7 inhabitants to the square mile, which is no more than one twenty-third part of that of the opposite country of Bantam, the least populous part of Java. The chief export is black pepper; and the others consist of the produce of the forest, such as rattans, and damar or resin. In former times, the country formed a part of the dominions of the kings of Bantam, from whom it has descended to the government of the Netherlands.

LAMUNGAN. The name of a mountain in the eastern part of Java, between the provinces of Prabalinga and Besuki, and an active volcano which rises to the height of 6500 feet above the level of the sea.

LANDAK. The name of a small Malay state on the western side of Borneo, situated on an affluent of the river of Pontianak. It lies about 40 miles north of the equator, and in a straight line about the same distance from the coast, but 70 miles by the windings of the river. Landak is only remarkable for being, unlike others, an inland Malay state, and being situated in that part of Borneo most remarkable for the production of gold and diamonds. Respecting its population we have no detailed knowledge, but it is certain that it is very inconsiderable. Besides

Malays, it consists of some Chinese, and of aborigines or Dayaks. The name in Malay and Javanese signifies "a porcupine;" but why so called is unknown.

LANGKA, the mythic name of Ceylon in the Hindu poem of the Ramayana, and as such, well known to the more advanced nations of the Archipelago. The popular name for it, however, is Selan, evidently taken from the Arabs, who probably made the island first known to the Malayan nations.

LANGKAT. The name of a Malay state on the north-eastern side of Sumatra, constituting the northern limit of the Malay nation, who have here to the north of them the Achinese, and westward and inland, the Batak nation. The entrance of the river, called also Langkat, on which is situated the principal village, bearing also this name, is in north latitude 4° 1′, and east longitude 98° 29′. At its mouth, the river is 800 yards broad, but obstructed by a bar of several miles in depth, on which there is little more than from a fathom to a fathom and a half of water, so that it is only navigable for large boats. The total population of Langkat has been estimated not to exceed seven or eight thousand, composed of Malays and dependent Bataks. Its chief produce is black pepper, which it is said to export to the yearly amount of from two to three millions of pounds. The country is part of the great alluvial plain, which extends nearly along the whole north-eastern side of Sumatra, and is washed by the waters of the Straits of Malacca.

LANGKAWI, called in our charts Lancava, is a considerable island, on the western coast of the Malay peninsula, having several smaller ones contiguous to it to the south, named the Ladas, which signifies the pepper-islands, so called more probably from their number than their produce. Langkawi and all the islands contiguous to it form part of the territories of the prince of Queda. They lie between the sixth and seventh degrees of north latitude, and the ninty-ninth and one hundredth of east longitude. Langkawi is about 25 miles in length from east to west, and about 10 from north to south. The land of all the group is high and level, and the geological formation, like that of the adjacent continent, plutonic, consisting of granite and mountain limestone. Both Langkawi and the larger islands of the group are inhabited by a Malay population.

LANGUAGE. In Malay and Javanese, there are the following words for language or speech, tutur, lidah, bahasa, chara, bâchara, and kata. Tutur and lidah are native words, the last, literally "tongue," not of frequent use. All the others are Sanscrit, the two first of them signifying also way or manner, and the two last talk or discourse. In the present state of our knowledge, the languages of the Malay and Philippine Archipelagos may safely be said to be innumerable, and even those ascertained to exist are very numerous. In this respect the Indian Islands more resemble Africa, and America, than continental Asia. As in America too, and, indeed, it may be said in every country, the languages in different parts of the country are numerous in proportion to the rudeness of their inhabitants. The Malay peninsula alone is in this respect an anomaly, for, with the exception of the languages of its dwarf negros, it has but one tongue, the Malay, having had seemingly no indigenous brown population, until occupied by men speaking that tongue. Java is the most civilised island of the two Archipelagos, and it has but two languages. Bali and Lomboc have each but one tongue. In Sumbawa, there are six. In Celebes, there are four languages of the more civilised nations, besides those spoken by rude tribes; in Floris six, and in Timur and its adjacent islets at least as many. In Sumatra and its islands, there are not fewer than ten, and in Borneo fifty have been counted, and this certainly falls far short of the actual number. It is the same in the Philippines. In Luzon, six languages of the civilised nations are spoken, and thirteen of the rude tribes of the Malayan race, besides the languages of the Negritos. In Panay, besides the Bisaya, four languages of tribes of the Malayan race are spoken, and, at least, one of the Negritos. The languages of Mindano, although we have no specification of them, are stated to be even more numerous than those of Luzon.

All the languages, both of the Malay and Philippine Archipelagos, are of simple grammatical structure, that is, they are tongues in which prepositions and auxiliaries take the place of inflexions, and there is no evidence to show that their simplicity of form has arisen from the breaking down of ancient languages of complex structure, for no vestige of such complex language is discoverable. The only remains of an ancient and obsolete language that exist is that of Java, and this proves on examination to be equally simple as the vernacular tongues. Notwithstanding this general agreement in grammatical character, there is still sufficient difference, both in this respect and in their phonetic character, to admit of our arranging them into classes, of which there are, perhaps, three. The first class will comprise the languages from Sumatra to Borneo, and Lomboc eastward; the second, those from Celebes to the Moluccas inclusive, and the third, those of the Philippine Archipelago. This arrangement, of course, refers only to the languages of the nations and tribes of the Malayan race, for of the Negritos and Papuan negros we know far too little to enable us to attempt a classification. But if we extend our enquiry to the utmost bounds to which words of the Malayan languages extend, we must add two more classes, one for the Polynesian languages, but not including the negro tongues of the Pacific, and one for the language of Madagascar. Between these classes, there are considerable differences in grammatical structure, but the widest difference relates to their phonetic character. In the first class the range of consonants extends to nineteen and the vowels to six, whereas in the second, the consonants are but sixteen and the vowels but five. The phonetic character of the second or Celebesian class of languages distinguishes it remarkably from the first. This character is accompanied by much commutation of consonants and much elision. No word or syllable can end in a consonant, saving the nasal *ng*. The consequence of this peculiarity is that words of the first class of languages, as well as foreign ones, when adopted, become so altered as not to be easily recognised. Thus, mawar, a rose, in Malay, is changed into mawara; ratus, hundred, into ratu; laksa, ten thousand, into lasa; and bintang, a star, into witoëng. The grammatical structure of the languages of the second class is equally simple with that of the first, but the prepositions used in the formation of cases, and the auxiliaries employed in that of the tenses and moods of verbs, are wholly different. The phonetic character and grammatical structure of the third class of languages, the Philippine, differ most materially from those of the two first classes. It has five vowels and sixteen consonants, but among the consonants it has two sounds, which are absent in the first and second class, while it wants no fewer than seven of those of the first class. In the two first classes no two consonants come together without the intervention of a vowel, unless one of them be a liquid or a nasal. No such rule exists in the Philippine languages, and the consequence is that many combinations of sound are found in them, which are never heard from the mouths of those that speak the languages of the two first classes. Another distinction in the pronunciation of the Philippine tongues consists in the frequent occurrence of an aspirate at the beginning of words and syllables, but never at their termination, which is the very reverse of what obtains in the languages of the two first classes. Accent in the languages of the two first classes is a very simple matter. In bi-syllabic and tri-syllabic words it is, with rare exceptions, on the penultimate, and in polysyllables there are two accents, one on the first syllable and one on the penultimate. On the contrary, accent in the Philippine tongues is a very complex matter. Some of the Spanish writers, on Philippine grammar, make them only two, while others run them up to seven, the more usual estimate being four. The accent in these cases, however, includes quantity. Two examples may be given. The word baga, with what is called the long penultimate, signifies "a live coal," and with the short penultimate, "chance." Sala, with the long penultimate, means "sin," and with the short, "desirous" or "anxious." The words now given are, in their first meanings, Malay or Javanese, that is, belong to the first class of languages; and to suit them to the genius of Philippine pronunciation, they have been changed from barak and salah to what we find them, by eliding the final aspirate, in both words, and substituting a *g* for an *r*, the last of these being a letter which does not exist in the Philippine languages. The grammatical structure of the Philippine languages, although essentially simple, differs very materially from that of the two first classes of languages. Relation is expressed, not by prepositions, but by articles, and of these there are two kinds, one for proper names and one for appellatives. A plural, instead of being formed, as in the first and second class of languages, by an adjective following the noun, is formed by prefixing to it a particle appropriated to this particular use. The formation of the personal pronouns in the Philippine languages is very remarkable. They alone have cases expressed by inflexions, and they have no fewer than three plurals. The verb is of considerable complexity. Time is expressed by inseparable particles affixed to the root, and not by auxiliaries, —moods by auxiliaries and in several different manners, according to the conjugations, of which there are three, instead of one, as in the first and second class of languages, and this, too, besides compound ones, which are numerous. There are no means of distinguishing transitive and intransitive verbs, as in the two first classes.

The Polynesian class of languages is broadly distinguished from those now described, both in phonetic character and grammatical structure. The consonants, according to dialects, run from seven to ten only, and when they rise to fifteen it is from an intermixture of the languages of the negro tribes, as in the case of the Tonga and Fiji tongues. Another peculiarity is the paucity of liquids. The Maori and Tonga have only two; the Tahiti and Sandwich Island but one each, and the Marquesa none at all. The scarcity of liquids is compensated for, not by the variety, for there are but five, but by the frequency of vowels. No two consonants can occur in the same syllable, and every word must terminate in a vowel. The accent differs from that in the previous classes, for it may be on the first, the last, or the penultimate, and a polysyllabic word may have as many as three different accents. The grammatical structure resembles that of the Malayan languages, in being simple, but the simplicity is of a different character. The noun has a definite and an indefinite article. The relations of nouns are expressed by prepositions, a plural by a particle placed before the noun, gender by adjectives, two for man and two for the lower animals. In all these cases, the particles employed differ wholly from those of the previous classes. The formation of the personal pronouns is the most singular part of Polynesian grammar. These have each a singular, and no fewer than four plurals. Each pronoun has three different forms of a genitive case, the other cases being formed as in the noun by prepositions. The verb is also sufficiently distinguished from that of the previous classes.

The Malagasi, or language of Madagascar, is still more distinct than even the Polynesian, from those of the three first cases. Instead of having only from seven to ten consonants, like the Polynesian, or nineteen, like the Malay and Javanese, or sixteen, like the Philippine languages, it has twenty-one. It wants five of the Malay and Javanese system, but has six which do not belong to it. It has only two liquids, and of these, one only, *r*, coalesces with another consonant, or is a semi-vowel, and even this, only with the letters *d* and *t*. With this exception, no consonant can follow another in a word or syllable without the intervention of a vowel, unless one of them be a nasal. Words and syllables frequently begin with an aspirate, but never end with one, a rule the reverse of that which obtains in Malay and Javanese. As to grammatical form, the Malagasi has one article, the definite. Relation is expressed by prepositions, and gender and number by adjectives, the words employed being wholly different from those used in the four first classes. The verb is the most complex part of the grammar. There are no fewer than 450 roots or radical words, from which are formed thirteen conjugations, some of the derivate formations running to the cumbrous length of eight syllables.

Written language is of immemorial antiquity in the Indian Islands, and in every case the characters are phonetic, and not emblematical; for of the latter, no trace has been discovered. There are, in all, no fewer than seven current native alphabets in the two archipelagos, namely, four in Sumatra, one in Java, which extends to Bali, Lomboc, and Palembang in Sumatra, one in Celebes, which extends to all the more cultivated languages of that island, and to those of some islands near it, as Boeton and Sumbawa, and one in Luzon, which is used by some of the more advanced nations of that island, and some of the other Philippines. But besides these current alphabets there are, at least, four obsolete ones, one in the country of the Sundas, in Java, one in Celebes, one in Sumbawa, and one in the Philippines, that of the Bisaya nation, so that, in all, there appear to have been invented among the rude tribes of the Indian Islands, no fewer than eleven different systems of phonetic writing, whereas Western Europe with its energetic races, Italy excepted, invented none at all. All these alphabets have the appearance, to judge by the form of their letters, of having been separate and independent inventions,—not borrowed by one tribe from another, but seemingly invented in the spots where we now find them. Neither have they the appearance of having been borrowed from any foreign source. Notwithstanding the disparity in the form of the characters, all the insular alphabets are framed on the same principle, with, at the same time, a wide difference in the manner in which that principle has been carried out. In all of them the writing is from left to right, as with Europeans, and in all of them the consonants only are considered as substantive letters, with the single exception of the vowel *a*, as an initial, the other vowels being looked on as merely supplemental characters, or, as the Malays call them, the "armour," and the Javanese, "the clothing" of the consonants. Every consonant has in it the inherent vowel, *a*, annexed, or in fact is a syllable, when there is no orthographic mark eliding it. The letters of the Sumatran alphabets consist simply of one or more straight strokes or lines standing vertically, horizontally, or diagonally, and those of the alphabet of Celebes, segments of circles, generally running in a horizontal direction. Those of the Javanese alphabet alone are regularly and symmetrically formed. This and the

Tagala or Philippine alphabet, as the most perfect and the rudest, may be briefly described as examples. As to the Javanese, the vowel *a* is inherent in every consonant, unless there be a mark of elision, or the sign of another vowel which supersedes it, and thus, every consonant is a syllable ending in *a*, and even the initial *a* itself becomes another vowel when accompanied by the mark or sign of one. This produces the necessity of a contrivance to elide the terminal vowel *a*. At the end of a word this is effected by a peculiar orthographic mark, but in the middle of one by supplemental secondary consonants corresponding in number with their primitives. Their presence implies the elision of the inherent vowel. Most of them are written under the primary characters, and differ from them in form. The liquids alone are joined to the primary characters. The nasal *ng*, as in the Hindu alphabets, preceded by a vowel, is expressed by a dot over the primary letter, and the aspirate always following a vowel, and ending a word or syllable, is expressed by an orthographic mark only, as in the case of the vowels. The Javanese alphabet is, beyond all doubt, the most perfect of all the insular alphabets, and has every appearance of an original alphabet, invented where it is now chiefly used. Although Hindu influence was far greater in Java than in any other country of the Archipelago, it has not adopted the aspirated consonants, nor, as some ruder alphabets have done, the metrical arrangement of the Hindu alphabets,—perhaps, indeed, taken nothing from the Hindus, unless the character for eliding the inherent vowel at the end of a word, the sign for the nasal by a dot over the consonant, and the character for the aspirate after a vowel.

The substantive letters of the Tagala or Philippine alphabet amount to sixteen, but three of those are vowels, namely, a character which represents *a*, one which represents either *e* or *i*, and another which expresses indifferently an *o* or an *u*. Instead of five vowel marks, as in the Javanese, there are but two, one being a dot above, and another a dot below the consonant, the first representing either *e* or *i*, and the last either *o* or *u*. There is no character to represent an aspirate. No liquid in this class of languages coalesces with a consonant except *l*, and the alphabet has no sign to indicate when this takes place. The Tagala has been described as a writing as easy to read as it is difficult to comprehend, because you have always to guess, both at sense and pronunciation. Examples have been given of a combination of the same letters which admit of seven, or even eight, different pronunciations and meanings, whereas in the Javanese alphabet, which has characters to represent every sound in the language, —in which every letter is pronounced, and in which the same letter has always the same sound, a word can be pronounced only in one way. From the rudeness of the one alphabet to the perfection attained by the other, there is a very wide interval, but probably not a greater than existed in the social condition of the nations using them when first seen by Europeans.

It will be observed that the invention of written language is confined to three islands, Sumatra, Java, and Luzon, or, at the utmost, to four, if we include the obsolete character attributed to Sumbawa. These are all among the larger islands, and no writing is known to have ever sprung up in any small one, or even in some of considerable extent, as Floris and Timur in the Malay, and Panay, Leyte, and Samar in the Philippine Archipelago. Even some of the largest have produced none, as Borneo, Mindano, and New Guinea. It is a product of civilisation, and civilisation could not easily spring up in the sterile soils and unauspicious circumstances of these last islands.

The languages of the Malay and Philippine archipelagos have received more or less of an admixture of foreign tongues. These are, Sanscrit, Arabic, Telugu, Persian, and Portuguese, but of the two first only to any considerable amount. The proportion in which they exist is greatest in the most cultivated languages, while there is hardly a vestige of them in the ruder. It is also greatest in the countries nearest to the sources from which they have been derived, Hindustan, Arabia and Persia, that is, in the western parts of the Indian Islands, while they are gradually diminishing as we recede from them in an easterly, northerly, and southernly direction. Thus the amount is large in Malay and Javanese, trifling in the languages of the Philippines, and no words of them are found at all in the languages of the islands of the Pacific.

A singular fact respecting the dissemination of one or more of the Malayan languages themselves is well attested. Satisfactory traces of them have been discovered in most of the languages of all the islands from Easter Island, in the Pacific, to Madagascar, close to the continent of Africa, and from Formosa, in the northern, to New Zealand in the southern hemisphere. This wide field includes the languages of men of the Malay and Polynesian races, with brown complexions and lank hair, and of Negrito, Papuan, Polynesian, and African negros with dark complexions, frizzled hair and snouty faces. The generally adopted explanation of this wide dissemination of language amounts to this, that the many existing tongues were originally one language, through time and distance split into many dialects, and that all the people speaking these supposed dialects are essentially of one and the same race of man. But as this hypothesis could not well be maintained in the face of a negro population, the negros and their languages have been specially excepted on the erroneous supposition that no words of the common tongue exist in their languages. Some of the objections to this theory, exclusive of the palpable and now well-ascertained one of the existence of Malayan words in all the negro languages, are sufficiently obvious. It supposes, for example, that languages and races are identical, taking it of course for granted that men are born with peculiar languages, as they are with peculiar physical conformations, and that both are alike unchangeable. Many well-known events of authentic history sufficiently refute this notion. It is quite certain that within the Malayan Archipelago respecting which our information is most complete, no languages exist derived from a common stock, and standing to each other, in the relation of sisterhood, as Italian, Spanish, and French do to each other, and from the existence of which such a parent tongue might be inferred, as Latin is to these languages. Another insuperable argument against the theory of one original tongue is found in the nature of many of the words of the imagined derivative dialects. These abound in terms, very widely diffused, indicating an advanced state of society; as, for example, a comprehensive system of numeration, terms connected with agriculture, navigation, the useful arts, and even with letters. The people that possessed a language with such terms must necessarily have been in a tolerably advanced state of civilisation,—such a one, for example, as we find the principal nations of Java and Sumatra to be now. Instead of this, many of the tribes which the theory supposes to be derived from the imaginary nation in question, not only did not maintain the civilisation of the fancied parent, but have fallen into the condition of mere savages —a result at once improbable and contrary to the usual history of society. Others, again, have native terms of their own to express the class of words to which we have alluded, as in the case of the numerals. If the alleged parent nation had ever existed, we ought surely to have been able to trace it to its locality. The name of the language, and the name and habitation of the people who spoke it, ought to have been known and traced, and certainly would have been so had such a people or language ever existed.

The tests applied by the supporters of the theory to prove the existence of a common original language, have consisted in the essential identity of a few words, and in a supposed agreement in grammatical structure. The last of these tests has been chiefly relied on by recent German writers. I cannot, however, attach much importance to them; particularly when applied to languages generally of very simple structure, and therefore presenting few salient points for comparison. Even here, however, there is so broad a difference between the languages of Sumatra, of the Philippines, of Madagascar, and the Polynesian Islands, that no one can reasonably think that they can be brought under the same category. With respect to the test by identity of words, it is certain that the number and the particular description of words are alone entitled to any weight; and that the existence of a small number of words common to the languages in question, is no more a proof of their derivation from a common tongue, than the existence of Teutonic words in the languages of the south of Europe, that they are derived from a German tongue and not from Latin.

It has been imagined by some writers, that when the class of words expressing the first and simplest ideas of mankind, happen in some cases to be the same in two or more languages, such languages may be concluded to be derived from one stock. This certainly does not accord with my experience of the Malayan languages; for I find that easily pronounced words of any class readily find admission into them, the simplicity of their structure affording facility for adoption. Instead of words of simple ideas being excluded, I should, on the whole, owing to the frequent and familiar use of the ideas they express, consider them the most amenable to adoption. Accordingly, such words will be found either to have supplanted native words altogether, or to be used as familiar synonyms along with them. Thus, to give some examples: in Malay, the most familiar words for the head, the shoulder, the face, a limb, a hair or pile, brother, horse, elephant, the sun, the day, to speak, and to talk or converse, are all Sanscrit. From the same language, we have in Javanese: the head, the shoulders, the throat, the hand, the arm, the face, father, brother, son, daughter, woman, horse,—to say nothing of synonyms for the hog, the buffalo, and dog, the sun, the moon, the sea, and a mountain. In the principal Philippine language, although the whole number of Malay words in it does not exceed one-fiftieth part, we find the following Malay or Javanese terms,—head, brain, hand, finger, elbow, hair, child, feather, sea, moon, rain, to speak, to die, to give, to love. In the Maori, or New Zealand,—the words forehead, sky, great, stone, fruit, to drink, to die, are Malay or Javanese, although of these two tongues there are not above a hundred in the whole language. As to the personal pronouns, which have often been referred to as evidence of a common tongue, in so far as concerns the languages under examination, they are certainly the most interchangeable of all classes of words, and cannot, therefore, be received as evidence. Some of them, for example, are found in the Polynesian dialects, where, in a vocabulary of five thousand words, there are not above a hundred that are Malayan. The numerals are clearly out of the category of early invented words; for they imply a very considerable social advancement, and seem to belong to the class most likely to be adopted from strangers by savages of tolerably natural capacity and progressing in civilisation. The Australians are not savages of this description; and, although with opportunities of borrowing the Malayan numerals, they have not done so, and no tribe of them counts beyond "two." On the other hand, all the Polynesian nations, and even the Papuan negros of New Guinea, have adopted them to a greater or less.

The words which appear to me to afford the surest test of the affiliation of languages, are those which are indispensable to their grammatical structure,—which constitute, as it were, their frame-work, and without which they cannot be spoken or written. These are the prepositions which represent the cases of languages of complex structure, and the auxiliaries which represent times and moods. If a sentence can be constructed by words of the same origin in two or more languages, such languages may be considered as sister tongues; to be, in fact, dialects of, or to have sprung from one stock. In applying this test, it is not indispensable that the sentence so constructed should be strictly grammatical; or that the parties speaking sister dialects should be intelligible to each other. The languages of the south of Europe can be written with words common to them all, derived from the Latin, without the assistance of any of the foreign words which they all contain. The common stock, therefore, from which they are derived, is Latin; they are sister tongues, and the manner in which they have been broken down, and made to assume their present forms, is satisfactorily explained by Adam Smith, in his beautiful Essay on Language. English can be written with great ease with words entirely Saxon, and without any French word, although French forms a sixth part of the whole body of its words; but no sentence can be constructed with words exclusively French. The parent stock of our tongue, therefore, is Saxon, and not French or Latin. By the same test, Irish and Gaelic are proved to be virtually the same language; and the Welsh and American to be sister dialects of one tongue. But it will not prove that the Welsh and Irish are sister dialects of one tongue, although they have many words in common. In Italian there are a few well-known passages, in which the construction is equally Latin and Italian, notwithstanding the complexity of the one tongue and the simplicity of the other. In our own tongue, containing a much larger proportion of French than the southern languages do of Germanic words, passages now and then occur in our classic writers wholly Teutonic, such as the following in the well-known dialogue between Queen Katherine and her Secretary, in King Henry the Eighth:

"His overthrow heaped happiness upon him;
For then, and not till then, he felt himself,
And found the blessedness of being little."

Applying this last proof to the Malayan languages, it will be found that a sentence of Malay can be constructed without the assistance of Javanese words, or of Javanese without the help of Malay words. Of course, either of these two languages can be written or spoken without the least difficulty, without a word of Sanscrit or Arabic, which stand to them in the same relation that French does to English, or German to the languages of the south of Europe. The Malay and Javanese then, although a large proportion of their words be in common, are distinct tongues, and not sister dialects. But when we apply the test to languages of the South-Sea Islands spoken by the brown-complexioned, lank-haired race, we find an opposite result. A sentence in the Maori or New Zealand, and the Tahitian, can be written in words common to the two, and without the help of one word of the Malayan, which they contain; just as a sentence of Welsh and Armorican, or of Irish and Gaelic, can be construed without a single word of Latin; although, of this language, all of them contain a much larger proportion than the Polynesian tongues do of Malayan words.

After as careful an examination as I have been able to make of the many languages involved in the present inquiry; and duly considering the physical and geographical character of the wide field over which they are spoken, with the social condition of its diversified inhabitants, I come to the conclusion, that the words which are common to so many tongues, have been chiefly derived from the languages of the two most civilised and adventurous nations of the Malayan Archipelago, the Malay, and Javanese.

This conclusion is certainly in accordance with what we know of the manner in which foreign languages have been intermixed with vernacular ones in other parts of the world. It is the way in which Greek came to be intermixed with the languages of ancient Italy; Latin with those of Southern Europe, the Teutonic language with the latter, Latin with the Celtic tongues, Arabic with the languages of Central Asia and of some parts of Europe, Persian with the languages of Hindustan, and Sanscrit with these as well as with the languages of the countries between Hindustan and China, and those of the Indian Islands. In these cases, the strange languages have found their way by various means,—sometimes by colonisation or settlement, sometimes by conquest and settlement, and sometimes through the agency of religious conversion. In the case of the Malay and Javanese languages, the intermixture seems to have been chiefly effected through settlement originating in commercial intercourse, and not, improbably, sometimes in buccaneering expeditions. Independent of their superior civilisation, the grounds for fixing on the Malay and Javanese nations as the instruments of the wide diffusion of language under consideration, are :—that when we have the earliest authentic information of the Indian Islands through the arrival of the Portuguese, they alone were found conducting the whole carrying trade, their adventures extending from the Peninsula and Sumatra to the Moluccas and Philippines;—that the language of one of them was then everywhere the medium of intercommunication;—that colonies of one or the other were found in various parts of both Archipelagos; and, above all, that their languages may be distinctly traced, not only in all the tongues of those Archipelagos, but also in the language of Madagascar, and in the dialects of the islands of the Pacific. Of the general prevalence of the Malay trade and language throughout both Archipelagos, before the arrival of Europeans, we have the most unquestionable evidence. By means of a Malay interpreter in the fleet, the companions of Magellan were everywhere understood in the Philippines by all parties concerned in trade with strangers, although not by the mass of the people. This same language served them afterwards in Borneo and the Moluccas. De Barros tells us that in Sumatra and the Moluccas it was the only medium of communication between different tribes. Speaking of the last of these, he says: "Two facts give reason to believe that the inhabitants of these islands consist of various and diverse nations. The first is the inconstancy, hatred and suspicion with which they watch each other; and the second, the great variety of their languages; for it is not with them as with the Bisayans, where one language prevails with all. The variety, on the contrary, is so great, that no two places understood each other's tongue. Even the pronunciation differs widely, for some form their words in the throat: others at the point of the tongue; others between the teeth; and others in the palate. If there be any tongue through which they can understand each other, it is the Malay of Malacca, to which the nobles have lately addicted themselves since the Moors have resorted to them for the clove."—Decade III. Book V., c. 5.

The proportion of Malay and Javanese to be found in the languages with which they are intermixed, varies with the facilities or difficulties of communication, between the Malay and Javanese nations and the other tribes. Generally, the proportion is greatest towards the western part of the Archipelagos and diminishes as we recede from them. A few examples may be given. In a thousand words of the Lampung, a language of Sumatra, intermediate between the Malay and Javanese, there are 555 words, of these two languages; in the Sunda of Java there are 530; in the Bali 470; in the Bugis of Celebes 226; in the Kayan of Borneo 114; in the Tagala of the Philippines 23; in the Madagascar 20; and in the Maori or New Zealand 16. Of the two languages, namely the Malay and Javanese, the proportion of words in the different foreign tongues is always largest of the first, except in the languages in the immediate neighbourhood of Java, such as the Lampung, the Sunda, the Madurese and Balinese. This refers, however, only to words exclusively Malay or exclusively Javanese, for the greater portion of the words belong equally to both tongues. The prevalence of Malay words was what might naturally be looked for, since it was found on the arrival of Europeans what it still continues to be, the common medium of intercommunication from Sumatra to the Philippines.

The infused words have undergone some alterations in sense, but still more in form, and the amount of corruption in both respects is generally great in proportion as we recede from Java and Sumatra, the seats of the adopted languages. The following are examples. In Malay and Javanese, kâris is a poniard or dagger; in the languages of the Philippines the word is pronounced kalis, and signifies a sword. In Malay, bungah, is a flower, but in the languages of the Philippines, deprived of its aspirate, it signifies fruit. Bli, in Malay, means, to buy, but in the Philippine tongues it signifies to buy and sell, that is, to traffic. Bânua, in Malay, signifies country or region, but in the languages of Polynesia, land, earth, or soil. Jaran is a horse in Javanese, but in the Bugis of Celebes, it is converted into añarang. Rice in the husk, in Malay, is padi, in Javanese, pari, and in the Madagascar it is vari. Ñur, in Malay, and ñu, in Javanese, is the coco-nut palm: in the Madagascar, it is büañu, the first part of the word bua being the Malayan word for fruit without its aspirate, and the last the proper name of the palm. In Malay and Javanese, sândawa is saltpetre, but in the Bugis the word is converted into sunrawa, while in the Philippine tongues it is sunyava, and made to mean, not saltpetre, but sulphur. The verb to sew or stitch is in Malay and Javanese jait, and in the Madagascar it is sait, to which is annexed a favourite particle, ra. Tânun, in Malay and Javanese, means, to weave. This in the Bugis is pronounced tönungi, and in Madagascar, tenuna, signifying, in this last language, a web of cloth. In Javanese, the numeral three is tâlu, and we have the four following versions of it in as many dialects of the Polynesian, tulu, toru, kulu, and kolu. Of the Javanese numeral seven, pitu, we have in the same dialects also four versions, fitu, witu, kitu, and kiku, and of the numeral eight, wolu, of the same tongue, we have in the same dialects, in like manner, four versions, walu, valu, waru, and vau. In the first class of languages, or those of which the Malay and Javanese are the type, the corruptions of sound are much fewer and less extravagantly divergent, while of the sense there are hardly any at all.

LANSIUM. Botanists have given this name to a genus of plants of the natural order of Meliaceæ, which consist of moderately sized trees, bearing fruits peculiar to the islands of the Malay Archipelago, and, according to the taste of Europeans, ranking next to the Mangostin. The fruit springs in racemes from the naked trunk and branches, and is about the size of a pigeon's-egg, having a tough white skin of a bitter taste. The edible part is the pulpy semi-transparent envelope of the seed. There appear to be two permanent cultivated varieties, if they be not, indeed, distinct species of this genus, the duku and the langseh, called also langsat by the Malays and Javanese: the first, which is that most esteemed, is of a globular shape, and the last of an oblong one.

LANUN. This is the name given by the Malays to the boldest, stoutest, and most dangerous of all the piratical nations of the Archipelago. They are the same people called by the Spaniards of the Philippines Illano, but whether either of these be the proper name of the nation is not ascertained. From all accounts, the native country of this people is at the head of the great bay, which deeply indents the southern side of the great island of Mindano, the second in size of the Philippine group. From this locality, these rovers issue in fleets of stout, well-armed praus, and scour the whole extent of the Malay and Philippine Archipelago, their cruises often extending to a whole year. On the northern coast of Borneo, they have formed settlements, as well as on some of the smaller islands north of it. At one time, they had done so as far west as Banca, and even on some of the islands at the eastern end of the Straits of Malacca, which, in all probability, would have been permanent, but for the presence of the European nations. The Philippine islands north of Mindano, are even more infested by them than those of the Malayan Archipelago, and here their piracies are coeval with the first settlement of the Spaniards.

The predatory habits of the Lanuns, beyond the Philippines, seem to be of comparatively modern origin, for certainly their piracies are not mentioned by early European writers. On the contrary, the faithful Dampier, who sojourned six months in Mindano, and close to the present locality of this people, describes them as an inland nation, without any allusion to their predatory habits. "The Mindanao people more particularly so called," says he, "are the greatest nation in the island, and trading by sea with other nations, they are, therefore, the more civil. I shall say but little of the rest, being less known to me, but so much as has come to my knowledge, take as follows. There are, besides, the Hilanoones (Lanuns), as they call them, or the mountaineers, the Sologues, and the Alfoores. The Hilanoones live in the heart of the country. They have little or no commerce by sea, yet they have proes that row with twelve or fourteen oars a piece. They enjoy the benefit of the gold mines, and with their gold buy foreign commodities of the Mindanao people. They have, also, plenty of bees-wax, which they exchange for other commodities. The Sologues inhabit the north-western end of the island. They are the least nation of all. They trade to Manila in proes, and to some of the neighbouring islands, but have no commerce with the Mindanao people." It is probable from this account that Dampier had a personal knowledge only of the Mindanayans and Lanuns, the habits of both of which have certainly greatly changed since he saw them in 1686, for the first hold, at present, little commercial intercourse with the other islands in their neighbourhood, and the last, from being an inland people, have become notorious rovers. The nation which he calls Sologues, and which he supposes to be a people of Mindano are, no doubt, the inhabitants of the neighbouring Suluk islands.

LAUT. This is the most general name among the nations of the Archipelago for the sea or ocean,—the most common, even with the Javanese, who have besides three synonyms for it. It is found in composition in the names of places, as Pulo-laut, "sea island," Tanak-laut, "sea-land or sea-board-land," and Laut-kidul, "the south sea," the name which the Javanese give to the sea south of their own island.

LAUT-PULO. The words, contrary to the usual rule of Malay syntax are, in this instance, reversed, on what grounds I do not know. This name is given to a considerable island, about 55 miles in length, and from 10 to 15 in breadth, lying off the south-eastern angle of Borneo, and separated from it by a narrow channel, navigable only for boats. The land on the eastern side of this island, or that which faces Celebes, is of moderate height, but the western side consists of high mountains. The most northern extremity of the island is ascertained to be in north latitude 3° 23′, and east longitude 116° 41′. Laut-pulo is, for the most part, covered with forest, very scantily inhabited by Malays, and belongs to the state of Banjarmasin.

LAWANG, or KULIT-LAWANG, the clove-bark of commerce. This is the bark of a species of cinnamon, the Cinnamomum sinto of botanists, and takes its commercial name from having a clove flavour. It is a produce of Borneo, and an object of export to China.

LAWU. The name of a mountain in the interior of Java, and in the province of Madiyun, 10,750 feet high, and with an active volcano. On one spur of it, and at an elevation of 3525 feet, are the Hindu ruins of Suku, the remains of a rude architecture, and on another at the height of 4220 feet, those of Chato of the same age and character. The first bears an inscription with the year of Salivana 1361, and the last of 1354, corresponding respectively with the years of Christ 1439 and 1434.

LEAD, in Malay, Tima-itam, that is, "black tin," is known to the natives of the Archipelago, only as an article introduced from abroad. No ore of this metal has, as yet, been found in any part of the Archipelago, although, most probably, such will eventually be discovered, as was the case with antimony, which was unknown until the year 1823. Some ancient coins of it have been found in Java, the metal having probably been imported from China, a country from which are also brought the red and white oxides of this metal for painting.

LEDANG. This is the Malay name of the highest mountain of the Malay Peninsula, one of the two which the Portuguese thought proper to call Ophir, the other of far greater elevation being in Sumatra. Ledang lies inland from the town of Malacca at the distance of about 40 miles. It is chiefly of granitic formation, boulders of granite being found on its very summit. In recent times it has been repeatedly ascended to the top by European travellers, and its height has been ascertained to be 4320 feet above the level of the sea. Fahrenheit's thermometer at night falls at the summit to 64°.

LEGASPI. Don Miguel de Legaspi, the conqueror of the Philippines, and their first Spanish governor. The command of an expedition for the conquest of the Philippines, after two such enterprises had proved unsuccessful, was entrusted to Legaspi, and fitted out in New Spain. It consisted of five vessels only, most of them of small size carrying, soldiers and sailors inclusive, no more than 400 men. Such was the expedition which achieved the conquest of countries far more extensive than the kingdom of Spain itself. In it was Padre Urdaneta, a Dominican monk, who had visited the Philippines in the last of the previous expeditions, accompanied by other ecclesiastics of the same order, parties who turned out the most effective agents of the conquest. Legaspi sailed from the port of Natividad, in Mexico, on the 21st of November, 1564, and crossing the Pacific, reached the body of the Philippines on the 13th of February, 1565. Then began the conquest, four and forty years after the discovery by Magellan, and five and twenty after the conquest of Mexico by Cortez, an event which greatly facilitated the subjugation of the Philippines. Legaspi was a man of talent, firmness, and prudence, equal to the great enterprise entrusted to him. He possessed, moreover, all the zeal and enterprise which distinguished the discoverers and conquerors of new regions in the sixteenth and seventeenth centuries. Like several of them he had sold his patrimony in order to supply funds for fitting out the expedition. After an administration of seven short years he died in Luzon on the 20th of August, 1572, having virtually achieved the conquest of the large islands Çebu, Panay, Leyte, Mindoro, and Luzon, and also discovered all of them, except the first. "To his disinterestedness, prudence, constancy, and loyalty," say the Spanish writers of the Geographical Dictionary, "Spain is indebted for the rich jewel of the Philippines." The conquest of these islands was effected with more facility and less bloodshed than that of any part of America, and no doubt this is in some measure ascribable to the merits of the conqueror. Still it must not be forgotten that there were peculiar circumstances which greatly contributed to his success. The Philippines contained no one considerable nation, united by language and institutions. They possessed no religion with a powerful priesthood to resist the new faith that was offered to them, and that this was a material element in the success of the conquerors is made evident from the total want of success of the same people in those parts, even of the Philippines themselves, where such a religion existed, as in the examples of Mindanao and the Suluk group, to say nothing of the neighbouring island of Borneo. The Philippine islanders, too, it may be added, were equally ignorant with the nations of America of the use of fire-arms, although by the possession of the useful metals, and of one of the larger animals for labour, they were, in some respects, superior to them in civilisation, as evinced by their possession of alphabetic writing.

LEPROSY, or ELEPHANTIASIS. In Malay, untal and kudal; in Javanese, kudig, and in both languages from Sanscrit, kusta, is a disease not unfrequent in all parts of the Archipelago. In Java, especially, the only beggars to be seen are the unfortunate persons labouring under this incurable malady.

LEYDEN, JOHN. This remarkable man, who was born of peasant parents, whom I had the pleasure of seeing long after the death of their distinguished son, was born in the parish of Cavens and county of Roxburgh in 1775, and is mentioned in this work on account of his researches into the history and languages of the Malay nations. In 1803, after distinguishing himself at the University of Edinburgh, and enjoying the friendship and intimacy of his great cotemporary Sir Walter Scott, he proceeded to Madras in the Indian Medical Service, and there received the liberal patronage of the Governor-General the Earl of Minto, near whose estate he was born. In 1811 he accompanied this nobleman on the expedition which effected the conquest of Java and of most of its dependent islands, and was eventually destined to proceed on a mission to Japan. Unhappily, however, he had exposed himself in his literary pursuits to the malaria of Batavia, and caught the fever which on the 27th of August carried him off in the 36th year of his age. I had seen and conversed with him the day before his death, labouring under the complaint, but without any appearance of eminent danger. Leyden's oriental erudition, more particularly as relating to Malayan literature, was more multifarious and surprising than accurate, as might reasonably be expected from the number and rapidity of his acquisitions. He published at Calcutta a copious vocabulary of the Malay, Burmese, and Siamese languages, and after his death appeared a small work entitled "Malay Annals;" but the most remarkable of his publications was an essay in the tenth volume of the Asiatic Researches on the languages and literature of the Hindu-Chinese nations (he was the first that made use of this designation) in which he gave a rapid sketch of the chief languages, continental and insular, of all the nations between Hindustan and China. His political views were wild, speculative, and scholastic, as is sufficiently attested by a published letter of his to his friend Sir Stamford Raffles, at the time about to undertake the administration of the Indian Dutch possessions. "We must," says he, "have a general Malay league in which all the rajahs must be united, like the old ban of Burgundy or the later one of Germany, and these must all be represented in a general parliament of the Malay States like the Amphyctyonic Council of the Greeks, and this council should meet in the island of Madura, or some celebrated ancient place, and under the protection of the Governor of Java. In short we must make a great and mighty noise, for we will compel his lordship (the Earl of Minto) to be a greater man than he would wish to be if left alone." Memoirs of Sir Stamford Raffles, page 25.

LEYTE. The name of one of those Philippine Islands called by the Spaniards the Bisayas. It lies west of Samar, east of Bohol and Çebu, and north of Mindano, between north latitude 9° 49′ and 11° 34′, and east longitudes 124° 7′, and 125° 9′. Its extreme length is 102·6, and its greatest breadth 46·8 geographical miles. Its computed area is 3641 geographical square miles, and it has a coast line with many bays, creeks and harbours, of 342 geographical miles. Its surface is generally mountainous, but it contains, notwithstanding, several large and fruitful valleys. The prevailing geological formation is volcanic, and several of the mountains are the extinct craters of volcanos, in which are found sulphur and other products of volcanic action, with, it is stated, quantities of fossil shells of brilliant hues. As, however, gold and iron ore are said to abound in the island, it seems probable that a portion of it is of Plutonic and sedimentary formation. The mountains are covered with forest, among the trees of which is that which yields damar, the "brea" or pitch of the Spaniards, for the production of which Leyte is the most remarkable of the whole Philippines. All the kinds of game and all the larger wild animals of the other large islands—the buffalo excepted—are found in the forests of Leyte. The climate although hot and liable to hurricanes is healthy. The rivers are small and unfit for navigation, but extensively applied to irrigation. There are two considerable lakes, that of Bito, with a circumference of 5½ leagues in latitude 10° 50′, and that of Jaro with one of 4½ in latitude 11° 8′. The chief productions of Leyte are rice, wheat in the higher lands, cotton, abaca, indigo, black pepper, coffee, cacoa, and sugarcane.

Leyte is also the name of one of the 34 provinces of the Philippines, which, besides the island of this name, includes the small ones Panamao, Maripipi, Pantahon, and Biliran, with the Camotes Isles. The whole of the inhabitants of this province are of the Bisaya nation, speak the language which goes under this name, and with the exception of a few tribes of mountaineers of the principal island, are of the Malayan race and have long been converted to Christianity. In recent times the progress of population has been very remarkable. In 1735, although the province then included the large island of Samar, the whole population was no more than 53,239, and in 1798, still including Samar, it had decreased to 52,955. This was in consequence of the frequent incursions of the Mahometan pirates of Mindano, Borneo, aud Suluk, by which the property of the inhabitants was pillaged or destroyed and themselves carried into captivity. In 1798 however Samar was parted from Leyte, and erected into a separate province, and the population which then remained to Leyte was 35,433. In 1818 this number had increased to 40,623, in 1845 to 89,322, and in 1850 to 112,937, making an increase of better than 200 per cent. in 52 years, ascribable to the vigorous measures taken by the Spanish government for the suppression of Moorish piracy, and the scope which a fertile soil and abundant land afforded for a rapid development of population. The province consists of 14 townships, and has 24,916 persons contributing to the poll-tax, which in 1850 amounted to 249,160 reals of plate. The seat of the local administration is Tacloban, a town of 2494 inhabitants, situated at the north-eastern angle of the main island, and on the shore of the very narrow strait which divides it from the island of Samar. The best harbour of Leyte goes under its own name, and is at its northern extremity, between it and the island of Panamao.

LIGNUM ALOES, OR EAGLE-WOOD. See AGILA.

LIGOR, is the Malay name of a Siamese province, called by the Siamese Lâkon. It is the portion of the Siamese territory which lies nearest the country of the Malays on the western side of the Peninsula, bordering there on the principality of Queda. Geographically, indeed, it forms a portion of the peninsula, as does Sungora, another Siamese province, on its eastern side. The population is scanty and poor, the majority consisting of Siamese, with a considerable number of Malays, and a mixed race of these two called in Malay Samsam, with a few Chinese.

LIMASAGUA, the name of an islet lying in the Straits of Suriago, or the channel which lies between the islands of Leyte and Mindano. This is the Massana of Pigafetta, and the first place in the Philippines, at which Magellan touched and where he was hospitably received. Although cultivated and peopled at the time of the discovery, it is now an uninhabited desert. From its position, so far south, it is evident that Magellan must have passed through the greater number of the Philippine islands, without seeing them, or being aware of their existence.

LINAO. The name of a considerable lake in the interior of the island of Mindano, which discharges itself by a large river, the Butuan, which falls by two mouths into the bay of this name at the north-western side of the island, and in the Spanish province of Caraga. A Spanish settlement, consisting of about 120 houses, with a church, has been formed on the lake at the issue of the Butuan from it, the object of which was to prevent the descent of the Moorish robbers to the low country by the river, as well as to check the incursions of the wild mountaineers of the neighbourhood, called Manubo, who, however, have of late years begun to embrace Christianity.

LINGAYEN. The name of an extensive bay on the western side of the island of Luzon, between the 16th and 17th degrees of north latitude, and within the provinces Pangasinan and Zambales. It is 34 geographical miles in extent from north to south, and 37 from east to west, with a coast line of 99 miles. Within it are many small islands.

LINGAYEN. The name of the chief town of the province of Pangasinan, in the island of Luzon. It is situated on the southern shore of the gulf of the same name above-mentioned, near one of the mouths of the river Aguo-grande, in north latitude 16° 1′, and east longitude 115° 55′, distant from Manilla 35 leagues. It contains 3459 houses, and in 1845 had a population of 20,972 souls, of whom 2856 paid tribute which amounted to 28,560 reals of plate. Lingayen is one of the largest towns in the Philippines, and is a place of considerable trade.

LINGIN,—in Malay, correctly, LINGGA. The name of one of the largest of the multitude of islands by which the eastern end of the Straits of Malacca is crowded. It extends from the equator to 20 miles south of it, and is estimated to have an area of 286 square geographical miles. Its highest mountain rises to the height of 3755 feet, and is consequently the most elevated land of any of the islands within the Straits of Malacca. Nearly the whole island is covered, like the others in its neighbourhood, by an ever-verdant forest, the inhabitants consisting, on the coast, of a few Malay fishermen and in the interior, of some wandering tribes of savages of the same nation. Lingin forms a part of the territories of the kings of Johore, and is consequently under Dutch protection.

LION, in Malay and Javanese, SINGA, from the Sanscrit, just as our own name is from the Latin. The lion is a mere myth to all the inhabitants of the Archipelago. The word is chiefly found in composition in the names of places and the titles of persons, as in the examples Singapura, "lion city," the name of the British emporium; Singasarï, "lion flower," the name of some ancient Hindu ruins in Java; and Singanagara, "lion of the city," the name of one of the public executioners under the native governments of Java.

LITERATURE. All the nations of the Malay and Philippine archipelagos possessing a written character, have some writings which may be called a literature; but as far as is known to Europeans, the Javanese, the Balinese, the Malay, and the Bugis of Celebes, are the only people that have a considerable number of written compositions. Those of the Javanese are certainly the most remarkable. They exist in two different languages, or perhaps rather dialects,—an ancient and recondite one, and a modern or popular. The first is commonly known under the name of kawi, a Sanscrit word signifying "narrative." The second, its correlative, goes under the name of jawi, a rhyming form of the word Jawa or Javanese, which in contradistinction to the recondite language, may be translated the vulgar tongue.

All Javanese literature is in verse; that in the recondite language being in Sanscrit metres, and that in the vulgar tongue in rhyming measures peculiar to Java. Prose writing is unknown to the Javanese except in epistolary writing, grants of land, and the like. Most Javanese works are narratives, and of the character of romances, the names by which they are known, indeed, which are the native word konda, and the Sanscrit charitra, signifying a tale or story. Their subjects are taken either from the mythology of the Hindus, or from the ancient and almost mythic history of Java. Of the first description are paraphrases of the celebrated Hindu epics, the Mahabarat and Ramayana; the first containing the wars of the descendants of Barat, and the last the adventures of the demigod Rama. These two poems are to the Javanese and Balinese, and even to the Malays and other nations of Sumatra, what the Iliad and Odyssey were to the Greeks and Romans, the chief source of their ancient mythology. Of the tales founded on local story, the main subjects are the adventures of certain princes called Panji. But besides mere romances founded on Hindu or ancient native story, the Javanese possess narratives of their modern history, of somewhat more authenticity. These are known by the two names of sâjarah, and babad; the first signifying annals or chronicles, and the last the cutting down and clearing of a forest. Works on judicial astrology are also frequent subjects of Javanese literature, under the name of pawukon. To these may be added a few ethical works, and songs known by the name uran-uran, and rârâpen, the last seldom, however, committed to writing. Two ancient manuscripts only have been discovered in Java. These are in the ancient character and language, but their dates have not been satisfactorily determined; and the ancient inscriptions on stone and brass must be considered as the earliest specimens extant of the literature of Java, and they will carry us back only to the 12th century of our own time.

The greatest part of Malay literature, like that of Java, consists of romances, known under the Sanscrit name of charitra, or the Arabic one of hikayat. Their subjects are taken from the Hindu epics already mentioned,—from the local legends of Java,—from the Mohammedan legends of Arabia, and from the story of Malay princes hardly less fabulous. Such compositions differ, however, in this respect from those of the Javanese, that the greater number of them are in prose. The Malays are possessed of no ancient manuscripts, nor inscriptions on stone or brass. Their whole literature, all in the Arabic character, is certainly not of greater antiquity than their conversion to the Mahommedan religion: indeed, the earliest recorded specimen of it is the vocabulary of the Italian Pigafetta, collected in the Moluccas in the year 1521, during the first navigation round the world.

The literature of Bali is in the Kawi, or recondite language of Java, and no doubt borrowed from that of the larger island. The Bugis of Celebes have a considerable body of literature, consisting like that of the Javanese and Malays, for the most part, of romances, some of them founded on local legends, while others are paraphrases of Javanese and Malay works. Very little, however, is known of the literature of this people, as no competent European has hitherto made their language his study. The literature of the nations of the Philippine Archipelago, the rudest of all the people of the Indian islands who had invented letters, is said to be confined to a few songs. Examples of these, but without translations, have been given by Spanish grammarians, so that their merits or demerits cannot be tested.

LOKON. The name of a mountain 5250 feet high, and with an active volcano in the northern peninsula of Celebes, and in north latitude 1° 25′.

LOMBATA. The name of a considerable island lying between Floris and Timur, and containing an area of 396 square geographical miles.

LOMBOC. This is the second island due east of Java, and lies between the islands of Bali and Sumbawa, divided from the first by a strait from four to five, and from the last by one from two to three leagues broad, respectively called the Straits of Lomboc and of Alas. To the north, Lomboc is washed by the Sea of Java, and to the south by the Pacific. The name of Lomboc, or as he writes it, Lomboch, is mentioned by Pigafetta, in 1522, or within eleven years of the first appearance of Europeans in the waters of the Malay Archipelago. He had not seen it, and simply enumerates it with other islands, such as Endé or Flores, Bouton, Sumbawa, and Java Minor, or Bali, and evidently from the information of the native pilot who accompanied the companions of Magellan from the Moluccas. From this it may be concluded that it was, at the time, a name for the island known to native traders, although it has been generally believed to have been imposed by European navigators. There are two small villages of this name which in Javanese is literally that of the capsicum, from one or other of which that of the island was probably taken. At present it is not known to the natives or their neighbours in this sense, and the usual name is Sasak, which in the Malay and Javanese languages signifies "a raft," and sometimes a temporary bridge. Another name, which is occasionally used, particularly in connection with the titles of the princes of the island, is Selaparang. The first part of this compounded word, Sela, is a synonym for stone or rock, in Javanese, borrowed from Sanscrit, and parang, in Javanese, is the name for a kind of calcareous rock. If this be the correct etymology, the name may be taken from one of the ranges of the mountains of Lomboc, which is principally composed of recent limestone.

Lomboc lies between south latitudes 8° 10′ and 8° 45′, and east longitudes 115° 42′ and 116° 46′, and has an area of 1,656 geographical square miles. Its prevailing geological formation is volcanic. Two mountain ranges pass through it from east to west, the one wholly volcanic, lying towards the northern, and the other of recent calcareous formation, lying towards the southern side of the island. Between these, and occupying the centre of the island, is an extensive plain, intersected in one place, and to the length of ten miles, by a line of volcanic hills, many in number, and not above 100 feet above the level of the sea. The northern or volcanic range consists of two groups, the western being composed of several mountains, and the eastern of one great one. This last is the Gunung Rinjani, or Mount Rinjani, the same which is called by mariners the Peak of Lomboc. This rises to the height of 12,375 feet above the level of the sea, and is consequently the highest land in the whole Archipelago. The mountains of Lomboc contain no volcanos in activity, but many extinct craters. Nearly the whole island is covered with a bed of ashes which proceeded from the celebrated eruption of Tambora, in the neighbouring island of Sumbawa, in April 1815, distant twenty leagues. This was felt with great severity at the time and long after, the depth of ashes which fell having varied, according to the nature of the locality, from one to two feet in depth. This not only destroyed the growing crops, but for some years prevented the sowing of corn, and the result was famine, disease, and the cutting off of much of the population. The after-effects, however, have proved beneficial, much land before incapable of cultivation having been fertilised and rendered productive by the volcanic ashes.

The rivers of Lomboc are numerous, but small, and generally unfit even for boat navigation. By their application to the purpose of irrigation, they are, however, the main cause of the great productiveness of the island. Lomboc also has numerous mountain lakes, like Bali, and these, by furnishing a perennial supply of water, contribute to the same object. One of these lakes, named the Danu, that is, "the lake," or Sagara-anak, literally "child-sea," is of considerable extent, and computed to be 8813 feet above the level of the sea. These lakes are, no doubt, extinct volcanic craters.

The vegetation of Lomboc resembles that of Java. The teak tree, however, is absent, as in Bali, and, generally, the timber trees, although ornamental, are not of good quality for economical uses. The Fauna differs very much from that of Java. In Java, for example, there are three species of ape, but in Lomboc only one. The tiger, the leopard, and all the other large feline animals found in Java are wanting in Lomboc. The elephant, the rhinoceros, and the tapir, are all wanting, and of this family of animals the wild hog alone is present. The wild ruminants are numerous, as different species of deer, the Sunda ox, and the common buffalo become wild. In the domestic state are found the ox of the same variety as the cattle of Bali, but differing from those of Java, the buffalo, the goat, the hog, the dog, and the horse, the latter much inferior to that of the neighbouring island of Sumbawa. Among birds, the peacock of Java does not exist in Lomboc, but it has one beautiful species of parrot, peculiar to itself, and a cockatoo, a bird not found in any island west of it. The poultry are the common fowl of the game breed,—the people of Lomboc as well as the Balinese being great cock-fighters,—and the duck, an ugly, lean, penguin-like animal, kept in great quantities, chiefly for their eggs, which, as in Java, are, when pickled, a favourite food of the people.

The natives of Lomboc, who call themselves Sasak, are a distinct people from the Javanese and Balinese, speaking a language essentially different from those of these two people, although containing many words in common with them. It is written in the Javanese character, on palm leaves. The entire population has been estimated at about 400,000, in the following proportion of nationalities, namely,—Sasaks, 380,000; Balinese, 20,000; and natives of Celebes, 5,000. To this may be added four or five Europeans, and a very small number of Chinese.

The ordinary arts, as they are practised by the natives of the Archipelago, have acquired a considerable degree of advancement among the Sasaks, especially the art of agriculture, in which irrigation is said to be practised with even more skill than in Java. Their iron is all imported, but manipulated at home into implements of agriculture, and tools, swords, spears, and fire arms, with no inconsiderable skill. Agriculture is, however, the special pursuit of the people of Lomboc. They are, indeed, almost exclusively a rural and a home-keeping people, seldom engaging in external trade, and never in piracy. This traffic is in the hands of the natives of Celebes, who, as already stated, are computed to amount to 5,000, all settled at the places of foreign trade, on the coast. The exports of Lomboc consist of raw agricultural produce, namely, rice, cotton-wool, pulses, horses, with ox and buffalo hides. The rice, the chief export, is reckoned to be not less than 16,000 tons, a large quantity for so small an island, and probably more than is at present exported from the great island of Java, once the granary of the whole Archipelago. Much of this, and of the pulses and hides, are sent to the market of China. The imports consist of salt, which the island itself, from the form of its coasts, does not produce,—of iron, cutlery, fire-arms, cotton cloths of Europe and the neighbouring islands, with gold and silver, and the small money of China, the last the principal currency of the island, as was the case with the whole Archipelago, except to some degree with Java, before the arrival of Europeans. The chief place of trade is Ampânan, on the western coast, and shore of the strait which divides Lomboc from Bali, although but an open road. Labuhan Tring (probably Labuhan-pring, "bamboo harbour"), on the same coast, is a land-locked harbour, and secure against all winds, but cannot be used, except occasionally as a port of refuge, on account of its insalubrity, a quality which within the tropics belongs to most harbours of the same nature. The town of Ampânan consists of four different quarters, or kampungs, called after their respective inhabitants, the Sasaks, the Balinese, the Bugis, and the Malays. Shipping obtain at it, in abundance and cheapness, wood and water, with refreshments, consisting of oxen, hogs, poultry, rice, farinaceous roots, and excellent fruits. Whalers, and other European and American shipping repair to it for this purpose.

The Sasaks have adopted the Mahommedan religion, but when, or by whom they were converted they cannot tell. Before its adoption they had professed the same kind of Hinduism as the people of Bali now do, and as did the Javanese up to the close of the 15th century. They are, however, very far from being rigid Moslems, as evinced by their decided predilection for strong potations, a license in which they agree with the Hinduised population of Bali.

At the beginning of the present century, Lomboc, which had been divided into four native principalities, was subdued by the princes of Karang-asam, in Bali. In order to effect the conquest, it was only necessary to cross the narrow channel which divides the two islands. Although no longer subject to the state that effected the conquest, the Sasaks are still ruled by a prince of the family of Karang-asam, and the Balinese are the ruling nation of the island, holding the Sasaks in subjection, although near twenty times their own number,—an unique example of a people professing Hinduism conquering and holding in permanent subjection one professing Mahommedanism. The residence of the Balinese king of Lomboc is called Mataram, the name of a metropolitan province of Java, once of considerable reputation. It is situated about three miles inland from the port of Ampânan, and two from the nearest part of the western coast. Most of the Balinese are settled in or near it, and if this be the case, and their numbers are correctly given, its population would not be less than 20,000. M. Zollinger, who visited the place, and from whom I take most of my account of Lomboc, gives the following account of it:—"The present capital of the kingdom is Mataram, three miles distant from Ampânan, and two miles in a straight direction from the coast. From the last-named place we proceed along the coast, and then cross a river, when we find ourselves on a beautiful road more than forty feet broad, planted with an avenue of wild fig trees, which runs all the way to Mataram. This town is surrounded by a bamboo hedge. The four entrances or principal gates are closed during the night with a kind of bamboo barricade, such as the Dutch call Friesland horses. All the streets and paths intersect each other at right angles, and the two main ones cross each other in the very centre of the town, and between the two palaces of the Raja. These so-called palaces are built of brick, and have externally nothing peculiar or impressive. The other houses are in large squares, parted from each other by mud walls. The houses themselves are built of the same material, and agree entirely with those of the island of Bali. They are thatched with grass or palmetto leaf." "To the north of Mataram, at a distance of two miles, we find Gunung-rata (level-mount) at the foot of a range of mountains. This is a fine large park, with a small pleasure house, a deer paddock, beautiful gardens, fruit trees, and woods planted on hills—all the work of men's hands."

LOMPO-BATANG. The name of the highest mountain of Celebes, situated in the province of Boelocomba, in the south-western peninsula of the island, about 40 miles from the town of Macassar, and in south latitude 5° 12′. Its computed height is 8000 feet above the level of the sea, which is by about one-third short of that of the highest mountains of Sumatra, Java, Bali, and Lomboc.

LONTAR. The Malay name of the Palmyra palm, or Borassus flabelliformis. This is a slight corruption of the Javanese one, rontal, compounded of the native word ron a leaf, and tal or tar, the Sanscrit name of this palm. The compounded word is equivalent to the Hindu one, talpat. The name of the tree is evidently derived from the leaf which was the writing material of all the nations of the Archipelago before the introduction of paper, and still continues to be so of some of them.

LOORY, but correctly Nuri in Malay, and Nori in Javanese, is the generic name for "parrot." The sub-family of parrots, to which naturalists have given the name of Lorius, is not found in any island of the Archipelago west of New Guinea, nor at all in the Philippines. The loories of naturalists are, in fact, confined to New Guinea and its adjacent islands.

LOS BANÕS, in Spanish "the baths," is the name of a town in the province of the Laguna in the island of Luzon. It lies near the southern shore of the great lake of Bay, and at the skirt of the mountain Maquiling, in north latitude 14° 9′ 40″. By the natives it goes under the name of Mayit, signifying "hot." Early in the history of the Spanish Philippines, the Franciscan friars brought these hot springs into notice, and they soon came into repute for their sanative qualities. A convent and an hospital were in time built near them. The heat of the water at its issue from the springs, for there are many of them, is 67° of Reaumur, and the chief chemical contents of the water, are muriates of lime, of magnesia, and of soda, with a small quantity of iron, the muriate of lime forming 60 per cent. of the whole matter in solution. The country in the neighbourhood of the springs is naked, mountainous, sterile, and hardly fit for any kind of cultivation, so that the common necessaries of home have to be brought to the town, which in 1845 had a population of 1859 souls. Fishing on the lake is the principal employment of the inhabitants.

LUBANG. This is the name of the largest of a group of small islands lying off the western coast of Luzon, and off the north-western end of the large island of Mindoro, with which and other islands it constitutes the province of Mindoro. Its town, of the same name, contained in 1845 a population of 6040 souls, of which 1139 contributed to the poll-tax, which amounted to 11,395 reals of plate. The inhabitants cultivate rice, cacoa, coffee, and pepper, and find some employment in the collection of the eggs of the turtle, an animal that much frequents their coast. From the large population of this very small island compared to that of the large one of Mindoro, to which it is annexed, and from the immediate neighbourhood to it of the small islet of Ambil, which is an active volcano, it is to be suspected that its soil is volcanic and fertile, and the interior being mountainous, most probably well supplied with water for irrigation. It may be remarked that the names Lubang and Ambil are both Malay, and do not belong to the Philippine languages unless by adoption. The first means a hole, cavity, or excavation, and the last "to take or seize." They may have been imposed by the pirates who have immemorially harassed the coasts of Mindoro.

LUSÉ. The name of the highest mountain of Sumatra, 11,250 feet above the level of the sea, and situated in north latitude 3° 40′ towards the western side of the island and in the territory of Achin.

LUZON. The largest island of the Philippine group, and after Java the most fertile and populous of all the islands of the Asiatic Archipelago. The name is thus generally written by the Spaniards; sometimes, however, as Luçon, which in our maps and charts has been converted into Luconia. Luzon is probably derived from the Malay and Javanese word lâsung, "a mortar," borrowed by the Philippine islanders, and by them pronounced, losong. There is a tradition that when the Spaniards first arrived in the island they asked its name, and the natives fancying they asked that of a rice mortar which was before them at the moment, replied accordingly, and hence the name. There is no ground, however, it is obvious, for this whimsical etymology. The Spaniards did not land on Luzon until 1569, or until 48 years after the discovery of the Archipelago, and as they had heard of its existence, for it is expressly stated they had done so, it is impossible they could have fallen into so ridiculous a mistake. Besides this, the island must have been familiar to them, and must have precluded the necessity of asking its name when they reached it in force, to effect its conquest. The name, indeed, seems to have been known to Europeans from the time of their first arrival among the eastern islands. Thus De Barros in enumerating the nations trading with Malacca before the arrival of the Portuguese, names the Luçoes as one of them, and even Pigafetta, one of the first discoverers, although he had not seen or described the island, tells us in his account of Borneo that the fleet of the king of that place "was commanded by a son of the King of Luzon," a name which could not well refer to any other place. In all probability, therefore, the name of Luzon, or as the Malays would pronounce it, Lâsung, was imposed by this people, and given by them in the first instance not to the whole island but to the country about the great bay of Manilla, with which they traded, and a few of the inhabitants of which they had even converted to Mahommedanism before the arrival of the Spaniards, to whom, moreover, they were as Pigafetta informs us, the early interpreters. It may even be conjectured that the Malayan name was given from the most remarkable feature of the country that presents itself in entering the bay; the peninsula which forms its western barrier, and the most conspicuous promontory of which still goes under the name of Lozon, or "the mortar." That the natives of the island itself, divided as they were into many nations and tribes, speaking different languages, should have had a common name for their country, of which, in all likelihood, even the insularity was unknown to them, is highly improbable.

Luzon lies between north latitudes 12° 10′ and 18° 43′, so that it is in the same climate as a large portion of southern continental India. To the north and west it is bounded by the China Sea, to the east by the north Pacific, while to the south it has all the greater islands of the Philippine group as far as Borneo, the northern limit of the Malayan Archipelago. Its form has been compared to that of a bent arm—"brazo doblado" and its outline is very irregular. Its most striking character is its distinct division into two peninsulas, a northern embracing the main body of the island, and a southern or smaller, the first called by the Spaniards the upper or Luzonia, and the last the lower or Camarines. The whole island measured in a straight line is about 420 miles long, but by its bends as much as 550. Its greatest breadth is about 135 miles, but in other parts, excluding the isthmus, it does not exceed 30. The isthmus called that of Tayabas is about 50 miles in length, and varies in breadth from 10 to 20 miles. The area of Luzon is computed at 52,328 geographical square miles, so that it does not want much of being twice the size of Ireland. A range of mountains runs throughout the whole of it, from north to south, branching out in different directions so as to give the island a decidedly mountainous character. This range goes under the general name of the Montes Caraballos, and according to their localities are called northern, southern, or central. The branching of the mountains, proceeding northward, commences in about the 16° of latitude. One branch beginning here and terminating at the promontory of Engaño, at the northern end of the island, being the most elevated land of the island, goes under the name of Sierra Madre or Gran Cordillera. All the mountains included under the name of the Caraballos are thought to occupy an area of 250 square leagues, or about one-eighteenth part of the surface of the island. In its widest part the range is 15 leagues broad, but diminishes gradually as it runs south. The great mass of it extends to the eastern coast, where it forms generally a bold and almost inaccessible shore, exposed to the whole force of the north-eastern monsoon. The heights of the mountains of Luzon is a subject which has received very little attention. It is tolerably certain, however, that they do not generally exceed one-half the altitude of those of Sumatra, Java, Bali, and Lomboc. One mountain only, and that reckoned the highest in the island, has been actually measured. This is Banajao, called also Mujayjay, in latitude 14° 2′, and longitude 121° 14′, and this is reckoned to be 2233 varas and 34 pulgadas, or about 6214 English feet above the level of the sea. Snow, certainly, never falls on the highest peaks of the mountains of Luzon, notwithstanding their comparative distance from the equator. Between the mountain ranges are innumerable dales, valleys, and plateaus, but the only plains of much extent are those of Cagayan, Abra, and Agno, all in the larger or upper peninsula.

The rivers of Luzon are almost innumerable, most of them disemboguing on the western coast or on the northern end of the island, and having a comparatively short course with a rapid current. Apparently the largest river of the island runs through the province of Cagayan, taking its name from it, but being also known as the Aparri, and the Tajo or Tagus, from the celebrated Iberian stream. This, after a course of 55 leagues disembogues at the northern end of the island. It is navigable to a considerable distance for small craft, and for boats still further, but during the floods of the rainy season the navigation is dangerous from the quantity of floating timber drifted down. Through the same plain of Cagayan there passes another considerable river called the Abulug, which also debouches at the northern end of the island further west than the Tajo. Two rivers of considerable size called by the Spaniards the Chico and Grande of Pampanga, pass through the fruitful province of the last name, and unite before falling into the sea in the Bay of Manilla. The Chico, or little river, is the source of the united stream, and issues from the great lake of Canaren. The united stream is computed to have a course of three and twenty leagues. Another large river is called the Abra, from the province of this name. This has its origin in the Western Caraballos, in latitude 16° 47′, and after receiving many affluents falls into the sea by three branches near the headland of Namagpacan, on the western coast. This river and its branches are navigable for small vessels. The Agno-grande is one of the largest rivers of the island, and has its source in the range of mountains called the Central Caraballos, disemboguing in the gulf of Lingayen.

Luzon, contrary to what is the case with Java and the other large islands of the Malayan Archipelago, abounds in lakes, some of which are of great extent. By far the largest is the Lago de Bay, already described, after which come those of Täal, Canaren, and Cagayan. But besides lakes, there are great periodical collections of water, called in the native languages Pinag, produced by the overflowing of the rivers in the low country during the rainy season, and which in the dry, either disappear or are reduced to moderate sized lakes. The most extensive of these is the pinag of Candava in the province of Bulacan, which, in some parts, is eight leagues broad at the height of the rains, while in the dry season the greater part of it is dry land, yielding rich pastures for numerous herds of cattle. Another of these periodical lakes is that of Mangabol in the province of Pangasinan, and this has a circumference of five leagues.

The coast line of Luzon is much broken by gulfs, bays, creeks, and estuaries. Among the most remarkable bays on the western side are those of Lingayen, of Manilla, of Balayan, of Batangas, of Ragay, and of Sorsogon. On the eastern coast, we have those of Difun, of Lamon, of St. Miguel, of Lagonoy, and of Albay. Some account of these will be found under their respective heads.

The geology of Luzon has not been explored by men of science, but it is certain that a volcanic formation is very prevalent, although, not as in the case of Java and several of the islands immediately east of it, where that formation is almost the exclusive one. This is to be inferred by the existence, in considerable quantities, of such minerals as iron, gold, copper, lead, coal and marble. The southern part of the island, and especially the peninsula of Camarines, would appear, however, to be for the most part volcanic, and here may be counted no fewer than nine different volcanos, which, since the conquest, have been in a state of more or less activity. The most formidable irruptions have proceeded from the mountain of Mayon in the province of Albay, and from that of Täal or Bombon in that of Batangas. The lava which has flowed from these has overwhelmed neighbouring towns, and the earthquakes accompanying the irruptions have proved destructive, even in remote parts of the island as well as in their neighbourhoods. See Bombon and Mayon. In some instances mountains of considerable height have been swallowed up and disappeared, as was the case in 1627 with one of the highest peaks of the Caraballos range in the province of Cagayan, towards the northern end of the island.

The climate of Luzon may be inferred by its geographical position. It is exposed to the full influence of the monsoons that blow north of the equator. The north-east prevails from November to March both inclusive, and corresponds with winter, and the south-west from April to October, corresponding with summer. On the western side of the island the rainy season begins in the middle of June and extends to the middle of September, as in the greater part of continental India. On the eastern side, on the contrary, the rains occur with the north-east monsoon, in consequence of the great chain of the Caraballos, which produces, in this respect, the same results as the chain of the Ghauts in Southern India. The annual fall of rain on the western side of Luzon is very great. At Manilla it has been ascertained to be not less than 84 inches, nor to exceed 114, although the average fall throughout the island is thought to exceed the medium of these numbers. At the same place, the thermometer of Reaumur seldom rises above 29° or falls below 19°, so that the range is 10°. Between the southern and northern ends of the island, there must be a considerable difference of temperature, as the difference of latitude exceeds six degrees. The high lands also give rise to a considerable difference. Thus, in a beautiful mountain valley called Benguet, about 12 leagues from the city of Manilla, Fahrenheit's thermometer falls from 47° to 45°. Two instances only are known of hail having fallen in Luzon, viz., in May 1749 and in February 1803.

It is at the change from one monsoon to the other that typhoons or hurricanes occur, and their violence is nowhere greater than in Luzon and the other more northerly Philippines. In one of these, for example, which was felt at Manilla in 1831, several vessels were carried by the waves far above the beach inland, and a corvette of 600 tons burthen, which lay in the port of Cavité, was actually cast on the ramparts of the fort, while sheets of lead from the house-tops of Manilla were carried by the force of the wind across the river Pasig.

The climate of Luzon is not an unhealthy one, nor is the greatest heat experienced even equal to that of the summers of some temperate regions. Thus, Spaniards who have had experience of both, assure us that the greatest heats of Manilla are short of those of the summers of Madrid. The greatest climatic inconvenience of Luzon arises from the excessive fall of rain. The wet season lasts for five months, and it is alleged to rain at times, without intermission, for 15 days. At this season the lower parts of the country are inundated, forming sheets of water, as far as the eye can reach,—the rivers overflow their banks, forming temporary lakes, and the public roads become impassable, so that communication can be carried on, in some parts, only by boats. The most frequent diseases are dysenteries and cutaneous disorders, from the most simple affections of the skin up to leprosy, or elephantiasis, which is of frequent occurrence.

The vegetation of Luzon is of the luxuriance to be looked for from much heat and moisture, acting on a soil usually of great fertility. The mountain sides and, indeed, generally the greater portion of the country, are covered with a deep forest, many of the trees of which furnish strong and durable timber fit for house and ship-building. Among these the Molavé and Dongon are considered by the Spaniards to be superior even to the Teak, the first being used for all crooked timbers, and the last for planks and spars. Other trees called the mangachapiü, the yeal, the quitaquita, and the Banaba, are thought to be little inferior. Extensive plains, not under cultivation, furnish pastures for numerous herds of horses, oxen, and buffalos, none of which are natives of the country, but which notwithstanding have run wild to an extent unknown in any of the great islands of the Malayan Archipelago, a fact which would seem to attest the superior quality of the grasses of Luzon. The only cereals cultivated are rice, maiz, and in some of the higher lands wheat, all of them exotics, and the two last certainly introduced by the Spaniards. The farinaceous roots cultivated are the yam, known by its Malay name ubi, and the batata, generally known by the native name of Camote, probably an indigenous plant. Several species of pulses are cultivated. The plants cultivated for the production of saccharine matter and spirits are the sugar-cane, the cocoa palm, the buri palm (Corypha gebanga), and the nipa palm (Nipa fruticosa). Oil is yielded by the cocoa-nut, and by the sesame. The nipa yields materials for thatch, for matting, and for distillation. For fibrous materials, the plants cultivated are cotton, the abaca banana, and the piña, or pine apple. Indigo, coffee, and cocoa are the comparatively recent introductions of European industry. The principal esculent fruits are the banana, of which the Spaniards reckon no fewer than fifty-seven varieties,—the mango, the orange, the pine-apple, and the musk melon. The mango is described as of excellent flavour,—in the estimation of a Spanish writer who had visited other parts of India, superior to that of any of them, and, indeed, he adds, superior to all fruits, except the melon of Valentia. Besides these, Spanish writers enumerate a hundred other fruits, most of them, however, either worthless or of small account. Neither the mangostin nor the durian, the choice fruits of the Malayan islands, are found in Luzon, the rather boisterous climate of which is probably unsuited to them.

The most remarkable wild animals of Luzon are several species of monkey and of deer, with horses, oxen and buffaloes, become wild. The tiger and leopard, so frequent in the western islands of the Malay Archipelago, do not exist in Luzon, which, of the feline family, possesses only one, called by the Spaniards gato de montes. Of the weasel family there are two species, the Viverra musanga, known by its Malay name musang; and one civet cat, both probably introduced. Of the family of Pachydermata, the hog is the only native, but of what species that native one is, has not been ascertained. The rhinoceros, the tapir, and the elephant, are all wanting. Spanish writers have come to the conclusion that the elephant must, at one time, have existed, from their discovering a name for it in the native languages. This supposed native name is, however, the Sanscrit one, gajah, evidently borrowed from the Malays and Javanese, with whom it is in universal use, even where the elephant is indigenous. This is like concluding that the lion was once a denizen of England, because we have a name for it taken from the Latin.

The largest of the birds of Luzon is the gigantic crane, so well known to the English in India under the name of the Adjutant, the Ciconia argela of naturalists. It produces also the swallow which furnishes the esculent nest, the common fowl in the wild state, and a great number of species of the pigeon and parrot families, as yet for the most part, undescribed. Among serpents, there are several which are poisonous, and a python equal in size to those of any other part of India. Alligators and tortoises are numerous, and among the latter both the esculent and that which yields the shell of commerce. Of all the countries of the east, Luzon seems to be the most abundant in fish, both of the sea and fresh water. They are especially abundant in the lakes and rivers,—even, indeed, in the flooded fields during the periodical rains. Spanish writers enumerate ten different kinds of esculent fish, as being the most abundant. Of these, the dalag, a fresh-water fish, is in great repute, and much used, both fresh and cured. Some of the fish enter the rivers and lakes from the sea, for the purpose of spawning like salmon, and are then taken in great numbers. In the lake of Taal, a fish of such habits called the sabalo, of the size of the salmon, is taken in weirs, and by other contrivances in which the natives display much ingenuity. In the shallow bays, the tripang or holothurion is taken, and cured for the Chinese market. "The facility with which fish is produced," says the author of the 'Informe sobre el estado de las Islas Filapinas,' "is wonderful. Sometimes a piece of dry land, after being flooded for a few hours, is found full of fish. On the 23rd of September, 1767, there appeared on the plain near Manilla, and for the space of a quarter of a league, such a quantity of dead fish as was sufficient to load twenty large waggons. This fish came, already dead, from the lake of Bay, by the river Pasig, and after the above quantity was carried away, much remained to infect the air or to be carried off by the current, and again thrown on the coast by the waves. This phenomenon is supposed to have been caused by hurricanes, but there may be other causes, for it is to be observed that occasionally great quantities of living fish in a state of terror come down the river from the lake, when they are easily caught."

As to insects, flights of locusts occasionally devastate Luzon, but these are always destroyed by the hurricanes to which it is liable. Mosquitos and ants are numerous and troublesome, but in requital, the common fly, as in other countries not distant from the equator, is not frequent, and fleas and bugs are nearly unknown.

Two distinct races of man inhabit Luzon,—the Malayan and the Negrito. The first of these is socially divided into two classes, namely,—the civilised inhabitants, occupying the coasts, plains, and larger valleys, and forming the bulk of the population; and the rude tribes inhabiting the mountain sides and narrow glens of the interior. The civilised inhabitants consist of six distinct nations, speaking different languages, and are as follow,—the Tagalog, or Tagala as they are called by the Spaniards; the Iloco; the Pampanga; the Pangasinan; the Cagayan, and the Vicol. The uncivilised of the Malayan race consist, according to the Spanish enumeration, of no fewer than fifteen different tribes or nations, speaking, as far as is known, distinct languages. The greater number of these are in the hunter state, a few of the more advanced only practising a rude husbandry, whereas all the civilised inhabitants are agriculturists. The Negritos, like the rudest of the Malayan race, seem to be divided into many tribes, speaking distinct languages, but of their names or their tongues we have no information.

The first enumeration of the inhabitants of Luzon which we possess was made in 1735, or 164 years after the conquest, and this made their number 410,300. It has certainly advanced with vast strides since that time, for a census made in 1800 brought it up to 990,864; one in 1818 to 1,407,422; and one in 1850, to 2,534,613. In the course, therefore, of 215 years, it would appear from these statements, that the population had increased more than six-fold. It is to be observed, however, that these different enumerations, framed chiefly from the registers of the capitation-tax, include only the inhabitants subject to the Spanish rule, and generally those who have embraced Christianity. As the different nations and tribes were subdued, they were included in the enumerations, so that these statements represent, not only the natural increase of population, but also the progress of conquest and conversion. According to the registers kept by the clergy, the number of marriages in 1850, was 20,614 or 1 in 123 of the population; of births 84,328, or 4·09 births to a marriage. The registered deaths were 61,188, and the surplus of the births over these would make the doubling period about 27 years. The increase, however, is certainly not so great as this rate, for in the thirty-two years which had elapsed between 1820 and 1852, it was no more than 80 per cent. It is, notwithstanding, very large, and more resembles the increase in a prosperous Anglo-Saxon colony in the New World than that of an old Asiatic country. Like Java and the British possessions on the continent of India, it owes this rapid increase to the fertility of its soil, to the abundance of it, and to the peace and order secured by European government.

The relative population of Luzon will give between 48 and 49 inhabitants to the square mile, which, as to density, is about one-fifth part of that of Java. If Luzon, therefore, were as populous as that island, instead of containing little more than two millions and a half of inhabitants, it ought to contain, at least fourteen millions. Although, therefore, it is probable that Luzon contains more sterile and unreclaimable land in proportion to extent than Java, or a less relative extent of fertile land, there can be no question but that it has still ample room for a large increase of population, and that the rapid augmentation which has been in progress is likely for a long time to continue.

The population of Luzon is very unequally distributed over its area, as is also the case, although not to the same degree, in Java. Thus the province of Bulacan, lying on the northern shore of the bay of Manilla, and one of the most fertile of the island, has an area of no more than 49 square leagues, and a population of 293,455, or 5927 to the square league. The province of Laguna, although it includes the area of the great lake of Bay, has a population of 137,083, for an area of 108 square leagues, or 1269 to the league. On the other hand, the province of Cagayan, situated towards the boisterous and remote northern extremity of the island, and including a large share of mountain land, has a population of no more than 62,127 inhabitants for an area of 650 square leagues, or only 95 inhabitants to the square league.

The population of Luzon in 1850 is stated to have consisted of the following elements, namely,—Aboriginal inhabitants subject to the poll-tax, 2,373,765; European and Creole Spaniards (it may be presumed, exclusive of the army and navy), 319; Mestizo Spaniards, 5242; Chinese of the pure blood, 9372; Mestizo Chinese, 56,000; and subdued wild tribes, 89,944. Of the unsubdued tribes, of course, no account can be rendered, but it is certain that their aggregate number must be inconsiderable.

The state of industry in Luzon may be briefly described. Agriculture is, of course, the most important of the arts. The wild land is the property of the state, but the reclaimed, occupied by the native inhabitants, is virtually a private, heritable, and vendible property, although, in theory, they have only the use of it,—so long as they shall continue to cultivate it. Convents, and other pious foundations, and European settlers, hold their lands on a somewhat different tenure. They pay to the crown a tithe of the produce, but this tithe is the same as when first levied, so that the amount of the impost is almost nominal, or but a trifling quit-rent. The smaller proprietors cultivate their own lands, but the larger are farmed on a "metairie" system, as in the southern countries of Europe. The husbandry, like that of other Asiatic countries, is rude and unskilful. The plough, drawn by a single buffalo, consists of a single piece of crooked timber, which forms at once, the handle, beam and share. The last is tipped with iron, but there is neither a coulter or a mould-board. Before ploughing, the ground is levelled by a harrow, consisting of a square frame of bamboo with teeth, on which a heavy weight is placed, and which, like the plough, is drawn by a single buffalo. In dry-land culture, the rice seed is sown broad-cast at once, but in irrigated land, it is first sown in beds, and from these transplanted, as in Java. The thrashing is performed by the treading of a buffalo, and the husking in that kind of wooden mortar, the lâsung, in the Tagala losong, which, by accident, has given its name to the island. The most usual carriage is a car without wheels, or a sledge. There are wheel-carts, however, drawn by a pair of buffalos, which will carry about half a ton, or about half the load of a single horse on a tolerable English road. The system of irrigation, notwithstanding the abundant command of water, seems to be very rude, and much inferior to that of Java, Bali, and Lomboc. The husbandry of Luzon has, however, one great advantage over that of most other parts of the East,—the higher reward of labour. A native porter in Manilla earns a quarter of a dollar, or thirteen pence a-day, and the wages of labour are proportionably high in the country. This rate is probably twice as much as in Java, and three times what it is in British India, while all the necessaries of life are, at least, as cheap as in either of these countries.

The land in Luzon, as in the other Philippines, is subject to no direct public impost. All such imposts are embraced in the tribute or poll-tax, which for state and municipal purposes amounts to about half-a-crown, payable by all males from 20 to 60 years of age, and by all females from marriage or 25 years of age up to 60; the whole contribution of a family in this manner being, generally, no more than five shillings a-year. Land, as in other warm countries, is divided into irrigated and non-irrigated, with the usual wide difference in value in favour of the first of these. The effect of a fixed tenure of land and of freedom from land-tax on the value of land is very striking, and favourably contrasts with the results which arise in Java and continental India from the greater part of rent being taken as tax, and this too frequently in the form of a variable impost. The author of the Estado de las Islas Filipinas, gives us the usual prices at which land is sold in different parts of the island of Luzon, his quotations referring to lands of the highest value, that is, to such as are irrigated and fenced, and which are situated in the most fertile and populous provinces of the island. In Pangasinan, the price of a quiñon of land, a measure of 1000 square fathoms, is from 220 to 250 Spanish dollars; in South Ilocos, 300 dollars; in Laguna, from 250 to 300 dollars. In Pasig, near the city of Manilla, and also in Bulacan, it is occasionally as high as 1000 dollars. These prices range from about 22*l.* to 125*l.* for an English acre, and are, probably, ten times as high as those of Java or continental India, in parts of these where a variable land-tax prevails. The chief obstacle to cultivation in Luzon, as in all countries similarly situated, consists in clearing and grubbing up the forest, and in forming the dikes and trenches in the case of irrigated land. The most valuable wild lands are, consequently, stated to be those without timber trees or underwood, but covered with ferns, and these, from the increase of population, have become scarce. With lands of this description, all that is necessary is to burn the fern in the dry season, and proceed at once to form the dikes and trenches for water-field. From the high price of land in Luzon, I imagine it must be concluded that the amount of fertile land easily available to profitable cultivation must be much smaller than in Java, for even with the advantage of freedom from land-tax, the price would not have been what it is, had the good land been abundant in proportion to the area of the island. Next in value to irrigated land, is the dry-field fit for the growth of sugar-cane, of maiz, cotton, the abaca banana, and tobacco. The sugar-cane, coffee, cocoa, and indigo, are raised to a considerable extent in Luson, but chiefly by small proprietors, as tea is in China, because the high price of labour and the minute subdivision of landed estates is adverse to raising these commodities in a large way. "The whole of the productions of the islands," says Mr. Mackmicking, who had resided several years in Luzon, "are raised by the poor Indian cultivators, each from his own small patch of land, which they till with very simple, though efficient, implements of agriculture."

Besides agriculture, the inhabitants of Luzon have acquired considerable skill in the manufacture of textile fabrics, the raw materials of which are cotton, the fibre of the abaca banana, and that of the pine-apple, with silk chiefly brought from China. That the manufacture of these is comparatively large, is attested by the fact that besides a considerable exportation, between two and three millions of people at home are principally clothed with them. They are carried on to a greater or less extent in every part of the island, but most extensively in the provinces of Ilocas, Camarines, and Tondo, Ilocas alone being reckoned to have no fewer than 20,000 looms. Matting, including hats, is also a considerable branch of industry, both for home consumption and exportation, the principal raw materials being the ratan with fibres the produce of the Buri palm (*Corypha gebanga*). Very fine cordage from the coarsest sorts of the abaca is largely manufactured, and so much esteemed in Europe and America, as to fetch a higher price than that of the best Riga hemp. The art of dyeing is but in a rude condition, the colours produced being neither brilliant nor durable. The knowledge of the art is, indeed, confined to the use of a few native colouring materials, and a few simple mordants; the first consisting chiefly of sapan-wood and indigo, and the last of alum imported from China. In the art of dyeing, the natives of Luzon are far below the Hindus; and of printing, immemorially practised by the latter, they are entirely ignorant. Embroidery, chiefly on the piña cloth, is executed by women with extraordinary skill and patience. "Probably," says Mr. Macmicking, "the piña (pine-apple) cloth manufactured in the Philippines, is the best known of all the native productions, and it is a very notable instance of their advance in the manufacturing arts. There is, perhaps, no more curious, beautiful and delicate specimen of manufactures produced in any country. It varies in price according to texture and quality; ladies' dresses of it costing as low as twenty dollars (88*s.* 4*d.*) for a bastard sort of cloth, and as high as fifteen hundred dollars (325*l.*) for a finely worked dress. The common coarse sort, used by the natives for making shirts, costs them from four to ten dollars a shirt."

Lime is generally obtained from shells fished up from the rivers, or procured by excavation, and not by the burning of any kind of limestone. The art was probably introduced by the Javanese, for I find the native name to be only a corruption of the most usual one in the language of that people, apog for apu. Salt is obtained either by solar evaporation or the boiling of sea-water. The principal place for the manufacture in the first manner is the province of Pangasinan, on the western coast, and as this is a Javanese word signifying "place of brine," it would seem likely that the art of making salt by the process of solar evaporation was taught by the Javanese, the only people of the Malay Archipelago who practise it. The necessity of having recourse to boiling, and especially of making salt from burning vegetables containing that article would seem to imply that either the soil or climate, or both, are generally ill-suited to the manufacture of this necessary of life. It is not taxed, or a subject of monopoly in Luzon, or any other of the Philippine islands, its cost having probably saved its consumers from this calamity.

The manipulation of the metals is in general but imperfectly practised by the inhabitants of Luzon. The iron used is, for the most part, English or Swedish.

Some trinkets of gold, however, in the form of filagree work, and especially in neck-chains, are made of such beauty as to be much sought after by strangers. All the goldsmiths are women, a singularity in the arts which is confined to the Philippine islands. Turning and carpentry are exotic arts of recent introduction, the last entirely in the hands of the Chinese. The houses and public buildings of the natives of Luzon are wholly composed of such frail and perishable materials as wood, canes, palmetto, and grass; and every building in the island of solid materials is of Spanish origin. In a word, the best architecture of Luzon is wholly Spanish, the city of Manilla, indeed, more resembling an European town than any in Asia,—greatly more so than Batavia, Calcutta, Bombay, or even the very modern town of Singapore. Boat-building is an art long and extensively practised by the inhabitants of Luzon, but ship-building is entirely one of European introduction. Large ships have been built in the ports of Luzon, of timber of such durable quality, that they are estimated to last forty years, which is probably equal to the durability of those of teak itself.

The inland commerce of Luzon is considerable, although it has many difficulties to contend with. During the five rainy months of the year, much of the low country is turned into lakes, so that all communication is nearly put an end to; and when the waters draw off, they leave behind them, for a time, such a deposit of mud, as makes it impossible to use the small horses of the country for travelling, and the slow heavy buffalo is had recourse to instead. The roads are, besides, intersected by frequent rivers and brooks, over which there are but few stone bridges; while the wooden ones are frequently carried away by the torrents of the periodical inundation, so that the passage over them has to be effected on cane rafts. In going from either end of the island to Manilla, it is said that no fewer than one hundred of these rafts must be had recourse to. The coasting trade of Luzon is very considerable, enhanced by the difficulty of the transit by land, and by the law which makes Manilla the sole emporium of all foreign trade. Even the coasting voyage is attended with serious difficulties from the hurricanes of the equinoxes, and from the monsoons themselves, which make one voyage only practicable for native craft for half the year. Owing to this last difficulty, it not unfrequently happens that no communication is held between Luzon and the islands lying west of it for whole months. Another obstacle to commerce, even more pernicious than the hostility of the elements, presents itself. The ill-paid governors of provinces are themselves traders, and, of course, use all their influence to exclude competitors. Most of the inland and coasting trade is attracted to Manilla by the central and convenient nature of the port; by its market of a hundred and fifty thousand consumers; as well as from its being the constituted emporium of the foreign trade. Still there is a good deal of traffic between the different provinces. The most fertile furnish corn to the least productive. Pangasinan furnishes salt, oil, and sugar to the neighbouring provinces: the raw cotton of Ilocos is conveyed to all parts of the island; the provinces of Bulacan and Laguna furnish the rest with indigo; and the other provinces receive their piña and abaca cloths from the two Camarines. The trade in timber and canes is very considerable. These are obtained in the mountains during the dry season, and floated to the coast on rafts during the rains, by the nearest river, to which they are dragged by buffalos. The foreign trade of Luzon includes that of the whole Philippine group, and will be adverted to under that head.

The Spaniards divide Luzon into three great sections, which they call the Costa, the Contra-Costa, and the Centro; meaning, respectively, the western side, the eastern, and the centre or interior of the island,—a vague division of little practical value, and having reference chiefly to the times in which the different portions of the island were brought under the Spanish dominion, and to their relative importance. The present civil divisions are into provinces, which, by subdivision of the larger, have been raised from twelve to twenty. Their names, with their populations in 1850, are as follow: Tondo, 280,130; Bulacan, 290,455; Pampanga, 155,697; Nueva Ecija, 32,704; Lambales, 22,394; Batuan, 38,642; Cavité, 117,230; Batangas, 217,594; Laguna, 137,083; Ilocos sur, 189,477; Ilocos norte, 136,868; Abra, 28,971; Pangasinan, 228,418; Cagayan, 62,127; Nueva Viscaya, 22,192; Batanes, 10,433; Camarines sur, 102,527; Camarines norte, 10,382; Albay, 219,740; and Tayabas, 81,098. Some account of all these will be found under their respective heads.

It is hardly necessary to say that Luzon was as unknown to the Europeans of antiquity or of the middle ages as Cuba or St. Domingo. Indeed, it was not actually reached until three quarters of a century after these two islands had been discovered. Legaspi, its conqueror, had been five years in the Philippines before the Spaniards landed in Luzon. The first of them that did so was Juan de Salcedo, the nephew of

Legaspi, who was sent to Manilla in 1569, with a detachment of eighty soldiers, in pursuit of pirates. Legaspi himself did not reach the island and begin its conquest until 1571, fifty years after the discovery of the group by Magellan. Luzon, however, although wholly unknown to Europeans until towards the end of the 16th century, had been long known and frequented by the Malays, the Javanese, the Chinese, and Japanese, for the purpose of trade. The intercourse of the two first must have been of long standing, to judge by the considerable number of words of their languages found in all the cultivated tongues of Luzon, as well as by the character of these words. Thus we find many nautical and commercial terms to be Malayan, such as vessel, sail, ballast, anchor, plummet, with the names of nearly all weights and measures. In Luzon, as in the other Philippine Islands, the Malay language had become the common medium of communication between the natives and strangers, and was spoken by all persons connected with foreign trade. Through the Malayan nations, the Hindu religion first, and then the Mahommedan, had made some slight progress. When the Spaniards first arrived, they found, on the site of the present city of Manilla, a prosperous Mahommedan community (un rico pueblo de Moriscos). This village, for such without doubt it was, had a wooden stockade, on which were mounted twelve pieces of cannon; a place, it may be safely inferred, of no great strength, or not well defended, since the Spaniards easily captured it with eighty men. It was the haunt of the denounced pirates of Juan de Salcedo.

Both the Chinese and Japanese appear to have traded with the inhabitants of Luzon before the arrival of the Spaniards, although there is no direct evidence of their having done so. Soon after that event, both nations invaded the island in the character of corsairs. The Chinese did so in 1574, only three years after the Spaniards had settled in the bay of Manilla. A pirate, of the name of Lim-ma-hon, had ravaged the coast of China, with a fleet of ninety-five war-junks, and having been pursued by an Imperial fleet of a hundred and thirty sail, carrying 40,000 men, he fled towards Luzon, and hearing of the small number of the Spanish garrison of Manilla, he attacked it, and was defeated by a force which, at the time, did not exceed sixty soldiers. The condition of the Chinese Empire, which gave rise to the extensive system of piracy indicated by this numerous fleet, was probably not unlike what it is in our own time, and, indeed, has been, more or less, for the last forty years. It was most likely in that state of anarchy which portended the overthrow of the native dynasty of the Ming, an event which was brought to a crisis forty-five years later by the invasion of the Manchu Tartars. In 1581, ten years after the first Spanish settlement, the Japanese invaded the northern end of the island, occupying the present province of Cagayan, from which they were expelled, not without danger and difficulty.

With all these obstacles, the facility and rapidity with which the essential conquest of Luzon was effected is very remarkable. A few short years were sufficient to bring under the Spanish rule four out of the six advanced nations of Luzon, with little bloodshed. The two principal heroes of these exploits were Juan de Salcedo, the nephew of Legaspi, and Martin Goiti. The first of these, with forty-five soldiers and a few priests, marched from Manilla to near the northern end of the island, and afterwards to near its southern extremity, subduing and converting as he marched. These triumphs, indeed, were at least as much owing to spiritual as temporal arms, the Augustine and Franciscan monks always accompanying and aiding the troops, a politic course which has been invariably persevered in ever since. The priests who in this manner contributed to the easy conquest, not only of Luzon, but of the other Philippine Islands, are said not to have exceeded forty or fifty in number. No such cruelties were perpetrated in Luzon as the Spaniards are charged with having committed in America and its islands. On the contrary, the conduct of their chiefs seems to have been politic, and humane.

It must, however, be observed that the state of society in Luzon was highly favourable to the enterprise of the Spaniards. The more advanced populations, as already stated, were divided into six different nations, with as many different languages. But each of these nations again, did not form an united people. Those even who spoke the same language, were themselves divided into small independent tribes called, in the languages of the country, barangay, and headed by a chief, with a native name varying with the nation to which he belonged, but also frequently called by the Malay name of datu, which may be translated "an elder." Besides being thus broken down by division, even the most advanced of the nations of Luzon were, in civilisation, far below the Malays, and especially the Javanese, of the same time. They possessed a knowledge of malleable iron, but made small use of it,—most probably from its scarcity. The only other metal they were acquainted with was gold, which they sometimes used by weight as a medium of exchange, although their mercantile transactions were usually carried on by barter. The horse and ox possessed by the cotemporary Malays and Javanese, were unknown to them, and their only beast of draught and burden was the heavy and sluggish buffalo, and even this they had received from the Malayan nations. Their knowledge of letters was confined to the possession of a written character, far more rude and imperfect than those of any of the nations of the Malayan Archipelago. Their religion was crude and unsystematic, and their temples, unlike those of Java, were mere hovels of perishable materials. Neither the Hindu nor Mahommedan religions had made any serious impression on them, or conduced in any material degree to their advancement. Of the use of fire-arms, they were nearly as ignorant as the Aztecs or Peruvians, although the Malayan nations, their neighbours, had been in possession of them long before the arrival of Europeans. With all this, the principal inhabitants of Luzon were not a wild race of wandering savages, but, on the contrary, an agricultural people, fixed and attached to the soil. They were a superstitious and credulous, but not a sanguinary people; the only cruel rite alleged to have been practised by them being the occasional sacrifice of a slave. A people in this state of society were prepared for subjugation, and for the reception of the new religion which they so readily adopted. The Spaniards found the inhabitants of Luzon and the other principal nations of the Philippines far below the chief nations of the Malay Archipelago in civilisation, and they have the merit of having made them what they now are, upon the whole, superior to any of them. They are, indeed, the only people of the Indian islands who have made a sensible advance in civilisation in the three centuries and a half which have elapsed since the arrival of Europeans among them. See PHILIPPINES.

M.

MACASSAR, in the language of the country Mangkasara, and in Malay Mangkasar, is properly the name of a people of Celebes, inhabiting the extreme end of its south-western peninsula, one of the two civilised nations of the island, and speaking a peculiar language of its own, with a written character. When Celebes was first visited by the Portuguese, in 1525, the Macassar nation was rising into notice, and soon became the paramount one of the island, having brought the Bugis tribes under its yoke. It was the first to embrace the Mahommedan religion, and even on the first arrival of the Portuguese they found a few converts to this faith, but it was not until 1606, or about eighty years later, that their general conversion was effected, and this was brought about by Malay and Javanese missionaries. The Macassars became, in time, involved with the Dutch, and in 1669 were wholly subdued, since which time the Dutch influence has been paramount over the greater portion of Celebes, although in remote parts it be little more than nominal, and nowhere assuredly profitable.

Popularly, the name of Macassar is confined to the Dutch town and fortress of Rotterdam, lying on the western shore of the peninsula above-named, and in south latitude 5° 7′ 45″, and east longitude 119° 21′ 31″. The town is a small one, of European construction, and the port a mere roadstead, yet, considering the low latitude in which it lies, and consequent freedom from storms, affording, like Singapore, somewhat similarly situated, safe anchorage, in almost any season. When I visited Macassar in 1813, it was, in an European sense, a place of very small importance. It was always, however, a port of considerable native trade, and four hundred praus are now said to belong to it, trading with almost every commercial place from Sumatra to New Guinea, and carrying on the fishery of tripang or holothurion, on the northern coast of Australia, with Chinese capital. In 1847 the Netherland Government made Macassar a free port to all nations, in imitation of the British ports in the Straits of Malacca, and this enlightened measure will, no doubt, be attended with as much success as can be reasonably looked for from a place not lying in the highway of general commerce.

MACTAN, the name of a small island lying adjacent to the eastern coast of Çebu, one of the principal Philippines, and parted from it only by a very narrow strait. It has an area of 26 square geographical miles, and is described as fertile and well peopled. But the place is chiefly of note for having been the scene of the death of the celebrated Magellan, who, on the 26th day of August, 1521, was killed in a foolhardy affray with the natives, who, with pointed bamboos, defeated his fifty Spanish cavaliers clad in armour.

MADAGASCAR. This great island, reckoned to have an area of 195,000 square geographical miles, or to be thrice the size of Britain, three thousand miles distant from the nearest part of the Malayan Archipelago, and not inhabited by a Malay but a negro race of men, is mentioned in this work only on account of the singular fact of a considerable number of Malayan words being found in its language. How came they to be there? In their grammatical structure and phonetic character, the Malagasi and the Malayan languages are as widely different as Latin is from the Teutonic languages, or Sanscrit from the Semitic, while the vast majority of their words entirely disagree. The theory, therefore, of the languages being cognate tongues has no foundation. In another work I have endeavoured to account for the presence of such terms in the following words :—"Monsoons, or periodical winds, blow between them to the south of the equator, namely, the south-east and north-west monsoons,—the first in the Austral winter, from April to October, which is the dry and fair season of the year, and the last in the Austral summer, from October to April, which is the rainy and boisterous season. The south-eastern monsoon, with which we are chiefly concerned in this inquiry, is, in fact, only a continuation of the trade wind that blows in the same direction with it, to the south of the equator. A native vessel, or a fleet of native vessels, sailing from the southern part of Sumatra, or from Java, must, of course, sail with this monsoon in order to have the least chance of reaching Madagascar. Undertaking the voyage, however, such vessel or fleet would have a fair wind all the way, and the sailing distance from the straits of Sunda would be 3300 miles. Making only at the rate of 100 miles a day, a vessel or a fleet of praus would reach the eastern shore of Madagascar in 33 days. But it may be asked how Malays or Javanese, who never quit the waters of their own Archipelago, could come to contemplate such an enterprise? I suppose the adventurers to have been composed of one of those strong fleets of rovers that, in all known times, have ranged the seas of the Archipelago, and which do so, from one extremity of it to another, even at the present day. I suppose them, while either in quest of booty or adventure, to be driven into the south-eastern monsoon or trade wind by a tempest. Unable to regain the shores of the Archipelago, they would, from necessity, and after some struggle, put before the wind, and make for the first land. That land would be Madagascar, for there is no other. In civilisation, the adventurers would be superior to the natives; their numbers would be too few for conquest, but their power, from superior civilisation, might be adequate to secure a compromise. They would settle, amalgamate with the inhabitants, and convey some instruction to them along with a portion of their languages. It is not necessary to limit such an enterprise to the single adventure of one nation, for in the course of ages there may have occurred several accidents of the same description. One, however, might have sufficed, for the roving fleets of the Archipelago, like our own buccaneers, have crews of several nations, among whom several languages would be spoken, but the most general, the Malay and Javanese,—those which we find in the Malagasi."

The proportion of Malayan words found in the Malagasi is but inconsiderable,—about one-fiftieth of the whole language. These, however, are important, such as, the numerals, the names for rice, yarn, cocoa-nut, mango, capsicum, iron, to sew, to weave, sea and land as correlatives, bow and stern, billow, cape or headland, rock, island, skies, storm, month, year, people. Of such words, some belong exclusively to the proper Malay, and some to the Javanese, while some are common to these two languages. "A fleet that had been above a month at sea, going it knew not where, is not likely to have saved any domesticated animals, even supposing it originally to have had such, and consequently we find no domestic animal with a Malayan name in Madagascar. It is not only possible, however, but highly probable, that from its stock of provisions, it would save a few grains of rice, a few cocoa-nuts, and a few capsicums,—perhaps, even, some yams and mango seeds, and all these, as just mentioned, bear in the Malagasi, Malayan names, and these only."—A Dissertation on the Affinities of the Malayan languages, prefixed to a Grammar and Dictionary of Malay.

MÂDANG, or MÂNDANG-KAMOLAN. The name of a mythic kingdom of Java, and the same as Koripan, the locality of which is placed by the Javanese in the modern district of Grobogan, in the country of the proper Javanese nation. There are, however, no remains to show that such a state ever existed. The foundation of this state is ascribed to a colony of Hindus, but as both its names are Javanese and not Sanscrit, this is highly improbable. Some of the factitious chronicles of the Javanese assign for its foundation the year of Salivana 525, corresponding to the year of Christ 603. Such a kingdom, most likely, did exist, but nothing is known of it but its name.

MADIOEN, or, in a more correct orthography, Madiyun, is the name of a province of Java, in the proper country of the Javanese nation. It is composed of one of the seven principal valleys or plains of the island,—that which lies between the mountain of Lawu to the west, 10,750 feet high, an active volcano, and that of Wilis, to the east, 7,957 feet. The area of this province is computed at 1580 square miles, and by a census made in 1850, its population was made 307,029, so that it has 194 inhabitants to the square mile,—all Javanese, except 1059 Chinese, 113 Europeans, or their descendants, and 120 Arabs, and natives of Celebes. The number of oxen and buffalos, in 1843, was 103,500, and of horses, 18,000. Its teak forests are valuable, and so extensive as to amount to 510 square miles, or to cover near one-third of its whole surface. Its natural staples are rice, pulses, cotton, and tobacco, but the Dutch, to whom it was surrendered in 1830, have introduced the forced culture of the sugar-cane, coffee, indigo, and even of cinnamon and tea.

MADRÉ (SIERRA DE), or the Gran Cordillera. This is the name given by the Spaniards to the highest portion of the mountain chain which runs from south to north through the island of Luzon. The Sierra Madré is reckoned to commence in latitude 16°, and to end at Cape Engaño, at the northern end of the island, in latitude 18° 37′, its length being estimated at fifty leagues. It is of great breadth, the whole area occupied by it being reckoned at 250 square leagues, but it seems nowhere to exceed 6000 feet high. In its fastnesses are found many of the wandering tribes, both of the Negro and Malayan race. Its forests abound in fine timber, and contain many wild animals, as the hog, ox, and buffalo.

MADURA. The name of the island which from its proximity, its geological formation, its vegetable products, and the manners and character of its inhabitants, forms almost an integral part of Java. The name is derived from the Hindu legend, which represents it as the kingdom of the hero and demi-god Baladewa. It is but a corruption of the Sanscrit Mathura, a name familiar to the English reader. Towards its western end, but embracing only a small part of its coast line, Madura is separated from Java by a strait of from a mile to two miles broad, having a deep, navigable, but narrow channel. Elsewhere a gulf divides the two islands, ranging from 30 up to 50 miles broad, but not navigable for vessels exceeding 300 tons burthen. The greatest length of the island is about 90 miles, and it is computed to have an area of 1556 geographical miles. Its geological formation resembles that of Java, or is volcanic. A low chain of calcareous mountains runs through it from north to south, but it contains no mountain of considerable elevation, and compared with Java its soil is either sterile, or rendered so by want of facility for irrigation.

The inhabitants of Madura are of the same race as the Javanese, and generally in the same state of civilisation, with a little less refinement, and a little more hardihood. The language of Madura is different from that of Java, and divided into two dialects, at least as different as Spanish and Portuguese. One of these is spoken in the eastern portion of the island, and the other in the western, the last being commonly called the Madura, and the first the Sumanap. An analysis of the language of Madura gave the following results: "A thousand words of it are found to be composed of the following lingual elements—Madurese, 250 words; Javanese, 170; Malay, 145; common to the Malay and Javanese, 360; Sanscrit, 40, and Arabic, 35. From this analysis it will appear that one-fourth part of the Madurese only is original." (Dissertation on the Affinities of the Malayan Languages.) The Madurese have no other literature than that of Java, and when they write their language it is in the Javanese character, and there exists no evidence of their ever having had, like the Sundas, one of their own.

In 1815 the population of Madura was reckoned to be 218,660; in 1845, 295,748; and in 1850 it had risen to 316,370; so that in 36 years the augmentation was about 44 per cent. The density of population gives about 204 to the square mile. Neither increase or density, then, are comparable to what these are in some of the richest provinces of Java. Much of the land is at the same time unreclaimed, and the whole is comparatively poor. But the Madurese have found a convenient outlet for their surplus population in the rich provinces of Java which lie directly opposite to their island. Depopulated as these had been by foreign invasion and civil war, the Madurese for a century back have been migrating to and occupying them. These Javanese provinces contain at present near 900,000 inhabitants, the great majority of whom are

Madurese, still speaking their own language and following their own customs. In this manner it is probable that the Madurese in Java are at least three times as numerous as those of the parent country, and thus the whole Madurese people will, in reality, exceed a million. There have been emigrations within the Archipelago on many occasions, but they have originated in general from the roving habits and love of adventure of the maritime tribes, and this Madurese emigration is the only known one which can be traced to the pressure of the means of subsistence, and it could only have taken place under the peculiarly favourable circumstances which presented themselves, and especially under the auspices of an European government, for under a rude and fickle native one, the migrating population would not have sprung up nor the settlers, in their new country, received protection had it done so.

MAGELLAN (FERDINAND), or, correctly, in his native tongue, Fernando Magalhães, the first circumnavigator of the globe, and the discoverer of the Philippines, was a native of the province of Alemtejo, in Portugal, and born about the year 1470. He served five years in India, and was with Alfonso Alboquerque when he captured Malacca and sent Antonio d'Abreu to discover the Moluccas. He was at this time above 30 years of age, but among the many officers whose names are recorded with approbation by De Barros, his is not mentioned. This author, however, afterwards mentions his death, and has a passage respecting his companions worth transcribing. "When," says he, "Antonio de Brito was preparing to return from Banda to Malacca, Don Garcia Henriques arrived at that place with four vessels, his own and three junks. Don Garcia had come to seek for a cargo of spices, as the commanders from Malacca were wont yearly to do. These came along with a junk from Java, also in search of spices. From this, he received intelligence that a white people like ourselves had lately come into the country, and that they had furnished the junk with a letter of safe conduct in case it should meet at sea with any of their countrymen. Antonio de Brito having seen the letter found it was in Castilian, and given by Castilians in the name of the King of Castile, and that it was as pompous and abundant of words as that nation is wont to be in its writings when treating matters they are fond of expatiating on." Decade 3, book iii., chapter 6. It was at this time that he acquired his knowledge of the Moluccas, although it is not asserted that he visited them. What moved him to offer his services to Charles the Fifth is not known, but most probably disappointment of promotion and distinction in the service of his own country. The project of sailing round the world is said to have been rejected by Don Manuel, on which he proceeded to Spain and presented himself before Charles the Fifth, who was at the time at Valladolid. He was accompanied on his journey by the great cosmographer Ruiz de Tallero, and patronised by Fonseca, bishop of Burgos, minister for the Indies. Pigafetta expressly states that the project of reaching the Moluccas by sailing westward was suggested to Magellan by his relation and intimate friend Francesco Serano. This person employed at the time in the Moluccas, Pigafetta says, was in the habit of corresponding with Magellan when the latter was at Malacca, and he adds that Don Emanuel, King of Portugal, having refused to increase his salary, even by a single "testone," he applied to his sacred majesty Charles the Fifth, and got whatever he asked for. The proffered service being accepted, he was placed in command of a squadron of five small vessels of from 60 to 130 tons, with crews amounting in all to 234 persons, soldiers and mariners included. The squadron left Seville on the 10th of August, 1519, and San Lucar on the 20th of September. It cleared the straits which go under the great navigator's name, and entered the Pacific on the 28th of November 1520. On the 6th of March, 1521, it reached the Ladrone or Marian Islands; on the 18th of the same month sighted Samar, the first seen of the Philippine Islands; reached the little island of Massana, correctly Limasagua, on the coast of the large island of Leyte, on the 28th of March, holding a friendly intercourse with its inhabitants. On the 7th of April Magellan entered the harbour of Çebu, called by Pigafetta Zubu, and on the 27th of the same month he was killed in a wanton and fool-hardy affray with the rude natives of an islet close to the eastern shore of Çebu, called in the narrative Matan, but correctly, Mactan. See MACTAN.

Magellan, as a navigator and discoverer, ranks next to Columbus, but surely, whether as to their achievements or the merits of the men themselves, at a long interval. Magellan was but following up the original notion of Columbus, that of getting to the East Indies by sailing westward. He had also the advantage of all the discoveries of seven-and-twenty years over his predecessor, during which even the Spice Islands, the main object of research, had been reached. He himself had either seen these islands or was not far from them when they were discovered, and

Barbosa, who had described with surprising accuracy all the maritime countries of the East, except Japan, was his relative, his friend, and the companion of his voyage. The object of Columbus' adventure was to get at the rich countries of the East, and especially at China and Japan, of which he had read in his guide, Marco Polo. That of Magellan was confined to getting to the Moluccas by a route that should enable the Spaniards to wrest them from his countrymen, the Portuguese, for even he, like the rest of his cotemporaries, attached the highest importance to the spice trade, one which in our times is of far less importance than the traffic in rags, in oranges, in pullets' eggs, or the dung of certain sea-fowl. Notwithstanding these drawbacks, it must still be admitted that in some respects the adventure of Magellan was a more arduous one than even that of Columbus. The voyage of the latter from Spain to the nearest American land was but of 70 days' duration, and from the Canaries, already long discovered, it was but 36 days. That of Magellan from Spain to the Ladrone Islands lasted 533 days, and was performed in ruder climates, and through a more perilous navigation. The very voyage across the Pacific lasted 116 days, or more than three times as long as that of Columbus, counting the latter from the Canaries. The hardships which Magellan and his companion underwent in this last portion of the voyage are well described by Pigafetta. "On Wednesday, the 28th day of November, 1521, we issued from the strait, ingulfing ourselves in the ocean, in which, without comfort or consolation of any kind, we sailed for three months and twenty days. We eat biscuit which was biscuit no longer, but a wormy powder, for the worms had eaten its substance, what remained being fetid with the urine of rats and mice. The dearth was such that we were compelled to eat the leather with which the yards of the ship were protected from the friction of the ropes. This leather, too, having been long exposed to the sun, rain, and wind, had become so hard that it was necessary to soften it by immersion in the sea for four or five days, after which it was broiled on the embers and eaten. We had to sustain ourselves by eating sawdust, and a rat was in such request that one was sold for half a ducat." Primo Viaggio, page 43. Nineteen of the crew of the admiral's ship died of the scurvy, and twenty-five more were ill with it when they arrived in the Ladrone Islands.

Magellan's Italian companion Pigafetta, who was present in the action in which he had lost his life, calls him, after describing that event, "the mirror, the light, and the true guide" of the expedition. His narrative is addressed to Philip de Villiers Lisle Adam, Grand Master of the Knights of Rhodes, and it is curious to see the writer entreating this person, whose own name is hardly known to posterity, to see that the memory of the great navigator shall not be forgotten: "I see reproduced in him," says Pigafetta, "the virtues of a great captain. Among these was his constancy in the most adverse fortune. In the midst of the ocean, he endured hunger better than any of us. Skilled in the knowledge of nautical charts, he understood the true art of navigation better than any one else: the sure proof of this is, that by his own genius and courage, and without any precedent to guide him, he attempted and nearly accomplished the circumnavigation of the globe."

Magellan was beyond all doubt a great man, and possessed many of the qualities necessary for the direction and government of mankind. Yet his firmness had in it a taint of ferocity, even beyond the measure of his own times, while his courage amounted to rashness, and his religion to intolerance and fanaticism. Of all this, there is abundant evidence in the narrative of his friend and companion. The four other commanders of his squadron were Spaniards, and Pigafetta says, they hated him for no other reason than that they were Spaniards and he a Portuguese. They entered, as is alleged, into a conspiracy to take his life in the Port of St. Julian, on the coast of Patagonia. They were apprehended and three of them put to death. Their execution might have been indispensable to the success of the expedition, but the manner of it in two of the cases could not have been so. The inspector of the squadron was quartered (fu squartato il veador), and the treasurer stabbed to death (trucidato a pugnalate il tesoriere). One of the commanders was pardoned because his appointment was made directly by the emperor, but he being charged in a few days after with conspiring afresh, was, along with a priest his accomplice, turned out of the ship and abandoned to the tender mercies of the savages of Patagonia.

The inhabitants of the first land that Magellan made after crossing the Pacific Ocean committed thefts on board his squadron, as did those of the Society Islands on the ships of Cooke. He burnt their dwellings, and named their country the "Robber Islands" (Islas de los ladrones). On his arrival in Çebu, the only large island with which he held any considerable intercourse, he began the work of a conversion and subjugation which were equally nominal. In eight days' time, (from the arrival of the squadron) all the "inhabitants of this island were baptised, and also some of those of the neighbouring islands. In one of the latter, we set fire to a village," because the inhabitants would obey neither the king (of Çebu) nor himself. "Here," says Pigafetta, "we planted a wooden cross, as the people were Gentiles. Had they been Moors, we should have erected a stone column, in token of their hardness of heart, for the Moors are more difficult of conversion than the Gentiles." Viaggo intorno al Globo, p. 89. In fifteen days after these supposed conversions, and in three after the death of Magellan, the supposed converts entrapped and murdered four-and-twenty of the Spaniards, including their new commander, the experienced Barbosa, and the astrologer or astronomer of the fleet, San Martino of Seville.

The circumstance which led to the death of Magellan affords ample proof of his rashness and fanaticism. In the little island of Mactan, lying close to the eastern shore of Çebu, there were two chiefs, one of whom offered to embrace Christianity and to submit to the Spanish rule, but was prevented by the other. Magellan resolved to bring the recusant to reason by force of arms. His friends attempted to dissuade him from risking his own person in the enterprise, but he persevered and left Çebu on the night of the 26th of April with a force of sixty Spaniards and some native auxiliaries. Waiting for daylight, he landed with forty-nine men, leaving eleven in charge of three boats that had conveyed the party. In order to get on firm land, they had to wade knee-deep for the distance of two good bow-shots. The natives of the island, to the number, as Pigafetta says, of 1500, met the Spaniards and their allies boldly, with bows and arrows, bamboo spears, of which the points were sharpened and hardened in the fire, swords, stones, and even clods of earth. Their resistance was more vigorous than was reckoned on. Magellan commanded a retreat, which became a rout, and he was left with six or eight persons,—surrounded, cut down by a sword-wound in the thigh, and killed, in the fortieth year of his age. Eight Spaniards and four friendly natives lost their lives in this inglorious affray. This is the account given of it by Pigafetta, who was himself present and wounded in the action. The name of Magellan is venerated in the Philippines and especially among the people of Çebu, and it is still the reproach of the inhabitants of Mactan that their forefathers slew him.

MAGNET. The name for the magnet in Malay and Javanese is batu-brani, and it extends to all the languages of the Asiatic Archipelago, including those of the Philippines. The literal meaning of the word is "dare-stone," or "venture-stone;" a term similar to our own of load or leading-stone, although less expressive. See Compass.

MAHABARAT. This is the proper name of the renowned Hindu epic which narrates the wars of the Pandus and Kurus, the descendants of Bharata. The original poem and its name are unknown to the Malays and Javanese; but the latter have, both in the ancient and modern language, an epitome of it under the name of the Bratayuda, which may be rendered "the war of the descendants of Bharata," this last word being corrupted into Brata. The heroes and adventures of the Mahabarat are as familiar to the Javanese as those of the poems of Homer were to the Greeks and Romans. See Bratayuda.

MAHOMETANISM. The Mahometan religion is known to the natives of the Archipelago by its usual Arabic name of Islam, to which they generally prefix the Sanscrit word agama, religion. All who have adopted it are of the same professing orthodox form as the Arabians, by whom, directly or indirectly, they were converted. The history of the conversion of the islanders of the Archipelago may be briefly told. The missionaries who effected the conversion were not, for the most part, genuine Arabs, but the mixed descendants of Arab and Persian traders from the Persian and Arabian gulfs, parties who, by their intimate acquaintance with the manners and languages of the islanders, were far more effectual instruments. In the course of several ages, Arabian and Persian merchants, and Mahomedan merchants from Gujrat and other parts of India, had settled in various parts of the Archipelago. Unaccompanied by their families, they intermarried with the native inhabitants, and from this union sprang the apostles of Islam. The earliest recorded conversion was that of the people of Achin, in Sumatra, the nearest part of the Archipelago to the civilised parts of western Asia. This happened in 1206 of our era. When the Malays of Sumatra were converted is not fixed, but probably about the same time as their neighbours the Achinese. The Malays of Malacca adopted Mahometanism in 1276; the Javanese in 1478; the inhabitants of the Moluccas about eighty years before the arrival of the Portuguese; and the general conversion of those of Celebes did not take place until after their arrival. The progress of conversion, as might be expected, was generally from west to east, and took several centuries to accomplish. In a north-eastern direction, the furthest point to which conversion reached was the island of Mindano and the Suluk group. It had just begun to make some impression in the chief island of the Philippines on the arrival of the Spanish conquerors, but was quickly overpowered by Catholic Christianity. The dates and times quoted for the conversion of the different people refer to that of their rulers and not of the people generally. Many converts had in every case been made long before the periods quoted, and many had still to be made.

De Barros, in his account of Sumatra, gives a very satisfactory account of the manner in which many of the inhabitants of that island were converted, and it is probably applicable to most of the other nations of the Archipelago. "The land," says he, "has two classes of inhabitants,—Moors and Gentiles. The last are natives of the country; the others, in the beginning, were strangers who, in the way of trade, began to people the sea-coast, until multiplying, little more than 150 years ago, they came to make themselves masters of the country and to assume the name of kings." De Barros wrote his 3rd Decade, which contains this statement, in 1563, which would carry the Mahomedan conversion of the people of Sumatra no further back than the beginning of the 15th century.

From Sumatra to Mindano, all the more civilised nations,—all those possessed of the art of writing, have adopted the Mahomedan religion, with the exception of those of Bali. All the ruder populations within the same limits have resisted its introduction. The conversion, it will be seen, was slow and gradual, and bore no resemblance to the rapid conversion by the Arabs of the nations of western and central Asia, and which, within the first century of the Hegira, embraced most of the nations from Persia and Transoxiana to Spain. The conquest of the Archipelago was never attempted by the Arabs. It was an enterprise wholly beyond the strength of a people whose maritime skill never enabled them to subdue effectually even the countries on the lower Indus, so much nearer to them. So slow was the proselytism of the Malayan nations, that a period of no less than 572 years had elapsed from the death of Mahomed to the first national conversion, that of the Achinese. None of the nations of the Archipelago are strict Mahomedans, often mixing up local customs or old superstitions with its precepts and practice. The Malays are the most strict, and the Javanese, probably, the least so. All of them still look up to the Arabs as their spiritual guides, as they once did to the Hindus.

MAIL-ARMOUR. In Malay, baju-rantai, and in Javanese, rasukan-kâre or kâlambe-kâre. The sense of the terms, in both languages, is the same, namely, "chain-coat," or jerkin, and agrees exactly with our own definition of the term, as given by Johnson, "A coat of steel net-work for defence." This coat, and a morion or casque, called katopang, both being native words, are the only kinds of defensive armour which were used by the Malayan nations. They are now rarely seen, and from the high price of iron and the impediments they would throw in the way of the free use of the favourite weapons the spear and the dagger, were probably never in general use.

MAIZ. The Zea maiz of botanists is at present well known and much cultivated in all the islands of the Asiatic Archipelago, taking among several corns the next rank to rice. The Malay name for this plant is jagung, which appears to be a native word, but it is not traceable to any root. The same name is found for it in many of the other languages, and extends to the Javanese, which, however, has a synonym, jali, which signifies also a horn, possibly from the ear or cob bearing some resemblance in form to this object. In several of the languages of the islands further east, the name is different. Thus in the Bugis of Celebes, it is bâröleh, which seems to signify "found" or discovered, and to be a corruption of the Malay word bârulih, which has this meaning. These native names would encourage the belief that maiz was an indigenous plant, but after all, there is no solid foundation for this, and there can be little question of its being a native of America, introduced most probably by the Portuguese. Pigafetta, who gives an enumeration of the cultivated plants of Massana and Çebu in 1621, does not mention maiz as one of them, although he mentions rice, millet, and panick grass. A Spanish pilot of the name of Juan Gaetano, whose narrative is to be found in Ramusio, and who visited Mindano in 1642, one-and-twenty years after its discovery, is still more satisfactory: "In a certain part of that island," says he, "ruled by the Moors, there are some small artillery, and hogs, deer, buffalos and other animals of the chase, with Castilian fowls (common poultry), rice, palms and cocoa-nuts. There is no maiz in that island, but for bread, they use rice, and a bark which they call Sagu, from which also they extract oil, in like manner as they do from palms." Vol. i. p. 376. The hardihood of maiz, the facility with which it is propagated, and the extent of the geographical range in which it thrives, have probably contributed to throw obscurity on the history of its introduction into the different countries in which it has been naturalised. In the first volume of Ramusio, published in 1550, there is a very accurate wood-cut of an ear of maiz, which is thus described: "The wonderful and famous seed called maiz of the Western India on which one half the world is fed. The Portuguese call it Miglio Zaberto, and some of it has already come into Italy, both red and white. Above Polosene de Brigo and Villabona, whole fields of both colours, red and white, are cultivated." From this, it would appear that within little more than half a century after the discovery of America, maiz was already an object of extensive cultivation in some parts of Italy. Maiz grows in unirrigated land, and is cultivated in places that do not admit of being watered. In the Archipelago, however, it is nowhere converted into meal and baked as bread, but boiled and eaten as with us peas and beans.

MAJAPAIT. The name of the last kingdom of the Javanese professing Hinduism, and the subversion of which is considered the era of triumph of the Mahomedan religion in Java. The ruins of the capital of this state are to be seen in the district of Wirasaba (in Sanskrit "hall of heroes") and province of Japan. Maja in Javanese, is the name of a kind of coarse fruit of a sweetish taste, the Ægle marmelos of botanists, and pait signifies bitter, the compound forming an imaginary fruit. In the ceremonial language, the first part of the name is turned into Maos, and hence some persons, converting the last part of the word into the Sanscrit pati, a lord, have come to the conclusion that Maospait is a corruption of Maospati, which, in Hindu legend, is the name of the kingdom of the hero and demigod Arjuna. This is a fair sample of the fancifulness of some etymologies. The state of Majapait is supposed to have been founded about the year 1221 of Salivana, or 1299 of Christ, and was certainly overthrown by the Mahomedans in 1400 of the first-named era, and 1478 of the last, so that its duration was in all, but 179 years. In this time five princes only are said to have reigned, which would give about 36 years to each reign, far too long a duration for any state of society. That all of these were Hindus, however, is attested by their Sanscrit names, as Ardi-wijaya, "mountain of victory," and Mârta-wijaya, "life of victory." It has been asserted that the kings of Majapait ruled over all Java, but for this, it is certain, there is no evidence, but the contrary; for within the same period, Pajajaran certainly existed in the country of the Sundas, and Jangala close to Majapait itself, is proved to have done so by the evidence of an inscription on stone, containing the name of its king and bearing the date of 1242. The ruins of the city of Majapait afford evidence both of power and civilisation. Among these is a cistern 1000 feet long by 600 broad, of which the well-built walls are 12 feet deep. Some of the gates of the Kadaton or royal palace also remain, and although in a ruinous state are beautiful specimens of native architecture, the style and workmanship being equally commendable. All the remains of Majapait are of well-baked large bricks, skilfully put together, and not like most of the ruins in other parts of the island, of hewn trachyte.

MAJINDANO. The largest island of the Philippine group is thus frequently written in our maps, but on what authority is not known. See MINDANO.

MALACCA, in more correct orthography, Mâlaka, the name of the well-known town and territory on the western side of the Malay peninsula, washed by the Straits which bear its name, and which are here but five-and-twenty miles broad. The town is in north latitude 2° 14′, and east longitude 102° 12′. The territory extends along the shore of the Straits for 40 miles, and is considered to have a mean breadth inland of 25, so that its area is 870 geographical or 1000 square statute miles, which makes it about the same size as the East Riding of the county of York. To the north and the south, respectively, it is bounded by the Malay states of Salangor and Jehor, and inland by the very petty ones of Rumbo and Jehol. The geological formation of the territory of Malacca, consists chiefly of granite rocks, overlaid in several places by the red cellular clay iron-stone, called by geologists laterite. Many of the low plains are alluvial, the soil composed of decayed vegetable mould intermixed with sand. The metallic ores are iron, gold and tin. The surface generally is undulating, consisting of low, round ridges and narrow valleys, the only mountain of considerable elevation being the Ledang of the Malays, and the Ophir of the Portuguese, 4320 feet above the level of the sea, or less than one-half the height of the principal mountains of the volcanic islands of Java, Bali and Lomboc, or those of the partially volcanic neighbouring island of Sumatra. The rivers are numerous, but all small, and navigable for boats only to a short distance from their mouths. The largest are the Lingi and the Kasang, the first dividing Malacca from Salangor, and the last from Jehor. The other larger streams are the Batu-paat (Chisel-rock) which is the Rio-formoso of the Portuguese, and Muar which is of some local renown. The river which runs through the town of Malacca itself, is but a mere streamlet.

The climate of Malacca, as to temperature, is such as might be expected in a country not much more than 100 miles from the equator, lying along the seashore,—hot and moist. The thermometer in the shade ranges from 72° to 84° of Fahrenheit, seldom being so low as the first of these, and not often higher than the last. The range of the barometer is only from 29·8 to 30·3 inches. Notwithstanding constant heat, much moisture and many swamps, the town at least, is remarkable for its salubrity, and with the exception of the early period of its occupation by the Portuguese, has always enjoyed this reputation.

Some English writers have dwelt on the eminent fertility of the soil of Malacca, apparently judging it by the luxuriance of its vegetation, a test of useful productiveness of about the same value as a profusion of weeds in a neglected field. Facts contradict such a flattering notion of it. In a practical sense, a country can only be considered fertile when it produces the Cereal grasses, that is, the best human food with comparatively little labour, and this proof is eminently wanting in Malacca. It has no chain of high mountains yielding a perennial supply of water for irrigation, in such a climate an indispensable requisite for the production of cheap corn, and assuredly the main cause of the abundant harvests of Java, Bali, Lomboc, and several of the larger islands of the Philippine group. With Malacca, the result of this absence is, that it has not only never exported corn, but never even furnished enough for the maintenance of its own scanty population, always,—even down to our own times, importing it, first from Java, then from Bali and Siam, and now from Arracan. The Portuguese conquerors had formed a far juster estimate of the capabilities of the soil of Malacca than ourselves. De Barros expressly calls the country a "barren land" (terra esteril), and informs us that, immediately after the conquest, a dreadful famine ensued, in consequence of the junks which brought the usual supplies of food from Java being stopped and seized by the expelled Malays, while the Portuguese themselves were prevented by an adverse monsoon from repairing to that island for a supply. "The monsoon," says he, "was adverse for going to Java in quest of provisions, for Malacca and all the neighbouring countries depend on that island for them."—Decade 3, book vi. chapter 1. The same fact is stated by the historian Castaghneda. "All provisions," says he, "they bring from other parts by sea, for in the land there is nothing else but what I have mentioned." What he had mentioned consisted of the durian and some other fruits. The Dutch historian, Valentyn, who wrote above two centuries after the Portuguese conquest, expresses the same opinion of the soil of Malacca. "The neighbourhood," says he, "is not very productive in provisions, except fish and some fruits, so that everything besides has to be brought from other places. The country, for productiveness, will not bear comparison with Coromandel, Bengal, or Ceylon." It is in vain to plead for the unproductiveness of Malacca, the mal-administration of former national administrations, for Malacca has been, with little interruptions, nearly 60 years under British rule, while Arracan, in less than half the time, under the same government, competing with its immediate neighbour Bengal, has become one of the principal granaries of India.

The zoology of Malacca is that of the peninsula generally, and the larger animals may be briefly enumerated. They consist of nine species of Quadrumans, the tiger, leopard, and several smaller feline animals; several species of Viverra, as the musang or Viverra musanga, and the binturung or Ictides ater. Among Pachydermata, there are the elephant, a one-horned rhinoceros, the Asiatic tapir, or tânuk of the Malays, found here for the first time in 1816, after more than three centuries occupation of the country by Europeans, by my friend the late Col. Farquhar; several species of deer, and two species of wild ox, the Bos sondaicus, and another called by the Malays the sâladang, not yet described.

In 1847, the population of the whole territory of Malacca was reckoned to be within a fraction of 55,000, which, on the estimated area, gives 55 inhabitants to the square statute mile, the majority, however, being comprised within the narrow compass of the town and its vicinity, which consequently leaves the greater portion of the country, either very thinly inhabited or a mere jungle. The population is a very heterogeneous one, consisting of the following ingredients, 2784 Europeans and their descendants; 10,589 Chinese and their descendants; 33,473 Malays; 6875 natives of Hindustan and their descendants, and about 1000 natives of the islands of the Archipelago. The remainder consist of a few Arabs, Siamese, and African negros. In 1828, the population was estimated at no more than 28,000, so that in about twenty years time it must have nearly doubled, if these figures be correct. The land of Malacca, as to populousness, is at present, probably, not very different from what it was when first seen by Europeans in the beginning of the 16th century. De Barros thus describes it :—" Not only is the site of the city of Malacca marshy, but so is the whole region to which it belongs, because from its vicinity to the equinoxial, the climate is hot, and the vegetation so rank, as to make it unhealthy, and consequently ill-peopled. To such an extent does this go, that from the point of Cingapura to Puloçambilam (Pulo-sâmbilan, the Nine isles), being the whole length of the kingdom, and estimated at 90 leagues, there is no place of importance save the city of Malacca. The shores of a few creeks only are inhabited by fishermen, and inland there are a few hamlets; and what is more, some of the miserable inhabitants sleep on the tops of the highest trees they can find, in order to escape from the tigers, which can leap to prey upon them to the height of twenty palms (vinte palmas). These animals are in such numbers that they even enter the city at night; and since our own occupation of it, one night they leapt over a wooden fence, broke a part of it, and carried off three slaves. Besides this, in the recesses of the great forests there exist large and ferocious animals, which cause the land to be ill-peopled and ill-cultivated."—Decade 2, Book vi. Chapter 1.

The husbandry of Malacca consists chiefly in the growth of rice, the coco-palm, for which the coast is well adapted, black pepper, and the indigenous fruits, particularly the mangostin, durian, and shaddock, which are produced in perfection and abundance. A little coffee has been grown, and the culture of cinnamon and the nutmeg have been tried with some success.

In an industrial view, the only mineral products of the Malacca territory are gold and tin. The gold is trifling in amount, not exceeding 1500 ounces; but the tin has of late years become of importance, and along with that of the neighbouring countries forms the staple export of the country. Mines of this metal, as elsewhere alluvial or stream-works, were not opened until 1793, and even after that, were long neglected. In 1847, the quantity produced was about 5000 cwts., and it is yearly increasing. The chief miners are the Chinese, whose numbers are said to amount to between three and four thousand. The whole quantity produced between Malacca and the Malay states in its immediate neighbourhood, is stated not to be less than 1000 tons, and all the Chinese employed in producing it are said to amount to 8000.

The trade of Malacca is, the greater part of it, with the neighbouring British settlements of Penang and Singapore, and especially with the latter. In 1853, the imports were valued at 248,385*l.*, and the exports at 337,058*l.*, the greater part of the last consisting of tin. The port of Malacca is a mere roadstead, but variable winds and calms only being felt, and the monsoons not reaching it, it is equivalent in safety to an ordinary harbour. Small vessels lie within a mile of the shore, and large within two; but there is little convenience in landing on a shallow and muddy shore. It was its advantageous geographical position which made Malacca, for so many ages, and even under a rude Malay government, a considerable commercial emporium; and such it would have continued to be, had its trade not been cut off at both ends by the superior convenience of Penang and Singapore, but especially of the latter. The extent of the commerce, which that position assured to it, is highly spoken of by all the early Portuguese writers, and according to the measure of the 15th and 16th centuries, it was undoubtedly considerable, although it would make but a poor figure in our times.

The revenue of Malacca is derived from the same sources as that of the other British, and generally of the Dutch, possessions in the Archipelago, namely, from excise licenses for the vend of opium, spirits, wine, and the like. The only article in which it differs consists in a seignorage of a tithe on all the tin that is smelted,—an improving revenue, which produced in 1847 the net sum of 2340*l.* As elsewhere, the revenue is realised on the principle of farming, the farmers being always Chinese. As at Penang and Singapore, no custom duties, or any other charge on ship or cargo exists. In 1847, the total net revenue amounted to 19,272*l.*, of which 3427*l.* consisted of a tax on the rent of houses assessed for municipal purposes. This amounts to a tax per capite of better than 8*s.*, which is more than the rate paid in any part of continental India, and chiefly ascribable to the Chinese, who, although the minority in numbers, are the principal contributors. The expenditure is enormous, having amounted in the same year to no less than 51,783*l.*, or 168 per cent. beyond the receipts, a state of things calling loudly for reformation. It must be stated, however, that a very considerable portion of this expenditure is factitious and extrinsic, such as the expenses of convicts from continental India, the salary and establishment of a non-resident governor, and a share of the charge of two war steam-ships engaged in the protection of the general trade of India from piracy. These items which have no business where they are, amount to near 12,000*l.* a-year. Besides this, the blunders of a former governor have fixed, in perpetuity on the reveuue of Malacca, a charge of 1000*l.* a-year. The fee-simple of the lands of Malacca had for the most part been alienated by the Dutch government to private parties, on the condition of exacting no more from the occupants than a tithe of the gross produce. This, of course, reduced the virtual proprietors to the condition of mere lords of their respective manors, receiving quit-rents, while it raised the occupants who were irremoveable to that of copy-holders. Mr. Fullerton, the governor in question, a man of sense and integrity, happened, however, to be an apostle of the once-cherished ryotwarrie fiscal system of Madras, and resolving that as, under that system, no one should stand between the state and the cultivator, he bought up the tithes for more than they were worth, and hence an inheritance to the Malacca treasury of the payment for ever of a thousand a-year. This in itself inconsiderable circumstance, is only adverted to as an example of the mischief which may flow from the adoption of a false system, and an entire misunderstanding of the state of society in the country for which this kind of legislation was adopted.

Under the Portuguese administration, according to the historian Faria y Sousa, the net revenue paid into the Malacca exchequer, was no more than 70,000 crowns, which I suppose would be about 14,000*l.*; but he adds that the perquisites of the Portuguese officers amounted to 150,000, so that the whole revenue would, in this manner, amount to no less than 44,000*l.* In 1779, when the Dutch had no competitors, and no European war to interrupt their trade, the Malacca revenue amounted to 26,600*l.*, which, however, exceeded the expenditure by 5150*l.* In 1807, in our own occupation, and without any local rival, the revenue was only 39,433*l.* In 1831, all custom duties having been abolished, it fell to 10,400*l.* As already stated, it had risen in 1847 to 19,272*l.*, without any increase in the rate of old taxes, or any new taxes, except the seignorage on tin. Thus, there was an improvement in sixteen years time of 85 per cent., obviously arising from increased prosperity, and leaving, therefore, no rational grounds for the lamentations that have been made of imagined decadence. Meanwhile that trade of which it was once the sole emporium has been multiplied by at least tenfold beyond what it ever was when it had a monopoly.

Malacca, with Penang and Singapore, form a small government, with a governor, having under him at each settlement, a lieutenant-governor, under the name of a resident counsellor. It shares also with Singapore, a Queen's court, being that of a Recorder. A very moderate garrison suffices to maintain order in a community, however heterogeneous, peaceable and docile.

The native history of Malacca is as usual full of obscurity. Two Malay manuscripts, known by Arabic and Malay titles which signify "the Crowns of all kings," that is, the reigns of all Malay kings, and their genealogies give the following account of the foundation of the state. About the year 1160 of our time, a certain chief of Palembang in Sumatra, with his followers, established themselves in Singapura. Here he and his successors continued until 1252, when they were expelled by an invasion of the Javanese of the kingdom of Majapait, and next year established themselves at Malacca. The third prince, in succession to the fugitive who founded this last place, ascended the throne in 1276, and was the first who embraced the Mahometan religion. It was the twelfth prince in descent from the founder of Singapura, and the seventh from the founder of Malacca, that was driven from his throne by the Portuguese in 1511. There is too much reason to believe that the greater part of this story is a fabrication of comparatively recent times, and, indeed, there is sufficient internal evidence of its being so. I have never seen the manuscripts in question myself, nor am I aware of any cotemporary that has. They were first made known in the Introduction to a vocabulary printed at Batavia, in 1667, and abstracts of them were furnished by the Dutch historian, Valentyn, in 1726. The manuscripts, however, are as usual anonymous and without dates. The five princes who reigned in Singapore give an average duration for a reign of little more than 18 years, while the eight of Malacca, including among them the founder who had also reigned three years in Singapore, give the improbable average of 32 years, far too long even for peaceable and civilised communities. Yet one of these eight princes is described as having reigned only two years, while another was assassinated seventeen months after he had ascended the throne. To make up for these brief reigns, another prince is described as having reigned 73 years! Another discrepancy consists in giving to the two first kings, Arabic, that is, Mahommedan names while they were still pagans; and it may further be objected to the narrative, that dates are assigned to reigns for 116 years before the conversion to Mahommedanism, that is, for more than a century before the Malays are known to have been possessed of any era. These objections seem to me to be fatal.

There is more consistency and verisimilitude in the account rendered by the early Portuguese writers, who, as they tell us themselves, derived their information from the Malayan cotemporaries of the conquerors, men who were by near three centuries and a-half closer the events than inquirers of our own time. "Concerning the time," says Debarros, "in which Malacca was founded, or respecting its early inhabitants, no writing has come to our knowledge, but there is a common belief among the people themselves, that little more than two hundred and fifty years had elapsed since the place was first peopled." He gives no dates, nor does he furnish the names or the number of the line of kings. This, however, is done in the Commentaries of Alboquerque, which give six kings, all but the first with Arabic names, and in such a corrupt orthography as would have made them utterly unintelligible, had we not possessed a clue to them. Of this orthography, the second name in the list, Xaquem Darxa, for Sekandar Shah, or King Alexander, is a sufficient example. The x of the Portuguese orthography represents our sh, and the last syllable of the first part of the name being added to the second, the whole is wrapt in almost inextricable obscurity.

De Barros' account of the foundation of Malacca is as follows:—"A fugitive from Java, whose name he writes Paramisura, and which is probably the Javanese compound, taken from the Sanscrit, Prama-sora, meaning "valiant hero," arrived in Singapore, then ruled by a chief named Sansinga. This prince received him hospitably, but in requital was assassinated by him, with the aid of his Javanese followers, and of a certain people called Cellates. The assassin seized the government and retained it for five years, when he was expelled by the Siamese, not by the Javanese of Majapait, as he is represented to have been in the Malay manuscripts. On his expulsion he is represented as having fled and sought refuge at Pago, on the river Muar, distant, according to De Barros, forty-five leagues from Singapore, and five from Malacca. Eventually, along with 2000 Javanese followers, he settled at Malacca, on the invitation of some of the Cellates, who had themselves taken refuge on the banks of the river of that place.

Who these Cellates were is certain enough. The word is a Portuguese formation, from the Malay word Sâlat, a strait or frith, and at full length in this language would be orang-sâlat, or men of the narrow seas, in reference to the numerous straits among the many islands between the Peninsula and Sumatra. The Cellates were, in fact, the well-known orang-laut, or "men of the sea," of the present time, famous all over the Archipelago for their piscatory and predatory habits. They are correctly described by De Barros, who calls them "a people who dwell on the sea, and whose occupation it is to rob and to fish (cujo officio he rubar e pascar)." Such of this people as had fled with the Javanese from Singapore, and had formed their encampment about the river of Malacca, found there, not far from it, as they would find at the present day, an inland people, of the same race, and speaking the same language with themselves, with whom they intermixed. "The first settlement," says De Barros, "which they (the Cellates) made was on a hill above the fortress which we now hold, where they found some people of the land, half savages in their manner of living, whose language was the proper Malay, which all these people used, and with which the Cellates also were acquainted. But as in the beginning of intercourse, there was some alienation caused by difference in their modes of life, concord was established through the women, in which the Cellates were deficient, each party, however, still following the mode of life to which they had been accustomed—the Cellates living by the produce of the sea, and the Malays by the fruits of the earth. And as both these people knew that the place where Paramisora dwelt was confined, they invited him to join them. Finally, Paramisora, having seen the place, quitted his residence in Pago, and came and dwelt among the people of the plain of Beitam."—Decade I., Book 6, Chap. 1.

It was the son of Paramisora, according to De Barros, that commenced the building of Malacca. "And," continues he, "as the Cellates were a low and vile people, and the natives of the country half savages, Paramisora and his son, in order to make them faithful allies in their labours, and especially, in order to avail themselves of their services in building the intended city, they ennobled them by intermarriages with distinguished persons of those whom they had brought with them from Java, and thus the native Malays became all of them Mandarijs (mantri, in Sanscrit a counsellor or noble), and these are now the nobles of Malacca, in virtue of the privileges conferred by former kings on them, as being the first inhabitants of the city."

The account given in the Commentaries of Alboquerque is essentially the same. "Paramisura (so spelt in the Commentaries) was so well contented with the country, that, on account of the service which the fishermen (the Cellates) had rendered in bringing him to the place, he made them Fidalgos and mandaris (mantris) of his palace. Water being abundant, and the port good, with many other advantages, in four months' time from his arrival, he built a town of 100 families (vezinhos), where now stands the city of Malacca. The pirates who roved over the sea in their lancharas (lanchang, barges), and came to Malacca for water, on account of the favour and kindness with which they were received by King Paramisura, began to fix their dwelling here, and to bring hither the merchandise which they had plundered. This was the cause of such increase of trade that, in two years' time, a town of 2000 families was built, and commerce began."—Chap. 17, p. 353.

On one point, all parties seem to agree, that not only the founders of Malacca, but even of Singapore, were Javanese and not Malays, for even the Malayan account is substantially to this effect, since it brings the emigrants who established themselves in Singapore from Palembang, which was a Javanese settlement. This view receives some countenance from the etymology of the names of the persons and places concerned, which, for the most part, are either Sanscrit or Javanese, evidence of the first of these languages, it should be observed, being frequent only in countries to which the influence of the Javanese people had extended. According to the Malay manuscript, one of the leaders of the migration from Palembang to Singapore has the name of Dâmang Lebar daun, literally, "Chief of the broad leaf." In this case, the title is Javanese, and not Malay. The principal leader of the migration is called Sri Turi-Buwana. The first and last words of this compound are Sanscrit, and the second the name of a flowering forest tree, equally Malay and Javanese. The title may be translated "Illustrious Turi tree of the world." The second prince who reigned in Singapore is called Paduka Pikaram-wira, or, correctly, Prakrama-wira. Here the first word is equally Malay and Javanese, and may be translated "Highness." The two last are Sanscrit, and signify "valiant hero." The name of the third prince, Sri Ramawikaram, is entirely Sanscrit, the last of these words being, correctly, in that language, vikrama, signifying valiant, and being of frequent use in the composition of names of persons. The name may be rendered "The illustrious Rama the valiant." The name of the fourth prince is, also, entirely Sanscrit. Sri Maha-raja, signifying "The illustrious great king." The name of the Javanese refugee who, according to the statements given to the early Portuguese writers, seized, first the government of Singapore, and afterwards founded Malacca, is written by De Barros, Paramisora, and in the Commentaries of Alboquerque, Paramisura. This is most probably the Apramasya-sura of the Sanscrit, and which the Javanese pronounce Prameya-sura, signifying "incomparable hero." The King of Singapore, assassinated by the Javanese refugee, is called Sangesinga, and this name, omitting the medial *e* in the Portuguese orthography, would mean, literally, "flower of lions," the first part of the word, Sang, an honorary title, frequently prefixed to the names of persons, being Javanese, and the last Sanscrit. My guide in these etymologies, as he has often been on other occasions, is my friend Professor Horace Hayman Wilson, without implicit confidence in whose judgment and learning, I should not have ventured, as I now do, to submit them.

In De Barros and the Commentaries, the name of Malacca is alleged to be connected with the foundation of the state. There can, however, be no doubt but that it is derived from that of the Malaka plant, Phyllanthus emblica, a shrub said to be abundant in the locality. Mr. Marsden, after quoting De Barros, observes that, "an error so palpable (as that Malacca, in Javanese, means an 'exile') throws discredit on the whole narrative." This, however, is not correct. The passage, as he quotes it, runs thus: "They again descended the river, in order to enjoy the advantages of a sea-port, and built a town which, from the fortunes of his father, was named Malaca, signifying an exile." But the passage at full length is as follows: "Xaquen Darxa (Sekandar

Shah) now ruled the people, because his father was very old, and in order to avail himself of the sea through which he hoped to attain eminence, he resolved to make Malaca a city, to which he gave this name in memory of the banishment of his father from his native country. For, in his own language (Javanese) it means an exile (homem desterrado), and hence, also, the people call themselves Malaios."—Decade 1, Book 6, Chap. 1. In the Commentaries of Alboquerque, the founding and naming of the town are ascribed, not to the son, but to the fugitive Javanese himself, and the account they give is this. "Parimisura gave the town the name of Malaka, because, in the language of Java, they call Palimbao (Palembang, which the writer in another place says is in Java, instead of Sumatra), to which he fled, Malayo, and because he came a fugitive from the kingdom of Palimbao, of which he was king, he named the place Malaca. Others say it was called Malaca on account of the many peoples that came to it from one or other country in so brief a time, for Malaca also means to meet or assemble (encontrar)."

In the Javanese language the word malayu signifies not only Malay, but also "to run," and "a fugitive;" and this is, no doubt, the source of the derivation at which the Portuguese writers, imperfectly instructed by their informers, were aiming, while in all probability Malacca, from a certain similarity of sound, is made to be a derivative from Malayu. The derivation of the name of the Malay people, from the Javanese verb "to run," or its participle, "fugitive," is very likely only fanciful, yet it is more reasonable than that of the Malayan manuscript adopted by Mr. Marsden, which traces it from "the river Malayu, which flows by the mountain Maha-meru," seeing that no such river as the Malayu is known in Sumatra, to which it is thus ascribed, and that the mountain alluded to is no other than the Olympus of Hindu mythology.

The great probability, then, is, that the founders, both of Malacca and Singapore, were not Malays, but Javanese, the only nation that, in comparatively early times, is proved by monuments to have attained such an amount of civilisation as would be equal to the formation of commercial communities of a reasonable prosperity. This view receives some countenance from the numbers, wealth, and consequence of the Javanese settlers of Malacca at the time of the conquest. De Barros states that they were subject only to their own chiefs, two in number, one of which had under his authority 10,000 persons. He gives the names of these chiefs, and even enumerates the provinces of Java from which they emigrated. The Malays, whether "men of the sea," or "men of the land," were either half savage and very rude, as, indeed, are those among them who continue their original modes of life, down to this day. The foundation of the civilisation which they eventually attained was laid by the first Javanese colonists, and improved and extended by intercourse with the maritime nations of Arabia, Persia, and Hindustan.

But the language of the people of Malacca was not Javanese but Malay, and it may be asked how this is to be accounted for. The obvious explanation seems to be that in a mixed population the easy language of the majority prevailed over the more difficult one of the minority. What took place in our own country, and also in northern India, in both of which the languages of the few were absorbed or displaced by those of the many, are examples in illustration. Castaghneda's account of the Malay, as a language of intercommunication, is perfectly accurate. "The people" (of Malacca), says he, "speak a language called Malaya, which is very sweet (muy doce), and easy to acquire."—Vol. ii. p. 335. The Malay spoken at Malacca contains a large infusion of Javanese, as English does of Norman-French, and Hindi of Persian.

Of the supposed expulsion of the founders of Malacca from Singapore by the Javanese of Majapait, there is no allusion in the Portuguese writers, and certainly there is no mention of it in the native chronicles of Java. Both De Barros and the author of the Commentaries of Alboquerque, state that the expulsion was effected by the Siamese, and the latter expressly asserts that the prince of Patani, at present the next Malay state to Siam on the eastern side of the peninsula, was the instrument employed, as he was the brother of the king of Singapore who had been assassinated by the future founder of Malacca. The subjection of Malacca to Siam seems, indeed, to be admitted by all parties. Four of the most northerly of the states of the peninsula are still subject to it, while a claim of supremacy is made for, at least, three more. The author of the Commentaries of Alboquerque giving a greater extension to Malacca than De Barros, thus describes it and its subjection to Siam. "The kingdom of Malacca on one side borders on Queda, and on the other on Pam (Pahang). It has 100 leagues of coast, and inland extends to a chain of mountains where it is parted from Siam, a breadth of 10 leagues. All this land was anciently subject to Siam. It was, more or less, ninety years before the arrival of Alfonso D'Alboquerque that the country became independent, and that the kings became what they called themselves, Çoltois (Sultans), which among them is equivalent to Emperor."—Chap. 17, p. 353.

Of the time in which the Mahommedan religion was embraced by the people of Malacca, there is no precise statement. The Malay account assigns the event to the reign of a prince, called Sultan Mahomed Shah, who ascended the throne in 1276, and this seems probable, since so remarkable an event is likely enough to have been chronicled (as indeed it has been in other countries of the Archipelago), by a people proud of the event, and now in possession of an era to reckon by. The Javanese founders might, indeed, have possessed the era of Salivana, but certainly no mention is made of it in this case if they did. The statement of De Barros respecting the conversion is as follows: "The greatness of Malacca induced the kings, who followed Xaquem Darsa (Sekândar Shah), to throw off their dependency on the kings of Siam, and this chiefly, since the time when induced by the Persians and Gujrati Moors, who came to Malacca and resided there, for the purpose of trade, from Gentiles, to become converts to the sect of Mahommed."—Decade II., book vi. chap. i.

The amount given by the Portuguese historian Diogo De Cauto differs materially from all the other statements. He says that the conversion of the King of Malacca was effected by a cazee from Arabia, who gave him the name of Mahommed after the prophet adding that of sá (shah) to it, and that this took place in the year 1388, or 112 years later than the date assigned to this event by the Malay manuscript. Including the converted prince, he gives the names of the five kings who reigned down to Alboquerque's conquest, and these agree substantially with those of the other statements. This account, then, which would give from 22 to 23 years to each reign is, after all, perhaps, the most probable. Decade IV. book ii. chap i.

The flourishing condition of Malacca, at the time it was attacked by the Portuguese, has, no doubt, been much exaggerated, but making every abatement, enough will remain to show that it was a place of considerable commercial importance, judging it by the ideas of the beginning of the 16th century, and by the peculiar value then attached to some of the commodities of which its trade consisted. "In matters of trade," says De Barros, "the people (the Malays) are artful and expert, for, in general, they have to deal with such nations as the Javanese, the Siamese, the Peguans, the Bengallis, the Quelijo (Chulias or Tâlugus), Malabaris, Gujratis, Persians and Arabians, with many other people, whose residence here has made them very sagacious. Moreover, the city is also populous, owing to the ships that resort to it from the country of the Chijs (Chinese), the Lequios (Japanese), the Luçoes (people of Luzon in the Philippines), and other nations of the Orient. All these people bring so much wealth, both of the East and the West, that Malacca seems a centre at which are assembled all the natural products of the earth and all the artificial ones of man. On this account, although situated in a barren land, it is, through an interchange of commodities, more amply supplied with every thing than the countries themselves from which they come." Decade II. book vi. chap. i.

The same author, in the same place, describes the general aspect of the town as follows. "Our people, although they did not see majestic structures of stone and mortar, or ramparts, or towers, or, indeed, any other kind of defence, beheld, notwithstanding, a town, extending along the beach for a good league, and ranged along the shore, many merchant vessels. But if the town was almost entirely built of wood, and the houses thatched with palm-leaves, in other places there were towers, walls, and some examples of a better architecture. Its real defences were a numerous people, and a multitude of ships."

The account given of Malacca by the author of the Commentaries of Alboquerque is less moderate. Thus, he asserts that the predecessor of the last king had accumulated a treasure of 140 quintals of gold, and that the town, in his time, contained 40,000 dwellings (vezinhos). According to him, it contained, including its precincts, 100,000 dwellings, when Alboquerque attacked it. "It is truly believed," says he, "according to the information we have of Malacca, that if another world and other navigations were discovered, all parties would still resort to it, for here come every sort of drugs and spices of the world that can be named, because its port is the most convenient in all monsoons of any from and within Cape Comorin." Chap. 18.

Castaghneda's account is less extravagant. "The city," says he, "at the time of its capture, was as long as from Dexobragas to the monastery of Belem, but narrow. It might contain about 30,000 hearths (fogos). The river divides it into two parts, the communication between them being by a wooden bridge. The houses are of wood, and principally by the sea-side, but in other directions, they are of stone and mortar, very noble. In the quarter which lies to the south stand the king's palace and the large mosque, and here dwell all the nobility. On the northern side dwell the merchants, and here the city is most extensive." Vol. II. p. 335.

According to the most moderate of these accounts, Malacca is made to contain a population of 150,000 inhabitants, and although narrow, inland, to have extended for three miles along the shore. It is evident, however, that it was for the most part a mere assemblage of thatched huts, and with the exception of temporary breastworks, it is certain that it had no kind of fortification such as the Portuguese themselves had found in other parts of Asia.

The reputation of Malacca had reached the Portuguese as soon as they had arrived in Calicut, and in 1508, ten years after that event, King Emanuel fitted out a fleet in Portugal in order to establish a trade with it. This was under the command of Diogo Lopez de Sequiera and reached the city in the following year. Here, through the representations of the Mahommedan merchants of Western India trading with Malacca, an attempt was made to cut him off, and some of his people were killed, and others taken prisoners. The ill conduct of the Portuguese, indeed, had been such, since their arrival in India, that an act of perfidy to cut them off is easily credible on the part of a semi-barbarous people. De Barros after describing the flourishing condition of Malacca, gives the following account of the effects which the depredations of his countrymen had produced on it. "This busy trade," says he, "lasted until our arrival in India, but the Moorish, Arabian, Persian and Guzrati ships, fearing our fleets, dared not, in general, now undertake the voyage, and if any ship of theirs did so, it was only by stealth and escaping our ships. The king, Mahommed of Malacca, immediately began to experience a loss in the duties which he levied on trade. As from the great number of ships which had frequented the port, a large revenue had been realised, and now from a few there was but a small one, he began to recompense himself for his loss by plundering the resident merchants, and they, consequently, began to leave the place." Decade II. book vi. chap. 2.

According to De Barros, the conduct of Sequiera was, at least, as barbarous as that of the Malay king. "Finally," says he, "seeing so many inconveniences to arise, they agreed that it was expedient to quit the place, and by way of proclaiming their future intentions, Diogo Lopez commanded that a man and woman, who had come on board the ships the day of the affray, should have an arrow passed through their skulls, and thus they were landed in one of his boats as a present to the king, who was thus informed through these his subjects, that unless he kept a good watch the treason which he had perpetrated would be punished with fire and sword." Decade II., book ii. chap. 4.

It was to punish the act of perfidy practised towards Sequiera and his companions, that Alfonso Alboquerque, then governor-general of India, fitted out the expedition which effected the conquest and which he himself commanded in person. This fleet consisted of nineteen sail, and, according to De Barros, the Portuguese troops amounted to no more than 800 men, with 200 Malabar auxiliaries, the latter armed only with swords and shields. The fleet anchored in Malacca roads on the first day of July 1511, near a small island, the usual station of the Chinese junks, of which three had already arrived. The first care of Alboquerque was to enter into a negociation in order to rescue the prisoners of Sequiera's fleet, in which he succeeded, and with the information which they furnished, he resolved to attack the city. In his first attempt, however, he met with such resistance that he was either beaten back, or found it prudent to retire to his fleet, and it was only in the second assault that he succeeded, and then, in a good measure, through a kind of blockade, which lasted nine days, and by which the Malays were starved into quitting it. "In the attack," says De Barros, "Alboquerque confined himself to capturing the bridge, at which he entrenched his troops. In this position he maintained himself for nine days, until the Malays were wearied out and forced to abandon the town. Among them, there was such hunger that in order to pilfer a little rice from houses in which they knew there was a store, they preferred risking their bodies against our steel to losing their lives through want of food." Chap. 6.

The preparation for and commencement of the first attack is thus mentioned by De Barros. "Next day, which was the vesper of St. Jago, before dawn and to the sound of the trumpet, the captains in their boats repaired to the admiral's ship, and having received absolution from the priest, they instantly made for the land, Alfonso Alboquerque making for the mouth of the river in order to capture the bridge, and the other commanders proceeding to the different points assigned to them. Alboquerque giving the word 'St. Jago,' the trumpets sounded the signal to engage, and the soldiers set up a shout. Some artillery, brought in the boats, replied to the cannon which the Malays had on the bridge. On this, the air was rent with a confusion of noises, so that the trumpets, the cannon, and the shouts, could not be distinguished from one another, the whole forming a doomsday of fear and terror." The arms of the Malays consisted of cannon (bombardas), hand-guns (espingardas), bows and arrows, blow-pipes for discharging small-darts, swords, daggers, spears and bucklers. Among other means of attack by the Malays were elephants, and with the usual result to those that employ them. "The king and his son," say the Commentaries, "who were mounted on elephants, seeing themselves pressed by our men, turned back, with 2000 men that accompanied them, but some of our men meeting them at the end of a street resolutely attacked the elephants with their lances. The first to do this is said to have been Fernão Gomes de Lemos. As elephants bear ill to be wounded, they turned backwards and fell on the Moors, throwing them into confusion. The elephant on which the king was mounted, feeling the pain of its wound, seized the 'negro' that guided it with its trunk and dashed him to the ground, on which the king, wounded in the hand, dismounted, and not being recognised, effected his escape." Chap. xxiii. p. 369.

In the first attack the Portuguese set fire to both quarters of the city. "From the stockades which he had erected," say the Commentaries, "Alfonso d' Alboquerque, directed Gaspar de Paiva, with 100 men, now that the sea-breeze had set in, to fire the commercial part of the town, and Simão Martinez, with an equal number, to do the same to the king's palace. When the fire took effect it consumed a great part of the city, and the Moors, in consequence, kept at a distance from our people." P. 369.

As soon as the Portuguese had become masters of the town, Alboquerque, as a reward to his troops, gave a general order to sack it, making an exception only in favour of the natives of the Malabar coast, and of the Javanese and Peguans, who had favoured his enterprise. No account is given of the total loss sustained by the Portuguese in the capture, but in the first attack the number of the wounded is stated at seventy. "Of the Moors," say the Commentaries, "men, women, and children, an infinite number perished by the sword, for no one was spared."

De Barros estimates the value of the plunder taken at 500,000 crusados which would amount to no more than 62,200*l.* but Castaghneda reduces it to no more than two fifths of that sum. All the authorities seem to agree that the number of cannon captured was 3000, most of them, in all probability, mere wall-pieces. This is the amount given in the Commentaries. "There were captured 3000 pieces of artillery, 2000 of them of brass, and among these, was one large gun presented to the king of Malacca by the king of Calicut. The rest were of iron. All this artillery with its appurtenances was of such workmanship that it could not be excelled, even in Portugal. There were also captured matchlocks (espingardas), blow-pipes for shooting poisoned arrows, bows and arrows, lances of Java, and divers other weapons, which excited, the wonder of the captors. Besides these arms, much merchandise of many kinds was taken. All this, and much besides not stated to avoid prolixity, Alfonso Alboquerque ordered to be divided among the commanders and crews of the fleet, taking to himself only six large brass lions which he reserved for his tomb. These with a bracelet, some children of all the nations of the land, and some tributes to be presented to King Don Emanuel and Queen Doña Maria were all lost in the ship Flor del Mar in returning to India. Let no one be surprised in perusing this narrative, that in Malacca there were taken 3000 pieces of artillery, for Ruy de Arrujo (a prisoner of Sequiera's fleet), Ninachetuan (chief of the Talingas), and Alfonso Alboquerque stated that in Malacca there were 8000, and this may be believed for two reasons, first, that in that town, there was much copper and much tin, with smelters as good as in Germany, and in the second place, that the city was a league in length, and that when Alboquerque was effecting a landing he was fired upon from all parts, from which it will appear that the number of guns was even small for the extent that had to be defended." Chapter xxviii. p. 380.

The Portuguese certainly considered the capture of Malacca one of the most glorious of their Asiatic conquests. Castaghneda, speaking of the point at which the chief resistance was experienced says of it, "And surely until this day, from the time we began the conquest of India, was no enterprise undertaken so arduous as the affair of that bridge, nor one in which so much artillery was employed or in which so many were engaged in the defence. Moreover, from the play of the enemy's artillery, we received much damage before we had effected a landing."

Vol. iii. p. 195. The enemy that Alboquerque had to contend against was certainly both braver and more skilful and better armed than the American nations over whom a few years later Cortez and Pizarro gained their victories. The inhabitants of Malacca, however, when attacked, divided as they were into several different nations, were not unanimous. Thus shortly after capturing the city, Alboquerque pursued the king to Muar, and his force is described as having consisted of 400 Portuguese, 600 Javanese and 300 Peguans. In his meditated attack on the city, the commanders of the Chinese junks anchored in the roads near his fleet, volunteered their assistance in the storm, but it was declined with thanks, and the reason is characteristic, although not consistent with the help he afterwards accepted. "The Portuguese never accepted assistance when they fought against Moors, for God, through his apostle, had commanded them to fight them. But he (Alboquerque) requested them to look on and see how the Portuguese fought." De Barros—Decade 2d, Book 6, chapter iv.

The Portuguese held Malacca for 130 years, a period of disaster throughout, in which with the exception of courage and daring, they exhibited none of the qualities fit to rule an Asiatic people. Their subjects were Mahomedans, most of those with whom these maintained commercial relations were of the same religion, and against the Mahomedan religion the Portuguese declared a crusade from their first appearance in the Indian seas. Their main object, too, was the establishment of a commercial monopoly, and they made a piratical war on all who opposed them in its prosecution. This policy necessarily raised against them a host of enemies. The expelled Malays made war upon them during their whole occupation of Malacca, and finally assisted in extruding them. They had hardly got possession when they were nearly losing it by famine brought on by their own acts. This was immediately followed by an invasion from Java, and from the kingdom of Achin in Sumatra, Malacca was invaded no fewer than eight different times. Besides these attacks by the natives of the different countries of the Archipelago, a far more formidable enemy, the Dutch, continued to assail them for 40 years, until they at last supplanted them by the capture of the city.

The Portuguese resisted all these enemies with extraordinary courage and fortitude. The Dutch had besieged Malacca in 1606 and 1608, and were defeated on both occasions, and it was not until 1641, and after a blockade, a siege, and an assault that they succeeded in capturing it, the siege having in all lasted nine months. The Dutch force had amounted to 1500 men with Malay auxiliaries to the same number, the storming party to 650. The Portuguese garrison on the capture was found reduced to 200 Europeans and 400 natives. This was the end of the proud conquest of Alboquerque and his companions. The Dutch held possession of Malacca until 1795, or for 154 years, when during the war of the French revolution, it was surrendered by capitulation to the British government, by which it was occupied until 1818, when it was restored to the Netherland government, which exchanged it for Bencoolen in 1824. Down to 1813, the principles on which all the three European nations governed the country, were those of an exclusive commercial monopoly, and the result of this mode of government was, that the country was far poorer than it had been under its native rulers three centuries before.

MALACCA, city or town, lies in north latitude 2° 14′ and east longitude 102° 12′, and on a small river, little better indeed now than a brook. This divides it into two parts as it did the ancient native town. In 1832, it contained about 12,000 inhabitants, and now about 20,000, or above one-third part of the population of the whole territory. Immediately behind the town, there is a hill about a hundred feet high, and on this are the ruins of the Portuguese monasteries of St. Paul and of the Hermanos de leche with the church of the Madre de Dios, in which once reposed the ashes of the celebrated apostle of the Indies, St. Francis Xavier, afterwards transferred to Goa. The fortifications had been complete down to 1807, when they were most barbarously destroyed by the British government, which at the time had the absurd intention of transferring the whole population to Penang, 300 miles distant, and far less convenient as the resort of shipping. Many of the dwellings are tall many-storied houses of the architecture of the 16th centuries. The town embraces a circuit of about a mile. The church on the hill and the original fortifications were built by Alboquerque, and the conqueror was not scrupulous as to the sources from which he drew his materials. "Alfonso Alboquerque," says De Barros, "found stone in the country to burn for lime, and he obtained much hewn stone from some ancient tombs of the gentiles—those who occupied the hill before the arrival of the Cellates. Moreover, he built a church dedicated to our Lady of the Annunciation, the chapel of which he crowned with the capital of a king's tomb which he transported to its place by means of elephants. It was of wood, and skilfully worked. In these works, he availed himself of the services of a people of the town called Ambarages (âmba-raja) which signifies, slaves of the king, as in truth they were. Of these the king of Malacca had 3000, and to these when he employed them, he gave daily rations, and when he did not, they earned wages for themselves, their wives and children." Decade 2d, book vi. chap. vi.

The town of Malacca is distant from the nearest shore of Sumatra about 45 miles. The port is but an open road, but notwithstanding safe at all seasons, not being within the latitude of hurricanes, nor within the influence of either monsoon; or as the Commentaries of Alboquerque express it, "It is the beginning of one monsoon and the end of another." In the roads there are two islets about a mile from the shore, called by the Portuguese Ilha de Pedras, and Ilha de Naos—Stone and Ship Island. It was near these that Alboquerque with his armada cast anchor in 1511, and at which also were wont to anchor the largest caraques of the Portuguese in five and six fathoms' water. This part of the roads is now accessible only to small craft, owing to the growth of an extensive mud bank dry at low water, and the anchorage of vessels of burthen is at the inconvenient distance of two miles from the shore.

MALACCA STRAITS. This is the name given to the Channel which separates the Malay Peninsula from the island of Sumatra, but the Malays have no name for it, for it is not consonant to their practice to give the appellation of strait (sâlat) to so large a body of water, whatever its form. The Straits of Malacca form in fact almost a land-locked sea, in which variable winds prevail, and in which the monsoons are felt only for a few miles at both extremities. Their extreme length is about 500 miles, and their breadth varies from 40 up to 300. At their western end there are many islands, chiefly towards the Malayan shore, half-a-dozen of which, including Penang, are of considerable size. At the eastern end they are almost innumerable, about a dozen of them, including Singapore, being large. The Straits of Malacca form the usual channel through which is carried on all the intercourse of the countries of Asia east and west of them. The dangers which impeded the navigation in the middle of the passage from sand-banks, and at the eastern entrance from countless islands, have of late years been obviated by the construction of two fine lighthouses by the British Government. The first notice we have of these straits is by Ludovico Barthema, a native of Bologna, who seems to have visited Malacca about 1503, or six years before the visit of Sequiera, and he would seem to have taken them for a salt river. "Opposite to that city (Malacca)," says he, "there is a very great river (Fiumara), than which we had never seen a larger. It is named Gaza (?) and appears to be about 15 miles broad." Ramusio, vol. i., p. 166.

MALANG. The name of a district of the province of Surabaya, in Java. The word in Javanese signifies across or athwart, and figuratively "unlucky." Malang is a valley from 1000 to 1500 feet above the level of the sea, having to the east the mountains of Tengar, Brama, and Sumiru, and to the west those of Kawi and Arjuna, some of the highest of the island. It is a fertile, populous, and beautiful country, and is remarkable for containing some of the most extensive Hindu ruins of Java, particularly those of Singasari.

MALAY. The word is correctly Mâlayu, in the language of the Malays themselves, in Javanese, and indeed in all the languages of the Archipelago. A people of the brown complexioned race, with lank hair, speaking the Malay language is found in greater or lesser number all over the Archipelago, from Sumatra to New Guinea, and from the Peninsula to Timur. It is however only in Sumatra, the Malay Peninsula, and islands adjacent to its coasts, and in Borneo that they exist in large numbers, and have a distinct independent nationality, for everywhere else they are found only as settlers or sojourners among indigenous populations. In Sumatra they are thought to possess about one-half the area of the island, including the whole of the eastern coast, a part of the western, and some of the most fruitful parts of the interior, their number being here estimated at about a million. With the exception of a few wandering negritos, they form the entire population of the Malay Peninsula and its adjacent islands, and their number here has been estimated at about a quarter of a million. In Borneo they occupy nearly the whole sea-coast, without penetrating far into the interior, which is inhabited by men of the same race, but speaking languages distinct from Malay. The Bornean Malays may, perhaps, be as numerous as the Malays of the Peninsula and its islands, and thus, without including settlers scattered over the other parts of the Archipelago, the whole Malay population may be estimated at about a million and a half. In this number, however, is no doubt included many not of the original Malay stock, but who, adopting their language, manners, and religion, came in process of time not to be distinguishable.

The Malay nation may be divided naturally into three classes—the civilised Malays, or those who possess a written language, and have made a decent progress in the useful arts; the gipsy-like fishermen, called "the sea-people," and the rude half savages, who, for the most part, live precariously on the produce of the forests. The civilised Malays consist of the inhabitants of the eastern side of Sumatra, of much of the interior of that island, and of those of the sea-boards of Borneo and the Malay Peninsula. The sea-gipsies are to be found sojourning from Sumatra to the Moluccas, but are most numerous among the narrow seas of the many islands lying between Sumatra and the peninsula towards the eastern end of the strait that divides them. The only habitations of this people are their boats, and they live exclusively by the produce of the sea or by the robberies they commit on it. The most usual name by which they are known is orang-laut, literally, "men of the sea," but they are also sometimes called rayat-laut, or "sea-subjects," the Arabic word for subject being here used to express their dependence on the princes of the civilised Malays. Another name for them is Sika, and a very frequent one Bajau, which seems to be only the Javanese word, bajo, a robber, with a Malay termination. The rude wandering class, speaking the Malay language, is found in the interior of the Malay Peninsula, in Sumatra, and in the islands lying between them, but in no other part of the Archipelago. In Sumatra they are known under the names of Lubu and Kubu, or orang-utan, men of the woods, wild men or savages. The most general name for them is orang-bânua, that is, "men of the soil," or Aborigines, but in some parts they are called sakai, which means followers or dependents. These are all of them names given by the civilised Malays, for among themselves the many tribes into which they are divided are known only by the names of the localities which they frequent, as Udai, Jakun, Sabimba, Bâsisi, &c.

These three classes of Malays existed near three centuries and a half ago, when the Portuguese first arrived in the waters of the Archipelago, just as they do at the present day. That people describes them as having existed also for two centuries and a half before that event, as without doubt they did in times far earlier. Thus De Barros describes the first class of Malays as men "living by trade, and the most cultivated of these parts:" the second as a "vile people," whose "dwelling was more on the sea than the land," and who "lived by fishing and robbing," and the third as "half savages" (quasi meios salvages), while the Malay language was common to all of them.

The question of the parent country of a people so widely spread over the Archipelago, which has exercised so large an influence over the other population of the same region, and of whose tongue clear and unquestionable traces are found, not only in those of the Philippines, but of the South Sea Islands, and even of remote Madagascar, has been much debated, but certainly not settled, nor, indeed, likely ever to be precisely determined. The Malays themselves, like all people in the same state of society, have no true history. The books, which have been called their Annals, are, in reality, romances, and indeed so called by themselves. The quality of these productions may be judged from the example of one of them translated by the learned Dr. Leyden, and which is deemed the most authentic. It is called Sâjarah Mâlayu, which is rendered "Malay Annals," and stated to have been composed in 1612 at Malacca, of course under the government of the Portugese. This was framed from a Malay manuscript which had been brought from Goa, and entitled a hăkayat, the Arabic word which the Malays use in common with the Sanscrit one, charitra, for a tale or romance. Even the name given to these annals themselves is not Malay, but Javanese, and mis-spelt in adoption. They are without a single date, and indeed, for the period of Malay history which preceded the conversion to Mahommedanism, there could hardly have been any dates, as the Malays are not known to have had an era from which to reckon. The narrative is a wild tissue of fable often drawn from Hindu and Arabian mythology, and the personages that figure in it not unfrequently Arabians and Hindus. It is conclusive of the worthlessness of such writings that the Malays have long ago converted even the events of the Portuguese conquest of Malacca into a mere romance.

In order to conjecture what may have been the parent country of the Malays, and to form some notion of their early history, nothing better than a reasonable hypothesis can be offered. The name of the people gives little assistance in this enquiry. The word Mâlayu is an adjective which requires to have a noun prefixed in order to give the sense required, as Orang Mâlayu, a Malay or Malays; Tanah Mâlayu, the "Malay land," or land of the Malays; and Bahasa Mâlayu, the Malay language. In Javanese Mâlayu has the same meaning, but it also signifies to run away or flee, and fugitive, or fleeing. Hence a derivation of the name of the Malayan people in reference to the founders of Malacca who were fugitives from Java. This derivation, most probably given to the Portuguese by the Javanese of Malacca, has probably no better foundation than the accidental coincidence of sound in the two words. Mâlayu is no doubt the name of the original tribe or nation, and its source is as obscure and untraceable as those of Jawa, Javanese, Sunda, Sundanese, Wugi, Bugis, and many others. We need not, indeed, go further than our own language for a name as obscure for Angle as applied to ourselves, our country and our language is as difficult to trace as Mâlayu applied to those of the Malays.

It is natural to look for the parent country of the Malays where this people are most numerous, and least intermixed with other nationalities; and this locality can be no other than either Sumatra, the Malay Peninsula or the islands lying between them. The Malays themselves call the peninsula Tanah Mâlayu, that is, the "Malay land, or country of the Malays;" and they designate its wild inhabitants, speaking the Malay language, as the Orâng bânua, literally "people of the soil;" or as we should express it, "aborigines." The term "land of the Malays" is, however, given to the Peninsula by the civilised Malays, perhaps only on account of its being the only country almost exclusively peopled by Malays; whereas in Sumatra and Borneo they are intermixed with other populations. The term "men of the soil," applied by these civilised Malays may in the same manner, be used by them only to distinguish the rude natives from themselves claiming to be foreign settlers. The expression, however, would seem to imply that the civilised Malays considered the wild tribes, speaking the same language with themselves, as the primitive occupants of the land. But the same wild tribes, speaking the Malay language, although not distinguished as "men of the soil," exist also in Sumatra, and more especially on its eastern side opposite to the Peninsula: and they are found also, in several of the islands lying between those countries, extending even to Banca and Billiton.

The first seat of the Malayan nation may, therefore, be either the Malay Peninsula, Sumatra, or the islands lying between them; and, as in the instance of the Polynesian people of the islands of the Pacific, where we find men speaking the same language and of the same race, from the Sandwich Islands to New Zealand and from the Friendly Islands to Easter Island, it is difficult or impossible to determine on a particular locality for an original seat. The origin of Malay civilisation, however, is quite a distinct matter from that of the nation; and we may be tolerably sure that this did not spring up in the Peninsula, or islands adjacent to it, for no civilisation has ever sprung up in any part of the globe in a country of such a physical character,—in a region covered with an obstinate tropical forest, destitute of open plains, composed of mountains without table-lands, without natural facilities for irrigation, and with a stubborn or sterile soil. Such obstacles would be insuperable in the early and feeble stages of society, and, indeed, in the Peninsula, have not been conquered even in a more advanced one. The only Malay state within it that ever acquired any degree of eminence was Malacca; and it owed it to the strangers who founded it, and to the convenience of its position as a commercial emporium,—assuredly not to the fertility of a soil, which never raised sustenance enough for its inhabitants, many of whom still continue in the condition of mere savages.

All the civilised Malays of the Peninsula claim their origin from Sumatra and from Menangkabo, the most powerful state of that island; but they do not pretend to state the time, or the cause of their migration. Some of the states of the interior even call themselves "men of Menangkabo," their chiefs receiving an investiture from that place. Indeed the migration from Menangkabo to the Peninsula, although in dribblets, goes on down to the present time. The Malays of Borneo, in like manner with those of the Peninsula, claim their descent from the same Menangkabo.

This claim of Malays beyond Sumatra of being colonies from a country in the heart of that island, is probably, after all, no better than a myth founded on a desire to claim a descent from a country which had, at one time, acquired more power and distinction than any other inhabited by Malays. The apocryphal Malay Chronicle, for such without a doubt it is, referred to in the article on Malacca, does not, however, refer to Menangkabo, but to Palembang, as that part of Sumatra from which

Singapore first, and afterwards Malacca, was founded. This, probably, arose from the real founders of both, as has been attempted to be shown elsewhere, not having been Malays but Javanese. Even, however, supposing the emigrants in these cases to have been Malays, and the statement to be trustworthy, the mere peopling of two small places, and this too at a time by near a century posterior to the Norman conquest of England, would be neither an account of the parent country of the Malay nation, nor a history of its migrations.

To account for the civilisation and migration of the Malays, (to fix their original seat is hopeless,) the most probable supposition seems to be, that the wandering tribes of the Sumatran coast, or of the Peninsula, or of the islands between them, after they had learned the construction of boats,—after they had acquired some nautical skill and enterprise,—after they had, in a word, become the sea-gypsies which some of them still continue to be; in process of time, reached lands more promising than their own and there settled, abandoning to some degree, their habits as fishermen, and addicting themselves to agriculture. By such a progress they would, in due course, become what most of the civilised tribes of Malays are at the present day, half-fishermen and half-husbandmen. Of such tribes there existed in Sumatra, at the time of the arrival of the Portuguese, no fewer than nine-and-twenty; while in the Peninsula there were, at least, eight. All of these were at or near the coast, and invariably at the mouth, or on the banks of a river. The maritime character of the Malay nation is, indeed, impressed on its language, and discoverable in the copiousness of its meteorological and nautical vocabulary. Thus, the compass is divided into sixteen points with specific names, all native; and there are peculiar idiomatic terms for windward and leeward, signifying literally, "above the wind," and "below the wind." The river, the favourite and familiar locality of the Malay nation, affords room for a curious variety of expression. Kuwala, and muwara signify "the mouth," and ulu "the source" of a river. Ilir is to "descend," mudik to "ascend" it, these last terms signifying, at the same time, "the interior," and "the sea-board." Tâluk means "a bight," or "cove," and rantau, "a reach;" but they also signify a district of country, which is moreover frequently called anak-sungai, "child of the river."

There is but one country eminently favourable to the development of an early civilisation, in which we find the Malay nation planted—Menangkabo, so often referred to in Malay story. This is in the centre of Sumatra, among the fertile valleys of volcanic mountains rising to a height exceeding 10,000 feet,—in short, in a locality of similar features to Java, and the islands immediately to the east of it. The late Sir Stamford Raffles, who had visited Menangkabo, declared that it was as populous and well cultivated as any part of Java that he had seen, which is assuredly what cannot be asserted of any other country whatever inhabited by Malays. The great probability then is, that this country was peopled by the Malays of the eastern coast of Sumatra, penetrating into the interior of the island by the principal rivers which have their source in it. This, indeed, is distinctly asserted in the traditions of the Malays themselves. In this favorable position they would naturally acquire a degree of power which the same people have certainly nowhere else reached. It is, no doubt, the possession of this comparative power which has caused the maritime Malay states to look to it with respect, and to claim their origin from it. Malay tradition, however, by no means asserts that Menangkabo was the primitive seat of the Malayan nation; but, on the contrary, affirms that it was itself peopled from Palembang, in the same island.

The Javanese, as already intimated, appear to have had no inconsiderable share in the civilisation of the Malays; and although there is certainly no historical record of it, there is satisfactory proof. As stated in a former article, the Javanese would seem to have been even the founders of Malacca. Monuments, which prove the presence of this people in the country of the Malays, have even been discovered. Thus, Sir Stamford Raffles, when he visited Menangkabo, found there inscriptions on stone in the ancient character of Java, such as are frequent in that island; and he was supported in his conclusion that they were so, by the learned natives of Java who accompanied him in his journey. The settlement of the Javanese in several parts of Sumatra, is, indeed, sufficiently attested. In Palembang they have been immemorially the ruling people; and although the Malay language be the popular one, the Javanese, in its peculiar written character, is still that of the court. In the state of Jambi, which borders on Palembang, Hindu images, identical with those of Java in all respects, except that the material is granite instead of trachyte, have been discovered. Probably as much as one-fourth part of the Malay language is equally Javanese, and in a good many instances of compounded words, their Javanese origin is satisfactorily made out through their elements, themselves without significance, in the Malay language. One example will suffice. The founder of the states of Menangkabo, who is stated by Malay tradition to have come from Palembang, is called Sang Sapurba. The word sang is not Malay but Javanese, and signifies, literally, "a flower;" but is frequently prefixed to the titles of personages of distinction, as sang-prabu, or sang-aji, "a king;" sang-yogi, "a devotee;" and sangywang, "a god" or "deity." Sapurba is composed of the article sa, "one," and the Sanscrit purba, "first" or "beginning." The name, in fact, has much the appearance of one fabricated for the occasion. To these evidences of Javanese influence, it may be added, that Malay literature has nothing original of its own; being, when not drawn from Arabic sources, borrowed from the fictions of Java, or the mythology of the Hindus, such as the latter was in that island.

It is remarkable that De Barros, drawing his information, no doubt, from the traditions furnished by natives to the Portuguese conquerors, expsessly states that the Sumatrans themselves considered that the Javanese were once masters of their island. "It is held by themselves," says he, "that the Javanese (Jaōs) had been once masters of their great island, and that prior to the Chinese, (Chijs). they conducted its commerce, as well as that of India."—Decade, III., book v., chapter 1. The authority of De Barros, in this case, no doubt, suffers some depreciation from his asserting afterwards, that the Javanese themselves were a people of Chinese origin, a derivation which he founds on their supposed imitation of the policy of the Chinese, and of their skill in the mechanic arts. This assertion, however, is but an hypothesis of his own.

The reliable history of the Malays began only with the arrival of the Portuguese. As already stated, the maritime Malays, without including those of Borneo, were at this time divided into near forty petty states. With the Malays of the interior of Sumatra, the Portuguese did not come into communication. Menangkabo is simply named, but certainly not, as it has been very absurdly called by some European writers, as a great empire, which undoubtedly it never was, unless we are contented to accept assertion for proof. The Portuguese found the maritime Malays, in common with the Javanese, conducting the carrying trade of the Archipelago, including, at the time, the most important branch of it, the spice trade. Along with their trade, they propagated the Mahommedan religion. Many of the inhabitants of Borneo, of the southern Philippines, and most of those of the Moluccas, they had converted before the arrival of the Portuguese. In most of the sea-coasts of the islands of the Archipelago, we find traces of the settlement of Malays. Both for trade and propagandism, this language was the medium of communication, and for such a purpose it is certainly peculiarly well suited, from the simplicity of its structure and facility of its pronunciation and acquisition. From Sumatra to the Philippines and Moluccas, it was in general use for this purpose. "The Gentiles of the interior, as well as the Moors," says De Barros, "who dwell on the coast, although they differ from each other in language, nearly all speak the Malay of Malacca, being the most common in these parts." When Magellan discovered the Philippines, he had no difficulty in communicating with the inhabitants through a Sumatran slave that he had brought along with him. The same state of things continues to the present day from Sumatra to New Guinea.

But the Malay language, besides being the common medium of communication, has been infused, to a greater or less extent, into all the languages of the Archipelago, and clear traces of it are to be found even in the languages of tribes with which the Malays of our time hold no communication, and even of whose existence they are wholly ignorant, as in the case of the languages of the islands of the Pacific and of Madagascar.

MALAY PENINSULA. This, or Peninsula of Malacca, is the name given by European geographers to the long spit of land which forms the most southerly extremity of the continent of Asia,—the supposed Golden Chersonesus of the ancients. The Malays, although seldom giving names to such large masses of land, occasionally call it Tanah-Malayu,—the "Malay land," or "country of the Malays." For a peninsula, which it truly is, they have no name. Although the existence of this country was really unknown to Europe until the arrival of the Portuguese in India, it is remarkable how early its peculiar form became known to the latter. Barbosa, whose work is dated at Lisbon in 1516, and who must have seen Malacca before its conquest, describes it as "a great piece of land which juts into the ocean, ending in a promontory, and having the sea, as well in the direction of China as towards the west."

By far the best account of the Peninsula has been given by Mr. Logan in his Journal, and I take him as my principal guide in attempting to give a sketch of it. In the widest sense, the Peninsula extends from the parallel of the head of the gulf of Siam, in latitude 13° 30′, to Cape Romania, the Tanjung-bulus, or "naked headland" of the Malays, in latitude 1° 41′, or only 74 miles from the equator. Its extreme length is about 800 miles; its least breadth about 60, and its greatest about 150. Generally, it is about ten times as long as it is broad. The area of the entire Peninsula is reckoned to be 83,000 square miles, which makes it about equal in extent to Britain. But the country inhabited by the Malays, which does not include the northern portion of it, has an area of no more than 61,560 miles, and is, therefore, about half as large again as Java, single provinces of which, such is the difference between the natural capabilities of the two countries, contain more fertile land, more cultivation, and more inhabitants than the whole of it. The northern part of the Peninsula, forming a narrow isthmus, running nearly due north and south, to the length of 140 miles, contains an area of 21,600 square miles, and is inhabited by the Siamese, or a cross between them and the Malays, known to the latter by the name of Sansam. Except at its base, where it forms a portion of the Siamese territory, the Peninsula is every where surrounded by the sea,—to the east by the Sea of China and Gulf of Siam, and to the west by the Bay of Bengal and the Straits of Malacca, the latter washing that portion of it inhabited by the Malays.

Along the shores of the Peninsula lie many islands, not included in the area above given. On the western side, and fronting the portion inhabited by the Malays, we have, besides many smaller ones, Trutao, Langkawi, Penang, Singapore, Batam and Bintang. On the eastern coast the islands are fewer and smaller. All these littoral islands are of the same character as the main land, and when inhabited at all, are so by the same race of men, the Malayan. Their superficies may probably be not less than 5000 square miles, to be added to the continental portion of the "land of the Malays."

The geological formation of the Peninsula is granitic, overlaid most generally by sandstone, and frequently also, by laterite or cellular clay iron-stone, and to the north by lime-stone. A granitic mountain chain runs along the whole length of the Peninsula, and on both sides of it, but particularly on its western one, or that sheltered by Sumatra, there are extensive alluvial plains, little above the level of the sea. The highest mountains are Pulai, in the territory of Jehor, 2152 feet above the level of the sea; Jerai, in the territory of Queda, 3894 feet, and Ledang, the continental Ophir of the Portuguese, 4320. Thus it will be seen that the mountains of the Peninsula are not above one third part of the height of those of Sumatra, Java, Bali, or Lomboc. Thermal springs exist within the territory of Malacca, but no trace of a volcanic formation has any where been discovered.

The prevailing metals are iron, tin, and gold. "Iron ores," says Mr. Logan, a skilful geologist, "are everywhere found, and in the south they exist in vast profusion. In some places the strata have been completely saturated with iron, and here the naked surface of the ground, strewed with blackish scoriform gravel and blocks, presents a strange contrast to the exuberant vegetation of the surrounding tracts, appearing as if the ground had been burnt and blasted by subterraneous fires. Much of the ordinary forms of iron-masked rocks are so common, and so little regarded for their metallic contents, that in Singapore they are used to macadamise the roads, although containing nearly 60 per cent. of pure metal." The Peninsula, with the islands adjacent to it, certainly contain by far the most extensive tin fields in the world, extending as they do over seventeen degrees of latitude, or from Tavoy, in north latitude, 14°, to the island of Billiton, in south latitude, 3°. "Seeing," observes Mr. Logan, "that tin is procured in all parts of the Peninsula where it is sought for, and in proportion to the enterprise and labour which are devoted to the search, we may consider the entire zone as a great magazine of tin. It is, in fact, incomparably the greatest on the globe." He gives examples of the extent of its distribution. Within the territory of Jèhor, forming the southern extremity of the Peninsula, it was not thought to exist until 1846, when it was found in several places. In 1845, the whole quantity produced in the territory of Malacca was about 13 tons; in 1846, it rose to 84 tons; and in 1847, when there were fifty different mines open, to 260 tons; and this result proceeded entirely from the application of the skill and enterprise of the Chinese, for tin was not discovered in the Malacca territory until 1793. The intelligent writer who furnishes these details estimates the whole produce of the Peninsula in 1848 at 2400 tons. This is constantly increasing,—forms a large portion of the consumption of Europe, China, and India, and is the great staple product of the Peninsula and its islands. The whole ore is "stream," or alluvial, and as yet the metal has not been traced to its veins in the rock. Gold is much less abundant in the Peninsula than in Sumatra, Borneo, or Celebes, and its whole produce is thought not to exceed 20,000 ounces a-year, less than the weekly produce of a single locality in Australia.

The Peninsula is remarkably deficient in lakes. I have heard but of one of any extent,—that which is called Brau, lying between Malacca and Penang, but I have seen no account of it. The rivers are numerous, but small, and navigable, even for craft of little draught, only as far as the reach of the tide. Towards their embouchures their banks are low, muddy, and lined with mangroves, and sand-bars impede navigation at their entrances. On the western side, the most considerable amount to six, of which the largest are those of Perak and Jehor. The Muar, about six leagues to the south of Malacca, has attained a Malayan celebrity from being the locality where the Javanese refugees first established themselves after their expulsion from Singapore, and that to which their descendants first fled when driven out of Malacca by the Portuguese.

The botany of the Peninsula is a very wide field, as yet but partially explored. The plants put to economical uses are, however, sufficiently known. Of the great many species of forest trees, about half-a-dozen only yield good durable timber, but there is not one that is fit for the higher purposes of ship-building, for the teak does not exist. The forests yield ebony, sapan, and eagle wood, but none of them of the best quality, or in much abundance. They yield, also, ratans, bamboos, the nibung, and the nipa palms, all constituting the main materials of Malayan architecture. But their most remarkable and valuable product is the guttah-percha, a few years ago used only for Malay horse-whips and knife-handles, but by the help of which the English and Irish channels, the Mediterranean and the Euxine, are now crossed by the electric telegraph. It was from the Peninsula, in fact, that this article was first made known to Europeans, more than three centuries after the country had been frequented by them. This was in 1843, and in justice to my relative, the late Dr. William Montgomerie, I am bound to mention that he first made the discovery, and was rewarded for it by the gold medal of the Society of Arts. The chief products of agriculture are rice, the coco, and areca palms, yams, the batata, and the sugar-cane. The esculent fruits are numerous, abundant, and some of them excellent. Incomparably the most esteemed by the natives is the durian, which attains perfection without culture; and by Europeans the mangostin, which is the most delicate fruit in the world. The exotic ananas, with little or no care attains the same perfection as the best pines of our hot-houses, and is hardly dearer than Swedish turnips. The same soil brings such luxuries as these to perfection, which is unfruitful in the production of the necessary food of man.

The zoology of the Peninsula is a very wide field. The following is a brief view of some of its most remarkable animals. The quadrumanes, or apes, amount to nine, eight monkeys, each species having a distinct name, and a sloth, the Lemur tardigradus of naturalists, called by the Malays the kukang, and occasionally kamalâsan, that is, "the lazy," or "the slothful." Of bats, there are several species, but the most remarkable is the vampire, or kalung of the Malays. This flies high in great flocks, and but for larger size and slower flight, flocks of them might easily be mistaken for those of crows or rooks. The kalung is a great enemy to the best esculent fruits. The only plantigrade animal is a small bear, peculiar to the Peninsula and Borneo. Of viverra, or weasels, there are four species, the largest and most singular of which is the binturung of the natives, and the Ictides ater of naturalists. Of the feline family there are seven, including the royal tiger and the leopard, both of them far too numerous. The domestic cat exists, and as in Siam and the country of the Peguans, the Burmese, and even the Japanese, always with a tail half the usual length, as if it had been amputated. The domestic dog, the anjing of the Malays, exists in the same vagrant state in which it is found in most Asiatic countries; and a wild dog is said to exist in the woods. The otter, the mâmbrang of the Malays, exists, but seems to be scarce, which is not easily accounted for considering the abundance of fish. The Pachydermata, or thick-skinned family, consist of four, the elephant, the one-horned rhinoceros, the same with that of Sumatra, the Malay tapir or tânau of the Malays, and the hog. Elephants are numerous, but whether of the same species with that of Sumatra, or with the ordinary Asiatic one, has not been ascertained. That they are equally capable of domestication as either is certain, for they are used as beasts of burden in the northern parts of the Peninsula, and occasionally exported to the coast of Coromandel. The hog is found both in the wild and domestic state, and numerous in the first, constituting the chief animal food of the nomadic races, as no doubt before their conversion to Mohammedanism, it did of the cultivated Malays. No animal of the Equine family is known in the Peninsula, for the horse itself is not found even in the domestic state. A country covered with forest or marsh, and where it would be difficult to find a mile of firm open land, is eminently unsuited to it. The ox or the buffalo takes its place. Even in Malacca, under the Malays, the horse seems not to have been used; at least the early Portuguese make no mention of it. In Sumatra, however, where there are extensive open plains, the horse is frequent, although even here, it may be suspected to be exotic, since there is no name for it, except the corruption of a Sanscrit one. The species of Ruminants are nine in number, namely, four deer, the goat, the buffalo, and three species of ox. Two of the deer are smaller than the European hare, a third about the size of a fallow deer, and the fourth as large as an elk. The domestic goat is a small mean-looking animal, of little value; and there exists in the forest a wild one, the same with that of Sumatra. The buffalo attains its greatest size in the Peninsula, and is larger than that of Java, or of Cochin-China, both of which far exceed the buffalo of Italy, and in a still greater degree that of Continental India. The domestic ox is a short-legged, compact, strong and hardy animal. The wild species are two, the Sunda ox of Java and Borneo, and an undescribed one called by the Malays sâladang, and which would seem to be peculiar to the Peninsula. The sheep is known to the Malays of the Peninsula only by its Sanscrit name biri, and as a partially acclimated stranger. The hare is wholly unknown, and the rabbit only in the domestic state, introduced by the Portuguese, the name tarwelu and kuwelu being probably a strange corruption of the Portuguese conejera.

The most remarkable birds of the Peninsula are those of the gallinaceous and pigeon families. Of the first, there are the peacock, or mârak of the Malays, the same as that of Java, but differing from that of India, and never seen in the domesticated state; the double.spurred peacock, smaller than the European pheasant, a beautiful but shy and timid bird; three species of pheasant, including the Argus, or the kuwau of the Malays; a partridge, the Perdrix Javanica; and the cock in the wild and domestic state, the last a small bird but of great courage. The species of pigeons are very numerous, from those of the size of a thrush to that of the European ring-dove, the prevailing colour being green, and some of them being probably migratory. Snipes are numerous, and quails rare. In the wild state, there is but one duck, a teal, and no goose. The only poultry of the Peninsula, in so far as the Malays are concerned, is the common fowl and the duck. The goose is known only by its Sanscrit name, angsa; and the peacock and rock pigeon have not been domesticated. The parrot family, in Malay nuri, the same word which we have converted into loory, is numerous, but none of the species equal in brilliancy of plumage to those of New Guinea, and its adjacent islands. The esculent-nest-making swallow, the lawit of the Malays, exists in the caves of the coast of some of the islands, but is not numerous. The birds of prey are numerous, and consist of kites, alang, and hawks, alapalap, in Malay. The vulture does not exist, and there is no hawk of a size to entitle it to the designation of an eagle.

The reptiles consist of the alligator, the iguana, and several species of small lizard, and of probably at least forty different species of snakes, of which not more than one in ten are poisonous. Among the innoxious snakes is a python, and among the poisonous ones a cobra. Both the seas that wash the shores of the Peninsula, but more especially the comparatively shallow and sheltered one which parts it from Sumatra, abound in fish, which form the principal animal sustenance of the great mass of the inhabitants. Among fish the seal and the whale do not exist, the latter being known to the Malays only by a Sanscrit name, gajah-mina, which signifies "elephant fish." The only cetaceous animal is the duyong, which our naturalists by the mistake of a single letter have converted into dugong. This animal, not very frequent, lives in the shallow waters, feeding on submarine plants, and its flesh is esculent, being much superior to that of the green turtle. The fresh water fish are not abundant, nor held in much esteem by the natives, but some of those of the sea are of excellent flavour; and the white pomfret, the bawal of the Malays, is certainly one of the most delicate fishes in the world to the European palate, being less rich than the turbot, and higher flavoured than the sole.

As to climate, that of the Peninsula is hot and moist. These qualities necessarily belong to a region that reaches to within 74 miles of the equator, that in so far as the proper country of the Malays is concerned, is not above 6° distant from it,—that is almost surrounded by the sea, and seldom more than 50 miles away from it; and the vastly greater portion of which is covered with a dense and ever-verdant forest. The whole Peninsula is, alternately, protected from both monsoons by its own mountain range, and by the more elevated ones of Sumatra, with the exception of its eastern side, and even this is exposed only to the north-eastern monsoon. Every where else, and at all seasons, land and sea-breezes, calms and variable winds, prevail, interrupted to the north by occasional squalls from the north-west, and throughout by heavier ones from the south-west, not exceeding an hour or two's continuance, known to mariners from the direction from which they blow as "Sumatras."

At Penang, in latitude 5° 15′ north, the mean annual temperature, at the level of the sea, is nearly 80°, and the mean range from 70° to 90°. At the height of 2410 feet, the mean of the year is 70°, and the range 10°, from which we may infer that the average temperature of the year at the highest elevation of the peninsula, Mount Ophir, is rather less than 40°. The average number of rainy days in the year is 182; a rainy season being but indistinctly marked. Heavy dews fall in all clear nights throughout the year, and fogs, although not dense ones, are frequent, especially during the most rainy season. At Malacca, in latitude 2° 14′, the mean temperature of the year is 80°, and the range 15°. At Singapore, in latitude 1° 17′, the average heat of the year is 82°, and the range from 68° to 92°. The fall of rain here is frequent, generally every third day, although a continuous drought of ten or fourteen days occasionally occurs. A rainy season is scarcely distinguishable. Generally, the climate of the peninsula, notwithstanding its heat and moisture, is not insalubrious, although a few ill-ventilated spots here and there occur with most pestiferous malaria.

With the exception of a few nomad negritos in the mountains of the northern portion of the peninsula, the Sâmang of the natives, the whole of the inhabitants of the peninsula, not strangers, are of the Malay race and speak the Malay language. Besides the settled and cultivated Malays, they consist of land, river, and sea nomads. The first practise a rude agriculture, and have dwellings of some permanency: the second live on fish, and wild roots, dwelling entirely in their boats without quitting the rivers; and the third are the sea-gypsies, who rove over the whole archipelago. The two first classes are divided into many small tribes, frequently designated by the names of the localities which they chiefly frequent. The names of at least a dozen of these tribes have been given by Mr. Logan and others, such as Jakun, Udai, Sakai, Bâsisi, Sabimba, Mintira, &c. For an example of the manners and condition of these rude people generally, I shall transcribe the very graphic and well-written account of a river-tribe given by Mr. J. D. Thomson, in an article in the "Journal of the Archipelago." This tribe takes its name, Saletar, from a creek in the island of Singapore, on the narrow strait which divides it from the main land, not above eight miles distant from the flourishing and civilised British emporium. Its numbers are about 200, living in forty boats or canoes, and their range in quest of subsistence does not exceed thirty square miles. "Their language," says Mr. Thomson, "is the Malayan, and considerable pains were taken to elicit any words foreign to that language, but without success. As a proof of their possessing the same language as the Malays, I may mention that the children were heard, when playing, to converse in this language, and were perfectly understood by the Malays amongst our crew. They are possessed of no weapons, either offensive or defensive. Their minds do not find a higher range than necessity compels; the satisfying of hunger is their only pursuit. Of water they have abundance without search. With the sârkab, or fish-spear, and the parang, or chopper, as their only implements, they eke out a miserable existence from the stores of the rivers and forests. They neither dig nor plant, and yet live, nearly independent of their fellow men; for to them, the staple of life in the East, rice, is a luxury. Tobacco they procure by the barter of fish, and a few marketables collected from the forests and coral reefs. Of esculent roots, they have the prioh and kalana, both bulbous, and not unlike coarse yams. Of fruits, they eat the tampüi, kledang, and buroh, when they come in season; and of animals, they hunt the wild hog, but refrain from snakes, dogs, iguanas, and monkeys. On their manners and customs I must need be short, as only long acquaintance with their prejudices and domestic feelings, could afford a clue to the impulse of their actions. Of a Creator, they have not the slightest comprehension, a fact so difficult to believe, when we find that the most degraded of the human race, in other quarters of the globe, have an intuitive idea of this unerring and primary truth imprinted on their minds, that I took the greatest care to find a slight image of the deity within the chaos of their thoughts, however degraded such might be, but was disappointed. They know neither the god or the devil of the Christians or Mahommedans, although they confessed they had been told of such; nor any of the demi-gods of Hindu mythology, many of whom were recounted to them. In the three great epochs of their individual life, we consequently find no rites or ceremonies enacted. At birth, the child is only welcomed to the world by the mother's joy: at marriage, a mouthful of tobacco and one chupah (gallon) handed to one another confirm the hymeneal tye: at death, the deceased are wrapped in their garments, and committed to the parent earth. 'The women weep a little, and then leave the spot,' were the words of our simple narrator. Of pâris, dewas, mâmbangs, and other light spirits that haunt each mountain, rock, and tree, in the Malayan imagination, they did not know the names, nor had they anything to be afraid of, as they themselves said, than 'the pirates of Galang,' who are men like themselves. With this I was forced to be contented, and teased them no more on the subject. They do not practise circumcision, nor any other Mahommedan rite. Their women intermarry with the Malays, which appears not to be unfrequent: they also give their women to the Chinese; and an old woman told us of her having been united to individuals of both nations at an early period of her life. Their tribe, though confining its range within the limits of 30 square miles, may still be considered of a very wandering kind. In their sampans (canoes), barely sufficient to float their loads, they skirt the mangroves collecting their food from the shores and forests as they proceed, exhausting one spot and then searching for another. To one accustomed to the comforts and artificial wants of civilised life, theirs, as a contrast, appears to be extreme. Huddled up in a small boat hardly measuring 20 feet in length, they find all the domestic comfort they are in want of. At one end is seen the fire-place: in the middle are the few utensils they may be in possession of, and at the other end beneath a mat, not exceeding six feet in length, is found the sleeping apartment of a family, often counting five or six, together with a cat and a dog. Under this, they find shelter from the dews and rains of the night, and heat of the day. Even the Malays, in pointing out these stinted quarters, cried out 'how miserable!' But of this the objects of their consideration were not aware. In them they have provided for all their wants. Their children sport on the shore in search of shell-fish at low water; and during high water, they may be seen climbing the mangrove branches, and dashing from thence into the water with all the life and energy of children of a colder clime, at once affording us proof that even they have their joys. The personal appearance of these people is unprepossessing, and their deportment lazy and slovenly, united to much filthiness of person. The middle portion of the body of men and women is generally covered by a coarse wrapper made from the bark of the trap tree (a species of Artocarpus), which extends from the navel to the knee. The women affected a slight degree of modesty at first approach, which soon gave way. The locks of the men are bound up with a tie of cloth, and sometimes by the Malay sapu-tangan (kerchief); those of the women fall in wild luxuriance over their face and shoulders. Their children go entirely naked until the age of puberty."

The same intelligent writer gives an account of a tribe of forest nomads, called Sabimba, in a still more miserable condition, and whose numbers did not exceed eighty persons. With respect to the origin of these wild tribes, so justly called half-savages near 350 years ago by the early Portuguese writers, he observes, "As I before stated, they speak the language of the Malays with much less difference in pronunciation than may be found in our own tongue in stepping from one county of England to another. They may, therefore, be said, with little fear of contradiction, to be merely unconverted Malays, properly so called." The epithet "uncivilised" would probably be better than unconverted, and with this slight alteration, the conclusion at which Mr. Thomson has arrived seems to me inevitable. Mr. Logan, however, whose opinion on such a subject is entitled to great respect, thinks that the Bânua, or aboriginal inhabitants of the peninsula, once spoke a distinct language of their own, superseded through their long intercourse with the Malays; and he draws this inference from their speech, being rude and ungrammatical in sound and structure, and its containing words no longer known to the present Malay language. It is no doubt possible that the Aborigines may have had a language of their own, but the probability is much against it. Similar arguments might be adduced against the universality of our own Anglo-Saxon tongue over England, for the mass of our people speak it rudely and ungrammatically; while many words are in common use in different parts of the country which have long ceased to be considered as part of the English language. The case of Borneo is against Mr. Logan's hypothesis. In the interior of that island, of which the coasts, like those of the peninsula, are occupied by Malay settlements, it is not one but many tongues that are spoken by the aboriginal inhabitants; and in the few instances in which these tribes, to the supersession of their own, have adopted the Malay language, it has happened in consequence of the parties having adopted the religion, manners, and habits of the Malays, which the rude inhabitants of the peninsula have not done.

The states of the civilised Malays on the western side of the peninsula amount to three, or if we include the British territory of Malacca, of which the bulk of the inhabitants are Malays, four, namely, Queda, Perak, Salangor, and Malacca. Those on the eastern side amount to four, namely, Patani, Kalantan, Tringano, and Pahang. Towards the extremity of the peninsula, both the eastern and western sides, and all the islands adjacent to them, except those in possession of the European governments, form the principality of Jehore. In the interior, and between the second and third degrees of latitude, we have the three small states of Rumbao, Jehole, and Jompol. The actual population of all these states is unknown, but it is well ascertained to be very small, and conjectured, excluding the wild inhabitants and those of the British and Dutch territors, not to exceed 200,000, which would give between four and five inhabitants to the square mile. The British possessions in the same country, the oldest of which is not above seventy years standing, contain at present not less than a quarter of a million of inhabitants, or about 250 inhabitants to every square mile, a striking example of the different effects resulting from barbarism and civilisation.

MALÁWAR. The name of a mountain of Java, in the country of the Sundas, one of the chain which bounds the plain of Bandong to the south. It rises to the height of 7500 feet above the level of the sea, but has no active volcano.

MÂMPAWA. The name of a Malay State, on the western side of Borneo, the chief town of which, of the same name, is situated on a small river, twenty-five miles north of the equator, and in east longitude 109° 15′. The territory is tributary to the Netherland Government, and forms a portion of its "Residency of the West coast." Of its extent and population no account has been given. The inhabitants consist of Malays, Dyaks, and Chinese.

MAN. For the generic name Man, or human being, the term seems to be derived, in all the languages of the Malay Archipelago, either from the Javanese wong, as in the example of the Malay, where we find it as orang, or from the Sanscrit, as in the case of the Balinese, where it is jana, corrupted into janma and jalma. In our inadequate knowledge, it is very difficult to determine the varieties of the human race that exist within the Malay and Philippine Archipelagos, but I imagine they are not fewer than five, that number into which some writers on the natural history of Man would fain compress all the inhabitants of the earth. These are the race of which the Malay nation is the type; the Sâmang, or dwarf negros of the Malay peninsula; the Negritos, or Aetas of the Philippines; the large negros or Papuas of New Guinea, and a race intermediate between these last and the Malayan, which may be called the Negro-Malay. Some account of all these will be found under their respective heads, or under the title Archipelago.

The tribes of which the first enumerated race consist, although living in climates very similar, are found to be in very different states of social existence, some not rising above the level of the rudest savages of America, while others have attained a civilisation far exceeding that of any nation of that continent at the time of its discovery. A few remarks on the causes which have conduced to this disparity will not be without interest. The question of race may be soon dismissed. Whatever is entitled to be called civilisation has originated with the brown, lank-haired, or Malay race; and the woolly-haired, whether the pigmy negritos of the Malay Peninsula and the Philippines, or the stouter Papuans of New Guinea and its adjoining islands, have risen little beyond the condition of mere savages. Wherever the Negro comes into collision with the Malayan race, as in some of the Philippine Islands, it seems to retreat, much as wild animals retreat before man, and appears to be saved from utter destruction only by seeking shelter in the recesses of inaccessible mountains. Even in New Guinea and its adjacent islands, where a more vigorous negro race has the whole land to itself, the progress which it has made is hardly equal to that of the rudest of the Malay under the least favourable auspices.

Although there be several subsidiary causes to be subsequently noticed, which have contributed to the disparity of civilisation which is found to prevail among the several tribes and nations of the Malay race, the most material are certainly, differences in the quality of the localities they happen to occupy. Wherever the soil is fertile, irrigation easily practised, and the land not encumbered with heavy timber, an indigenous and independent civilisation will be found everywhere to have sprung up, and where these conditions are absent, we are sure to encounter rudeness and barbarism. A rapid survey of the condition of society in the various parts of the two Archipelagos will afford ample evidence of the truth of these positions. The invention or possession of phonetic writing may be considered a fair criterion of civilisation, and density of population evidence of the relative extent to which it has been carried.

We have an example of the highest civilisation which has ben reached in the Indian islands, in the cases of Java and the three islands adjacent to it, Madura, Bali, and Lomboc. These have a volcanic soil of great fertility, a perennial irrigation easy and abundant, with plains and valleys unencumbered with heavy forest. Immemorially they have possessed the art of writing, and although embracing less than one-tenth part of the Archipelago, they contain full seven-tenths of its whole population, and this, too, without any admixture of the rude and wandering tribes to be found in all other parts of it.

Even in these islands, however, where civilisation has attained its highest point, the degree of it is not equal throughout, the amount being in proportion to the causes which gave rise to it. Thus, in the western mountainous part of Java, the country of the Sundas, the soil is less fertile, and the facilities for irrigation fewer than in the central and eastern portions of the island, and hence an inferior civilisation, and as usual in such cases, a smaller density of population. The island of Madura, although so close to Java, is much inferior to it in soil, and still more so in capacity for irrigation. Its social condition is consequently inferior to that of Java, and much of its civilisation has palpably been derived from the larger island. This observation applies, also, to the islands of Bali and Lomboc, although in a lesser degree. In all the three islands we discover, in language, writing, manner and religion, ample evidence of their obligations to Java.

Mere fertility of soil, unaccompanied by capacity for easy irrigation, is not sufficient for the production of any considerable amount of civilisation. The island of Sumbawa forms part of the same volcanic chain as the three last-named islands, and is separated from the most easterly of them only by a narrow strait. Yet, wanting a copious irrigation, its inhabitants are in a ruder state, than those of the islands above mentioned, some of them, indeed, little better than savages. Its area is nearly double that of Bali and Lomboc united, and yet its population is little more than one-fourth that of these two islands.

The Malay Peninsula has, perhaps, the most stubborn and intractable soil of all the large countries of the Archipelago. Its geological formation is exclusively sedimentary, plutonic, and alluvial, and it is destitute of any peculiar facilities of irrigation. It is rich in tin, iron, and even gold, but its soil is either sterile or stubborn. The consequence is that its mountains, valleys, and plains are, with the exception of a few patches, covered with a stupendous primeval forest. Its inhabitants throughout are of the Malay nation, with the exception of a few pigmy negros. Many of these inhabitants are still in the rude condition of mere nomads, and even the strangers who have settled in it hold no very respectable position in the social scale. No indigenous writing has ever originated in it. The Peninsula, in its widest extent, is better than double the size of Java, but certainly does not contain one-fortieth part of its population.

Sumatra, in respect to its capacity to generate civilisation, may be considered in a condition intermediate between the Peninsula and Java. The greater portion of it consists of sedimentary and plutonic formations, with an extensive alluvial tract, but a small part of it also is of volcanic formation, and well watered. Much of the island is still covered by a rank primeval forest embracing nearly the whole of the great alluvial plain which covers one side of it nearly from one extremity to the other. Five different indigenous civilisations have sprung up in this island, by far the most remarkable of which is that of the Malay nation, and this had its origin in the well-watered volcanic portion. The lowest civilisation is that of the Bataks, who have invented phonetic writing, but are, at the same time, occasional cannibals. These occupy some of the poorest of the plains and table-lands of the interior. The inhabitants of the great alluvial plain of the eastern side of the island are little better than fishermen, with the predatory habits and other vices of a nomadic state of society. The mere obstruction of the forest seems to have hindered them from advancing beyond this condition. Sumatra is about three and a-half times the extent of Java, but does not contain probably above one-fifth part of its population, and much of this, too, in the very rudest state.

Many of the islands on the western side of Sumatra afford striking illustrations of the position which I am endeavouring to establish. Thus, the island of Nias has a fertile and well-watered soil, and the result is a peaceable agricultural population of 200,000, while the other islands in its neighbourhood are for the most part still covered with forest, and have a rude or savage population, not estimated at above one-twentieth part of that number. Even the large island of Banca, rich in iron and tin, but poor in soil, and destitute of perennial irrigation, has a native population not exceeding one-tenth part of that of the small island of Nias, and this population, too, a very abject one.

Borneo, so far as it is known, is destitute of volcanic formation, and composed of sedimentary, plutonic, and alluvial formations. It is rich in minerals, such as gold, iron, antimony, and coal, but either of a poor or a stubborn soil, and with few exceptions covered by a forest unsurmountable by a rude infantine labour. It has, consequently, never produced an indigenous civilisation like the civilisations of Java and Sumatra, the whole of its native inhabitants being, up to the present time, sheer savages, while even its foreign settlers have made no material advancement since their first establishment. It is between five and six times the extent of Java, but its estimated population certainly not one-tenth part, to say nothing of the rudeness of the one and the civilisation of the other. It seems probable that the vast solid mass of Borneo, unbroken by deep bays or inlets which would afford facilities for intercommunication, have contributed, with its stubbornness of soil, its want of easy irrigation, and its unconquerable forests, to hinder the development of that civilisation which has sprung up at so many other points in several of the other large islands.

The civilisation of Celebes is of a much higher order than that of Borneo, and this it owes to its superior fertility, and in some degree, no doubt, to its form, deeply indented by large bays, so as to make it to consist of several peninsulas. With the exception of a small portion of the extremity of its northern peninsula, which is volcanic, the formation everywhere else is sedimentary, plutonic, or alluvial. The civilisation of Celebes is confined to its south-western, and seemingly most fertile peninsula, and to this is confined the invention and use of written language, the party with which it originated being the people speaking the Wugi or Bugis language. Most of the rest of the island is inhabited by rude tribes, the greater number, indeed, as rude as those of Borneo. Celebes is by one-half larger than Java, but is not supposed to contain above one-seventh part of its population. But, on the other hand, it is only between one-third and one-fourth the extent of Borneo, while it is computed to have double its population. The race, the Malayan, is one and the same in the three islands.

The two considerable islands of Floris and Timur afford curious illustrations, not only of the effects on social progress, of soil and water, but also of race, for they are inhabited, not by a Malay or Negro race, but by an intermediate one,—that with brown complexion and frizzled but not woolly hair growing in tufts. Floris is of the same volcanic formation as Java, Bali, and Lomboc, but seemingly without their capacity for irrigation. Its native inhabitants are in a very rude state, divided into independent tribes speaking different languages, who have neither invented nor adopted written language. It is about two and a-half times the size of the civilised island of Bali, but its computed population is about one-thirtieth part.

The large island of Timur is destitute of all trace of volcanic formation, and has a soil eminently sterile, and no mountains of sufficient elevation to secure a perennial supply of water for irrigation. In physical configuration and natural productions, it has, in fact, more the character of an Australian tropical than of a Malayan country. Its inhabitants are in a very rude state, and divided into innumerable petty tribes, speaking many different languages. They have neither invented letters themselves, nor adopted foreign ones. Timur is almost six times the extent of Bali, and is thought not to have above one-seventh part of its population.

If we turn to the Philippine Archipelago, we shall find ample confirmation of the proposition, that fertility of soil and ready means of irrigation are the causes which have given rise to an indigenous civilisation. The geological formation of the most remarkable of the islands, as for example, that of Luzon, is partly sedimentary and plutonic, and partly volcanic, none of them being like Java, entirely volcanic. It is in these only that any considerable amount of civilisation has sprung up, all those destitute of volcanic formation being inhabited by tribes in the very infancy of society. The climate of the Philippines, more rude and tempestuous than that of the Malayan Archipelago, is probably less favourable to the production of an early indigenous civilisation. About ten different nations of the Philippines may be stated to have acquired some degree of civilisation when they were first seen by Europeans, while a far greater number, both of the Malay and Negrito race were, and some still continue to be, in the condition of savages. Alphabetic writing, instead of having been invented at many points, as in the Malayan Archipelago, was invented at one only in the Philippine, and even this of a far ruder description than the most imperfect of the Malayan alphabets.

Civilisation in the Philippines themselves is proportioned to fertility of soil and means of irrigation. Luzon, in which letters were invented, stands highest, and is followed by

Panay, Çebu, Negros, Samar, and Leyte. But close to the great and fertile island of Luzon, and parted from it only by a narrow channel, is that of Mindoro, mountainous, destitute of volcanic formation, and sterile. Its most advanced inhabitants are fugitives or other settlers from Luzon, its own inhabitants consisting of squalid savages. Between Luzon and Mindoro lies the small but fertile island of Marinduque, which in fact forms part of the province of Mindoro. It is about one-eighth part of the size of Mindoro, but has an industrious and docile population of double its amount. The great island of Mindano is partly of sedimentary and plutonic and partly of volcanic formation. The northern portion of it seems generally sterile, but parts of the southern are fertile, and in these have sprung up the Mindano and Lanun nations, who have attained a considerable amount of civilisation, while the sterile southern portion is inhabited by innumerable very rude tribes. The large island of Palawan is wholly of sedimentary and plutonic formation, and eminently sterile, and the consequence is, that all its inhabitants are even in a more abject condition than the Dayaks of Borneo.

One fact is certain, whether as regards the Philippine or Malayan Archipelago, that no considerable indigenous and independent civilisation has ever originated in a small island; and independent of the sterility, which is their normal condition, the reason seems obviously to be, that they afforded no room for the growth of a nation of sufficient strength to secure its own independence, and hence to afford the security and leisure indispensable to the pursuit of the arts of peace. It is only in the large and fertile islands of Sumatra, Java, Celebes, and Luzon, that phonetic writing, the highest proof of advancement, has been invented. Many of the smaller islands of both Archipelagos are not even inhabited at all, and some very considerable ones, on account of their sterility, are peopled only by rude tribes, as Gilolo, Boeroe, Ceram, and several of the islands between the Malay peninsula and Sumatra, which included Singapore before it was occupied by ourselves.

The subsidiary or accessory causes which contributed to raise the indigenous civilisations to the point to which they had reached on the arrival of Europeans, were, the possession of iron, of cereal corn, of the larger domesticated animals, and intercourse or intermixture with strangers more civilised than the natives. Without the possession of iron no nation of the Malay or Philippine Archipelago has attained any respectable amount of civilisation. All of the nations that have possessed the art of phonetic writing, have also possessed a knowledge of this metal. The same may be said of bread-corn, in this case rice, which in these regions has the same rank with wheat in temperate ones. It is the universal bread of all the civilised nations from Sumatra to Celebes and Luzon. Those tribes that live on sago, which embraces the wide region east of Celebes, including New Guinea, are either illiterate, or rude and savage, whether belonging to the Malay or Negro race. The cause is obvious. Sago is produced with little labour, and this of the rudest description: it is for the countries in which it grows the lowest quality of farinaceous food on which man can subsist; it has little exchangeable value, and holds out no inducement to its consumers to ameliorate their condition by the practice of economy. The yam, the batata, the banana, and the bread-fruit labour under similar disadvantages.

The possession of the larger domesticated animals, seems equally indispensable as iron and cereal corn to civilisation. All the nations, therefore, which were found in a state of considerable advancement,—all that had attained the art of writing, were found in possession either of the ox or buffalo, or both. Some of the natives of Sumatra were found in possession of the buffalo only, and such was the case also, even with the most civilised of those of the Philippine Islands; but the Malays and Javanese were in possession of both these animals, and even of the horse. The rude and unlettered tribes, on the contrary,—the consumers of sago or of farinaceous roots, were like the inhabitants of the South-Sea Islands in possession only of the hog and dog, and therefore without any animals adapted for labour.

Intercommunication with strangers, although not the primary cause of the civilisations of the two Archipelagos, contributed largely to increase them. The communication in these cases was effected not by invasion and conquest, but by commercial intercourse and partial settlement. The earliest strangers who contributed to the civilisation of the Indian islanders, of which we have any evidence, were the Hindus, and the extent of their influence is testified by language, religion, architectural monuments and inscriptions. Java was the chief seat of this influence, the popular language of which contains in 1000 words, full 120 which belong to the languages of the Hindus. Religion and Commerce were the principal channels through which this influence was exercised. Thus we find the following religious terms to be Sanscrit,—a god or deity, religion, prayer, heaven, infernal region, to which many others of the same class might be added. In this class may be included terms connected with the kalendar, and even a well-known Hindu epoch. Of commercial terms, we find such words as price, profit, capital, ship, and emporium, to be all of Hindu origin, while the names of such objects as copper, quicksilver, sugar, black-pepper, cotton, silk, indigo, camphor, aloes-wood, nutmeg, pearl, and pearl-oyster, have a similar origin.

The other foreigners who have contributed to promote the civilisation of the Indian islanders, are the Arabs and other nations of Western Asia, converted by them. The effects produced by these have been, not through the medium of the Javanese, but of the Malays, whose language contains a far larger proportion of Arabic than any other of the Archipelago. This nation indeed has even adopted the written character of the Arabs to the abandonment of its own, and has been the chief instrument in propagating the Mahometan religion among the other nations and tribes.

But the Malays and Javanese stood themselves in the relation of strangers to all the other nations of the two Archipelagos, and communicated to them, according to their opportunities, more or less of the civilisation which they had themselves attained, whether native or derived from foreign sources. It was through them, and not by direct intercourse with Hindus or Arabs, that Hindu and Arabian improvement was communicated to the other tribes. This is testified by the Hindu and Arabic words found in their languages being always the same,—by these being used in the same sense, although differing from their original meanings in Sanscrit and Arabic, to the extent even of copying errors, and by the proportion of such foreign words diminishing in proportion to distance from Java and Sumatra. Thus in the case of the Sanscrit language, while in the popular tongue of Java there are in 1000 words about 120, in the principal language of Celebes, there are but 17, and in that of Luzon 2. Beyond this they disappear altogether.

But the greatest improvement which has been imparted by the Malays and Javanese to the other nations, has been derived from their own native resources. This is proved by an examination of language, from which it will be seen that the proportion of Malay and Javanese is always largest in the neighbourhood of Sumatra and Java, and is constantly decreasing as we increase our distance from them. The degree in which imitation as to the form or meaning of words obtains holds the same proportion. Thus, in the language of Bali there are in 1000 words, 470 that are Malay and Javanese; in the principal language of Celebes only 226; while in the chief tongue of Luzon, the number falls as low as 22.

Among the words communicated by the Malays and Javanese to less civilised tribes are the numerals; some terms connected with the kalendar, as year and month; the names of the domesticated animals, as of the hog and buffalo; of cultivated plants, as rice and the yam; of all the metals, except gold; of utensils and weapons, and terms connected with trade. These observations apply more especially to the more cultivated languages of Celebes and of the Philippines, and show the extent to which the people speaking them are indebted to the civilisations of the Malays and Javanese.

Tribes less civilised than those just referred to, have received into their languages similar, although smaller infusions, of the languages of the Malays and Javanese, the influence of which have even penetrated to the languages of the South Sea Islands, and to the language of Madagascar. Thus, we have in the Polynesian dialects, the numerals, the names of the coco-palm, of the sugar-cane, of the yam, and of the Taro or Caladium esculentum. But the names of the domesticated animals of the South-Sea islanders are not to be traced to the Malayan languages, nor had any of the metals known to the Malayan nations reached the Polynesian. Indeed, the proportion of Malayan words in the Polynesian languages, does not at the utmost exceed 20 in 1000.

In the language of remote Madagascar, we find the names of four cultivated plants to be Malayan, namely, rice, the coco-palm, the yam, and capsicum pepper; but the names of the domesticated animals have not this source; and iron is the only metal bearing a Malayan name. The proportion of Malayan words, the minerals included, is nearly the same in the Malagasi as in the Polynesian languages. These facts have been stated elsewhere, but for convenience are here repeated.

Two examples of the direct effect of the commercial intercourse of strangers in civilising the people of the Archipelago deserve to be specially quoted, namely, Malacca and the Molucca islands. The first of these, although established in a barren land, which drew all its supplies of food from what was a remote country to its semi-barbarous inhabitants, Java, yet became from its central position, and by sheer virtue of commerce, one of the first commercial emporia of the Indies. For this fact we have the unvarying testimony of the Portuguese, previously acquainted with Calicut and the other emporia of Western India. The progress made by the petty Moluccas was equally striking. They consisted of fine islets of barren land, incapable of producing corn, and without a neighbourhood to yield any. Notwithstanding, from the mere accident of their producing, and almost exclusively, the article of cloves, a spice in demand by remote nations, their inhabitants became numerous and had attained a considerable amount of civilisation. Although their own islands were but mere specks on the coast of Gilolo, they had conquered and were masters of that large island. They were even lords of a portion of Celebes, and of part of New Guinea, and its adjacent islands. Both in the Moluccas and Philippines, it should not be forgotten that on the first arrival of Europeans the Malay language had obtained, in the course of a long commercial intercourse, such a footing that it was the common medium of communication, being preferred for this to any of the native tongues.

From the facts now stated, it will appear that the causes which have contributed to the advancement or retardment of civilisation in the Indian islands, have been mainly the same as in other parts of the world. Wherever the conditions have been propitious, indigenous civilisations have spontaneously sprung up, in a degree proportioned to their favourableness. An indigenous civilisation sprang up in the rich valleys and plains of Java, just as it had done in the valleys of the Nile, the Assyrian rivers, the Ganges, and the great rivers of China. What then, it may be asked, hindered civilisation in Java from attaining the same maturity as in these localities—for that it never did so is unquestionable? The solution will probably be found in the inferior intellectual capacity of the races occupying the Malayan Archipelago, for it is difficult to find any other. Even among the insular races themselves, there exists the greatest disparity in the progress they have made. Not one of the tribes belonging to any of the woolly-haired races have gone beyond the condition of naked savages, and whatever of civilisation is found is confined to the lank-haired or Malayan race. Even the highest degree of this is far below that of the ancient Egyptians or Assyrians, of the Hindus or of the Chinese, all of them people who had been over-ran, subdued, and domineered over by foreign conquerors, a disadvantage to which neither Malays nor Javanese had ever been subjected. The close resemblance in physical geography between the Malay Archipelago and Greece and Italy, will probably occur to the reader. The soil is equally fertile; the climate, for those born to it, alike temperate and healthy; and the seas even more tranquil and easy of navigation. Neither is there the smallest ground for imagining that the one country was more early occupied than the other. To what cause, then, but difference of race, can it be ascribed that Greeks and Italians had attained to a far higher civilisation five hundred years before the Christian era, than the most advanced of the Malayan nations had done two thousand years later, when they were first observed by Europeans?

MANA, or MANNA, correctly Manak. This is the name of a district on the south-western side of Sumatra, the town of the same name lying in south latitude 5° 30′. The district is described as the best cultivated and most populous of the western side of Sumatra, which Mr. Marsden ascribes to the pressure of necessity, arising from the exhaustion of the pepper-lands. Its superiority, however, is more likely to proceed from the fertility of its soil, or, which is nearly the same thing, facility of irrigation. The mountains Patak and Dompo, respectively 5250 and 10,000 feet high, lie in its neighbourhood inland, and the volcanic soil and abundant water, which cause its fertility, are most probably derived from these.

MANCHANÂGARA. A name given by the princes of Java to the provinces of their dominions lying at a distance from their capitals. The name taken from the Sanscrit signifies literally "far lands," that is, districts remote from the capital.

MÂNDANG-KAMOLAN. The name of an ancient kingdom of Java, in the present province of Mataram. Tradition states that four princes reigned in this country, and the most probable account assigns its foundation to the year of Salivana 658, or of Christ 736.

MANDHAR. The name of a country of Celebes, forming the most southern portion of the main body or nucleus of the island, and terminating in a Cape bearing the same name, which is in south latitude 3° 35′ and east longitude 119°. To the north Mandhar is bounded by Kaili, to the east by the Bugis countries of Masenreng and Pulu, and to the west by the broad channel which divides Celebes from Borneo.

The country is hilly, without, however, any mountain of considerable elevation. The soil, judging by its productions, is sterile. It produces no rice, its principal products being maiz, the coco-palm, and cotton. Its exports are coco-nuts and their oil, with cotton cloths, but no gold, which is exported from the neighbouring country of Kaili. The inhabitants of Mandhar are a distinct nation, speaking a language peculiar to themselves. Those of the sea-board have been converted to the Mahommedan religion, but many of those of the interior are still pagans. The chief food is maiz and the banana, the last eaten fresh after being roasted.

MANDUR, or correctly Tumandur, is the name of a district on the western side of Borneo, and situated on an affluent of the Kapuwas, or river which falls into the sea below Pontianak. The town or village lies about 15 miles north of the equator, and in east longitude 109° 20′. Mandur is a principal station of the Chinese gold-diggers, and forms part of the Dutch "Residency of the western coast" of Borneo.

MANGARAI. This is the name of a place of trade on the northern side of Floris, and that by which the whole island is generally designated by the Malays and Bugis.

MANGO, the Mangifera Indica of botanists, is at present cultivated by all the civilised inhabitants of the Indian Islands, and is of as many varieties as in Europe, the pear or apple. As is the case with most other fruits, the mangostin and durian excepted, the fruit varies in quality as widely as a crab-apple from a New Jersey pippin. The finest sorts are an excellent fruit, and the ordinary kinds a very indifferent one. The name mango, or correctly mangga, is not Malay, but Sunda, and in this language, only that of a wild species of the same genus. Our early traders took the word from Bantam, which is in the country of the Sunda nation. Although several species of Mangifera are found in the Indian Islands, the cultivated mango cannot be traced to any of them, and is, most probably, an exotic introduced from the continent of India. This is to be inferred from its names, which are generally corruptions or abbreviations of the Sanscrit, maha-pahala, or, according to the Telingas, maha-pahalam, that is, "the great fruit." Thus, in Malay, it is mâmpâlâm, in Javanese, pâlâm, and in Lampung, kapâlâm. Into many of the islands it was certainly introduced by Europeans. Thus, Rumphius tells us, that it was unknown in the Moluccas, until introduced by the Dutch in 1655. Pigafetta makes no mention of its existence in the Philippines in 1521, but it is now abundant, and known only by the adopted name of Europeans, manga. The same may be said of the remote island of Madagascar, where its name is the same.

MANGOSTIN. This famed fruit is the first in rank of all tropical fruits, in the opinion of Europeans, but second only to the durian in that of the natives of the Archipelago. The plant which produces it is about the size of a cherry-tree, very handsome, and one of a score of the genus Garcinia of botanists, that which yields gamboge being one of the number. To none of these, however, is the cultivated mangostin traced as the parent stock. In Malay, the name of the tree and fruit is manggusta, from whence the European name. In Javanese it is manggis, and in the languages of all the other countries of the Archipelago in which it is found, it has either this name or a modification of it. Thus in Bali it is manggis, in Sunda, mangu, in Lampung, manggos, and in Bugis, manggisi. Even in Siamese, the name is the Malay one. The mangostin, in suitable situations, grows in perfection, as far as 14° north of the equator, and 7° south of it. On the shores of the Bay of Bengal, the tree will not bear fruit further north than the 14° of latitude, but in the inland country of Siam, I was assured that it bore as far north as between the 16° and 17° degrees. At Bangkok, in Siam, in 13° north latitude, I found the fruit equally good and abundant as in Batavia in 6° south latitude. All attempts to propagate it on the continent of India have failed: it has partially succeeded in Ceylon, but not in any of the West India Islands. The only one of the Philippines in which it will produce fruit is the most southerly, Mindano, where also its constant companion, the durian, is grown. Even here, however, the mangostin must have been of comparatively very recent introduction, for Dampier, who visited the island in 1685, in giving an account of its cultivated plants, although he names and describes the durian, takes no notice of the mangostin which he so full and accurately describes in his account of Achin. A congenial proportion of heat and moisture throughout the year, seems much more requisite for the successful growth of this fruit, than soil or latitude, since we see it thrive equally well in the volcanic soil of Java, the stiff clays of Malacca, and the deep rich alluvion of the valley of the Menam in Siam, and over a range of, at least, fourteen degrees from the equator. In suitable localities, the fruit grows with little skill or care: it does not sport into varieties like many other cultivated plants, and when grown at all the fruit is always nearly equally good.

MANGROVE, the Rhizophora of botanists. The generic name of this tree in Malay is manggi-manggi, from which is probably taken our popular one, as well as the trivial one of mangil used by botanists. One species of it goes under the name of kayu-api-api, literally fire-wood, from its being used as fuel. This is the Rhizofera gymnorhiza. The bark of the common or black mangrove, Rhizofera mangil, is used in tanning, and the wood of one species for giving a red dye. The tree forms a striking feature in the physical geography of the Archipelago, as it does, indeed, of all tropical countries, for a belt of it, as deep as the reach of the tide, is always found wherever there is a shallow and muddy shore. The tree which rises to the height of forty or fifty feet is invariably found in such situations, constituting a dense, and almost impenetrable, forest. Each tree stands on a cradle of its own roots from five or six feet high, bare at low water, but at high water covered so as to give the appearance of trees growing in the sea. The mangrove jungle is the favourite resort of mosquitos and alligators, and affords a convenient and almost inaccessible retreat to the pirate.

MANILLA. The capital of the Philippines is the most ancient European town in India, after Goa, and the largest, after Calcutta, Madras and Bombay. It is situated on the eastern side of the spacious bay of the same name in the island of Luzon in latitude 14° 36′ north, and longitude 120° 52′ east. It lies at the mouth of the small but rapid river, the Pasig, which after a course of thirty miles, discharges into the sea the waters of the great lake of Bay. The city of Manilla consists of two parts, a fortified town lying on the south or left bank of the river, and of suburbs on the north or right bank, connected by a narrow but neat stone bridge of ten arches, about 200 Spanish fathoms in length. The circumference of the fortified town which has the form of an irregular triangle, of which the sea forms one side, the land a second, and the river the third, is 1234 Spanish fathoms, or 2288 English yards. The walls are of solid masonry, and on the land and sea faces, have bastions with embrasures, and a deep, broad ditch, double on the land side. On the river side, there is but a curtain with a few weak bastions in barbette, while the river, not above two hundred fathoms broad, has its opposite bank lined with houses of solid masonry, giving abundant shelter to an assailant. It has six gates, two to each face, all furnished with draw-bridges, except one. The principal fortification is strengthened by several out-works, the chief of which is the fort of San Ignacio at the mouth of the river, and forming the north-western angle of the works. The river, which forms the fosse on the northern side of the fortifications, has a bar at its mouth, on which, at spring tides, there is a depth of 10 or 11 feet. Besides the weakness of the fortifications on the river face, it is to be observed that the largest ships of the line have sufficient depth of water to come within two miles of them, and frigates within a mile. Manilla, therefore, although impregnable against a native power, is defenceless against an European one having the command of the sea.

The walled town or city consists of eight straight narrow streets, running in one direction, with an equal number at right angles to them, and one small square. Within its precincts are contained all the public buildings, such as the palaces of the governor-general and archbishop, the town-house, the court of justice, the cathedral, the arsenal, and the military barracks. The total population within the walls is estimated at from 10,000 to 12,000.

The mass of the population is in the suburbs, and these are reckoned to have 130,000 inhabitants. The warehouses, shops, and manufactures, are all in these, and all strangers reside in them. Outside the walls on the land side, there is a handsome promenade consisting of an avenue of trees. In the same direction there is a spacious and handsome burying-ground for the Catholic population, the most meritorious public work of Manilla. Churches and convents abound, and it is thought that one-third part of the area within the walls is occupied by the latter.

Manilla has more the character of an European town than any in India, but is by no means distinguished for the beauty of its architecture. The most remarkable building is the cathedral, equally distinguished for the ugliness of its exterior, and the gorgeous richness of its inside. The original building was erected by Legaspi, the conqueror of Luzon, and no time assuredly was lost by him, for this happened in 1571, the very year of the conquest. His original rude structure was of bamboo, thatched with palmetto leaf. Within seven years of its erection, the church was raised to the dignity of a cathedral by Pope Gregory the 13th, on the petition of

Philip the Second. In due time it had been built of substantial materials, but in this shape having been repeatedly destroyed by fire or earthquakes, the existing structure was built in 1654, in the pontificate of Innocent the 10th. Some of the private buiidings are large, but not well-arranged: they consist of two storied houses of solid materials, the upper one of which only is inhabited, the ground-floor being frequently let as shops or warehouses. To the street fronts they are furnished with a balcony, glazed with thin plates of mother-of-pearl shells in moveable panels, and the walls are daubed with grotesque paintings in flaring colours, such as red, yellow, and blue.

Manilla is a corporate town, having received a municipal form of administration from its founder, Legaspi, in 1571, the very year of its foundation, and Philip the Second having confirmed it three years after. The total population of the city and suburbs is reckoned at 140,000, which makes it about half as large again as Batavia, and about one-fourth of the size of Bombay. Its inhabitants are composed of an extraordinary variety of races and nations, consisting of the five principal nations of the Philippines, of Chinese, of Creole and mestizo Chinese, with Spaniards Creole and mestizo; and representatives of all the commercial nations of Europe and America. The most numerous class are the Tagalas, or Tagalogs, the nation in whose territory the Spanish colony was planted. The Chinese with their descendants, pure or mixed, are next in number. The Spaniards with their Creole descendants are said not to exceed 5000, or one twenty-eighth of the whole inhabitants. These are exempt from the capitation-tax, but the Chinese and their descendants, in common with all natives of the country, are subject to it in one form or another. A few of the genuine Chinese, and most of the mestizos of this nation, have embraced Christianity. The different classes of inhabitants speak their own native tongues, and consequently, there is no part of the world in which so great a diversity of languages prevails; not even the Dutch and British settlements in the Archipelago. The Spanish language, however, spoken with more or less purity, is the prevailing one in the city and its immediate neighbourhood, while at a distance the predominant one is the Tagala.

The name of Manilla is that of the native town or village on the site of which the Spaniards built the city, and which Legaspi, contrary to the usage of the Spaniards in such cases, adopted. It is said, with some probability, to be composed of two Tagala words, abbreviated by syncope. These are mairon, "to be, or to exist," and nila, the name of a shrub growing among the mangroves, and which abounds on the shore of the bay. The happy locality of Manilla, with its spacious bay, its good anchorage, and its navigable river, communicating by a brief course with the great lake, did not fail to fix the early attention of the conquerors, and Legaspi performed the ceremony of laying the foundation of the future city on the 15th of May, 1571, almoss immediately after his arrival.

MANTAWI. This is a name given by the Malays to the people who inhabit the islands on the western coast of Sumatra from the equator to the third degree of south latitude, namely, Sibatu, Sibiru, Sipora and the two Pagais. Mr. Logan in his account of Sumatra, estimates the area of all these islands at 6640 square miles, and their population at 5000, which is less than one inhabitant to a square mile, and this is probably its utmost amount. The people are rude, but simple and inoffensive, and have not adopted the Mahommedanism of the opposite coast of Sumatra.

MÂRAPI. The name of a mountain of Sumatra, with an active volcano, as its name, a derivative from api "fire," implies. It is situated towards the south-western side of the island, and about 27 miles south of the equator. Its height has been reckoned at 9800 feet above the level of the sea.

MÂRAPI. The name of a mountain of Java, lying between the provinces of Samarang and Kadoe to the north-west, and Pajang to the south. It is an active volcano, and rises to the height of 9250 feet above the level of the sea. There is no record of any great eruption of this mountain, although both its eastern and western acclivities furnish abundant evidence of ancient ones. At present, many parts of it are cultivated up to two-thirds of its height.

MARATUWA. The name of a considerable island on the eastern coast of Borneo, having with the smaller adjoining islands an area of 336 geographical square miles. The inhabitants are Malays.

MÂRBABU. The name of a mountain of Java contiguous to that of Mârapi, and forming with it the western boundary of the great plain of Pajang, as the mountain-chain of which Lawu is the principal, forms the eastern. It rises to the height of 10,500 feet above the level of the sea, but has no active volcano. Like Mârapi it is cultivated to a great height, and its valleys and slopes are found peculiarly well adapted to the cultivation of coffee.

MARIANES. The Marian or Ladrone Islands form an Archipelago of seventeen different groups of islets in the Northern Pacific, lying between the latitude of 12° and 17°, the 140° meridian running through them. The largest islands are seventeen in number, of which the most considerable are San Juan or Guajan, the Guam of our maps, Rotaz, Saipan, and Tinian. The geological formation of the whole Archipelago is volcanic. Many extinct craters exist, and there are some volcanos in a state of activity. All the islands are mountainous, and subject to violent earthquakes, of which, in the months of January, February, and March, 1819, no fewer than 125 shocks were experienced in the island of Guajan. The climate is healthy, and the soil represented as fertile. The cultivated productions are the coco-palm, the bread-fruit, called by the natives rima, the batata, the sugar-cane, the banana, and the water-melon. The islands when discovered were without any domestic animals, but a few have been introduced by the Spaniards. The native inhabitants are stated to be of the same race as the brown-complexioned and lank-haired inhabitants of the Philippines, and to speak a language resembling the Bisaya, but both assertions seem very doubtful. The first of them is more especially so, as would appear from Dampier's excellent description of their personal appearance, which differs very materially from that which he afterwards gives of the inhabitants of Mindano, who are certainly of the true Malayan race. "The natives of this island," says he, "are strong-bodied, large-limbed, and well shaped. They are copper-coloured like other Indians. Their hair is black and long, their eyes meanly proportioned. They have pretty high noses, their lips are pretty full, and their teeth indifferent white. They are long visaged and stern of countenance, yet we found them to be affable and courteous." Vol. i., page 297. At present they are slothful and poor, but inoffensive and hospitable. All of them have been converted long ago to Christianity. Down to the close of the last century they went almost stark naked, but are now decently clad. The essential portion of their food is the bread-fruit. In 1735, their whole numbers were but 2697. In 1801 they amounted to 7555, and by the census of 1850, to 8569, so that in half a century's time the increase was little more than 13 per cent.

The Marians form a distinct province of the Philippines, subject to the Governor-General of these islands. The seat of administration is in the island of Guajan, where is the town of San Ignacio de Agaña, which, with its district, contains 5620 inhabitants, or the majority of the population of the Archipelago. This is divided in all, into fourteen districts. The islanders pay no capitation tax, and seem to yield no revenue, their whole expenses being defrayed from the treasury of the Philippines.

The discoverer of the Marians was Magellan. They were the first lands which he reached after his painful passage across the Pacific in 1521. This is Pigafetta's account of the inhabitants as they first presented themselves to Europeans. "They go entirely naked. Some of them have long beards, with black hair reaching to their reins, although some tie it in a knot on the head. On their heads they wear little caps of palm leaves, in form like those of the Albanians. They are as tall as ourselves and well shaped. Their colour is an olive, but when born they are white. Their teeth are made by art red and black, for this they esteem a beauty. The women are handsome, of a slender form, and more fair and delicate than the men. Their hair is jet black, dishevelled, and so long as to be able to reach the ground. They too, go naked, with the exception of a modesty piece, consisting of a narrow band of bark, as thin as paper, made from the inner bark of the palm" (the reticulated material at the insertion of the fronds of the coco palm?). They do not till the land, but are found in their houses weaving mats and baskets of palm leaf, with other articles for domestic use. They eat birds, flying-fish, batatas, figs a palm long (bananas), sugarcane, and other things. They anoint their hair and their whole body with the oil of the coco-nut or that of the sesame. Their houses are of wood, covered with planks, over which are spread fig (banana) leaves two cubits long. In their houses they have chambers and garrets, with windows. Their beds are covered with beautiful mats made of palm cut into shreds, minute and delicate. They have no other arms than spears pointed with fish-bones. They are poor, but artful, and above all thieves, on which account we named these three islands 'Isles of Thieves.' Their amusement consists in going with their women in their little boats on excursions. These resemble the gondolas, which are used between Fusine and Venice, only that they are narrower. All of them are painted either black or red, and have latine-shaped sails made of palm-leaves stitched together. On the opposite side to the sail there is a beam, supported by transverse ones, the object of which is to preserve the equilibrium of the boat in sailing. The helm is in the shape of a baker's shovel, that is, a pole with a board at one end. This helm serves also for an oar, and the stern and bow of the boats are of the same make. These islanders swim and leap in the water like dolphins, from wave to wave. From the signs of wonder which they exhibited, we concluded that before seeing us they believed that besides themselves there were no other men in the world." Primo Viaggio, page 51.

From this faithful account of the personal aprearance and manners of the Marian islanders, when first seen by Europeans, and before their intermixture with other races, they would seem to have been a people much more nearly allied to the Polynesian islanders than to the people of the Philippines. Instead of being short, like Malays, they were as tall as Europeans. Their habits were maritime, like those of the South Sea Islanders. Like them they were thievish in character: like them, too, they knew neither iron nor any other metal, and like them they fed chiefly on the bread-fruit, the banana, and fish. They were, however, inferior to the Polynesians in the absence of tillage, the want of the hog, dog, and common fowl, and of every kind of clothing. The only evidence of foreign intercourse on the part of the Marian islanders consists in their possession of the Malayan numerals, although in a very corrupt form.

The first appearance of the Spaniards was not auspicious. "The Captain-General," says Pigafetta, wished to remain some time at the largest island (Guajan), in order to obtain refreshments and provisions, but he could not, for these islanders came on board the ships and stole one thing after another, so that we could not protect them. In the long run they attempted to lower the ship's sails, in order to run our vessels aground, and then with great dexterity they robbed us of the boat which was attached to the admiral's ship. The Captain-General, irritated on this account, landed with forty armed men, set fire to from forty to fifty houses and many boats, killing seven of the islanders. We then recovered our boat and quickly took our departure from the islands, pursuing the same course as before. Before landing, some of our people, who were sick, told us, that in the event of our killing an islander, man or woman, we should bring the entrails on board, being persuaded that if they possessed them, they would be restored to health. When we wounded any of these people with an arrow that passed through and through a limb, they endeavoured to extract it, first pulling one way and then another, and looking at it with wonderment. The same did such as were struck in the chest and died of their wounds. This did not fail to excite our compassion." Page 50.

The Marian Islands were taken possession of for the crown of Spain by Legaspi, the conqueror of the Philippines, in 1565, four and forty years after their discovery. The subjugation of the poor but warlike natives was, however, a work of considerable difficulty, for they resisted for a period of four-and-twenty years. The name which Magellan had given to them, Islas de los Ladrones, or "Isles of thieves," which is still continued as a synonym, was changed to the Marianes, which is an abbreviation of Maria Ana, the name of Mary Anne of Austria, Queen of Philip IV.

MARINDUQUE. One of the Philippine Islands, forming a part of the province of Mindoro. It is a long narrow island lying between Mindoro and Luzon, opposite to the isthmus of Tayabas in the latter, between latitudes 13° 11′ 10″, and 13° 33′ 30″, and longitudes 121° 45′ and 122° 5′. Its length is about 29 geographical miles, its utmost breadth 20, and its area 373 geographical square miles. The land is elevated and even mountainous, the mountain of Marlanga at its southern end, forming the Cape of the same name, being of considerable although unascertained height. From the well-known fertility of the soil of Marinduque, and the vicinity of the island to the most volcanic portion of Luzon, the geological formation is probably the same. The natural fertility of the soil is enhanced by the existence of many brooks applicable to irrigation. The chief production is rice, of which it exports a considerable quantity. The port of Malagi on its southern coast is a safe and convenient harbour for the colonial craft that carry on the coasting trade between Luzon and the Bisaya Islands. The population of Marinduquo in 1850 was 19,969, giving a density of near 50 to the square league.

MARIVELES. The name of a chain of high mountains,—of a small town,—and of a sea-port in the province of Bataan, and island of Luzon, in the Philippines. All of them are situated on the peninsula which forms the western boundary of the great Bay of Manilla. The sierra of Mariveles, which is a spur of one of the Cordilleras, runs in a direction from north to south, to the length of about twenty miles.

The town is in latitude 40° 27′ 40″, and lies between two small rivers which disembogue at the port, and opposite to the island which once bore the same name, but is now called Isla de Corregidor. The town has 233 houses, and a population of 1402 inhabitants. The chief productions of the neighbourhood are rice, maiz, sugar-cane, cotton, and the abaca banana; but fishing is the chief occupation of the inhabitants, who have constructed weirs and stews in which great quantities of fish are taken or preserved.

MARRIAGE. The only terms for marriage in Malay are the Arabic and Persian ones, respectively, nĭkah and kawin, the native ones having probably been displaced by these and forgotten. In Javanese we have, besides these, the native words, krama and rabi. Owing to the youth of the parties in a first marriage, the negociation is almost always conducted by the parents. The courtship among the Malays and other nations of Sumatra, consists in the lover sending his mistress a present of areca and betel pepper, the ceremony, from the name of the first of these, being called pinangan. Children are frequently betrothed at an early age, and this goes under the name of tunangan.

The conditions of the marriage contract vary considerably among the different nations of the Archipelago; but generally there is more or less of a purchase of the bride by the bridegroom, or more correctly by his parents. The most frequent form of marriage among the Sumatrans goes under the name of jujur, and implies a complete purchase of the wife, when she becomes the servant of the husband and his family. Among the Javanese the money paid for the bride is, virtually, of the nature of a marriage settlement on her, and is called, in the vulgar tongue, the patukon, literally the "purchase money," and in the polite, the srahan, or "deposit," but more generally than either, the srikawin, which is in reality a dowry or settlement. In Sumatra, however, it is, in a few cases, the husband and not the wife that is bought. This happens when the parents of the wife are of higher rank than those of the husband. This is called the marriage by ambil-anak, which, literally translated, signifies "adopting as a son." In this case, the husband becomes the servant of the family adopting him. Among the civilised nations of the Philippines, the purchase of the wife takes a ruder form than even a money payment, for the lover has to serve the parents of his mistress for a period of three or four years, much after the manner of the ancient Hebrews.

The marriage ceremony is everywhere a religious one; and Sir Stamford Raffles gives the following translation of that in Java as pronounced by the priest. "I join you, Raden-mas, in wedlock with Satiya, with a pledge of two reals weight in gold. You take Satiya to be your wife for this world. You are obliged to pay the pledge of your marriage, (srikawin), or to remain debtor for the same. You are responsible for your wife in all and everything. If you should happen to be absent from her for the space of seven months on shore, or one year at sea, without giving her any sustenance, and are remiss in the duties you owe to your sovereign, your marriage shall be dissolved, if your wife demand it, without any further form of process; and you will, besides, be subject to the punishment which the Mahommedan law ordains."

Marriages within certain degrees of consanguinity are prohibited; but as with the Jews, a man can intermarry with the widow of a brother, and then becomes liable for all the obligations of the deceased husband. Polygamy and concubinage are legal throughout the Malay Archipelago; but these are, from the nature of things, only the riotous indulgences of the few rich and powerful. The first married wife being, generally, the person of highest birth, takes, in Java, rank of the rest. In Sumatra, the highest rank belongs to her for whom the highest price has been paid.

Divorce, in Malay, charaïan and sarakan; and in Javanese, pâgatan and pisahan,—all of them signifying "a parting,' or "a separation," are easily obtained. In Java, as already seen, a seven months' absence by land, or a year's by sea, without provision for the wife, is declared to be a virtual divorce, should the wife demand one. Among the simpler inhabitants of the Archipelago, divorces are of rare occurrence; but not so in Java, where they are frequent.

MARSDEN, (WILLIAM),—the author of the "History of Sumatra," was born in Dublin, the son of a merchant of that city, and the second in descent from a Derbyshire gentleman, which had settled in Ireland in the last years of the reign of Queen Anne. After the usual school education in Dublin, he received a civil appointment for Bencoolen, at sixteen years of age; proceeded to that place in 1771; remained there eight years only, and returned to England in 1779. In 1782, he published his "History of Sumatra," which established his reputation as an oriental scholar, and a man of clear and sound judgment. His well-earned reputation obtained for him, first, the situation of Under Secretary; and, ultimately, of Chief Secretary to the Admiralty; and these offices he discharged with great credit for the twelve years from 1795 to 1807, when he retired, and returned to his favourite studies. The fruits of these were his Grammar and Dictionary of the Malay language, the first deserving the name which had been published in England, and the best which had been published anywhere. This work had engaged more or less of his attention for six-and-twenty years. In 1811, a new edition of his "History of Sumatra," which had been translated into French and German, was called for and published. In 1817, he published, with copious and valuable notes, his translation of the celebrated travels of Marco Polo,—that singular work which gave the hints that led to the discovery of the New World. In 1823, he published his "Numismata Orientalia, or Description of Eastern Coins," a valuable collection of which had fallen into his hands; and in 1834, in his seventy-eighth year, he gave to the world his last work, a "Collection of Essays," the most valuable of which consists of a dissertation on the "Polynesian and East Insular" languages. By his will he bequeathed his valuable collection of Oriental coins, medals, and manuscripts to the British Museum; and his library to King's College, London.

Mr. Marsden's long and meritorious career terminated on the 6th of October, 1836, when he had nearly completed his eighty-second year. He was the first literary and scientific Englishman who, with the advantages of local experience, treated of the Malayan countries; all our knowledge before him being confined to the crude narratives of mariners and voyagers unacquainted with the language, through which, alone, accurate knowledge could be obtained. He was the cotemporary of Sir William Jones, of Colebrooke, and of his own relative, Sir Charles Wilkins; and while they were studying the philosophy of Continental Asia, he was doing the same thing for its islands. The chief characteristics of his writings are laborious care and scrupulous fidelity, ever under the control of a sound judgment, qualities in which he has not been excelled, or even equalled, by any writer on the subjects he treated of, foreign or native. He is, in fact, the model and example of all that has been done since his time;—sometimes with more knowledge than he could have possessed, but never with more care or integrity.

MARTABAN. Situated at the confluence of three fine rivers in the country of the Mon, or Peguan nation, and now a portion of the British territory in India, is called by the Malays, Maritanan. This place, which is in latitude 16° 28′, was, probably, the most northern limit of the navigation of the Malays. The Portuguese name, Martabané, or Martavané, is most likely taken from the Malay one, for it is not a Peguan word. That considerable intercourse subsisted between the Peguans and Malays, before the arrival of Europeans, is testified by the fact, that the Portuguese found a considerable number of Peguans settled at Malacca when they captured it. This is asserted by all the narrators of that transaction; and in the "Commentaries of Alboquerque," it is expressly stated, that they formed part of the auxiliaries that accompanied the Portuguese commander when he went in pursuit of the fugitive king, after his expulsion from the town. "Alphonso Alboquerque," say they, "learning that the king of Malacca had fortified himself on the river Muar, sent against him seven of his captains with a force of 400 Portuguese, 600 Javanese under Utemuta raja, and 300 Peguans under their native chiefs."—Page 383. No Peguan settlers now exist either at Malacca, or any other European settlement in the same quarter; nor do they seem to have done so at any time after the overthrow of the Malay government.

MARUWI. This is the name given by the Malays to the natives of the group of islands on the western coast of Sumatra, lying between the third and fourth degrees of north latitude, and of which the principal are Simalu and Sibañah. Mr. Logan conjectures that the area of this group may be about 600 square miles; and their population about 3000, or five inhabitants to the square mile.

MASA. This is the name of a considerable island lying off the western shore of Sumatra; one of the group called by the Malays Pulo-batu, or the "rock islands," and the most northerly of which touches on the equator. The word masa signifies "time," in Malay and in Javanese, but it is taken from the Sanscrit language, and is one of a good many names of places having the same origin. It is certain, however, that these were not imposed directly by a people speaking or using the Sanscrit language; but by the Malays or Javanese who had borrowed them, and incorporated them in their own languages.

MASBATE. One of the Philippine islands lying between north latitudes 11° 49′ and 12° 36′, and east longitudes 123° 1′ and 123° 49′. It has Luzon to the north, Samar to the east, and Panay, Negros, and Çebu to the south. Between it and Luzon are the two smaller islands of Burias and Ticao, the last of which forms with it a distinct government. Through the whole of Masbaté there runs a crescent-shaped chain of mountains, most probably of plutonic formation, since the rivulets of the island bring down a sufficient quantity of gold to make it worth while to wash their sands for it. Its area is estimated at 2334 square geographical miles; and in 1846, its population amounted to 5489 souls, giving, therefore, no more than 2·3 inhabitants to the mile. Along with the smaller island of Ticao, the entire population of the province in the same year was 7994, distributed in four townships, three of them in Masbaté and one in Ticao. That in this last island, named San Jacinto, lies on a good harbour and is the capital of the province. The extent of Masbaté under cultivation is very trifling, as may be judged by the small amount of the population. The probability is, that the soil is sterile, and the island without natural facilities of irrigation.

MASENRENG is the name of an inland country of the Bugis or Wugi nation of Celebes, situated at the base of the south-western peninsula of that island, and between the Bay of Boni and country of Mandar.

MASOY, correctly Misoi, is the aromatic bark of a large forest tree of New Guinea and its adjacent islands, the Cortex oninus of Rumphius. It is a considerable article of trade, being much used by the Malays, Javanese, and Chinese as a cosmetic, and sometimes medicinally as an external application.

MATAN. This is the name of a Malay State on the western side of Borneo, and forming, at present, part of a province of the Netherland Government. The town of Matan is situated about a degree south of the equator, and in east longitude 110° 35′, and by boat about three days and three nights sail up a considerable river of the same name, which, at its mouth, has a hard sand-bar, with very little water. It consists of about 300 houses, its population being almost entirely Malay, while that of the rest of the country consists of Dayaks or Aborigines, in this instance, a harmless people, not addicted to head-hunting. To Matan belongs the island of Carimata, or correctly Kurimata, inhabited or rather sojourned at by the seafaring fishermen, or sea-gipseys, called orang-laut, said to amount to about 300 in number.

MATARAM, or in the polite dialect Matawis, is the name of a province of Java, in the country of the proper Javanese, and about equi-distant from the eastern and western extremities of the island. It is bounded to the north by the province of Kadu, to the east by that of Pajang, to the west by Baglen, and to the south by the sea. The mountains Mârapi and Sumbing lying northward of it; the first, 9250, and the last 10,500 feet high, furnish this province with a perennial supply of water for irrigation, and the result is that nearly the whole of it is one sheet of cultivation, including the slopes of Mârapi, to the height of 4000 feet, there being usually two corn harvests within the year. Mataram has been twice over the seat of a native principality. The first was founded in 1508, and the last, which still subsists, in 1756. Mataram forms the principal part of the dominions of the chief who has the title of Sultan, and the population of whose territories was estimated in 1846 at 348,354.

MATARAM. The same word as the last, and most likely borrowed from it, is the name of a place in the island of Lomboc. It is at present its chief town, and is situated on the western side of the island, or that which is opposite to Bali, three miles inland from the port of Ampânan. A well constructed road, being an avenue of fig trees, leads to it. The town consists of streets running regularly at right angles to each other, the two palaces of the Raja being in the centre. The houses consist of mud walls, thatched with the lalang grass or palmetto leaf, and the town is surrounded by a quickset hedge of bamboo, and a barricade after the manner of chevaux-de-frise. The population consists for the most part of Balinese, the dominant nation, but no account is given of its amount. See LOMBOC.

MAYA (Pulo). This is the name of an island lying off the western side of the larger one of Obi, and between this last and the large island of Gilolo or Halmahera. I mention it only on account of its name, which is Sanscrit, with the Malay or Javanese word Pulo prefixed, the compound signifying "illusion" or "Deception Island," without doubt given to it by the Malay or Javanese spice-traders, who would probably encounter it in their route to the Clove islands.

MAYON. This is the name of an active volcano in the province of Albay, in the island of Luzon, which has produced formidable irruptions since the arrival of the Spaniards in the Philippines. The crater is in latitude 13° 14′ 40,″ and longitude 123° 34′ 10.″ The mountain itself is of considerable elevation, being part of the great Cordillera. One of the most formidable irruptions of this volcano took place on the 23rd of October, 1766, which totally destroyed one town, that of Malinao, and did great injury to Albay, the capital of the province, along with four other towns. Besides lava, a torrent of water was discharged, which after a course of two leagues fell into the sea. A typhoon raged during the eruption which increased the destruction caused by it. In 1814 an equally terrific eruption took place which destroyed the entire town of Albay.

MEGA-MÂNDUNG. The name of a mountain of Java in the district of Chanjur, and country of the Sundas, 5000 feet above the level of the sea. The first part of the name is Sanscrit, meaning a cloud, and the last, Javanese, signifying "lowering." It is not much more than one half the height of the neighbouring mountain of Gâde, or "the great mountain."

MELON. The only cucurbitaceous cultivated plants that thrive well in the Indian and Philippine Archipelagos are the cucumber and gourd. The humid climate of these countries does not seem well adapted to the growth of the common or the water-melon, the first being, indeed, little known, and the last much inferior in size to that of northern India and Persia. The cucumber is known in all the languages by the name of antimun, or some slight variation of it, and may be presumed to be a long-cultivated native plant, since the name is not traceable to any foreign tongue. The gourd is known in all the languages of the Archipelago by the one name of labu, and as far as can be inferred from this, is indigenous. The water-melon is known in Javanese and most of the other languages by the name of sâmangka, but in the Lampung it is called lamuja. In Malay, besides sâmangka, it has also the name of pâtaka, which appears to be a native word, and mândiki and tâmikai, both of which are Telinga. The name, therefore, will not direct us to its origin, but it is most probably a stranger, brought from the eastern coast of the Peninsula of India.

MENADO. The name of a port and town on the northern peninsula of Celebes, on its northern coast, and towards its extremity, in north latitude 1° 30′, and east longitude 124° 56′. This place, and the territory annexed to it, form part of the Netherland possessions, and have been so since the year 1677. In 1848 it was declared along with Kema on the opposite coast of the same peninsula, a free port, exempt from all imposts on ship or cargo. The town and fort called Amsterdam, are situated on a spacious bay, which affords shelter only during the eastern monsoon, being a lee-shore in the western. The anchorage in from 30 to 40 fathoms depth is within a cable's length of the shore, and near a fresh-water stream with good potable water. See MINAHASA.

MENANGKABAU, or more correctly Mânangkabo, is the name of an inland country of Sumatra, in which the Malay nation seems to have at one time attained a greater amount of civilisation and power than in any other part of the Archipelago, and to which the chiefs of some of the other Malay tribes take a pride in tracing their origin. It extends generally from the equator to a degree south of it, and Mr. Logan describes it as composed of a series of mountain valleys, 60 miles long and 50 broad, or containing an area of 3000 square miles. Southward, it has the mountain Talang, 10,750 feet high, with Singalang and Mârapi, each 9800, while to the north it has that of Sago of 5000 feet. Talang and Mârapi are active volcanos, and indeed the name of the last of these signifies as much. The geological formation is partly volcanic and partly plutonic and sedimentary, these different formations appearing here to meet. Within this small territory there is a lake about 15 miles in length and 5 in breadth, abounding in fish. The soil of the valleys is described as fertile, and the land is well supplied with water for irrigation, the result of which is that the country is highly cultivated and populous. The late Sir Stamford Raffles, who visited it, gives the following glowing picture of it. "As far as the eye could distinctly trace was one continued scene of cultivation, interspersed with innumerable towns and villages, shaded by the cocoanut and other fruit-trees. I may safely say, that this view equalled anything I ever saw in Java. The scenery is more majestic and grand, population equally dense, cultivation equally rich." Sir Stamford estimated the population of one small district of this country, not exceeding 50 square miles, at a million, or 400 inhabitants to each mile; but as this far exceeded the populousness of the best inhabited parts of Java in his time, the estimate seems evidently greatly in excess. Still, there can be no doubt but that the valleys of Menangkabo are cultivated and peopled to a degree unknown in any other part of Sumatra.

Of the history of Menangkabo no details are known, and most probably none exist. No time is assigned for its foundation, nor is it even known when or how its inhabitants were converted to the Mahommedan religion. Some European writers have, notwithstanding, described it as having been once a great and powerful empire of which the rule extended over the whole of Sumatra, an assumption for which there is not a grain of evidence, native or European. It may be safely asserted, indeed, that the Malays have never attained that degree of civilisation which could have enabled them to acquire and to hold together so large a dominion, especially in a forest-clad country like Sumatra, and of which, independent of rude tribes, the more advanced nations alone amount to five in number, speaking distinct languages, and having different customs. De Barros tells us that when the Portuguese arrived in India the sea-coast of Sumatra was divided into no fewer than nine and twenty distinct independent kingdoms, and as he furnishes a list of them, we can see that all but one of them were Malay. As to Menangkabo, it is not included in the number, and mentioned only as a country that furnished some gold, and was famous for its manufacture of arms, a reputation which it still maintains.

With local advantages of soil and water, it is certain that Menangkabo must have attained an amount of population and power beyond the less favourably circumstanced Malay States, and this would naturally induce the latter to look up to it with respect, and make it a point of pride to trace their origin to it. It seems however more than probable, and indeed to a certain extent admitting of proof, that the natural advantages of Menangkabau were promoted by the intercourse and settlement of strangers. I take these strangers to have been Javanese, already imbued with some portion of the civilisation and religion of the Hindus, and most probably finding their way from Palembang, where they are still settled, and have been so immemorially.

The names of persons and places afford evidence of the presence of the Javanese. Thus by one set of legends, the founders of Menangkabo are represented to have been two brothers, called Papati-si-batang and Kayi Tumângung. The first word in the first of these names is Sanscrit, with a Javanese prefix, and signifies lord, and the last is Javanese, meaning the shaft of a spear. Both words in the second name are Javanese, the last of them borrowed by the Malay, but the first the title of a class of Javanese nobility, and signifying "respectable," and unknown to the Malay. According to another legend found in the manuscript translated by Dr. Leyden, and which he called "Malay Annals," the founder of Menangkabau was a personage called Sang Sapurba, represented to have come from Palembang, that is, from a Javanese colony. The name is a mixture of Javanese and Sanscrit, the first part of it being a Javanese title prefixed to the names of gods and ancient kings, and the last the Sanscrit word purba, "first," with the abreviated Javanese numeral "one" prefixed. Another party concerned in this supposed adventure is called Sang Nila Utama. The first word here is that just explained, and the two last are Sanscrit, signifying in their order, "blue" and "excellent."

The evidence afforded by the names of places is perhaps more satisfactory. The name of Mânangkâbo itself may perhaps be Javanese, for the two words of which it is composed are capable of being rendered without alteration in that language, "the victory of the buffalo," that is, it may be presumed, the victory of the buffalo over the tiger, such being the usual result of the contest between these two animals. The first place in which the fabled brother founders established their government, is called Prayangan. This is Javanese and not Malay, and signifies "place of wood-spirits or fairies," and still exists as the name of an extensive region of Java. The name of the mountain Mârapi, signifies a volcano, and is the Javanese but not the Malay form of the word. Ringgit is the name of another mountain, and this word which signifies a puppet, or marionnette, is exclusively Javanese. A place in the country of Menangkabo, is called Ayar-angat, it may be presumed, from the existence of a thermal spring, for this is the native name for one. The first word in this case, is modern Malay, signifying water, but is also found in the ancient language of Java: the last is exclusively Javanese not Malay, signifying "hot." Pagarrayung, the name of a district of Menangkabo, has its first part common to the Malay and Javanese, but its last wholly Javanese, being the name of a species of aquatic grass, and the entire word meaning literally fence, or inclosure made of the grass in question. Linto is the name of another district of the same country, the word having no signification in Malay, but in Javanese meaning "exchange or barter," probably from its being the site of an established fair or market. Jambi is the name of a Malay state and of a large river on the eastern side of Sumatra. The word is the Javanese for the areca palm, and is equivalent to pinang in Malay. Mâdang and Koripan are the names of towns or villages in the south-eastern part of Sumatra, and are evidently taken from the names of the seats of two ancient principalities of Java. Then we have Preng and Trap, Javanese words signifying "bamboo," and "command or order" for the names of two rivers, and we have Rino signifying "day" in Javanese, for the name of a river islet. Bañu, the Javanese for water, or river, we find in Bañu-asin, Salt-river, the name of the most westerly of the four branches of the Palembang river as it debouches in the sea. Again, we have the name of the country of Palembang itself, correctly Palimbang, a word derived from the Javanese verb limbang, which signifies "to drain off a fluid." The complete word, probably here abbreviated, would be Palimbangan, of which the sense would be, the vessel or place from which water or other fluid is drained off, and, no doubt, has reference to the subsidence of the inundation, in the territory named, one of the most striking phenomena belonging to it. In the countries of the Rejang and Sârawi, as if on the road from Java to Menangkabo, we have equally decisive evidence of Javanese settlement in the names of places. A lake with a district to which it gives name, is called Ranu, which in Javanese signifies water or a lake. Another district has the name of Padang-ratu, which in Javanese signifies "king's plain:" and a third is Surabaya, the name of a province of Java, a word half Sanscrit and half Javanese, signifying "heroic difficulty." Indragiri, mountain of Indra, and Indrapura, city of Indra, are examples of names of places entirely Sanscrit, and Bumi-agung and Gunang-raja, "great land" and "king's mount," of those in which the two languages are combined. These Sanscrit and Javanese names, it should be remarked, are frequent only in the south-eastern part of Sumatra, or that which is in proximity to Java.

Better evidence, however, than even these words, of the presence of the Javanese in Menangkabo, exists in actual monuments of this people. Sir Stamford Raffles, in his visit to it, found a stone inscription in the ancient character of Java, exactly like those he had been familiar with in that island, and accompanied as he was by learned Javanese, he could not well have mistaken the writing for any other character. The inscription was on a slab of basalt, and my friend Dr. Horsfield who accompanied Sir Stamford, showed me a fac-simile of the writing which leaves no doubt of its identity with that of Java. It is remarkable that when the Portuguese became first acquainted with Sumatra, a tradition of the former presence of the Javanese still prevailed among its inhabitants. There is a passage in De Barros to this effect worth quoting, "The people of the coast as well as of the interior," says he, "are of a tawny colour, have flowing hair, are well proportioned, have a goodly aspect and are not of the appearance of the Javanese although so near to them. From this fact it deserves to be noted how so small a distance may change the nature of things. And more especially, as all the natives of Sumatra are called by the common name of Jauiji (Jawi), for it is held by Sumatrians as certain that the Javanese had once been masters of this great island." Decade 3, Book 5, Chap. 1. The word Jawi here employed belongs still to the Malay, and implies a mixture of what is partly native and partly foreign, a sense in which it is especially applied to the language as now written.

About the year 1807, there sprang up in Menangkabo a new and conquering religion, being a professing reformation of the Mahommedan. It is called that of the Padris or Rinchis, names given to the parties who first propagated it, and who were three native pilgrims recently returned from Mecca. The first name mentioned is evidently the Portuguese designation of the Roman Catholic ecclesiastics, and the last is an abbreviation of Korinchi, the district in which the reform first sprang up. The converts to the new sect were called by the Malays orâng-putih or "white men," in reference to the dress they wore. The following account is given by Mr. John Anderson of this singular religion, the only original one that has ever been known to have sprung up within the Archipelago. "The Rinchis," says he, writing in 1822, "are the chiefs of a religious sect in the kingdom of Menangkabo in the interior of Siak, who have been gradually extending their power and their influence during the last twelve or fifteen years. They are most rigorous in preventing the consumption of opium, and punish with death all who are detected in this indulgence. They prohibit coloured cloths of any description from being worn, and allow only pure white. Tobacco and betel, articles in such general use in all Malay countries and considered so essential to comfort, are not permitted. Every man is obliged to shave his head and wear a little skull-cap. No man is permitted to converse with another's wife, and the women are obliged to cover their faces with a white cloth having only two small holes for their eyes." Mission to the East Coast of Sumatra, 1826, p. 343. The reformers, in time, became conquerors,—subdued a large portion of the interior of Sumatra, and had they not come into collision with the Dutch at Padang would most probably have succeeded in mastering a large portion of the island. In 1837 they were attacked by the Netherland troops, made a brave and fanatical resistance, but after a war of three years' continuance were wholly subdued in 1840. The religion of these Moslem puritans was far too rigorous in its exactions for the easy and lax Malays, and consequently, the Padris were very unpopular with them. See PAGAR-RUYUNG.

METALS. There is no word for this general term in Malay, Javanese, or any other language of the Archipelago. Sometimes the word Lâburan signifying the "melted object" is used by the Malays. The metals immemorially known to the natives of the Archipelago are gold, (mas), iron (bâsi), tin (tima), silver (perak and salaka) and copper (tambaga). The only alloys known to them are those of gold with copper (suwasa), and those of copper with tin (loyang and kuningan). The three first-named metals only are native products and have native names. Silver has also native names, the origin of which cannot be traced, but the metal is certainly a foreign one, and De Barros informs us that before the arrival of the Potuguese, the Malays of Malacca received their supply of it from Siam, to which De Barros tells us, it had been brought from Lao. The probability, however, is that most of it must have come from China. The name for copper is the corruption of a Sanscrit one, and the knowledge of this metal was probably made known by the Hindus, but at the arrival of of the Portuguese, the market of Malacca was supplied from China. Quicksilver was probably, like copper made known to the Malays and Javanese by the Hindus, for the only name for it, rasa, is Sanscrit. Lead is known by a name which signifies "black tin," and is probably of Chinese introduction. The inhabitants of the Philippines know it only by the Spanish name of plomo. Down to the year 1824, when it was first made known to them by Europeans, the natives of the Archipelago were as ignorant of antimony which abounds in their country, as were the natives of Europe four centuries before. I was present when the first button of the regulus was obtained from the ore of Borneo, a result which surprised the Chinese and Malays who witnessed the operation, some of whom pronounced the metal to be tin and others silver.

MINAHASA.—This is the name of a province or district of the island of Celebes, embracing the extreme end of its northern peninsula, between the first and second degrees of north latitude. It appears to be about 60 miles in length by 20 in average breadth, and thus to have an area of about 1200 square miles. The whole is a volcanic region, the great volcanic band embracing this small portion of the Celebes only. Minahasa is a romantic region of volcanic mountains, several of them in a state of activity, of valleys, table-lands, and lakes. Several of the mountains rise to the height of 4000 and 5000 feet above the level of the sea, and the highest of them, Klobat, to that of 6133 feet, so that the mountains of Minahasa are little more than one-half the height of those of Java. One of these, the active volcano of Sempo, is well described by a Dutch traveller who ascended it, and whose narrative is contained in the Journal of Netherland India, published at Batavia. "To keep ourselves warm," says he, "we walked to the right and left on a dry flat, while the dense mist prevented us from seeing to any distance. But what an image of desolation and violence met the eye when the mist cleared up! As far as the eye could reach, nothing was visible but a dry sandy desert, the ground being formed of lava, and having much resemblance to the cinders of burnt coal, and on which only small tufts of grass grew here and there. This is the crater Rañu-asâm (in Javanese "the sour-water or meer"). It is all a congeries of valleys, or basin-formed hollows, probably formed, as the volcanic action has consumed and heaved up the ground under the surface of the earth. We find here no sign of living things, except wild oxen, whose tracks are so abundant that at one place we lost the direction of the proper path through them. Shuddering, we approached this chaos of desolation. At some distance from the margin of the crater, we began to creep, so that we might in safety receive the full impression of all the terrible but grotesque features of this work of nature. A noise struck our ears, much resembling that produced by opening the valve of a steam engine. This is audible at a great distance. It came from the sulphur-pool at the bottom of the crater. At first the sulphurous vapour hindered us from distinguishing objects, but after half-an-hour it was driven off by the wind, and the whole basin was exposed to view before us. The first impression was fearful. A boiling pool, about 500 feet in diameter, is surrounded by a steep rocky wall. We endeavoured to cast stones into the middle of the crater: for this purpose we fastened a tolerably heavy stone to the end of a rope of about 110 fathoms long, and threw it forward, but it ran out 100 fathoms without the stone reaching the pool. We saw no living beings, save some swallows which wheeled above the pool. We observed, also, traces of wild oxen which had descended into the crater. What they seek there is a mystery, for neither in the crater nor in its immediate vicinity is a single blade of grass to be found."

The table-lands of Minahasa are generally from 2000 to 2500 feet above the level of the sea, and on them are many lakes, seemingly the craters of former volcanos. The largest of these is that of Tondano, which is three leagues long, and from a mile to a league broad, with a depth of from 90 to 100 feet. On this an Englishman of the name of Davis, has constructed some small sloops with which he navigates it. The lakes abound in fish of six different species, and their fisheries furnish a considerable part of the subsistence of the native inhabitants. The discharge of their waters gives rise to several magnificent cascades, and that of Tondano is especially remarkable for its picturesque beauty. The rivers of Minahasa are all small, and none of them navigable.

The cultivated productions of the country are rice, maiz, the American potato in the high lands, ground pulse (Arachis hypogæa), the Gomuti and sago-palms, tobacco, coffee, and the cacoa (theobroma). This last is produced to the extent of about 250,000 pounds yearly; and Minahasa is the only country of the Malay Archipelago, in which this rather delicate plant has been successfully cultivated. The coffee is of a very fine quality, and considered superior to the best of Java. The annual produce is about 1,500,000 pounds, but it is rather falling off than increasing, which is not to be wondered at, since it is a monopoly of the government, which requires the delivery to it of all that is produced at the price of 15s. a cwt., payable in a depreciated small copper change. The fertility of the soil is remarkable, as is the case generally in the volcanic formation, and water available for irrigation to develop it seems not to be wanting. Notwithstanding the absence of the plough, the harrow, and the buffalo, and that the labours of husbandry are performed by human hands only, the country produces more rice than it consumes, and exports about 40,000 cwts. The usual fruits of the western islands of the Archipelago, including the durian and mangostin, are produced, but little attention is given to them by the rude and careless natives.

None of the larger ferocious animals exist in Minahasa; and, indeed, no large animals in the wild state at all, except oxen become so, most probably, from the domesticated state. The domesticated are the ox, the hog, the goat, and the horse. The buffalo has not been introduced. The ox is abundant, the pastures of the high lands being well suited to it. The hog forms the principal flesh used by the native inhabitants. The horse is evidently a stranger, for it is known only by a corruption of its Portuguese name (cavayo), and has none in the native language.

The native inhabitants of Minahasa are of the same Malayan race as all the other inhabitants of Celebes, but they speak a distinct and peculiar language, and in civilisation, are far below the Bugis and Macassar nations. They are a simple, inoffensive, but indolent, dirty and poor people. Their chief subsistence is sago, always evidence of poverty. The total population of the province is reckoned to be 96,218 souls, of whom 92,332 are aborigines, 3375 Malays or Bugis, and 510 Chinese. This gives about 80 inhabitants to the square mile, a denser population than that of any other part of Celebes, a result which must be ascribed to the salubrity of the climate and the fertility of the soil.

On the arrival of the Portuguese, the country was subject to the little island of Ternate, one of the Moluccas, and the people had not then, nor have they since, adopted the Mahommedan religion. The Portuguese occupied it, in virtue of their conquest of the Moluccas, and they were expelled by the Dutch in 1677. The country is now a province of Netherland India, and is divided into 26 districts, containing 286 villages.

MINDANO. This is the most southerly of the Philippine islands, and next to Luzon, the largest of them. It lies between north latitudes 5° 31′ and 9° 49′ 30″, and east longitudes 121° 44′ and 125° 44′. Its general form is an irregular triangle, having one side to the north-west, one to the east and one to the south. The whole coast is extremely irregular, and on its north-western and southern sides, it is indented by several deep bays, of which Butuan and Yligan are the largest on the first, and Illano or that of Lanun on the last. Those of Yligan and Lanun indent it opposite to each other to such an extent as to make the land between them an isthmus not exceeding 35 geographical miles broad, making the island, in fact, to consist of two peninsulas, a larger or eastern and a smaller or western. The extreme length of Mindano is reckoned to be 283 geographical miles, and its breadth about the same. Its area is about 37,000 square geographical miles, or about one-third part larger than Ireland. Its geological formation would seem to be, like that of Luzon, partly sedimentary and plutonic, and partly volcanic. The surface is considered to be generally mountainous and uneven, but, probably, contains some extensive plains. Of the height of the mountains nothing is known. Several of them, however, are active volcanos, from which have proceeded formidable irruptions, since the island became known to Europeans. It contains several lakes, as those of Linao or Mindano, of Lanao, of Buguey, of Lingasin, Buloan, Selangan, and Sapongan. By far the largest of these is the first-named, which Spanish writers describe as being by its extent a real inland sea. It is situated towards the eastern side of the island and about 8 leagues inland from the bay of Baganga in north latitude 7° 35′. This is emptied by the considerable river which falls into the sea in the bay of Butuan on the north-western coast. It is from this lake that the island is supposed to have received its Malay and European name, its two last syllables forming a word signifying "lake." The Lanao or Malano is situated towards the isthmus between the bays of Lanun and Yligan, and discharges its waters into the latter by a river called the Ninanton. The lake of Buguey is situated in the western peninsula, and gives rise to a considerable river, which falls into the bay of Kamaladan on the southern coast. Very little, however, beyond an enumeration of names, is known of the greater part of the interior of Mindano, which has certainly never been trodden by the foot of an intelligent and instructed European. The rivers are numerous but small, and fit only for the navigation of native craft. As far as is known, the largest is the Butuan on the north-western coast, and the Salangan, which falls into the bay of Illanun on its eastern side, and fronting the island of Bunwut. It is at the mouth of this river that stands the chief town of the prince called the Sultan of Mindano, and which bears the same name.

The climate of Mindano is hot and humid, and is under the influence of the monsoons of the northern hemisphere, the north-east and south-west, but unlike the other islands of the Philippine group, it is beyond the reach of typhoons. The mineral products of the island applicable to economical uses, are, iron, gold, sulphur, and, it is said, mercury. Among many unknown forest-trees we find here the well-known Teak (Tectona grandis), Mindano being, except Java, the only island of the Malay and Philippine Archipelagos that is known to produce it in any considerable abundance,—a fact which indicates the presence of a calcareous formation, this being the one in which it flourishes. The cultivated plants are rice, maiz, sugar-cane, the esculent and the abaca banana, the coco, the areca, and the sago palms, with the usual fruits of the Malayan countries, including the durian, but, as far as is known, not the mangostin. Dampier, who tarried six months on the southern coast, and is the most accurate and intelligent European that ever visited and described the island, speaks thus of the soil: "The mould, in general, is deep and black, and extraordinarily fat and fruitful. . . . The valleys are well moistened with pleasant brooks, and small rivers of delicate water."—Vol. i. p. 310. No doubt in the interior of the island, and in the vicinity of the volcanic mountains, fruitful and well-watered valleys will be found, well fitted for the growth of corn. Although the classes of the inhabitants in easy circumstances use rice, a great proportion of the people feed on sago, groves of the palms producing which are said by Dampier to extend along the marshy banks of the rivers to the extent of five and six miles. The eastern side of the island appears to be mountainous, and generally barren, and the Spanish portion, lying chiefly on the north-western side, seems, generally, to be more remarkable for sterility than fertility.

As far as is known, and it seems very probable, none of the larger ferocious animals exist in Mindano. The elephant, the rhinoceros, and the tapir are also absent, and the only known animal of the family to which they belong is the hog, which is very abundant, and from the description given of it, it would seem to be the same as one of the species of Java, the Sus verrucosus, with an excrescence over the cheeks. Monkeys and deer are also very plentiful, but the species unknown. Dampier, who went on a hunting party with a native chieftain, thus describes the abundance of deer:

"This savannah abounds with long grass, and it is plentifully stocked with deer. The adjacent woods are a covert for them in the heat of the day, but mornings and evenings they feed in the open plains, as thick as in our parks in England. I never saw, anywhere, such plenty of wild deer, though I have met with them in several parts of America, both in the north and south seas."—Vol. i. p. 347. The wild hogs are equally numerous, according to the same authority, "yet," says he, "there are wild hogs in the island, those so plentiful that they will come in troops out of the woods, at night, to the very city, and come under the houses, to romage up and down the filth that they find there. The natives, therefore, would even desire us to lye in wait for the hogs, to destroy them, which we did frequently by shooting, and carrying them presently on board, but were prohibited their houses afterwards."—Vol. i. p. 343. Wild oxen are also numerous, but whether a genuine wild race, or the domestic become so, is not known. The domesticated animals are those usual among the Malays, the ox, the buffalo, the goat, and the horse. The poultry consist of the common fowl and duck. Fish, as in these regions generally, are abundant in the seas, lakes, and rivers.

The inhabitants of Mindano appear to be all of the true Malayan race, without, as in some other islands of the Philippine group, any negritos. They are composed of many distinct tribes, speaking distinct languages, but of which no specimens have, that I am aware, been produced. "This island," says Dampier, "is not subject to one prince, neither is the language one and the same, but the people are much alike in colour, strength, and stature." He then describes those with whom he held most communication, and this with a simple, graphic fidelity which cannot be excelled. "The Mindanayans, properly so called, are men of mean stature, small limbs, straight bodies, and little heads. Their faces are oval, their foreheads flat, with black small eyes, short low noses, pretty small mouths, thin lips, and their teeth black, yet very sound; their hair black and straight; the colour of their skin tawney, but inclining to a brighter yellow than some other Indians,—especially the women."—Vol. i., p. 324, 325. As to language, what Dampier says of it is true to our own time. "In the city of Mindano (Selangan) they speak two languages indifferently,—their own Mindanao and the Malay,—but in other parts of the island they speak only their proper language, having little commerce abroad."—Vol. i. p. 330. Many of the inhabitants of the island are little better than utter savages, but the people of the southern side, and the Mindanese and Lanuns would appear to be nearly in the same state of social advancement as the Malays, and superior to the Malays of our time in enterprise and audacity, since from among them proceed the most daring and most dangerous pirates of the Archipelagos, the men that infest it by their cruises from one extremity to the other.

Mindano was discovered by the celebrated Magellan, on Easter Sunday of the year 1521, and, landing on its northern coast in the bay of Butuan, he took possession of it in the name of the King of Spain. The more civilised inhabitants have all been long converted to the Mahommetan religion, but with respect to the time or manner in which the conversion was brought about, nothing is known with certainty. Spanish writers, however, assert, with some show of probability, that it was effected from Borneo. It does not appear that the inhabitants had, like those of Sumatra, Java, Celebes, and Luzon, invented or used alphabetic writing before their conversion, but at present they follow the Malays in writing in an adapted Arabic character. No ancient monuments of any description are known to exist in the island.

The southern portion of Mindano is subject to the prince, who calls himself Sultan, and the whole northern, with a portion of the eastern and western, to the Spaniards, much of the interior being still in the occupation of wild tribes whose very names are unknown. The Spanish provinces amount to four,—Caraga, Nueva Guipuscoa and Misamis on the northern, and Zamboanga on the western side. The area occupied by these is stated at no more than 3617 square geographical miles, or less than one-tenth of that of the island, and their population, in 1841, was reckoned at 8000. The same rate for the whole island would give between 800,000 and 900,000 inhabitants, about 23 to the square mile, which is probably fully as much as it contains.

MINDORO. One of the large islands of the Philippine Archipelago, and of these by far the poorest and least populous, lies between north latitudes 12° 12′ and 13° 31′, and east longitudes 120° 12′ and 121° 29′. It is 89 geographical miles in length, and 56 in its greatest breadth, and is computed to have an area of 2917 square geographical miles. At its north-eastern end, it is separated from Luzon by a strait of about four miles broad, in the middle of which is the islet called Isla Verde. To the south-west it has the Calamianes group, the channel between them being that called by our mariners the Straits of Mindoro, while the Spaniards give this name to the narrow sea which divides Mindoro from Luzon. South of it lies the fine island of Panay, distant about forty miles, and to the east of it Marinduque and Isla de Tablas.

Mindoro is a mountain mass composed of a triple range running from north to south, some peaks of which are of considerable but unascertained elevation, especially that called Calavite at its north-western extremity, with another on its northern coast, fronting Luzon and four leagues from the coast. The ranges decline in height southward, until they terminate in the southern extremity of the island called Buracan or Punta del Diablo. A narrow belt of low land, of about thirty leagues in length, runs along the northern and eastern shores. The whole coast-line, extending to about seventy leagues, is unbroken by bays or inlets of any extent; but on the western side, and towards the southern extremity, there is one small and safe harbour, called Marguirin, close to the islands Ambolon and Ylin, and on the northern coast fronting Luzon there is another affording safe anchorage for small vessels, called Puerto galera, from its being the station for the galleys that cruise after pirates. The inland valleys are narrow, but one of them contains a lake between six and seven leagues in circumference, and distant about two leagues from the eastern coast. The geological formation of Mindoro has not been described, but it seems tolerably certain that it contains no volcanos, notwithstanding its proximity to Luzon, which abounds in them. The most remarkable geological phenomena connected with it are those produced by the action of water on its coasts. A very interesting account of these is given in a description of the island contained in the Diario de Manilla, for 1847, and of which Mr. Logan has published a translation. "The valley," says the Spanish writer, "which crosses from north to west, from Abra de Ilog to Paluan and Mamburao, is passable during the dry months; but that which crosses from north to east, from Calapan to Bongabon is not to be traversed at any time except by the wild inhabitants of the interior. In the centre of this last named valley, between the towns of Naujan and Pola, and at a distance of two leagues from the sea, there is a lake of six or seven leagues in circumference, fed by the waters which fall from the principal mountain chain. Those rivers which do not pursue their course until they collect in this lake, or the water which overflows from the lake itself in the rainy season, flood the entire valley, depositing in the lower grounds so abundant a sediment, that when the waters retire, and the ground dries up, the land becomes six or seven inches more elevated. The church of the old town of Naujan, situated in the immediate neighbourhood of the lake, has, in the course of less than fifteen years, become buried in the mud, as far as the key-stone of the arched door, and the inhabitants have found themselves obliged to remove to the sea-side. Nor is this the only change that the surface of the island of Mindoro has undergone. Every year the embankments of the small rivers which run into the sea change their position, overcome by the combined action of the wind and sea. The bay of Pola (at the extreme eastern point of the island) is formed by the submersion of a portion of the coast, in 1695, according to the chronicles of the religious orders. The town of Balalacao, in the southern part of the island, was founded less than ten years ago, upon a hill of a perfectly conical form in the middle of a green plain well cultivated. The hill is now an isolated mount, and the plain has become an inlet of the sea in which small vessels can anchor."—Journal of the Indian Archipelago, Vol. iii., p. 765.

The climate of Mindoro is hot and moist, but in general equal in salubrity to the rest of the Philippines. Some of the close valleys, however, are pregnant with intense malaria, producing their usual effects on the human constitution. "The deep and marshy valleys we have described," says the writer above quoted, "covered with dense forests which preserve a perpetual humidity, are constantly exhaling miasma, which prove prejudicial to health. The wind follows the direction of the valleys and empoisons the air of the narrow gullies, through which it makes its exit. At Abra de Ilog which is situated at the mouth of one of these valleys, a stranger cannot set his foot down, especially during the south-west monsoon, without catching a putrid or tertian fever. The inhabitants, taught by experience, have removed their parish church to Puerto Galera, and when they visit Abra de Ilog, they scarcely dare to pass a single night there. We frequently hear that the crew of a vessel which has anchored for only two or three hours in this dangerous spot, has become thoroughly infected with fever, and a great part has died in the course of three or four days. It is on this account that the labourers of the neighbouring provinces of Luzon will not go to the coasts of Mindoro for any amount of wages."—Ibid.

Nearly the whole island is covered with a dense forest. among which are found ebony and sapan wood, with many timber-trees affording wood suited to house and ship-building. The soil of the interior would seem to be generally stubborn or sterile, and the alluvial lands of the valleys and sea-coast intractable from rankness of vegetation and malaria. The products of the soil are the usual ones of the climate. The culture of rice is carried on but to a small extent, and generally not by irrigation, but by the rude and laborious one which consists in snatching an occasional crop from the forest lands, by felling and burning the trees, and dibbling the seed, a practice everywhere a sure indication of rudeness and poverty. Yams and manioc (Jatropha) are cultivated on the mountain sides, and the principal palms in culture are the coco and gomuti. From the last, and not from the true sago-palm, a sago is extracted which forms a main part of the subsistence of the people. Mindoro does not appear to produce any of the metals for economic use, and the only large wild animals ascertained to exist in the forests are hogs.

The inhabitants of Mindoro consist of two classes,—those of the coasts, and those of the interior. The first, now constituting the greater part of the population of the island, are the descendants of vagabonds and fugitives from the neighbouring provinces of Luzon, their language, which is the Tagala, being sufficient evidence of their origin. The most numerous people of the interior, of the same Malayan race with the other nations and tribes of the Philippines, are most probably the aboriginal inhabitants of the island. By the natives of the coast they go under the common name of Manguianos, but they are divided into many tribes, and speak at least one language (probably several), differing from any other language of the Philippines. They are almost naked, and wholly miserable, yet inoffensive savages. The Spanish writer already quoted gives the following lively account of their manners:—"The appearance they present is, in general, filthy and repugnant. Almost all are disfigured by the cutaneous disorder from which they constantly suffer. Those who are affected in a lesser degree are covered with a kind of white scurf, formed by the constant excitation of the skin, and the absence of cleanliness. Many of them suffer from chronic ulcers; others from large excrescences; some have a foot or a hand enormously swollen, while the leg or arm appertaining to it is withered or shrunken. . . . . They have no fixed domicile. They plant, here and there, tobacco, buyo (areca), sweet potatoes, and several other descriptions of edible roots; and pass the night under trees or in the hollows of rocks. For the infirm or sickly they have couches formed of trunks of small trees, parallel to one another, with one laid across to serve as a pillow. If they scatter a few dried leaves over the trunks, they consider this as constituting a very desirable bed. They have villages which contain two or three houses, if a shed with one side resting on the ground, or at best on a floor of bamboo, and the other elevated by means of two stakes or poles, deserve the name of house. In these hovels, which are only twelve or fourteen feet square, fifteen or twenty of these people shelter themselves, huddled together, without distinction of sex, age, or relationship. It is to this custom of sleeping pressed close together, and to squatting all day on their hams, that their peculiar mode of walking may be attributed. They advance very timidly, especially the women, with the body stooping forwards, precisely like an ape whose hands have been tied behind him, and who is consequently obliged to walk on his hind feet."—Ibid. p. 759. Besides these people of brown complexion and lank hair, there seems also to exist a race of negritos, or small negros, of whom, however, no description has been given.

The total number of the Manguianos or wild inhabitants of Mindoro has been estimated at 6000. By the census of 1850, the inhabitants of the coasts, distributed in six small towns amounted to 8921 souls, the greater number on the northern and eastern coasts opposite to Luzon. Calapan, the chief town, contained 2878 inhabitants, and Naujan, 3191. The number contributing to the poll-tax was 1910, and the amount of the tax 19,105 reals of plate. The total population, including the wild tribes, would be about 15,000, giving 5 inhabitants to the square mile, a miserable rate for a country so extensive and so favourably situated, and which proclaims its poverty and essential sterility.

Mindoro was discovered and taken possession of by Miguel Lopez de Legaspi, the conqueror of the Philippines, who deputed his nephew Juan de Salcedo to conduct the enterprise, which he accomplished with 30 Spaniards and a crowd of natives. This transaction must refer to the pirates of Mindano and Sulu, who had immemorially infested the Philippines, and formed their stations on the coast of Mindoro, and not to the native inhabitants of the island, who have never been subdued, because never thought worth while subduing. In 1570, Legaspi himself touched on this shore of Mindoro on his way from Pamay to the conquest of Luzon, and then imposed a poll-tax or tribute on the conquered inhabitants, being the first example of this tax in the Philippines. Its form, on this occasion, was an impost of 8 reals of plate on every family. Ever since its occupation by the Spaniards, Mindoro has continued to be scourged by the pirates of Mindano and Sulu, who afflicted it in the 16th century. They seem, even in the last century to have had their regular stations on its coasts, shifting them according to the monsoons, Mamburac on the western coast affording them shelter in the north-eastern monsoon, and Balete on the eastern during the north-western. Steam navigation will in all likelihood, put an end to this hereditary freebooting.

MINDORO, from the name of the island just described, is that of one of the provinces of the Spanish Philippines. It is composed of Mindoro, Lubang, Ylim and other small islands, and of the considerable one of Marinduque, although the latter be much nearer to Luzon. The province consists of ten towns, and in 1850 had a population of 35,136 of which 6445 paid the tribute amounting 64,450 reals of plate. In 1735 its population amounted to no more than 10,170; in 1801, to 15,845, and in 1818 to 18,796. The Island of Marinduque which is about one-eighth part of the size of Mindoro, contains a good deal more than double its population.

MINTO, correctly Muntok, is the name of the small town which is the seat of administration of the island of Banca. It is situated on the shore and towards the western end of the strait which parts the island from Sumatra, and opposite to the river on which lies Palembang, the capital of the princes to which Banca once belonged. It lies in a sandy plain, and a small river passes through it. In 1813, it contained a population of 1547, which in 1847 had risen to 3000. South latitude 2° 2′ 45″, and east longitude 105° 10′ 50″.

MISAMIS is the name of one of the four Spanish provinces of the great island Mindano, the most southerly of the Philippines. It lies on the north-western side of the island, having the province of Caraga to the east, and that of Zamboanga to the west with the territory of the Sultan of Mindano to the south. It has a coast line of 27 geographical miles, extends inland to from 20 to 27, and has an area of 1400 square geographical miles. The climate is hot and damp, but not unhealthy. Most of the country is covered with forest of unusual density. The woods contain such wild animals as the buffalo, hog, deer and monkeys. Several considerable rivers run through the province, affording facilities for irrigation, not taken advantage of. These and the bays and coves of the coast abound in fish, which determines the localities of the population. The washing of gold-dust from the sands of the rivers is one of the principal occupations of the inhabitants, a poor and indolent people composed of several indigenous tribes. In 1801, the population is stated to have amounted to 56,390, but in 1818, owing to the depredations of the pirates of the southern side of the island, it had fallen off to 30,164. In 1850, however, it had increased to 47,388. On account of their poverty, most of the inhabitants are exempt from the poll-tax which, in 1850, amounted to no more than 45,120 reals of plate. The total number of towns, or more correctly, of villages in the province is 30. The chief place, called like the province Misamis, is situated on the western side of the great bay of Yligan in north latitude 8° 23′ 10″, and east longitude 123° 46″. This, in 1850, contained 3,830 inhabitants.

MISOL, or MYSOL, but correctly Mesiial, is an island of the Molucca sea, lying west of New Guinea, and north of Ceram. Its most westerly point is in south latitude 1° 57′, and east longitude 129° 41′. It is 40 miles in length, and about 15 in average breadth, and therefore has a superficies of 600 square miles. The population of the interior is said to be negro, and that of the coast a mixture between the negro and Malay. Beyond these alleged facts nothing is known of this considerable island.

MOA, one of the Sarawati islands or group of islets which lies off the western end of Timur and towards New Guinea. It is in south latitude 8° 19′ and east longitude 128° 8′. The people are of the Malayan race, and are understood to speak the same language as those of the neighbouring island of Kisa.

MOAR or MUAR. This is the name of a river of some note in the history of the Malays, a place situated on it being that to which the Javanese founder of Malacca fled when driven out of Singapore, and where his descendant first took refuge when driven from Malacca by the Portuguese in 1511. The place is about ten leagues south of Malacca. At its embouchure, the river is 600 yards wide, and

18 miles up diminishes to one-sixth part of this breadth. A sand bar obstructs its mouth on which there is no more than three-quarters of a fathom of water. The whole country is an extensive primitive jungle. The district, which takes its name from the river, is subject to the Malay chieftain of Segamat, himself a nominal tributary of Jehor. The little state consists of about seven principal villages with a computed population of 2,400. Its productions are the usual ones for such a country,—most of them spontaneous products of the forest, as ivory, ebony, bees-wax, rattans, &c. The interior, however, yields a little gold and tin.

MOENA, correctly Muna, called also Pangasané, is the name of a large island, lying between Boeton and the south-eastern peninsula of Celebes. The channel between it and Celebes is about 15 miles broad in its narrowest part, and is interspersed with numerous islets. That between it and Boeton is from three-quarters of a league to a league in breadth, and full fifty long, and notwithstanding its narrowness, is navigable for large ships, having generally a depth of from 10 to 12 fathoms. Moena is about 105 miles in length, and 30 in average breadth, and is computed to have an area of 744 square geographical miles. The principal town, of the same name as the island, is in the interior, but the only port of any traffic is at the northern end fronting Celebes, and called Tiworo, giving name to the strait between the two islands. The inhabitants are of the Malayan race, like all those of Celebes, and speak a dialect of the language of Boeton, to the Sultan of which the island is subject. The Bajaus, orang-laut, or sea gypsies, fish tripang on the coasts of the island, and this article is the staple of its trade. The few traders are the Wajus of Celebes.

MOLUCCAS. The proper Moluccas, although the name has been extended to all the islands east of Celebes and west of New Guinea, consist only of five islets lying in a chain running north and south, on the western side of the large island of Gilolo or Halamahéra, and extending to about five-and-forty miles on both sides of the equator. Their names, beginning from the north, are Ternate, Tidor, Mortier, Makian, and Batjian; or in a more correct orthography, Târnati, Tidori, Mortir, Makiyan, and Bachĭan. These constitute the native country of the clove; the celebrated islands which mainly prompted the European nations of the 15th century to the discovery of the New World, and of a navigation which made known to them a portion of the old one, equal to the New in extent. De Barros tells us, that their ancient names were respectively, in the language of the natives, Gapé, Duco, Montal, Mara, and Sequé. But the meaning of neither old or new names is known; for the latter, which might be expected to be Malay or Javanese, are not so. The collective name, which the Portuguese write Maluca, and is correctly Maluka, is equally unknown, although said to be that of a place and people of the island of Gilolo. No such name is, at present, known to exist in that island. There can be no doubt, however, but that this word was used by the Malays and Javanese, who conducted the spice trade, before it fell into the hands of the Portuguese; for it is employed by Barbosa, who visited the Archipelago before the conquest of Malacca: and again in 1521, by Pigafetta, who writes the word Malucco. All that De Barros tells us of the name is, that it is a collective one for all the islands, as the Canaries and Cape de Verde are with European nations for these groups.

By far the largest of the Moluccas is Bachĭan, the most southerly. The rest are mere volcanic cones, springing from the sea; and Ternate, the most northerly and important of them, as well as the seat of the Dutch administration, is an active volcano, which has produced more eruptions since the first arrival of Europeans than any other in the Archipelago. This is De Barros' description of these famed islands as they were first seen by his countrymen. "The land of these islands," says he, "is ill-favoured and ungracious to look at, for the sun is always very near,—now going to the northern, and now to the southern solstice. This, with the humidity of the climate, causes the land to be covered all over with trees and herbs. The air is loaded with vapours, which always hang over the tops of the hills, so that the trees are never without leaves. Generally the acclivities of the hills, from their elevation, are healthy; but the coast, particularly in the case of Bachĭan, is unwholesome. The soil, for the most part, is black, coarse and soft; and so porous and thirsty, that however much it rains, forthwith the water is drunk up. And if a river comes from the mountains, its waters are absorbed before they reach the sea."—Decade 3, Book 5, Chapter 5.

The same writer's account of the state of society among the islanders is graphic and reliable. "Although," says he, "they have some millet and some rice, all the inhabitants of these islands eat a nutriment which they call sagum (sago), the pith of a tree resembling the palm, except that its leaves are more tender and their green of a darker hue. . . . And although the inhabitants have animals which serve for food, as hogs, sheep (?) and goats, with various wild animals, they prefer fish to flesh. In these islands there are no metals, although some allege that there is gold, which, however, we never saw. The people are of a tawny complexion,—have lank hair,—are robust in person,—strong limbed and addicted to war. In everything but war they are slothful; and if there be any industry among them in agriculture or trade, it is confined to the women. They are agile on land and still more so on water; for in swimming they are fish, and in fighting, birds. Altogether they are a malicious people, false and ungrateful, but expert in learning anything. Although poor in wealth, such is their pride and presumption that they will abate nothing from necessity; nor will they submit, except to the sword that cuts them, and through the blood of their bodies. Finally, these islands, according to the account given by our people, are a warren of every evil. and contain nothing good but their clove tree."—Decade 3, Book 5, Chapter 5. It is to be observed, that when this unfavourable picture of the inhabitants of the Moluccas was written, the Portuguese had been engaged in hostilities with them, resisting the imposition of the monopoly of the intruders.

With respect to language, De Barros observes, that the inhabitants spoke many different ones, so that the language of one place was not understood in another. These tongues, he adds, differed entirely, even in pronunciation, some "forming the word in the throat, others at the tip of the tongue, others between the teeth, and others again in the throat." "And," he adds, "if there be any common tongue through which they can understand one another, it is the Malaya of Malacca, to which the nobles have addicted themselves of late, and since the Moors have resorted to them for the clove."—Ibid.

Before the arrival of the Portuguese in India, all that was known of the Moluccas to the nations of Europe, amounted simply to the fact, that certain remote parts of India produced cloves; and this became known to the Romans about the end of the second century, when the clove came to be an article of import into the Roman provinces. The first true account of them is given by Barbosa, whose manuscript is dated in 1516. He names the five islands correctly; describes the growth and preparation of the clove, and the manner in which the trade in it was carried on. "From the city of Malacca," says he, "there go many ships to the islands of Maluco to load with cloves; and as merchandise they carry thither, cloths of Cambaya, and other cotton and silk stuffs; with commodities of Pulicaté and Bengal, and quicksilver, tin, unwrought copper, and copper made into bells, (gongs), with a money of China resembling a denier, (bagatino), but having a hole through the middle, (the pitis or pichis), and black pepper, porcelane, garlick, onions, with drugs of Cambaya. And of all these things they take great quantities."—Ramusio, Vol. i., p. 317. "At the time," says De Barros, "that we arrived in India, these two nations, the Javanese and Malays, carried on the whole of the spice trade, bringing all the spices to the famous emporium and fair of Malacca, now in our possession."

De Barros' account of the conversion of the inhabitants to the Mahometan religion is as follows: "Before the arrival of the Moors, the people of Maluca had no division of the year, and no weights and measures; and lived without knowledge of one god, or indication of any certain religion. Only some of them worshipped the sun, the moon and the stars; while others adored the powers of the earth, which some of them still do, the sea coast only being in the power of the Moors." . . . . . "And now, in the Maluco islands, many persons have been converted to the sect of Mahommed. . . . The Javanese and Malays themselves already converted, trading to the Maluca and Banda islands, converted the inhabitants of their coasts with which they held commercial intercourse. Of fourteen kings which the Maluca islands have had, the first who became a Moor was the king of Ternate, named Tidoré Vongué, father of king Boleifo, who entertained Francisco Serrão. According to the account given by the inhabitants themselves at the time of our arrival, little more than eighty years had elapsed since that pest entered the Malucas; and when Antonio de Brito arrived in Ternate, there still lived a Caçiz who gave it that hellish doctrine, (infernal doctrina)."—Decade 3, Book 5, Chapter 5.

The account given by De Barros of the time in which the inhabitants of the Moluccas were converted to Mahometanism, would carry it back to about the year 1440. Pigafetta, however, makes it a good deal later; but it must be observed, that he speaks of the island of Tidore, while De Barros refers to that of Ternate. "Scarcely fifty years have passed away," says the former, "since the Moors conquered Maluco and dwelt there. Before then, these islands were inhabited only by Gentiles, who set no value on cloves. There are still some Gentile families who have fled to the mountains, where also the clove grows."—Page 161. This would bring the conversion down to 1470.

The trade and intercourse of the Malays and Javanese with the Moluccas is certainly of a far higher antiquity than is to be inferred from the expressions of De Barros and Pigafetta. This is attested by the prevalence of the Malay language as a common medium of communication,—by the frequency of Malay and Javanese words in the native tongues, intermixed with Sanscrit; such as the current names of the spices themselves, articles not used by the natives even now, any more than they were in the time of Pigafetta, as condiments; and which, therefore, could only be raised to exchange with strangers.

The Portuguese, by the conquest of Malacca, were at once in the best position to obtain full information respecting the spice islands, and quickly availed themselves of it. "Alfonzo Albuquerque," says De Barros, "having, as already stated, taken the city of Malacca in the year 1511; and seeing that it was the mart at which was assembled all the trade of the east and of the west, as well as of so many neighbouring provinces and of thousands of islands, and feeling the importance of preserving it, since it was now in our power, resolved to make known to all the places in question, that they might resort to it without fear, and be treated with justice and favour. In order to further this measure, he despatched Antonio de Miranda to Sião, (Siam); Ruy d'Acunha to Pegu and Jaüa, (Java); and Antonio d'Abreu to Maluca. Before the last of these set out, he sent on before him one Nakhoda Ismael in a trading junk belonging to some Moorish Javanese and Malays of these parts, in order that when he arrived in the ports of Maluca he should be well received. As our name was wonderful in these parts, there seemed no risk of his not having a good reception. Antonio d'Abreu having sailed with three ships, proceeded on his voyage by way of Java, taking with him, besides his own Portuguese pilots, some Malays and Javanese who had before made the voyage. The first port he touched at was Agaçim, in Java, (Gressik), and from thence he proceeded to the island of Amboino, (Amboyna), which now belonged to the lordship of Maluco, from which it was distant about sixty leagues."—Decade 3, Book 5, Chapter 5. D'Abreu did not quit Malacca until the end of December, 1511, so that the actual discovery was not made until 1512, twenty years after Columbus had attempted it.

D'Abreu, however, went no further than Amboyna, a recent conquest of the kings of the Moluccas, and to which they had carried the culture of the clove. It was not until the year 1521, the same in which the companions of Magellan visited them, that the Portuguese presented themselves in the true Moluccas, and commenced their conquest under Antonio de Brito. They held them in all about eighty years, a period of anarchy and disorder. In 1602, the Dutch conquered Amboyna and Tidore under their admiral, Stephen Van der Hagen, and the other islands quickly followed. The same power has held them ever since with two short and profitless interludes of British occupation during the war of the French Revolution, amounting, jointly, to about twelve years.

MONEY. The current and convenient principal coin of the Malay and Philippine Archipelagos is at present, and has long been, the hard Spanish dollar, the peso duro of the Spaniards; and that with globes and pillars, containing 370·9 grains of pure silver, and worth in sterling money 51·79 pence, has an universal preference. The English rupee and Dutch guilder are but of local currency, and always, more or less, at a discount. The dollar, in the native languages, is known by various names. The Malays usually call it real, which is, no doubt, an abbreviation of the Spanish real de a ocho, or "piece-of-eight." The common name with the Javanese is ringgit, which literally means "scenic figure." Such figures had been represented on their own ancient coins; and the impressions on the Spanish coin appearing to resemble them, probably given rise to the name. They call it often also angres, that is, "English," probably from its being the money in use by English traders. Both Malays, Javanese, and Bugis call it very frequently pasmat, which is a corruption of the Dutch Spanish-mat.

A great variety of small coins of brass, copper, tin and zinc are in circulation throughout all the islands. The most frequent of these is the Dutch doit, of which about 300 ought to go to a Spanish dollar. The intrinsic value of all such coins, however, having no relation to their assumed one, and being usually over-issued, they are generally at a heavy discount. The small coins of Palembang, Achin, Bantam, and Queda are of tin. Those of the latter place go under the name of tra, which is, however, only the word "stamp" or "impression." Of these 160 are filed on a filament of ratan, of which 8 strings or 1280 coins are considered equivalent to a hard dollar. In Bali and Lomboc the currency consists of Chinese zinc coins with a hole in the middle for filing them on a string, each string having 200, and five of these called a siah, that is, "one thousand," being the highest denomination of money in the reckoning of the inhabitants of these islands. Their value rises and falls in the market according to the supply, like any ordinary article of merchandise; so that a Spanish dollar will sometimes buy 800 of them, but often as few as 500 only. All these small coins are generally known by the Javanese name of pichis, corrupted pitis by the Malays, a name which had extended to the Philippines. This was the name of the ancient coin of Java, and is now a frequent appellative for money in general, as well as for small change. Chinese coins of this description were found in the ruins of the ancient Singapore, of as early a time as the 10th century, as will be presently stated; and we have the authority of the first Europeans that visited Borneo Proper, the companions of Magellan, that they were the only money of that part of the Archipelago. "The money," says Pigafetta, "which the Moors use in this country is of brass, with a hole for filing it. On one side only there are four characters, which represent the great king of China. They call it picis."—Primo Viaggio, p. 121.

The only native country of the Archipelago in which a coin of the precious metals seems ever to have been coined, is Achin. This is of gold of the weight of nine grains, and of about the value of 14*d.* sterling; to which European traders have given the name of a mace, a corruption of the Malay mas, itself a corruption of the Sanscrit, masha, the name of an Indian weight. All the coins of this description that have been seen are inscribed with Arabic characters, and bear the names of the sovereigns under whom they were struck, so that they are comparatively modern.

With the exception of the gold coin now mentioned, evidently suggested by the Hindus, none of the nations of the Archipelago had any coin of the precious metals. When serving in Java between 1811 and 1817, a small earthen vase of silver coins was excavated in the province of Samarang, of which I received specimens. These consisted of small button-shaped pieces convex on one side and concave on the other, and having rude characters on both sides, but too much defaced to be legible. Mr. Marsden, to whom I presented them, and who was at the time engaged in preparing his work on Oriental coins, pronounced them to bear much resemblance to some ancient Hindu coins in his own possession.

Previous to the arrival of Europeans, the natives of the Archipelago generally, had no other coin than the small bits of copper, brass, tin, or zinc, already named. The Javanese appear to have coined some of their own money, as we find from many examples excavated from old temples and other places. These contain impressions of scenic figures, such as are still represented in their dramas called wayang or shadows, but having no dates, and, indeed, no written character, until after the adoption of Mahometanism. But besides these native coins there have been found in Java and elsewhere ancient Chinese and even Japanese coins. In Singapore, after our occupation, there were excavated some Chinese coins from among quantities of Chinese pottery. One of these bore the name of a Chinese emperor, whose death corresponded to the year of our time 967; of another to 1067, and of a third to 1085, so that it may be confidentially asserted that an intercourse, direct or indirect, existed between China and Singapore as early as the 10th and 11th centuries.

The absence of all other current coin than such as are now mentioned previous to the arrival of Europeans is testified by the early Portuguese historians, and this, even in Malacca, the most considerable trading emporium of the Archipelago. The enterprising Alboquerque before he quitted that place after its conquest, proceeded at once to supply this deficiency, actuated at the same time, in a good measure, by his hostility to the religion of its previous rulers. "Having," says De Barros, "done these things for the security of the city (built a fortification and a church from materials furnished by the tombs of ancient Malay kings), he did other things for its grandeur and for its commerce, and this, as if at the request of the people. With this view, he ordered money to be coined, for in the country, gold and silver passed only as merchandise, and during the reign of King Mahommed, there was no other coined money than that made from tin, which served only for the ordinary transactions of the market." Decade 2, Book 2, Chap. 2. Castaghneda is more full in his account of the transaction. "As," says he, "there was no money in Malacca except that of the Moors, the governor-general ordered some to be coined, not only that he might extinguish the Moorish coin, but also in order that a coin might be struck with the stamp and arms of his royal master. And taking on this subject the opinion of the Gentile Chetins (the Talinga Hindus), and other honourable men, dwellers in the city, he commanded forthwith, that a tin coinage should be struck. Of the one small coin called caixa (cash), he ordered two to be made into one, to which he gave the name of dinheiro. He struck another coin, which he named soldo, consisting of ten dinheiros, and a third, which he called bastardo, consisting of ten soldos. And as there existed no coin of gold or of silver, for the merchants made their sales and purchases by weighing the precious metals, the governor-general resolved, with the advice of the persons above-mentioned, to coin gold and silver money. To the gold coin he gave the name of Catholicos, and it weighed 1000 reas, and to the silver that of Malaques. Both were of the purest metal that could be smelted." Vol. 2.

Even the small coin now described seems to have been confined to the more advanced nations, for many of the ruder tribes had no money at all. In this state were the inhabitants of Celebes, some of whom now understand its use so well,—most of the people of Borneo and all those of the Philippine islands. It is remarkable, indeed, that the Malays of Brunai, or Borneo Proper, even to the present day, have no other money than the small tokens already mentioned, using blue cloths of Bengal and Madras as their larger standard of exchange. Some employed salt, cakes of bees-wax, and similar commodities, as a standard of exchange; but most of the civilised nations used gold dust, estimated by weight and touch, a practice in which it is evident from the derivation of the terms connected with them, that they were initiated by the Hindus, most probably the Telingas of the Coromandel coast. Thus, we have the scarlet weighing-bean rakit, from the Sanscrit raktaka, mas from masha, tail from talaka in the same language, with mutu the touch of gold, from the Telinga. The values of the denominations are all Hindu. Thus 24 of the scarlet beans each 2¼ grains troy make a mas, and 16 mas make a tail, while the touch is a scale of 10, like that of the Hindus. A colony of the Hindus of Telingana still exists in Malacca, whose profession it is to try gold by the touch and to refine it.

In the collections of the customary laws of the Malays, the mulcts imposed are always specified in the denominations thus named. The following are examples taken from the collection of those of Malacca, supposed to have been compiled under the direction of the first prince that adopted the Mahommedan religion. "If a man attempt to seduce a married woman, and her husband make complaint, the magistrate shall cause the offender to humble himself before the husband by making to him an obeisance in open court, and if he refuse, then he shall be fined 10 tails and one päa, (¼) or less, at the option of the magistrate. If a man attempt to seduce a married woman and the husband kill him, the slayer shall be fined 5 tails and 1 päa, for the offender only attempted to seduce, which is not a justifiable cause of homicide, excepting always, however, in the case of men of exalted rank. If a man attempt to seduce an unmarried woman, and her parents complain, the offender shall be fined 2 tails and 1 päa, and if the parties appear a suitable match, the magistrate shall cause them to be married, the offender paying to the parents the customary pecuniary consideration. If a man attempt to seduce a female slave, the property of another, he shall be fined 5 mas, but should he have cohabited with her, the mulct shall be double that amount. If a man deflower the slave of another, he shall be fined 10 mas, for he has committed violence. If a man deflower a free unmarried woman, the magistrate shall call the offender before him, and direct him to marry her, which, if he refuse, he shall be fined 3 tails and 1 päa, and pay to the parents, moreover, the customary consideration."

There is no word for "coin" in any of the languages of the Archipelago. For money, the Malay and Javanese name is uwang, abbreviated wang, but the Sanscrit word bânda is used in both languages, and yatra, also Sanscrit, in Javanese. Uwang or wang, in Malay, signifies also "the palace," and may, possibly, be the source from which the term for money is derived, in something like the manner in which our own coin is called "a sovereign." Both the Malays and Javanese use also the name of their small coin pitis or pichis for money generally, but wang is the common name throughout the Malay Archipelago. In the Tagala of the Philippines, however, money is expressed by the word salapa, and in the Bisaya of the same group by pilak, the first of these words being, no doubt, the salaka of the Javanese, and the last the perak of the Malays, both signifying silver. This is exactly the same proceeding as that of the modern European languages that use the Latin word for silver for the same purpose.

MONKEY or APE. I do not believe there is any genuine name to express the Quadrumanes or four-handed family of animals in any tongue of the Archipelago. In the different languages, each species has its own proper name, and the family is referred to generally by the name of the most familiar species, as kârá in Malay, and kâtek in Javanese. In Malay, there are names or synonyms for, at least, nine different species, and in Javanese for at least twelve, one or two of the last, as palgusa, being taken from the Sanscrit. The distribution of this family over the Archipelago is singular. In Sumatra and Borneo, there are for each ten species; in Celebes four; in Singapore and Banca three each; in Java four; in Bali two, and in Lomboc only one. In Mindano, Luzon, and the other large islands of the Philippine Archipelago, there are several species. East of Celebes no ape is found, the family being entirely wanting even in the large islands of Gilolo, Ceram, Timur and New Guinea. It is not less remarkable, that the greater number of species differ from each other in the different islands. Thus the four species of Java are not to be found in Sumatra, nor any of the ten of Sumatra in Java, although these islands lie within a few miles of each other. On the other hand, a few of the species of Sumatra and Borneo, as the orang-utan, the most manlike of all apes, agree, although these islands are 500 miles apart. It is probable that in the Malay and Philippine islands, there are, in all, not fewer than 50 distinct species, from the size of a cat to that of a child of ten years of age.

MONSOON. This is a corruption of the Arabic word musim, "season," which the Portuguese received from their first instructors in Indian navigation, the Arabs and other Mahometan navigators, and which they corrupted into mução, whence the form of our own term. The word in the sense of the Indian periodical winds occurs in De Barros, who wrote his history in the middle of the 16th century. Thus, when he is giving an account of the famine which took place in Malacca immediately after its capture, he ascribes it to the supplies of corn from Java being intercepted by the fleets of the expelled Malays, and by the impossibility of the Portuguese ships going for them themselves in consequence of the monsoon (mução) being adverse, that is, the south-east monsoon prevailing.

The word musim is in use among all the maritime nations of the Archipelago, but only as a synonym for the Sanscrit words kutika and masa, "time" or "season." To complete the sense, the words east or west, timur and barat in Malay, or wetan and kulon in Javanese, must be added. There is a peculiar idiom of the Malay language connected with the monsoons, which requires a short explanation. The Malays call all countries west of their own, "countries above the wind," and their own and all places east of it, "countries below the wind," the Malay words being atas angin and bawa angin. The expression is really equivalent to "windward" and "leeward," the west representing the first and the east the last. The origin of the phrase admits of no explanation, unless it have reference to the most important of the two monsoons, the western, that which brought to the Malayan countries the traders of India. It is at least as old as the 16th century, and no doubt, a great deal older. De Barros describes it, but mistaking east for west, he gives an explanation of the phrase which is necessarily erroneous. "For," says he, "before the foundation of Malacca, which by its position ought to be the Saba of Ptolemy, it was at Çingapura that the navigators of the western seas of India and the eastern seas of Siam, China, Champa, Camboja, and of the many thousand islands which lie to the eastward, assembled. These two different quarters (the east and the west), the natives of the country (the Malays) call Dybanangim (dibawa-angin), and Atazangim (atas-angin) which mean below the wind and above the wind, that is, the west and the east. For as the chief parties that navigate these seas proceed from two great gulphs, that of Bengal and that which extends towards the land of China reaching to a high northern latitude, it is in reason to call the one high and the other low." Decade 2, Book 6, Chap. 1. De Barros adds, by way of confirmation, that the expression may also have reference to the rising and setting of the sun in the east and west, and that it is consequently equivalent to the Levante and Ponente, or orient and occident of European nations, a plausible theory founded, however, on a mis-statement of facts.

The monsoons which blow over the Malayan Archipelago, are not two, but in reality four in number; namely, the north-east and south-west to the north, and the south-east and north-west to the south of the equator. To the two first are subject, the northern part of Sumatra, of Borneo and of Celebes, with the whole Malay Peninsula, and all the Philippine islands. The chief countries subject to the two last, are the southern parts of Sumatra, Borneo, and Celebes, with all the islands, from Java to New Guinea inclusive, south of the equator.

MONTRADOK. This is the name of the chief town of the Chinese gold-diggers of the western coast of Borneo. It is situated about 45 miles north of the equator, and about 25 from the coast, and in a wide plain within the territory of the decayed Malay chief of the principality of Matan. The Chinese of Montradok are settlers from the Chinese province of Canton, a rude but industrious people, all issuing from the labouring classes of society. Coming without their families, they intermarry with the Aboriginal inhabitants, and hence the population of Montradok is a mixed one. The manners, religion and dress of the parent country are preserved by them unchanged, and they preserve also the oral language of their province, few of them acquiring any knowledge of Malay. The washing of gold and occasionally of diamonds, with the raising of food for the miners, are their chief occupations. Of their number nothing is really known. They themselves estimate it at 110,000, but probably with exaggeration. Nothing is known of the manner or time of their first settlement, but probably the latter is of no very remote date. Since the restoration of their possessions in the Archipelago to the Dutch, they have brought the Chinese of Montradok under their authority, but this has been followed by several rebellions, making the conquest of more than doubtful advantage.

MORTAI or MORTY. This is the name of an oblong island about 60 miles in length, and 15 in its greatest breadth, lying off the northern end of the large island of Gilolo or Halmahera in the Molucca sea. Its length is from north to south, and lies between 1° 40′, and 2° 44′, north latitude, its northern cape being in longitude 128° 29′. The land of Mortai is described as high and forest-clad, abounding in deer and wild hogs, but of its human inhabitants nothing is recorded.

MORTIER or MOTIR. This is the name of one of the five true Moluccas, the smallest, and lying about 45 miles north of the equator. Like the others, it is a volcanic cone, but since the extirpation of the clove trees from the group to which it belongs in 1650, it has become of no importance.

MUSIC. There is no word for Music that I am aware of in any language of the Archipelago. In Malay the term buñi-buñiàn, a derivate from buñi "sound," is occasionally used to express it, but its real meaning is "musical instruments," the cause and effect being confounded. In Javanese the word tâmbang is sometimes employed for it, but the true meaning of this word is "song." In both languages the Sanscrit word lagu is used, but this really signifies, "air" or "time." Fine musical ears often occur among all the nations and tribes of the Archipelago, and in this respect they are favourably distinguished from the Hindus, and still more from the discordant Chinese. They are all passionate lovers of their own music and capable of acquiring considerable skill in European. Like all rude nations, their music is composed in a single common enharmonic time, the sounds produced by their instruments being the same as those by the black keys of the harpsichord. They have wind and stringed instruments and instruments of percussion.

Of the first of these, the most singular is a sort of gigantic Æolian pipe, frequently referred to in the poetry of the Malays under the name of buluh-pârindu, literally "the languishing bamboo," and occasionally of buluh-ribut, or "the bamboo of the storm." By far the best account of it has been given by Mr. Logan, in the narrative of his journey into the interior of the Malay Peninsula. It is as follows: "On our right there was a succession of neat cottages, amongst coco-nut trees, forming the village of Kandang. On nearing one of these, our ears were saluted by the most melodious sounds, some soft and liquid, like the notes of a flute, and others full like the tones of an organ. These sounds were sometimes interrupted or even single, but presently, they would swell into a grand burst of mingled melody. I can hardly express the feelings of astonishment with which I paused to listen to and look for the source of music so wild and ravishing in such a spot. It seemed to proceed from a grove of trees at a little distance, but I could see neither musician nor instrument, and the sounds varied so much in their strength, and their origin seemed now at one place, and now at another, as if they sometimes came from mid-air, and sometimes swelled from amidst the dark foliage, or hovered faint and fitful around it. On drawing nearer to the grove of trees, my companions (Malays), pointed out a slender bamboo which rose above the branches of the trees, and from which they said the music proceeded, and when the notes had died away in the distance, our ears were suddenly penetrated by a crash of grand and thrilling tones which seemed to grow out of the air that surrounded us, instead of pursuing us. A brisk breeze which soon followed, agitating the dark and heavy leaves of the fronds of the gomuti palms explained this mystery, while it prolonged the powerful swell. As we went on our way the sounds decreased in strength, and gradually became faint, but it was not until we had left 'the bamboo of the wind' far behind us, and long hidden by intervening trees and cottages that we ceased to hear it." The instrument which produced these fine effects was a bamboo cane, "rough from the jungle," from thirty to forty feet long, perforated with holes and stuck in the ground. This is certainly a very simple contrivance, but would not have occurred to any people who had not a natural taste for music. Certainly the Hindus and Chinese have, as well as the Malays, been living for ages among forests of bamboo without making such an invention.

But it is in the fabrication and use of certain instruments of percussion that the people of the Archipelago, or more correctly the most advanced of them, the Javanese, especially excel. These consist of the well-known gongs, a native word, and of bars of wood or of brass laid over wooden troughs, or suspended over them by cords. The gongs are used separately in the manner of drums; but smaller ones are also suspended over troughs, in the same manner as the bars. Both these form so many keys, in the manner of an harmonicon; and are struck by the musician sitting down, with a small stick armed with elastic gum. A competent judge, the late Dr. Crotch, after seeing the fine collection of Sir Stamford Raffles, said of these instruments, that he "was astonished and delighted with their ingenious fabrication, splendour, beauty, and accurate intonation." A full band of such instruments used to cost in Java up to 500*l*.

A band of music goes in Javanese under the name of gamâlan, a word of unascertained derivation; and from the Javanese it has passed into several other languages of the Archipelago. For every instrument of the band there is a specific name; and of the bands themselves there are no fewer than seven different sorts, each with its proper name. But there is no native name for a musician, except that which is formed by placing the word "artist," (tukang), before the band or instrument played on, the same idiom that is followed in forming the term for carpenter or blacksmith. Sometimes the word niyaga, which signifies musician in Sanscrit, is used. The native word, bâduwan, means, not a musician generally, but a public singer, which always supposes also a public dancer.

MYSOL. See Misol.

MYSORY. This is the Schouten Island of European geographers, and lies at the entrance of the great bay of Geelvink, on the northern side of New Guinea, penetrating the island so deeply as to convert it into two peninsulas. All we know about Mysory is, that it is about 60 miles in length, and 12 in its greatest breadth, that its western end is but 25 miles south of the equator, that it consists of high land, and that it is inhabited by negros, who have acquired sufficient skill in navigation to have, at one time, proved dangerous pirates to the Dutch possessions in the Spice Islands.

N.

NAGA. This word, in Sanscrit the name of a fabulous snake or dragon, is of frequent occurrence, singly or combined with other words, in all the cultivated languages of the Archipelago, and in those of the Philippines we see it in the names of places in composition, while standing alone it is the term for the prow or figure-head of a vessel.

NANING. This is the name of a small Malay State, lying inland from Malacca, and subject to it. It has a mean length of 40 and a mean breadth of 10 miles, and consequently an area of 400 square miles. In 1836 its population, consisting almost wholly of Malays, divided into ten tribes, or in the native language suku, amounted to 5881, but was increasing. Naning formed a portion of the territory of the ancient kings of Malacca, and from 1511 has been dependent successively on the Portuguese, the Dutch, and the English. It is a poor unprofitable possession, for the most part covered with jungle, and containing only from fourteen to fifteen inhabitants to the square mile.

NARANJOS (Islas de los), literally, "the Orange Islands." These are six small islands, lying between the extreme southern point of Luzon and the islands of Ticao and Samar. Their names are San Andres, the most northerly and the largest, Medio, Raso, Darsena, Escarpada and Agnada. San Andres is three leagues in length, by half a league in breadth, and its centre is north latitude 12° 23′. The Naranjos forms part of the province of Albay in Luzon.

NATAL, correctly NATAR, meaning ground, surface or foundation, is the name of a place on the western coast of Sumatra. The inhabitants are Malays of Menangkabo mixed with Achinese, but those of the interior are of the Batak nation. The town is on the shore of an unsafe roadstead, not far from a small rivulet. It is an emporium for the gold, camphor, and benzoin of the inland country, and for the iron, cotton fabrics, and opium given in exchange for them. North of Natal, and distant about 30 miles from it, is the mountain Siduwa-duwa (double mount), 7000 feet high, and east of it, at the distance of 75 miles, the volcanic mountain of Seret-bârapi ("fiery flounce"), estimated to be of the height of 5200. The settlement of Natal formed by the English in 1762, is now a Dutch possession. Latitude north, 32′ 30″, and longitude east 99° 5′.

NATUNA. This is the name given by navigators to three groups of islets in the China Sea, and lying between Borneo and the Malay peninsula, extending from north latitude 2° 28′ to 4° 56′, and from east longitude 107° 57′ to 108° 15′. The names given to them in our maps are the Grand, the Northern, and the Southern Natuna, which in the Malay language are respectively Bungoran, Sarasan, and Pulo-lant. The origin or meaning of the name Natuna is unknown, but was probably imposed by the Portuguese. All these islands consist of mountainous land, and the highest part of the Grand Natuna, which is visible from a ship at 15 leagues distant, must be from 2500 to 3000 feet above the level of the sea. This island is the only one of the three groups which is of considerable extent. Its form is round, and 15 miles in breadth, probably, therefore, containing an area of about 460 geographical square miles. The South Natuna, or Sarasan of the Malays, has an area of no more than 64 geographical miles. The larger of the Natuna Islands have the following wild quadrupeds, pigmy deer, but none of the larger species, hogs, and buffaloes; and all the islands, monkeys, squirrels, and the musang (Viverra musanga). The larger islands have also a few domestic oxen and goats, with poultry, consisting of the common fowl and a few ducks. All the islands are deeply forest-clad, their soil is sterile, and their cultivation consisting only of a few patches of rice without irrigation, maiz, the coco and sago palms. The larger islands only are inhabited, and by a population entirely Malay. According to native information supplied to me in 1824, the Grand Natuna had then a population of 600, the Northern group 300, and the Southern 400, making a total of 1300. The Natunas, in common with the Anambas, form part of the territory of Jehor, owning allegiance to the prince who lives under British protection in Singapore. The people of these islands exchange their fish, raw sago, and coco-nut oil at the European settlements in the Straits of Malacca for rice, clothing, and iron.

NAVIGATION. The name for this in Malay, layaran, or pâlayaran, taken from layar, a sail, is a literal translation of our own Anglo-Saxon word "sailing." Most of the inhabitants of the thousands of islands of the Archipelago are eminently maritime in their habits,—a real seafaring people. The Malays are more especially so, and this character is strongly impressed on their language. A few examples of this may be given in illustration. The words mudik and ilir, two peculiar verbs, not I believe found in any other language, respectively signify, to ascend and to descend a river, or to go against, and with the stream or tide. The same words employed as nouns signify the interior and the sea-board. Kuwala and muwara are terms which signify the embouchure of a river, either at its disemboguement in the sea or at its junction with another river, and such places will be found often the residence of the Malays. Anak-sungai means, literally, "child or offspring of the river;" tâluk, is a bight or cove, and rantau, the reach of a river; but these words also, from their being the frequent localities of Malay settlements, signify a district of country. The very structure of the Malay houses has reference to the accustomed localities of this people. They are all built on posts of 10 or 12 feet high, often half-submerged at flood tides, whereas the habitations of the agricultural nations, such as the Javanese, have their foundations on the ground. Sâbrang is a preposition which means across the water, and when turned into a verb, to cross the water, and into a noun, the opposite side. The Malay compass is subdivided into sixteen points, each of which has a specific name, all but one, and this Sanscrit, being native terms. The monsoons, or periodical winds, are distinguished by specific names by the Malays, and by them only of all the nations of the Archipelago. For every part of a vessel and her equipment, the Malay language has a specific name, and the names of the different kinds of vessels are very numerous—prau, that which is most familiar to Europeans, being the general one for all vessels. The language has also terms for the different modes of sailing, such as to luff, to go free, and to tack.

When Europeans first became personally acquainted with the Archipelago in the last years of the fifteenth and first of the sixteenth century, they found the Malays navigating it from one extremity to the other,—from Sumatra to Luzon northward, and from the same island to Timur eastward. The course of their navigation and trade is thus described by Barbosa, such as they were before the arrival of the Portuguese. After describing the voyage of the native traders of Malacca to the Moluccas for cloves, he adds, "They trade also at many islands on the way, as far as Timur, from which they bring white sandal of which the Indians (Hindus) consume much. In return for it, they give iron, needles, knives, swords, cloths of Pulicat and Cambay, copper, quicksilver, tin, lead, and paternosters of every sort coming from Cambay (carnelian beads). With such things they purchase the sandal-wood, and also honey, bees'-wax, and slaves. Then, they go to the Banda Isles for nutmegs and mace, for these are the places that produce them, and they give in exchange for them the merchandise of Cambay. They go also to Sumatra and other islands, whence they bring black pepper, silk in hanks (?) benzoin, fine gold, camphor, and aloes-wood, which are afterwards conveyed to Tanasori (Tennaserim), Bengal, Pulicat, Coromandel, Malabar, and Cambay." Barbosa in Ramusio, vol. i., p. 317.

At the time in question the Javanese were found to be conducting the carrying trade of the Archipelago in common with the Malays. This is expressly stated by all the Portuguese historians. Indeed, the Javanese at the arrival of the Portuguese were the most wealthy resident merchants of Malacca. Their trade, however, was not confined to this place, for it was carried on from several emporia of their own island, as Bantam, Jacatra, and Gressik. Both nations were found equally in possession of the mariners' compass, the name of which is derived from the Javanese word for a needle, dom, the derivative being pandoman, or the object with the needle. According to Ludovico Barthema they also used charts, but it is more than probable that they received both these and the compass from the Arabs in comparatively recent times, these people themselves having borrowed them from Europeans, as without doubt they did gunpowder and fire-arms.

It was not however to charts or the compass that the Malays and Javanese were indebted for their power to perform long voyages, but to the monsoons, and to the physical geography of the Archipelago, consisting of innumerable islands, each of which was a land-mark in its navigation. The periodical winds blowing steadily for several months from one quarter, and for a like number from the opposite one, enabled them to perform, without serious difficulty or danger, voyages outward and inward, which in any other seas would have been wholly impracticable to a people in the same state of society. Over 10° latitude of this navigation on each side of the equator, the adventurers were even safe from the equinoxial gales that vex regions beyond these limits.

The prevalence of the easy language of the Malays, as that of intercommunication with strangers in every part of the Malayan Archipelago, and even in the Philippines before their occupation by Europeans; the existence of Malay colonies or settlements on the coasts of most of the islands remote from the parent country of this people, and the infusion of more or less of the Malay and Javanese languages into all those from Sumatra to New Guinea and Luzon, are sufficient proofs, even of the antiquity of Malay navigation, for such effects are not the result of a few years' intercourse, but of that of ages.

Malayan navigation, although it probably embraced an area of not less than a million and a half of square leagues, it is certain never extended much beyond the bounds of the Malayan waters. The exceptions to this are few, and limited to places at a very moderate distance from them. It extended as far as Martaban on the Bay of Bengal, to the north, and to the south as far as the northern coast of Australia, for the fishery of tripang and tortoiseshell as it still does. In the China Sea the Malays went as far as the 10° of north latitude, planting a colony in Kamboja, the limit of the region which is free from the equinoxial storms. That Malayan influence, although not navigation, extended far beyond these limits, is sufficiently attested by the presence in the language of Madagascar, and in the languages of all the islands of the Pacific, of words of the Malay and Javanese tongues. On this obscure and mysterious intercourse, which more resembles the changes which have taken place in the physical geography of the globe than the civil history of man, I have offered some remarks in a Dissertation to another work which need not here be repeated.

The natives of Celebes have, in the navigation of the Archipelago, to a great extent, taken the place which the Malays and Javanese occupied before the arrival of the Portuguese. These consist of two nations, the Macassar and Bugis, but especially the latter. It is singular that Barbosa, who describes so correctly the trade which the Malays and Javanese conducted from Malacca, does not even name the people of Celebes as being present at that place. The first account we have of them is in the native annals of Ternate, as given in the "History of the Moluccas" by Argensola, where they are described as having frequented that island in 1338. The earliest notice we have of them in the annals of the Malays is in the reign of a prince called Mansur Shah, who ascended the throne of Malacca in 1374, and died in 1447. They are, in this case described, not as traders but as freebooters that harassed the trade of Malacca, under the leadership of a notorious pirate of the name of Samerluk, whose title of Kraing shows that he was of the Macassar, and not the Bugis nation. When the Portuguese first became acquainted with the inhabitants of Celebes, they had not yet been converted to the Mahommedan religion, and it seems to have been subsequent to their conversion that they acquired that industry and spirit of enterprise which has continued ever since to distinguish them. The account which Barbosa, in the beginning, and De Barros about the middle of the 16th century, gave of the people of Celebes, is probably greatly exaggerated, and indeed, is hardly credible of a people possessed as they were of the art of writing, and even of a literature. That they were, however, in a rude state, and possessed none of the enterprise which now distinguishes them, is certain. It seems probable that their comparative freedom from the depressing influence of European nations which has acted so injuriously on the Malays and Javanese, has been one of the chief causes that favoured the development of their character, and promoted their progress in civilisation.

The vessels in which the most distant voyages of the most civilised nations of the Archipelago are performed, are all of small size, seldom exceeding the burden of 50 or 80 tons. What they want in size is, in some degree, made up in numbers. The number of foreign and native vessels which yearly frequents the port of Singapore, and it includes the junks of China, Cochin China, and Siam, gives an average burden to each vessel of no more than 30 tons, their number being about 2400. All native vessels continue to use the oar as well as the sail. The larger vessels of the Malays and Javanese go under the name of jung, the same word which the Portuguese write junco, and which we have corrupted into junk, and apply to the huge unwieldy vessels of the Chinese. Neither of them have any name for a ship in our sense of the word, except the foreign one, kapal, which they have borrowed from the natives of Coromandel, who have immemorially traded with the western parts of the Archipelago in vessels that have some right to this name. Each nation of the Archipelago has its own form of construction, both as to hull and equipment, and by this their nationality is readily known. Flags, in so far as shipping is concerned, have been taken from the Portuguese, as the sole name, bandera, implies. Such rude native vessels as are here referred to are to be seen in the same harbours with the sailing ships and steamers of European nations,—with the unwieldy stereotyped junks of China, and with the lighter and more manageable ones of Siam and Cochin China,—all affording true types of the respective social conditions of the people to whom they belong.

The war-boats of the Indian islanders are but their merchant-vessels, built for speed, furnished with bulwarks, and better armed and manned. For open war, the presence of three powerful European nations has wholly superseded them, and the present vessels of war of the insular nations are only piratical praus. Speed is, in this case, the main object, and for this purpose, the hull is often built on a model which rivals that of our fastest steamers. In this fashion are constructed the praus of the most notorious corsairs of the Archipelago, the Lanuns of Mindano.

In the early period of European intercourse with the nations of the Archipelago, we find them in possession of large fleets of vessels of the description just referred to. Thus, the king of Malacca, after his expulsion from his capital, was still in possession of a fleet that in a good measure blockaded the town, interrupting the supply of corn from Java, so as to produce a famine in the recent conquest, and this in despite of the fleet of Alboquerque, who was himself still in the roads of Malacca. A still more remarkable instance was presented in a fleet which had been prepared by certain Javanese chiefs, for the purpose of wresting Malacca from the Malays, an enterprise which was persevered in, even after it was known that it had fallen into the hands of the Portuguese. Castaghneda gives the following account of this singular expedition :— "Fernâo Perez, admiral of the Malacca Sea, observing that the city was secure from attack, resolved to return to India. With this intention, he sent a message to the governor of Malacca, informing him that he would depart with the monsoon in January, taking along with him the merchant ships of Diego Mendez. Just as he was making preparations to leave, news came to the fortress that Pate Unus, lord of Japara, in the island of Java, had passed through the Straits of Sábáò (Sabon, one of the narrow straits leading through the islands at the eastern entrance of the Straits of Malacca), with a great fleet, and such turned out to be in reality the case. This Pate Unus was a Moor, a valorous cavalier, and not a vassal of the Gentile king of Java, against whom on the contrary, he and other Moorish lords had rebelled, calling themselves kings. Before the Governor-General (Alboquerque) had quitted Malacca, news had come, that Pate Unus had fitted out a great fleet, not only with his own means, but with the assistance of other lords, his friends and relatives, with the intention of attacking Malacca, and taking it from the Malay king, who was then still in possession of it. With this object in view, he sent many Javanese to reside in Malacca, in order to have them at his service when he should arrive there. Pate Unus had entered into a league with Mutaraja, the same whom the Governor-General had put to death, and this person had promised him his entire assistance. This fleet having been prepared, he did not desist from his enterprise, even although he knew that Malacca was now in our possession, for he was told that we were few in number, and might be easily overcome by the strength of his armada, which was very powerful, consisting, between juncos (jung), lancharas (lanchang, a barge), and calalenzes, of three hundred vessels. The fleet, equipped as I have now said, sailed for Malacca, and passing the Straits of Sábáò, was seen by certain people of the town of Malacca, who brought information of it to the Governor, Ruy de Brito, who forthwith communicated the news to the Admiral, Fernão Perez, in order that he might ascertain what fleet it was, and whether it was as great as it was represented."—Decade II., book 9, chap. 5.

Castaghneda's account of one of the ships that formed this fleet is curious :—"Pate Unus," says he, "gave orders to construct a ship which should be of the size of ours, 500 tons. In building her, he commanded that a second layer of planking should be placed over the first, and so on, to the number of seven coats. And between each layer of planking there was put a coating consisting of a mixture of bitumen, lime and oil. Each layer of planking they called lapis (in Malay, "fold" or "lining.") In this manner the sides of the junco were three palms in thickness, so that, wherever she might be placed, she would serve for a tower or bastion."—Decade II., book 9, chap. 4.

A part of this expedition made an effectual landing, but quickly re-embarked, and fled. It was pursued, attacked, and discomfited by five Portuguese ships, none of which could have exceeded the size of an ordinary corvette. This is the historian's account of the flight and pursuit :—"At sight of the flight of the enemy, our people were so overjoyed that they shouted 'Victory, victory, they fly!' Fernão Perez, making sail, gave the signal, 'Saint Iago, at them!' and it was marvellous what every one then achieved. It would be difficult to describe the daring, the courage, which every man displayed in this action. Suffice it to know, that our few ships appeared among the multitude of those of the enemy like so many wolves amid a flock of sheep. Our people had only to reach their little vessels to set fire to them with the materials we had prepared beforehand, and to pass on. The enemy, without means of defence, and without even attempting to take refuge in the river Muar, saw the vessel of Pate Unus himself turning her head in flight towards the Straits of Sábáò, and followed her. He himself, when he saw one part of his fleet burnt, and another sunk, ordered the vessels that were near him to come closer, in dread of being boarded, or sunk by our artillery, notwithstanding his many-coated ship."—Decade II., Book 9, chap. 5.

NEGRITOS, or Little Negros, a name given by the Spaniards to the negro race of the Philippines. See AETAS.

NEGRO. Races bearing a great resemblance to, yet very materially differing from, those of Tropical Africa, occur, from the Andaman Islands, in the Bay of Bengal, in the ninety-third degree of east longitude, to the Feejee Islands, in the hundred and eightieth, and from Luzon, in the Philippines, in the nineteenth degree of north, to New Caledonia in the twenty-first of south latitude, or over a space of eighty-eight degrees of longitude, and forty of latitude. Over this vast surface however, they are strangely and almost capriciously distributed. Of the Andaman Islands they are the sole inhabitants, while the Nicobar group, but thirty leagues distant from them, is occupied by a different race. We next find them in the mountains of the interior of the Malay Peninsula. But there is no trace of them in Sumatra, or in any of the islands lying between it and the Peninsula. They are absent in Borneo, in Java, in Celebes, and in all the islands east of them until we reach New Guinea, and the islands near its coast, where they form the only inhabitants, as they do of all the islands of the Pacific, east of it as far as the Feejees, and south as far as New Caledonia. After these two limits they disappear, and are not to be found in any of the islands of the northern or southern Pacific. In the Philippine Archipelago they form a scanty portion of the population of four islands only, namely, Negros, Panay, Mindoro and Luzon. These are all large islands, and they exist in no small one.

While these Negros differ widely from those of Africa, they are themselves far from being a homogeneous race, some of them even differing more from each other than others do from the African negro. Thus, all of them to the north of the equator, consisting of those of the Andamans, of the Malay Peninsula, and of the Philippines, are pigmies whose average stature does not exceed four feet eight inches, while those of New Guinea, and of the Feejee Islands are, at least, half a foot taller. Some of the negros of New Guinea, both as to stature and features, might be taken for Africans, which the most careless observer could not do with the puny negros north of the equator. Even in the Austral Negro, there are wide differences. Those of Malicollo and Tana are a diminutive people, while those of the Feejees and New Caledonia are a tall one. Even in complexion there is much variety. All are dark, although never of the ebony black of a Congo negro. The inhabitants of the Andamans are black, while those of the Philippines are described as of the colour of over-burnt coffee. The people of New Guinea are of a deep brown, with a bluish tinge. The hair of the head in all of them grows in separate spiral tufts, but in the negro of New Guinea, and in some of those of the Pacific Islands, it attains such a length that the wearer converts it into a huge turban, from whence Europeans have given them the name of mop-headed Indians. The hair of the Boreal negros, also grows in spiral detached tufts, but is short and incapable of the same elongation, and in this respect more resembles that of the African.

When the test of language is applied, in so far as we can judge from the few fragments we possess, all these negros seem widely different from each other. Of the grammatical structure of their languages we know nothing, but their phonetic character is often different, and their vocabularies never agree, except in a very few instances in which tribes are adjacent to each other, or when they have borrowed the same Malayan words. This was the result of an examination of from fifty to sixty words of seven languages, which I made myself in the Dissertation to a Malay dictionary, and it is confirmed by Mr. Windsor East, a writer who, by his knowledge and experience of these races, is by far the most competent judge. In his "Papuans" he has given a list of fifty-six words of four of the languages of New Guinea. Examining these, I find, as to indigenous terms, that the word for water, although differing materially in form, may possibly be the same in three languages, with some suspicion that all of them may be derived from the same Malay or Javanese word. The name for man and for the verb to speak agree in two languages. This is the sum of agreement in four languages, in so far as native words are concerned. The Malay words amount to six, namely, those for bird, tree, root, moon, fire, and dog; but besides these, there are the numerals in two of the languages. These last, are indeed, much altered in form, and after a fashion of which there are examples in the languages of nations of the Malayan race, as in the instance of those of the remote island of Timur. Thus, to the numeral one in Malay, sa, is added mosi, which, most probably, signifies a stone or pebble, and is the equivalent of the sawatu, "one pebble," the usual form of this numeral in Javanese, abbreviated satu in Malay. The four next numerals are corruptions of the Malayan, but after these, instead of adopting the common Malayan numerals, they combine the lower numerals with that for five, as five and one for six, and five and two for seven, and so on. As to the languages of the Boreal negros, they have absolutely not one word that I can detect, in common with those of the Austral, except in the instance of the language of the Sâmangs or negros of the Malay Peninsula, and here the similarity exists only through the common medium of the Malay. In so far, then, as the test of language is concerned, there may be as many different races of negros as there are tongues, and in the present state of our knowledge, these are not countable. The languages of the negros towards the eastern side of the Malay Peninsula, are stated to be entirely different from those of tribes towards the western. The languages of the innumerable tribes of the Negritos, or little negros of the Philippines, are stated to have no resemblance to each other, except in so far as they have borrowed a few words from the languages of the civilised brown complexioned people of the same islands.

In point of capacity, tested by social advancement, there is an immense difference between the different negro races. The negros of the Andamans are abject savages, in no way superior to the Australians, and, indeed, hardly on a level with them; and those of the Malay Peninsula and the Philippines are erratic savages, living on the precarious produce of the forest, and very little superior to them. Most of the negros of New Guinea, on the contrary, have fixed habitations, some knowledge of agriculture, and have domesticated the hog; and those of the Feejee group in the Pacific are on a par with the most civilised of the brown Polynesian race. In the present state of our information, then, the only conclusion we can reasonably come to is, that there are many different races of Asiatic Negros, wholly unconnected with the negros of Africa or Madagascar,—equally so with the Australians, and not traceable to any common origin. See AETA, PAPUA, SAMANG.

NEGRO-MALAYAN RACE. By this name may be designated a variety of the Man of the Malay Archipelago, certainly distinct from the Malay and the Papuan, but intermediate between them, or partaking of the characters of both. The stature is the same as that of the Malay or Papuan. The complexion is deeper than that of the first, but a good deal lighter than that of the last. The hair of the head does not grow, as in the Papuan, in separate tufts, nor is it long and lank as in the Malay. It is uniform over the scalp, and either curls or frizzles. This race embraces the aboriginal inhabitants of all the islands of the Archipelago, east of Sumbawa and Celebes, and west of New Guinea, with the exception of those of a few on the immediate coasts of the latter, peopled by negros. This includes, besides small islands, Floris, Timur, Gilolo, and Ceram, excluding Sumba or Sandal-wood island, which is inhabited by the Malay race. In some of the smaller islands, the character is less distinctly pronounced, as in the example of the five Molucca islets, where, by emigrations of Malays, Javanese, and natives of Celebes, there is a considerable admixture of the Malayan blood. No one has had personal experience of the inhabitants of the islands to which I have referred, without being struck with the difference which exists between them and the Malays. A judicious writer, who had long resided in Timur, in giving an account of this island, and some of the adjacent ones, thus describes the physical characteristics of its inhabitants: "The natives are generally of a very dark colour, with frizzled bushy hair, but they incline less to the Papuans than the natives of Ende (Floris). They are below the middle size, and rather slight in their figure. In countenance they more nearly resemble the South-Sea islanders than any of the Malay tribes." The inhabitants of Solor, Sabrao, Pantar, Ombay, and Wetter are described by him as resembling the people of Timur, "having the same kind of frizzled hair, and very dark colour." Of Solor he adds, "This island and Floris appear to be the most westward islands in which the natives have frizzled hair, as the people of Sumbawa, and of the islands to the westward of it, have invariably straight hair. The form of countenance of the last, also, is entirely different, and their manners and customs much less savage and ferocious."—Notices of the Indian Archipelago, by J. H. Moor, Singapore, 1837. The few of the aboriginal inhabitants of Floris, whom I had myself occasion to see in Singapore, certainly agreed with the character given by this intelligent writer, whose account was corroborated by the statements made to me by Bugis merchants, settlers in Floris. Of these statements, I find the following memorandum in a note-book, of the date of 1823: "Near half of the tribes have woolly or curly hair, and negro features, but not in the same decided degree as the inhabitants of New Guinea."

Of the existence of the physical characters thus described there can be no question; but it may be alleged to have arisen from an admixture, in the course of ages, of the Malay and Papuan races. This is, no doubt, possible, but we do not observe any such admixture in progress,—and from the repugnance of the races it is not likely to have proceeded to any considerable extent. On the contrary, the coasts of several of the islands are occupied by strangers of the Malay race, who hold themselves distant from the aboriginal inhabitants of the interior, while the line of demarcation which separates the Negro-Malayan race from the Malayan to the west, and from the Negro to the east, is sufficiently well defined. It may even be remarked, that it is the inhabitants of the islands which are nearest to those inhabited by the Malayan race, as in the case of Floris, that most nearly approach to the Negro character, while it is those of the islands nearest to New Guinea, as in the example of Timur, that partake least of the Malay, the very reverse of what would have been the case from an admixture of the two races. One strange anomaly, however, deserves notice. The inhabitants of one small island, that of Rotti, in the very centre of those which I have described as peopled by a Negro-Malayan race, is really inhabited by a Malayan people. "The inhabitants," says the anonymous writer, before quoted, "are below the middle stature, and considerably darker than the people of Celebes (the Malayan race), but are remarkable for having long lank hair, whilst nearly the whole of the inhabitants of the surrounding islands have frizzled hair. Their features are much more prominent, and they bear a stronger resemblance to the natives of India than to those of the Eastern islands. The women are much fairer than the men, and have, many of them, very pleasing countenances. They are esteemed a mild-tempered people, and are certainly not a jealous one."—Notices of the Indian Archipelago, by J. H. Moor. The resemblance to the Hindu features here supposed, implies, probably, nothing more than a strong contrast with the half-Papuan ones of the inhabitants of Timur, to which the writer was most accustomed.

NEGROS (ISLA DE). The island of Negros, so called from the number of the Negritos or Aetas found in it by the Spaniards, is one of the Philippines called the Bisayas. It lies between Panay to the north-west and Çebu to the east, divided from them by narrow straits from a league to three leagues broad. South from it is the island of Mindano, distant about 30 miles. Negros is 37 leagues long by from 6 to 10 leagues in breadth, and is computed to have an area of 260 square leagues, or according to other estimates 3827 square miles. Its coast is very little broken by bays or inlets, and does not contain any good harbour. A central chain of mountains runs through it from north to south, which attains its greatest height towards the latter point. The rivers are but of small size and unfit for the navigation of vessels of burthen. The largest is the Ilog, which falls into the sea on the western side of the island, and on which lies the chief town of the same name. The forest-clad mountains contain deer, hogs, and buffalos, with monkeys. The chief inhabitants are of the Bisaya nation, the same which peoples Panay, Çebu, and Leyte. The Augustine monks began early to convert them to Christianity, which was completed by the Jesuits who entered on the task in 1623. On their expulsion, the Dominicans succeeded them.

Negros forms, at present, a province by itself, although formerly united to Çebu and to parts of Panay. By the census of 1850, it contained 31 townships or districts, and a population of 58,773 inhabitants, exclusive of the Negritos or other wild tribes, of whom the Spanish writers give no account. Out of this population 12,856 were subject to the poll-tax or tribute, which amounted to 128,360 reals of plate. The density of population is little more than 15 to the square mile, a small rate, which would seem to prove that Negros is one of the poorest of the larger islands of the Philippines. The chief products of the soil, which although mountainous is fertile, are, rice, cotton, and abaca, with the coco and gomuti palms. The first of these articles is exported, and from the second and third, various tissues are woven for export, and cordage is manufactured from the gomuti.

NEIRA, correctly, Pulo-NERA, that is, in Malay, "Palm-wine Island," is the name of one of the islets which form the little group of the Banda or nutmeg islands. Neira, although much smaller than Lontar or the Great Banda, is the seat of the Dutch local administration and the most populous of the whole group, having had, by an enumeration made in 1840, besides slaves and convicts, 1225 inhabitants.

NEW GUINEA. The most northerly part of this vast island is only twenty miles south of the equator, while its most southerly is in latitude 8° 22′ south. From east to west, it is 1400 miles in length. It is conjectured to have an area of 200,000 square miles, which would make it about twice the extent of all the British islands put together. To the south, it is divided from Australia by a sea only 80 miles broad, and to the north it is washed by the Pacific Ocean, while to the west it has Ceram and the other islands of the Molucca Sea. New Guinea is composed of two peninsulas, an eastern and a western, the first by far the largest. This is effected by the deep gulf of Geelvink, which penetrates it so deeply from the northern side, as to leave an isthmus not exceeding 20 miles in breadth. Indeed, the island may be said to consist of even three peninsulas, for the western or smaller one is itself so deeply penetrated from the south by Mackluer's narrow gulf, as to make an isthmus between it and the western side of the bay of Geelvink, which does not exceed 40 miles broad. Of the whole island we know but a little, and this confined to a few spots of its sea coast. Of the interior, we know no more than Dampier and his contemporaries of the 17th century knew of that of Australia. That interior has never been trodden by the foot of an European, and, considering the nature of the country, of the climate, and of the inhabitants, many generations will probably pass away before it is explored.

The geological formation of New Guinea, from its extent, will be found, no doubt, to embrace almost every kind of formation. As yet, however, it has not been ascertained to have any active volcano, nor, indeed, any volcanic formation, slate and limestone being the rocks chiefly met with. A range of mountains running from east to west, is visible from both the north and south coasts, and which, having the appearance of being snow-clad, are computed not to be less than 20,000 feet above the level of the sea. On the southern side of the smaller peninsula, and forming the back-ground to the place which is called Triton bay, in latitude 3° 12′, and where a settlement was attempted in 1828 by the Dutch, there is a mountain trigonometrically measured, which proved to be only 2460 feet high, and exclusive of the great central range, the highest land even on the north side of the island is not thought to exceed 3200 feet.

The rivers of New Guinea are unknown, the embouchures of a few only having been seen, but it is presumed from the height of the great interior mountain range and the distance of the water-shed from the coasts, that there must exist some considerable ones. At a place called Oetenata on the western coast and on the larger peninsula in south latitude 5° and longitude 137° 30′ east, the Dutch discoverers of 1828, examined the mouth of a river which they estimated at four-fifths of a mile broad, but at a short distance above its debouchement it was found to branch off into three different streams. No lakes have been seen or even heard of.

The whole island, as far as it has been seen is one uniform and luxuriant forest, many of the trees of which run up to the height of 150 and 180 feet. The economical use of the timber of these huge trees has not been determined, but the forests of New Guinea produce three plants which have been immemorially in demand by the nations of the Malayan islands, namely, the true nutmeg (Myristica moschata) the missoy or masui (Cortex oninus) and the pulasari (Alyxia stellata). If the timber should prove to be of good quality, it is probable that it may come to be in demand with the European colonies of Australia, when these attain a dense population.

The character of the zoology of New Guinea partakes more of that of Australia than of the Malayan Archipelago, but in part it does so of both. Every one of the larger mammiferous land animals is wanting, except the hog. No animal of the bovine or equine families exist; no deer, no monkey, and no ferocious animal. The able and indefatigable Dutch naturalists, who pursued their researches on the southern coast for three months in 1828, found no more than six mammifers, and all of them belonging to the marsupial or pouched class. Three of these were new species, two of them kangaroos distinguished from all others of the same name by their singular habit of living in trees. French naturalists had before discovered another marsupial on the northern coast, and this with the hog, make the total mammiferous animals of New Guinea, as yet ascertained, no more than seven species. The paucity of mammiferous animals is in some degree balanced by the number of species of birds. The Dutch, on a few points of the southern coast, collected 119 species belonging to 60 genera. Among these, birds of prey were rare, and the family of pies altogether wanting. The most prevailing families consisted of the insect-eaters, parrots, and pigeons. Among the first were the birds of paradise, confined to the country of the Papuan negros. Among the parrots, were some from the size of a sparrow to that of the cockatoo. One of these, among the most frequent, was remarkable by its snow-white plumage, which, at a distance, gave a tree on which a flock of them lighted, the appearance of a profusion of white blossoms. Aquatic birds were numerous, both web-footed and waders, but more especially the latter. Among the birds met with were the helmet-headed Cassowary, the suwari of the Malays, and the megapodius which leaves its eggs to be hatched in earthen tumuli.

Of reptiles, the Dutch naturalists collected on the southern coast six and twenty different species, namely, fifteen lizards, five serpents, five frogs, and one tortoise. Fish appears to be abundant along the coast of New Guinea, many of the species esculent.

The men of New Guinea may now be safely pronounced to be one and the same throughout the island, a variety of the oriental negro. No other indigenous race has been found in any part of the coast, and the captives brought from the interior as slaves are found to be essentially of the same race. The negro of New Guinea, then, and in this matter the Dutch voyagers to the north, as well as to the south, agree, are men below the middle stature of Europeans, or about the same as that of the Malay, that is, from five feet three to five feet six inches high. The complexion varies from a deep brown to a black; the nose is more or less flat with wide nostrils; the mouth is large, the lips thick, the teeth fine and not obliquely set; the iris of the eye is black or brown, and the sclerotic coat tinged with yellow. The hair of the head grows in spiral detached tufts to the length of, at least, nine inches or a foot. The beard and whiskers partake, more or less, of this quality, and are ample. This is, in fact, the negro of tropical Africa, the complexion less dark, the facial angle less exaggerated, the stature shorter, and a woolly hair growing in separate tufts to a considerable length, instead of being spread equally over the scalp and short. Even with respect to the detached spiral tufts of the hair of the head, the Papuan is not singular, for the hair of the Hottentot grows in the same manner.

With respect to the state of society, a very wide difference seems to exist in different parts of the island. The inhabitants of the coast of the western peninsula and of the bay of Geelvink, for ages in communication with the western nations of the Archipelago, and especially with the people of the Moluccas, have been imbued with a considerable portion of their civilisation. These have good dwellings, are decently clothed, have large rowing and sailing vessels, a knowledge of iron, a little agriculture, and two domestic animals, the hog and the dog. That most of these improvements have been derived from strangers is attested by the evidence of language. Thus, the names for iron, rice, the banana, the yam, the coco and sago palms, are all taken, in such of their languages as have been examined, from Malay and Javanese. Terms implying commercial intercourse are from the same source. The names for silver and for bees-wax are Javanese, and all the numerals are Malayan. As we proceed eastward, or remove to a distance from the nations of the western part of the Archipelago, the tribes of New Guinea become more and more barbarous; there being some of those of the interior and even of the coast, that had never even seen the face of a stranger. When the Dutch, in 1828, visited the southern coast, opposite to the western angle of the Gulf of Carpentaria in Australia, they encountered, instead of the peaceable inhabitants of the coasts of the western peninsula, a tribe of naked and hostile savages, every attempt to hold intercourse with which proved vain. They had canoes, but neither iron, nor domesticated animals. The point at which these men were seen was in south latitude 7° 28′, and east longitude 138° 58′, and there is no ground for supposing that the inhabitants of the remaining five degrees of longitude to which the island extends eastward, whether of the coast or interior, are more advanced than these arrant savages. Of even the most improved of the negroes of New Guinea, it may be safely asserted, that in civilisation they are much below the aboriginal inhabitants of Borneo. At the same time, even the rudest of them must be admitted to be more respectable savages than the negros of the Andamans, of the Malayan peninsula, or of the Philippines, and still more so than their neighbours the Australians.

As far as they are yet known, the inhabitants of New Guinea are divided into small, independent, and generally, hostile tribes speaking different distinct languages. Both on the north and south coast, the Dutch discoverers of 1828 and 1835 required fresh interpreters as they moved on but a few miles. The population of a country of which the inhabitants are in such a condition must be small, but this is all that can be safely affirmed respecting its amount. Five inhabitants to a square mile would give New Guinea a million of inhabitants, but one-fifth part of this number is far more probable. Such, then, is the condition of a vast island, a large portion of which is within the same latitudes, subject to the same monsoons, and having the same temperature as Java, with its industry, its ancient civilisation, and its ten millions of inhabitants. The contrast must be ascribed to difference in the fertility of the soils of the two islands, to difference in locality, and most probably also to difference in the quality of the two opposite races which inhabit them.

New Guinea was certainly discovered by the Portuguese. Antonio d'Abreu was sent by Alboquerque from Malacca in 1511, in order to find out the Moluccas, but went only to Amboyna, from whence he proceeded to Banda. It is not certain whether he actually visited New Guinea, but he could hardly have failed to hear of a country immemorially visited by the inhabitants of the Moluccas, and not more than 170 miles distant from Banda, where he most probably saw negro slaves brought from it. The Portuguese called the country New Guinea, from the palpable resemblance of its inhabitants to those of Guinea in Africa, at the time well known to them. The Malays and Javanese call it Tanah puwah-puwah, which Europeans have corrupted into Papua. This word is a Malay or Javanese adjective, meaning "woolly or frizzly," and is applied to any object having this quality. The term at full length would be

Tanah orâng Puwah-puwah, that is "the land of frizzly or woolly-haired men." The name is applied by the western nations of the Archipelago, not only to New Guinea, but to all the islands near it inhabited by the negro race. Some recent geographers have thought proper to give the great island the name of Papua, but an innovation which is correct neither in sound, sense, or orthography, seems to possess no advantage over one which it has borne for now nearly three centuries and a half. No European nation had ever attempted to form a settlement in New Guinea until the Dutch did so on its southern coast in 1828, in the bay of Oetenata, in the 5° of south latitude, and 138° 30′ of east longitude; and this ended in a total failure. It required seven weeks time to clear a spot for a small redoubt, and when this was effected the insalubrity of the place was at once developed, and continued for several years until necessity compelled its abandonment. A country, indeed, without any other inhabitants than a few scattered savages, and in so far as concerns Europeans, having neither aptitude for pastoral or agricultural husbandry, no known native products of much value for exchange, and no near and convenient market, holds out no conceivable advantage for an European establishment. The future discovery of mines of gold, silver, copper, or tin, might tempt the settlement of Chinese, but not of Europeans in tropical and forest-clad New Guinea.

NIAS, or in Malay Nia, is the name of an island on the western side of Sumatra, and of the people inhabiting it, as well as of some others of the group called the Batu, or "Rock Islands." The principal part of the island of Nias is in north latitude 1° 22′, and east longitude 97° 31′, and the island itself is distant from the shore of Sumatra about 30 geographical miles. Its length is about 65 miles, its greatest breadth about 17; and it is computed to have an area of about 1200 square geographical miles. Its surface consists of mountain chains, nowhere rising above 800 feet, and of plains and valleys about 80 feet above the level of the sea. The rock formation is slate with sand and lime-stone, the decomposition of which with a considerable admixture of mould forms a soil of great fertility. Nias exhibits no evidence of volcanic formation, but is yet subject to violent earthquakes. One of these was experienced in 1843, which swallowed up a hill and a village, driving boats at anchor to the distance of 160 feet over the beach. This consisted of a single shock which lasted nine minutes, and is not stated to have been connected with any eruption of the volcanos of Sumatra. The botany and zoology of Nias have not been explored; but with respect to the latter, it is ascertained to have none of the larger ferocious quadrupeds. It wants also the elephant, rhinoceros, and tapir of Sumatra, its larger wild mammalia being confined to some deer, hogs, and monkeys.

The aboriginal inhabitants of Nias are of the Malayan race, and said to be a shade fairer than the nations of Sumatra, a circumstance from which some writers have very absurdly supposed them to be descended from Chinese, an hypothesis contradicted by their stature, which is the same with that of the Malays; by their manners, as well as by their language, which has nothing Chinese in it as to words or structure. In the "Malayan Miscellany," published at Bencoolen in 1822, there is a short vocabulary of the Nias, consisting of sixty-eight words, of which thirty-four are common to the Malay and Javanese, and six exclusively of that of the latter language, so that the native words amount to no more than eighteen. All the Malay and Javanese words are so altered and corrupted as to be very difficult of recognition. The inhabitants of Nias are a simple, mild, and primitive agricultural people. They have domesticated the ox, the buffalo, the hog, the dog, and common poultry, and in their husbandry use the plough and harrow. They practise a skilful irrigation, and raise rice, cotton, and other useful products. Their religion, without temples or images, consists in a belief in good and evil spirits, and it is remarkable of them that, although for centuries, in the neighbourhood of Mohammedans and even ruled by them, they have resisted the adoption of their faith. They live in villages in the interior of the island, these being surrounded by earthen walls and quickset hedges which, as their localities are well chosen, gives them a very picturesque appearance. While the other islands along the western side of Sumatra are inhabited by half savages, without skill or industry, the inhabitants of Nias are, in fact, a civilised people, an advantage for which they seem to be chiefly indebted to fertility of soil and facility of irrigation, the same conditions, although in a lesser degree, to which the islands of Bali and Lomboc owe their advancement. The result is shown in the extraordinary amount of the population, the total number of which has been computed at 169,500, which would give a relative one of better than 140 to the square mile, which far exceeds that of any island of the Malay or Philippine Archipelagos, except Java,

Bali, Lomboc, Luzon, and Panay. In the number of the population now named is included 350 natives of Achin, and about 3000 Malays inhabiting the coast, and living by trade and fishing. The Malays, notwithstanding their small number, are the dominant race, their chief town or village being on a bay on the northern shore of the island facing Sumatra. The island is claimed as part of the Dutch possessions.

NIBUNG AND NIPA. These are the names of two littoral palms, the Caryota urens, and Nipa frutescens, which are common to most of the islands of the Malay and Philippine Archipelago, and much used by the natives. The first forms the posts of houses and palings, and when hollowed out, water-pipes; and the leaf of the Nipa is the chief material of thatch with the inhabitants of the coasts. In the Philippines, but not that I am aware of anywhere else, the sap of the Nipa, a lowly plant, is used as a beverage, and for the manufacture of vinegar, and the distillation of spirits. On this account it yields a considerable part of the revenue of the Spanish government. Although a wild plant, for it is so abundant that its culture is not necessary, it is remarkable that its name should be the same in all the languages from Sumatra to the Philippines.

NITRE OR SALTPETRE. The only name for this salt in Malay and Javanese is sândawa; and it appears to be a purely native one, which has spread to all the languages of all the nations with whom the Malays and Javanese have held intercourse, although in some of them it be corrupted, as in the languages of Celebes, where it is sunrawa, and in those of the Philippines, in which we have it as sanyava. Saltpetre, in the Indian islands, is prepared from the decomposed dung of bats and swallows, accumulated in caves or old buildings; and is not, as in Hindostan, the almost spontaneous produce of certain soils. That it was known to the people of the Archipelago before they were acquainted with gunpowder, we may believe from their having a native name for a commodity which they only produced by art. But to what use they applied it, unless to the preparation of fire-works, for which also they have a native name, mârchun, it is hard to say. It is, at present, chiefly used in the manufacture of gunpowder, to which, in Javanese, it gives its name.

NUEVA ECIJA, or NEW ECIJA. This is the name of one of the provinces of the island of Luzon, in the Philippines, which had previously formed part of the large one of Cagayan. It consists of a portion of the eastern side of the island, or that called by the Spaniards the Contracosta. It is an extensive territory, which, with the exception of a few sheltered valleys, is for the greater part of the year, exposed to all the severity of the north-eastern monsoon. It extends in length to 240 miles; its greatest breadth being 48, and its area 5600 square geographical miles. The exposed mountains are either naked or have stunted trees, but the valleys are covered with forest. The climate, notwithstanding its tempestuousness, is considered salubrious. The land, although mountainous and generally sterile, contains some fertile and well-watered valleys. In 1850 the whole province, consisting of eighteen townships, contained a population, besides several wild races not brought under the Spanish rule, of 32,704, which gives the poor relative population of 5·8 inhabitants to the square mile, making it, therefore, the least populous and poorest province of Luzon.

NUEVA GUIPUSCOA. This is the name of a Spanish province of the great island of Mindano, created in 1850 out of the southern portion of that of Caraga, including the large but seemingly barren island of San Juan. No limits are stated by my authorities, but it seems to embrace all the eastern coast of Mindano between the latitudes of 7° and 9°. Neither is its population named; but it consists of eight townships, the most considerable being Davao, situated on a bay of the same name and the seat of the local administration. Here there is a small fort, the main object of which is, to afford protection against the pirates of Sulu and the southern coast of Mindano, the immemorial scourges of the Philippine islands.

NUEVA VISCAYA, or NEW BISCAY. This is the name of an under-peopled province in the centre of the island of Luzon, the chief of the Philippines. It was erected into a separate province in 1839, out of the southern portion of the extensive province of Cagayan. In 1850 it had sixteen townships; with a population, independent of several wild mountain tribes, of 22,192, of whom 5410 paid tribute. Its area may be taken at 2500, and hence its relative population will be no more than 8·8 inhabitants to the square mile, showing it to be one of the least populous and poorest of the great island to which it belongs.

NUMERATION. The Malayan decimal system of numeration with its terms more or less corrupted, although not universal, is very general, and this without regard to race, from Sumatra to the Philippines and to Easter Island, and from Formosa to New Zealand. It has even reached to Madagascar. The origin of this wide-spread system cannot, by any analysis of its terms, be traced to any particular nation; but as it is most perfect and comprehensive among the Malays and Javanese, and generally becomes less so as the distance from them increases, the presumption is in favour of its having had its source with one of these two nations. All the more civilised nations of the Malayan and Philippine Archipelagos adopt the whole system, which reaches to 1000; while the ruder or remoter tribes, such as those of the Pacific islands, have retained but a part of it; counting in it only as far as 100, and sometimes, indeed, only as far as 10. Of the corruptions which have taken place, a single example will be sufficient for illustration. In Malay and Javanese the numeral six is anâm, abbreviated nâm; and we have it thus in the languages of Sumatra, Java, Madura, Bali and Lomboc, but after this it assumes some strange shapes. In the Bugis of Celebes the initial *a* is turned into a peculiar vowel resembling the German *ö*, and the final *m* is converted into *ng*, the only consonant with which a word or syllable can end in that language. In the languages of Timur and its adjacent islets, it becomes näen. In one language of Floris it is ana by the elision of its final consonant; but in another it is lima-sa, which in Malay and Javanese means "five and one." In the language of Sangir, one of a chain of islands lying north-east of Celebes, the word becomes nong; and in Saparua, one of the Amboyna group, it is noï; so that in these two tongues all that remains of the original is a single consonant. In one language of the Philippines the word is anim, in another anum, and in a third unum; and these are written tongues, although in a very imperfect alphabet, especially as regards the vowels. When we get into the Pacific, we find the Malayan anâm converted by these languages in which no word can end in a consonant into ono, as in the Sandwich Island, the Tonga, and Feejee; while in the Maori, the medial consonant is turned from an *n* to an *m*. In the language of the Marian or Ladrone islands, we have the strange corruption of gurum; and in the Madagascar it becomes enind. Finally, in the language of the negros of Triton Bay, on the southern coast of New Guinea, the term is rim-sa-mosi, which means "five and one;" and is most probably equivalent to lima-suatu in Malay, and Sawatu in Javanese, which signifies literally, "five and one stone, or pebble."

But there are tribes even of the Malayan Archipelago who had invented a decimal system of their own, not superseded by the Malayan. Of this we have examples in the language of Tambora, in the island of Sumbawa; of Ternate, one of the true Moluccas; and in that of an inland tribe of negros, on the southern side of New Guinea, quoted by Mr. Windsor Earl. In all these cases there is not a vestige of the Malayan system: one example will be sufficient in proof. In all the languages which have adopted the Malayan system, the numeral five is expressed by the word lima, varied into lema, lim, rim, and nim. In the Tambora it is kutelon; in the Ternate, nomatoa; and in the Papuan tongue, siworo. An equal disagreement exists in the other nine digits.

Many of the ruder languages, appear only in part to have adopted the Malayan numerals, retaining some of what appears to have been a native system. This is shown especially in the first digit. In Malay and Javanese this, in its simplest form, is asa, abbreviated sa, to which the Malay adds in an abbreviated form, batu a stone or pebble, and the Javanese, also abbreviated, siji, a seed or corn, or tungil "alone" or "only." In the language of the Kayans of Borneo, the Malayan asa or sa is je; in the language of Kisa, one of the chain of islets extending from Timur towards New Guinea, it is ida; in the Manatoto, a language of Timur, it is nëe; in the Ceram, tăkura; in the language of the Aru islands, itu; in the Madagascar, trai; in the Marquesa and New Zealand, tahi, and in the Caroline island tot. In all these cases there is certainly not only no agreement with the Malayan word, but a very rude divergence among the quoted tongues themselves. In some instances, the Malayan digits seem to go no further than "five," some of the higher numbers being framed by adding the lower ones to it. We have an example of this in the Endé, a language of the western part of the island of Floris, in which the term for six and for seven, are literally "five and one," and "five and two." Even here, however there is an anomaly, for the term for "four" is a native word, and the number "eight" is framed by adding to it the Malayan numeral two, so as literally to make the term "two-fours," which would seem to indicate the remains of a native binal scale. We have another example of this in the negro language of Triton Bay, already referred to. Here all the units, up to five, are Malayan, although in a very corrupt form, while the numbers above it are formed by combining the lower ones with them up to nine. Among the digits of the Aru islands, close to New Guinea, "two" and "five" only are Malay, the rest being native, and in all the Polynesian tongues, while the units are Malayan, the tens, hundreds and thousands, are expressed by native words.

The languages of the negro races, equally with those of the fairer ones, have frequently adopted, in part or wholly, the Malayan numerals. The Sâmangs or diminutive negros of the Malayan Peninsula have adopted the whole, with the exception of the two first units, which are native, so that it is probable that before their intercourse with the Malays, they counted, like the Australians, no further than "two," The Papuans of the north and south coasts of the western peninsula of New Guinea and its adjacent islands have also, in general, adopted the Malayan numerals, for I find them in no fewer than five of their languages, which in all other respects differ from each other. One tribe, an inland one of the southern coast, has not done so, but has its own numerals up to five, the higher ones being formed by combining these with the lower digits in the manner already mentioned as being practised in some cases with the Malayan numerals.

I have supposed the wide-spread Malayan numerals to have originated with the Malay or Javanese nations, but to decide with which of these two, is difficult. In the languages of these two people, the terms for the numbers two, four, five, six, ten, hundred and thousand, substantially agree, while for the numbers seven, eight, and nine, they are wholly different. Now, in the cases in which these languages disagree, it is the Javanese and not the Malay form of the words that has been adopted by remote nations. This applies to the languages of Bali, Lomboc, Sambawa, Celebes, Floris, Timur, the Philippines, and even of remote Madagascar. The conclusion to be deduced from this is, that the Malayan system of numerals, most probably, originated in Java. But with the single exception of lima "five," which signifies also "the hand," (and even this, although it exists in some of the neighbouring islands as Bali, is obsolete in Javanese), the etymology of the numeral terms cannot be traced: the utmost that can be safely affirmed is, that the wide-spread Malayan numerals had, in all likelihood, their origin with the Javanese, the most cultivated people of the Archipelago. Certain it is that so complete a system never originated with any people that had not attained a considerable measure of civilisation, and that to ascribe the Malayan to a savage or rude people would, therefore, be unreasonable.

The Malayan numeral system, in so far as it is native, extends only to a thousand, the higher number being taken from the Sanscrit. The first step in this process is a blunder, consisting in making the term for 100,000 to stand for 10,000 only, and it is to be remarked, that the error has been copied by all those nations that count as far as 10,000, which includes all the nations of the islands of Sumatra, Bali, Lomboc, Celebes, the Philippines, and even of Madagascar. The only people of the Archipelago who have native characters to represent the numerals are the Javanese, and ancient monuments, both in brass and stone, carry the existence of these very satisfactorily as far back as the year of Salivana or Saka 1220, or of 1298 of Christ, that is to the last years of the 13th century, although it is probable that they are of a far higher antiquity.

NUSA, or NUSWA. In Javanese an island, the same as Pulo which equally belongs to it and to the Malay language. Nusa, like Pulo, is prefixed to the names of small but not of large islands, and by it we may trace the navigation of the Javanese eastward and westward from their own island, as in such names as Nusa-laut, "sea-island;" Nusa-niva, correctly Nusa-nîba, "fallen island," in the Amboyna group; and Nusa-telo, correctly Nusa- tâluh, "magic island," near the Banda group. Except on the coast of Java, however, the word is of rare occurrence.

NUSA-KAMBANGAN, literally, "Duck Island," is the only island of considerable extent to which the word nusa is always prefixed. It is a narrow island, about fifteen miles in length, and not exceeding three in breadth, lying on the south coast of Java, and separated from it by a very narrow strait, not navigable, except for boats. It is of considerable elevation, covered with forest, and almost uninhabited. It forms part of the province of Bañumas, the most westerly in this direction of the proper country of the Javanese, its western limits bordering on that of the Sundas. The western entrance of the strait which divides Nusa-kambangan from Java, called Cali-pujang (Kali-bujang, "bachelor's river"?) is a good harbour for vessels of burthen, and the only one along the whole extent of the southern coast of Java. The forced culture of coffee has of late years been introduced into the island by the Dutch.

NUSINGAN. The name of a large lake in the interior of the island of Mindano, in the territory of the Illanos or Lanuns, and in the centre of the isthmus formed by the Bay of Iligan to the north, and that of Illanos to the south. It is said to communicate with the lake of Apo, which discharges itself by a river into the lagune of Panguil, a continuation of the Bay of Iligan.

NUTMEG. This is the fruit of the Myristica moschata, the true nutmeg, a tree of the natural order of Myristicaceæ. It is an evergreen, bearing a general resemblance to the laurel or bay, and in its native climate growing to the height of forty or fifty feet. It is a diœcious plant, or bears male and female flowers on separate trees, but when cultivated, it has a tendency to become monœcious, or to produce both flowers on the same plant. The species of the genus Myristica are numerous and wide-spread, for some are found in all the islands of the Archipelago, in several parts of Hindustan, in the Hindu-Chinese countries, in the Philippines, in Australia, and in tropical America. As a spice, however, the moschata or aromatic is the only one of which the nut or mace is of any value, and of this the geographical limits are comparatively narrow, being comprehended between the 126th and 135th degrees of east longitude, and the 3rd degree of north, and the 7th of south latitude. It is, or has been, found wild in the proper Moluccas, in Gilolo, Ceram, Amboyna, Boeroe, Damma, the north and south sides of the western peninsula of New Guinea, and in all its adjacent islands. It certainly does not exist in its wild state in any of the islands west of these, nor in any of the Philippines. Wherever the soil and climate are suitable for its growth, the aromatic nutmeg is raised with great facility. It is even transported to remote parts, and the seed is disseminated by birds that feed on the mace dropping the nut. These birds consist of two species of pigeon, Colomba perspicillata and ænea, which prey on the nutmeg as our own wood-pigeons on the acorn.

In its native country the nutmeg tree comes into full bearing in its ninth year, and lives to seventy-five. In shape and size, the ripe fruit resembles a peach, or rather a nectarine. When ripe, the fleshy outer substance bursts, the nutmeg in its black shining shell is seen through the interstices of its reticulated crimson envelope, the mace, which last amounts to about one-fifth part of the weight of the whole dried fruit. These two articles, the nut and mace, constitute the spices which for so many ages have been in request among the nations of Europe and Asia, although never used as a condiment by the inhabitants of the countries that produce it.

The Hindus, who had traded for ages with the western parts of the Archipelago, such as Jacatra, Bantam, Malacca, and Achin, appear at these places, to have obtained the nutmegs, which they have immemorially used as a condiment. The Portuguese, on their arrival in the Archipelago, furnish us with the first accurate account of the nutmeg, and of the course of the trade by which it was conveyed from the place of its growth to western Asia and Europe. The Malays and Javanese, as stated elsewhere, carried on the interior trade of the Archipelago, and brought the nutmegs, as well as the cloves to the western ports, where they were purchased by the merchants of Continental India, and in later times also by the Arabs and Persians. The Banda, and not the true Molucca Islands, formed, latterly at least, the emporium to which the Malays and Javanese resorted for the purchase of both the clove and nutmeg, although they yielded the latter only. "From Amboyna," says De Barros, "Antonio D'Abreu, (the Portuguese discoverer of the Spice Islands) proceeded to the Isle of Banda, losing on his way the ship of Francisco Serrão, but, by God's blessing, saving the crew. And as the Moluccas comprehend five islands, so under the name of Banda, there are also five, each with its appropriate name. In truth, the chief of them is called Banda, to the principal port of which, called Lutatam," (possibly a misprint for Lontar, the name of the principal island,) "all ships resort that come for nutmegs. . . . . . Every year, there repair to Lutatam the Malay and Javanese people to load cloves, nutmegs, and mace. This place is in the latitude most easily navigated, and as the cloves of the Moluccas are usually brought hither, it is not necessary to go there to seek for them. In the five islands above alluded to, grow all the nutmegs and mace which are conveyed to every part of the world, in the same way as in the five Moluccas are grown all the cloves."—Decade II., book 5, chap 5.

This account of the course of the spice trade is confirmed by the current names of objects of trade, as well as by the names of places, all of which are either Malay, or Javanese; or Sanscrit through one of these tongues. Thus, in the case of the nutmeg itself, it had a native name in the language of the inhabitants of the Banda Islands,—galago; but this was unknown beyond the locality, and the current name for it was pala, as it still continues to be, and this has every appearance of being a corruption and abbreviation of the Sanscrit jatipahla. In the same manner we have Sanscrit names for sugar, black pepper, sandal-wood, and even for the clove, which seems to point to the fact of these commodities being chiefly wanted for the consumption of Hindus. As to the names of places, we have that of the whole group, which is properly Pulo or Nusa-bânda, literally, "Islands of wealth," and Lontar, which is half Javanese and half Sanscrit, and signifying, "the leaf of the Palmyra palm." In or near to the islands of the Molucca Sea, we have the following Javanese names of places:—Nusa-laut, "sea-island," Nusa-niva (niba), "fallen island," and Nusa tânuh, "magic island." As to Malay names of places, or names common to it and the Javanese, they are innumerable within the navigation embraced in carrying on the internal spice trade.

Barbosa, in his price current, gives us the cost of nutmegs in the market of Calicut in the beginning of the 16th century, before the native trade was interrupted by the conquests of the Portuguese, and as far as can be made out from the weights and moneys to which he refers, it seems to be about three pence half-penny a pound. But as the nutmegs in this case were, no doubt, in the shell, the actual price of clean nutmegs may be stated at about five-pence. The cost of nutmegs in Europe at the same time, enhanced by land and sea transports, and many imposts, was about four shillings and six-pence a pound, or close upon eleven times their prime cost at the nearest port of India to Europe. The present average price in the European market, although aggravated still by a monopoly in the genial land of production, does not exceed, exclusive of duty, above one-third of what it did before the discovery of the route by the Cape of Good Hope, a striking illustration of the difference between the Indian trade of the 16th and the 19th century.

The Banda or Nutmeg Islands, as elsewhere stated, were reached in 1512, by the Portuguese, under Antonio D'Abreu. From this time, until they were expelled by the Dutch in 1621, they were in possession of the monopoly, having driven away the Malay and Javanese traders, and changed the whole course of the trade. The aim of their successors, the Dutch, was exactly the same as theirs,—an exclusive monopoly. In the course of their efforts to carry this into operation, they were immediately involved in war with the natives, represented as a warlike and independent people, and the end of the war was the extermination of the inhabitants of all the Banda Islands, and the re-peopling of these islands by slaves and convicts. After a lapse of between two and three centuries, the monopoly still continues. This is certainly absurd enough in our times, but in justice to the Dutch nation, it must be stated that any other European nation would have, at least, in the earlier periods of the spice trade, pursued the very same policy they did. Our own was, above all others, solicitous to do so, and when even, in very recent times, it had twice over an opportunity of abolishing the monopoly, it left it untouched.

The result of the monopoly as to production is instructive. In 1708, after the Portuguese and Dutch had been for close on two centuries tampering with the trade, the total annual produce of mace and nutmegs was 870,000 pounds. In 1786, or in 70 years, it had fallen to 760,000, and at present is stated not to exceed 530,000 pounds, or by 340,000 less than it was about a century and a half ago, and indeed singularly enough, exactly the same quantity which is supposed to have been the consumption of all Christendom before the discovery of the route to India by the Cape.

The English, after the unsuccessful efforts of two centuries, succeeded at length in participating in the nutmeg trade, in consequence of having occupied the Spice Islands in 1796. In 1798 the nutmeg was introduced into Bencoolen and Penang, and in 1819 into Singapore, and at these places it is now largely cultivated, but certainly under the disadvantage of growing a not readily acclimated exotic. In countries native and congenial to it, the nutmeg is reared with great ease, requiring little care beyond shelter from the sun and weeding. In the countries to which it has been transplanted, the young trees require artificial shade, rich dressings of manure, and a fastidious care and attention in every stage of cultivation. With this expensive husbandry the trees will yield the same quantity and the same quality of fruit as in their native country, but will not attain above half the size or live above half the time. This is certainly very remarkable, and proves that the nutmeg is a peculiarly delicate plant, for the latitudes and monsoons of the countries of the western parts of the Archipelago to which it has been transferred are, generally, the same as those of its parent countries, nor can the soils be always dissimilar, for although those of the Banda Islands be volcanic, those of New Guinea and its islands are certainly not so, but probably much the same as those of Bencoolen, Penang, and Singapore. The growing of nutmegs, therefore, in countries not so congenial to it as its native ones, is somewhat like the attempt to grow maiz or the vine in the northern, in competition with the southern countries of Europe. Were the monopoly therefore abolished in the Dutch possessions, the probability is that the cultivation would cease in the British. But as the nutmeg even in its native country is always inferior in its wild to its cultivated state, a considerable amount of skill and labour must continue to be exercised in producing it even there; and as in the remote and rather rude countries most congenial to it, this is not likely soon to happen, it is probable that the culture in the British settlements may continue to be carried on for a long time.

In 1850 the total produce of mace and nutmegs in their parent country was, as already stated, 530,000 pounds, exclusive of wild ones, of which no estimate can be given. In the countries to which the culture has been transferred within the Archipelago (in every other region than this in which it has been tried it has failed for marketable purposes), the whole produce in the same year was estimated at about 470,000, making a total produce of 900,000. This, with the exception of wild nutmegs, which are not considerable, forms the whole consumption of the world "from China to Peru." The amount exceeds that of 1708 by no more than 30,000 pounds. As early as 1615, and while the Portuguese and Dutch were struggling for the monopoly, the consumption of our own country was estimated at 115,000. In 1850 it was short of 200,000. The consumption of black pepper in 1615 was no more than 450,000 pounds, and in 1850 had increased to near 3,200,000. Thus, in a period of 235 years, our consumption of mace and nutmegs had barely increased by 74 per cent., while that of black pepper, to say nothing of the correlative condiments of capsicums and pimento, had multiplied by no less than 611 per cent. When we consider these facts, and advert to the vast increase which has taken place in the wealth and population of the world during the last two centuries, it must, I think, be concluded that the taste for nutmegs in the middle ages, and in the earlier periods of the Indian trade, was a fashion which has been long on the decline, and that the article is at present the mere luxury of a very small number. This view of the taste for it having been in early times in some measure a caprice, seems to be confirmed by the recent change which has taken place in the relative estimations of the mace and nutmeg, which have qualities so near to each other that they cannot easily be distinguished, and which also, are always produced in the same proportions to each other. In former times the mace bore what may be called a fancy price, and sold for double the price of the nutmeg, or even more, whereas at present it is hardly equal to it in market value.

With respect to the nutmeg as an article of husbandry, it is hardly necessary to observe that it can have no possible advantage over any other commodity except in so far as it may be more suitable to a particular soil and climate. Within its own natural limits, very wide ones as it happens, it ought when not interfered with by legislation, to be always a staple product, for the obvious reason that it can there be reared with less labour than anywhere else. Beyond these it is certain that its culture must be conducted with manifest disadvantage, and that more congenial products ought to be preferred to it. The factitious value once put on it and on the clove, and which it is evident they owed to the caprice of fashion and their rarity, ought to be utterly discarded as simply irrational.

O.

OBY, correctly, PULO-UBI, that is "Yam island." This is the name of several islets in the Archipelago, but that which is best known to navigators is one on the coast of Cambodia, and at the entrance of the Gulf of Siam in north latitude 8° 25′, and east longitude 104° 54′. It is a mass of granite from 300 to 400 feet high, covered with a forest of stunted trees. When I visited it on my way to Siam in 1821, its inhabitants consisted of about a dozen poor Cochin-Chinese cultivating a few patches of vegetables. The soil is thin and sterile, and the place of consequence only as a land-mark, and for the wooding and watering of the junks trading between Siam, Cambodia and the Malayan countries. A large wild yam seems to be plentiful in the woods, from which, most probably, the island takes its name. Its only wild quadruped is a squirrel, and the most abundant birds are the white shore pigeon, Columba littoralis.

OBY MAJOR, a translation by the Portuguese of the Pulo ubi bâsar of the Malays, that is "Great Yam Island," the epithet being intended to distinguish it from an islet near it called Oby latta, or correctly, Pulo ubi lata, "Creeping Yam Island." Oby major is a considerable island of the Molucca Sea, between 30 and 40 miles south of Gilolo and the true Moluccas. Its extreme length from east to west is about 40 miles, its greatest breadth about 15, and its area 624 geographical miles. Around it are several small islands, as Gomona, Lukisong, Oby latta, Pulo-maya (Deception Island), and Pulo-pisang (Banana Island). Beyond these few particulars nothing is known of the island, and nothing at all of its inhabitants.

OLANGO. This is the name of a long narrow islet on the eastern side of Çebu, one of the principal Philippines. Maktan, the scene of the death of Magellan, lies between it and the main island. It is in north latitude 10° 15′, and in east longitude 124° 46′, distant about three leagues from Çebu.

OMBAY, correctly PULO-OMBAI (in Malay "fringed island"), is the furthest east, and the largest of the five islands which lie between the large ones of Floris and Timur. It is separated to the west from Pantar, correctly Putar, by a strait five miles broad, and to the east from Timur by one of fifteen at its narrowest part, the last well known to navigators as the Ombay Passage. Its extreme eastern point is in south latitude 8° 9′ 40″ and east longitude 125° 6′; and its extreme western in latitude 8° 9′, and longitude 124° 27′. Its greatest length, which is from east to west, is 45 miles, its greatest breadth about 10, and its area computed at 732 square geographical miles. At its western extremity it is indented by a deep bay. The land is high and bold, and the formation volcanic, although it is not ascertained to contain any active volcano. From the accounts given of them the inhabitants appear to be of the Negro-Malayan race, having dark brown complexions, thick lips, flattened noses, and frizzled or curling hair. They are a rude people, whose arms consist of bows and arrows, spears, and krises, and who have no knowledge of fire-arms. Like the rudest inhabitants of Borneo and Celebes, they are head-hunters, contenting themselves, however, with preserving, as a trophy, the lower jaw-bone, instead of the whole skull. They seem to have some acquaintance with iron, to practise a rude husbandry, and to have domesticated the ox, hog, dog, and common fowl. Such is the account given of them by the companions of M. Freycinet, who visited the island in 1817. Some of the natives of the coast, however, seem to have adopted the Mahommedan religion.

OIL, in Malay miñah, and in Javanese lânga, both of them words of extensive currency throughout the Malay and Philippine Archipelagos. The plants from which fatty oils are chiefly extracted are the coco-palm, the ground pea, the sesame, and the palma-christi; the first for edible use, and the three last for the lamp. In the islands of the Molucca Sea, a fine esculent oil is expressed from the nut of the kanari tree (Canarium commune). I am not aware that oil is expressed in any of the islands from cruciform plants, nor is flax reared for this purpose. Animal oils are hardly used in any shape: essential oils are obtained from the clove, the nutmeg, the kayu-puti (Melaleuca cajeput) and in great abundance and cheapness from the Malay camphor-tree (Dryobalanops camphora).

ONION (ALLIUM). The Malay and Javanese name for the onion is bawang, the latter tongue adding for the polite dialect, brambang. The word bawang is almost universal in the other languages of the Archipelago, wherever the plant is known. As in many other cases, however, it is a generic term, the epithet "red" being given to the common onion (Allium cepa), and "white" to garlic, the only two species of the family known in the Archipelago. The onion, a small variety, is largely cultivated in Java, but only at an elevation of three or four thousand feet above the level of the sea, so that although bearing a native name, or at least one not traceable to any foreign source, it is probably an exotic. It forms an article of inland traffic, and has long been exported. Thus we find Barbosa enumerating it as one of the articles brought by the Javanese to Malacca before the Portuguese conquest.

OPHIR. Among the many places to which this name has been whimsically given, there are two mountains, in the Archipelago to which the Portuguese have applied it,—one in the Peninsula, and one in Sumatra. The last of these is in the interior of the island, and towards its southern coast, inland from Pasammah. Its summit is computed to be 9200 feet above the level of the sea, but it is exceeded in height by six other Sumatran mountains. For the Peninsular OPHIR see LEDANG.

Of the celebrated place itself nothing is said in Scripture that will enable us to determine its geographical position. It is simply said to be one with which the Jews, with the assistance of the Tyrians, carried on a lucrative trade for about a century, but more especially during the reign of Solomon. We are, therefore, left to judge of its locality by the character of the people who conducted the trade with it, by the place from which it was conducted, and by the nature of the commodities brought from it.

In the time of Solomon, about eight and twenty centuries ago, the Jews were an inland people, partly agricultural, and partly pastoral. They were unskilled in the arts, as we find from the necessity they were under of bringing skilled artisans from Tyre and Sidon. They were unacquainted with iron, and the only metals known to them were gold, silver and brass, or rather bronze, the last of these received either from the Tyrians or Egyptians.

Neither do they seem to have possessed any maritime commerce until David effected the conquest of Edom or Idumea, when they became possessed of a small portion of the coast of the Red Sea, the Gulf of Eloth, now called Akaba, at the north-east part of its head. On this gulf was situated the port of Ezion-geber, which is expressly stated to have been "beside Eloth, on the shore of the Red Sea, in the land of Edom." Some, at least, of the ships with which the trade to Ophir was carried on were built at this port, for it is distinctly stated that the king "made a navy of ships in Ezion-geber," which, with the help of Tyrian mariners and pilots, performed the voyage to Ophir. Solomon is even stated to have visited Ezion-geber in person, a journey of no great difficulty, since it is not, in a straight line, above 120 geographical miles from Jerusalem.

The cause of Solomon's engaging in the trade to Ophir was evidently his having become possessed of a portion of the shore of the Red Sea, and his alliance with the Tyrian king. The conquered Edomites of the coast were at least fishermen, and most probably, as they are described as a people considerably advanced, carried on some traffic along the coasts of the Red Sea. The Jews themselves could have had no maritime skill, and the probability is that the Idumeans formed the bulk of the crews of Solomon's commercial navy. Even these, however, would be destitute of the skill necessary to conduct a fleet on the distant voyage to Ophir, and hence the necessity of employing the pilots and mariners of Tyre, already familiar with the voyage. It was not, however, pilots and mariners alone that the Tyrian king furnished, for he also supplied ships. "Hiram sent him by the hands of his servants ships and servants that had knowledge of the sea, and they went with the servants of Solomon to Ophir."

But the Jewish navy that traded with Ophir is also called a navy of Tarshish. This Tarshish must in all probability have been a Tyrian port or emporium on the shore of the Red Sea,—most likely on the Gulf of Suez, and would be the port of departure for the Tyrian fleet for Ophir, as Ezion-geber on the Gulf of Eloth, was for the Jewish. Both fleets would appear sometimes to have joined at Tarshish before taking their departure. Thus in Chronicles, the kings of Judah and Israel combine to build ships for the Ophir trade at Ezion-geber, in order to proceed to Tarshish. They were foiled in this project, however, for as the text says, "the ships were broken" (that is wrecked) "so that they were not able to go to Tarshish." The Tarshish thus referred to must have been on the same sea with Ezion-geber, and nothing could have been more natural than that the Jewish fleet should before starting, take advantage of the superior skill and safe convoy of the Tyrian. To suppose Tarshish, from its accidental resemblance in sound to have been, as some have done, a port on the coast of the Mediterranean, would be to make the Jewish fleet of Ezion-geber to sail over the Isthmus of Suez, since in Solomon's time there was no canal connecting the Red Sea with the Nile: nor even if there had been, could it be supposed that the boats suited to a canal would be fit to navigate an open sea. Tarshish, then, we may conjecture with considerable probability, was one of, and perhaps the principal of the emporia or factories which the Egyptians, not themselves a maritime people, granted to the enterprising Phœnicians on the Red Sea.

The Jewish trade with Ophir is said to have been conducted, not by Jewish merchants, but by the king, perhaps in the rude state of society which existed at the time, the only party competent to do so. This is at all events quite consonant to the practice of all the small rude and despotic countries of the East, as for example, of the Malayan princes. It was even so as late as in the Indian trade of the Portuguese, the monopoly of which was in the king's hands. That the government of Solomon was a rude and arbitrary one is sufficiently proved from the fact that the Temple was constructed, as such edifices always are in the East, by corvée, or forced labour, and that for want of skill in his own people, the labour was carried on under the direction of the Tyrians and Sidonians, whose services were paid for in corn and oil.

With respect to the length of the voyage from the gulfs at the head of the Red Sea to Ophir, some writers have inferred that it must have been to a very distant country from the following expression from the text of Scripture, "For the king had at sea a navy of Tarshish with the navy of Hiram. Once in three years came the navy of Tarshish, bringing gold, &c." This would not seem to imply that the voyage occupied three years, a length of time which the voyages of no rude people ever did occupy. With the Tyrians, the voyage to Ophir was most probably, as in all similar cases, an annual one, regulated by the periodical winds in the Red Sea, and the monsoons in the Indian ocean. The expression used would seem only to imply that the Jews, who were new to the trade, engaged in the enterprise but once in three years, having probably not the means of carrying it on regularly. Even what they did effect, they were enabled to accomplish, only through the friendship of the Tyrians. It is, indeed, impossible not to suspect that the so-called friendship of Hiram for Solomon was dictated by policy on the part of the Phœnicians, a small commercial people with distant factories, who would stand naturally in fear of the Jews, who had not only subdued all the nations of Palestine, but also the Idumeans, thus becoming their immediate neighbours at home on the Mediterranean coast, and also coming into close contact with their settlements on the Red Sea.

We may next consider the character of the Jewish trade with Ophir, from the nature of the commodities of which the cargoes of the ships consisted. Of the outward investment, nothing is said in Scripture, but we may suppose it to have consisted of Egyptian and Tyrian manufactures, since the Jews had none of their own fit for exportation. These would consist of linen, pottery, utensils, tools, lamps, musical instruments of bronze, and arms. Such commodities as these would have been indispensable for the payment of the gold and other articles which were brought from Ophir, unless we suppose the Jews to have been pirates, and the collection of a sufficient assortment of them might have occupied the long period which elapsed between each voyage.

The imports from Ophir consisted, according to our translation, of the following commodities, namely, gold, silver, precious stones, ivory, apes, peacocks, and almug-trees. The quantity of gold brought is in one place called 420, and in another 450 talents. The smallest of these amounts would make, according to the usual estimate of the Jewish talent, 573,720 ounces, at 4*l.* the ounce equal to 2,294,880*l.* This is an enormous and improbable sum, and most probably there is a mistake in the transcription of the numbers, and this is the more likely when we find the quantities differing in the two statements of it given. It is not, however, stated that the quantity of gold brought was the result of each adventure, and it is even more probable that it was the whole quantity brought from Ophir during the whole reign of Solomon. He is stated to have reigned twenty-four years, and as he is said to have inherited the trade from his father David, he may have made as many as eight voyages during his life-time. This would reduce the quantity brought in each adventure to the average of 71,715 ounces, or 286,860*l.*, still a sum far too large for a trade conducted by so rude a people as the Jews were some eight-and-twenty centuries ago. The countries which would furnish the largest supply of gold to the Tyrians and Jews would be the eastern coast of Africa, such as Senna and Sofala, where it is still found; and in this early period the washings or diggings may have been as productive as we have recently found them in California and Australia, a supposition which would diminish our surprise at the large quantity stated to have been brought by Solomon's fleets.

The same parts of Africa that furnished gold would furnish both apes and ivory, for the first exist there in numbers, and the elephant still abounds. They would not, however, produce the silver which was brought from Ophir, for these countries are not known to produce any, and if they did, it is not probable that the rude Africans would have understood the art of reducing the ore. As to the "precious stones" which were brought from Ophir, it is impossible to identify them under so general a term with any country. With so rude a people as the Jews, such things as agates, blood-stones, carnelians, garnets, and amethysts, would probably be considered as precious stones, and it is, indeed, highly improbable that they brought from Ophir, or obtained from any quarter, real oriental gems, such as the diamond, emerald, sapphire, and ruby.

What the almug-trees were, it is difficult to conjecture. They appear to have been foreign timber, known, however, to the Jews, for it had been previously imported both by themselves and the Tyrians. The navy of Hiram is expressly stated to have brought from Ophir along with gold, "great plenty of almug-trees." The uses to which the almug timber was put, show that it was in greater esteem than the cedars and firs of Lebanon. Solomon "made of the almug-trees pillars for the House of the Lord, and for the king's house,—harps also and psalteries for singers. There came no such almug-trees, nor were seen unto this day." Some commentators have supposed the almug to be sandal-wood, or the Santalum album of botanists; but this, from the uses made of it, and the omission to notice its perfume, its most remarkable quality, is highly improbable. The sandal-wood is a small tree, not much exceeding in size a large myrtle; while it is much branched, and the wood crooked. The sandal, in short, would not afford pillars for a temple which was thirty cubits high, nor is the timber at all suited for the manufacture of any kind of musical instruments, an use to which it is never put. In another place it is stated that Solomon made terraces, that is floors, of the almug-trees. But setting aside the cost, it is certain that planks for terraces could not have been sawn or hewn out of crooked wood, not above two or three feet long, or exceeding three or four inches in diameter. We may conclude, then, that the trees which would make pillars for a temple and palace, and terraces for the first, must have been of very considerable size, and hence that the vessels which imported them must have been of considerable burden, while the voyage could not have been very distant that would admit of so bulky an article being imported to profit. Solomon, indeed, might have imported them without regard to cost for the Temple, but the Tyrians, who seem to have imported them as a regular article of trade, would not have done so. If the almug-trees were really sandal wood, this would suppose a trade,—from the nature of the commodity, even a direct one,—with India, Malabar being the nearest country to the Red Sea that produces sandal-wood. That the almug or algum was a hard wood admitting of a polish, is to be inferred from some of its uses. It was, probably, the high polish of which it was susceptible, that recommended it in preference to fir and cedar as ornamental pillars for the temple. The Jewish psalteries are described as a kind of staccatos with wooden keys, apparently similar to the gambangs of the Javanese; and if so, the keys of these would require a hard and sonorous wood, which no native tree of Syria or Egypt might have afforded in the same perfection as the foreign wood called almug.

According to the Latin version of the Scriptures, and to our own and those of other modern European nations, "Peacocks" are among the things brought from Ophir. The Greek version, however, passes by the word which we so render altogether, the translators having been evidently unable to make up their minds what it meant. The original Hebrew word is "tuchiïm," which, as a name for the peacock, cannot certainly be traced to any foreign tongue. The nearest country to Egypt and Syria in which the peacock is indigenous is Hindustan, and hence it has been concluded that Ophir was in some part or other of that continent. The Hebrew word, at least, will give no countenance to this supposition, for it bears no resemblance to the name of the bird in any language of that continent or its islands. Thus, in Sanscrit, the name for the peacock is "manyura," changed in the ancient and recondite language of Java into "mañura." My friend, the learned and accomplished Professor Wilson, has furnished me with the names of the peacock in eight of the principal languages of Hindustan. In Hindi, Bangali, and Gujrati, they are merely corruptions of the Sanscrit name. In the languages, however, of the nations of the south, or that portion of India which the Phœnicians and Jews are most likely to have frequented for trade, the terms are different, and seemingly native. Thus in the Tamil and Malayalam, the name is "mayil," and in the Telugu and Kanarese, "nemali." Not one of these, however, bears the remotest resemblance to the "tuchiïm," of the Hebrew. In Malay and modern Javanese, the name is "mârak," evidently a native and local word, and neither Indian nor Semitic.

The Persians appear early to have received the peacock in the domestic state from India, and from Persia it would appear at an early period to have been received in Greece, a fact which seems to be corroborated from the Persian and Greek names, "täus" or "tawus" being essentially the same. Even the Arabs seem, although probably at a much later time, to have received the peacock through Persia, since the Arabic name of the bird is identical with the Persian.

But there are other facts which make it highly improbable that the Hebrew word, tuchiïm, should mean the peacock. Independent of its great size, this bird is of delicate constitution, which would make it nearly impossible to convey it in small vessels, and by a long sea-voyage, such as that from Gujrat or Malabar to the head of the Red Sea. Another argument still more cogent may be urged, that the tuchïm or peacock is never mentioned, before or after, in any part of the Old Testament; nor, indeed, is it at all likely that the early Jews should be acquainted with this bird, seeing that they were even ignorant of the hardy, useful, and easily transported Common Fowl, like the peacock a native of India. The pigeon, indeed, seems to have been the only bird which the Jews had domesticated before their conquest by the Greeks.

It seems far more probable that parrots were meant by the word tuchiïm. These hardy and long-lived birds are easily conveyed by long sea-voyages. Many of them, and of several species, are brought yearly as objects of traffic in small vessels all the way from New Guinea to the most westerly parts of the Malay Archipelago, a voyage which the peacock would not survive. It may even be added that the Persian and Arabic name for parrot, tuti, bears a nearer resemblance to the Hebrew word, than any Indian one of the peacock.

All the commodities forming the imports from Ophir, could not well have been the native products of one and the same place, and hence it is to be inferred that Ophir was an emporium at which the different articles enumerated were collected. Africa would certainly furnish gold, ivory, and parrots, but it is not celebrated for its precious stones; and with the addition of the double voyage, which would be implied by conveying them through an emporium, is not likely to have furnished the timber-trees, called almug. It could not have furnished the silver which formed part of the homeward investment, since it is not known at any time to have possessed silver mines; while, even possessing them, the rude natives cannot be supposed possessing the art of smelting the ore. Another objection to placing Ophir in any part of the eastern coast of Africa, is to be found in the incapacity of its savage inhabitants to consume the valuable manufactures which, of necessity, the Tyrians and Jews must have given in exchange for the rich cargos which they brought back. Ophir certainly cannot, with any show of probability, be placed in any part of India or its islands, since none of the peculiar products of India, sandal-wood and peacocks being the only ones supposed, are shown to have been so. The great distance of that country, a direct voyage to which from the Red Sea would be incompatible with such skill as we are warranted in attributing to the early navigation of the Phœnicians, makes it very improbable that Ophir was in that country.

All the enumerated commodities of the ophir commerce might easily have been collected at an emporium convenient for all the parties engaged in the trade; and the most probable station for it would be on the southern coast of Arabia, or even within the Arabian Gulf itself, on its eastern shore. The enterprising character of the Sabæans, or early Arabians, would determine an emporium to such a locality. With the help of the monsoons, these Arabians might have traded not only to Ethiopia, but even to India. With the first of these countries they are expressly stated to have traded, and they could easily have brought from it gold, ivory, and parrots to their own country. The monsoons would, in such a voyage, afford a fair and steady wind outward and homeward; and even if the voyage extended beyond the entrance of the Red Sea and as far as the southern shore of Arabia, it would not equal in length that which is yearly performed at present, and has been performed for ages, by Malay praus between New Guinea and Sumatra under similar auspices.

The Arabs might even have extended their navigation eastward as far as India, although from the nature of the commodities constituting the exports from Ophir, there is no evidence that they did so, no mention being made of any of its peculiar products. If the Tarshish of Scripture was, as I have supposed it, situated on the Gulf of Suez, the commodities which that place furnished to Tyre were probably brought from India to Ophir, and thence by the Phœnicians to Tarshish, to be conveyed by a short land journey and a brief coasting voyage to Tyre. They consisted, according to Ezekiel, of silver, iron, tin, and lead. India Proper could only furnish of these commodities iron, while the tin must have been brought to the emporia of Malabar from the Malay Archipelago; and as to the silver and lead, China, and the countries immediately west of it, could alone have furnished them,—if they really were Asiatic products. The lead might have come from the same countries through the Malayan, Malabar, and Sabæan ports; and the diffusive precious metal through many channels.

It seems probable that the Phœnicians themselves never went beyond Ophir, or some other Arabian emporium, trusting to the Arabians to bring thither the commodities of India. This, at least, is consonant to what we know of the course of trade among all rude nations. Thus, on the arrival of the Portuguese at the end of the 15th century, the Malayan nations carried on the internal commerce within their own waters, but never went beyond them. The Chinese from the east, and the nations of Hindustan from the west, frequented only a few emporia of the Malay Archipelago, and seldom went beyond them. The intercourse between India and the Arabian Gulf was then in the hands of the Arabs, the descendants of the same men who conducted a portion of it in the time of Ezekiel, about 587 years before the birth of Christ, but now in possession of astronomical instruments and the compass.

The character of the Tyrian shipping carrying on the trade of Ophir, and of the Jewish which were an imitation of them, may be readily imagined. They must of necessity have been of inconsiderable size to have enabled them to carry on a coasting voyage, in the course of which it would often be necessary to put into small creeks for shelter against bad weather, as well as for wood, water, and provisions. They must have been equally adapted for the sail and the oar, the last indispensable to save them from being wrecked on a lee shore. They must have been built of fir, the only timber abundant in Syria and the other countries in the neighbourhood of the Red Sea; and it may be conjectured that the largest of them would not exceed 100 tons burden.

If the Tyrian and Jewish fleet proceeded no further than Mokha, this would itself be a voyage extending over 18° of latitude. At Loheia, in latitude 15° 30′, the fleet would encounter the monsoons. If Ophir was on the Arabian coast, at such a place, for example, as the bay of Kanin-kanin, into which runs the river Shab, the voyage would extend over 21° of latitude and 13° of longitude, and in a straight line be not less than 1320 miles in length. In the northern parts of the Red Sea, northerly winds prevail for eight months in the year. If the fleet for Ophir sailed towards the end of these winds, they would take them to Loheia, where, in the middle of June, they would meet the south-west monsoon; which, after quitting the Straits of Bab-al-mandab, would be a fair wind along the whole southern coast of Arabia.

From all that has now been stated, I think it may be concluded that the Ophir of Scripture was a commercial emporium, situated either close to the entrance of the Red Sea on its Arabian side, or not far east on the southern coast of Arabia. The nearest of these localities to the head of the Arabian Gulf, would assuredly have been a long and difficult voyage even for the small coasting craft of the Phœnicians, and still more so for the confessedly inexperienced Jews; without supposing voyages to India, or far south on the coast of Africa.

The celebrated German orientalist, Lassen, however, has placed Ophir somewhere about the debouchement of the river Indus; a locality which would have yielded no gold, except as an emporium, and which, in that capacity, could have received it from no country nearer than Sumatra, about 2500 miles of a coasting voyage distant. His hypothesis is founded on some supposed resemblance between the Hebrew and Sanscrit names of the commodities brought from Ophir. The nearest resemblance is in the words for an ape, that in the Hebrew being koph or kof; and in Sanscrit, kâpi or kepi. The similitude then consists in the initial letters being the same, and in the second consonant being one amenable to transmutation, while the vowels are different, and the word in one language a monosyllable, and in the other a bi-syllable. It is far more probable then, that the remote resemblance between the two words is purely accidental, than that one should be a corruption of the other. The resemblance between the Hebrew and Sanscrit names of other commodities is still more remote. Thus, the Hebrew word which is supposed to represent the peacock, has been sometimes written sukhim, and this is fancied to be derived from the Indian word, sikhi; but this last word, although taken from Sanscrit, is the name of the bird in the language of Bengal, and not of any tongue of Western India, being, moreover, only an epithet signifying "crested." The German hypothesis, too, supposes that Sanscrit was the vernacular language of the Indians that traded with the Phœnicians, which is not probable, since it is not even ascertained that that tongue was ever the living speech of any Indian nation, and was, assuredly, always a foreign one in Southern India.

OPIUM, the inspissated juice of the poppy, is known to all the nations of the Archipelago by no other name than its Arabic one, afyun; from the absence of the letter *f* in all the cultivated languages, pronounced apyun. Neither is the poppy cultivated for its juice, or its oil, in any part of the Archipelago, so that there can be no doubt but that the Malayan nations were first made acquainted with opium, directly or indirectly by the Arabs, the same people that made them acquainted with ardent spirits, and gave them a religion that denounces the use of both. The earliest account we have of its use, not only for the Archipelago, but also for India and China, is by the faithful and intelligent Barbosa. He writes the word "amfiam," and in his account of Malacca, enumerates it among the articles brought by the Moorish and Gentile merchants of Western India, to exchange for the cargos of the Chinese junks, and such is, in some degree, the course of the trade even in the present day. He also tells us that it was an article of import from Arabia into Calicut, besides being brought to that place from Cambay, and he quotes its various prices. His account of it runs thus :—"Opio (the orthography here varies from that in his account of it given under the head of Malacca), which comes from Adem (Aden), and is prepared there, is worth in Calicut, each farazuola, from 280 to 320 fanoes (fanam), and another sort which is made in Cambaya, from 200 to 250." The farazuola, he informs us, is a weight equal to twenty-two pounds six ounces and a half of Portugal; and the fanoes he reckons to be of the value of a silver real, probably about fourpence halfpenny. With these data, the value of the Arabian opium, most probably Turkish, brought by the route of Aden, would be from 4*s.* 8*d.* to 5*s.* 6*d.* the pound avoirdupois; and that of the Indian, most probably from Malwa, from 3*s.* 4*d.* to 4*s.* 5*d.* The average of these prices would make the value of a chest of Turkish opium, weighing about 134 pounds, 157 hard Spanish dollars; and one of Indian of 148 pounds, 132 dollars. These prices are about one-third part the cost of Indian opium at present. But it is probable that Barbosa's opium of the beginning of the 16th century paid little or no duty, while that of our times, either through duty or monopoly, is subject to a very heavy impost.

Opium, is at present, largely consumed in the Malayan islands, in China, in the Indo-Chinese countries, and in a few parts of Hindustan, much in the same way in which wine, ardent spirits, malt liquor, and cider, are consumed in Europe. Its deleterious character has been much insisted on, but, generally, by parties who have had no experience of its effects. Like any other narcotic or stimulant, the habitual use of it is amenable to abuse, and as being more seductive than other stimulants, perhaps more so; but this is certainly the utmost that can be safely charged to it. Thousands consume it without any pernicious result, as thousands do wine and spirits, without any evil consequence. I know of no person of long experience and competent judgment who has not come to this common-sense conclusion. Dr. Oxley, a physician and a naturalist of eminence, and who has had a longer experience than any other man of Singapore, where there is the highest rate of consumption of the drug, gives the following opinion : "The inordinate use, or rather abuse, of the drug most decidedly does bring on early decrepitude, loss of appetite, and a morbid state of all the secretions; but I have seen a man who had used the drug for fifty years in moderation, without any evil effects; and one man I recollect in Malacca who had so used it, was upwards of eighty. Several in the habit of smoking it have assured me, that, in moderation, it neither impaired the functions, nor shortened life; at the same time fully admitting the deleterious effects of too much." There is not a word of this that would not be equally true of the use and abuse of ardent spirit, wine, and, perhaps, even of tobacco. The historian of Sumatra, whose experience and good sense cannot be questioned, came early to the very same conclusion. The superior curative virtues of opium over any other stimulant are undeniable, and the question of its superiority over ardent spirits, appears to me to have been for ever set at rest by the high authority of my friend Sir Benjamin Brodie. "The effect of opium, when taken into the stomach," says this distinguished philosopher, "is not to stimulate but to soothe the nervous system. It may be otherwise in some instances, but these are rare exceptions to the general rule. The opium-eater is, in a passive state, satisfied with his own dreamy condition while under the influence of the drug. He is useless, but not mischievous. It is quite otherwise with alcoholic liquors."—Psychological Inquiries, p. 248.

It may be worth while to show what is really the relative consumption in those countries in which its use is alleged to be most pernicious. In the British settlement of Singapore, owing to the high rate of wages, and the prevalence of a Chinese population, the consumption is at the rate of about 330 grains, or adult doses, a year for each person. In Java, where the Chinese do not compose above one in a hundred of the population, and where wages are comparatively low, it does not exceed 40 grains. Even in China itself, where the consumption is supposed to be so large, it is no more than 140 grains, chiefly owing to the poverty of the people, to whom it is for the most part inaccessible. It must not be forgotten, that some of the deleterious qualities of opium are considerably abated in all the countries in question, by the manner in which it is prepared for use, which consists in reducing it to a kind of morphine, and inhaling its fumes in this state. Moreover, everywhere consumption is restricted by heavy taxation. The opium of India pays, in the first instance, a tax which amounts to three millions sterling. The same opium, in Singapore, with a population of 60,000, pays another impost of 30,000*l.*; and in Java, with a population of ten millions, one of 800,000*l.* Not the use, then, but the abuse, of opium is prejudicial to health; but in this respect it does not materially differ from wine, distilled spirits, malt liquor, or hemp juice. There may be shades of difference in the abuse of all these commodities, but they are not easily determined, and, perhaps, hardly worth attempting to appreciate. There is nothing mysterious about the intoxication produced by ordinary stimulants, because we are familiar with it; but it is otherwise with that resulting from opium, to which we are strangers. We have generally only our imaginations to guide us with the last, and we associate it with deeds of desperation and murder; the disposition to commit which, were the drug ever had recourse to on such occasions, which it never is, it would surely allay and not stimulate.

ORÂNG. In Malay, a man or human being, in the singular or plural; also people. It is probably the same word which appears in the popular language of Java as wong.

ORÂNG-GUNUNG. A mountaineer; and hence, a rustic or clown. The Malays apply the phrase to any people less cultivated than themselves.

ORÂNG-LAUT, literally men of the sea, or sea-people. This is the most frequent name given by the Malays to that rude class of their own nation whose permanent dwelling is their boats, without any fixed habitation on shore. They are also called rayat-laut, or, abridged, rayat; literally, "sea-subjects," the last word being only a slight corruption of the Arabic word with the same signification, the phrase meaning the sea-subjects of the kings of Malacca or Jehor. Occasionally, too, they go under the name of Sika, the meaning of which I do not know; and more frequently of Bajau, which is probably the same as the Javanese word, bajag, a pirate or sea-robber, a name to which they have often earned a title. Some English writers, from their wandering habits and suspicious modes of life, have, with a good deal of propriety, called them "sea-gypsies." The native locality of this people, for it cannot well be called country, is the straits or narrow seas of the many islands between Sumatra and the Malay Peninsula, towards the eastern end of the straits of Malacca. There, at least, they are congregated in the greatest numbers, and own allegiance at present to the kings of Jehore, as in former times they did to those of Malacca. From this locality they appear to have spread themselves, most probably step by step, to the shores of Banca, Billiton, some of the islands on the eastern and western coasts of Borneo, the coasts of Celebes, and even of Boeroe and other islands of the Molucca sea, from which again they make voyages to the northern coast of Australia, in search of tripang and tortoise-shell. "At Pulo Tinggi (on the eastern coast of the Malay Peninsula, in north latitude 2° 17′) we found," says Mr. Thomson, a very intelligent traveller, "many orâng-laut, or sea-gypsies, assembled. A large crop of durians, this season, had attracted tribes of them from the coasts of the Peninsula, as well as from the islands of the Jehore Archipelago. Six boats from Mora, an island of that group (about fifty miles north of the equator), we found on their way to Pulo Tinggi. They had travelled by sea a distance of 180 miles to partake of the fascinating fruit. This would appear incredible were it not explained, that these people live in their boats, changing their position from the various islands and coasts according to the season. During the south-western monsoon, the eastern coast of the Peninsula is much frequented by them, where they collect as they proceed, rattans, damar, and turtle, to exchange for rice and clothing. The attractions of Pulo Tinggi are also of a more questionable kind, by its offering, during the season that the Cochin-Chinese visit Singapore in their small unarmed trading junks, considerable facilities for committing occasional quiet piracies on that harmless class of traders. Prior to the introduction of steam-vessels by the English and Dutch governments, these sea-gypsies were notorious for their piratical propensities, though less formidable than the Illanuns (people of the southern side of Mindano), owing to the smallness of their praus, which, while it rendered them harmless to European shipping, did not cause them to be less dangerous to the native trade, which is generally carried on in vessels of small burden."—Journal of the Indian Archipelago, Vol. 5, p. 140.

This singular people, who are in fact maritime nomads, are, wherever found, in race and language genuine Malays. Some of them have been converted to a kind of superficial Mohammedanism, while others are still Pagans. A few of their tribes have more industry than others, and a few are more attached to particular localities than the rest, even practising a little husbandry, and intermarrying with the more civilised Malays. What seem the original inhabitants of Banca, Billiton, and some of the islands on the coast of Borneo and Sumatra, are only the same Malays in the same rude state, the only difference being that they have the land instead of the sea for their habitation. One can hardly, indeed, help conjecturing that even the more advanced Malay States of the Peninsula, Sumatra, and Borneo, of whose history we have no record, may have sprung from the same people, seduced by circumstances favourable to social advancement to abandon their roving habits and precarious mode of existence for a fixed life.

The first notice of the sea-gypsies that we possess is by De Barros, who describes them at the beginning of the 16th century, very much as they are at the present day. He calls them Cellates, which is only a Portuguese corruption of sâlat, a strait or narrow sea, the Malay idiom requiring orâng, or people, to be prefixed, making "people of the straits," a name by which they are still occasionally called by other Malays. He describes them as a people whose life was passed rather on the sea than the land, whose children were born and reared on the sea without hardly landing; and as a low and mean people, whose livelihood was gained by "fishing and robbing." Besides all this, he expressly states that, like other Malays, they spoke the Malay language. See MALACCA and MALAY.

ORANG-UTAN, literally signifies man of the wood or forest, but its current sense is "wild man," or "savage." The man-like ape to which Europeans give this name, is never called by this name by the natives, but said to be known to the Malays of Borneo, under that of mias.

ORANGE. The species of the genus Citrus of botanists, cultivated in the Indian and Philippine Archipelagos are, the orange of several varieties, the pumplenoos or shaddock (Citrus decumana), the lime (Citrus limetta), and the sweet lime (Citrus lumia). In Malay and Javanese the name for fruits of this family is jâruk, and to this generic term an epithet is affixed for the species or varieties, as Jâruk-manis, the orange, and Jâruk-machan, the shaddock, literally, the sweet and the tiger orange. For the native generic term, there is frequently substituted by the Malays, limo, lemon, from the Portuguese. A sweet orange, with a thick skin adhering closely to the pulp and green, even when ripe; the shaddock and the lime are, most probably, indigenous, for they thrive at the level of the sea, and this from the equator to the twentieth degree of latitude. The epithets applied to other species or varieties imply that they are exotics, as Jâruk-China, or Jâruk-Jâpun, orange of China or Japan, applied to the mandarin orange, which, moreover, attains perfection only at an elevation of 3000 feet above the sea-level. The native name jâruk extends to all the languages west of Celebes, but in this last island we have the Portuguese word limo, and in the Philippines we have the native words, delandan, and kahil. The orange was found, at the time of their discovery, to be cultivated in several of the islands of the Pacific, and here we find it with native, and not Malayan names. Thus, in the languages of the Marquesas and Sandwich Islands, it is called tiporo, and in the dialect of Tonga, moli. The inference to be drawn from these facts is, that the Orange family, in its cultivated state, is indigenous in the Malayan, Philippine, and Polynesian islands, and that in the western parts of the first of these, it was probably disseminated from one point, which very likely was Java. The orange in all the Indian islands is generally of inferior quality to the varieties cultivated in the south of Europe, the Azores, and Northern India. The shaddock, however, when carefully cultivated, as in the neighbourhood of Batavia, is far superior to any other fruit of this name. It seems to have been conveyed to the continent of India from Java, in very modern times, as its name, "the Batavian orange," implies. Its name in the West Indies, also, implies that it was carried thither in recent times, for it took it from one Shaddock, the master of a trading ship of the time of Queen Anne, who brought it from Java.

ORDEAL. There is no name for this, except sumpah and supata, an oath or imprecation; each kind of ordeal being designated by an annexed epithet, as the trial by fire, by boiling oil, by melted tin, and by submersion in water. It must have been, at least in former times, in use, as it is referred to in the Malayan collections of written laws called Undang-undang, which may be translated "edicts." The collection of Jehor has the following reference to it:—"If one party make an accusation, and another deny its truth, the magistrate shall direct both to contend by diving under water, or by immersion of the hands in boiling oil, or molten tin. The party who is worsted in this contest shall be deemed the guilty one, and be punishable with death or otherwise, according to the custom of the country."

ORPIMENT, or sulphuret of arsenic, is not a native product of any part of the Malay or Philippine Archipelagos, but it is, notwithstanding, well known to the inhabitants, and immemorially imported, being the produce of Lao, and coming direct from Siam and Pegu. The name by which it is known is wârangan, from the Javanese wârang, a collyrium, of which it was, most probably, an ingredient.

OX (BOS). Exclusive of the buffalo, which is doubtful, two species of the ox are found in the wild state. One of these, called by the Malays, sâladang, is sufficiently well ascertained to exist in the forests of the Malay Peninsula, although not as yet described by naturalists. The other is the Bos Sondaicus, or Sunda ox, which exists in Java, the Peninsula, and Borneo, but, singularly enough, not in Sumatra, or in Celebes, or any island of the Philippine Archipelago. It is a large, massive, and powerful animal, of a light brown colour, with the hips and legs of the male of a clear white. It is the same species which is found in the forests of Pegu, up at least as far as Martaban.

The common ox, varying in race in the different countries, is found in the domestic state in the Peninsula, and in all the considerable islands of the Malay Archipelago, up to Timur; but although now existing in great herds in all the larger islands of the Philippine group, it did not, like the buffalo, exist on the arrival of the Spaniards. The source of the domesticated ox of the Malayan Islands is as obscure as its origin everywhere else. The Sunda ox cannot be the source from which it has sprung, as, according to the statements of recent Dutch naturalists, it has been ascertained, after many trials, to be as incapable of domestication as the American bison. It is, notwithstanding, certain, that a fertile cross between it and the domestic cattle has been long propagated, and forms a distinct breed, known by the same name as the wild cattle. This is also the breed which is found in Bali and Lomboc. In Malay and Javanese, there are two names for the domestic cattle, sapi and lâmbu, and wherever the ox is domesticated, it goes under one or other of these, but most frequently under that of sapi, which is peculiarly Javanese. Beyond the Malayan Islands, however, neither name extends. Thus, in the language of Madagascar, which has many Malayan words, the ox is called ombai. In the Javanese, the wild bull is called banteng, and the cow jawi. The Malay has no specific name for the wild cattle to which they give the same as to the domestic, adding the epithet utan, or wild. The Javanese name for the wild cow, jawi, the Malays use for neat cattle, generally. All these words are native, and afford no clue to the origin of the domesticated cattle. Some have fancied them to have been originally imported from the country of the Hindus, but this is mere conjecture, without evidence. The Javanese, have, indeed, a Sanscrit name for the ox, andaka, signifying "the blind;" but it is only an obsolete synonym of their recondite language. Images of the ox, in stone and brass, and representations of it in bas-relief, on temples, are frequent in Java, but in all these cases the animal is the zebu, or humped ox of the Hindus, and not the native ox, so that from this fact, nothing as to the origin of the domestic cattle can be inferred.

The oxen of the Indian Islands are of considerable size, generally in good condition, and multiply rapidly, showing that the pastures are congenial to them. Their chief use is in husbandry, being, on account of their greater activity, preferred on light, dry uplands, to the more powerful buffalo, better suited to the low irrigated lands. Like cattle everywhere near the equator, they give very little milk, which forms no part of the food of the inhabitants. According to the statistics of the Dutch government, the number of oxen in Java in 1842 was 431,357 head; and as they are greatly on the increase, it is probable that they now exceed half a million, which, however, is but one-third of the number of buffaloes in the same island. In the Philippines, also, and especially in the great island of Luzon, they are very numerous, although only introduced by the Spaniards in the 16th century. So suitable are the pastures of Luzon to them that they have run wild, and, as in America, multiplied greatly in this state.

P.

PACIFIC OCEAN. This is the Laut-kidul of the Javanese, literally, the "South Sea," but of which they know no more than the little portion of it that is visible from the shore of their own island. Europeans knew even less about this part of the Pacific down to the middle of the 16th century. De Barros, in 1553, thus refers to it when treating of Java: "The length of the island of Java is 190 leagues, but respecting its breadth, we have no certain knowledge, for our people have not yet navigated its southern side. According to the information of the natives, the whole of the south side, on account of the great gulf of the ocean, has few harbours, and those who inhabit the northern portion of the island hold no intercourse with the gentiles who dwell on the southern coast."—Decade 2, Book 9, Chap. 3. This was written four-and-thirty years after the discovery and conquest of Mexico, and it is curious to mark the ignorance of Europeans respecting an island which probably at the time contained a larger population than Mexico and Peru put together, and, beyond all question, a more civilised one.

PACHITAN, probably from the Sanscrit chipta, corrupted chita by the Malays and Javanese, desire, wish, and signifying "place of desire." This is the name of a small district or province of Java, part of the Dutch possessions lying on the southern side of the island, bounded to the east by Kadiri, to the south by Madiyun, and to the west by Pajang. Its chief town, situated at the head of a small bay, open to the south, and affording little shelter to shipping, is in south latitude 8° 15′, and east longitude 113° 18. The area of Pachitan is 773 square miles, and its population, in 1850, was 88,278, all of the Javanese nation, with the exception of 30 Europeans, and about 100 Chinese. This gives about 114 inhabitants to the square mile, making this district, therefore, one of the least populous of the proper county of the Javanese nation, easily accounted for, by its remote position. Its chief product is rice, and to this the Dutch government has added the forced culture of coffee, black pepper, and cinnamon. Its horned cattle, in 1845, amounted to 58,000, and its horses to 9,300. It was ceded to the European power during the temporary occupation of Java by the British; and when I visited it, in 1812, was but a poor place.

PADANG, in Malay, signifies a plain or open field, and is the name also of the chief settlement of the Netherland government on the western side of Sumatra. The town lies 1° south of the equator, and in east longitude 100°, and is the seat of the Governor, or, correctly, Lieut.-Governor of the whole western coast of the island. It has a population of 10,000 inhabitants, consisting of Malays, Achinese, Bataks, and Chinese, with some European merchants, and is a place of considerable trade.

The total area of all the Netherland possessions in Sumatra has been estimated at 104,000 square geographical miles. The population has been called 4,000,000, which would give 38·4 to the square mile. But it is far more likely to be one-fourth of this amount, which would give only 9·6, a sufficient proportion for a country the greater part of which is known to be a primeval forest, with a people notoriously deficient in industry. In 1845, the gross revenue of this vast territory was only 200,000*l.*, and the expenditure only 122,000*l.*, leaving an apparent balance of 78,000*l.* This statement, however, will not bear examination. The income, for example, includes as revenue the value of the provisions and supplies received from Java, amounting to no less than 48,000*l.*, while Sumatra is not debited with its share of the metropolitan charges. A few facts in illustration will demonstrate the slender value of the European possessions in Sumatra, obtained at a great expenditure of life and treasure, while they will put the paucity and poverty of the inhabitants beyond all question. These possessions are about two and a-half times the extent of Java. The single item of the impost on opium of Java is about four-fold as much as all the Sumatran revenue put together, although in Sumatra, equally as in Java, opium is a subject of taxation, and the inhabitants equally addicted to its use. The land revenue of Sumatra is no more than one forty-fifth part of that of Java. In Java this tax consists of an impost on rent, because in that populous country a real rent exists. In thinly-peopled Sumatra, it cannot do so any more than in the wilds of America or Australia. It must inevitably, therefore, be a tax on the capital invested in clearing and cultivating the land, and hence a very impolitic and injurious one. The paltry amount of it for so vast a territory was, in 1845, no more than 18,700*l.* Under the English administration, the Sumatran settlements were even still more profitless than under the Dutch, for at all times, they were a heavy drain on the Indian treasury, without any corresponding advantage. The original object of them was the collection of pepper, an article of importance only in the early and rude periods of the Indian trade, and which had ceased to be so long before the pursuit was abandoned.

The total value of the exports of Padang and the other ports of the western coast of Sumatra, in 1854, was about 175,000*l.*, treasure included, and that of the imports 157,000*l.*, a large portion of the first consisting of coffee, the produce of forced culture, and of the last, of government provisions and stores.

PADRIES. This is one of the names given to the sect of Puritanical Mahommedans that sprang up in the interior of Sumatra about the beginning of the present century. See MENANGKABAU.

PAGARUYUNG. This is the name of the chief town of the Malay State of Menangkabo in the interior of Sumatra. According to Sir Stamford Raffles, who visited the place, it lies at the foot of the mountain called Gunung-bongsu (youngest child-mountain) at an elevation of 1800 feet above the level of the sea, and 50 miles inland from the coast settlement of Padang, in south latitude 14′ and east longitude 100° 20′. It was at the time of his visit a ruinous village, but contained some architectural remains, and near it were found a mutilated Hindu image, and a stone with an inscription in a character identical with the ancient Javanese, and such as are of frequent occurrence in the central and eastern parts of Java. In a correct orthography the name of the place is Pagar-rayung, which in Javanese would signify a fence of the rayung, which is the name of a tall aquatic grass.

PAGI, written also PAGEH and POGGY, is the name of two considerable islands with several islets on the western coast of Sumatra lying between south latitudes 2° 32′ and 3° 15′. In our charts the two largest islands are designated the north and south Pagi, which are parted by a navigable strait called that of Kakab, about two miles long and a quarter of a mile broad. The nearest point of the Pagis is distant from the coast of Sumatra, about 45 miles. Both islands consist of high land covered with large luxuriant timber. The most northerly and largest of the two islands is about 21 miles long and 10 broad, and the most southerly, sometimes called by Europeans Nassau, 27 miles long by about six in breadth. The principal cultivated products of the Pagis are the coco and sago palms. The last of these furnishes the sole bread of the inhabitants, for they are unacquainted with the culture of rice or other corn. Coco-nuts are the article which they exchange with strangers for implements of iron, but it is remarkable that they are unacquainted with the simple art of expressing their oil. Some of the coarser fruits of Sumatra are cultivated.

The wild quadrupeds of the Pagis consist of deer, hogs, monkeys, and squirrels, without any of the large carnivorous animals. The domesticated animals are the hog, the dog, and common fowl. The inhabitants are of the Malayan race, and along with those of the islands Sipora and Sibiru go under the common name of Mantawi, speaking a common language which contains a few words of Malay and Javanese, but has all the appearance of an original and peculiar tongue. The Mantawi are a simple, inoffensive, but very rude people. They live in villages, subsist chiefly by fishing, have no clothing but a slip of bark round the loins for mere decency, and no dress, except tattooing, which is general with them. Their arms are the bow and arrow, and they have neither adopted fire-arms nor Mahommedanism. The population of the two Pagis has been computed at 1400, and Mr. Logan, making the area of the country of the Mantawi nation 2240 square miles, computes the total number of its inhabitants at 5000, which would hardly give 2¼ to the square mile, yet probably fully as much as the population amounts to. The name if correctly written, Pagi or Pagai, would signify, with the usual prefix of Pulo, "Morning Islands." The names of the two northernmost Islands, Sibiru and Sibatu, are obviously enough, "The azure" and "the rock islands."

PAHANG, the Pam of the Portuguese, and, correctly, Päang. This is the name of a virtually independent Malay State on the eastern side of the Peninsula, bounded by that of Jehor, with very undefined limits to the west, and by that of Tringanu to the north. Along the shore its length is about 80 miles, and it embraces, besides the territory on the continent, two chains of islets running parallel to its coast, and generally at the distance of about 30 miles. The country of Pahang is mountainous, the highest peaks however rising to no greater height above the level of the sea than from 2181 feet to 3221. The geological formation consists of granite, sandstone, shale, and clays. Some of the islands, as Tioman and Tingi, consist partly or entirely of trap rock. The rivers are numerous, the Pahang and the Indau being the largest, but even these are fit only for the navigation of native craft.

The whole coast of Pahang, although but an uninhabited forest, is beautiful and picturesque, the result of a powerful sun, abundant moisture, and exposure to the easterly monsoon for ages. Mr. J. S. Thomson who surveyed the coast, and from whose judicious narrative a great part of this article has been taken, gives the following account of it. "I was much struck with the beauty of the scenery along the coast, particularly after entering the Sibu Channel. The Straits of Malacca on the opposite side of the

Peninsula have invariably called forth the admiration of travellers, but they must yield the palm to this side. Spacious bays and fine sandy beaches extend uninterruptedly along the coast, shaded by the high primæval forests, whereas on the opposite coast the greater part is fringed by mangroves and slimy mud-banks. The numerous islands outside the Sibu Channel also tend to impart great variety and beauty to the view, some high and mountainous, assuming fantastic shapes and rugged outlines, others low and diminutive, but in their turn presenting almost equally interesting features. By the exposure of their northern sides to the north-east monsoon, the action of the waves has beaten down the soil and worn the softer rocks into cliffs and caverns. While most of the islands are covered with lofty forests, others remain denuded, and where not barren and rocky, are covered with tufty grass, a circumstance uncommon in these latitudes." Journal of the Indian Archipelago, Vol. v., p. 147.

The vegetable products of Pahang, put to economical use, are its timber, ratans, gutta-percha, and damar; its minerals, iron, gold, and tin, the two last being washed both by Malays and Chinese, although not to the same extent as in the Malay states of Tringanu and Kalanteu, on the same side of the Peninsula. The wild Mammalia are the elephant, two species of rhinoceros, the tapir, the tiger and leopard, several species of deer and monkeys, the buffalo, and the wild ox, called by the Malays the sâladang.

The population consists of the more civilised Malays forming its bulk, several tribes of the same nation in the wild and unconverted state, and some tribes of the small crisp-haired negros. The wild tribes of the Malayan race are here known to the civilised Malays indiscriminately, under the names Sakai and Pungan. Mr. Thomson, furnishing details, has estimated the whole Malay population of Pahang, exclusive of the wild races and the Chinese, at 14,110 only. From other sources the Chinese are thought to amount to about 2000. It is probable, therefore, that the total population does not exceed 20,000; and if we estimate the area of the state at 3200 square miles, we shall have a relative population of little more than six inhabitants to the square mile. The chief town, which gives its name to the principality, lies on the left bank of a small river in latitude 3° 40′ north, and is a very poor place. On the opposite bank there is a village inhabited by the Chinese and other strangers. The river is about a quarter of a mile wide at its mouth, but full of islets and sand-banks, and navigable only for small native craft; and not by these, except during the south-west monsoon, for during the boisterous north-east it is almost inaccessible.

The rajah of Pahang is nominally a dependant of the sultan of Jehor, now a pensioner of the British government and residing in Singapore, but he is really independent. He holds the nominal office of bândara, "treasurer" or "first minister of Jehor;" as does the virtual sovereign of the western side of the Peninsula that of tumangyung, equivalent to that of "first magistrate." At the time of the conquest of Malacca by the Portuguese, the prince of Pahang appears to have been independent; for he is stated by their historians, under the name of the "king of Pam," as having been present in Malacca during the combat which ended in its capture, being there for the purpose of espousing the daughter of the king.

PAJAJARAN. This is the name of an ancient kingdom of Java, the capital of which was situated in the Sunda district of Bogor, about 40 miles east of Jacatra or Batavia. The site is indicated by the foundations of a palace, and by a monumental stone bearing an inscription, known under the name of the batu-tulis, literally "the inscribed stone." Pajajaran is the only ancient state known to have existed in the country of the Sundas,—all others having been in the proper country of the Javanese. The inscription is in an unknown character, a much ruder one than any of the ancient Javanese inscriptions, and, most probably, that in which the Sunda language was written before the adoption of the Javanese writing. The peculiarity of the character,—the locality of Pajajaran, and the names of the princes said to have reigned in it, lead to the belief that the state was Sunda and not Javanese. Of the time in which it flourished, nothing reliable is known,—one legend placing its foundation in 1078, and another, two whole centuries later. The name signifies "arrangement," or "place arrayed," from the verb jajar, "to put in order," or "arrange," in Javanese.

PAJANG. This is the name of a large, fertile, and populous province of Java, situated in the plain of the same name, which extends in a direction east and west, between the mountains Lawu and Mârapi, to a length of 75 miles. In it are situated the ruins of the old capital, Kartasura, and the modern town of Surakarta, or Solo.

Nearly the whole province is one sheet of cultivation, the greater part of it by perennial irrigation.

PAKALONGAN, or PAKALUNGAN, (Place of Kalung Bats or Vampires). This is one of the provinces of the alluvial northern side of Java, having that of Tâgal to the west, that of Samarang to the east, and that of Baglen to the south, with the sea to the north. It is divided from the two last-named provinces by high mountains, the peaks of which rise to from 7000 to 11,500 feet above the level of the sea. These mountains, bending to the south-east, leave between them and the sea an alluvial plain; which to the west, where it is widest, is from five to six leagues broad. From the mountains, there proceed many streams, eleven of which are of considerable size; and which, although not navigable, are extensively applied to irrigation, and are the main cause of the great fertility of the province. The coast is an unbroken line without harbour or bay. The chief town of the same name lies in south latitude 6° 55′, and east longitude 109° 40′.

The climate of Pakalongan is hot but healthy. The thermometer in the shade rises to 88° and 90° at the level of the sea; but on Prau, one of the mountains which bounds it to the south, it falls to 50°, and in the winter months of June and July thin ice and hoar frost are seen in the early morning. The sugar cane thrives at no greater height than 200 feet above the level of the sea; but indigo at 600, and rice and coffee as high as 3000. At this last height a few coco-palms are still to be seen, after which the gomuti, or Saguerus sacchariferus takes its place. The tea-plant flourishes at the height of 5000 feet.

Pakalangan has still 129 square miles of forest, containing some useful timber, but teak only in quantity sufficient for local use. In this forest are found the tiger and leopard, the wild dog of Java, deer, two species of hog, the rhinoceros, the Sunda ox, and the otter, with as usual, deer and monkeys. It also contains the two species of gallinaceous birds found in other parts of Java, Gallus Bankiva and Gallus furcatus. The vampire bat, from which is derived the name of the province, is to be seen in great numbers in the day-time hanging from the trees and at night preying on the orchards.

The staple product of Pakalongan is rice, but the Dutch, in recent times, have introduced the culture, by corvée labour, of indigo, sugar-cane, and the exotics, coffee, tea, and cinnamon, all which are produced in considerable quantity. The bulk of the population consists of true Javanese, with the usual sprinkling of Malays, Chinese, Europeans, and their respective descendants. In 1845, the census made the total population 235,539, and its area being 466 square miles, we have a relative one of 505 to the square mile, which makes it one of the most populous of Java. In 1850, however, the population would seem, even within the short period of five years, to have declined, for it is put down at no more than 223,852. In 1843, the number of its horned cattle was reckoned at 31,000, and its horses at 4000. Pakalongan was ceded to the Dutch in 1743, at the close of the long intestine war which followed the massacre of the Chinese at Batavia in 1740, and ten years later the Dutch fort was built, which still exists in the town.

PALAWAN, generally called by the Spaniards of the Philippines, Paragua, is the name of the most westerly of the Philippines, and after Luzon and Mindano, the largest of them. The name of Palawan, or correctly Palawang, is said to be taken from the Bugis language, and to signify a gate or sluice, in reference to its position, serving as a protection or barrier against the violence of the China Sea. It extends between north latitudes 8° 13′ and 11° 17′, in a direction south-east and north-west, to the length of about 230 miles. Its breadth varies from 10 to 25 miles, and its area probably does not exceed 4500 square miles. The northern end consists of a peninsula, or rather of two peninsulas, a larger and a smaller, formed by the intervention of the Bay of Malampaya. Towards its northern end, the coast is studded by numerous islands, the only ones of considerable size being Dumaran and Iloc. Palawan is distant from Borneo to the south, many islets intervening, about 90 miles; from Mindoro to the north-east, about 100; and from Panay, to the east, about the same distance; so that in this manner, it is remote from any of the other considerable islands.

The land of Palawan is represented as high, but the island does not appear to contain any mountain of considerable elevation, and of its geological formation we know no more than that its northern end consists of limestone rocks rising abruptly from the sea to the height of 200 and 300 feet, and containing many caverns. It is expressly stated to be, like the other Philippines, vexed by earthquakes, and we therefore conclude that it does not come within the limits of the great volcanic band, and, consequently, that no part of its formation is volcanic. The climate is hot, and the island within the latitudes of the typhoons, its western side being exposed to the action of the Sea of China. Its vegetable productions are stated to bear much resemblance to those of Borneo, and among them is the Malay camphor-tree (Dryobalanops camphora). Its canes are in great repute in Manilla. Its wild animals are deer, hogs, monkeys, the porcupine, a species of civet or polecat said to be peculiar to it, and it is alleged, one feline animal, a kind of leopard. The most marketable of its products are bee's-wax and the esculent nests of the swallow, which abound in its many caves, and in gathering which the natives exhibit much skill and courage.

The inhabitants of Palawan resemble those of the Bisaya islands in person, but are darker in complexion, with hair frizzling instead of lank. All of them not subject to the Spanish rule, are represented as naked savages, but inoffensive ones, living chiefly by the chase, and having no other arms than sumpitans or blow-pipes for discharging little arrows. The northern end of the island, which is the narrowest, is alone subject to the Spaniards, and forms part of their province of Calamianes. It is to this that the name of Paragua especially applies. It comprehends about 60 miles of the length of the island, with an area of 1000 square miles, and its whole population, most probably emigrants from the Bisaya islands, amounted, by the census of 1850, to no more than 1570, paying a capitation-tax of 5475 reals of plate. This gives about an inhabitant and a half to the square mile, distributed in eleven villages, and converted to Christianity. The Spanish part is represented, and no doubt truly, as the most populous portion of the island. Some part of its west end is claimed by the Sultan of Borneo, but the larger is occupied by the wild and independent aborigines, divided into numerous tribes. We shall not greatly err in pronouncing Palawan to be, although a great, yet an eminently sterile island, in this respect far even below Borneo.

PALEMBANG. This is the name of a kingdom of Sumatra, composed of the most southerly end of the great alluvial plain which lies between the central chain of mountains and the sea, from the western entrance of the Straits of Malacca to the eastern of those of Banca. It is bounded to the north by the state of Jambi, to the south by the country of the Lampungs, to the north-west by Limun, to the west by the central chain of mountains which are a part of it, and to the south-east by the sea which forms the Straits of Banca. Its area has been reckoned at 16,480 geographical square miles, or little short of half the extent of Java. It contains many rivers, the most considerable of which are the Musi, or Sungsang, and Bañuasin which are connected by a branch or natural canal, and falls into the sea by four different mouths.

The climate of Palembang, as might be expected so near to the equator, is uncertain and variable as to seasons. The monsoons which prevail are the same as those of Java, but less constant,—namely, the south-east and the north-west. The rainy season corresponds with the last of these, and during its continuance the rivers overflow their banks, and the lower country is extensively inundated. While this inundation is draining off, the quantity of water is so great that the flood-tide ceases to be felt in the rivers. This is the case from December to April inclusive. In the other months of the year it reaches for 100 miles up the Musi, or principal river. In the hottest season, Fahrenheit's thermometer stands at 80° in the morning, and at 92° at two o'clock, and in the coldest at 76° and 85°. The climate, notwithstanding the superabundance of heat, moisture, marsh, and forest, is remarked not to be unhealthy, the country being open and well ventilated.

Of the geological structure of the territory of Palembang, no account has been rendered. By far the greater portion of it, however, is an alluvial plain, but it contains, also, to the west, some mountain and hilly country, which has not been examined. Its forests yield ratans, dragon's-blood and benzoin, and its cultivated plants are rice, the sugar-cane, tobacco, gambir, indigo, coffee, and pepper. All the larger animals of the forests of the other parts of Sumatra are found here, as the tiger, the leopard, the elephant, and the rhinoceros. The chief domesticated ones are the buffalo, the goat, the hog, and common poultry. The sheep has been introduced, but the horse does not exist in this country of marsh and forest.

The inhabitants of Palembang consist of the descendants of Javanese,—of Malays,—of an aboriginal people called Kumring, and of a wild race known under the name of Kubu, with a few Arabs and Chinese. The total population has been estimated at 250,000, which gives about 15 inhabitants to the square mile. This is about one-seventeenth part of the rate of population of Java, a simple fact conclusive of the real condition of Palembang, and showing that it is in reality a forest, with a few scattered inhabitants on its river banks.

The town of Palembang which it is, as usually happens in such cases, that gives name to the whole kingdom, is situated on the river Musi or Sungsang, about fifty miles above its mouth, and in south latitude 2° 58′, and east longitude 105°. It lies on both banks of the river, which is here 400 yards broad, with a depth of from eight to nine fathoms, and a rise and fall of tide varying from 10 to 16 feet. All the way from the sea, and even for a mile or two above it, and until two affluents fall into it, the Musi is navigable for ships of burthen, and deserves therefore to be considered the most valuable of all the rivers of Sumatra. The town, in 1822, according to the account given of it by a judicious writer in the ninth volume of the Transactions of the Batavian Society of Arts and Sciences, contained a population of from 20,000 to 25,000, including, besides Javanese and Malays, 500 Arabs and 1500 Chinese, the most valuable parts of it. These strangers are the chief merchants and traders, but the native inhabitants are represented as skilful artificers in wood, iron, gold, and silver. Many of the houses of the town are built on moveable rafts moored to the shore, as in the Siamese capital: nearly all are of the perishable materials of wood, ratan, and bamboo. The only buildings of stone are the mosque and the tombs of the kings. The mosque is in the form of a parallelogram with a dome, is ornamented with pilasters, has casemated glazed windows, a marble floor and a stone pulpit. Near it is a minaret 50 feet high with a spiral stair. It deserves, therefore, to be considered the most considerable edifice ever erected in the Archipelago, not being European, since the conversion to Mahommedanism. Nothing is known about the time or manner in which it was built, but the architects, it may be presumed, were not natives, but most probably Arabs, in the same manner as were those of the ancient temples of Java, Hindus. The tombs of the kings about three miles below the town, are all of solid masonry, of a square form, with arched roofs, two of the sides of each tomb being of hewn stone. No ancient Hindu remains of buildings are known to exist. That they must have once done so is certain, but the probability is that they were destroyed by the Mahommedans, and that their materials now form part of the mosque and royal tombs in a country where stone is rare and must be brought from a great distance.

Palembang, notwithstanding its extensive alluvial land and its scanty population, does not produce even sufficient corn for its own consumption and receives a supply from Java. Some other necessaries of life and native luxuries, it yields, however, in great cheapness and abundance. In 1822, a moderately sized buffalo cost only 22 florins of 20*d.* to the florin, a large hog 44 florins, a sheep 17, a goat 11, a pullet 1½, and a pound of venison three doits. For a single florin might be had 6 pine-apples, or 16 durians, or 50 shaddocks, or 55 mangos, or 150 mangostins, or 400 oranges. The comparative cost of these different productions indicates the amount of labour necessary to produce them. A buffalo that lives in the marshes, feeds on their spontaneous produce and weighs probably 800 pounds, costs only one half the price of a stall-fed hog, of probably not one-eighth part of its weight. The sheep is within five florins of the cost of the buffalo, that will probably weigh 16 times as much. As to the five fruits above named, the soil and climate are represented as peculiarly suited to them and in no part of the Archipelago are they produced in such cheapness and perfection. The trade of the country is with Java, Banca, Siam, China and the European settlements in the Straits of Malacca, and when Banca with its tin formed a part of the territory it was very considerable.

The name of Palembang, or more correctly Palimbang, seems to be a verbal noun derived from the Javanese verb "limbang" to drain off or decant a fluid, as is done in the process of washing gold, which is performed in wicker baskets. The word at full length, namely Palimbangan, would signify, "the place or the implement in which or with which the operation of decanting or drawing off is performed." We have many examples of such a mode of formation in the Javanese, as, for example, pasarëan, a sleeping-place or bed, from sare, to sleep, and pakapuran, a place where lime is made, or a lime-kiln, from kapur, lime; nor does it always happen that the affix "an" is included. It is, probably, that the name may have been given from the drawing off or subsidence of the periodical flood, which is one of the most striking characteristics of the country.

That Palembang was a settlement formed from Java, and by the proper Javanese, and not the Sundas who are nearer to it, is placed beyond all doubt by the Javanese being still the spoken and also, in its own proper character, the written language of the Court, and by the titles of nobility of office, and often of names of places being in that language. Thus, we find the word ratu for king, priyayi and raden as the titles of classes of nobles, and bañu for a river, all of which are purely Javanese. But of the manner in which the immigration took place or the time in which it happened nothing worthy of credit is known. As Java is not likely, at any period of its history, to have been so overpeopled as to have encouraged emigration, the settlement is most likely to have been formed by fugitives fleeing for their lives after defeat in a civil contest. That an intercourse should afterwards have been maintained between the mother country and its colony is almost certain. It is very probable too, that the emigrants would look up with respect to the principal state in Java, compared to themselves, wealthy and powerful. According to Javanese tradition, therefore, it is asserted that Palembang was a settlement founded by the state of Majapait towards the last years of its existence, which, as that place was overthrown in the year 1478, would make its foundation about the middle of the 15th century. There is, assuredly, no ground for making its origin so recent an event, and, on the contrary, it can be shown to have been much earlier than even that of Majapait itself to which the Javanese ascribe the date of 1221 of Salivana or Saka, corresponding to 1299 of our time, making the whole duration of that kingdom, so famed in the history of the Archipelago, only 179 years. According to the accounts given by the natives to the Portuguese at the time of the conquest of Malacca, fresher by three centuries and a half than any thing we can now get from their descendants, Malacca had been founded little more than two hundred and fifty years before the arrival of the Portuguese. This would carry us back about a hundred years before the era of the foundation of Majapait, which is alleged to have given birth to Palembang the country from which, Singapore first, and then Malacca were colonised. According to the apocryphal Javanese chronicle, Palembang must have been founded from Java only 60 years before the arrival of the Portuguese. De Barros, however, enumerates it in a very correct Portuguese orthography, Palimbam, as one of the twenty-nine established kingdoms of the sea-board of Sumatra at the epoch in question, without any reference to its being a new establishment.

From the first appearance of the Portuguese to a very recent time, Palembang continued to be a virtually independent kingdom, ruled by a prince, who, like many others, assumed the Arabian title of Sultan, being, however, under treaty with the Dutch to deliver to them, at a low price, the tin of Banca, the staple produce of his dominions. In 1821, the kingdom of Palembang was subdued by the Netherland government, and now forms part of the sub-government of Sumatra. What led to this was an act of atrocity on the part of the reigning prince. When in 1811, Java and its dependencies were occupied by the British, the Dutch officials of Banca fell into the hands of this chieftain, and fancying, like a true barbarian, that he would do an acceptable service to the new rulers, he put the whole of them to death. He was undeceived by the British government sending an expedition against him, dethroning him and wresting Banca from him. At the restoration of Java, he resumed his authority and kept the Netherland government at bay for five years, having defeated one expedition, and a second of greater strength being necessary for his subjugation.

PALMA-CHRISTI, the castor-oil plant; the Ricinus communis of botanists. This is cultivated from Java and Sumatra to the Philippines inclusive; and Mr. Marsden says it is found growing wild on the sea coast of the western side of Sumatra. The name by which it is known in Malay and Javanese is jarak, and this is a very general one in the Malayan languages; but it is not the only, for in the Sunda and Maduresе it is called kaliki. Both words are native and not traceable to any foreign source; so that, as far as this kind of evidence is good, the plant must be considered as indigenous. In the languages of the Philippines the name is tangan-tangan, a word which, not reduplicated, signifies in Malay "the hand," no doubt given to it from the palmate form of the leaves. This may lead to the suspicion that the plant was introduced by the Malays, at least as an object of culture, for the name is Malay, but not that for the hand in the native languages of the Philippines. For the lamp, the oil of the palma-christi is less esteemed, or probably less easily produced, than that of the sesame or of ground pea, and hence its culture is not extensive. It is a coarse hardy plant, and easily reared in very indifferent soils. Its medicinal use is unknown to the natives.

PALMS. The palms cultivated in the Indian islands, and which form so considerable a branch of their husbandry, are :—the coco, (Cocos nucifera); the sago,

(Metroxylon sago); the gomuti, or cabo-negro of the Spaniards (Borassus gomuti); the Palmyra, or lontar, (Borassus flabelliformis); and the areca, or pinang, (Areca catechu). Those put extensively to economical uses, but not cultivated because spontaneously produced in abundance, are the nibung, (Caryota urens); the palmetto, or nipa, (Nipa fruticosa); the common ratan, (Calamus rotan); and the dragon's-blood ratan, (Calamus draco). Some account of all these will be found under their respective heads.

PALM-WINE. The sap of palms is called in Javanese, tuwak; and in Malay, nera and tuwak. The palm chiefly used for the production of this liquor in the Malay islands, is the gomuti, or sagwire; and in the Philippines, this and the nipa. The coco-palm is too valuable, on account of its oil, to be so employed. The sap of palms is, to the inhabitants of these islands and of other inter-tropical countries, what wine is to the countries of southern Europe; cider and beer to those of the northern; and the sap of the agave to the Mexicans. But it is in some respects more useful than any of these, for it is produced with less labour, and yields, by the simple process of boiling, the chief supply of sugar for native consumption.

PAMANUKAN, ("place of birds.") This is the name of a district of Java, in the country of the Sundas, and on the northern side of the island. During the British occupation, it contained 124 villages; and a computed population of 18,475 inhabitants, all of the Sunda nation, at present, probably, greatly increased. It forms part of the province of Krawang.

PAMARUANG. The name of a considerable island on the eastern coast of Borneo, with a computed area of 480 geographical square miles. It forms part of the delta of the Cootie river, and is mostly covered with jungle.

PAMPANGA. This is the name of one of the finest provinces of the island of Luzon, in the Philippines. It is bounded to the south-east by Bulacan, to the north-west by Pangasinan, to the west by Zambales, while the northern shore of the bay of Manilla forms its southern boundary. From north to south it is 68 miles in length, and from east to west 51 miles broad. Its area will probably be about 2260 geographical miles. The more elevated portion of the province enjoys a cool and delicious climate, but is under-cultivated and under-peopled. The lower is hot but healthy, highly cultivated and densely peopled. Here the principal crops are rice and maiz, the same land yielding one crop of the first of these and one crop of the last, sometimes even two within the year. The other chief crops are tobacco, sugar-cane, sesame, and cacoa. The coco-palm does not flourish so well as in some other provinces of Luzon. Great quantities of fruit are raised in it for the market of Manilla. In the mountains, good iron ore is found, and some gold is washed from the sands of the brooks. In the forest, deer, buffalos, and hogs are so numerous, that in a single year as many as 3000 have been killed. As far back as 1818, the number of oxen belonging to Pampanga was 13,000, of buffalos, 23,000, and of horses, 12,000. The inhabitants are of the same race with the Malayan Tagalas and Bisayas, but of a distinct nation from both, speaking a different language, called, like the province, Pampanga. The twenty-five townships of which Pampanga is composed, contained in 1818, a population of 106,381 souls, which, by the census of 1850, had risen to 156,272, making the relative population about 68 to the square mile. The chief town of the province is Bacolor, about 10¼ leagues distant from Manilla, and in latitude 15° 15′. This is in the interior of the province, on the right bank of a river of the same name; and contains a population of 8737 inhabitants, with 1456 houses, for the most part native huts of temporary materials. Pampanga was subdued by Martin Goiti, one of the lieutenants of Legaspi, as early as the years 1571 and 1572, and the conquest was effected by a force of 80 Spaniards, a striking proof of the feeble resistance made by the natives of the Philippines to their invaders.

PANAMAO. This is the name of a considerable Philippine island at the northern end of that of Leyte, and divided from it by a narrow strait, which forms a safe harbour with the land of the main island. It is inhabited, and forms a portion of the township of Leyte, and province of the same name.

PANAON. This is the name of an islet at the southern end of the Bisayan island, Leyte. It is described as being nine leagues long and three broad; and its centre to be in latitude 9° 33′, but no other facts are stated regarding it.

PANAY is the name of the largest of the Philippine islands after Mindano; and of the whole Archipelago the most fertile and densely peopled. It is separated from Negros to the east by a channel which, in its narrowest part, does not exceed four miles broad. To the west, nothing lies between it and the distant Calamianes Islands and Paragua or northern end of Palawan, except the little Cuyos Islands. To the north it is, at least, 90 geographical miles distant from the nearest part of Luzon, the islands Burias, Tablas, and Sibuyan intervening; while its southern part is about 130 miles from the nearest part of Mindano. The form of Panay is a triangle, of which the base is to the north, and the apex to the south. Its greatest length is 95 geographical miles, and its area has been computed at 3960 square geographical miles, or near double the size of the British island of Trinidad. A chain of high mountains runs through it from north to south, but of its elevation or formation we have no account.

The soil of Panay, well irrigated by abundant mountain streams, is eminently fertile, its staple products being rice, sugar-cane, cotton, coffee, tobacco, pepper, and cacoa. Its forests yield ebony and sapan-weed; and its shores and rivers abound in fish, including the mother-of-pearl oyster, the tripang, and tortoise. The mass of the inhabitants consist of the Bisaya nation, speaking a dialect of the same language as those of Negros, Çebu, and Leyte; but in the mountains there are negritos, or little negros, stated to be of the same race with those of Luzon and Negros, although nothing regarding them, beyond their bare existence, is really known; and that here, as elsewhere, they preserve their wild independence, in the inaccessible recesses of the mountains. In 1850, Panay contained a population of 566,957, equal to 145 inhabitants to the square mile. This makes it the most populous island of the Philippines, yet not above one-fourth part of the populousness of some parts of Java of the same extent, and full 100 short of the average density of that island. In 1799, it had a population of no more than 271,748, so that if these statements can be relied on, the population, in the course of half a century, had more than doubled itself. Panay exports rice, sugar, and its other staples to a considerable extent, to Luzon, and to some of the less productive islands in its neighbourhood. It was conquered, or at least occupied by Legaspi on his way to the conquest of Luzon. Here he found the supply of food which Çebu was incapable of furnishing. It is, at present, divided into three provinces, called Capiz, Iloilo, and Antiqne, having between them 46 townships. See these heads.

PANCHUR. This is one of four low alluvial islands, which seem at a distance to be but parts of the eastern side of Sumatra, being divided from it by a very narrow but navigable channel, called by European navigators Brewer's Straits, but by the natives Sâlat-panjang, or the long strait. The principal inhabitants of this and of its neighbouring islands are of the Malayan race and nation, speak a rude Malay language, are in a very low state of society, and like the inhabitants of the interior of the Malay Peninsula have not adopted the Mahommedan religion. Their chief employment is the cultivation of the sago-palm. The name Pulo-panchur signifies in Malay, "spouting or gushing island." It is subject to the Malay prince of Campar.

PAND·AN. This is the native name of a family of plants which botanists, Latinising, have adopted for a genus, and for the natural family of "screw pines." The name, and at least two species of the genus, prevail over all the countries from Sumatra to Luzon. One species, the Pandan-wangi of the Malays and Javanese, the Pandanus odoratissimus of botanists, yields the perfumed flowers which are as much in repute with the Malays as they are with the Hindus. The tough rigid leaves are used in mat and basket-making. The word "pandan" is both Malay and Javanese, and from them has spread to many other tongues. It has no other signification than the name of the plant. Some European writers tell us that its meaning is "to see or observe," but this is a mistake, arising from imperfect knowledge. The verb to see or observe is written with a dental d, and ends with the nasal ng, whereas the name of the plant has a palatal d, and ends with a nasal n, not to say that the last vowel of the two words differs. This is a good example of hasty etymology. Pand·an is a name frequently given to places, as Pulo-pand·an, or Pand·an Island, in the Straits of Malacca, and in the Philippines, I see it given to no fewer than eleven different places, none of them, however, of any importance.

PANGARANGO. The name of one of the highest mountains of Java in the district of Bogor and country of the Sundas, 10,500 feet above the level of the sea.

It is the sister mountain of Gâdeh, springing from the same base, but not, like it, an active volcano.

PANGASANÉ. The name of a very considerable island, lying off the south-eastern Peninsula of Celebes, called also Moena. See MOENA.

PANGASINAN, in Malay and Javanese, "place of salt," or "salt-pans," is the name of a province of Luzon in the Philippines, bounded to the south by Pampanga, to the north by Ilocos, to the west by Zambales, and to the east by the chain of mountains which takes its name from the wild tribes that occupy it, the Igorrotes, the Ilongotes, and the Alaguetes. It extends to 78 miles in length, and 44 at its greatest breadth, comprises 29 townships, and has an area of about 1240 square geographical miles. Its chief place is Lingayen, distant 120 miles north of Manilla, and in latitude 16° north. Close to this place is the port of Sual, a safe harbour for vessels of moderate burden. The whole country seems to be a well-watered valley, of eminent fertility, lying between the sierra of Zambales and that of the Igorrotes, down to the gulf of Lingayen, or Pangasinan. The torrents from the mountains bring down particles of gold, the washing of the sands affording occasional employment to the inhabitants, and the mountains themselves yielding sulphur and arsenic. The most considerable river of the province is the Ano, which affords means of transport for the produce of the forests of the range of the Igorrotes, from which it has its source. The inhabitants of Pangasinan consist of two distinct nations speaking different languages, namely, the proper Pangasinan and the Ilocos, and this, independent of the wild tribes of the mountains on its eastern borders.

In 1735, Pangasinan, which then included the province now called Zambales, (itself, at present, containing 95,260 inhabitants,) was computed to have a population of no more than 73,305 souls. In 1818, after the separation from it of Zambales, the population was 119,322. In 1850, five new townships, however, having been annexed to it, the inhabitants amounted to 224,180, of whom 48,321 were subject to the poll-tax. Its relative population gives 180 to the squire mile, making it one of the most populous provinces of the Philippines. Its chief productions are rice, maiz, pulses, and sugar-cane, and it produces on the coast, much bay salt, from which it takes its name. It is evidently one of the most fertile and productive provinces of the Philippines, although much wild land still remains unredeemed.

PANGOLIN. The scaly ant-eater, or Manis Javanica of naturalists, is found in most of the larger islands of the Archipelago, a sluggish animal of nocturnal habits, which, in self-defence, rolls itself up, and hence the Malayan name, which literally means "roller," from the verb guling, to roll or revolve.

PANJANG (PULO), literally, "long island." This is the name of several islands, or islets, all the way from Sumatra to Celebes. The largest of them is one of the four alluvial islands on the eastern side of Sumatra, and nearly opposite to Malacca. Of these, Panjang is the nearest to the Sumatran coast and hence the strait between them takes its name. It is chiefly inhabited, as are the other three islands near it, by wild unconverted men of the Malay nation, and speaking its language, or rather a rude dialect of it. Panjang is best known as producing the best crude sago, which is exported by the Malays to Singapore and Malacca to be refined by the Chinese.

PANJI. This is the name of an ancient king of Java who reigned in a country called Janggala, the capital of which was in the modern province of Surabaya. This personage, called also Ina-karta-pati, is the hero of many of the romances of the Javanese, and from them of the Malays, and is supposed to have flourished about the year 1300 of our time.

PANTAR. This is the name given in our maps to one of the little-known islands lying between Floris and Timur. I find it sometimes called by the Malays, Pulo-Putar, which would signify turning or twisting island, and sometimes Pulo-Pandai, which would literally be "artificer or blacksmith island." It consists of high land, most probably volcanic, and is about 8 leagues in length. The inhabitants are described as having dark-brown complexions with frizzled hair, and are, therefore, of the race that I have ventured to call the Negro-Malayan. A few of the inhabitants of the coast have adopted the Mahommedan religion, but the people of the interior are described as rude, half-naked heathens, armed with bows and arrows.

PANTUN. This word is Malay, and may be translated epigram. It is a quatrain stanza, in which the alternate lines rhyme, the two first containing a proposition, and the two last, its application. The application or point, however, must not be obvious, but obscure, so as to try the ingenuity of the party, to whom the pantun is addressed, so that, in fact, the pantun is a kind of enigma or riddle. These riddles are favourite pastimes of the Malays, to whom they are confined, for they are not known to the Javanese or other nations of the Archipelago. The following are translations of three of these: "The waves beat white on the reach of Katawan—day and night without cease. The garden is white with blossoms, but among the flowers, one only is love-inspiring." "The diamond falls in the grass, and there still glitters, but love is like dew on the grass. It vanishes when the sun appears." "The peacock nods its head; the peacock that perches on the battlement. When her locks wave, new beauties shine in her face."

PAPANDAYANG. This is the name of a mountain of Java, in the country of the Sundas, and of a district of the province of Cheribon called Sukapura (city of gladness, Sanscrit). It is an active volcano, of which the summit, which is also the crater, is 8000 feet above the level of the sea. My friend, Dr. Thomas Horsfield, has given an account of the last eruption of this mountain which is worth quoting, as being one of the few of the Archipelago satisfactorily authenticated. "The Papandayang, situated at the western part of the province of Cheribon, in the district of Sukapura, was formerly one of the largest volcanos of the island; but the greater part of it was swallowed up in the earth, after a short, but very severe eruption in the year 1772. The account which has remained of this event asserts that near midnight, between the 11th and 12th of August, there was observed about the mountain an uncommonly luminous cloud, by which it appeared to be completely enveloped. The inhabitants, as well about the foot as on the declivities of the mountain, alarmed by this appearance, betook themselves to flight; but before they could all save themselves, the mountain began to give way, and the greatest part of it actually fell in and disappeared in the earth. At the same time, a tremendous noise was heard, resembling the discharge of the heaviest artillery. Immense quantities of volcanic substances, which were thrown out, at the same time, and which spread in every direction, propagated the effects of the explosion through the space of many miles. It is estimated that an extent of ground of the mountain itself, and its immediate environs, fifteen miles long, and full six broad, was, by this commotion, swallowed up in the bowels of the earth. Several persons sent to examine the condition of the neighbourhood, made report that they found it impossible to approach the mountain, on account of the heat of the substances which covered its circumference, and which were piled on each other to the height of three feet, although this was the 24th of September, and full six weeks after the catastrophe. It is also mentioned that forty villages, partly swallowed up by the earth and partly covered by the substances thrown up, were destroyed on this occasion, and that 2957 of the inhabitants perished. A proportionate number of cattle was destroyed, and most of the plantations of cotton, indigo, and coffee, in the adjacent districts were buried under the volcanic matter. The effects of this eruption are still visible."—Transactions of the Batavian Societies of Arts and Sciences, vol. 9.

PAPAW FIG, (Carica Papaya). This coarse and little esteemed fruit is easily reared in very indifferent soils. It is evidently a plant of tropical America, introduced by the Spaniards and Portuguese, and most of its names, in the different languages, point at its being an exotic. The most frequent of these is papaya, which is the papayo of the Spanish. In the language of Bali it goes under the name of gâdang-castila, or the Castilian banana; and the people of Celebes, who probably received it directly from Java, call it the Javanese banana, in the same manner in which they sometime call the buffalo the horse of that island.

PAPER. The art of making a true paper from fibrous matter reduced to a pulp in water, has never been known in, or introduced into, any of the Indian islands. The usual name for it, in all the languages of those nations that are now acquainted with it, is the Arabic one, kărtăs, although they may have received it, before the arrival of the Arabians, from the Chinese, its original inventors. We possess Javanese inscriptions on stone and brass which carry us back six centuries, probably only a brief part of the time in which the Javanese wrote on these materials. But the current materials for writing on in ancient times, by all the nations of the Archipelago, as it still is of those that have little communication with strangers, was the leaf of the Palmyra palm, the lontar or rontal, a word half Javanese and half Sanscrit. The Javanese alone have a native paper, or more correctly, a kind of papyrus, prepared much in the same manner as that ancient and imperfect material, but made of a more plastic and manageable substance. This consists of the inner bark, or liber, of the paper mulberry, the Broussonetia papyrifera of botanists, the same plant from which the South Sea islanders make their clothing. In Javanese, the name of the plant is gluga; and of the fabric dâluwang in the vulgar, and dâlanchang in the polite tongue, both native words. This is of a yellow colour, strong, tough, but of rather uneven texture, very liable to be preyed on by insects, but surprisingly cheap considering the great amount of labour which must be bestowed on its manufacture.

PAPUA. This word is a slight corruption of the Malay word, which is written either papuwah, or puwah-puwah. It is an adjective, the meaning of which is crisped or frizzled, or of a woolly texture, as in the hair of the negro. Orâng-papuwah and Tanah-papuwah are terms which signify crisp or woolly-haired men, and country of crisped or wool-haired men. Some recent geographers have applied the word Papua to New Guinea, and Papuasia, derived from it, to itself and other neighbouring countries, but I see no advantage in such an innovation, neither definite nor comprehensive, that entitles it to supersede a name of three centuries and a half standing.—See NEW GUINEA.

PARADISE (BIRDS OF). The first mention made of these remarkable birds is by Pigafetta, who informs us that the king of Bachian, one of the true Moluccas, gave the companions of Magellan a pair of them, along with a slave, and two bahars, or near 1000 pounds weight of cloves, as a gift to the emperor Charles the Fifth. "He gave us besides," says he, "two most beautiful dead birds. These are about the size of a thrush, have small heads, long bills, legs a palm in length, and as slender as a writing quill. In lieu of proper wings they have long feathers of different colours, like great ornamental plumes. Their tail resembles that of a thrush. All the other feathers, except those of the wings, are of a dark colour. They never fly, except when the wind blows. They informed us that these birds came from the terrestrial paradise, and they called them Bolondinata, that is, 'birds of God.'"—Prima Viaggio, p. 156. The name of the bird, as given by Pigafetta in this account of it, is properly burung-dewata; and I have no doubt was correctly enough written by the author, but corrupted in transcription. It is the Malay name, and signifies "bird of the gods;" that is, of the Hindu deutas or deities. The name manuk-dewata is Javanese, and has exactly the same import. These are common names for a family of birds of which there are several species; but they are names given by the strangers who traded with the Spice Islands, to which the prepared birds were brought from their native country, New Guinea, as they still continue to be. The Spaniards or Portuguese evidently paraphrased the Malay or Javanese name into Ave de paraiso, conformably to Pigafetta's account of their origin, and hence the "birds of Paradise" of the European languages. Before the arrival of Europeans, the Malay and Javanese traders seem to have brought the birds of Paradise to the western emporia of the Archipelago from the Spice Islands, most probably for sale to the Chinese, for such an article would not have been in demand either by Hindu or Mahommedan consumers.

PARAGUA. This is the name of the northern part of the large island of Palawan, and frequently given by the Spaniards to the whole island. It forms part of the province of Calamianes. See PALAWAN and CALAMIANES.

PARI-PARI. The name of a place on the western side of the south-western peninsula of Celebes, in south latitude 4° 2′ 30″, and east longitude 119° 36′. It is situated on a bay which penetrates the land in a northern direction to the extent of some seven miles. This affords a safe harbour for native craft, and is a place of some external trade, carried on by the Bugis of Waju, and belonging to the prince of Sedenreng.

PÁSAR, which occurs not unfrequently prefixed to, and part of, names of places in Java, is, no doubt, a corruption of the well-known Arabic word, bazár, a market or market-place, the native word for which is pâkân.

PASIG. This is the name of a river of Luzon, in the province of Tondo. It is the canal which empties the surplus water of the Lago de Bay into the great bay of Manilla. At its issue from the lake it consists of five different branches, which quickly unite; and the river, after a brief course of sixteen miles, disembogues at the city of Manilla. It is navigable only for native boats, but might evidently be made so for vessels of considerable burden.

PASIG. This is the name of one of the largest towns in the Philippines, situated on the river to which it gives name, and in a fertile and populous country. In 1850 it contained 4000 houses, many of them of solid materials and Spanish architecture, and a population of 22,106.

PASIR, probably Tanak-pasir, "sand-land," is the name of a Malay state on the eastern side of Borneo, or that which fronts the south-western peninsula of Celebes. The principal town lying on a river, navigable only for small craft, the mouth of which is in south latitude 1° 44′ and east longitude 116° 26′ 30″, is about 45 miles up this stream. It was described to me in 1824, as containing about 400 native houses, but the banks of the river, along its whole course, as many as 4000; which, at the usual estimate, would give a total population of 20,000. The inhabitants consist of Malays; of Bugis settlers from Celebes, the most influential and enterprising part of the population; and of several tribes of Dayaks, or wild aborigines, the most numerous of which were described under the name of Madang. The products of this very rude and scantily-peopled tropical forest rather than country, consist of esculent swallows'-nests, bees'-wax, ratans, damar, and a little gold-dust, obtained from the wild inhabitants of the interior. The external trade is wholly conducted by the resident Bugis.

PASOEROAN, (pasuruhan, "place of the betel pepper,") is the name of a fine province of Java, embracing the western portion of that narrow part of the island which runs parallel to Madura. It extends from sea to sea,—is bounded to the west by the province of Surabaya, and to the east by that of Besuki. It is computed to contain an area of 1784 square miles; and by the census of 1850 had a population of 364,497, of which, 842 were Europeans or their descendants, and 2369 Chinese and their descendants. The native inhabitants consisted of Javanese, with settlers from Madura retaining their own language and customs. The relative population is about 204 inhabitants to the square mile, which is far below that of the central provinces of the island, and even below the average one of the whole island. In 1843, its horned cattle were reckoned to be 90,000, and its horses at 24,000. This Netherland province comprehends the native ones of Pasuruhan, Bangil, and Malang. Within it are some of the highest mountains of Java, as Arjuna, 12,000 feet; and Sumira, the highest peak of the whole island, 12,500 feet. Both of these are active volcanos, and it contains, besides, the Brama with its "sea of sand." Situated, also, in this province are the Hindu ruins of Singasari. The staple agricultural products are rice, pulses, cotton, and sugar-cane; to which the Dutch, for the upland soils, have added coffee. The northern parts of Pasoeroean were acquired by the Dutch in 1743 from the Susunans of Java as a result of the war of the Chinese insurrection, and the southern in 1777.

PASUNDAN; a derivative from Sunda, the name of the nation occupying the western part of the island of Java, signifies "place or country of the Sunda people;' and is a name given to it by the proper Javanese to distinguish it from their own country, which alone they designate Jawa or Java.

PATANI. The name of the most northerly of the Malay states on the eastern side of the Peninsula. It is situated between Kalanten and Sungora, the last the most southern province of Siam. Its chief town, or rather village, consists of a couple of hundred huts, lying on a shallow river, in north latitude 7°, and east longitude 101° 35′. The population of Patani, wholly Malay, is thought to have amounted in 1780, to 90,000; and in 1832 to have fallen off to 54,000, both figures, probably, greatly exaggerated. In the last-named year it underwent the last of many invasions by the Siamese, when several thousands of its inhabitants were carried into captivity. It is, at present, understood to be incorporated with Siam. Patani in common with every other state of the Malay peninsula, Malacca included, have been, at one time or another, more or less tributary to Siam; the degree of subjection depending on the relative power or weakness of the paramount state and its tributaries. From their propinquity, Patani on the eastern, and Queda on the western side of the Peninsula, have suffered most from the paramount state. Mr. Newboldt, in his history of the Malayan states of the Peninsula, furnishes the names of nineteen princes of two dynasties who reigned in Patani. At the usual estimate of 20 years to a reign, this would give a period of 380 years for the history of the state; but as it has, chronologically, neither a beginning nor an end, the statement is necessarily of little value.

PAT·I, (literally, "meal" or "farina.") This is the name of one of the four native districts, of which the Netherland province of Japara, on the northern side of Java, is composed. Of these it is the largest, and is a populous, fertile, and well-cultivated country, containing no fewer than 519 villages.

PATUWA, (literally, "ancient father,") is the name of a mountain of Java, without an active volcano, situated in the district of Bandong and country of the Sundas, and of which the summit has been computed to be 8000 feet above the level the sea.

PAYUNG in Malay and Javanese, and Songsong in Javanese only, an umbrella. This is the universal badge of rank from the prince to the humblest office-bearer among the civilised nations of the Malayan Archipelago, and stands instead of the crowns, coronets, stars and ribbons of the nations of Europe. The quality of the party is expressed by its size, colour, or material.

PEACOCK, in Malay and Javanese Mârak, and in the polite dialect of the latter Máñura, which is Sanscrit. The bird known by this name is the Pavo muticus of ornithologists, and a distinct species from the Indian one which is that of our poultry-yards. It appears to be confined to Java, Sumatra, and the Malay Peninsula, and has never been domesticated by the natives of the Archipelago.

PEARL, and MOTHER-OF-PEARL. Pearls worth fishing are found in the seas about the Arrow Islands, and in those of the Sulu Archipelago, but none in size or quality to be compared with those of the Menar or Persian gulfs. Mother-of-pearl oysters are found in the same situations and on the coasts of several of the Bisaya islands of the Philippines much more abundantly. From Manilla there are yearly exported about 200,000 pounds weight of them. Mr. Windsor Earl has given the following very satisfactory account of the fishing of the Arrow Islands on the coast of New Guinea. "But the great sources of wealth are the pearl and tripang banks which lie on the eastern side of the group, and are often several miles in width, being intersected by deep channels, some of which will admit vessels of burden. The pearl oysters are of several varieties; first, the large oyster with its strong thick shell from six to eight inches in diameter which furnishes the mother-of-pearl shell of commerce. These are obtained by diving and are highly prized, being nearly always in demand at Singapore for the European and Chinese markets. This oyster produces few real pearls, but gnarled semitransparent excrescences are occasionally found on the surface of the inner shell, which are so highly esteemed by the Chinese that they often fetch enormous prices. The other description is the small semi-transparent pearl oyster, having the inner surface of the shell of a bluish tint. The shell is of small value as an article of commerce, but the oyster itself often contains pearls which although individually of no great value, are so numerous, as amply to repay the labour of collection. Pearls of sufficient size to undergo the process of boring are sometimes found, but the greater portion are what go by the name of seed-pearls, and are only marketable in China, where they are much valued as a medicine when pounded and mixed with some liquid." Journal of the Indian Archipelago, vol. iv. p. 490. The names for the pearl in Malay and Javanese, muti, mutya, and mutyara, are all Sanscrit, and I am not aware that in any of the Malayan languages, there are native names for it. Occasionally the Persian word lulu is used. The name for the mother-of-pearl oyster, indung-mutyara, is exactly equivalent to our own, for the Malay word indung signifies mother or matrix. From this we may suppose that both the pearl and mother-of-pearl were most probably made known to the Malayan nations by the Hindus. It may be remarked, that the pearl-fishing of the Sulu Islands was certainly carried on before the arrival of Europeans, for they are mentioned by the indefatigable Barbosa. "Going on," says he, "in a northerly direction towards China, there is another island abounding in the necessaries of life called Solar (Sulu), inhabited by a gentile people, almost white, and in person well made. They have their own proper king and language. In this island is found much gold by washing the soil, and over against it, the people go to fish small pearls, and even find occasionally larger ones, fine as to colour and roundness." Ramusio, vol. i.

PEDIR is the name of a Malay state on the eastern side of Sumatra, and comprising that portion of the sea-board of the island which extends from Diamond Point, the Tanjung-pârlak of the Malays, to Achin. This portion of the Sumatran coast is known to European traders under the name of the "Coast of Pedir," and is noted for its large produce and export of the areca nut. In the beginning of the 16th century, Pedir was an independent state, one of the twenty-nine of the sea-board of

Sumatra, and De Barros enumerates it as such, in the orthography which it has ever since borne. It was the first spot in the Archipelago at which the Portuguese touched, and they found it carrying on some foreign trade, being frequented by ships from different parts of the continent of India. At present it is a place of no moment, except for its export of the areca-nut and a little pepper, which is carried to the British settlement of Penang. The principal town bearing the same name, is situated on a small river, a little east of a headland which is in north latitude 5° 29′ and east longitude 96°.

PEDRA-BRANCA, or the "White Rock" of the Portuguese navigators, a well-known land-mark 32 miles distant from Singapore, is thus well described by Mr. Windsor Earl. "Pedra-branca is a detached rock 24 feet in height above the level of the sea, situated nearly in the centre of the eastern entrance of the Straits of Malacca, which has been the leading mark for vessels entering or leaving the strait for ages past. The main channel which lies immediately to the north of the rock, is four miles wide in the narrowest part. A light-house of dressed granite 75 feet in height has recently been erected on the summit of the rock, which is probably the most perfect of the kind that has ever been constructed to the eastward of the Cape of Good Hope. The light which is regularly illuminated is on the revolving principle, attaining its greatest brilliancy once in a minute as the concentrated rays strike the eye of the spectator. It is visible from the deck of a ship at the distance of 15 miles, when it disappears below the horizon, but it may be seen much further from the mast-head, as its brilliancy is so great that the horizon is the only limit to its range. The reefs and dangers which beset the eastern entrance of the Straits of Malacca are all within the influence of the light as visible from a ship's deck."

PENANG, Pulo-Pinâng, that is "Areca palm island" in Malay. This is the island to which we gave the clumsy and unmeaning name of Prince of Wales Island, but which is fortunately becoming obsolete. This British settlement is situated towards the western end of the Straits of Malacca, separated from the main land of the Peninsula by a channel, about two miles broad, forming a safe and spacious harbour and distant from the nearest point of Sumatra about 150 miles. The insular shore of the harbour, the site of the fort and town, lies in north latitude 5° 25′ and east longitude 100° 21′. The island is about 15 miles long and from 7 to 8 broad, and is computed to contain an area of 139 geographical or 160 statute square miles, so that it is by 30 square miles less than the Isle of Wight. Annexed to it, however, is a territory on the opposite main of the Peninsula which goes under the name of Province Wellesley, and which has an area of 121 geographical or 140 statute square miles, so that the entire territory of the settlement amounts to 260 geographical or 300 statute square miles. With the exception of a plain of about three miles in depth fronting the mainland, the island is a mass of granite with narrow valleys. The highest peak is above 3000 feet above the level of the sea (2922). The territory on the main is, generally, an alluvial flat, but a few feet above the level of the sea.

The influence of the regular monsoons is more distinctly felt at Penang than in the more easterly part of the Straits of Malacca owing to the wideness of the latter to the west, and vicinity to the Bay of Bengal. During the north-easterly monsoon, from November to March inclusive, clear settled weather prevails, and in the south-westerly from April and October the rains take place. But neither rain nor drought are of long continuance. The average heat of the year at the level of the sea is 80° and at the height of 2410 feet, the highest inhabited point 70°, the annual range being about 20°. Wherever there is a free ventilation, the climate is equal in salubrity to that of any other tropical one, but in a few close valleys wanting this advantage the malaria is poisonous, and such localities, few in number, are not habitable by Europeans. Much of the island is still covered with its primeval forest of heavy timber trees, and even the cultivation, consisting as it does, for the most part, of tall evergreen plants, such as palms, bamboos, bananas, fruit trees, the clove and the nutmeg, has from its luxuriance much the aspect of a forest. There are plenty of brooks, a beautiful waterfall, an abundant supply of potable water, but no stream that deserves the name of a river.

Penang was taken possession of as a British settlement on the 17th day of July, 1786. The British government of India had been long desirous of possessing a commercial emporium, but above all a naval station at the eastern side of the Bay of Bengal, and the chief instrument it employed in carrying this object into effect was Francis Light, the master of a merchant vessel and a man of the same class of society, and the same profession as the Dampiers and the Horsburghs. The question of the formation of such a settlement was, on the representation of this gentleman, first entertained and resolved upon under the administration of the able, active, and ambitious Warren Hastings, although not carried into effect until that of his immediate successor. Mr. Light had been in the habit of trading with the Siamese possessions on the Bay of Bengal, and with Queda and other Malay states on the eastern side of the Peninsula. He first recommended for the locality of the future settlement the larger island of Junk Ceylon, the Salang of the Malays belonging to the Siamese, and finally, Penang an uninhabited island belonging to Queda, itself a tributary of Siam. A romantic story had long obtained currency that Mr. Light had married the daughter of the king of Queda, and received with her as a dowry the island of Penang, which he sold to the East India Company. There was no foundation of truth in this tale. The wife of the enterprising adventurer was neither a princess nor a Malay, but a mestizo Portuguese of Siam, and the raja of Queda did not give his desert island to any one, but sold it to the British government for the payment of a quit-rent of 10,000 hard Spanish dollars a year, which sum is at the present day paid to his descendant. Francis Light the agent in this transaction became the first governor under the title of superintendant, planted the colony and carried on its administration until 1793, when he died at his post.

When Penang was first occupied it was an entire forest throughout, without a rood of cultivation, or an inhabitant, with the exception of a family or two of migratory Malay fishermen, whose huts were on the beach near which stands now Georgetown. In 1800, the territory on the main was annexed to the island, having been purchased from the king of Queda for the consideration of 2000 Spanish dollars, about 430*l*. sterling, or little more than a penny an acre, which was probably fully as much as it was worth to the vendor.

That the founder of Penang was a man of comprehensive mind and forecast is testified by the extent to which his views have been realised by experience. In a despatch to the Indian government, he gives the following summary of the advantages to be expected from his colony, for such, in reality, it was. "A harbour with good anchorage, secure from bad weather, and capable of containing any number of vessels;—an island well watered, of excellent soil, capable of containing 50,000 people, and abounding in all necessary materials for their service and security;—a port favourable to commerce, the present imports amounting to upwards of 600,000 dollars per annum;—a place of refuge for merchant ships, where they may refit and be supplied with provisions, wood and water, and protected from the insults of enemies, and an emporium, centrically situated, where the merchants of all nations may conveniently meet and exchange their commodities."

Most of the anticipations here held out have been realised, and some of them have even exceeded the sanguine expectations of the founder. The only serious exception relates to the supposed excellence of the soil, which Mr. Light fancied was well adapted for the growth of corn, a vulgar error derived from the notion that the land, which grows huge forest trees, must, of necessity, be fertile and adapted to produce the staple necessaries of life. The soil of Penang, notwithstanding the luxuriant vegetation which, with the help of heat and moisture it produces, is anything but fertile, and found by experience very ill suited to the production of corn. It consists of a thin coat of vegetable mould over a sharp sand, or a stiff clay, both the produce of the decomposition of the granite, on which the soil rests. Fertility might with equal truth be predicted of the "barrens" of North America, or the mountains of Scandinavia, on account of the tall pines which they produce.

In 1792, or within seven years of its establishment, Penang had a population of 7000 resident inhabitants, or, including public establishments and sojourners, 10,000. By a census made in 1810, the population, which now included the annexed territory on the continent at the time of its occupation, nearly as destitute of inhabitants as was the island itself, amounted to 31,600. In 1827, it rose to 55,354, and in 1851, sixty-five years after its foundation, to 111,096, this last extraordinary augmentation having been, in a good measure, caused by migrations from the neighbouring Malay state of Queda, laid waste by Siamese invasion. The relative population is, according to the statements now given, at the rate of 370 inhabitants to the square mile, and yet by far the larger part of the country is still unoccupied, and a mere forest. Thus, of the territory on the continent, the most fertile and available for cultivation, not above one-fourth is reckoned to be reclaimed from the jungle.

In 1789, or within three years of its establishment, its founder reported the imports of Penang to be of the value of 130,000*l*. In 1854, or in sixty-five years' time, they were of the value of 581,240*l*. But in the first of these years, Penang was the only British port in the Straits of Malacca, and its imports represented, therefore, the whole British trade of the Straits. In 1854, it was competing with two other British settlements, as an emporium, the joint imports of the three settlements in that year having amounted to 4,923,237*l*., or to near thirty-eight fold what they were three years after the foundation of Penang. These figures represent the progress which British commerce has made in this remote quarter in little more than sixty years time.

The products of the soil of Penang include none of the staple articles of food, its rice and pulses being all imported. It produces the coco and areca palms, nutmegs, cloves, and in perfection all the Malayan fruits. At one period of its history, no less than three millions and a-half of pounds of black pepper were yearly produced by Europeans and Chinese, but, in time, it was found out that this article could be produced far cheaper in the wide lands, and with the cheap labour of Sumatra and other places, and the culture has now been wholly abandoned. On the territory on the continent the sugar-cane is largely cultivated, and several thousand tons of sugar are yearly exported. Sheep cannot be reared, but are imported, nor is the pasture fit for rearing oxen, the only useful domestic animal that flourishes being the dull, coarse, but useful buffalo. Poultry is chiefly imported, but abundant, and fish is of finer quality and more abundant than in any other part of India.

Penang at present forms with Singapore and Malacca what is called the Straits' government, which is, in fact, a Lieutenant-Governorship, subject directly to the Governor-General of India. The laws administered from its first foundation have been those of England, and the all-sufficient proof of their having, upon the whole, given satisfaction, is to be found in the constant immigration of strangers seeking their protection. Since 1807 they have been administered by a Recorder's Court.

In 1852-53 the gross revenues of Penang, drawn from excises on opium, spirits, and intoxicating drugs, quit rents, and sale of waste lands, &c., &c., amounted to 18,236*l*. This, however, does not include the municipal revenue or rates imposed on police purposes, which is considerable. As at the other Straits' settlements, there is an entire exemption from all imposts on ship or cargo.

PEPPER (BLACK). Piper nigrum. This commodity, although now compared to others, such as sugar, coffee, cotton, and indigo, all of them either unknown, or little known, in the early period of the Indian trade of Europe, of very little importance, formed for many ages the staple article of it. The great Vasco Di Gama did not think his achievement complete, until he had loaded his ships with cargos of it, and for three centuries after his time, the maritime nations of Europe contended with each other for the possession of the monopoly of it, forming costly establishments in India that had no other object in view.

The pepper vine grows readily in very indifferent soils, which consist of dry upland. Heat, moisture, and some shade are alone indispensable to it. Unlike the sugar-cane, indigo, and even coffee, the careless husbandry of the Malays is sufficient to rear it in perfection. Sumatra is the principal Malayan country which produces it, but it is also produced in the Peninsula, Borneo, Java, and to a small extent in some of the Philippines. Thus we find it growing from the seventh degree of south, as far as the eighteenth of north latitude. In an easterly direction, however, its cultivation, within the Malay Archipelago, is not known beyond Java and Borneo. The soils most favourable to it seem to be those of sedimentary and plutonic formations, and it does not succeed equally well in the richer volcanic ones, such as those of Java.

There is no doubt but that black pepper is an exotic in the Indian Archipelago, and as little, that it must have been introduced from Malabar, the only other country that produces it. It is not found wild in any of the Malayan islands, but abundantly so in the mountains and valleys of most of the countries of the western side of India, according to the testimony of an excellent botanist, Dr. Francis Buchanan Hamilton. This fact would be sufficient to prove its foreign origin, but it is corroborated by etymology. In Malay, the name of the plant, lada, which in the language of the Sundas of Java, among whom we may suppose the exotic to have been first cultivated, signifies "pungent," but it is a generic one, requiring the epithet "black," in fact corresponds exactly with our own name for it, and this, of course, proves nothing as to its origin. So it is with several other of the insular languages, but in Javanese the name is maricha, which is pure Sanscrit. The Javanese appear to have extended this Hindu name to the languages of Celebes, Bali, and Lomboc. In those of the Philippines, again, we have the Malay name, lada, corrupted lara, by the conversion of the palatial *d* into *r*, a very frequent commutation. Of the time in which the pepper vine was introduced into the Archipelago, we know nothing, but as a commercial intercourse had immemorially existed between Calicut and other emporia of Malabar and the Malayan islands, we can have no doubt about the channel by which it found its way.

The consumers of pepper may be said to be the whole world, with the singular exception of the parties that produce it, for, as in the case of the clove and nutmeg, these have no taste for it as a condiment. With the exception of salt, there is perhaps no condiment of such general use, and it has been an object of consumption among the civilised nations of Europe for probably not less than 2000 years. Pliny expresses his surprise that people should go all the way to India in quest of this commodity, which had nothing to recommend it but its acrimony (amaritudo).—Lib. xii. In his time the price of a pound of black pepper in the Roman market was about 3*s.* 9½*d.*, and of the same article, white or blanched, 6*s.* 7½*d*, for both sorts seem then to have been imported as they are now, and it is remarkable that their relative prices should be nearly the same at that time that they are at the present day. The cost of black pepper in Europe immediately before the discovery of the new route to India, appears to have been about 3*s.* 6*d.* a pound, or near the same which it had been in the time of Pliny, fourteen centuries before, which would seem to indicate that in this long interval, no material improvement had taken place in the mode of conducting the Indian trade. Neither did the facilities of the new route itself produce any diminution of price, owing to the rapacity of the European nations. During the period of near a century that the Portuguese had the trade of India to themselves, driving the Indians out of it, by a conduct not less than piratical, the European price of pepper seems to have been generally about 4*s.* a pound, or by 6*d.* more than before the discovery of the new route. The matter was not mended when the Dutch superseded the Portuguese, but, on the contrary, was greatly aggravated by their more stringent monopoly, for the cost of pepper in Europe rose to double what it had been under the Portuguese. The French and English, each with a monopoly of the market of their own country, quickly entered the field of Indian competition with the Dutch, and the price fell to 1*s.* 8*d.*, between which and 1*s.* it fluctuated for two centuries, when, towards the beginning of the present century, the monopoly having ceased by the awakening of the public, after a long dream, to common sense, the price fell to about 3*d.* a pound, or one-fifteenth part of what it was in the time of Pliny, and in the middle ages, and one-fourth of what it was when at the lowest, or least aggravated state of the monopoly. In the last year of our monopoly, 1813, our consumption of pepper fell short of a million of pounds a year; it is now about three millions and a-half, the result of lower prime cost, lower duties, and, in a less degree, to increased population.

As to the quantity of pepper actually produced, nothing better than an approximate estimate can be given. The smallest supply is furnished by the parent country, Malabar, and this, probably, does not exceed 1,000,000 of pounds a year. By far the largest supply is furnished by the western side of Sumatra, which exports it from no fewer than fourteen different ports, the entire quantity being estimated at 22,000,000. The produce of the eastern side of the same island has been computed at 9,000,000, making the whole produce of Sumatra 31,000,000. The Malay Peninsula, Borneo, and the western part of Java produce a considerable quantity which may probably equal 8,000,000 of pounds, making the total supply about 40,000,000. The total value of this quantity, at the wholesale Indian price is, at present, little more than half a million sterling. As the prices were far higher, and the consumers fewer, in the 15th and 16th centuries, the quantity and value could not have been even one-half of this. It was then, in order to establish for themselves a monopoly in an article of which the intrinsic prime cost was, at the utmost, not more than a quarter of a million sterling, that the nations of Europe, for three long centuries, made such a notable display of ignorance and rapacity. They fancied that a commodity naturally cheap, because produced with little labour, had a specific intrinsic value, because they had received it enhanced by the multiplied charges of a barbarous commerce. This notion is even discoverable in the very manner in which we quote its price. That of pepper, on account of its once factitious value, is always given in pounds, whereas coffee, an article of superior intrinsic value, but never a fit one for monopoly, is quoted by hundred-weights. For the same reason, we reckon tea by pounds, while the Chinese sell it to us by a weight of above one hundred and thirty times that amount.

The accurate Barbosa gives an account of the pepper trade, shortly after the arrival of the Portuguese in India, and this both at Calicut and Sumatra. This is his statement:—"Pepper is produced in the kingdoms of Malabar and Calicut, and a bahar sells in the latter at from 200 to 230 fanoes, each fanoe being worth a real of Spain, and the bahar being equal to four cantaros of the old weight of Portugal, at which all spices are sold in Lisbon. The duty paid to the King of Calicut is 12 fanoes on each bahar. The purchasers of pepper convey it to Cambay, Persia, Aden and Mecca, and thence to Cairo and Alexandria. Pepper also grows in the island of Sumatra in the neighbourhood of Malacca, which is finer and larger than that of Malabar, but not so good and strong, and this is conveyed to Bengal and China, and to some parts of Arabia, by contraband, and unknown to the Portuguese. This pepper is worth, in Sumatra, from 400 to 600 maravedis the cantaro of the new weight of Portugal, the difference between the old and new weights being two ounces,—the pound of the first being 14 ounces, and of the last 16."—Ramusio, Vol. i. p. 322.

The bahar, or Persian weight, so called, varies from 400 to 450 pounds, but by a note of Ramusio it would appear in this case to be 425, and the fanoes is certainly no other than the silver fanam of Calicut, of the intrinsic value of $4\frac{3}{4}d$. Assuming these data to be correct, the market price of pepper at the emporium of Calicut about the year 1500, ranged from 2·23*d.* to 2·57*d.* the pound avoirdupois. The Sumatra quotations are not so easily determined, but seem to be higher, and to take a higher range. I make them from 2·68*d.* to 4*d.* It is remarkable that the price of pepper, at the present day, and what it has steadily been for some years, at the British settlements in the Straits of Malacca, do not materially differ from those of Barbosa. I make them, in the Singapore market, from 2·32*d.* to 2·52*d.* a pound. The cause of this correspondence of prices, at an interval of near three hundred and fifty years, is, I think, obvious. At both periods the trade was free; at both the land fit for the production of pepper was practically boundless and consequently bore no rent, and in both periods the wages of labour were probably the same, or, in fact, the same amount of labour, under the same circumstances, being expended in the production of the article at two periods so distant, the price was necessarily the same. One very important inference may, I think, be fairly deduced from this fact, namely, that the popular belief that great depreciation in the value of the precious metals, with a corresponding increase in the cost of all other commodities, took place after the discovery of the mines of America, is without foundation. The depreciation in the value of gold has been supposed to have amounted, in the first fifty years after the influx of the precious metals from America, to one-fourth part of its previous value, which, if true, must have affected the cost of pepper proportionally, which it has not done any more than it has yet done by the still larger influx, in our own time, of gold from California and Australia. This view, taken from the prices of pepper, is corroborated by Barbosa's quotations of other commodities, not likely, any more than itself, to be affected by rent or variations in the wages of labour, compared with present prices. Opium, camphor, and stick-lac are examples, for in these three commodities the quality is not, probably, now different from what it was in the beginning of the 16th century, while their prices nearly correspond.

PEPPER (BETEL); Piper Betel. This plant, the leaf of which is in universal use as a masticatory, along with the fruit of the areca palm, is found cultivated among all the more civilised nations of the Malay and Philippine Archipelagos, but is not known to the ruder, and does not extend to the islands of the Pacific. In so far as can be judged by the names which it bears, and which are all native, and generally different in different languages, this plant, which grows freely in a rich soil, is probably indigenous. In the popular language of Java, it is called suruh, and in the polite, sâdah. In Malay, it is sirih, which is most likely the same word as the Javanese, but in the Bali it is basi, in the Lampung, chambai, and in the Tagala of the Philippines, buyo. Being an article of such general consumption, attempts have been made to make it, like tobacco, an instrument for levying a capitation-tax, but with little success, since the plant must be used in the fresh state, and not being capable of storing, an impost on it can be levied only in retail, and is, therefore, easily evaded.

PEPPER (LONG), Piper longum. This is the chabe of the Javanese, and the lada panjang of the Malays, which is a literal translation of our own and the botanic name. This commodity, is probably a native of Java, although now grown in other countries of the Archipelago. It is rather singular that it is not named by Barbosa, but there can be little doubt but that it must have been an article of trade in his time. It is, at present, about half as high-priced again in the Indian market as black pepper. If it be the pepper which Pliny calls "long," its cost in the Roman market was between three and four times the price of black pepper.

PEPPER (Cubeb). See Cubeb.

PERAK, is the name of the second Malay state of the western side of the Peninsula, counting from the north. It is bounded to the north by Queda, to the south by Salangore, and to the east by Tringanu and Pahang, the central mountain chain dividing them. The coast line of Perak is said to be 100 miles in length, and the depth of the country inland generally 50 miles, so that it may contain an area of 5000 square miles. Besides the territory on the mainland, the uninhabited Dending and Sambilan islands belong to it. The name Perak signifies silver, and is probably taken from that of the principal river of the country. This is a tortuous stream of intricate navigation, and accessible only to small craft, having its debouchement in the Straits of Malacca in north latitude 5° 10′. On the banks of this river are situated the bulk of the inhabitants, consisting of Malays and a few Chinese, while the mountains of the interior contain some wild and wandering tribes of the Malayan race, here known under the name of Sakai, and a few of the Negritos or Sâmang. The total population is a matter of conjecture. It has been reckoned at 15,000, and as high as 35,000, but 20,000 is supposed to be the most likely approximation, and this would give the scanty rate of four inhabitants to the square mile. The whole country is, in fact, a vast jungle, in which are scattered a very few villages. The principal cultivation is rice, of which about enough is produced for local consumption. The durian, mangostin, and rambutan (Nephelium lappaceum) grow in perfection. The productions of the forest for commerce are the usual ones, ivory, bees'-wax, rhinoceros' horns, ratans, and some perfume and dye-woods. Its tin, however, is the product which has always given some importance to Perak: this is, as usual, alluvial, the workings existing towards the foot of the mountain range, and being chiefly wrought by the Malays without the aid of Chinese, and consequently unskilfully and unproductively. The quantity of metal produced, and which is all exported to Penang or Singapore, has been estimated at from 500 to 600 tons.

When or how the state of Perak was founded is unknown,—a mystery, like the founding of all the other states of the Peninsula. At present, it is nominally subject to Siam, and in former times, had been occasionally so to Malacca, Jehor, Achin, and the Dutch. Virtually, it is entirely independent.

PHILIPPINE ARCHIPELAGO. This comprehends the many islands extending between the fifth and the twenty-first degree of north latitude, and is bounded to the east by the North Pacific Ocean, and to the west by the sea of China. It embraces about 16° of latitude, and 9° of longitude. To the north the nearest land to it is the island of Formosa, distant about 80 miles; to the north-west China distant about 300 miles; and to the south Borneo about 45 miles. According to this view, the long chain of the Sulu Islands form the southern boundary of the Archipelago, and the Bashis its northern; but these last can hardly be said to belong to it geographically, and probably, therefore, the Babuanes islands, in about latitude 19° 30′, ought more justly to be considered so.

According to the reckoning of Spanish writers, the Philippines amount to 408 islands, exclusive of rocks and uninhabited islets. Two islands are pre-eminently large, Luzon which is by more than one-half, and Mindano by one-fifth larger than Ireland. These are followed by seven islands, Panay, Negros, Çebu, Samar, Leyte, Mindoro, and Palawan, the smallest of which, Çebu, is about one-fifth, and the largest, Panay, about one-half the size of Sicily. After these come two considerable islands, Bohol and Masbate, of about one-half the extent of the smallest of the last-named group. Finally, we have about twenty such islands as Marinduque, Catanduanes, and Calamianes. The islands now named, about thirty in number, constitute the important part of the Archipelago. One island, Luzon, is pre-eminently superior to all the rest put together; and for extent, fertility, and other natural advantages, is, probably, the finest in the tropical world. The entire Archipelago may probably contain an area of about 200,000 square geographical miles.

The configuration of most of the larger islands is longitudinal, their length being in a direction north and south, and in all of them, a chain or range of mountains runs through them in this direction, seldom exceeding 6000 feet high, or about one-half the height of the mountains of the Sunda Islands. All the larger islands are abundantly, almost superabundantly, supplied with rivers flowing from these mountains, many of them contributing by irrigation to the fertility of the countries they water, but few to internal communication. The two largest islands contain some fine lakes,—Luzon four large ones, and Mindano five; the first, moreover, having periodical lakes of vast extent, which may be compared, for the fertility they bestow, to the inundations of the Nile and Ganges. The western side of Luzon alone contains safe and spacious harbours, but the southern portion of the Archipelago, out of the region of storms, stands in little need of them.

The geological formation of the Archipelago consists of almost every kind of rock. The basis of the mountain chains is considered to be granitic, but the most characteristic feature of the geology of the group, consists in the great volcanic band which begins in the bay of Bengal and ends with the Kurile Islands passing through it. This band, after proceeding from Sumatra and Java to the Banda Islands in the 130th meridian, in a direction nearly east, turns to the north-west, and after passing the Molucca islands and a small part of the north-eastern peninsula of Celebes, enters the Philippines at Mindano at the distance of about 220 miles. From Mindano, it extends through the whole Philippine Archipelago, (its western portion from Palawan to Mindoro excepted), as far as the Babuyan islands, so that its length here extends over about 280 leagues. Extinct volcanos are numerous in all the large islands, and active ones in Luzon and Mindano, in which, since the Spanish conquest in 1564, no fewer than eleven destructive eruptions are recorded as having taken place, the earliest being in 1627.

The metals ascertained to exist in the Philippines are gold, found in most of the larger islands but most abundant in Luzon and Mindano, iron, chiefly in the same islands, with copper, lead, and mercury, in Luzon. Sulphur is abundant in most of the islands, but especially in Leyte, Mindano, and the province of Albany in Luzon. Coal, a lignite, has been found and partially worked in the islet of Rapu-rapu on the eastern coast of Luzon, at the entrance of the great bay of Albany, and the two small islands at the southern extremity of Mindano called Sirangan, are stated to be nothing but coal beds, not improbably part of the same Bornean field, which crops out in Labuan, and is now worked by an English company in that island. Variegated marble is found in the province of Bataan in Luzon, and has been occasionally used in church building in Manilla. Carbonate of lime is widely disseminated, but gypsum sparingly.

The native vegetable products of the southern portion of the Philippines correspond, generally, with those of the Malayan Islands, but as the Archipelago extends by twelve degrees of latitude further north, there must be in many respects a material divergence. No fewer than 218 forest trees, chiefly of the more northern provinces, have been subjected to experiments in the arsenal of Manilla, and the relative strength, tenacity, and specific gravity, of the timber, ascertained for economic uses. For ship-building the following six are most in use, the Molave Vitex genicutala or V. pubescens, the Banaba, the Iacal, the Dongon a Sterculia, the Mangachapiu Vateria mangachapoi, and the Quita-quita. Of the timber of these, large ships have been built which are stated to have lasted 40 years, a fact which would place them on a level with teak or oak, which would not be asserted of any of the woods of the islands of the Malay Archipelago. The teak itself, it is singular, is found only in the island of Mindano, at the distance of 1300 geographical miles from Java and Sumbawa, the only two islands of the Malayan Archipelago, which yield it. It grows in Mindano, in such parts of that island as are in native occupation and is, consequently, not available to European use. The Philippine forests yield several dyewoods, the most valuable of which is the Sibucao of the natives, the sâpang of the Malays and our sapan-wood (Cæsalpinia sappan). This is largely exported, and in the foreign markets, is worth 50 per cent. more than the same article brought from Siam, or in other words, yields half as much more colouring matter. The author of the "Informe sobre el estado de las Islas Filipinas," furnishes a list of 600 wild plants, with names which have but a very small sprinkling of Malayan ones. Among these are some yielding dyes, gums, resins, and textile materials, which like the Indian-rubber and gutta-percha of the Malayan Archipelago, may be found of value in the arts. It seems not unlikely that in the southern portion of the Archipelago, even these articles themselves may be found.

The zoology of the Philippines has received but little attention from European naturalists. Among the larger mammalia, monkeys and deer of several species, and at least one species of hog are ascertained to be natives of most of the islands from Mindano to Luzon. The elephant, the rhinoceros, and the tapir of the Malayan Archipelago, are all absent. Some Spanish writers have supposed that the elephant once existed, because there is what they fancy to be a native name for it. This name, which is variously written garya, gadia and gadya, is only a corruption of the Sanscrit word gajah taken from the Malay or Javanese, so that the supposition in question is much on a par with supposing that the same animal was within the historical era, a native of Europe, because there are naturalised names for it, received very much after the same manner. All the large animals of the feline family, such as tigers and leopards, so abundant in the Malayan, are wanting in the Philippine Archipelago. One small wild cat and the musang of the Malays, known by this name also, in the Philippine tongues, the Paradoxus musanya of naturalists, are the only two mammalia of prey known in the Archipelago. Some domesticated animals, however, have become wild, and favoured by abundance of suitable pastures and freedom from beasts of prey, have greatly multiplied. This has been the case with the buffalo, the ox, and even the horse. Dampier saw wild oxen of this description in Mindano in 1686, and was present with a party that hunted them. It is to be observed, indeed, that the names of all the animals domesticated in the Philippines belong to foreign languages. This applies to the dog, the hog, the goat, the buffalo, the cat, and even to the domestic fowl and duck. The names of all these are either Malay or Javanese, while those of the horse, ox, and sheep, are Spanish. If these animals, as is most probable, were introduced by strangers, it follows that the inhabitants of the Philippines, before their intercourse with the civilised nations of the Malayan Archipelago, were far worse off in domesticated animals for food or labour, than even the more advanced nations of America, who had, at least, the lama, the alpaca, and the turkey. Of small mammalia, the Philippines have several species of bats and of squirrels, including among the latter the flying one of the size of an ordinary hare the krawak of the Malays, and Sciurus maximus volans of naturalists.

The largest bird of the Philippines is a species of heron, rising to the height, it is asserted, of five or six feet, called by the natives, pagala. This has a bag in front of the throat, and may be the same bird known in Bengal as the adjutant, or in the native language argala, and which, in that country, is migratory. Another of this family measuring from two to three feet high, called by the natives the tapol, is tamed and taught to dance to the sound of a flute or drum. In the forests of Luzon there is one species of pheasant, and the jungle fowl, Gallus bankiva, is widely disseminated over most of the larger islands. The most numerous birds are those of the parrot and pigeon families, among the first of which is said to be a cockatoo, a bird nearly unknown to the Malayan Archipelago, west of New Guinea. No species of peacock seems to exist. Among the Philippine birds is the tubon, which leaves its eggs in the sands of the sea-shore, to be hatched by the sun. The swallows which build the esculent nest, frequents the many limestone caves of the islands, and the nests are collected, as in the Malay islands, for the market of China. The bird is known in the Philippines under the native name of salangan. Wild ducks and geese which, as birds of passage are unknown in the Malayan islands, frequent the Philippines.

Among reptiles, serpents are numerous in the Philippines, and a few of them poisonous. A python exists and of such size as to be capable of destroying the calf of the buffalo. One of them, it is stated, was killed in the mountains of Cavité, near the bay of Manilla, measuring 18 Spanish yards, which would make it about 50 English feet in length. Alligators are numerous in all the lakes and rivers, and there are several species of land and sea tortoise, including that which yields the precious shell.

Fish, in reference to their utility to man form, perhaps, the most important branch of the zoology of the Philippines. They seem to be more abundant than in almost any other country, for they are not only numerous in the sea, but unlike the islands of the Malay Archipelago, are even more so in the fresh water,—in the rivers, in the permanent lakes, and in the periodical ones. Even the cultivated fields, during their temporary submersion, yield a supply. Some of these fish are migratory, entering particular rivers from the sea for the purpose of spawning, when great quantities of them are taken with little care or art. Of this description is one called the ipon or dolon, which frequents one of the rivers of the province of Ilocos in Luzon in the dry season from October to February, and which, it is alleged, can only be captured during the first five days of the moon's age. A fish called the sablao, of the size of a salmon, is peculiar to the lake Taal in Luzon, of volcanic origin. The Lago de Bay or lake of Manilla, produces a great variety of fish, of which those called the curbina and dalag are most abundant and most esteemed. Fish forms the principal animal aliment of all the inhabitants of the Philippines, and great quantities of them cured, form an important article of the internal native trade. One may form some notion of the abundance of fish, when it is stated that the retail price of a dalag fish, enough for six persons, is in the market of Manilla, no more than a real of plate or about 5 pence. On several of the shores of the Philippines the tripang, called in the native languages balaté, is fished for the market of China. On the same shores are also carried on the fishery of the pearl-oyster or mother-of-pearl-shell, of which the Philippines furnish to Europe and China, their largest supply.

Among insects, mosquitos, and various kinds of ants, including the termes, or white ant, are numerous and troublesome in all the islands. On the other hand, fleas and bugs are almost unknown, and the common fly is not frequent. Flights of locusts are experienced, but they do not appear to be very destructive.

The climate of the Philippines varies with latitudes which range from 5° to near 20° from the equator. At Manilla, in latitude 14° 36′, the difference between the longest summer and the shortest winter day is but one hour, 47 minutes, and 12 seconds. The monsoons are, the north-east and south-west, the first, as in all countries lying on the China Sea being the most violent, contrary to what is the case west of it. In the southern and western portions of the Archipelago the rainy season corresponds with the summer and autumn, but the case is reversed in the northern and eastern parts, occasioned by the ranges of mountains which run north and south, in the same manner as is the case on the eastern and western sides of Southern India. At the changes from one monsoon to another take place those terrible hurricanes so well known to mariners as typhoons. These are most severe at the autumnal equinox, and the month of October is the most remarkable for them. From these scourges all parts of the Archipelago within ten degrees of the equator are exempt, which include the island of Mindano and the long chain of islands extending between it and Borneo. The rainy season commences in May, and lasts to September inclusive. At Manilla, which is not far from the centre of the Archipelago, reckoning from north to south, the lowest annual fall of rain is 84 inches, and the highest 114, giving an average of 98. A vast quantity of rain falls within a comparatively short space of time, and the consequence is that much of the low country is submerged,—the rivers overflow their banks and periodical lakes of many leagues in extent are formed. At Manilla Fahrenheit's thermometer never falls below 72°, nor rises above 95°, so that the range is but 23°. In the mountain valley of Banhao, 6400 feet above the level of the sea, and but 12 leagues from the city, the thermometer stands at from 45° to 47°. The greatest heats are experienced from April to August in the fair season, but Spanish writers declare that those of Manilla never equal those of Madrid in severity, although they last longer. A fall of hail is recorded to have taken place in the Philippines twice only since the Spanish occupation—once in May, 1749, and once in February, 1803.

The Philippines are inhabited by two distinct races of men, the Malayan and the Philippine Negro; the first constituting the great mass of the inhabitants, and the last consisting only of a few tribes of mountaineers found only in four of the principal islands. The Malayan race is known to the Spaniards by the vague names of "Indians" and "natives," and among themselves, they have certainly no common denomination. Spanish writers thus describe their physical form—Stature, seven lengths of the head; facial angle, from 67 to 73; nose, broad, flat, and between the eyes hardly any relief; lips thick; inner angle of the eye depressed; head broader than that of the European; hair, harsh, rigid, and black; beard very scanty; complexion, olive coloured. There can be no doubt but that this is the genuine Malay. The negros, or as the Spaniards call them negritos or little negros, are in physical form diminutive Africans, the negro features less pronounced, and the complexion less black. Although of shorter stature, those who have seen them have been struck by their resemblance to the natives of Australia. Some writers have fancied the negritos to be the aboriginal inhabitants of the Archipelago and the fairer race to be intruders from some unknown couhtry, but for this hypothesis there is not a shadow of evidence, historical or lingual, and it must be regarded as the mere dream of the inventors. For anything known to the contrary, both the Malay and negro race have an equal claim to be considered as aborigines.

The Spaniards divide the fairer race into two classes, namely, the nations or tribes that have been subdued, who pay the capitation tax, and who have been converted to Christianity, and the rude independent people who are still, either pagans or Mahommedans. This division is, in fact, nearly equivalent to civilised and uncivilised. The first of these classes is divided, as they were at the conquest, into several distinct nations, speaking distinct languages. Of these there are in the great island of Luzon alone no fewer than five. It is asserted that one nation speaking one language inhabits all the islands lying between Luzon and Mindano. This has been called by the Spaniards the Bisaya, from a native word signifying to paint, derived from the circumstance of the inhabitants of those islands practising tattooing when first seen by the Spaniards. The fact, however, is not very clearly ascertained, for Pigafetta certainly takes no notice of it, while he describes the people of Çebu who are ranked with the Bisaya nation as speaking a very different tongue from those of Massana whom he had previously seen. Whether, however, the Bisaya language be substantially one and the same tongue throughout, there is no doubt but that it is divided into several dialects, so widely different that the parties speaking them are not mutually intelligible. They may really be practically considered as so many distinct nations, and thus among the more civilised inhabitants of the Philippines there are in all probably no fewer than a dozen distinct people.

In character the more civilised nations of the Philippines may be described as simple, docile, indolent, credulous, rather excitable, and very superstitious. The Spaniards affirm that they are as easily led by an European of good understanding that takes the pains to understand them, as the horse, the ox, or the buffalo. They are in fact led, guided, and virtually governed by the Christian priesthood, who may be truly said to have conquered them, and to have maintained them since in subjection. Of their wonderful credulity and proneness to imposition, some singular instances have been recorded. In 1672, a report was spread in one of the Bisaya islands that his majesty the King of Spain had gone on a fishing party,—that he was fallen upon and made prisoner by the Turks, and that for his ransom the inhabitants of a certain district were demanded. The people of the district in question abandoned their houses, fled to the mountains, and it was with the utmost difficulty that they were disabused of their delusion and induced to return. In the same year a silver mine was supposed to have been discovered in the district of Tanavan, but an impostor gave out that it could not be worked, unless the vein was first anointed with an unguent made of "old women's eyes" and similar ingredients. All the old women were immediately concealed by their friends,—the district was in a state of commotion and the ministers of religion had the greatest difficulty in reassuring its inhabitants. In 1832, a ship of war having brought 250 soldiers from Spain to Manilla, a report immediately got abroad among the women engaged in the state manufactory of tobacco, that the object of this force was to seize their children for the purpose of watering with their blood, in the manner of a charm, the gold and silver mines of Spain. The women fled from the manufactory, began to hide their children, and the men took up arms. To disabuse them in this case also was a work of some difficulty. But the most dangerous insurrection took place in 1820, when the Asiatic cholera made its first appearance in Manilla. The people ascribed its introduction to the foreign European resident or sojourning strangers. A commotion was the consequence, in the course of which several innocent persons were assassinated, among whom were some French naturalists, considered, on account of their preserved specimens, the greatest offenders.

Notwithstanding such weaknesses as these, the natives of the Philippines have many estimable qualities. They are a good-natured, cheerful, happy, and hospitable people. The Spaniards found them, on their first arrival, much inferior both to the Malays and Javanese in the social scale, and at present they must be considered, on the whole, superior to either of them. They are, indeed, the people of all Asiatic and American nations who have made the greatest advance in civilisation under European rule, if, indeed, others have not rather retrograded. Their education has not been neglected: many have acquired the use of the Spanish language, which has been encouraged, and it has been observed that more of the humbler classes can read and write than even among European nations. As mariners, in so far as skill and presence of mind are concerned, they excel the natives of Hindustan, as is shown by their frequent employment in British ships as quartermasters or steersmen, a duty which cannot be entrusted to any Hindu or Mahommedan of our own possessions.

In 1849, the total number of the civilised native inhabitants of the Philippines, subject to Spanish rule, was reckoned to be 3,698,730 souls. This statement is founded on the registers of the tribute or capitation tax to which all natives, with trifling exceptions, as well as all mestizo-Chinese are subject. The usual estimate is that one person in five pays the tributo or poll-tax, but it appears that in some cases the calculation is at the rate of one in four. Many parties, however, it is well-known evade paying the tax, and the general belief is that the population is understated. Several additions have to be made to the numbers even as here given. The wild independent tribes are estimated to amount in Luzon alone at 200,000, and in the Bisaya islands to 50,000. In the Spanish part of Mindano the independent idolatrous tribes have been estimated at 7500, and the Mahommedan at 70,000. This is, however, exclusive of the inhabitants of the same island, beyond the pale of Spanish rule, and these have been computed at 800,000. The negro population has been reckoned for Luzon at 7700, for Negros at 3476, and for Panay at 5400. This does not include those of Mindoro, or those asserted to exist in Mindano, and the usual estimate for the negros in the whole Philippines is 25,000. To these numbers have to be added parties not included in the registers of the native capitation tax, namely, Spaniards 1500, Creole Spaniards 3500, mestizo Spaniards 20,000, and Chinese of the pure blood, 8000. To complete the population of the entire Archipelago it would be necessary to add that of the Sulu and other islands, some of which are populous, extending from Mindano to Borneo, but for this we have no date whatever. Making allowance for this and for the admitted defects of the registers, the whole population of the Philippines in 1849 will probably not be exaggerated if we take it in round numbers at five millions, which after all is but one-half of that of the single island of Java.

The population is very unequally distributed, being usually in proportion to extent of fertile land in the different islands. According to the registers for 1849 the population of Luzon was 2,418,445, or near 65 parts in 100 of the whole of that of the Archipelago, giving about 42 inhabitants to the square mile. The population of Panay was 566,957, making 123 to the square mile, which is three times the rate of that of Luzon which has a great extent of mountain and sterile land, while Panay has comparatively little, and is in reality the most fertile and densely peopled island of the Archipelago. The relative population of Çebu is 113 to the square mile, that of Leyte only 24, of Samar, 18; and of Negros but 9.

According to the registers for 1849 the total number of marriages in a population of 3,698,730 was 34,055; of births, or as they are called "baptisms," which would include still-born children, 139,833, and of deaths, 83,986. The excess of births over deaths would, according to these figures, make the period in which the population would double itself about 45 years. This may be compared with the actual censuses as given by the public registers. The first census framed on these data is for the year 1735, and it makes the population of the then Spanish Philippines 837,182. In 1799 it was 1,522,224, and in 1849 it rose to the number already given. According to these figures the increase in the first period of 64 years was better than 80 per cent., and in the last 50 years no less than 148 per cent. This seeming discrepancy may be accounted for. The first period was one of disorder, insurrection, and commercial monopoly. It was within it that the English invaded the country, occupied its capital, and raised an insurrection of the natives and Chinese, which lasted for several years. The last period, on the contrary, has been one, for the greater part of it, of commercial freedom and most of it of uninterrupted tranquillity.

The increase of population, as expressed by the proportion of births to marriages, varies greatly in the different provinces. Throughout the great island of Luzon the doubling period is made to extend to an average of 76 years. In three of its twenty provinces, indeed, the deaths are in excess of the births. In the populous province of Tondo, which contains Manilla, the capital, the doubling period reaches to 195 years, whereas in North Ilocos, it is no more than 35. In the poor island of Mindoro, peopled in a good measure by emigrants of doubtful character from Luzon, the doubling period reaches to 187 years, while on the other hand, in the fertile islands of Panay and Çebu, it falls to twenty-five. These results are curious, and would be satisfactory, could we implicitly rely on the data.

As to the constitution of the inhabitants of the Philippine Islands, in so far as regards age of puberty, period of gestation, and length of life, there is no reason to suppose that they differ in any respect from the rest of mankind. According to the registers of population, there were living in 1848, sixty-two individuals whose ages exceeded 100 years. It is remarkable that four and twenty of these belonged to one province, Iloilo, the most populous one of the fine and fertile island of Panay. The senior of the whole, and who had attained the age of 137, was a native of the metropolitan province of Tondo in Luzon.

The agriculture of the Philippines, in so far as concerns the principal crop, rice, is in point of skill and ingenuity, greatly below that of the islands of Java, Bali, and Lomboc. The only material agricultural improvements which the European conquerors have made, consist in the introduction of some exotics, as maiz, tobacco, coffee and cacoa, and a better culture of the sugar cane and the rearing of the horse and ox. For the main corn crop, rice, the ground is prepared for the plough by levelling it with a small harrow armed with wooden spikes and loaded with a weight. The plough itself consists of a single piece of crooked timber tipped at the lower end with iron, being at once handle, beam and share, without coulter or mould-board. Like the harrow, it is drawn by a single buffalo, the horse and ox never being used in field-labour. After ploughing, the seed is sown broad-cast without any subsequent harrowing and transplanting as practised in the best husbandry of Java: the artificial irrigation, so extensively practised in that island is equally unknown; all seems to depend upon the periodical rains which, it is obvious, perform more than half the labour of tillage. The usual agricultural vehicle is a car without wheels, drawn by a single buffalo, and capable of carrying about 200 pounds weight. Occasionally, however, a cart with wheels is employed drawn by a pair of buffalos, and this will carry 1200 pounds, or little more than one half what a single English horse will draw on a good road.

The staple product of Philippine agriculture is, of course, rice. Next to it may be ranked maiz, of which two crops are yearly produced, the variety usually in cultivation coming to maturity in nine weeks. Then follow pulses, the abaca banana, cotton, the sesame, sugar-cane, coffee and cacoa, with the coco, areca, and gomuti palms, and all the fruits of the Malay Archipelago, the mangostin and durian excepted.

The soil of the Philippine Islands is exempt from all public and municipal imposts, a great advantage, which is owing to the existence of the poll-tax which takes the place of all other direct taxes. In the rude and under-peopled condition of these islands when they were conquered, unlike Java, Hindustan, China, and other populous countries of Atia, no proper rent existed, and consequently no source of a land-tax. The only means of raising a revenue was the rude one of a capitation tax, and the Spanish government imposed it much after the same fashion that the proprietor of a Russian or Polish estate imposes it upon his serfs. Over a land tax, it has undoubtedly the advantage of being fixed, invariable, and in this particular instance, of being really moderate in amount, and even economical and easy in collection. This tax affects only the native inhabitants and some of the mixed races descended from them. European proprietors and religious and charitable corporations pay the state a tithe of the produce of their estates, but this amounts to little more than a nominal quit-rent, for it is the same now as when the estates were first granted centuries ago. The theory in respect to such real property held by the natives is, that the sovereign is the proprietor, and that the occupant has only the usufruct of the soil, so long as he continues to till it. In practice, however, the actual possessor is the real owner; and land of whatever description is a heritable and vendible property like moveables. The effect of this, and of the increase of population is, that in many parts of the country, land bears a high price. Thus in the province of Pangasinan, a quiñon of land, which is a measure of 1000 square fathoms, each of three varas or Castilian yards (33·38 inches) sells at from 220 to 250 hard dollars; in the province of Laguna or that of the great lake, at from 250 to 300, and in the district of Pasig near the city of Manilla and in the province of Bulacan, sometimes as high as 1000 dollars. The places thus named are all in very fertile and populous districts, and the lands referred to, cleared and enclosed. The most valuable lands are those subject to periodical immersion, or in other words those fit for the growth of the great staple, rice. Dry uplands fit for the growth of sugar-cane, cotton, coffee and the abaca, are of inferior value as are all such lands in other tropical countries. The chief value of land in a country in which it is still abundant, is derived from the labour bestowed in clearing and bringing it into a state fit for cultivation. The amount of this is large, when a country, as is usually the case in an unpeopled one, is covered with a heavy forest. Hence, in the few cases in which it is not so, even fertile wild lands conveniently situated begin, with the progress of population, to fetch a considerable price.

The land in the Philippines, when not tilled by the proprietor, is everywhere cultivated on the métairie system, that is, half the produce going to the owner and half to the cultivator. The latter furnishes the plough, the buffalo, and his own labour, and the proprietor shares equally with him in the expense of sowing, reaping, and thrashing, in so far as concerns rice the main crop, for in the case of the less costly cultures of maiz, sesame, and pulses, the cultivator incurs the whole expense of labour, the proprietor still receiving half the crop. It is generally considered that in practice the actual shares of the two parties, are three-fifths for the tenant and two-fifths for the proprietor. The tenements or holdings, are all small, usually, the amount that a métayer and his family are able to cultivate, which is considered to be one quiñon. The métairie system is considered, and I think justly, as the best suited to the state of society in the Philippines. The wages of labour, for an Asiatic country, are very high: in Manilla and its neighbourhood, for example, they are, about a quarter of a dollar or thirteen pence a day, which is at least three times the day wages of an ordinary labourer in Calcutta or Bombay, and probably twice as much as in Java. Notwithstanding these high rates, and the large share of the crop received by the métayers, they are, with few exceptions, indolent, and needy,—frequently in debt and in the hands of money lenders,—in short, cheerful and contented sluggards.

The useful arts are certainly in a more advanced state among the Philippine islanders than among any of the Malayan nations, and this is, without question, the effect of Spanish rule; for before the conquest, they were in this respect, very far below them. The highest degree of skill is displayed in the manufacture of textile fabrics, the raw materials being cotton, the fibres of the abaca banana and of the pine-apple leaf, all of them domestic products, with silk imported from China. The manufacturers are women, and as in all other Asiatic countries, the manufactures entirely domestic. They extend all over the islands, but are more especially determined towards the provinces of which the raw materials are the staple products. Thus, in Ilocos which is remarkable for the growth and export of cotton, there are supposed to be no fewer than twenty thousand looms. Camarines and Albay in Luzon, and Iloilo in Panay, are the chief provinces for the production of the abaca, and here, also, are the principal manufacturers of it. Manufactures of cotton and abaca, as also of the piña or fibre of the leaf of the pine-apple, are carried on in the metropolitan province of Tondo. The finest cloths are made of the piña, and from it are produced fabrics which are as great curiosities as the muslins of Dacca, or the shawls of Cashmere. A single dress of piña richly embroidered, has sometimes been sold for the enormous sum of 325*l*. The art of dyeing is but very imperfectly understood. The materials are native vegetable products such as the sibucao or sapan-wood, and the colours produced are neither bright nor permanent. The art of calico-printing is unknown, as it is indeed to all Asiatics except the Hindus. The art of manufacturing cotton and abaca fabrics was certainly known to the Philippine islanders for many ages, and seems not to have been derived either from Malays or Europeans. This is sufficiently proved by the names of the cotton and abaca plants, and of all the terms connected with the art of weaving which are, in every case, native and not foreign words. The piña manufacture as its name implies, was evidently introduced since the Spanish conquest. The extent to which textile manufactures is carried may be judged by the fact, that with but a small exception for foreign fabrics, some five millions of people are clothed with them, and that there is even some considerable exportation.

The art of mat-making is carried to much perfection by the Philippine islanders, the raw material being palm-leaf and the ratan. In the shape of hats, cigar-cases, and the like, there is even a considerable exportation, besides a large domestic consumption of articles of this description. The highest degree of mechanical skill is probably exhibited in the manufacture of gold trinkets, consisting of works in filagree and necklaces. Some of the last under the name of bejuguillos are even highly appreciated in foreign countries. The goldsmiths, equally with the weavers, are women. The art of manufacturing a coarse unglazed domestic pottery has been immemorially practised, but all the earthenware of any value is brought from China. The manufacture of glass is altogether unknown. Salt is made both by solar evaporation and by boiling, and most probably in a climate so damp not economically, or it would as in other parts of the world, have been seized upon by the state as an instrument of taxation. The manufacture of malleable iron is very imperfectly understood, and the iron of inferior quality, and hence, the chief consumption is furnished from Europe. The building of boats and small coasting craft is carried on in several of the provinces, but more especially in Pangasinan.

The internal trade of the Philippines is carried on both by land and water. This is exempt from the nuisance of transit duties, but subject to many impediments, natural and factitious. One great obstacle, is the absence of good roads in a country immersed in water for several months of the year. Even for some time after the waters have abated, they leave such a deposit of mud on the highways, that it is impossible to travel over them with horses, and the buffalo is the only available conveyance. The roads are besides intersected by innumerable rivers and brooks, for the most part without bridges, or with wooden ones of which the materials must be removed in the rainy season lest they be carried away by the floods. In the absence of bridges, goods and passengers have to be ferried over on bamboo rafts, furnished by the corvée labour of the neighbourhoods. In passing from either end of Luzon to the capital, it is said that not fewer than a hundred of these rude ferries have to be crossed. In the few places in which good causeways exist, they require to be raised five feet above the level of the plains which during the inundation have the appearance of a sea or lake. Some of the periodical lakes must be crossed in boats, and that of Mongabol between Pangasinan and Pampanga, has at the height of the rains, a depth of 30 feet, so that the navigation is impeded by the tops of the trees.

The coasting trade is attended by hardly fewer difficulties. It has to encounter the storms and hurricanes of the equinoxes, and when the monsoons themselves set in, they cause either the outward or homeward voyage to be carried on with an adverse wind, often too strong to be encountered. The extensive introduction of steam navigation alone can obviate this difficulty. Another obstacle to the internal trade is the piracy of the southern tribes which has harassed the Archipelago from the conquest to the present day. But there is yet one more obstacle to it, the creature of European misrule. The petty governors of provinces and districts, have the privilege of carrying on trade to eke out their incompetent salaries, and of course use their whole authority to monopolise the commerce of their respective jurisdictions.

Notwithstanding those many impediments, the internal trade is more considerable than might be looked for. A weekly fair or market is held in every province or district, and considerable traffic results from the exchange of the peculiar products of the different provinces, the staple articles in which are rice, salt, oil, cattle, jerk-beef, stock-fish, indigo, and sugar. In the coasting-trade, there are employed about 240 vessels from 40 tons burthen and upwards, and above 300 of smaller size, exclusive of the craft that navigates the lakes and rivers, which are very numerous.

The whole foreign trade of the Philippines is by law confined to the single port of Manilla, an impolitic arrangement, since, in many cases, it subjects both exports and imports to the cost of a double transport. The port is free to all friendly nations, the duties being double under foreign flags. The countries with which the external trade is carred on are Spain, Great Britain, France, the Hanse Towns, the United States of America, China, Java, Singapore, and Australia. For a commercial intercourse with China, it is easy to see that, in so far as the navigation is concerned, the Philippines possess an obvious advantage over every other Asiatic country, the course being not with or against the monsoons, but across them, so that instead of one voyage, several can be performed within the year. The following are the staple exports,—rice, sugar, coffee, cotton, abaca hemp, tobacco, indigo, hides, sapan-wood, ebony, tortoise-shell, tripang, abaca-cloth, hats, and gold-dust. The imports consist of the silks of China, the wines of Spain, and the cottons, woollens, iron, and copper of Great Britain. In 1841, the latest year for which I have seen any account, the value of the exports was about 762,750*l.*, and the imports 400,757*l.*, the difference being made up by bills of exchange drawn on Europe, and chiefly on England.

The weights and measures of the Philippine islanders, and even their money, seem to have been chiefly derived from the Malays, and some of them are still in use. Thus we have the gantang or gallon, the chupak or quart, the pikul or load, the dâpa or fathom, the jânkal or span, and the pichis or farthing; respectively corrupted, ganta, chupa, pico, dipa, dangkal, and pitis. Without superseding these, the Spaniards have introduced their own weights, measures, and monies. The current weights are, the pound, which is 2 per cent. heavier than the English; the arroba, of 25 Spanish or 25½ English pounds; the pico (pikul) of 5½ arrobas, or 137½ Spanish pounds, equal to 140 English pounds, instead of being as with us 133⅓ pounds. To these is added a seeming native dry measure for corn, called the caban, which the Spaniards have defined to be equal to 3·47 cubic Castilian feet, and which in weight is about 105 pounds of rice in the husk. This name, which appears to be native, may however be the Malay word kawan, signifying company or assemblage, in reference possibly to this measure being, as it is, the complement or union of the lower Malay measures, the guantang and the chupak. The measures of length, besides the fathom and span, are the Spanish vara or yard of 33·38 English inches. The superficial measure is the quiñon, which is equal to 1000 square fathoms, each fathom of three Castilian varas or yards. The Malay kodi, the Hindu kori, and the English corge, that is, the "score," is in use, and written by the Spaniards of Manilla, corja. The current money is the peso-duro or Spanish dollar, which ought to contain grains 370·9 of fine silver, worth 51·79 pence. This is divided into 8 reals, and the real into 12 granos, represented by copper tokens.

The government of the thirty-four provinces of the Philippines, including the Marian Islands, is administered by a governor and captain-general, in whom is vested with little check, the whole civil, military, and naval administration. To carry on the executive details, he is assisted by three secretaries-general. There lies an appeal from his acts to the Real Audiencia, or exchequer, but it is rendered in a great degree nugatory by the prerogative which he possesses, of carrying his orders at once into operation, pending a reference to the crown, on the plea of urgency. The assessment and collection of the revenue is under the direction of an officer called the superintendant of the Real Hacienda, who, in extraordinary cases, refers for advice to a junta composed of the six principal fiscal functionaries. This officer is directly responsible to the home-government, and next to the governor-general and archbishop, is the first person in rank in the Philippines. In case of the death or absence of the governor-general, it is not he, however, but the commander of the forces that succeeds to the temporary government.

The Philippines are divided into provinces of very various sizes. The local administration of the larger of these is confided to officers named gobernador, and the smaller to functionaries called Alcalde mayor. Each province is divided into pueblos or townships, which are administered by chiefs called gobernador-chillos, or petty governors. The township itself is subdivided into barangays, each of which is composed of from 45 to 60 families, or rather, tribute-payers, with a headman known by the native name of manguinôo, or the Malay one of dato, which last signifies an "elder." This is an original native institution, and bears no inconsiderable resemblance to our Anglo-Saxon tithings and hundreds. The datos, or elders, appear to be hereditary, but it is remarkable in the institution of the townships and their subdivisions, that the petty governors are elective periodically, and that the electors are the elders, restricted however to the twelve seniors among them.

The revenue of the Philippines is derived from the following sources,—a capitation tax, corvées, a tobacco monopoly, an excise on palm-wine, licenses for cock-fighting, and custom duties. The capitation tax is of three kinds,—that paid by the natives, that paid by the Chinese mestizos, and that paid by the Chinese of the full blood. The native impost comes under three heads,—the contribution to the state which amounts to five reals of plate, that for municipal purposes which is one real, and that to the church which is three reals, making the entire poll-tax nine reals; or at sixpence to the real, four shillings and sixpence. The capitation of the mestizo Chinese is double that of the natives, or nine shillings. Both are paid by all males above twenty years of age, and by all females on marriage, or after the age of twenty-five. The Chinese of the full blood are divided into three classes according to their condition in life, and their lowest tax is twelve hard dollars, but the average is above seventeen, so that the assessment on the Chinese is about seventeen fold that on the natives. The parties exempt from the tribute or capitation-tax, are Spaniards and their mestizo descendants, all foreigners except the Chinese, all natives above the age of sixty, a few native families hereditarily on account of services rendered to the Spaniards by ancestors, and the gobernador-chillos or petty governors with their families while in office. The natives paying the poll-tax are reckoned at about 700,000. The tax was first imposed by the conqueror, Legaspé, and is of the same nature with that imposed by the Mahommedan conquerors on those who refused to accept their religion, with this difference that the Mahommedans imposed it on the infidels, and the Spaniards on the believers. It is not unlikely, indeed, that the Spaniards took the hint of the impost from the practice of the Arabian conquerors in Spain itself.

There is another kind of poll-tax, the amount of which cannot be stated in figures; this consists of corvées or forced labour, in making and maintaining roads, bridges, and ferries, in conveying the mail, and transporting the baggage of the military and of travellers, all which falls on the native inhabitants. The tobacco monopoly, which furnishes the largest branch of the Philippine revenue, is of the same nature. This is but a comparatively recent impost, for it was first established with much difficulty by the governor-general, José Basco, who administered affairs from the year 1778 to 1787. The monopoly extends only to the island of Luzon, and the production of tobacco is confined to a few of its most fertile districts. The whole crop is carried to Manilla and its neighbourhood, where it is stored for exportation, or made into cigars, in manufactories where from 3000 to 4000 persons, chiefly women, are employed.

An excise on palm-wine at one time yielded a considerable revenue, but from the year 1836, owing to the increased consumption of foreign wines and spirits, it has been constantly falling off. A tax on cock-fighting is another source of the Philippine revenue. A cock-pit, or rather stage, exists in every pueblo or township, licensed by the government. Stamp and customs duties, neither of them very productive, form the other branches of the revenue, the total amount of which, in 1841, was 3,480,000 Spanish dollars, or 754,000*l.* This is supposed to be at the rate of a dollar, or near 4*s.* 4*d.* a-head, for the population subject to Spanish rule, a lower rate of taxation than that of any portion of our own Indian dominions.

The supreme administration of justice in the Philippines is vested in a high court, the Real Audiencia, composed of a regent or president, with puisne judges administering the law of Spain. This is a court of primary jurisdiction for Manilla and its neighbourhood, and an appellate one for the provinces. The country judges are the Alcalde mayor or governors of provinces, and the native heads of townships called gobernador-chillos. In civil causes the jurisdiction of the first is limited to the value of 100 hard dollars, and of the last to two tails of gold, or 44 dollars; in both cases subject to appeal. In criminal matters, the authority of the heads of townships is limited to apprehending malefactors and taking informations. The power of the alcaldes, or provincial governors, extends to all criminal matters, but eight days detention is the limit of their power to punish, without the confirmation of the supreme court, or Real Audiencia. In the person of these functionaries, therefore, are united executive, fiscal, magisterial, and military authority. The parties thus empowered are generally military officers, and in all cases without legal education. At every step of a process, therefore, they have to refer to an assessor, a functionary not present, being an advocate of the supreme court residing at the capital. The salaries of the provincial governors are most inadequate, and to make up for their deficiency they enjoy the privilege of trading. Out of a list of 23 governors, or alcaldes, 17 receive salaries of 600 hard dollars, or about 130*l.* a-year; and this is the highest amount given, except in the single instance of Mindoro where it is 1000 dollars, or about 216*l.* Five of the governors receive only 300 dollars, or 65*l.* For the privilege of trading, these functionaries, moreover, pay yearly sums varying from 40 to 300 dollars. The privilege, however, during the six years to which the tenure of office is limited, is estimated to be worth from 40,000 to 50,000 hard dollars. This barbarous form of administration seems to unite every vice of a judicial system, in so far as the office of the alcaldes or provisional governors is concerned.

We may form some idea of the state of crime and the administration of justice in the Philippines, from the schedule of trials in the Real Audiencia. The trials in the five years ending 1841 amounted to 1607, of which the acquittals were 518, and the condemnations 1089. The offences were classed as follow,—rebellion and conspiracy, 2; homicide, 439; robbery, theft, and imposture, 270; incendiarism, 26; commotion and libel, 12; falsehood and perjury, 19; scandal and immorality, 212; injuries and misdemeanours, 227. The capital punishments amounted to 28, and the condemnations to penal servitude to 735. The minor punishments, such as deprivation of office and the like, amounted to 328. This was for a population of about three millions and a half in round numbers, and does not imply either a great amount of crime or a harsh administration of justice.

The ecclesiastical establishment of the Spanish Philippines consists of a metropolitan and three suffragans,—namely, the Archbishop of Manilla, and the Bishops of New Segovia, of New Carceres, and of Çebu. The metropolitan, besides his general superintendence, has under his immediate charge nine provinces, having 167 parishes, served by 95 regular and 72 secular priests. The Bishop of New Segovia's diocese consists of six provinces, with 92 parishes, served by 80 regular and 12 secular priests. The diocese of New Carceres consists of five provinces, with 84 parishes, served by 27 regular and 57 secular priests. The bishopric of Çebu extends over eleven provinces, which contain 143 parishes, served by 86 regular and 57 secular priests. The three first-named dioceses are wholly confined to the great island of Luzon; that of Çebu embraces all the Bisaya islands, with Mindano and the remote Marians.

We see from this statement that the number of parishes in the Philippines is 486, served by the same number of priests. The whole number of ecclesiastics, however, is computed at 1150, of whom 450 are Europeans, and 700 mestizo-Europeans, or mestizo-Chinese, or natives of pure blood. The capitation-tax for ecclesiastical purposes is three reals, of about 6*d.* each, on every taxable inhabitant. Reckoning the parties subject to this impost at 700,000, its produce will be 52,000*l.* per annum. But independent of this a large portion of the land belongs to the Church, or to conventual establishments, and the parochial clergy are maintained out of the special funds of the townships, or by fees, so that the income of a parish priest is estimated to be equal to a hard dollar a head for each tribute payer within his cure, so that if a parish should contain 1500 tribute payers, his income would amount to the same number of dollars, that is, to about 325*l.* a year. When the parish exceeds this number of tribute-payers, the priest is allowed an assistant, who, besides a house and provisions, is allowed an income varying from 35 to 40 hard dollars a month. The ecclesiastical establishment now sketched began with the conquest, and has been extended with it. The monastic orders have, however, been the most active instruments, not only in the religious, but virtually, also, in the civil conquest of the islands. The chief merit belongs to the Augustines, the Dominicans, and the Franciscans, for the Jesuits did not interfere until the main work had been accomplished. From the account now given, it will be seen that in their religious establishment, as well as in their other institutions, the Philippines bear a much nearer resemblance to an European colony than any of the Asiatic possessions of the other European nations, in which the ecclesiastical establishments are trifling, and the converts to Christianity, instead of being the majority, are but exceptions.

The education of the natives has, by no means, been neglected by the Spanish government. In every township there is a school of primary instruction maintained from the funds of the commune. "Elementary education," says the author of the Informe sobre las Islas Felipinas, "cannot be considered in a backward state. On the contrary, I really believe that there is a larger proportion of persons who can read and write in the Philippines than in Spain, or any other civilised country;" and this favourable opinion is confirmed by a very intelligent English traveller, the author of the "Recollections of Manilla and the Philippines." Beyond mere reading, writing, and a little religious instruction, however, education has made no considerable advance, and the Philippine islanders are certainly still as superstitious as any people of Asia, while their superstitions are of an excitable character, which leads to the commission of dangerous excesses. They still practise circumcision, because their forefathers did, to the great scandal of their present spiritual instructors, and they still believe in sorcery and witchcraft, notwithstanding the pains taken by these instructors to disabuse them.

The military of the Philippines consists of five regiments of regular infantry, a battalion of artillery, a regiment of cavalry, and an embodied regiment of militia. Besides this, there is the provincial militia, dispersed over the different provinces, under the orders of the Alcaldes, amounting to about 2000. The entire force amounts to 9200 infantry, 1000 cavalry, and a field-train of 24 guns. The rank and file of all these different arms is native, the commissioned and non-commissioned officers only being European, somewhat after the manner of our Indian sepoy force, but much inferior, from the inferiority of the native raw material of men, and for the cavalry, of the horses also, which are mere ponies. The force is one wholly incapable of defending the islands against the invasion of an European maritime power, which would easily capture Manilla, defeat the main force, and, if necessary, capture one island after another in detail, without any serious resistance. The climate, and the army of ecclesiastics, however, would offer a far more formidable resistance. No power, however, can have any interest in conquering, and still less in retaining, the Philippines, which will probably remain to Spain long after she has lost all her other colonies.

The Philippine local marine consists of about 68 small armed vessels, under the names of goletas, lamkas, faluccas, &c., with crews, in all, of about eleven hundred men. Their object is the protection of the trade and coasts of the islands from piracy and inroads of the Mahommedan marauders, that have harassed them from the first moment of the conquest. For this purpose their large draught of water and want of speed have rendered them very inefficient, and steam vessels, with great advantage, have been recently in great part substituted for them.

In so far as the civilised nations of Europe are concerned, the history of the Philippine Archipelago begins with the day of its discovery by Magellan, before which it was as unknown to them as the Columbian. "There being in this region," says Pigafetta, "many islands, and their discovery having been made on Sunday, the anniversary of St. Lazarus, we called them the Archipelago of San Lazaro." The day of the discovery was Passion Sunday, the 17th of March, 1521, nine and twenty years after the discovery of America, and two after the conquest of Mexico. The name given by Magellan was changed for its present one by Villalobos, the leader of the second unsuccessful expedition, in honour of the unworthy son and successor of Charles the Fifth, Philip the Second, who, at the time, was Prince of the Asturias. The Philippines, although wholly unknown to the Europeans of antiquity, or the middle ages, were not so to the Malays, the Javanese, the Chinese, and Japanese, who appear to have frequented them for ages, for the purposes of trade, and occasionally for settlement.

When the Spaniards arrived in the Philippines, they found the inhabitants everywhere divided into small, independent, and often hostile tribes, or hordes, governed by elective elders, and no state or principality existed of any extent, such as the Portuguese found in the islands of the Malay Archipelago. The name by which the tribe or horde was known was barangai, and their chiefs were called either manguinoo or dato,—the first a native, and the last a Malay word, signifying chieftain, or elder. The people were divided into three classes,—nobles, free labourers, and slaves. Of the origin of the inhabitants of the Philippines, nothing is or can be known. Spanish writers attempt to trace them to Borneo and the other islands of the Malayan Archipelago, but a wide difference in language, both as to structure, pronunciation, and words, shows, at once, that there is no foundation for this hypothesis. A sample of the manner in which it is supported may be given as an etymological curiosity. The name for a tribe, barangai, signifies, also, a particular kind of large boat, and is supposed by the authors of the hypothesis to have been bestowed on the tribe because the first settlers arrived in a boat of this description. But it happens that the word in question is native, and belongs neither to the Malay nor to any other cultivated language of the Malay Archipelago. By arguments equally baseless, some of the wild tribes are imagined to be descendants, some of Chinese, some of Japanese, and others of natives of the South Sea Islands.

The more civilised nations of the Philippines, when first seen by the Spaniards, were in a far ruder state than the cotemporary Malays and Javanese, but they were, at the same time, very far from being utter savages, like many of the American tribes discovered about the same time. They had cultivated corn and fruits, wore textile fabrics for clothing, were acquainted with malleable iron and with gold, had a few domestic animals for food and labour, and were in possession of a phonetic written character, although a far less perfect one than any of those of the Malayan Archipelago. Much of the imperfect civilisation of the Philippine islanders was undoubtedly imparted to them by the nations of the Malayan Archipelago, who not only carried on trade with them, but, most probably, also settled among them in considerable numbers. This is sufficiently attested by the presence, in their most cultivated languages, of a considerable body of Malay and Javanese words, amounting to from four to five hundred, or perhaps to a thirtieth part of their vocabularies. Among the words thus introduced are to be found Sanscrit and Arabic ones, which had been previously naturalised in the Malayan tongues. From the nature of the adopted words, some notion may even be formed of the amount of civilisation which the Philippine derived from the Malayan nations. Thus the names of most of the cultivated plants, as rice, yam, sugar-cane, coco-palm, indigo plant, are all Malayan. So are, without an exception, the names of all the domestic animals, the hog, the dog, buffalo, goat, the common fowl, and common duck. Among the metals, we find silver, copper, and tin, to be Malayan words. Of terms connected with the mechanic arts, however, one-third only are Malayan. Of commercial terms, again, the great majority are Malayan, as higgle, bargain, wages, profit, price, debt, cheap, dear, pledge, account, merchant, merchandise, with the names of weights and measures, and those of staple articles of foreign trade, such as black pepper, clove, pearl, mother-of-pearl, and indigo. To all these may be added the numerals, which, though much corrupted, are entirely Malayan. Of terms connected with war, a few only are Malayan, as fortress, arms, bow and arrow, and sword, the last being expressed by a corruption of the Malayan word for a dagger. The rude calendar of the Philippines, so far as it extended, seems to be taken from the Malayan, as in the words for month and year. Of literary terms, we have such words as to write, to read, story, and language. The religion of the Philippine islanders was a very rude and very superficial Hinduism, engrafted on many local superstitions, and was evidently derived directly from the Malayan nations. The words for deity, fortune, adoration, and place of worship, and of Avatar in its Malay and Javanese sense of a chief deity, are examples.

From the terms in the Philippine languages, which are native and not foreign, we may form some estimate of the amount of the civilisation of the Archipelago, which is purely indigenous. Thus, among cultivated plants, the only ones bearing native names are the banana, esculent and textile, with their many varieties, the batata, the bread-fruit, and the cotton-plant. Among the domesticated animals, not one bears a native name. Among the metals, the names for iron and gold alone are native. Terms connected with the ordinary mechanic arts, such as house, thatch, spin, weave, thread, woof, shuttle, cloth, are all native, while the tools and processes of manipulation in wood and metal, as hammer, chisel, saw, anvil, are Malayan. As to the Philippine alphabet it is far more imperfect than any Malayan one. Thus, instead of 20 consonants, like the Javanese, it has but 16, and for these but 14 characters, the same letters representing d and r, and p, and f. As to vowel characters, instead of having five, like the Javanese, it has only three, being mere dots, the sounds of which depend on their position. The vowel sounds, however, are really five in number, two of the characters representing one of them, either e or i, and the other o or u. The form of the characters is, moreover, wholly different from that of any Malayan alphabet, and the Philippine writing must, therefore, be deemed indigenous. As to religion, the titles of priests, of astrologers, and of all the local deities with the word for circumcision, were all expressed by native words. From all this it may be inferred, so far as the evidence of language can be trusted, that the Philippine islanders before their intercourse with the Malayan nations were a very rude people. They cultivated no corn, their vegetable food consisting of the banana and batata. They had no domesticated animals whatever. They were acquainted with malleable iron and gold, but had no knowledge of any other metal. They were clothed in domestic woven fabrics of cotton and the abaca. They had invented a native alphabet, and their religion consisted in a belief in good and evil spirits, in the practice of circumcision, and a belief in sorcery and astrology. They were superior to the Polynesian people of the South Sea islands in the possession of gold, malleable iron, and textile fabrics, but inferior to them, by wanting the tame dog, the hog, and domestic fowl.

With respect to the intercourse of the Chinese and Japanese with the inhabitants of the Philippines, previous to the arrival of the Spaniards, all that is known respecting it is, that these nations furnished them with silk tissues and raw silk, with utensils of porcelane, iron, and copper, and, probably, with the small currency of zinc, although known by a Malay name. In return, these nations received the esculent swallows' nests, the tripang and pearl-oyster shells, which are still staples of the trade with China. Besides, the Chinese and Japanese, other people of the Asiatic continent appear to have traded with the Philippines. Thus, Magellan and his companions found at Çebu a Moorish merchant of Siam, who had come from that country in his ship, and who is stated to have paid for liberty to trade, and in return for his merchandise to have received payment in "gold and slaves." With all foreigners, the medium of intercourse was the Malay language, which Pigafetta informs us, that all the native chiefs, that is, all the persons who held intercourse with strangers, understood, although the native languages were different.

In 1524, three years after the discovery of the Philippines the Emperor Charles the Fifth sent an expedition for their conquest under the command of Juan José Garcia de Loaissa, which ended in total failure. All that it saw of Magellans Archipelago of San Lazaro was the Ladrone Islands, and a small part of Mindano, its two extreme north and south limits, when it proceeded to the Moluccas, after losing three successive commanders. A second expedition in 1528 was undertaken by the same Emperor, of which the command was given to Alonzo de Saavedra, but this was equally unsuccessful. The third expedition was not undertaken until 1542. This was under the conduct of Ruiz Lopez de Villalobos, the person who gave the Archipelago the name which it has ever since borne, but this too was equally unfortunate with its predecessors. There was not one of these fruitless expeditions that was not as powerful as to equipment as that with which Columbus discovered America. It was not until 1565, four and forty years after the discovery, that the conquest was effectually commenced. The great leader in this achievement was Miguel Lopez de Legaspé, a man equal in enterprise, resource, and courage, to Cortez or Pizarro, and in humanity, far superior to them. His expedition consisted of no more than five vessels, his whole force, soldiers and sailors included, amounting only to 400 men. On the 21st of November, 1564, he sailed from the port of Natividad in New Spain,—in the beginning of February, 1565, reached the Marians, and on the 13th of the same month entered the proper Philippines, reaching a small island lying at the south-east end of Samar, which he called Bonseñal or "good omen," in commemoration of the event, a name which it still retains. It was not until the 27th of April that he reached Çebu. Legaspé was accompanied by a corps of Augustine monks, more effectual in the conquest of the Philippines than his soldiers. Its leader was a remarkable man, Andrea de Urdañeta, who had commanded a ship in the first expedition, twenty years before, and who had afterwards entered the order of the Augustines. Çebu was soon brought under subjection, and Legaspé then discovered the fertile island of Panay, where, even then, provisions were abundant. The natives of Çebu and Panay informed him of a still larger island than their own, and in 1569, four years after his arrival, he discovered Luzon, in two more founding the capital of Manilla. The subjugation throughout was effected, far more through the timid and credulous character of the inhabitants, and the skilful and politic character of the leaders of the conquest, than by the martial prowess of the Spaniards, although this, too, when an occasion offered for its display, was conspicuous.

A few examples will show with what facility the conquest was effected, and with what slender means. In 1569, Legaspé, while himself at Panay, having heard of the island of Luzon and of Manilla, described as "a rich Moorish town" with a wooden fort or stockade, defended by twelve cannon and several falconets, sent against it his two chosen captains with a force of 120 soldiers and some natives of Çebu. The Spaniards were at first favourably received, but some acts of treachery having been committed by the native chief, Soliman, a convert to the Mahommedan religion, the fort was attacked by 80 Spaniards, taken, burnt, and its artillery carried off. In 1571, the year of his death, Legaspi himself, undertook, and in a good measure achieved, the conquest of Luzon, a country not much short of twice the size of Ireland, with a force of 280 Spanish soldiers, with some thousands of auxiliaries from Çebu and Panay. During his short administration of six years, he brought under subjugation, the islands of Çebu, Leyte, Panay, Mindano, Masbate, and several nations out of the five which occupied Luzon, embracing provinces which now contain above a million and a half inhabitants.

Since the first conquests, the most prominent incidents of the history of the Philippines have been, the attempts made to subdue the Mahommedan tribes and nations of the southern islands of the Archipelago, or the Malayan countries bordering on them; the invasions and insurrections of the Chinese and Japanese, and the attacks or invasions of European nations. If the Spaniards found it a comparatively easy task to subdue the rude and simple pagan inhabitants of the northern islands of the Archipelago, they have found, by near three centuries experience, the subjugation of the more civilised Mahommedan tribes and nations of the southern islands wholly impracticable. Against the Sulu Islands and southern parts of Mindano not fewer than twelve different expeditions have been fitted out from Manilla, the earliest in 1577, and the last in 1850. To defeat these tribes, and to capture and destroy their strongholds was not a matter of much difficulty, but their permanent subjugation and religious conversion have hitherto been found impossible. It has been the same with the huge island of Borneo, the conquest of that portion of it to which this name especially belongs, having been attempted with a fleet of thirty sail as early as 1577. Instead of being able to subdue these tribes, the Spaniards have found them, from the first moment of the conquest to the present day, through their piracies, the greatest scourge of their possessions.

The Chinese and Japanese, as already stated, had carried on some commercial intercourse with the Philippines before the arrival of the Spaniards, but there is no evidence of their having formed any settlements within them. No sooner, however, had the Spaniards established themselves than we find both nations in great numbers, either as corsairs and invaders or peaceful settlers. In 1574, only three years after the foundation of Manilla, this place was attacked by a powerful corsair, called by the Spaniards, Li-ma-hong, said to have been a native of the province of Canton, and the son of a highway robber. By skill, courage, and good management, he had contrived to assemble a considerable piratical fleet, which plundered the coasts of China, and set the imperial navy at defiance, much in the same manner as Chinese pirates have often done in our own time. The corsair in question, in the course of his depredations, having heard of the supposed riches of the Spanish settlement, resolved to attack it, and accordingly made two different assaults on it, the first with a force of 400, and the last with one of 600 men headed by himself. He met with a very different reception from what he had been accustomed to on the coast of China, for he was beaten off by a mere handful of Spaniards, and afterwards pursued as far as the distant province of Pangasinan, where his whole force was either destroyed or dispersed. This event, it may be observed, took place about four and forty years before the conquest of the northern provinces of China by the Manchoo Tartars, and the piracy of Li-ma-hong was, no doubt, only part of the system of disorder in the government of China, which portended the revolution which overthrew the native dynasty of Ming, and substituted for it that of a foreign conqueror.

As early as 1603, or within two and thirty years of the foundation of Manilla, the Chinese were already settled in great numbers in the capital and its neighbourhood, and their numbers exciting the fear and jealousy of the Spanish authorities, they proceeded to measures of restriction. This brought on an insurrection, in which all the Chinese, with the exception of 2000, were involved. Twenty-three thousand are said, on this occasion, to have lost their lives, 100 of the actual insurgents only saving their lives, and those, on surrender, being condemned to the gallies. In 1639, or only thirty-six years after this event, the Chinese amounted already to 30,000, an increase, no doubt, caused, in a great measure, by the emigration, which the progress of the Tartar conquest, which had now reached the southern provinces of China, had produced. Measures of persecution on the part of the Spanish government, again drove them to insurrection, and this rebellion ended in the surrender of the survivors, amounting to no more than 7000. In 1759, in consequence of repeated commands from the court of Madrid, an order was issued for the total expulsion from the Philippines of all Chinese that had not adopted the Christian religion, and a locality was appointed, to which they might resort for the purposes of trade, after the manner practised by the Chinese towards the nations of Europe, and by the Japanese towards the Chinese and Dutch. The edict, however, so injurious to the Spanish colony itself, was never carried into effect, and three years after its promulgation, the English captured Manilla, when the Chinese, of course, heartily joined the invaders.

The Chinese in the Philippines are still placed under restraints and disabilities unknown in the possessions of the other European nations, and especially in those of the English; and hence, although the Philippines be far more conveniently situated for an intercourse with China than the possessions of the Dutch or English, the total number of Chinese in them, native and mestizo, does not exceed one-fourth of those of Java, and hardly equals that of the small island of Singapore. But for the accidental, and it must be added, fortunate presence of the Spaniards, it is certain that at this day the Philippines would have been principally peopled with Chinese, in the same manner as is now the case with the island of Formosa; and it is a mystery not easily explained how it came to pass that this did not happen both with Formosa and the Philippines long before the arrival of Europeans, considering the strong and decided tendency to immigration on the part of the Chinese which was evinced almost immediately on the occurrence of that event.

The Japanese, before their laws excluded them from all communication with the rest of the world, showed the same disposition to frequent and to settle in the Philippines as the Chinese, and in the early history of the Archipelago we find a considerable number of this people as settlers in Manilla. They were, indeed, encouraged in this by the Spanish authorities, on account of the fabrics of their native country which they imported, and which were found to be well suited to the once celebrated Acapulco trade. In 1603, they were settled in such numbers in Manilla, that the Spanish government, taking advantage of their well-known antipathy to the Chinese, employed them in counteracting the machinations of the latter. The Spaniards, however, found them equally unmanageable as the Chinese. Thus in 1581, a Japanese pirate with a large fleet, landed, encamped in, and took possession of the province of Cagayan, at the northern end of the island of Luzon, a place not less than 1000 miles distant from the nearest part of the Japanese Archipelago, yet an easy voyage at the height of the monsoons. "It was no easy matter," says the Spanish writer from whom I quote, "to expel them, for the Japanese fight with obstinacy, not retreating before fire-arms, but rushing to receive death on the points of our weapons."

The Portuguese first, and afterwards the Dutch, made some feeble efforts to dispossess the Spaniards, but the only serious invasion of the Philippines ever made by an European power, was that by the English in 1762, during the seven years' war. The attack was made from Madras, by a force of 2300 men, a part of it consisting of sepoys, a description of troops which, at this early period of our dominion in India, could not have been of a superior quality. The naval part of the equipment consisted of thirteen men-of-war and transports. Such was the force destined for the conquest of a vast Archipelago, in which it had taken the Spanish nation two centuries to establish their power and their religion. The Spanish authorities were taken by surprise, for they had not even heard of the war which England had declared against Spain the year before. The English expedition landed without resistance, besieged Manilla, battered, breached, stormed and captured the town within ten days of its landing. The citadel capitulated, the governor, an archbishop, engaging to pay a ransom of four millions of hard dollars, 862,500*l*., on condition that the sack should last only three hours. According to the Spanish accounts it lasted for four-and-twenty! The public treasure, a small sum, had been removed into the interior, and of the whole ransom a contribution levied on the city of Manilla, together with the confiscation of some church plate, yielded no more than a fourth part of the stipulated sum. The governor drew a bill for the balance on the Treasury of Madrid, which was very properly dishonoured. The commander of the expedition was Sir William Draper, celebrated for his controversy with Junius on this very subject. The Spanish troops composing the garrison of Manilla did not exceed 550 men, and therefore a force of 5000 Pampangas, supposed to be the bravest people of the Philippines, was called in as auxiliaries. With the help of these, two sorties were made against the British entrenchments, both easily defeated. It was no difficult enterprise to capture and hold Manilla, but the British conquest never extended beyond ten miles from its walls, and after a ten months' occupation, Manilla itself was restored by the Treaty of Paris. Its chief result was an insurrection of the Chinese population, followed by severe punishment. Some insurrections also took place among the native inhabitants, encouraged by a proclamation of the invaders promising to abolish the capitation-tax, which, had they acted on it, on achieving the conquest, would have left them devoid of revenue to carry on the administration, since at the time the other main branch of income, the tobacco monopoly, did not yet exist. The Manilla expedition must be considered a mere marauding adventure, conducted in a manner that would not be tolerated in our time. By the Spaniards of the Philippines, it is still considered as the most untoward event in the history of the Archipelago.

PIGAFETTA, ANTONIO, the companion of Magellan in the first circumnavigation of the globe, and the faithful narrator of his voyage, was a native of Vicenza, and of a patrician family, but the years of his birth and death are not known. He was only a volunteer in the celebrated expedition; and having leisure and industry he kept a journal, the work by which he is known. He accompanied Magellan in the rash adventure in which he lost his life,—was slightly wounded in it, and was one of the few survivors of the voyage that returned safe to Spain. He afterwards became a knight of the order of St. John.

The first published account of Pigafetta's Journal was in French, from an abridgment presented by the author to Louisa of Savoy, mother of Francis the First, and regent of France in the absence of her son in his unfortunate Italian campaign. From the French, this abridgment was rendered into Italian by Ramusio, and appeared in his celebrated Collection in 1550. The original work was found in the Ambrosian library of Milan; and published in 1800 by Amoretti, with some corrections as to language, indispensable from the coarseness of some of its descriptions. Pigafetta, although noble by birth, seems to have been but imperfectly educated, for his manuscript contains errors both of grammar and orthography; but these are more than compensated by his good sense and fidelity. For much of his information, it may be presumed, that he was indebted to his companions, Magellan and Barbosa, both of whom had passed several years in India before the last great adventure; and Barbosa's manuscript is dated in 1516, or three years before the expedition quitted Spain. He was, however, himself inquisitive, industrious, and intelligent; and his description of the manners, customs, religion, and productions of the Philippines and Moluccas are equal to those of our best modern travellers, and form a contrast to the obscure glimpses of knowledge which we get from his countryman, Marco Polo. After the Malay slave of Magellan, hitherto the interpreter, had absconded on his master's death, Pigafetta seems already to have acquired such a competent knowledge of the Malay language, that in Mindano, Borneo, and the Moluccas he was able to supply his place. The vocabularies, which form a part of his journal, are sufficient proofs of his industry. These are called respectively the Philippine and Molucca languages, but are, in fact, the Çebu dialect of Bisaya and Malay. The first amounts to 140 words, but the last to 450; and making due allowance for errors of transcription, it is wonderfully accurate. Independent of this, it is a great curiosity, being the most ancient specimen of Malay which we possess, for in that language there exist neither old inscriptions nor old manuscripts.

PILGRIMAGE. It is probable that pilgrimages were made in the times of Hinduism to some of the ancient shrines of Java, such as those of Brambanan and Singasari; but there is certainly no record of any such having been made, nor of pilgrimages having been performed to any of the sacred places of Hindustan, although such may also have occasionally taken place. Since the conversion to Mahommedanism, pilgrimages to Mecca have been frequent; the greater number of the pilgrims proceeding from Java, and a few from Sumatra and the Malay Peninsula. I was, myself, told by one of those who had seen the lists in Arabia, that the usual number present at Mecca was about 900. The annual number proceeding from Java alone is about 400. The performance of the pilgrimage, in Malay, Nayik-hāj, brings with it the same honors and consideration as did that of the pilgrimage to Jerusalem to the Europeans of the middle ages. The pilgrim wears for life the Arabian costume; is clothed in white,—is a person of importance, and sometimes a fanatic and an intriguer. It was, for example, persons of this description under the name of the Padris, who set up the puritanical Mahometanism that caused a civil war in Sumatra about the beginning of the present century.

PINE APPLE. The Ananassa sativa grows in great perfection, and with such facility as to be very abundant throughout every part of the Malay and Philippine Archipelagos. It may even be said to be produced with the facility of a native weed, and yet there can be no question of its being a native of tropical America, introduced by the Spaniards and Portuguese, although at what precise time is unknown. The name given to it, in nearly all the languages of the two Archipelagos, is but a corruption of that which was received from their European conquerors, ananasa. Thus, in Malay and Javanese it is nanas; in Balinese, manas; in Madurese, lanas; and in Lampung, kanias. In the languages of Celebes it is called pandang, which is but a corruption of the Malayan name for the Pandanus, given to it from the general resemblance between the two plants. The natives of the Philippines frequently give it the name of piña, the Spanish name of a pine-cone, which is equivalent to our own name. The fruit is considered by the natives a coarse one, and less esteemed even than the banana.

PIÑA. This is the name by which the cloth manufactured in the Philippines from the fibre of the leaf of the pine-apple is known. From the extraordinary facility and certainty with which the pine-apple is grown in the vicinity of the equator, it seems almost certain, that by the application of European skill to the process of separating the fibre from the pulpy matter of the leaf, a valuable raw material composed of it, might be obtained for the manufactories of Europe. The cloth made from the pine-apple fibre, by the rude industry of the Philippines, is well known to be of great strength, durability, and beauty. To show the facility with which the pine-apple is reared, I copy the following passage from a very intelligent writer. "This (that of the pine-apple) is a cultivation for which Singapore is famous. The beautiful islands and islets, to the west of the harbour, are covered with plots neatly planted with rows of this favourite fruit. The peculiar soil of these is said to impart the delicious flavour possessed by the Singapore pine-apples. The principal cultivators are Bugis. The produce, at times, far exceeds the consumption; and then, when bought at the gardens, is sometimes to be had at the rate of ten apples to a cent, (1000 for a hard dollar). The plant is hardy, and requires little care or cultivation. The principal labour is in collecting the fruit. The fibres of the leaf are prepared, to a small extent, for shipment to China."—Mr. J. T. Thomson, in the Journal of the Indian Archipelago. Vol. iv. p. 140. The production of fruit and of leaves in no manner, it should be remembered, interfere with each other, the leaves being fittest for fibre after the fruit has ripened, the reverse of what is the case with the poppy, which cannot produce both opium and oil; and with the coco-palm, which will not yield both sap and fruit.

PIRACY and PIRATE. There is no name in Malay and Javanese, or indeed in any other native language, for piracy or robbery on the high seas. There is, in fact, no word to distinguish the element on which the act of plunder is committed, a thing natural enough with a people who live as much on the sea as the land. Rompak is to rob or plunder generally; and from this is derived the most usual name for a pirate, pârompak; and for piracy, pârompakan. In a region like the Malay and Philippine Archipelagos, abounding in narrow seas, rivers, creeks, coves, and mangrove swamps, and often inhabited by rude and lawless tribes of fishermen, piracy must have existed as early as there was anything to plunder. It has so existed in every part of the world similarly circumstanced; as for example, in the Grecian Archipelago at various times, and in northern Europe, including our own islands, and the countries from which our forefathers sprang, in the middle ages. The account which Thucydides gives of the manners of the early Greeks, so closely resembles that of the Malayan nations in this respect, that it is worth quoting as an illustration. "The Greeks of former times," says he, "as well as the barbarians of the continent dwelling on the sea coast, and all the inhabitants of the islands, as soon as they had acquired the art of passing to and fro in their vessels, betook themselves to piracy under the leadership of the most able among them, for the purpose of enriching themselves and maintaining their poor. They landed,—surprised, and plundered unfortified towns and dispersed villages, and in this manner, chiefly, they gained a subsistence. In these times such an employment was, by no means, considered a subject of reproach, but rather a matter to glory in. Even to this day, some of the people of the continent attach credit to exploits of this nature, provided they be performed with decency and humanity. The inhabitants of the continent, also, exercised robberies on one another; and down to the present day, many people of Greece are supported by such practices, as, for example, the Ozolian Locrians, the Ætolians, and Acarnanians, with their neighbours. The custom of wearing weapons, introduced by this old life of rapine, is still retained among these people. It once prevailed, indeed, all over Greece; for as houses had no manner of defence, and travelling was full of hazard, the Greeks passed their whole lives in armour, like barbarians. A proof of this is the continuance still, in some parts of Greece, of those manners which were once general over the whole of it. The Athenians were the first who passed from this dissolute course of life to polite and elegant manners."

If the term, piracy, be restricted, as it ought, to robbery committed on the high or even the narrow seas, it is necessarily confined to the inhabitants of the sea coast, or of the rivers debouching upon it; and to such of these as have, by the possession of stout vessels, of fire-arms, and of skill in navigation, the power to commit it: and it would be an abuse of language to bestow the name on the depredations committed on each other by rude tribes, without other vessels than paddled canoes, or other arms than spears, with swords and bucklers. The boldest and most dangerous pirates of the Indian islands, at present, are two nations of the Philippines, well known to native traders as the Lanuns and Balanini; the first being a people of the great bay on the southern side of Mindano, and the last, of the group of the Sulu islands. These tribes, centrically situated and taking advantage of the monsoons, scour the coasts both of the Philippine and Malayan Archipelago from Luzon to Sumatra, in fleets of stout vessels of from fifty to one hundred tons burden, generally armed with a few cannon or wall pieces, with some muskets; and having a stout bulwark, called in Malay an ampilan, a mark by which they are sufficiently distinguished from merchant praus. Next to these come the Malay pirates, once the most formidable of all, but now comparatively few and feeble. Their principal seat, ever since the conquest of Malacca by the Portuguese in the beginning of the 16th century, had been the group of islands at the eastern extremity of the Straits of Malacca; and the principal parties concerned, the oràng-laut, or "men of the sea," the same race that is denounced by De Barros, as a people whose habitual occupation was "fishing and robbing." This class of pirates, if it has not wholly disappeared, has, at least, ceased to be dangerous, since the establishment, in the very centre of their haunts, of the British settlement of Singapore, and the Netherland one of Rhio, both of which localities had themselves, down to the year 1819, been favourite piratical haunts.

Besides the piratical tribes now named, there is hardly any other maritime people of the Archipelago, that at one time or another, has not had its pirates, such as those of Celebes and the Moluccas, and even of New Guinea. The people not addicted to piracy, or, at least, who have committed none in our times, are the Javanese, the people of Bali and Lomboc, all the nations of Sumatra, except the maritime Malays, and all the inhabitants of the Philippines subject to the rule of Spain, and these constitute the great majority of the population of the two Archipelagos.

The receivers of the stolen goods, or at least the sharers in the booty, have been many of the native princes, who, far from thinking piracy any discredit, have looked on its gains as a fair and regular branch of their incomes. Strangely enough, the government of the Philippines, which has suffered most from piracy, gives the practice, in one instance at least, a tacit countenance, most probably from necessity. "Yligan, in the province of Misamis, and island of Mindano," says the author of the Informe sobre las Islas Filipinas, "is a kind of stockaded place to which the Moors resort for trade, bringing, yearly, about 80,000 cavans of rice in the husk, from 20,000 to 30,000 cavans of cacoa, from 1200 to 1400 cavans of coffee, and from 50 to 60 tails of gold dust; with great quantities of fine cloths, mantlets, crises, and whatever they collect in their incursions in the interior, or their piracies at sea, including money, on which they set no high value. In return they receive earthen and hard-ware, chintzes, but above all, coco and areca nuts which are scarce in their country. The inhabitants of this town do not exceed 1500 souls; are constantly exposed to the attacks of the Moors; and it would be well to fortify the place with a rampart and fosse." The pirates here alluded to are the well-known Lanuns.

The only formidable piratical praus are those of the Lanuns and Balanini. These are vessels of from 40 to 100 tons, have crews of from 40 to 60, and carry half-a-dozen wall-pieces, with a supply of small arms, spears, cutlasses, and krises. They are furnished with oars or sweeps, as well as sails, and are made for speed. They are, in fact, the regular native war boats. To the native trading vessels they are irresistible, but utterly contemptible to the smallest European man-of-war, and it is seldom they have ventured to attack, even the smallest European merchant ship,—hardly ever, when manned by Europeans. The larger junks of the Chinese are equally safe from them, and it is only the smaller or the unarmed junks of the Cochin Chinese and native trading praus to which they are formidable.

Piracy, as already stated, has existed in the Malay and Philippine Archipelagos ever since they were known to Europeans, and without doubt had existed for many ages before. In the annals of the state of Malacca it is asserted, that the trade of that place was greatly harassed by pirates of Celebes, under the leadership of a Macassar chief whose name was Kraing Samerluk, in the time of Sultan Mansur Shah, whose reign commenced in 1374. The Spaniards, when they commenced the conquest of the Philippines in 1565, found the inhabitants of Mindoro carrying on piracy; and those of Mindano and Sulu soon after commenced those incursions which have continued to the present day, and often set the Spanish power at defiance. As early as the year 1589, or only eighteen years after the foundation of Manilla, the first attempt to conquer the Sulu Archipelago, and to suppress the predatory habits of its people was made, and many others have followed, the last of them as late as 1851. In reference to the first of these, the historian Zuñiga makes the following remarks: "From that time to the present the Moors have not ceased to infest our colonies. It is incredible what a number of Indians have been made prisoners; what villages have been destroyed; and what vessels they have captured."

The Malayan nations are not the only people that have committed, or now commit piracies in the waters of the Archipelagos. When disorder and civil war prevail in China, as always happens during its revolutions, it is sure to produce hordes of pirates; which, although they usually confine their depredations to the coasts of their own country, occasionally extend them to the Philippines, and to the northern portion of the Malayan Archipelago. Such piracies, as already stated, were rife during the revolution which placed the present Tartar dynasty on the throne; and they are, at present, rife pending that which threatens to overthrow it. The Chinese pirates, from the superior size of their vessels, and the superior skill of those that navigate them, are more formidable to native trading vessels than even the worst of the Malayan buccaneers. The piracy of the Chinese, a civilised people, will necessarily cease with the temporary causes which have given rise to it; but the utter extermination of Malayan piracy is as hopeless as that of theft and burglary in the best ordered states of society. It may, however, be greatly abated, and made not worth following as a profession, by a vigilant police exercised, not only over the plunderers, but the receivers of the plunder, by the European nations having territorial possessions in the two Archipelagos. The obvious means of pursuing the pirates are armed steam vessels of very small draught, which can pursue them into the shoals to which they resort, and from whose speed there is no escape. The destruction of the supposed haunts of the pirates by large and costly expeditions, seems by no means an expedient plan for the suppression of piracy. In such expeditions the innocent are punished with the guilty; and by the destruction of property which accompanies them, both parties are deprived of the future means of honest livelihood, and hence forced, as it were, to a continuance of their piratical habits. The total failure of all such expeditions on the part of the Spaniards, for a period of near three centuries, ought to be a sufficient warning against undertaking them.

PISANG, (PULO), literally "banana island," is the name of no fewer than six different islands, or rather uninhabited islets of the Malayan Archipelago, extending from Sumatra to the Moluccas. The name, pisang, is one peculiarly belonging to the Malay language, all the other tongues having their own separate names for this fruit; so that the word, applied to the names of places, points to the extent of Malay navigation. Except for navigation, the islands which bear this name are of no importance whatever.

POETARE, correctly PUTAR, which, in Malay, signifies "to turn," or "revolve," is the name of an island lying between Floris and Timur, computed to have an area of 209 square geographical miles.

POLILLO. The name of a considerable island lying on the eastern coast of the great island of Luzon. It is of a triangular form; in length about 25 miles, and in breadth 20 in its widest part. The chief town lies on its south-western side, bears the same name, and lies in north latitude 14° 30′. The island is mountainous and well watered, but seems indifferently cultivated, for its whole population is no more than 1214.

POLO, MARCO. The celebrated Venetian traveller passed through the Malayan Archipelago, in a voyage from Fokien in China to the Persian Gulf, performed by a fleet of fourteen Chinese junks. This happened about the year 1291, or 218 years before the first appearance of the Portuguese in the waters of the Archipelago. In so far as the Malayan countries are concerned, the work of Marco Polo is most meagre and unsatisfactory. It gives, in fact, but obscure glances, leaving us, in the matter of names, dates, and distances, to mere conjecture. The information communicated is, indeed, more like what might be expected from a Chinese than an European traveller, and the author who had gone to China at eighteen, and lived there for twenty years, was probably in his turn of thinking as much a Chinese as an European. In the voyage in question he must have chiefly associated with Chinese, or with the Arabian pilots which must have been present in a fleet bound for the Persian Gulf.

A few examples may be given of the nature of the information which he gives us. He is the first European author that names Java, but he had not seen it. His description of it, in reality, comprehends the whole Archipelago, except Sumatra, for he alleges it to produce gold, cloves, and nutmegs, as well as its own native products, and he asserts it to be of vast extent, making Sumatra but a lesser Java, under the name of Java Minor. The first Malayan land that the fleet reached after quitting Kamboja, or Champa, was an island that he calls Pentân, which is most probably the large island of Bentân, improperly Bintang, at the eastern entrance of the Straits of Malacca. Malacca itself seems to be indicated by the word Malacur, no doubt a corruption of Malayu, or Malay, and it is described as being at once an island, a state, and a town. "The people," he says, "are governed by a king, and have their own peculiar language. The town is large and well built. A considerable trade is there carried on in spices and drugs, with which the place abounds." According to the usual reckoning, Malacca at the time in question had been founded only forty years.

The fullest account given by the Venetian traveller is of Sumatra, not under this name, but that of Java Minor, evidently imposed by himself in order to distinguish it from all those other lands which he comprehended under the common name of Java. He describes the elephant and rhinoceros as natives of the island, and his account of the gomuti and sago-palms is correct, and the earliest ever given. He says that the majority of the inhabitants were idolators, and some of them, evidently referring to the Bataks, cannibals. In speaking of one of its kingdoms, which he calls Felech, and which is probably Pârlak, he says that "many of those who dwell in the sea-port towns had been converted to the religion of Mahomet by the Saracen merchants who constantly frequent them." The place referred to is in the territory of Achin, and the Achinese, by their own account, had been converted in 1206, or 85 years before the arrival of Marco Polo.

Sumatra is described as being divided into eight different kingdoms, each having its own proper language, but these alleged kingdoms, in so far as they can be identified at all with real names, turn out to be mere petty places, and all on the northern coast of the island. Marco Polo expressly described himself as having visited six out of these eight kingdoms, which, judging from another part of his narrative, is so improbable that we are obliged to consider the assertion as either a fiction or an interpolation,—most likely the latter. He was, he informs us, detained in one of the eight kingdoms, namely, that called Samara, the place supposed to be the present Sambalangan, for five months, waiting the return of the north-eastern monsoon in order to prosecute his voyage westward. "As it was necessary," says the narrative, "to continue so long a time at this island, Marco Polo established himself on shore, with a party of about 2000 men, and in order to guard against mischief from the savage natives who seek for opportunities of seizing stragglers, putting them to death and eating them, he caused a large and deep ditch to be dug round in such manner that each of its extremities terminated in the port where the shipping lay. The ditch he strengthened by erecting several block-houses or redoubts of wood, the country affording an abundant supply of that material; and being defended by this kind of fortification, he kept his party in complete security during the five months of their residence. Such was the confidence inspired among the natives, that they furnished supplies of victuals and other necessary articles, according to an agreement made with them." The place where this fortified camp was made is distant from two of the other kingdoms, supposed to be Kampar and Junbi, between 800 and 900 miles. How, it may be fairly asked, was it possible for Marco Polo to have visited these remote places without any protection, when the protection of his own fleet, and of an intrenched camp with a garrison of 2000 men were necessary in one locality to secure stragglers from being killed and eaten by the savage inhabitants?

Marco Polo's notice of the trade between China and the Archipelago is confined to mere hints. The first of these is to the following effect, in reference to Java, evidently including Borneo and the Spice Islands. "The quantity of gold collected there exceeds all belief. From thence it is that the merchants of Zaitun and Manji (the northern and southern provinces of China) in general have imported, and to this day import that metal to a great amount; and from thence also is obtained the greatest part of the spices that are distributed throughout the world." The second is this.—"It (Java Minor or Sumatra) contains abundance of riches and all sorts of spices, lignum-aloes, sappan-wood for dying, and various other kinds of drugs, which on account of the length of the voyage, and the danger of the navigation, are not imported into our country (Venice), but which find their way to the provinces of Manji and Kataia, (the southern and northern provinces of China.)" His own voyage, indeed, gives us but a very poor idea of the navigation of the Chinese in his time, compared even with its present imperfect condition. The first departure of the fleet was from Fokien, which produces now, and most probably did then, the most skilful and adventurous mariners of China. He could only have sailed with the north-easterly monsoon, and in all likelihood, only when it had set in steadily in the month of December. Yet by the time he had passed through the China Sea and the Straits of Malacca, and reached the north-western end of Sumatra, that monsoon was already expended, and he was obliged to await its return during five tedious months. It would not return earlier than the beginning of November. The monsoon with which he quitted China would end in the beginning of March, but the voyage through the Straits of Malacca would be performed with the variable winds which always prevail in them. The voyage, then, from Fokien to the port at the western entrance of the Straits, where the fleet was arrested by the south-western monsoon, occupied the six months from December to May inclusive, and it was detained in the port of Samara for the five months from June to October inclusive. The greatest difficulties of the voyage to large junks, and some of the fleet of Marco Polo were certainly of this description, for they had crews of 250 men, would be amongst the sand-banks of the Straits of Malacca. The voyage, which it took the Imperial fleet six months to perform in the thirteenth century, would now be performed in one-sixth of the time. A Fokien junk makes the voyage from Amoy to Singapore in 15 days, and probably would not take a longer time in passing from one end of the Straits of Malacca to the other.

It may be asked through what channel Marco Polo acquired his knowledge of the Malayan Archipelago, scanty as it is. He is described as being acquainted with three Tartar and one Chinese dialect, but these would not help him among the Malays, nor is it probable that his Chinese companions were themselves capable of rendering much assistance. The probability then is, that he had most of his knowledge from the Arabian pilots that, although not mentioned, must have been in the fleet, and this notion is confirmed by the Arabian and not Chinese stamp of the names of places. The words are, indeed, Malayan, but written just as an Arab would pronounce them. Thus the Champa of the Malays is converted into Siamba or Ciamba, the Arabs not having the sound ch. The name of Java is written nearly as Europeans now pronounce it, with the letter v, instead of with a w, as the natives themselves do, and this seems also taken from the Arabian pronunciation. It may be further mentioned that a derivative of this, namely, Jawi, or Javi, is a common term among the Arabs for all the countries and people of the Archipelago, and this is not unlikely to have been the source of Marco Polo's error in uniting so many countries under the common name of Java. Another example is found in the name of one of the six Sumatran kingdoms said to have been visited by the traveller. This he writes Felech, and is, correctly, the Pârlak, or Diamond Point of our maps, and with the exception of the letter r, the Arabs having no p, and always substituting an f for it, the pronunciation is what an Arab would give, and an Italian write from an Arab's pronunciation.

The amount of knowledge concerning the Archipelago communicated by Marco Polo, small as it is, yet is great in comparison with what Gibbon justly calls "the ignorance of the ancients." Still, the wonder is that, considering his opportunities, it should not have been greater, when we recollect the extensive and accurate knowledge obtained by such writers as Barbosa and Pigafetta, within a very few years of the first appearance of Europeans in the Indian waters. Much allowance, however, must be made for the short-comings and errors of his narrative, when it is considered that it was circulated in manuscript for a century and a half before it was printed, and that the author, as his judicious commentator, Mr. Marsden remarks, had no ready use of his own, or any other language, and was, in fact, although an enterprising, yet an illiterate traveller.

POLYNESIA. The Islands of the Pacific Ocean are referred to in the present work only on account of a certain connection by language which exists between them and the Malayan Archipelago. Their inhabitants may be divided into three great classes—those of the islands of the Northern Pacific, the Sandwich group excepted,—those of the islands extending west and east from the Tonga group to Eastern Island, and north and south from the Sandwich to the New Zealand islands; and those of the islands from New Guinea to the Fiji group, lying between the equator and the southern tropic.

The first class are supposed to belong to the Malayan race of man, or to be the same with the fairer inhabitants of the Malay and Philippine Archipelagos. The tribes inhabiting these islands, however, seem to speak languages not only differing from those of the Malayan nations, but also differing among themselves. The second class differ from the first in physical form, being a stout, athletic, handsome people whose stature exceeds that of the Malayan race by at least three inches. They speak a language which is essentially the same throughout, and differing in phonetic character, grammatical structure and vocabulary from those of the first class of inhabitants, as well as from all the languages of the Malay and Philippine Archipelagos. The third class of inhabitants are negros, woolly-headed, in complexion dark but not black, and of at least the average stature of the Malayan race. They differ, therefore, essentially from the pigmy negros of the Malay Peninsula and of the Philippines, and may be pronounced a peculiar and unique race of men. Their languages differ wholly from those of the two first classes of inhabitants, and as far as our information extends, would seem also to be entirely different among the different negro tribes themselves. From the account now rendered of the geographical distributions of the three classes, it will appear that they are not found territorially intermixed, as is the case in the Malay Peninsula and the Philippines, with the fairer race and the negros. Even the larger islands contain no intermixture. New Guinea is peopled only by negros, and New Zealand only by what has been called the great Polynesian family. Negros are only to be found south of the equator, and the islands of the Northern Pacific are, with the exception of the Sandwich group, wholly occupied by what is believed to be the Malayan race.

In all the languages of the islands of the Pacific, whether of the negros or of the fairer races, a small infusion of the Malayan languages is to be found, in the same manner as we find words of Norman French in English, of Teutonic words in the languages of the south of Europe; of Arabic in Spanish, Portuguese, Turkish and Persian; of Persian in the languages of Hindustan, and of Sanscrit in Malay and Javanese. The proportion of the Malayan ingredient in the languages of Polynesia is smaller, however, than in any one of the cases now quoted in illustration, not exceeding where it is largest above 200 words in 1000. It exists in the languages of the negros, equally as in those of the fairer races, although from greater barbarism and stronger antipathy of race, not generally to the same degree.

The nature of the Malayan words introduced into the Polynesian languages is a consideration of not less importance than the proportion in which they exist. The most frequent class consists of the numerals, which are always imperfect as to the number of them introduced, and always corrupted as to form. The South-Sea islanders, both of the fair and negro races are in possession of one or all of these domesticated animals, namely, the hog, the dog, and common fowl, but not one of these, in any of the Polynesian tongues that have been examined, is known by a Malayan name. So far then as language is good evidence, the Polynesian nations are not indebted to the Malayan for them. Not so with cultivated plants: the evidence of language shows, that the Polynesians have received from the Malay nations the yam, the coco-palm, and the sugar-cane, for all these are known by names which although greatly disfigured, are unquestionably Malayan. Some degree of instruction received by the Polynesian from the Malayan nations is to be inferred from the existence in their tongues of the following words which are of undoubted Malayan origin,—thatch, plank, comb, adze, weapon-point, mesh of a net, ladder, bow, year, and chieftain or lord.

This analysis reduces the advantages which the islanders of the Pacific have derived from Malayan intercourse to a very inconsiderable amount. The Malayan nations taught the islanders a convenient system of numeration; they introduced the culture of the yam, the coco-nut, and the sugar-cane, and bestowed, perhaps, some rude instruction in the mechanic arts. But they introduced no useful domestic animal, nor corn, pulse, or cotton. They did not instruct the islanders in the fabrication of iron, or in the manufacture of any textile fabric. Still less did they instruct them in law, in letters, or in religion.

But the interesting question arises, in what manner the small number of Malayan words came to be infused into the languages of the Polynesian Islands, the nearest of which is far beyond the usual limits of Malayan navigation. A few suggestions may be thrown out in explanation. In the course of the present work, it has been shown that the two leading nations of Sumatra and Java, the Malays and Javanese, have been for ages pushing their enterprises, whether commercial or predatory, as far as the Philippines, the Moluccas, and New Guinea, and, therefore to the very confines of the Polynesian islands to the west. It is from this quarter that it is natural to suppose that the Malayan words must have found their way into the Polynesian languages. The words certainly belong to these two languages, and it can be proved that they do. Thus in the 85 Malayan words existing in the Maori or language of New Zealand, 18 are Malay and 10 Javanese, the remaining 57 belonging equally to these two tongues, while they do not contain a word of any other Indian language.

The praus of the Malays and Javanese when at the eastern confines of the Archipelago, might seem, at first sight, to have their further progress eastward arrested by the trade winds. Such, however, is not practically the case, for in the first part of their voyage they would have the westerly monsoon in their favour, and in the Pacific itself, within a zone of about seven or eight degrees on each side of the equator, it is not trade winds but variable ones, blowing even more frequently from the west than the east, that prevail. By this track, then, Malayan praus might easily enough penetrate a considerable way, among the islands of the Pacific. They might do so either through the Southern Philippines, the Moluccas or Torres Straits, and most probably did so by all these channels. Were our vocabularies sufficiently copious, we might even be able to trace the progress of the Malayan nations among the Polynesian islands by the proportion of their languages found in the Polynesian dialects. Thus, supposing that the Malayan nations entered the Pacific by the route of Torres Straits, leaving out the negro nations on account of ferocity and incompatibility of race, the first of the fairer people they would encounter would be the inhabitants of the Tonga or Friendly Islands, and judging by the inadequate specimens of their language which we possess, it contains a far larger proportion of Malayan words than the languages of the remote Marquesas, Sandwich and New Zealand islands, although all be dialects of the same tongue.—See Preliminary Dissertation to a Grammar and Dictionary of the Malay language.

POMEGRANATE. (Punica Granatum.) The pomegranate is cultivated in the Indian Islands as an ornamental plant, on account of its flowers, but bears a poor fruit, hardly esculent. It is, without doubt, an exotic, but when or by whom introduced is unknown. It bears notwithstanding a native name, dalima, which is also that of "the ruby." The natives state that this word is derived from the numeral five, lima, in reference to the remains of the five segmented calyx on the top of the fruit. This opinion of the origin of the name seems confirmed by that given to the tree in the polite language of Java, gangsalan, which is a translation of the vulgar name.

PONTIANAK, or PONTIYANAK. This is the name of a Malay town and state of the western coast of Borneo. The town lies on the left bank of the river, usually called by the same name, about 15 miles from its mouth. The river, a navigable one for vessels of moderate burden, is formed by the junction of two considerable streams, the Kapuwas and the Landak. The town is almost on the equator, and in east longitude 109° 10′. Pontianak is at present the chief place of the Netherland administration of the Province of the west coast of Borneo, and contained in 1825, with the territory belonging to it, a population of 36,676, consisting of the following elements: Malays 3000, Dayaks or wild tribes, 13,391, Chinese 17,693, Arabs and their descendants 319, and Europeans 2273. The total population of the province of which it is the head, was computed, at the same time, at 590,000, the majority composed of the wild races.

PORCELANE and POTTERY. All the more civilised inhabitants of the Archipelago have possessed immemorially the art of fabricating a coarse unglazed pottery, much resembling that of the Hindus, but not borrowed from them, judging by the native names connected with the art. For either pottery or porcelane there is no common native term, but a great many names, to distinguish the vessel or utensil made from them, these often varying in the different languages. A coarse domestic earthenware is of much less general use among the islanders than the Hindus, its place being frequently taken by the coarse porcelane of China, which has been imported for ages. Fragments, or even entire vessels of it, have been found in ancient ruins in Java; and when Singapore was established by ourselves specimens were found along with ancient Chinese coins of the 10th and 11th centuries. It seems probable, too, that the sacred jars of the Dayaks of Borneo, known to these people under the name of pânaga, and undoubtedly Chinese, are of considerable antiquity, since none of the same description are at present manufactured.

PORCUPINE (Histrix). The porcupine of the Malayan islands, is found in most of the large islands, and differs but little from the African porcupine long naturalised in Italy. It is the landak of the Malays and Javanese. The Malays, however, assert the existence in the Peninsula and Sumatra of two species which they distinguish by the epithets of great and small.

PORTUGAL, PORTUGUESE. The Portuguese made their first appearance in the waters of the Archipelago under Sequiera in 1509, twelve years after their arrival in Calicut. The insults which they then received and undoubtedly provoked, led two years after, to the conquest of Malacca, and from that event is to be dated the commencement of their domination, which virtually terminated with the loss of the same place in 1641. Thus the supremacy of the Portuguese lasted in all but 130 years. Their territorial possessions comprehended only the principality of Malacca, and the Clove and Nutmeg Islands, but even in these, their sovereignty was never peaceably established, for throughout, they were involved in hostilities with their nominal subjects, or with neighbouring native states. Notwithstanding, however, their short and disputed power, it must be observed that they have left behind them more marks of their dominion than either the Dutch or English. The facts which attest this, are the number of words of their language which have been naturalised in the languages of the Archipelago, and the number of converts to Christianity which they have left. These results are most probably attributable to the greater congeniality of their manners and language with those of the Archipelago, and to the spirit of propagandism being far more active with them than with their successors in power.

POTATO. The American potato, Solanum tuberosum, the Ubi yuropa of the Malays, and the Kântang holanda of the Javanese, names equivalent to European and Dutch yam, was first introduced into Java by the Dutch, and in comparatively very modern times. It will produce fruit and tubers only at an elevation of not less than 4000 feet above the level of the sea, and consequently its production must always be confined to a few localities. In all the higher mountain valleys of Java, it is produced easily and of very good quality, chiefly for the consumption of Europeans, for with the natives it never can become a general article of food, as long as they have cheaper farinaceous roots in the yam and batata. It is also grown in some of the mountains of Celebes, and far more readily and abundantly in those of the Philippines.

PRAMBANAN. This is the native pronunciation of the celebrated Hindu ruins in Java, which Europeans, rightly or otherwise, write Brambanan. See BRAMBANAN.

PRANARAGA, or, as pronounced by the Javanese, Pronorogo, is the name of a native province of Java, situated south-west of the volcanic mountain Wilis, and towards the southern side of the island, in the proper country of the Javanese nation. This fine province abounds in relics of Hinduism, consisting of temples and images. In it was situated the kingdom of Däa, which appears to have flourished in the 12th century, and at which, in the reign of Jayabaya, was composed by a Bramin of the name of Ampusâdah, the paraphrase of the Hindu epic, the Mahabarat, called the Bratayuda. The name, Pranaraga, is Sanscrit, and signifies "the desire of life."

PRAU, is in Malay and Javanese the generic name for any vessel, whether rowing or sailing. The different sorts are distinguished by specific names, according to form, size, use, and nationality.

PRAU (Gunung), that is "boat or ship mountain," from its form, is the name of a mountain of Java with an active volcano, lying between the provinces of Kadoe and Pakalongan. It rises to the height of 6500 feet above the level of the sea, and its table-lands and valleys contain the ruins of many Hindu temples of hewn trachyte of the best architecture, but there exist no inscriptions to tell when or by whom they were built.

PRAYANGAN. This is a name given by the proper Javanese to certain of the Sunda districts of Java. It has been adopted by the Dutch with the corrupt orthography of Priyanger. Prayang, in Javanese signifies a ghost, or wandering spirit of the dead, and Prayangan is "country of ghosts.' The districts in question have been constituted a province by the Dutch, under the name of the Preanger Regencies. This embraces an area of 6077 square miles, and in 1850 had a population of 737,466, which gives little more than 104 inhabitants to the square mile, or not more than one-fourth part the density of some of the most fertile provinces of Java. The country, indeed, although in picturesque beauty equal to any in the world, is very mountainous, and relatively to other portions of the island, not fertile. The Preanger Regencies have been, since the first introduction of coffee, the chief locality for its forced cultivation.

PRINCE OF WALES ISLAND. This is the name which is given to Penang, or Pulo Pinang, by its English founders, an unmeaning piece of flattery to the Prince of Wales of the day, the future George the Fourth. See PENANG.

PROBOLINGO, or, as a Malay would pronounce it, Prabalinga, called also Bangâr, or "the Fetid," on what ground I do not know, is the name of a native district of Java, which now forms part of the Dutch province of Besoekie. The soil of the lower lands of this district, lying between the sea and the slopes of the mountains Tengger, Lamongan, and Iyang, all active volcanos, is of eminent fertility, and the best suited of any of the island for the growth of the sugar-cane, which is extensively cultivated. The great majority of the inhabitants are emigrants from Madura, who began to settle in this part of Java about the middle of the last century, and still continue to migrate to it. They have brought with them from their native island, whose language they continue to speak, that private hereditary right of property which has been nearly obliterated among the proper Javanese, although it exists among the Sundas. The name is, most probably, Sanscrit, the first part of it prabo or prabu, signifying "a lord," and the last linga, the Hindu priapus, an emblem of the worship of Siva, and the whole signifying a place where such an emblem was erected.

PULO, or in the pronunciaation of the Malays, pulao, is equivalent to the nusa of the Javanese, and signifies an island, or more correctly, an islet, for it is rarely applied to any of the larger islands, the idea of insularity in regard to which, is scarcely consistent with the state of knowledge, even of the more cultivated nations of the Archipelago. It is of very frequent occurrence from one end of the Malayan Archipelago to the other, and even where the Malay language is not vernacular, and points, of course, to the extent of the navigation that was familiar to the Malays. The name, however, does not extend to the Philippine Islands, nor to those of the Northern and Southern Pacific oceans.

PULOSARI is the name of a mountain of Bantam in Java, rising to the height of 4000 feet above the level of the sea, and an active volcano.

PULSES. The generic name in Malay and Javanese for all leguminous plants, is kachang, by adding an epithet to which we have the name of the species. Several species are regular objects of cultivation, as Phaseolus max, lunatus and radiatus; Dolichos kachang; Lablab vulgaris; Soja hispida; Cytisus cajan, and Arachis hypogæa. In Java, the greater number of these are cultivated in the dry season from irrigated land, which during the wet had yielded a crop of rice; that is, they form one of the two crops from the same land within the year. The last-named plant, the ground nut, is raised in inferior dry lands, and is the chief source of the lamp-oil consumed by the natives. Most of the cultivated leguminous plants may be judged by the epithets annexed to them to be exotics; thus, Phaseolus lunatus, is called Kachang-China, or Chinese pulse; and Soja hispida, the soy-bean, Kachang-Jâpun, or Japanese pulse; Phaseolus max has a Tâlugu or Telinga name annexed to it, kâdâlé.

Q.

QUEDA. The name of the most northerly of the Malay states on the western side of the Peninsula of Malacca. This is the Portuguese orthography of the name, correctly written Kâdah, and which, following the Portuguese, has been continued by other European nations. The word signifies in Malay "an elephant trap." Queda is bounded to the north by the Siamese territory of Ligor, to the east by the Malay state of Patani, to the south by the state of Perak, and to the west by the sea, and partially by the continental portion of the British territory annexed to Penang. Its length is about 150 miles, and its average breadth about 30, so that it is computed to have an area of 4500 miles. Besides this territory, a chain of many islands, including Lancavy, correctly Langkawi, and Trutao, of considerable size, run along its coasts and form part of it, so that its actual area is probably not much less than that of the county of York. Queda is distinguished from the other states of the Peninsula by the greater amount of its level land. The highest of its mountains is Jerai, an isolated one, which rises to the height of 3894 feet above the level of the sea. It contains no lake, but at least twenty-six rivers, six of which are of considerable size, but all of them obstructed at their mouths by bars, over which at spring tides there is not above 9 feet water. The most considerable of them is that on which the chief place stands, a mere village, and of this the embouchure is in latitude 6° 5′ north. Between the main land and Langkawi and the other islands, indeed, there lies an extensive mud bank, so that vessels of any considerable burden cannot come nearer the coast than four miles.

The geological formation of Queda, generally, is granite, which contains iron and tin, of the last of which near 150 tons used to be produced. The vegetable products are the usual ones of the Peninsula, and the country seems to be better fitted for the production of rice than any of the other states; for, besides feeding its own population, it used, in the time of tranquillity, to furnish Penang with 30,000 quarters of husked rice. All the peculiar Malay fruits, and especially the mangostin and durian, grow in it in great perfection. Among its wild animals, the elephant is very numerous, and is used as a beast of burthen,—even bred, and occasionally exported to the Coromandel coast. The ox, a small compact and hardy breed, and the buffalo of great size, are abundant in the domestic state. The horse does not exist. The whole coast is most abundant in fish, and some of them are of exquisite flavour, especially that called the bawal putih, or white pomfret of the English, which is less rich but more delicate than the turbot.

The inhabitants consist of Malays, of Samsams or Siamese converted to Mohammedanism, and speaking a mixed language of Malay and Siamese; of the peninsular Negritos, of mestizo Telingas speaking both Telugu and Malay, and of a very few Chinese. Before the Siamese invasion and conquest of 1821, the country is believed to have had a population of 50,000, which in 1839 was reduced to 21,000, the rest having been either killed in action, perished by disease and famine, or taken refuge within the British territory. The last of these numbers gives a relative population of less than five inhabitants to the square mile, and even the higher of one under twelve. Indeed, at all times, the greater part of the country seems to have been little better than a primeval jungle.

The history of this state, as of all the others of the Peninsula, unless we except Malacca, is involved in obscurity. The people themselves really know nothing of their origin. My friend, Col. James Lowe, translated a Malay manuscript, entitled "Annals of Queda," but this production is a dateless tissue of rank fable, from which not a grain of reliable knowledge can be gathered. Col. Lowe discovered in the forests some remains of temples, and some inscriptions in the Pali character, and which, consequently, indicated not Malay but Siamese occupation. It would appear that even in the beginning of the 16th century, the Malays had been but partially converted to Mohammedanism. The earliest authentic information we have of Queda is from the Portuguese writer, Barbosa, whose manuscript is dated at Lisbon in 1516, and he describes it as "a place of the kingdom of Siam." "Having," says he, "passed the aforementioned country of Tenassire, and proceeding along the coast of Malacca, there occurs a sea-port called Quedaa, to which an infinite number of ships resort trading in all kinds of merchandise. Here come many Moorish ships from all quarters. Here too is grown much pepper, very good and fine, which is conveyed to Malacca, and thence to China."—Ramusio, vol. i. p. 318. Queda, in common with all the other states of the Peninsula, has been immemorially tributary to Siam, and being with Patani the nearest to it, has been most subject to its direct influence. In token of its subjection, it sends once in three years an offering consisting of an artificial "flower of gold," which is the literal meaning of the name of this offering, Bunga-mas. Notwithstanding this dependence the raja, in 1785, alienated to the British government a portion of his dominions, namely, the island of Penang, and subsequently a further portion of it on the mainland, all without the sanction or even knowledge of his liege, the king of Siam; but still without the right of alienation being disputed. By the cession of Penang, the prince of Queda lost some of the native foreign trade which used to frequent his ports, but this was more than counterbalanced by the annual stipend paid to him by the British government, and by the demand which the new settlement gave rise to for the produce of his country. The revenue which the prince received, including a stipend from the British government had amounted in all to 82,000 Spanish dollars, or near 18,000*l.*, a large sum for a Malay prince. In 1821, the raja was either refractory, or alleged to be so, and the Siamese invaded his country, over-ran it, and after an occupation of several years, abandoned it after ruining it. The prince fled to the British for protection, but had by treaty no claim to assistance. He of course received an asylum.

R.

RÂBABU. The name of a mountain of Java, rising to the height of 10,500 feet above the level of the sea. It seems to be only a corruption or abbreviation of Mârbabu, which see.

RAFFLES, SIR THOMAS STAMFORD, was the son of the commander of a West India merchant ship, and born at sea off the island of Jamaica on the 15th of July, 1781. After a very imperfect education, he was entered as a clerk in the secretary's office at the East India House, at the early age of 15, an inauspicious training which would have made the object of it, under ordinary circumstances, a mere drudge for life. Fortune and his own abilities rescued Sir Stamford from this position, and raised him to eminence and distinction. In 1805, after serving nine years at the India House, he was appointed deputy-secretary to the absurd and extravagant government, with which the authorities at home thought proper then to overlay the little island of Penang, at the time with barely 30,000 inhabitants. This was certainly no field for the active mind of Sir Stamford, but it placed him in a position to obtain an elementary acquaintance with the Malay language, and to acquire the friendship of the celebrated orientalist, Dr. John Leyden, who had visited the island in quest of health, and there acquired himself that polyglot acquaintance with the Malayan languages which gained him so much distinction as an orientalist.

In 1811, it became known that an expedition for the conquest of Java, and the other possessions of the Dutch in the Archipelago, was preparing by the British government of India, and Sir Stamford Raffles repaired to Calcutta, was introduced to the governor-general, the Earl of Minto, by his friend Dr. Leyden, and tendered his services, which in the paucity of information respecting the Archipelago which then existed, were gladly accepted. Sir Stamford was appointed secretary to the Governor-General, who himself accompanied the expedition in person. In this capacity he acted until the conquest was completed, when he was appointed nominally lieutenant-governor, but in reality governor of Java and all its dependencies, with, as matters turned out, the unlucky exception of the Spice Islands, which had been captured the previous year, and placed under a distinct authority. In Java, Sir Stamford found the government still conducted on the old and vicious principle of commercial monopoly and forced labour, and intrepid innovator as he was, he overthrew the whole system. But he was not so successful in the more difficult task of reconstruction. Many errors were committed both by himself and by the officers who served under him, of whom I was one. The changes from one scheme to another were too frequent, the draughts on the treasury of British India became burthensome to it, and Sir Stamford, after an administration of four years, was removed by the government of the Marquess of Hastings, the successor of the Earl of Minto.

After his removal from the government of Java, he returned to England, and during his short stay there, published his History of Java, a work which, although hastily written, is replete with valuable information; and a lasting monument of his ability and industry, the more meritorious when it is considered that the materials for it were collected amidst the distractions of a most stirring and busy administration. In 1817, he was appointed to the government of Bencoolen, with the title of lieutenant-governor. This poor settlement, however, afforded no scope for his ambition and activity. He betook himself, therefore, to the study of natural history; made an enterprising journey into the interior of Sumatra, visiting a part of that great island which no European had ever seen before, and with the view of establishing a commercial emporium and free port in a convenient and central position, he proceeded to Bengal, and laid his scheme before the Marquess of Hastings. This gave rise to the establishment of Singapore in 1819, the most enduring monument of his reputation. In carrying his plan into execution, he encountered obstacles which would have discouraged and baffled a man of less determination, but he was rewarded with a success which was almost immediate, for in his last visit to it in 1823, he saw a miserable village of piratical Malay fishermen already converted into a prosperous commercial community.

Sir Stamford Raffles finally returned to England in 1823, and there, continuing the study of natural history, through his indefatigable activity, the Zoological Society and gardens were formed. His slender frame and weakly constitution contrasted with the energy and activity of his mind. His health had never been good, and in 1826 he died suddenly, from the effect of an abscess on the brain. Activity, industry, and political courage were the most remarkable endowments of his character. In the transaction of public business he was ready, rapid, and expert,—partly the result of early training, but far more of innate energy and ability. He was not, perhaps, an original thinker, but readily adopted the notions of others,—not always with adequate discrimination. Thus, without much time for examination, seeing it lauded by its partisans, he adopted, and at once carried into execution among the then five millions of inhabitants of Java, the fanciful and pernicious Indian revenue system called the Ryotwarry, and saw it break down even before he had himself quitted the administration of the island.

RAJA. This Sanscrit name for a king or sovereign prince is current nearly throughout the whole Malay Archipelago, usually as a synonym with a native word, or with the well known Arabic one of Sultan.

RAJANG. The name of a river of the north-western coast of Borneo, and described by Mr. Robert Burns, who had ascended it, as the finest and, perhaps, the largest of the island. It falls into the sea by six different mouths, the largest of which is in latitude 4° 40′ north. This is easy of entrance for ships of considerable burthen, having, on its bar at low water, a depth of three fathoms, and a rise and fall of tide of ten feet. Within the bar the depth increases to eight and ten fathoms, and it is navigable for large vessels as far as the tide reaches, which is up to the great rapids, or from 90 to 100 miles. The rapids are fully two miles in length, and are formed by the river in breaking through a range of hills. Their ascent is difficult and dangerous, from the many rocks and islets which intervene, around which the river rushes with fearful rapidity. These, unfortunately, offer, at present, an almost unsurmountable obstacle to the development of the extensive coal fields and deposits of iron ore which characterises the country above them. The country traversed by the Rajang is in the occupation of the Kayan nation, the most numerous, powerful, and civilised of the wild tribes of Borneo, but, with the exception of rare patches of cultivation, it is a continuous jungle.

RÂKAN, frequently written in our charts, Reccan, is the name of a river of the north-eastern side of Sumatra. The mouth of the Râkan is, at its widest part, about fifteen miles broad. Within are two islets, the largest of which is, in north latitude, 2° 10′ and east longitude 100° 36′ 50″. The channel between them, shallow, and never three miles wide, forms the entrance to the river. After ascending the Râkan for about eight or nine miles, its breadth contracts to four, and afterwards to two miles, when it is joined by a tributary to its right, and another to its left bank. Towards its debouchement, the Râkan, which seems here to be but an estuary, is almost a dry bed at low water spring tides. The navigation is extremely dangerous, owing to the excessive rapidity of the tides, which, at springs, run at the rate of seven miles an hour, the rise and fall of water amounting to thirty feet. The river moreover, like others in its neighbourhood, is subject to a bore or tidal wave which adds to the danger of its navigation. The country, on the lower portion of the Râkan, is in the possession of scattered Malay settlers, and the upper inhabited by the Batak nation.

RAMA. This Hindu demi-god, and all the personages of the Sanscrit poem which takes its name from him, with his own adventures in search of his stolen wife Sita, are nearly as familiar to the Malays, and more especially to the Javanese, as they are to the Hindus themselves. The Javanese have poems, both in the ancient and modern tongue, narrating the adventures of Rama, and from these have been formed romances in prose by the Malays. These adventures, too, form the most frequent subject of the drama of both people.

RAMBUTAN. The name of an esculent fruit, the produce of a tree of moderate size (Nephelium lappaceum). Like the durian and mangostin, it is peculiar to the Malayan Archipelago. The semi-transparent, subacid pulp which envelopes the seed is of grateful taste, but the quantity is too small to make the fruit be much valued. The native name is derived from the word rambut, the human hair of the head, taken from the shaggy rind of the fruit.

RAMI. This is the name of a species of nettle,—Urtica estuans, the fibre of which is of extraordinary tenacity, and used by the natives of the Archipelago in the fabrication of cordage, fishing lines, and fishing nets. It is supposed to be the same plant, or a species of the same genus which is used in several parts of continental India, for similar purposes, as well as that which is the material of the grass-cloth of China. It is not cultivated by the Malays or Javanese, but is abundant in the wild state.

RANUM is the name of a mountain of the eastern end of Java, and within the province of Besuki, 8500 feet high, but without an active volcano.

RANTAU, in Malay, signifies, literally, the reach of a river or of a narrow strait, and from thence a district of country. It is the specific name of one of four low islands close to the eastern coast of Sumatra, opposite to that portion of the Malay peninsula which lies between Malacca and Singapore. The island is about forty-five miles long and fifteen broad, in its widest part. The few inhabitants consist of Malays, and the chief, if not only produce for exportation is crude sago, sent to Singapore to be there manufactured by the Chinese.

RAPURAPU. The name of an uninhabited islet, one of several, at the entrance of the great bay of Albay, on the eastern side of Luzon, in the Philippine Archipelago. Latitude 13° 22′.

RAT. The common brown rat is frequent all over the Malay and Philippine Archipelagos,—wherever there is a considerable population. In Singapore, until the formation of the British Settlement, there were very few, but immediately after, they appeared in vast numbers, and I have nowhere seen them so numerous. The Malay and Javanese name for the rat is tikus, and it is the same for the mouse, for there is no distiction between them, except as large and small. The word is purely native, and there is no other, except in the recondite Javanese, the Sanscrit one musika. There is a name in Javanese, even for the young mouse, chindil. It seems probable that the word tikus belonged, originally, to the mouse only, as being indigenous, and that the brown rat was brought to the islands, as to other countries, from the continent of India, although there be no record of the time or manner of its introduction.

RATAN (Calamus). In Malay, rotan, an abbreviation of raotan, from the verb raot, to pare or trim, that is, the object pared or trimmed. Of this universal product of the forests of the islands, the name, as might be expected, is different in all the different languages. Thus, in Javanese, it is pânjalin, and in Sunda kowe. The plants which yield ratans are considered by botanists as a genus of the family of palms, which consists of many species, from the girth of a goose-quill to that of a stout walking-stick. They are abundant in all the forests of the Malay and Philippine Archipelagos, and are everywhere extensively used as cordage or ligatures, or in the manufacture of mats and basket-work. These singular plants creep along the ground or climb trees, and, according to the species, to the length of from 100 to 1200 feet. The principal places of production for the general market are Sumatra, Borneo, and the Peninsula. By far the most valuable, probably a distinct species, is brought from Banjarmassin on the southern coast of Borneo, for in the market they are worth about 150 per cent. more than any others. A vast quantity of ratans are exported from the Malay Archipelago to Europe, Hindustan, and China.

RAWA, literally, in Malay and Javanese, a morass or lake. It is the specific name of an inland country of Sumatra, drained by the great river Râkan, which disembogues in the Straits of Malacca. Its population is of the Malay nation, and Mr. Logan has estimated it at 25,000, occupying an area of 1600 miles, which gives from fifteen to sixteen inhabitants to the square mile, a poor rate for a people who have had for ages a knowledge of the common arts, and possessed the art of phonetic writing.

REJANG. This is the name of one of the most civilised nations of Sumatra, having a peculiar language in an original written character. The country of this people is bounded to the north-east by the territory of Palembang, to the south-east by that of the Lampung nation, to the north-east by the Malays of Anak-Sungai, and to the south-west by the sea. Mr. Logan has estimated the area of the country at 4500 miles square, and its population at 72,000, or at the rate of sixteen inhabitants to a square mile.

The Rejangs, like the Malays, are divided into tribes (suku), and every village is ruled by a head-man, called a Dupati, which, however, seems only a corruption of the Sanskrit Adipati, taken most likely from the Javanese. For the transaction of public affairs, all the chiefs of villages situated on the same river meet in council, and are then denominated proatins, which seems to be a native word, and not Malay or Javanese. Over this assembly presides a chief, with the Javanese title of pangeran or prince. It is from this people that Mr. Marsden has drawn his general character of the natives of Sumatra. "The Sumatran of the interior country," says he, "though partaking in some degree of the Malayan vices, and this partly from the contagion of example, possesses many exclusive virtues; but they are more properly of the negative than the positive kind. He is mild, peaceable, and forbearing, unless his anger be roused by violent provocation, when he is implacable in his resentments. He is temperate and sober, being equally abstemious in meat and drink. The diet of the natives is mostly vegetable. Water is their only beverage, and although they kill a fowl or a goat for a stranger whom, perhaps, they have never seen before, nor ever expect to see again, they are rarely guilty of that extravagance for themselves; not even at their festivals (bimbang), where there is plenty of meat, do they eat much of anything but rice. Their hospitality is extreme, and bounded by their ability alone. Their manners are simple; they are generally, except among the chiefs, devoid of the Malay cunning and chicane, yet endued with a quickness of apprehension, and on many occasions discovering a considerable degree of penetration and sagacity. In respect to women, they are remarkably continent, without any share of insensibility. They are modest, particularly guarded in their expressions, courteous in their behaviour, grave in their deportment, being seldom or never excited to laughter, and patient to a great degree. On the other hand they are litigious, indolent, addicted to gaming, dishonest in their dealings with strangers, which they esteem no moral defect, suspicious, regardless of truth, mean in their transactions, and servile. Although cleanly in their persons, they are dirty in their apparel, which they never wash. They are careless and improvident of the future, because their wants are few, for though poor, they are not necessitous, nature supplying, with extraordinary facility, whatever she has made necessary for their existence."—History of Sumatra, p. 208.

It was among the Rejangs that the English established themselves in the latter part of the seventeenth century, persevering for 140 years in the attempt to create wealth by the forced culture and monopoly of black pepper. Their chief station here was Bencoolen, in south latitude 3° 47′ 30″, and east longitude 102° 18′. This place, with the territory annexed to it, now forms a district of the Netherland territory of Sumatra, having been exchanged for Malacca in 1824. See BENCOOLEN.

REMBANG. The name of a province of Java, situated on the northern side of the island, its principal town, of the same name, lying in south latitude 6° 40′ 30″, and east longitude, 111° 16′40″. It contains an area of 1983 square miles, and in 1850 had a population of 536,478 souls, equal to 270 inhabitants to the square mile. Rembang contains some of the principal teak forests of Java, said to embrace one half its surface. Its staple products are rice, sugar, coffee, and tobacco. The fisheries on its coasts are considerable, and it produces bay salt to the yearly amount of about 10,000 tons. In 1845 its horned cattle were reckoned to amount to 116,000, and its horses to 16,800.

RESIN and Gum, in Malay and Javanese, damar. See DAMAR.

RETTEH, correctly **RÂTEH.** This is the name of a place situated on the left bank of a river on the eastern side of Sumatra, which falls into a bay opposite to the tin-producing island of Singkep, the most southerly of the numerous group which almost chokes up the eastern end of the Straits of Malacca. Retteh was, at one time, in the occupation of the Lanuns of Mindano, and prior to the establishment of the British settlement of Singapore and the Netherland one of Rhio, a noted haunt of pirates.

RHIO in the English, and **RIOUW** in the Dutch orthography, but correctly **RIYAU**, is the name of the Dutch settlement established by the government of the Netherlands shortly after that of Singapore by the English, and like it, and in imitation of it, a free port. It lies south of Singapore, and distant from it about 50 miles. It is situated on a strait formed by several small islands with the main land of the island of Bintang. The town lies on the northern shore of a promontory of Bintang called Tanjung Pinang, or Areca Point, but which, however, is almost insulated by a shallow strait. North of this promontory is the island of Singarang, and west of it that of Pâningat. The harbour of Rhio consists of an outer with a depth of four and five fathoms, and an inner one, not exceeding two fathoms. These are sheltered by the larger island of Bintang from the north-eastern monsoon, the only one that is felt heavily in this part of the Straits of Malacca. The small town is neat and clean, with a church and a small fort. The staple articles exported from Rhio are the black pepper and gambir of the large islands of Bintang and Batam, cultivated by the Chinese who are settled in great numbers on both. The soil of these two islands consisting, like that of the Peninsula, of decomposed laterite or cellular clay iron ore and granite, seems peculiarly favourable to the growth of the two plants in question, although ill adapted to that of corn or similar products. The establishment of Rhio, instead of proving unfavourable to that of the neighbouring one of Singapore, has contributed much to its prosperity, while it has itself gained largely by its supposed rival, with which, after Java, it conducts its principal trade. The port lies in latitude 54′ 40″ north, and east longitude 104° 23′.

RHIO-LINGGA ARCHIPELAGO. This is the name which has been lately given by Dutch geographers to the numerous group of islands, islets, rocks, and shoals which lie between Sumatra and the Peninsula towards the eastern end of the Straits of Malacca. When the Malays refer to it they usually call it Tanah-sâlat, that is the "land of straits." The equator runs through it; to the east it is washed by the China Sea, and to the south-east bounded by the island of Banca.

Dutch writers have divided this Archipelago into two parts, a northern and a southern, distinguishing each by the name of its largest island, namely, Bintang for the first, and Lingga for the last. The Bintang group comprises the following considerable islands, namely, the island of this name, Batam or Batang, Galang or Gallat, Bulang, Chumbul, Sugi, Durian, Krimun and Sagupong. Singapore also naturally belongs to it, but is not included by Dutch writers. The southern group comprises only two considerable islands, namely, Lingga, which gives it its name, and Singkep. Besides small straits, practicable only for boats, no fewer than nine navigable ones afford routes through this Archipelago. Of these, the most important and frequented are the Straits of Rhio, which lie between Bintang on the one side, and Galang and Batam on the other, and that of Singapore, having the island of this name and the Malay Peninsula to the north, with Batam and Bintang to the south.

The monsoons and seasons of rain are much more irregular and uncertain in this Archipelago than in places at a greater distance from the equator. The north-east monsoon prevails from November to April inclusive, and the south-west in the opposite half of the year. The influence of the monsoons which belong to the southern hemisphere are not felt. The greatest quantity of rain falls in the months of November and December, and in those of July and August. There is, in fact, no regular period of continuous rain, showers, seldom excessive, falling throughout the year.

The geological formation of all the islands of this Archipelago is the same as that of the Malay Peninsula, and consists of granite and sandstone, with laterite or clay iron ore. The metals found are iron and tin. The land usually rises from 100 to 200 feet above the level of the sea, and is generally hilly, the hills being round or table-topped. At a few points, however, it rises to the elevation of mountains. Thus the peak of Lingga is 3755 English feet above the level of the sea; the mountain called Lanjut in the island of Sinkep, 1597, and the Saddle-mount on Bintang, 1368 feet.

All the islands are with the exception of a very few rare spots in a state of nature, covered with a tall forest, impenetrable wherever the land is low and marshy, and not easily penetrated anywhere. The soil, usually a stiff clay, is unproductive of plants useful to man, with the exception of a few articles peculiarly congenial to it, the coco-palm, the black pepper vine, the gambir plant, and some fruits native or long acclimated. Of the gambir, now so useful in the arts, this Archipelago is the principal place of production. The forests yield the usual products, honey and wax, with some dyeing and aromatic plants. Mr. Kops, an officer of the Dutch Royal Navy, who has rendered the best account of the Archipelago, enumerates about 80 different forest trees either yielding timber of fair quality, or some other useful product. Among these are the trees which yield gutta-percha, India rubber, damar, and wood oil.

The aboriginal population of this Archipelago is the Malay nation, that is a people speaking the Malay language. This is divided into three classes, according to social condition, namely, men of the shore or dry land, having their dwellings on land and to a greater or less extent cultivating the soil; men of the sea, living exclusively in their boats, and subsisting by fishing, and men of the forests, or wild men, leading a wandering life in the woods, and subsisting on their spontaneous products. The native terms for these classes are orang-darat, orang-laut, and orang-utan, literally "men of the dry land," "men of the sea," and "men of the forest." The Chinese are, probably, at present not less numerous in this Archipelago than the native inhabitants, attracted to it chiefly by the suitableness of the soil for the growth of gambir and black pepper, of both which they are the chief cultivators. No estimate either of their number or of that of the native inhabitants has been given, but in proportion to the area of the land, it is certain that the amount of both is very inconsiderable.

RICE (Oryza sativa). This is the universal bread-corn of all the nations of both the Malay and Philippine Archipelagos that have attained any considerable amount of civilisation, and the existence of its culture among the wild tribes may be looked upon as the beginning of their social advancement. Rice bears the same relation to other corns among the natives of these islands as indeed it does with all the intertropical people of Asia, that wheat does to other corns among the nations of the temperate regions of Europe and Asia. As food, it is more esteemed than any other grain, and its cultivation demands more skill and labour than any other product of husbandry. It is only in the most fertile parts of both Archipelagos that more of it is grown than suffices for local consumption. The principal of these are Java, Bali, Lomboc, Luzon, and Panay, all of them countries of volcanic formation, of great fertility of soil, and supplied with easy means of irrigation. Many parts of the Archipelagos, indeed, do not produce rice enough for their own consumption, and a few, such as the Spice Islands, none at all. This corn, therefore, must have been from the earliest times the chief staple of the internal commerce of the islands. Thus, we find Malacca to have been wholly supplied from Java at the first appearance of the Portuguese. Such also was the case with the Spice Islands, and, indeed, continues to be so to the present day. Even now the European settlements within the Straits of Malacca, and in Borneo and Sumatra are in a great measure fed from Java, Bali, and Lomboc.

There is no evidence to show that rice is other than an indigenous product of the Malayan Archipelago, and I am disposed to think that its first culture is traceable to Java. Its own name in its different forms and all the terms connected with its culture are native and not foreign. Thus the name of the corn in the husk, the usual form in which it is presented, is universally native in every tongue, the only exception being the Sanscrit word, dahna, which belongs to the recondite language of Java. A few examples may be given. In Javanese the word is pari, and so it is in Sunda and Lampung, while in Malay, Bali, and Madurese, by turning the liquid r into a palatal d·, a frequent practice in the Malayan languages, it becomes padi, now almost naturalised in our own language. In the Philippine tongues the letter *r* not existing, an *l* or an *s* is substituted for it, as is the case in several other instances, and the Javanese pari thus becomes pali, or pasi. In the languages of remote Timur the initial letter is elided, and we have the word as ari. The Javanese name has extended even to far Madagascar, and here, by substituting one labial for another, we find it as vari. The name for husked or clean rice has also had a large, although not so wide a diffusion, being confined to the languages of the Malayan Archipelago. The Javanese name is băras, and this, with various corruptions, is to be found in at least twenty different languages. In Malay it is bras, in Sunda bias, in the Bugis of Celebes warasa and barasa. The term for artificially irrigated land is also very widely spread over the Malayan Archipelago, but confined to it, for the practice itself has not extended to the Philippines. In Javanese it is sawah, and so it is in Malay, while the sole variation I see in it is in the Lampung, where the labial w becomes the labial b. The name for the rice mortar, lăsung, extends over the whole Malayan Archipelago, and with the slight corruption of losong, is found also over the Philippine. No word whatever belonging to rice exists in any language of the islands of the Pacific Ocean, although in them are found the Malayan names for the coco-palm, the sugar-cane, and the yam. Such could not have existed, since the culture of this corn was unknown to their inhabitants when they were discovered by Europeans. Had it reached them, there certainly would have been no cannibalism, and they would have been in a much higher state of civilisation than that which they had attained when discovered.

The numerous varieties of rice in cultivation are proof that this corn has been for many ages in cultivation. Such varieties exist with all corns that have been for ages under culture, but probably they are more multifarious in the case of rice than of any other, for the Javanese reckon no fewer than forty-six, and the people of the

Philippines, who have a greater variety of climate, carry the number up to ninety. The only material distinctions in these consist in the sorts grown respectively in dry and in irrigated land, and those which take a longer or a shorter time to ripen. The dry and wet land corns differ only in the habit of growing with or without the help of irrigation, very much like the difference between our European corns which are sown as autumn or spring crops. In Java, when a single annual crop only is taken, the grain chosen is that which takes about seven months to come to maturity, but when two crops are taken from the same land within the year, the corn of more rapid growth, although less productive, is preferred. In all warm countries a broad distinction is drawn between irrigated and unirrigated land, and this distinction is widest when the object of cultivation is rice, to which a copious irrigation is more congenial than to any other crop. As a general rule, regularly irrigated land, as tested by the amount of rent, is from five to ten-fold more valuable than dry land of the same natural fertility. In Java the land is permanently laid out into small chequered fields of a perch or two each, surrounded by a dyke, not exceeding a foot high, to retain the water, which is frequently supplied by brooks and rivers. This is the kind of land known properly by the word "sawah," already mentioned. It is the most skilful exercise of Javanese husbandry, and is not known in the Philippines, where the copious periodical rains alone are relied on. Spanish writers quote this as evidence of the superior fertility of the Philippines, whereas it is, in fact, only proof of a ruder husbandry. The Javanese pursue the culture of their favourite crop with pleasure, and consider it more an enjoyment than a task. Such, also, is the case with the Philippine islanders. "It costs the Indian," says a Spanish writer, "no trouble. On the contrary, it is to him a source of pleasure, for he loves the water and the mud as much as the buffalo, the companion of his labour."

RICINUS COMMUNIS, the castor-oil plant, is cultivated throughout the Malayan Archipelago, but more especially in Java, and in so far as the natives are concerned, only for lamp-oil, its medicinal use being unknown to them. It is a hardy, prolific plant, growing in very indifferent dry lands, and with small care. The most frequent name for it is jarak, and such we find it in the Malay and Javanese, but in the Sunda and Madurese languages it is called kaliki. Both are purely native words, and there is no ground for believing that it was introduced from any foreign country. It is frequently found wild, but with a plant so easily propagated and so hardy, this is no sufficient proof of its being indigenous. As the oil is known to mix well with the alkalis, it is probable that, economically produced, it might be used in the manufacture of soap.

RINCHI. This is the most usual name by which the sect of purest Mahommedans, which sprung up in Sumatra about the beginning of the present century, is known. They are the same that are also called Padri and Orang-putih, "white men," that is, men dressed in white. I am unacquainted with the literal meaning of the word Rinchi. It is probably, however, an abbreviation of korïnchi. See MENANGKABO.

RINGGIT. This is the name of a mountain of Java, situated towards its eastern end, and in the district of Panarukuan, celebrated for the great and destructive volcanic eruption which took place from it in the year 1586, the last on a large scale which has occurred in Java. The mountain is of no great height, rising only to 4200 feet above the level of the sea. The name in Javanese signifies a scenic figure or puppet. See VOLCANO.

ROMA. This is the name of the largest of a cluster of islets lying east of Wetter, and north-east of Timur, in south latitude 7° 30′. It is about six leagues in circumference, and consists of high land. The inhabitants are of the Malayan or brown-complexioned race, inoffensive, industrious fishermen, and have been converted to Christianity. Roma produces good timber, and furnishes bees'-wax, and tortoise-shell for exportation.

ROMANIA POINT. This is the name given in our maps to the most southerly point of the Malay Peninsula, and consequently, of the Continent of Asia. It is in north latitude 1° 22′ 30″. The origin of the name is unknown, but probably Portuguese. In Malay it is called Tanjung-pañusu, literally "wet-nurse cape." The whole country near this last joint of the tail of Asia, the fertile mother of so many civilisations, is a continuous forest, without human inhabitants, and the abode of the tiger and wild boar.

ROTTI, is the name of a small island lying off the western end of Timur, and distant from it about twenty miles. Its length is about 60 miles, its greatest breadth about 38, and its area 492 geographical square miles. The surface of the island is rugged, rocky, full of fastnesses, and easily defensible against an enemy, but scantily supplied with water. The objects of culture are, a small quantity of rice, maiz, millet, yams, and sweet potatoes, with the lontar-palm for its sugar. The principal domestic animals are the horse and buffalo, the first considered a superior breed. The only articles of export are horses and the sugar of the lontar or Borassus flabelliformis. The inhabitants of Rotti are distinguished from those of Timur and of the neighbouring island of Savoe, by a darker complexion, more prominent features, and lank instead of frizzled hair. Their houses, instead of being like those of Timur, built on the ground, are raised on tall posts, in the Malay manner, and under them they bury their dead. A few of the inhabitants have been converted to Christianity, the rest remaining pagans. Their language is peculiar, with an intermixture of Timurean, Malay, and Javanese words. The whole island is divided into petty independent states, of which no fewer than fifteen are enumerated,—an order of society seemingly arising from the physical aspect of the country. Rotti forms a dependency of the Netherland government of Coepang in Timur.

RUMBOWE (correctly **RÂMBAU**), is the name of a very small inland Malay state of the Peninsula of Malacca, lying between Salangor to the north, and Malacca to the west. The Malay population is computed not to exceed 9000, divided into eight tribes or sukus, each ruled by elective chiefs called batin, who form a council of government presided over by a chief, also elective, with the title of Pângulu, literally "headman." Rumbowe, besides its Malay inhabitants, has several wild tribes, such as the Udai, the Jakun, and the Sakai, but no negritos.

RUMPF (GEORGE EVERARD); Latinised **RUMPHIUS**. The celebrated author of the "Hortus Amboinense" was, like several other persons who acquired distinction in the Indian service of the Dutch, a German, having been a native of Solms, in Hesse Cassel. He was born about the year 1626, and educated as a physician at Hanau. At the age of twenty-eight he proceeded to India, and arriving at Batavia, entered the civil, or rather mercantile service of the East India Company, in which he attained the rank of a senior merchant, being stationed at Amboyna, where he passed the remainder of his life. At the age of forty-two, when contemplating a return to Europe, he was struck blind by gutta serena, yet continued in that state to prosecute his researches in natural history. He died at Amboyna in 1693, at the age of sixty-seven. The naturalists of the French Expedition of D'Entrecasteaux are stated to have discovered his tomb, after the neglect of a century. Yet the English, after occupying the island twice over for several years, and making diligent search, were unable to find it. The first literary performance of Rumphius was a civil history of the Moluccas, still in manuscript, and of which there exist several copies besides the two in the Dutch archives, one of them deposited by myself in the Library of the Advocates in Edinburgh. His great work, the "Herbarium Amboinense," was not published until forty-eight years after his death, when it was rescued from the Dutch archives by Burman, and the original, which was in Latin, printed along with a Dutch translation. Rumphius' account of plants contains many which are not peculiar to the little island of Amboyna, and embraces their names and synonyms, their botanical description, their flowering seasons, their habitats, their uses, and the modes of culture of such as are objects of cultivation. He is stated not to have been a professed botanist, but having received a medical education, which necessarily included a certain acquaintance with plants, he was probably as much so as most of his cotemporaries in an age when botany hardly existed as a science.

Rumphius was evidently a man of talents, sound sense, and indefatigable industry. Much of his information was obtained through the natives of the country, and his work affords ample evidence of his familiarity with their language. It was he that taught the natives of Amboyna the improved process for preparing sago, which is still followed by them, and for which his name is still remembered.

RUPAT. The name of a considerable island, divided from the mainland of Sumatra by a very narrow strait, and lying nearly opposite to the town of Malacca, the straits here not exceeding twenty-five miles broad. The island is, for the most part, a sheer jungle, having a few Malay fishermen on its coast, with some of the wild unconverted people of the same race, called Sakai in the interior.

S.

SACRIFICE. In Malay and Javanese the word sâmbâlih signifies "to sacrifice with religious rites," and sâmbâlihan, a derivative from it, is a "sacrifice or immolation." These words, which are native, are now used for the slaughter of animals with the forms of the Mahommedan religion, but what kind of sacrifice they referred to before conversion to this faith, it is difficult to conjecture. It cannot have been the self-sacrifice of the widow or concubine on the funeral-pile of the husband, for that is known by a different name,—bela, signifying "expiation or atonement." The Arabic word for a sacrifice or atonement,—kurban, is occasionally employed.

SADDLE. Although the horse was unknown to the inhabitants of the Philippines before it was introduced by the Spaniards, the people of Java, Celebes, and the interior of several parts of Sumatra, with Bali, Lomboc, and Sumbawa, had been in possession of it immemorially, using it, however, only for the saddle. In Javanese the name for the saddle is a native one,—kâkapa, while that in Malay is pâlana, which is Persian, with the frequent use of sela, a corruption of the Portuguese silla. The bridle, always a snaffle or plain single bit, is called in Javanese kândale, and in Malay kakang, abbreviated kang. At present, at least, the stirrup, although unknown, as is believed, to the Greeks and Romans, is in use among all the islanders, but except in the language of the Sundas of Java, I can discover no name for it. The Sunda one is sanggawâdi, a compound word, which literally signifies "guard-fear," from which there may be ground to suspect that it is only of recent introduction. The women of Java, it may be noticed, ride on horseback with the same seat as the men.

SAFFLOWER; the Carthamus tinctorius of botanists. This plant, which has a geographical distribution, extending from the South of Europe and Egypt to the equator, is well known in the Malayan Archipelago, being cultivated for the colouring matter of its flowers, but not for the oil of its seeds. Bali is the place in which it is chiefly grown, and from whence it is distributed, as an article of trade, to other parts of the Archipelago. The name by which it is universally known, kasumba, is Sanscrit; and the Malays, to distinguish it from arnotto, the Bixa orellana, add the epithet Jawa or Javanese, giving to the latter that of kling, or the safflower of Telingana. There can, therefore, be little doubt of its being an exotic, and introduced, like indigo, by the Hindus; but when, or how, is unknown.

SAGO, in Malay, Javanese, and all the other languages of the Archipelago, sagu, most probably a word of one of the languages of the Moluccas. It is, probably, the name of the farina or meal, for each species of the genus of palms producing it has its own specific name. Of these there are supposed to be five, the most frequently cultivated of which are the râmbiya, Sagus Konigii or Metroxylon sago, and the bamban or Sagus lævis. All the species much resemble each other, and all yield an immense quantity of farina, the wood being a mere shell, containing a mass of medulla. Sago trees are found in every part of the Malayan Archipelago and Philippines, as far as Mindano, wherever there is a genial soil for them, and this soil consists of a marsh or bog, composed of decayed land vegetables, near the sea, but excluding tidal action. They are most abundant in the eastern parts of the Malay Archipelago, as the Moluccas and neighbouring islands, with New Guinea and Borneo, and in the Philippines, Mindano. In all these, they are more or less the bread of the inhabitants. From these countries, they are believed to have been introduced into Sumatra and the Malay Peninsula.

The sagos differ from all other palms in two important particulars. They propagate themselves by lateral shoots, as well as by seed, like the banana, and they die after producing fruit. From the first of these properties, a sago plantation once formed is perpetual. The trees are cultivated in small patches, and a man and his family are thought, without much care, to be equal to the management of a plantation of 100 square fathoms, which will contain 400 trees. The trees are cut down immediately before bearing fruit, which is usually about the age of 15 years. "When," says Mr. Logan, who has given by far the best and fullest account of the culture and manufacture that has ever been published, "a plantation has once arrived at maturity, there will be a constant harvest, because the natural mode of growth secures a continued succession of new plants from the time those first planted have begun to extend their roots, and this succession can be regulated by the knife in any manner the planter desires. The sago-tree when cut down and the top severed from it is a cylinder about 20 inches in diameter, and from 15 to 20 feet in height. Assuming 20 inches as the diameter and 15 feet as the height of the trees, the contents will be nearly 26 bushels, and allowing one half for woody fibre, there will remain 13 bushels of starch, which agrees very closely with our previous calculation of 700 pounds for each tree or 12½ bushels. It may give some idea of the enormous rate of this produce, if it be considered that three trees yield more nutritive matter than an acre of wheat, and six trees more than an acre of potatoes. An acre of sago, if cut down at one harvest will yield 5220 bushels, or as much as 163 acres of wheat, so that according as we allow 7 or 15 years for the growth of a tree, an acre of sago is equal in annual produce to 23 or to 10 acres of wheat." Journal of the Indian Archipelago, vol. 3. p. 312.

Sago is the sole bread of the inhabitants of the Spice Islands and of New Guinea, and its neighbouring islands, but of no other part of the Archipelago. In the Malay countries it is only the food of the wild tribes, and is hardly used by the Malays themselves. In Mindano it is consumed only by the poorer classes, and in Java, Bali, and Lomboc, fertile in rice, it is altogether unknown as an article of food. It is far from being either so palatable or nutritious as it is prolific, and is never preferred, even where it is most abundant, to rice. It has the obvious disadvantage of being the lowest quality of farinaceous food, and living on which it is impossible to fall back on any other. In this respect it is like the potato or the banana, although over the first of these it possesses the advantage of the crop being less liable to failure; if, indeed, liable to it at all. One thing is certain, that no nation of the Archipelago, of whom it has been the chief vegetable diet, has ever acquired any respectable amount of civilisation. Those doing so, who had attained the greatest degree of it, were the inhabitants of the small islands producing spices, and they owed their advancement to the trade they carried on in these commodities, but even these had neither a kalendar nor a written language, and received the useful metals and their clothing from the nations of the west.

The granulated farina of sago, of a dirty brown colour, used to be exported from the Archipelago in small quantities, under the old system of monopoly, but about the time when the trade with Europe was first thrown open in 1814, the Chinese of Malacca began to prepare a much superior article, known in commerce under the name of pearl sago. Of this and of sago flower, or the ungranulated starch, Singapore is, at present, the chief place of manufacture and principal mart, the Chinese being the sole manufacturers, and the raw material being brought from various neighbouring countries, but chiefly from the north-western coast of Borneo, and the north-eastern of Sumatra with its adjacent islands from Siak to Indragiri. In the year 1847-48 the quantity of sago exported from Singapore was about 80,000 cwt., worth on the spot about 45,000*l*.

SAKA. This is the name of a celebrated personage of Southern India, and the same as Salivana, the founder of an era that is called after him, and which the Hindus introduced into the Archipelago. It dates 78 years after Christ, and stills exists in Bali, and nominally in Java, for here, in consequence of the adoption of lunar time in A.D. 1633, the years no longer correspond. The Javanese, prefixing the word Aji, signifying in their language king, to the name of Saka, fable this personage to have arrived with a colony from India in the first year of his own time, and to have been the introducer into their island of letters and civilisation. This is a good example of the manner in which the early chronology of this people is fabricated.

SAKAI. This is one of the most frequent names given by the civilised Malays to the rude tribes unconverted to Mahommedanism inhabiting the interior of the Malay Peninsula from Perak southward, as well as the opposite coast of Sumatra and its islands. These are of the same race and apparently of the same nation as the Malays themselves, for they speak a rude dialect of their language. Generally, they are an inoffensive and simple people, living by hunting, but occasionally practising the culture of rice, or the sago palm. The Malays, according to their localities or states of civilisation, divide them into forest or wild, and tame or docile, expressed in their language by the words utan and jinak. See ORANG-LAUT.

SALAWATI. The name of an island lying off the western point of New Guinea, having the island of Balanta to the north-west. It is computed to have an area of 528 square geographical miles.

SALAYAR. The name of a considerable island lying off the end of the south western peninsula of Celebes. Its length runs from north to south, and is about 40 miles, but its breadth is small, and its whole area, including some neighbouring islets annexed to it is but 720 geographical square miles. In 1824, the whole population, including that of dependent islets, was 30,524, so that it is one of the most populous parts of Celebes. It raises, at present, a sufficiency of food for its own maintenance, although before a burthen to the Dutch treasury, and this revolution has resulted from the abolition of monopolies. The teak tree has been introduced into Salayar from Java, and appears to flourish. The straits which divide it from the main-land of Celebes are the highway to and from the Spice Islands, and in them is first experienced the change of seasons, between the western and eastern halves of the Archipelago, in which the rainy season is reversed, and by which they conform, to the west with the north-westerly, and in the east with the south-easterly monsoon.

SALIBABO. See TALANT.

SALT. The name for culinary salt in Malay is garâm, and in Javanese uyak, the last of these words, with trifling corruptions extending to all the languages of the countries in the neighbourhood of Java, as Bali, Madura, and the country of the Lampungs in Sumatra. I know no place in the Malay and Philippine Archipelago, in which salt is made by the cheap process of solar evaporation, except some parts of the northern coast of Java, and the province of Pangasinan on the western side of Luzon; and this, no doubt from the absence of land suited for the formation of salt-pans, and the want of sufficient heat accompanied by drought for evaporation. From all we know of the coasts of the other islands, the land is either too elevated or it is skirted with mangroves, or the shore is so flushed with fresh water, so as to render them wholly unfit for this process. In Borneo, the ashes of littoral plants are lixiviated in order to obtain from them an impure muriate of soda, and the same practice seems to be followed in several of the Philippine Islands. Generally, however, the islands of both Archipelagos are supplied from Java or Luzon, and to a large extent from foreign countries producing a cheap bay-salt, especially the Coromandel coast of India, Siam and Cochin-China. On some parts of the southern coast of Java an impure salt is obtained, from boiling a concentrated brine, obtained by mixing with common salt water sea-sand impregnated with salt previously watered from the sea, as a gardener would water a flower-bed. With the exception of a small quantity employed in curing fish, all the salt of the islands is used only as a common condiment. It is everywhere subjected to a custom duty, but it forms nowhere the subject of an excise tax or a monopoly, except in Java, where it realises to the Netherland government an annual revenue of about 400,000*l*.

SALTPETRE. The name for this commodity in Javanese and Malay, indeed, with some corruptions, in all the languages of the Malay and Philippine Archipelagos, is sândawa. It is obtained from the decomposed dung of birds and bats in caves. To what purpose it was applied before the knowledge of gunpowder, is uncertain, but, probably, to the manufacture of fire-works. It is the name which the Javanese apply to gunpowder, and it is entirely a native word.

SÂMANG. This is the name which the Malays give to the race of small negros found in the mountains of the Malay peninsula. See NEGROS and NEW GUINEA.

SAMAUW or SAMAO, is the name of a small island lying off the western end of Timur, separated from it by a safe navigable passage, three miles broad, with good anchorage and shelter in the south-west monsoon, when there is none in the road of the Dutch settlement of Coupang opposite to it. The island is 20 miles in length and 7 in breadth, with an area of 134 square geographical miles. The interior and south-eastern side consist of a chain of mountains of moderate height,—the rest of the island of a sandy, bare, and sterile plain, formed of decomposed lime-stone and fossil shells. The mountains are of lime-stone, and covered with a coat of sulphur and sulphuret of iron. Here there are two hot springs, strongly impregnated with sulphuret of iron, and close to them is a remarkable banian or fig-tree—the Ficus benjamina, which has above 3000 stems, and, of which the spread would afford shelter to a small army. It is an object of worship by the natives. Samao is the residence of the raja or native prince of Coupang, and has been so from the year 1616, when the Dutch, by the expulsion of the Portuguese, took possession of the western part of Timur. The inhabitants are the same dark-complexioned, frizzle-haired race as those of Timur, and amount to 3000.

SAMAR. This is one of the names of Bima, one of the heros of the Hindu poem of the Mahabarat, of which the Javanese epitomes go under the name of Bratayuda, or the War of the Descendants of Brata. Samar is a noted personage of the Javanese drama taken from the poem.

SAMAR, formerly called Ibadeo, one of the larger Philippine islands, called by the Spaniards the Bisayas or of "painted men." It lies north-east of the island of Leyte, and south-west of the extreme eastern end of Luzon,—the peninsula of Camarines, and separated from the first by the narrow strait of San Juanico, and from the last by that of San Bernardino. It lies between north latitudes 11° 1′ and 12° 36′, and east longitudes 124° 7′ and 125° 37′, and has an extreme length of 140 miles, its greatest breadth being 45. It has a coast line of 376 miles, and an area of 4574 geographical square miles, which would make it about 300 miles larger than the island of Porto Rico in the Columbian Archipelago. The island, generally, is mountainous, but contains some fine plains under culture.

Down to the middle of the last century, Samar formed with Leyte one province, but was then separated from it, and has since formed an independent one. In 1818 it contained 27 townships, and a population of 57,922; and in 1850, its townships were 28, and its population had risen to 110,103, of whom 22,023 paid the capitation-tax,—that is, were genuine natives. These are of the Bisaya nation, speaking a dialect of the language which goes under this name. It has no negritos like Luzon, Negros, and Panay. Samar is one of the islands which, from its position, is most harassed by the Mahommedan pirates of the south; and as a protection against them, the coast is studded with numerous small forts, garrisoned only by the inhabitants themselves, serving as places of refuge to them when invaded.

SAMARANG. This is the name of one of the finest provinces of Java, and of its principal town. The province lies on the northern coast, about midway between the eastern and western end of the island, and towards the eastern angle of the wide bay or indentation of the coast, which extends for about 130 miles, from the Point of Indramaya to that of Japara. It is computed to have an area of 1425 square miles. Some portion of this along the sea is a low alluvial plain, but to the south the country rises to the height of 2000 feet, forming a plateau, containing several mountains, the highest of which is Ungarang, attaining the elevation of 4970 feet above the level of the sea. To the south-west the province is bounded and separated from that of Kadoe, by the high volcanic mountains of Màrapi and Râbabu, rising respectively to the heights of 9250 and 10,500 feet above the sea level. It is well watered by numerous small rivers, but none of them navigable except for boats, and even this only to the reach of the tide. A good highway passes through it from east to west, and another from north to south; the latter extending across the island, here about 70 miles broad. In 1845, the population of this province amounted to 753,315, composed of the following elements: Javanese, 732,098; Chinese, and their mixed descendants, 9057; Arabs, and natives of Celebes, with their descendants, 2277; and Europeans, with their descendants, exclusive of military, 2883. The relative population gives no less than 426 to the square mile, which is by far the densest of any portion of the Malay or Philippine Archipelagos, except that of the island of Bali, less correctly determined. It is to be observed, however, that this population had been exaggerated, or has since declined; for by the census of 1850, we find it to be no more than 624,874.

In 1845, the number of horned cattle in the province was reckoned at 110,000; and of horses at 7500. In the same year, exclusive of corn, it produced for exportation, about 82,000 cwts. of coffee; 50,000 of clayed sugar; and 1,200,000 lbs. of tobacco, besides some tea and cochineal. The town is situated on a river about a mile from the sea, in south latitude 6° 57′ 20″, and east longitude 110° 20′ 30″. It constitutes, with Batavia and Surabaya, the only three towns of Java that can be properly called European; and is a place of considerable population, but I have not been able to ascertain its present amount. It is the entrepôt of all the commerce of the interior of the island lying behind it, thus embracing the richest and most populous provinces of the island. The fishery is so large, that about 5000 of the indabitants are supposed to find employment in it. Besides numerous native trading praus, it has an European coasting craft of thirty vessels.

SAMBAS, is the name of a Malay state on the western side of Borneo, and now forming the most northerly district of the Netherland province of the west coast of that island. To the north, it is bounded by the territory of the sultan of Borneo at

Tanjung Datu, literally "Elders' promontory." Inland, it is bounded by the country of various wild tribes, and to the west by the sea. The town of the same name is situated on the tributary of a considerable river, about 50 miles from the embouchure of the main stream, which embouchure is itself in north latitude 1° 12′ 3″, and east longitude 108° 58′ 30″. Sambas is purely a Malay town, the houses being raised on posts along the river side, or standing on rafts moored to the shore, after the manner of the town of Borneo, and the Siamese capital, Bangkok. There is not a furlong of road in the whole country, nor a single beast of burthen, all communication being by boat. With the exception of a few patches of cultivation, the whole country is, in fact, a low primeval jungle. The population, the number of which is not stated, consists of Malays, various wild tribes or Dayaks, and a considerable number of Chinese engaged in gold-washing, for it is with Sambas that the gold-fields of Borneo commence.

SANDAL WOOD, (Santalum album). The wood called in commerce white sandal is the produce of a lowly tree bearing a general resemblance to a large myrtle, although belonging to a different natural family of plants. It is a native of several of the islands of the Malay Archipelago, but more especially of Timur, and of the island which takes its European name from it. From these it extends to the South Sea Islands, having been found abundant in the Fiji, Marquesa, and Sandwich groups. It is, therefore, a very widely-distributed tropical plant, since it is also found in the forests of Malabar. The only name by which it is known to the Malays and Javanese is a Sanscrit one, although, no doubt, it has native ones in the languages of the countries in which it is indigenous. This name is chandana, which the natives of the Philippines write sandana, but apply to a different tree. It may be inferred from this, that as in the case of the clove and nutmeg, its use was first made known to the natives of the Archipelago by the Hindu traders, who had immemorially frequented the islands. Barbosa mentions it as an article of native trade, before the arrival of the Portuguese, and quotes it in his "Calicut Price Current," as follows: "Sandal-wood, white and cedar-coloured, which grows in an island called Timur, costs the Farazuola from 40 to 60 fanoes." The foreign consumers of sandal-wood, to be used as a perfume, an incense, or a fancy wood, are the Hindus and Chinese, but especially the last, with whom the consumption is still large.

SANDAL-WOOD ISLAND, called by the natives of Celebes and the Malays, Sumba, is a considerable island of the Malayan Archipelago on its southern outskirts, lying south of the western end of Floris, and distant from this island about 30 miles. The tenth degree of south latitude runs through it, and except Timur and the islands adjacent to it, it is the most southerly land of the Archipelago. The country is mountainous, and like the neighbouring ones is, most probably, volcanic. Its area is estimated at 3786 geographical square miles. The inhabitants are of the Malayan race, but a distinct nation, speaking a peculiar language. They have made considerable progress in civilisation, cultivating rice and maiz, the last being their principal bread corn. They possess the goat, buffalo, and horse, the last in considerable numbers, and said to be the largest and best of the whole Archipelago. They are clothed in cottons, not their own, but received in exchange for sandal-wood, bees'-wax, swallows' esculent nests, and tortoise-shell. Like the Javanese, and people of Bali and Lomboc, their houses are not raised on posts, but built on the ground, showing that they are not a maritime but an agricultural people. They do not, indeed, go abroad, and have no vessels larger than their fishing boats, their trade being carried on by the Bugis. Of the number of the inhabitants nothing is known.

SANGIR is the name of an island surrounded by many smaller ones, situated between Celebes and Gilolo to the south, and Mindano to the north. The usual anchoring ground for European ships is on the western side of Sangir and lies in north latitude 3° 28′, and east longitude 125° 44′. The area of this island is computed at 208 geographical square miles. It is of volcanic formation, containing many extinct craters and several active volcanos, so that by it, we trace the great volcanic band from the Malay to the Philippine Archipelago. The inhabitants of Sangir are of the Malay race, but seem a peculiar people, speaking a peculiar language. Sir Stamford Raffles has given a list of forty-eight words of it, in which, the numerals excepted, I can find but eight that are Malay or Javanese. The people have acquired some amount of civilisation, and are simple and inoffensive. Before the arrival of the Portuguese, the Sangir islands had been conquered by the people of Ternate, one of the Spice Islands.

SANSCRIT. Although all the more cultivated languages of the Indian Islands contain more or less of this ancient dead tongue, and the Javanese, even a great deal; and although ancient inscriptions in it exist in Java, the name is wholly unknown. That name is not, indeed, as in the case of other languages, derived from that of a people, but a mere epithet, apparently of no very remote invention, and given after the name and even the locality of the people who spoke it, as their vernacular tongue, had been forgotten.

SAPAROWA, called by the natives **HONIMOA.** Correctly written it is probably Sapurwa, or Sapurba, from the native numeral, *sa*, standing as an article, and the Sanscrit, purwa, "first," or "source." This name was, probably, like several others, imposed by the ancient Malay and Javanese spice traders. Suparowa is one of the Amboyna group of islands lying off the south-western end of Ceram. It has a population of 12,000, and produces more cloves than all the other islands of the same group put together. To the residency or district to which it gives name, are annexed the smaller islands of Nusa-laut or Sea Island, and Melano, which added to it make the total population 20,000. The district contains twenty-two villages, all of which are inhabited by Protestant Lutheran Christians, except two, of which the people are Mahommedans. After the restoration of the Spice Islands by the English to the Dutch in 1817, a rebellion broke out in Saparowa, which involved nearly the whole island, and which it required the efforts of two years to suppress. The leaders in it were, it is remarkable, all Christians.

SAPI, or SAPPY. This is the name given by navigators to the strait which divides the islands of Sumbawa from Floris; and within or near to which are the islands of Gunung-api, Gilibanti, and Comodo. It is one of the highways between the seas of the Malay Archipelago and the Pacific Ocean, the navigable passage being between the last-named island and Sumbawa. The word sapi, in Malay and Javanese, signifies "kine," or "oxen," and seems to be taken from the name of a bay on the Sumbawa shore of the strait.

SAPONGAN. This is the name of a lake in the Spanish province of Caraga on the northern side of the island of Mindano. A river proceeds from it which shortly after quitting it, divides into three branches, and falls by as many mouths into the bay of Butuan. Of the extent of the lake, nothing is stated beyond its being large.

SAPPAN-WOOD. (Cæsalpinia sappan.) This dyeing material, the wood of a lowly tree, is found in many parts of the Malay and Philippine Archipelagos but is most abundant in the island of Sumbawa, and in the provinces of Iloilo in Panay and Pangasinan in the great island of Luzon. In 1850, there were exported, chiefly to Europe and America, no less than 11,000 tons of this article from the port of Manilla. The sappan-wood is the wild produce of the forests, and that it is indigenous wherever it grows there can be little question. It has, like many indigenous products a distinct name in the different languages, the only agreement, and this not perfect, being between the Malay and the Javanese, in the first of which it is called sâpang, the origin of the European commercial and scientific names, and in Javanese sâchang. In one language of the true Moluccas we have it as samya, and in another as roro, while in Amboynese it is lolan, and in the Tagala of the Philippines sibukao. It seems probable, however, that the Cæsalpinias which produce the dye-wood of countries which extend from the 9th degree of south to the 19th of north latitude, may be distinct species. The sappan-wood of Luzon is by from 40 to 50 per cent more valuable than that of Siam, that is, yields by so much more of colouring matter. In this respect all the Asiatic Cæsalpinias rank far below those of Brasil.

SAPUTU. The name of one of the mountains of the northern Peninsula of Celebes, with an active volcano. It rises to the height of 5800 feet above the level of the sea.

SARASAN is the name of one of the many islets off the eastern coast of the Malay Peninsula. Like all the rest, it is inhabited by the orang-laut, or sea-gypsies, amounting to about 300. The people of Sarasan had, at one time, the reputation, not without good foundation, of being habitual pirates. Since the establishment of Singapore, however, they have taken to peaceable pursuits, and bring their birds-nests and coco-nuts to the British settlement to exchange for corn, salt and clothing.

SARAWAK, is the name of the most southerly district of the western sea-board of Borneo, and of the territory of the sultan of that island, bounded to the south by Sambas, at the projecting head-land called by the Malays Tanjung Datu, meaning "elders" or "chieftain's promontory." It is described by its present possessor as extending along the coast for sixty miles with an average breadth of fifty, so as to give it an area of 3000 square miles, which would make it by about one-fifth part larger than the West Riding of York. With the exception of a few specks, it is a vast forest, without any sign of having ever been otherwise, with the ape, the deer, and the wild boar for its most numerous inhabitants. The climate is moist and hot, the average temperature of the year being 83° of Fahrenheit. The geological formation consists of sandstone and granite, but it possesses neither the gold of the southern districts of the island, nor the coal of the northern, its only discovered mineral hitherto, being antimony. This previously little known country, was brought into notice in 1824, by the accidental discovery within it of the richest, the most easily worked, and the most easily transported supply of sulphuret of antimony in the world, and which has ever since furnished Europe and America with their principal supply. There are three considerable rivers within the territory, or forming its boundary. The chief of these which bears the name of the place itself, is formed by the union of two streams proceeding from the mountains of the interior, which after their junction pass in a course of 20 miles. through the territory, and at 12 miles from the sea divide into two branches entering it by the same number of considerable mouths with several small ones. The eastern of these channels called the Morotabas is the navigable one, and is about three quarters of a mile broad, with a depth of from 3½ to 4 fathoms at low water spring-tides, which makes it to a short distance navigable by large ships. On the banks of this river stood the only Malay settlement, distant about fifteen miles from the sea. This was called Kuching (the cat), and contained a population of about 2000, of a rather miserable kind. It is now the town of Sârâwak, with a population of 15,000. The primitive inhabitants of the soil are the wild tribes known to the Malays under the common appellation of Dayaks. These are not a homogeneous people, but however small the tribes, really distinct and independent nations. "There are," says Sir James Brooke, "twenty tribes in about fifty square miles of land." All these, although with a little occasional admixture, speak really distinct languages, which exhibits a state of society far more resembling that of Africa or South America than of Asia. The Malays, by virtue of superior civilisation, became the rulers of the land, as in other parts of the coast of Borneo, and the Dayaks, in so far as they came within their reach, their Helots."

In 1841, Sir James Brooke an English gentleman, a man of great enterprise, strong will, and ample courage and ability, obtained a grant of Sârâwak, from its little more than nominal lord, the Sultan of Borneo, and has ever since governed it as a virtually independent sovereign, under the Malay title of Raja, taken from the Hindus, and literally signifying "king." The result has been a great accession of population by immigration, consisting of Malays, Dayaks, and Chinese, and a large augmentation of trade, for in 1854, its exports are stated to have amounted to the value of a million of Spanish dollars, and its imports to eight hundred thousand. Such a result, indeed, in these rude and anarchical countries, never fails to follow from any administration which gives a fair amount of security to life and property, and examples of it now and then occur, even under native governments, although the effects, in such cases, are necessarily temporary.

SARAWI, is the name of a nation of the western side of Sumatra, whose locality is between that of the Rejang and Palembang. They speak a peculiar language, but write it in the same character as the Rejangs. Their country includes Pasâmak-ulu and Pasâmak-lebar, that is "inland" and "broad" Pasâmak, with Manah. Mr. Logan estimates the territory occupied by the Sarawi at 5000 square miles, and the population at 16,000, giving consequently 32 inhabitants to the square mile, a large proportion for Sumatra. The Sarawi must be considered as among the civilised people of the island.

SAVAGE. The only term for savage in any of the languages of the Malay Archipelago is equivalent in English to "man of the woods, or forests." This in Malay, is orâng-utan, our well-known orang-utang, and in Javanese wong-alas. The word dayak seems more especially restricted by the Malays to the wild people of Borneo, Sumatra, and Celebes.

SAVOE or SAWEE is the name of a small island lying west of Timur and distant from it about 75 miles. It is computed to have an area of 180 geographical square miles. The surface of the country is mountainous and rocky, with a very scanty supply of water. In ordinary years, however, the inhabitants raise a sufficiency of maiz, millet and yams, for their own subsistence, and in times of scarcity, obtain a living from the banana, and the sugar of the lontar palm (Borassus flabelliformis), both of which are abundant. The island produces a small quantity of tobacco reputed to be of a very fine quality. Thus we find two American plants, among the staple products of this sequestered island, namely, maiz and tobacco. The principal domesticated animals of Savoe are the buffalo and horse, both of which are abundant. In personal appearance, the people resemble those of Timur, but are said to differ materially from those of the neighbouring island of Rotti, that is, they are short, dark complexioned, and have frizzled hair instead of lank. Their language is peculiar, although intermixed with some words of the dialects of Timur and with Malay and Javanese. The women go naked with the exception of a short petticoat, and the men wear no other dress than a bit of cloth wrapped round the loins. The whole population is reckoned at 5000, and the island, with the neighbouring ones, are dependencies of the Netherland government of Kupang in Timur.

SEA, the Ocean. The Malay has three words for the sea, namely, laut and tasik, which are native words, and luji which is Arabic, the last of rare use. The Javanese has five, namely, the two Malay ones, and samudra and sâgara which are Sancrit, with sâgantàn, a derivation from the last of these for the polite dialect. The native words laut and tasik are of very wide currency, being found in nearly all the languages of the Malay Archipelago, and extending even to the languages of the Philippines, although in these accompanied by native synonyms. They do not extend to the languages of the islands of the South Sea, nor to the language of Madagascar, yet in the last, the sea is expressed by a Malayan compounded word, ranumasina (ranu-masin), which signifies "salt water." In Malay all that is connected with the sea, as might be expected with the language of a peculiarly sea-faring people, has a copious phraseology. Thus, we have specific terms for interior and sea-board, for going with or against the current, for current, tide, ebb and flow, for cove, islet, strait, various kinds of shoals, dry land the correlative of sea or water; not to mention the enumeration of winds, which amount to no fewer than sixteen.

SERWATI, or SELAWATI, is the name of a chain of islets extending from the large island of Timur, towards the considerable one of Timur-laut, the most westerly of which is Kisser or Kissa, and the most easterly Sermata. The inhabitants are of the Malayan race, speak a peculiar language, and are a peaceable and industrious people raising yams and sweet potatos, the lontar palm for its sugar, and rearing poultry and hogs. Mr. Windsor Earl who visited them, describes the people as divided into three castes, namely, lords or rulers, proprietors of the land, and serfs or labourers.

SHADDOCK, or PUMPLENOOSE. The Citrus decumana of botanists, the kadangsa of the Malays, and the jâruk-machan, or tiger-orange of the Javanese, is very generally disseminated over the whole Malay Archipelago, but unlike the mangostin and durian, is a fine fruit only when well and carefully cultivated, as it is at Batavia and Malacca, where it attains a perfection which, in these regions, no other of the orange family reaches. It is, most probably, a fruit originally peculiar to the Malay Archipelago, and the names which it bears in other countries shows that in these it is an exotic. Thus in the continent of India it is called the "Batavian orange," and in our West Indian islands the shaddock, which it takes from the name of the commander of a merchant ship that carried it from Batavia to these islands. As Batavia was only founded in the year 1619, and Captain Shaddock lived in the reign of Queen Anne, it is certain that the introduction of the fruit into both the countries named is of comparatively modern date.

SHAFEI. The patronymic of a celebrated Mahommedan doctor, the founder of one of the four sects considered by the Arabians as orthodox. All the Mahommedans of the Indian Islands belong to his sect. He was a native of Syria, and flourished in the eighth century, or about three centuries before the earliest conversions of the inhabitants of the Archipelago to Islam. These know little about him or his doctrines.

SHARKS. These predatory fish, which are numerous, and of great size in the seas of the Archipelagos, are only named here on account of their fins being a regular article of trade for the market of China, where they are prised for their real or imaginary stimulating and restorative qualities. The name for the shark in Malay and Javanese is Iyu, or, abbreviated, Yu, and this has a very extensive currency, for it is even found in some dialects of the islands of the Pacific.

SHASTRE. This celebrated Sanscrit word is unknown to the languages of the Malay Archipelago, in its sense of a scripture or sacred writing. In the form of sastra, it signifies, in Malay, an alphabetic character, and written language, as distinguished from oral.

SHEEP. This animal is undoubtedly an exotic in all the islands of both Archipelagos, the moist and hot climates of which are ill suited to it. It exists only, and in small numbers, in a few places where the Hindus or Europeans have settled, as Achin, Java, and Luzon in the Philippines. They are most numerous in the latter country, particularly in the province of Ilocos, introduced by the Spaniards, most probably, through America. The wool, however, is coarse, and the natives will not eat the flesh. The name by which it is known to the Malays and Javanese is the Sanscrit one, biri, although they occasionally call it "the European goat."

SHIELD, or BUCKLER. This arm seems to have been universal over the Malay and Philippine Archipelagos before the introduction of fire-arms, and is still continued by all the ruder tribes. In Malay, there are no fewer than seven different names for it, four of which are native,—two taken from the Javanese, and one from the Tâlugu. These names, however, rather refer to the different forms of it, than constitute synonyms.

SHIP. The name for a large trading vessel in Malay and Javanese is jung, which the Portuguese converted into junco; and we, improving on this corruption, into junk. This is the word which we apply to the large trading vessels of the Chinese, which the Malays and Javanese call by the name of wangkang. The natives of the Archipelago have not now, and seem never to have had a square rigged vessel. The people of the Coromandel coast, the Telingas, who traded immemorially with the Archipelago, had vessels of this class, and from them the Indian Islanders borrowed, and naturalised the name for them, namely, kapal.

SHRIMPS AND PRAWNS. These are very numerous along the coasts of the islands of both Archipelagos, under the name of udang in Malay, and urang in Javanese. They form, almost everywhere, a very material portion of the animal food of the people. The form in which they are commonly used is that of a paste, formed by mashing them,—well known to the Malays under the name of bâlachan, turned by Europeans into balachong, and to the Javanese by that of trasi. This is used as a condiment, and forms a very material article of native trade between the coasts and interior.

SIAK, or SIYAK, is the name of a Malay state on the north-eastern side of Sumatra, as well as of its principal river and town. The river, the finest in Sumatra, has its origin in the central chain of mountains, and, after passing through an extensive alluvial plain, disembogues in the Straits of Malacca, nearly opposite to the island of Bungkalis, and at the northern end of Brewer's Strait, in north latitude 1° 30′, and east longitude 102° 10′. The mouth of the river is about three-quarters of a mile wide, but almost closed by a sand-bank, in some places dry at low water, and leaving a very narrow navigable channel only, but still a safe one for vessels of considerable burden. After passing this bar, the water deepens to five fathoms, and fifteen miles from the mouth of the river, there are still from seven to nine fathoms. The river is, in fact, navigable for vessels of large burden for eighty miles up, and for a hundred for vessels not exceeding 200 tons. Altogether, including boat navigation, its navigable course is not less than 150 miles, so that it may be considered the most useful stream in Sumatra. The town of Siak is about eighty miles from the mouth of the river, and described as a considerable place, but no details are given. Neither have we any account of the extent or population of the state itself. Siak, under the name of Ciaca, is one of the twenty-nine states mentioned by De Barros as occupying the sea-board of Sumatra when the Portuguese first appeared in the waters of the Archipelago.

SIAM. This name for the kingdom and its people is taken directly from the Malay, in which it is Siyâm, and this again is said to be derived from the ancient Siamese name of the country and its principal inhabitants, Sayam. The present Siamese, however, call themselves Thai, a word which, in their language, means "free." It is probably equivalent to Franks, or freemen, and was probably first used to distinguish the ruling and privileged nation from subjected tribes. It is also applied to the Laos, with the epithet "great," while the Siamese themselves bear that of "little," terms, however, which, probably, signify no more than elder and younger.

The kingdom of Siam extends from about the 4° to the 22° of north latitude, or to the length of 1080 geographical miles. Its breadth is very irregular, varying from 150 to 360 miles. Its entire area, tributary states included, has been estimated at 12,330 geographical leagues, or 111,000 geographical miles.

To the north Siam is bounded by the territory of the Burmese in one quarter, and by the British in another; to the west by the British territory and the Bay of Bengal; to the south by the Malay States of Perak and Jehor, and by the Gulf of Siam, and to the east by the territories of Cochin China. The essential parts of the kingdom, however, seem to lie between the 14° and 17° of latitude. and embracing about 36,000 geographical square miles, do not much exceed in extent the island of Java.

The coast line of Siam, on the gulf of its own name, extends to about 1000 miles, but on that of Bengal, to not more than 200. It contains no deep bays or inlets, but on the Siamese gulf, the embouchures of several large rivers. The Gulf of Siam extends from between the 8° and 9° of north latitude to between the 13° and 14°, and all its upper or northern coast is in possession of the Siamese. Along its coasts the depth of water is usually from nine to ten fathoms, and in the centre from fifty to sixty. A current at the rate of three miles an hour prevails in the gulf running from north to south during the northern monsoon, and in the opposite direction during the southern. It is beyond the reach of the region of hurricanes, and usually its navigation is safe and easy. Both its eastern and western coasts contain many islands,—a few of them thinly inhabited, and all of them green, wooded, but sterile.

The mountain chains of Siam have a direction from north to south, and seem to be three in number, but of their height and geological formation we have no reliable information. The most westerly range seems to be a continuation of the great central one, which runs through the Malay Peninsula. Some of the highest points of this rise to the height of 5000 feet. Up to the 14° of latitude, this range yields iron, tin, and gold, and no doubt the formation is sedimentary and plutonic.

The Menam, the Mekong, the Meklong, the Petriü, the Tachin, and the Chantibun are the principal rivers of Siam. The first of these, of which the literal meaning is "mother of waters," is by far the most important, in so far as regards Siam itself. It is said to have its source in the Chinese province of Yunan, and is computed to have a course of 300 leagues. Between the 17° and 18° of latitude it receives a large affluent, the Phitsalok, and in about the 16° it divides into several branches, producing an extensive system of irrigation. At the ancient capital Yuthia, it receives another affluent, and nine leagues from the sea, above the modern capital Bangkok, all the branches unite, and thus debouche at Paknam, literally "the river's mouth." From the ancient capital to the sea, the Menam is navigable for large vessels, having, from bank to bank, a depth varying from six to nine fathoms, and at Bangkok it is half-a-mile broad, a spacious river and convenient harbour. A bar, composed of mud and sand, however, obstructs its entrance, about ten miles in breadth, on which the depth at low water does not exceed three feet, nor at high, even during spring tides, above fourteen. The three rivers, the Meklong, the Petriü, and the Tachin, all of short course, have their distinct embouchures at the head of the gulf, but are connected with the Menam, or principal river, by natural canals, which contribute to extend its irrigation and navigation. All these together inundate the lands in their neighbourhood, from June to November, and, by their deposit, fertilise a plain which is considered to be about sixty leagues in length, by twenty-five in breadth, or having an area of 6750 geographical miles. In the month of August the water overflows the banks of the Menam, rising to the height of forty inches above its ordinary level in the dry season, in some years having even an elevation of double this amount. It is remarkable, however, that this inundation does not extend to the lands which border the river for eleven leagues inland from the sea, which are so high as not to be affected by it. The valley of the Menam is obviously of modern creation, for even at the city of Bangkok, at the depth of twenty-five feet below the surface, abundant débris of sea-shells and crustaceæ are found, and the water reached is stated to be as salt as that of the gulf.

The river of Chantibun, which is of short course, disembogues on the eastern coast of the gulf, between the 12° and 13° of latitude, and is stated to fertilise a narrow plain twelve leagues in length. The Mekong, or great river of Kamboja, is said to have a course of 500 leagues, and must be reckoned one of the greatest rivers of Asia. A small portion of it only passes through the territory of Siam,—that which is inhabited by the tributary Laos and Kambojans.

Lakes do not seem to be numerous in Siam, or at least not to be of great extent. One, however, is described as existing in the tributary part of Kamboja. This is called Talesap,—said to be situated between the 11° and 12° of latitude,—to be twenty leagues in circumference, and to abound in fish.

As to climate the year in Siam as in other Asiatic countries within the same latitudes, is divided into two seasons, a wet and a dry, the first of which extends from the middle of June to the middle of October. The south-west monsoon during this time blows over the country, and for the rest of the year, the north-east. At the capital, Bangkok, Fahrenheit's thermometer ranges in the months of December and January from 50° to 53°, and in March and April, the hottest months, from 86° to 95°. Over the great alluvial plain the ventilation is as complete as in the open sea, and hence the country equal in salubrity to any tropical one. But in many of the confined and thickly wooded valleys the climate is deleterious from malaria.

The mineral products of Siam of economical use are iron, lead, tin, gold, zinc, and antimony. Iron is chiefly manufactured in the little town of Thasung on the Menam in about latitude 16° 30′. The ore obtained in the western range of mountains and said to be of good quality, is brought to the place of manufacture by a small river, and being smelted by the Chinese is sent in pigs to be cast into those caldrons which are so generally used in the country itself, and largely exported to the Malayan countries. Tin is described as the produce of four different provinces, exclusive of the tributary Malay States which also yield it. These provinces extend from about the 8° to the 15° of latitude, and seem to be part of the same formation which extends to the Malay peninsula and its islands as far as Banca and Billiton. Lead, zinc, and antimony are found in the ranges of mountains which lie on the western borders of Siam between the 13° and 14° of latitude, but no mines of them seem ever to have been worked, and, indeed, although the two first metals are well known to the Chinese, they are unacquainted with the last. Gold is produced only in the same localities which yield tin, the most noted mines being at a place called Bang-tapan, at the base of the range of mountains called the "Three hundred peaks," close to the western shore of the gulf, and between the latitudes of 11° and 12°.

The only remarkable gems found in the Siamese territory are the ruby and sapphire, said to be found in the valleys among the mountains of Chantabun or Chantaburi, on the eastern side of the gulf between the 12° and 13° of latitude. These precious stones, however, would seem to be much less abundant than those of the Burmese mines in the country of the Shans or Laos. Long ranges of limestone mountains exist in the western part of the Siamese territory. Culinary salt obtained by solar evaporation is largely produced near the sea on the banks of the river Meklong. This which is in unusually large crystals of great purity, furnishes the whole kingdom, and is the commodity which chiefly supplies the Malayan countries, with the exception of Java.

The useful spontaneous or cultivated vegetable products of Siam are, with a few exceptions, the same as those of the Malayan Archipelago, and especially of Java, although there be a difference of some eight degrees of latitude between them. The cereal corns are rice, the great staple of the country, of which no fewer than forty varieties are reckoned to be cultivated, and maiz, of course, as a plant of American origin of comparatively recent introduction. The chief pulses grown are the Phaseolus radiatus, or Soy bean, and the Arachis hypogæa or ground pea, the first but not the last being an article of exportation. The chief cultivated palms are the coco-nut, the areca, and the palmyra. The first yields the principal supply of oil for home consumption, and is a large article of export, and the last, the sugar, for domestic use. The sugar-cane has been immemorially known to the Siamese, and the historian, Diogo de Cauto states that both sugar and spirits were made from it when the Portuguese first visited Siam towards the commencement of the sixteenth century. This, however, seems to have ceased for a long time, and it was not until about the year 1810, or about eleven years before my own visit to the country, that the Chinese settlers began to cultivate the cane for the manufacture of sugar. After Bengal, Java and the Philippine island of Luzon, Siam is, at present, the principal sugar-producing country in Asia, and the produce is of a very high quality and well-known in the markets of Europe.

Cotton is extensively cultivated in upland regions, but not within the tract of inundation. It supplies not only the whole domestic consumption, but is to some extent exported to China. Its Siamese name, fai, would seem to imply that it is a native and not an exotic. Black pepper is confined to the district of Chantabun or Chantaburi on the eastern side of the gulf and between the 11° and 12° of latitude.

Its native name prik-thai, literally Siamese pepper, makes it probable that it is an indigenous product. Tobacco, known to the Siamese under the name of "medicine" or "physic," is of course an article introduced directly or indirectly by Europeans, most probably by the Portuguese, but at what particular time or under what circumstances is not known. The plant is very generally cultivated, and it may be said to be of universal use.

The following are the products of the Siamese forests put to economical use, the teak, or Tectona grandis; sappan wood, Cæsalpinia sappan; a kind of red wood called by the resident Portuguese Pao-rosa or rose wood; Agila or eagle wood; and a kind of benzoin differing from that of Sumatra, more abundant, but inferior in quality; two species of cardamom, seemingly different from the Amomum cardamomum of Malabar, with the gamboge of commerce, the produce of a Garcinium confined to that portion of Siam conquered from Kamboja. In various parts of the kingdom, especially of its southern districts, the tree or trees yielding the valuable gutta-percha, have been recently discovered and the gum exported. From all accounts teak forests are not found in any part of Siam further south than the 16° of latitude, which will correspond with the locality of our own in Pegu and Mantaban. As in Java they will probably be found confined to the limestone formation. The timber is brought down to the capital by a long navigation, and being largely used in the construction of temples, monasteries and ship-building, little probably remains for exportation to foreign countries.

The most conspicuous of the wild mammalia of Siam are the elephant, the rhinoceros, the hog, the ox, several species of deer, the hare, the otter, the royal tiger and leopard, with some smaller feline animals, and some species of viverra. The dog is stated, on native authority, to exist in the wild state, but the hyena, wolf, jackal and fox are all absent. Elephants are abundant in all the wildest parts of Siam, including Lao and Kamboja, and are largely domesticated as beasts of burden, the finest being esteemed those of the province of Suphan, lying west of the river Menam, and in about the 16° of latitude.

The domesticated quadrupeds, besides the elephant, are the ox, the buffalo, the horse, the hog, goat, and dog. The ox is used for labour only, and this confined to the dry uplands; the buffalo, the same powerful and unwieldy animal as that of the Indian Islands, is the only beast of draught employed in the deep and marshy irrigated tracts. The domesticated hog is of the Chinese breed, and largely reared by the Chinese. The Siamese horse, like that of all the countries south-east of India as far as China, is a pony, not exceeding 13 hands high, and is in general use only in the uplands, being rarely seen within the tract of inundation. The dog, as in all other eastern countries west of Cochin-China, is an unowned vagrant in towns and villages.

The ornithology of Siam is a subject for future naturalists. The most conspicuous birds are an eagle, a vulture, the carrion crow, all numerous about the capital, because attracted to it by the disgusting character of some of the Siamese funerals, and from religious motives, they never being either killed or disturbed. The common Indian peacock, and the beautiful double-spurred one are to be seen in the woods, as well as the common fowl, and several species of pheasant. The common house-sparrow, which, as a native, is unknown in the Malay and Philippine Archipelagos, is very frequent in the Siamese capital. The domesticated poultry are nearly confined to the common fowl and duck, the goose being rare, and the turkey unknown.

The reptiles of Siam are numerous, consisting of various tortoises, lizards, and snakes. Not only the eggs of turtles, but also of alligators, are used by the Siamese as food. The snakes are of many species, but few of them poisonous. A python, of which I saw an example when in the country, measured 12 feet long. Both the sea-coasts and rivers of Siam abound in fish, the latter more especially in the period of inundation. Dried fish is, indeed, a considerable article of export, besides forming the largest part of the animal food of the people. A sauce or rather a paste made of crushed and pickled prawns is an article of universal consumption. This, which the Siamese call kapi, is the blachan of the Malays, and the trasi of the Javanese.

Among insects the most useful are the honey-bee, only wild, and the lac insect. The stick-lac of Siam is in the quantity and quality of its colouring matter, the best in the east, and continues to be an article of export. At the capital, the mosquito was not found more troublesome than in other hot and damp countries, but towards the mouth of the Menam, they exceeded in number anything I had ever experienced elsewhere. The common fly is by no means frequent or troublesome in Siam, and it is rather remarkable that lice, bugs, and fleas are nearly unknown, as is the case also in the Philippines.

The man of Siam, including all the nations and tribes which inhabit it, is the same with the Burmese and Kambojan. It is the race which prevails from Bengal to China, a peculiar one that has not been much commingled with other races. The average stature of the male sex is about five feet three inches, which is about an inch taller than the stature of the Malay, and an inch and a half shorter than that of the Chinese. The complexion is a light brown, nearly the same with that of the Malay, but considerable darker than that of the Chinese. The hair of the head, is black, lank, course, and abundant. That of every other part of the body scanty, the beard consisting only of a few scattered piles. The nose is short, round at the point yet never flat. The upper part of the forehead is narrow, and the face broad at the cheekbones, giving it a lozenge instead of an oval form. It is not difficult to distinguish a Siamese from a Malay or a Chinese, when the parties are present to the observer, but by no means easy to convey by words the difference between them.

The dominions of Siam are inhabited by four distinct nations,—the Siamese proper, or Little Thai, the Lao, or great Thai, the Kambojans, and the Malays, and of three rude tribes,—the Karieng, the Chong, and the Lawá. All these have their separate languages, and are more or less distinct in manners and customs.

The proper Siamese, or ruling nation, as far as our imperfect knowledge extends, inhabits from the seventh degree of latitude to the twentieth, and from the shores of the Bay of Bengal to about the one-hundred-and-second degree of east longitude. This embraces the whole fertile tract of the inundation of the Menam, and other rivers which debouche at the head of the Gulf of Siam, and to this favourable locality is, no doubt, to be attributed their supremacy. The Lao nation lies north of the Siamese, extending eastward as far as the Mekong, or great river of Kamboja. The Laos are composed of several petty states, governed by their own princes, and paying tribute to the Siamese. There is no record of their having existed as an independent people, their states being subject either to the Siamese, Burmese, or Kambojans. The Kambojans, called by the Siamese, Khmer, inhabiting the Siamese territory, occupy a considerable portion of the country on the eastern side of the Gulf, from between the tenth and eleventh degree of latitude up to about the sixteenth.

The wild race of the Chong inhabits the mountains to the east of the province of Chantibun, on the eastern side of the Gulf, and the Kariengs have their locality to the north of them. The Lawá are found in the range of mountains lying between the Menam and the river of Martaban. In reference to the Siamese, the Lao, and Kambojans, those three rude tribes stand in the same relation as do the mountaineers of Hindustan to the civilised Hindus, or those of the Philippine Islands to the advanced inhabitants of the lowlands. They are not without some knowledge of agriculture and the useful arts, but have not adopted the religion of their masters, to whom they, notwithstanding, pay tribute.

Besides the native nations of Siam, a large number of strangers are permanently settled in it, retaining their own languages and manners. These are chiefly Chinese, from the maritime provinces of that empire, with some Peguans, and Cochinese or natives of Anam. M. Pallegoix, in his recent work, makes the whole population of the kingdom, tributary states included, 6,000,000, composed of the following elements,—namely, proper Siamese, 1,900,000 ; Laos, 1,000,000 ; Malays, 1,000,000 ; Kambojans, 500,000 ; Peguans, 50,000 ; and rude tribes, also 50,000. As the area of the whole kingdom is estimated at 111,000 square geographical miles, the relative population, by these dates, is about 54 inhabitants to a mile. The statement, however, is not only suspicious on account of its round numbers, but also from no data whatever being furnished of the principle on which the estimate has been formed. That portion of it which relates to the Malay population is, beyond doubt, a monstrous exaggeration, since we know that English writers, with far better means of information, do not make the population of the four tributary Malay states to exceed 180,000. Their estimate, however, does not include the Malays living within the proper Siamese territory, but if we make these 20,000, the exaggeration will still amount to 800,000, which must be deducted from the total population of the kingdom.

In the estimate of M. Pallegoix, the proper Siamese population is put down at 1,900,000, which is probably not overrating it. The territory occupied by them is the fertile inundated plain of the Menam, and its affluents. Estimating the area of this at 24,000 square miles, it would give, excluding Chinese and other strangers, a relative population of near 80 to the square mile. The population of the Laos is given at 1,500,000, and considering that the territory they occupy is extensive, and that they are a peaceable and rather a civilised people, it may not be over-rated. The Kambojans are set down at 500,000, but we know so little of them and their country, that no means exist for checking the statement.

The presence of a large Chinese population is certainly a singular fact in the history both of China and Siam, and the more so since the emigration is of comparatively recent origin, for at the close of the 17th century, according to the statements of the missions sent by Louis XIV. the number did not exceed 5000. M. Pallegoix gives it at 1,500,000, which I have no doubt is over-rating it. In 1826, it was stated to myself at about half-a-million, and supposing it to have since increased by one-half, the number will be 750,000, which far exceeds the number of this people to be found in all the other countries put together to which this people has migrated. They are chiefly confined to the fertile part of the country occupied by the Siamese, attracted to it by trade, and the manufactures of iron and sugar. Adding them, therefore, to the Siamese we shall have a total population for an area of 24,000 square miles of 2,650,000, or 110 to the square mile, which in density is one-half that of the island of Java, and scarcely a third of that of the plain of the Ganges.

With the deductions now made, the total population of Siam will amount to 4,450,000, which would give about 40 inhabitants to the square mile. Most of the country, indeed, consists of mountain and forest, and even the most fertile portion of it is under-peopled. The people are rude, and have never enjoyed any other than a barbarous and arbitrary government. The country is now, and has been for the last half-century, better governed than perhaps in any other period of its history. It has the example and the labour of a large body of industrious Chinese, and is no doubt from all this, more populous than it ever was before. The abundance and cheapness of corn and the other necessaries of life, show that much fertile land is yet unoccupied, and still abundant room for a rapid increase of population.

The country of the proper Siamese nation is divided into forty-one provinces, named, after the manner of the Chinese, from their chief towns. The tributary Malay states amount to four, namely, Trânganu, Kalanten, Patani, and Queda, which are described under their respective heads. The tributary Lao states amount to seven, and the Kambojan to five. It is only where their own language is vernacular that the Siamese administer government directly.

As to towns, the Bishop of Siam renders some account of twenty-four, most of which he had himself visited, and which, exclusive of the capital, contained populations varying from 4000 up to 80,000, giving a total between them of 330,000, or, including the capital, of about 730,000. This, according to the estimate of the population of the kingdom which I have attempted, would make the town inhabitants to amount to one-sixth part of the whole, a result highly improbable in a rude state of society, and in a country which, with the highest estimate of its population, is very thinly inhabited.

By far the largest and most important of the towns of Siam is Bangkok, the modern capital, in north latitude 13° 38′, and east longitude 100° 34′. It lies on both banks of the river Menam, where it is about half-a-mile broad, and about eight leagues from the sea, its site being within that portion of the lower valley of the Menam, which, as already stated, is elevated above the level of the annual inundation. The present reputed population of Bangkok is 404,000, composed of the following nationalities, namely, Siamese, 120,000; Laos, 25,000; Malays, 15,000; Peguans, 15,000; Kambojans, 10,000; Cochin-chinese, 12,000; Burmese, 3000; Portuguese Christians, 4000; and Chinese of the whole, or mixed blood, 200,000.

There is no doubt but that Bangkok is a populous and busy place, but the probability is, that this estimate of the number of its inhabitants is greatly in excess. The number given would make its population equal to that of Calcutta or Bombay, which, considering the difference of government, and that these towns are of earlier foundation than itself, is highly improbable. The town is described as occupying an area of twenty-five square miles, but this includes the river, the palace which has a circumference of three-fourths of a league, and many temples with their courts. Most of the houses, too, consist only of the ground-floor, or if there be a second, the lower is uninhabited, owing to the insuperable repugnance of the Siamese to have any one over their heads. The Chinese, it will be seen, form near one-half the population, and to them is entirely due its commercial prosperity. The Menam within the town, and indeed for many miles above and below, forms a safe, spacious, and commodious harbour. Bangkok was founded in the year 1769, after the destruction of Yuthia by the Burmese, and in the long period which has since transpired, has never suffered by foreign invasion or serious insurrection.

Yuthia, or Ayuthia, a corruption of the Sanscrit Ayudya, the name of the country of the Hindu demi-god, Rama, the ancient capital is situated on the river Menam, fifty-four miles above Bangkok, and seventy-eight miles from the sea, and lies in latitude 14° 38′. It is within the tract of inundation, surrounded by water, and intersected by canals. Its present population, consisting of Siamese, Laos, Chinese, and Malays, is computed at 40,000. The ruins of this old capital are very extensive, and several of the temples still standing, although neglected.

Changmai, or in Portuguese orthography, Xiengmai, is a town of Lao, and the capital of a principality of the same name, situated apparently in latitude 20° 46′. It lies at the foot of a mountain, but has an extensive fertile plain near, and is close to the Menam. The town, surrounded by a double wall and fosse, is said to occupy an area of 1000 toises in length by 900 in breadth, and to have a population of 50,000.

The only other large town in the Siamese dominions is Luang Phra-bang. This is also a town of Lao, and the capital of a tributary state. It is situated on the Mekong or great river of Kamboja, in latitude 17° 50′, and is a flourishing place, supposed, although probably with much exaggeration, to have a population of 80,000.

Of all the people inhabiting the Siamese territory, the Thai, or proper Siamese, have attained the highest degree of civilisation, and it is of them only that the state of our knowledge will enable us to speak with any confidence,—the Malays alone excepted. Siamese civilisation is intermediate between Hindu and Chinese, but much below either of them. It has received a good deal from both these sources, but in the main is indigenous, nor is there any reasonable ground for concluding that it sprang up in any other locality than that in which it at present exists. Considering the extent, the fertility, and easy communication by water possessed by the country occupied by the Siamese, it is difficult to account for their inferiority to the Hindus on one side, and to the Chinese on the other, except by supposing the race an inferior one. That race although undoubtedly a different one, is, probably, intellectually not superior to the Malay, as may be seen where the latter has had a fair opportunity of development, as in the example of Java, for it cannot be asserted that the Javanese are in any respect a less civilised people than the Siamese.

For the character of the Siamese, we may safely take the description given of it by M. Pallegoix, who resided 20 years among them. He represents them as a lively, mild, timid, and inconstant people, disliking wrangling, and whatever savours of anger or impatience. They are scandalised, for example, when they hear a priest express himself with any degree of vehemence in delivering a homily. They are indolent; and above all, great beggars. Thus, if they see anything curious in the possession of a stranger, they do not hesitate to ask for it, yet will express their thanks on receiving it, by giving some trifle in return. They are of a very charitable disposition, and never suffer a beggar to pass without giving alms in some shape or another. In their relations with the female sex, they are very reserved, and on this head their laws are severe. The smallest caress bestowed on another man's wife or daughter, will often incur the risk of a law-suit, which may end in the offender's being sold as a slave. The Siamese are greatly addicted to games and amusements, and it may be truly said that one-half the year is passed in them. Mildness and humanity are, according to the bishop of Siam, characteristics of the nation. In the populous capital serious quarrels are of rare occurrence; and a murder is so uncommon an event, that a whole year will sometimes pass without the occurrence of a single case. In this respect the Siamese are favourably distinguished from most of the Malay nations, and even from the heterogeneous populations of our own insular possessions. The Siamese have this mark of a civilised people that they do not wear side-arms; and this, with a very phlegmatic temperament, must contribute materially to the infrequency of broils and homicides.

The Siamese exhibit the most profound respect for all superiors, from the king, whom they reverence almost as a deity, to the humblest of his officers. Europeans, indeed, would call their submission not respect but abject servility. Reverence to parents, and, generally, to old age, are held in great respect. The bishop observes, that among the resident Chinese, suicides are not unfrequent, while they are scarcely ever known among the Siamese; but this is an observation not applicable to the Siamese alone, but to all the Asiatic nations, not of the first rank of civilisation.

The most remarkable feature of the Siamese character is a national vanity, which is excessive. This was observed to distinguish it by the French travellers of the 17th century, and equally distinguishes it at the present day. One of these travellers the Abbé Gervaise, observes of them, that "they commonly despise other nations, and are persuaded that the greatest injustice in the world is done to them when their pre-eminence is disputed." This delusion no doubt arises from their having immemorially domineered over the small and inferior nations surrounding them; and their having no political equal. The presence of a large body of Chinese living among them, and superior to them in laboriousness, ingenuity—even in personal strength and stature—has by no means contributed to disabuse them. In so far as security of life and person, and to some degree, even of property is concerned, the Siamese are a safe people for strangers to live among, but they are by no means an agreeable one. The chief instrument for maintaining subordination and order, is the rod, administered very freely to all ranks, and its infliction held to be no disgrace by any, a matter in which they agree with the Burmese, Cochin-Chinese, and Chinese, but differ wholly from the Malays, who are as impatient of a blow as the most sensitive Europeans.

Among the Siamese, the distinction of castes has no existence, and in so far as religion is concerned, there is no hereditary privileged order. Except official rank, which is entirely personal, the only civil distinctions among them are of freemen and slaves. Slavery is an established institution, and it is thought that about one-third part of the whole Siamese nation are bondsmen. These are of three descriptions, namely, prisoners of war, parties sold for a consideration by their parents under a written contract, and parties who mortgage their services in liquidation of a debt. The second class is the only one not redeemable, and the last the most numerous. We are assured by the bishop of Siam, that the Siamese treat their slaves with kindness and humanity, exacting from them no severe labour, and treating them rather as domestic servants than bondsmen.

Marriages are contracted by the Siamese at from 15 to 17 years of age, that is, after the attainment of the age of puberty, rather a late period for an eastern people. When the time is delayed by parents over-anxious for favourable matches for their daughters, elopements are not unfrequent, the law afterwards enforcing a marriage if the parents should not be voluntarily reconciled. The husband has a right to sell a wife that he has purchased, but not otherwise. Generally, wives are well treated, not immured even among the higher classes, but among the lower performing much drudgery. In Siam the wages of labour are comparatively high, that is, high in proportion to the labour performed. Hence, a large family is not a burthen but an advantage, parents being even enabled to dispose of their children by sale to advantage. This is a state of things that was to be expected in a fertile country underpeopled, and it is what has led to the extensive immigration of the Chinese, who find no difficulty in obtaining Siamese wives, or wives from the half-caste settlers of their own country. It is the paucity of inhabitants, too, that has no doubt led to the existence of slavery, found in every underpeopled country of Asia, but hardly perceptible in such populous countries as Bengal, China, and Java.

In the common and necessary arts, the Siamese have made but slender progress. Immemorially they have been possessed of a knowledge of the useful and precious metals. They have grown their own cotton, and manufactured their own clothing. They manufacture coarse pottery, and they make bricks and tiles, but in no art have they attained any marked eminence. The women are the spinners and the weavers of their tissues, as among all the less civilised nations of Asia. The smelters and workers in iron are the resident Chinese; and the raw silk which their women weave is imported from China, for they have none of their own; nor, indeed, do they possess any native textile material except cotton.

The only remarkable exhibition of Siamese skill in the arts is shown in their architecture, and this is almost wholly confined to their religious edifices, among which may be included the royal palaces. One temple, or rather many temples with one large central one, which I visited myself in 1821, was contained within a square, the wall of which measured at each side 650 English feet. All the temples within the inclosure contained 1500 images of Buddha, some of them of most gigantic size, while the number of priests was 500, and of neophites 750. In one temple out of the many within the inclosure, there was an inscription which stated that it was built in the year of 2338 of the sacred era, corresponding with the year 1795 of our time, and that it cost 465,440 ticals, or about 58,180*l*.

The lower part or ground storey of a Siamese temple is of ordinary brick and mortar, and all ornament is reserved for the upper portion and roof, which are composed of solid teak-wood, richly and elaborately carved, and richly gilt both inside and out, or covered with a coat of bright vermilion. The statues are of brass, or of mortar, but in either case richly gilt.

Attached to the temples are the monasteries, and always near to them certain pyramidal spires, usually containing a single image of Buddha. These are of solid brick. The most remarkable of these is to be found still standing within a league of the old capital. This is computed to be 400 feet in height, and is said to have been built in the year 1387 of our era. Like many other ancient buildings of the Buddhists it is utterly neglected, and its gigantic gilt bronze statue of Buddha has, according to M. Pallegoix, for its sole worshippers, some thousands of bats.

The agriculture of Siam owes more to peculiarity of situation, rich alluvial land, and periodical inundation, than to the skill of the people. The country contains no great works of irrigation like those of Southern India, nor does the practice of transplanting rice prevail as in Java. In the month of May the land for rice is carefully weeded by means of a rude harrow, and with the first fall of rain in June, the seed is sown, after a ploughing with a very simple one-handed implement. The crop keeps pace in growth with the rise of the inundation, and as this abates and the land becomes dry, the grain ripens, and is reaped in January. As in other countries where rice has been immemorially cultivated, the varieties are very numerous, but the principal cultivated within the tract of inundation is a large and fruitful one, as is shown by its taking seven months to come to maturity. Of this, forty seeds are considered an average return. The horticulture of Siam, and especially of that portion of the valley of the Menam which is within about 10 or 11 leagues of the sea, and not periodically flooded, is distinguished for successful culture, producing most tropical fruits in perfection, and some of the most distinguished of the Malay fruits which refuse to grow in any similar latitudes, in any other part of the world in which the trial has been made.

The Siamese language is peculiar, differing materially from those of the neighbouring nations, except the Lao, which is said to be fundamentally the same tongue. The Siamese call it phasa-thai, that is, "the language of freemen." The first word in this term, however, it is evident is only a corruption of the Sanscrit bahasa, "tongue," or "speech." The Siamese consists of two dialects, the vulgar and the court. The sacred language is a distinct tongue, that is, the Pali or Pakrit, common to all the nations which have embraced the Buddhist religion, and brought along with them from Hindostan, the parent of both. The alphabet in which the vulgar and court languages are written is peculiar in the form of its letters, which, however, are arranged according to the organic classification of the Hindus. It forms a complex, but for its own purpose, a complete system. Thus it has no fewer than 12 vowels, 3 diphthongs, and 5 semi-vowel characters or liquids united to vowels. Its whole vowel characters, therefore, amount to no fewer than 20,—some long and some short, and some very long and some very short. The consonants amount to no fewer than 43, divided into gutturals, palatals, linguals, dentals, and labials; with a miscellaneous class composed of liquids, sibilants, and aspirates. As in the Sanscrit alphabet, in the first four classes, each simple consonant character has a corresponding aspirated one, with its own peculiar nasal. Thus, the entire system consists of no fewer than 63 characters, which approaches to three times the number of the letters of the Roman alphabet, excluding double ones from the latter. The Siamese alphabet is described by M. Pallegoix, who studied the language as ingenious and comprehensive; adding, that when recited in all its combinations, it forms a complete dictionary of the language. This, however, must refer only to the native portion of it, which is wholly monosyllabic, and cannot include its polysyllabic ones which are foreign, and chiefly Pali.

The Siamese is not of easy acquisition to a stranger, on account of the difficulty of pronouncing certain of its sounds,—of its different accents, which amount to five in number, and of its frequent idioms. It has, properly, no inflections of nouns to express gender, number, or case, nor of verbs to express time or mode; the first being effected by modals or adjectives, and the last by auxiliaries. In fact, it is a language of very simple structure; and considering that the great body of its words are monosyllables, it could hardly be otherwise.

The Siamese write on long sheets of native paper, nearly of the texture of pasteboard, and folded zig-zag. It is either white or black, the writing being with a pencil of chalk of the opposite colour. Their sacred books are, however, written on slips of palm-leaf, gilt at the edges, the characters being scratched with an iron style, and rendered distinct by lamp-black. Thirty or forty narrow palm slips, loosely connected by a silk cord, make a volume, and a library of such books belongs to every monastery. Books on religion, it is singular, are not written in the Siamese character, nor in the Pali as with the Cingalese and Burmese, but in the character of Kamboja.

The literature of Siam is in the form of both prose and verse, and is divided into sacred and profane; the first being in the vulgar tongue, and the last in Pali. M. Pallegoix has given translations of some specimens of the popular literature. The following are examples of Siamese proverbs. "When you go to the forest, do not leave your axe behind you."—"Do not place your bark across the current of the river."—"The elephant, although he have four legs, yet sometimes trips; and a man, however learned, is liable to make mistakes."—"If you land, you may encounter a tiger; if you continue in your boat, you may fall upon a crocodile."—"Nobility implies but pedigree, but manners the man."—"If a dog bite you, do not bite the dog in return."—"Why should a man fear the rain who dwells under the sky."

The following is a Siamese fable. "Avarice is an enemy to prosperity and may even lead to death. A certain hunter was in the practice of shooting elephants, for the nourishment of his wife and children. One day he discharged his bow at an elephant, which, struck by his arrow and maddened by the pain of the wound, pursued him in order to kill him. The hunter, in order to escape, ascended a white ant-hill, on which lay a snake that bit him. Enraged, he slew the snake. The elephant continued to pursue, but the arrow, by which he had been struck, being a poisoned one, he fell dead close to the ant-hill; and the hunter himself died of the bite of the snake, leaving his bow still strung. Meanwhile a wolf, in search of prey, came to the spot, and rejoiced exceedingly at what he saw before him. 'Behold me rich, for this turn,' said he, 'for good fortune has befallen me. The elephant will last me three months,—the man seven days,—and I will make two meals of the snake. But,' added he, 'why should I allow the bow-string to be wasted? Better that I eat it first to appease my hunger.' Thus meditating, he bit the string; and the bow rebounding broke his skull, and he perished on the spot."

The following is given as the translation of a Siamese poem. "The pains which men endure in this world are a thousand-fold less than those the wicked shall undergo in the infernal regions;—there the king of hell shall torment them cruelly.—The wicked man shall be immured and loaded with an iron ruff and fetters, on account of the crimes he committed in this world, when, pitiless, he cast others into fetters.—He shall be made to lie on a bed of red-hot iron,—he shall be transfixed, and die, and be born again seven times in a day.—Rapacious of bribes, he has not feared lying; his tongue shall be torn out, because he had judged unjustly.—When he was a judge on earth, he used menaces to extort gold; and obtaining it, he decided in favour of the guilty, making falsehood pass for truth.—When he dies, assuredly he shall not escape vengeance; he has not spoken truth, and for this he shall be thrown into hell, there to remain for a long duration.—He has not seen his own crime; he has despised the laws of his forefathers, and on this account, dogs of the size of an elephant, and crows and vultures shall devour his flesh."

Among the Siamese, the only branches of knowledge with which they are acquainted, that can be called science, refer to their calendar, their money, and their weights and measures; and these are of such a character as entitles them to rank in the third class of Asiatic civilisation. They have two eras, a sacred and a civil. The first of these they reckon from the death of Buddha, which they place 543 years before the birth of Christ. The second corresponds with the year of our era, 638, and is said to have been instituted by an ancient Siamese king. It probably, however, dates from the introduction of the Buddhist religion into Siam, an event which, it may be remarked, nearly corresponds in time with the origin of the Mahommedan in Arabia. The Siamese year is lunar, the alternate months being of 29 and 30 days. The calendar, however, is solar, and the time adjusted by adding a month to every third year. The week consists of seven days, and has been obviously borrowed from the Hindus, since its days are named after the same objects, as Sunday, Monday, &c., although the names be Siamese translations of the Sanscrit. For religious observances, however, the month is divided into two parts: a bright or increasing, and a dark or waning moon. The Siamese have two cycles, a smaller of 12 years, and a greater, which is its multiple by 5. Each year of the lesser cycle is named after some familiar animal, as the ox, the horse, the dog, the ape, &c., and the greater cycle is divided into 6 decades.

The Siamese have the advantage over the Burmese in possessing coined money. Indeed, in this matter, they are above even the Chinese, who have no coined money, except tokens of base metal. This advantage is probably no more than a matter of pure accident. The standard Siamese coin is known by the name of a bat; and is the same which is known to Europeans as a tical, a word of unknown origin. The coined fractions of the tical are halves, quarters, and eighths; and its own value about three

French francs, or 2s. 6d., which makes it about one-fifth more valuable than the Indian rupee. For small change, cowrie shells are used as in Hindustan; and of these, 1200 are considered to be equal to the lowest denomination of silver money, the fûang, or eighth of the tical, namely, about 15 farthings.

The smallest Siamese weight is called in the native language a hun, and weighs 45 centigrammes, or grains 6·943. Above this, and up to the bat or tical, the weights have the same denominations as the coins, the tical itself being of the weight of 18 grammes. What may be called the Siamese pound, weighs 720 grammes; and the Siamese quintal 72 kilogrammes. These two weights, however, are in much less use than the Chinese cattie and picul, which are of one-half their weight; making the first 9333 grains, and the last the multiple of it by 100, or 133⅓ pounds avoirdupois.

The standard Siamese long measure is the fathom, which is two French mètres, or 78·74 English inches. It is composed of 4 cubits, each cubit consisting of two measures, called empangs or feet. These consist of 12 parts or inches, and the inch is divided into 4 parts, known by the native term of kabit.

The lowest denomination of road measure is the fathom already mentioned, 20 of which make a sen, or 40 French mètres; and 400 sen, equal to 16,000 mètres, make a yot. This last measure is, probably, the Sanscrit yojana, which is nearly equal to 10 English miles. The other measures seem to be local.

The lowest measure of capacity is the coco-nut, and this, by law, ought to be equivalent to half a French litre, or 31·10 cubic English inches. Twenty of these make the measure called a thang, and 25 a set; and 80 thangs, or 100 sets make the largest measure, which is called a kien.

The religion of the Siamese is the same as that which prevails in Ceylon,—which is universal from Arraccan to the western frontiers of Anam,—which, in a modified form, is the worship of Tibet, and of the nations of Tartary, and which is partially established in Anam, China, and Japan. The Siamese ascribe its origin to the prince of a kingdom within the valley of the Ganges, which they name Kabilaphat, no doubt the Kapilawastu of the Sanscrit. This prince was Gautama, named Buddha, or the sage. They consider him a prophet and law-giver of incomparable wisdom, but not a god; for they describe him as dying in the 80th year of his age, and before Christ, 543, which would place his birth in 623, only 297 years before Alexander's invasion of India.

The leading characteristics of Buddhism are the existence of a priesthood living on the eleemosynary gifts of the laity, practising a rigid celibacy and exclusively devoted to religion,—the transmigration of souls,—a professed tenderness for all animal life,—a belief in a future state of rewards and punishments, and as the last reward of super-excellent piety and virtue, annihilation, or at least, absorption into the essence of the deity. Some European writers have described such a religion as a virtual atheism, for which, however, it is obvious that there is no ground. The religion of Buddha, although in theory more mild, and less monstrously superstitious than the Hindu, does not seem to have contributed to humanise or civilise its votaries. With the exception of Japan and of China in which it is not in much esteem, all the nations professing it are less advanced than those professing Hinduism.

The soil, climate, physical geography, and geographical position of Siam, make it a country well adapted for trade. The most active part of the internal trade is carried on by the Chinese, who are spread over every part of the kingdom where gain is to be made, much facility being afforded to their enterprise by the principal rivers, their branches and affluents. The main part of the foreign trade is with China, the traders, mariners, and the shipping at least, as to form, being Chinese. The next most important branch of the foreign trade is with the Malay islands, and this is confined to the Dutch and British settlements, and is of very modern origin, having originated with free trade and abolition of European monopolies in European commerce. This branch also is, for the most part, in the hands of the Chinese, as to capitalists, mariners, and shipping.

The articles of export from Siam are very various, no fewer than fifty-three native products being enumerated. The principal articles are as follows, rice, pulses, coconut oil, wood oil, resin, cane-sugar, palm-sugar, cardamoms, black and long pepper, sappan-wood, a certain yellow dye-wood, mangrove bark, gamboge, teak-wood, rose-wood, benzoin, eagle-wood, cotton-wool, liquid indigo, stick-lac, iron in the form of caldrons, tin, lead, horns, and hides, of the ox, buffalo, deer, and rhinoceros, ivory, jerked beef, salt, and saltfish. Coffee has, of late years, been cultivated and exported, and, as the climate and many localities of the kingdom are well suited to its growth, it promises to become a large article of export.

The principal imports are the productions of China, chiefly for the consumption of the large resident Chinese population. These consist of coarse pottery, paper, fans, umbrellas, raw and wrought silks, and tea. From Hindustan the staple imports are cotton fabrics and opium, and from Europe, mostly from British Indian settlements, cotton and woollen fabrics, glass-ware, cutlery, arms and ammunition.

The government of Siam is as thorough a despotism as can well be conceived. The sovereign is looked upon as a sort of demigod, who, after many migrations, is on the high-way towards final absorption into the essence of the Creator. His courtiers dare not look him straight in the face and so speak to him. They approach him in the crawling attitude of the lower animals, their knees and elbows being absolutely cicatrised by the long habit of this practice. When he appears abroad, which is seldom, every one prostrates himself as he passes, and all persons, even passing the royal palace, make a reverential obeisance to it. His real name, during his life-time, is never uttered, but he is alluded to under such titles or epithets as the following,—the most reverent, the perfect one, the godlike feet, the descendant of ancient kings, the descendant of angels, and the lord of perfect justice.

Siamese nobility is wholly personal and official, although from the nature of things, often heritable in families. It consists of five orders. Two persons only belong to the highest order, the two first ministers of state, one of whom is superintendant of the northern or interior provinces, and the other of the southern or maritime. In fact these functionaries constitute two distinct prime ministers, having each a moiety of the kingdom for his province. To the second class of nobles belong five ministers, namely, the governor of the palace, the treasurer, the minister of agriculture, the chief of the royal guards, and the superintendant of the Mon or Peguan resident inhabitants of Siam. The third order amounts to twenty-five in number, and are either the deputies of the officers of the two first classes, or holders of subordinate offices. The nobles of the fourth and fifth class are very numerous, and usually subordinate to those of the third.

The different provinces have each their own governors, and are named after their chief towns as in China. According to their importance, they are divided into four orders, the Siamese capital and the chief towns of the tributary princes, constituting the first. Muang, in Siamese, is a town or a country, and by affixing to it the numerals we have the degree to which each belongs. It may be remarked that the numerals employed for this purpose are not those of the vernacular language but the Sanscrit ones, or rather the corruptions of these in the Pali or sacred tongue, namely, ek, tho, tri, chateva.

A tolerable notion of the character of Siamese government and society may be formed from the manner in which public services are rewarded. Disbursements for this purpose are made yearly from the royal treasury in the month of November, the operation usually lasting about twelve days. The royal princes and the seven principal ministers receive each a sum equal to 200*l.* a year. Functionaries of the third class are paid, according to the importance of their charges, at the rate of from 7*l.* 10*s.* to 120*l.*: officers of the fourth class have salaries of from 7*l.* 10*s.* to 15*l.*, and inferior officers of from 2*l.* to 15*l.* Common soldiers, police officers, medical practitioners, artisans, and the like, are paid according to merit, at the rates of from 25*s.* to 30*s.* a year. These rates of remuneration are sufficient provocations to the extortions, peculations, and evasions, which are known to be generally practised.

The revenue of the kingdom is stated by M. Pallegoix at the sum of 26,964,100 ticals, equivalent to 3,370,512*l.*, probably a great exaggeration. It consists of poll-taxes, land-taxes, monopolies, and custom duties, of all of which a brief account will be satisfactory. With the exception of the Chinese of the pure blood, that is, of emigrants direct from China, all the inhabitants subject to the direct government of Siam, excluding, of course, the tributary states, are amenable to the performance of corvée labour to the crown, commuted when the services are not exacted into a money payment. This varies for a slave, from two to four ticals, and for a freeman from four to six ticals. The total amount of the commutation is stated at 12,000,000 of ticals, or 1,500,000*l.* At the medium rate of 4 ticals a head, the contributors to this tax would amount to 3,000,000 of persons.

The Chinese are also subject to a capitation tax, but at a higher rate. A census of them is taken every three years, and then every male of the age of 20 and upwards pays a tax of 5 ticals. The total amount of this tax is stated at 2,000,000 of ticals or 250,000*l.* The amount of the tax would make the number of the contributors 400,000, and if these constitute one-third part of the population, the total Chinese inhabitants of Siam would amount to 1,200,000*l.*

The tax on land is of three different descriptions, namely, an impost on land, yielding rice by irrigation,—one on such lands as produce such articles as sugar-cane, pepper, and tobacco, and a third on garden lands. The first of these imposts is a fixed tax of one tical for a measure equal to an arpent, and, if we consider this as an English acre, we have a moderate fixed impost of half a crown the acre. The produce of this tax is said to be only 2,000,000 of ticals, or 250,000*l.* The actual extent of land under water-field cultivation is, according to this estimate, only 2,000,000 of acres, but this, of course, excludes the lands of all the tributary states. The tax on lands yielding such products as sugar-cane and tobacco, is said to yield a sum of 500,000 ticals or 62,500*l.*, but the principal on which it is assessed is not stated. The tax on garden lands and orchards is far more productive than either of the other two, for it is stated as yielding 5,545,000 ticals, or 692,750*l.* This is a tax on every fruit tree or other tree, the produce of a garden or orchard, and it includes even the bamboo. The Durian pays the highest tax, namely, a tical, or 2*s.* 6*d.* on each tree, while the mangostin, the mango, and the jack, pay no more than one-fourth part of that sum. This impost is assessed at the beginning of each reign, and throughout, it is invariable, without reference to increase or diminution in the number of trees cultivated. This is, of course, an excise or a tax on the produce of the land, and not on the land itself. The other two taxes on the land are, no doubt, of the same nature, for in a country so under-peopled as Siam, no true land tax, or impost on rent, can correctly speaking exist.

Many royal monopolies exist in Siam, and the most considerable of these are farmed, and yield a considerable part of the public revenue. The monopoly of the retail vend of opium yields 50,000*l*, of rice-spirit 62,500*l.*, of tobacco 18,888*l.*, of gaming 62,500*l.*, of the fishery of the Manam 8888*l.*, of the public markets 12,500*l.*, and of the floating shops on the Menam 18,888*l.* The total of these farmed monopolies amounts to 231,664*l.* The practice of farming such taxes has been introduced only of late years, and has evidently been borrowed from that of the neighbouring European governments.

Inland duties appear to be levied on many articles, exclusive of those imposed on the land, and of custom duties. Thus, the tax on coco-nut oil, a staple product, is stated at the sum of 62,500*l.*, that on sapan-wood at 25,000*l.*, that on cane and palm sugar at 32,500*l.*, and that on black pepper at 50,000*l.*

The customs, including measurement duty on European and Arabian shipping, yield only 47,500*l.* excises and inland duties, having, in fact, anticipated them. Besides the taxes now enumerated, there are some peculiar ones which deserve notice. Thus, there is a lottery which produces 25,000*l.*, and a tax on public prostitutes, which yields 6250*l.*

Some particular articles are monopolised by the government, or received by it as tribute paid in kind. Thus, esculent swallows' nests are stated at 12,500*l.* Tin at 7500*l.*; iron, probably a royalty, at the same sum; gamboge, at 3000*l.*; eagle-wood, at 5625*l.*, and rosewood at 5000*l.* Besides the various sources of revenue now stated, the King of Siam is himself a merchant, trading to a considerable extent to China and the Malay Islands, but the extent of his profits in these unsuitable enterprises, if any, is unknown. The revenue derived by the Siamese government from the tributary states would appear to be but small, for that of the northern ones, or Lao, is set down at no more than 6250*l.*, while that of the southern, or Malay and Kambojan, amounts only to 5000*l.*

As to laws, the Siamese possess a written code in forty volumes, divided into three parts, the first of which contains the titles and attributes of all legal functionaries, the second the institutes of ancient kings, and the third the modern laws, dating from king Phra Naret, who ascended the throne in the year of our time, 1564. This last and most important part of the code consists of the following titles, namely, theft and robbery, slavery, marriage contracts and debts, inheritance, and finally forms and proceedings. M. Pallegoix, who states that he read the code, affirms it to be conformable to natural justice, and well suited to the genius of the people for whom it was framed. All the chief officers charged with the administration of justice are bound by law to be possessed of a copy of it, and daily to peruse some pages. He adds, however, that the laws are hardly ever followed, and he gives an example. They ordain that no suit or trial should exceed in duration three days, notwithstanding which they are frequently drawn out to the length of two and three years!

The Siamese, in the administration of the laws, make no distinction between judicial and executive functions, both being in the hands of the same parties. There are three classes of tribunals, the lowest that of the governors of provinces, the second that of princes and ministers at the capital, of which there are several, and third, that of the king. No causes of importance are tried by the first, and it is only the last that exercises unlimited jurisdiction. Every court has its assessors, and all proceedings are taken in writing. In criminal cases the punishments are occasionally of extreme severity. Thus, a thief who melts down a gold or silver idol stolen from a temple is condemned to be burnt alive. Adulterers are branded on the cheek, and Talapoins, or priests, convicted of a breach of chastity are stripped of their sacerdotal dress, scourged, and condemned for life to cut grass for the royal elephants, a punishment considered infamous, and for which there is no pardon. According to law, capital punishment ought to be inflicted for murder, and several other crimes, but at present it is confined to high treason and rebellion. Sentence of death is passed by the tribunal, but usually commuted by the crown for a smaller punishment. When the extreme sentence of the law is carried into effect, it is by decapitation, or by binding the malefactor to a post, and transfixing him with spears, the body in either case being left to be devoured by birds of prey. In the case of criminals of the royal family, their blood must not be shed, and with them the mode of execution is to sew them in leathern bags and sink them alive in the Menam. In cases of murder and of suicide, neighbourhoods within a radius of fifty fathoms are made responsible under the penalty of a heavy fine. When quarrels take place, therefore, the neighbours take much pains to prevent their ending in death; and acts of suicide, lest they should be construed into murders, are carefully concealed.

The Siamese prisons appear to be most execrable dungeons. The prisoners are all chained together at night, and in the day subjected to hard labour, while throughout their incarceration, they have no other food than a little rice and salt, while they are subject to the ill-usage and extortion of the jailers. Prisoners for debt, however, are usually set free in no long time by the interference of their relatives. A Siamese who had been confined in these dungeons observed to the Bishop of Siam, that he could not imagine hell itself to be worse.

The art of war, as may well be imagined, is in a very low state among the Siamese. By the accidents of position they are an agricultural and by no means a warlike people. The masses go unarmed, a mark of civilisation which distinguishes this people from the Malays and other rude nations of the same class. The strength, however, which a civilisation derived chiefly from the advantages of locality has conferred upon the Siamese, has immemorially enabled them to subdue and hold in subjugation most of the smaller nations of their neighbourhood not so favourably situated, as well as to hold their own with their equals in power and civilisation, the Burmese, Peguans, and Kambojans. The Siamese have never, indeed, been permanently conquered, although their country has frequently been invaded and over-run.

When the King of Siam declares war he issues a proclamation to the princes, chiefs, governors, and tributary states, to furnish the quotas of their respective followers, prescribed by custom. Each soldier is clothed, and supplied with one month's rations, the state furnishing arms. Such is the constitutional army of Siam; but within the last twenty years a sort of standing army, disciplined and formed on the European model, has been organised, under the instruction of some Englishmen. This consists of infantry and artillery, and is said to number 10,000. The route of a Siamese army is usually by water, and when it lands, in the absence of all roads, its artillery is conveyed on elephants, and its small baggage on the backs of the soldiers and camp-followers. In former times, and in wars with the Burmese, Peguans, and Kambojans, a Siamese army is said to have sometimes amounted to 100,000 men, and 1000 elephants. Such a rabble host could only have subsisted, and subsisted miserably, too, on the plunder and devastation of the country it invaded.

The Siamese marine is a good deal more respectable than the land force. It consists of 120 war boats, furnished both with oars and sails, some carrying two and some four guns, these being in the bow and stern only, so that in action each must be alternately swept round by oar, to bear on the enemy. In addition to these boats, the present king has built no fewer than six frigates and sixteen corvettes, on European models, and these are commanded by Europeans.

The Arsenal, for security against insurrection or rebellion, is within the inclosure of the royal palace, and amply stocked with small arms and cannon, kept in good repair. These are of foreign, chiefly English manufacture, but the gunpowder is of Siamese make, coarse and weak. Towards the mouth of the Menam, there have been erected, since my visit in 1822, several fortresses, well constructed of earth, and on European principles, some of which mount as many as 100 guns. These seem to be, with the exception of the weak wall round the king's palace, the only fortifications in the kingdom, for in this respect Siam, as well all the other Indo-Chinese countries, differ widely from Hindustan, which abounds in fortified places.

The Siamese are said to treat prisoners of war with humanity. This is probably a matter of policy. The paucity of population seems to be felt, and the prisoners are hence adopted as citizens, and planted as colonists, under a leader of their own nation. In this manner we find settlements of Peguans, Kambojans, Cochin Chinese, and Malays. The exception to this rule of good treatment are captured rebellious chiefs, who are exposed, in iron cages, to the insults of the populace, and then immured in dungeons. An example of this took place as late as 1829, under the late king, when the Lao prince of Vieng-chan was brought prisoner to Bangkok, exposed in an iron cage, and soon after died from the ill treatment to which he was subjected.

The history of Siam is divided by the Siamese themselves into two parts, an early and mostly fabulous, and a modern and comparatively authentic one. In the first, the founders of the kingdom are described as having been two Bramins, who were cotemporaries of Buddha, or who lived 543 years before Christ. The first date, however, which is, quoted for any event, is 950 of the sacred era, corresponding with 407 of Christ. Siam, at this time called Sayam, for it had not yet taken the name of Thai, was tributary to Kamboja, but threw off the yoke under a prince called Arunârat, said to have been born in the year in question. To his time is ascribed the invention of the Siamese alphabet, and the restriction of the Kambojan to religious purposes, as at present. In the year of Christ, 638, was established the civil era, and this is ascribed to a king called Phaya Krek. It is probable, however, that this era is contemporary with the first introduction of the Buddhist religion into Siam. At whatever time this last event happened, we must conclude that the Siamese must have been already a tolerably civilised people when they were capable of adopting a system of worship so refined as that of Buddha, with its transmigration, its priesthood supported by voluntary alms, its temples and its monasteries.

The modern or authentic history of Siam dates from the establishment of the seat of government in Yuthia, evidently a corruption of the Sanscrit Ayudhya or Oude. This happened in the civil year, 712, corresponding to 1350 of our time, under a prince named Phaya Uthong. This event, then, took place only 161 years before the arrival of Alboquerque at Malacca, when the name of Siam became first known to Europeans. From that time to the accession of the reigning king, 475 years have transpired, during which there have reigned twenty-nine kings, which gives an average of between sixteen and seventeen years for each reign. Some of the princes reigned only a few months, and others even only a few days. Some were assassinated by brothers, uncles, and ministers, and four different dynasties have occupied the throne. The country within the period named was repeatedly invaded by Peguans, Burmese, and Kambojans, even the capital having been taken, sacked, and its inhabitants carried into captivity. In the year 1583, one of the best of the Siamese kings, Phra Naret, in retaliation of an invasion of his own country, invaded Kamboja, captured its capital, and took its king prisoner. He had made a vow that he would bathe his feet in the blood of the Kambojan monarch, and he kept his word, for he caused his prisoner to be assassinated in his own presence, and went through the ceremony to the sound of cymbals and other musical instruments.

In 1656, a prince called Phra Narai, who on his accession took the title of Phra Châo Champhuok, ascended the throne. He was the second of his dynasty, for his father had been a noble who had usurped the government by the assassination of his predecessor. Phra Narai was the ally of Lewis XIV., and the same who sent missions to France and received ambassadors from that country. The intercourse was brought about by an adventurer of the name of Constantine Falcon, a Greek of the island of Cephalonia. This person had been the steward of an English East Indiaman, but had the talents and dexterity to raise himself to the post of first minister of Siam, and is justly quoted by Voltaire as a signal example of the superiority of the European over the Asiatic races. His master and protector, however, dying in 1688, Falcon was deposed and put to death, and with him ended the prospect, at one time promising, of establishing French influence in Siam.

In the 80 years between the death of the ally of Lewis XIV., and the year 1767, no fewer than five different sovereigns reigned in Siam, most of them usurpers. In 1758, the celebrated Birmese king, the conqueror of Pegu, and known to Europeans as Alomprah, invaded Siam, laid siege to Yuthia, but dying during the siege, his army retreated. The Siamese capital, however, was captured and sacked by his son and successor in 1766. Next year the son of a Chinese by a Siamese mother, seized the throne on the death of the reigning prince and expelled the Burmese.

This is the king known by the Siamese title of Phaya Tak. He appears to have ruled the country with ability and equity for fifteen years, but having incurred the hostility of the nobles, he flew to the asylum of a monastery in 1782, from which he was dragged and assassinated by one of the nobility who ascended the throne and was the first prince of the reigning dynasty. He was succeeded by his son in 1811, the prince, who was on the throne during my mission in 1822. On his death in 1825, the throne was seized by one of his sons by a concubine to the prejudice of the legitimate heir, the present king, who ascended the throne in 1851, under the name of Somdet Phra and several others. During the lifetime of his brother, he had lived in a monastery and worn the yellow garb of a talapoin for protection. Here he had studied for twenty years, and apparently to good purpose, for he appears to be the most intelligent and liberal monarch that ever ruled Siam. Along with him reigns his brother, as seind, or junior king.

SIAOW, or SIYAO, is the name of a small island lying off the Sangir chain which extends from the end of the north-eastern or volcanic peninsula of Celebes towards Mindano. This islet contains a mountain which rises to the height of 6000 feet above the level of the sea, and is the most elevated point of the chain to which it belongs. It is a volcano which has produced many eruptions.

SIBIRU (Pulo), literally "the blue" or "the azure isle" is one of the largest of the islands lying off the western coast of Sumatra, between 2° 15′ and 4° 5′ south latitude. It is sometimes called also Mintao. Sibiru is in length from north to south, about 50 geographical miles, but of unequal breadth, and has been computed to have an area of 480 geographical miles, or 16·5 myriometers. In its centre it has an active volcano. Its inhabitants belong to the Malayan race and speak the same language, and are of the same nation as the people of the islands immediately south of it, Pora and Pagi.

SIBUYAN. A considerable island lying between the Philippine Islands of Masbaté to the east and Isla de Tablas to the west, and north of the large island of Panay, to the province of Capiz in which it belongs. It is five leagues in length and three in breadth in its widest part. It is mountainous but fertile. The inhabitants are chiefly fishermen, and amounted, in 1848, to 5634 souls.

SILK. This commodity is known to the Malays and Javanese by the name of Sutra, which is the Sanscrit for thread or yarn, the form in which it was probably first made known to the Indian Islanders. The same name, with more or less corruption, is that by which it is called all over the Malay and Philippine Archipelagos. In most of the languages, it is, letter for letter, the same as in Malay and Javanese, but we find it in the Lampung of Sumatra as Sutagha, and in the Tagala and Bisaya of the Philippines, respectively Sutla, and Sukla, and in the Tagala, accompanied by a native synonym. Silk may probably have been first made known to the inhabitants of the Indian Islands by the Hindus, if we are to judge from its Sanscrit name, but in all times known to us, they have been supplied with this article raw and wrought by the Chinese, the original inventors of silk. Pigafetta, in 1521, found not only the king of Borneo and his courtiers clad in silk, but the very housings of the royal elephants made of it. The same thing was found to be the case at Malacca on its capture ten years before, and Barbosa expressly names raw and manufactured silks as among the articles brought by the Chinese junks, to Malacca. From the raw silk of China, the Malays and Javanese always wove and still continue to do so, some strong and often rich domestic fabrics suited to their own peculiar tastes. The culture of the mulberry and the rearing of the silkworm have never been practised by the natives of the Archipelago, whether from the unsuitableness of this branch of industry to the climate, or to the state of society, is not ascertained. De Barros, indeed, after enumerating, with great correctness, the commodities produced by Sumatra, such as gold, camphor, and pepper, says, "It produces, also silk, in such quantity that there are cargos of it sent to many parts of India," but this is probably an error on the part of that usually reliable writer. I am not even aware that wild silk is produced in any of the insular forests such as it is found to be in many of those of Hindustan. The only country of the two Archipelagos in which the rearing of the silkworm has been attempted is Luzon. In 1786, a governor-general of the Philippines caused four millions and a half of mulberry trees to be planted in the province of Camarines. Their culture, however, being voluntary, and the natives showing no disposition to attend to this branch of industry, the project wholly failed. It has since, more than once, been renewed, and very good silk produced, but still the rearing of the silkworm as a branch of industry has not succeeded, and most probably from being uncongenial to the habits of the natives and incompatible with the relative high price of labour.

SILVER. No veins of this metal have hitherto been discovered in any of the islands of the Malay or Philippine Archipelagos, many of which contain such abundant stores of iron, gold, tin and antimony. A small quantity of it, however, appears to be contained in all the gold of these countries. In Malay the name for silver is perak, and in Javanese sâlaka. Both are native words of which the origin has not been traced, and both have a very wide currency, for the Malay word is found as far as the Philippines in the slight disguise of pilak, and the Javanese without any alteration, in all the languages from the southern parts of Sumatra to Celebes inclusive. In some of the ruder languages, however, as those of Timur, Floris, and Madagascar, it goes under the name of "white gold," while gold itself is distinguished from it by the epithet of "red."

The silver with which the Indian Islanders were supplied before their intercourse with Europeans, was most probably derived from Tonquin, China, and Lao. Indeed, De Barros expressly states, that the silver which Alboquerque coined money from at Malacca in 1511, came from the last-named of these countries through Siam. Ever since, or at least since the discovery and conquest of Mexico and Peru, they have been furnished from America in the course of trade, and their favourite form is the column dollar or "piece of eight" of the old coinage.

SINGALANG. The name of one of the highest mountains of Sumatra, rising to the height of 9800 feet above the level of the sea. It lies in the inland part of the Netherland province of Padang towards the western side of the island and about 30 miles south of the equator.

SINGAPORE, correctly SINGAPURA, from the Sanscrit singa, lion, and pura city. This is the name of an island, which with the exception of a single village ot poor and predatory Malay fishermen, and that only formed in 1811, was covered with a primeval forest down to the 6th day of February, 1819, and is now the fourth in rank of the European emporia of India, ranking after Batavia. De Barros gives a whimsical etymology of the name "Anciently," says he, "the most celebrated city which existed in the land of Malacca, was called Cingapura, which, in the language of the country signifies 'false delay' (falsa demora)." This derivation must have come through the Malays who, no doubt were then, as they now are, ignorant of the true meaning of the name, and indeed, even of the fact that it is derived from the sacred language of the Hindus.

Singapore is the most northerly of the large islands of the almost countless group that in a great measure blocks up the eastern end of the strait which divides the Peninsula from Sumatra, leaving but narrow channels for navigation, and forming as it were, a region of straits. It is about thirty miles distant from the southern extremity of the Asiatic continent, and separated from the mainland by a strait generally about a mile broad, but in some parts little more than three furlongs. This is the Sâlat tambrau (strait of the tambrau fish), of the Malays and the "old Straits of Singapore" of European navigators. It was the old passage into the China Sea, but has long been abandoned for that by the southern side of Singapore. I went through it in a ship of 400 tons, and found the passage tedious but safe. Singapore in its greatest length from east to west, is 25 miles long, and in its greatest breadth 14, having an area of 206 square geographical miles, which will make it 70 miles larger than the Isle of Wight. To the north, it is bounded by the territory of Jehore, the limit between them being the continental shore of the narrow strait already mentioned. Everywhere else, the British settlement extends to 10 miles from the shore of the main land, and within this distance are contained no fewer than 75 islets of various sizes, embracing an area of 17 square miles, so that the superficies of the entire British settlement amounted to 223 square miles.

Viewed from a distance, Singapore presents no marked elevations, but has the unvarying aspect of one continuous forest. The surface, however, is undulating; consisting, generally, of rounded hills of from 80 to 120 feet high, with narrow valleys not above 15 or 20 feet above the sea level. A chain of rather higher hills runs through the island from east to west, making the water-shed in one direction to the north, and in the other to the south. The culminating point of the land is a hill, nearly in the centre of the island, called Bukit-timah, that is, "tin-hill," and this rises to the height of 519 feet above low water-mark spring tides.

The geological formation of Singapore consists of the same rocks as the Peninsula generally, and is plutonic and sedimentary ; the first consisting of granite, and the last, which embraces the greater portion of the island, of sand-stone, slate, and clay iron-ore. The only metallic ore that exists in abundance, and this is very rich, is that of iron. The island lies also in the formation most favourable for the existence of tin, namely, between the junction of the granite and sand-stone, but no ore of it has as yet been discovered. The blue clays furnish an excellent material for bricks and tiles; and the decomposed feldspar of the granite the finest kaolin which has yet been seen in India, but it has not been applied to the manufacture of porcelane. Some portion of the island, as that which is the site of the town, is of alluvial formation, chiefly sand with a very thin covering of vegetable mould.

The climate of the island is well described by Mr. Thomson, in the Journal of the Indian Archipelago. "Singapore," says he, "though within 80 miles of the equator, has an abundance of moisture, either deposited by the dews or gentle refreshing showers, which keeps its atmosphere cool, prevents the parching effects of the sun, and promotes continual verdure. It never experiences furious gales. If more than ordinary heat has accumulated moisture and electricity, a squall generally sets in, followed by a heavy shower of rain; such squalls seldom exceeding one or two hours in duration. According as the monsoon blows, you will have the squalls coming from that direction. But the most severe and numerous are from the south-west, called 'Sumatras,' and these occur, most frequently, between 1 and 5 o'clock in the morning. The north-east monsoon blows from November to March; after which the wind veers round to the south-east and gradually sets in the south-west, at which point it continues to September. The north-east blows more steadily than the south-west monsoon. The temperature is by one or two degrees cooler in the first than in the last." The average fall of rain is found, from the observation of a series of years, to be 92·697 inches; and the average number of days in the year in which rain falls is found to be 180, thus dividing the year almost equally between wet and dry; the rain not being continuous, but pretty equally distributed through the whole year, January, however, being the month in which the greatest quantity falls. The mean temperature of Singapore is, at present, 81°·247, the lowest being 79°·55 and the highest 82°·31, so that the range is no more than 2°·76. It would appear from this that the temperature of the island is by 9° 90′ lower than that of many other localities in the same latitudes. Comparing the temperature now stated with that which was ascertained 20 years earlier, and in the infancy of the settlement, it would appear that it had increased by 2° 48′, a fact ascribable, no doubt, to the increase of buildings, and to the country having been cleared of forest for three miles inland from the town, the site of the observations. The general character of the climate as to temperature is, that the heat is great and continuous, but never excessive, and that there is little distinction of seasons; summer and winter differing from each other only by one or two degrees of the thermometer. Thunder showers are of frequent occurrence, but the thunder is by no means so severe as I have experienced it in Java, and seldom destructive to life or property. "That interesting and wonderful phenomenon, called a water-spout," says Mr. Thomson, "is often to be seen in the seas and straits adjacent. They ought more properly to be called whirlwinds charged with vapour. They occur, generally, in the morning between the hours of eight and twelve, and rise to the height of half a mile, appearing in the distance like large columns supporting the heavy masses of cumuli above them. I noticed in October, 1841, six of these attached to one cloud, under action at the same time. In August, 1838, one passed over the harbour and town of Singapore, devastating one ship and sinking another; and carrying off the corner of the roof of a house in its course landward. No other atmospherical disturbances of any moment occur. The typhoons of the China Sea and Bay of Bengal do not reach those parts, nor are there hot winds to parch the land. The equable and quiet state of the atmosphere and seasons of these regions, consequently create analogous properties in the face of indigenous vegetation. Evergreens abound; few trees shed all their leaves at the same time; and many of the fruit trees produce all the year round. Such as have their seasons of fruit will produce crops out of season, bearing small irregular ones at intervening times. This continual verdure is, perhaps, more grateful to the stranger than to those who have been accustomed to it. To the former it bears the pleasant appearance of exuberance and fecundity,—of a region where the lofty forest not only hangs over the beach, but clothes the mountains to their tops, so unlike the sterile barrenness of higher latitudes. To the latter, the continual sameness palls the senses. They want variety, and call for a sterile winter, only that they may renew, with doubly keen perception, their acquaintance with the beauties of returning summer, a season that always here reigns."

Notwithstanding its heat and its monotony, the climate of Singapore is even remarkable for its salubrity; and with, perhaps, the exception of a few little-frequented spots in the interior, it is certainly free from the malaria which often infects countries, apparently more favourably circumstanced. This advantage it seems to owe to its perfect ventilation by the monsoons,—by land and sea-breezes,—and by frequent squalls. That this is the main cause is proved by the eminently pestiferous air of a land-locked harbour at the western end of the island, and not above two miles distant from the town.

A popular view of the botany of Singapore has been given by Dr. Oxley, a man of science, and long familiar with the place. "If nature," says he, "has been frugal in her gifts of the higher orders of the animal kingdom in Singapore, she has lavished with unsparing prodigality, the riches of the vegetable one. Notwithstanding the infertility of the soil, climate more than compensates for the loss: heat and moisture cover the lean earth with unceasing verdure; and we realise, what fancy paints as the most desirable of all climates,—an eternal spring. But independently of its position, the botany of this place possesses several other interesting considerations. Being a connecting link between the Indian and Australian forms, we have types of both, and many genera of either region. We observe the Indian forms in the natural families Palmæ, Scitamineæ, Aroideæ, Artocarpeæ, Euphorbiaceæ, Apocyneæ, Guttiferæ, Convolvulaceæ, Leguminosæ, all numerous. The natural families Casuarineæ, Myrtaceæ, particularly Melaleucæ and Proteaceæ, connect us with Australia."

"The plants," he observes, "which usually spring up when the primeval forest has been cut down; and where the bane of all the rest of the vegetable kingdom, the Andropogon caricosum, or Lalang grass, has not taken possession, belong to the following genera: Melastoma, Myrtus, Morinda, Solanum, Rubus, Rottlera, Clerodendrum, Commersonia, Ficus, and Passiflora. The jungle, with the exception of its outskirts, is unexplorable, without great risk, from the number of tigers; but I have collected between forty and fifty orchideous plants, including epiphytal and terrestrial, and about the same number of ferns. Fici are extremely numerous. Of palms I have not seen more than twenty species, although, I believe, there are a much greater number. The most interesting of these, in an economic point of view, are the coco-nut, the Areca catechu or pinang, the Areca sigillaria or nibung, the Sagus lævis or râmbuja, the Nipa fruticans or nipa, and the Gomutus or iju. Of the natural families which most abound, the Asclepiadeæ, Euphorbiaceæ, Scitamineæ, and Urticaceæ are the chief." The forest contains an immense number of species of timber trees, most of them of great height and growth. Above two hundred have been collected, and of these about half-a-dozen afford good timber for house and boat building. The teak is not of the number. The forest, also, produces the two species which yield the useful gutta-percha, and a fig which affords an elastic gum. But for use these articles, as well as timber, are not obtained from Singapore itself, but from the wider and more accessible forests of the neighbouring continent.

The zoology of Singapore is that of the neighbouring continent, to the exclusion of some of the larger animals, as the elephant, the rhinoceros, the tapir, and the ox. The largest feline animal indigenous to the island is a small leopard, called by the Malays arimau-dàan, that is "the branch" or climbing tiger. But the tiger, an animal unknown to the island in the earlier years of the British settlement, made its first appearance five or six years after it was formed, and is now too abundant. It seems to have crossed over from the continent, attracted no doubt by the sound of human voices and the lowing of cattle. It has multiplied greatly, and is supposed to destroy, yearly, from two to three hundred persons, proving the greatest bane of the settlement. Large rewards have been offered for the destruction of tigers, and a good number have been captured by pitfalls, but all attempts at their extermination have been unsuccessful and are likely long to prove so in this still forest-clad island, parted from a region in which the tiger is abundant by a channel of no more than a few furlongs broad. The channel between Penang and the main is two miles broad, and this has been sufficient to exclude the tiger, for although there have been examples of individuals having crossed over, it has been in an exhausted state, and they have been immediately destroyed.

Of the natural family of Mustelidæ, there are two in Singapore, the musang of the Malays, Paradoxurus musanga, and the binturung, Ictides ater, of the size of a badger. Otters are occasionally seen along the coasts, but are rare. The wild hog is frequent, and there are five species of deer, the usual ones of the Peninsula and Sumatra, from the Rusa of the size of a heifer to the kanchil, which is hardly as large as a rabbit. Among mammals, one species of bat is often to be seen, the same which is so frequent in almost all parts of the Archipelago, the kalong or Pteropus javanicus. This is about the size of a raven, and a troop of them in flight has very much the look of a flock of crows, and by a stranger may be easily mistaken for one. "I may add," says Dr. Oxley, "In rendering a sketch of the zoology of Singapore, several species of the bat tribe, and among them that most destructive one to all fruits, the flying fox or Pteropus. Fortunately, however, they are as yet scarce, but at no distance from us they are numerous beyond count. I have seen a flock of them while anchored in the Straits of Malacca, so large as to take several hours in passing. A colony is at present located in a mangrove creek at the head of the estuary of the Jehore river. In the day they are seen asleep hanging in millions from the branches of the mangrove. At sunset they begin to stir, and presently they ascend into the air and wing their way to the south-east in one vast uninterrupted cloud. They pass the whole night in the jungle and plantations devouring fruit, and as soon as dawn begins to appear, they mount the air again and return to their roosting-place at the head of the estuary. Their flesh is eaten by the natives, but no real fox smells to my mind half so rank as they do. Methinks a rat would be palatable food compared with them." These bats, in so far as the orchard is concerned, are the locust of the country, in which flights of the insect itself as far as I am aware are unknown. The Pteromys, or flying squirrel, the krawak of the Malays, is very frequent in Singapore, and so are three different species of monkey.

As with the larger quadrupeds, the larger birds of the Peninsula and Sumatra are not found in Singapore. It has neither their peacocks, nor their pheasants, and the only birds of the Rasorial family which exist in it are two species of quail. Nearly all the web-footed birds, whether indigenous or of passage, are not to be seen. There are six different species of pigeon, from the size of our wood-pigeon to that of a thrush. Parrots are frequent, but the species only two or three. The only bird that can be called game is the snipe, which seems a stranger to no country in the world that has marshes. The birds of prey of four different genera are sufficiently numerous, and Dr. Oxley remarks that among birds of this family is "that perfect type of the true falcons, the beautiful little Falco cærulescens, which, although not much larger than a sparrow, will kill and carry off a bird the size of a thrush."

Among reptiles, alligators are common in the salt water creeks, and along the shores of the island, but having an abundant supply of fish, are not troublesome to man. The Iguana lizard, the bewak of the Malays, is not unfrequent, but the noisy house lizard or tokay, the tákó of the Malays, so common in Penang and so much more so in Siam, is not found in Singapore. The esculent turtle is very abundant along the shores of Singapore and the neighbouring islands, and being, as food, restricted to the European and Chinese population, is the cheapest animal food in the market, one of the largest weighing several hundred weights selling for six or seven shillings. "Snakes," says Dr. Oxley, "are not numerous. The most common is a dark cobra. I believe this with a trigonocephalus are the only well-authenticated venomous species on the island. The first possesses the peculiar property of ejecting venom from its mouth. The Malays say there is no cure for its bite. I have seen it prove fatal to a fowl in two or three minutes, but have not observed its effects on large animals. Those I have killed have measured from 4½ to 5¼ feet in length. This reptile being slow and sluggish is easily overtaken and killed. When attacked, it erects the body and dilates the skin on either side of the head, uttering a noise like that of an irritated cat. If attacked it throws, to the distance of from six to eight feet, a venomous fluid of a most poisonous quality." Fish and crustaceans are in great plenty, and Dr. Oxley has enumerated forty species of them as seen by himself. About half-a-dozen of these are excellent for the table, fully equal to the best fish of our own coasts. Among these the best is the white pomfret of Europeans, the bawal-puteh of the Malays, of richer flavour than our soles and less luscious than the turbot.

The agriculture of Singapore, although conducted with sufficient spirit and activity, is limited to a small number of objects, and nearly excludes all the cereal grasses and pulses constituting the staple articles of human food. The soil of the island, with very few exceptions, is like that of the adjoining peninsula, unfertile,—there is no natural, and therefore no cheap source of irrigation, and hence the land is incapable of furnishing a cheap supply of the main necessaries of life, which are yielded only within the Archipelago by rich volcanic or alluvial soils, assisted by a copious perennial irrigation. For such plants as rice, the sugar-cane, the indigo-plant, pulses, maiz, tobacco, cotton, the soil must be considered as ill-suited. Besides want of fertility of soil, Singapore wants sufficient elevation to give a climate fit for the production of coffee. Even the nutmeg thrives only when forced by rich dressings, and the clove does not succeed at all. On the other hand, all plants which depend more on heat and moisture than on soil, flourish luxuriantly, such as the coco and areca palms, with the Uncaria gambir, which is indigenous. Black pepper, which is a long-naturalised exotic, although it answers well, yet even it requires some manuring. In 1854, the quantity of pepper produced amounted to 3,116,533 pounds, and the betel or areca nut to above 40,000 cwts. Among the plants congenial to both soil and climate are most of the intertropical fruits, whether indigenous or exotic. Among these the most easily reared, and even cheaper than the banana is the pine-apple, equalling in size and flavour the finest productions of our hot-houses. Besides fruits, the soil and climate are well adapted to the production of the yam and igname, and to that of the coarse pot-herbs which belong to the latitude.

The following judicious remarks are made by Mr. Logan on the soil of Singapore: "The soil is much more varied than it was supposed to be in former years, and so far from consisting entirely of decomposed sandstone and clay-iron ore, it contains a plutonic (granitic) tract of about sixty square miles, and another in which shales predominate. Although the soils have not the fertility of the volcanic and calcareous ones which occur in many parts of the Indian Archipelago, they are covered with an indigenous vegetation of great vigour and luxuriance, supporting numbers of animals of different species. The hills of plutonic rock support dense and continuous forests composed of more than 200 species of trees, many of which are of great size. So long as the iron is not in such excess as to recompose the clay into stone, or render it hard, those soils which contain most iron are most fertile. The purely, or highly felspathic are the worst. But even felspathic soils, when intermixed with a sufficient proportion of quartz, are, in this estimate, capable of producing an abundant vegetation. Although it is obvious to every observer that there is no kind of soil in the island for which nature has not provided plants, that flourish luxuriantly in it, yet it must not be hastily concluded, as some have done, that this exuberant vegetation indicates a general fertility in the soil. It is found, on the contrary, when the native plants are destroyed, and the land is employed for agriculture, that there are very few soils in which cultivated plants not indigenous to the region, but whose climatic range embraces it, will flourish spontaneously. While the coco-nut, areca, sago, gomuti, and the numerous Malayan fruits succeed with little care, the nutmeg and clove are stunted, and almost unproductive, unless carefully cultivated and highly manured. Yet the climate is perfectly adapted to them. Place them in the rare spots where there is naturally a fertile soil, or create one artificially, and the produce is equal to that of trees in the Molucca plantations. With respect to indigenous plants, gambier, pepper, and all the fruits flourish on the Plutonic hills, provided they are not too deficient in iron and quartz. The hills of violet shale, where they are not too sandy, are equal to the best Plutonic soils,—those, namely, in which there is a sufficient proportion of hard granules to render them friable, and sufficient iron to render them highly absorptive of water, without becoming plastic. Of all the sedimentary soils, the sandstone and very arenaceous shales furnish the worst. Of the alluvial soils, the sand, particularly when it contains a mixture of vegetable matter, or triturated shells, is the proper soil of the coco-nut and the vegetable mud of the sago. When the country has been better and longer drained and cultivated, the latter soil will become a rich mould. At present it is too wet and sour to make a fertile soil. Rice is grown on some patches of it. The bluish sea mud contains good ingredients, but the clay is in excess, and the animal matter in it appears to assist in rendering it hard and intractable, when it is not saturated with water. Even for such soils, however, nature has provided plants useful to man, for the areca and some of the indigenous fruit trees grow well in it with little cultivation. Although there are cultivated plants adapted to every kind of soil in the island, and it has indigenous tribes of man who can live exclusively on its yams, sago, fish, and wild animals, it is incapable of feeding a population of the more civilised races, and the latter must always be dependent on other countries for the great necessary of life—rice."

In the husbandry of Singapore, neither plough, harrow, nor spade are employed. All is done with the hoe and mattock. The whole is, in fact, a garden culture, in which no great crop is cultivated giving scope for the plough, and which is perhaps best performed by the hoe, the congenial and habitual implement, for this purpose, of all Asiatic nations. With respect to tenures, wild lands, when alienated by the government, are granted in fee simple, on payment of thirty shillings an acre, if within two miles of the town, and of one-half that amount, if beyond this distance. At this simple arrangement the government arrived at last, after the higgling and blundering of a quarter of a century, and the expenditure of vast quantities of ink and paper.

The only manufacture deserving this name that is carried on in Singapore, is that of sago, and for this, it is the workshop of nearly all that at present appears in commerce. This amounts to about 8000 tons yearly, of the value of about 30,000*l.* Great quantities of tools, implements, swords, and wall-pieces are manufactured by the Chinese, and there is some manufacture of furniture, with some boat and ship-building, but not to any great extent, for wet and dry docks remain yet to be constructed, although there be localities well adapted to them.

But every branch of industry is merely subsidiary to trade. Singapore, is, in fact, a great commercial emporium, in which are warehoused for future distribution, the staple products of Europe, Asia, and America. The town, the seat of this commerce, lies in north latitude 1° 17′, or only seventy-seven miles from the equator, and in east longitude 103° 50′ 47″. Its locality is on the southern side of the island, on a salt creek, into which falls the brook called the river of Singapore; the commercial part of it being on the western bank, and the public buildings and private houses on the eastern, which spreads into a sandy plain, a little above the level of the sea. There is, properly, no harbour, but the bay which fronts the town, and which is also the highway through the Straits of Malacca, is a roadstead equivalent to a harbour in a region never vexed by storms. Ships of the largest burdens lie in good anchoring-ground at the distance of two miles from the shore, those of moderate draught of water, within a mile, and small craft close to it. The salt creek, which has a quay on the commercial side, is navigable at all times for lighters up to the warehouses of the merchants.

In 1826, or seven years after the British occupation of Singapore, the population of the island, in round numbers, had already amounted to 13,000. In 1850, it had risen to nearly 60,000, of which 26,000 were in the town. The ingredients of this population were very heterogeneous, and composed of no fewer than fifteen nationalities. The most numerous party were the Chinese, forming fifty-three parts out of a hundred, or better than one half of the whole. Then followed the Malays, or proper natives of the country, forming twenty-three parts, or less than a fourth; natives of the Continent of India, chiefly of Bengal and the Coromandel coasts, forming fourteen parts, natives of Celebes four parts, and Javanese three parts. The coloured descendants of Europeans amounted to no more than 922, and the Europeans themselves, the rulers, only to 360. The languages spoken are, at least, as numerous as the nationalities. The Chinese speak three different tongues, the people of Continental India four, and those of Celebes and Java two each. Then come English, Arabic, and Persian. But the common medium of intercommunication, the language which unites all classes of inhabitants, and prevents such a variety of tongues from making a Babel of the place, is the liquid, easily-acquired Malay, of which all strangers acquire at least an useful smattering.

One peculiarity of the population of Singapore deserves special notice,—the extraordinary inequality of the sexes. This applies, more or less, to every class of the inhabitants. In the whole, the females form little more than one-seventh part, or to six men there is but one woman. But the disproportion is far greater in the Chinese population, for here the females form but one-nineteenth of the whole number, so that there is but one woman to eighteen men. This arises from the peculiarity of Chinese emigration which, with rare exceptions, and those very recent ones, is confined to the male sex, and this too, of men in the prime of life. Even the few females classed as Chinese, are not really so, but the offspring of native women married to Chinese or their mestizo descendants. This state of things, especially in regard to the Chinese inhabitants, forming too the majority of the population, is a source of much immorality and disorder, but it is hard to say how it can be remedied.

The commercial intercourse of Singapore is carried on with most of the European ports carrying on a distant foreign trade;—with the ports of Continental Asia, from the Red almost to the Yellow Sea, including those of Arabia, Persia, Hindustan, Siam, Cochin-China, and several of China; with all the ports of the Malay Archipelago, from Sumatra to New Guinea; with the capital of the Philippines; and with several of the east and west coasts of America. In the public returns of exports and imports, these places are classed under two-and-thirty different heads. The most important branch of the trade is that with the United Kingdom, and then follow respectively the trades with China, with British Continental India, and with Netherland India. In 1855, the whole imports amounted to the value of 21,267,696 Spanish dollars, and the exports to 17,504,398 Spanish dollars. This, as at all our Indian ports, included treasure as well as merchandise. The number of square-rigged vessels which arrived in the same year was 892, the departures 825. The number of junks and native praus was 2513, and the departures 2615. The staple imports from Europe are, cottons, woollens, and metals; from the continent of India, opium and cotton-wool for the Chinese market, and from China, coarse porcelain, silk, tea, camphor, and cassia. An ordinary price-current will contain at least forty different articles of the Malay and Philippine Archipelagos, with the countries immediately in their neighbourhood, as Tonquin, Cochin-china, Kamboja, and Siam. Among these, the staples are, rice, sugar, pepper, coffee, tin, gold, antimony, tortoise-shell, and fossil coal. The first appearance in commerce of several of the articles of this branch of the trade may said to be almost coeval with the foundation of the settlement, or to have appeared in consequence of its existence, such as the abaca or banana hemp, gutta-percha, Indian-rubber, vegetable tallow, pearl and flour sago, hides and horns.

Singapore is in every sense a free port, open to the flags of all nations upon equal terms, and has continued so nearly from its foundation. There is no impost whatever, on ship or cargo, saving a small charge for the light-house on the rock of Pedra-branca, and even from this, all native vessels are exempt. This freedom, and its highly convenient position, with security for life and property, are the causes of its rapid prosperity,—a prosperity of which there is no other example in the east, and which far more resembles that of an American than an Asiatic settlement. The example of Singapore has been followed by the Netherland government at several points of its vast possessions in the Archipelago, and with great, although not equal success.

In 1853, the number of dwelling-houses, shops, warehouses, and public buildings, constructed for the most part of brick, and roofed with tile, was 4719. A municipal tax of 10 per cent on the rental, yielded 5224*l*., which would make the yearly rent 52,240*l*., and reckoning house property at fifteen years' purchase, the value would be 783,600*l*. But as the rating for the assessment is low, this probably falls greatly short of its actual worth.

The executive government of Singapore is exercised conjointly with that of the two other British settlements in the Straits, Malacca and Penang, distant respectively about 90 and 400 miles, by an officer who has the title of Governor, but who is virtually but the lieutenant of the Governor-General of India, in whom is vested the essential attributes of government,—those of making laws, and directing their administration. Under the Governor, at each of the three settlements, is an officer, with the title of Resident Councillor. The laws are those of England, modified, in so far as concerns the native inhabitants, by an attention to their respective laws of inheritance and domestic usages. They are administered by the Court of a Recorder. There is also a Small Debt Court and a Court of Petty Sessions always sitting.

The public revenue is derived from excises, chiefly on the consumption of opium, spirits, and wine; the rent of public markets the property of the government; the sale of wild lands, the quit-rents on lands within the town held on long leases, namely, some for ninety-nine years, and some for ten times that time; fees and fines in the courts; and the post-office. In 1852–53, the gross amount of this revenue was 45,720*l*., and the chief branches of it being farmed, and always by the Chinese, the nominal charge of collection was but three-and-a-half per cent., which was, in fact, for the most part, the cost, not of collecting, but simply of receiving the amount. The expenditure in the same year, was 44,234*l*., or by 1486*l*. less than the income. The balance in favour of the last ought to have been much larger, but for certain charges which are preposterously debited to the settlement, such as a naval establishment for the general suppression of piracy, in which all India is equally interested, and the maintenance of the convicts of British continental India. These two items alone amount to near 10,000*l*., or close on one-fourth of the whole expenditure. In 1854–55, the public revenue had increased by the sum of near 10,000*l*. The main part of it is derived from excises on articles of luxury, and from the rents of public markets, the property of government. These taxes, with their amounts, were as follow in the year in question :—opium, 32,520*l*.; ardent spirits, 11,412*l*.; palm wine and hemp juice, 670*l*.; and public markets, 3372*l*., making a total of 47,874*l*., exclusive of the sale of public lands.

Besides the public revenue, there is a municipal one, under the management of a committee composed of public officers and merchants, or rate-payers, being justices of the peace. From this fund are maintained the police, roads, bridges, watering and lighting. It is derived, as already stated, from a rate of ten per cent. on the rent of houses, of five per cent. on the value of agricultural produce, and a tax on horses and carriages. In 1853, it yielded a gross sum of 8892*l*.

The ancient history of Singapore is, as usual, in all that relates to native story, full of obscurity. It has been stated in native writings, quoted by the Dutch writers, Van der Worm, and Valentyn, but which I have never seen, nor am I aware that any one else of our times has, that Singapore was founded by a colony of Malays from Palembang in Sumatra in the year of Christ 1160, and abandoned by them in the year 1253. The first palpable objection to this statement is that Palembang is not now, and is never known to history, as having been a country occupied by the Malays, the mass of its inhabitants being a distinct nation called the Sarawi, and its rulers immemorially Javanese. Another palpable objection is, that we have a Christian era given, without the Asiatic era from whence it is reckoned, and, indeed, what Asiatic era would it have been calculated from, for the Malays had none of their own, nor could they be supposed to have adopted the Arabian, since they did not embrace the Mohammedan religion until 116 years after the supposed date of the establishment of Singapore? If the first settlers of Singapore came from Palembang—and from its vicinity and the superior civilisation of its rulers, it is not improbable they did—they must have been Javanese and not Malays. This opinion gains some support from the fact that, for the most part, the names and titles of the princes who are stated to have reigned in Singapore, not to mention the name of the place itself, are either Javanese or Sanscrit,—such names, in a word, as the modern Javanese would, under similar circumstances, have imposed.

The account given by De Barros, and which he states to have been derived from the natives, makes the colony, which fled from Singapore and eventually established itself in Malacca, to have been Javanese, which is, in fact, virtually the same as the assertion of the Malays themselves, that it came from Palembang. The relics, very rude ones, discovered on the ancient site of Singapore, which is also that of the modern town, afford some corroboration of this opinion. The most remarkable of these is an inscription on a great mass of unhewn white sandstone. This nodule has been split in the centre, the two fragments lying opposite to each other, at about an angle of forty degrees, and at the base not above a couple of feet apart. The writing is on the two opposing faces of the rock, which itself seems to have been adopted for this purpose on the very spot where it lay, being still surrounded by several other masses of the same description. Nothing of the kind can be ruder. By time and the decomposition of the rock, most of the writing has been obliterated, although here and there a few letters are sufficiently distinct. These are, in form, rather round than angular, and, making allowance for the material and the rudeness of the execution, they bear the greatest resemblance to Kawi or the ancient writing of Java, the same which is found in most of the old monuments of that island. At all events, they bear no resemblance whatever to the Rejang of Sumatra, the character used by the majority of the people of Palembang, nor to the Korinchi, that in which the Malays most probably wrote before their adoption of the Arabic letters.

The other relics discovered are equally rude with the inscription. These were, the remains of an earthen wall, a fosse, a sepulchre, and a supposed temple on the hill behind the town, on which now stands the government house. Some old Chinese coins, such as formed the currency of all the civilised nations of the Archipelago, and still continue to do of some of them, were found among the ruins. The oldest of these bears the name of a Chinese emperor, who died in 967 of Christ, which carries us back to some 200 years before the supposed foundation of Singapore in the year 1160.

The remains discovered in Singapore are certainly not such as to convey a high opinion of what De Barros calls "the celebrated city of Cingapura, to which resorted all the navigators of the western seas of India, and of the eastern of Siam, China, Champa, and Camboja, as well as of the thousands of islands to the eastward." Earth, brick, unhewn sandstone, and wood, seem to have been the only materials made use of, and there is not a vestige of the granite which abounds in the neighbourhood and is now so largely employed.

From the time of its subversion down to the year 1811, or for a period of about five centuries and a half, there is no record of Singapore having been occupied, and it was only the occasional resort of pirates. In that year, it was taken possession of by the party from whom we first received it, an officer of the government of Jehore called tho Tumângung. This person told me himself that he came there with about 150 followers, a few months before the British expedition which afterwards captured Java passed the island, and this happened in the summer of 1811. The history of the formation of the British settlement is as follows. After the restoration of the Dutch possessions in the Archipelago, it was seen that no provision had been made for the freedom of British commerce, and various projects were suggested for the establishment of emporia within the seas of the Archipelago to obviate this inconvenience. One of these was submitted to the Marquis of Hastings, then governor-general of India, by Sir Stamford Raffles, and adopted by him in 1818. This, Sir Stamford proceeded to carry into effect, and with the courage and promptitude which belonged to his character. Many local obstacles, by nameless parties vested with a little brief authority, were thrown in his way, but he overcame them all, and the result has been such as has been described in this article. The convenience of a port at the eastern end of the Straits of Malacca was too obvious to escape observation, and to this quarter Sir Stamford Raffles directed his attention; but in the first instance the island of Singapore did not occur, either to himself or any one else. Yet, it is remarkable that in what was called a century and a half ago a "New Account of the East Indies," it is expressly pointed out in the following unmistakable words, "In the year 1703," says the author, Captain Hamilton, "I called at Johor on my way to China, and he (the king of Johor) treated me very kindly and made me a present of the island of Singapore, but I told him it could be of no use to a private person, though a proper place for a company to settle a colony on, lying in the centre of trade, and being accommodated with good rivers and safe harbours, so conveniently situated that all winds served shipping both to go out and come into these rivers." But this striking recommendation of Singapore was at the time unknown to Sir Stamford and his cotemporaries. He had hence to grope for a suitable locality. The first place thought of was Rhio, but it was found to be already in the occupation of the Netherland government. The next was the Carimon Islands, out, however, of the convenient tract of navigation, and here Sir Stamford and his expedition tarried three days, but found the place unsuitable. The river of Jehor was then thought of, but on the way to it, the expedition touched at Singapore to make enquiry, and then for the first time, the advantages and superiority of its locality presented themselves. A cession of a small portion of the island, to the extent of two miles along the shore, and to the distance of the point-blank range of ordinary cannon, inland, was obtained from the resident chief. This was afterwards confirmed by the Sultan of Jehore, or the person whom we found it convenient to consider as such, who on our invitation quickly repaired to the place. The inconveniences of a state of things, which, with the exception of the patch on which the town was to stand, left the sovereignty of the whole island, with its adjacent islets to the Malay princes, were quickly experienced, and obviated by a treaty which I drew up in 1824 under the direction of the Earl of Amherst, then governor-general, and this convention continues to be the tenure on which we hold the main island, with the islets and seas surrounding it, such as I have already described the limits of the British settlement.

SINGASARI. The name of certain Hindu ruins in the eastern part of Java. These are situated in the district of Malang, and in the elevated valley which lies between the Tengar range and the mountain of Arjuna, at a height of from 1000 to 1500 feet above the level of the sea. They consist of temples dedicated to the worship of Siwa, of whom, as well as of the personages and objects connected with him, such as his consort Durga, Ganesa the Indian Pluto, and the bull Nandi, there are well sculptured images. The material of the temples, instead of being brick or trachyte, as in other parts of the island, is here a firm calcareous stone, but the style of building is equally fine as in the temples of Brambanan. On one of the images, that of Siwa, there is an inscription in the Dewanagri character, or that in which Sanscrit is usually written, but it has not been translated, and is probably a mere Hindu scripture text. To the time in which these temples were constructed, the enigmatical memorial words, in which dates are most usually written, give the various years of Salivana or Saka, 818, 846, and 1082, but an inscription, found at no great distance from Singasari, and seemingly belonging to the same class of buildings, in numeral characters, gives only 1242. Seventy-eight years added to all these give the year of Christ. The name Singasari is composed of Singa, "a lion," which is Sanscrit, and of Sari, "a flower," or "beautiful," which is Javanese. Most probably, however, it is not the original name of the temples themselves, but rather of the place in which they were built.

SINGKEL. This is the name of the largest river of the western side of Sumatra. Its embouchure, about three-quarters of a mile broad, is in north latitude 2° 15′, opposite to the group of islands called by the Malays Pulo-bañak, or "the many isles." The course of the river is of considerable length, with abundant depth, and the place which gives name to it is said to be sixty miles distant from its debouchement. At its mouth, however, there is a bar, over which, even at spring tides, there is no more than twelve feet water. The country through which it passes forms a portion of the territory of Achin, although chiefly inhabited by the Batak nation, and on the coast by Malays. The river of Singkel used to be a place of export for benzoin, camphor and gold-dust.

SINKEP, is the most southerly of the larger islands constituting the Archipelago, at the eastern end of the Straits of Malacca, and is not above twenty miles distant from the shore of Sumatra. Its geological formation is the same as that of the Malay Peninsula and Banca, from which last it is distant about eighty miles. Its area is reckoned to be 152 geographical square miles. Mines, or washings of alluvial tin are found and worked in Sinkep, with this peculiarity, that in some situations the ore exists within high-water mark, and is collected by the Malays by a kind of rude dredging. The inhabitants are Malay fishermen. Nominally, Sinkep is part of the territory of Jehore, and consequently subject to the Netherland government.

SIPORA is the name of one of the considerable islands which form a chain from between the third and fourth degrees of south to the third degree of north latitude, along the western coast of Sumatra. It lies between the Pagi Islands and Sibiru, its northern extremity being in south latitude 56′, and its southern in 2° 25′. Its extreme length is about 45 miles, and its extreme breadth about 15, and with its adjacent islets it is computed to have an area of 1200 geographical miles. The inhabitants are the same people, and speak the same language as those of the Pagi Islands, namely, the nation called by the Malays Mantawi. Sipora has been sometimes called by European navigators "Good Fortune Island," which does not very well accord with its Malay name, that seems to mean "Pretender, or Simulation Island."

SIWA, OR MAHADEWA, one of the three personages of the Hindu triad, the destroying power, is not often called by either of these names, even among the Javanese, but images of himself and of the personages and objects connected with his worship are frequent in Java, and his sect appears to have been the most prevailing form of Hinduism throughout the Malay Archipelago, and, to some extent, to have reached even as far as the Philippines. He is the Batara-guru of the Javanese and Malays, and the Batala of the Philippine islanders. Batara is an obvious corruption of the Sanscrit "Avatara," and guru is "spiritual guide."

SLAMAT, OR SÂLAMAT (GUNUNG). The name of the mountain in Java usually called by Europeans that of Tegal, from the district within which it is chiefly situated. It is an active volcano, and its height above the level of the sea has been calculated at about 11,500 feet.

SLAVERY. In Malay there are six different names for a slave, and there is even one for the "slave of a slave." In Javanese, there are also several, but the most frequent in Malay is âmba, and in Javanese kawula. These, as well as all the others, are used as pronouns of the first person in addressing a superior. Slavery exists in every state of society in the Malay Archipelago, and in every country of it, except Java, where it is not found even in a predial form. This peculiarity has, no doubt, arisen from an experience of the superior economy of free labour in a populous country. To breed and maintain slaves was useless when the labour of freemen was cheaper, and slavery thus came to be naturally extinguished. Slavery, however, still exists in Bali and Lomboc, equally populous with Java. But this extends only to parties sold to strangers, and condemned as slaves, for some real or supposed offence, and slavery, as an institution, cannot be said to exist even among the people of these islands. In Malacca, when first discovered, all labour appears to have been performed by slaves, a fact which not only implies a very rude state of society, but also a paucity of population in relation to the land, or, in other words, comparative high-priced labour. "The Malay nation," says De Barros, "as they live by trade and no other pursuit, so are they the most luxurious people of these parts, and the proudest in their sentiments. All with them is nobility, and this proceeds to such a length that you will not find a native Malay who will carry on his back his own or any other man's property, however much you may offer him for doing so."—Decade 2, Book 6, Chapter 1.

Slaves are of two classes in the Archipelago, bondsmen and bond-debtors,—the first called, in Malay, tâbusan, which signifies the object purchased or redeemed, and the last iringan, which means a follower, or retainer. The distinction between the slave and the freeman (mârdeka), is distinctly enough drawn by the Malays, but yet the line is not so offensively drawn as to view the first as a mere chattel, for the slave can possess and inherit property,—purchase his freedom, and has in other respects, his prescribed rights. The only description of slaves that had not the power of redeeming themselves, appears to have been those of the king. The real condition of the slave may be seen from incidental notices of them in collections of the customary laws, and the following are examples from those of Jehor. "If a slave cut and wound a freeman, he shall be condemned as a slave for life to the king." "If a freeman wound a slave, he shall be fined to the extent of one-half the value of the slave, or, if very poor, in the sum of ten mas." "If a slave give a freeman a blow on the face, the offending hand shall be cut off." "If a freeman give a slave a blow on the face, without any provocation on the part of the slave, he shall be fined,—if poor, five, and if rich ten mas. But if the slave have been insolent, the freeman in such a case, shall be held blameless." "If a slave, whether male or female, strike another slave a blow on the face without offence given by the latter, the offender shall be fined to the extent of half the price of the slave assaulted." "If a slave give abusive language to a freeman, he shall receive a blow on the face, or have a tooth extracted." "If a slave commit a murder, it shall be lawful for a third party to put him to death, provided the act shall have taken place in a remote part of the country, where there is difficulty in securing the person of the offender. But if the crime be perpetrated near a public authority, the slayer shall be fined five tails and one paä, because he has killed the slave without leave of his owner or the permission of the public authorities. However, in this last case, should the slave have been mortally wounded, it shall be lawful to put him to death."

"If a freeman kill a slave of the king (âmba-raja) he shall be fined the value of the slave seven times seven-fold, and if he cannot pay the fine, he may be either put to death, or be condemned to be for ever, with his family and relations, slaves to the king. But, if the slayer of the king's slave be a man of high rank, he may not be put to death, but fined to the extent of one kati and five tails, of gold. In case, however, such great personage shall have killed the slave for some crime, then no notice shall be taken of the matter." "If a slave commit a theft, and is seized and put to death in the act, the slayer shall pay a mulct equal to half the value of the slave, to be shared equally between the master of the slave and the magistrate, for the offence of the slayer consists in not informing the magistrate."

One circumstance, probably, mitigates the condition of slavery among the people of the Indian Islands, that the master and slave are almost always of the same race,—that there is no broad disparity in their conditions, such as exists in civilised communities, and that the severe labour of a calculating taskmaster is never exacted.

SLING. In Malay Ali-Ali, and in Javanese Bandreng, although used, does not seem to have been a favourite weapon with any class of the inhabitants of the Malay or Philippine Archipelagos. One is tempted to suspect that this may have arisen from the scarcity of pebbles in countries covered with forest, and of which the shores consist of mangroves or sand. The blow-pipe for shooting arrows, and the bow and arrow, the materials for both of which are so constantly at hand, seem naturally to have taken its place.

SMALL-POX. This epidemic is well known to the inhabitants of both the Malay and Philippine Archipelagos, and of all the maladies with which they are afflicted, it has proved the greatest scourge. The Javanese call the disease by the two names, chachar and plânting, both native words, of which the origin is not traceable. By the Malays it is called chachar and also katumbuhan, the last of these signifying a sprouting or efflorescence, evidently taken from the eruption. Of the origin of the small-pox, or its first appearance among them, the people themselves, as might be expected, are wholly ignorant, and from the names we learn nothing, except that being purely native, they do not point to a foreign origin for the disease. Some European writers have fancied that it was introduced by the Arabian traders, but had this been the case, it is probable it would have had an Arabian name, or, at least, such a name as would give some indication of its being exotic.

SOLDIER. In all rude states of society, every man capable of bearing arms is alike a soldier, and the military profession, as a distinct one, is, of course, unknown. This is the case with all the people of the Indian Islands, and hence, there is no name in the languages of the Archipelago for a professional soldier, except soldado, which has been taken from the Portuguese. We find, however, words for a warrior, as in

Javanese prajurit, of which this is the literal sense, the word being corrupted in Malay pânjurit. Satriya or chatriya from the Sanscrit is also used, and has the same sense.

SOLO, according to Javanese, and Sala, according to Malay pronunciation, is the name of the largest native city of Java, and capital of the tributary prince who has for some generations assumed the religious title of Susunan, or "object of adoration," and is called by Europeans, "Emperor of Java." The town is situated in the province of Pajang, on a river of the same name. It contains a large palace, a Dutch fort and a large Javanese population with a suburb, inhabited by Europeans or their descendants, but I have not seen any statament of the total number of its inhabitants. Solo was founded only in the year 1742, after the previous capital, a few miles to the west of it, had been abandoned as unlucky, in consequence of having been captured by Chinese insurgents, although retaken by the Dutch and their allies the Madurese. The name of the abandoned capital had been the Sanscrit one, Kartasura, which signifies "work of gods or heroes." The word having essentially the same meaning was reversed in position, and the proper name of the new capital becomes Surakarta, Solo being only the name of the village, the site of which the town now occupies. The entire native principality embraces an area of 1803 square miles, and in 1850 was computed to have a population of 603,759, or 334 to every square mile. The bulk of the inhabitants is of the pure Javanese nation, the number of Europeans and Chinese being inconsiderable, the first no more than 863, and the last 1649.

SOLO RIVER. This is the largest and most useful river in Java. It has its source in the range of mountains which runs along the southern side of the island,—passes through the rich and extensive valley of Pajang, by the city of Surakarta, through the districts of Sukawati, Jagaraga, Blora, and Rembang, and disembogues between Sidayu and Gressik in the strait which separates Java from the western end of Madura. From Surakarta to the sea, a distance of about 200 miles, it is navigable for large cargo boats, and affords cheap transport for rafts of teak timber, large forests of which it passes through.

SOLOR. The name of one of several islands between Floris and Timur, lying close to the eastern coast of the first and to the south of the isle of Adenara, the strait between these two being the navigable passage called the Straits of Floris. It is computed to have an area of 80 geographical square miles. The island is of volcanic formation and barren. The inhabitants of the coast are the far-spread Malays called orang-laut, or men of the sea, but those of the interior, the aborigines, have dark complexions and crisped hair, resembling in their persons the aborigines of Timur. These are certainly savages, and have been represented as being even cannibals. The inhabitants of the coast are fishermen and pursue a small whale of about twenty feet long, from the blubber of which they extract the oil by the heat of the sun, collecting it in rude gutters. They profess Mahometanism, for the most part, but a few have adopted Christianity. The Dutch drove the Portuguese from Solor as early as 1613, and have a small fort and garrison on it, for the purpose of maintaining their right to what appears of very small value.

SOOLO, or SOELOE, and in Malay correctly Suluk, is called by the Spaniards Jolo. The Soolo Islands, usually called an Archipelago, extend from the most easterly extremity of Borneo, the promontory of Unsang to the most westerly of Mindano, that of Zamboanga, a distance of above 200 miles. They are said to be no fewer than 150 in number, most of them, however, uninhabited islets. They are divided into four groups, named from the largest island of each, namely, Tawi-tawi, Sooloo, which gives name to the Archipelago, Basilan and Cagayan Sooloo, the last, however, forming no part of the chain, for it lies 120 miles to the north-west of it, although inhabited by the same nation. The Archipelago lies between the fifth and seventh degrees of north latitude.

SOOLO, called by the natives Sug, and by the Malays Suluk, from which our own word is derived, is the name of the principal, although not the largest of the four chief islands of the Archipelago to which it belongs, and that which gives name to it. Its length is about 35 miles, its greatest breadth 12, and its computed area 288 geographical square miles. Its general aspect is hilly and undulating, without any mountain of great elevation. Respecting its geology, we have little or no information, but it will probably be found to consist of sedimentary rocks, chiefly limestone and sandstone. The only metallic ore ascertained to be abundant is that of iron, although gold is reported to exist. The face of the island is, as usual in these latitudes, covered with tall trees, having, however, it is stated, many open or cleared spots, which give the island a very picturesque appearance, that distinguishes it from most others in the same latitudes. The teak-tree has been reported to exist, but this seems very doubtful. The ascertained larger wild animals are the hog and several species of deer. Dalrymple names the elephant, but this is very improbable in so small an island.

Soolo, as well as the whole Archipelago to which it belongs, is within the influence of the north-east and south-west monsoons, which, however, interrupted by so many islands, do not blow with the same regularity as in the open sea, and calms, and variable winds, are not unfrequent. It is not within the range of hurricanes and experiences no storms. The thermometer rarely rises above 87° or falls below 75°, so that the range of temperature is reduced to 12°. But the seasons are unequal as to the fall of rain, and droughts, with their concomitant scarcity of food, occasionally occur.

The inhabitants of Soolo are of the Malayan race, and have attained a considerable amount of civilisation, cultivating rice, and rearing the buffalo, the ox, the goat, the horse, and common poultry, and all of these in abundance and cheapness. They also write their own language in the Arabic character like the Malays. That language is peculiar, but seems to partake of the character of the Philippine tongues, and sounds harsh to those accustomed to the soft Malay. Of this last language it contains a considerable proportion, but much corrupted. The principal people of Soolo, besides their own tongue, speak also Malay, as did those of the Philippines before the Spanish conquest. In a list of about 170 words of the Soolo language, given by Dalrymple, 65 are Malays, but these are not a fair specimen of the language, for they include the numerals, the names of the winds, of weights and measures, and of objects of commerce, the majority of which are Malayan in most of the insular languages. The orang-laut, bajaos, or sea-faring migratory Malays, are found on the coasts of Soolo, as well as of others of the Archipelago, and, no doubt, have had some share in communicating their language to the native inhabitants.

Of the number of the population nothing is known that can be relied on. A Mr. J. Hunt who visited, and for some time resided in the island in 1811, and whose account was printed by Sir Stamford Raffles in the Batavian Transactions for 1812, states that he had access to the sultan's archives, and that these made the whole population 200,000. This would give to a society of buccaneers, for such are the people of Soolo, near 700 inhabitants to the square mile, or about double that of the most populous provinces of peaceful and industrious Java. Of course it is purely fabulous, and even the more usual estimate of 60,000 is most probably an exaggeration.

The principal articles of commerce furnished by the Soolo and neighbouring islands are the usual ones of the rudest of the Malay and Philippine Archipelagos, such as tortoise-shell, tripang and esculent swallows'-nests, to which are to be added two which are in a great measure peculiar, pearls and pearl oysters. The principal place of commercial resort is the seat of the native government, exercised by a prince who like other petty sovereigns, has long assumed the title of sultan. This is situated in a bay, the anchorage being a mere road towards the north-western end of the island in north latitude 6° 1′ and east longitude 121° 12′.

The people of Soolo have been long converted to the religion of Mahomed, but are very far from being rigid Mahometans. When they were converted, or by whom is uncertain, but the great probability is, that the Malays and the Arabs of the half-blood were the instruments of conversion, and that as Soolo is far removed from Sumatra, where the Mahometan religion was first propagated among the Malayan nations, and from which it was disseminated over other parts of the Archipelago, it is not likely that its inhabitants were converted earlier than those of the Spice Islands, who adopted Mahomedanism only eighty years before the arrival of the Portuguese in 1512. In 1521, the people of Cagayan-Soolo were certainly Mahometans, for Pigafetta mentions them as such, when the companions of Magellan touched at it on their course from Çebu to Palawan and Borneo. "Quitting that place (a port in Mindano)," says he, "and pursuing a course between west and south, we arrived at an island almost uninhabited, which we afterwards learnt was called Cagayan. The few whom we saw were Moors and robbers from an island called Burné." Primo Viaggio, p. 109. Of the early history of the people of Soolo, nothing is known. The island is stated to have been, at one time, subject to Sukadana on the southern side of Borneo, which was a Javanese settlement, and this notion certainly receives some countenance from the existence in its language of words which are Javanese, without being at the same time Malay. The first authentic notice of Soolo is by Barbosa. After describing Celebes and an island which he calls Tendaya, possibly

Sangir, he says, "Proceeding in a northerly direction towards China, there occurs another island most abundant in the necessaries of life, called Solor, inhabited by a civilised people of fair complexions and good dispositions. They have a king, and a language of their own. In this island much gold is found by washing the earth, and in the sands of rivers. Opposite to it small pearls are fished, and even large ones occasionally found, fine as to colour and roundness." Rumusio, vol. i. p. 320. It is evident from this description that the island alluded to, notwithstanding the orthography, is Soolo, or Suluk, and not Solor between Floris and Timur, and to which the description in no respect applies. Barbosa's account was written at Lisbon in 1516, and evidently refers to a time four or five years at least earlier. In 1521, the surviving companions of Magellan passed the Soolo Archipelago, in their route from the Philippines to the Moluccas, and Pigafetta names Soolo, writing it Solo, the Jolo of the Philippine Islanders and Spaniards. "We turned back," says he, "after leaving Borneo proper, between the island of Cagayan (Cagayan-Soolo), and the port of Cipit (in Mindano), pursuing a course a quarter east of south in order to discover Malucco (the Moluccas). We passed through certain islets, around which we found many plants (marine), although there was a great depth of water. Having passed through these islets, it seemed to us as we were in a different sea. Leaving Cipit to the east, we saw to the west two islands, called Zolo and Taghima (Suluk and Basilan). Near these islands grow pearls. The two pearls of the king of Borneo, of which I have spoken, were found here." (Primo Viaggio, p. 125.)

Owing to some cause or other, there has sprung up in Soolo, a civilisation and power far exceeding those of the surrounding islanders. A superior fertility of the soil, and better means of maintaining a numerous and concentrated population, has probably been the main cause of this superiority, but whatever be the cause, it has enabled this people not only to maintain a paramount authority over the whole Archipelago, but to extend it to Palawan and to the northern coasts of Borneo and islands adjacent to it. It was from them that we ourselves obtained a cession of one of the islands off the coast of Borneo, Balambangan, twice taken possession of,—once driven out of it by the very parties who had made the grant, and once finally abandoned by us. The only reputation that the people of Soolo have ever obtained, is not an enviable one, that of being with the Lanuns of Mindano, the most daring habitual pirates of the Malayan seas. Both these nations are now, indeed, the only freebooters that are seriously troublesome. Their predatory fleets extend their cruizes from one end of the Malay Archipelago to the other, but the chief theatres of their depredations are, and have always been, the Philippines. These they have continued to infest nearly from the first establishment of the Spanish dominion down to our own times. The first expedition against them by the Spaniards took place in 1629, only 58 years after the foundation of Manilla, and it has been followed by many others even to the present time. Their strongholds have been captured and their villages burnt, but they have proved mere razzias which left the robbers irritated but not suppressed, and the Spanish government of the Philippines has never found it prudent to take possession of and occupy them.

Our accounts of the principal island of the Soolo Archipelago is extremely imperfect, for the islands comprising it have been rarely visited by intelligent Europeans with opportunity of collecting information. The best account of them is that of Mr. Alexander Dalrymple, afterwards hydrographer to our Admiralty; but this is near a hundred years old, the author having visited Soolo in 1759 and 1761, although publishing his account of it in his Oriental Repertory as late as 1792. The chief value of this work rests on its hydrographical information. In other matters, the author's statements are trivial, for he possessed neither the means nor accomplishments necessary to accurate inquiry, trusting much to native information. He gives himself with much frankness an example of the manner in which this led him into error. He was anxious to obtain accurate information respecting the history of the country, and at length obtained a manuscript which purported to be history, but when he displayed his treasure to competent judges in England, the pretended history turned out to be a collection of Arabian fables, and not in the Soolo or Malay languages, but in Arabic. At an interval of half a century, Mr. Dalrymple was followed by Mr. Hunt already noticed, and he either copied his predecessor, or added only loose gratuitous assertions of his own.

SORSOGON is the name of a bay, a harbour, and a town on the western side of the island of Luzon in the peninsula of Camarines and province of Abbay. The bay is both spacious and secure as a harbour. It is 14 leagues in circumference and 4½ in breadth, having at its entrance the islets of Poro and Malacimbo. Next to Cavité in the great Bay of Manilla, it is the best port in the Philippines. The town of Sorsogon is situated at the head of the bay and on its shore between two rivulets at their debouchement, in north latitude 12° 30′ 30″, and east longitude 123° 41′. It contains a population of 7315 inhabitants. Behind it is a high peak, but of which the height has not been ascertained.

SPEAR, LANCE, JAVELIN. Weapons of this class from their simplicity and the abundance of materials for them, must in the Indian Islands, have been, after clubs, the earliest weapons used, and notwithstanding the introduction of fire-arms, they still continue in present use, even among the most civilised tribes. The half savage inhabitants of the little island of Maktan in the Philippines encountered, defeated and slew Magellan and several of his companions, with no other weapon than bamboo spears, sharpened at the end and hardened in the fire, and long spears were the chief weapons of the Javanese when they made a show of encountering the British troops in 1811, near three centuries later. The Javanese spear or lance is about twelve feet long, and is armed with a simple iron pike. In the hands of resolute men, disciplined, and acting in unison, this would have been a formidable weapon; but it is probable that the effectual discipline never existed. A phalanx of men thus armed resists the spring of the tiger, as I have frequently witnessed with great ease and without any risk. The most general name for the spear in all the languages of the Malay Archipelago, but not extending to the Philippines is tumbak, which I take to have been originally Javanese, the people of Java having been, as we find from Barbosa, the great manufacturers of warlike weapons, even for the Malays, before the arrival of Europeans. In describing the trade of Malacca, after enumerating other commodities imported by the Javanese vessels, he says, "They also bring many kinds of arms for sale, such as spears, shields, and swords with handles worked in marquetrie (kris ?)." In the polite language of Java, the name for the spear is the same which expresses 'steel,' and in the languages of Celebes, it is the same which in Malay and Javanese expresses 'iron,' the reference, in both cases, being to the principal part of the weapon, the pike. For the javelin or half-pike, the Javanese and Malays have the same name, which is lâmbing.

STEEL. The art of converting iron into steel has been immemorially known to the more civilised nations of the Malay Archipelago, and they have native names for it. These are, in Javanese, waja and mâlela, abbreviated lela, and in Malay baja, the same word as the first Javanese, with the exchange,—a frequent one between those languages,—of one labial for another, and kâluli, a synonyme taken from the Tâlugu or Telinga, but not of frequent use. These names do not extend to the Philippines nor to Madagascar, for in the languages of the first, the Spanish word acero has been introduced, and into the last the French acier, corrupted isi. It may be inferred from this, that steel was not known to the rude people of the countries in question until made acquainted with it by Europeans. The probability is that, with the more civilised nations, steel was a native invention, and that it originated with the Javanese, the principal manufacturers in iron for the other nations of the Archipelago. There is, at all events, no evidence of its having been made known by strangers.

SUBIG. The name of a bay and of a township situated on its shore, on the western side of Luzon. The bay, which is one of no great extent, is a safe harbour for vessels of small draught, and the town, in north latitude 14° 32′ 58″, and east longitude 122° 8′ 30″, has a population of 3836 inhabitants. A high peak of the Cordillera of Zambales lies inland from the town at the distance of six leagues.

SUGAR-CANE and SUGAR.—(Saccharum officinalis). The cane is called in Malay and Javanese tâbu, with the accent, as usual, on the penultimate. This name is universal, and there is no other popular one throughout the Malay and Philippine Archipelagos. Indeed, there is no synonym at all, except in the polite dialect of the Javanese, where it has the factitious one of rosan, which signifies literally "the jointed object," that is, "the cane." But the word tâbu has a still wider extension, for we find it in the languages of all the islands of the Pacific in which the sugar-cane was grown when they were discovered by Europeans. No doubt the word has been, more or less, corrupted in all the ruder languages, but still there can be no doubt of its identity. Thus, in the language of the Philippines, it is tubu; in the Kayan of Borneo, tuvo; in the languages of Floris, tau; in the Polynesian Tonga also, tau; in the Tahiti and Marquesa, to; and in the Sandwich Islands, ko. This essential conformity of name, and that name too a native one, and not as is the case with its product sugar, taken from a foreign source, leads to the belief that the plant is indigenous, and was disseminated by one people directly or indirectly. What people that was, it is impossible to determine, but it is most natural to conclude that it was one of those in whose language the word appears in its most perfect or least corrupted form. This would limit us to the Malays and Javanese, and I should incline to the last as the people who had made the greatest progress in agriculture, as in every department of civilisation.

With respect to the names for sugar, the case is just the reverse of what it is with the cane, for every one of them is foreign, with the exception of those of the polite language of Java, namely, kara and gâudis. The ordinary Javanese name is gula, a slight corruption of the Sanscrit gura or gud'a, which properly applies to the crude article before separation from the molasses. This name has extended to almost every tongue of the Malay Archipelago, but has not reached the Philippines, where sugar was unknown in any form when discovered by Europeans, although palm-wine which it is made from in the Malay Archipelago was copiously used, as we find from the narrative of Pigafetta, and this beverage too, designated by its Malayan name, tuwak. Another name for sugar in Javanese, but confined to that language, is sakara, with its abbreviation kara. This, too, is Sanscrit, the original word being sarkara, the probable origin of the Arabic word săkar, from which all our European names are undoubtedly derived. In Javanese, however, the word sakara belongs to the recondite language, and is equally applied to honey as to sugar, the popular synonym for honey, namely, madu; being, it is singular enough, also Sanscrit, while the comb, the wax, and the hive are all expressed by native terms.

But it by no means necessarily follows that the sugar of the Indian islands with Sanscrit names, was the produce of the cane. On the contrary, the great probability is that the sugar to which these originally applied was the product of the sap of palms. This, and not the sugar of the cane, forms the saccharine consumption, not only of the Indian islands, but of most of the people of tropical Asia, as of the Cochin-chinese, the Siamese, the Burmese, and all the nations of Southern India, including that particular one, the Telingas, from whom the Malayan nations received the Sanscrit names, and from whom most probably they acquired the art of making sugar, even that from the sap of palms. The islanders obtain their palm-sugar from the gomuti (Borassus gomuti), and the people of the continent from the Palmyra (Borassus flabelliformis). Sugar, it should be observed, is obtained from the sap of palms, by a far simpler and easier process than from the cane. This consists in mere boiling in small earthen vessels, and no attempt is ever made at any kind of refining, although the crude product is equally capable of it as that of the cane.

The sugar-cane, in so far as native industry is concerned, is grown everywhere luxuriantly in the Indian Islands, in small patches near the dwellings of the inhabitants where rich dressings are easily available, but nowhere as a branch of husbandry. It is grown, in fact, only to be used as a kind of sweet-meat to be masticated in its fresh state, and never for the production of sugar, an art which, there is every reason to conclude, was unknown to the natives until taught by the Chinese. To grow the cane profitably on a large scale as a branch of husbandry, for the manufacture of sugar, is quite another matter. In this view it can be produced only in rich volcanic or alluvial lands, such as exist in some provinces of China, in some parts of Java, in some of the Philippine Islands, in parts of Cochin-china, Siam, and the valley of the Ganges. Even in these, it is excluded from the perennially irrigated lands, on which it is more profitable to grow rice. In general it may be said that, for native use, sugar is only produced from the cane in countries where palms cease to be abundant, which is the case in every country of Asia without the tropic. Hence it is grown for this purpose, as it were by necessity, in the upper valleys of the Jumna and Ganges, as well as in the greater part of China.

The sugar of the Indian Islands, therefore, to which the Sanscrit names were applied, we may safely conclude was that of palms and not of the cane, and this commodity must always have been, as we see it now, in its crudest form mixed with its molasses. The Javanese press out the sap of the cane to use it in its fresh state as a beverage, and have a specific name for it,—juruh 'but beyond this very simple proceeding they have not gone. The name gula is applied alike to the palm and cane sugar, but to distinguish the last from thefirst, the word is added which makes cane-sugar, gula-tâbu. The names given to the sugars made from the cane have even a modern air, consisting simply of the generic name with epithets, clayed sugar meaning literally "sand sugar" (gula paser); and candied or crystallised "stone sugar" (gula batu). In the early intercourse of Europeans with the Archipelago, it may be added that sugar is never once mentioned as an article of commerce, whether of the cane or palm. Barbosa gives an enumeration of above fifty different articles to be found in the emporium of Malacca, naming, for example, such inconsiderable commodities as safflower and cubebs, but he makes not even an allusion to sugar.

I strongly suspect that the same remarks apply to the sugar of the Hindus, their gura and sarkara, namely, that it consisted of a coarse unrefined article, the produce of the Palmyra palm; and, indeed, the first of the names mentioned, even now expresses only the ugly unrefined mass of sugar and treacle which is the form in which the natives of Hindustan still consume sugar,—the jaggory of Europeans, a name which is a corruption of the Kanara word sharkari, itself a corruption of the Sanscrit sarkara. The modern names, too, of cane-sugar, both clayed and candied, are certainly foreign,—the first, chini, signifying Chinese, and the last, misri, Egyptian. This would lead to the belief that the Hindus were unacquainted with the art of refining sugar in any manner until instructed by their Turkish and Persian invaders, themselves instructed by the Arabs, the same people who taught the nations of southern Europe. This notion is strengthened by the account which the Emperor Baber gives in his Memoirs of the very rude condition of the Hindus when he himself invaded India, which was twenty years after the arrival of the Portuguese at Calicut. It may be considered a further corroboration of this opinion, that Barbosa, in his price-current of the merchandise of that emporium, although it amounts to near thirty articles of several countries, such as indigo, borax, cinnamon of Ceylon, Chinese rhubarb, the clove and nutmeg, does not enumerate sugar in any shape, and Barbosa's manuscript is dated ten years earlier than the last successful invasion of Baber. The only early notice of cane-sugar in any Asiatic country except China that I have seen, relates to Siam, in which De Cauto (1548) expressly states "that, near the capital, Odia (Ayudya) much cane was grown, and sugar and spirits made from it, but the Chinese had been immemorially settled in Siam."—Decade 8, chapter 22. No doubt there was palm-sugar in the markets both of Malacca and Calicut in the time of Barbosa, but the article was evidently too coarse and rude a commodity to bear the cost of distant transport, even after the discovery of the route by the Cape of Good Hope, and hence would not be an article capable of competing in the European markets with the cane sugars of Sicily and Egypt.

With respect to the Indian Islands, then, the conclusion we must come to is, that sugar made from the cane was wholly unknown to their inhabitants, until introduced by the Chinese, and not even by them until exercising their industry under the protection of European governments. Down to the present day they are the sole manufacturers, not only in the Malay Archipelago, but in the Philippines, Cochin-China, and Siam; the origin of this branch of industry in the two last-named countries, or at least its revival, being an affair of our own times.

With respect to the Hindus, there is, at least, no evidence to prove that they manufactured a marketable sugar before the invasion of their country by the Mahommedan nations, in the 11th century. The probability then, is, that the Chinese were the inventors of the processes of making clayed and candied sugars from the cane. But the Greeks and Romans of antiquity were acquainted with sugar as a commodity which came to them in the course of the oriental trade, and Pliny describes it as a product of Arabia and India. This is his account of it, such as, we may presume, it appeared in the market of Rome in the 1st century: "Saccharon is a honey, which forms on reeds, white like gum, which crumbles under the teeth, and of which the largest pieces are of the size of a filbert."—Book 12, Chapter 8. The account of Dioscorides, a little earlier in the same century, gives the article the same name, and adds, that "in consistence it was like salt," that is, like salt of solar evaporation, or in large crystals, the kind known to the Greeks and Romans. Pliny's account seems to be a very fair one, of sugar-candy, the only mode of refining from clayed sugar known to the present day by all the eastern nations. But it is to Chinese sugar-candy, which is in distinct white crystals, and not to Indian, which is in the form of a confused brown crystallised mass, a very inferior article, to which it is applicable.

Had the sugar-cane existed in northern India, and sugar been made from it, as it now is, it is not likely that so remarkable an object should have escaped the Macedonian and Bactrian Greeks so long in communication with that part of the country, or that they should have failed in giving an unmistakable account of it. As soon as it was actually seen by Europeans, and this was by the Crusaders in Syria, in the beginning of the 12th century, their historians not only describe the plant, but the process of manufacturing sugar from it, in a manner which leaves no room for misapprehension. In the philological part of this account, I have been assisted, as I have often been before on similar subjects, by a great oriental scholar, my friend Professor Horace Hayman Wilson.

With respect to the native country of the sugar-cane, like wheat and other long cultivated corns, it has never been found in its wild state. The probability, however, is, that its original habitats had a wide range. There are, besides many varieties, three distinct species, or at least as many well-ascertained permanent varieties, of it;—the Indian saccharum officinarum, the ukk of the Hindi, and the ikshu of the Sanscrit; the plant immemorially cultivated in Hindustan, brought from thence by the Arabs to their own country, to western Asia, to southern Europe, and ultimately carried by Europeans to America; the Chinese Saccharum sinensis, probably as long cultivated as the Indian; and the Otaheite, Saccharum violaceum, brought within the last sixty years to Asia and America. This last kind I presume to be the same as the Malayan cane, or at most a variety of it. The cane originally cultivated by the Malays, before the introduction by Europeans of foreign species, or varieties, is a large luxuriant plant with a dark purple cuticle, differing materially in appearance from the Indian and Chinese canes, and much resembling the Polynesian species. That they are, indeed, the same seems corroborated by the essential agreement in their names already alluded to.

From these facts it may be safely inferred that Hindustan, China, and the Malay Archipelago, taking for granted that the Polynesian tribes received their cane from the latter, may all be considered parent countries of the sugar-cane. Although the cane has been immemorially cultivated in all three, the great probability is, that the Chinese were the sole discoverers of the processes of making a clayed and crystallised product from it.

SUKADANA. The name of a place, once the seat of a Javanese state on the western coast of Borneo, in latitude 1° 15′ south. It forms part of the Netherland province of the west coast of that island, but is at present a poor place of no consequence. The name, imposed no doubt by the Javanese, is Sanscrit, and signifies "Parrot's gift."

SUKAPURA. The name of one of the districts of the Sunda part of Java, called by the Javanese Prayangan, or "land of ghosts." The name is Sanscrit, and signifies "city of gladness."

SUKAWATI is the name of a district of Java in the country of the proper Javanese, and situated in the extensive and fertile plain of Pajang. The name in Sanscrit signifies "gladness-possessing."

SUKU AND CHÂTTO. These are the names of some singular ruins in Java, situated in the districts of Pajang and Sukawati. They stand on the acclivities of the volcanic mountain Lawu, 11,000 feet above the level of the sea. They are but a few miles apart, Suku 3525 feet, and Châtto 4220 feet above the level of the sea. These buildings are composed of blocks of trachyte, but the design and execution are rude, and some of the objects represented, grotesque and grossly obscene,—wholly differing, in this respect, from all the other ancient monuments of Java, implying that the Javanese themselves were the builders, without assistance from strangers. They consist of a series of terraces, one rising higher than the other, the communication between them being by flights of stairs. On the terraces are the remains of temples and gateways. There are no Hindu images, but instead, representations of monsters, snakes, birds, and tortoises. The temples were dedicated to the worship of the Linga, or Hindu Priapus, not as usual obscurely represented, but in its naked and grossest form. An inscription on the Suku temples in Javanese numeral characters, gives the date of 1361 of Saka, and one on those of Châtto in the same form, 1356, which correspond with the years of Christ, 1439, and 1434, so that the earliest of them dates but 44 years before the destruction of the Hindu capital of Majapait, the era of the final extinction of Hinduism in Java.

SULPHUR, in Malay bâlirang, and in Javanese wâlirang, essentially the same word. This name extends from Sumatra up to Celebes, when we find a new one for it, cholok. In one of the languages of the Philippines, the Tâgala, strangely enough, the name is sanyaya, which is, no doubt, a corruption of the Malayan word sandawa, saltpetre. In the Bisaya, as well as in the Tâgala, the name for gunpowder is maliling, doubtless a corruption of the Malay and Javanese name for sulphur. In the Madagascar, the name for it is sulifara, a corruption of the French soufre, from which it may be safely inferred that the article was unknown to the natives of this non-volcanic island until brought to their knowledge by Europeans. It is hard to say to what use the natives of the Malay Archipelago could have put sulphur, before the introduction of fire-arms, unless to the manufacture of fire-works, known by the native names of mârchun and rabok. The Malay and Philippine Archipelagos, the most extensive volcanic region in the world, must necessarily contain a vast supply of sulphur, but hitherto it has been very little availed of for economic use. From the Philippines alone it is exported, the export being to China only, and at the price at Manilla usually of about a Spanish dollar of 4*s.* 2*d.* a cwt. Among these islands, those which most abound in it are Luzon and Leyte, but particularly the last, where the article is of the best quality. A Spanish writer asserts that the quantity is such at the volcano of Taal, or Bombon, in the province of Batangas in Luzon, that many ships might be loaded with it. The difficulty, in all these cases, of obtaining a cheap supply, must arise from the absence of good roads, and the consequent costliness of transport.

SULTAN. This Arabian title, first taken by the celebrated Mahommed of Ghizni, the early Turkish conqueror of India, fell quickly into disesteem even among the Turks themselves, having been assumed by many of their petty princes, as we find from Mr. Erskine's accurate and excellent history of the House of Timur. Many of the native princes of the Malay Archipelago assumed it, after their conversion to Mahommedanism, in lieu of the Sanscrit name of raja, or the native ones of ratu and pangeran. Thus, De Barros informs us that the petty princes of Pasé and Pedir, in Sumatra, had assumed it before the arrival of the Portuguese, and so had three of the petty princes of the Moluccas, although, when the Portuguese saw these islands first, their inhabitants had been barely eighty years converted to Mahommedanism. The Javanese princes of Mataram took it in 1535, and maintained it for some time, and it is still the title of one of the two native princes of the interior of the island. It was taken, also, by the princes of Bantam, and the only considerable independent Malay prince of Borneo now goes by it.

SULUK. The Malay name of the island and Archipelago which the natives call Sug, the Spaniards Jolo, and we Soolo, or Sooloo, or Soeloe. See Sooloo.

SUMATRA. This great island, even to its very name, was, down to the arrival of the Portuguese in India, as unknown to the European world as Cuba, before the first voyage of Columbus. Its pepper and its frankincense were very likely consumed by Europeans, but of the place which produced them, they were certainly as ignorant as of the still remoter countries where grew the clove and nutmeg. In so far as its name is concerned, even to the present day, it is like the other large islands of the Archipelago, Java perhaps excepted, without a name familiar to the inhabitants. Ludovico Barthema, an Italian of Bologna, is the first writer who gives the name as we now write it. He had visited Malacca and Pedir, in Sumatra, in 1505, that is seven years after the arrival of the Portuguese at Calicut, and four before their first appearance in the waters of the Archipelago. He had touched at the places in question in his voyage from Tennasserim to the Moluccas, and he thus describes Sumatra, fancying it to be the Taprobane of Ptolemy: "Next day we embarked in a ship, and proceeded to a city called Malacha, which lies in a south-eastern direction, and in eight days arrived there. Near that city is a great strait (fiumara), than which we had never seen a larger. It is called Gaza, and appears to be above fifteen leagues broad. And on the opposite side of that strait (fiumara), there is one very great island, called Sumatra, and its inhabitants say that it is four thousand five hundred miles in circumference."—Ramusio, Vol. i. page 166. Barbosa, whose manuscript is dated at Lisbon, in 1516, and whose description appears to refer to a period preceding the Portuguese conquest of Malacca, in 1511, writes the name like Barthema, or, in the same orthography as we do now, and as usual his account is far more precise and accurate than that of his predecessor. "Having," says he, "passed the above-mentioned island" (Novacar, that is, Nicobar), "there is a very great island called Sumatra, which is in circuit seven hundred leagues, or two thousand miles, as reckoned by the Moors, who have sailed all round it. It runs in a direction from north-west to south-east, the equinoctial line passing through the middle of it."—Ramusio, Vol. i. p. 318. Forty years later, however, we find De Barros writing the name as Çamatra.

Barbosa tells us plainly from whom his information was derived, and in all probability, the name, as we now have it, was derived from the same parties,—namely, the Arabian, the Persian, and the Mahommedan navigators of India, who conducted the external trade of the Archipelago, and who, we are assured by the early Portuguese writers, possessed astrolabes, quarter-staffs and charts. Eleven years after the arrival of the Portuguese in the Archipelago, Pigafetta writes the name Samatra, but he mentions it only incidentally, and his information was most probably obtained from his better informed ship-mate, Barbosa. "On the night of Tuesday and Wednesday, the 11th of February, 1522," says he, "quitting the island of Timur, we entered the great sea called Laut-chidol (Javanese, Laut-kidul, the south sea), and taking our course between west and south, we left to the right hand, and in a northern direction, for fear of the Portuguese, the island Samatra, anciently called Taprobana."—Primo Viaggio, p. 179. It is remarkable that the name of Sumatra had not reached Marco Polo, although he was six months wind-bound at the island, and in communication with the natives. That of Java, the only large territory of the Archipelago, familiarly called an island by the natives, had done so; and he called Sumatra, knowing it to be an island, but ignorant of its relative extent, Java Minor. About two centuries and a quarter, therefore, before the arrival of the Portuguese, the name of Sumatra was not known to the Chinese of Marco Polo's fleet, nor even to its Arabian pilots, or it would hardly have escaped the Venetian traveller.

As to the first origin of the name Sumatra, or Samatra, as employed by the Moorish merchants trading to the Archipelago, and borrowed from them by the Portuguese, it has certainly hitherto baffled etymologists, but is very probably of Hindu or Sanscrit origin. Sumatra is the nearest part of the Archipelago to the country of the Hindus, and is, moreover, that part of it which is now, and has at all times been, most frequented by them for the purposes of trade. That trade was carried on from the eastern coast of the southern part of Hindustan, being also that part of it from which the islanders are reasonably believed to have derived the Hindu religion, and their languages their admixture of Sanscrit. The first syllable of the name of the island, when written with the vowel *u*, signifies, in Sanscrit, good, or excellent, but of the remaining two, no reasonable conjecture can be formed. Is it not probable, then, that the original word may have been Samudra, the sea, or ocean, in Sanscrit, and thence, in Javanese? The Hindus would add dipa, and hence we should have "sea-island, or sea-land," and traders, dropping the last named word, might easily have corrupted Samudra into Samatra. This seems at least as probable as any other conjecture that has been offered on the subject, for it is not unreasonable to fancy that the Hindus would call the nearest land to them sea-ward, by such a name, —that land from which, directly or indirectly, they drew their supplies of gold, tin, spices and incenses, and which they had immemorially supplied with salt and cotton fabrics.

But there are two other names which have been occasionally given to Sumatra—Indalus and Pulo-pârchah. Both are more mythic than real, and the first can neither be traced in sense or derivation. The last means, literally, rag, or patch island, but unluckily for it, the word pârchah is neither native nor Sanscrit, but Persian, and hence, however given, must of necessity be a comparatively recent one, since no ancient communication between the Archipelago and Persia is traceable.

Sumatra is the most westerly island of the Malay Archipelago, forming its barrier to the west against the Indian Ocean and Bay of Bengal. Its length is from north-west to south-east, and it stretches across the equator, which bisects it, leaving about an equal part in the northern and southern hemisphere, its most northerly point being, in north latitude 5° 45′, and its most southerly, in south latitude, 5° 55′. To the east it has the Malay Peninsula, and the chain of islands which extend to Banca inclusive. To the west, the nearest land is the continent of India, about 1000 miles distant. To the south, there is no land near it, except at its southern extremity, where it approaches within twelve miles of Java.

Sumatra is about 1000 miles in length, its extreme ends are its narrowest parts, and its centre its broadest. Its area is reckoned at 128,560 geographical square miles. Thus it is the largest island of the Malay or Philippine Archipelago, except Borneo. It is above three times the size of Java, or of Cuba, and better than half as large again as Great Britain.

The geological formation of Sumatra consists of sedimentary, plutonic, and volcanic rocks. "The circumstance," says Mr. Logan, in an excellent sketch of the island, "of the mountain belt being partly plutonic and partly volcanic forms its peculiar character. Its configuration is, in fact, a combination of that of the Malay Peninsula with that of Java, with this difference, that its middle region is more elevated and expanded than any part of the Peninsula, several of its masses being about thrice the height of the summits of the peninsular mountain range. If a number of volcanic mountains rose, here and there, among the peninsular groups, and in greatest number where the Peninsula is broadest, it would be identified, in character, with Sumatra.

The greater elevation of the mountains of the latter is, however, accompanied by a greater expansion of the plains and valleys which lie among them. In crossing it anywhere, save towards its northern and southern extremities, three, and sometimes more, principal ranges are found, with wide table-lands, plains, or valleys between them, watered by numerous streams, and in some places containing lakes . . . The most western ranges form the water-shed, and as the land to the west of it, chiefly hills, is not more than twenty-five miles broad, about one-fifth only of the waters of the island fall into the Indian Ocean,—the Straits of Malacca and the Java Sea receiving the remainder, in nearly equal proportions, as regards the drainage of the mountains, but with a large excess to the latter, from the wide plain traversed by the rivers which disembogue in it. The western margin of the mountain belt, washed by the strong waters of the Indian Ocean, has retrograded to the eastward, the sediment of the rivers and the débris of the coast being carried away, instead of being deposited. The northern part of the coast, exposed to the assault of the Bay of Bengal, has retained its ancient dimensions, if it has not contracted, but as soon as the open sea is exchanged for the Straits of Malacca, the mountain belt begins to retire from the coast, and a great alluvial belt commences."

The highest mountain in Sumatra appears to be Lusé, in the territory of Achin, and in north latitude about 4° 20′, and this rises to the height of 11,000 feet above the level of the sea, but there are at least six more which attain the elevation of 10,000, or better. Of the mountains of Sumatra, five only are active volcanos, while the volcanos of Java amount to fifteen. In fact, the volcanic portion of Sumatra seems to be confined to a small part of its central region,—the volcanic band, afterwards continued in Java and the islands east of it, appearing here to be limited to a zone comprised within about a degree on each side of the equator. One of these volcanos, Talang, rises to the height of 10,250 feet, an elevation equal to the average of the heights of the volcanos of Java, Bali, and Lomboc. Two of them, Bârapi, 6000, and Mârapi, 9500 feet high, indicate their character by their names, which signify volcano.

The plains, table-lands, and valleys of the mountain region, are many of them of considerable extent, such as those of Korinchi, Menangkabo, Tobah, Pertibi, and Mandaling. Some of these, especially of the volcanic formation, are fertile, while others, and by far the greater number, are sterile and ungenial. Mr. Willer, a Dutch writer, has given a very spirited account of the two last-named plains, which are in the country of the Bataks, but now forming parts of the Netherland dominions. He thus describes Pertibi, remarkable for its sterility, and presenting an appearance little to be expected by those accustomed to the luxuriant seaboards of Sumatra: "It is otherwise when we descend Gunung-Tuah (old mountain), and cast our eye downwards from the top of Sipopol. There we see unrolled a plain without horizon and without variety. The lalang grass (the rank and worthless Andropogon caricosum) makes the only diversity. On this plain not a single living creature appears to move; a tree is a rarity, and has an appearance of stunted dwarfishness. At the distance of miles we may descry, as an oasis in the desert, an insignificant thicket, or a small strip of brushwood, along the banks of a marsh, or brook. A fell scorching wind blows, for months together, and, from the numerous conflagrations, spreads a dull glow, through which the sun-light scarcely forces itself,—wavering and heavy. In a word, all nature appears to have gone to an eternal sleep. Such is the appearance of Padang-luwas (spacious plain), and of the greater part of Pertibi." "The naked and flat *terrain* of Padang-luwas offers no other diversity than the ravines and morasses with which it is intersected. The upper soil is of the most meagre and unfruitful kind, and is seldom more than six inches in depth. Beneath it, we soon come to layers of white clay, limestone, sandstone, and other formations. The climate, although not exactly unhealthy, is extremely rough. Frequently, we have in the afternoon a temperature of from 27° to 29° of Reaumur, and in the night of from 14° to 15°. The heat is accompanied by great dryness. The violent gânding, which blows over Probolingo, in Java, can give but a faint idea of the storm which, for the greatest part of the year, day after day, bellows from the west over Padang-luwas. Like the *mistral*, this wind has a strong desiccating power, cracking the ground, and, in a few minutes, removing all traces of mud and rain."

The neighbouring district of Mandeling offers a totally different aspect, and is thus described by the same writer: "The appearance of Mandeling is as luxuriant and varied as that of Pertibi is arid and monotonous. True, the southern ulu (interior) consists of high and naked mountains, over which the lalang grass again spreads its monotonous mantle. Here hamlets and cultivated tracts appear to be stuck on frightful steeps, where unfruitfulness and poverty have established their hungry seat.

True, also, the northern Ankola exhibits some dry and desert places like those of Padang-luwas. But for the rest, the district consists of one chain of beautiful valleys, hemming the banks of the Batang-gadis (Virgin River), which runs between the central mountains of Sumatra. These valleys, like the river itself, become wider and wider as we proceed to the north and west. The high chains of mountains are covered to their summits with stately woods, which afford abundance of good timber and other valuable articles. On the lower mountains, too, woods are here and there dispersed, and these are commonly adorned with the wild Aren palm (Saguerus sacchariferus), yielding a wine; while some bare red spots indicate the existence of gold mines, which, however, can seldom be considered as signs of true prosperity. We may more safely give way to satisfaction when we see the well-watered rice-fields, which in small valleys, like amphitheatres, climb up a considerable portion of the acclivities, and in the distance, extend to an invisible boundary. Nowhere does the landscape weary. The eye rests constantly on ornamental groups of bamboos and various trees, or on the small clumps of fruit-trees in which the villages lie concealed, their position especially marked by the abundance of coco and areca palms. Towards evening, we observe near the villages numerous herds of buffalos, oxen, and goats; while men, well-fed and well-clothed, and what is more, a superabundance of children, prove that in this favoured region, the greatest prosperity has reigned for some years."

The great alluvial plain of the eastern side of the island, generally but a few feet above the level of the sea, is 600 miles in length, and from 60 to 110 miles in breadth, giving an area of about 42,000 square miles, equal to better than half that of Great Britain. This, with the rare exception of a few patches in the river banks, and usually beyond the reach of the tide, is covered with a stupendous forest, probably older than the races of men that inhabit it, or wander over it. No doubt much of this vast territory is of ample fertility, and suited to the growth of most of the useful products of intertropical countries; but to clear and cultivate it effectually has always been a task far too difficult and gigantic for the rude and unskilful races of men who occupy it.

Sumatra, as far as can be asserted of a country, many hundred square miles of which have probably never been trodden by the foot of an intelligent European, is like the other great islands of the Malay, but not those of the Philippine Archipelago, deficient in lakes. The largest is described as being the source of the river of Indragiri, and is called the Danau Singkara, or the "Lake Singkara." This is described as being 20 miles in length, by from 12 to 15 in breadth, with a depth of 24 fathoms. Another lies near the foot of the mountain Mârapi, and goes under the name of the Danau Sapuluh kota, or "Lake of the ten forts." Two others are situated in the country of the Korinchi Malays. These last were visited, in 1804, by an English gentleman, Mr. Charles Campbell. The largest of them was described by him and his companions, as a beautiful and clear expanse of water, abounding in fish, and about seven miles broad. Another lake exists in the country of the Lampungs, towards that part of the island which fronts Java. This is called the Ranu, a word which, in Javanese, is a synonym for water, and probably the same word as danu, a lake. Two English gentlemen visited this lake in 1820, and estimated its length to be about 16 miles, and its breadth 8. It is surrounded in every direction by steep mountains, ranging from 1200 to 3000 feet high, and abounds in fish and water-fowl.

The coast-line of Sumatra is not broken by any great bay or deep inlet, as is that of Luzon or Celebes. Tapanuli on the western coast is the most extensive bay in the island, and contains behind the shelter of the islands within it several harbours, but with this exception, the anchorages of Sumatra are mere roads. In a sea without storms, however, the absence of harbours is comparatively little felt.

The principal rivers of Sumatra are those of its eastern side, and this, owing to the wide alluvial plain over which their course runs in their way into the Straits of Malacca. Beginning from the north-west, they are as follow: the Assahan, the Baruman or Bila, the Rakan, the Siak, the Kampar, the Indragiri, the Jambi, and the Palembang. These, it should be observed, are only the names by which they are known to Europeans, for generally, both here and in other parts of the Archipelago, no great river throughout its course is designated by the natives by a common name, each portion of it having a different one, generally taken from the place by which it flows. On the western coast, the only considerable stream is the Singkel. Disemboguing in the Straits of Sunda, we have the Mas-uji and the Pagadungan. All the Sumatran rivers have bars of mud or sand at their mouths, which preclude their navigation by vessels of burden; and the greater number of those of the eastern coast are subject to the bore or tidal wave. The finest of the rivers of Sumatra are those of Siak and

Palembang, the mouths of which are protected, the first by a low island close to it, and the last in a good measure by the island of Banca. These are navigable by vessels of considerable burden.

The mineral products adapted to economical use hitherto discovered in Sumatra, are fossil coal a lignite, sulphur, naphtha, granite, marble, iron, and gold. Indications of copper have been discovered, but no mines of it have ever been worked. Tin might be expected in a country so near to the Peninsula and Banca, and much of which is of the same formation, but I have not heard of its being anywhere worked except in the interior of Kampar, which is opposite to Malacca. It is certain, however, that it is nowhere abundant, or the ore would have been washed as in the Peninsula and Banca. The iron ore is described as of fine quality, and iron and steel have been immemorially made from it by the workmen of Menangkabo, who have attained a local reputation for the manufacture of tools and weapons. Gold is found in many parts of the interior, but seemingly not in such abundance as in Borneo, the Peninsula, or Celebes. Mercury, zinc, and antimony may be fairly looked for when the country is explored.

The vegetable products of Sumatra include none, as far as economic botany is concerned, which distinguish them from those of the Peninsula, and especially of Borneo. The island produces all the corns, pulses, farinaceous roots, and esculent fruits which belong to other portions of the western part of the Archipelago. Its eastern coast, and the islands lying off it, are the chief source of the sago of commerce. Benzoin and Malayan camphor are peculiar to it and Borneo. Sumatra is the great source of black pepper, producing far more than all the other countries of India put together. Of late years, coffee has been grown in larger quantities than in any other island except Java, and this production has even extended to the native cultivators, so that the island promises to furnish an almost unlimited supply. The sugar-cane has never been cultivated for the production of sugar, which here, as in most other places, is furnished by the sap of palms. The teak, the finest timber tree of the Indies, is not a product of the forests of Sumatra, although so abundant in the neighbouring island of Java. The ratan, producing the dragon's-blood, is, I believe, peculiar to the island.

The surprising dissimilitude of the zoologies of Sumatra and Java, islands parted from each other only by a narrow channel, has been already noticed. The elephant, and the tapir of Sumatra have no existence in Java. Even the rhinoceros and wild hog of Sumatra differ in species from those of that island. The orang-utan is found in Sumatra, but not in Java, while the Sunda ox of Java does not exist in Sumatra. The dissimilitude extends even to the birds of the two islands, and especially to those of the gallinaceous and pigeon families. Thus, the Argus pheasant of Sumatra does not exist in Java, nor the pea-fowl of Java in Sumatra. Even when the species of the feathered tribe are the same, the birds are larger and their plumage brighter in Sumatra. These curious facts we have on the authority of a great ornithologist, M. Temminck.

The aboriginal man of Sumatra is uniformly of one race, however different in manners, customs, language, and social condition. This is the Malayan. There is no diminutive negro, as in the neighbouring peninsula; nor an intermediate race between the Malayan and Negro, as in Floris, Timur, and the islands adjacent to them. Fifteen different nations, speaking as many distinct languages, inhabit Sumatra and the islands adjacent to it, of which eleven are found in the main island and four in the islets. Six of the nations of the main island have made considerable progress in civilisation, being possessed of the art of writing, and made respectable advances in the mechanic arts and agriculture. These are the Malays (Mâlayu), the Achinese (Aché), the Battas (Batak), the Palembangs, the Rejang and the Sarawi. Four tribes, the Lubu, the Kubu, the Abung, and the Kumring,—for these are the names by which they are called by their more civilised neighbours,—are in the same wild and rude condition as the least advanced of the Dayaks of Borneo, or the Bânuwa of the Malay Peninsula.

Mr. Logan has given an approximate estimate of the number of these different tribes and nations, the most reasonable as it is the most moderate which has ever been published, and the following is the substance of it. The first in power, in number, and civilisation is the Malayan nation. Its number he estimates at 898,650, occupying an area of 59,050 square miles, or at the rate of 15 inhabitants to the square mile. These are the conquerors of the island, and the same people who have spread themselves or their language as far as the Philippines and New Guinea, and even to the islands of the Pacific Ocean, or to within no great distance of the western shore of America.

Next to the Malays in number and, perhaps, equal to them in civilisation, are the Achinese, with a population of 450,000, occupying 22,000 square miles, and giving 20 inhabitants to the square mile. This is the nation which is nearest to the continent of India, which has held most intercourse and intermixed most with Asiatic strangers, and which was the first in Sumatra to embrace the Mahommedan religion. After this nation comes the Palembang, amounting to 201,000, occupying a territory of 13,400 square miles, which gives 15 inhabitants to each square mile. This people is partly Javanese and partly Malay, and is equal in civilisation to the Malays and Achinese. The Sarawi, a neighbouring nation to Palembang and an inland people, are computed to amount to the number of 160,000, and to occupy an area of 4875 square miles, which gives a relative population of 32 to the square mile. The number of the Rejang nation is computed at 72,000, and the territory it occupies at 4500 miles, giving 16 inhabitants to the square mile. This is the people among whom we planted our black pepper settlement of Bencoolen; and who have been described so graphically and so truthfully by Mr. Marsden, in his well-known History of Sumatra. They are, notwithstanding, a small obscure people, who have made no figure even in the local annals of Sumatra. The Lampung nation, occupying that part of Sumatra which faces Java, is an equally small and obscure people. Their number is put down at 92,000, and the territory they inhabit at 8280 square miles, giving 11 inhabitants to each mile. The last of the civilised nations is the Batak, the occasional cannibals who had invented what neither Aztecs nor Peruvians had done—phonetic writing. Their number is set down at 311,860, occupying 15,800 square miles, which gives nearly 20 inhabitants to the square mile. Mr. Logan makes the wild tribes of the main island no more than 6000, which, as they are spread over a vast surface, and as he has not included anywhere the inhabitants of the low islands of the eastern coast, for the most part, of the same class, is probably under-estimating them. He makes the population of the islands of the western coast 294,900, on an area of 5040 square miles, giving 48 inhabitants to the square mile.

From these data, the total population of the main island is reckoned at 2,486,410, or 19 inhabitants to the square mile, which is about one-fifteenth of the relative population of Java. From these statements, which are, probably, as near approximations to the truth as the nature of the subject would admit, it will appear that the greater portion of the surface of Sumatra is what the best part of it is well known to be, a sterile or intractable wilderness; for in the rude state of society which exists in the Malay Archipelago, it must never be lost sight of, that population and civilisation are commensurate with fertility of soil, accompanied by adaptation of the land to easy culture. This is tested by comparing Sumatra with Java, and Borneo with the little islands of Bali and Lomboc; or even Sumatra itself with the sterile and poorly-peopled Peninsula and Borneo. Even in comparing one part of Sumatra with another, we are furnished with an illustration of the same fact. The Malays of Menangkabo, inhabiting the volcanic valleys and plains of the interior of the mountain region, the cradle of Malayan power and civilisation, have a relative population of 128 to the square mile. On the western coast the same people amount only to 80 to the square mile; and in the great plain of the eastern coast, covered by unconquerable forest, the rate falls to 20, and even to 5 to the square mile.

The agriculture of Sumatra differs in no respect from that of Java, except that it is less skilful; and that, with few exceptions, it has to contend with an unfruitful soil. The same corns, pulses, palms, and fruits are cultivated as in that island. In the culture of black pepper and of the coco and areca palms only, it seems to excel Java; for, for these plants, the poor soil of its coasts seems peculiarly adapted. A country so extensive necessarily possesses a great variety of soils. Thus, the plains and valleys of Menangkabo, situated among the mountains of the volcanic band, are in fertility and capacity of perennial irrigation not, perhaps, inferior to the finest provinces of Java; and Sir Stamford Raffles, who personally visited this part of the island and was well acquainted with Java, asserts that the country was as extensively cultivated and well-watered as the finest part of that island. This gifted portion of Sumatra, however, constitutes evidently but a small part of its surface; and although, no doubt, many other fertile spots exist, the best known parts of the island are ascertained to be the reverse of fertile. Mr. Marsden's account of the soil of such parts of the western coast as he had an opportunity of observing, proves it, instead of being fruitful, to be both sterile and stubborn. "I cannot," observes this faithful writer, "help saying, that I think the soil of the western coast of Sumatra is, in general, rather sterile than rich. It is, for the most part, a stiff red clay, burnt nearly to the state of a brick, where it is exposed to the influence of the sun. The small portion of the whole that is cultivated is either ground from which old woods have been recently cleared, whose leaves had formed a bed of vegetable earth some inches deep, or else ravines into which the scanty mould of the adjoining hills has been washed by the annual torrents of rain."—History of Sumatra, p. 78. Even the land of the neighbourhood of Bencoolen, to which this description more especially refers, is fertile, if compared to the plains of Pertibi, in the centre of the island, already described. Many parts of the great alluvial plain of the eastern side of the island have an abundantly fertile soil; but covered as they are by a mighty forest, and as very probably they were before the creation of man, the labour of clearing and cultivating them is as much beyond the power of the present race of inhabitants, as that race would be to cover them with a net-work of railways. Sumatra would certainly be a more valuable territory if it wanted this huge plain altogether.

Of the ancient history of Sumatra we know little; and this is not to be wondered at when we advert to the state of society, even of the most advanced of its nations, —a state in which no reliable records have ever been preserved by any race of man. The very little that we do know is derived, not from the people themselves, but from the strangers that held intercourse with them, or from the evidence of language, much in the same manner as we derive our knowledge of the ancient Britons, the Gauls, and the Iberians. The people of Sumatra had certainly adopted a kind of Hinduism, and this is sufficiently attested by an examination of their languages, and even by a few monuments and inscriptions. The more civilised nations of Java seem, also, to have mixed with the Sumatrans, and to have had a considerable share in the formation of their manners. This is shown by the existence, even to the present time, of the Javanese language in Palembang,—by inscriptions in Menangkabo in the ancient character of Java,—and by many purely Javanese names of places in both the countries thus named. What De Barros says on this subject is worth quoting, since his information could only be derived from the natives themselves; and since he wrote by three centuries nearer the events than our times. "The people of the coast, as well as of the interior of the island, are all of a yellowish-brown colour (baço),—having flowing hair,—are well-made,—of a goodly aspect, and do not resemble the Javanese, although so near to them, a fact which shows how a small distance may alter the forms of nature. And this is the more remarkable, since all the natives of Sumatra are called by the common name of Jäuij (Jawi); for it is held by themselves as certain, that the Javanese had been once masters of this great island, and that before the Chijs (Chinese), they conducted its commerce as well as that of India."—Decade III. Book V. Chap. 1. The inference of a Javanese connection with the word Jäuij, as it is written by De Barros, but correctly Jawi, is most probably a mistake; for it is a common term applied by the Arabs to all the natives of the Archipelago, but more especially to the Malays; although, no doubt, it is a corruption of the word Jawa, Java, or Javanese.

The most remarkable event in the history of the people of Sumatra is the conversion of the most civilised of them to the Mahommedan religion, but even this is not correctly determined. De Barros states that the conversion took place about 150 years before the arrival of the Portuguese, which would carry us back, only to about the year 1360. Marco Polo, however, found the people of the eastern side of the island already Mahommedans, about 1290, or 70 years earlier than the time specified by De Barros. The account which this last author gives of the manner in which the conversion was effected, has every appearance of verisimilitude, and is worth extracting. "The inhabitants of the coast," says he, "follow the sect of Mahomet. The princes of the maritime ports were originally Moors, Persians, Arabs,—Moors of the kingdoms of Gujrat, India (Southern), and Bengal, who, in pursuit of trade, came to the ports of this country. These men observing the state of the country,—its great extent,—that the inhabitants were without law, and well disposed to receive their own religion,—they converted many of them, took their daughters in marriage, making themselves masters of the country, and in time assuming the title of kings." —Decade III. Book viii. Chap. 1.

The attempts of the Portuguese to establish their power in Sumatra, were productive only of petty wars and massacres, and never had the least prospect of success, nor are they worth narrating, affording only evidence of fanaticism and bootless courage. The Dutch and English petty establishments had only in view the paltry object of monopolising black-pepper, a mean and profitless one, which they both pursued with much assiduity for two whole centuries. It was not until the restoration of their possessions in the Archipelago to the Dutch in 1816, and, especially, since the convention with the English in 1824, that the government of the

Netherlands began to pursue a course of territorial conquest in Sumatra, through which they have become masters, at least nominally, of the whole of its coasts and islands, from Kampar on the Straits of Malacca to Singkel on the western coast, bordering on the territory of Achin, with much also of the interior of the island. The territory thus acquired, exclusive of the islands in the Straits of Malacca, and of Banca and Billiton, amounts to 6939 geographical leagues, or 3642 myriametres, which is little short of three times the extent of Java. The value of this acquisition to its masters may be easily judged. In 1843, the expense of maintaining it amounted to 290,000*l.*, and the revenue which it yielded was 165,000*l.*, which was about one-twentieth part of the revenue of Java, of one-third its size. No better result could reasonably have been anticipated from a country, generally unfertile, thinly inhabited by savages or by turbulent semi-barbarians, and without any true rent to yield a land-tax. The Netherland conquests in Sumatra, then, may be quoted as a flagrant example of the ambition of territorial extension run wild.

SUMBA, the proper name of Sandalwood Island, lying south of Sumbawa and Floris, out of the line of the Sunda chain, and in the same parallels as Timur. See SANDALWOOD ISLAND.

SUMBAWA. The name given by strangers, and taken from that of its principal nation, to the fifth island of the Sunda chain, reckoning from Sumatra inclusive. It lies between Lomboc to the west and Floris to the east, being about a degree further south than Java. Among the islands of the Malay Archipelago, it ranks in magnitude with Gilolo and Ceram, but in real importance, is far below Bali and Lomboc, which are not much more than one-third part of its size. The form of the island is oblong, its southern or exposed coast forming an unbroken line, while its northern or sheltered is broken by several bays, two of them of great extent, and one of them but penetrating the island to the extent of 20 miles, so as to make its eastern end a peninsula. Its length is 140 miles, its greatest breadth 50, and its computed area 278 square geographical leagues, or 152·5 myriameters, so that it is somewhat larger than Jamaica.

The geological formation of Sumbawa is eminently volcanic, and it contains both active and quiescent volcanos. Generally the height of its mountains is inferior to those of Java, Bali, and Lomboc, usually not exceeding 5500 feet, but the mountain of Tomboro is computed to rise to the height of 9250 feet above the level of the sea. It was from it, that took place in 1815, the greatest eruption recorded in history, and which is supposed to have caused, directly or indirectly, the death of 12,000 of the inhabitants of the island.

Sumbawa contains a good many small valleys of considerable fertility, but compared with the three islands to the west of it, it must be deemed a very unproductive land, less most probably from want of fertility of soil than the absence of what is even more necessary in a hot climate, an abundant perennial supply of water for irrigation, which so eminently distinguish Java, Bali, and Lomboc. The following account of the physical character of the neighbourhood of Bima by Mr. Zollinger is probably applicable to a large portion of the island. "Like every country of the Indian Archipelago," says he, "which occupies the sides of an old volcanic mountain, this country consists of a great number of trachytic ridges, which descend divergently to the Bay of Bima, and which are separated by ravines often very deep, and of which the sides are frequently perpendicular. In these ravines, run streams very impetuous in the rainy season, while their beds are nearly empty in the dry." Such is the case in a country which the Dutch have been masters of for a period approaching two centuries. The water is abundant, and it is seems only necessary that it should be husbanded and stored for use in reservoirs. Nature does this, with very little care on their own part, for the people of Java, Bali, and Lomboc, but it does not do so for those of Bima, and they are too weak and rude themselves to supply the want.

The only remarkable forest products of Sumbawa for economic use are sandal and sappan wood. The teak, it is singular, is a product of this island, after ceasing to be so in the intermediate islands of Bali and Lomboc, but it is either scarce or not accessible. The elephant, the tiger, and all the larger animals are wanting, and there are no considerable mammalia except deer and the hogs, but the island is remarkable for the number and beauty of its small horses, the most esteemed of all those of the Archipelago, and largely exported to Java, the native breed of which island is very inferior to it.

Before the great volcanic eruption of 1815, Sumbawa is thought to have had a population of better than 170,000, distributed among six different states, as follows,

Bima, 90,000; Sumbawa, 60,000; Dompo, 10,000; Tombora, 6000; Sangar, 2200, and Popekat 2000. By an estimate made in 1847 this population would seem to have decreased in the course of 32 years to 74,500, two of the smaller states seeming to have disappeared altogether, according to the following statement—Bima, 45,000; Sumbawa, 26,000; Dompo, 3000; and Sangar, 500. In this last enumeration, the total number of Europeans, exclusive of the military, was 70, and of Chinese but 6, while of Malays and Balinese there were 2000, of settlers from Celebes 8000, and of those from Floris, Timur, and Sumba 1000.

In manners and language, the inhabitants of Sumbawa bear a nearer resemblance to those of Celebes than of Java and Sumatra, but are inferior to them in energy and enterprise. The more advanced of them are composed of six different nations, speaking as many languages and forming separate states, of which the two most considerable, as will be seen from the estimates of population, are Sumbawa, which gives name to the island, and Bima, where the Dutch establishment exists;—for the whole island is subject to the government of the Netherlands and has been so since the year 1676. All the more civilised inhabitants have adopted the Mahommedan religion, and probably did so about the same time as those of Celebes, which was about the epoch of the first arrival of the Portuguese. Many of the mountaineers, a rude and simple people, are still unconverted. Attempts at their conversion are however in progress, and, according to the statements of Mr. Zollinger, a very intelligent traveller, these are of rather a singular description. "For some time past," says he, "Hajis (pilgrims) and fanatic Arabs have endeavoured to convert the Orang Dongo (mountaineers) to Mahommedanism, but they have not had much success. They do not adopt a very attractive method. They traverse the villages of the mountaineers, rod in hand, and crying, 'Dogs, do you wish to pray, or not?' The converts, for there are some, continue as they were before, except that they wear a scrap of cotton handkerchief on the head, do not eat pork any more, unless in secret, and construct their houses like the people of the plain. They call the stones which they worshipped before Nabi-Mahomed, or Dewa, a god in Sanscrit, putting their confidence in them as they have always done."

SUMBING. The name of one of the highest mountains of Java situated in the provinces of Kâdu and Bañumas, and in the most fertile and cultivated part of the island. It rises to the height of 11,250 feet above the level of the sea, forming with Sundara the mountains called by mariners "the Brothers."

SUMERU. The name of the highest mountain in Java, for its height is 12,500 feet above the level of the sea. It is situated in the western part of that narrow portion of the island which fronts Madura, and within the districts of Malang and Besuki. The name is Sanscrit, Su signifying good or excellent, and Meru, the Olympus of the Hindus.

SUNDA. This is the name of the people who occupy the western portion of Java, and who differ in language, and to a considerable extent in manners, from the Javanese, who occupy the centre and eastern end of the island. The proper Javanese call the country in contradistinction to their own, which alone they denominate Java, or more correctly the land of the Javanese, Pasundan, signifying the place or country of the Sundas. It is reckoned to count from the extreme western portion of the island up to Cheribon, which is itself partly Sunda and partly Javanese. It consists of what, before the arrival of Europeans, constituted the kingdoms of Bantam and Jacatra. Among the European nations, the name was first made known by the Portuguese, and it has been since applied by geographers to the Strait which divides Java from Sumatra, and to the whole chain of islands from Sumatra up to Timur. The entire country occupied by the Sunda nation embraces about 12,000 square miles, or about 30 parts in 100 of the whole island of Java, and has been computed to contain a population of 2,389,475. This is exclusive of some part of Cheribon, but includes the city of Batavia and its environs, containing a large population of foreign origin. The rate of population therefore is barely 200 to the square mile, while that of the country of the Javanese is about 270. The country of the Sundas is, in fact, of inferior fertility to that of Java, and although it contains some rich valleys and fine plains is more mountainous than that of the Javanese. It may be said to bear the same relation to Java proper that Wales does to England, or the Highlands to the Lowlands of Scotland, or the Basque provinces to the rest of Spain.

The only native state of any importance ever established in the country of the Sundas was Pajajaran, literally "place arranged or put in order." This stands in the district of Bogor (the mat or carpet) and near the present country-residence of the governor-general of Netherland India and about 40 miles from Batavia.

It is alleged to have been founded in the year of Saka 1084, and to have been overthrown or abandoned in 1221 of the same era, years which correspond with 1162 and 1299 of Christ, the last date being some nine years later than the time when Marco Polo passed through the Archipelago, and made known to the European world by its proper name that such an island as Java existed in the world.

The Hindu religion was certainly established in the country of the Sundas, as well as in that of the Javanese, but it contains no ruins of temples. Even the images which have been discovered are few in number, and of small size, yet sufficient to prove that the sect of Hinduism which prevailed was that of Siwa, or the power of destruction. The earliest attempt to convert the Sundas to the Mahommedan religion was made in the year of Saka 1250, corresponding with that of Christ 1328. But the real conversion did not begin until the year of our time 1480. According to De Barros many of the people were still Hindus when in 1522, Henrique Lemé, deputed by Jorge Alboquerque from Malacca, first visited Sunda Kalapa or Jacatra (the modern Batavia) and Bantam. This is the account of the state of the people given by De Barros, writing only thirty years after the mission of Lemé. "The people are not very warlike, but much addicted to their own idolatries, on which account they have many temples. They wish ill to the Moors, and the more so since one Sanque de Pate of Dama (Sang Adipati of Damak ?) conquered them. There can be bought here four or five thousand slaves on account of the poverty of the people, for the law allows of fathers selling their children for any trifling necessity. The women have a goodly appearance, and the nobility are very chaste, but not so the common people. They have convents for women who preserve a perpetual virginity, and this more out of vanity than devotion. The nobles, when they cannot marry their daughters to their liking, place them in the convents against their wish. As to the married women, when their husbands die they have to die with them, as a point of honour. But if they fear to die, then they must repair to the convents and pass their lives as nuns." —Decade III. book i. chapter 12.

De Barros' account of the country of the Sundas is a curious mixture of fact and error, and shows how little the Portuguese knew of Java, the most important island of the Archipelago, even forty years after their arrival at Malacca. "A third part of the island of Java, embracing its western portion, is called Sunda," says he, "and its inhabitants hold it to be an island separated from Java by a river little known to our navigators, which they call Chiamo or Chenano (Chi-manuk, literally, 'bird-river,' which is the river of Indramaya). This intersects the whole island from sea to sea in such a way that when the people of Java describe their own country, they say that it is bounded to the west by the island of Sunda, the aforesaid river Chiamo parting the two countries. The people hold that whoever passes this strait (the river Chiamo) into the South Sea is carried off by violent currents and unable to return. For this reason they do not navigate the South Sea, in like manner as the Moors from Caffraria to Sofala never pass the Cape on account of the great currents which there prevail. The inhabitants of Sunda, in praise of their own country, and boasting of its superiority over Java, say that God established the aforesaid division of the river Chiamo between the two countries. The island of Sunda is more mountainous in the interior than Java, and has six notable sea-ports, namely Chiamo, at the extremity of the island, Xacatra (Jacatra, that is, Jayakarta, 'work of victory') called also Caravam (Krawang, a different place), Cheguidé (Chaigâde, literally, 'great river,' but probably meant for Chitarum, 'indigo or blue river'), Pondang (Pontang), and Bintam (Bantam, properly Bantân). These are places of great traffic on account of the trade of Java as well as of Malacca and Sumatra. The principal town of Sunda is Daio, situated a little in the interior, and which, when Henrique Lemé was in the country, was thought to have 50,000 inhabitants, while in the whole kingdom there were 100,000 men capable of bearing arms." Decade III. book i. chapter 12. What place Daio was, if such a place existed at all, it is impossible to conjecture, as no place resembling it occurs in Javanese topography. The locality would point to the ancient capital of Pajajaran, although that is described as having been abandoned long before the first visit of the Portuguese.

SUNDARA. The name of one of the highest mountains of Java, and an active volcano, lying between the provinces of Kâdu and Bañuwangi, and rising to the height of 10,500 feet above the level of the sea. With the neighbouring mountain Sumbing, it forms one of the two called by European mariners "The Brothers."

SUNGAI, in Malay, a river, and equivalent to the Javanese Kali, or the Sunda Chai. As rivers, nearly throughout the Malay Archipelago, have no specific names, but take them from the places through which they pass, and as the Malayan nations dwell almost always on rivers, the word is of very frequent occurrence in the names of places.

SUNGORA is the name of the most southerly province of Siam, and consequently that which borders on the Malayan states of the Peninsula, and it is to it that the government of Siam entrusts the charge of its four Malayan tributaries.

SURABAYA. This is the name of a large province of the Netherland Government of Java, and of its chief town. The province includes also the island of Madura. The first part of the name Sura is Sanscrit, meaning brave or valiant, and the last, Baya, Javanese, danger or difficulty. Its area in Java is 2029 square miles, and in Madura, 1557, the population of the first being computed at 936,868, and of the last 295,748, making the total 1,232,616 inhabitants. Thus we have a density for the Javanese portion of 460, and for the Madurese of only 189 to the square mile. This is accounted for by the great fertility of that part which is in Java, and the very inferior one of that in Madura. By the census taken in 1850 the population of the Javanese portion of the province had risen to 967,889, or in five years sustained an increase of about 2¾ per cent.

The river of Surabaya is, next to that of Solo, the largest in Java. It has its source in the southern range of mountains, passes diagonally across the island, receives in its course many tributaries, runs through the fine provinces of Rawa and Kediri, and falls into the sea in the Straits of Madura by five separate and distant branches. It is one of these branches that passes by the town of Surabaya, and disembogues in the narrowest part of the channel which separates Java from Madura. Throughout a great part of its course the river is navigable for large boats, but has nowhere sufficient depth for shipping.

The town lies on the left bank of the river, about a mile from the sea. It was but an inconsiderable place in 1815 when I had civil charge of the province, but it has since, from its advantageous position, become of much importance, and by the census of 1845 contained a population of 82,203 inhabitants. This, however, included surrounding villages over an area of 45 square miles. The harbour is properly the only one in Java, the rest being mere roadsteads, unless we except the little frequented one of Châlachap on the southern coast. It is accessible both from the east and west, the channel in the latter direction being however a very narrow one.

SURAKARTA. See SOLO.

SURIGAO. The name of the chief town of the Spanish province of Caraga in the island of Mindano. It lies in a plain on the banks of a river called the Tomunday, which falls into a beautiful bay, but on account of strong currents difficult of access to shipping. Surigao is situated at the most northern extremity of Mindano, where it forms with the island of Leyté the Straits of Surigao, the passage for all ships trading between the Philippines and the western coast of America. The town consists of 1400 houses, chiefly native huts, and has a population of 7417 inhabitants, of whom 1568 are subject to the capitation tax. Latitude 9° 29′ north, and longitude 125° 24′.

SURIGAP. The name of a group of islands, thirty in number, lying off the north and north-east end of Mindano, and in the strait of Surigao, which separates that island from that of Leyté. The largest of them, which gives name to the rest, is 3½ leagues in length, 2 in breadth, and inhabited.

SWORD. The usual common term for this weapon in Malay and Javanese is pâd·ang, written with a palatal d, but for modifications of form there are other names, as lamâng and klewang, which may be translated hanger and cutlass. All the names for sword seem to be native and not foreign words. The most general, padâng, extends to all the languages of the Malayan but not of the Philippine Archipelago, for in the last the sword is called kalis, an obvious corruption of the Malayan kâris, a dagger. The spear and dagger, and not the sword, were, and indeed still are, the favourite weapons of the Indian islanders. De Barros does not include the sword at all among the weapons used by the Malays in defending Malacca when attacked by the Portuguese in 1511. "The arms," says he, "which they use are daggers, of from two palms and a half to three palms long, straight and two-edged. Along with these they employ bows and arrows, javelines for throwing, and blow-pipes from which they discharge very small darts, barbed and poisoned. These blow-pipes they have borrowed from the Javanese. They have two kinds of bucklers with which to shield themselves, a large one which protects the whole person, and a smaller."—Decade II. book vi. chapter 1.

In the generally meagre and obscure chronological lists of the Javanese, it is remarkable that the first use of swords and javelins is stated to have taken place in the year of Saka or Salivana 1502, which would correspond with the year of Christ 1580. This was about 70 years after the first arrival of the Portuguese in Malacca. It is possible, then, that the Portuguese may have introduced the sword into the Archipelago, and the Malayan word, pâd·ang, may be no more than a corruption of the Portuguese espada, a word difficult of pronunciation to a Malay, and which would certainly be altered in some way or another, as in the example of 'esgingarda, a matchlock, converted into satinggar, or even tinggar. Yet the sword, a straight one, is very clearly represented in the sculptures of some of the ancient Hindu temples of Java, and especially in those of the splendid one of Boro-budor, which is believed to have been built in 1338 of Christ. To be represented in a myth, and to be "used," for that is the expression in the Javanese chronicle, are, however, two very different things.

T.

TAAL. The name of a lake in the province of Batangas and island of Luzon, called also the lake of Bombon, or Bongbon. It is situated between latitudes 13° 52′ and 14° 6′; is in length from north to south 5 leagues, with a breadth from east to west of 3 leagues, and a circumference of 15. It is of such depth that, in some parts, it has not been fathomed. In every direction it is surrounded by a ridge of hills, so as to give it, according to the description of Spanish writers, the semblance of a huge caldron filled with water. In the midst of the lake stands an islet which goes under the name of "the volcano," and which, at a distance, has the look of a partially submerged mountain. It is of a triangular form, and has a circumference of three leagues, and a height above the level of the sea of 600 Spanish varas, or 1667 English feet. At its summit is a volcanic crater, within which is a lake of about a league in circumference, on a level with the lake of Taal, and of great depth. The whole surface of the islet is incrusted with a coat of hard lava about two inches thick, except in a few spots where it has been washed away by the action of the periodical rains. In such spots grows the only plant which the island produces. This is called by the natives cogon (Imperata Koenigii, a species of cane allied to saccharum, or sugar), grows to the height of a man, and affords food for deer, jungle fowl, and pigeons.

The island of the volcano had been cultivated with crops of cotton and other products down to 1716, when, on the 24th of September in that year, a terrible volcanic eruption took place from it. This was accompanied by detonations resembling the sound of heavy artillery, which were heard in the city of Manilla, 50 miles distant, and by shocks of earthquake which produced a commotion in the lake as if it had been agitated by a hurricane. This state of things lasted during Thursday, Friday, and Saturday, and did not cease until Sunday. All the fish in the lake, large and small, were killed and thrown on the shores in a state as if they had been boiled. On Sunday, being the fourth day since the commencement of the eruption, the sun became again visible, and then the water of the lake was seen "black as ink," says the Spanish narrative of the catastrophe. In 1754, a still more violent eruption took place from the same volcano, for on this occasion the towns of Sala, Lepa, Tamapan, and Taal were destroyed by it. This eruption was accompanied by a total darkness, and the ashes from it fell abundantly in the streets of Manilla, and were carried even as far as the provinces of Bulacan and Pampanga. No eruption since 1754 has taken place, now above a hundred years. The fishery of the lake of Taal is valuable, and is successfully prosecuted by the natives, who make use of wears and stakes after the manner of the Chinese. Some of the fish, weighing from six to seven pounds weight, are considered to be the most delicate of all those of the Philippines. They are chiefly caught in the river by which the lake discharges its waters in the sea, and, it is said, on their way to spawn in the latter, although the contrary seems more probable.

TAAL DE BOMBON. This is the name of the town which was built after the destruction of the first of the same name, which was situated on the borders of the lake. It stands on the shore of the bay of Balayan; this site, for safety, having been chosen as far as practicable from the scene of the volcano. The country around it is described as of great fertility, much of it highly cultivated, and the rest affording pasture, which supports herds of oxen, horses, and hogs. The town of Taal seems to be the largest in the Philippines, next to Manilla, for by the census of 1849, it contained a population of 41,347, of whom 8546 were subject to the capitation tax.

TABANAN. The name of one of the states of the island of Bali. See BALI.

TAGALA, but correctly Tagalog, is the name of one of the six principal nations and languages of the island of Luzon. The nation speaking this tongue embraces the province of Tondo, with its capital Manilla, with the provinces of Bulacan, Bataan, Batangas, Laguna, Nueva-Ecija, Tayabas, and Cavité. The Tagala language is also spoken in Mindoro, the province of Zamboanga in Mindano, and the Marian Islands. The language and nation therefore amounts to a population of 1,170,000, or to near one-third part of the native inhabitants of the Spanish Philippines.

TALAGA, from the Sanscrit taraga, a pond, tank, or reservoir, is the name of a district of the Sunda country of Cheribon in Java, which it takes from a beautiful lake which has the epithet bodas, in the Sunda language signifying "white."

TALANG. The name of a mountain of Sumatra, rising to the height of 10,500 feet above the level of the sea. It lies inland from the Netherland settlement of Padang, the most fruitful part of the Dutch possessions in the island, distant about 25 miles.

TALAUT, called also Tubour, is the name of a group of islands lying about half-way between the Moluccas and the Philippine island of Mindano, and to the north-east of the Sangir group, at the distance of 22 leagues. Three of them, called Karkelang, Salibabo or Lirong, and Kabruang, are of considerable size and inhabited,—the rest mere islets. The first of these is the largest, being about nine leagues long from north to south. M. Melville de Carnbée estimates the superficies of the whole group at 18 geographical square leagues, or 9·9 myriametres. The people appear to be a simple race, with some amount of civilisation, for they rear yams, batatas, and coco-nuts, and breed hogs, goats, and the common fowl. Of their languages nothing is known, but in race they are Malayan. The Dutch claim, without apparently exercising sovereignty over this group.

TAMARIND (TAMARINDICUS INDICUS). A frequent name for this tree in Javanese is asâm, which, however, signifies also, sour or acid, either as a noun, or adjective. Its more appropriate name in the same language is kamal. The Malays call the tree and fruit Asâm-Jawa, that is, the acid of Java. The name asâm, which may here be rendered "the acid," has extended to almost all the languages of the Malay Archipelago, the only exception being the Lampung of Sumatra, where the tree is called by the Javanese one, kamal. Both words are native, and not foreign, and therefore, as far as we can trust to language, the plant is indigenous, at least in Java. The tree, a handsome one, is very extensively planted in Java, both for its wood and fruit. The last serves the natives for all the purposes of vinegar. "The Sundas," says De Barros, "have abundance of ordinary flesh, much venison, and abundant corn, with tamarinds, which serve them for vinegar."

TAMBALAN. The name in our maps of a group of Islands. See TIMBALAN.

TANAH, most probably from the Sanscrit thana. This is the most frequent word to express, land, earth, or ground; and also country, land, and region, both in Malay and Javanese. Placed before the name of a people, it represents the country they inhabit, as Tanah-Jawa, the land of the Javanese, or that portion of Java occupied by the proper Javanese. Tanah-Sunda, the country of the Sundas, or that part of the same island inhabited by the Sunda nation, Tanah-Bugis, the land of the Bugis, or country of this nation, frequently extended to the whole island of Celebes, because the Bugis are its chief nation; and Tanah-Kling, the land of the Kalinga nation, or Tâlugus, often extended to the whole country of the Hindus, because the Tâlugus were the people of Hindustan best known to the inhabitants of the Malayan Archipelago. This is very much the manner in which the name of our own country is formed.

TANAH-LAUT, literally, "sea-land," is the name of the most southern portion of Borneo, lying east of Banjarmasin, and opposite to the distant islands of Bali and Lomboc. The name is most probably derived from its character of being flooded by the sea.

TANAHKEKE. The name of an islet in South latitude 5° 30", lying towards the extreme end of the coast of the south-western peninsula of Celebes. The name, partly Malayan and partly Macassar, signifies "land of sorcerers."

TANGAMUS (GUNUNG). The name of a mountain of Sumatra, in the country of the Lampung nation, which has an elevation of 7500 feet above the level of the sea, but of which the geological character has not been ascertained.

TANGKUBAN-PRAU is the name of a mountain of Java, in the country of the Sundas, and district of Bandong. It is an active volcano 6500 feet high, with three separate craters, called, respectively, Kawah-ratu, Kawah-badak, and Kawah-upas, signifying respectively, kings, rhinoceros, and poison caldrons. An eruption of this mountain took place in 1829, and another as late as 1846. These have been accurately and scientifically described by Dutch writers.

TANJUNG. In Malay, but not in Javanese, a headland, point, cape, or promontory,—any land, whether high or low, projecting into the sea, or a river. The word is of very frequent occurrence in the geography of Malayan countries, and examples are abundant, as Tanjung-datu, Tanjung-api, and Tanjung-sâlatan, literally, "elders," "fire," and south-points,—names of Bornean headlands.

TAPANULY. The name of the only extensive bay in the island of Sumatra, and situated on its western coast, in the country of the Bataks. It contains many islands, and within it are several well-sheltered coves and harbours, with ample depth of water for ships of burden. One of the islands towards its entrance, called Ponchong-kâchil, or little Ponchong, was one occupied by the English, and is in north latitude 1° 43′ 50″, and east longitude 98° 45′. This spacious bay, however, has never been a scene of industry, or much frequented, for the inhabitants on its coasts, few in number, are barbarous, and the country itself, with few exceptions, a mere forest.

TÂPARANG. This is the name of a Bugis country, situated nearly in the centre of the south-western peninsula of Celebes, but the name is also frequently applied to its most remarkable feature, the Tâparang-danau, or lake of Tâparang, called, also, the Lake of Labaya. According to the accounts given to me by intelligent merchants, inhabitants of its shores, this lake, by far the largest in Celebes, is twenty-four miles in length, from north to south, and about half this breadth. It is fed by many streams, at the disemboguement of each of which there is usually a village. Its superfluous water is carried off by the river Chinrana, which falls into the bay of Boni, in about south latitude 4° 15′. The Chinrana is navigable up to the lake for vessels of twenty tons burthen, and the lake itself is also navigable, having a depth of from two to three fathoms in the dry season, and in the wet as much as eight. It abounds in fish, and its shores are populous and well cultivated.

TAPIR (TAPIRUS MALAYENSIS), in Malay, Tânok. The tapir was thought to be exclusively a native of the New World, until it was found, also, to belong to the old one, and, strange to say, not until the beginning of the present century. It had been seen in Sumatra as early as 1772, but thought to be a hippopotamus. In 1803, a specimen was obtained in Penang, from the opposite side of the Peninsula, but it excited no attention, and the first account of it was rendered, in 1816, by my friend the late Colonel Farquar. The Portuguese, the Dutch, and the English had been, therefore, one or other of them, in Sumatra and the Peninsula, the only countries of the Archipelago in which the tapir exists, for three centuries without discovering that they produced one of the larger mammalia, the animal being all the while well known to the natives, and having a specific name.

TARAKAN. The name of one of the many islands in the bay which is included between Cape Unsang and Cape Jarum, on the eastern side of Borneo.

TASMAN (ABEL). This great and enterprising Dutch navigator and discoverer is noticed here on account of his having sailed from Java under the auspices of its Governor-General Van Diemen. His two voyages were performed in 1642 and 1644, and in these Tasman's principal discoveries were Van Diemen's Land, New Zealand, and the Friendly Islands. The first of these, in honour of him, has lately received, and it is hoped will retain, the name of Tasmania. Even the dates of the birth and death of this man, who equalled Dampier and Cook, and whose discoveries preceded those of the first by 50 years, and of the last by 130, are unknown.

TATTOOING. The practice of making indelible stained figures in the skin, by way of ornament or distinction, is called, in Malay, chachah, a word which also signifies to chop, or mince. It obtains only among the rudest tribes, such as some of the

Dayaks of Borneo, but is unknown to all the more civilised races, nor is it ascertained to have existed among the latter in any period of their history. It appears to have been general among one far-spread nation of the Philippines at the time of the Spanish conquest. These are the Bisaya, whose name, signifying "to paint," is said to be derived from this custom.

TAWALI is the name of a small island lying close to the north-western coast of Bachian, the largest of the five true Molucca or Clove Islands. Its most southerly point is thirty-three miles south of the equator, and in east longitude 127° 9′ 30″.

TAWI-TAWI. This is one of the three most considerable islands of the Sulu-Archipelago, and the largest, although not the most fruitful of them. Its area is 416 square geographical miles. Of the large islands of the Archipelago, it is the nearest to Borneo, being distant from the Point of Unsang not above twenty miles. Its inhabitants belong to the same Malayan race as those of the chief island, Soolo, speak the same language, and have, as rovers, the same evil reputation as the people of that island.

TAYABAS. The name of one of the provinces of the island of Luzon, bounded to the north by the great lake and province of Bay,—to the east by the Gulf of Lamon, and to the west by the province of Batangas. To the south, it is composed of the narrow isthmus which makes Luzon to consist of two peninsulas. The general character of the province is rugged and mountainous, yet it contains several plains and rich valleys, well adapted to the culture of rice, or which contain good pastures, in which are bred horned cattle and horses, the last of high reputation in other parts of the Philippines. The inhabitants of Tayabas are of the Tagala nation. In 1735, the population was only 10,000. In the first year of the present century, it was 39,690; in 1818, it rose to 48,676, and in 1845, to 80,110, of whom 17,347 paid the capitation tax.

The chief town of the province bearing the same name stands in north latitude 13° 37′ 30″, and east longitude 121° 30′, in a plain, and on a small river near its disemboguement, opposite to the island of Marinduque. It consists of 1800 houses, and a population of 22,265 souls, of whom 4712 were subject to the poll-tax. Taking the area of the province at 1575 geographical square leagues, the rate of population is 50·8 to the square mile.

TEA. The Chinese name for tea, adopted by the Indian Islands, is the same as our own, teh, and as we received our earliest supply from Bantam, it is probable that the English name comes directly from the Malay. This commodity must have been introduced into the Indian Islands with the first commercial intercourse of the Chinese with them, but, most probably, at first in very small quantities, and for the use only of the Chinese sojourners themselves. It is certainly not mentioned as an article of trade by the early Portuguese writers. Thus, Barbosa gives a list of seventeen different articles imported by the Chinese into Malacca, such as porcelain, raw and wrought silks, iron, silver, musk, rhubarb, but there is not a word about tea. It was not until 1600, or ninety years after the arrival of the Portuguese, that tea was first seen by them in the market of Malacca, and the first sample was imported into England, not until 1662, a century and a half after the conquest of that place. The upper class of the Javanese drink tea occasionally, although they have no taste for coffee, now so cheaply produced in their own country.

Of late years, among other factitious projects for increasing the wealth of Java, the Dutch have introduced the cultivation and preparation of tea, by corvée labour. All the chances are, I think, against the ultimate success of such a scheme, and this for reasons which are transparent. No good tea has been produced hitherto in any country within the tropics—not even in China itself, where all the requisite knowledge, skill, and low-priced labour exist, and it is not probable, therefore, that it should be produced within seven degrees of the equator, where equal knowledge, skill, or cheap labour do not exist. It may be pleaded that elevation above the level of the sea will furnish the requisite average temperature. No doubt it will do so in a great many parts of Java, but it cannot, there or anywhere else, supply the summer and the winter that may be necessary to the successful growth of tea. A moderate elevation furnishes the necessary climate for coffee, which, although a native of Abyssinia, is successfully grown at the equator. A long experience has proved that coffee may be grown in any tolerable soil in any country within the tropics, but it cannot be inferred from this that tea, a plant of a different natural family, can be so. On the contrary, we have known tea nearly as long as coffee, and after the lapse of near two centuries have never succeeded in growing it for commercial purposes, China, being now, as in the time of Charles the Second, the only country to furnish the vast consumption of the world. Moreover, coffee is produced with less agricultural skill than even wheat, and tea demands a great deal more. Coffee requires less manipulation than the same corn, and tea a great deal more than any other vegetable product used as food. To conclude, the successful growth of a few thousand pounds of tea, supposing such to be the case, by a government, with the help of corvée labour, would be no evidence of a successful culture of the same article as a legitimate product of free labour and private enterprise.

TEAK (TECTONA). In Javanese and Malay the name of this celebrated tree, which yields at once the strongest and the most durable timber of all Asiatic, and perhaps, also, even of all European or American woods, is Jati,—a word which, in Javanese, signifies also "true, real, genuine." This tree, abundant in a few places, is confined to a very few localities, both on the continent and islands. In the latter, it is unknown to Sumatra, Borneo, and the Peninsula, and is limited to part of Java, Sumbawa, and Mindano, which last is the only one of the Philippines that produces it. Java is the only one of these that is known to yield it abundantly, or at least in which it is accessible for use in any abundance.

TEGAL, or, in the orthography assumed in this work, Tâgal, which in Javanese means "a field," is the name of one of the provinces of the proper country of the Javanese, situated on the northern sea-board of Java, bounded to the east by the province of Pakalongan, to the west by that of Cheribon, and to the south by that of Bañumas. It is separated from the last by a mountain chain, the culminating point of which is the mountain which is usually known to Europeans by the name of the province, but is correctly Sâlamat. Next to Sumeru and Arjuna, it is the highest mountain in Java, being 11,250 feet above the level of the sea. The greater part of the province is a fertile alluvial plain, the whole of it containing an area of 850 square miles, with a population of 293,996, or 345 inhabitants to the square mile. The census of 1850, however, represents this population to have amounted to no more than 250,739, or to have fallen off by 43,257. In 1845, the number of its horned cattle was estimated at 38,000, and of its horses at 8000. Its staple vegetable products, in the same year, were estimated as follow,—namely, rice in the husk, about 250,000 quarters, equal to about one-half that quantity of clean corn; coffee, 4,488,000 pounds; sugar, 4,615,000 pounds; and tea, to the same extent as sugar.

TELINGA, OR KALINGA, in Malay and Javanese Kâling, the name of the nation of Southern India with which the Indian islanders have at all known times held most intercourse, and through whom, it is believed, they received, in ancient times, the Hindu religion, and some of the civilisation which belongs to those who profess it. See KLING.

TENGAR, OR TÂNGAR MOUNTAINS. The name of a group of mountains in the eastern part of Java, situated in the provinces of Surabaya and Pasuruhan. The name signifies "wide, spacious." My old and greatly esteemed friend, Dr. Thomas Horsfield, has given the following excellent description of this singular mountain, or rather cluster of mountains: "This mountain," says he, "constitutes one of the most remarkable volcanos of the island. It rises from a very large base by a gentle slope, with gradually ascending ridges. The summit, seen from a distance, is less conical than most of the other principal volcanos, varying in height at different points, from 7000 to 8000 feet. The crater is not at the summit, but more than 1000 feet below the highest point, and consists of a large excavation of an irregularly circular form, surrounded on all sides by a range of hills of different elevations. It is by far the largest crater in the island, and probably exceeds in size every other crater existing on the globe. It constitutes an immense gulf, the bottom of which is level, and denominated by the natives the dasar (the floor). This is naked of vegetation, and covered with sand throughout. In one portion, in the middle, the sand is loose, and blown by the wind into slight ridges. To this the natives give the name of Sagarawâdi, literally, 'sea of sand.' The largest diameter of the entire crater is, according to my estimate, full three miles. From the interior, near the middle, rise several conical peaks, or distinct volcanos. The chief of these, the mountain Brama (in Sanscrit, the god Brama, or fire), is a perfectly regular cone, and still in partial activity, with occasional eruptions. It is surrounded, on one side, by the sea of sand above mentioned. Adjoining it stands another conical peak, more than 1000 feet high, named Watangan (the Javanese Campus martius), or Widadaren (abode of celestial nymphs), covered externally with sand, quite naked, and, on account of its steepness, the top has never been examined. At a small distance from the Brama rises a smaller cone, called Butak ('the bald'). The two last have not exhibited any activity in recent times." To this account of the volcanic phenomena, Dr. Horsfield adds the following observations on the soil and productions of the Tângar valleys: "The soil of the Tenger hills is extremely fertile, consisting of a deep vegetable mould, accumulated for many ages on the sand and debris thrown up from the mountain. Vegetables of northern latitudes, potatoes, cabbages, onions, &c., &c., are planted by the natives in great abundance, for the supply of the markets of Pasuruhan and Surabaya. European fruits, as apples and peaches, are also raised, as well as wheat, and other northern grains. Rice refuses to grow, and the coco-nut produces no fruit."—Geographical Preface and Postscript of Plantæ Javaniæ rariores. 1852.

TENIMBER. This is a name of unknown origin or derivation given to a group of islands in the Timur Sea, of which the only large island is Timur-laut. The group forms the termination of the long chain of islets which extends east of Timur towards the Aroes. It is composed of many islands, but five only are of considerable size, namely, Timur-laut, Larat, Verdaté, Moeloe, and Cerva. The first is incomparably the largest of these, being about 90 miles long by 30 broad in its widest part. The area of the entire group has been reckoned at 2400 square geographical miles. They are all low, coral or madrepore-formed land, surrounded by reefs, without harbour or shelter for shipping. The natives are of the Malayan race, with goodly persons, and possess a considerable share of industry, raising farinaceous roots and the coco-nut, and rearing hogs, goats, and the common poultry. They are skilful fishermen, their seas abounding in fish. The Tenimber Islands form, at least, nominally, part of the dominions of the Netherlands. The population of the group has been reckoned at 22,000.

TENNASSERIM, in Malay TANAHSRI. Our name for this part of Pegu is taken, directly, from the Portuguese Tanaseri. All our popular names for those countries inhabited by the Burmese, Peguans, and Siamese seem to have come to us through the same quarter, the original source being Malay, such as Siam from Siyâm, Ava from Awak, Pegu from Paigu, and Martaban from Muritanau. At the time of the arrival of the Portuguese in Malacca, a very considerable commercial intercourse is described as existing between that place and the nearest parts of Pegu, then an independent monarchy. Peguans are even described by De Barros as being settled in Malacca, and among the auxiliaries who went to Muar in pursuit of the fugitive king of Malacca, we find 300 Peguans. This state of things soon ceased under the government of the Portuguese, nor has it, for reasons not easily understood, been renewed under their European successors.

TENURE OF LAND. With the exception of the populous islands of Java, Bali, Lomboc, and a few parts of the Philippines, the land is so superabundant, and the population so small in relation to it, that the greater part of it has, in reality, no saleable value at all. With the exceptions thus enumerated, no real or theoretic rent exists, and the only value of the land is derived from the labour invested in clearing it of forest, in making it amenable to irrigation, in digging wells, and in the fruit trees planted on it. All lands which have received a value from labour so invested, are a private heritable property, or an heir-loom,—in the languages of the Malays and Javanese, pusaka. If any public tax be imposed on such lands, it is taken in kind, and does not exceed a tithe. Even the rude laws of the Malays proclaim this private property in cultivated or reclaimed land, as the few following extracts from those of Jehore will satisfactorily show. "Land is of two descriptions, appropriated and unappropriated. The last has no owner, and therefore cannot be a subject of litigation." "He who reclaims forest land, or builds upon it, shall not be molested in his possession." "The proofs of land being appropriated are the presence of wells, of fruit trees, or marks of tillage, and if any one intermeddle with such lands, he shall be amenable to prosecution." "If any one trespasses on such appropriated lands, he shall be fined ten mas, more or less, at the discretion of the magistrate, according to the extent of the land." "If a man builds a house, and makes a garden upon the appropriated land of another, not knowing that it had an owner, and the owner return, he shall be entitled to one-third part of the produce." "If a man cultivate the irrigated land (sawah) of another, not knowing it had an owner, he shall pay such owner, as in the last case, one-third of the produce of the land." "If a man take possession of the land of another, after it has been prepared for upland culture (umah), he shall pay a fine of ten mas, and if a man seize upon such land forcibly, he shall be fined one tail and one päa." "If neighbours unite for the purpose of clearing, cultivating, and fencing a portion of forest land, and one out of the number neglecting the portion of the fence assigned to him, and cattle or wild hogs enter and destroy the crop, such person so neglecting shall be compelled to make good the crop which has been destroyed." "If a man steal the materials of a fence, and the owner of it meet him, it shall be lawful for him to seize and bind the thief, to take from him such articles as krises, hangers, or spears, and to carry him, if a free man, to the magistrate, or if a slave, to his master." "If a man go to hunt with toils, or nets, or decoys, or to fish in rivers or lakes, it shall not be lawful for the chief in authority over the land to hinder him, for the game he is in quest of are wild animals." "If however a person rob a beehive on another's land, without the knowledge of the owner, it shall be lawful for the owner to seize and take such hive from him, and the offender shall be further fined to the extent of half a tail. It is true that bees are wild animals, but the hives had yielded the owner of the land a regular and certain revenue."

But the tenure of land stands on a very different footing in the populous islands of Java, Bali, and Lomboc, and in the better peopled parts of the Philippines. In Java, it far more resembles its state in several parts of Hindustan than that now described. Here, a true rent, independent of the labour invested in the soil, has immemorially existed. In the most fertile and populous part of the island, the proper country of the Javanese nation, the greater part of this rent has, as in Bengal, been absorbed by the state in the shape of a land-tax, under the native governments usually taken in kind. In this manner little remains to the actual occupant or cultivator beyond the right of cultivating, and the sovereign is virtually the proprietor. In the mountainous and less populous country of the Sunda nation, a true rent also exists, but by custom less of it is taken by the state as tax, and enough remains with the occupant to make the land a saleable and heritable private property, which it seldom is in the country of the Javanese.

It is only in the Philippines, however, that the land is a private property in the sense in which that is understood in Europe, and unless in China, it is probably the only populous country of eastern or central Asia in which such a tenure exists. It was of course introduced by the Spanish conquerors, who found the country under-peopled and occupied by rude tribes, with the greater part even of the best lands, as yet, unreclaimed and wild. In such a state of society there was no rent, and consequently no source of a land-tax, such as has immemorially existed in the old and civilised countries of Asia. In lieu of it, the conquerors had recourse to a capitation tax, which has been continued ever since, and no attempt has ever been made to impose a tax on the land in any form whatsoever. The result of this is that land has a value in the most improved parts of the islands, unknown in any other country of Asia. Thus in the province of Laguna in the island of Luzon a quiñon of land, a measure of 1000 square fathoms, each of three varas of Castille, sells for from 220 to 300 hard Spanish dollars, in that of Pangasinan at from 120 to 250, in South Ilocos at 300, in that of Tondo, near Manilla, and in Bulacan at 1000, and in Balinag at 500.—Informe solne el Estado, p. 629 and 633.

TERNATE, correctly **TÂRNATÉ**, one of the five original Molucca or Clove Islands. It lies on the western coast of the large island of Gilolo or Halmahera, 48 miles north of the equator, and in east longitude 127° 24′. This mere islet has an area of no more than 11·5 square geographical miles. It is, in fact, the mere pedestal on which stands the active volcanic mountain of the same name, and which rises to the height of 5750 feet above the level of the sea. De Barros gives a very good account of this volcano on the authority of Antonio Galvão, who was captain of the island in 1538. It has produced during the Dutch occupation no fewer than fourteen different eruptions, beginning with the year 1608, and ending with 1840. In the eruption of 1840 the earthquakes lasted from the second to the fifteenth of February, with intervals of a few hours only. The inhabitants fled to the sea-beach or took to their boats. Every stone building in the town was overthrown, and the people were on the point of abandoning the island altogether, a resolution to this effect having been come to by the public authorities of the place, afterwards overruled at Batavia. The loss of property amounted to 85,000*l.*, a large sum for a very small place. By a census taken in 1840, the population of the island amounted to 6710 souls, of whom 4071 were natives of the island, 1216 settlers from Celebes, 401 Chinese, 412 Europeans with their mixed descendants, and 581 slaves. But, besides the inhabitants of Ternate itself, there was dependent immediately on it a population of 18,918, namely, in Gilolo, 3686; in Makyan, 6730; in the Xulla Islands, 10,769; making a total of 36,397. Ternate is the seat of the Dutch administration of the Moluccas. As is sufficiently known, the only staple product of its soil, the clove, that which brought it trade and civilisation, has been long extirpated. Sago is now, as it immemorially has been, the bread of the inhabitants, for rice is as much a foreign and imported article as it is in Britain.

TEXTILE MATERIALS. As these are mentioned in their respective places, it will only be necessary here to enumerate them. They are—cotton, the abaca or textile banana, the pine-apple fibre, the rami or urtica estuans, the fibres of the coco and gomuti palms, the paper mulberry or Broussonetia papyrifera, the bara or wara (Paritium tileaceum), and, perhaps, the universal ratan. No animal fibre is ever employed for textile purposes, except silk, and that is always imported.

TICAO. The name of one of the Philippine Islands forming, with the larger one of Masbaté near it, a distinct, although small province. Ticao lies off the coast of the extreme southern end of Luzon and nearly opposite to the fine bay and harbour of Sorsogon, between the 12th and 13th degrees of north latitude. Its length is about 25 miles and its extreme breadth about 10. It is mountainous, and to judge by its population, 2312, not fertile. Its chief town is named St. Jacinto.

TIDOR, correctly TIDORI, is one of the five original Molucca or Clove Islands. It is situated off the western coast of the large island of Gilolo or Halamahera, and immediately south of Ternate. It is larger than that islet, but I have seen no statement of its actual area. Like Ternate, too, its formation is entirely volcanic, and the mountain of which it is chiefly composed rises to the height of 6000 feet above the level of the sea, its extinct crater being 39 miles north of the equator and in east longitude 127° 24′. The population of Tidor itself, according to a census made in 1840, was 5924, of the territory belonging to its prince in Gilolo 3937, and in New Guinea and its adjacent islands 10,000, making the total population subject to this petty tributary of the Netherland government 19,861 souls. Tidor was the Clove Island visited by the companions of Magellan, at which they were so hospitably received, and at which the celebrated ship "Victoria," that accomplished the first circumnavigation of the globe, obtained the cargo of spices which she succeeded in conveying to Spain. This was in 1521, about 10 years after the arrival of the Portuguese in the Moluccas. The people of Tidor had, at this time, been but recently converted to the Mohammedan religion, in which, however, they have since persevered after a lapse of more than three centuries. This is Pigafetta's account of the transaction: "Hardly fifty years have elapsed since the Moors conquered (converted?) Malucco and dwelt there. Previously, these islands were peopled by Gentiles only, who did not appreciate the clove. There are still some families of these fugitives in the mountains exactly where the cloves grow."—Primo Viaggio, p. 161. This statement is, in some respects, not quite correct. It is true that the natives set no value on the clove as a condiment, which is the case even at the present day, but for ages it had been an article of trade with strangers, and gave their whole importance to the petty islands which produced it, and without which, they would have been inhabited only by a few wretched fishermen.

TIGER. This dangerous animal is too frequent in the peninsula, Sumatra, and Java, but wholly unknown in all the other large islands of the Malay Archipelago, nor does it even exist in the small islands near those mentioned, except where accident has introduced it, as in the case of Singapore. In the Philippine Archipelago it is wholly unknown. The tiger of the Malayan countries is the same as that of India. In Malay, the name for it is arimau, and by elision of the initial vowel, a frequent practice of the language, rimau. In Javanese, the most frequent name for it is machan, occasionally used also by the Malays, but it has four others, sima, from singah, a lion, sridula and mong. The three first of these are Sanscrit, and the last native, probably taken from the roar of the animal. But the royal tiger is the type which, in the native languages, furnishes the generic name of all the larger feline animals, the others being designated by adding an epithet. Thus, the leopard is called by the Javanese machan tutul, or the "spotted tiger," and the Malays call a kind of tiger cat arimau-akar, which may be rendered "the scandent or climbing tiger." The tiger itself, to distinguish it from the rest of the family, is designated arimau-tunggal, which signifies "the unique tiger, or the tiger itself."

TIMBALAN, written in our charts Tambalan, is the name of a small group of islands lying nearly midway between the eastern end of the Straits of Malacca and Borneo, in north latitude 1° 1′. The largest of them seems to be a mass of granite covered, for the most part, with a heavy forest. The whole group is computed to have an area of 112 geographical square miles. The inhabitants are Malay fishermen, about 750 in number, occupying a village in a cove at the eastern side of the island. The productions exported from it are coco-nuts, coco-nut oil, palm sugar, and salt fish, for which they receive in exchange at Singapore, rice, clothing, and utensils. Pulo Timbalan, in Malay, means literally, balance, equipoise, or requital island, but why this name, has not been explained. It forms with all the other islands between the Peninsula and Borneo, at least nominally, part of the territory of the principality of Jehor.

TIMOAN and TIMUN, correctly, in Malay, Tiyoman, a word, however, with the origin of which I am unacquainted. This is the name of the largest of a chain of islets, lying off the eastern coast of the Malay peninsula, and towards its southern extremity, belonging to the petty state of Pahang. It lies between north latitudes 2° 44′ and 2° 54′, is about ten miles long, and from five to six broad, and, as far as examined, consists of a mass of trap rock, bold and precipitous, presenting views not only picturesque but grand. Such is the account given of it by a most intelligent and judicious writer in the Journal of the Indian Archipelago, Mr. J. Thomson, who visited it in 1849. Several of its peaks rise to the height, above the level of the sea, of from 2394 to 3444 feet. "On the southern shore of Tioman," says Mr. Thomson, "are two remarkable peaks, or pinnacles, called by the English, the Ass's Ears," and by the Malays, Chula-naga (chula, a horn, and naga, the fabulous snake or dragon of the Hindus). They rise out of the spur of one of the southern mountains, at about 1500 feet above the level of the sea, and from this height, on one side, they spring perpendicularly 1000 feet. They form a most magnificent feature in the aspect of the island, and cannot be beheld without wonder and awe, even by the most unsusceptible." In another place he observes, "Tioman being mountainous and bold in its configuration, and abounding in lofty pinnacles, peaks and precipices, naturally inspires feelings of wonder not unmixed with awe, when closely approached. These emotions may be occasionally heightened, if the observer, when nearing it, experience, as was the case with us, a heavy squall, which covers the towering masses, wrapping the whole in gloom, exaggerating their apparent heights, when these can occasionally be discovered through the lurid haze. It is, therefore, not to be wondered at, that we find this island to be the subject of mythic tradition. The feelings which the scene inspires in the breasts of the simple races that inhabit these parts have sought expression in figurative language, what it would be otherwise difficult to explain, or which would, at least, have required a lengthened description. Tioman has been pictured as a dragon, the most hideous and powerful monster of tradition. Whether the myth had or had not its origin in a metaphor, the native now literally appeals to the peaks and ridges, in which he seeks to discover a similitude to the various parts of the monster, in order to give evidence to the traditions which spring from the prior idea."

Tioman produces nothing for exportation but swallows' esculent nests, ratans and damar, all wild products of the rocks or forests. About 30 years ago, according to information furnished to myself by some of its natives, the whole population of this comparatively sterile island amounted only to 50 souls. Most of these were seized and carried off as slaves by the corsairs of Mindano, and the remainder abandoned the place. About 1839 it was re-occupied, and during Mr. Thomson's visit, ten years after, the population was reckoned to be 200, or about one-seventh part of that of the smaller but more fertile Pulo Aoar.

TIMUR. This is the Malay name of the eighth in number, reckoning from Sumatra, of the more considerable of the chain of islands which geographers have called the Sunda. It is, however, out of the direct line of these, extending to near the 11th degree of south latitude,—differs from them in geological formation, and in animal and vegetable products, and, therefore, ought not to be classed with them. To the west, the nearest large island to it is Floris, with many islets intervening, and to the east the nearest extensive land to it is New Guinea, with which it is almost connected by a chain of islets, although the distance be 440 miles. To the south, Australia is not above one half that distance with nothing between but ocean. Timur is about 370 miles long, about 50 broad in its widest part, and is computed to contain an area of 9808 geographical square miles, so that it is about one-fourth the size of Java, and about double that of our island of Jamaica.

The geological formation of Timur, instead of being, like that of the islands from

Java to Floris, volcanic, is, on the contrary, plutonic and sedimentary, the principal rocks consisting of clay schists and especially of madreporic limestone, containing many caves and caverns. Notwithstanding the absence of volcanic formation, the island is subject to frequent earthquakes, and a particularly destructive one took place in 1794, which overthrew the church and other buildings of the Dutch settlement of Koepang. A chain of mountains runs through the length of the island from east to west, the highest points of which are from 4000 to 4500 feet above the level of the sea. The surface of the island generally consists of hills and narrow steep valleys, but there are a few plains of considerable extent, such as that of Koepang at the western end, which is about 10 miles square. The only metals, besides iron, that have been found are gold and copper, but neither of them in any great quantity. The rivers are numerous, but from the formation of the land they are but precipitate brooks of short course, and not navigable, even for boats, above the reach of the tide, generally not exceeding 400 yards. There are no lakes. The only two harbours in the island are Dili, the Portuguese establishment on the north-eastern side, and Koepang at the western end, and both are imperfect ones.

The vegetation of Timur, instead of being luxuriant like that of the western islands of the Archipelago, is comparatively thin, meagre, and sombre, more in the character of that of the northern part of Australia. The Cassuarinas, especially, remind the observer of the Australian vegetation. The palms are few in number, the only species that is frequent being the Gâbang, or the Corypha gebanga of botanists. The coco-nut is scarce, and the rich fruits of the western islands, the durian, the mangostin, and the duku do not exist. The zoology is scanty like the botany. None of the largest mammiferous animals, as the elephant, the rhinoceros, the ox, the buffalo, the tiger, or even the leopard exist. The largest animal, and the only deer of the island is the same as that of the Moluccas (Cervus Moluccensis). There is one undescribed species of wild hog, differing from those of Java, Borneo, and Sumatra. There is but one marsupial animal, an opossum, the Phalangista cavifrons, and there is also but one monkey, the Cercopithecus cynomologus, being the same as that of the Moluccas, and the only ape which reaches so far eastward. The squirrels and porcupines of the western islands are all wanting, and the only representative of the class of gnawers is the common brown rat. There is one species of the feline family only, and this is new, a small cat, Felis megolotis. The family of bats is numerous, and some of the species either rare or altogether new. Among birds, crows, jays, and birds of Paradise are wholly absent. There exist two gallinaceous birds, one of them resembling the Gallus bankiva, the supposed original of our domestic poultry. Among reptiles which are not numerous, the most remarkable is that crocodile, named by naturalists biporcatus, but a variety from that of Java and the other western islands. Even the fish of the seas of Timur are not abundant, nor do the natives possess any skill in taking them.

The domesticated animals of Timur are the horse, the buffalo, but not the ox, the goat, the sheep introduced by Europeans, the dog, the domestic cat, the common fowl, goose, and duck, but except the horse and buffalo none of them abundant. It is evident from the number of the two last that are bred, and their low price, that Timur is better adapted for pasture than for tillage.

The inhabitants of Timur seem to be of a race intermediate between the Malay and Papuan negro, but partaking most of the first. It is far more likely to be an aboriginal and distinct race than an admixture of these two, since it is difficult to imagine how such admixture could have taken place, as no negro race exists nearer than New Guinea, between four and five hundred miles distant, the intermediate islands being all peopled by the Malayan. They are thus described by the well-informed but anonymous author of an account of the island contained in a compilation called Moor's Indian Archipelago, being a collection of articles from the first newspaper published in Singapore, a considerable number of which were contributed by myself. "The natives," says he, "are generally of a very dark colour, with frizzled bushy hair, but less inclining to the Papuan than the natives of Endé (Floris). They are below the middle size, and rather slight in their figure. In countenance they more nearly resemble the South Sea Islanders than any of the Malay tribes." Compared with the principal nations of the western portion of the Archipelago, the people of Timur stand very low in the social scale. They seem to be divided into many small tribes, speaking different languages, among which two, the Manatoto and the Timuri, are the most prevalent. The first of these tongues is spoken in the north-eastern part of the island, and the last used as a medium of communication among several tribes in the south-western part. Alphabetic writing has never been invented by the people of Timur, nor have they ever adopted the written characters of any foreign people. The rude state of the country is attested by the condition of the arts. The plough, although the buffalo be abundant, and here of great size, strength and docility, is unknown and the only agricultural implements of the aboriginal inhabitants is a wooden hoe, and a stick sharpened at the end. Owing to the hilly nature of the land, and probably also its sterility, rice is little cultivated, and irrigation but rarely had recourse to. Maiz is the chief bread-corn of the Timurians, and as this is an undoubted American plant, introduced by Europeans, it is certain that the people must have been even poorer and fewer in number than they are now, before the arrival of Europeans. Their fishing is conducted in the same fashion, and this is the account given of it by the anonymous writer already quoted. "Fish," says he, "can scarcely be considered as an article of subsistence, as there are hardly any of the natives who will venture into a canoe. And almost the only method they have of taking them is by building successive walls of stone, one without the other, and within the reach of the tide, in places where the coast is flat enough to admit it, so as to prevent the return of the fish when the water ebbs."

The religion of the people of Timur seems to be a kind of demonology, and is well described by the writer just quoted. "The religion of the island," says he, "is pagan. Most of the princes, however, profess Christianity, but are at the same time entirely guided by their pagan priests and customs. There does not appear to be a single convert to Islamism on the island. Their deities are represented by particular stones and trees, and although the same stones or trees are generally worshipped by successive generations, instances are said to occur of their changing them. They style these Nieto, or evil spirits, considering the sun and moon as the good spirits, the latter as the superior. They conceive it to be impossible that their good spirits should occasion them any harm, and therefore deem it unnecessary to pray to them. But they pray to the Nietos to avoid the evils they are otherwise liable to suffer. Sacrifices are common, generally, of buffaloes, hogs, sheep, or fowls, but sometimes of a human being. An annual sacrifice of a virgin used to be made to the sharks and alligators close to the town of Koepang, until the interference of the Dutch government put a stop to it about 30 years ago. At the interment of a sovereign prince a male slave is to the present day buried alive with him, to be ready to wait on him in the world to come. This used to take place immediately in the neighbourhood of Koepang, but has also been put a stop to by the Dutch. It still exists throughout the interior. The natives place great reliance on auguries, particularly from the inspection of the entrails of animals, and, indeed, never embark in any undertaking without first obtaining a lucky omen. On occasions which concern the State, a buffalo is generally slain, but on private account, usually a chicken. The liver is the part chiefly attended to." If to these accounts we add "head stealing," which is practised, it is certain that the people of Timur are not more advanced than the savages of Borneo, and, indeed, are not even on an equality with some of these.

With respect to the population of Timur it is evident, from its social condition, that nothing better than reasonable conjecture can be offered. We may be quite sure, however, that in relation to extent it must be very small. The population of the district of Koepang, so long under the administration of the Dutch, numbers only 7000. It is asserted, however, that subject to the government of the Netherlands, there are 40,000 more. This would make 47,000 for the Dutch part of the island, which is the most populous and undoubtedly the best governed, and it is supposed to embrace half the whole island. Of the population of the Portuguese portion we know nothing, but supposing it, which is not likely, to be equally populous with the Dutch, the entire population of the island would be no more than 94,000, or 9·58 to the square mile. The population in this case would be about one-eighth part of that of the little island of Bali, which is barely one-sixth part of its size. Such is the vast difference in the results of eminent fertility on the one side, and to say the least, the absence of it on the other.

Timur appears to have been well known by this name before the arrival of the Portuguese in the Archipelago, and the Malays and Javanese to have extended their trade to it. It was probably the furthest limit of their ordinary trade in a south-easterly direction, and hence most likely the name which in Malay, but not in Javanese, signifies "the East." Barbosa, evidently on native authority, for his countrymen had not yet penetrated so far east in the Archipelago, thus refers to it in describing the course of native trade. "Passing the island of Java Major," (the real Java and not Sumatra, the Java Major of Marco Polo), "there occur many other islands, great and small, inhabited by Gentiles speaking their own proper languages. In Timur is produced much white sandal wood, and those who go to buy it, take thither iron, needles, large and small knives, swords, cloths of Cambay and Pulicate, porcelain cups, beads of all sorts, tin, quicksilver, and lead. Besides sandal wood they take away from that island honey, bees'-wax, slaves, and some little silver which is found in it." With the exception of the silver, which ought to have been gold, this is a correct account of the trade of Timur, such as it was conducted for three centuries after Barbosa wrote, and indeed with little difference, such as it is at the present day. The companions of Magellan touched at Timur on their return to Spain in 1522, and Pigafetta's account of it is surprisingly correct. "All the trade in sandal-wood and bees'-wax, conducted by the people of Malacca and Java is carried on at this place (Cabanaza ?), and, in fact, we found here a junk which came from Luzon for the purchase of sandal wood, for white sandal grows only in this country."—Primo Viaggio, p. 171. The Mahommedans never appear to have gained any footing in Timur, nor to have made any conversions. The inhabitants, indeed, seem to have been too rude and poor to have been capable of receiving any strong religious impression whatever. Christianity itself, has fared not much better, for in the Dutch half of the island, the total number of native Christians is no more than 1200. It is probable they are more numerous within the Portuguese territory, but on this subject we are without information. When it was that the Portuguese first formed establishments in Timur I am not aware, but in 1613 they they were driven by the Dutch from the western end of the island, and owe their possession of the eastern, only to the accident of the peace concluded between the two nations on the separation of Portugal from Spain and the restoration to the throne of the first, of the house of Braganza.

TIMUR-LAUT (Pulo), literally, "sea-ward Timur," or rather sea-ward Timur Islands. See TENNIMBER ISLANDS.

TIN, in Malay and Javanese timah. The word, however, is used as a generic term for both tin and lead, the epithet "white," or "flowery,"—putih and sari, being given to tin itself, and that of "blank," itam, to lead, a metal with which, being entirely a foreign product, the Malayan nations are but little acquainted. The word timah, without any change, extends to all the languages of the western portion of the Archipelago, and is, no doubt, the same which appears in the languages of the Philippines, as tinga. It is even probably the tumöra of the languages of Celebes. In the ruder languages, however, such as those of Floris and Timur, it has names distinct from the Malayan, probably epithets, as it is not likely that the metal should have original and specific names in countries which do not produce it, and the inhabitants of which know it only as a foreign and imported commodity. In the polite language of Java, the name for it is râjasa, which is the Sanscrit adjective "bright," or "shining." The people of Madagascar have no name for it but what signifies "white iron," vi-futsi, both of which words are, most probably, corruptions of the two Malayan words, with the same meaning, bâsih-putih.

What may be called the Malayan tin district, or tin field, is, beyond all comparison, the most extensive and the richest in the world, for it stretches from Tavoy, in the 14° of north latitude, to Billiton, in the 3° of south latitude, that is, over seventeen degrees of latitude, and ten of longitude. Tin has been found or worked in a great many localities within these wide bounds, as in the British territory of the Tennasserim coast,—in the Siamese island of Junk-Ceylon,—in various parts of the continental territories of the Malayan States, and in several of the islands at the eastern end of the Straits of Malacca. The ore would seem only to become the more abundant as it approaches its termination at Banca and Billiton. The localities richest in tin are ascertained to be those near the junction of the sandstone with the granite, and all the countries rich in tin are also observed to be so in iron. All the ore heretofore worked, it should be noticed, has been found in the alluvion, or detritus of ancient mountains,—what is called in mining language "stream-works,"—obtained, in fact, by washing the soil in the same manner as, for the most part, gold in Australia and California; for no ore has ever been obtained by mining the rock containing veins of it, although it has been traced to them. It must also be remembered that the greater part of the tin district is covered with an immense forest, and has not been explored, so that tin may reasonably be expected to be found in many situations which have hitherto remained unexamined. The supply of tin from the Malayan countries promises to last for at least as many ages as that of the coal of England. It is produced, in fact, in quantity proportionate to the labour and capital invested in working it, and without restriction from any other cause. With partial exceptions, the Chinese are at present the effectual miners and smelters, and the increase which has taken place in the quantity produced is remarkable. In the beginning of the present century the quantity yielded by Banca did not exceed 560 tons, and at present, increasing yearly, it is not less than 5540 tons. Yet the mines of Banca have now been worked for near a century and a-half, being stated to have been first discovered only in the first years of the eighteenth century. The tin mines of Malacca were not worked at all, until as late as 1793, and not effectually by Chinese until 1840, but in 1848 they yielded, paying a seignorage of a tenth to the state, better than 250 tons. The production in the neighbouring Malay states had also greatly increased, so that the whole quantity exported from Malacca amounted in that year to above 960 tons. Mr. Logan estimates the whole quantity produced in the Malay Peninsula at about 2350 tons, exclusive of the produce of the Siamese territory; and when this is added to the produce of Banca, namely, 5540 tons, we have an aggregate annual yield of 7890 tons, or, making but a moderate allowance for the produce of the Siamese mines, of which we have no estimate, probably not less than double the amount of the tin of Cornwall. Probably, not less than five-sixths of this amount have been brought into existence in the course of the present century. The price has not fallen with this new supply to the market, and as in the case of the gold of California and Australia, it may be asked how this has happened, and the answer must be the same, that new sources of consumption have been found, increased wealth and population keeping the demand equal to the supply.

Barbosa mentions tin among the commodities taken by the Malay and Javanese traders to the Moluccas and other eastern islands from Malacca; but in a detailed list of the articles taken by the junks to China, and amounting to ten in number, tin is not found. Neither does he name it in his Calicut Price Current of thirty articles, although among them there be several, the peculiar products of the Malayan countries, such as the clove, nutmeg, white pepper, agila-wood, and benzoin. De Barros names the metal as one of those found in the market of Malacca, but calls it, erroneously, a product of Sumatra. The tin referred to by these writers, was, no doubt, the produce of rude Malayan industry, for in their time the Chinese had not yet settled in any part of the Archipelago. It would, consequently, have been small in quantity, and, as it is, at present at least, by twenty per cent. less valuable than that smelted by the skilful Chinese. Malay tin must have reached Hindustan at an early period, for it is otherwise difficult to understand from whence the Hindus, who have none of their own, could have obtained their supply of a metal which is largely used by them in the formation of alloys. In the Periplus of the Erythræan Sea, tin is named as an article to be found at the emporia of the western side of India, namely, Barugaza, supposed to be Baroach, and Baraké, believed to have been Nilcunda. From both places it is said to have been exported, and from the first to have been brought from Ozené, or Ougein. Dr. Vincent is of opinion that this tin was British, but it is far more likely to have been Malayan, part of it, probably, brought overland from the Coromandel coast. The most usual Sanscrit names for tin, vanga, and ranga, seem to be Indian, and to have no relation to the Malayan word timah.

TINGI (Pulo), literally, "High Island," is the name of the most southerly of a group of islets, close to the eastern coast of the Malay Peninsula, towards its extreme end, and belonging to the State of Pahang. It is a mass of trap and porphyry, rising to the height of 2046 feet above the level of the sea, and covered with forest. Along with the islets near it, it contains a population of 300 Malay fishermen. North latitude, 2° 17′.

TOBACCO (Nicotiana), in Malay and Javanese tambako, a slight corruption of the Spanish and Portuguese, tabaco. In the polite dialect of the Javanese, it has the whimsical name of sata, which signifies a "fowl," or "cock." According to a Javanese chronicle, tobacco was first introduced into Java in the year 1601, which was ninety years after the conquest of Malacca by the Portuguese. It was, most probably, introduced by this nation, for at the time alluded to, the Dutch had as yet formed no establishment in the island, and, indeed, had appeared there as traders only four years before. Of the time when it was first introduced in other parts of the Malay and Philippine Archipelago there is no record. It was, most probably, earliest introduced into Malacca, and could not have been introduced into the Philippines sooner than 1565, the date of the first settlement of the Spaniards in these islands. As in other parts of the world, the culture and use of tobacco became, throughout both Archipelagos, rapid and universal. For home use, it is grown almost everywhere, but it is only in the most fertile islands, as Java, Bali, and Luzon, that it is produced largely as an article of trade. The tobacco of Java and Luzon are extensively consumed in the respective Archipelagos to which they belong, and that of the latter, in the form of cigars, is exported to the continent of India, and to Europe and America. Tobacco is not a taxed article in any part of the Malay Archipelago, but it is a monopoly of a Spanish government of the Philippines, confined, however, to the island of Luzon, where, in 1839, it yielded a net revenue of 1,280,283 Spanish dollars, or 277,343*l.*, being the largest branch of the public revenue.

TOMAIKI. The name given to a great bay which divides the eastern from the south-eastern peninsula of Celebes. At its entrance, reckoning from the island of Wowoni to the Cape of Tolabi, it is not less than 180 miles wide, but does not penetrate the land to a greater depth than 120. Its coasts are rude, little known countries, without any evidence of industry or civilisation. Such a name as this and others given to the other great gulfs of Celebes, it should be recollected, are unknown to the natives of the Archipelago, and have been imposed by European navigators, although the terms which designate them are of native origin.

TOMBORO, the name of the mountain in the island of Sumbawa, in which, in the month of April, 1815, took place the greatest and most destructive volcanic eruption of which there is any record. The crater of this mountain is in south latitude 8° 14′ 30″, and east longitude 117° 55′ 30″, and the mountain itself rises to the height of 9000 feet above the level of the sea. The year preceding the eruption, I accompanied an expedition to Macassar in Celebes, and in our course we passed close to the coast of Sumbawa, and even then the volcano of Tomboro was in a state of great activity. At a distance, the clouds of ashes which it threw out blackened one side of the horizon in such a manner as to convey the appearance of a threatening tropical squall. In fact, it was mistaken for one, and the commander of the ship in which I was, took in sail, and prepared to encounter it. As we approached, the real nature of the phenomenon became apparent, and ashes even fell on the deck. When the great eruption took place, I was in civil charge of the province of Surabaya, in Java, distant from Tomboro about 300 miles. The noises proceeding from the volcano at this distance much resembled, at first, a distant but heavy cannonade, and the illusion, indeed, was so complete that gun-boats were ordered out, under the supposition that a merchantman was attacked by pirates in the Straits of Madura. The same deception respecting the detonations extended to Yogyakarta, 180 miles further west than Surabaya, or, in all, 480 miles distant from the volcano, for there my friend the late Colonel Dalton, marched out with his battalion to the relief of a fortress eighteen miles east of that place, which he imagined had been attacked, and had got half way to it before he was undeceived. The day after the sounds and shocks of earthquake which accompanied them were heard at Surabaya, the ashes began to fall, and on the third day, up to noon, it was pitch dark; and for several days after I transacted all business by candle-light. For several months, indeed, the sun's disk was not distinct, nor the atmosphere clear and bright, as it usually is during the south-east monsoon. The explosions of the volcano were heard, and even ashes fell, as far as Bencoolen, a thousand miles distant from the volcano; and the same evidence of the eruption was experienced in the Banda Islands, at the distance, in an easterly direction, and against the monsoon, of 750 miles. The total number of persons supposed to have lost their lives from the immediate effects of the eruption has been reckoned at twelve thousand, but its indirect effects extended much further, for the ashes fell so thick in Lomboc, Bali, and the eastern end of Java, as to destroy or injure much of the growing rice crops. The future effects of the ashes, however, were, in some places, evidently beneficial, for I see it stated that, in some parts of Lomboc, where, from its proximity, they fell heaviest, they had greatly increased the fertility of some districts.

TOMBORO is also the name of a native state of Sumbawa, which probably gives its name to the volcanic mountain. Before the eruption of the volcano in 1815, this was computed to have had a population of 6000, but in 1847, I do not find it named as a state at all, and most probably it had disappeared as the result of the catastrophe.

TOMINI. This is the name of the great gulf, which penetrating the island of Celebes to the depth of 220 miles, divides its northern from its eastern peninsula. At its entrance, it is about 65 miles wide, and in its broadest part about 90. At its extreme western end, an isthmus, not above 20 miles broad, divides it from the Straits of Macassar, which separate Celebes from Borneo. On the northern shore of the gulf is the Dutch settlement of Gorongtalo, a name which has been also, occasionally applied to the gulf itself.

TONDO, the name of one of the provinces of the island of Luzon, and that which contains the capital, the city of Manilla. It is bounded to the west by the bay of Manilla, and the province of Bataan, to the east by the provinces of Nueva Ecija and Laguna, to the south by those of Cavité and Laguna, and to the north by the province of Bulacan. It is considered to have a circumference of 95 geographical miles, and an area of about 300 square miles. A rocky ridge of hills passes through it, from north to south, with the exception of which it is a fertile plain, well watered, and adapted to the culture of rice, and of most other tropical products. It is, in fact, in a high state of cultivation. The mass of the inhabitants are of the Tagala nation. In 1735, the population amounted to no more than 31,805. In the first year of the present century, it had risen to 100,000; in 1818, to 149,951; in 1845, to 254,015, and in 1850, to 281,499. Deducting the population of the city of Manilla, 140,000, the relative one for the rest of the province is 471·6, which is equal to that of the finest parts of Java. Thus, in half a century, the increase was above 180 per cent., arising from immigration from other provinces and the advent of strangers, attracted by the commerce of Manilla. The chief town, having the same name as the province itself, is distant from the city of Manilla about half a league only, and is situated on a river which had passed through the provinces of Pampanga and Bulacan, and over which, at the town, there is a handsome stone bridge, one of the few in the Philippines. The town is built in the Spanish fashion, contains some fine buildings, and in 1850 had a population of 29,257, being one of the largest in the Philippines after Manilla, for Binondo in the same province is considered but a suburb of the capital. It contains 4855 houses of all descriptions, many of them of solid masonry, among the most remarkable of which is the government manufactory of cigars, in which 8000 work-people of both sexes are employed. The town of Binondo communicates with Manilla by a fine stone bridge of 149 Spanish varas, or 138 English yards span. The population in 1850 was 29,211, of whom 4817 paid the capitation tax, amounting to 48,170 reals of plate. Binondo is the commercial part of Manilla, and the residence of the foreign merchants.

TORTOISE-SHELL, in Malay, Sisik-pâñu, literally, "tortoise scales." The only part of the sea tortoises or turtles held of much value by the natives of the Indian islands is the shell. Tortoises are found in all the seas of the Malay and Philippine Archipelagos, but the imbricated kind that yields the finest shell is most abundant in those of Celebes and the Spice Islands, as far as the coasts of New Guinea. The parties chiefly engaged in their capture are the Bajaus, or Malay sea-nomadic hunters, of whom the turtle is the principal game. These people distinguish four species of sea-turtle, to which they give the names of kulitan, akung, ratu, and boko. The last is the pâñu of the Malays and the green esculent turtle, of which the carapace is of no use, the animal being valued only for its flesh to sell to the Chinese and Europeans, for among the Mahommedans it is unlawful food. The three first-named species all yield a marketable shell. The ratu, which signifies king or royal turtle, is said to be of great size, measuring from five to six feet in length, but is not often taken, and the shell is of inferior value. All the finest shell is afforded by the first, the kulitan, the name, in fact, signifying "shell turtle." A very interesting account of the turtle fishery of Celebes, contained in the 16th volume of the Transactions of the Batavian Society of Arts and Sciences, describes the animal as follows. "The first named" (the kulitan) "is the kind which, on account of its costly shell, is the most prized. It is the so-named *caret* tortoise. The shell or back of this creature is covered with thirteen shields or blades, which lie regularly on each other in the manner of scales, five in the centre of the back and four on each side. These are the plates which furnish such costly tortoise-shell to the arts. The edges of the scales of the back are further covered with twenty-five thin pieces, joined one to another, which, in commerce, are known under the appellation of 'feet' or 'noses' of the tortoise. The value of the tortoise-shell depends on the weight of each 'head,' by which expression is understood the collective shell belonging to one and the same animal. Such is the article of commerce so much in request, both for the Chinese and European markets. Shells, which have white and dark spots that touch each other, and are, as much as possible, similar on both sides of the blade, are, in the eyes of the Chinese, much finer, and, on that account, more greedily bought by them than those which want this peculiarity. On the contrary, shells which are reddish rather than black in their dark spots, which possess little white, which are more damasked than spotted; in a word, of which the colours, according to Chinese taste, are badly distributed, are less valued. The caprice of the Chinese makes them sometimes value single 'heads' at unheard-of prices, such for example, as go under the name of 'white heads,' for the varieties of which they have peculiar names. It is impossible to give an accurate description of these varieties, and their sub-divisions, for these depend on many circumstances unappreciable to our senses. It is enough for me to observe that such heads as possess the above named qualities, that is, are very white in their blades, and have the outer rim of each blade, to the depth of two or three fingers, wholly white, and the weight of which amounts to two and a half catties, qualities that are rarely found united, may be valued at 1000 guilders or even more (above 24*l.* per pound, avoirdupois). The 'feet' or 'noses' of the tortoise-shell are in demand only in the Chinese market. Whenever the two hinder pieces of these have the weight of a quarter of a catty (between 5 and 6 ounces), which is seldom the case, they may reach the value of fifty guilders, or more. The whole shell of a tortoise seldom weighs more than three catties (four pounds), notwithstanding, it is asserted, that there occur 'heads' of four and five catties. Tortoise-shells are sometimes found of which the shell, instead of thirteen blades, consists of a single undivided one. The Bajos call this, which is rarely met with, loyong (brass?). The usual modes by which these people catch the tortoise are the adang (intercepting), the harpoon, and the net. To these, we add the simplest of all, namely, falling on the females when they resort to the strand to lay their eggs. This is also the most usual, I may say almost the only way, by which the inhabitants of the coast catch this animal. They need nothing more than, as soon as they have got the creature in their power, to turn it on its back, when, unable to turn itself again, it lies helpless. It sometimes, also, falls into the hands of the dwellers on the coast, through means of their fishing stakes, into which it enters like the fish, and from which it can find no outlet, but remains imprisoned in the innermost chamber. When the Bajos have caught a tortoise, they kill it immediately by a few blows on the head. They then take its upper shield, or the back itself off, being the only thing about the animal that has value. But as the shells adhere fast to each other, there would be danger of tearing them, if they at once pulled the plates asunder, they usually wait three days, in which time, the soft parts become decomposed, and the plates are loosened with very little trouble."

The Indian islands furnish, I believe, the largest supply of tortoise-shell for the European and Chinese market, the chief emporia being Singapore, Manilla, and Batavia, from which are exported yearly about 26,000 pounds: one half of this quantity is from Singapore.

TOWN. There is no word in Malay or Javanese for town or city, except such as are Sanscrit, namely, nâgri or nâgara, pura and praja, with kut·a, which signifies, literally, "a fortress." The application of the word praja to a town is rather singular, for in Sanscrit it signifies "subjects" or "inhabitants," that is, the inhabitants of the town are taken by the Javanese for the town itself. I state this on the highest authority I can quote, that of my friend Professor Wilson. It is not, therefore, an unreasonable conclusion to come to, that towns were unknown before the arrival of the Hindus, even to the most civilised nations of the Archipelago.

TRADE, COMMERCE. In Malay and Javanese, and, generally, in the other languages of the Archipelago, the most usual word for these is an abstract noun, derived from the word which signifies "a stranger," dagang. In Malay bãrniyaga or bârniyagan is a synonym of frequent use, and this is Sanscrit. The simple native expression, jüal-bli, "selling and buying," is of frequent use also. To sell, to buy, to be in debt, are all expressed by native words. Interest of money is expressed by the figurative phrase, "flower of gold," which also signifies "tribute." Mercantile profit is usually expressed by the Sanscrit word laba, but sometimes by the native figurative word bunga, flower or produce, and, occasionally, by the word untung, which signifies, "luck." The only word for capital or stock is modal, which is from the Telinga. The most usual expression for money is mas-perak, that is, gold and silver, or pichis, which is the name of the small tin or zinc coins borrowed from the Chinese. Another word is uwang or wang, which also signifies "a palace." The Javanese use the Sanscrit words arta and yatra for money. For a merchant, the most usual native word is the same which signifies a stranger. Another native name, juragan, means, literally, the master or commander of a vessel. Two others are Sanscrit, bopari, and santri, the last being literally scholar or priest, and a fifth ,sudagâr, is Persian.

TRINGANO, correctly **TRINGGANU**, is the name of the second Malay state on the eastern side of the Malay Peninsula, counting from its southern extremity. It is bounded on the south by the principality of Pahang, to the north by that of Kalantan, and to the west by that of Perak, the central range of mountains parting it from the last. Of its area nothing certain is known, nor does it seem of much consequence that there should be, since nearly the whole is one continuous jungle, in its present state of very little use to man. The inhabitants consist of the dominant people, or Malays converted to Mahommedanism,—some wild tribes of the same race unconverted,—a few of the Negritos in the mountains, and a few Chinese engaged in trade or in tin-mining. The total population of the state has been computed at 37,500. Of this number, the town of the same name, situated on a small river not far from the sea, has been estimated to contain from 15,000 to 20,000 inhabitants, or about one-half the population of the state. Among the inhabitants of the town are about 600 Chinese settlers. A little gold, some black pepper, and some tin are the staple products of Tringano, the tin being by far the most important, and said to amount yearly to about 480 tons. This state is one of the hereditary tributaries of Siam, but has long, and at present successfully, resisted the assumed supremacy of the Siamese.

TRIPANG, the name of a species of Holothuria, is found in most of the shallow seas of the Malay and Philippine Archipelagos. The word tripang is Malay, and the animal is called by the people of Celebes, süala, which our traders write swalloe. It is the bêche de mer, or sea-worm of the Portuguese, and our own "sea-cucumber," for in appearance and shape, although not in colour, for it is a dirty brown, it greatly resembles a cucumber. The esculent holothuria is by no means confined to the seas of the Archipelago; it is found in the upper part of the Gulf of Siam, and is so abundant on the northern coast of Australia, that the people of Celebes, receiving advances from the resident Chinese, have been long in the habit of making annual voyages thither in quest of it. Gutted, dried in the sun and smoked, it is considered cured, and fit for its only market, that of China, to which many hundred tons are yearly sent for the consumption of the curious epicures of that country.

The fishery of the tripang is to China what that of the sardine, tunny, and anchovy is to Europe. It is, for the most part, caught by hand, for it has little power of locomotion, but in deep water sometimes by diving. This is the account given by Mr. Windsor Earl of the fishery on the shores and banks of the Aroe Islands, where this animal appears to be very abundant. "But the great sources of wealth are the pearl and tripang banks, which lie on the eastern side of the group. These extend the entire length of the islands, and are often several miles in width, being intersected by deep channels, some of which will admit vessels of burthen. The tripang, or sea-slug, is of several varieties. The greater portion is caught in shallow water, where it can be picked up off the bank without diving."—Journal of the Indian Archipelago, Vol. 4, p. 480. The tripang, although an article of considerable importance in the trade of the Indian Islands, is never found in the printed price-currents of an European emporium, because never dealt in by Europeans, which arises from nice or rather capricious distinctions in their quality, which no European is competent to appreciate. I can discover no mention of the tripang in the early Portuguese writers; which seems to be another proof that the Chinese, who carry on the trade and advance the funds, had not yet settled in the Archipelago when the Portuguese first appeared in it.

TROTTO (Pulo), correctly **TRUTAO**, is the name of one of the numerous islands at the western end of the Straits of Malacca, close to the coast of the Peninsula, and belonging to the state of Queda. It is barren, covered with forest, and uninhabited.

TRUBU. This is the name of a fish, the scientific appellation of which I have not ascertained, but of which the salted and dried roes form a very considerable article of trade in the western parts of the Malayan Archipelago. It seems to be local, and like salmon and some other fish, to frequent rivers for the purpose of spawning. Its favourite resort is the muddy eastern coast of Sumatra, and more especially the narrow strait which divides Bancalis and some other low islands from the main land, and into which the river of Siak disembogues. At a place called Bukit-batu (rock-hill), a considerable fishery of the trubu is carried on, which is thus noticed by Mr. Anderson :—"The river of Bukit-batu is a very small stream, close to the mouth of which stands the town of Bukit-batu, which is a place of considerable trade, the grand staple being roes of the trobo-fish, or telur-trobo (trubu roes, or eggs), as they are called. Here there is a very extensive fishery, and three or four hundred boats, with two and three men in each, often go out at a time to the fishery, which is outside the Straits of Tanjung-Jati" (teak-tree promontory).—Anderson's Mission, p. 335. The fishery of the trubu is of immemorial antiquity, and is referred to by De Barros as existing on the arrival of the Portuguese just as it does at present. "The rivers" (of Sumatra), says he, "contain a great variety of fish, and in some of them, such as that of Siaca (Siak) they catch small shads (saves), of which the people of the country use the roes only, and of these they have a greater abundance than we have of the fish themselves."—Decade 3, Book 5, chap. 1.

TUBAN. The name of a district, and formerly of an ancient province of Java, and now forming part of the Netherland province of Rembang.

TURAJA. The name of a mountainous country in the very centre of the island of Celebes. The inhabitants are described as savages who have not adopted the Mahommedan religion, and in the same social condition as the Dayaks of Borneo. By the Malays, indeed, they are called Dayaks. Little is known about them, as they seem never to have been visited by Europeans.

TURKEY. This bird has been long naturalised in Java and the Philippines, but is bred only by Europeans and their descendants, for, preposterously, the Mahommedans consider its flesh unlawful food, although the bird was unknown to any of them for near nine centuries after the time of their prophet. The prejudice arises, it is said, from the tuft on the breast, which bears some resemblance to a hog's bristles. The name given to the turkey by the natives sufficiently points to the source from which they derived it,—ayam-Yuropa and ayam-Holanda, the "fowl of Europe," and the "fowl of Holland."

TUWAJU, or WAJU, is the name of a tribe of the Bugis or Wugi nation of Celebes, by far the most industrious and enterprising people, not only of that island but of the whole Malay Archipelago. Their parent country is in the centre of the south-western peninsula, between the third and fourth degrees of south latitude, its sea-board being on the Gulf of Boni, and its boundary to the south, the great lake of Labaya. But they are, at present, found as settlers in almost every trading port of the Archipelago, native and European, having in some of the ruder countries, as Floris and Borneo, independent settlements. In Singapore, although of such recent origin, they already number from 2000 to 3000. Besides this, they perform voyages from one end of the Archipelago to the other,—to the eastward as far as New Guinea, and to the westward as far as Sumatra. In fact, they conduct most of the native carrying trade, and seem, in this respect, to occupy now the same position which the Malays and Javanese did before the arrival of Europeans. I can find no mention whatever of them in the early Portuguese writers, and therefore conclude that their rise, as a mercantile people, is of comparatively very recent origin. I copy the following account of this people in their own country, from notes which I took in 1823, from communications made to me by respectable members of the tribe trading to Singapore:—"There are large Waju villages on the banks of the great lake (Labaya), all of which carry on a considerable foreign trade. The trading praus are tracked up the stream of the Chinrana river, the voyage being performed in about thirty-six hours, while that from the lake to the sea does not occupy above one half that time. The depth of water in the river is abundant during the rainy season for the largest praus, but not so in the dry. The tribe of Waju consists of a confederation of forty princes. By these, assembled in council, the general affairs of the whole nation are conducted, and the council, like an English jury, must be unanimous. Its chief is elected by the other members, and holds his place during good conduct. He goes under the title of Arung-matuwa, which may be rendered 'the prince-elder.' Six of the princes, under the name of Bati-lumpo, literally 'great banners,' form a select council to advise and assist the president in his ministerial functions. These councillors are hereditary in particular families, the choice of the individual being made by his own particular tribe. The Waju people pay no taxes, direct or indirect, being even exempt from import or export duties. The princes are supported from their own domains, the Arung-matuwa, or presiding prince, alone receiving three days' corvée labour,—one at the time of ploughing, another at that of planting, and a third at harvest. The Waju men of all ranks, unlike the rest of the Bugis people, have full liberty to go abroad and to return at pleasure, at once a cause and effect, it may be presumed, of their independence, enterprise, and prosperity."

TYPHOON, it is to be presumed from the Arabic word tufan, a storm. This is the name by which those frightful equinoctial gales are known to Europeans, which vex sea and land about the tropics, and down as far as to 10° from the equator. The whole Malayan Archipelago is excluded from their sphere, while the whole of the Philippine is within it, the island of Mindano alone excepted. The following account of one of these visitations is by an eye-witness. "The change of the monsoons does not take place peacefully. The two winds seem, as it were, to struggle with each other, until one of them yields the ground. The tornados, on such occasions, are sudden and violent. Torrents of rain fall so copiously, that he who is overtaken by them in the open country can hardly draw his breath. If the tempest take place at night, the scene presented is grand. The obscurity is intense, the flashes of lightning, broad and bright, overspreading earth and sky. The thunder-claps are tremendous, some of them bursting within doors with a force which strikes one dumb. Others resound in the firmament with a report prolonged for eight and ten minutes, with various sounds, now diminishing, and now redoubling, and finally dying away in the noise of the storm. Sometimes the tornados continue with little interruption for fifteen days. When these storms are of the most violent kind, they take the name of hurricanes (huracan), which the Chinese call ti-fan, and the Philippine islanders bagui. Towards the end of the year 1831, one of these took place, when several ships were cast far inland from the beach, and the frigate 'Union,' of 600 tons, was driven from her anchors in the harbour of Cavité, and thrown on the ramparts of the fort. Whole galleries were torn from the houses of Manilla, and sheets of lead from their roofs carried by the force of the wind across the river Pasig. The flood in the great lake was such as to carry off houses on its banks, along with their inhabitants, sweeping them into the river. On such occasions, the ends of posts and canes are seen with a flame playing on them, as if they were so many torches; this magnificent illumination proving the vast quantity of electricity with which the air is charged."—Informe sobre el estado de las Islas Filipinas.

U.

UJUNG, in Malay and Javanese, signifies point, or sharp end, and is also frequently applied to a point of land, or head-land, promontory, or tongue. It occurs frequently in the geography of the Malay Archipelago, as in Ujung-tanah, which is frequently applied to the land's end of the Malay Peninsula, or at least to the most salient point of it. We have another example of it in the name of the island called by Europeans Junk-Ceylon; and which is in reality the name of a promontory of that island, called by the Malays Ujung-Salang, or the point of Salang.

UMBRELLA, in Malay and Javanese, payung, and in the latter, also, songsong. To use an umbrella at all, or rather to have it carried over one, for no native carries an umbrella himself, is a mark of rank, and its quality implies the degree of that rank. The sovereign alone uses one which is gilt throughout. In Java, a small umbrella, called a bawat, is the special badge of the higher nobility, called by the Sanscrit title of bopati. This is not made use of to screen from sun or rain, but carried by a retainer, before the party.

UNGSANG is the name of the most southern easterly part of the island of Borneo, which is a kind of peninsula, a large bay to the north, and a still larger to the south, making of the intervening land a kind of isthmus. Very little is known of this peninsula, which has hardly ever been visited by an European, but it seems to be a barren wilderness, claimed by the Sultans of Sulu, whose insular dominions approach within twenty miles of it. The elephant, escaped most probably from the domesticated state, is now well known to exist in this remote corner, although in no other part of Borneo.

UPAS, in Javanese "poison," or "venom." The sap of some plants of the Malay and Philippine Islands yields poisonous juices, which, by concentration, produce a poison of considerable activity, which has been sometimes employed by the ruder natives to render their weapons deadly. The most potent of these plants in Java are the Anchar, the Antiaris toxicaria, a large forest tree, and the Chetek, strichnos tienté, a climbing shrub. In all these cases, the poison, even when fresh, is far less active than that of the cobra snake, for the most powerful will take an hour to kill a dog, which the venom of the hooded snake would certainly accomplish in half the time. To effect a fatal purpose, too, it is necessary that the poisoned weapon should be left in the wound, and not withdrawn, so that the probability is that few human beings have ever lost their lives by means of these poisons.

V.

VALENTYN (FRANCIS). The author of the great work on the Dutch Possessions in India, was a clergyman of the Lutheran church, and born in Dordrecht, about the year 1660. In the year 1685 he proceeded to India, in his capacity of minister, and in the following year reached Batavia. After exercising for a short time his professional functions at Japara, on the northern coast of Java, he was transferred to Amboyna, the future field of his ministry and literary labours. He applied himself diligently to the study of the native languages, and with such success that in a few months' time he was able to preach in Malay. After twelve years' residence in Amboyna and the other Spice Islands, his health obliged him to return to Europe in 1694. After a stay in Holland of eleven years, he returned a second time to India in 1705. On this occasion, he remained in Java two years, and then proceeded to Amboyna, where he continued for seven years, and finally returned to Holland in 1714. He then began to arrange for publication the vast mass of materials which, during his Indian residence, he had so industriously collected. His work was published from 1724 to 1726, in eight folio volumes, with plates. It embraces not only an account of the Dutch possessions in the islands of the Archipelago, but of all those from the Cape of Good Hope to Japan. The most valuable part of it is that which relates to those places of which he had personal experience, Java and the Spice Islands, but especially the last. The rest consists of mere compilation, and relates to matters now obsolete, and never of much public interest. The time of the death of this eminent person is unknown, but he must have been in his sixty-sixth year when he completed the publication of his most laborious work.

VARELA (Pulo). This is a name given by navigators to several islets in the western part of the Malayan Archipelago,—one, for example, in the group of islands at the eastern extremity of the Straits of Malacca, another on the north-eastern side of Sumatra, and a third in the little chain which lies close to the Malay Peninsula on its eastern coast, and towards its extremity. The word is a Portuguese corruption of the Malay bârala, which signifies an idol, or image.

VENEREAL. There can be no doubt but that it was the Portuguese who first introduced this malady into the Malay, and thence into the Philippine Archipelago. The companions of Magellan, on their return from the Moluccas to Spain, touched at the island of Timur, and Pigafetta thus refers to the subject on quitting it :—"In all the islands of this Archipelago which we visited, the malady of San Giobbe was prevalent, and more here than anywhere else. They call it For-franchi, that is, the Portuguese disease." Some have fancied that the disease of St. Job might mean leprosy, but that indigenous disease would certainly not have been called a Portuguese malady, nor would the small number of persons labouring under leprosy, a non-contagious disease, have attracted the special attention of the companions of Magellan. The passage in Pigafetta is dated in 1522, and at this time the Portuguese had been already above ten years in the Archipelago, and frequented many parts of it, from Sumatra to the Moluccas. During all this time, too, there were no Europeans in the Archipelago but themselves. In twenty-eight years' time, then, from the discovery of America, the malady had already pervaded the remotest islands of the Archipelago, but had not reached the Philippines, unless left there by the companions of Magellan, for Pigafetta takes no notice of its existence in that Archipelago.

VILLAGE, in Malay and Javanese d'usun, and desa, the last being from the Sanscrit. A small village or hamlet is called dukuh. The word kampung is frequently used for a village, but it properly signifies a close, or place enclosed by a fence, which the village generally is. The habitations of the Indian islanders, for the obvious purpose of protection, are grouped into villages, as, indeed, in all other countries of the east. Each cottage composing it is surrounded by fruit or ornamental trees and shrubs, so that the village is, as if it were embosomed in an orchard, and the cottages, in a good measure, hidden from view. Even a town of several thousand inhabitants is no more than an aggregation of villages, divided into a number of closes or inclosures, the only conspicuous building in it being the chieftain's dwelling. In Java, Bali, and other agricultural countries of the Archipelago, the village is a corporation almost as complete as in Hindustan. It has its head-man, known by various names, such as bâkâl, lurah, patingih, and pângulu,—the two last signifying, respectively, the highest or most elevated, and the head-man. The head-man has his assistant, and a scribe or accountant, with a priest, complete the office-bearers. The actual village, which might more correctly be called a township, with its houses and orchards, are the private property of the several occupants, and not held collectively, as in some of the Hindu countries. The adjacent corn-lands alone are subject to the land-tax, whether the whole rent has been absorbed under that name or a part of it still remains as the private property of the cultivator.

VISCAYA (NUEVA). The name of a province of the island of Luzon. See NUEVA VISCAYA.

VOLCANOS. The Indian islands contain the largest volcanic region in the world. The band of this formation begins with Sumatra, passing through a considerable portion of the central part of it. It embraces the whole of Java, and all the islands east of it as far as Ombay, in longitude 125°. From this it takes a course north of east, and presents itself in the Banda Islands. It thus extends in an easterly direction over 30° of longitude. The band, if it really be the same, then takes a northwesterly course, and shows itself in the Moluccas, or true Clove Islands, and again, at the extremity of the northern peninsula of Celebes, opposite to them. We have it next in the most southerly of the Philippines, and it passes through the whole of this Archipelago to the Babuyanes Islands, over 13° of latitude. With the exception of a part of Sumatra, there is no volcanic formation in the Malay Archipelago, north of 6° south latitude. Thus the Peninsula, Borneo, and the greater part of Sumatra and Celebes, with the great island of New Guinea, are non-volcanic. The Philippines embrace the plutonic and sedimentary formations as well as the volcanic.

The number of extinct volcanos in the two Archipelagos is very great, and even the active ones are numerous. Of the last, there are in Sumatra five, in Java twenty, in the islands immediately east of it about seven; in the Banda and Molucca Islands three, and in the Philippines at least ten. There is no record, that I am aware of, of any destructive eruption in Sumatra, and although there have been several minor eruptions in Java of late years, the last great one in that island took place as long ago as the year 1586. This was from the mountain Ringgit (puppet), a peak only 4200 feet above the level of the sea. (See RINGGIT). In the Javanese chronicles an eruption is stated to have taken place in Java, without naming the mountain, as early as 1273 of Saka, or 1351 of our time. In the Moluccas the eruptions have been numerous since the arrival of Europeans. In the Philippines, also, there have been some very destructive ones, but hardly on so great a scale as that of Ringgit in Java, or Tomboro in Sumbawa. One of these took place in 1645, in the province of Cagayan, when a whole mountain sunk into the earth, carrying with it an entire village and its inhabitants. The succession of earthquakes which accompanied it is said to have lasted during two months, and although the city of Manilla be at least two hundred miles distant from Cagayan, every stone building in it was levelled to the ground, with the exception of the churches of the Augustins and Jesuits, and 600 of the inhabitants perished under the ruins.

W.

WAIGIOE. The name of a considerable island off the north-western end of New Guinea. It lies between five miles and seventy-five miles south of the equator, and stretches as far east as longitude 131° 16′. Its area has been estimated at 960 geographical square miles. Waigioe is mountainous in the interior, with a low and marshy coast. The officers of the French discovery-ship Coquille gave to the highest peak of the island the name of the Cone de Beuffle, and made it 480 toises, or 1516 feet above the level of the sea. The climate appears to be moist and hot. The inhabitants of the coast are represented as a cross between the Malay and Papuan negro, and most probably those of the interior are pure Papuan. The bread of the inhabitants, like that of all those of the neighbouring islands, is sago, and the culture of rice is unknown.

WAJU. The name of a tribe of the Bugis nation of Celebes. See TUWAJU.

WAR. The most frequent name for this in both Malay and Javanese is pârang, or abbreviated, prang; but the Javanese has also two native words peculiar to itself, jurit and laga, with the Sanscrit one yuda. The chief force of the agricultural nations is an infantry, but the people of Java, Bali, and Lomboc have also a cavalry, mounted on ponies, seldom thirteen hands high, and therefore little formidable. To the maritime tribes the prau is what the horse and the camel united are to the Arabs and Tartars, and their armies, in fact, are fleets. An army in the Malayan countries is, as in all rude states of society, a mob composed of the followers and retainers of the chiefs, every adult being supposed to be a soldier. The words for an army are Sanscrit, bala and balatantra, which signify "a host," or "the people." Between a fleet and an army there is no distinction. Both are expressed in Malay by the word angkatan, which literally means a lifting or rising. For a soldier, the Javanese have the derivative word prajurit, from jurit, war, but this signifies only a warrior. They have also the Sanscrit chatriya, and the Malays, with some corruption, have adopted the first of these. For a soldier by profession they have adopted the Portuguese soldado. For military exercise, after the European manner, the term is baris, which literally signifies "a row or line."

WAX (BEES'). In Malay and Javanese lilin, but in the latter more frequently malam. This last word, it is singular enough, is to be found in some of the Papuan languages of New Guinea, where the negros have had an intercourse with the Malayan race, but generally there are distinct native words for it in each language. This is also the case with the bee; but for honey it is curious to find the general name, madu, to be Sanscrit, the Javanese adding another from the same language, sakara, or abbreviated, kara, which is properly sugar. Wax has always been a considerable article of exportation from the Indian Islands, chiefly the produce of the wilder parts of it. Barbosa names it as one of the chief articles obtained by the Malay and Javanese traders in Timur and the other islands on the route to the Spice Islands. It is always the produce of the forests, for the bee has never been domesticated in the Malay or Philippine Islands, and in a region where there are flowers throughout the year, and consequently no inducement to form a large store, its domestication would probably be difficult. The honey is always thin, poor, and flavourless, compared to that of more temperate climates. Although the bees be wild, their hives, once appropriated, are considered as private property, which other productions of the forest, whether animal or vegetable, are not, and the ground of this distinction is explained in the following law of the Malays. After declaring that game and fish are not private property, it says;—"If, however, a man rob a bee-hive without knowledge of its owner, such owner meeting him may take the honey from him, and bring him before a magistrate, who shall further fine him in the sum of half-a-tail. It is true that bees are wild animals, but their hives afford the owner of the land in which they are a regular and certain revenue."

WAY (Pulo). There are three islands of this name in the Malay Archipelago, —one in the Roads of Achin, one in the Gulf of Siam, and one near the Banda Islands. The word wai, or we, is probably a corruption of ayâr in Malay, or er in Javanese, "water," for in this form we find it in the languages of Celebes, and even in those of the South Sea Islands. If this be true, Pulo Way means simply "water island."

WAYANG signifies in Malay and Javanese a scenic figure, and also an actor, or player, and the drama. The word is probably the same as bayang, a shadow and an apparition, and most probably taken from it.

WAYANG (GUNUNG). The name of a mountain of Java, between the districts of Bandong and Sukapura, in the country of the Sundas, an active volcano, and rising to the height of 6000 feet above the level of the sea. The name signifies "mountain of the drama or scenic exhibition."

WEAVING. The weaving of cloth from some raw material or another seems to have been immemorially practised by all the more advanced nations of the Malay and even of the Philippine Archipelago. There is no ground for believing that this is an art which the inhabitants were taught by strangers, for nearly all the terms connected with it in the two leading languages, the Malay and Javanese, are native words, as, to spin, antih; yarn, bânang or lawe; warp, lungsen; woof, pakan; to weave, tânun; shuttle, turah and balera; loom, pâkakas-tânun (literally weaving apparatus); distaff, räat; bow for clearing cotton, busor; and cloth, kain in Malay and sinjang in Javanese. The only exceptions are, the name of the principal raw material now employed, cotton, which is kapas, from the Sanscrit karpasa; and that of the spinning-wheel, also Sanscrit, jantra, signifying "a machine." What raw material would have been employed before the introduction of cotton from India, it is not easy to understand, although there are several native textile fibres on the spot which were available, such as the fibre of the banana, and of several urticas, or nettles.

As nearly all the terms now enumerated are found in all the languages of the Malay Archipelago, it is natural to conclude that the art of manufacturing woven cloth from thread was the invention of one country, and not unreasonable to fancy that country to have been Java, the one in which civilisation earliest sprung up, and in which it made the greatest progress. Although the terms connected with the art of weaving a textile fabric have extended to all the languages of the civilised nations of the Malay, they have not extended to those of the Philippine Archipelago, which have their own peculiar ones, and even a native word for cotton, along with the Sanscrit one, received, like other words of the same tongue, through the Malayan languages. The art of weaving a cloth, as is well known, had never spread to the tribes of the islands of the Pacific, and this is one of the many facts which show how little they really received through the Malayan nations. It is remarkable, however, that the Malayan words for weaving and sewing should have found their way into the language of remote Madagascar. All the cloths manufactured by the inhabitants of the Malayan islands are strong, coarse, and durable fabrics, and the fine textures woven by the Hindus are wholly unknown to them. The native manufactures are purely domestic, and the women the only manufacturers. The best are the fabrics of Celebes and Java, and these continue to form a considerable article of external commerce, although competing with the manufactures of Manchester and Glasgow.

WEIGHTS and MEASURES. The original measures of the Malays and Javanese were evidently by capacity (takâr) and not by weight, for which there are no words in their language, except such as signify heaviness or balance. The lowest denomination for a measure of capacity among the Malays goes under the name of chupak, most probably taken from the shell of the coco-nut or the joint of the bamboo. Of this, 4 make a gantang, and 800 of the last a koyan. These are native words, with the literal meaning of which, however, I am unacquainted. The measures of length, as with other people, are taken from the members or parts of the human body, as finger-length, span, foot, pace, fathom, with the length from the foot of one side to the tip of the outstretched hand on the opposite one. Superficial or land measure is still more rude. Thus the Javanese, in reference to their irrigated land, the only description on which they set a special value, have, for the largest measure, what they term a jong, which, literally signifies a ship, and this divided into halves called kikil, or a leg, and into fourths called bau, which means a shoulder. Another admeasurement of land goes under the name of chachah, of which gawe-ning-wong is the synonym, the first word signifying "count" or "census," and the last, "a man's work," that is, the quantity of irrigated land that a family of peasantry can till. This last term is of the same nature as our own "plough-land."

All such weights and measures are vague and uncertain, and vary, not only in the different countries of the Archipelago, but often in districts of the same country. Strangers have in some degree contributed to give them precision by the introduction of their own, the native names being generally preserved. To judge by the name, the Persians seem to have introduced the balance (trazu), and the Chinese, probably, the steelyard (d'achin). The weighing of gold was, of course, an important operation, which required to be conducted with nicety in a country producing gold, and where all large payments were made in this metal by weight and assay. It seems, immemorially, to have been conducted, as it still is, by the Telingas, and these people introduced the Hindu gold weights. The denominations of these correspond in value with the Indian, although in some places, having native terms, as the saga or "counting bean," the mayam, the bungkal, and the kati. In others they are expressed by corruptions of the Sanscrit ones. Thus the scarlet bean is called rakât, from the Sanscrit raktaka; the weight of 12 beans, a mas; from maska, andthe tail or 16 maskas, from the tolaka or tola. For long measure the Hindu hasta or cubit has generally superseded the native measures, at least for commercial purposes. The only weight introduced by the Arabs is the bahar, usually considered as equal to three pikuls, and this was in use even as far as the Moluccas, when the Portuguese first arrived.

The business-like Chinese have introduced their own well-defined weights, although under native names. Thus we have the tail or weight of 23 drams, avoirdupois, the kati, consisting of 16 tails, and the piknul, which literally signifies a man's load or burden, composed of 100 katis or 133⅓ pounds, avoirdupois. The weights and measures of the Malays, with their denominations, have not only extended over the whole Malay Archipelago, but are also prevalent in the Philippines. In the settlements of European nations the weights and measures of the natives have been fixed with precision.

WETTER. The name of a considerable island on the northern side of Timur, and towards its eastern end. Its most northerly point is in south latitude 8° 6′, and east longitude 125° 58′. Its length from east to west is 60 miles, with a breadth of about 25 miles. The northern coast is mountainous, but the southern has some open plains and valleys. The inhabitants are of the same race as those of Timur, that which is intermediate between the Malay and Negro. The conjectural population is made to amount to 82,000, probably an exaggeration, since it would give not less than 70 inhabitants to the square mile, a proportion not to be looked for in a poor mountainous country, and in a very rude state of society. The bread-corn of Wetter, like that of Timur, is maiz and the principal export, bees'-wax.

WHEAT. This corn, known to the natives of the Indian Islands only by its Persian name of gandum, or its Portuguese of trigo, is cultivated in small quantities for the consumption of European settlers in Java and Luzon, with a few other parts of the Philippines, at an elevation above the level of the sea of from 4000 to 6000 feet.

WIDADAREN. The name of a mountain of Java, with an active volcano rising to the height of 8000 feet above the level of the sea. It is one of a range which divides the districts of Besuki and Bañuwangi, the last forming the eastern extremity of the island. The name signifies place or abode of the Widari, a class of celestial nymphs, according to the local mythology of the Javanese.

WILIS. The name of a mountain of Java, without an active volcano, 7957 feet above the level of the sea. It forms the eastern boundary of the plain of Madiyun, as Lawu does the western. The name in Javanese signifies "green," but for what reason does not appear, since every mountain of the island is equally verdant.

WOWONI. The name of an island lying north of that of Boeteon, and divided from the south-eastern peninsula of Celebes by a strait about two miles broad. As laid down in the maps, it appears to be about seventeen miles in length, and ten in its broadest part. I can discover nothing recorded about it, and suppose it to be almost unknown to Europeans.

WRITING, in Malay and Javanese tulis, but in the last of these it has two synonyms, chiri and tanu. All these are native words, but in both languages the Arabic surât is also of frequent use. All the native words signify "to paint" as well as to write. See LANGUAGE.

X.

XULLA. This, with an epithet to each, is the name given in our maps to three islands, which, with a fourth, much smaller, form a group lying east of Celebes, and west by north of Boeroe, in the Molucca Sea. They lie from one to two degrees and a half south of the equator, and run as far east as longitude 126°. The group extends over thirty-six leagues, and has been estimated to contain an area of 1808 square geographical miles. Respecting the natural history of these islands, or the condition of their inhabitants, I have seen no notices. That they were discovered and named by the Portuguese, there can be little doubt. The odd orthography can, I think, be explained. The initial x, in Portuguese is equivalent in power to our sh, or the French ch, but such a sound is not known in any of the Malayan languages, and the real one intended was most probably our own, and the Spanish ch, which would make the xula, chula, a word which in Malay and Javanese signifies a horn, or a horny protuberance, like the horn of the rhinoceros. The name of one of the islands, Xulla-bâsi, would, in this case, be Chula-bâsi, literally, "iron horn." Another of the islands is called Xulla-mangola, and this is probably meant for Chula-manggala, which, in Javanese, would be literally "elephant horn," for in that language manggala is one of several synonyms for the elephant. The name of the third, Xulla-taliabo, is not so clear, but it may be meant for Chula-târlabuh, or Chula-tâlabuh, which would literally be, "horn let fall" or "horn at anchor."

Y.

YAM (DIOSCOREA). This plant is universally cultivated among all the tribes, and generally most so where rice is least abundant, but it no where forms the chief bread of the people, as rice, maiz, or sago do. The batata, indeed, and I think justly, is preferred to it. The Malay and Javanese name, ubi or uwi, extends not only to the languages of the Malay and Philippine Islands, but to those of the Pacific, and to Madagascar. In the Philippine languages the name is identical with that in the Malay; in the Tonga it is ufi; in the Tahiti eüi; in the New Zealand the same as in Javanese, namely, uwi; in the language of New Ireland u, and in the Madagascar uvi. With all these varieties of pronunciation there can be no doubt of the virtual identity of the name. It is probable that several species of Dioscorea are natives of the Malayan Archipelago, but that the culture originated with one people, and was directly or indirectly disseminated by them, seems likely from the universality of the name. It may be remarked, that in the language of Madagascar, a wild yam is called uvi-ala, which is, without doubt, the Uwi-alas— the wild or forest yam of the Javanese, with the elision of the final consonant, conformably to the genius of Malagasi pronunciation. The word ubi, besides being applied specifically to the yam, is used as a generic for farinaceous roots. Thus the batata, or Convolvulus batatas, is called by the Malays Ubi-jawa, or the Javanese yam, to distinguish it from the Dioscorea.

YAMORA. The name of a mountain on the north-eastern side of Sumatra, within the territory of Achin, and not far from the western end of the island. It is the Golden Mount, or Queen's Mount of our navigators, and, rising to the height of 5250 feet above the level of the sea, is a conspicuous land-mark to the mariner.

YOGYAKARTA, OR AYOGYAKARTA is the name of the capital of one of the two native princes of Java, who still retain the administration of their own territories, —the same party who assumes the title of Sultan. The town is situated in the plain which extends from the volcanic mountain Mârapi to the southern coast, from which it is distant about twelve miles. It consists of the Kraton, or walled palace of the prince, which is in itself a considerable town, and of several quarters or closes, being an aggregate, in short, of large villages, with wide streets, or rather roads, dividing them from each other. When I represented the British government at the court of the prince in question, in 1816, the population amounted to about 35,000, much of it consisting of retainers and followers of the court and chieftains. I have seen no recent account of it, but, as there have been since, large cessions of territory to the European power, it is probable that the population has not much increased. By the census of Java, made in 1850, the population of the whole territory of the Sultan was computed to be 364,045, and the area of the principality being 926 square miles, we have a relative population of better than 393 to the square mile. Yogyakarta, or, as the Dutch write the name, with a clumsiness and inaccuracy not usual in their orthography of Malayan words, Djocjacarta, was founded only in 1755, when a long rebellion was brought to a close by a compromise, in which the territories of the Susunan, or Emperor of Java, as he has been called by some European writers, were partitioned between two princes of the same family. The name is Sanscrit, the first part of it, Ayugya, being a corruption of Ayudya, the kingdom of the Hindu demi-god Rama, and the same which we ourselves write as Oude. The last part, karta, means labour or work.

Z.

ZAMBALES. The name of the most westerly province of the Island of Luzon. It is washed by the sea of China, and extends from latitude 14° 45′ to 16° 24′, and from longitude 119° 34′ to 120° 18. To the north, it includes the western shore of the great Gulf of Lingayen, and to the south the bay of Sulig. This last penetrates the island to the depth of forty miles, and at its mouth, its width is but five miles, while within it widens to double that breadth. This bay, protected at its extremity, forms a safe harbour against all winds except the south-west. The province forms a strip of land along the foot of the range of mountains called Zambales, and which run in a direction north and south, ending to the north in the conspicuous promontory of Bolino. Its length is a hundred miles, and its greatest breadth about twenty, but its area does not exceed 1200 geographical miles. The inhabitants of Zambales speak a peculiar language of their own, but in manners, customs, and social state, resemble the other civilised nations of Luzon. On the arrival of the Spaniards, they were found in possession of a written language, and some poetical compositions. The Zambales range of mountains, and its valleys, are occupied by some tribes of Negritos, and by the brown or Malayan tribes called Igorrotes and Cimmarones. The mountains themselves are steep and rugged, but the land between them and the sea, forming the main part of the province, is fertile, well watered, and suited to the growth of rice, the sugar-cane, and even to wheat in its more elevated parts. In 1818, Zambales contained a population of no more than 18,841, and this, in 1846, had increased to the extraordinary number of 95,260, of whom 8494 paid the capitation tax. The relative population is but seventy-nine to the square geographical mile. The chief town of Zambales is Iba, or Yba, in north latitude 15° 19′ 45″, and east longitude 119° 51′. It is situated on a river navigable for small craft only, and distant from its mouth about three quarters of a league.

ZAMBOANGA. The name of a Spanish province of Mindano, forming the south-western extremity of that island. The climate is described as hot, but healthy, being a good deal tempered by regular land and sea breezes. It is beyond the region of typhoons, and is, strictly speaking, the only part of the Spanish Philippines that is wholly so. Water is abundant, and the soil described as fertile, but neither its exported produce or number of inhabitants afford satisfactory evidence of this. The area of the province has not been stated, and most probably has never been ascertained. The greater part of the territory is inhabited by wild tribes, not included in the registers of its population. The inhabitants subject to the Spanish rule amounted, in 1801, to 5162; in 1818, to 8640; but in 1847 to no more than 8281; so that in thirty years, instead of an increase, as in the better islands of the Philippine Archipelago, there was a positive falling off. The principal town bears the same name, and contains the bulk of the population of the province. It has a quadrangular fort, with four bastions.—The Island of Basilan, one of the largest of the Sooloo Archipelago, has been lately annexed to the province. This is four leagues distant from the town of Zamboanga, but has only the miserably small population of 424 souls. The chief purpose of the province of Zamboanga is as a defence to the northern islands of the Philippines against the piracy of the natives of Soolo and Mindano.

INDEX.

C.

D.

E.

F.

G.

T.

U.

V.

W.

X.

Y.

Z.

THE END.